COLLEGES
WORTH
YOUR MONEY

COLLEGES WORTH YOUR MONEY

A Guide to What America's Top Schools Can Do for You

5TH EDITION

Andrew Belasco, Dave Bergman, & Michael Trivette

ROWMAN & LITTLEFIELD

Lanham • Boulder • New York • London

Published by Rowman & Littlefield
An imprint of The Rowman & Littlefield Publishing Group, Inc.
4501 Forbes Boulevard, Suite 200, Lanham, Maryland 20706
www.rowman.com

86-90 Paul Street, London EC2A 4NE

Distributed by NATIONAL BOOK NETWORK

British Library Cataloguing in Publication Information Available

Library of Congress Cataloging-in-Publication Data Available

ISBN 9781538191873 (paperback) | ISBN 9781538191880 (ebook)

♾™ The paper used in this publication meets the minimum requirements of American National Standard for Information Sciences—Permanence of Paper for Printed Library Materials, ANSI/NISO Z39.48-1992.

About the Authors

Andrew Belasco, Ph.D., a graduate of Georgetown University and Harvard University, is a higher education researcher, counselor, and CEO of College Transitions, an educational consulting firm. His work has been published in the nation's top higher education journals and featured in dozens of media outlets, including *The New York Times, Washington Post, Time, Boston Globe, Forbes, The Chronicle of Higher Education*, and NPR, among others. Andrew is also the co-author of *The Enlightened College Applicant: A New Approach to the Search and Admissions Process* (Rowman & Littlefield, 2016).

Dave Bergman, Ed.D., earned his doctoral degree from Temple University and has fifteen years of professional experience that includes work as a teacher, high school administrator, adjunct professor, researcher, and independent educational consultant. As a co-founder of College Transitions, Dave oversees the collegetransitions.com blog and Dataverse, reaching an audience in excess of five million readers annually. Dave is also the co-author of *The Enlightened College Applicant: A New Approach to the Search and Admission Process* (Rowman & Littlefield, 2016).

Michael Trivette, Ph.D., a graduate of the University of Georgia Institute of Higher Education, has over fifteen years of experience in the higher education field, including college admissions, enrollment management, intercollegiate athletics, student support services, and student life. A co-founder of College Transitions, he also has experience working within the University of North Carolina System and the University System of Georgia. His research has been published in *Educational Policy, Review of Higher Education, The Journal of Higher Education*, and the *Journal of Education Finance*.

Contents

Introduction & Methodology

Before the birth of the modern internet, savvy teens seeking information on prospective colleges cracked open the latest Yellow Pages-thick college guidebook, eager to soak in school-specific admissions data that felt like classified information. Possessors of such guidebooks were the true insiders of the day, privy to admissions statistics that simply could not be found within the glossy brochures delivered to the masses via snail mail. By 2024-25, those oversized volumes have been rendered far less essential. Basic admissions data such as SAT ranges, grade point averages, tuition costs, and acceptance rates are available via fast and free Google searches. Everyone is now—at least in 1980s or '90s terms—an insider.

The formula for these annual editions is simple. Easy-to-find admissions and tuition data points are complemented by blocks of heavily anecdotal text designed to reveal something about the campus milieu: the quality of the food, the architectural style of the buildings, the political leanings of the student body, and the subjective like (don't worry, we've included a sprinkling of that fun stuff in CWYM as well). While these books all serve as useful starting points for your college search (we read them ourselves each year), they fail to acknowledge the seismic shift taking place in the national conversation about higher education—the idea that students should stop obsessing over gaining admission into the most prestigious schools that will accept them and instead ask, "What can a given college do for me?" If students/parents are going to pony up $200,000 or more in tuition alone, they should first demand to see outcomes data, return on investment (ROI) figures, and a statistically backed account of unique opportunities for undergraduates. That's where the college guide you're holding comes into play.

Why do I need this guide?

There are two main reasons:

(1) Given the absurd cost of a college education, finding a school that will provide an acceptable ROI has never been more challenging.

(2) Your prospective colleges are likely to be more selective than they were only a few years ago; greater information gathering/strategic planning will be required to successfully gain admission.

Let's begin with the issue of price. As we get older, it's easy to fall into a nostalgic trap on the subject of how much things cost. For example, "When I was a boy, you could feed a family of four for a Buffalo nickel." Yet when it comes to lamenting rising college expenses, there is actual data to back up the sticker shock. In 1950, the University of Pennsylvania charged $600 per year to attend—roughly $6,000 in 2022 money. Today, Penn's annual cost of attendance is over $89,000. By 1960, most private institutions charged an annual fee of $1,500–$2,000, which equates to $12,000–$16,000 today. In the current marketplace, a $50,000 annual tuition is considered "reasonable." This is hardly just a private school phenomenon. The University of North Carolina at Chapel Hill's current in-state tuition cost of $9k is one of the best bargains in all of higher education. Of course, that pales in comparison to the in-state tuition of thirty years ago—only $504 per year. (No, that's not a typo).

Turning to the matter of increased selectivity, you don't need to look back to the '50s, '60s, or even '70s to find a college admissions landscape vastly different from today's hyper-competitive environment. In 1980, nearly half of all applicants were accepted into prestigious Swarthmore College while the Class of 2026 had a 7% acceptance rate. As recently as the 1990s, the University of Chicago accepted 60–70% of those who applied, but for applicants to the Class of 2026, only 5% were successful. Less drastic but still significant changes have proliferated as the overwhelming majority of desirable public and private schools have grown more selective in recent years. As of the publication of this book, many of the most prestigious schools in the country boast single-digit acceptance rates, including all of the Ivy League schools, Stanford University, Johns Hopkins University, Duke University, Bowdoin College, Pomona College, Northwestern University, Vanderbilt University, Rice University, and Massachusetts Institute of Technology, among others. Other elite schools including NYU, Georgetown University, and the University of Southern California all have inched closer to the single-digit club and will likely join it soon.

The reasons for this increased level of selectivity include an influx of highly qualified foreign students applying to US colleges, the Common App making it easier for top students to apply to as many elite schools as they wish, and a greater number of applicants paying for services, such as private SAT tutors, that ultimately enhance their academic profiles.

How to use this guide:

We hope the above statistics have convinced you that the college selection and admissions process has never been more of a high-stakes game. Parents/students who are about to essentially take out another mortgage to finance their own or their teen's college education should, at the very least, first perform the equivalent of a home inspection. Just as it is easy to fall in love with a house based on a Zillow photo, many select a college based on surface observations: the campus is pretty, the school colors would look nice on a bumper sticker, or they've heard good things from other parents in their social circle. Think of this guidebook as an inspection report with no crawlspace left unexplored.

Each profile includes six statistically rich narrative sections and two tables containing in excess of seventy additional data points. The following is a brief overview of the information included for each school and why it is important for prospective college students (and their parents) to know.

Inside the Classroom

We begin each profile by discussing what makes a given institution academically unique. Some schools have a core curriculum that dictates three semesters of study; others have an entirely open curriculum. Some mandate foreign language, physical education, a freshman seminar or two, and a senior thesis; others have no such requirements. Statistics on class size, undergraduate research opportunities, study abroad participation, and—when possible—institutional survey data regarding professor availability and the quality of classroom instruction are included. In this section, we also highlight particular programs/departments that have standout reputations as well as how seniors fare in landing nationally competitive postgraduate scholarships.

Outside the Classroom

Words such as "vibe," "feel," and "atmosphere" may sound like flaky reasons to pick one college over another, yet when formulating college lists, future applicants absolutely should be mindful of their fit at a given school. The key is to properly size up the vibe/feel/atmosphere through more than merely a brief and heavily sanitized campus tour.

Some traits of a given school are easy to spot, and the contrast between institutions can be stark. For example, attending a small liberal arts school is going to be a wholly different social experience than attending a flagship state university with ten times the enrollment. However, there are many small liberal arts schools with high percentages of student-athletes where Greek life dominates the social scene. While this section is certainly our most anecdotal, we use statistics to dig beyond mere generalizations wherever possible.

For instance, if—like at Wake Forest University—85% of the student body participates in National Collegiate Athletic Association (NCAA), club, or intramural sports, and you hate sports, that information may help you cross the school off your list. If you are dead set on joining a fraternity or sorority, Bucknell University's 40-50% rate of participation in Greek life will be more attractive than the single-digit pledge rate at Wesleyan University. If volunteer work is important to you, you may wish to target a school filled with kindred spirits, such as the College of William & Mary, where thousands perform community service every year. If a cappella is an essential creative outlet for you, a school such as Amherst, where one can barely count the number of established singing groups on two hands, may be appealing.

Undoubtedly, any personality type can find at least a few like-minded souls at any of the 3,000 four-year colleges in the United States, but it's important that teens find schools where they can develop a true sense of belonging. Research has consistently demonstrated that college students who feel connected to their school experience far greater academic success than those who do not.

Career Services

In an effort to entice applicants, college brochures are usually filled with group shots of smiling students on picturesque quads, amenities such as Olympic-size pools and rock climbing walls, and dining halls that look like five-star restaurants. Those images are usually accompanied by some hollow catchphrase such as "Where leaders are born." Yet you likely won't find much (if any) information about the career services offerings — one of the most overlooked but important offices within a university. In reality, the professionals who provide individual career counseling, arrange internships, engage in corporate recruiting, and plan job fairs will do far more for your future than that towering rock climbing wall.

We answer the questions that students should ask when they evaluate their prospective colleges: What is the student-to-counselor ratio? What percent of students engage with career services? Does this happen in freshman year or does counseling only get utilized by seniors? We'll provide information on job fairs, networking events, corporate recruiting on campus, and how helpful staff are with arranging internships. In utilizing this section, you will discover which schools actually give rise to tomorrow's leaders vs. those whose public relations departments merely thought up an empty marketing slogan. And, yes, on occasion we will briefly note rock climbing walls or exceptionally delicious cuisine because, well, those things are nice to know as long as they aren't one of the top reasons you pick School A over School B.

Professional Outcomes

We'll look at how recent graduating classes are faring six months after graduation. In examining the list of companies that hire the most alumni, you'll see which schools serve as a pipeline to many of the nation's premier employers. Geographic information will allow you to see where the largest pockets of alumni settle — a factor that may assist your networking efforts. You'll also be able to identify which undergraduate institutions send large numbers of students to elite graduate and professional schools. Universities that have notable success preparing their students for admission into law and medical schools are highlighted.

Admissions

As wonderful as many high school guidance counselors are, even the best are pulled in a million different directions over the course of the day. To quantify that phenomenon, counselors in public high schools report spending only 22% of their time on college-related counseling while their private school counterparts spend a far healthier 55%. In either setting, given their breadth of responsibilities, even knowledgeable counselors may not be able to keep track of the latest admissions-related news at every one of the top postsecondary institutions in the country.

Given the aforementioned escalation in selectivity over the last few years, schools that may have been considered *safety schools* when you were a freshman may now be closer to *reach schools*. A multitude of applicants to the University of California's branch campuses discovered that reality the hard way just a few short years ago. It's important to consider the way a given school is trending from a selectivity standpoint, which is why we include our unique "five-year admissions trend" metric that shows the degree to which the school has become more/less competitive in recent years. Further analysis of that number will reveal whether the decreasing acceptance rate is simply the result of an influx of borderline applicants or whether the profile of the average accepted student is actually shifting. We also will identify whether an admissions edge can be gained by applying early, the impact of legacy status, and the factors each admissions office values most.

Worth Your Money?

The worth of a college degree is almost always context-dependent. Plenty of students attend unspectacular universities and go on to incredible levels of success; conversely, plenty of young people have attended prestigious institutions and struggled in their careers. A school that may be an incredible value for an in-state electrical engineering major may be a terrible choice for out-of-state students concentrating in sociology.

The intent of this section is to (a) give you an overview of how generous (or stingy) particular schools are with financial aid; (b) inform you about cost of attendance, in-state vs. out-of-state tuition rates, and the amount of debt students graduate with; and (c) give an assessment of the circumstances in which one might want to be wary of paying the full sticker price for a given school. Think of this as an introductory counseling session that will get you thinking about whether a school's cost makes sense for *you*.

Data Tables

In addition to the data-heavy narrative section, each profile is accompanied by two tables brimming with useful and often underappreciated statistical information.

But first, a quick note on missing data points

Missing data points fall into one of three different categories: Not Applicable, Not Offered, or Not Reported.

Not Applicable or NA – Used when the data point in question is not applicable to this specific institution. For example, the admission rate for men at a women's-only college will be listed as "Not Applicable."

Not Offered – Used when an institution does not offer the admission plan or activity listed. For example, if an institution does not offer an Early Action application plan, "Not Offered" is indicated.

Not Reported or NR – Used when the institution does not make the data point available to the public.

Now, let's get to the data! The following data points are included for each of the 200 institutions listed in this guide:

Admissions Data

Admission Rate
The overall percentage of the total application pool that is offered admission.

Admission Rate - Men
The overall percentage of male applicants that are offered admission.

Admission Rate - Women
The overall percentage of female applicants who are offered admission.

Early Action Admission Rate
The percentage of applicants admitted during the early action (EA) or single-choice early action (SCEA) rounds.

Early Decsion Admission Rate
The percentage of applicants admitted during the early decision (ED) round.

Early Decision Admits as a Percentage of Total Admits
The percentage of total admits who come by way of early decision (ED).

Admission Rate (five-year trend)
This is the percentage change in the acceptance rate from five years ago. For example, if a school's acceptance rate was 32% in 2017 and 27% in 2022, the five-year trend would be -5%.

Percent of Admits Attending (yield rate)
A school's yield rate is the percentage of accepted students who ultimately elect to enroll in the freshman class divided by the number of accepted applicants. For example, if 5,000 students were accepted and 1,000 chose to enroll, the yield rate would be 20%.

Transfer Admission Rate
The overall percentage of the total transfer applicant pool that is offered admission.

SAT Reading/Writing (middle 50%)
The 25th-and 75th-percentile reading/writing SAT scores for first-year students.

SAT Math (middle 50%)
The 25th-and 75th-percentile SAT math scores for first-year students.

ACT Composite (middle 50%)
The 25th-and 75th-percentile composite ACT scores for first-year students.

Percent in Top 10%, 25%, and 50% of High School Class
Among enrolled freshmen who reported their class ranks, the percentage who finished in the top tenth, quarter, and half of their graduating classes.

Demonstrated Interest
Whether an applicant's demonstrated interest is considered in the admissions process.

Legacy Status
Whether an applicant's familial ties to the institution is considered in the admissions process.

Racial/Ethnic Status
Whether an applicant's race/ethnic background is considered in the admissions process.

Interview
Whether a college offers an alumni, on-campus or virtual admissions interview.

Enrollment Data

Total Undergraduate Enrollment
The number of undergraduate students attending the institution.

Percent Full-Time
The percentage of undergraduates classified as full-time students during the academic year.

Percent Male/Female
The percentage of males and percent of females that comprise the undergraduate student body.

Percent Out-of-State
The percentage of domestic (U.S.) students who are not residents of the state in which the college is located.

Percent Fraternity/Sorority
The percentage of undergraduates who are members of Greek organizations.

Percent on Campus (All Undergraduates)
The percentage of all undergraduates living on campus in the most recent school year.

Freshman Housing Required
Whether or not the institution requires that freshmen live on campus.

Ethnic/Racial Demographics
The percentage of undergraduate students who identify as African American, Asian, Hispanic, and white.
A separate category is also provided for "other."

Percent International
The percentage of foreign students enrolled at an American university who are studying through a temporary visa.

Percent Low-Income
The percentage of students who meet the US Department of Education standard for "low income" (for a family of four, that figure is $41,625 per year). Students meeting this criteria are Pell Grant-eligible.

Academics

Studendent-to-Faculty Ratio
The number of undergraduate students divided by the number of full-time faculty members.

Percent of Classes under Twenty Students
The number of undergraduate course sections with an enrollment under 20 divided by the number of undergraduate course sections.

Percent of Classes between Twenty and Forty-Nine Students
The number of undergraduate course sections with an enrollment between 20 and 49 divided by the number of undergraduate course sections.

Percent of Classes with Fifty Students or More
The number of undergraduate course sections with an enrollment of 50 or more divided by the number of undergraduate course sections.

Percent of Full-Time Faculty
The percentage of faculty members who are full-time professors at a given institution.

Percent of Full-Time Faculty with Terminal Degree
The percentage of full-time professors who possess the highest possible degree in their field (typically PhD).

Top Programs
This is not purely a list of the most popular majors by volume. While that is factored into our algorithm, so are other metrics including selectivity, student-to-faculty ratio, class size, peer assessment, graduate earnings (by major), and PhD productivity. (More details are included later in this section.)

Retention Rate
The percentage of freshmen who return to the same institution the following fall to begin their sophomore year.

Four-Year Graduation Rate
The percentage of enrolled undergraduate students who graduate in four years or fewer.

Six-Year Graduation Rate
The percentage of enrolled undergraduate students who graduate in six years or fewer.

Curricular Flexibility

Many colleges have a "core curriculum" and "distributional requirements" that dictate what specific courses and/or general categories of courses all undergraduates must complete in order to graduate. We awarded schools one of three grades: Very Flexible, Somewhat Flexible, or Less Flexible, depending on the extent and specificity of their curricular mandates.

Academic Rating

To construct an academic rating for each college, we rely on ten different indicators of academic quality, namely the average SAT/ACT composite of incoming students, the percentage of incoming students ranked in the top 10% of their high school class, student-to-faculty ratio, class size, the percentage of faculty who are full-time employees, the percentage of faculty with terminal degrees, mean faculty salary, freshman retention rate, six year-graduation rate, and graduation performance. This last variable compares an institution's actual graduation rate with its predicted graduation rate, after controlling for SAT/ACT scores of incoming students as well as the percentage of undergraduates receiving a Pell Grant (a grant primarily given to low-income students). Both variables are very strong predictors of graduate outcomes.

After collecting data, we normalize and subsequently sum values across all ten indicators, assigning each institution a total score, and by extension, its academic rating. Academic ratings range from one to five stars (institutions receiving a rating of lower than three stars are not featured in this book), with a rating of five stars assigned to colleges and universities receiving the highest total scores. We opted to use a discrete variable (a "star" rating) instead of each college's total numerical score because incorporating the latter would presume that our assessment is precise. It is not. An institution's academic environment and offerings can never be captured by a single number. That said, we do believe the ratings assigned can prove useful when comparing the academic climates and offerings of the colleges featured in this book.

Financial

Institutional Type
Indicates whether the school is a public or private institution.

In-State Tuition
For public schools, the annual cost of full-time tuition for one academic year charged to state residents. For private schools, we list the general tuition here.

Out-of-State Tuition
For public schools, the annual cost of full-time tuition for one academic year charged to state residents. For private schools, we list the general tuition here.

Room & Board
The annual cost for university-owned housing and meal plans.

Books and Supplies
The average figure students pay for one academic year's worth of books purchased through the university bookstore.

Average Need-Based Grant
Of students who qualified for need-based aid, the average dollar amount the institution awarded.

Average Percentage of Need Met
Of students who qualified for need-based aid, the average percentage of the demonstrated need that the institution met.

Average Merit-Based Award
Among incoming freshmen without financial need who received a merit-based award, the average annual award that was granted.

Percent Receiving Merit-Based Awards – Freshmen without Need
The percentage of incoming freshmen who received some degree of non-need-based aid.

Average Cumulative Debt
Among students who took out loans to pay for a given college, the average cumulative debt owed upon graduation.

Percentage of Students Borrowing
The percentage of students who are taking out loans in order to fund a portion of their educational expenses.

Career

Who Recruits
A list of high-profile companies that regularly recruit on campus.

Notable Internships
Collected from institutional data sources, this is a list of employers who regularly provide meaningful internships to undergraduate students.

Top Industries
According to LinkedIn data, a list of the sectors where the highest number of recent graduates find employment.

Top Employers
According to LinkedIn data, the companies/organizations that employ the largest number of graduates.

Where Alumni Work
According to LinkedIn data, the cities where the largest concentration of alumni currently live.

Earnings
In an effort to give you the most complete picture of alumni earning possible, we include three data points. They are as follows:

College Scorecard (10-YR Post-Entry): earnings of former students who received federal financial aid at 10 years after entering the institution.

PayScale (Early Career): The median salary of individuals with 0-5 years of work experience, based on the responses of 3.5 million survey respondents.

PayScale (Mid-Career): The median salary of individuals with 10+ years of work experience based on millions of survey respondents. This figure tends to be higher than the other two because it includes professionals in mid-to-late career, when earnings are typically highest.

PayScale (20-Year ROI): This value represents the difference between 20-year median pay for a bachelor's graduate and 24-year median pay for a high school graduate minus the total four-year cost of attendance.

Rankings

Money Ranking
Money provides a 5-star ranking system where colleges are rated according to the following formula: quality of education (30%), affordability (40%), and outcomes (30%). The number provided represents the amount of stars received from Money. For example, 4.5 represents four and a half stars.

<u>US News & World Report Ranking</u>
A college's ranking by *US News & World Report (US News)*, which is determined via the following formula: outcomes (35%), faculty resources (20%), expert opinion (20%), financial resources (10%), student excellence (10%), and alumni giving (5%).

<u>Wall Street Journal/Times Higher Education Ranking</u>
A college's ranking by *The Wall Street Journal/Times Higher Education (THE)*, which is determined via the following formula: resources (30%), engagement (20%), outcomes (40%), and environment (10%).

<u>Washington Monthly Ranking</u>
A college's ranking by *Washington Monthly*, which is determined via the following formula: social mobility (33.3%), research (33.3%), and community and national service (33.3%).

Overgeneralizations

Okay, it's time to put down our calculators and loosen up the collars of our 1950s IBM employee-style short-sleeved white dress shirts for just a brief moment. We are calling this category "overgeneralizations" to poke fun at ourselves for including a category that is a bit off-brand for a trio of data nerds. Still, for this new edition of CWYM, we felt it was important to give readers a sense of how the student body is most frequently described by actual undergraduate students.

To bring a bit of validity to this inherently anecdotal endeavor, we scoured multiple student review sites & surveyed counselors and current students ourselves to see which descriptors of the student body appeared most often. That said, we encourage you to take all of these with a grain of salt. After all, every campus is populated by a diverse group of individuals with all types of backgrounds, interests, and beliefs. You can find your social niche anywhere, but ultimately, it can still be valuable to have a sense of the prevailing student body traits.

Overlaps

Five schools with which a particular college shares applicants and important institutional characteristics, such as selectivity, academic quality, location, and majors/programs of strength and emphasis.

Where did this data come from?

Admissions Data

Our primary source for SAT and ACT middle-50% ranges is the Common Data Set (CDS), a collaborative effort of data providers in the higher education community in which most institutions participate. We gathered superscoring policies from institutional websites and, in the many cases where nothing was listed publicly, from direct contact with admissions offices. We also gathered regular and early decision (ED) acceptance rates and waitlist statistics from a combination of the CDS and institutional websites.

Enrollment Data

We took enrollment and demographic data directly from each school's CDS. If the school did not publish a CDS, we collected that information from alternative institutional reports.

Academics Data

We pulled class sizes, student-to-faculty ratios, and graduation/retention rates from the CDS or other available institutional publications.

Top Programs Within Colleges

Our methodology for determining each college's top academic programs incorporated the following four factors:

1. Major Emphasis
Indicates the number of students at an institution studying a specific major. If a high percentage of students at a particular college are studying a major, it is likely that the major attracts a relatively large portion of the institution's resources. To measure major emphasis, we relied on data collected by the National Center for Education Statistics as reported by The Integrated Postsecondary Education Data System (IPEDS).

2. Student-to-Faculty Ratio and Class Size
Research consistently shows that class size as well as student–faculty interaction and collaboration lead to better learning and career-related outcomes. We collected data for these indicators from the US Department of Education, institutional websites, and surveys of college administrators.

3. Peer Assessment
To derive a peer assessment score, we relied on questionnaires distributed to both college admission experts (including school counselors, independent education consultants, and college admission officers) and higher education administrators, and then compared responses with "strong programs" data published by *US News & World Report*, Niche, and other reputable sources that rank colleges within a specific discipline (e.g., *CSRankings.org* for computer science, *The Hollywood Reporter* for film, *Foreign Policy* for international relations, etc.) Alone, peer assessment surveys are subject to a fair amount of bias. However, when evaluated in sum and considered along with more objective data—such as that examining major emphasis and class size—they can provide more complete and corroborative insight into the strength of a particular program/major.

4. PhD Productivity
While most undergraduates have no intent to pursue a doctoral degree, the rate at which a department/program produces Ph.D. recipients arguably reflects how well the program promotes academic rigor and prepares students to tackle advanced coursework. When available, we used data provided by the National Science Foundation in order to assess which programs graduated the highest percentage of students who later completed a PhD degree.

Top Programs Across Colleges ("Top Colleges for America's Top Majors")

When choosing which majors to feature in this section, we considered both professional prospects (i.e., which majors result in high salaries and ample job opportunities) and popularity of discipline (i.e., how many students pursue the major). In order to identify the top colleges for each major, we relied on the same variables used to select the top programs within each college, as well as three additional variables, namely those for institutional selectivity, major share, and graduate earnings (see descriptions of variables below). It is also important to note that for some areas of study (e.g., actuarial science, information systems), we list colleges that do not offer a formal major, but that possess offerings (within a minor or informal concentration) so strong that they warrant inclusion.

1. Institutional Selectivity
Though selectivity is not a perfect proxy for college or major/program quality, it is highly correlated with student ability/achievement and institutional expenditures per student, which both contribute significantly to the undergraduate learning experience. We looked at a college's freshman admission rate and average SAT/ACT score (as reported by each institution's CDS) to measure selectivity.

2. Major Share
If a college enrolls a relatively high percentage of all students in the United States studying a particular major, it is likely that the college has been identified by prospective students, employers, and other stakeholders as a leader in that subject area. Though this assumption may result in bias against smaller institutions or programs, it is important to account for the fact that larger programs often have the ability to attract more tuition revenue, meet fixed costs, and reinvest the major's offerings. To measure major share, we relied on data collected by the National Center for Education Statistics as reported by IPEDS.

3. Graduate Earnings

To measure graduate earnings, we relied on salary data provided by PayScale, both of which indicate early-career and mid-career wages of students by college. We analyzed early-career and mid-career wages because the former is typically an indicator of how employers perceive the quality of a particular major/program, while the latter indicates how well a major/program may have prepared students for work.

In addition, when able, we used data indicating graduate earnings by field of study, as doing so provides a more accurate measure of the relationship between a specific academic program and graduate earnings. For example, PayScale provides salary data for a student attending Boston University and majoring in engineering, which is different from salary data for students attending Boston University and majoring in business.

Financial Data

Financial data is taken directly from each school's CDS. If the school did not publish a CDS, we collected this information from alternative institutional reports.

Career/Salary Data

There are two main sources for information related to the most popular industries and the companies at which alumni have the most representation. LinkedIn is an excellent resource for gathering data on how many alumni of all ages are working for a particular employer. Reports that colleges produce for each recent graduating class—often called "First Destination Surveys"—receive high response rates and offer a glimpse into where the Class of 2021 is headed. If your aim is to work at a relatively new mega-company such as SpaceX, Uber, or Airbnb, it may be more helpful to know where recent graduates have landed. Where possible, we included this data in the narrative sections of the profiles.

No one source of salary data is perfect, so we sought to give you as many data points as possible for each college. As previously mentioned, the salary figures provided in each data table come from PayScale. We also included First Destination Survey data in instances where reliable institutional data could be reported. This sometimes offers a glimpse at the average or median starting salary for a school's recent graduates; certain universities provide a breakdown of starting salary by major.

Rankings

Taken at face value, a school's rank in a given publication can be unhelpful or even misleading to your unique college search. For instance, the fact that the 2023 *US News & World Report* rankings list Emory University as 22nd and Tufts University as 32nd doesn't mean that one school is superior to the other; Emory and Tufts happen to be two of the finest schools in the country, and assigning any value to a fraction of a point in a ranking algorithm would just be plain silly. However, when considered in proper context and across several different rankings systems utilizing different algorithms, one can get a general idea of a school's reputation in the eyes of graduate schools and top employers. Collectively, we believe that these rankings can provide a degree of insight as you ponder your postsecondary future.

Why some colleges made the cut and others did not.

We wish to be fully transparent about an important issue: There is no definitive algorithm that would determine the dollar-for-dollar "best colleges for your money." Sure, you could base your rankings solely on return-on-investment figures and just list the top 200 schools in terms of median salaries. However, doing so would pretty much produce a list of the colleges that produce the greatest percentage of business, computer science, and engineering grads because those fields generally pay the best. You could also concoct a pseudoscientific formula with dozens of inputs that would spew out a concrete score that would serve as a defense as to why one school made the top 200 and others were left out in the cold.

In truth, selecting these schools was as much art as science. In aiming to create a useful college guide, we drew on our collective experience of having guided thousands of students through the application process over the past decade. In seeking quantifiable evidence of value, we also examined every available report on earnings, social mobility, academic rankings, and school-specific outcomes. In the end, we were genuinely surprised by some of the lesser-known schools that stood out by those metrics and were equally surprised by some big-name schools that fared poorer than expected. Ultimately, we are extremely confident that every institution included in this book does admirable work on behalf of its undergraduates.

On the other hand, there are not only 200 schools that are, in our professional opinion, "Worth Your Money." So before alums or representatives from omitted schools start penning nasty emails to us, this book is not being intentionally exclusionary—200 is an arbitrary cutoff because—well—you have to have an arbitrary cutoff. Depending on one's circumstances (again, all higher education value is context-dependent), there may be hundreds more schools that could serve as fine postsecondary destinations from which to springboard into a successful career/life. Our hope is that this book will help give you the tools and mindset to evaluate any prospective institution, whether or not you find that college in the pages that follow.

Final Thoughts

Before you turn to the profiles section of this book, consider the following startling facts:

- Barely half of current college students can provide an accurate estimate of their freshman year cost of attendance.
- Less than 65% of undergraduates nationwide finish their degree within six years.
- For those who do graduate, the average debt load is more than $37,000.
- Studies estimate that over 40% of college grads end up working in jobs that do not require a college degree.
- Over half of college grads ultimately wish they had chosen a different school, degree program, or major.

If picking the right college was easy, the numbers above wouldn't be nearly so bleak. Selecting a school that will put you on the right side of those unfortunate statistics takes a great deal of hard work and planning. Applicants are often so swept up in the quest to gain admission into a given school that they fail to stop and consider exactly why their dream school became their dream in the first place.

A dream college—or to be less hyperbolic, a good-fit college—should check boxes in terms of the availability and quality of academic programs of interest, the extracurricular opportunities and aspects of campus life that will promote a sense of connectedness, the level of career services you will need to get on the path to the right career/graduate school, a demonstrated history of positive outcomes for graduates, and should also be a place where you have a genuine chance of being accepted.

Whether you are a parent or a high school student, rest assured that by carefully examining the profiles that follow, you are about to become a more knowledgeable college consumer than your adult or teenage peers. Ideally, you will enter the pages that follow with an open mind and be willing to consider disconfirming data about a school you previously thought was perfect for you as well as new, unexpected information about a school you would never have considered before. While the college search and admissions process is rife with challenges and stressors, eschewing the cacophony of unhelpful voices in favor of data will result in increased confidence and focus as you make this extremely important life decision.

Enjoy the journey ahead!

Agnes Scott College

Decatur, Georgia | 404-471-6285

ADMISSION
Admission Rate: 67%
Admission Rate - Men: Not Applicable
Admission Rate - Women: 67%
EA Admission Rate: Not Reported
ED Admission Rate: 88%
ED Admits as % of Total Admits: 1%
Admission Rate (5-Year Trend): +1%
% of Admits Attending (Yield): 22%
Transfer Admission Rate: 35%

SAT Reading/Writing (Middle 50%): 590-700
SAT Math (Middle 50%): 540-650
ACT Composite (Middle 50%): 24-31

% Graduated in Top 10% of HS Class: 29%
% Graduated in Top 25% of HS Class: 62%
% Graduated in Top 50% of HS Class: 93%

Demonstrated Interest: Considered
Legacy Status: Considered
Racial/Ethnic Status: Not Considered
Admission Interview Offered: Yes

ENROLLMENT
Total Undergraduate Enrollment: 1,006
% Full-Time: 100%
% Male: Not Applicable
% Female: 100%
% Out-of-State: 38%
% Fraternity: Not Applicable
% Sorority: Not Offered
% On-Campus (All Undergraduate): 79%
Freshman Housing Required: Yes

% African-American: 32%
% Asian: 6%
% Hispanic: 14%
% White: 37%
% Other: 2%
% International: 2%
% Low-Income: 39%

ACADEMICS
Student-to-Faculty Ratio: 11 to 1
% of Classes Under 20: 75%
% of Classes 20-49: 25%
% of Classes 50 or More: 0%
% Full-Time Faculty: 70%
% Full-Time Faculty w/ Terminal Degree: 96%

Top Programs
Business Management
Astrophysics
Creative Writing
Mathematics
Neuroscience
Political Science
Psychology
Public Health

Retention Rate: 83%
4-Year Graduation Rate: 69%
6-Year Graduation Rate: 74%

Curricular Flexibility: Somewhat Flexible
Academic Rating: ★★★✔

#CollegesWorthYourMoney

The most acclaimed member of the unofficial "Seven Sisters of the South," Agnes Scott College (ASC) is among the most innovative undergraduate teaching-focused schools in the country. With just over 1,000 undergraduate students, ASC is a single-sex, liberal arts college conveniently situated in suburban Atlanta. A loyal and generous alumnae have led to the school accruing an endowment of over 200 million dollars. The college's largesse is directed toward highly impactful targets like the massive amounts of merit aid awarded to every student (more details later) and the Mary Brown Bullock Science Center, which is loaded with state-of-the-art instrumentation that would turn many research universities green with envy.

Inside the Classroom

Agnes Scott has one of the more uniquely tailored sets of general education requirements you'll find. Consisting of 25-45 credits that focus on global learning, leadership development, and intellectual breadth, the school's primary mission is to mold its students into global leaders who are proficient in five leadership-related areas: critical thinking, digital literacy, public speaking, teamwork, and writing. In addition, all students need to demonstrate proficiency in a non-English language and may need up to four courses to do so. There are 34 majors to choose from.

The First-Year Experience at ASC is robust and multifaceted as freshmen are assigned a SUMMIT Peer Advisor, enjoy Scotties Week of Welcome, attend a Student Organization Fair, and receive academic advising, all before the calendar turns to September. Therefore, it is unsurprising that over 84% of freshmen return for their sophomore year, an achievement undoubtedly made possible by the highly supportive faculty and administration plus an 11:1 student-to-faculty ratio that results in 75% of courses enrolling 19 or fewer undergrads; the average class size is 18 students. The hands-on opportunities for learning are exceptional with 52% of graduates completing a research mentorship or creative project and 46% studying abroad.

Undergrads spread across the available majors fairly evenly, but for the Class of 2022, the greatest number of degrees conferred were in the social sciences (19%), biology (14%), psychology (13%), health professions (9%), English (8%), and business (8%). The college's math and science departments have a terrific reputation, as does the major in creative writing. On the national fellowship front, three students were named a Fulbright Scholar in 2023, and it is not uncommon for ASC to have two or three winners in a typical year. ASC also produces a fair number of Marshall Scholars.

Outside the Classroom

Approximately two-thirds of undergrads are from Georgia, but 87% percent of freshmen and 79% of all students live on campus. Located northeast of Atlanta, Decatur is a town of roughly 25,000 that features a solid array of historical landmarks, museums, eateries/breweries, and arts/theater venues. There are no sororities permitted at Agnes Scott, but many students participate in the 60+ student-run organizations that include The Profile, a student newspaper; The Aurora, a literary magazine; Model UN; the community orchestra; and nine religious organizations. Over 80% of students participate in community service. ASC is one of the most environmentally sustainable campuses in the country, boasting a campus arboretum, renewable energy installations, and a history of reducing its carbon footprint year after year. The school also boasts one of the more beautiful campuses around and receives strong reviews on the condition of its dorms and the quality cuisines available at the Evans Dining Hall. Sports-minded students may compete on one of six NCAA Division III teams or utilize the open-access, Olympic-sized swimming pool, six tennis courts, or 24-hour fitness and cardio center.

Career Services

The Office of Internship & Career Development has eight professional employees who work as career coaches, internship coordinators, and employer relations experts. That works out to a 125:1 student-to-advisor ratio, in the superior range when compared to other schools featured in our guide. The office masterfully uses this favorable ratio to reach every student with its highly personalized guidance. All undergraduates are "invited to join at least one of the following career communities led by four career coaches," and "each community convenes for skill-building workshops, career panels, and recruitment events." The five areas of focus are (1) Health and Science; (2) Business & Technology; (3) Nonprofit, Arts, Social Impact & Sustainability; (4) Digital and Visual Communications, Education; (5) Government, Policy, Pre-Law, and International Affairs.

The office facilitated 2,538 student interactions in a single recent academic year, including 700+ 1:1 sessions. Seventy percent of graduates complete at least one internship and one-third complete two or more. Over $100,000 is available annually to support students in unpaid internships and research endeavors. Alumnae are also more than happy to lend a hand, to the point that 80% of graduates say a former student played a role in helping them achieve their postgraduate goals. Opportunities to attend career panels and shadow an alumna are ample. Even as a small school, Agnes Scott hosts its own annual Internship & Job Fair as well as a Graduate School Fair.

Professional Outcomes

Based on the most recent outcomes data available, 87% of job-seekers quickly found their first employment opportunity. Exiting seniors were hired by Amazon, AT&T, the Georgia Bureau of Investigation, Deloitte, and E&J Gallo Winery. With only a couple hundred graduates per year, Agnes Scott does not send massive numbers of students to any one company, but it does have more than ten alums working at the Centers for Disease Control, Emory Healthcare, Children's Healthcare of Atlanta, and Wells Fargo. Many graduates stay in the Greater Atlanta Area, but sizable numbers head to Washington, DC; New York City; Chicago; and San Francisco.

Of the 17% of the Class of 2022 who applied to graduate and professional school, 100% of applicants obtained at least one acceptance. Over the past five years, that figure has never dipped below 90%. Notable acceptances included Columbia University, Emory University, Northeastern University, Tufts University, and the University of Michigan. With a significant number of premeds, ASC churns out loads of biology majors and also offers a post-baccalaureate program for medical school hopefuls that leads to a 75% acceptance rate. Surveys of Agnes Scott alumnae reveal that they feel their school prepared them for the working world, graduate school, and social, civic, and social engagement far better than the average American college graduate.

Admission

This is not a college that will intimidate you with its admissions numbers. Of the 1,879 applicants to the Class of 2026, a healthy 1,250 were accepted for a 67% acceptance rate. The applicant pool does tend to be self-selecting and mostly consists of accomplished young women. To that point, the average GPA of enrolled 2022-23 freshmen was 3.76. Twenty-nine percent placed in the top decile of their high school graduating class with 62% in the top quartile and 93% in the top half. On the standardized test front, the middle-50% range was 1140-1340 on the SAT and 24-31 on the ACT.

Agnes Scott values rigor of secondary school coursework and GPA above all others. Rated as "important" are standardized test scores, essays, recommendations, extracurricular activities, and talent/ability. The college has been test-optional for more than a decade but still values test scores when submitted—33% of applicants to the Class of 2026 included an SAT result and 22% included an ACT score. Few students apply early decision to this school, but those who do are almost universally successful—14 of the 16 ED applicants last cycle were accepted. In sum, ASC is relatively easy to gain acceptance into with solid high school grades, particularly when considering the immense quality of the educational experience at stake.

Worth Your Money?

Tuition at Agnes Scott was $47,820 for the 2023-24 academic year; the official total cost of attendance was $61,775. Fortunately, 99% of undergrads pay far less than that thanks to the Agnes Scott guarantee that all admitted students will receive a renewable, merit-based scholarship of at least $20k; many students receive even more with the average annual aid package reaching $41k. With that level of generosity being the norm and the uniquely personal nature of the undergraduate program, Agnes Scott is worth your money no matter who you are or what academic/professional area you intend to pursue

FINANCIAL
Institutional Type: Private
In-State Tuition: $48,150
Out-of-State Tuition: $48,150
Room & Board: $13,375
Books & Supplies: $1,000

Avg. Need-Based Grant: $34,202
Avg. % of Need Met: 85%

Avg. Merit-Based Award: $31,849
% Receiving (Freshmen w/o Need): 27%

Avg. Cumulative Debt: $35,702
% of Students Borrowing: 63%

CAREER
Who Recruits
1. EY
2. Federal Reserve Bank of Atlanta
3. National Wildlife Federation
4. Red Ventures
5. UPS

Notable Internships
1. Prudential
2. BMG Records
3. Morgan Stanley

Top Employers
1. Centers for Disease Control
2. Emory University
3. Children's Healthcare of Atlanta
4. AT&T
5. Georgia Tech

Where Alumni Work
1. Atlanta
2. New York City
3. Washington, DC
4. Netherlands
5. Chicago

Earnings
College Scorecard (10-YR Post-Entry): $49,314
PayScale (Early Career): $50,400
PayScale (Mid-Career): $88,700
PayScale 20-Year ROI: $135,000

RANKINGS
Money: 4
U.S. News: 63, Liberal Arts Colleges
Wall Street Journal/THE: Not Ranked
Washington Monthly: 50, Liberal Arts Colleges

OVERGENERALIZATIONS
Students are:
Ethnically diverse
Less likely to party
Economically diverse
Collaborative
Passionate about social justice

COLLEGE OVERLAPS
Barnard College
Emory University
Scripps College
Smith College
Wellesley College

American University

Washington, District of Columbia | 202-885-6000

Located in the heart of our nation's capital, American University's highly desirable location and access to an abundance of government/corporate internships and networking opportunities have contributed to the university becoming far more selective than it was a decade ago. AU presently plays host to 7,917 undergraduate students as well as over 5,900 graduate and law students. There are 60+ undergraduate degrees for students to choose from at AU across six colleges: the College of Arts & Sciences, the Kogod School of Business, the School of Communication, the School of Education, the School of International Service, and the School of Public Affairs.

Inside the Classroom

All undergrads are exposed to a recently adopted core curriculum that focuses on enhancing students' metacognitive abilities. Requirements include more than thirty credits of study in courses such as Complex Problems, Quantitative Literacy, Ethical Reasoning, Creative-Aesthetic Inquiry, and Written Communication. As the school itself explains, the "AU Core general education program offers a four-year, inquiry-based liberal arts education, beginning with a Complex Problems seminar (small, 19-person seminars that include co-curricular experiences), bridging to essential habits of mind and integrating these skills and habits with the student's major, and culminating in a capstone." The American University Experience Program is designed to provide first-years with the advising and experiences that help students adjust to the academic rigors and social challenges that arise with the transition to college.

A low 12:1 student-to-faculty ratio allows 58% of offered courses to be capped at nineteen students; the average undergraduate class size is 23. Undergraduate research opportunities are taken advantage of by 50% of first-year students and 40% of seniors. For the last 15 years, AU has hosted an Undergraduate Research Symposium at the end of each year where students can present their research. Students here are not afraid to hop on a plane and pursue a semester's worth of education in a foreign land. A substantial 52% of undergrads take a semester abroad, with the most popular destination points being the United Kingdom, Italy, Spain, Kenya, and Belgium.

American's School of International Service (SIS) is one of the top-ranked programs in the country—its Public Affairs program also receives universally high marks. In terms of sheer popularity, the most commonly conferred degrees are in the social sciences (35%), business (17%), and journalism (11%). Graduates fare quite well in securing service-oriented awards and scholarships. Among medium-sized universities, AU is the number two producer of Peace Corps volunteers in the country. It also boasts the most Boren Scholars, awarded to students who wish to study language for the purpose of national security. AU saw 11 alumni capture Fulbright Scholarships in a single recent year.

Outside the Classroom

This 90-acre campus receives accolades as one of the most beautiful urban campuses in the country. Off campus, Northwest DC is a happening place, containing a number of other large schools (Georgetown, GW, Howard, and Catholic) and Capital One Arena, home to the Wizards, Capitals, and countless concerts. All of the dining, cultural, and museum experiences the District of Columbia offers can be accessed car-free via the Metro. For a flat fee, students receive a University Pass entitling them to unlimited Metro rides. The undergraduate population is more than 60% female, which certainly influences social life on campus. Fraternities and sororities attract less than 10% of students. The Eagles play Division I sports in the Patriot League (except for wrestling) and boast six men's teams and eight women's teams. Another 25 club teams provide opportunities for athletic participation. For the less athletically inclined, 150 student organizations are available including student government, political clubs, charitable groups, and those dedicated purely to recreational pursuits. Facilities for student use include three gymnasiums, an aquatic center featuring two eight-lane pools, a two-mile fitness trail, and a beautiful outdoor athletic complex with basketball and tennis courts.

Career Services

The AU Career Center is staffed by 24 full-time professional employees who serve as career counselors, employer relations specialists, merit awards program coordinators, and alumni career coordinators. That works out to a phenomenal student-to-advisor ratio of 330:1, better than the average midsize institution included in this book. It's no wonder that 99% of surveyed undergraduates are happy with the school's career advising services.

AU does an exceptional job hooking up students with internship opportunities; 89% of grads had such an experience. Being located in DC is a boon to internship opportunities, as the leading host agencies include the Departments of Education, State, and Homeland Security, DC Public Schools, and the Public Defender Service for the District of Columbia. The Employer-in-Residence program brings organizations including Deloitte, the CIA, CNN, and Google on campus for one-on-one networking opportunities with undergrads. Student-Alumni Networking Receptions in areas such as human security, public health, education, and energy, the environment, and sustainability allow current students to network with alumni working in their area of interest. In one recent academic year, 500+ employers recruited at AU, over 230 hiring organizations attended career fairs, and over 500 on-campus interviews were conducted. Among the employers that recruited on campus in that same time were the CIA, Politico, Booz Allen Hamilton, the Washington Nationals, the US Department of Defense, EY, Bloomberg, and Yelp

Professional Outcomes

Within six months of graduation, 90% of AU grads have found employment, are enrolled in grad school, or both. There is a 60/40 split on landing jobs in the private sector versus finding employment in the nonprofit/government arena. A healthy percentage of grads are attracted to public service in the form of Teach for America and the Peace Corps as both organizations are among the top five employers of recent grads. Ernst & Young, Deloitte, and the US Army round out the list. Across all graduating years, more than 100 alumni presently work for the US House of Representatives, the US Department of State, Booz Allen Hamilton, Google, EY, IBM, PwC, and Accenture. With a heavy concentration of grads flowing into the public sector, starting salaries are not eye-popping—54% start above $50k, and 83% start above $40k. Many remain in DC but others flock to New York City, Boston, San Francisco, Los Angeles, and Philly in substantial numbers.

Many of the most popular grad school destinations are only a Metro stop away. George Washington, Georgetown, Johns Hopkins, and American itself head the list. Nineteen percent of recent grads went straight into graduate school. Slightly more than 50 graduates apply to medical school each year, but some have had success in recent years gaining acceptance into schools including the Georgetown University School of Medicine, the University of Massachusetts Medical School, and Upstate Medical University. Recent grads pursuing a legal education have done so at the University of Pennsylvania, the University of Miami, Villanova University, and, of course, American's own Washington College of Law.

Admission

American University had a 26% acceptance rate in 2016; it ticked up to a far friendlier 64% for the Class of 2025. The Class of 2026 acceptance rate was in between the high- and low-water marks at 41%. 30% of recent freshmen placed in the top decile of their high school class, 60% were in the top quartile, and 92% were in the top half. The mid-50% GPA range for admitted students was 3.7-4.2. The median test scores for those who went on to enroll were a 31 on the ACT and a 1360 on the SAT.

However, it is important to note that American is test-optional, having been one of the earlier competitive institutions to jettison test scores almost a decade ago. The strongest emphasis is placed on the rigor of one's course load, GPA, and, most interestingly, an applicant's interest. Since AU is a popular backup, the school very much wants to know if it is one of your top choices. This idea is supported by the school's early decision acceptance rate. In the 2021-22 admissions cycle, the school accepted 746 of 868 ED applicants, an overwhelming 86%. American is a quality institution situated in a city that is a highly desirable destination for young people. AU remains accessible to good but not top-of-the-class students who view the school as their number one choice.

Worth Your Money?

Spending big money on tuition to attend American University can be a wise decision, but it really depends on your financial circumstances and academic area of interest. The annual cost of attendance is $76k, but approximately 80% of undergraduates qualify for some form of financial aid totaling almost 100 million dollars per year. Still, over three-fifths of students take out loans to attend, and the mean amount of debt is close to the average college grad in the US. Yet, if you want a school that opens doors to jobs in politics, government, and major consulting firms, AU may be worth the expense.

FINANCIAL
Institutional Type: Private
In-State Tuition: $56,544
Out-of-State Tuition: $56,544
Room & Board: $17,012
Books & Supplies: $1,000

Avg. Need-Based Grant: $29,340
Avg. % of Need Met: 93%

Avg. Merit-Based Award: $13,293
% Receiving (Freshmen w/o Need): 18%

Avg. Cumulative Debt: $31,794
% of Students Borrowing: 53%

CAREER
Who Recruits
1. Central Intelligence Agency
2. Politico
3. Yelp
4. Government Accountability Office
5. AARP

Notable Internships
1. United States Senate
2. Smithsonian
3. American Foreign Service Association

Top Employers
1. U.S. State Department
2. Deloitte
3. Booz Allen Hamilton
4. U.S. House of Representatives
5. IBM

Where Alumni Work
1. Washington, DC
2. New York City
3. Boston
4. Philadelphia
5. San Francisco

Earnings
College Scorecard (10-YR Post-Entry): $75,354
PayScale (Early Career): $59,900
PayScale (Mid-Career): $113,600
PayScale 20-Year ROI: $601,000

RANKINGS
Money: 4
U.S. News: 105, National Universities
Wall Street Journal/THE: 132
Washington Monthly: 118, National Universities

OVERGENERALIZATIONS
Students are:
Dressed to impress
Politically active
Politically liberal
Career-driven
Less likely to party

COLLEGE OVERLAPS
Boston College
Boston University
Georgetown University
George Washington University
Northeastern University

Amherst College

Amherst, Massachusetts | 413-542-2328

ADMISSION
Admission Rate: 7%
Admission Rate - Men: 7%
Admission Rate - Women: 7%
EA Admission Rate: Not Offered
ED Admission Rate: 32%
ED Admits as % of Total Admits: 20%
Admission Rate (5-Year Trend): -6%
% of Admits Attending (Yield): 43%
Transfer Admission Rate: 6%

SAT Reading/Writing (Middle 50%): 700-760
SAT Math (Middle 50%): 720-790
ACT Composite (Middle 50%): 32-35

% Graduated in Top 10% of HS Class: 90%
% Graduated in Top 25% of HS Class: 96%
% Graduated in Top 50% of HS Class: 100%

Demonstrated Interest: Not Considered
Legacy Status: Not Considered
Racial/Ethnic Status: Considered
Admission Interview Offered: No

ENROLLMENT
Total Undergraduate Enrollment: 1,898
% Full-Time: 100%
% Male: 48%
% Female: 52%
% Out-of-State: 85%
% Fraternity: Not Offered
% Sorority: Not Offered
% On-Campus (All Undergraduate): 97%
Freshman Housing Required: Yes

% African-American: 11%
% Asian: 14%
% Hispanic: 16%
% White: 38%
% Other: 2%
% International: 11%
% Low-Income: 22%

ACADEMICS
Student-to-Faculty Ratio: 7 to 1
% of Classes Under 20: 66%
% of Classes 20-49: 31%
% of Classes 50 or More: 3%
% Full-Time Faculty: 81%
% Full-Time Faculty w/ Terminal Degree: 94%

Top Programs
Biochemistry and Biophysics
Economics
English
History
Law, Jurisprudence, and Social Thought
Mathematics
Neuroscience
Statistics

Retention Rate: 95%
4-Year Graduation Rate: 85%
6-Year Graduation Rate: 94%

Curricular Flexibility: Very Flexible
Academic Rating: ★★★★★

#CollegesWorthYourMoney

One of the premier liberal arts colleges in the country—and one of the most selective—Amherst College is an Ivy-equivalent institution that offers its brilliant student body a one-of-a-kind academic experience. A mere 1,898 undergraduates grace this picturesque rural campus located seventy-five miles west of Boston. Yet, a small-town location is not at all indicative of an isolated existence. If the 41 majors and ample course offerings on campus aren't enough, Amherst belongs to the Five College Consortium that allows students to take any course offered at Mount Holyoke, Smith, Hampshire College, or UMass Amherst—collectively, this puts 6,000 courses at your disposal.

Inside the Classroom
Similar to Brown's "Open Curriculum," Amherst operates its "New Curriculum" that requires no specific courses or distribution of credits. Students have the flexibility to pursue their areas of passion and interest from the very start of their collegiate experience. With no burdensome requirements, double majoring is commonplace with over 30-40% of the student body electing to study at least one additional discipline. The college encourages students to "take full responsibility for their intellectual growth, in the same way they will take responsibility for important choices later in life."

If you crave face time with your professors, Amherst delivers. A 7:1 student-to-faculty ratio allows for 66% of courses to have fewer than twenty students and 32% to have single-digit enrollments. That level of intimacy pays off with the forging of student-faculty relationships. By senior year, 98% of seniors report feeling close enough to a faculty member to ask for a letter of recommendation. The eight-to-ten-week Summer Science Undergraduate Research Program is available for students as are plenty of grants aimed at funding original student research projects. A sizable number of students study abroad, 45% to be precise, in just about any country you can name from Namibia to Trinidad. The school's student body has become increasingly diverse in recent years, now boasting double-digit percentages of African American, Latino, and first-generation students.

A true liberal arts college, Amherst possesses strong offerings across the board, most notably in economics, English, history, mathematics, and law (through its one-of-a-kind major in Law, Jurisprudence, and Social Thought). Amherst also boasts one of the most esteemed (and highest-paid) liberal arts faculties in the country. The social sciences account for 22% of degrees conferred, while 14% are in mathematics, 11% in biology, and 7% in computer science. Students are always competitive for postgraduate awards and fellowships. The college has been recognized as one of the top producers of Fulbright Scholars for over a decade; it had seven winners in 2023 to go along with two Watson Fellows in 2022.

Outside the Classroom
Ninety-seven percent of undergraduates reside in school-owned housing. There are no Greek organizations, but a colossal 35-38% of Amherst students are rostered on one of the college's twenty-seven NCAA Division III sports teams, which means that many are dedicating a good portion of their time to athletics. For everyone else, over 200 student organizations are operating on campus. The school's six a cappella groups and four-ensemble Choral Society play a notable enough role to have earned the school the nickname "The Singing College." Membership in the Five College Consortium opens the door to a variety of other clubs and activities within close proximity. However, it is important to note that the other four campuses are not adjoining—UMass and Hampshire are about a ten-minute drive, and Smith and Mount Holyoke take twenty minutes to reach by car. Guest speakers are regularly on campus. Each year, the Amherst Leads organization brings up to twenty-five well-known athletes, business leaders, and writers/journalists to speak on campus. Dorms, food, and other amenities generally receive positive reviews. For students who want to be in touch with nature, a 500-acre wildlife preserve is located on campus, and it can be freely hiked and explored.

Career Services
Unlike at just about every other institution of higher education, the vast majority of the Amherst student body actually takes advantage of the Career Center's offerings. In fact, the Loeb Center for Career Exploration and Planning advises more than 1,400 students and alumni each year for a total of more than 6,000 sessions. That prodigious output comes from the office's 18 full-time staff members who focus on either career advising or employer relations. Loeb's 105:1 student-to-advisor ratio is among the best of any school featured in this guide.

Amherst does a superb job recruiting companies to campus with more than 175 visiting per year and close to 450 interviews taking place on campus, which is roughly the size of the graduating class. Other programs, such as Career Treks, involve organized trips to Boston, New York City, and Los Angeles. Those trips allow students the chance to meet with alumni in the areas of finance, government, entertainment, education, and philanthropy. The Pathways program facilitates hundreds of additional mentoring relationships between alumni and current students each year. Nearly one-quarter of freshmen are enrolled in the Amherst Select Internship Program, which allows first-year students to jump directly into a hands-on learning opportunity.

Professional Outcomes

Whether you are interested in going directly into the workforce or continuing into graduate school, Amherst's reputation and connected alumni network will open doors. Six months after graduation, 93% of the Class of 2022 had already found its way into the world of employment, graduate school, or a volunteer organization. The highest number of recent grads went into financial services (15%), with education (14%), healthcare (12%), and consulting (11%) next in popularity. Recent graduates found jobs everywhere from Bain Capital to the United Talent Agency to the US Department of State. The largest employers of Amherst grads make up a high-end list including Google, Deloitte, Morgan Stanley, and Goldman Sachs. The average starting salary for Amherst graduates is among the highest-paid liberal arts grads in the country. That is even more impressive when you consider that Amherst doesn't even have an engineering program, the profession that usually bolsters starting salary figures.

Amherst grads fare well at gaining acceptance to elite schools. It regularly sees 50% or more of applicants get into law schools like those at Georgetown, Columbia, Harvard, Berkeley, and Stanford, more than twice those schools' overall acceptance rates. In total, the schools where the highest number of Amherst grads can be found pursuing advanced degrees include the University of Cambridge (UK), MIT, Dartmouth, and the University of Pennsylvania. Fifty to sixty Amherst grads apply to medical school each year, and the acceptance rate hovers around 75-80%. As with law schools, students attend many of the finest medical institutions in the world. In order, the greatest number of alumni settle in New York City, Boston, Washington, DC, and San Francisco.

Admission

Amherst accepted under 7% of applicants to the Class of 2026. This cohort had a gaudy mid-50 percent standardized test score range of 1450-1550 on the SAT and 32-35 on the ACT. However, this incredible degree of selectivity is nothing new as Amherst has long been one of the most selective liberal arts schools in the country, so the landscape hasn't changed all that much. The college has had an acceptance rate of under 16% for more than a decade. Unsurprisingly, a high percentage of admitted students finished in the top 10% of their high school class—90% at last count; an impressive 22% of another recent incoming class were valedictorians.

The admissions office lists seven categories as having the highest level of influence on admissions decisions. That list includes talent/ability, character/personal qualities, recommendations, and extracurricular activities. While the process is holistic and genuinely committed to increasing the underrepresented minority and first-generation presence on campus, Amherst remains one of the most selective liberal arts colleges in the United States. If Amherst is your top choice, applying ED can give you a sizable edge; 32% of the 2022-23 ED applicants were accepted. Many of Amherst's varsity athletes are also admitted early; the school claims that fewer than seventy admitted athletes per year are given preferential admissions treatment, a figure that equates to a sizable 15% of the class. Successful applicants will be near (or at) the top of their high school class, have earned standardized test scores in the top 1-2%, and possess unique gifts/intangibles that help separate them from a mass of similarly qualified peers.

Worth Your Money?

The full annual cost of attendance at Amherst is between $85k and $88k, a figure that many wealthy families pay as this school does not offer merit aid awards. However, for those who qualify for financial aid, Amherst meets 100% of their demonstrated need, which works out to an average of $68k per year, making the school quite affordable. Amherst is an Ivy-level school that is worth attending for most as it will legitimately play a role in opening any and all employment or graduate school dreams you could conjure up.

FINANCIAL
Institutional Type: Private
In-State Tuition: $67,280
Out-of-State Tuition: $67,280
Room & Board: $17,560
Books & Supplies: $1,000

Avg. Need-Based Grant: $66,393
Avg. % of Need Met: 100%

Avg. Merit-Based Award: $62,733
% Receiving (Freshmen w/o Need): <1%

Avg. Cumulative Debt: $18,397
% of Students Borrowing: 26%

CAREER
Who Recruits
1. Hulu
2. FiscalNote
3. T. Rowe Price
4. RBC Capital
5. Fox Sports

Notable Internships
1. National Center for Health Research
2. U.S. House of Representatives
3. NY State Division of Human Rights

Top Employers
1. Google
2. Goldman Sachs
3. JP Morgan
4. Massachusetts General Hospital
5. Citi

Where Alumni Work
1. New York City
2. Boston
3. San Francisco
4. Washington, DC
5. Springfield, MA

Earnings
College Scorecard (10-YR Post-Entry): $81,855
PayScale (Early Career): $68,700
PayScale (Mid-Career): $133,400
PayScale 20-Year ROI: $676,000

RANKINGS
Money: 5
U.S. News: 2, Liberal Arts Colleges
Wall Street Journal/THE: 8
Washington Monthly: 7, Liberal Arts Colleges

OVERGENERALIZATIONS
Students are:
Athletic
Self-driven
Preppy
Intense about their academics
Crazy about the Mammoths

COLLEGE OVERLAPS
Brown University
Dartmouth College
Harvard University
Princeton University
Williams College

Arizona State University

Tempe, Arizona | 480-965-7788

ADMISSION
Admission Rate: 90%
Admission Rate - Men: 88%
Admission Rate - Women: 91%
EA Admission Rate: Not Offered
ED Admission Rate: Not Offered
ED Admits as % of Total Admits: Not Offered
Admission Rate (5-Year Trend): +6%
% of Admits Attending (Yield): 25%
Transfer Admission Rate: 89%

SAT Reading/Writing (Middle 50%): 560-670
SAT Math (Middle 50%): 560-700
ACT Composite (Middle 50%): 19-27

% Graduated in Top 10% of HS Class: 27%
% Graduated in Top 25% of HS Class: 56%
% Graduated in Top 50% of HS Class: 85%

Demonstrated Interest: Not Considered
Legacy Status: Not Considered
Racial/Ethnic Status: Not Considered
Admission Interview Offered: No

ENROLLMENT
Total Undergraduate Enrollment: 65,492
% Full-Time: 92%
% Male: 51%
% Female: 49%
% Out-of-State: 29%
% Fraternity: 8%
% Sorority: 10%
% On-Campus (All Undergraduate): 24%
Freshman Housing Required: No

% African-American: 4%
% Asian: 9%
% Hispanic: 26%
% White: 45%
% Other: 3%
% International: 7%
% Low-Income: 30%

ACADEMICS
Student-to-Faculty Ratio: 19 to 1
% of Classes Under 20: 40%
% of Classes 20-49: 44%
% of Classes 50 or More: 17%
% Full-Time Faculty: 73%
% Full-Time Faculty w/ Terminal Degree: 83%

Top Programs
Art
Business
Communication
Computer Science
Criminology and Criminal Justice
Earth and Space Exploration
Engineering
Industrial Design

Retention Rate: 86%
4-Year Graduation Rate: 54%
6-Year Graduation Rate: 66%

Curricular Flexibility: Somewhat Flexible
Academic Rating: ★★★

#CollegesWorthYourMoney

It may be surprising to see one of the largest universities in the country—one that sports an 88% acceptance rate—included in this guidebook. Yet, Arizona State University has flourished across its five desert locations (including the ASU Colleges at Lake Havasu City), enhancing its offerings and academic quality in recent years. Serving over 65,000 undergraduate students, ASU offers a staggering 400 academic majors. The renowned Barrett Honors College enrolls an incredible 7,100 students compared to the average honors college size of 1,200. Barrett attracts a talented bunch, enrolling more National Merit Scholars than several Ivy League schools combined.

Inside the Classroom
All students must complete a minimum of twenty-nine credits in General Studies courses. Courses can be used to meet more than one requirement at a time but, ultimately, boxes must be checked in the areas of literacy and critical inquiry; mathematical studies; humanities, arts and design; social-behavioral sciences; and the natural sciences. Three "awareness areas" also must be satisfied: Cultural Diversity in the United States, Global Awareness, and Historical Awareness.

The faculty-to-student ratio is a fairly high 19:1, but not all classes call for stadium seating. In fact, 40% of course sections seat fewer than twenty students. You'll find classes of over fifty students 17% of the time, not unreasonable for a university of this unmatched size. There are plenty of opportunities for experiential learning as close to half of undergrads engage in research, land an internship, or have a practicum experience as part of their academic program. The school also has above-average study abroad rates, ranking in the top ten in the nation by sending approximately 2,600 students to 250 programs in 65 countries each year.

Business is the concentration in which 22% of total bachelor's degrees are conferred. Engineering (9%), biology (9%), and the health professions (7%) are the next three most popular. The WP Carey School of Business offers many highly ranked programs as does the Fulton Schools of Engineering. In the last decade, the number of Sun Devils winning competitive national fellowships has skyrocketed. ASU produced an outstanding 12 Fulbright Scholars in 2022. It also is becoming a regular producer of Marshall, Gates-Cambridge, Truman, Goldwater, Udall, and Boren Scholarships. Over the past five years, over 100 graduates have been awarded National Science Foundation Graduate Research Fellowships.

Outside the Classroom
Young people don't typically come to ASU to live a hermetic existence. While the university has begun to shed its "party school" label in recent years, it remains a vibrant, extremely connected campus. Athletics are popular with ten NCAA Division I men's teams and fourteen women's teams. Sun Devil football stadium plays host to 71,000 raucous fans on game days. In addition, ASU fields forty club teams, and at least 6,000 additional students take part in competitive intramural sports leagues. Greek life attracts 8% of men and 10% of women, giving it substantial influence on the social scene. There are more than 1,000 clubs operating across the five campuses with the ASU Outdoors Club and the school's seven identity-based student coalitions drawing large memberships. Interestingly, only 24% of the undergraduate student body lives on campus—however, 71% of freshmen do opt for that experience. Due to large numbers of students renting apartments/houses in surrounding neighborhoods, ASU hosts an Off-Campus Housing Fair and provides free advice to undergrads seeking a place to reside. In addition to living in the surrounding communities, Sun Devils like to get involved in volunteer work. Collectively, the student body contributes 1.8 million hours of community service each year. There is plenty to do in the cities of Phoenix, Tempe, Mesa, and Scottsdale, all a short drive from one another.

Career Services
ASU's Career and Professional Development Services (CPDS) has offices in its Tempe, Downtown, Polytechnic, and West locations. When you boast 65,000 undergraduate students across your four metropolitan campuses, things can only be so personalized, but ASU does a solid job making services available on a mass scale. Amazingly, it claims close to 100,000 annual interactions with students through job fairs, workshops, and networking events.

Over 30,000 jobs and internships are posted each year on Handshake, and the school has been selected as a top choice for recruiting talent by more than one hundred companies including Marriott International, Microsoft, General Mills, Charles Schwab, Geico, Ford, FedEx, and Yelp. For such a behemoth of an institution, ASU has a fairly impressive level of internship participation.

Fifty to sixty percent of undergraduates have at least one internship, and 56% of those are paid opportunities. Having an alumni base of over half a million Sun Devils is great for networking. It is an active and proud bunch that presently has over 125,000 members who donate annually to the university. Thanks to this strong alumni base, a wealth of employer partnerships, and a strong internship participation rate, the CPDS succeeds in helping the great majority of its graduates swiftly arrive at their next destination soon after receiving diplomas.

Professional Outcomes

A healthy 83% percent of ASU graduates looking for work are employed within six months of earning their degrees. As you would expect from a large school offering 400 majors, the most prolific employers of Sun Devils represent a broad array of corporations and nonprofit entities. Among the school's top fifty employers are Amazon, Apple, Intel, The Vanguard Group, Walt Disney Company, a number of local school districts, and Arizona-based government organizations. In total, the five industries most frequently entered by alumni are healthcare, K-12 education, higher education, internet/software, and government. Arizona also ranks eighth in the nation among large universities for graduates entering the Peace Corps. The median salary for an ASU grad is roughly $55,000; for engineering students that rises to $69k. The majority (62%) of newly minted grads were working in Arizona with California (10%) next in popularity.

Approximately one-fifth of recent grads enrolled in graduate school. Similar to employment, the size and scope of the university lead to many graduate pathways. Many grads continue at ASU itself, but some continue at various prestigious institutions. For example, Yale Law School typically claims at least one ASU alum in its 1L class. From 2010-14, ASU sent 375 graduates to medical school; today, close to 450 apply each year. The school's Mayo Medical Scholars program exclusively offered to Barrett Honors College students can open doors for future doctors. While the majority of ASU grads continuing their education do not enter prestigious graduate or professional programs, getting strong grades at ASU absolutely puts them in a position to be strong applicants at any university in the country, including the elites.

Admission

While ASU's reputation for academics has been climbing in recent years, the school is still only slightly selective, accepting 88% of those who apply. Considering that friendly acceptance rate, the academic profile of the typical Sun Devil may surprise you. The average GPA is over a 3.5 and 27% percent of Class of 2026 freshmen ranked in the top 10% of their high school class while 56% were in the top quartile, and 85% were in the top half. The average SAT score for enrolled freshmen is now over 1200; only a decade ago, the 75th percentile SAT score was 1210, meaning that despite the high acceptance rate, ASU is attracting a more academically superior crop than in the past. Among the students presently enrolled in the superb Barrett Honors College, the average SAT score is around 1350 and the average unweighted GPA is a 3.81.

As you might expect at one of the nation's largest universities, admissions officers will not be agonizing over every detail of your application, carefully weighing the merits of your essay, recommendations, and extracurricular resume. In fact, none of those factors are even considered at ASU. Grades and class rank are considered "most important," and the rigor of your secondary school record is "important." State residency is "considered." Getting into Arizona State is a straightforward proposition; those who bring a solid transcript and test scores to the table will be invited to join this thriving institution. Admission into the Honors College requires another level of achievement.

Worth Your Money?

Competitively priced for both in-state and out-of-state students, it's no wonder students from around the globe flock to Arizona State. Those from the Grand Canyon State pay around $31,000 per year cost of attendance while nonresidents cough up $52,000, not that much more than the in-state rate for many public schools on the East Coast. Further, ASU awards merit aid to a substantial number of undergraduates; the average amount for freshmen is $10k, and the average need-based grant is $14k. Thanks to those extremely reasonable prices (we don't utter that phrase often without major qualifiers), this university produces graduates who carry a below-average debt load relative to their peers. Whether you're a local majoring in American Indian Studies or an out-of-stater learning cybersecurity, your tuition dollar goes far at ASU.

FINANCIAL
Institutional Type: Public
In-State Tuition: $12,051
Out-of-State Tuition: $32,193
Room & Board: $16,091
Books & Supplies: $1,320

Avg. Need-Based Grant: $12,781
Avg. % of Need Met: 61%

Avg. Merit-Based Award: $9,550
% Receiving (Freshmen w/o Need): 30%

Avg. Cumulative Debt: $23,515
% of Students Borrowing: 41%

CAREER
Who Recruits
1. Amazon
2. Aetna
3. ExxonMobil
4. Ticketmaster
5. General Motors

Notable Internships
1. Intel
2. Geico
3. Phoenix Suns

Top Employers
1. Intel
2. Wells Fargo
3. Amazon
4. American Express
5. Apple

Where Alumni Work
1. Phoenix
2. Los Angeles
3. San Francisco
4. New York City
5. Seattle

Earnings
College Scorecard (10-YR Post-Entry): $58,967
PayScale (Early Career): $58,900
PayScale (Mid-Career): $106,600
PayScale 20-Year ROI: $515,000

RANKINGS
Money: 4
U.S. News: 105, National Universities
Wall Street Journal/THE: 72
Washington Monthly: 33, National Universities

OVERGENERALIZATIONS
Students are:
Ready to party
Diverse
Crazy about the Sun Devils
Independent
Social

COLLEGE OVERLAPS
Michigan State University
San Diego State University
University of Arizona
University of California, Santa Barbara
University of Oregon

Auburn University

Auburn, Alabama | 334-844-6425

ADMISSION
Admission Rate: 44%
Admission Rate - Men: 45%
Admission Rate - Women: 43%
EA Admission Rate: Not Reported
ED Admission Rate: Not Offered
ED Admits as % of Total Admits: Not Offered
Admission Rate (5-Year Trend): -40%
% of Admits Attending (Yield): 27%
Transfer Admission Rate: 46%

SAT Reading/Writing (Middle 50%): 620-690
SAT Math (Middle 50%): 620-700
ACT Composite (Middle 50%): 25-31

% Graduated in Top 10% of HS Class: 40%
% Graduated in Top 25% of HS Class: 71%
% Graduated in Top 50% of HS Class: 94%

Demonstrated Interest: Not Considered
Legacy Status: Not Considered
Racial/Ethnic Status: Not Considered
Admission Interview Offered: No

ENROLLMENT
Total Undergraduate Enrollment: 25,379
% Full-Time: 91%
% Male: 50%
% Female: 50%
% Out-of-State: 40%
% Fraternity: 27%
% Sorority: 44%
% On-Campus (All Undergraduate): 17%
Freshman Housing Required: No

% African-American: 4%
% Asian: 3%
% Hispanic: 4%
% White: 83%
% Other: 0%
% International: 3%
% Low-Income: 12%

ACADEMICS
Student-to-Faculty Ratio: 20 to 1
% of Classes Under 20: 35%
% of Classes 20-49: 49%
% of Classes 50 or More: 16%
% Full-Time Faculty: 85%
% Full-Time Faculty w/ Terminal Degree: 87%

Top Programs
Animal Science
Business
Engineering
Industrial Design
Interior Design
Kinesiology
Supply Chain Management

Retention Rate: 92%
4-Year Graduation Rate: 56%
6-Year Graduation Rate: 80%

Curricular Flexibility: Somewhat Flexible
Academic Rating: ★★★

#CollegesWorthYourMoney

In east central Alabama, the town of Auburn is home to Auburn University, Alabama's top-ranked public institution. With just under 25,000 undergraduates and over 6,000 graduate students, Auburn is the second-largest college in the state, with about 60% of its student body hailing from the Heart of Dixie. While it has undergone four different name changes since 1856, Auburn's commitment to its land-grant traditions—defined as the mission to improve the lives of others through "forward-thinking education, life-enhancing research and scholarship, and selfless service"—remains steadfast. An institution on the rise, this Southern gem is well-regarded for its strong academic programs and innovative offerings.

Inside the Classroom

All undergraduates must complete Auburn's core curriculum, the purpose of which is to "foster the knowledge, skills, and perspectives that are the hallmarks of an Auburn graduate." This extensive undertaking includes English composition, humanities (including mandatory literature and fine arts), science (including lab), mathematics, and social sciences. The exact classes required will depend on one's major, but in total, the core curriculum accounts for about 30% of the credits required to graduate.

The faculty-student ratio is 20:1, but only about 35% of classes enroll fewer than 20 students. The majority—50%—offer a mid-sized learning environment of 20-50 students. The university encourages undergraduate research; the Undergraduate Research Fellowship Program can be undertaken for a single semester or an entire year and provides a stipend to accepted students. There is also a yearly undergraduate research symposium. About 20% of Auburn students study abroad, and over 130 programs are offered on every continent.

Overall, undergraduates can choose from over 150 majors across 12 colleges, which include highly regarded business and engineering programs. In 2022, the greatest number of degrees conferred were in business (24%) followed by engineering (18%), biological/life sciences (10%), and health professions (6%). The "forward-thinking education" part of Auburn's mission is evident in majors like Professional Flight and Geospatial and Environmental Informatics as well as the School of Hospitality Management, which offers one of the country's only four-year Culinary Science degrees. Majors in architecture, apparel merchandising & design, and interior design receive high marks, as does nursing; over 99% of students pass the NCLEX on their first try. Service-learning is built into many curriculums. While postgraduate fellowships are not a major focus, several recent students have won Fulbright, Udall, Truman, and Goldwater Scholarships. There are five Rhodes Scholars in the school's history.

Outside the Classroom

"The Auburn Family" is a real thing; Auburn consistently ranks highly on "happiest campus" lists. In addition to over 500 student organizations, Greek life has a powerful presence, with approximately 40% of undergraduates joining a sorority and 20% joining a fraternity. School pride is off the charts, from the ubiquitous "War Eagle" greeting to the tradition of "rolling" (i.e., toilet papering) Toomer's Corner after big wins. Auburn fields nineteen varsity teams in 13 sports, including top-ranked teams in swimming and diving, golf, and of course, football—the Auburn Tigers regularly fill Jordan-Hare Stadium's 88,000 seats and play in the annual Iron Bowl against notorious rival the Alabama Crimson Tide. Not a DI athlete? There's a robust club and intramural sports program along with a 240,000-square-foot Recreation and Wellness Center, complete with an indoor track, two rock climbing walls, and a leisure pool. Although 60% of freshmen live on campus, approximately 80% of undergraduates ultimately migrate off-campus; Auburn is integral to the surrounding community's identity and vice versa. Residents are fervent Auburn supporters and students frequent the local downtown area, including Toomer's Drugs, a circa-1800s landmark beloved for its fresh lemonade.

Career Services

While the main Career Discovery and Success office consists of 17 professionals, six colleges have their own designated career services departments, bringing the total number of advisors to a friendlier 46 and resulting in a student-advisor ratio of 717:1 (including graduate students). Although this number is below average, career services runs an outstanding number of events. In one recent two-month span, the main office held a grad school expo, multiple informational panels and breakfasts with local companies and alumni, part-time job and summer experience fairs, career fair prep and resume review workshops, and an on-campus interview event, among others. College-specific career services also held their own slate of specialized events.

In addition to drop-in and appointment-based career guidance, professional skill development, internship resources, and personality tests, career services runs the popular Career Closet, a collection of borrowable business-casual attire for job fairs and interviews. Undecided students can take advantage of Auburn's unique Exploratory Major, where they work closely with academic advisors and career services professionals to determine a major while staying on track to graduate. Nearly 500 students participate in Auburn's paid co-op program. Networking opportunities are limitless as the 240,000 living Tiger alumni are actively involved with their alma mater; there are over 120 Auburn alumni groups across the country.

Professional Outcomes

Within six months of graduating, 58% of the Class of 2022 were employed full-time. 23% had entered graduate programs, 15% were seeking employment or a continuing education program, and 2% had entered military service. However, outcomes varied by college—70% of business and engineering majors were employed full-time while nearly half of College of Science and Math graduates pursued continuing education. Companies that employ the greatest number of post-2019 Auburn grads are Auburn University, Lockheed Martin, and the US Army. Significant numbers also went on to work at UAB Hospital, J.B. Hunt, Brasfield & Gorrie, Amazon, and Deloitte. 43% of those working full-time elected to stay in Alabama; the next most popular destinations were Georgia, Texas, Kentucky, and Florida. In 2022, the average starting salary was $58,708; engineering graduates enjoyed the highest average starting salary ($71,656) while education majors pulled in the lowest ($42,362).

Of the students continuing their education, 59% were pursuing master's degrees, 28% professional degrees, and 4% doctorates. The health professions were the most common continuing education destination (23%), followed by business, management, and marketing (17%), and engineering (11%). Of students who reported outcomes, 43% enrolled in one of Auburn's graduate programs—whether working full-time or continuing your education, it's a popular choice to stay at or near Auburn. At least ten recent grads can be found at each of Vanderbilt, Emory, Columbia, Georgia Tech, NYU, and Johns Hopkins. Recent Auburn graduates have been accepted to law school at an 83% rate and enjoyed medical school acceptance rates of 70-75%, 30 points higher than the national average.

Admission

For the past decade, the admissions rate hovered quite comfortably between 70-80%. However, the number of applications for the Class of 2026 absolutely skyrocketed, with over 45,000 applications being submitted and an all-time low acceptance rate of about 44%. (For reference, in 2021, the school received less than 30,000 applications.) In 2021, the mid-50th percentile test scores were a 1310 on the SAT and a 27 on the ACT. The average GPA was 4.07. It's safe to say that Auburn's admitted student profile has grown much more competitive—ten years ago, the average GPA was 3.74 and the mid-50th percentile SAT was around 1100.

Auburn has four early action deadlines, any of which are smart choices as Auburn may have reached capacity for the freshman class by the regular decision deadline. Factors most important to the admissions committee include academic GPA and standardized test scores, both ranked as "very important." Auburn is "test-preferred"—in 2022, only 9% were admitted under the test-optional pathway. Course rigor is "important" and state residency is "considered," with in-state students gaining acceptance at nearly twice the rate of out-of-state students. Otherwise, all other factors are "not considered," including application essays, recommendations, extracurricular activities, and demonstrated interest. Acceptance to Auburn, while more difficult now than it has ever been, remains a fairly straightforward endeavor—strong grades and test scores as well as a rigorous course load are your best ticket.

Worth Your Money?

Last year, 33% of undergraduates were determined to have financial need, and 48% of need was met with an average scholarship/grant award of $9,189. However, even without aid and regardless of major, Auburn is an excellent deal for in-state students—the total sticker price cost of attendance is just over $35k per year. Out-of-stater? That number climbs to about $56k. Auburn's student debt load is slightly under the national average, so it may be well worth the investment if you're entering a profession with a higher starting salary, such as business or engineering. Otherwise, you'll want to carefully weigh your prospective major's general outcomes alongside your aid package and offers from other institutions.

FINANCIAL
Institutional Type: Public
In-State Tuition: $12,536
Out-of-State Tuition: $33,944
Room & Board: $15,396
Books & Supplies: $1,200

Avg. Need-Based Grant: $9,728
Avg. % of Need Met: 58%

Avg. Merit-Based Award: $7,739
% Receiving (Freshmen w/o Need): 25%

Avg. Cumulative Debt: $31,893
% of Students Borrowing: 38%

CAREER
Who Recruits
1. Lockheed Martin
2. Amazon
3. Deloitte
4. J.B. Hunt
5. UAB Hospital

Notable Internships
1. Haworth Inc.
2. Hormel Foods
3. Smithsonian

Top Employers
1. Regions Bank
2. Delta Airlines
3. The Home Depot
4. Amazon
5. Deloitte

Where Alumni Work
1. Atlanta
2. Birmingham, AL
3. Nashville
4. Dallas
5. Charlotte

Earnings
College Scorecard (10-YR Post-Entry): $61,042
PayScale (Early Career): $59,100
PayScale (Mid-Career): $111,000
PayScale 20-Year ROI: $522,000

RANKINGS
Money: 4
U.S. News: 93, National Universities
Wall Street Journal/THE: 174
Washington Monthly: 257, National Universities

OVERGENERALIZATIONS
Students are:
Politically conservative
Crazy about the Tigers
More likely to rush a fraternity/sorority
Religious
Career-Driven

COLLEGE OVERLAPS
University of Alabama
University of Georgia
Clemson University
University of Florida
University of Tennessee

Babson College

Babson Park, Massachusetts | 781-239-5522

With an unmatched entrepreneurial ethos, tiny but powerful Babson College in Wellesley, Massachusetts only has one offering on the menu–a BS in business administration–but it is expertly prepared. Instead of offering a smorgasbord of majors, Babson students pick from 24 areas of concentration including business analytics, global business management, and statistical modeling that offer more curricular flexibility than a traditional major. Babson was an all-male college until 1969, but it has completely transformed as women now comprise 42% of the school's 2,700+ undergraduate population. Of equal interest is the college's status as one of the best schools for international students; over one-quarter of the population hails from outside the United States.

Inside the Classroom
The Babson experience kicks off with a one-credit first-year seminar designed to help you "better understand your identity, your classmates' identities, and what it takes for all of you to be successful students in the diverse Babson community." While you'll unavoidably spend a good portion of your time swimming in business-related curriculum, roughly half of the courses you will take will be in the liberal arts, on engaging subjects such as Art and Ecology; Imagining Nature, Imagining Ourselves; Sports and Literature; Literature and Philosophy of Madness; Constructing and Performing the Self; and Global Pop. One of the many unique experiences at Babson is Foundations of Management and Entrepreneurship, a freshman requirement. Teams of students are loaned up to $9,000 in start-up money to launch and run an actual business. They concurrently take part in the Coaching for Teamwork and Leadership Program, working with staff and alumni coaches to enhance personal development, problem-solving skills, and ethical decision-making.

This school's exceptionally interactive and hands-on approach to undergraduate education is evident from the moment students step foot on campus. While a fair number of courses are large—87% seat between 20 and 49 students—the nature of the instruction is highly interactive with professors and with peers. It is simply not possible to be an anonymous student at Babson. Around one-half of the undergraduate population spends time studying abroad in one of the college's 100+ programs spread across 40+ countries. While Babson is more about doing than spending time in the ivory tower, students are encouraged to assist with faculty-led research or propose an independent research study of their own (for credit).

It's little surprise that a business school like Babson has done an excellent job of branding. It is regularly ranked at the top of any list of best colleges for entrepreneurship and business. Babson also ends up toward the top of any list that looks at return on investment, as its graduates fare well on the job market. This institution usually produces one or two Fulbright Scholars per year, but the vast majority of graduates are champing at the bit to enter the workforce.

Outside the Classroom
Babson's classrooms are filled with entrepreneurial spirits, and that obsession doesn't disappear when students leave the academic setting. Of the one hundred or so clubs and activities at the college, a large number have the words "investment," "business," or "banking" somewhere in their titles. The school does run 23 varsity sports teams, but it does not offer athletic-based scholarships, so while its men's soccer and basketball teams have captured NCAA Division III titles in recent years, sports hardly dominate life at Babson. Seventeen percent of men and 24% of women partake in Greek life, and the number of sorority and fraternity members has grown in recent years. Over three-quarters of undergraduates live in one of the 18 on-campus residence halls, and some socialize in the surrounding suburb of Wellesley, but with Boston a short T ride away, jaunts into the city are commonplace. The demographic makeup of the student body continues to grow more and more diverse as 27% of the Class of 2026 is international–coming from 43 countries–and almost half of US students are nonwhite.

Career Services
The Hoffman Family Undergraduate Center for Career Development (CCD) at Babson is dedicated solely to the college's undergraduates; a separate career services office exists for MBA students. With 10 full-time, professional staff members, Babson operates with a 276:1 student-to-advisor ratio, far better than the average school featured in this guide. The career center facilitates a number of corporate sponsorships with major companies including PepsiCo, Boston Scientific, EY, and PwC. Events sponsored by the office occur frequently, at least once per week, and are well attended by the student body. These include regular Industry Spotlights where corporate guests present to and network with students as well as Career Expos.

A global alumni network of more than 43,000 graduates spread across 115 countries and all 50 US states as well as the Babson Connector, an online resource, help connect current students with alumni. As a result of this type of engagement, a staggering 87% of the Class of 2022 embarked on at least one internship during their four years of study. Further, thanks to the diligent, hands-on work of this career services office, less than 2% of graduates are still looking for employment/grad school within six months of graduating. Considering its well-staffed office and excellent track record for helping graduates find internships and high-paying employment options, Babson's career services is worthy of a great deal of praise.

Professional Outcomes

Babson students are a group of young people with exceptional drive and direction. Within six months of graduation, 98.7% of the Class of 2022 were already employed or in graduate school. The largest numbers flock to finance, technology, accounting, and consulting, with the highest concentration of recent graduates ending up at EY, PwC, Dell, and Wayfair. Many alumni also work at Fidelity Investment, IBM, Deloitte, Google, Amazon, Siemens, and Accenture. Keeping with the entrepreneurial philosophy of the college, 4% of recent Babson grads started their own businesses soon after graduation. Starting salaries averaged $71,385 for the Class of 2022. The highest average salaries await those entering the oil, financial services, and accounting industries while the lowest average salaries go to those in the sports/entertainment, staffing, and media/publishing fields. Even though only one-quarter of domestic undergrads hail from Massachusetts, many put down roots nearby after graduation, and over 12,500 alumni are clustered in the Boston area.

While many pursue MBAs down the road, only 10-15% enter a grad program right out of undergrad. Babson students typically enter excellent institutions once they do decide to pursue a graduate or professional track. Recent grads have entered law school at the likes of Harvard, Tulane, Boston University, UVA, and UC San Diego. Alumni going the MBA route have attended top programs, including those at the London Business School, Yale, Columbia, Boston College, USC, and Northwestern.

Admission

Babson is a school whose national and international reputation is on the rise, and with that has come shrinking acceptance rates. As recently as six years ago, 40% of applicants were accepted. For students entering in the 2022-23 academic year, that number was only 22%. Women fared better than men, gaining acceptance 29% of the time versus 18% for their male counterparts. The caliber of students admitted has risen with the school's selectivity. For those offered a place in the Class of 2026, the mid-50% SAT range was 1370-1480 and 30-33 on the ACT. Five years back, a 30 on the ACT would have placed you in the 75th percentile of attending students.

Successful Babson applicants do not have to have perfect grades, but they need to have performed in the B+/A-range within a rigorous high school program. Interviews are not required but are evaluative in nature and would be a good idea for any applicant with borderline statistics. The process is genuinely holistic as admissions staff want to see evidence of leadership and extracurricular involvement during your high school career. Those committing to Babson via early decision were admitted at a 39% clip, making ED a wise choice, particularly for those on the admissions bubble. In general, Babson is undoubtedly getting more selective year by year, but students with excellent grades, strong standardized test scores, and a burning passion for business should still fare well in the application process.

Worth Your Money?

With business being the dominant area of focus in the classroom, the $80,242 annual cost of attendance is not as terrifying as it might otherwise be. The school also offers students the chance to apply for various merit scholarships ranging from the Weissman Scholarship, which covers full tuition, to a Dean's Scholarship worth $5,000 per year. If you're committed to a career in business, Babson is worth your money thanks to its distinctive brand of education, industry connections, and solid starting salaries that would allow students to comfortably pay back some level of student loans.

FINANCIAL
Institutional Type: Private
In-State Tuition: $56,032
Out-of-State Tuition: $56,032
Room & Board: $20,786
Books & Supplies: $1,292

Avg. Need-Based Grant: $46,062
Avg. % of Need Met: 100%

Avg. Merit-Based Award: $23,148
% Receiving (Freshmen w/o Need): 5%

Avg. Cumulative Debt: $39,255
% of Students Borrowing: 37%

CAREER
Who Recruits
1. Boston Scientific
2. AXA Advisors
3. RxAdvance
4. Applause
5. PepsiCo

Notable Internships
1. Mid-Market Securities
2. CoreAxis Consulting
3. PepsiCo

Top Employers
1. Fidelity Investments
2. PwC
3. EY
4. Dell
5. IBM

Where Alumni Work
1. Boston
2. New York City
3. Sao Paulo, Brazil
4. San Francisco
5. United Kingdom

Earnings
College Scorecard (10-YR Post-Entry): $111,604
PayScale (Early Career): $77,800
PayScale (Mid-Career): $155,400
PayScale 20-Year ROI: $1,094,000

RANKINGS
Money: 4.5
U.S. News: Not Ranked
Wall Street Journal/THE: 10
Washington Monthly: Not Ranked

OVERGENERALIZATIONS
Students are:
Wealthy
Preppy
Competitive
Career-Driven
Ambitious

COLLEGE OVERLAPS
Bentley University
Bryant University
Boston College
Boston University
Northeastern University

Bard College

Annandale-On-Hudson, New York | 845-758-7472

Something of a Star Wars bar in the collegiate landscape (meant purely as a compliment), Bard College is the remote meeting spot for an incredibly diverse set of young people, many of whom may have felt out of place anywhere outside this small-town New York school. Each fall, 1,800+ undergraduates descend on the shores of the Hudson River where Bard College's picture-perfect campus is situated to join kindred spirits who are about as intellectual, artistic, and individualistic as it gets. Ethnic and socioeconomic heterogeneity is also present at Bard, and the diverse Class of 2026 included 17% international students and 19% Pell Grant recipients.

Inside the Classroom

Bard's academic experience is both open-ended and interdisciplinary while simultaneously setting high standards for completing a traditional liberal arts education. First-year students have numerous requirements, including an intensive three-week course called The Language and Thinking Program that freshmen complete in August. From there, all first-years enter a two-semester seminar course centered on a thematic topic that enhances critical thinking skills through ample discussion-based and written assignments. During the winter break, freshmen return for a two-week course called Citizen Science where the ability to pursue answers to a given question through scientific inquiry is developed.

Class sizes at Bard are wonderfully small. A student-to-faculty ratio of 9:1 allows the school to offer close to 90% of classes with an enrollment of fewer than 20 students. Upper-level classes are particularly intimate, and the Senior Project that begins in the junior year involves working closely with a panel of three faculty members. There are 35 areas of academic concentration across six divisions: The Arts; Languages and Literature; Science, Mathematics, and Computing; Social Studies; Interdivisional Programs and Concentrations; and the Bard Conservatory of Music. The majority of undergraduates elect to study abroad for a semester.

All academic programs at Bard are rigorous and respected in intellectual circles, but none towers above the rest. Once primarily an enclave of artists, the school now sees its fair share of biology, economics, and computer science majors. Competitive scholarships are within reach for qualified Bard students. Seven students were awarded Fulbright Scholarships in 2023. Bard also boasts a fairly long list of Watson Scholarship winners with two seniors capturing the award in 2022.

Outside the Classroom

A vast 1,000+ acre expanse of land on the Hudson that is surrounded by the Catskill Mountains, Bard's campus offers endless natural beauty. Situated 90 miles from New York City, social life is mainly confined to the area around the school—not a bad thing, considering the wealth of activities on the school's grounds. Three-quarters of undergraduates live on campus. There are no fraternities or sororities, but there are more than 150 student clubs to select from, including a number of performing arts groups. The Fisher Center for the Performing Arts, a 63 million dollar, 100,000+ square foot complex, routinely hosts opera, dance, musical, and theatrical shows. Volunteering is popular through the Trustee Leader Scholar Program, which has an output of 750 community service hours per week. Bard may seem like the antithesis of a "jock school," but it fields 19 NCAA Division III teams. For those seeking casual fitness outlets, the Stevenson Athletic Center is replete with amenities such as a six-lane swimming pool, squash courts, and 12,500 square feet of gym space. Other notable campus features include a 125-acre, fully operational farm that produces food served in the dining halls.

Career Services

With six professional staff members serving the 1,852 Bard undergrads, the Career Development Office (CDO) has a 309:1 student-to-advisor ratio, which is within the average range compared to the other schools featured in this guide. Annually, the office hosts over 80 events designed to help students engage in career exploration and the development of professional skills. These include anything from site visits to top NYC-based companies to resume workshops to employer information sessions on campus.

Bard hosts several smaller recruitment events throughout the year and participates in two outside events for students attending selective liberal arts schools—the Fall Recruiting Consortium (FRC) and the New York Recruiting Consortium (NYRC). In terms of individual services, the CDO engages in 900 one-on-one career counseling sessions. As a staple of its career counseling the office relies on two assessments it administers with regularity: the Myers-Briggs Personality Assessment and the Focus 2 Career Planning model. BardWorks is a three-day boot camp designed to help rising seniors ready themselves for the networking process, develop interviewing skills, and advance early-career development that will help launch graduates into the workforce.

Professional Outcomes

Seventy-five percent of 2022 grads found a home in the workforce six months after graduating while 17% directly entered graduate school. Only 8% of this cohort were still seeking employment or grad school at that juncture. With a sizable portion of students majoring in the fine/studio arts, English literature, and the social sciences, popular employers of Bard graduates include many museums, publishing houses, and charitable organizations. As a result, it is unsurprising that salary data for Bard graduates early in their careers lags behind many other highly selective colleges. Employers that have ten or more Bard alumni working for them include Google, Morgan Stanley, JPMorgan Chase, and Amazon.

Within a decade of leaving Bard, approximately one-third of alumni have completed an advanced degree. Graduate schools attended by recent alums include everything from the Ivies to close-by members of the CUNY and SUNY systems. Since 2000, Bard has seen alumni gain acceptance into Yale Law School, Harvard Law, and Columbia Law. Recent students also have pursued advanced degrees at Stanford, Oxford, Julliard, and the London School of Economics. Bard students who have applied to medical schools have enjoyed a 78% acceptance rate and have matriculated to institutions that include Johns Hopkins Medical School, George Washington School of Medicine, and Tufts University School of Medicine. Perhaps even more impressively, Bard grads average an MCAT score in the 96th percentile.

Admission

The epitome of a self-selecting school, Bard sports a relatively high acceptance rate of 60%, but that statistic is not indicative of the academic profile of the average attending student. Although Bard is a test-optional school, according to the most recent data available, the mid-50% SAT range of attending students is roughly 1300-1470, and the ACT range is 28-33. A fair number of admitted applicants boast extremely strong transcripts with one-third earning a place in the top 10% of their high school class. However, only two-thirds placed in the top 25%, meaning that Bard will consider bright students with B averages.

While there is a degree of flexibility with assessments and in-class results, Bard firmly wants to see more than just a smattering of AP and honors courses on an applicant's transcript. In its own words, Bard seeks "ambitious, independent thinkers" and "students who will take full advantage of all that the Bard community has to offer." Uniquely, high school juniors and seniors can elect to apply early via the Bard Entrance Examination, which entails composing four 2,500-word essays. The admissions committee at Bard is open-minded and takes a holistic approach, even by small, liberal arts school standards. Personality and fit are extremely important aspects to both getting into and succeeding at this proudly unorthodox college.

Worth Your Money?

With its focus on the visual and performing arts and humanities, Bard isn't going to stand out on any set of ROI rankings. Rather, the value of a Bard education has more to do with the one-of-a-kind learning community and wealth of personalized connections the school offers its undergraduates. Those who can afford the school are paying for an innovative curriculum and potentially life-changing experience, but that doesn't mean this is a sound choice for everyone. On the positive side, the blow of Bard's $83,000 cost of attendance is softened by an average scholarship of $47k+ offered to the majority of those who enroll. As a result, cumulative debt accrued by Bard alumni rests slightly below the national average.

FINANCIAL
Institutional Type: Private
In-State Tuition: $60,270
Out-of-State Tuition: $60,270
Room & Board: $17,180
Books & Supplies: $1,100

Avg. Need-Based Grant: Not Reported
Avg. % of Need Met: Not Reported

Avg. Merit-Based Award: Not Reported
% Receiving (Freshmen w/o Need): 3%

Avg. Cumulative Debt: $27,714
% of Students Borrowing: 63%

CAREER
Who Recruits
1. Google
2. Morgan Stanley
3. Mount Sanai Health System
4. The Metropolitan Museum of Art
5. U.S. Department of State

Notable Internships
1. CBS
2. Human Rights Watch
3. Council on Foreign Relations

Top Employers
1. NYC Department of Education
2. New York University
3. Amazon
4. Google
5. Morgan Stanley

Where Alumni Work
1. New York City
2. Los Angeles
3. Boston
4. San Francisco
5. Washington, DC

Earnings
College Scorecard (10-YR Post-Entry): $42,825
PayScale (Early Career): $54,900
PayScale (Mid-Career): $94,400
PayScale 20-Year ROI: $327,000

RANKINGS
Money: 3
U.S. News: 72, Liberal Arts Colleges
Wall Street Journal/THE: Not Ranked
Washington Monthly: 81, Liberal Arts Colleges

OVERGENERALIZATIONS
Students are:
Politically liberal
Unique
Free-spirited
Critical
Intellectual

COLLEGE OVERLAPS
New York University
Oberlin College
Reed College
Skidmore College
Vassar College

Barnard College

New York, New York | 212-854-2014

Affiliated with Columbia University, this all-women's college serves 3,442 accomplished young women in the heart of Manhattan's Upper West Side. The institution's cosmopolitan locale is appropriately populated by a diverse student body—47% of current undergrads identify as women of color, and 18% of the Class of 2026 are first-generation college students. Roughly fifty majors are offered, including crossover programs with Columbia such as the 3:2 engineering program or five-year programs that lead to a BA plus a Master of International Affairs or Master of Public Administration. Barnard also has partnerships with The Jewish Theological Seminary and The Juilliard School.

Inside the Classroom

The recently adopted Foundations curriculum has refined an already rigorous educational tradition at the college. Freshmen must tackle a first-year writing course and a first-year seminar that emphasizes persuasive writing/speaking. In subsequent years, students must fulfill six Modes of Thinking courses that focus on local NYC history, global inquiry, social difference, historical perspective, quantitative and empirical knowledge, and technological thinking. Distributional requirements in a foreign language, arts/humanities, social sciences, and the hard sciences also must be fulfilled. Regardless of major, seniors must complete a semester or year-long thesis/project that is publicly presented or displayed.

All of this unfolds in an academic environment in which students will work closely with professors. Barnard has a 10:1 student-faculty ratio, and a sensational 71% of courses are capped at nineteen or fewer students; 18% have fewer than ten. Many get the chance to engage in research alongside a professor as 240+ undergraduates are granted such an opportunity through the Summer Research Institute each year. Many students also take advantage of the more than 100 study abroad programs spread over 65 countries. Over one-third of students elect to take a semester in a foreign country.

Barnard's most popular majors, by number of degrees conferred, include economics, English, political science, history, psychology, neuroscience, and computer science. Offerings in the performing arts program are outstanding and among the best anywhere. With a strong emphasis on global perspective and public service, it makes sense that the school produces a disproportionately high percentage of Fulbright and Truman Scholars. In 2023, fourteen graduates and alumni won Fulbright Scholarships. Additionally, a handful of Barnard grads were named National Science Foundation fellows in recent years.

Outside the Classroom

Outside the classroom is where Barnard's affiliation with Columbia really comes into play. The school doesn't have its own athletic teams, so Barnard students are recruited to play for Columbia's NCAA Division I teams. Barnard has seventy clubs of its own, most of a fairly serious nature (pre-professional and performance-oriented), but the bulk of opportunities for campus engagement come from Columbia's more than 500 student organizations that are open to Barnard students. Parts of dorm life are also a shared experience. For the 74% of students who decide to live on campus, two buildings serve as co-ed dorms where Barnard students are mixed with Columbia students, and meal plans for all dorm residents can be utilized at either school's cafeterias. Of course, being located in the heart of New York City, opportunities for fun and excitement are hardly limited to the Barnard and Columbia campuses. Within a single mile of their dorm rooms, students can enjoy multiple parks, theaters, music venues, diners, and countless other attractions.

Career Services

Barnard has 17 professionals, a number of peer advisors, and a handful of administrative assistants working in the offices of Beyond Barnard, the recently reorganized/renamed career services center. In past years, complaints about the lack of hands-on assistance from the career services office were voiced by the student government and school newspaper. The college responded by beefing up its offerings, and the work being done today is impressive by any quantifiable measure. Beyond Barnard's 202:1 student-to-advisor ratio is superior to most other colleges featured in this guide, and it puts that staffing to good use. From 2018-23, they conducted 22,000 one-on-one appointments; 80% of current students have completed at least one session.

The school hosts career and internship fairs in the fall and spring. Fairs are attended by 1,000 students and approximately 150 employers visit campus, including Brown Brothers Harriman, Uber, and Hearst Magazines. Those sessions also are open to Columbia students, and there is some degree of reciprocity with Barnard students being allowed to attend a good number of Columbia-hosted events. Three-quarters of Barnard grads complete at least one internship during their four years at the school. The New York Network mentoring program saw 140 alumni work in person with current students, and an additional seventy individuals participated in a Virtual Mentoring program. Beyond Barnard helps fund internships by offering summer stipends of $4,500; it funds 300+ internships per year. Students interned at exciting locations including The New York Times, the US House of Representatives, Comedy Central, and Christie's.

Professional Outcomes

Six months after graduation, 91% of 2022 Barnard grads had found employment or were enrolled in a graduate program. The school is known for producing women with a wide array of interests, so it makes sense that grads disperse into many different fields. Financial services was the field of choice for 18% of 2022 grads and healthcare & biotech was second, accounting for 14% of graduates. JP Morgan, Goldman Sachs, Blackrock, Citibank, and Morgan Stanley all appear on the list of the top fifteen employers of Barnard alumni. The journalism, government, and education sectors are next in popularity. Across all fields, companies employing twenty-five or more Barnard alums include the NYC Department of Education, Google, IBM, Accenture, and the Metropolitan Museum of Art. By leaps and bounds, New York City remains home to alumni with small clusters of graduates forming in San Francisco, Boston, Los Angeles, DC, and Philadelphia.

It is rare for a student to call it an academic career after finishing her bachelor's. Within ten years of graduation, over 80% of Barnard alums eventually enroll in graduate school. Those entering graduate school flock in large numbers to Columbia, with 112 heading there over the last three years. The Class of 2022 also sent six students to NYU and four to Harvard. Medical schools where recent grads enrolled include St. Louis University School of Medicine, Icahn School of Medicine, and Jefferson College of Health. During the previous five years, applicants with a minimum 3.5 GPA and 510 MCAT score have been accepted to medical school at an 84% clip.

Admission

The last six years have seen the admission rate at Barnard fall from 24% (2014) to an all-time low of 9% for those entering the Class of 2026. The middle-50% SAT range of attending students is 1430-1530; for the ACT, the range is 32-34. In 2014, the 25th percentile was a far friendlier 1240 SAT/28 ACT. Therefore, it is safe to conclude that Barnard is trending in a more selective direction.

The average weighted high school GPA of a Barnard student is typically over 4.0, and 95% finished in the top 10% of their high school class. That aligns with the school's stated beliefs that rigor of secondary record and GPA are among the admissions committee's strongest considerations. Also making this list are more holistic factors including the essay, recommendations, and character/personal qualities. The early decision acceptance rate is around 30%, so that may be an avenue worth exploring for those dead set on attending this fine institution. As at many selective colleges, gaining acceptance into Barnard is more difficult than ever. Sterling grades, solid test scores, and winning personal attributes are the right combination to receive serious consideration at one of, if not the best women's college in existence.

Worth Your Money?

A sizable portion of Barnard students come from families that fall in the top 5% of income earners in the United States. Those individuals will almost always be asked to pay the full $90,000 cost of attendance as merit aid is nonexistent at this school. Those on the lower end of the income scale see 100% of their demonstrated need paid for by the college through an annual grant of $64k. Thanks to this equitable process, the average debt carried by a Barnard graduate is far less than the average college graduate. In addition to its generous financial aid, Barnard is worth the price for the incredible employment and graduate school networks it will open for you post-graduation.

FINANCIAL
Institutional Type: Private
In-State Tuition: $66,246
Out-of-State Tuition: $66,246
Room & Board: $18,028
Books & Supplies: $1,150

Avg. Need-Based Grant: $57,173
Avg. % of Need Met: 100%

Avg. Merit-Based Award: $0
% Receiving (Freshmen w/o Need): 0%

Avg. Cumulative Debt: $24,784
% of Students Borrowing: 37%

CAREER
Who Recruits
1. Harlem Arts Alliance
2. 826NYC
3. Bank of America
4. Mastercard
5. Hospital for Special Surgery

Notable Internships
1. U.S. Embassy
2. MacMillan Publishers
3. Prudential

Top Employers
1. NYC Department of Education
2. Google
3. JPMorgan Chase
4. Citi
5. IBM

Where Alumni Work
1. New York City
2. San Francisco
3. Boston
4. Los Angeles
5. Washington, DC

Earnings
College Scorecard (10-YR Post-Entry): $74,415
PayScale (Early Career): $64,300
PayScale (Mid-Career): $129,300
PayScale 20-Year ROI: $554,000

RANKINGS
Money: 4.5
U.S. News: 11, Liberal Arts Colleges
Wall Street Journal/THE: 211
Washington Monthly: 61, Liberal Arts Colleges

OVERGENERALIZATIONS
Students are:
Politically liberal
Driven
Politically active
Diverse
Dressed to impress

COLLEGE OVERLAPS
Brown University
Bryn Mawr College
Columbia University
New York University
Wellesley College

Baruch College (CUNY)

New York, New York | 646-312-1400

ADMISSION
Admission Rate: 50%
Admission Rate - Men: 42%
Admission Rate - Women: 56%
EA Admission Rate: Not Offered
ED Admission Rate: Not Offered
ED Admits as % of Total Admits: Not Offered
Admission Rate (5-Year Trend): +21%
% of Admits Attending (Yield): 20%
Transfer Admission Rate: 55%

SAT Reading/Writing (Middle 50%): 457-663
SAT Math (Middle 50%): 505-755
ACT Composite (Middle 50%): Not Reported

% Graduated in Top 10% of HS Class: 70%
% Graduated in Top 25% of HS Class: 94%
% Graduated in Top 50% of HS Class: 99%

Demonstrated Interest: Not Considered
Legacy Status: Not Considered
Racial/Ethnic Status: Not Considered
Admission Interview Offered: Yes

ENROLLMENT
Total Undergraduate Enrollment: 15,896
% Full-Time: 79%
% Male: 50%
% Female: 50%
% Out-of-State: 3%
% Fraternity: Not Offered
% Sorority: Not Offered
% On-Campus (All Undergraduate): 2%
Freshman Housing Required: No

% African-American: 9%
% Asian: 36%
% Hispanic: 27%
% White: 18%
% Other: 3%
% International: 7%
% Low-Income: 38%

ACADEMICS
Student-to-Faculty Ratio: 19 to 1
% of Classes Under 20: 21%
% of Classes 20-49: 62%
% of Classes 50 or More: 17%
% Full-Time Faculty: 45%
% Full-Time Faculty w/ Terminal Degree: 88%

Top Programs
Accounting
Business Administration
Computer Information Systems
Corporate Communication
Finance
Real Estate

Retention Rate: 87%
4-Year Graduation Rate: 51%
6-Year Graduation Rate: 73%

Curricular Flexibility: Less Flexible
Academic Rating: ★★★

#CollegesWorthYourMoney

Locating a certifiable commuter school with a highly selective admissions process and an outstanding academic reputation sounds about as realistic as stumbling upon a unicorn on your way to the grocery store. Amazingly, there may be only one institution in the country that perfectly fits that description. Baruch College, a gem within the CUNY system, shines bright in the eyes of employers, even those New York City juggernauts with a taste for Ivy League grads. Of course, not every commuter school is situated in Midtown Manhattan, a primo location for high-level internships and flourishing corporate connections. Baruch students take full advantage; of the three undergraduate schools within the college, the Zicklin School of Business attracts a mind-boggling three-quarters of the student population.

Inside the Classroom
All students at Baruch have to complete a 45-credit sequence of required courses, but there is some choice within the broad boxes that need to be checked. The nonnegotiable courses are Writing I & Writing II, Speech Communication, Mathematics, and Foreign Language. Students also need to choose classes that fulfill requirements in fine and performing arts, history, literature, philosophy, natural sciences, anthropology/sociology, economics, politics and government, and psychology. Those who are part of the Honors Program complete an honors thesis as a culminating academic experience during their senior year.

With a 19:1 student-to-faculty ratio and more part-time than full-time faculty, one-on-one bonding time with your professors is at a premium. Single-digit classes are a rarity, and only 21% of courses have 19 or fewer enrolled students. That being said, Baruch does offer many courses in the 20- to 49-student range; 62% of sections fall in that span. Tapping into undergraduate research projects is tough at a business-oriented commuter school. Procuring those opportunities requires initiative, but it can be accomplished through connecting with individual faculty members. Those who do make such a connection eventually share their research at the college's Creative Inquiry Day. Studying abroad is an option at any of the CUNY system's 160+ programs in 50+ countries.

Zicklin is not only a great business school for the money, it's a great business school period. Popular majors within this well-respected and well-connected institution include accounting, finance, marketing, and business communication, and, as we will cover later, leading companies in those fields have a strong affection for Baruch graduates. With so many entering the job market postgraduation, prestigious scholarships and fellowships are an afterthought, but the school does produce an occasional Fulbright winner.

Outside the Classroom
Only 2% of undergraduate students live on campus, and no—that is not a typo—it is simply a reality for this school of 15,896 undergrads set on three Manhattan acres. Baruch is not going to provide a typical college campus experience, and for some, that's not a bad thing, but it's just important to go in with the right expectations. The surrounding area is not a college town in any way, shape, or form. As a result, the typical student is there for one purpose—to earn a degree. This "nose to the grindstone" ethos shapes campus life. There are no Greek organizations, although there are thirteen NCAA Division III sports teams that play as the Bearcats. While most time spent on campus is time spent in the classrooms themselves, there are ways to get involved through 130+ clubs and activities. The weekly newspaper, The Ticker, and the student-run radio station, WBMB, have lengthy histories. Most clubs meet at specific times during the early afternoon while people are actually on campus, and most of those meetings are held in the Newman Vertical Campus, a seventeen-floor architectural wonder that was erected twenty years ago for $327 million. (For a CUNY school, Baruch has some very wealthy donors.)

Career Services
The Starr Career Development Center (SCDC) employs 15 professional staff as well as four part-time staff members. Full-timers play roles such as career counselor, internship coordinator, and employer relations director. Including full-time and adjunct career coaches, Baruch sports a half-decent 1,060:1 student-to-advisor ratio, but the service delivery exceeds expectations.

More than 40 companies traveled to Baruch's campus for recruiting purposes in 2022 including KPMG, McKinsey, Accenture, and PwC. In excess of 3,600 students attended those events. Overall, 71% of Baruch students land at least one internship; 66% of that group actually had two or more. Five or more recent graduates interned at each of KPMG, EY, Citi, Deloitte, and JP Morgan. The SCDC provided 4,188 career consultations in 2021-22; for perspective, that is greater than the number of total graduates annually. It also conducted over 1,700 resume reviews, posted 8,000+ jobs online, and facilitated 1,200+ on-campus interviews with employers. The online system, cleverly named Starr Search, is utilized by roughly 80% of the undergraduate student body, and it offers countless opportunities for those aggressive and motivated enough to follow leads.

Professional Outcomes

Within six months of graduation, 96% of the Class of 2022 were already employed or in full-time graduate programs; this was a huge improvement from the 80% mark achieved two years earlier. Given that over three-quarters of graduates possess business-related degrees, most first jobs are in the realms of accounting, finance, real estate, management, and marketing. Baruch is one of the few accessible public institutions that is a direct feeder to many of Wall Street's top banks. In fact, the top employers of 2022 grads were KPMG (22), Morgan Stanley (17), JP Morgan (16 grads), Accenture (12), and Bank of America (11). The average salary for Arts & Sciences grads was $53,000 while Zicklin School of Business grads earned $61,000. Just about everyone graduating from this college remains in New York City, although some alumni head to Miami, DC, San Francisco, or Los Angeles, but only in dribs and drabs.

Graduate studies are not usually the immediate step after receiving one's diploma from Baruch—only 5% of those finishing their bachelor's go right into another degree program. There are few students majoring in the hard sciences at this school, so you don't see a ton on the premed path, but sophomores do have the option of applying for early admission to the Icahn School of Medicine at Mount Sinai through the FlexMed program. Of the alumni who decide to go the law school route, even if they do so years later, many attend local NYC schools like Pace or Brooklyn Law School, but a handful of recent grads have been welcomed to the law schools of the University of Michigan, Tufts, Fordham, and Cornell.

Admission

Baruch admitted 50% of the 25,671 students who applied for admission into the Class of 2026; that is significantly higher than the 23% acceptance rate the college registered a decade prior. Part of the change is that the school's enrollment has grown during that same period, increasing by a few thousand undergraduates even though admissions standards have become more rigid. Today, 70% of entering freshmen are top 10% finishers at their respective high schools; in 2009, only 32% held that distinction. Further, the 75th percentile SAT score from ten years ago is close to the 25th percentile score today.

The Baruch College Admissions Office considers GPA and rigor of curriculum above all else. Recommendation letters and essays sit alone in the next rung of important categories. This is a school that can be forgiving of a bad grade or two. In fact, in one recent incoming class, 51% earned under a 3.5 in high school, and 3% had under a 3.0. It's hard to find a school as exceptional as Baruch that is willing to accept late-bloomers and, in some cases, bright AP/honors kids who earned B's and C's throughout high school.

Worth Your Money?

New Yorkers pay under $7,500 in tuition for a school with an alumni network with deep ties to a number of major Wall Street players. This school is unequivocally worth every cent for Big Apple denizens. Outsiders pay a reasonable $19k per year in tuition—of course, there is the small matter of finding an affordable place to live. Once again, that's about as likely as spotting that unicorn.

FINANCIAL
Institutional Type: Public
In-State Tuition: $7,461
Out-of-State Tuition: $19,131
Room & Board: $21,788
Books & Supplies: $1,500

Avg. Need-Based Grant: $9,629
Avg. % of Need Met: 58%

Avg. Merit-Based Award: $5,934
% Receiving (Freshmen w/o Need): 9%

Avg. Cumulative Debt: $4,836
% of Students Borrowing: 10%

CAREER
Who Recruits
1. BBC Worldwide Americas
2. FDM Group
3. Home Advisor
4. NYS Department of Civil Service
5. Yelp

Notable Internships
1. PwC
2. RBC Capital Markets
3. Atlantic Records

Top Employers
1. JPMorgan Chase
2. Citi
3. NYC Department of Education
4. Morgan Stanley
5. EY

Where Alumni Work
1. New York City
2. Miami
3. Washington, DC
4. Los Angeles
5. San Francisco

Earnings
College Scorecard (10-YR Post-Entry): $71,078
PayScale (Early Career): $62,800
PayScale (Mid-Career): $116,600
PayScale 20-Year ROI: $686,000

RANKINGS
Money: 4.5
U.S. News: 9, Regional Universities North
Wall Street Journal/THE: 47
Washington Monthly: 85, Master's Universities

OVERGENERALIZATIONS
Students are:
Diverse
Less likely to party
Open-minded
Independent

COLLEGE OVERLAPS
Binghamton University (SUNY)
Brooklyn College (CUNY)
Hunter College (CUNY)
Queens College (CUNY)
Stony Brook University (SUNY)

Bates College

Lewiston, Maine | 207-786-6000

The nation's second adopter (1984) of a test-optional admissions policy, Bates College has always prided itself on a commitment to egalitarian education—even back to its official founding in the middle of the Civil War when it proudly admitted students regardless of race, religion, or sex. Today, the school is once again on the cutting edge of higher education, advocating a curriculum that honors the liberal arts tradition but also prepares students for "purposeful work" that is both personally meaningful and societally relevant.

Inside the Classroom
Toward those aims, Bates students are required to complete (a) three "writing-attentive" courses; (b) three courses focused on scientific reasoning, lab experience, and quantitative literacy; and (c) two four-course concentrations revolving around a particular issue or area of inquiry. General education at Bates is intended to ensure "depth of knowledge" and a "comparative appreciation of how the several disciplines function and what they can teach us." Distinctive features include a mandatory first-year seminar, senior thesis requirement, and a Short Term at the end of the academic year that provides students the opportunity to focus exclusively on one course, field project, internship, or study abroad opportunity. For those wishing to save money and/or fast-track their undergraduate education, the college offers a three-year option that allows students to graduate in three years, provided they register for five courses (as opposed to four) each semester and one course during each Short Term.

Thirty-four percent of courses at Bates have a single-digit enrollment, and 63% of classrooms contain nineteen or fewer students, allowing for this process to unfold in an intimate academic atmosphere. Additionally, the student-to-faculty ratio is 10:1, and not a single graduate student is present to vacuum up professorial attention. Students interested in research will find opportunities across all disciplines, many of which culminate with a presentation at the Mount David Summit, an annual campus-wide celebration of undergraduate research and creative works. Bates has one of the highest percentages of study abroad participation of any college in the country, typically sending over 60% of each class to one of 200+ global destinations.

Twenty-eight percent of all degrees earned at Bates are in the social sciences, and psychology (14%), biology (13%), and the physical sciences (7%) are next in popularity. Though strong across many disciplines, Bates boasts exemplary programs in biochemistry, English, political science, and philosophy. The college has produced 70+ Fulbright Scholars in the last five years and is recognized as a top recipient of prestigious academic fellowships, even among highly selective institutions. In 2023 alone, Bates produced 12 Fulbright Scholars.

Outside the Classroom
Outside the classroom, Bates places a particularly strong emphasis on community and civic engagement, facilitating numerous volunteer and civic leadership opportunities, primarily through the Harward Center. More than half of all Bates students participate in community-engaged learning (for academic credit). Aside from community service, Bates offers more than 100 officially recognized student organizations, including a nationally ranked debate team and an active investment club. Athletic opportunities also abound at the Division III varsity level and within the college's extensive intramural program that encompasses club sports ranging from equestrian to rugby. There are no fraternities or sororities at Bates, and 92% of students live in one of the dorms or school-owned Victorian homes that accommodate ten to thirty students each. Lewiston is the state's second-most populous city, yet that isn't saying much in Maine because Lewiston is a post-industrial town with only 38,000 residents. Portland, the state's largest city, can be reached in about forty minutes by car.

Career Services
The Center for Purposeful Work features 11 full-time staff and a student-to-advisor ratio of 163:1, a superior level of support when compared to most other institutions included in this book. Services offered by the center include career/interest assessment, interview preparation, and a guest lecture series. The Center for Purposeful Work hosts an annual graduate and professional school fair (with Bowdoin and Colby), as well as a number of its own networking events throughout the year, one example being a presentation from Google/Pinterest on tech careers for liberal arts majors. Organizations such as The Beacon Group, Analysis Group, Barclays, and the CIA have recruited on campus in recent years. Over 350 interviews are conducted on campus by sixty-five companies in a single academic year.

The Purposeful Work Job Shadow Program affords undergrads the opportunity to job shadow a Bates alum in a field of interest. Roughly 250 Bobcats take advantage of that program each year. The Purposeful Work Internship Program helps fund the living expenses of students interning more than 300 summer hours. Despite Bates' location in Maine, internship opportunities are plentiful, particularly in Boston and smaller cities throughout the New England region. During one recent summer, Bates students worked in over 130 companies and organizations throughout the United States and internationally, including at JP Morgan, the Institute of Infectious Diseases, the Conservation Law Foundation, Amazon, and the Sloan Kettering Cancer Center.

Professional Outcomes

Within six months of graduation, 99% of the Class of 2022 were either employed, enrolled in graduate school, or otherwise meaningfully engaged in a fellowship or internship. The most frequently entered fields were healthcare (17%), education (16%), finance/banking (14%), and technology (7%). Popular employers included Accenture, Fidelity Investments, Google, Wayfair, and Liberty Mutual Insurance whereas common employment destinations of Bates graduates were concentrated primarily in the Northeast, namely Boston, New York, and Portland, Maine. However, sizable numbers of Bates alumni also can be found working in the Washington, DC, and San Francisco areas.

According to the Bates Career Development Center, within ten years of graduation, approximately 13% of Bates graduates are in, or have completed, law school whereas 7% enroll in medical school. Some years, every single law school applicant is accepted into at least one school. Grads in 2022 were accepted into med school at an 84% clip and attended the likes of the Brown University Warren Alpert Medical School, Dartmouth College Geisel School of Medicine, and Tufts University School of Medicine. In addition, Bates is currently among the top producers of graduates who eventually go on to enroll in PhD programs in the social sciences, especially economics and sociology. By mid-career, Bates alumni are most frequently found working in the professional fields of business development, education, and community and social services.

Admission

Of the 8,273 applicants to join Bates College's Class of 2026, just 1,137 were admitted which works out to a 14% acceptance rate, far lower than the 24% admit rate back in 2014 and also lower than the 17% figure for the Class of 2025. The mid-50% standardized test score ranges are approximately 1340-1500 on the SAT and 31-33 on the ACT. Students typically ranked high in their graduating high school class, with 55% in the top 10% and 89% in the top quartile.

Aside from grades, class rank, and course rigor, Bates places significant emphasis on an applicant's essay, letters of recommendation, extracurricular profile, talent/ability, and character/personal qualities. Demonstrated interest also plays a considerable role. Of course, the ultimate declaration of love is the submission of an early decision application. Those who go the binding ED route enjoy an acceptance rate almost three times higher than those who apply in the regular cycle (48% for ED). A massive 61% of the 2022-23 freshman class was admitted via early decision, making it a wise strategic maneuver for anyone serious about attending Bates.

Worth Your Money?

Upper-income families will likely pay the full $81,000+ annual cost of attendance. For the 40% of students who do qualify for need-based financial aid, Bates delivers in a big way. The college meets 100% of the demonstrated need for every qualifying student with grants averaging $53k each year. Not only do Bates grads generally find solid-paying jobs after graduation, but they also have far less debt, on average, than their peers receiving diplomas from other institutions.

FINANCIAL
Institutional Type: Private
In-State Tuition: $63,478
Out-of-State Tuition: $63,478
Room & Board: $17,904
Books & Supplies: $900

Avg. Need-Based Grant: $52,925
Avg. % of Need Met: 100%

Avg. Merit-Based Award: $0
% Receiving (Freshmen w/o Need): 0%

Avg. Cumulative Debt: $28,397
% of Students Borrowing: 26%

CAREER
Who Recruits
1. Chevron
2. Hulu
3. Oppenheimer & Co.
4. athenaHealth
5. Owl Cybersecurity

Notable Internships
1. CNN
2. United States Senate
3. Morgan Stanley

Top Employers
1. Fidelity Investments
2. Massachusetts General Hospital
3. Liberty Mutual Insurance
4. Google
5. Amazon

Where Alumni Work
1. Boston
2. New York City
3. Portland, ME
4. Lewiston, ME
5. Washington, DC

Earnings
College Scorecard (10-YR Post-Entry): $65,860
PayScale (Early Career): $62,800
PayScale (Mid-Career): $136,600
PayScale 20-Year ROI: $709,000

RANKINGS
Money: 4.5
U.S. News: 24, Liberal Arts Colleges
Wall Street Journal/THE: Not Ranked
Washington Monthly: 39, Liberal Arts Colleges

OVERGENERALIZATIONS
Students are:
Collaborative
Outdoorsy
Wealthy
Accepting
Involved/invested in campus life

COLLEGE OVERLAPS
Bowdoin College
Colby College
Dartmouth College
Middlebury College
Tufts University

Baylor University

Waco, Texas | 254-710-3435

ADMISSION

Admission Rate: 46%
Admission Rate - Men: 52%
Admission Rate - Women: 42%
EA Admission Rate: Not Reported
ED Admission Rate: 30%
ED Admits as % of Total Admits: 1%
Admission Rate (5-Year Trend): +7%
% of Admits Attending (Yield): 18%
Transfer Admission Rate: 89%

SAT Reading/Writing (Middle 50%): 620-700
SAT Math (Middle 50%): 610-710
ACT Composite (Middle 50%): 28-33

% Graduated in Top 10% of HS Class: 40%
% Graduated in Top 25% of HS Class: 72%
% Graduated in Top 50% of HS Class: 95%

Demonstrated Interest: Considered
Legacy Status: Considered
Racial/Ethnic Status: Not Considered
Admission Interview Offered: No

ENROLLMENT

Total Undergraduate Enrollment: 15,213
% Full-Time: 98%
% Male: 40%
% Female: 60%
% Out-of-State: 39%
% Fraternity: 20%
% Sorority: 34%
% On-Campus (All Undergraduate): 29%
Freshman Housing Required: Yes

% African-American: 5%
% Asian: 9%
% Hispanic: 16%
% White: 61%
% Other: 1%
% International: 3%
% Low-Income: 13%

ACADEMICS

Student-to-Faculty Ratio: 15 to 1
% of Classes Under 20: 49%
% of Classes 20-49: 42%
% of Classes 50 or More: 9%
% Full-Time Faculty: 73%
% Full-Time Faculty w/ Terminal Degree: 89%

Top Programs
Accounting
Biology
Communication
Design
Entrepreneurship
Exercise Physiology
Finance
Nursing

Retention Rate: 89%
4-Year Graduation Rate: 68%
6-Year Graduation Rate: 80%

Curricular Flexibility: Less Flexible
Academic Rating: ★★★

#CollegesWorthYourMoney

A private Christian university in Waco, Texas, the "mission of Baylor University is to educate men and women for worldwide leadership and service by integrating academic excellence and Christian commitment within a caring community." The oldest continually operating university in the state of Texas has 15,213 undergraduates along with another 5,496 graduate/professional students. In offering 125+ majors and minors, the school captures high marks for everything from undergraduate teaching to hands-on research opportunities, and applicants have taken notice. Baylor is a far more selective school than it was in the first decade of the millennium when four-fifths of applicants got in. Today, only 46% make the cut.

Inside the Classroom

Structured freshman experiences at Baylor have received national attention for their inside-the-classroom offerings, like New Student Experience courses that help give students tools and support to have a successful first year. The core curriculum, revamped five years ago, includes the following required courses: Chapel, Creative Arts Experience, American Literary Cultures, The United States in Global Perspective, The US Constitution, Christian Scriptures, and Christian Heritage. There are also distributional requirements one must fill in the areas of communication and media literacy, contemporary social issues, fine arts, foreign language and culture, and scientific methods, among others. All told, those requirements can account for up to 56 credits toward a Baylor degree, a sizable chunk of one's overall coursework.

Class sizes at Baylor generally range from small to medium, with 48% of sections containing fewer than 20 students and 76% enrolling fewer than 29. This solid level of support enables the school to truly encourage undergraduates to collaborate with professors on research "as early as the first semester of their freshman year." The Undergraduate Research and Scholarly Achievement (URSA) office does a superb job connecting students with a research opportunity in their field of interest. The school also pushes overseas experiences in the form of an internship, academic semester, or mission trip. Baylor offers signature programs in Scotland, the Netherlands, and Ireland.

Far more Bears major in business/marketing (25%) than the second-place finisher, health professions (19%). Other popular academic pursuits are biology (12%) and communication/journalism (7%), both of which are very strong. The Hankamer School of Business is highly respected across the country, particularly for accounting, entrepreneurship, and finance. Baylor, as a whole, does well capturing prestigious scholarships and fellowships. Ten 2023 graduates captured Fulbright Scholarships, and others won Goldwater Scholarships and Truman Scholarships as well.

Outside the Classroom

In a standard academic year, almost every single freshman at Baylor lives on campus, but the same is true of only 29% of the total undergraduate population. There are seven freshmen residence halls that each seek to establish a cohesive community for first-year students. Greek life draws in a large percentage of the student body, with one-fifth of men joining fraternities and one-third of women entering sorority life. Overall, there are 40 national and local Greek organizations and 350 other clubs and activities. The spirit of volunteerism is strong as the undergraduate student body contributes a collective 150,000 hours of community service each year. There are 19 varsity sports teams that compete at the Division I level within the Big 12 Conference. School spirit is strong at this university, even on non-game days. Perhaps this is best exemplified by the fact that there are actually two live bears on campus! Other traditions include a well-attended Family Weekend, weekly Dr. Pepper Hours (the soft drink was invented in Waco), epic Christmas celebrations, and two mandatory trips per week to Chapel, a gathering where spiritual and philosophical issues can be discussed in depth. Waco is not the most celebrated college town, but it is situated 1.5 hours south of Dallas and roughly the same distance from Austin for those seeking big-city adventure on the weekends.

Career Services

The Career Center at Baylor University is staffed by 26 professional staff members who serve in various capacities including, most notably, as career success professionals who advise students within a particular academic discipline. The Career Center's student-to-advisor ratio of 585:1 is within the average range when compared to other colleges selected for inclusion in this guidebook. Simply by looking at a random week's career services programming, one learns a great deal about how hard this office works on behalf of students. For example, in one single day, the office presented a workshop on standing out as a graduate school applicant, a Q&A with professionals in the consulting field, a JPMorgan Chase information session, a Google resume workshop, a seminar on the career of financial advising, and four additional events.

Major companies recruit and interview on Baylor's campus with great frequency and are eager to attend Baylor's two campus-wide career fairs every fall and spring. The office goes to great effort to engage freshmen and sophomores in beginning the process of career exploration early in their academic careers. They encourage students to meet with them every single year in a 1:1 capacity to utilize career discovery tools and seek assistance with lining up internships and alumni connections. The mix of Baylor's personal touch and wide network of employer connections leads to very positive postgraduate results for its undergraduates.

Professional Outcomes

At the 180-day post-graduation point, those who earned their diplomas from Baylor had entered the world of full-time employment at a 50% clip, and 28% had entered a graduate or professional degree program. At this six-month juncture, 6% of graduates were still seeking employment. Large numbers of recent grads were scooped up by many of the most desirable employers in the country including Dell (19), EY (16), and Oracle (16). The average starting salary was $59k. Remaining in Texas after graduation is a popular choice, with Dallas, Houston, Waco, Austin, and San Antonio containing the greatest number of alumni.

Among recent grads, the most commonly attended graduate school was Baylor itself (125), followed by Texas A&M (12), University of North Texas (9), and Texas Tech (8). Substantial numbers also matriculated into elite institutions such as Johns Hopkins (5), NYU (4), and Vanderbilt (4). Baylor produced 429 applicants to medical schools during 2021-22. Twenty members of the last two classes are presently students at the renowned Baylor College of Medicine while others entered the Saint Louis University School of Medicine, the Long School of Medicine, and the UT Southwestern Medical Center. Of the 101 recent grads who entered law school, 11 did so at Baylor while others entered their legal training at the likes of Texas Tech, Washington and Lee, and Tulane.

Admission

The Class of 2024 had a friendlier-than-usual 69% acceptance rate, likely, in large part, due to the onset of the pandemic. By the time they were selecting the Class of 2026, that figure fell back to 46%. Freshmen entering the university in fall 2022 possessed a middle-50% SAT score of 1170-1360 and an ACT range of 25-31. Forty percent of this group finished in the top 10% of their high school class while 72% finished in the top 25%. Fifty-four percent of freshmen resided in the state of Texas. Other states sending a significant number of students to Baylor were California (344), Colorado (111), and Illinois (86).

The admissions committee gives preference to the hard facts of an application, granting "very important" status to the rigor of one's course load, GPA, and standardized test scores. Essays are "important" and factors like class rank, recommendations, extracurricular factors, legacy status, work experience, talent/ability, character/personal qualities, and demonstrated interest are "considered." Borderline candidates who do not have much financial need should strongly consider applying early decision; in 2021-22, the ED acceptance rate was 76%. Strangely, this dipped to 30% in 2022-23. Having a familial connection can also be beneficial as roughly 30% of undergrads have an alum in their family.

Worth Your Money?

The estimated cost of attendance for a student living on campus is $75k with $55k coming in the form of annual tuition. The university does cover 66% of the demonstrated financial need for qualifying students and awards average merit aid packages totaling $18k annually. However, the school does not fare well when it comes to the average debt load that students carry with them after graduation. For the over 50% of students who borrow, the average amount of debt is just shy of $50k, about $20k more than the national average. Like many schools included in our book, Baylor is only "worth your money" if you are taking advantage of one of its premier programs like finance or accounting, and have a clear pathway to a solid starting salary. We would not recommend selecting Baylor if you have a significant level of financial need and are uncertain about your academic/professional pathway.

FINANCIAL
Institutional Type: Private
In-State Tuition: $54,844
Out-of-State Tuition: $54,844
Room & Board: $15,318
Books & Supplies: $1,438

Avg. Need-Based Grant: $27,496
Avg. % of Need Met: 72%

Avg. Merit-Based Award: $17,909
% Receiving (Freshmen w/o Need): 43%

Avg. Cumulative Debt: $46,992
% of Students Borrowing: 48%

CAREER
Who Recruits
1. Goldman Sachs
2. Oracle
3. Bank of America
4. Hershey
5. Allstate

Notable Internships
1. Texas Legislature
2. Methodist Healthcare System
3. MTV

Top Employers
1. US Army
2. Baylor Scott & White Health
3. EY
4. AT&T
5. PwC

Where Alumni Work
1. Dallas
2. Houston
3. Waco
4. Austin
5. San Antonio

Earnings
College Scorecard (10-YR Post-Entry): $62,913
PayScale (Early Career): $59,700
PayScale (Mid-Career): $110,400
PayScale 20-Year ROI: $448,000

RANKINGS
Money: 3.5
U.S. News: 93, National Universities
Wall Street Journal/THE: 331
Washington Monthly: 357, National Universities

OVERGENERALIZATIONS
Students are:
Politically conservative
Religious
Crazy about the Bears
Friendly
Goal-oriented

COLLEGE OVERLAPS
Southern Methodist University
Texas A&M University - College Station
Texas Christian University
Texas Tech University
The University of Texas at Austin

Waltham, Massachusetts | 781-891-2244

ADMISSION
Admission Rate: 58%
Admission Rate - Men: 55%
Admission Rate - Women: 63%
EA Admission Rate: Not Offered
ED Admission Rate: 78%
ED Admits as % of Total Admits: 6%
Admission Rate (5-Year Trend): +14%
% of Admits Attending (Yield): 20%
Transfer Admission Rate: 54%

SAT Reading/Writing (Middle 50%): 618-690
SAT Math (Middle 50%): 640-730
ACT Composite (Middle 50%): 28-32

% Graduated in Top 10% of HS Class: 34%
% Graduated in Top 25% of HS Class: 67%
% Graduated in Top 50% of HS Class: 94%

Demonstrated Interest: Important
Legacy Status: Considered
Racial/Ethnic Status: Considered
Admission Interview Offered: Yes

ENROLLMENT
Total Undergraduate Enrollment: 4,131
% Full-Time: 99%
% Male: 61%
% Female: 39%
% Out-of-State: 47%
% Fraternity: 14%
% Sorority: 26%
% On-Campus (All Undergraduate): 76%
Freshman Housing Required: No

% African-American: 4%
% Asian: 10%
% Hispanic: 11%
% White: 57%
% Other: 1%
% International: 14%
% Low-Income: 15%

ACADEMICS
Student-to-Faculty Ratio: 12 to 1
% of Classes Under 20: 23%
% of Classes 20-49: 77%
% of Classes 50 or More: 0%
% Full-Time Faculty: 54%
% Full-Time Faculty w/ Terminal Degree: 83%

Top Programs
Accounting
Data Analytics
Finance
Management
Managerial Economics
Marketing
Professional Sales

Retention Rate: 92%
4-Year Graduation Rate: 84%
6-Year Graduation Rate: 89%

Curricular Flexibility: Less Flexible
Academic Rating: ★★★★

#CollegesWorthYourMoney

Situated just west of Boston, Bentley University is one of the premier business-focused institutions in the country. Rival Babson College is only ten miles away geographically, but the two schools used to be a much greater distance apart in reputation and prestige. That gap has closed quickly in recent years. The school's 4,131 undergraduate students traversing this attractive 163-acre Waltham, Massachusetts, campus are, somewhat surprisingly, exposed to a top-notch liberal arts education while working toward a BA or BS in a business-related field.

Inside the Classroom
Of the 29 majors and 35+ minors to choose from, a handful are non-business concentrations such as English, philosophy, and history. These students typically supplement their education with a healthy number of business courses. The majority take the opposite path, majoring in business and supplementing their studies with liberal arts courses. Always innovating, the school recently started three cutting-edge majors in data analytics, professional sales, and creative industries. Regardless of one's major, the core curriculum consisting of sixteen mandatory courses must be tackled. That includes a first-year seminar, information technology and computer system concepts, a sequence of two expository writing classes, and courses in math, the hard sciences, government, and history.

Earning a Bentley degree is far from a passive experience. The average undergraduate class is comprised of 26 students, and academics are intense. Roughly 20% of the student body is double majoring, tacking the liberal studies major onto their business concentration. Approximately half of Bentley students elect to study abroad in one of 80 programs spread across 25 countries. Just about everyone lands an internship; the majority of students complete two. Undergraduate research participation has increased in recent years as the school has joined The Council on Undergraduate Research. While not a focal point of the school, it is possible to land a position assisting a faculty member with a research project at some point during your four years on campus.

Bentley is a school on the rise. Having just celebrated its one-hundredth anniversary, it has become a highly-respected name in the corporate world and possesses an international reach. The most popular majors are all within the business domain and include finance, business, management, marketing, accounting, and poetry—just kidding about that last one. Bentley is a one-trick pony, and that's not a bad thing when you examine the outcomes data for recent graduates (more ahead).

Outside the Classroom
A bastion for extroverts, 90% of Bentley undergrads belong to at least one student organization; one-third consider themselves "highly involved." Over 100 clubs and activities are available with a multitude of options in the academic, cultural, religious, arts and media, and recreational realms. Participation in athletics is high. The Falcons compete in eleven men's and ten women's sports in NCAA Division II (men's ice hockey is the lone Division I team). Intramural and club sports are popular, including ultimate Frisbee, sailing, rugby, and equestrian. More than 1,700 students participate in an intramural sport each year. With 76% of students living in school-owned housing, most social events are centered on campus. Fraternity and sorority life attract 14-26% of undergraduates. Additionally, some students live in defined communities—residential housing for those passionate about areas such as women's leadership, social justice, or service-learning. Waltham, also home to Brandeis University, is a historic and pretty New England town with plenty of bars, restaurants, and other attractions. The university is only thirteen miles from downtown Boston, and the school provides free public transportation to and from Harvard Square.

Career Services
The Pulsifer Career Development Center at Bentley has 11 professional staff members who work with the college's undergraduates. That equates to a 376:1 student-to-advisor ratio, placing the university in the average range compared to other schools featured in this guide. Career services may be average in this category, but it is exceptional by just about every other metric. For example, the staff does an incredible job facilitating meaningful internships. An astonishing 97% of Bentley students complete an internship; 74% complete more than one. Further, 98% of Class of 2022 grads stated that they got their job through the Career Development Center. On-campus recruiting events led another 14% of employed graduates to their first employment destination, and a sizable number of students also found their way through alumni networking, school-organized career fairs, and referrals from the school. The school has developed close corporate partnerships with companies including Dell, Fidelity Investments, Liberty Mutual, and United Technologies, all of whom hire their fair share of graduates each year.

Offerings include career development seminars that begin freshman year; 95% of first-years sign up for the introductory class. Those seminars are part of the school's larger Hire Education Program that helps students formulate career goals, hone job-readiness skills, and build professional networks. The Mentor Marketplace is an online tool that helps connect current students with alumni who work in a relevant field to serve as a career resource. In addition to the full internships taken advantage of by the bulk of the student body, Bentley also offers micro-internships in which alumni can bring in undergraduates to work on short-term, impactful projects within their company. Taking into account the breadth and quality of its services as well as the stellar outcomes achieved by its graduates, Bentley has as high quality a Career Development Center as you will find anywhere in the country.

Professional Outcomes

A superb 99% of 2022 Bentley grads were employed or in graduate school six months after receiving their diplomas. The financial services and technology sectors each account for almost one-quarter of new hires. Most job functions are in the areas of finance, sales, accounting, analytics, marketing, consulting, and operations/logistics. A hub of entrepreneurship, the school typically sees 5-10% of its graduating class start their own businesses right out of college. Companies employing the highest number of alumni include Fidelity Investments, PwC, EY, Dell EMC, and Wayfair. The median starting salary for 2022 graduates was $68,000, a strong figure compared to other universities of its ilk. By mid-career, Bentley grads have a median income similar to Harvard and Tufts alumni.

Bentley does not see a high number of graduates directly entering graduate school—roughly 10% in any given year. While many pursue MBAs or other advanced business degrees later in their careers, those in this field typically gain work experience prior to attending graduate school. Recent graduates have ended up in advanced degree programs at elite business schools like Wharton (Penn), Stern (NYU), Columbia Business School, Yale School of Management, Sloane School of Management (MIT), and the Tuck School of Business (Dartmouth). Whether entering graduate school or chasing their first job, the vast majority of Falcons stay in the Boston area.

Admission

In building the Class of 2026, Bentley accepted 58% of the 9,662 who applied; three years ago, it was a much stingier 47% for the Class of 2023. Members of the Class of 2026 earned a median SAT score of 1340 and a median ACT of 29. Looking at class rank, 34% were in the top decile, 67% finished in the top quartile, and 94% placed in the top half. The university views the level of rigor of an applicant's course load to be "very important" in making admissions decisions.

Grades (including an emphasis on senior year grades), test scores, essays, and two letters of recommendation are among the "important" admissions factors. Rigor of secondary school record is labeled as "very important". Class rank and an on-campus interview are "considered" components of the admissions process. While the interviews are not mandatory, they can be an excellent opportunity to highlight interpersonal skills and intangible attributes that a top business school like Bentley is seeking. With a relatively low yield of 20%, Bentley is competing with many other rival institutions for the same pool of students. Thus, it makes sense that the school accepted 78% of those who applied through its binding early decision program last year. Bentley is a competitive business school and is a notch easier to gain admission into than comparable Babson.

Worth Your Money?

More than 70% of attending students receive some type of financial aid. Forty-six percent of undergraduates receive need-based aid averaging $41k which helps to alleviate the pain of the $80,670 per year cost of attendance. Even at that high cost, Bentley is worth the money for most applicants. The school rates very well in terms of pure salary—both starting and mid-career—and it rates well for social mobility, allowing those from poor-to-modest backgrounds to climb the economic ladder.

FINANCIAL
Institutional Type: Private
In-State Tuition: $58,610
Out-of-State Tuition: $58,610
Room & Board: $19,200
Books & Supplies: $1,300

Avg. Need-Based Grant: $39,857
Avg. % of Need Met: 89%

Avg. Merit-Based Award: $19,672
% Receiving (Freshmen w/o Need): 31%

Avg. Cumulative Debt: $34,626
% of Students Borrowing: 51%

CAREER
Who Recruits
1. Cognex Corporation
2. Boston Scientific
3. Grant Thornton LLP
4. P&G Gillette
5. Lincoln Financial Group

Notable Internships
1. Liberty Mutual Investments
2. KPMG
3. L'Oreal

Top Employers
1. Fidelity Investments
2. PwC
3. Liberty Mutual Insurance
4. EY
5. State Street

Where Alumni Work
1. Boston
2. New York City
3. Hartford
4. San Francisco
5. Providence, RI

Earnings
College Scorecard (10-YR Post-Entry): $111,896
PayScale (Early Career): $72,500
PayScale (Mid-Career): $127,900
PayScale 20-Year ROI: $859,000

RANKINGS
Money: 4.5
U.S. News: 1, Regional Universities North
Wall Street Journal/THE: Not Ranked
Washington Monthly: 60, Master's Universities

OVERGENERALIZATIONS
Students are:
Career-driven
Politically conservative
Wealthy
Ambitious
Social

COLLEGE OVERLAPS
Babson College
Boston College
Bryant University
Fordham University
Villanova University

Berea College

Berea, Kentucky | 859-985-3500

ADMISSION

Admission Rate: 25%
Admission Rate - Men: 22%
Admission Rate - Women: 26%
EA Admission Rate: Not Offered
ED Admission Rate: Not Offered
ED Admits as % of Total Admits: Not Offered
Admission Rate (5-Year Trend): -10%
% of Admits Attending (Yield): 65%
Transfer Admission Rate: 45%

SAT Reading/Writing (Middle 50%): 578-673
SAT Math (Middle 50%): 558-625
ACT Composite (Middle 50%): 23-27

% Graduated in Top 10% of HS Class: 31%
% Graduated in Top 25% of HS Class: 70%
% Graduated in Top 50% of HS Class: 96%

Demonstrated Interest: Considered
Legacy Status: Not Considered
Racial/Ethnic Status: Considered
Admission Interview Offered: Yes

ENROLLMENT

Total Undergraduate Enrollment: 1,433
% Full-Time: 100%
% Male: 40%
% Female: 60%
% Out-of-State: 55%
% Fraternity: Not Offered
% Sorority: Not Offered
% On-Campus (All Undergraduate): 96%
Freshman Housing Required: Yes

% African-American: 19%
% Asian: 4%
% Hispanic: 15%
% White: 44%
% Other: 0%
% International: 8%
% Low-Income: 83%

ACADEMICS

Student-to-Faculty Ratio: 8 to 1
% of Classes Under 20: 84%
% of Classes 20-49: 16%
% of Classes 50 or More: 0%
% Full-Time Faculty: 67%
% Full-Time Faculty w/ Terminal Degree: 88%

Top Programs
Agriculture and Natural Resources
Business
Communication
Computer and Information Science
Economics
Education Studies
Peace and Social Justice Studies
Sociology

Retention Rate: 84%
4-Year Graduation Rate: 51%
6-Year Graduation Rate: 66%

Curricular Flexibility: Somewhat Flexible
Academic Rating: ★★★✦

#CollegesWorthYourMoney

It's a sad reality that many moderately selective private colleges lack endowments substantial enough to meet the full financial need of their students, but that's not the case with Berea College in rural Kentucky. In fact, this school won't even accept you if your parents can afford to send you elsewhere; 96% of current students were Pell Grant Recipients. Amazingly, tuition costs are 100% covered. In exchange, the 1,433 undergraduate students must work a set number of hours per week and are held strictly accountable for their academic performance. Only the College of the Ozarks and Deep Springs College are at all comparable institutions.

Inside the Classroom

The Labor Program at Berea has existed, in some form, since 1859, and it continues to be a core feature of the school today. Students work between 10 and 15 hours per week and are evaluated on their performance. Of course, this is all done to help finance the true academic purposes for which students come to the school. On the academic front, a number of courses must be completed regardless of a student's area of concentration. Those include Understandings of Christianity, Scientific Knowledge and Inquiry, Seminar in Contemporary Global Issues, and two writing seminars. Students must also dip their toes into the Six Perspective Areas: Arts; Social Science; Western History; Religion; International; and African Americans', Appalachians', Women's.

The student-to-faculty ratio in 2022-23 was only 8:1, and the average class is just 14. With such favorable numbers, plenty of opportunities exist to connect with faculty outside the classroom. Each summer, 8-10 Berea students head to paid research programs in the biological sciences at Vanderbilt, CU-Denver, and Pitt. By the time students graduate, 93% have taken a semester abroad, landed a paid internship, conducted research alongside one of their professors, or engaged in a formal service-learning program.

There are 30+ fields of study at Berea, and students are spread fairly evenly across the disciplines. Over the last five years, the most commonly conferred degree was in computer science. Next in line were business administration, biology, psychology, and communication. The Agriculture and Natural Resources Department is well regarded and is one of the few of its kind to be housed inside a liberal arts college. Berea does a phenomenal job of assisting students in applying to prestigious national fellowships. Among colleges with fewer than 5,000 students, Berea placed first in the country in the number of Gilman Scholars in 2022-23, setting an all-time record with 21 students selected.

Outside the Classroom

Among all presently enrolled students, just under three-fifths are female, and 70-80% come from the Appalachian Region of Kentucky. Campus is a 140-acre plot of land in a rural setting, and 96% of the student body resides there. Louisville, KY; Knoxville, TN; and Cincinnati, OH, are a bit more than two hours away by car, but Lexington, KY, is only 40 miles north. If there is an opposite of a "party school," Berea is it. The vibe at this school is different than at your typical college where some students participate in work-study while others are free from financial responsibilities. At Berea, students pick from 100 campus positions and need to balance their work schedules with their academic ones. This is also an exceptionally "green" campus, and the school runs an Office of Sustainability that keeps data on the amount of trash created, the school's recycling percentage, and total greenhouse gas emissions. For a small college, there are plenty of student organizations to join—180+ are active. Sixteen varsity teams compete at the NCAA Division III level, and plenty of intramural and recreational sports programs can be found inside the Seabury Center, which offers a pool, an indoor track, racquetball courts, and other amenities.

Career Services

The Office of Internships and Career Development (ICD) has eight professional employees including two dedicated to internship coordination and three focused on career development. There are also four student staff members plus an administrative assistant. Counting only professional employees, the student-to-counselor ratio is 179:1, an excellent figure for any institution. Philosophically, the office breaks down its process of guidance into three realms: Articulation, Discernment, and Navigation, and within each realm action steps are delineated and geared for both under- and upperclassmen.

Being a small school in a rural location, Berea's ICD does not host gigantic career fairs, but it does bring employers to campus for information sessions and routinely offers workshops related to career exploration, the job search, and internship procurement. Looking at one recent cohort of graduates, 96% who completed an internship felt it helped them become better prepared to enter the world of work, and 75% received full funding from the college to cover expenses related to the experience. The ICD also offers a formal seven-week course in graduate school preparation that includes help with interview prep, personal statements, and the applications themselves.

Professional Outcomes

After graduation, many students remain in Kentucky in the Lexington and Louisville areas. Many others cluster in Knoxville; Cincinnati; Atlanta; and Washington, DC. Alumni also reside in 94 countries with the greatest numbers in Asia, Africa, and Europe. With small graduating classes each year, you won't find swarms of Berea alumni in any one company, but more than one grad can be found employed at Norton Healthcare, Humana, EY, PepsiCo, PwC, the US Department of Justice, Procter & Gamble, and the Ford Motor Company. The most common occupations for alumni are (1) teaching, (2) educational administration, (3) nursing, (4) management, (5) computing, (6) social work, and (7) medicine.

The average American may not have heard of Berea College, but those in the know—namely graduate and professional schools—think highly of the school. Berea has a pre-medical/pre-dental and pre-law pathway that provides academic and extracurricular support to those aiming to continue their studies in a professional program. Recent grads have been admitted into medical schools that include the University of Louisville School of Medicine and the University of Kentucky College of Medicine and law schools including the University of Mississippi and the University of Memphis.

Admission

The level of academic preparation among applicants varies, and Berea welcomes that, understanding that many students have not had access to top-notch educational resources. Yet, the school is still highly selective with an acceptance rate for the Class of 2026 of only 25%, a figure that was identical to the previous cycle. In a typical year, more students submit ACT scores than SAT results, and the average composite score is 24. The average high school GPA is 3.6, and 31% of freshmen placed in the top decile of their high school class while 70% were in the top 25% and only 4% finished outside the top half.

A different kind of school deserves a different kind of admissions process, and that's exactly what you'll find at Berea College. The only factor rated by this committee as "very important" is the interview, which is an opportunity to make the case for Berea as the perfect college for you. As part of a holistic review, Berea will consider factors including "a properly completed application, official academic records, test scores, and financial eligibility" as well as "recommendations and endorsements, admissions counselor conversations, extracurricular and cocurricular activities (e.g., music ensembles, athletics, theatre), community service, character and personal qualities, social maturity, and demonstrated interest in the college."

Worth Your Money?

As with the service academies, there is not much doubt as to the value of a free college education. It is estimated that the Tuition Promise Scholarship awarded to each undergraduate student has a four-year value of over $200,000. If you come from a low-income background (which all who are admitted do), Berea is an unbelievable, life-changing opportunity that you should seize. If you also happen to have exceptionally high test scores and a stellar academic resume, it would still be worth applying to highly selective schools known for meeting 100% of a student's demonstrated need. This would be the only scenario in which an applicant might find a comparably terrific deal.

FINANCIAL
Institutional Type: Private
In-State Tuition: $726
Out-of-State Tuition: $726
Room & Board: $7,892
Books & Supplies: $700

Avg. Need-Based Grant: $51,676
Avg. % of Need Met: 98%

Avg. Merit-Based Award: Not Reported
% Receiving (Freshmen w/o Need): Not Reported

Avg. Cumulative Debt: $5,208
% of Students Borrowing: 39%

CAREER
Who Recruits
1. U.S. Department of Veterans Affairs
2. Lexmark
3. Walmart
4. Humana
5. Sodexo

Notable Internships
1. Trane Technologies
2. Kentucky Educational Television
3. Amazon

Top Employers
1. University of Kentucky
2. Amazon
3. Commonwealth of Kentucky
4. Walmart
5. US Dept of Veterans Affairs

Where Alumni Work
1. Lexington, KY
2. South Africa
3. Louisville
4. Cincinnati
5. Knoxville, TN

Earnings
College Scorecard (10-YR Post-Entry): $40,738
PayScale (Early Career): $45,100
PayScale (Mid-Career): $74,000
PayScale 20-Year ROI: $37,000

RANKINGS
Money: 5
U.S. News: 30, Liberal Arts Colleges
Wall Street Journal/THE: 150
Washington Monthly: 2, Liberal Arts Colleges

OVERGENERALIZATIONS
Students are:
Service-oriented
Diverse
Independent
Resilient
Always working

COLLEGE OVERLAPS
Centre College
College of the Ozarks
University of Kentucky
University of Louisville
Warren Wilson College

Binghamton University (SUNY)

Binghamton, New York | 607-777-2171

Created in the GI Bill era to accommodate the influx of returning soldiers entering college, SUNY Binghamton (a.k.a. Binghamton University) is the shining star of the State University System of New York. Considered a "Public Ivy," the 14,402 undergraduates are an accomplished bunch (median SAT is 1430), and the excellence of the academic offerings is commensurate with the student body. It's no wonder that 92% of freshmen return to campus the next fall, a retention rate that is unparalleled among non-flagship public institutions.

Inside the Classroom
The university offers over 130 areas of concentration across its five undergraduate schools: the Harpur College of Arts and Sciences, the College of Community and Public Affairs, the Decker School of Nursing, the School of Management, and the Thomas J. Watson School of Engineering and Applied Science. General education requirements include foreign language (except for engineering majors), creating a global vision, the liberal arts (aesthetics, humanities, laboratory sciences, social sciences, and mathematics), and a series of physical activity and wellness classes. Unlike many state universities, there is no long list of required courses awaiting you. Rather, the mandated categories of coursework are broad enough that you'll have plenty of room for exploration.

The student-to-faculty ratio is on the high side at 19:1, but class sizes are reasonably small with 48% of sections containing fewer than twenty students. Only 14% of courses are held in large lecture halls with 50+ students. Research opportunities are available, with the Freshman Research Immersion program being one shining example. This program welcomes students to college with a year-long authentic research experience in the sciences and engineering. The Office of Undergraduate Research is adept at connecting students in all fields, not just STEM, to research opportunities alongside faculty members. The school's own undergraduate research journal, Alpenglow, gives students the chance to publish scholarly as well as original creative works. Study abroad opportunities are available at over fifty worldwide locations, and roughly one-fifth of undergraduates spend a semester in a foreign country.

In the spring of 2022, Binghamton awarded the greatest number of degrees in business (17%), biology (15%), the social sciences, (11%), engineering (11%), and health professions (7%). The School of Management is renowned for its accounting program and is well-known by NYC-based companies. Programs in chemistry, psychology, and nursing are also well respected. The university's graduates are somewhat competitive in procuring prestigious postgraduate fellowships—a handful of recent students have been named Fulbright Scholars.

Outside the Classroom
Just over half of undergrads reside on campus in dorms or residential college communities designed for 200 to 1,000 students each, and all have their own distinct personalities. Most off-campus apartment dwellers reside in the city's West Side neighborhood, but some end up in small towns a ten- to twenty-minute drive away. With 45 fraternities and sororities and thousands of participants, you might think that Greek life would be a dominant presence, yet only around 15% of students pledge, leaving the majority to carve out their own social scene. The Binghamton Bearcats field twenty-one varsity sports teams in NCAA Division I. However, with no football team, the university is not a sports-centered campus. There is much to do within the university's 930 acres of grounds that include a 190-acre nature preserve, a 156,000-square-foot multipurpose center, two fully equipped gyms, two pools, twenty-six tennis courts, and a 1,200-seat theater for art/speaking/musical events. Over 2,000 students participate in 40 recreational and club athletic teams, and another 3,000 play intramural sports. There are 300 other clubs and activities. From their high-achieving speech and debate squad to a plethora of political, cultural, academic, and religious clubs, all 14,000+ undergrads can find some way to connect. There are also eighty-five organizations focused on community service and volunteer work. Green initiatives are popular on campus, including energy efficiency, local food sources, recycling, and the bike-share program.

Career Services
The Fleishman Center for Career and Professional Development is not your average state school career services office. Consisting of 21 professional employees (including the School of Management's office) and fifty peer assistants and interns, the 686:1 student-to-advisor ratio (only counting the professionals) is more supportive than it appears. In a single recent year, Fleishman staff conducted 4,705 one-on-one counseling sessions. More than 5,300 unique students connected directly with career services, a sizable portion of the undergraduate population.

Approximately 750 students earn academic credit for internships each year and 270 current students were matched with alumni mentors last year alone. The hireBing platform (run by Handshake) sees 50,000 job and internship postings annually. SUNY Binghamton's Fall Job Fair attracts more than 120 corporate, government, and nonprofit employers including Teach for America, Geico, Wayfair, and Raytheon Company. In total, 240+ employers and 1,400+ students attended in-person/virtual job fairs in one recent year. The school's recently launched Washington, DC, Employer Site Visit Program complements its successful New York City Site Visit Program. Having increased its staffing, outreach, and technological capabilities in recent years, Binghamton's career services is on the rise.

Professional Outcomes

The Class of 2022 saw 50% of job-seeking graduates land their first professional job and 49% enter grad school within six months of commencement. Those entering the technology & computing fields found homes at companies like Facebook, IBM, Apple, and Microsoft in large numbers. Graduates entering finance careers were successful in finding employment at firms like Morgan Stanley, JPMorgan, Goldman Sachs, and CitiGroup. In the accounting/consulting realm, the most popular employers of Binghamton grads were EY, PwC, Deloitte, and KPMG. The average starting salary procured was $72,438, well above the national average for college grads. New York City is, by far, the most common landing spot for Binghamton graduates, but many also remain in Upstate New York or travel to Washington, DC; Boston; San Francisco; Philadelphia; and Los Angeles.

Of the Binghamton grads seeking to transition directly into graduate studies, 91% were already enrolled in a program six months after graduation. Many SUNY branch campuses were among the most popular graduate school destinations, but many prestigious universities also graced this list including Cornell, Columbia, NYU, UPenn, and Georgetown. SUNY Binghamton's reputation also helped open the doors to law school as it enjoys an 85% acceptance rate. The school's early admission med school program (during sophomore year) creates a pipeline into SUNY Upstate Medical University. In the most recent year, medical school applicants were accepted at a rate 10% higher than the national average.

Admission

SUNY Binghamton received 41,642 applications for the Class of 2026 and accepted 42%. That acceptance rate was similar to acceptance rates at this selective state university over the past decade, but the profile of the average enrolling freshman indicates that the school is becoming significantly more competitive. Entering freshmen in 2022-23 had an average GPA of 3.89. The mid-50% range on the SAT was 1340-1510 and 29-24 for the ACT. Ten years ago, the SAT range was 1190-1350. Even with SAT score inflation, it is safe to say that the average student at this school today is a higher achiever than the average student of a decade ago.

The factors that are considered above all others in admissions decisions are grades and rigor of secondary curriculum. Class rank and the essay make up the second tier of important considerations. With such a massive applicant pool, interviews are not offered. SUNY Binghamton is a special value, especially by the standards of today's higher education marketplace. With an annual in-state tuition and fees of just over $10,000, this excellent public research university continues to draw more and more qualified applicants each year. The admission formula falls far short of rocket science. Solid grades in AP/honors classes rule the day.

Worth Your Money?

You simply won't find a better combination of quality and price anywhere on the East Coast than Binghamton University. With a total annual cost of attendance of $30,577 (much lower for those who commute) for an in-state student, this SUNY school is worth anyone's money, no matter your major or career path. More than half of students qualify for financial aid and receive an average grant package of almost $11k, making an already affordable school nothing less than a ridiculous bargain.

FINANCIAL
Institutional Type: Public
In-State Tuition: $10,363
Out-of-State Tuition: $28,203
Room & Board: $17,506
Books & Supplies: $1,000

Avg. Need-Based Grant: $10,848
Avg. % of Need Met: 68%

Avg. Merit-Based Award: $8,887
% Receiving (Freshmen w/o Need): 6%

Avg. Cumulative Debt: $25,975
% of Students Borrowing: 51%

CAREER
Who Recruits
1. AMETEK Aerospace and Defense
2. NYS Department of Transportation
3. Dick's Sporting Goods
4. AXA Advisors
5. Mirabito Energy Products

Notable Internships
1. United Health Services
2. Cushman & Wakefield
3. Deloitte

Top Employers
1. IBM
2. EY
3. JPMorgan Chase
4. PwC
5. Morgan Stanley

Where Alumni Work
1. New York City
2. Ithaca, NY
3. Washington, DC
4. Boston
5. San Francisco

Earnings
College Scorecard (10-YR Post-Entry): $77,436
PayScale (Early Career): $65,200
PayScale (Mid-Career): $120,900
PayScale 20-Year ROI: $752,000

RANKINGS
Money: 4.5
U.S. News: 73, National Universities
Wall Street Journal/THE: 82
Washington Monthly: 126, National Universities

OVERGENERALIZATIONS
Students are:
Diverse
Working hard and playing hard
Less concerned with fashion or appearance
Independent
Driven

COLLEGE OVERLAPS
Boston University
Cornell University
New York University
Stony Brook University (SUNY)
University at Buffalo (SUNY)

Boston College

Chestnut Hill, Massachusetts | 617-552-3100

Along with Notre Dame, Georgetown, and Villanova, Boston College, home to 9,484 undergrads, is among the most academically renowned Catholic universities in the world. The college offers roughly 60 majors across four schools that award undergraduate degrees: the School of Management, the School of Education, the School of Nursing, and the Morrissey College of Arts & Sciences. Certain majors that one takes for granted as being offered at a large research institution, such as engineering, do not yet exist at BC. However, the school recently completed a new $150 million science facility and launched its engineering program in 2021-22.

Inside the Classroom

The core curriculum lays out an extensive series of academic requirements that includes two courses in the natural sciences, social sciences, history, philosophy, and theology as well as one course in the arts, cultural diversity, math, and writing. All told, the core curriculum accounts for three full semesters of coursework. The breadth of the requirements is far from accidental—BC's program is designed to expand students' intellectual horizons and build character at the same time.

This odyssey unfolds in a caring and personal atmosphere. Approximately half of the college's sections contain nineteen or fewer students; there are some larger lecture hall classes, but those are fairly rare. Working closely with their professors pays off for students. In their own self-assessment, 95% of graduates reported learning how to think critically at BC, and 93% said they learned how to write clearly and effectively. Fifty percent of BC grads pursued a semester abroad in one of 200+ locations around the globe, and 90% cited the experience as a source of personal growth.

BC offers highly respected programs in communications, psychology, and business through the renowned Carroll School of Management. Other popular and well-regarded majors include economics, communication, and chemistry. Graduates fare decently in procuring prestigious awards, especially in the realm of fellowships to study abroad. Thirteen members of the Class of 2023 won Fulbright Scholarships, and BC holds the distinction as one of the top twenty Fulbright-producing research universities over the past decade.

Outside the Classroom

Unlike Boston University, BC is not located in the heart of its namesake city. Fortunately, downtown Boston is only six miles away and easily accessible from the Chestnut Hill section of Newton, where BC's main campus is located. With 70% of students identifying as Catholic, it is little surprise that religion and spirituality are a big part of campus life. Clubs in this arena are well represented among the 300+ student organizations on campus, but there are a multitude of pre-professional, special interest, performing arts, and political offerings as well. There are no Greek houses at BC, a void that is filled by tightly knit groups with common interests. One such galvanizing force is the school's athletic teams. The Eagles compete in 31 NCAA Division I and over 40 intramural sports. The men's ice hockey team is always in the national spotlight, regularly appearing in the Frozen Four. For those seeking charitable opportunities, the Volunteer & Service Learning Center connects students with a plethora of organizations all over the country. One of the most popular of those experiences is the Appalachia Volunteers Program, which sends around 500 students each year on spring break to forty impoverished cities and towns in the United States.

Career Services

The Career Center is manned by 23 professionals whose specialty areas include career counseling, exploration, and employer engagement. Not counting the graduate assistants and peer coaches who also are available to work with undergraduate students, this calculates to a student-to-advisor ratio of 412:1, about average when compared to the pool of institutions included in this book.

The better news is that the office is effective at what is most important—helping students achieve positive career and graduate school outcomes. Over 200 companies recruit on campus each year with most offering in-person interviews. A solid 80% of recent grads landed an internship during their undergraduate years and 67% of 2022 grads stated that they used a BC Career Center resource to secure employment. Career fairs occur throughout the year; some events are general while others cater to specific areas of interest including public accounting, government, and sports and entertainment. The Career Center regularly offers job shadowing opportunities, networking nights, Career Treks, workshops covering a host of topics, and the Eagle Intern Fellowship, which provides a $3,500 stipend to selected students pursuing unpaid internships. The alumni network is 188,000 strong and is generally very active and willing to help current students.

Professional Outcomes

Within six months of graduation, 96% of the Class of 2022 had landed at their next destination, whether that was employment, graduate school, a fellowship, or a volunteer position. The most favored industries were financial services and real estate (26%), health care/science (20%), and business/consulting (16%). More than twenty newly minted alumni found employment at Ernst & Young, Oracle, Citi, and PricewaterhouseCoopers. Notable numbers also flocked to Mass General, Deloitte, and KPMG. Across all graduating years, more than 150 alumni also work at each of Deloitte, Google, Morgan Stanley, and Goldman Sachs. The median starting salary for a 2022 BC grad was $67,000. By a wide margin, the locale where the most alumni settle is the university's home state of Massachusetts; New York City also draws a sizable number of BC grads.

Eighteen percent of the Class of 2022 entered graduate schools including Brown, Columbia, the University of Chicago, and Yale. Examining the Class of 2022 data, 16% entered law school, and 14% pursued some other type of doctoral degree. Of the law school attendees, the greatest number continued in BC's own program. BC was also, by far, the most common graduate choice for those pursuing advanced degrees in education and business. Tufts was the No. 1 target for medical school and the natural sciences. Graduates also enjoyed acceptances into other elite medical schools including Dartmouth, Harvard, and Boston University.

Admission

Boston College received over 40,000 applications for the Class of 2026, and the acceptance rate fell to 17%. However, selectivity is nothing new for BC. A decade ago, acceptance rates were in the 26-27% range. What is changing is the academic profile of the average student being offered a spot at this high-end Catholic university. The mid-50% SAT score for the Class of 2026 was 1435-1530; ten years ago, that 1435 would have had you above the 75th percentile. In the 2022-23 academic year, 90% of freshmen placed in the top decile of their high school class.

They recently introduced an early decision admission plan and, last cycle, 28% were accepted, filling 53% of the Class of 2026. No matter when you apply, BC places a high value on writing ability and requires completion of the Boston College Writing Supplement. There are no interviews as part of the admissions process. BC attracts some of the most gifted Catholic students in the country as well as a fair number of non-Catholics. SAT scores in the 1400s and A/A- grades in a rigorous curriculum will put applicants on solid footing.

Worth Your Money?

In 1990, Boston College had an annual cost of attendance of around $15,000. Today, you will owe $86,000+ per year for the privilege of attending this fine institution. While this jump in price far outpaces the rate of inflation, so goes the entire higher education marketplace. The good news is that BC awards healthy amounts of financial aid to those unable to pay full freight as eligible undergraduates receive more than $52,000 per year, making the cost far more palatable. The university meets 100% of demonstrated need. If you were in a situation where you had to take on massive loans to study at BC, it would likely be a good investment if you planned on going the finance or consulting route but less so if you planned to study education.

FINANCIAL
Institutional Type: Private
In-State Tuition: $67,680
Out-of-State Tuition: $67,680
Room & Board: $18,475
Books & Supplies: $1,250

Avg. Need-Based Grant: $49,761
Avg. % of Need Met: 100%

Avg. Merit-Based Award: $22,433
% Receiving (Freshmen w/o Need): 1%

Avg. Cumulative Debt: $24,579
% of Students Borrowing: 45%

CAREER
Who Recruits
1. MullenLowe Mediahub
2. Oracle
3. Epsilon
4. Liberty Mutual
5. Accenture

Notable Internships
1. NBC Sports Boston
2. Pfizer
3. IBM

Top Employers
1. PwC
2. EY
3. Deloitte
4. Morgan Stanley
5. Citi

Where Alumni Work
1. Boston
2. New York City
3. Washington, DC
4. San Francisco
5. Los Angeles

Earnings
College Scorecard (10-YR Post-Entry): $96,325
PayScale (Early Career): $69,000
PayScale (Mid-Career): $126,800
PayScale 20-Year ROI: $821,000

RANKINGS
Money: 4.5
U.S. News: 39, National Universities
Wall Street Journal/THE: 45
Washington Monthly: 41, National Universities

OVERGENERALIZATIONS
Students are:
Preppy
Athletic
Working hard and playing hard
Religious
Crazy about the Eagles

COLLEGE OVERLAPS
Boston University
Georgetown University
New York University
Notre Dame University
Villanova University

Boston University

Boston, Massachusetts | 617-353-2300

ADMISSION

Admission Rate: 14%
Admission Rate - Men: 16%
Admission Rate - Women: 13%
EA Admission Rate: Not Offered
ED Admission Rate: 25%
ED Admits as % of Total Admits: 14%
Admission Rate (5-Year Trend): -11%
% of Admits Attending (Yield): 31%
Transfer Admission Rate: 29%

SAT Reading/Writing (Middle 50%): 660-730
SAT Math (Middle 50%): 690-770
ACT Composite (Middle 50%): 31-34

% Graduated in Top 10% of HS Class: 87%
% Graduated in Top 25% of HS Class: 99%
% Graduated in Top 50% of HS Class: 100%

Demonstrated Interest: Considered
Legacy Status: Considered
Racial/Ethnic Status: Considered
Admission Interview Offered: No

ENROLLMENT

Total Undergraduate Enrollment: 18,459
% Full-Time: 99%
% Male: 42%
% Female: 58%
% Out-of-State: 73%
% Fraternity: Not Reported
% Sorority: 10%
% On-Campus (All Undergraduate): 65%
Freshman Housing Required: Yes

% African-American: 5%
% Asian: 20%
% Hispanic: 11%
% White: 33%
% Other: 4%
% International: 23%
% Low-Income: 19%

ACADEMICS

Student-to-Faculty Ratio: 11 to 1
% of Classes Under 20: 60%
% of Classes 20-49: 28%
% of Classes 50 or More: 13%
% Full-Time Faculty: 70%
% Full-Time Faculty w/ Terminal Degree: 91%

Top Programs
Biomedical Engineering
Business
Communication
Hospitality
International Relations
Music
Neuroscience
Theatre Arts

Retention Rate: 94%
4-Year Graduation Rate: 83%
6-Year Graduation Rate: 89%

Curricular Flexibility: Somewhat Flexible
Academic Rating: ★★★★✦

#CollegesWorthYourMoney

Growing more selective each year, Boston University is a private research institution playing host to 18,459 undergrads as well as an additional 18,255 graduate students. It's hard to imagine a more dynamic locale than BU's sprawling campus that shares a neighborhood with Fenway Park, the Museum of Fine Arts, MIT, and countless culinary and cultural enticements. In total, the university offers more than 300 programs of study, 100+ of which are distinct undergraduate degrees spread across ten schools/colleges.

Inside the Classroom

Unique programs include the Kilachand Honors College, which welcomes 130-150 new students each year and offers an original, integrated four-year curriculum thematically centered on global challenges and practical solutions. Not shockingly, it's tough to pin down course requirements with so many colleges within the larger university. College of Arts & Sciences students must satisfy basic requirements in foreign language, mathematics, and writing as part of their 128 credits. Engineering students, on the other hand, must complete sixteen credits in mathematics and twelve in the natural sciences. First-year experience courses are available but not required.

Many classes at BU are reasonably small—60% contain fewer than twenty students; only 19% contain more than forty. The student-to-faculty ratio is 11:1, quite an achievement for a school of its size. BU's Undergraduate Research Opportunities Program (UROP) funds 650 students per year, and many additional students participate in BU's research for credit, volunteer, work-study, and other independent opportunities. Over 70 study abroad sites in 15+ countries are available for those seeking a global experience. Participation is quite high, with 40% of students completing a semester on a foreign campus.

The greatest number of degrees are conferred in social sciences (16%), business/marketing (15%), communications and journalism (15%), biology (11%), engineering (9%), and health professions/related sciences (7%). The Questrom School of Business and the College of Engineering are highly regarded as well as the university's College of Communication and College of Health & Rehabilitation Services. Over the last five years, BU has produced at least five Fulbright Scholars annually. In 2022, grads took home 16 Fulbright Scholarships; they often produce multiple Goldwater Scholarships and Critical Language Scholarships as well.

Outside the Classroom

Sixty-five percent of the undergraduate student body and 99% of freshmen reside on campus. Greek life has a modest presence at BU—roughly 10% elect to pledge one of the school's eight frats and twelve sororities. Nicknamed the Terriers, BU is represented by 24 teams in NCAA Division I, highlighted by its perennially stellar men's ice hockey team. In an odd move for a school of its size, BU dissolved its football program in 1997. The basketball team makes an occasional appearance in March Madness. For those a bit less serious about/ skilled at sports, 7,000 students participate in intramural athletics. With 450+ student organizations and offerings from improv to synchronized swimming, just about everyone can find their niche. The student-run Daily Free Press is recognized as one of the top in the country and claims the fourth-highest circulation of any paper in Boston. Volunteer spirit runs rampant at BU—the Community Service Center has a volunteer base of over 1,500 students and contributes 75,000 hours of service to the Boston-area community each year. Being located in the heart of Boston, students have limitless choices for nightlife and culture and can conveniently hop aboard the Green Line to explore the farthest reaches of the city.

Career Services

Seventeen counselors, recruiters, and outreach coordinators comprise the BU Center for Career Development (CCD). They also have additional professional staff embedded within their various colleges and schools which brings the total to 27. This equates to a student-to-advisor ratio of 684:1, below average when compared to the pool of institutions included in this book. Despite limited personnel for a school so large, the office is successful at working with those who engage with them. In fact, students who regularly utilized the career center reported 22% higher earnings than their peers. In a single year, staff conducts 2,500+ one-on-one advising sessions. Remarkably for a school of BU's size, the CCD helps 85% of students complete at least one internship over their four years of study.

Every spring and fall, the CCD organizes an All-Majors Career Fair with over one hundred guest employers; individual colleges within BU also host discipline-specific career fairs in business, engineering, nonprofit leadership, and public health. In total, 600 employers attend BU fairs and 750+ recruit on campus in a given academic year. Freshmen are encouraged to attend a seminar called Career Directions: Starting Your Journey, which gives tips on how to maximize one's educational experience with an eye on life beyond college. Through the Career Advisory Network, the CCD also works to connect students with over 6,000 participating alumni who are employed in a wide spectrum of fields. Even with a less-than-ideal number of counselors, BU's career services staff works hard to reach students through seminars, job fairs, and online resources.

Professional Outcomes

Six months after graduation, 90% of BU grads have found their way into the world of employment or full-time graduate study. A recent survey of corporate recruiters with international companies revealed that Boston University alums have the sixth-highest employability ranking, directly behind the likes of MIT, Caltech, Harvard, and Stanford. Recent graduating classes have seen more than ten graduates join employers like EY, PwC, Deloitte, and TJX Companies. Healthy numbers of engineering grads found their way to Amazon, IBM, Lockheed Martin, and Pfizer. Across all graduating years, companies employing more than 350 BU alums include Google, Oracle, Accenture, IBM, and Amazon Web Services. Starting salary data is highly dependent on which school within BU one attended. Recent grads of the Questrom School of Business earned a starting salary of roughly $65k, College of Engineering grads average $74k, and Arts & Sciences students come in just shy of $58k.

Respect for the BU degree comes from more than just the corporate world. Of the one-quarter of grads who move directly into graduate school, many are welcomed onto the campuses of elite graduate programs. For example, engineering students found new academic homes at MIT, Stanford, Carnegie Mellon, and Columbia. Most top law schools have some level of representation from BU alumni including BU Law itself, a top 20 institution that accepts a significant number of its own undergraduates. Those aiming to become medical doctors can apply for the Seven-Year Liberal Arts/Medical Education Program that leads directly to study at the BU School of Medicine. Overall, the university saw 334 undergraduates apply to med school in 2022-23 alone. Whether attending grad school or starting their careers, the greatest number of BU grads remain in Boston with New York City, San Francisco, Los Angeles, DC, and Philadelphia next in popularity.

Admission

Almost 81,000 applications rolled into BU for spots in the Class of 2026, and 14% gained acceptance. For historical context, 46% of applicants were accepted in 2012 and close to three-quarters in 2005. The average member of the Class of 2026 finished with a 3.88 unweighted GPA and the SAT range was 1370-1480. Back in 2012, the 75th percentile on the SAT was 1390, an indicator that gaining acceptance into BU is considerably more difficult than in the not-too-distant past. Most BU students finished in the upper echelon of their high school classes—87% were in the top 10%, and 99% were in the top quartile. On a 4.0 scale, 99% had unweighted GPAs of 3.5 or higher.

The only three admissions criteria rated as "very important" for all applicants are the rigor of one's high school course load, GPA, and talent/ability. Factors in the second rung of importance are class rank, recommendations, essays, extracurricular activities, and character/personality. Those who demonstrate the most fervent interest and commitment by applying early decision receive a nice boost, gaining acceptance at a 25% clip. It is critical to remember that this isn't your mother's or father's BU—it's not even your older sibling's BU. Far more highly selective than even a few years ago, Boston University hopefuls need to bring top-tier credentials in order to be offered admission at this fine private research institution.

Worth Your Money?

At nearly $87,000, Boston University has a hefty list price cost of attendance, a sum made slightly more manageable for undergraduates who receive an annual merit-based award of $28k or some level of need-based financial aid. BU does award need-based aid to approximately two-fifths of its undergraduates, and now meets 100% of all demonstrated need for all students. If attending BU would necessitate taking out large loans, your decision should come down to whether you intend to major in a field with a high enough starting salary so you can comfortably make the monthly payments.

FINANCIAL
Institutional Type: Private
In-State Tuition: $65,168
Out-of-State Tuition: $65,168
Room & Board: $18,110
Books & Supplies: $1,000

Avg. Need-Based Grant: $53,029
Avg. % of Need Met: 95%

Avg. Merit-Based Award: $28,069
% Receiving (Freshmen w/o Need): 4%

Avg. Cumulative Debt: $38,263
% of Students Borrowing: 36%

CAREER
Who Recruits
1. Marriott
2. Turner Broadcasting System
3. TJX
4. General Electric
5. Bloomberg LP

Notable Internships
1. Amazon
2. Boston Scientific
3. BuzzFeed

Top Employers
1. IBM
2. Google
3. Amazon
4. Microsoft
5. Oracle

Where Alumni Work
1. Boston
2. New York City
3. San Francisco
4. Los Angeles
5. Washington, DC

Earnings
College Scorecard (10-YR Post-Entry): $80,582
PayScale (Early Career): $66,400
PayScale (Mid-Career): $128,700
PayScale 20-Year ROI: $750,000

RANKINGS
Money: 4.5
U.S. News: 43, National Universities
Wall Street Journal/THE: 200
Washington Monthly: 77, National Universities

OVERGENERALIZATIONS
Students are:
Politically liberal
Diverse
More likely to venture off campus
Academically driven
Anxious to meet new people and
have new experiences

COLLEGE OVERLAPS
Cornell University
New York University
Northeastern University
Tufts University
University of Michigan

Bowdoin College

Brunswick, Maine | 207-725-3100

Set on 215 lush acres in the quaint town of Brunswick, Maine, Bowdoin College serves 1,915 undergraduate students. This quintessential, elite New England liberal arts college is steeped in history and tradition; its oldest buildings date to the late eighteenth century, and the curriculum is guided by a poem, "The Offer of the College," penned by the school's president in 1906. Does it get any more New England liberal-artsy than that?

Inside the Classroom
Among its core beliefs, Bowdoin offers a flexible and broad liberal arts education. Polar Bears can choose from one of thirty-three academic programs or get more creative through an interdisciplinary or student-designed major. One-size-fits-all requirements are minimal. All must take a freshman seminar in an area of interest such as Personal Genomes, The Moral Economy, or The Supreme Court and Social Change. Bowdoin students are required to take one course from each of five distribution areas: (1) mathematical, computational, or statistical reasoning; (2) inquiry in the natural sciences; (3) difference, power, and inequality; (4) international perspectives; and (5) visual and performing arts.

Class sizes are small—64% contain fewer than twenty students—and 21% have fewer than ten students. The student-faculty ratio is 9:1, which leads to ample and meaningful interaction and guidance in and out of the classroom. More than half of Bowdoin undergrads report interacting with a professor outside of regular class time at least once per week. Professors have a reputation for being extremely dedicated to their teaching. Students also enjoy a plethora of study abroad opportunities with 55% electing to spend a semester learning in a foreign locale.

The greatest percentage of degrees are conferred in the social sciences (30%), biology (13%), area/ethnic/gender studies (8%), computer science (7%), and mathematics (7%). Economics and Government and Legal Studies are two of the more popular majors within the social sciences. Bowdoin is one of the strongest in the country for those on a premed track (more later). The school is also a prolific producer of fellowship/scholarship winners. In 2023 alone, 17 graduates and alumni were named Fulbright Scholars—the highest total from any one school. Graduates also routinely win other prestigious awards including National Science Foundation Graduate Research Fellowships, Boren Scholarships, Watson Fellowships, and Critical Language Scholarships awarded by the US State Department.

Outside the Classroom
By sheer numbers, athletics are a driving force of life outside the classroom. An insanely high 40%+ of undergrads are varsity athletes who compete on one of thirty NCAA Division III teams. And that doesn't include those who play on one of the six club teams or participate in one of ten intramural sports, each of which has an A, B, and C level. Over one hundred non-sports clubs are also active, including the Outing Club, which boasts over 400 members and takes over 150 nature-themed excursions per year. Greek life was disbanded around the turn of the new millennium and replaced with a system of eight college houses that serve as the backbone of the campus residential experience. Each house has its own student government and hosts special events throughout the year. The dining halls are known to prepare extravagant meals that receive rave reviews across the board. 95% of students live on campus, and certain annual events like the Gala and Ivies concert bring together the whole student body. Among the most favored off-campus destinations is Portland, Maine's largest city, which is less than half an hour away.

Career Services
Bowdoin's Career Exploration and Development (CXD) office is staffed by an impressive 12 professionals who specialize in areas like discipline-specific career advising and employer relations. That works out to a student-to-advisor ratio of 160:1, among the very best of any institution included in this book. Students are always welcome to schedule a one-on-one counseling session or mock interview or drop by between noon and 2 p.m. each weekday, unannounced, with a quick question. In a single year, the office planned over 200 programs with over 5,200 attendees, more than two-and-half times the size of the student body. Incredibly, the staff managed to work, in some capacity, with 80% of students and 99% of the senior class.

The school combines some events with Colby and Bates; the Graduate & Professional School Fair, which is held every October and the annual Maine Employers Career Fair are two examples. The school's outreach efforts pay off with an overflow of companies recruiting on campus each year including all of the major financial and consulting firms as well as government entities like the US Treasury Department. Bowdoin also distributes close to a quarter of a million dollars in grants to support unpaid internships each year. Two-thirds of graduates complete some type of internship. To provide further assistance in carving out career pathways, 200 alumni and parents of current students come to campus to help students with career exploration and networking.

Professional Outcomes

An examination of three recent years' worth of outcomes data reveals that one year after graduation, between 73 and 77% of recent grads have found full-time employment, and 15% have gone directly into graduate school. Only 2-8% are still seeking employment. Prominent corporations across all sectors love Bowdoin grads. Recent alumni have found positions at Apple, IBM, Goldman Sachs, Google, HBO, and Microsoft. Other companies that employ more than a dozen alumni are Fidelity Investments, Morgan Stanley, Amazon, Google, and Goldman Sachs. The cities attracting the greatest numbers of graduates include Boston; New York City; Portland, Maine; San Francisco; DC; and Los Angeles.

Of those entering graduate school, 48% were enrolled in master's programs, 23% in PhD programs, 13% in law school, and 8% in med school. The top twenty graduate schools attended, by volume, in the last five years make an exclusive list including six Ivies along with Duke, MIT, Johns Hopkins, Northwestern, and Stanford. Boston College and Boston University are also two of the largest recipients of Bowdoin grads. Those aiming for medical school fare exceptionally well with 87% typically earning acceptance into at least one institution. Recent grads are presently studying medicine at Tufts, Harvard, Boston University, NYU, and the University of Michigan.

Admission

Already a highly selective school, Bowdoin has become even more difficult to get into in recent years. The acceptance rate for applicants to the Class of 2026 was a paltry 9% compared to 20% back in 2012. An examination of the middle-50% ranges on standardized tests for attending students suggests there is little evidence that the school is accepting a higher caliber of student than it was just a handful of years ago. In 2013-14, Bowdoin freshmen scored 1360-1510 on the SAT and 30-33 on the ACT. In 2022-23, those SAT figures were almost identical at 1340-1520 while the ACT range was slightly higher at 32-36. Bowdoin is famous for becoming the first test-optional school in the country (1969). Nevertheless, 58% of the Class of 2024 submitted SAT scores, and 30% shared ACT scores. A decent number of students submitted results from both tests, so it is fair to conclude that the vast majority of successful applicants elected to submit standardized test scores.

Being in the top 10% of your high school class is almost required—83% of freshmen held that distinction, and 95% were in the top 25%. The school also ranks essays, recommendations, talent/ability, personal qualities, and extracurricular activities as "very important" in the admissions process. Although Bowdoin is, technically, a test-optional school, it pays to have high SAT/ACTs. The acceptance rate may be shrinking, but the average student profile has held relatively steady. Those with the best chance of acceptance will be near the top of their high school class and possess standardized test scores above the 95th percentile. Applying early decision also will provide a great boost for your prospects; 26% of ED applicants were accepted last admissions cycle.

Worth Your Money?

Bowdoin's annual cost of attendance is $85,100, and merit aid awards are practically nonexistent. Fortunately, the school is generous with need-based aid, meeting 100% of the demonstrated need for qualifying students. At present, undergraduates who can demonstrate need receive an average annual grant of $61k. If you come from a family making an income in the top 5% nationwide—it is estimated that nearly half of all Bowdoin students do—you can expect to pay full price. In the end, the average graduate takes out less than the national average in loans, which isn't bad for the privilege of attending one of the nation's most elite institutions.

FINANCIAL
Institutional Type: Private
In-State Tuition: $64,910
Out-of-State Tuition: $64,910
Room & Board: $17,690
Books & Supplies: $840

Avg. Need-Based Grant: $59,010
Avg. % of Need Met: 100%

Avg. Merit-Based Award: $1,000
% Receiving (Freshmen w/o Need): 0%

Avg. Cumulative Debt: $20,652
% of Students Borrowing: 23%

CAREER
Who Recruits
1. Barclay's
2. Deutsche Bank
3. Prudential
4. Cornerstone Research
5. Teach for America

Notable Internships
1. Athena Global Advisors
2. eBay
3. CBS News

Top Employers
1. Unum
2. Fidelity Investments
3. Massachusetts General Hospital
4. Google
5. Morgan Stanley

Where Alumni Work
1. Boston
2. New York City
3. Portland, ME
4. San Francisco
5. Washington, DC

Earnings
College Scorecard (10-YR Post-Entry): $68,211
PayScale (Early Career): $67,200
PayScale (Mid-Career): $135,900
PayScale 20-Year ROI: $710,000

RANKINGS
Money: 4.5
U.S. News: 9, Liberal Arts Colleges
Wall Street Journal/THE: 89
Washington Monthly: 11, Liberal Arts Colleges

OVERGENERALIZATIONS
Students are:
Politically liberal
Always studying
Outdoorsy
Wealthy
Involved/invested in campus life

COLLEGE OVERLAPS
Brown University
Colby College
Carleton College
Dartmouth College
Yale University

Brandeis University

Waltham, Massachusetts | 781-736-3500

Unlike many other elite Boston-area universities, this institution does not have 300-400 years of history and tradition. Founded in 1948 by a group of Jewish donors only a few weeks before the modern State of Israel was established, Brandeis has been a nonsectarian university open to talented students of all backgrounds and faiths. Home to almost 3,700 undergraduates with a female-heavy split (57/43), Brandeis offers 43 majors, the most popular of which are in the social sciences (18%), biology (17%), business (10%), psychology (8%), public administration (8%), and computer science (7%).

Inside the Classroom

An ethos of high academic standards and intellectual curiosity permeates this Waltham, Massachusetts, campus. An awe-inspiring 50%+ of Brandeis undergraduates double major. Core requirements for all students include a university writing seminar; one qualitative reasoning course; one diversity, equity, and inclusion course; one difference and justice in the world course; three semesters of a foreign language; and at least one class within each of the schools of humanities, science, social science, and creative arts.

Professors at Brandeis are committed to undergraduate education and will interact with you in close enough quarters that you can rest assured they will learn your name. The student-faculty ratio is 11:1, and 60% of courses contain nineteen or fewer students. Invitations to assist faculty members with academic research are common, even for undergraduates. In the Chemistry Department alone, 260 undergrads have coauthored and published papers with their professors in the last fifteen years. International experiences also abound, whether you are interacting with the 20% of the student body who are citizens of another country or decide to travel abroad for a semester, which 40% of undergraduates do in one of 160 approved destinations.

Departments with a particularly strong national reputation include economics, international studies, and sociology as well as all of the traditional premed pathways including biology, chemistry, and the Health: Science, Society, and Policy program. More than 200 students work each year with the school's Office of Academic Fellowships to apply for sponsored opportunities to pursue their intellectual passions after graduation. Many have successfully landed Fulbright, Boren, and Critical Language Scholarships, among others.

Outside the Classroom

With over 200 student organizations, the club scene plays a prominent role at Brandeis. A cappella, Jewish groups, intramural sports, and theater are among the most popular. Opportunities to volunteer in the local community abound, and many take advantage; over 60% accrue more than 300 service hours over their four years. Fraternities and sororities do operate on campus and have a genuine presence, although they are unrecognized by the university. The Brandeis Judges (the school is named for famed Supreme Court Justice Louis Brandeis) compete in NCAA Division III and field nineteen teams (10 for women, 9 for men). The school also has nineteen club teams that include Brazilian Jiu-Jitsu, archery, and sailing. With a plethora of activities in which to participate and a generally active social scene, you don't need to venture off campus in order to fill your days with excitement. Of course, with Boston less than ten miles away, many do stray away from Waltham on the weekends. Over three-quarters of undergrads (and 99% of freshmen) choose to live on campus; Brandeis' nineteen dorms are often ranked highly on lists of best collegiate housing.

Career Services

The Hiatt Career Center is staffed by 15 professionals with expertise in career counseling, giving it a 246:1 student-to-advisor ratio, which is better than average compared to other schools featured in this guide. It deploys its resources effectively, connecting with more than 50% of undergrads through counseling appointments, workshops, or job fairs. One-on-one counseling is available to all students as often as once per week, and the center encourages developing a relationship with one particular counselor over your four years of study.

E-mail: admissions@brandeis.edu | Website: brandeis.edu

Specialized counseling is available for those considering pursuing an MD or other healthcare-related positions after undergrad. Walk-in hours are more generous than most universities and can be utilized for quick questions that require fifteen minutes or less of interaction. Career Services connects students with internship/employment opportunities by a variety of means. Industry Meetups bring Brandeis alumni to campus from a host of fields. Brandeis Networking Nights are held over winter break each year in Washington, DC, and New York City. It also hosts area-specific fairs for students concentrating in computer science, careers with a social impact, or volunteer and internship opportunities; over 40% of recent grads attended at least one job fair. On-site interviews are conducted at fall and spring career fairs. This adds up to almost all graduates finding their next destination within months of leaving the university.

Professional Outcomes

Within six months of graduation, 98% of the Class of 2022 had found their way to employment (59%), graduate school (35%), or another full-time activity like travel or volunteer work (4%). The most common industries entered by Brandeis grads are (in order): healthcare, science/research, computer science, education, and finance/banking. Three of the largest employers of recent grads are in the healthcare sector: Boston Children's Hospital, Massachusetts General Hospital, and the Dana Farber Cancer Institute. Nonprofits such as Teach for America, City Year, and the Peace Corps are also well represented. Members of the Class of 2022 were hired by Red Hat, Deloitte, Nasdaq, NPR, and McKinsey & Company. The average starting salary for recent grads is $61k. The greatest number of graduates remains in Boston but many flock to New York City, DC, San Francisco, Los Angeles, and Philadelphia.

A large contingent of grads elects to continue at Brandeis for graduate school. The next most commonly attended graduate/professional schools over a recent three-year period included BU, Columbia, Duke, Harvard, and Yale. That list is a good indication that Brandeis' reputation for academic excellence leads to positive outcomes for those applying to elite graduate schools. Those applying to medical school are remarkably successful, gaining acceptance between 65 and 75% annually, 20-30 points higher than the national average.

Admission

Brandeis is one of the rare, elite New England liberal arts schools that has not experienced an admissions rate freefall over the past decade. Typically, 30-35% of applicants find success, the same range as five years ago; the Class of 2026 was admitted at a 39% clip. The average SAT and ACT scores of accepted students have increased, but that is likely more a result of the school going test-optional in 2013 than an indicator that the applicant pool has become more competitive. Those who submitted traditional standardized test scores generally earned high scores. The mid-50% SAT range for a member of the Class of 2026 was 1360-1500 and the composite ACT score range was 31-34.

Excellent performance in the classroom is valued most strongly by the admissions committee, with 83% of Brandeis undergrads in the top 25% of their high school class and 57% in the top 10%. The average GPA was 3.88 and only 7% earned lower than a 3.25. The other categories that qualify as "very important" to the committee are class rank, first-generation status, and the rigor of one's high school curriculum. The rate of acceptance for early decision was 64%, which means that borderline applicants should strongly consider that option.

Worth Your Money?

Given the annual cost of attendance of $86k, you may be pleasantly surprised to learn that Brandeis is known for being quite generous, meeting 94% of demonstrated need. The school does prioritize enrolling an economically diverse student body, awarding need-based grants of $47,000 to qualifying undergraduates. Due to that generosity, many lower-to-middle-income students have the opportunity to attend this school. However, graduates do hold slightly more debt than the average college graduate in the United States. With solid financial aid offerings (as well as a bit of merit aid) and positive graduate outcomes, Brandeis University is typically worth its net price.

FINANCIAL
Institutional Type: Private
In-State Tuition: $62,722
Out-of-State Tuition: $62,722
Room & Board: $17,092
Books & Supplies: $1,000

Avg. Need-Based Grant: $50,325
Avg. % of Need Met: 97%

Avg. Merit-Based Award: $15,172
% Receiving (Freshmen w/o Need): 21%

Avg. Cumulative Debt: $28,061
% of Students Borrowing: 44%

CAREER
Who Recruits
1. TIBCO
2. Analysis Group
3. John Hancock
4. Sun Life Financial
5. Kayak

Notable Internships
1. Uber
2. Symantec
3. Goldman Sachs

Top Employers
1. Dell
2. Google
3. IBM
4. Morgan Stanley
5. Amazon

Where Alumni Work
1. Boston
2. New York City
3. Washington, DC
4. San Francisco
5. Los Angeles

Earnings
College Scorecard (10-YR Post-Entry): $73,676
PayScale (Early Career): $64,500
PayScale (Mid-Career): $135,700
PayScale 20-Year ROI: $650,000

RANKINGS
Money: 4
U.S. News: 60, National Universities
Wall Street Journal/THE: 223
Washington Monthly: 161, National Universities

OVERGENERALIZATIONS
Students are:
Economically diverse
More friendly
More quirky
Passionate about social justice
Less concerned with fashion or appearance

COLLEGE OVERLAPS
Boston University
Brown University
Cornell University
New York University
Tufts University

Brigham Young University

Provo, Utah | 801-422-2507

An almost exclusively Mormon student body of more than 31,400 undergraduates occupies Brigham Young's high-altitude campus in the mountainous and breathtaking area of Provo, Utah. In addition to living by a strict honor code guided by the LDS Church (more on this later), students come to BYU for its 195 undergraduate majors and reputation for academic excellence.

Inside the Classroom

Required coursework for BYU undergraduates includes a number of courses in the Mormon faith including Teachings & Doctrine of the Book of Mormon, Christ and the Everlasting Gospel, Foundations of the Restoration, and The Eternal Family. Mandatory courses in American heritage, global and cultural awareness, first-year writing, advanced oral and written communication, foreign language, and the social, biological, and physical sciences are all part of the core curriculum that supports BYU's larger mission "to provide an education that is (1) spiritually strengthening, (2) intellectually enlarging, and (3) character building, leading to (4) lifelong learning and service."

A 21:1 student-to-faculty ratio translates to some undergraduate sections being a bit large. Thirteen percent of sections contain more than fifty students. However, those lecture hall courses are balanced with classes of more modest size; 47% of courses have nineteen or fewer students. Despite the size of the university and some classes, the school does an excellent job getting undergraduate students involved in hands-on research. In the Department of Chemistry and Biochemistry, 88% of students worked with a faculty mentor on a research project. Additionally, the school offers 200+ approved study abroad programs in 61 countries; over three-fifths partake.

The areas where the most degrees were conferred in 2022 were business (14%), biology (12%), engineering (8%), health professions (7%), and the social sciences (7%). The programs with the strongest national reputations are those within the Marriott School of Business and, to a slightly lesser extent, the Ira A. Fulton College of Engineering. Brigham Young alumni do occasionally win highly competitive post-graduation recognition, but in 2017, the National Scholarships, Fellowships, and Programs office was shut down, and those duties now fall under the purview of the Honors College. Students can still apply, but this is certainly a program in transition. However, in 2022, BYU was named the top school in the nation for Boren Scholarships.

Outside the Classroom

While not a requirement, a fair number of freshmen (83%) live in on-campus dorms. In total, only 22% live on campus, but over 23,000 students live in BYU-contracted housing in the immediate area. There is no Greek life; rather, the LDS Church is at the center of much of student life outside the classroom. The school is governed by an Honor Code that includes clauses about facial hair, foul language, chastity, and abstaining from the consumption of caffeinated beverages. A good number of recognized student organizations are related to religion, volunteer work, or professional associations. One of the more recognizable and typical elements of BYU college life is the passion displayed for the school's sports teams. The Cougars send 21 athletic squads into high-level competition in NCAA Division I and have seen ten NCAA titles, a Heisman Trophy winner, and over 1,000 All-Americans. Football games draw 56,000 fans to LaVell Edwards Stadium. Over 12,000 students participate in intramural sports each year on this extremely athletically-inclined campus. Outdoor activities are also emphasized and are aided by the overwhelming natural beauty surrounding the school's 550+ acre campus situated at the edge of the Rocky Mountains.

Career Services

Brigham Young's University Career Services Office employs 20 professionals (not including office managers) who are responsible for career development and counseling. That works out to a counselor-to-student ratio of 1,550:1. BYU's Career Services staff believes that a career is more than just a job; it is a calling to which one is deeply dedicated. To help students find their path, the office offers free assessments such as the Myers-Briggs, the Strong Interest Inventory, and TypeFocus. The university even offers a credited course called Career Exploration intended to help undergrads learn their strengths, define their interests, and begin seriously thinking about a vocation.

Three 2022 career fairs were attended by a total of 192 companies and 1,182 students. Hundreds of companies interview on campus each year. All students are able to utilize Handshake accounts that allow them to connect with potential employers for jobs and internships. One of the school's greatest career services strengths is the tight-knit network of alumni who are always willing to help a fellow Cougar. While this office is understaffed, it does excel in the areas of graduate school placement and career development that are uniquely tailored to this mostly LDS-affiliated population.

Professional Outcomes

The average age of a BYU graduate is nearly twenty-five, a result of the eighteen months to two years of missionary work members of the LDS Church are required to complete. The most popular fields entered are business management, education, operations, engineering, sales, and information technology. By a wide margin, the two largest employers of BYU alums are the university itself and the LDS Church. However, there are hundreds of Cougars working at major corporations including Adobe, Google, Microsoft, and Goldman Sachs. The median salary of a 2022 grad was $62,500. Unsurprisingly, Provo and the Greater Salt Lake area see the highest concentrations of BYU alumni. Major cities outside of Utah with significant numbers of graduates include San Francisco, Phoenix, LA, and Seattle.

Brigham Young is in the same league with Berkeley, Cornell, the University of Michigan, and the University of Wisconsin in terms of producing future PhDs. Over the past decade, more than 3,000 alumni have gone on to earn doctoral degrees. Many grads pursuing advanced degrees do so at BYU, yet plenty of others relocate to pursue educational opportunities at institutions such as MIT, Vanderbilt, and the University of North Carolina. In 2022-23, there were 367 BYU students who applied to allopathic medical programs; 40-50% are accepted in a given year, a slightly better mark than the national average. Those who attend law school flock to BYU's own well-regarded Reuben Clark Law School, but 2022 grads also matriculated into law school at Stanford, UPenn, and Harvard.

Admission

Despite a 67% acceptance rate, gaining admission to BYU requires a strong academic profile. The high rate of acceptance is attributable to the school's uniquely self-selecting applicant pool. Unless you are a member of the Church of Jesus Christ of Latter-day Saints, you likely aren't placing the university on your college wish list. Most students who apply favor the ACT over the SAT, and among 2022-23 freshmen, the middle-50% ACT range was 27-32. Those who submit SAT scores have a middle-50% band of 1280-1450. Roughly 60% typically finish in the top 10% of their high school class. On a 4.0 scale, 88% had a GPA of 3.75 or higher and the average GPA was 3.90.

Even with over 10,500 applications to read, BYU employs a holistic review of each one. It values eleven factors as being "very important" in influencing admissions decisions. In addition to the usual factors of rigor of curriculum, grades, recommendations, essays, and test scores, the university also places great importance on religious affiliation, volunteer work, work experience, character/personal qualities, talent/ability, and extracurricular involvement. High-achieving LDS teenagers frequently see BYU as their top or, perhaps, even their only choice for postsecondary education. Those who fit the mold will gain acceptance. Only rarely do non-Mormon individuals attend BYU; they comprise less than 2% of the student body.

Worth Your Money?

Similar to an in-state and out-of-state rate, BYU charges different tuition to Latter-day Saints than it does to non-Latter-day Saints. Members of the LDS Church pay an annual tuition of only $6,496, an unheard amount in the third decade of the twenty-first century. The total annual cost of attendance is barely over $23k, and the majority also receive some type of merit aid with the average award being over $4,000. For members of the LDS Church, BYU is an amazing fit and worth every penny. For the limited number of non-LDS members who apply, Brigham Young University is still an exceptional value, even at a higher cost.

FINANCIAL
Institutional Type: Private
In-State Tuition: $6,496
Out-of-State Tuition: $6,496
Room & Board: $9,720
Books & Supplies: $1,040

Avg. Need-Based Grant: $6,073
Avg. % of Need Met: 34%

Avg. Merit-Based Award: $4,538
% Receiving (Freshmen w/o Need): 27%

Avg. Cumulative Debt: $15,049
% of Students Borrowing: 20%

CAREER
Who Recruits
1. Podium
2. Qualtrics
3. Domo, Inc.
4. Pluralsight
5. Lucid

Notable Internships
1. Adobe
2. Bain Capital
3. Utah Jazz

Top Employers
1. LDS Church
2. Intermountain Healthcare
3. Qualtrics
4. Adobe
5. Vivint Smart Home

Where Alumni Work
1. Provo, UT
2. Salt Lake City, UT
3. Phoenix
4. San Francisco
5. Los Angeles

Earnings
College Scorecard (10-YR Post-Entry): $74,630
PayScale (Early Career): $63,400
PayScale (Mid-Career): $120,100
PayScale 20-Year ROI: $752,000

RANKINGS
Money: Not Ranked
U.S. News: 115, National Universities
Wall Street Journal/THE: 20
Washington Monthly: 25, National Universities

OVERGENERALIZATIONS
Students are:
Politically conservative
Less likely to party
Service-oriented
Religious
Crazy about the cougars

COLLEGE OVERLAPS
Arizona State University
Brigham Young University - Hawaii
Brigham Young University - Idaho
University of Utah
Utah State University

Brown University

Providence, Rhode Island | 401-863-2378

ADMISSION
Admission Rate: 5%
Admission Rate - Men: 7%
Admission Rate - Women: 4%
EA Admission Rate: Not Offered
ED Admission Rate: 15%
ED Admits as % of Total Admits: 35%
Admission Rate (5-Year Trend): -3%
% of Admits Attending (Yield): 67%
Transfer Admission Rate: 5%

SAT Reading/Writing (Middle 50%): 730-780
SAT Math (Middle 50%): 760-800
ACT Composite (Middle 50%): 34-36

% Graduated in Top 10% of HS Class: 93%
% Graduated in Top 25% of HS Class: 97%
% Graduated in Top 50% of HS Class: 100%

Demonstrated Interest: Not Considered
Legacy Status: Considered
Racial/Ethnic Status: Considered
Admission Interview Offered: No

ENROLLMENT
Total Undergraduate Enrollment: 7,639
% Full-Time: 99%
% Male: 49%
% Female: 51%
% Out-of-State: 94%
% Fraternity: 7%
% Sorority: 4%
% On-Campus (All Undergraduate): 70%
Freshman Housing Required: Yes

% African-American: 8%
% Asian: 19%
% Hispanic: 12%
% White: 38%
% Other: 3%
% International: 12%
% Low-Income: 14%

ACADEMICS
Student-to-Faculty Ratio: 6 to 1
% of Classes Under 20: 68%
% of Classes 20-49: 20%
% of Classes 50 or More: 12%
% Full-Time Faculty: 92%
% Full-Time Faculty w/ Terminal Degree: 95%

Top Programs
Applied Mathematics
Computer Science
Economics
Engineering
English
Geology
History
Neuroscience

Retention Rate: 97%
4-Year Graduation Rate: 85%
6-Year Graduation Rate: 96%

Curricular Flexibility: Very Flexible
Academic Rating: ★★★★★

#CollegesWorthYourMoney

Founded in 1764, Brown University holds the distinction as one of the oldest colleges in the United States and, of course, as a member of the vaunted Ivy League. Yet, much like its Rhode Island home, Brown possesses an uncommon blend of tradition and extraordinary commitment to the celebration of individuality. Toward that aim, Brown's Open Curriculum has long been the guiding academic force at the university, perfectly capturing its spirit and core values. The 7,639 undergraduates who chose (and were chosen by) Brown fit the school's ethos and relish the chance to be the architects of their own educational journey.

Inside the Classroom
Students must choose one of 80+ "concentration programs," but there are no required courses. In essence, the guiding philosophy is that students should take control of their learning, pursue knowledge in areas that they are truly passionate about, and learn to integrate and synthesize information across disciplines. Specialized programs include the Brown/RISD five-year Dual Degree program that leads to a bachelor's from Brown as well as a BFA from the famed Rhode Island School of Design. Teens committed to the medical field even before exiting high school can apply for entry into the program in Liberal Medical Education that allows students to graduate in eight years with an MD from Brown's Warren Alpert Medical School.

This one-of-a-kind experience transpires with a student-faculty ratio of only 6:1, and 100% of faculty members spend time teaching the undergraduate population. Class sizes tend to be small—68% have fewer than twenty students—and 35% are comprised of nine or fewer students. Student surveys reveal an unsurpassed level of satisfaction with the quality of instruction and professor availability. Undergraduates give favorable reviews in those areas at an overwhelming 92-97% clip. Undergraduate research is a big part of the Brown experience for many students; 50% conduct research alongside a faculty member and 43% complete an independent study. As is typical in the Ivy League, the majority of students stay grounded on (or near) campus for all four years. However, each year, 470 students do travel abroad.

Biology, economics, computer science, mathematics, and engineering are among the most popular areas of concentration at Brown; however, it is hard to distinguish any one program, because Brown possesses outstanding offerings across so many disciplines. Computer science is a growing department, conferring 14% of the school's degrees in 2022; applied math and English are notably strong. Graduates are a scholarly lot and experience high levels of success at procuring prestigious academic fellowships. In 2023 alone, the school produced 30 Fulbright Scholars, and graduates and alumni earn as many as 30 National Science Foundation Graduate Research Fellowships in a given year. Brown has produced the seventh most Rhodes Scholars of any institution in history.

Outside the Classroom
The Main Green, surrounded by iconic buildings and located at the heart of campus, is almost always a lively hub of activity. There are more than 500 clubs and activities available to what tends to be a highly involved student body. Performance-based groups such as a cappella, improv, music, and theater draw large numbers of participants. A thriving student-run media scene includes the Brown Daily Herald, the nation's second-oldest collegiate daily, and two award-winning campus radio stations. Brown fields an unusually large number of varsity athletic teams—37—which compete in NCAA Division I. The Brown Bears claim 18 women's teams, the largest number of any school in the country. Greek life plays a moderate role on campus with a 4% participation rate for women and a 7% rate for men. Last year, 70% of students (99% of freshmen) lived on campus in one of forty-nine residence halls as old as 1822 and as new as 2023. Off-campus housing and a multitude of cultural and entertainment options exist in Providence, including the bustling Thayer Street that runs through campus.

Career Services
The CareerLAB ("LAB" stands for Life After Brown) has 13 full-time staff members who focus on career advising, pre-professional advising, employer relations, marketing, and BrownConnect, which connects current students with alumni. The 588:1 student-to-advisor ratio is slightly higher than the ratio for other midsize schools featured in this guide. However, the LAB is extremely effective at outreach and has a measurable impact on student success. Remarkably, more than three-quarters of Brown undergrads reported engaging with CareerLAB last year.

In a single recent academic year, career services staff counseled 3,600 students and brought 240 employers to campus, leading to 900 job interviews. Freshmen engaged at an extremely high rate of 69%, which has been an institutional goal. Keeping busy, Brown manages to put on more than one hundred career programs and one hundred employer information sessions per year. Its career fairs, alumni events, and workshops drew almost 20,000. If you can name a corporation, chances are it will be visiting Providence at some point this upcoming year. Help finding internships is always available as the school provides 600+ funded opportunities per year. The CareerLAB deploys its resources well in order to meet the needs of its talented population, and it receives high praise from our staff.

Professional Outcomes

Soon after receiving their Brown diplomas, 69% of graduates enter the world of employment. The university has placed significant numbers of recent graduates in top companies within the following fields: the arts (CAA, Lincoln Center), consulting (every major firm), finance (every major investment house), government (United Nations, Federal Reserve Board), technology (Amazon, all major tech companies), and the list goes on and on. Companies employing the greatest number of Brown alums include Google, Microsoft, Goldman Sachs, Amazon, Morgan Stanley, Apple, McKinsey & Company, and Bain & Company. New York, Boston, Providence, San Francisco, and DC are the five cities attracting the greatest number of Brown alumni. That makes sense given that the two most popular areas of employment are in technology and finance, and many such firms are based in those urban areas.

The Class of 2022 saw 27% of graduates go directly into graduate/professional school. Right out of undergrad, Brown students boasted an exceptional 81% admission rate to med school (the national average was 43%) and an 81% admission rate to law school (national average was 70%). A decade after graduating, 80% of Brown alumni have earned an advanced degree and 88% say that their degree prepared them for their current career. Frequently attended institutions include all of the Ivies plus Stanford, Duke, Carnegie Mellon, the London School of Economics, Oxford, Johns Hopkins, Berkeley, UCLA, and UVA. In sum, you can rest assured that if you do well at Brown, there are few graduate or professional schools on the planet that will not welcome you with open arms.

Admission

In selecting their Class of 2026 from a pool of 50,649 applicants, Brown accepted only 5.1%, and 93% of those who went on to enroll were in the top 10% of their high school class. A decade earlier, the admit rate was just shy of 16%, but it has been in the single digits since 2014. Back in 2014, the middle 25th-75th percentile range for Brown freshmen was 1330-1550 compared to the current range of 1500-1560. Even with a degree of SAT score inflation, those numbers indicate that the university has become even more competitive in recent years. Ninety-four percent of freshmen in the Class of 2026 scored better than a 700 on the math portion of the SAT.

The admissions office lists seven areas that are considered most important in determining admission: rigor of courses, grades, class rank, recommendations, essays, talent/ability, and character/personal qualities. In a typical year, close to half of admitted students were either the valedictorian or salutatorian of their high school class. Those applying early are accepted at a much higher rate than in the regular round. The Class of 2026 saw 896 seats filled through ED with an acceptance rate of 15%. The 896 admits account for roughly 52% of the total class. In short, those looking to come to Providence should be individuals at the top of their class who are intellectually curious and open-minded, and who possess intangible qualities that would allow them to flourish in Brown's unique academic program.

Worth Your Money?

With an $84,828 annual cost of attendance, Brown University will cost a great deal for anyone who does not qualify for financial aid. For the current students who receive need-based grants, 100% of their demonstrated need will be covered. That equates to an average grant of more than $60,000 per year. Despite the cost, Brown is the type of school worth its hefty price tag. Not only will the Ivy League credentials benefit you in graduate/professional school admissions and the world of employment, but the quality of the educational experience, the flexibility of your coursework, and the chance to take many small, seminar-style classes with distinguished faculty are of incredible value.

FINANCIAL
Institutional Type: Private
In-State Tuition: $68,230
Out-of-State Tuition: $68,230
Room & Board: $16,598
Books & Supplies: $1,300

Avg. Need-Based Grant: $60,190
Avg. % of Need Met: 100%

Avg. Merit-Based Award: $19,306
% Receiving (Freshmen w/o Need): <1%

Avg. Cumulative Debt: $26,272
% of Students Borrowing: 21%

CAREER
Who Recruits
1. Boston Consulting Group
2. Oracle
3. Millenium Management
4. BlackRock
5. Teach for America

Notable Internships
1. Google
2. Etsy
3. Apple

Top Employers
1. Google
2. Microsoft
3. Facebook
4. Goldman Sachs
5. Amazon

Where Alumni Work
1. New York City
2. Providence
3. Boston
4. San Francisco
5. Washington, DC

Earnings
College Scorecard (10-YR Post-Entry): $87,811
PayScale (Early Career): $74,700
PayScale (Mid-Career): $142,400
PayScale 20-Year ROI: $992,000

RANKINGS
Money: 5
U.S. News: 9, National Universities
Wall Street Journal/THE: 67
Washington Monthly: 43, National Universities

OVERGENERALIZATIONS
Students are:
Intellectually curious
Politically liberal
Politically active
Wealthy
Service-oriented

COLLEGE OVERLAPS
Columbia University
Cornell University
Duke University
Harvard University
University of Pennsylvania

Bryn Mawr College

Bryn Mawr, Pennsylvania | 610-526-5152

Eleven miles west of Philadelphia and situated on the swanky Main Line rests an immaculate, 135-acre campus that serves as the educational home to 1,409 brilliant, politically active, and fiercely independent young women. Bryn Mawr College, still an all-female institution, used to serve as the sister school to Haverford College, which was all-male until the late 1970s. The two schools still retain a degree of partnership. In fact, Bryn Mawr, Haverford, and Swarthmore (collectively known as the Tri-Co) all run on the same academic calendar so students can take courses at all three schools. Additionally, Bryn Mawr undergraduates can opt to take up to two courses at Penn each semester. There are more than 3,000 cross-registrations exercised each year.

Inside the Classroom
On the home campus, undergraduates can choose from 35 majors and 50 minors. Roughly 35% of the student body earns degrees in the natural sciences or mathematics, a figure four times the national average for women. However, as a true liberal arts school, all students must take courses in each of Bryn Mawr's four "Approaches": critical interpretation, cross-cultural analysis, inquiry into the past, and scientific investigation. Additional courses in quantitative reasoning and a full year studying one of ten foreign languages round out the mandated coursework. The college does point out that "within this structure, variety abounds," noting that students averse to the hard sciences can fulfill their scientific investigation requirement through the likes of anthropology or psychology.

An 8:1 student-to-faculty ratio leads to small class sizes with 74% of sections having fewer than twenty students, and 24% of sections enrolling nine students or fewer. The median class size is just 14 students. This type of academic setting leads to close mentoring from professors. Over 500 undergraduates collaborate on research and independent projects with faculty each year. Those electing to study abroad have more than seventy programs to choose from and, in recent years, 33% of students have spent a semester in thirty countries across six continents.

This elite liberal arts school offers a number of excellent academic programs that receive national recognition from employers and graduate schools. By volume, the most popular majors are mathematics, psychology, biology, English, and computer science. Nationally competitive fellowship/scholarship programs also look favorably upon Bryn Mawr alumni. Recent graduates have been successful in procuring Boren, Fulbright, and Watson Fellowships.

Outside the Classroom
Bryn Mawr's breathtakingly beautiful and historic campus is where 100% of freshmen and 90% of the overall student body reside. Sororities are not permitted at Bryn Mawr as the college prefers participation in the 100+ nonexclusive student organizations presently active. Clubs in music/performing arts and community service are among the most popular. Student government is also strong as elected members are dedicated to carrying out the institution's Honor Code. This is a tradition-rich school with events such as Parade Night, Lantern Night, and May Day all taken seriously by the student population. The Owls participate in twelve NCAA Division III sports, and casual athletic participation is always an option as the school boasts a 50,000-square-foot gymnasium, Olympic-size swimming pool, and outdoor tennis courts. While there is plenty to do on campus, nearby Haverford College, Swarthmore, and Villanova University provide Bryn Mawr undergrads with additional social scenes to explore. The college's proximity to Philadelphia means that restaurants, concerts, sporting events, museums, and theaters are only a short drive away.

Career Services
The Career and Civic Engagement Center is staffed by 13 professionals who specialize in areas like career counseling, prelaw advising, and employer relations. With an eye-popping 108:1 student-to-advisor ratio, Bryn Mawr rates among the very best when compared to other colleges featured in this guide. That provides undergraduates with ample opportunity to work closely with a career counselor on resume development, internship hunting, and networking. This level of attention resulted in 78% of recent graduates landing at least one internship.

In terms of employer relations, rather than hosting their own events, the college tends to rely more on partnerships with other Seven Sisters schools and the Tri-College Consortium (TCC) with Haverford and Swarthmore. The Fall Policy & Government Career Fair is held at the University of Pennsylvania and is open to members of the TCC. Spring events held at Haverford College include the Tri-College STEM Recruiting Day and the Philadelphia Career Connection, which attracts forty employers. Students can find internship and job opportunities online through Handshake or via the Selective Liberal Arts Consortium, which can facilitate off-campus interviews. Bryn Mawr has a low student-to-counselor ratio and has an excellent track record for helping its students gain acceptance into top graduate schools. However, its alumni salary figures lag behind its peers, and its on-campus recruiting opportunities are somewhat limited.

Professional Outcomes

One year after receiving their diplomas, 57% of Bryn Mawr graduates had found employment and a robust 28% had already entered graduate school. Among those who are employed, the five most popular fields are business, education, health/medicine, science, and communications/media. With graduating classes of under 400 students, there are no massive numbers of alumni clustered in particular companies as is the case at many larger institutions. Most of the organizations employing the greatest number of alumni are universities and hospital systems, although Google, Accenture, JPMorgan Chase, and Vanguard do employ a fair number of Bryn Mawr graduates. Median mid-career salaries are on the low side by elite college standards, in part due to the heavy concentration of students pursuing lengthy graduate programs.

Among recent grads pursuing further education, 63% were in master's programs, 13% were already working on their PhD, 10% were in medical school, and 2% were in law school. Again, due to the minuscule class sizes, it's rare that multiple graduates flock to particular institutions for graduate school. However, to get a sense of the prestigious programs accepting Bryn Mawr alumnae, one can simply examine the higher education destinations of recent graduates. Those included Brown University, Sciences Po, MIT, Stanford University, Harvard University, Oxford University, and Yale University.

Admission

Bryn Mawr accepts 31% of those who apply, making it more selective than Mount Holyoke, comparable to Smith, and less selective than Barnard and Wellesley. Freshmen at Bryn Mawr possessed middle-50% SAT scores of 1300-1470 and 30-35 on the ACT. A healthy 63% finished in the top 10% of their high school class; 86% were in the top quarter. Fifty-nine percent of those accepted into the Class of 2026 were from public schools and 16% were first-generation college students.

The admissions office places the greatest emphasis on the rigor of an applicant's high school curriculum, essays, and recommendation letters. Grades, class rank, extracurricular activities, and character/personal qualities are next. While Bryn Mawr is a test-optional school, 56% submitted SAT results, and 29% submitted ACT scores, so tests do still play a role in shaping the overall admissions picture. Early decision is the right choice for those who have the school atop their college list. Bryn Mawr fills a large portion of its freshman class in the early round and accepts 57% of those who apply (in the most recent year reported). A highly selective destination point for high-achieving young women, this member of the Seven Sisters Colleges is tougher to get into than its acceptance rate would imply. Known as a supportive, collaborative, and academically excellent school, Bryn Mawr draws brilliant and accomplished applicants from around the globe. An impressive resume is needed, and applying early can give you an edge.

Worth Your Money?

Despite a list price above $80,000, Bryn Mawr is generous with aid, leading to graduates who possess lower-than-average debt. Seventy-eight percent of freshmen in 2022-23 received some form of financial aid with the average need-based package (for eligible students) exceeding $61k. This school meets 100% of each student's demonstrated need, helping to make Bryn Mawr more accessible to those of varying socioeconomic backgrounds. The average cumulative debt for graduates is slightly below the national average.

FINANCIAL
Institutional Type: Private
In-State Tuition: $62,560
Out-of-State Tuition: $62,560
Room & Board: $18,690
Books & Supplies: $1,000

Avg. Need-Based Grant: $57,712
Avg. % of Need Met: 100%

Avg. Merit-Based Award: $18,728
% Receiving (Freshmen w/o Need): 38%

Avg. Cumulative Debt: $30,234
% of Students Borrowing: 50%

CAREER
Who Recruits
1. FDIC
2. Moody's Corporation
3. Philadelphia Museum of Art
4. Vanguard
5. Northwestern Mutual

Notable Internships
1. Whitney Museum of Art
2. JetBlue
3. Citi

Top Employers
1. Penn Medicine
2. Children's Hospital of Philadelphia
3. Vanguard
4. Accenture
5. Google

Where Alumni Work
1. Philadelphia
2. New York City
3. Washington, DC
4. Boston
5. San Francisco

Earnings
College Scorecard (10-YR Post-Entry): $72,117
PayScale (Early Career): $59,800
PayScale (Mid-Career): $103,700
PayScale 20-Year ROI: $362,000

RANKINGS
Money: 4
U.S. News: 30, Liberal Arts Colleges
Wall Street Journal/THE: Not Ranked
Washington Monthly: 10, Liberal Arts Colleges

OVERGENERALIZATIONS
Students are:
Intellectually curious
Politically liberal
Less likely to party
Passionate about social justice
Always studying

COLLEGE OVERLAPS
Barnard College
Brown University
Haverford College
Mount Holyoke College
Smith College

Bucknell University

Lewisburg, Pennsylvania | 570-577-3000

Approximately 3,700 undergraduate students grace this gorgeous, 450-acre campus in bucolic Lewisburg, Pennsylvania. While technically a "university," the number of graduate students is nominal, and, academically, the school functions more as a liberal arts college with a strong engineering program. Socially, with its focus on athletics and Greek life, the "university" label may start to feel more apt.

Inside the Classroom

Over 60 majors and 70 minors are on tap across three undergraduate schools: the College of Arts & Sciences, Freeman College of Management, and the College of Engineering. Required core curriculum coursework for A&S and Freeman is identical and must include multiple classes under the umbrella categories of intellectual skills, disciplinary perspectives, tools for critical engagement, and a culminating experience that involves research and/or independent study. The College of Engineering keeps the vast majority of its requirements concentrated in the areas of math, science, and engineering. Before classes even commence, all first-year students attend a five-day new student orientation centered around scholarship and community. Further, all freshmen take a foundation seminar course, and that instructor serves as the faculty adviser until the student declares a major in the sophomore year. That supportive environment helps the school maintain a superb 91-92% retention rate.

Getting well-acquainted with your professors is easy with a 9:1 student-faculty ratio, and class sizes are reasonably small. Slightly more than half of courses at Bucknell unfold in a classroom of no more than nineteen students, and 88% of all sections enroll fewer than twenty-nine students. All of Bucknell's 405 full-time professors spend some of their time teaching undergraduates. Last year, almost 300 students took advantage of summer research opportunities on campus. An additional 175 typically engage in research for academic credit during the regular school year. Study abroad semesters are available at over 130 sites across six continents, and 42% of the student body takes advantage of that (compared to 10% nationally).

The greatest number of degrees are conferred in the areas of the social sciences (26%), engineering (14%), business (14%), biology (11%), and psychology (9%). The Freeman College of Management and College of Engineering have the most prominent national reputations, but Bucknell is a well-regarded institution across the board. With a career-focused student body, this is not a college that produces a sizable number of postgraduate fellows or scholars, but three Class of 2022 Bucknell grads were awarded Fulbright Scholarships, and the school has averaged one Goldwater Scholar per year over the last five years.

Outside the Classroom

The vast majority of the student body, 88%, reside in university housing on campus. Many join the school's thriving Greek life with 30% of men and 41% of women becoming members of one of the school's eight fraternity or ten sorority chapters. For a university of Bucknell's modest size, athletics are massive in scale. The school fields 27 teams that play in the Patriot League of NCAA Division I. On top of that, intramural and club sports attract a high level of participation. Over 200 student clubs run on campus and enjoy small but loyal followings, thanks to the energy pouring into fraternities and athletics. Many Bucknell students also make time for volunteer work; three-quarters perform some degree of community service over the course of their four years. With no major city within a quick driving distance, students seeking some semblance of nightlife settle for Main Street in quiet Lewisburg. Central Pennsylvania does offer limitless opportunities for those who love the great outdoors with camping, hiking, kayaking, and similar activities available in abundance.

Career Services

Manned by 13 full-time professionals with expertise in career counseling, internship coordination, and company recruitment, the Center for Career Advancement offers a 288:1 student-to-advisor ratio, which is better than average compared to other schools featured in this guide. Each year, the Center for Career Advancement hosts a fall Job Expo attended by up to one hundred employers and 750 students. Attendees include corporations like Deloitte, Coca-Cola, and Hershey Entertainment & Resorts. Additionally, it organizes a separate internship/job fair in the spring, the Health & Law School Fair, the Engineering Career Network Event, and several off-campus events in New York and DC to afford Bucknell students the chance to meet with additional companies in the finance and government realms. More than 200 employers attend school-sponsored career fairs each year.

Corporations, including the likes of ExxonMobil and Procter & Gamble, appear regularly on campus to conduct job interviews. In a single year, 670 on-campus interviews were conducted with Bucknell seniors. Annually, the Center for Career Advancement helps over 500 students secure summer internships, which was cited by grads as frequently leading to their maiden jobs. In a given year, 57-74% of graduates complete at least one internship. With generous staffing and a track record of helping students, Bucknell's career services does a strong job preparing its undergraduates for the real world.

Professional Outcomes

Nine months after graduation, 94% of the Class of 2022 had launched their careers or entered graduate school. Financial services is the most common sector for Bucknell grads to enter, attracting 24% of alumni. The largest concentration of recent grads can be found working at Accenture, Sloan Kettering Cancer Center, PwC, Amazon Robotics, Yelp, and Axis Group. Across all graduating years, more than 75 Bucknellians are presently working at Goldman Sachs, Google, Merck, JPMorgan Chase & Co., Morgan Stanley, and EY. Across all disciplines, the average salary for a Class of 2022 grad was $69,540. Mid-career salaries for Bucknell grads fare well when compared to other liberal arts colleges.

Bucknell saw 18% of 2022 grads go directly into an advanced degree program. Bison alumni heading to graduate school predominantly pursue degrees in the medical field, social sciences, business, or engineering. Recent graduates have found their way into top med schools (e.g., Dartmouth, Penn State, and Duke) and to top engineering schools (e.g., Carnegie Mellon, Princeton, Stanford). Seven percent of this group decided to pursue a legal education. Law schools attended by recent grads include Temple University, Pepperdine, and UCLA. Geographically, most Bucknell grads remain concentrated in Pennsylvania, New York, New Jersey, and the DC metro area.

Admission

Bucknell admitted 33% of the 11,708 applicants into the Class of 2026. Surprisingly, the university received more applications five years prior and had a significantly lower acceptance rate of 25%. Admission into the well-regarded engineering programs is far more difficult than it is for the College of Arts & Humanities. The middle 50% SAT range for the Class of 2026 was 1180-1390; the ACT range was 27-32. A solid 59% finished in the top 10% of their high school class, and 84% were in the top quarter. The average unweighted GPA was a 3.63, and 40% of attending students earned better than a 3.75.

Rigor of classes, GPA, extracurricular activities, talent/ability, character/ability, and essays headline the most important factors for acceptance into Bucknell. Admissions staff members have stated that they keep a six-minute timer on their desks while they examine each application as a team. Thus, we know that your measurable achievements need to be within range in order for your intangibles/outside-the-classroom activities to become serious factors in admission. Those who apply early decision enjoy a major edge; last year, 54% of ED applicants were accepted. Being a legacy also gives you an admissions boost. The school regularly hosts events for children (or grandchildren) of alumni, and legacy students comprise 6-9% of the average freshman cohort.

Worth Your Money?

An $80,890 list price cost of attendance is made slightly less onerous by the average need-based grant package awarded of $46,000. Those falling in between financially—not qualifying for aid but not well-off enough to pay full freight—will need to consider whether their intended major/future career is likely to make loan payments worth the cost. If you were on a budget and studying to be a teacher, Bucknell may not prove a wise choice. If you were in the same financial boat but studying engineering or business, attending this school absolutely could be worth your money. Average debt loads accrued rest right around the national average.

FINANCIAL
Institutional Type: Private
In-State Tuition: $64,772
Out-of-State Tuition: $64,772
Room & Board: $16,118
Books & Supplies: $900

Avg. Need-Based Grant: $42,325
Avg. % of Need Met: 92%

Avg. Merit-Based Award: $24,895
% Receiving (Freshmen w/o Need): 11%

Avg. Cumulative Debt: $37,632
% of Students Borrowing: 38%

CAREER
Who Recruits
1. Exelon
2. Horizon Media
3. Nielsen
4. Ralph Lauren
5. Southwest Airlines

Notable Internships
1. NBCUniversal
2. CBRE
3. Bloomberg LP

Top Employers
1. PwC
2. Deloitte
3. Morgan Stanley
4. IBM
5. Merck

Where Alumni Work
1. New York City
2. Philadelphia
3. Washington, DC
4. Boston
5. Williamsport, PA

Earnings
College Scorecard (10-YR Post-Entry): $86,631
PayScale (Early Career): $72,000
PayScale (Mid-Career): $136,900
PayScale 20-Year ROI: $869,000

RANKINGS
Money: 4.5
U.S. News: 30, Liberal Arts Colleges
Wall Street Journal/THE: 109
Washington Monthly: 59, Liberal Arts Colleges

OVERGENERALIZATIONS
Students are:
Athletic/Active
Ready to party
More likely to rush a fraternity/sorority
Wealthy
Preppy

COLLEGE OVERLAPS
Colgate University
Lafayette College
Lehigh University
Pennsylvania State University - University Park
Villanova University

California Institute of Technology

ADMISSION
Admission Rate: 3%
Admission Rate - Men: 2%
Admission Rate - Women: 4%
EA Admission Rate: Not Reported
ED Admission Rate: Not Offered
ED Admits as % of Total Admits: Not Offered
Admission Rate (5-Year Trend): -5%
% of Admits Attending (Yield): 50%
Transfer Admission Rate: 6%

SAT Reading/Writing (Middle 50%): Test-Blind
SAT Math (Middle 50%): Test-Blind
ACT Composite (Middle 50%): Test-Blind

% Graduated in Top 10% of HS Class: 96%
% Graduated in Top 25% of HS Class: 100%
% Graduated in Top 50% of HS Class: 100%

Demonstrated Interest: Not Considered
Legacy Status: Not Considered
Racial/Ethnic Status: Considered
Admission Interview Offered: No

ENROLLMENT
Total Undergraduate Enrollment: 982
% Full-Time: 100%
% Male: 55%
% Female: 45%
% Out-of-State: 64%
% Fraternity: Not Offered
% Sorority: Not Offered
% On-Campus (All Undergraduate): 93%
Freshman Housing Required: Yes

% African-American: 4%
% Asian: 4%
% Hispanic: 6%
% White: 80%
% Other: 1%
% International: 1%
% Low-Income: 15%

ACADEMICS
Student-to-Faculty Ratio: 3 to 1
% of Classes Under 20: 70%
% of Classes 20-49: 21%
% of Classes 50 or More: 9%
% Full-Time Faculty: 94%
% Full-Time Faculty w/ Terminal Degree: 99%

Top Programs
Biology
Chemistry
Computer Science
Engineering
Geological and Planetary Sciences
Physics
Mathematics

Retention Rate: 97%
4-Year Graduation Rate: 81%
6-Year Graduation Rate: 93%

Curricular Flexibility: Somewhat Flexible
Academic Rating: ★★★★★

#CollegesWorthYourMoney

The setting of television's The Big Bang Theory, the California Institute of Technology is, as suggested by the show's focus on a group of socially awkward physicists, a collection of some of the most brilliant science and engineering minds in the world. Situated in gorgeous Pasadena, California, Caltech enrolls a mere 982 undergraduates, affectionately known as "Techers," very few of whom got a single question wrong on the math portion of the SAT. As tough as it is to gain admission, coursework at the school is perhaps an even more rigorous and consuming process.

Inside the Classroom
The university's common core is, not surprisingly, STEM-heavy with requirements that include Freshman Mathematics, Freshman Physics, Freshman Chemistry, and Freshman Biology. However, students also must conquer 36 units of the humanities and social sciences, nine units of physical education, and one course in scientific communication in which undergrads write a paper for submission to a peer-reviewed academic journal. There are six academic divisions: biology and biological engineering; chemistry and chemical engineering; engineering and applied science; geological and planetary sciences; the humanities and social sciences; and physics, mathematics, and astronomy, each with more options for specialized concentrations. Across all divisions, there are 28 distinct majors.

Possessing an absurdly favorable 3:1 student-to-faculty ratio, plenty of individualized attention is up for grabs. Class sizes are not quite as tiny as the student-to-faculty ratio might suggest, but 70% of courses enroll fewer than twenty students, and 28% enroll fewer than ten. Summer Undergraduate Research Fellowships (SURF) enjoy wide participation with 90% of undergraduates partaking, and 20% of that group going on to publish their results. Six approved study abroad programs are available at Cambridge University, University College London, University of Edinburgh, Copenhagen University, the University of Melbourne, and École Polytechnique in France.

Computer science is the most popular major, accounting for 38% of all degrees conferred. Engineering (30%), the physical sciences (20%), and mathematics (6%) also have strong representation. Grads find a high level of success in obtaining prestigious scholarships for graduate study including Watson, Fulbright, and Hertz Fellowships. The school also sees an incredible number of students win National Science Foundation (NSF) Graduate Research Fellowships as an astounding 50 Caltech seniors and 9 alumni captured awards in 2023.

Outside the Classroom
Despite its small undergraduate population, campus is a spacious 124 acres, and 93% elect to live in one of the university's eleven residences; freshmen are required to do so. Greek life was long ago banished in favor of a coeducational residential house system. Each house has its own vibe and traditions, and students go through a two-week rotation period (in place of a pledging process) to find the best fit. On the athletics front, the Beavers field 13 teams to compete in intercollegiate sports, mostly at the NCAA Division III level, although they are more noted for insanely long losing streaks than anything else (the baseball team once lost 228 straight games). Four-fifths of undergrads participate in some kind of organized athletics, and the high rate of involvement isn't limited to sports. Roughly 65% of students also play a musical instrument, and many join one of the more than one hundred student-run organizations on campus. There are plenty of pre-professional and tech-oriented club options as well as groups like Magic: The Gathering Club or the Anime Society. While students generally report that academic pursuits plus a club or two generally take up 100% of their waking hours at Caltech, gorgeous Pasadena and nearby downtown Los Angeles provide limitless opportunities for those seeking some degree of socialization.

Career Services
Caltech's Career Advising and Experiential Learning (CAEL) office has six full-time professional staff members working on career counseling, internship coordination, and employer recruiting. That equates to a 164:1 student-to-advisor ratio, which is among the best of any university featured in this guide. Caltech hosts two large career fairs per year, one in October and one in January. Anywhere from 150-200 companies attend those fairs, which is a massive number when considering the school has fewer than 1,000 undergraduates. Small events take place pretty much weekly, and samples of those regular offerings include visits from the likes of Harvard Business School, Bain & Company, Yahoo, and the Google Women's Focus Group.

Caltech students have little trouble procuring summer internships in engineering, computer science, or business/finance. Unlike most schools where undergrads compete for internships at top companies, the top companies typically have to compete to attract Caltech students. (Its website offers advice for companies in that regard.) Similarly, on-campus recruiting is strong with companies constantly visiting campus to try to snag young talent. That list includes NASA, Goldman Sachs, Oracle, and SpaceX. Based on its low student-to-counselor ratio, prodigious on-campus recruiting efforts, placement of more math/science PhD candidates than any university in the country (adjusted for enrollment size), and unmatched starting salaries for graduates, Caltech's CAEL easily earns the highest praise from the College Transitions staff.

Professional Outcomes

Caltech is a rare school that sees six-figure average starting salaries for its graduates; in 2022, the median figure was $120,000. Forty-three percent of recent grads went directly into the workforce and found homes at tech giants such as Google, Intel, Microsoft, Apple, and Facebook. Engineering students are routinely courted by the likes of Boeing, Lockheed Martin, SpaceX, and Northrop Grumman. The school also has a strong alumni representation at NASA. Those who go the academic/research route ultimately end up on the faculty at schools such as Stanford, MIT, USC, and Caltech itself. Networking as a Caltech alum is a dream. The university has 25,500 alumni, many of whom are leaders in the tech world, including seventeen living Nobel Prize winners and countless founders/execs of major corporations.

Not surprisingly, the largest number of alumni remain in California, settling into careers in Silicon Valley. A healthy 46% of those receiving their diplomas in 2022 continued directly on the higher education path, immediately entering graduate school. Ninety-seven percent of these students were admitted to one of their top-choice schools. Caltech is the number one per capita producer of math/science PhDs in the country. Many continue their education at Caltech or other elite STEM graduate programs. After attaining graduate degrees, careers in research and higher education are popular pursuits. While engineering is where the largest number of grads eventually land, higher education is a close second.

Admission

With an acceptance rate of 2.7%, Caltech occupies the same uber-selective air as MIT. In a normal year, it would be hard to get into Caltech with an ACT/SAT score in the 99th percentile. However, in 2020, Caltech enacted a multi-year moratorium on the consideration of SAT/ACT scores. This test-blind policy will continue for at least the 2024-25 admissions cycle. On the class rank front, 96% of the Class of 2026 finished in the top decile of their graduating high school class.

Directly from the admissions office, four factors carry the heaviest weight in the process: rigor of secondary curriculum, essays, recommendations, and character/personal qualities. Caltech does not offer early decision, but its nonbinding early action round does offer better odds of gaining acceptance. In previous cycles, the regular round saw 5% admitted, but 10% of those who applied by Nov. 1 found success. Caltech is among the most competitive universities in the world and is a top choice for many of the most brilliant young minds seeking to study computer science, the hard sciences, and engineering. Flawless grades in a rigorous curriculum are necessary but not sufficient for admissions consideration; those whose intangibles shine brightest gain an edge in this highly competitive process.

Worth Your Money?

Anything beyond a simple "Yes" here feels superfluous but, nevertheless, we'll offer a few statistics to back up the claim. While the school does not offer merit aid, the majority of students do not pay anything close to the almost $87,000 annual cost of attendance. Need-based aid is awarded to more than half of the undergraduate population and carries a mean value of $60k. Regardless of what you have to pay to attend this institution, it will be well worth the cost. As we highlighted previously in the profile, students' average starting salaries right out of Caltech are in the six figures.

FINANCIAL
Institutional Type: Private
In-State Tuition: $63,255
Out-of-State Tuition: $63,255
Room & Board: $19,503
Books & Supplies: $1,428

Avg. Need-Based Grant: $58,169
Avg. % of Need Met: 100%

Avg. Merit-Based Award: $0
% Receiving (Freshmen w/o Need): 0%

Avg. Cumulative Debt: $17,219
% of Students Borrowing: 27%

CAREER
Who Recruits
1. Goldman Sachs
2. Southern California Edison
3. Amazon
4. Facebook
5. Intel

Notable Internships
1. Facebook
2. Adobe
3. Apple

Top Employers
1. Northrop Grumman
2. Google
3. Boeing
4. NASA Jet Propulsion Laboratory
5. Apple

Where Alumni Work
1. Los Angeles
2. San Francisco
3. New York City
4. Boston
5. San Diego

Earnings
College Scorecard (10-YR Post-Entry): $104,209
PayScale (Early Career): $93,100
PayScale (Mid-Career): $153,100
PayScale 20-Year ROI: $1,294,000

RANKINGS
Money: 5
U.S. News: 7, National Universities
Wall Street Journal/THE: 18
Washington Monthly: 35, National Universities

OVERGENERALIZATIONS
Students are:
Always studying
Diverse
Intellectual
Quirky
Less likely to party

COLLEGE OVERLAPS
Harvard University
Massachusetts Institute of Technology
Princeton University
Stanford University
University of California, Berkeley

California Polytechnic State University, San Luis Obispo

San Luis Obispo, California | 805-756-2311

Nestled between San Francisco and Los Angeles, California Polytechnic State University-San Luis Obispo is the more competitive of the state's two public polytechnic schools, Pomona being the less selective branch. Home to close to 21,000 undergraduate students, Cal Poly churns out a jaw-dropping number of engineers each year, but it is far from a unidimensional university.

Inside the Classroom

Cal Poly is comprised of six undergraduate schools: the College of Agriculture, Food & Environmental Sciences, College of Architecture & Environmental Design, College of Engineering, College of Liberal Arts, College of Science & Mathematics, and the Orfalea College of Business. Across all divisions, there are 60+ majors and 80+ minors offered. While academic requirements vary by college and program, there are a number of general graduation must-haves that apply to all Mustangs. They include 72 units of general education, demonstration of writing competency, and the completion of a senior project.

You won't find many small, liberal-arts-style learning spaces—only 4% of classes have a single-digit enrollment. Yet you also won't find many classes that enroll one hundred or more students; only 4% do. The majority of courses–59%–fall between twenty and forty students. Cal Poly's student-to-faculty ratio is a high 18:1, but such is the cost of an uber-affordable STEM degree from an excellent institution. Still, faculty receive extremely favorable reviews for their accessibility, and opportunities to work intimately with professors are built into the curriculum in many programs. For example, all students in the College of Science & Mathematics are required to participate in faculty-directed research and complete a senior project in order to graduate. One-quarter of students take advantage of the school's robust study abroad program that offers learning opportunities in over seventy-five countries.

The School of Engineering is the university's crown jewel. Over one-quarter of all degrees conferred (22%) are in engineering, and Cal Poly gets recognition in many specialty areas of the field including industrial engineering, mechanical engineering, aerospace engineering, computer engineering, and civil engineering. The Orfalea College of Business also receives strong national recognition and is recognized as one of the better ROI business degrees one can find; 18% of undergrads earn a business degree. Other popular majors include agriculture (11%), the social sciences (5%), and biology (4%).

Outside the Classroom

While more students than ever are living on campus—the university has added 5,600 beds since 2003—only 40% of undergraduates presently reside on campus. Twenty percent of women and 16% of men sign up for Greek life. The 38 total Greek organizations completed 120,000 community service hours last year. With twenty-one NCAA Division I sports on tap, there is always an opportunity to cheer on the Mustangs. Across all men's and women's sports, Cal Poly squads have captured fifty Big West Conference championships. Twenty-seven club sports, from rodeo to surfing, are available, and the massive intramural program attracts 10,000 participants each year. There are an additional 400 student-run clubs, including a heavy dose of pre-professional organizations. San Luis Obispo is known as "The Happiest City in America" for a reason. Located on the coast, students have access to the beach and the natural beauty of Big Falls Trail. Outdoor concerts, an art museum, and the Thursday night farmer's market offer a taste of the effervescence of the surrounding town.

Career Services

The Cal Poly Career Services Office has 19 full-time professional staff members working on career counseling, employer relations, and employer recruiting. That includes three counselors—the Freshman Focus Team— who are dedicated solely to first-year students. The office also employs 20+ student assistants. Overall, the school's 1,103:1 student-to-advisor ratio does not fare well against other colleges featured in this guide. In spite of the high student-to-counselor ratio, the office does accomplish impressive things on behalf of students. Each year, Cal Poly hosts ten major career fairs, including three large, non-major-specific events in the fall, winter, and spring that draw 150+ employers each. Additional fairs cover fields that include teaching, architecture and environmental design, computing, and construction management.

This active office initiates 16,000+ unique contacts per year, posts 37,500 jobs on MustangJOBS (powered by Handshake), and draws almost 20,000 individuals to 500+ workshops, presentations, and group counseling sessions. Amazingly, the Freshman Focus Team engaged 100% of the 4,348 first-year students in a single recent school year. Further, the office has forged official employer/university partnerships with 300+ companies, creating excellent networks for current undergrads to lean on while pursuing employment. In the fall of 2020, they launched Career Curriculum Modules which are embedded into academic classes. By virtually any measure, Cal Poly is doing exceptional work on behalf of its undergraduates.

Professional Outcomes

Within nine months of graduating, 91% of graduates are "positively engaged" in their next life activity. Top employers of Cal Poly grads include many of the top tech, consulting, engineering, and financial firms in the country such as Google, Deloitte, KPMG, Microsoft, Northrop Grumman, Adobe, EY, and Apple. Overall, grads enjoy a terrific median starting salary of $72,000. Given that the in-state tuition is only $11k per year, this makes the university one of the best ROI schools in the country. An overwhelming majority—81%—remain in California upon graduation. Washington, Texas, and Colorado are the next three most popular destinations.

Of the 14% of alumni who directly enter graduate school, the six most commonly attended schools are all in California. By far, the greatest number continue their studies at Cal Poly. UC Davis, USC, UC San Diego, Stanford, and Berkeley also draw more than a handful of graduates each year. Many graduates of the Orfalea College of Business pursue master's degrees in accounting. The highest number of engineering students pursued MBAs or master's degrees in specific branches of engineering. Pursuing a legal education is a frequent choice of liberal arts graduates, and the University of San Diego, USC, and UCLA are the most commonly attended law schools.

Admission

Cal Poly accepted 29% of the freshmen applicants who applied for membership in the Class of 2025, a less friendly figure than the 38% for the Class of 2024. Like many California public universities, Cal Poly has become more competitive in recent years. While acceptance rates have remained steady, other indicators strongly suggest this trend. A startling 15,600 students with 4.0 GPAs (or higher) were denied entry in one recent cycle. Of equal interest is the fact that Cal Poly (like all CSU schools) will be test-blind moving forward. This means that they will not consider SAT or ACT results when evaluating applicants.

Freshman applicants apply to one of six colleges within the university, and some are more competitive than others. For example, the acceptance rate into the College of Engineering is 22%; those aiming for the School of Agriculture, Food & Environmental Sciences enjoy a 48% acceptance rate. No matter the college to which you apply, Cal Poly is mainly interested in two factors when making admissions decisions: the rigor of your secondary curriculum and GPA. Things like extracurricular activities, work experience, and first-generation status also carry a small amount of weight. Getting into Cal Poly is a straightforward, albeit increasingly challenging, proposition. Candidates with sparkling grades earned in advanced coursework should fare well. Those aiming to study engineering, business, or science and mathematics will need stronger credentials than those applying to other colleges.

Worth Your Money?

Annual in-state tuition and fees to attend Cal Poly remain just a hair above five figures, an astounding value in today's higher education marketplace. Including room, board, and all other expenses, the cost of attendance for California residents sits at $32,000. Out-of-staters pay an annual COA of $53,000, not at all an unreasonable sum for the quality of education one will receive at this university. The school does not award large sums of need-based or merit-based aid; however, the net price most students pay still remains relatively low given the school's modest sticker price.

FINANCIAL
Institutional Type: Public
In-State Tuition: $12,924
Out-of-State Tuition: $26,970
Room & Board: $17,220
Books & Supplies: $1,089

Avg. Need-Based Grant: $13,893
Avg. % of Need Met: 76%

Avg. Merit-Based Award: $1,955
% Receiving (Freshmen w/o Need): 14%

Avg. Cumulative Debt: $18,665
% of Students Borrowing: 34%

CAREER
Who Recruits
1. Lockheed Martin
2. NBCUniversal
3. Greystar
4. The Raymond Group
5. Cushman & Wakefield

Notable Internships
1. Nike
2. EY
3. Oracle

Top Employers
1. Apple
2. Google
3. Cisco
4. Oracle
5. Amazon

Where Alumni Work
1. San Francisco
2. San Luis Obispo
3. Los Angeles
4. San Diego
5. Orange County, CA

Earnings
College Scorecard (10-YR Post-Entry): $85,801
PayScale (Early Career): $70,500
PayScale (Mid-Career): $130,800
PayScale 20-Year ROI: $893,000

RANKINGS
Money: 5
U.S. News: 1, Regional Universities West
Wall Street Journal/THE: 116
Washington Monthly: 37, Master's Universities

OVERGENERALIZATIONS
Students are:
Self-motivated
Decided upon their chosen major
Collaborative
Hands-on (like to learn by doing)
Independent

COLLEGE OVERLAPS
Cal Poly, Pomona
San Diego State University
University of California, Davis
University of California, Irvine
University of California, San Diego

Carleton College

Northfield, Minnesota | 507-222-4190

ADMISSION
Admission Rate: 17%
Admission Rate - Men: 17%
Admission Rate - Women: 17%
EA Admission Rate: Not Offered
ED Admission Rate: 22%
ED Admits as % of Total Admits: 18%
Admission Rate (5-Year Trend): -4%
% of Admits Attending (Yield): 37%
Transfer Admission Rate: 10%

SAT Reading/Writing (Middle 50%): 710-770
SAT Math (Middle 50%): 720-780
ACT Composite (Middle 50%): 32-35

% Graduated in Top 10% of HS Class: 75%
% Graduated in Top 25% of HS Class: 94%
% Graduated in Top 50% of HS Class: 99%

Demonstrated Interest: Not Considered
Legacy Status: Considered
Racial/Ethnic Status: Considered
Admission Interview Offered: Yes

ENROLLMENT
Total Undergraduate Enrollment: 2,034
% Full-Time: 99%
% Male: 50%
% Female: 50%
% Out-of-State: 81%
% Fraternity: Not Offered
% Sorority: Not Offered
% On-Campus (All Undergraduate): 96%
Freshman Housing Required: Yes

% African-American: 7%
% Asian: 10%
% Hispanic: 9%
% White: 52%
% Other: 3%
% International: 10%
% Low-Income: 14%

ACADEMICS
Student-to-Faculty Ratio: 8 to 1
% of Classes Under 20: 70%
% of Classes 20-49: 30%
% of Classes 50 or More: 0%
% Full-Time Faculty: 80%
% Full-Time Faculty w/ Terminal Degree: 98%

Top Programs
Biology
Chemistry
Geology
Mathematics
Political Science & International Relations
Physics
Psychology
Statistics

Retention Rate: 95%
4-Year Graduation Rate: 88%
6-Year Graduation Rate: 92%

Curricular Flexibility: Somewhat Flexible
Academic Rating: ★★★★★

#CollegesWorthYourMoney

One of the top liberal arts schools (if not the top) in the Midwest, Carleton has the reputation as a destination point for studious young people who love to learn for learning's sake. Located in fairly remote Northfield, Minnesota, the college still manages to be a magnet for the academically gifted and intellectually curious from coast to coast. Carleton is a small institution of 2,034 undergraduate students. It offers 33 majors, the most popular of which are within the disciplines of the social sciences (19%), the physical sciences (14%), biology (11%), computer science (11%), mathematics (10%), and psychology (8%).

Inside the Classroom
Mandated coursework is extensive and includes an argument and inquiry seminar for first-year students, a global citizenship requirement, a class in international studies as well as domestic studies, and three writing-intensive courses. Undergrads also must take a stroll through the usual liberal arts categories of humanistic inquiry, literary/artistic analysis, the arts, science, statistics, and social inquiry. All of this is done via three ten-week terms per academic year during which most students take only three courses per term.

Students work closely with their professors, and the college is routinely rated atop lists of best undergraduate teaching institutions. Small classes are the norm with the average being only sixteen students; in 14% of your classes, you will be surrounded by no more than nine of your peers. Faculty-mentored research is embedded into many courses, independent study opportunities abound, and full-time supervised research is available during summer and winter break. Over three-quarters of the student body elect to study abroad in one of 130 programs offered in sixty countries. Furthermore, 70% of students spend a semester studying in another part of the globe.

All academic programs at this elite liberal arts school are well-regarded, particularly by other universities where an exceptional percentage of Carleton grads later pursue doctoral degrees (more on this below). Consistently named a top producer of Fulbright Scholars, the college enjoyed four award recipients in 2023. The Peace Corps also ranked Carleton thirteenth on its list of Top Volunteer-Producing (Small) Colleges.

Outside the Classroom
With 96% of students living on campus and no Greek life at Carleton, the dorms take on the role of the preferred social setting. Fourteen theme houses also play a big role on campus, allowing people with aligned interests to live communally. These include the WHOA House for campus activists, the Culinary House for those committed to gastronomic pursuits, and the Q&A House for the LBGTQA community. Over 300 student-run clubs offer a multitude of niche activities to suit this fairly eclectic student body. The Ravens' eighteen varsity athletic teams are split evenly between men and women, and they all compete in NCAA Division III. Club and intramural sports are popular with ultimate Frisbee in the lead by a wide margin. Northfield is a small town, but it has its share of social/cultural offerings as well as neighboring St. Olaf's College, which opens additional social opportunities. Those looking for more action than Northfield can provide will be pleased to find that the bustle of Minneapolis and St. Paul are both less than fifty miles away. Students seeking natural beauty do not have to look any further than the on-campus Cowling Arboretum, a 900-acre wooded area perfect for hiking or cross-country skiing.

Career Services
The Career Center is staffed by six full-time professionals, just about all of whom have director, assistant director, or manager in their title. However, at such a small school, most of these individuals do work directly with students in some capacity, and that results in a student-to-advisor ratio of 339:1, better than the average institution included in this book.

The major career/internship/graduate school fairs that are open to Carleton students are joint efforts with other Minnesota-based universities, yet many companies, nonprofits, and government entities do make the trip to Northfield to directly recruit this talented cohort of undergraduates. Those companies include Amazon, Ernst & Young, Meta, Google, and Microsoft. The 30 Minutes Program brings current students face-to-face with alums who work in a field of interest for quick (hence the name) informational/networking sessions. Externships with alumni allow students to shadow alumni in their place of employment for one to three weeks. Alumni remain extremely engaged with the school as evidenced by an extremely high percentage who donate. The area in which the career services office truly excels is advising students on graduate school pathways, an area we will explore further in a moment.

Professional Outcomes

Carleton does not track the activities of every graduating class, but when it last administered a senior survey roughly five years ago, nearly three-quarters of soon-to-be grads were headed into the workforce with the most common job functions being business analyst, project manager, research assistant/associate, software engineer, and medical scribe. There are thirty-five companies that employ more than ten Carleton alums. Many are prestigious academic institutions including the University of Chicago, the University of Michigan, Columbia, Stanford, Northwestern, and Penn; the University of Minnesota is the largest employer of Knights with over 150 alumni in its ranks. Target, Epic Systems, Google, Wells Fargo, and Amazon all employ more than 40 alumni. Geographically, the greatest number of students remain in the Minneapolis-St. Paul area, but many also head to New York City, San Francisco, Chicago, DC, Boston, and Seattle.

Carleton is a breeding ground for future scholars as a ridiculously high number of graduates go on to earn PhDs. In fact, by percentage, Carleton is one of the top five producers in the country of future PhDs. They produce an incredible number of doctoral degree holders in the areas of economics, math, political science, sociology, chemistry, physics, biology, and history. In recent years, 20-25% of graduates immediately entered graduate school; within ten years, 75% of graduates have enrolled in or completed an advanced degree program. Over the past five years, medical school applicants have enjoyed an 82% success rate.

Admission

The 8,583 applications submitted for the Class of 2026 doesn't sound like an overwhelming number, but for tiny Carleton, that figure is more than double the number of applications received at the turn of the millennium. Only 17% of those applicants received an offer of admission, a tiny decrease from last year's 18% figure. Those presently enrolled at Carleton almost exclusively finished near the top of their high school classes; 75% of those admitted into the 2022-23 freshman class were in the top 10%, and the school typically attracts around 30-50 National Merit Scholars each cycle. The 25th percentile SAT score was 1430, and the 75th percentile marker was 1540. A larger number of applicants submitted ACT scores to Carleton with a middle 50% range of 32-35. Most Carleton admits were active in their high school communities; 67% played varsity sports, 44% studied music, and an overwhelming 87% participated in some type of volunteer work.

The college lists eight factors as the most significant in the admissions process: rigor of secondary curriculum, GPA, class rank, essays, recommendations, extracurricular activities, talent/ability, and character/personal qualities. With such a low number of applications, those from remote areas of the country may particularly benefit from the quest for geographic diversity; four states sent zero students to the Class of 2026. Early decision can also provide a slight advantage to those targeting the college as their number one choice. With two rounds of early decision offered, they admitted 23% of ED applicants into the Class of 2026. Carleton is among the most highly selective liberal arts colleges not located on the East or West coasts. Its remote location keeps application numbers in check, but the applicant pool tends to be self-selecting.

Worth Your Money?

With little merit aid and an $84,900 estimated annual cost of attendance, there are many Carleton students who will be paying $340k for their bachelor's degree. The good news is that current undergraduates with demonstrated financial need see 100% of that need met, which averages to a $60k grant. While Carleton's excellence isn't directly reflected in the early-to-mid career salaries of its graduates, the tiny classes, professor quality, extensive career services, and preparation for those aiming for prestigious graduate schools make this school very much worth your money.

FINANCIAL
Institutional Type: Private
In-State Tuition: $65,457
Out-of-State Tuition: $65,457
Room & Board: $16,710
Books & Supplies: $938

Avg. Need-Based Grant: $53,106
Avg. % of Need Met: 100%

Avg. Merit-Based Award: $5,597
% Receiving (Freshmen w/o Need): 3%

Avg. Cumulative Debt: $18,677
% of Students Borrowing: 37%

CAREER
Who Recruits
1. U.S. Bank
2. Anderson Corporation
3. Lewin Group
4. SPS Commerce
5. UnitedHealth Group

Notable Internships
1. Moody's Analytics
2. Smithsonian
3. Federal Reserve Bank of St. Louis

Top Employers
1. Google
2. Epic
3. UnitedHealth Group
4. Target
5. Wells Fargo

Where Alumni Work
1. Minneapolis
2. New York City
3. San Francisco
4. Chicago
5. Washington, DC

Earnings
College Scorecard (10-YR Post-Entry): $70,334
PayScale (Early Career): $62,100
PayScale (Mid-Career): $125,200
PayScale 20-Year ROI: $510,000

RANKINGS
Money: 4.5
U.S. News: 9, Liberal Arts Colleges
Wall Street Journal/THE: 218
Washington Monthly: 36, Liberal Arts Colleges

OVERGENERALIZATIONS
Students are:
Always studying
Academically driven
Intellectually curious
Quirky
Politically liberal

COLLEGE OVERLAPS
Brown University
Bowdoin College
Grinnell College
Macalester College
Pomona College

Carnegie Mellon University

Pittsburgh, Pennsylvania | 412-268-2082

ADMISSION
Admission Rate: 11%
Admission Rate - Men: 9%
Admission Rate - Women: 15%
EA Admission Rate: Not Offered
ED Admission Rate: 13%
ED Admits as % of Total Admits: 15%
Admission Rate (5-Year Trend): -11%
% of Admits Attending (Yield): 44%
Transfer Admission Rate: 7%

SAT Reading/Writing (Middle 50%): 720-770
SAT Math (Middle 50%): 770-800
ACT Composite (Middle 50%): 34-35

% Graduated in Top 10% of HS Class: 90%
% Graduated in Top 25% of HS Class: 100%
% Graduated in Top 50% of HS Class: 100%

Demonstrated Interest: Not Considered
Legacy Status: Not Considered
Racial/Ethnic Status: Important
Admission Interview Offered: No

ENROLLMENT
Total Undergraduate Enrollment: 7,509
% Full-Time: 98%
% Male: 49%
% Female: 51%
% Out-of-State: 66%
% Fraternity: 14%
% Sorority: 11%
% On-Campus (All Undergraduate): 46%
Freshman Housing Required: Yes

% African-American: 4%
% Asian: 32%
% Hispanic: 10%
% White: 21%
% Other: 5%
% International: 24%
% Low-Income: 15%

ACADEMICS
Student-to-Faculty Ratio: 6 to 1
% of Classes Under 20: 70%
% of Classes 20-49: 20%
% of Classes 50 or More: 11%
% Full-Time Faculty: 91%
% Full-Time Faculty w/ Terminal Degree: 93%

Top Programs
Artificial Intelligence
Business
Computer Science
Drama
Design
Mathematics
Physics
Statistics

Retention Rate: 97%
4-Year Graduation Rate: 76%
6-Year Graduation Rate: 92%

Curricular Flexibility: Somewhat Flexible
Academic Rating: ★★★★★

#CollegesWorthYourMoney

Founded by steel baron Andrew Carnegie in 1900 as an eponymous technical school, CMU's rise to its present position as one of the best research universities in the country is as much a Horatio Alger story as that of its original namesake. Despite its humble roots and gradual ascension into a regional powerhouse, Carnegie Mellon today is home to 7,509 brilliant undergrads and an additional 9,270 graduate students who come from all over the world to reap the benefits of a top-notch educational experience.

Inside the Classroom
Carnegie Mellon is unique in a number of ways; it is both highly segmented by area of study and, at the same time, interdisciplinary. Students are admitted to one of six colleges: the College of Engineering, College of Fine Arts, Dietrich College of Humanities and Social Science (which houses the popular information systems program), Mellon College of Science, Tepper School of Business, and the School of Computer Science. There are a combined 80+ undergraduate majors and 90 minors available across the six schools, but young people simply do not come to CMU as "undecided." CMU students are expected to be well-rounded, and that philosophy is reflected in departmental requirements. For example, Dietrich students are required to take courses on data and computer science as freshmen, and students in the College of Engineering must take courses in writing and expression and foreign language.

Impressively, particularly for a school with more graduate students than undergrads, CMU boasts a 6:1 student-to-faculty ratio and small class sizes, with 36% containing single digits and 70% having an enrollment of nineteen or fewer. In a given school year, 800+ undergraduates conduct research through the University Research Office, and many others participated through various outside arrangements. Between 500-600 students study abroad for a semester each year in such countries as Japan, China, and Germany.

The most commonly conferred degrees are in engineering (21%), computer science (16%), mathematics (12%), business (10%), and visual and performing arts (9%). CMU boasts a number of programs that have a stellar worldwide reputation. In fact, it's hard to think of a university that accrues such high praise across such a broad spectrum of disciplines. The School of Computer Science is one of the best in the country, perennially ranked right next to (or above) the likes of MIT, Caltech, and Stanford. Also of note: it enrolls women at two or three times the national average. Tepper is recognized as one of the top undergraduate business schools by corporations around the globe. The drama program is a constant producer of top talent and, amazingly, three alumni won Tony Awards in 2022 alone. The School of Engineering and the information technology program are also regulars in any top ten list. In 2022, CMU students captured nine Fulbright Scholarships and three Goldwater Scholarships.

Outside the Classroom
CMU undergrads are known for being so consumed with academics that some might ask, "What life outside the classroom?" Yet, there is plenty of activity, both on campus and in the surrounding Oakland section of Pittsburgh. In 2022-23, all freshmen and 46% of the entire student body lived on campus. There are over 400 student organizations including the famed Scotch'n'Soda, one of the oldest student theater groups in the country. It regularly puts on professional quality plays and musicals. More than sixty of the clubs on campus are pre-professional in focus, such as the popular Society of Women Engineers, but there are plenty of options in the LGBTQ, spiritual, and tech-hobby realms as well. Fraternities and sororities have twenty-three chapters on campus, and a substantial but not overwhelming 14% of men and 11% of women participate in Greek life. Star speakers from all walks of life can frequently be heard on CMU's campus. Attending sports events is not among the most favored CMU pastimes, but the Tartans do compete in eight men's and nine women's sports in NCAA Division III. Plenty of club sports are available as well, including badminton, cricket, and Alpine skiing.

Career Services
The Career and Professional Development Center at Carnegie Mellon produces enviable results for its students. A fantastically high number of graduates find their first jobs through internships (26%), career fairs (14%), Handshake (12%), or directly through their career advisor (11%). The university pours ample resources into career services, employing 27 full-time consultants, experiential learning coordinators, and employee relations specialists. That equates to a student-to-advisor ratio of 278:1, which is better than average when compared to the other institutions included in this book.

The office does a strong job of engaging with students, whether in person or virtually. Over three-quarters of undergrads log in to Handshake to view the roughly 12,000 job and 5,000 internship postings. Many job search-related events focus on specific sectors such as the Civil & Environmental Engineering Career Fair, Energy Industry Career Fair, or Tepper Meetup (for business students). Multiple members of each class intern at companies that include Amazon, Deloitte, and JP Morgan Chase. In a single year, an impressive 500 companies recruited at the university and conducted 5,900 on-campus interviews. Close to 80% of undergraduates complete at least one internship. Possessing a heavy arsenal of industry connections and hands-on offerings, CMU's Career and Professional Development Center provides exemplary service to its undergraduates.

Professional Outcomes

By the end of the calendar year in which they received their diplomas, 66% of 2022 grads were employed, and 28% were continuing to graduate school. The companies that have routinely scooped up CMU grads include Google, Meta, Microsoft, Apple, Accenture, McKinsey, and Deloitte as well as Pittsburgh-based PNC Bank. Starting salaries for CMU grads are exceptionally high, due in part, of course, to the high number of engineering and computer science diplomas it awards, yet all Tartans tend to do well financially. With an average starting salary of $105,194, CMU grads outpace the average starting salary for a college grad nationally ($55k) by a wide margin. Some majors offer even better remuneration, such as computer science ($135k) and electrical and computer engineering ($122k). While some do remain in Pittsburgh, graduates flock in large numbers to San Francisco, New York, and DC.

Of those pursuing graduate education, around 20% typically enroll immediately in PhD programs. A perusal of the schools where recent grads have decided to continue their education is a who's who of the Ivy League and includes MIT, Caltech, and Stanford as well as Carnegie Mellon itself (a popular choice). In 2023, there were 69 CMU applicants to medical school. Recent grads have gone on to medical institutions at Harvard, Rutgers, Temple, UMass, and SUNY Downstate Medical Center. Those entering law school are currently studying at elite schools including UVA, Columbia, Penn, Yale, and Georgetown.

Admission

Carnegie Mellon received 34,261 applications for the Class of 2026, almost triple the number that applied a decade ago. The overall acceptance rate for the Class of 2026 was 11%; however, since applicants apply to one of the six schools within the university, it's essential to examine a school-specific breakdown. Acceptance rates vary greatly from program to program. For example, in selecting the Class of 2024 (most recent available), only 7% of applicants were accepted into the School of Computer Science (SCS) while 26% were accepted into the Dietrich College of Humanities and Social Sciences (DC). Within the DC, School of Architecture applicants enjoyed a robust 34% admit rate while among School of Drama applicants, the percentage admitted was an infinitesimal 4%. You can apply to more than one program at CMU, but you must fill out separate applications, pay the fee for each, and meet the unique requirements for every school you apply to.

The 50% SAT range for students enrolled in the university is roughly 1500-1560 and the average unweighted GPA is 3.9; 90% were in the top decile of their high school class. Successful applicants to CMU have taken the most rigorous high school schedules available to them, and the school also lists character/personal qualities, volunteer work, and extracurriculars among the most important factors for admission. Additionally, it is worth highlighting the fact that women fared much better than their male counterparts, being admitted at a 15% rate versus less than 9% for men.

Worth Your Money?

A Carnegie Mellon education carries an annual cost of attendance of $83k+ that, for most attendees (except fine arts and many humanities students), will be less than their starting salary when they graduate. While it does not meet 100% of the demonstrated financial aid for all qualifying students, it comes very close. Of the 37% of students who receive financial aid, grant awards average $50k. With few exceptions, a degree from Carnegie Mellon is worth taking on a bit of debt. The average amount owed by graduates is right around the average college debt nationwide.

FINANCIAL
Institutional Type: Private
In-State Tuition: $63,829
Out-of-State Tuition: $63,829
Room & Board: $17,468
Books & Supplies: $1,000

Avg. Need-Based Grant: $49,845
Avg. % of Need Met: 100%

Avg. Merit-Based Award: $41,651
% Receiving (Freshmen w/o Need): 5%

Avg. Cumulative Debt: $30,334
% of Students Borrowing: 34%

CAREER
Who Recruits
1. PNC
2. Uber
3. Epic
4. Google
5. Goldman Sachs

Notable Internships
1. GoDaddy
2. Microsoft
3. Chicago Trading Company

Top Employers
1. Google
2. Microsoft
3. Facebook
4. Amazon
5. Apple

Where Alumni Work
1. Pittsburgh
2. San Francisco
3. New York City
4. Washington, DC
5. Boston

Earnings
College Scorecard (10-YR Post-Entry): $111,064
PayScale (Early Career): $84,000
PayScale (Mid-Career): $143,400
PayScale 20-Year ROI: $1,066,000

RANKINGS
Money: 4.5
U.S. News: 24, National Universities
Wall Street Journal/THE: 70
Washington Monthly: 38, National Universities

OVERGENERALIZATIONS
Students are:
Always studying
Nerdy
Self-motivated
Decided upon their chosen major
Career-driven

COLLEGE OVERLAPS
Cornell University
Massachusetts Institute of Technology
Princeton University
University of California, Berkeley
University of Michigan

Case Western Reserve University

Cleveland, Ohio | 216-368-4450

A private, midsize institution in Cleveland, Ohio, Case Western Reserve University (CWRU) is a school whose reputation and selectivity are among the fastest risers in the nation. Long an engineering powerhouse with a rich history of technical education, there has been a recent, sharp rise in the caliber of students clamoring to join this undergraduate student body of 6,017. In fact, the university granted acceptance to close to three-quarters of applicants a mere decade ago; today, that figure is sliding toward one-quarter.

Inside the Classroom
Unlike many schools of its ilk, CWRU has a single-door admission policy. Those accepted into the broader university are free to pursue any of the nearly one hundred areas of concentration. All students must complete four seminars called SAGES (one first-year seminar, two university seminars, and one in the major), and two semesters of physical education. From there, most requirements are school/major-specific. In their final year, students must conquer the senior capstone, which can take many forms but must be designed in consultation with a faculty member.

Sporting a 9:1 faculty-to-student ratio, the university does a nice job keeping classes on the small side, with 50% of course sections capped at nineteen and only 13% of courses having fifty students or more. An exceptional 86% of students have the opportunity to participate in undergraduate research as the school places heavy emphasis on experiential learning. The same goes for international experiences. Case Western has a high rate of undergraduates who elect to study abroad; 38% spend a semester in a foreign land.

The Weatherhead School of Management and the Case School of Engineering have stellar reputations within the worlds of employment and academia. Engineering is the most commonly conferred undergraduate degree at 27% followed by biology (15%), computer science (10%), and health professions (8%). In a typical year, Case Western produces between two and four Fulbright Scholars as well as Churchill Scholars and NSF Fellowship recipients. The school counts sixteen Nobel Prize winners among its alumni and faculty, past and present.

Outside the Classroom
The main campus covers 155 acres, not including a verdant 389-acre, university-owned farm located only ten miles away. Freshmen and sophomores are required to live on campus, and 75% of the overall undergraduate student body resides on the university's grounds. First-year students live in one of four residential colleges designed to foster a sense of community and belonging. Greek life is thriving, with 27 fraternities and sororities attracting 17% of men of 22% of women. An academically focused student body does not pay a ton of attention to the school's nineteen NCAA Division III sports teams. There are over 200 student-run groups, including plenty of opportunities for intramural athletics, volunteer work, and faith-based connections. CWRUbotix, the school's robotics team, has placed near the top of various national competitions in recent years. Case Western's proximity to downtown Cleveland makes off-campus excursions popular even though the immediate surroundings of East Cleveland are less than ideal. An endless array of restaurants, museums, concerts, and professional sporting events are easily within reach for those willing to take an occasional break from studying.

Career Services
The Career Center at CWRU includes 15 full-time staff members, equating to a student-to-advisor ratio of 401:1, slightly higher than the average institution included in this book. The office is guided by a Four-Phase Plan designed to cultivate career-oriented thinking from freshman through senior year. CWRU has implemented the Student Success Initiative in which each freshman is assigned to a "navigator," a single staff person who remains the student's contact throughout the student's time at the school. Workshops are regularly offered on basic topics such as resume development, internship search strategies, interviewing, and graduate school preparation. Two major career fairs take place each year: the University Career Fair held in October and the Get Experienced! Internship & Career Fair held in February.

Annually, more than 300 employers, from global corporations to start-ups, conduct on-campus interviews with undergraduates. Case Western has fifteen official career center partners including IBM Watson Health, GE, Progressive Insurance, and Yelp. Thanks to a strong emphasis on hands-on education, 99% of graduates report having the opportunity to engage in some type of experiential learning. Those opportunities include both traditional internships (70%) and more structured 560-hour practicums. In a given year, more than a handful of Case Western students land internships at organizations including NASA, Procter & Gamble, Amazon, and Deloitte.

Professional Outcomes

Fifty-six percent of 2022 CWRU graduates head into the world of professional employment upon receiving their diplomas; only 3% were still looking for work six months after leaving the university. More than half of the Class of 2022 enjoyed a starting salary of at least $65,000. The employers of the greatest number of graduates included the Cleveland Clinic, University Hospitals, Accenture, Microsoft, Deloitte, and Google. Many alumni also presently work for IBM, Medtronic, EY, and PwC. Nearly 24% work in the engineering field, 16% pursue information tech, 13% find employment in the research realm, and 11% enter nursing. A good number of alumni stay in the Cleveland area, but San Francisco and New York are other common destinations.

Of the 37% of graduates who decide to enroll in an advanced degree program after completing their undergraduate work, many are accepted by elite graduate schools. In 2022, four or more grads were accepted to continue their studies at the likes of NYU, Columbia University, Johns Hopkins University, WashU, and the University of Michigan. However, the most popular option is to continue studying at Case Western as 170 of those going on to graduate school in a single recent year elected to stay on the CWRU campus. Among the Class of 2022, 18% entered medical school and 6% pursued a legal education.

Admission

Case Western received a record 38,701 applications for admittance into its Class of 2026 and accepted 27%. For comparison, only a decade ago Case Western received a little over 7,300 applications and accepted 73% of those students. SAT/ACT scores in the 75th percentile for incoming freshmen back then would barely crack the 25th percentile now. Freshmen in 2022-23 boasted a middle-50% SAT of 1420-1520 and a 32-35 on the ACT. Sixty-three percent of successful applicants finished in the top 10% of their high school classes and 91% placed in the top 25%.

This increasingly selective admissions committee ranks four factors as "very important": rigor of secondary school record, class rank, GPA, and extracurricular activities. Essays, recommendation letters, interviews, volunteer work, ethnic status, talent/ability, and personal qualities comprise the second tier of considerations. The school is test-optional. Case Western offers an early action as well as ED I & ED II rounds. Those applying early find success at a slightly higher rate than regular round applicants, earning acceptance 32% percent of the time. We often see schools make massive jumps in selectivity over the course of a generation where a warning of "This isn't your mother's/father's fill-in-the-blank university" would be apt. Yet, with CWSU, "This isn't your older sibling's Case Western" is a far more accurate statement. Exponential leaps in the profile of the average accepted student have created an extremely competitive environment.

Worth Your Money?

A Case Western degree will cost you $86k per year if you do not qualify for any need-based or merit aid. Fortunately, there aren't many students who fail to qualify for some sort of tuition reduction as 80%+ receive some level of need-based/merit aid. When all is said and done, graduates possess reasonable levels of postsecondary debt relative to the national average. Higher-than-average starting salaries make repaying those loans a doable task.

FINANCIAL
Institutional Type: Private
In-State Tuition: $62,234
Out-of-State Tuition: $62,234
Room & Board: $17,040
Books & Supplies: $1,200

Avg. Need-Based Grant: $42,504
Avg. % of Need Met: 100%

Avg. Merit-Based Award: $26,072
% Receiving (Freshmen w/o Need): 41%

Avg. Cumulative Debt: $28,085
% of Students Borrowing: 51%

CAREER
Who Recruits
1. Progressive Insurance
2. Lubrizol Corporation
3. Rockwell Automation
4. Amazon
5. The MetroHealth System

Notable Internships
1. Merck
2. Deloitte
3. MITRE

Top Employers
1. Cleveland Clinic
2. University Hospitals
3. Rockwell Automation
4. IBM
5. Microsoft

Where Alumni Work
1. Cleveland
2. New York City
3. San Francisco
4. Washington, DC
5. Chicago

Earnings
College Scorecard (10-YR Post-Entry): $81,346
PayScale (Early Career): $72,100
PayScale (Mid-Career): $126,600
PayScale 20-Year ROI: $830,000

RANKINGS
Money: 4
U.S. News: 53, National Universities
Wall Street Journal/THE: 238
Washington Monthly: 224, National Universities

OVERGENERALIZATIONS
Students are:
Academically driven
Competitive
Diverse
Less likely to party
Intellectually curious

COLLEGE OVERLAPS
Carnegie Mellon University
The Ohio State University - Columbus
Purdue University - West Lafayette
University of Michigan
University of Rochester

Danville, Kentucky | 859-238-5350

ADMISSION
Admission Rate: 62%
Admission Rate - Men: 61%
Admission Rate - Women: 64%
EA Admission Rate: 77%
ED Admission Rate: 73%
ED Admits as % of Total Admits: 5%
Admission Rate (5-Year Trend): -14%
% of Admits Attending (Yield): 23%
Transfer Admission Rate: 21%

SAT Reading/Writing (Middle 50%): 595-710
SAT Math (Middle 50%): 600-760
ACT Composite (Middle 50%): 26-34

% Graduated in Top 10% of HS Class: 44%
% Graduated in Top 25% of HS Class: 75%
% Graduated in Top 50% of HS Class: 96%

Demonstrated Interest: Considered
Legacy Status: Considered
Racial/Ethnic Status: Considered
Admission Interview Offered: Yes

ENROLLMENT
Total Undergraduate Enrollment: 1,357
% Full-Time: 100%
% Male: 48%
% Female: 52%
% Out-of-State: 39%
% Fraternity: 36%
% Sorority: 40%
% On-Campus (All Undergraduate): 97%
Freshman Housing Required: Yes

% African-American: 6%
% Asian: 4%
% Hispanic: 7%
% White: 73%
% Other: 1%
% International: 5%
% Low-Income: 21%

ACADEMICS
Student-to-Faculty Ratio: 10 to 1
% of Classes Under 20: 72%
% of Classes 20-49: 28%
% of Classes 50 or More: 0%
% Full-Time Faculty: 97%
% Full-Time Faculty w/ Terminal Degree: 99%

Top Programs
Anthropology/Sociology
Biochemistry & Molecular Biology
Economics & Finance
International Studies
Mathematics
Politics
Psychology
Spanish

Retention Rate: 89%
4-Year Graduation Rate: 85%
6-Year Graduation Rate: 85%

Curricular Flexibility: Somewhat Flexible
Academic Rating: ★★★★⭑

#CollegesWorthYourMoney

The global pandemic hit many small liberal arts colleges especially hard, chipping away at enrollment numbers and tightening many budgets. Fortunately, this is not the story at Centre College in Danville, KY, which saw its largest freshman cohort ever put down deposits to join the Class of 2026. Founded in 1819, the college has established a reputation as a top liberal arts school, and yet getting in is infinitely easier than most academically and experientially comparable schools in the Northeast; over three-quarters of those who apply receive an offer of admission.

Inside the Classroom
On the academic end, there are 50+ majors, minors, and dual-degree programs to pursue, or you can design your own. Centre requires all students to complete a First-Year Studies course, two courses in the humanities, two in social studies, one in life science, one in physical science, one religion-themed course under the umbrella of Fundamental Questions, and one additional philosophy/religion course. Proficiency in a foreign language is required and can be checked off by taking two courses or by testing out. You'll also need a course in advanced math as well as computer science. Meeting all Gen Ed requirements will entail 10 to 14 courses over your four years of study.

The average size of a Centre class is just 18 students, a reality made possible by a 10:1 student-to-faculty ratio and zero graduate students. While anecdotal, surveys of alumni have found Centre grads to be among the most pleased in the whole country with the personal attention they received from faculty. Over 40% of undergrads participate in either on-campus or off-campus research projects. Opportunities for undergraduate research are available as early as freshman year and take place via summer research apprenticeships, independent studies, or formalized 400-level classes. With 85% of students studying abroad at some point, Centre College ranks among the top schools for creating global citizens.

The most commonly pursued degree at Centre is economics; 15% of degrees awarded are in this discipline. Biology, psychology, international studies, and behavioral neuroscience are next in order of popularity. Many top banking institutions pull sizable numbers of econ majors into their ranks, and graduate schools generally look favorably upon graduates of all disciplines. Highly competitive fellowship organizations also regularly accept Centre seniors. The college has produced 50+ Fulbright Scholars since 1990, and it has produced a number of National Science Foundation Graduate Research Fellows in recent years. With such an international focus, it is no surprise that those applying for Critical Language or Boren Scholarships also fare well.

Outside the Classroom
It's not unusual for the vast majority of freshmen to dwell on campus; it is a bit rarer to find a school where 99% of all undergraduates do so, but Centre is one such institution. The percentage of students who participate in fraternity and sorority life is over 50%, making it one of the most Greek-focused schools in the country. Overall, there are six fraternities and five sororities at Centre. Approximately two-fifths of the student body participates in at least one varsity sport; the Colonels compete at the NCAA Division III level. There are 80+ organizations on campus that collectively host 2,000 events annually. Highlights include Best Buddies, the Cento student newspaper, and a number of religious groups for all faiths. Over 80% of Centre students participate in service through organizations like Alpha Phi Omega or Alternative Spring Break. Danville is a charming and walkable small town with a population of just over 17,000. The closest big cities are Lexington (less than an hour away), Louisville (1.5 hours away), and Cincinnati (2+ hours away).

Career Services
The Center for Career & Professional Development (CCPD) is staffed by seven professional employees including an employer relations specialist and career counselors who specialize in math and science, social studies, and the humanities. The 194:1 student-to-counselor ratio is in the above-average range for a liberal arts college featured in this guidebook. The CCPD staff prides itself on working intimately with students throughout their four years on campus and has many scheduled events designed to draw underclassmen, including the annual Career KickStart for sophomores.

The CCPD also hosts monthly Career Chats, a monthly series called "Emerging Professionals," and regular campus information sessions hosted by employers. The school participates in the larger Spotlight Career Fair that brings together 20 colleges in the region to meet with premier employers. It's hard to find a Centre senior who has yet to experience an internship, and recent Colonels have landed positions with US senators, M&T Bank, the Kentucky Environmental Coalition, and a host of other impressive organizations/employers. In total, 87% of recent grads landed at least one internship experience. Many also procure internship positions abroad including as a financial manager in Honduras, a human rights advocate in Guatemala, and a vocal performance teacher in India.

Professional Outcomes

One year after leaving Danville with their diploma, 64% of the Class of 2022 had found employment, 34% had entered graduate school, and just 2% are still seeking employment or are underemployed. Twenty-two percent of recent graduates have entered the financial services field followed by education (12%), research (9%), and medicine/healthcare (8%). The organizations that employ the greatest number of Centre grads include Humana, Fidelity Investments, AT&T, PNC, Edward Jones, Republic Bank, and the Commonwealth of Kentucky. Nearby Louisville and Lexington are the cities possessing the highest concentration of Centre-affiliated adults. Next in line are Cincinnati; Nashville; Atlanta; and Washington, DC.

Among members of the Class of 2022 who enrolled directly in an advanced degree program, 29% were studying in a healthcare-related field, 14% headed to law school, and 1% were pursuing a master's or doctorate in the hard sciences. Members of this cohort enrolled in graduate programs at the likes of Columbia, Duke, Georgetown, Kings College (London), and Vanderbilt. Recent medical school applicants earned acceptance 83% of the time, one of the best rates of any college in the country. Recent premed majors have gone on to study at Dartmouth College, Emory University, Stanford University, and the University of Virginia. Those applying to law school have been successful at a 94% clip and have been admitted to top institutions including Cornell, the University of Chicago, Notre Dame, NYU, Penn, and USC.

Admission

Centre's Class of 2026 was comprised of 407 members who hailed from roughly 50 Kentucky counties and 28 US states. Last year, the acceptance rate at this school was 62%, making it a terrific option for any student with solid but imperfect bona fides. The ED acceptance rate is even higher; it was 73% for the Class of 2026. The vast majority of attending students did place in the top quartile of their high school class, and the average unweighted GPA was 3.8. The mid-50% SAT score was 1195-1470, and the mean ACT range was 26-34; the ACT is, by far, the more frequently submitted exam.

The school began a test-optional pilot program at the start of the pandemic; they then made the policy a permanent switch. The two most important factors in the school's admissions decisions remain the rigor of an applicant's course load and GPA. The next most important items are class rank, test scores, essays, and recommendations. Centre does not consider demonstrated interest.

Worth Your Money?

Given that 90% of students receive some type of financial aid at Centre, only a few pay the $63k total cost of attendance. The school ranks inside the top ten in the country for awarding merit aid, giving more than $41 million in scholarships and grants last academic year. The average debt accumulated by students at this institution falls slightly below the national average. Those who may need to take on a bit more debt to attend would likely still get their money's worth, especially if they planned to take advantage of one of Centre's top programs, such as economics.

FINANCIAL
Institutional Type: Private
In-State Tuition: $50,550
Out-of-State Tuition: $50,550
Room & Board: $13,040
Books & Supplies: $1,200

Avg. Need-Based Grant: $41,084
Avg. % of Need Met: 93%

Avg. Merit-Based Award: $33,557
% Receiving (Freshmen w/o Need): 38%

Avg. Cumulative Debt: $23,918
% of Students Borrowing: 52%

CAREER
Who Recruits
1. PNC
2. Humana
3. Fidelity Investments
4. AT&T
5. Norton Healthcare

Notable Internships
1. C-SPAN
2. USAID
3. Pilot Flying J

Top Employers
1. University of Kentucky
2. Humana
3. University of Louisville
4. US Army
5. Fidelity Investments

Where Alumni Work
1. Lexington, KY
2. Louisville
3. Cincinnati
4. Nashville
5. Boston

Earnings
College Scorecard (10-YR Post-Entry): $60,447
PayScale (Early Career): $53,100
PayScale (Mid-Career): $89,200
PayScale 20-Year ROI: $360,000

RANKINGS
Money: 4.5
U.S. News: 51, Liberal Arts Colleges
Wall Street Journal/THE: 163
Washington Monthly: 71, Liberal Arts Colleges

OVERGENERALIZATIONS
Students are:
Working hard and playing hard
Preppy
Involved/invested in campus life
Driven
Homogenous

COLLEGE OVERLAPS
Davidson College
Furman University
Rhodes College
Sewanee - The University of the South
Washington and Lee University

Claremont McKenna College

Claremont, California | 909-621-8088

Start with your average elite liberal arts college in the Northeast, cut the size of the student body in half, replace stuffy Gothic edifices with a modern California feel, and physically connect the campus to four other elite schools whose premier offerings can all be shared communally. That's the recipe for Claremont McKenna College (CMC), a liberal arts school that is home to 1,386 bright and motivated undergraduates and is a founding member of the Claremont Consortium that is comprised of four additional undergraduate institutions: Pomona, Pitzer, Scripps, and Harvey Mudd.

Inside the Classroom
CMC offers 33 majors and 11 "sequences," series of courses that can be completed across the neighboring schools in addition to one's major. Registering for courses in one or more of the other Claremont Colleges is a staple of academic life at CMC; 99% of undergrads do so. An academically focused group, one-third of the student population ends up completing a double major. No matter your academic pursuit, required courses will include a first-year writing seminar, a humanities seminar, multiple semesters of a foreign language, a laboratory science, a math or computer science course, physical education, and—of most significance— a senior thesis.

The college boasts an average class size of eighteen, and 82% of course sections have fewer than twenty students. With an 8:1 student-to-faculty ratio and only one graduate program offered (an MA in finance), undergrads benefit from ample professor attention. In a typical school year, an incredible three-quarters of CMC students had the chance to conduct research with a faculty member, and the school has eleven partner research institutes and centers that provide graduate-level research experiences. Studying abroad is another popular pursuit as CMC offers approved programs on each of the world's six populated continents. Almost half of all undergrads spend time at one of 100+ approved programs in forty countries.

Economics, government, international relations, biology, and psychology are the most popular majors, and among the strongest. Interdisciplinary majors such as Environment, Economics, and Politics (EEP) and Philosophy, Politics and Economics (PPE) also carry outstanding reputations. Claremont graduates annually have representation of Fulbright, US Department of State Critical Language, and Luce Scholarships. Per capita, it is often among the top ten in Fulbright production, boasting four winners in 2022.

Outside the Classroom
Academically, students attending any of the Claremont Colleges are used to crossing campuses to take courses at one of the other schools. Those permeable borders apply to life outside the classroom as well. Pomona, Pitzer, Scripps, Harvey Mudd, and CMC are all located on the same 560-acre property, and many activities are joint efforts between members of the consortium. Even Claremont McKenna's 21 NCAA athletic teams are combined squads with Harvey Mudd and Scripps student-athletes; it has won over 300 conference championships since its founding in 1958. Not everything is a shared venture; there are 50+ CMC-exclusive student-run organizations of the academic, identity-based, service, sports, or music/arts nature. The Model UN team wins the world championship pretty much every year. An endless flow of public speakers graces the stage at the Marian Miner Cook Athenaeum, which presents guest lectures four nights per week. With 85% of CMC students electing to live on campus and no fraternities or sororities, campus life is an open and vibrant experience. Most facilities are shared among the members of the consortium, including the eight-lane pool; Roberts Pavilion, which includes a 2,200-seat arena and a state-of-the-art fitness center; and the Collins Dining Hall, which garners solid culinary reviews. Situated 35 miles east of Los Angeles, all of the culture and excitement you could want is never more than a relatively quick car ride away. The SoCal beaches are about an hour's drive as are Disneyland and Joshua Tree National Park.

Career Services
The Claremont McKenna Career Services Office has 14 full-time professional staff members working on grad school/career advising, employer relations, and internship procurement. That equates to a 99:1 student-to-advisor ratio, which is superior to just about every college featured in our guidebook. The college aims to provide individualized career coaching to all of its students and begins that process freshman year. It even has a counselor solely dedicated to the school's 350 first-year students, and that counselor is able to meet with more than 90% of that cohort each year. Annual fall career expos attract representatives from more than one hundred top employers. Events like company information sessions, two-to-five-day networking treks, and job shadowing experiences take place frequently throughout the year.

Employers recruiting at CMC include Google, Deloitte, Bain, the CIA, NASA, Goldman Sachs, and the National Football League. A phenomenal 90% of students participate in at least one internship. Many of those are financially supported by the Sponsored Internship Experiences Program, which provides between $500 and $6,000 grants for hundreds of undergrads. In a single school year, staff conducted 3,000 one-on-one counseling appointments, enticed forty-four employers into recruiting on campus, and facilitated 500+ on-campus interviews, more than one per member of the senior class. Thanks to that focus on hands-on experience, strong employer relations, and ample resources (including personnel), Claremont McKenna's career services easily earns the highest praise from the College Transitions staff.

Professional Outcomes

Eighty-eight percent of 2022 graduates found employment within six months of graduation, and only 4% were still looking for work. Financial services/accounting, consulting, and technology are the most frequently entered sectors. Companies employing the highest number of graduates include Accenture, Ernst & Young, Goldman Sachs, Amazon, Deloitte, and JP Morgan. The median starting salary for a 2022 Claremont grad is $87,000, a particularly impressive figure for a liberal arts college.

You name the prestigious graduate/professional program and, chances are, a recent CMC grad (or two or three) is presently studying there. Since 2001, more than 120 alumni have enrolled at USC and UCLA. More than 60 grads have headed to UChicago, Columbia, and Stanford. In the last five years, students have been accepted to medical schools at Stanford, Emory, Harvard, Johns Hopkins, and Penn. Students also have enjoyed law school acceptances at institutions including Columbia, NYU, Berkeley, the University of Chicago, and Yale. The list of MBA and other graduate programs attended by alumni is similarly eye-popping. Ten years out, 15% of the total alumni have earned a law degree, 10% an MBA, 5% a PhD, and 4% have completed a medical degree.

Admission

CMC's acceptance rate dipped into the single digits in recent cycles but came in at 10% for the Class of 2026. The mid-50% test scores of freshmen entering in 2022-23 were a 1450-1540 on the SAT and a 33-35 on the ACT. The median SAT score was 1500 and the median ACT score was 34. However, we must point out that the school is test-optional and many take advantage as over half of the Class of 2026 applied without SAT or ACT scores. The majority of students—68%—placed in the top 10% of their high school class, and 89% landed in the top quartile.

The process is a holistic one with six factors deemed "very important" by the admissions committee: rigor of secondary coursework, class rank, GPA, recommendations, extracurricular activities, and character/personal qualities. First-generation status is listed as a factor that is merely "considered," yet 18% of undergrads meet that criterion. Applying early decision is a worthwhile strategic maneuver as the ED acceptance rate tends to be 3-4 times that of the regular cycle; in 2022, thirty percent of the 742 ED applicants were admitted. To gain admission into CMC, applicants should bring exceptional credentials, as expected at any highly selective liberal arts college.

Worth Your Money?

Meeting 100% of demonstrated financial need, families earning less than $100,000 per year typically receive aid packages in the $65-75k range, a huge help at a school with a sticker price of $86,500. Those who can pay full price at Claremont McKenna likely will, and there are plenty of wealthy applicants capable of handling the bill. Whether you're a full-paying student or the recipient of generous aid, CMC's strong academics, sterling reputation, and incredible career service offerings will more than justify your investment in this top-notch liberal arts school.

FINANCIAL
Institutional Type: Private
In-State Tuition: $64,150
Out-of-State Tuition: $64,150
Room & Board: $19,650
Books & Supplies: $1,200

Avg. Need-Based Grant: $58,735
Avg. % of Need Met: 100%

Avg. Merit-Based Award: $18,491
% Receiving (Freshmen w/o Need): 6%

Avg. Cumulative Debt: $20,978
% of Students Borrowing: 32%

CAREER
Who Recruits
1. Cloudfare, Inc.
2. United Talent Agency
3. Whittier Trust Company
4. Boston Pharmaceuticals
5. Morgan Stanley

Notable Internships
1. BlackRock
2. Adidas
3. House of Representatives

Top Employers
1. Deloitte
2. Google
3. Microsoft
4. EY
5. Accenture

Where Alumni Work
1. Los Angeles
2. San Francisco
3. New York City
4. Seattle
5. Orange County, CA

Earnings
College Scorecard (10-YR Post-Entry): $97,174
PayScale (Early Career): $75,700
PayScale (Mid-Career): $151,200
PayScale 20-Year ROI: $1,003,000

RANKINGS
Money: 4.5
U.S. News: 11, Liberal Arts Colleges
Wall Street Journal/THE: 9
Washington Monthly: 12, Liberal Arts Colleges

OVERGENERALIZATIONS
Students are:
Career-driven
Athletic/active
Working hard and playing hard
Politically active
Wealthy

COLLEGE OVERLAPS
Georgetown University
Pomona College
University of California, Berkeley
University of California, Los Angeles
University of Southern California

Clark University

Worcester, Massachusetts | 508-793-8821

Founded as a graduate-only institution in 1887, Clark has been a cutting-edge undergraduate institution for the last 119 years, from hosting a series of lectures by Sigmund Freud to being at the forefront of AIDS research to starting the first PhD program in Holocaust and Genocide Studies. Today, Clark University continues to beat its own drum, with a unique liberal arts program focused on experiential learning, community service, and the pursuit of a meaningful life's work. With an undergraduate enrollment of just 2,389, this school offers the intimacy of a liberal arts college with the research emphasis of a university.

Inside the Classroom

Freshmen must begin their collegiate experience with a First-Year Intensive (FYI) course capped at 16 students and designed to forge close relationships with students and a professor with similar academic interests to your own. This FYI professor then becomes your academic advisor for the rest of your time at Clark. All students complete eight Program of Liberal Studies courses over their four years and must take one course (each) categorized as verbal expression, formal analysis, aesthetic perspective, global comparative perspective, historical perspective, language and culture perspective, natural scientific perspective, and values perspective. As seniors, students will complete a capstone project that "addresses a significant issue, problem, or theme" in their field of study.

Class sizes are fairly small with 23% containing fewer than 10 students and 63% having an enrollment of under 20. The average undergraduate class size is exactly 20 students. As a result, strong working relationships with faculty routinely develop. An impressive 67% of students participate in undergraduate research at some point in their four years of study. Opportunities exist to publish in the Scholarly Undergraduate Research Journal (SURJ). Fifty study abroad programs are available in 20+ countries.

Psychology and geography are two standout departments at Clark, and psychology (14%) is actually the school's most commonly conferred degree. Overall, 21% of degrees are conferred within the social sciences realm and many also earn degrees in biology (11%), the visual & performing arts (9%), business (8%), and communication technologies (8%). Clark's reputation with employers and grad schools is solid, and alumni also tend to fare well in the procurement of prestigious postgraduate scholarships and fellowships. In recent years, multiple students have won Critical Language Scholarships while others landed Fulbright, Boren, Goldwater, and Princeton in Africa Fellowships.

Outside the Classroom

Sixty-three percent of undergrads at Clark live off campus; however, among first-year students, 95% reside in university-owned housing. The university does not allow fraternities or sororities on campus, which leads to a less cliquish, fairly cohesive student body. Clark undergrads crack many lists of "happiest students" and tend to be, in general, an extroverted and liberally inclined bunch. With 17 (7 men's, 10 women's) NCAA Division III sports teams (the Cougars) and 130 student-run organizations, most Clarkies are involved in some type of extracurricular activity. The volunteering spirit is huge at Clark; 20 student groups based on volunteering as well as the school's own Community Engagement Office help connect undergrads to charitable efforts in the Worcester area. The Worcester area, previously a deterrent to many college applicants, now provides a surprising number of recreational opportunities—Shrewsbury Street is lined with more than 40 restaurants offering any type of cuisine imaginable. The CitySquare area recently received a $500 million transformation and is now brimming with retail and dining options. For those up for a longer trip, downtown Boston is just an hour away, and New York City is about a three-hour car ride from campus.

Career Services

The Career Connections Center is staffed by eight professional staff members who specialize in advising students in the various majors; one counselor works with students applying to prestigious scholarships or fellowship programs. This student-to-advisor ratio of 299:1 is lower than the average institution included in this book. Individualized support is offered in the form of career advising sessions, resume development, interest inventories, and networking assistance. Beyond these traditional career services offerings, this office is guided by its stated mission to provide students with experiential learning opportunities in an effort to help them parlay their academic studies into "a meaningful life and career."

E-mail: xadmissions@clarku.edu | Website: clarku.edu

Clark's annual Fall Career and Internship Fair is on the small side, with roughly 25 employers attending, including notables such as the FBI, Booz Allen Hamilton, and Fidelity Investments. It also hosts the On-Campus Job & Internship Fair each February with approximately 35 organizations in attendance. Clark students are also encouraged to attend off-campus job fairs such as the career fair at Worcester State University. Overall, career center staff engage with over 250 employers per year. This networking pays off immensely as 84% of undergrads ultimately land an internship or similar experiential opportunity.

Professional Outcomes

Six months after graduation, 97% of Cougars have clawed their way into gainful employment or full-time graduate programs. Sixty-three percent enter private industry, 32% enter the nonprofit/education world, and 5% are employed by government entities. The companies and organizations that employ the largest number of Clark grads include Amazon, the Clinton Foundation, Google, IBM, Microsoft, National Geographic, and Fidelity Investments. Sectors employing the greatest number of alumni are business development, education, and information technology. The bulk of Clark diploma holders stay in the Greater Boston area. New York City and Washington, DC, are next in popularity.

Of the 44% of freshly minted alumni who enrolled in graduate school, a good number continued their education at Clark or at nearby universities such as UMass Amherst, Boston College, and Boston University. Recent grads also found homes in highly selective graduate programs such as Brown University, NYU, Penn, USC, and the University of Cambridge. Clark does not produce a large number of students who go on to prestigious law schools; however, recent grads have earned acceptances into UNC's and Notre Dame's law programs. Those applying to medical school do have a strong track record of finding a home—Clark claims an acceptance rate of around 75%.

Admission

Clark received approximately 8,787 applications for a place in the Class of 2026 and accepted 50% of applicants. Although Clark is a test-optional university, freshmen who submitted standardized test scores had a middle-50th percentile range of 1260-1430 on the SAT and a 28-33 on the ACT. Perfect grades and being positioned at the top of your high school class are not prerequisites at Clark—just 37% ranked in the top decile, 73% in the top quartile, and 93% in the top half. The mean GPA for the Class of 2026 was 3.68. The school attracted students from 40 US states and 27 countries into the last three freshmen classes. The largest number of students come from Massachusetts followed by New York, Connecticut, California, and Maine.

Clark assigns the most weight to three factors: rigor of coursework, GPA, and letters of recommendation. The next tier of factors in terms of importance are essays, extracurricular activities, talent/ability, character/personal qualities, and volunteer work. Early decision and early action are both options for those with a strong interest in the university; however, the acceptance rate for those early rounds is typically comparable to the regular cycle. A realistic landing spot for those with a B average in a rigorous high school course load, Clark's test-optional status makes it an attainable destination for solid, but less-than-perfect, applicants.

Worth Your Money?

Clark's list price cost of attendance (COA) is $67,277, but 65% of students receive some need-based grants, and the average total financial aid package (including merit aid) awarded is $30k. The university awards merit scholarships at four different levels with annual values of $14k, $17k, $20k, and full COA. Even the full sticker price is equal to the tuition alone at many private schools in the state of Massachusetts, making it a relative bargain. With 97% of graduates finding their next stop very quickly, it is no shock that the loan default rate for Clark alumni is less than half of the national average. With some level of institutional aid, the cost of attending Clark can be well worth it for the small class sizes, undergraduate research opportunities, and personalized career services offerings.

FINANCIAL
Institutional Type: Private
In-State Tuition: $55,187
Out-of-State Tuition: $55,187
Room & Board: $11,690
Books & Supplies: $900

Avg. Need-Based Grant: $34,600
Avg. % of Need Met: 96%

Avg. Merit-Based Award: $19,599
% Receiving (Freshmen w/o Need): 30%

Avg. Cumulative Debt: $38,035
% of Students Borrowing: 66%

CAREER
Who Recruits
1. Reliant Medical Group
2. Eaton Vance
3. Microsoft
4. Fidelity
5. Dana-Farber Cancer Institute

Notable Internships
1. American Red Cross
2. Mountain Health
3. IBM

Top Employers
1. Fidelity Investments
2. UMass Medical School
3. Public Consulting Group
4. Dell EMC
5. IBM

Where Alumni Work
1. Boston
2. New York City
3. Washington, DC
4. San Francisco
5. Hartford, CT

Earnings
College Scorecard (10-YR Post-Entry): $55,982
PayScale (Early Career): $56,600
PayScale (Mid-Career): $120,400
PayScale 20-Year ROI: $381,000

RANKINGS
Money: 3.5
U.S. News: 142, National Universities
Wall Street Journal/THE: 367
Washington Monthly: 296, National Universities

OVERGENERALIZATIONS
Students are:
Politically liberal
Service-oriented
Open-minded
Passionate about social justice
Less likely to party

COLLEGE OVERLAPS
American University
Boston University
Northeastern University
University of Massachusetts Amherst
University of Vermont

Clarkson University

Potsdam, New York | 315-268-6480

ADMISSION
Admission Rate: 78%
Admission Rate - Men: 80%
Admission Rate - Women: 76%
EA Admission Rate: Not Offered
ED Admission Rate: 81%
ED Admits as % of Total Admits: 3%
Admission Rate (5-Year Trend): +12%
% of Admits Attending (Yield): 12%
Transfer Admission Rate: 94%

SAT Reading/Writing (Middle 50%): 580-680
SAT Math (Middle 50%): 610-690
ACT Composite (Middle 50%): 25-30

% Graduated in Top 10% of HS Class: 38%
% Graduated in Top 25% of HS Class: 72%
% Graduated in Top 50% of HS Class: 95%

Demonstrated Interest: Considered
Legacy Status: Considered
Racial/Ethnic Status: Not Considered
Admission Interview Offered: No

ENROLLMENT
Total Undergraduate Enrollment: 2,668
% Full-Time: 100%
% Male: 69%
% Female: 31%
% Out-of-State: 34%
% Fraternity: 14%
% Sorority: 9%
% On-Campus (All Undergraduate): 86%
Freshman Housing Required: Yes

% African-American: 3%
% Asian: 3%
% Hispanic: 6%
% White: 80%
% Other: 1%
% International: 3%
% Low-Income: 24%

ACADEMICS
Student-to-Faculty Ratio: 12 to 1
% of Classes Under 20: 58%
% of Classes 20-49: 30%
% of Classes 50 or More: 12%
% Full-Time Faculty: 69%
% Full-Time Faculty w/ Terminal Degree: 90%

Top Programs
Biology
Civil Engineering
Environmental Engineering
Environmental Science and Policy
Global Supply Chain Management
Innovation and Entrepreneurship
Mechanical Engineering

Retention Rate: 85%
4-Year Graduation Rate: 64%
6-Year Graduation Rate: 76%

Curricular Flexibility: Somewhat Flexible
Academic Rating: ★★★

#CollegesWorthYourMoney

Among the lesser-known of the Upstate New York schools, Clarkson University is even further north than Syracuse, Rochester, or Buffalo. For perspective, it would take a six-hour drive to reach Potsdam from New York City. The good news is that Clarkson's remote location makes getting in much easier than at comparable small, engineering-heavy schools like Lehigh University, Lafayette College, or Union College. The student body is made up of 2,668 undergraduate students pursuing more than 50 programs in engineering, business, the arts, education, and sciences and health professions.

Inside the Classroom
All Golden Knights are required to complete the Common Experience Curriculum, which includes a First-Year Experience course on adjustment to college life, the Clarkson Seminar, which is an introduction to college-level thinking and writing, and five courses that adequately cover the six broad areas of knowledge: cultures and societies; contemporary and global issues; imaginative arts; science, technology, and society; economics and organizations; and individual and group behavior. The four common threads in all of the introductory coursework are communication, diversity, ethics, and recognizing how technology can better serve humanity. Students in the business and engineering schools have a fairly rigid schedule of courses during the first two years of study. For instance, all business students take Principles of Microeconomics their first semester and Principles of Macroeconomics second semester.

A student-to-faculty ratio of 12:1 translates to reasonable undergraduate class sizes. Fifty-eight percent of sections enroll fewer than 20 students, but there are also 50-100+ students in some introductory courses. Undergraduate research is embedded in the Honors Program, which admits 40 to 50 students each year. Everyone else can apply to programs like the Research Experience for Undergrads (REU), which offers a ten-week apprenticeship funded by the National Science Foundation. Within the Biology Department, for example, all students are strongly encouraged to engage in research during their four years via the REU program, departmental connection, or by completing a senior thesis and presenting the findings at the Clarkson Symposium for Undergraduate Research. The school also offers 50+ study abroad programs in 27 countries but, as at most engineering-focused schools, the participation is low.

An overwhelming 63% of undergraduate degrees conferred are in engineering and 6% are in biology. Overshadowed by large research institutions in most ranking systems, the School of Engineering is, nevertheless, a stud whose quality is fully recognized by big-time employers well outside the region. The National Science Foundation frequently awards one or more students/alums a Graduate Research Fellowship each year.

Outside the Classroom
Clarkson students tend to be proud nerds. As the admissions office states, "If the idea of working all night on an animated video for physics class sounds more like fun than work, you'll fit right in at Clarkson." This school has a 69% male student body, which impacts the make-up of the social scene. The presence of SUNY Potsdam and its 61% female student body does help even the town's gender divide a bit. Four in five undergrads live on campus in one of eight dorm buildings or in one of the four apartment complexes. Additional Living-Learning Communities bring together students with common interests in areas like robotics, gaming, or women in engineering/business. There are nine fraternities and four sororities that, together, attract 9-14% of students. The school's 200+ intramural teams draw an incredible 80% of the student body into recreational athletics. NCAA Division I ice hockey is huge as this tiny powerhouse has produced approximately thirty NHL players in its history; the other ten teams participate in Division III. Overall, there are 250 student-run clubs and activities from which to choose. Like the woods? If so, you're in luck. Not only do you get to enjoy the 640 wooded acres on which the campus is set, but the grounds are adjacent to Adirondack Park, which adds another six million acres (not a typo). Like to spend time in a major metropolitan area? You're not so lucky on that front—Ottawa and Montreal, Canada (both around a two-hour drive), are closer to Clarkson than any major American city.

Career Services

The Clarkson Career Center (CCC) is staffed by three professionals with expertise in career coaching, employer relations, and graduate school advising. That works out to an 889:1 student-to-advisor ratio, which is in the higher range compared to other schools in this guidebook. Despite its distance from major American cities, the CCC still manages to entice companies to campus with regularity, and 200+ come to the annual career fairs. Even more impressive are the office's efforts in arranging internship and co-op experiences; the rate of participation was 96% for the Class of 2022, and many undergrads procure two or more placements. It's no wonder 95% of Clarkson grads end up finding a job directly related to their area of study.

A proactive office, the Clarkson Career Center has a reputation for seeking to connect personally with every student. Whether you are a freshman or a senior, staffers are equally happy to have you stop by to take a personality assessment, discuss career options one-on-one, work on your resume, or arrange an employer site visit. They conducted more than 1,000 one-on-one meetings in a single recent year. Golden Knights have a powerful alumni base to tap when it comes time for the job hunt. According to the university, among its 44,000 alumni, "One in five is already a CEO, senior executive, or owner of a company." Thanks to a thriving internship/co-op network that leads to fantastic employment/salary results for grads, the CCC gets high marks as an efficient and effective career services office.

Professional Outcomes

Within six months of graduation, the Class of 2022 enjoyed a job/grad school placement rate of 96% and an average starting salary of $69,024. Annually, 170+ employers snatch up Clarkson seniors. Top employers of recent grads include BAE Systems, Amazon, IBM, General Electric, Lockheed Martin, and Pratt & Whitney. Other companies that historically hire large numbers of Golden Knights include GlobalFoundries, Corning Incorporated, Xerox, Siemens, Accenture, and Intel. While a fair number of graduates stay in Upstate New York—Utica, Syracuse, Albany, and Rochester rank as the third through sixth most popular cities—the Greater New York and Boston areas are the most common alumni destinations.

Only 15% of Class of 2022 members were pursuing advanced degrees immediately after completing their undergraduate education. Students from recent cohorts were admitted into graduate school at institutions including Duke, MIT, Cornell, and NYU. Medical school is usually the direction of choice for around ten graduates each year. Medical school-bound students often attend SUNY schools, including SUNY Upstate Medical University, SUNY Stony Brook Medical School, and SUNY Buffalo Medical School. Recent grads also have landed at Dartmouth, Johns Hopkins, and Penn State. Remaining at Clarkson for graduate study is an option many also pursue, and the school offers approximately forty advanced degree programs.

Admission

In evaluating 6,594 applicants for membership in the Class of 2026, Clarkson ultimately admitted 78% of the pool—pretty nice considering that your average engineering school of this quality typically possesses an admit rate that is a mere fraction of those generous figures. Still, many top students choose Clarkson as 38% of freshmen hailed from the top decile of their high school class, and 72% finished in the top 25%. The average high school GPA was 3.8, and the mid-50% test score ranges were 1190-1370 on the SAT and 25-30 on the ACT.

Two factors reign supreme in the minds of admissions officials—GPA and a rigorous high school curriculum. Factors on the next rung of importance include class rank, extracurricular activities, recommendations, and volunteer work. The early decision acceptance rate is even friendlier than the regular round as 81% of ED applicants were admitted during the last cycle. A personal visit to Potsdam as well as a face-to-face informational interview with an admissions counselor is highly recommended. Clarkson remains a rare, strong engineering school that is open to B students with less-than-perfect test scores.

Worth Your Money?

The focus on engineering unsurprisingly raises starting salaries into a higher stratosphere than most schools of Clarkson's size. The list price of this university is roughly $76,000, including room and board, but merit and need-based aid are distributed generously; nine out of ten students receive financial aid. Middle-class families can expect to pay closer to $30-35k per year in total costs which, depending on one's academic track, can lead to a terrific return on investment.

FINANCIAL
Institutional Type: Private
In-State Tuition: $57,950
Out-of-State Tuition: $57,950
Room & Board: $17,792
Books & Supplies: $1,560

Avg. Need-Based Grant: $39,913
Avg. % of Need Met: 90%

Avg. Merit-Based Award: $37,934
% Receiving (Freshmen w/o Need): 20%

Avg. Cumulative Debt: $28,000
% of Students Borrowing: 79%

CAREER
Who Recruits
1. Procter & Gamble
2. General Dynamics
3. Tecnica Group
4. Whiting-Turner
5. Novelis

Notable Internships
1. Salesforce
2. Siemens
3. Hewlett Packard

Top Employers
1. IBM
2. Lockheed Martin
3. GLOBALFOUNDRIES
4. Corning Incorporated
5. GE

Where Alumni Work
1. New York City
2. Boston
3. Utica, NY
4. Albany, NY
5. Syracuse, NY

Earnings
College Scorecard (10-YR Post-Entry): $86,334
PayScale (Early Career): $70,700
PayScale (Mid-Career): $139,900
PayScale 20-Year ROI: $914,000

RANKINGS
Money: 4.5
U.S. News: 142, National Universities
Wall Street Journal/THE: Not Ranked
Washington Monthly: 135, National Universities

OVERGENERALIZATIONS
Students are:
Career-driven
Homogeneous
Not afraid to work hard
Collaborative
Hands-on (like to learn by doing)

COLLEGE OVERLAPS
Rensselaer Polytechnic Institute
Rochester Institute of Technology
St. Lawrence University
Syracuse University
Worcester Polytechnic Institute

Clemson University

Clemson, South Carolina | 864-656-2287

ADMISSION
Admission Rate: 43%
Admission Rate - Men: 41%
Admission Rate - Women: 44%
EA Admission Rate: Not Offered
ED Admission Rate: Not Offered
ED Admits as % of Total Admits: Not Offered
Admission Rate (5-Year Trend): -4%
% of Admits Attending (Yield): 20%
Transfer Admission Rate: 58%

SAT Reading/Writing (Middle 50%): 610-700
SAT Math (Middle 50%): 610-710
ACT Composite (Middle 50%): 28-32

% Graduated in Top 10% of HS Class: 54%
% Graduated in Top 25% of HS Class: 88%
% Graduated in Top 50% of HS Class: 99%

Demonstrated Interest: Not Considered
Legacy Status: Considered
Racial/Ethnic Status: Not Considered
Admission Interview Offered: No

ENROLLMENT
Total Undergraduate Enrollment: 22,566
% Full-Time: 97%
% Male: 47%
% Female: 53%
% Out-of-State: 40%
% Fraternity: 9%
% Sorority: 19%
% On-Campus (All Undergraduate): 41%
Freshman Housing Required: Yes

% African-American: 5%
% Asian: 3%
% Hispanic: 8%
% White: 77%
% Other: 2%
% International: 1%
% Low-Income: 14%

ACADEMICS
Student-to-Faculty Ratio: 16 to 1
% of Classes Under 20: 37%
% of Classes 20-49: 44%
% of Classes 50 or More: 18%
% Full-Time Faculty: 73%
% Full-Time Faculty w/ Terminal Degree: 87%

Top Programs
Agriculture
Animal Sciences
Construction Management
Design
Environmental Engineering
Industrial Engineering
Nursing
Sport Management

Retention Rate: 93%
4-Year Graduation Rate: 66%
6-Year Graduation Rate: 85%

Curricular Flexibility: Somewhat Flexible
Academic Rating: ★★★

#CollegesWorthYourMoney

Championship-caliber sports teams, thriving Greek life, and a passionate and generally happy undergraduate population of 22,566 young people define the Clemson experience—not to leave out the strong academic reputation, which becomes more pronounced with each passing year. A highly selective school for out-of-staters, Clemson caters to those residing within its home state of South Carolina. Nearly two-thirds of the student body are South Carolina-born and bred, and locals enjoy more relaxed entry requirements (not to mention one-third the tuition costs) than those from out of state.

Inside the Classroom

There are seven undergraduate colleges within the larger university: the College of Forestry and Life Sciences; the College of Architecture, Arts, and Humanities; the College of Business; the College of Engineering, Computing and Applied Sciences; the College of Education; the College of Science; and the College of Behavioral, Social, and Health Sciences. All Tigers, regardless of their academic program, must tackle 33 hours of required coursework that includes six credits in communications, ten in mathematical, scientific, and technical literacy, six in arts and humanities, six in social science, three in cross-cultural awareness, and three in science and technology in society. Most degree programs also require coursework in a foreign language.

Class sizes are mixed, and many sections are smaller than you would expect for such a large university where the student-to-faculty ratio is 16:1. Fifteen percent of classes have single-digit enrollments, and 55% contain fewer than 30 students; 18% of courses are larger, playing host to fifty or more undergraduates. More than half of Clemson students participate in some type of undergraduate research, a strong percentage given the size of the school. Each year over 1,400 students elect to study abroad in one of Clemson's own programs or one offered by a third party.

Business and engineering are the two programs with the highest profiles, and the university's highly selective Clemson University Honors College (formerly named Calhoun Honors College) regularly draws national attention and praise. Business and engineering also are the most popular majors with a 21% and 18% market share of diplomas, respectively. The next most frequently conferred degrees are in biology (9%), the social sciences (7%), and health professions (7%). With such an emphasis on professional career tracks, there is not a strong emphasis on winning prestigious postgraduate fellowships; however, Clemson had four Fulbright Scholars in 2023.

Outside the Classroom

Only 41% of undergrads, mostly underclassmen, reside on Clemson's 1,400-acre campus. Yet, that figure is not indicative of a dull social scene. Athletics are a galvanizing force as the Tigers compete in eight men's and nine women's NCAA Division I sports. Over 81,000 pack Memorial Stadium, nicknamed "Death Valley," on Saturdays to watch their highly-ranked football squad; Clemson won the national title in 2016 and again in 2019. Other sports draw large audiences as well. Greek life is almost a way of life at Clemson as 9-19% of undergrads are fraternity or sorority-affiliated. As at many Greek-heavy institutions, there has been increased scrutiny of those organizations in the wake of some incidents of sexual assault and hazing. Other opportunities for involvement abound as Clemson has over 500 student-run organizations. The school's thirty-four club sports attract widespread participation as does the intramural program. The town of Clemson offers plenty of enjoyable bars and restaurants within walking distance. Hiking trails and botanical gardens offer nature lovers everything they could ask for. Greenville, only 40 minutes away, provides a more exciting downtown feel.

Career Services

Clemson's Center for Career and Professional Development employs 38 full-time staff members who function as counselors, recruiters, and internship coordinators. That equates to a student-to-advisor ratio of 594:1, above average compared to the other institutions included in this book. Despite a less-than-ideal ratio, Clemson's staff garners much-deserved praise for its dedication to student success through the sheer scope of their offerings. Fall and spring career fairs attract roughly 600 employers and more than 5,400 students annually. The school's online database features over 12,000 job and internship postings each year. The center has forged corporate partnerships with twenty-four large corporations including Home Depot, Vanguard, Bosch, and General Electric.

Even more impressively, the CCPD personally reaches a massive number of students, claiming more than 28,000 engagements in the last school year. There were almost 3,000 one-on-one career counseling sessions held. Additionally, the CCPD put on 245 workshops that drew a total of 7,324 students. An astonishing 100% of those attending information sessions or individualized career counseling rated the experience favorably. Over 940 students participated in the University Professional Co-op/Internship Program with the school's 450 employer partners; 97% reported being satisfied with the experience. As a result, 96% of those receiving diplomas believe their resumes demonstrate marketable skills.

Professional Outcomes

Within six months of graduation, 92% of 2022 grads had already entered the working world or were pursuing a graduate degree. The top employers of newly-minted diploma holders include Michelin, Amazon, Vanguard, and Wells Fargo. Including all alumni, the most frequent employers include Bank of America, GE Power, Deloitte, IBM, and Microsoft. Recent graduates of the College of Engineering, Computing and Applied Sciences reported a median starting salary of $62,000. College of Business graduates enjoyed median earnings of $60,000. Graduates of the College of Architecture, Arts, and Humanities also averaged $60k while those completing degrees in the College of Science brought in a university-low $50k per year. Over two-fifths of graduates remain in South Carolina, and most stay in the Southern United States with North Carolina, Georgia, Texas, and Florida being the next most popular destinations.

Of the 19% of recent graduates directly entering graduate or professional school, the largest number retained their Tiger stripes by continuing their studies at Clemson. The next most frequently attended institutions were the Medical University of South Carolina, the University of South Carolina, the University of Georgia, the University of Florida, and Wake Forest University. Clemson grads also enjoyed three or more acceptances to prestigious graduate schools including Duke, Penn, Emory, Vanderbilt, and the University of Virginia. Among all alumni pursuing advanced degrees, 15% were in PhD programs, and a robust 23% were pursuing professional degrees in law or medicine.

Admission

The number of applicants to Clemson has rapidly risen in the past decade as 52,819 students applied last year compared with 15,542 in 2008. In that time, the average SAT score of attending students has climbed from 1221 to over 1310; the ACT mid-50% range is 26-31. The acceptance rate for the Class of 2026 was 43%. Most successful applicants—88%—finished in the top 25% of their high school class, and 54% were in the top 10%. The average weighted high school GPA for entering students was over a 4.0, and 91% earned a 3.75 or higher. Those applying to the Honors College need to be even stronger. On average, admitted honors students have a 1480/32 and are ranked in the top 4% of their class.

Over 50% of first-year students in 2022-23 were from South Carolina, but including transfers, home-state students comprise an even larger percentage of the student body. Being a South Carolina resident is listed among the five most important criteria for admission along with rigor of secondary coursework, GPA, class rank, and standardized test scores. Soft factors like essays, recommendations, and extracurricular activities comprise a distant second tier. Legacy status is also considered at Clemson. There is no early admission round at Clemson, but those who apply by the priority deadline of December 1 will receive an answer by February 15. This desirable Southern public university is friendlier toward in-state applicants than outsiders. Applicants not from South Carolina will need to bring above-average standardized test scores and strong grades in honors and AP courses to gain acceptance.

Worth Your Money?

The cost of attendance for South Carolina residents is under $35,000 per year, making Clemson a fantastic bargain for them. For nonresidents, the price is $59k, not a fortune relative to the out-of-control higher education marketplace at large, but not the steal that it is for those from the Palmetto State. Overall, close to 90% of students receive some form of financial assistance. In-state, attending Clemson is worth your money no matter what you are studying. If you hail from outside the state, a little bit of financial aid can keep the university affordable and a strong educational investment.

FINANCIAL
Institutional Type: Public
In-State Tuition: $15,558
Out-of-State Tuition: $39,502
Room & Board: $12,350
Books & Supplies: $1,388

Avg. Need-Based Grant: $11,196
Avg. % of Need Met: 48%

Avg. Merit-Based Award: $4,708
% Receiving (Freshmen w/o Need): 22%

Avg. Cumulative Debt: $34,307
% of Students Borrowing: 46%

CAREER
Who Recruits
1. Bank of America
2. ScribeAmerica
3. Global Lending Services LLC
4. Insight Global
5. TD Bank

Notable Internships
1. BMW
2. Booz Allen Hamilton
3. Capital One

Top Employers
1. Michelin
2. Fluor Corporation
3. Bank of America
4. Wells Fargo
5. Amazon

Where Alumni Work
1. Greenville, SC
2. Charlotte
3. Charleston, SC
4. Atlanta
5. Columbia, SC

Earnings
College Scorecard (10-YR Post-Entry): $69,479
PayScale (Early Career): $62,100
PayScale (Mid-Career): $111,500
PayScale 20-Year ROI: $620,000

RANKINGS
Money: 4
U.S. News: 86, National Universities
Wall Street Journal/THE: 81
Washington Monthly: 158, National Universities

OVERGENERALIZATIONS
Students are:
Ready to party
Politically conservative
Religious
Crazy about the Tigers
Preppy

COLLEGE OVERLAPS
Auburn University
College of Charleston
North Carolina State University
University of Georgia
University of North Carolina at Chapel Hill

Colby College

Waterville, Maine | 207-859-4828

Situated within the natural splendor of Waterville, Maine, Colby College's location may be remote, but the alluring sheen of this liberal arts gem is spotted each year by a growing number of top students from around the globe. Over the past decade, applications to Colby have tripled, and the school has become commensurately more selective. The 2,299 undergraduates presently on campus are, by far, the highest-achieving group the school has seen in its 210+ years.

Inside the Classroom

Offering 56 majors and 35 minors, Colby provides a classic liberal arts education with a high degree of flexibility and room for independent intellectual pursuits. Dual engineering degrees with Dartmouth and Columbia, independent majors of your own creation, and a strong premed track are among the bevy of options. Academic requirements for all Colby undergraduates include a freshman writing seminar, three semesters of a foreign language, two natural science courses (including one lab science), two courses dealing with diversity, and one course each in historical studies, literature, quantitative reasoning, history, and social sciences.

A 10:1 student-to-faculty ratio is put to good instructional use as roughly two-thirds of courses have fewer than 19 students. The school's "Jan Plan" tacks on a truncated semester during which students can conduct research alongside faculty, pursue internships, or take an accelerated course; 90% of undergraduates participate. An exceptionally high 70% of students study abroad at some point during their four years at Colby. The college runs three of its own off-campus study programs and allows participation in hundreds of programs in 60 total countries.

Being a true liberal arts school, Colby has strengths across many disciplines, but biology, economics, and global studies draw especially high praise. These programs along with government and environmental science—both of which are also very strong—attract the highest number of students as well. Unlike many of its elite Northeastern liberal arts counterparts, Colby does not produce a significant number of fellowship/scholarship winners, but in 2023, two graduates were named Fulbright Scholars. The previous year, Colby also had three Davis Projects for Peace winners and multiple Watson Fellowship finalists.

Outside the Classroom

The vast majority of students (96%) live on campus with a smattering of undergraduates living off campus in the surrounding town of Waterville. Colby ditched fraternities and sororities in the 1980s, but underground Greek-like organizations still exist. The Colby Mules field 32 NCAA Division III athletic teams (16 men's, 15 women's, 1 co-ed) as well as extensive intramural and club sports programs. An incredible one-third of undergraduates are members of a varsity athletic team. Of the one hundred student-run clubs and activities, the Colby Outing Club has the largest membership, catering to an outdoorsy student body. Wildlife trails and a pond perfect for ice skating are only two of the many natural treasures found on the school's 714-acre campus. In fact, the outdoor life is impossible to avoid as all freshmen participate in an outdoor bonding experience prior to the start of the fall semester. Manmade features of note include three libraries, the Colby College Art Museum, which features more than 6,000 works, and an Olympic-size pool. Getting to major cities from Colby will require the use of planes, trains, or automobiles. Portland, Maine, is 78 miles from the college, Boston is 180 miles away, and New York City is a lengthy 390-mile trip.

Career Services

Davis Connects, the office that facilitates employer recruiting and provides Colby students with career counseling and internship procurement, features 16 full-time professional staff members and a student-to-advisor ratio of 144:1. That figure is among the very best when compared to the other institutions included in this book. Career services staff members do an excellent job of directly engaging the undergraduate population, reaching roughly 1,200 students per year in more than 3,300 counseling sessions. The office also runs a job shadowing program, hosts an interview boot camp, and facilitates the Colby Connect program that hooks undergraduate students up with alumni-parent mentors in their fields of interest.

Due to its small size and remote location, Colby hosts an annual joint career fair with fellow elite Maine-based schools Bowdoin and Bates. However, many companies do host information sessions directly with Colby undergrads, and those employers include Google, Prudential, Epic, and Citigroup. Davis Connects has increased its number of credited internship opportunities in recent years, now facilitating close to 300 summer/winter experiences at Lockheed Martin, Goldman Sachs, Citigroup, Time, Massachusetts General Hospital, and others. Organizations that have formal partnerships with Davis Connects include PwC, Goldman Sachs, Accenture, Hearst Magazines, the US Department of State, and IBM. Overall, with strong graduate school advising, employer relations, and job placement rates, Colby's career services receive high marks from our staff.

Professional Outcomes

Within six months of graduation, 93% of the Class of 2022 had either obtained jobs or were enrolled full-time in a graduate program. Eighteen percent of graduates enter the financial industry and large numbers also start careers in education, with government/nonprofit, STEM, and healthcare next in popularity. Organizations hiring recent Colby grads were an eclectic bunch that included Teach for America, Barclays, Harvard Medical School, HBO, Deutsche Bank, Google, Fidelity Investments, and the United States Olympic Committee. Boston is the most frequent postgraduate destination followed by New York City; Portland, Maine; Lewiston, Maine; Washington, DC; and San Francisco. By mid-career, Colby grads enjoy a median salary of $100,000.

The Medical school acceptance rate over the past five years is 68%, nearly double the national average. In that time, multiple graduates have enrolled at prestigious medical schools including Tufts University School of Medicine, Emory University School of Medicine, Dartmouth Medical School, and University of Michigan Medical School. A solid 87% of law school applicants also find success. Law schools where multiple recent alumni have studied include the University of Pennsylvania, Georgetown University, Boston College, and Cornell University.

Admission

In the 2020-21 admissions cycle, the number of applicants to Colby reached almost 17,000, an all-time high. Such has been the pattern at Colby in recent years. A decade ago, Colby attracted fewer than 5,000 applicants and had an acceptance rate greater than 30%; the Class of 2014 enjoyed a 28% acceptance rate. In stark contrast, those seeking a place in the Class of 2026 were accepted at a paltry 8% clip. The average standardized test scores of this cohort were a 1485 SAT and a 33 ACT, and 82% of students graduated in the top 10% of their high school class. Just five years ago, a 1485 SAT/33 ACT would have placed you in the 75th percentile of attending students.

Among the factors rated as most important by the admissions committee are rigor of secondary curriculum, grades, recommendations, and character/personal qualities. In the fall of 2018, Colby became a test-optional institution. Serious applicants should strongly consider early decision as the ED rounds usually allow more generous acceptance rates, often more than three times as high as the regular round. Colby has become exponentially more competitive in recent years and shows no sign of slowing down. Applicants who would have been accepted a mere five years ago may quickly end up on the rejection pile. Those dead-set on Colby should apply early to gain a much-needed edge in this now hypercompetitive admissions process.

Worth Your Money?

While priced at the level one would expect for a premier New England liberal arts school—the current cost of attendance is over $86,000—Colby College is generous when it comes to need-based financial aid. In fact, all undergraduates with demonstrated financial need—approximately 40% of Colby's student body—have the full amount of their need met, with the annual grant averaging more than $65,000. Those grants are balanced by the many wealthy families who send their children to the college and pay full price for the pleasure. That makes possible the school's new policy that says, "Families with a total household income of $60,000 or less and typical assets may expect a parent or guardian contribution of $0." Overall, given its excellent reputation and generous need-based aid, Colby proves a sound investment for most.

FINANCIAL
Institutional Type: Private
In-State Tuition: $66,600
Out-of-State Tuition: $66,600
Room & Board: $17,120
Books & Supplies: $850

Avg. Need-Based Grant: $63,002
Avg. % of Need Met: 100%

Avg. Merit-Based Award: $611
% Receiving (Freshmen w/o Need): Not Reported

Avg. Cumulative Debt: $23,958
% of Students Borrowing: 18%

CAREER
Who Recruits
1. CGI
2. Market Axess
3. Analysis Group
4. Ocean Spray
5. Boston Medical

Notable Internships
1. Morgan Stanley
2. Boston Red Sox
3. Vertex Pharmaceuticals

Top Employers
1. Fidelity Investments
2. Morgan Stanley
3. Goldman Sachs
4. Massachusetts General Hospital
5. Google

Where Alumni Work
1. Boston
2. New York City
3. Lewiston, ME
4. Portland, ME
5. Washington, DC

Earnings
College Scorecard (10-YR Post-Entry): $84,482
PayScale (Early Career): $64,900
PayScale (Mid-Career): $111,000
PayScale 20-Year ROI: $690,000

RANKINGS
Money: 4.5
U.S. News: 25, Liberal Arts Colleges
Wall Street Journal/THE: 50
Washington Monthly: 13, Liberal Arts Colleges

OVERGENERALIZATIONS
Students are:
Environmentally conscious
Outdoorsy
Wealthy
Tight-knit (possess a strong sense of community)
Working hard and playing hard

COLLEGE OVERLAPS
Bates College
Bowdoin College
Brown University
Dartmouth College
Middlebury College

Colgate University

Hamilton, New York | 315-228-7401

When the sons of toothpaste/soap magnate William Colgate bailed out the penniless, struggling seminary/college known as Madison University in the late 1800s, the school had no idea that, from that point on, it would bear the family's name and rise to become one of the most respected liberal arts colleges in the country. Today, Colgate University is just that—one of the finest schools of its kind and home to 3,130 high achievers in the rustic, hilly town of Hamilton, New York.

Inside the Classroom
Fifty-six majors are on tap at Colgate, including all of the expected liberal arts concentrations. No matter your discipline, students must work through the extensive core curriculum. The requirements start with five classes that everyone must complete by the end of sophomore year: Legacies of the Ancient World, Challenges of Modernity, Communities and Identities, Scientific Perspectives on the World, and Global Engagements. An additional six courses from a range of the usual disciplines round out the mandated components of the curriculum as well as foreign language and physical education requirements.

With a student-faculty ratio of 9:1 and an average class size of 16, Colgate undergraduates work intimately with their instructors. Undoubtedly, the resulting connections help to explain the school's sterling 94-95% freshman retention rate. It is commonplace for Colgate students to research alongside professors. Each summer, the school funds over 200 undergraduates who assist with research projects, and, year-round, it maintains a useful database of professors who are seeking research across all disciplines. Raiders study abroad in overwhelming numbers with a 60-70% participation rate in one hundred programs that operate in 50 countries.

The social sciences account for 35% of all degrees conferred and, within that umbrella, economics, political science, and English are among the most popular and most well-regarded majors. International relations and neuroscience are also very strong. Other commonly issued degrees include biology (11%), psychology (8%), and computer science (5%). Compared to other elite liberal arts schools, Colgate students have only begun, in recent years, to pursue competitive fellowships at a high rate. However, they did see seven students win Fulbright awards in the 2022-23 academic year.

Outside the Classroom
Rural Hamilton is not exactly a hotbed of activity, leading many to spend a great deal of time within the bubble of the university's grounds. Fortunately, those grounds happen to be a lush, 575-acre paradise that often receives accolades as one of the most beautiful colleges in the country. The university's eight Greek organizations, dating as far back as 1856, attract 21% of males and 33% of females and play a leading role in defining the university milieu. Overall, 92% of students live on campus. The sports tradition at Colgate is rich as the Raiders field twenty-five teams that compete in NCAA Division I. The ice hockey team is particularly exceptional and has produced many NHL players. Also competing are club teams in 40 sports including Aikido, juggling, and Nordic skiing. Including those who play in varsity, club, and intramural sports, a majority of undergraduates find themselves involved in some level of athletic competition. For everyone else, there are 200+ student-run organizations with a fair representation of environment-oriented clubs. That aligns with the university's status as one of the more eco-friendly campuses as it runs almost exclusively on hydroelectric power and places a strong emphasis on organic food, sustainable energy, and increasing the use of bicycles on campus.

Career Services
The Career Services staff at Colgate is comprised of 14 professionals with expertise in career advising, employer relations, and alumni engagement. That works out to a 224:1 student-to-advisor ratio, which is better than average compared to other schools featured in this guide. Further, this staff deploys its ample resources effectively, engaging with 90% of students each academic year, including 93% of seniors and 88% of freshmen.

The CCS holds over 10,000 individual meetings with more than 3,000 current students and recent alumni per year. On-campus workshops and programs attract over 11,000 attendees. The office also excels in employer relations, having forged formal recruiting partnerships with 175+ companies/hiring institutions, which leads to roughly 600 on-campus interviews per year (close to one per senior). Premier employers include many of the top banking, accounting, and consulting firms in the country. The university supplies generous funding to students who wish to take low-paying or nonpaying internships, financially supporting close to 200 students per year. Job shadowing opportunities with alumni are arranged for more than 300 undergrads and 4,500 jobs and internships are posted exclusively for Colgate students each year. Displaying proficiency in undergraduate engagement, recruiting, and generating positive graduate outcomes, Colgate's career services rates among the best anywhere in the country.

Professional Outcomes

Nine months after graduation, only a small number of Colgate alumni are still looking for work; in 2022, that group represented less than 2% of the graduating class. A substantial 80% had already landed full-time jobs. Business, communications, consulting, and sales are the most commonly entered sectors. Employers hiring the most Colgate grads included Bank of America Merrill Lynch, JP Morgan, EY, Wayfair, and the NIH. Including alumni of all ages, the strongest concentrations of Raiders can be found roaming the corporate offices of Google, Goldman Sachs, JPMorgan Chase & Co., Deloitte, Citi, UBS, PwC, and Amazon. A sizable portion of alumni set up shop in the Greater New York City area. Boston and DC are the next most popular locales.

According to the most recent data available, 85-95% of law school applicants are accepted into one of their target institutions. The medical school numbers were even more impressive with 100% of graduating seniors (who were recommended by the school) gaining acceptance into at least one med school. The other most commonly pursued areas of graduate study are biology, business, engineering, public affairs and policy, and the social and behavioral sciences. Over the last five years, the most frequently attended graduate schools were primarily elite institutions that included Columbia, Cornell, Georgetown, NYU, Northwestern, and the University of Pennsylvania.

Admission

Colgate received 17,540 applications for a place in the Class of 2026 and the acceptance rate for a spot in this cohort was 12%, down five points from the prior year. The mid-50% standardized test scores of enrolled students in the Class of 2026 were 1118-1510 on the SAT and 32-34 on the ACT. The average unweighted GPA was 3.86. Among freshmen in the 2022-23 school year, 73% finished in the top 10% of their high school class while 94% were in the top 25%.

The admissions office ranks only three factors as being "very important": rigor of coursework, GPA, and class rank. Standardized test scores are optional through at least 2026-27. Though Colgate claims that demonstrated interest is not a factor, 60% of the Class of 2026 was admitted through early decision, so the school does "want you to want them." Those who applied early for the Class of 2026 got in at a far more generous 25% acceptance rate than those who applied in the regular cycle. Children of alumni, so-called legacies, obtain an even more favorable rate of over 50%. Over the past decade, Colgate's admit rate has declined and the average admitted student today possesses superior credentials to Raiders of the recent past.

Worth Your Money?

While the majority of students come from upper-income homes, those from less fortunate backgrounds are showered with need-based aid. That helps make the $84k cost of attendance a bit easier to swallow. The 37% of freshmen who qualify receive a combined package (merit + need-based aid) of approximately $60k, meeting 100% of their demonstrated need. One way or another, people are pleased with their decision to invest their time and money in Colgate University.

FINANCIAL
Institutional Type: Private
In-State Tuition: $67,024
Out-of-State Tuition: $67,024
Room & Board: $16,790
Books & Supplies: $1,524

Avg. Need-Based Grant: $61,929
Avg. % of Need Met: 100%

Avg. Merit-Based Award: $0
% Receiving (Freshmen w/o Need): 0%

Avg. Cumulative Debt: $25,631
% of Students Borrowing: 26%

CAREER
Who Recruits
1. NYU Langhorne Medical Center
2. Revlon
3. Guidepoint Global
4. AlphaSights
5. Zipcar

Notable Internships
1. ESPN
2. Wells Fargo
3. Barclay's

Top Employers
1. EY
2. Morgan Stanley
3. Google
4. Goldman Sachs
5. JPMorgan Chase

Where Alumni Work
1. New York City
2. Boston
3. Washington, DC
4. San Francisco
5. Syracuse, NY

Earnings
College Scorecard (10-YR Post-Entry): $86,737
PayScale (Early Career): $73,800
PayScale (Mid-Career): $152,600
PayScale 20-Year ROI: $983,000

RANKINGS
Money: 4.5
U.S. News: 21, Liberal Arts Colleges
Wall Street Journal/THE: 40
Washington Monthly: 20, Liberal Arts Colleges

OVERGENERALIZATIONS
Students are:
Working hard and playing hard
Wealthy
Preppy
Career-driven
Athletic/active

COLLEGE OVERLAPS
Boston College
Brown University
Cornell University
Hamilton College
Tufts University

The College of New Jersey

Ewing, New Jersey | 609-771-2131

ADMISSION
Admission Rate: 64%
Admission Rate - Men: 62%
Admission Rate - Women: 67%
EA Admission Rate: Not Offered
ED Admission Rate: 97%
ED Admits as % of Total Admits: 5%
Admission Rate (5-Year Trend): +16%
% of Admits Attending (Yield): 24%
Transfer Admission Rate: 71%

SAT Reading/Writing (Middle 50%): 570-670
SAT Math (Middle 50%): 570-680
ACT Composite (Middle 50%): 24-30

% Graduated in Top 10% of HS Class: 33%
% Graduated in Top 25% of HS Class: 67%
% Graduated in Top 50% of HS Class: 94%

Demonstrated Interest: Important
Legacy Status: Considered
Racial/Ethnic Status: Considered
Admission Interview Offered: No

ENROLLMENT
Total Undergraduate Enrollment: 7,039
% Full-Time: 97%
% Male: 43%
% Female: 57%
% Out-of-State: 5%
% Fraternity: 21%
% Sorority: 22%
% On-Campus (All Undergraduate): 46%
Freshman Housing Required: No

% African-American: 6%
% Asian: 11%
% Hispanic: 18%
% White: 60%
% Other: 3%
% International: 1%
% Low-Income: 21%

ACADEMICS
Student-to-Faculty Ratio: 13 to 1
% of Classes Under 20: 42%
% of Classes 20-49: 58%
% of Classes 50 or More: 0%
% Full-Time Faculty: 45%
% Full-Time Faculty w/ Terminal Degree: 90%

Top Programs
Accounting
Business Administration
Biology
Criminology
Communication Studies
Education
Nursing

Retention Rate: 92%
4-Year Graduation Rate: 75%
6-Year Graduation Rate: 86%

Curricular Flexibility: Somewhat Flexible
Academic Rating: ★★★✦

#CollegesWorthYourMoney

Let's lead off with a telling factoid: The freshman-to-sophomore retention rate at the College of New Jersey is 94%, better than at the majority of selective private schools. As one of only eight public colleges in the country to maintain a four-year graduation rate above 75%, the school is in the esteemed company of such institutions as UVA, Michigan, and UNC-Chapel Hill. Central Jersey may not draw a flood of applicants from the far reaches of the globe (only 5% of the student population comes from out of state), but TCNJ, a midsize state school with 7,039 undergraduate students, is simply one the best bargains you can find in the Northeastern United States.

Inside the Classroom
There are more than 50 majors, but whether you're studying art history or computer science, there are an identical series of general requirements known as Liberal Learning awaiting you, beginning as a freshman. As part of the Intellectual and Scholarly Growth phase of your education, new arrivals participate in a First-Year Program, a seminar-style course centered on one of seventy engaging topics. Students also complete an online, not-for-credit course on Information Literacy. A second language requirement exists for the School of Humanities and Social Sciences and selected programs with the arts and sciences, business, and science schools. While you can test out of the introductory course, three writing-intensive classes are on the menu, including a senior capstone. Additionally, you must choose a collective eight courses that fulfill your breadth requirements in the areas of the arts and humanities, social sciences and history, and natural science and quantitative reasoning.

TCNJ sports a 13:1 student-to-faculty ratio and an average class size of twenty-one; 42% of sections contain fewer than 20 students. While you won't find many seminar-style courses with single-digit enrollments, there are plenty of ways to personally connect with faculty thanks to the school's serious commitment to facilitating undergraduate research. In fact, the Council on Undergraduate Research awarded TCNJ its signature honor, the Campus-Wide Award for Undergraduate Research Accomplishment. In addition to plenty of research opportunities in the hard sciences, this school has invested in specialized facilities that include twenty psychology research labs, a digital humanities lab, and a fully equipped quantitative studies lab for criminology and sociology students. The College of New Jersey may not attract many from outside its state borders (although they have plans to double the number in the coming years), but it certainly helps its own expand their global horizons as 25-30% of undergrads participate in one of 500 study abroad programs.

Sixteen percent of degrees conferred are in education as many attend TCNJ to become teachers and the School of Education is widely considered the finest in the state. The most popular degree is actually business/marketing (19%), followed by engineering (9%), and health programs (8%). Jersey- and New York-based employers think highly of the school, which also has strong programs in biology, criminology, accounting, and nursing. Recent TCNJ students have won or placed as finalists for Fulbright, Marshall, Gates, Goldwater, and Truman awards.

Outside the Classroom
In the 2022-23 school year, just under half of the undergraduate student body resided on the 289-acre, well-maintained grounds of this suburban campus in Ewing. The College of New Jersey's fourteen residence halls do accommodate 90%+ of freshmen. Greek life does have a noticeable presence on campus with 21% of men pledging fraternities and a nearly identical 22% of women entering sororities. Aikido, knitting, and broadcasting on WTSR 91.3 are only three of the diverse 230+ active clubs available. A strong Division III athletics program features nine men's and nine women's teams that, since 1979, have captured 40 team and 50 individual NCAA championships. The Student Recreation Center features an indoor track, tennis courts, and a dance studio for those wanting to stay in shape, and there are plenty of intramural sports on tap at that same location. TCNJ is only five miles from the state capital of Trenton, ten miles from Princeton, and an hour's drive from Philly or New York City.

Career Services
A small office, the Career Center at the College of New Jersey employs only five full-time professional staff, not counting secretaries, office assistants, interns, or peer career educators who assist with things like resume reviews and career fair organization. The student-to-counselor ratio of 1,408:1 isn't terribly strong, but it's clearly enough staffing to make plenty of positive things happen for the school's undergraduates.

Over 400 employers recruit on campus, a phenomenal number given that there are fewer than 7,000 undergrads. A solid 67% of surveyed graduates reported having at least one internship, with 70% of that group having procured a paid internship. In large part due to the efforts of the Career Center, 30% of graduates say the school did an excellent job in preparing them for entering the workforce, 44% rate the center's efforts as "above average," and fewer than 5% of respondents gave a mark of "below average." The large presence of graduates, recent and otherwise, in the offices of many top companies and banks around the country speaks to the superb employer engagement efforts of this school.

Professional Outcomes

Checking in with TCNJ grads one year after receiving their degrees, 93% had entered the working world or started an advanced degree. The list of companies employing significant numbers of recent alumni includes Johnson and Johnson, JP Morgan Chase & Co., Bank of America, Bloomberg LP, MetLife, EY, and PricewaterhouseCoopers. Factoring in all alumni, the school also has a huge presence within Verizon, Merrill Lynch, Merck, and Bristol-Meyers Squibb. The starting salary after exiting the College of New Jersey was an impressive $57,720, more than the national average for college grads. School of Arts & Communication grads earned $50,000 while School of Business degree-holders took home $61,000. The most popular geographic destinations were New Jersey, New York, and Pennsylvania.

The most frequently attended graduate schools by recent grads included Rutgers, Georgetown, and Stevens Institute of Technology. Recent graduates entered law schools including William & Mary, Hofstra, Penn State, and Rutgers. Young alums have also attended an array of excellent medical schools including Johns Hopkins, the Icahn School of Medicine at Mt. Sinai, NYU, Drexel, and Penn State University. Many also attend Rutgers via the 7-Year Combined BS/MD Program with Rutgers New Jersey Medical School. Overall, undergraduates enjoy a 60-65% medical school acceptance rate, roughly 20 points higher than the national average.

Admission

The College of New Jersey is a rare school that isn't exceptionally hard to get into—the acceptance rate for 2022-23 freshmen was 64%—but still provides a superior and supportive academic experience to its undergraduates. One-third of the Class of 2026 placed in the top 10% of their high school class, 67% were in the top 25%, and 94% were in the top 50%. The mid-50% standardized test score ranges were 24-30 on the ACT and 1160-1330 on the SAT. In a higher education world where many schools have experienced massive spikes in selectivity in recent years, TCNJ remains fairly steady; the profile of an accepted student five years ago is similar to today's freshman.

At the top of the list of "very important" admissions factors sits participation in a rigorous course load, class rank, extracurricular activities, and, most interestingly, volunteer work. The essay, teacher recommendations, GPA, talent/ability, character/personal qualities, and state residency are all in the next tier of "important" factors. However, given that the overwhelming majority of TCNJ students come from inside New Jersey, out-of-state applicants should enjoy a slight advantage. This reality is made more evident by the fact that TCNJ offers an application fee waiver to all students applying from out of state. Finally, applying early decision may also offer a notable edge–of the 354 submitting ED applications in 2022, 97% were accepted. Those accepted through early decision comprised 22% of the entire freshman class.

Worth Your Money?

Garden State residents will pay around $41,000 per year in tuition and fees, and while the school isn't as cheap as it used to be (what is?), TCNJ represents a decent bargain for an East Coast public school with a tremendously successful alumni base. Few out-of-state students seek out this college, but the price is not unreasonable, particularly for those wishing to study business or a STEM field.

FINANCIAL
Institutional Type: Public
In-State Tuition: $17,980
Out-of-State Tuition: $30,774
Room & Board: $15,112
Books & Supplies: $1,200

Avg. Need-Based Grant: $12,960
Avg. % of Need Met: 40%

Avg. Merit-Based Award: $5,854
% Receiving (Freshmen w/o Need): 10%

Avg. Cumulative Debt: $39,795
% of Students Borrowing: 58%

CAREER
Who Recruits
1. Target
2. Withum
3. NJM Insurance Group
4. Cenlar
5. Johnson & Johnson

Notable Internships
1. U.S. Department of Education
2. Prudential Financial
3. Lockheed Martin

Top Employers
1. Johnson & Johnson
2. Merrill Lynch
3. Bristol-Myers Squibb
4. Merck
5. Prudential Financial

Where Alumni Work
1. New York City
2. Philadelphia
3. Washington, DC
4. Boston
5. Los Angeles

Earnings
College Scorecard (10-YR Post-Entry): $70,578
PayScale (Early Career): $63,700
PayScale (Mid-Career): $106,200
PayScale 20-Year ROI: $651,000

RANKINGS
Money: 4.5
U.S. News: 4, Regional Universities North
Wall Street Journal/THE: Not Ranked
Washington Monthly: 21, Master's Universities

OVERGENERALIZATIONS
Students are:
Career-driven
Competitive
Hardworking
More likely to go home on the weekends
Always admiring the beauty of their campus

COLLEGE OVERLAPS
Pennsylvania State University - University Park
Rutgers University - New Brunswick
University of Delaware
University of Maryland, College Park
Villanova University

College of the Holy Cross

Worcester, Massachusetts | 508-793-2443

ADMISSION
Admission Rate: 36%
Admission Rate - Men: 35%
Admission Rate - Women: 38%
EA Admission Rate: Not Offered
ED Admission Rate: 81%
ED Admits as % of Total Admits: 16%
Admission Rate (5-Year Trend): -4%
% of Admits Attending (Yield): 35%
Transfer Admission Rate: 10%

SAT Reading/Writing (Middle 50%): 640-720
SAT Math (Middle 50%): 620-710
ACT Composite (Middle 50%): 28-32

% Graduated in Top 10% of HS Class: 43%
% Graduated in Top 25% of HS Class: 75%
% Graduated in Top 50% of HS Class: 98%

Demonstrated Interest: Considered
Legacy Status: Considered
Racial/Ethnic Status: Considered
Admission Interview Offered: Yes

ENROLLMENT
Total Undergraduate Enrollment: 3,233
% Full-Time: 99%
% Male: 45%
% Female: 55%
% Out-of-State: 61%
% Fraternity: Not Offered
% Sorority: Not Offered
% On-Campus (All Undergraduate): 88%
Freshman Housing Required: Yes

% African-American: 4%
% Asian: 4%
% Hispanic: 12%
% White: 71%
% Other: 3%
% International: 3%
% Low-Income: 15%

ACADEMICS
Student-to-Faculty Ratio: 10 to 1
% of Classes Under 20: 62%
% of Classes 20-49: 38%
% of Classes 50 or More: 1%
% Full-Time Faculty: 91%
% Full-Time Faculty w/ Terminal Degree: 96%

Top Programs
Biology
Chemistry
Economics
English
History
Political Science
Psychology
Sociology

Retention Rate: 93%
4-Year Graduation Rate: 89%
6-Year Graduation Rate: 92%

Curricular Flexibility: Somewhat Flexible
Academic Rating: ★★★★⬩

#CollegesWorthYourMoney

The oldest Catholic college in all of New England, the College of the Holy Cross in Worcester, Massachusetts, offers an exceptional liberal arts education with a strong Jesuit influence that permeates the service-oriented undergraduate student body of 3,233. The college offers thirty traditional majors as well as additional subjects in which one can pursue a student-designed major. Hands-on learning, interdisciplinary connections, a genuine quest for meaning and value, and faculty guidance that extends beyond the classroom are all staples of academic life for all Crusaders.

Inside the Classroom

All undergraduate students must work through a comprehensive but straightforward list of required coursework. Mandatory areas of study include one course each in religion, philosophical studies, arts, literature, history, and cross-cultural studies. Two courses are required in language studies, social science, and natural and mathematical sciences. All freshmen complete a year-long seminar called Montserrat that is centered on an interdisciplinary topic and designed to help students "develop broad foundational skills, including critical thinking, strong writing, and effective communication."

The average class size is a manageable 19 students, and 62% of courses have enrollments lower than that. An undergraduate-only institution, Holy Cross offers ample individualized attention and guidance from faculty. Each year, one hundred students participate in the intensive Weiss Summer Research Program that offers STEM majors the opportunity for one-on-one mentorship from a professor. Across all disciplines, research apprenticeships are available to undergrads as early as the sophomore year. Study abroad figures were understandably modest during the pandemic (7%), but roughly a quarter typically take advantage.

There are no majors that undergrads flock to in overwhelming numbers, but the most popular are the social sciences (29%), psychology (14%), history (7%), and biology (6%). All of those popular departments also rank well nationally. Biology and chemistry are very strong as well. Highly competitive postgraduate fellowships are frequently pursued by seniors. In fact, Holy Cross is one of the nation's top Fulbright producers, having had seven named in 2023.

Outside the Classroom

Thanks to a campus regularly voted as one of the country's most beautiful, few undergraduates wish to flee the grounds. Guaranteed housing is available for all four years in one of eleven residence halls, and 88% of students elect to live in college-owned housing. The nine campus eateries also receive acclaim and leave students with little reason to seek off-campus dining options. Those seeking the typical university experience of Greek parties and big-time athletics will find themselves batting .500. There are no fraternities or sororities on campus, but with 27 Division I squads, twenty-two club teams, and eleven intramural sports on the menu, it seems like most of the student body participates in some form of athletic competition. The Hart Center is replete with amenities including a six-lane swimming pool, ice rink, and a 2,800-square-foot facility dedicated to cardiovascular and strength training. There are 100+ student organizations, including a healthy dose of clubs in the performing arts, service, and multicultural realms. While Worcester isn't a town that teems with alluring activities, recent investment in the city's downtown area has provided an increasing number of dining and entertainment options. In addition, the college is located only 44 miles west of Boston and 61 miles northeast of Hartford.

Career Services

The Center for Career Development (CCD) is staffed by ten professional employees (not counting office assistants), resulting in a 323:1 student-to-advisor ratio that is in the average range when compared with other schools featured in this guide. The CCD believes in a "three-stage model of career development: self-assessment, exploration, and implementation." Individualized attention is available to undergraduates at each stage of their education, whether it involves discussing the results of an interest inventory, preparing a resume, engaging in a mock interview, or applying to graduate/professional school.

Fall and spring career fairs attract approximately 40-60 employers and 300+ students. Well-known employers such as City Year, GE, EY, PepsiCo, and the FBI are regular attendees. The office excels in coordinating student internships as an impressive 73% of graduates end up with at least one such experience. A few years ago, the school ponied up more than $200k to help defray the costs of eighty-two undergrads completing unpaid summer internships. Students who completed internships enjoyed better job placement rates and higher starting salaries than those who did not. Through the Career Advisor Network, current students can link up with alumni in fields of interest to arrange a job-shadowing experience or to receive career advice. Thanks to a high level of student engagement and strong employment/graduate school results (more on this in a moment), the Center for Career Development is performing admirably on behalf of its undergraduates.

Professional Outcomes

Six months after moving their tassels to the left, 68% of the Class of 2021 (most recent stats available) were employed, 19% were in graduate school, 6% were engaged in volunteer work, and only 3% were still seeking full-time employment. The industries drawing the most Holy Cross grads were financial services (18%), health care (12%), education (10%), and government (9%). Organizations employing more than one recent graduate include Fidelity Investments, JP Morgan, Goldman Sachs, Massachusetts General Hospital, Deloitte, EY, PwC, Oracle, and Dell. Large numbers of alumni also can be found at State Street, Morgan Stanley, and the Dana Farber Cancer Institute. The average salary is $59k. New England is the most popular home, keeping over 50% of grads in the area with the Mid-Atlantic region soaking up an additional 30%. Boston and New York City are the two most common destinations.

Among those enrolled in graduate school, 14% were in law school, 14% were pursuing degrees in a health profession, and 6% were in PhD programs. Boston College and Fordham are among the most frequently attended law schools. Recent graduates have earned spots in medical schools such as Tufts and acceptances into dental school at the University of Pennsylvania and Boston University. Overall, Holy Cross graduates enjoy a 92% acceptance rate to law schools and a 72% acceptance rate to medical schools. Grads have been accepted into master's and doctoral programs at elite schools including Georgetown, Johns Hopkins, Princeton, Harvard, the University of Chicago, and Columbia.

Admission

A competitive pool of 7,036 applicants vying for a place in the Holy Cross Class of 2026 encountered a 36% acceptance rate. This is in the same ballpark as the acceptance rates over the last five years. Holy Cross is test-optional and, of the Class of 2026, only 35% submitted SAT scores, and 19% submitted ACT scores. Given that a fair number of applicants are likely to have submitted both, it is reasonable to assume that a healthy percentage of the class was admitted sans standardized test scores. Among those who did submit scores, the mid-50% range on the SAT was 1270-1420 and 28-32 on the ACT. Forty-three percent of Crusaders finished in the top 10% of their high school class and 75% fell within the top quarter.

According to the admissions committee, six factors rise above the rest when evaluating applicants: rigor of secondary school record, GPA, essays, recommendations, the interview, and character/personal qualities. Extracurricular activities and talent/ability are the only other factors labeled as being "important." Those dead-set on attending this school shouldn't think twice about applying early decision as the ED acceptance rate was 81% last cycle. The two most notable items related to admissions at the College of the Holy Cross are its test-optional admissions and incredibly generous ED acceptance rate. Serious applicants are advised to strongly consider the latter.

Worth Your Money?

Holy Cross helps to mitigate the impact of its $77k sticker price by meeting 100% of demonstrated need for every single student who qualifies for financial aid. At the end of the day, the majority of students receive some form of aid and the average cost after aid is $36k. Holy Cross is an excellent school, but you won't get a huge income boost from attending so you may not want to go deep into debt to afford a full-price tab, especially if you're considering a lower-paying field.

FINANCIAL
Institutional Type: Private
In-State Tuition: $60,850
Out-of-State Tuition: $60,850
Room & Board: $17,750
Books & Supplies: $1,000

Avg. Need-Based Grant: $42,303
Avg. % of Need Met: 100%

Avg. Merit-Based Award: $21,323
% Receiving (Freshmen w/o Need): 10%

Avg. Cumulative Debt: $24,617
% of Students Borrowing: 60%

CAREER
Who Recruits
1. Dell
2. General Electric
3. Peace Corps
4. Wayfair
5. Deloitte

Notable Internships
1. National Football League
2. McCann
3. MetLife

Top Employers
1. Fidelity Investments
2. PwC
3. Deloitte
4. EY
5. Morgan Stanley

Where Alumni Work
1. Boston
2. New York City
3. India
4. Washington, DC
5. United Kingdom

Earnings
College Scorecard (10-YR Post-Entry): $83,583
PayScale (Early Career): $65,600
PayScale (Mid-Career): $127,100
PayScale 20-Year ROI: $715,000

RANKINGS
Money: 4.5
U.S. News: 27, Liberal Arts Colleges
Wall Street Journal/THE: 60
Washington Monthly: 34, Liberal Arts Colleges

OVERGENERALIZATIONS
Students are:
Service-oriented
Religious
Preppy
Homogenous
Driven

COLLEGE OVERLAPS
Boston College
Fordham University
Providence College
University of Notre Dame
Villanova University

College of William & Mary

Williamsburg, Virginia | 757-221-4223

Brimming with tradition, the College of William & Mary is one of the oldest public institutions in the country (some contend the oldest), the alma mater of three US presidents, and a school that has long been a member of the "Public Ivy" club. Nearly two-thirds of the 6,700+ undergraduates on this spectacularly beautiful Williamsburg campus hail from in-state, and members of the student body known as "the Tribe" tend to be an intellectual and passionate lot who adore their school. Of W&M's 100,000 living alumni, you'll rarely meet one who doesn't have a strong affinity for their school.

Inside the Classroom

Forty undergraduate programs are available with the most popular being business, psychology, economics, biology, and government. All undergraduates must work through the College Curriculum, the school's liberal arts core, including two first-year seminars, four COLL 200 courses covering a variety of topics, COLL 300 (that often involves studying abroad), and COLL 400 as a senior, which requires the production of original research. Additional requirements include taking courses in three "knowledge domains" and demonstrating proficiency in mathematics and foreign language.

William & Mary has a 13:1 student-to-faculty ratio. Class sizes are rarely tiny seminars, but 44% do enroll fewer than twenty students, and only 9% contain more than fifty. An extremely high percentage of undergrads study abroad for a semester; by graduation, roughly half of the class has done so, traveling to one of more than 60 countries. Undergraduate research opportunities are widely available. In the Chemistry Department, for example, 80-90% of students complete independent/professor-assisted research with many becoming coauthors of studies alongside faculty. Across the college, 80% of undergraduates participate in research by the time they graduate.

Among the college's most notable academic programs are (1) government and (2) international relations, both of which serve as pipelines to Washington, DC, employers. The Mason School of Business is highly regarded in the corporate world. The social sciences (20%) and biology (11%) are the areas in which the greatest percentage of degrees are conferred. With a notable service-minded ethos, William & Mary is the top producer of Peace Corps volunteers among midsize universities. In 2023, the college had ten Fulbright Scholarship winners. They typically produce multiple Boren Fellows each year as well.

Outside the Classroom

The campus is large and lush with over 1,200 acres, including an amphitheater, Lake Matoaka, and College Woods, the latter two of which can be freely enjoyed by nature-loving students. William and Mary's grounds easily make any list of the most beautiful college campuses in the country. Sixty-eight percent of students live on campus, which includes a sizable number of Greek houses. Greek life first appeared at W&M in 1776, and the tradition is still alive and well today. Presently, 32-36% of undergrads participate, with higher numbers in the school's sororities than fraternities. More than 450 student clubs in every area imaginable are available with volunteer organizations drawing large numbers—3,500+ each year. That spirit of involvement carries over into athletics as well with an 85% participation rate when including the school's twenty-three NCAA Division I teams and thriving intramural and club sports. Nightlife in the surrounding Williamsburg area is generally pretty tame unless you happen to be a colonial-era history buff. Most students enjoy a social life more centered around campus activities and dorm life.

Career Services

The Office of Career Development & Professional Engagement employs 19 full-time staff members, not counting graduate assistants or administrative assistants, giving it a student-to-advisor ratio of 353:1, which is slightly higher than the average school profiled in this guide. The office does arrange several well-attended job fairs each year including the Government & Nonprofit Career Expo that features ninety employers as well as large-scale career and internship fairs in the fall and spring that are attended by as many as 1,000 undergrads. In a typical year, roughly 400 employers attend William & Mary career fairs.

In a single school year, the office completed 2,680 total advising contacts, put on 191 programs with 4,308 total attendees, and brought 94 employers to campus for information sessions, which attracted over 1,400 students. For those interested in graduate school, representatives from more than one hundred programs across the academic spectrum attend the annual Graduate & Professional Fair. Partnerships with Deloitte, PwC, KPMG, EY, and Accenture lead to on-campus recruiting and interviewing with those giants of the accounting and consulting fields. Over 285 on-campus interviews were arranged last year with W&M seniors. A respectable 60% of grads participate in at least one internship, externship, or research project. The office does a solid job guiding undergraduates toward meaningful work as 94% of recent grads found first jobs that aligned to some degree with their career goals.

Professional Outcomes

The Class of 2021 (the most recent class for which data is available) saw 52% of its cohort join the workforce, and 36% enter graduate school within six months of graduation. Over 500 employers snatched up at least one member of the Tribe. Companies hiring at least four 2020 grads included Accenture, Booz Allen Hamilton, KPMG, and Deloitte. More than fifty alumni across all graduating years can be found in the corporate offices of Capital One, PwC, Microsoft, Google, Amazon, and Deloitte. Starting salaries varied significantly by industry. The average salary for those entering STEM careers was $55k, business was $68k, and education was $38k. The vast majority of alumni remain in the Mid-Atlantic region; the Northeast is a distant second.

Many of those opting for immediate entry into graduate school stayed at their alma mater and the next most frequented universities included Columbia, Duke, Harvard, Northwestern, and the University of Chicago. Recent grads have been admitted to law schools such as Emory, USC, Georgetown, Notre Dame, and Yale. Most impressively, William & Mary graduates gain acceptance into medical school at a rate twice the national average.

Admission

Of the 18,087 applicants vying for a seat in W&M's Class of 2026, just under 6,100 received the proverbial thick envelope. That calculates to an acceptance rate of 33%, down from 42% two years prior. Like UNC-Chapel Hill, but not to nearly as extreme a degree, in-state applicants have an easier pathway to acceptance at William & Mary. The acceptance rate for out-of-state students is typically significantly higher than for out-of-staters. Of those who enrolled in the Class of 2026, the SAT middle-50% range was 1375-1520, and the ACT range was 32-34. (A far greater number of applicants submit SAT scores.) Seventy-seven percent of enrolled freshmen hail from the top 10% of their high school class, and 95% placed in the top quartile. The average high school GPA was 4.33.

The admissions office ranks a dozen factors as being most important in the admissions process. In addition to the obvious factors of grades, test scores, and class rank, the college also prioritizes state residency status, volunteer work, work experience, character/personal qualities, and talent/ability. Applying early decision can work to your advantage as 50% of ED applicants get positive results, and ED admits comprised 36% of the 2022-23 freshman class. William & Mary is a highly selective school, but even more so for non-Virginia residents. The school maintains a 65/35 split of in-state versus out-of-state students.

Worth Your Money?

High-achieving residents of Virginia are lucky to have two Ivy-level public schools at their disposal. Like UVA, William & Mary comes at a bargain price for those living in Virginia. The cost of attendance is roughly $40,000 in-state and $64,000 out-of-state, and the school tries to meet 100% of demonstrated financial need for Virginia residents. The average amount of debt for a W&M graduate is slightly less than the national average. For in-state students, attending this school is a no-brainer. Prospective out-of-state students have to factor in the amount of loans they would need and the starting salaries typical of the field they eventually wish to enter.

FINANCIAL
Institutional Type: Public
In-State Tuition: $25,041
Out-of-State Tuition: $48,841
Room & Board: $14,555
Books & Supplies: $1,080

Avg. Need-Based Grant: $20,853
Avg. % of Need Met: 81%

Avg. Merit-Based Award: $9,065
% Receiving (Freshmen w/o Need): 6%

Avg. Cumulative Debt: $27,866
% of Students Borrowing: 33%

CAREER
Who Recruits
1. Central Intelligence Agency
2. National Institutes of Health
3. The Carlyle Group
4. Aldi
5. Navigant Consulting

Notable Internships
1. Booz Allen Hamilton
2. Vanguard
3. NFL Films

Top Employers
1. Capital One
2. Booz Allen Hamilton
3. Deloitte
4. EY
5. IBM

Where Alumni Work
1. Washington, DC
2. Norfolk, VA
3. New York City
4. Richmond, VA
5. Boston

Earnings
College Scorecard (10-YR Post-Entry): $69,897
PayScale (Early Career): $63,400
PayScale (Mid-Career): $120,800
PayScale 20-Year ROI: $644,000

RANKINGS
Money: 4.5
U.S. News: 53, National Universities
Wall Street Journal/THE: 212
Washington Monthly: 69, National Universities

OVERGENERALIZATIONS
Students are:
Politically active
Academically driven
Service-oriented
Less likely to party
Nerdy

COLLEGE OVERLAPS
Georgetown University
James Madison University
University of North Carolina at Chapel Hill
University of Virginia
Virginia Tech

The College of Wooster

Wooster, Ohio | 330-263-2322

New York Times columnist and bestselling author Ron Lieber devoted an entire chapter of his excellent book, *The Price You Pay for College*, to the College of Wooster. The chapter is entitled "How the College of Wooster Puts It All Together," referring to the school's many admirable features, including its remarkably transparent financial aid process and one-of-a-kind mandatory independent study program. You might expect that a school receiving so much attention for its exemplary undergraduate program would be extraordinarily hard to get into, but this liberal arts college of 1,967 students in northeastern Ohio accepts significantly more students than it rejects.

Inside the Classroom
A Wooster education is bookended by two highly regarded rites of passage: a first-year seminar in critical inquiry and three independent study courses, one taken in the junior year to learn research skills and two senior-year courses to work one-on-one with a faculty mentor. Twenty-eight other classes are required to earn a BA, and those will include one or more courses in writing; global and cultural perspectives; religious perspectives/social justice; quantitative literacy, history, and the social sciences; mathematical and natural sciences; and the arts and humanities.

The College of Wooster receives high marks across the board in undergraduate teaching, senior capstone, undergraduate research, innovation, and value. With no graduate students, the faculty is wholly committed to undergraduate education; an 11:1 student-to-faculty ratio and an ability to form mentoring relationships via the Independent Study Program ensures that everyone gets individualized attention. An exceptional 52% of course sections enroll a single-digit number of students, and only 6% contain more than 30 students. Wooster is one of the few schools that can genuinely state that every graduate is afforded a supervised research experience. In addition, 35% of Scots participate in an international experience.

The most conferred degrees last year were in the social sciences (19%) and biology (17%). Next in popularity were psychology (6%), the physical sciences (6%), mathematics (6%), communication/journalism (6%), visual/performing arts (6%), and computer science (5%). No one major holds a reputation far above the others. Prestigious national scholarships love Wooster grads; the 2022-23 academic year saw three Fulbright winners as well as multiple alumni selections for National Science Foundation Graduate Research fellowships in recent years.

Outside the Classroom
This 240-acre campus rests in the town of Wooster, population 27,000, which is located 55 miles southwest of Cleveland. The majority of students—69%—hail from outside Ohio, and 96% of undergrads live in university housing. The makeup of the student body is relatively diverse with 24% of US students being nonwhite, and 17% of the total student body being international students. For a liberal arts school, the College of Wooster has a fairly substantial Greek presence with 12% of women joining sororities and 12% of men entering fraternity life. Wooster has 23 varsity sports teams (11 men's and 12 women's) that are known as the Fighting Scots; over 30% of students are members of a varsity team, and the intramural sports program has a mind-blowing 80% participation rate. There are also 120 student-run clubs, including many popular volunteer organizations like the Wooster Volunteer Network, COW 4 Kids, and Circle K. Almost one-third of undergrads partake in choir, symphonic or marching band, jazz ensemble, or one of four a cappella groups. The town itself offers quality restaurants, a year-long farmer's market, the Wayne Center for the Arts, and all the hiking and mountain biking trails anyone could desire.

Career Services
Traditionally, career services at the COW have been part of the larger APEX Center that more broadly addresses all facets of advising, planning, and experiential learning. In 2021 it launched the Scots Career Hub, an online platform full of virtual resources and information.

There are four professional employees devoted to the career-related elements of APEX's mission, including counselors who specialize in pre-health and prelaw advising. This 492:1 student-to-counselor ratio may be on the high side for a small liberal arts school, but this is a department committed to continuous improvement. In addition to the aforementioned virtual tool, the college is also developing a Pathways Program "designed to help integrate intentional career planning into the full student experience."

Wooster does bring employers to campus for information sessions, on-campus interviews, and an annual Grad School Fair, but for larger fairs/expos it relies on its membership in several consortia and regional/state events. There are presently hundreds of job postings, many of them local, to help connect students and alumni to prospective employers. One of the coolest features of the Scots Career Hub is that it features alumni mentors who are open to working with current students in 10 disciplines/fields from communications to finance and corporate to STEM.

Professional Outcomes

Within six months of leaving Wooster, 96% of job-seeking individuals had landed a job, and 72% were employed in their preferred field. Organizations hiring at least one recent grad include Bank of America, Ernst & Young, the FBI, Morgan Stanley, and Northrop Grumman. More than 10 alumni can also be found in the offices of Amazon, PNC, the Cleveland Clinic, and KeyBank. Those entering the banking, finance, and insurance fields netted an average starting salary of $59k while those in the K-12 education, government, communications, or nonprofit fields started at approximately $40k. Many alumni remain in the Cleveland, Akron, or Columbus areas, but large numbers also can be found in Washington, DC; New York City; Chicago; Boston; and Pittsburgh.

Over the past few years, 97% of graduate school applicants were accepted into their top-choice institution. Among recent grads, 54% left to pursue a master's degree, 27% entered doctoral programs, 8% matriculated into medical school, and 3% began law school. Eight of the 19 medical school applicants (including alumni) gained acceptance to at least one institution in one recent cycle. Recent enrollments include the Duke University School of Medicine, the Philadelphia College of Osteopathic Medicine, and the Ohio State University College of Medicine. Recent graduates have attended many top law schools including Boston University, Georgetown, the University of Chicago, Stanford, and the University of Michigan.

Admission

In accepting 4,080 of the 7,251 applicants for a place in the Class of 2026, the College of Wooster sported a 56% acceptance rate, roughly double that of rival Ohio-based liberal arts standouts Kenyon, Oberlin, and Denison. The middle-50% test score ranges were 1260-1430 on the SAT and 27-32 on the ACT. Forty-six percent of enrolled 2022-23 freshmen placed in the top 10% of their high school class, but there was plenty of room for those lacking A averages; 71% were in the top quartile, and 90% were in the top half. The average weighted GPA for the Class of 2026 was 3.73, and 18% earned a GPA below 3.25.

The rigor of an applicant's secondary record and the GPA earned are the only two factors viewed as "very important" by the Wooster Admissions Committee. In its own words, the committee gives "due consideration to many different expressions of a student's qualities and abilities: scholastic achievements, extracurricular activities, character, and promise to contribute to the intellectual and social life of our distinct academic community." In 2020, Wooster adopted a test-optional policy. While the timing of this adoption matched the start of the pandemic, it represented a genuine philosophical shift that took root well before the spread of COVID-19. Fifty-six percent of the 143 ED applicants for the Class of 2026 were accepted, a figure similar to the percentage accepted in the regular round.

Worth Your Money?

A liberal arts school like the College of Wooster that sends large numbers of students into the nonprofit world and PhD programs is not going to pop on any ROI metrics alone. Instead, Wooster is a good investment because of the uniqueness and quality of the academic experience and the straightforwardness of the financial aid process. Need-based aid was awarded to a whopping 70% of freshmen in the 2022-23 academic year, and 85% of students received some type of assistance. The school even offers a human-calculated financial aid estimate (as opposed to a generic net price calculator) before you apply. All of that transparency and generosity make the intimidating $74,000 list price cost of attendance irrelevant to the vast majority of prospective students.

FINANCIAL
Institutional Type: Private
In-State Tuition: $59,050
Out-of-State Tuition: $59,050
Room & Board: $14,000
Books & Supplies: $1,250

Avg. Need-Based Grant: $42,878
Avg. % of Need Met: 96%

Avg. Merit-Based Award: $34,133
% Receiving (Freshmen w/o Need): 34%

Avg. Cumulative Debt: $26,785
% of Students Borrowing: 52%

CAREER
Who Recruits
1. Amazon Web Services
2. Huntington National Bank
3. PNC Bank
4. Lubrizol Corp.
5. Charles River Laboratories

Notable Internships
1. Microsoft
2. Dow AgroSciences
3. National Park Service

Top Employers
1. Ohio State University
2. Cleveland Clinic
3. Case Western Reserve University
4. JPMorgan Chase
5. Amazon

Where Alumni Work
1. Cleveland
2. Washington, DC
3. New York City
4. Columbus, OH
5. Chicago

Earnings
College Scorecard (10-YR Post-Entry): $54,485
PayScale (Early Career): $51,600
PayScale (Mid-Career): $102,600
PayScale 20-Year ROI: $310,000

RANKINGS
Money: 4
U.S. News: 75, Liberal Arts Colleges
Wall Street Journal/THE: 316
Washington Monthly: 114, Liberal Arts Colleges

OVERGENERALIZATIONS
Students are:
Politically liberal
Always studying
Diverse
Accepting
Collaborative

COLLEGE OVERLAPS
Case Western Reserve University
Denison University
Grinnell College
Kenyon College
Oberlin College

Colorado College

Colorado Springs, Colorado | 719-389-6344

ADMISSION
Admission Rate: 14%
Admission Rate - Men: 17%
Admission Rate - Women: 16%
EA Admission Rate: Not Reported
ED Admission Rate: 44%
ED Admits as % of Total Admits: 24%
Admission Rate (5-Year Trend): -1%
% of Admits Attending (Yield): 42%
Transfer Admission Rate: 29%

SAT Reading/Writing (Middle 50%): 640-730
SAT Math (Middle 50%): 620-750
ACT Composite (Middle 50%): 29-33

% Graduated in Top 10% of HS Class: 72%
% Graduated in Top 25% of HS Class: 95%
% Graduated in Top 50% of HS Class: 99%

Demonstrated Interest: Considered
Legacy Status: Considered
Racial/Ethnic Status: Considered
Admission Interview Offered: Yes

ENROLLMENT
Total Undergraduate Enrollment: 2,180
% Full-Time: 98%
% Male: 43%
% Female: 53%
% Out-of-State: 78%
% Fraternity: Not Reported
% Sorority: Not Reported
% On-Campus (All Undergraduate): 77%
Freshman Housing Required: Yes

% African-American: 3%
% Asian: 5%
% Hispanic: 11%
% White: 66%
% Other: 1%
% International: 7%
% Low-Income: 14%

ACADEMICS
Student-to-Faculty Ratio: 9 to 1
% of Classes Under 20: 63%
% of Classes 20-49: 37%
% of Classes 50 or More: 0%
% Full-Time Faculty: 80%
% Full-Time Faculty w/ Terminal Degree: 78%

Top Programs
Art
Economics and Business
Environmental Studies
Geology
International Political Economy
Organismal Biology and Ecology
Political Science
Sociology

Retention Rate: 93%
4-Year Graduation Rate: 83%
6-Year Graduation Rate: 86%

Curricular Flexibility: Very Flexible
Academic Rating: ★★★★✦

#CollegesWorthYourMoney

With the Rocky Mountains visible from Colorado College's 90-acre campus, the school's 2,180 undergraduates find themselves in rarefied air—in more ways than one. A magnet for high-achieving, civic-minded, and generally liberally inclined young people, CC is ideally located seventy miles south of Denver and within a reasonable car ride of seven national parks and ten ski resorts. The student body is geographically diverse with about one-quarter hailing from the Northeast, one-quarter from the West Coast, and a sizable representation from the Midwest and the South.

Inside the Classroom

Rather than the typical semester schedule, Colorado College operates on the "block plan," a series of eight three-and-half-week periods during which students take only one course. Requirements are broad, affording undergraduates the opportunity to chart their own course. That course, however, must stay within some boundaries that include a first-year seminar, a foreign language, and courses fitting under the umbrellas of global cultures, social inequality, quantitative reasoning, and scientific investigation of the natural world.

You won't find a more intimate liberal arts college than CC. Classes have a cap of 25 students, and no more than a handful of courses exceed that figure. The average class consists of 16 students, and 17% of offerings have single-digit enrollments. Face time with your professors is a certainty as the school boasts a solid 10:1 student-faculty ratio. Although it does offer master's programs for teachers, this is a teaching college that focuses on undergraduate education. In faculty-wide surveys, the vast majority of professors report that quality of instruction is properly factored into their evaluations. Research opportunities are built into the academic program as 20% of CC classes involve some degree of undergraduate research. Another 6% of students receive stipends to conduct research. Tigers appear unafraid to go into the world and immerse themselves in other cultures as a healthy 74% study abroad.

Regularly ranked among the top liberal arts schools in the country, Colorado College has an excellent reputation. Environmental studies, art, and sociology are considered very strong, but CC doesn't necessarily offer programs that clearly stand above the rest. In its own words, "The most popular majors at CC are those that are popular nationally." In terms of sheer volume, most degrees are conferred in the social sciences (28%), biology (17%), natural resources and conservation (8%), and physical science (6%). This institution is a regular producer of Watson and Fulbright Scholarship winners. It also ranks 13th in the nation for the number of Peace Corps volunteers produced, which is especially impressive given the modest size of each graduating class.

Outside the Classroom

One hundred percent of freshmen live on Colorado College's campus, and 77% of the total undergraduate student body remains in school-owned housing. There is a Greek presence, but it in no way dominates the social scene. There are 80 active student clubs and organizations available, the most popular being the Outdoor Recreation Committee. That makes sense given the natural splendor surrounding campus that is conducive to hiking, skiing, cycling, and the like. Students have the dual benefit of attending what is, technically, an urban campus situated in Colorado Springs, which is, by area, the largest city in the state. Dorms, food, and campus facilities all receive generally favorable reviews from the student body. Community service projects are inclusive with an 80% undergraduate participation rate. While no one would mistake CC for a jock school, it does have sixteen total men's and women's sports teams competing in NCAA Division III, except for the highly competitive Division I ice hockey squad.

Career Services

The Career Center has nine full-time staff members who focus on either career advising or employer relations. Titles include career coach, health professions advisor, and prelaw advisor. The 242:1 student-to-advisor ratio is superior to many schools featured in this guide. The center puts its personnel to excellent use, having conducted a remarkable 1,700 one-on-one counseling sessions in a single recent year.

E-mail: admission@coloradocollege.edu | Website: coloradocollege.edu

Colorado College is a member of the nine-school Selective Liberal Arts Consortium that is comprised mostly of elite schools on the East Coast such as Vassar and Haverford College. This organization hosts off-campus interview days based in New York City and DC as well as video interviewing days with a host of high-caliber employers. The Career Center also arranges so-called "Tiger Treks" in which current students travel to a major city to meet with alumni in a variety of job settings. On-campus recruiting and interviewing are not a regular occurrence; only twenty-two companies recruited on campus last year. Internship opportunities are available, but assistance in landing one is limited. Last year, 62% of graduating seniors reported having participated in at least one internship.

Professional Outcomes

Among the Class of 2022, an impressive 99% arrived successfully at their next destination within six months of earning their diploma. Being a small school, Colorado College does not send massive numbers of graduates to any one company or organization, but there are employers that have wrangled their fair share of Tigers. That list includes Adobe, Wells Fargo, CBRE, Amazon, Google, and the Democratic National Committee. The largest number of graduates who pursue employment end up in the fields of education, technology, health care, the arts, and government. Ten years after entering college, CC alumni have lower average salary figures than one might expect. Again, this is attributable to many graduates pursuing careers in nonprofit sectors and the relatively low number of STEM majors. Further, as we will discuss in a minute, seemingly all graduates of this school continue their educational journeys, a choice that typically delays financial rewards. Roughly one-quarter of grads stay in the state of Colorado while the majority migrate to major cities across the United States with San Francisco, New York, Seattle, and Los Angeles among the most popular destinations.

The bachelor's degree earned at Colorado College is unlikely to be the last degree a graduate will earn. Five years after graduation, the typical cohort sees 70-90% of its members having either completed or finishing an advanced degree. Over half of that group are in PhD or professional programs with an average of 25% going to medical school. Recent graduates pursuing legal training have matriculated at a wide range of law schools including UVA, Columbia, NYU, Fordham, the University of Colorado, Temple, and Vermont Law School.

Admission

With an acceptance rate of only 16%, Colorado College unquestionably qualifies as a highly selective school. That figure has decreased considerably over the past decade as the number of applicants continues to soar. The good news is that the profile of the average admitted student has remained fairly steady. The mid-50% SAT range is 1270-1460 and the ACT range is 29-33. Scores around the 50th percentile will put you on solid ground if accompanied by a strong academic transcript.

Colorado College's testing policy used to be as unique as its academic calendar. However, starting in 2020, the school made the shift from test-flexible to full-blown test-optional. Superb grades in a challenging high school curriculum are a must as "rigor of secondary school record" is the sole category rated by the admissions staff as "very important." The data suggests that the school means what it says: 13 members of one recent cohort were the valedictorians of their graduating class; 72% of the Class of 2026 finished in the top decile. Applying via early action or early decision can have a profound impact on your chances of gaining admission. In the 2022-23 admissions cycle, ED applicants were accepted 44% of the time. Early action applicants also enjoy an edge, but the percentage of regular decision applicants admitted is typically minuscule. In short, Colorado College is an institution with a low acceptance rate but a clear idea of what type of applicants it is looking for. While highly selective, those who performed at the top of their high school class can expect to be welcomed here, even if they didn't score perfectly on the SAT/ACT.

Worth Your Money?

The affluent make up a sizable portion of the undergraduate population at Colorado College, rendering the $87,000 annual cost of attendance of less concern to many considering the school. For those who are concerned about the price tag, Colorado College comes through strong for qualifying applicants, meeting 100% of demonstrated need for every financial aid recipient. The average annual value of those grants is roughly $60,000, helping make the school a worthy investment to students coming from more modest economic backgrounds. Students coming from families who make too much to qualify for significant need-based aid, but who make too little to comfortably cover CC's hefty price tag, are encouraged to consider their career and/or graduate school plans before committing.

FINANCIAL
Institutional Type: Private
In-State Tuition: $65,028
Out-of-State Tuition: $65,028
Room & Board: $14,376
Books & Supplies: $1,240

Avg. Need-Based Grant: $60,186
Avg. % of Need Met: 100%

Avg. Merit-Based Award: $11,758
% Receiving (Freshmen w/o Need): 9%

Avg. Cumulative Debt: $26,093
% of Students Borrowing: 29%

CAREER
Who Recruits
1. US Olympic Committee
2. El Pomar Foundation
3. Accenture
4. SunShare Community Solar
5. Amazon

Notable Internships
1. National Science Foundation
2. Late Show with Stephen Colbert
3. Accenture

Top Employers
1. Denver Public Schools
2. Microsoft
3. Amazon
4. Google
5. Charles Schwab

Where Alumni Work
1. Denver
2. Cororado Springs
3. San Francisco
4. New York City
5. Seattle

Earnings
College Scorecard (10-YR Post-Entry): $61,590
PayScale (Early Career): $58,300
PayScale (Mid-Career): $107,700
PayScale 20-Year ROI: $433,000

RANKINGS
Money: 4
U.S. News: 33, Liberal Arts Colleges
Wall Street Journal/THE: 339
Washington Monthly: 68, Liberal Arts Colleges

OVERGENERALIZATIONS
Students are:
Outdoorsy
Wealthy
Politically liberal
Free-spirited
Less concerned with fashion or appearance

COLLEGE OVERLAPS
Colby College
Lewis & Clark College
Middlebury College
University of Colorado Boulder
University of Denver

Colorado School of Mines

Golden, Colorado | 303-273-3200

Less than a half-hour ride from Denver and a neighbor of the Coors factory, the Colorado School of Mines, commonly referred to as "Mines," is a public technical institute with an ever-increasing undergraduate enrollment of 5,733, over 1,000 more students than a decade ago. The majority of students are Coloradans taking advantage of the reasonable $19,500 in-state tuition. However, the school is becoming more of a draw for out-of-staters and international students. Presently, there are representatives from all 50 states and 80 countries on campus.

Inside the Classroom

There are around 20 bachelor of science degree options to choose from as well as additional areas of specialization. The vast majority of undergraduates are pursuing engineering degrees in areas such as petroleum engineering, mining, mining engineering, geological engineering, mechanical engineering, and chemical engineering. In short, you don't come to Mines to read Tolstoy or intensively study Picasso's Blue Period. That being said, the university does demand that all undergrads complete its core curriculum that does include a smidgeon of work in the humanities and social sciences with an emphasis on "fundamental technical, mathematical, and writing skills."

Classes are rarely small as Mines possesses a student-to-faculty ratio of 17:1. The average class has 34 students, and only 27% of sections have an enrollment under twenty. Yet, that does not translate into a lack of hands-on opportunities. All Mines students must take a two-semester sequence of courses called EPICS (Engineering Practices Introductory Course Sequence) in which they tackle an open-ended design problem as part of a small team. Freshmen also take Cornerstone Design, in which teams of students must solve re-al-world design problems. In a given year, roughly 125 students are awarded Mines Undergraduate Research Fellowships and work as research assistants on faculty-led projects.

The largest number of degrees are conferred in mechanical engineering and petroleum engineering. In fact, 78% of all earned degrees are classified under the engineering umbrella. However, any degree from the Colorado School of Mines, thanks to its terrific academic reputation and extensive alumni base, will open doors in the world of industry. Prestigious postgraduate fellowships are within reach even though they are not pursued in large numbers; five Mines students and alumni were awarded National Science Foundation Graduate Research Fellowships in 2022.

Outside the Classroom

The 373-acre campus is populated by mostly modern, recently renovated buildings, but only five residence halls that mostly house freshmen—who are required to live on campus. Just about everyone else lives off campus in apartments in Golden, nearby Lakewood, or in Greek houses. Greek life is prevalent, but not overbearing, with seven fraternities and three sororities attracting 6% of men and 6% of women. The Orediggers compete in 18 NCAA Division II sports and generally place well within the Rocky Mountain Athletic Conference. Club and intramural programs enjoy widespread participation. There are 200+ registered student clubs and endless opportunities for outdoor recreation. The school's official Outdoor Recreation Center lends equipment for hiking, biking, or rock climbing. A practice rock climbing wall prepares students for organized climbing trips to the Rockies. "E-Days" are campus-uniting events held multiple times per year that feature activities like carnivals, boat races, concerts, and fireworks shows. Golden, Colorado, which many know only through beer commercials—"Brewed in Golden, Colorado"—is a place of natural beauty where the Great Plains meet the Rocky Mountains. In addition to natural splendor and ample outdoor recreational opportunities, Golden has a nice downtown replete with shops, restaurants, and cafes. Denver is only a quick fifteen-mile car ride away, making Mines' location anything but remote.

Career Services

The Colorado School of Mines Career Center has nine full-time professional staff members working on career counseling and employer relations. That equates to a 637:1 student-to-advisor ratio, which is slightly higher than many schools featured in this guide. Yet, that statistic is not at all telling of the level of career services the school provides. For a moderately sized institution, Mines' career fairs draw an exceptional number of companies to campus. They draw 450+ unique hiring organizations to their Fall and Spring Career Days as well as 3,800+ students.

The 2021-22 school year saw 1,300 companies visit the school to recruit undergraduate students on campus. Last year, there were 900+ interviews held virtually and on campus. A commendable three-quarters of students engage with the Career Center each year. Over 60 small-group workshops are held on topics related to career skill acquisition and job and internship search strategies. A fantastic 69% of 2022 graduates had at least one hands-on internship or co-op experience.

Professional Outcomes

Members of the Class of 2022 landed industry jobs or full-time graduate school positions at a clip of 93%. The largest number of recent grads entered the aerospace/defense/transportation industry (17%); construction (16%), oil and natural gas (14%), and information technology (13%) were next in line. Companies employing massive numbers of Mines' grads include Lockheed Martin, BP, ExxonMobil, Halliburton, Chevron, and Shell. Those finding employment enjoyed an average starting salary of $81,000. Petroleum engineering majors averaged $79k and had offers as high as $110k. After graduating, 64% of Mines Class of 2022 grads remained in Colorado. Texas and California were the next most popular destinations.

Nineteen percent of freshly printed diploma-holders directly enter graduate school, and the most popular institution is Mines itself, which is the choice of 82% of those pursuing advanced degrees. Other universities attended by recent graduates include Baylor College of Medicine, Boston University, Carnegie Mellon, Columbia University, Imperial College London, Kyoto University, Rice University, and Stanford University.

Admission

Accepting 58% of the 10,886 who applied for a spot in the Class of 2026, Mines may not sound as highly selective as it actually is. Acceptance rates can fluctuate greatly at this school from year to year. For instance, in 2015, only 38% of applicants were admitted. Freshmen in 2022-23 sported ACT middle-50% ranges of 30-33 and 1340-1460 on the SAT. Fifty-seven percent finished in the top 10% of their high school classes and 87% were in the top 25%. The average GPA was 3.85 and 23% had a perfect 4.0. The profile of the average freshman today is similar to previous years, whether 58% or 38% of applicants were admitted.

There is nothing complicated about the admissions process at Mines. The committee considers two cut-and-dried factors to be "very important" in evaluating applicants: rigor of secondary school record and GPA. The only factors labeled as "important" are essays and recommendations. With almost 70% of the student body being male, being a qualified female applicant can yield a significant admissions edge. The acceptance rate for women is 66% compared to 55% for men. A touch over half of the student body hails from the Rocky Mountain State, and being a resident can give you a slight boost. No early round is offered, but students should aim for the priority deadline of November 1 to maximize their chances. Mines uses about as straightforward a formula as you will find to make its admissions decisions. That makes self-assessment of one's chances for admission simple. Strong grades in rigorous courses + standardized test scores in the 90th percentile = probable acceptance.

Worth Your Money?

With the annual cost of attendance of roughly $42,000 for Colorado residents and $65,000 for out-of-staters, Mines is a good value for everyone, especially given that the average starting salary is roughly $81k. The news only gets sunnier when you look at the fact that approximately 40% of undergraduates receive an annual need-based grant with a mean value of $6k. Whether you live in the Centennial State or not, the Colorado School of Mines is a wonderful place to study engineering or computer science. You will have no trouble finding well-compensated work after you earn your diploma.

FINANCIAL
Institutional Type: Public
In-State Tuition: $20,040
Out-of-State Tuition: $42,120
Room & Board: $16,110
Books & Supplies: $1,500

Avg. Need-Based Grant: $5,644
Avg. % of Need Met: 67%

Avg. Merit-Based Award: $8,153
% Receiving (Freshmen w/o Need): 44%

Avg. Cumulative Debt: $31,046
% of Students Borrowing: 54%

CAREER
Who Recruits
1. Rio Tinto
2. Chevron
3. Phillips 66
4. Procter & Gamble
5. Occidental Petroleum

Notable Internships
1. ExxonMobil
2. Cigna
3. Chevron

Top Employers
1. Lockheed Martin
2. Chevron
3. Aramco
4. BP
5. National Renewable Energy Laboratory

Where Alumni Work
1. Denver
2. Houston
3. San Francisco
4. Colorado Springs
5. Dallas

Earnings
College Scorecard (10-YR Post-Entry): $95,887
PayScale (Early Career): $79,300
PayScale (Mid-Career): $148,700
PayScale 20-Year ROI: $1,204,000

RANKINGS
Money: 4.5
U.S. News: 76, National Universities
Wall Street Journal/THE: Not Ranked
Washington Monthly: 101, National Universities

OVERGENERALIZATIONS
Students are:
Career-driven
Decided upon their chosen major
Nerdy
Homogenous
Hardworking

COLLEGE OVERLAPS
Colorado State University
Purdue University - West Lafayette
Texas A&M University - College Station
University of Colorado Boulder
The University of Texas at Austin

Columbia University

New York, New York | 212-854-2522

ADMISSION
Admission Rate: 4%
Admission Rate - Men: 4%
Admission Rate - Women: 3%
EA Admission Rate: Not Offered
ED Admission Rate: 12%
ED Admits as % of Total Admits: 35%
Admission Rate (5-Year Trend): -2%
% of Admits Attending (Yield): 65%
Transfer Admission Rate: 11%

SAT Reading/Writing (Middle 50%): 730-780
SAT Math (Middle 50%): 770-800
ACT Composite (Middle 50%): 34-35

% Graduated in Top 10% of HS Class: 96%
% Graduated in Top 25% of HS Class: 100%
% Graduated in Top 50% of HS Class: 100%

Demonstrated Interest: Not Considered
Legacy Status: Considered
Racial/Ethnic Status: Considered
Admission Interview Offered: No

ENROLLMENT
Total Undergraduate Enrollment: 6,668
% Full-Time: 100%
% Male: 50%
% Female: 50%
% Out-of-State: 79%
% Fraternity: 10%
% Sorority: 11%
% On-Campus (All Undergraduate): 88%
Freshman Housing Required: Yes

% African-American: 7%
% Asian: 17%
% Hispanic: 15%
% White: 32%
% Other: 4%
% International: 18%
% Low-Income: 23%

ACADEMICS
Student-to-Faculty Ratio: 6 to 1
% of Classes Under 20: 58%
% of Classes 20-49: 28%
% of Classes 50 or More: 15%
% Full-Time Faculty: 50%
% Full-Time Faculty w/ Terminal Degree: 48%

Top Programs
Chemistry
Computer Science
Economics
Engineering
English
History
Mathematics
Political Science

Retention Rate: 98%
4-Year Graduation Rate: 89%
6-Year Graduation Rate: 96%

Curricular Flexibility: Less Flexible
Academic Rating: ★★★★

#CollegesWorthYourMoney

Attending an Ivy League school that also happens to be located in Manhattan is, for many, an opportunity to have your cake and eat it too. It's no wonder that this particular "cake," Columbia University, is one of the most selective schools in the country. It's also one of the most rigorous in the classroom. The 6,668 exceptional students who make it through a treacherous admissions gauntlet are spread across two schools: Columbia College and the Fu Foundation School of Engineering & Applied Sciences. They also have another 2,200+ non-traditional undergrads who study in the General Studies program. Combined, those schools offer 100+ unique areas of undergraduate study as well as a number of pre-professional and accelerated graduate programs.

Inside the Classroom
The academic experience at Columbia is driven by the famed Core Curriculum that lays out an extensive to-do list that includes highly specified courses rather than categorical requirements. Those courses include Introduction to Contemporary Civilization in the West, Masterpieces of Western Art, Masterpieces of Western Literature & Philosophy, Frontiers of Science, University Writing, and Music Humanities. Additional science, global core, foreign language, and physical education mandates add seven courses to the core as well as two activities (for phys ed). School of Engineering & Applied Science students only tackle approximately half of the core curriculum (depending on your major). Columbia College students will spend roughly a year and a half slogging through this considerable scholarly workload.

Class sizes at Columbia are reasonably small and the student-to-faculty ratio is favorable; however, in 2022, it was revealed that the university had been submitting faulty data in this area. It is presently believed that 58% of undergraduate courses enroll 19 or fewer students. More than 570 students per year participate in the Columbia Overseas Program. A little over one-quarter of the students leave Manhattan for a foreign country during their four years of study. Undergraduate research is taken seriously by the university, which offers multiple avenues through which students can work side-by-side with faculty on their projects or pursue funding for their own original research ideas. Recent student projects included the following: "Analyzing Sediment Levels in New York Harbor to Examine Urban Growth" and "Examining Chemical Pathways in Stimulating Ovarian Follicle Stem Cell Renewal." Those who participate in a ten-week Summer Undergraduate Research Fellowship present their findings the following spring at a school-run symposium and can publish their work in a number of undergraduate academic journals affiliated with the university.

The greatest number of degrees are conferred in the social sciences (22%), computer science (15%), engineering (14%), and biology (7%). The Engineering School as a whole can be found near the top of most national rankings, along with nearly every other department and program. Fewer students pursue prestigious postgraduate fellowships at Columbia than at its Ivy-League brethren; however, 16 Columbia College affiliates won Fulbrights in 2023. If earning a Clarendon, Gates Cambridge, Schwarzman, US State Department Critical Language, or Truman Scholarship is your aim, it can certainly be done at Columbia.

Outside the Classroom
Morningside Heights is a quiet, relatively safe section of New York City, and while Columbia is not situated in the traditional heart of the city like NYU, there are plenty of restaurants and cultural experiences within the immediate vicinity of campus. Unusual for an NYC university, 88% of the student body lives in college-owned housing. (Try to rent a place in Manhattan at your own risk—or your wallet's.) A decade ago, Greek life was flatlining with a minimal number of participants, but in recent years, it has undergone a rebirth, and now 10-11% join a fraternity or sorority. The Lions field 31 NCAA Division I teams and an additional 40+ club squads, including a number of recent strong performers. Columbia has won seventeen Ivy League titles in the last five years. A full cornucopia of opportunities awaits through the school's more than 500 student-run organizations. With thirteen a cappella groups, twenty-three dance troupes, thirty-one student-run media outlets/publications, and forty political organizations, everyone can find a place to explore their passions at Columbia. The volunteer spirit is also strong with the Community Impact organization attracting more than 950 members who work in 25 community service programs throughout New York City.

Career Services

The Columbia Center for Career Education (CCE) has 27 professional staff members who are dedicated to undergraduate counseling, employer relations, and other functions related to undergraduate career/graduate school exploration. That 326:1 student-to-advisor ratio is in the average range compared to other schools featured in this guide. The CCE is a well-oiled machine that provides meaningful guidance and experiential opportunities from freshman year through graduation. In one recent academic year, staff engaged in 6,436 one-on-one counseling sessions (98% of students reported those as helpful) and posted more than 71,000 jobs and internships on the LionSHARE database. Hosting over 400 events that attracted 3,200 students, the CCE is dedicated to bringing a range of large-scale career fairs as well as industry showcases where students with targeted interests can learn from professionals in fields such as book publishing, fashion, sports marketing, and healthcare technology.

Columbia does an excellent job with outreach, but its internship numbers are, perhaps, even more impressive. A staggering 98% of undergraduates complete at least one internship. In part, that phenomenal participation rate is due to Columbia's relationships with hundreds of major employers. Thanks to its high level of undergraduate engagement and superb employer relations efforts, the Center for Career Education receives high praise overall from our staff.

Professional Outcomes

Examining the most recent graduates from Columbia College and the Fu Foundation School of Engineering & Applied Science, 73% had found employment within six months, and 20% had entered graduate school. Investment banking, internet & software, and consulting were the three most favored industries. The companies hiring the largest number of Lions in 2021 were among the most desirable employers in the world including Amazon, Goldman Sachs, Morgan Stanley, Google, Citi, McKinsey, and Microsoft. The median starting salary for graduates of Columbia College/Columbia Engineering is above $80,000.

Those moving on to graduate/professional school were welcomed in large numbers into other universities of Columbia's ilk. In addition to remaining at Columbia (the most popular choice), the top ten institutions attended were Stanford, Harvard, NYU, Yale, Carnegie Mellon, UChicago, Oxford, Princeton, and MIT. A significant number of students from each graduating class also generally secure spots at elite law and medical schools that include the university's own top five law school and the esteemed Vagelos College of Physicians & Surgeons.

Admission

Columbia received 60,374 applications for a spot in the Class of 2026 and only 2,255 were offered admission, which works out to a 4% acceptance rate, the second lowest in the Ivy League (only Harvard was lower). Infinitesimal chances at admission are not a new phenomenon here—the acceptance rate hasn't been in the double digits since 2011. The profile of the average accepted student is impressive. Entering 2022-23 freshmen had a middle-50% SAT of 1500-1560, and the ACT range was 34-35. Ninety-six percent were in the top 10% of their high school class.

Straight from the admissions office, there are seven main factors that are given primary importance as part of the university's holistic process: rigor of curriculum, class rank, grades, essays, recommendation, extracurricular activities, and character/personal qualities. Columbia is definitely a school where it is advantageous to apply early decision as ED admit rates are typically at least three times higher than in the regular round; it was 12% for the Class of 2026. The university fills over 50% of its freshman class through the early round. The aforementioned admitted student bona fides should give you an idea if you have a puncher's chance at success, but no one is a sure thing when only one of every 20 high school superstars is welcomed aboard.

Worth Your Money?

All qualifying students at Columbia receive an aid package that meets 100% of their demonstrated need and averages over $65,000. Columbia does not offer any degree of merit aid, so those without financial need will end up paying the full annual cost of attendance of $86k per year. While $340,000+ for a bachelor's degree sounds (and probably is) insane, Columbia certainly has a number of degree programs that will lead you into a high-paying job right out of college. It's also hard to undervalue the social capital accrued by spending four years at Columbia, which makes spending a massive amount of money on undergraduate tuition a less onerous proposition.

FINANCIAL
Institutional Type: Private
In-State Tuition: $65,524
Out-of-State Tuition: $65,524
Room & Board: $16,800
Books & Supplies: $1,392

Avg. Need-Based Grant: $65,756
Avg. % of Need Met: 100%

Avg. Merit-Based Award: Not Reported
% Receiving (Freshmen w/o Need): Not Reported

Avg. Cumulative Debt: $26,531
% of Students Borrowing: 19%

CAREER
Who Recruits
1. eBay
2. Memorial Sloan Kettering
3. Boeing
4. Calgene
5. Arup

Notable Internships
1. Mount Sinai Hospital
2. Google
3. Glassdoor

Top Employers
1. Google
2. Morgan Stanley
3. Citi
4. Goldman Sachs
5. JPMorgan Chase

Where Alumni Work
1. New York City
2. San Francisco
3. Los Angeles
4. Washington, DC
5. Boston

Earnings
College Scorecard (10-YR Post-Entry): $97,540
PayScale (Early Career): $78,200
PayScale (Mid-Career): $138,200
PayScale 20-Year ROI: $1,113,000

RANKINGS
Money: 5
U.S. News: 12, National Universities
Wall Street Journal/THE: 5
Washington Monthly: 7, National Universities

OVERGENERALIZATIONS
Students are:
Politically active
Always studying
Competitive
Diverse
More likely to venture off campus

COLLEGE OVERLAPS
Cornell University
Harvard University
Princeton University
Stanford University
Yale University

Connecticut College

New London, Connecticut | 860-439-2200

Founded as a school for women in the early twentieth century, Connecticut College, known affectionately as Conn College, went co-ed in 1969 and operates today as a unique liberal arts school in the sleepy seaport town of New London. Conn College Camels can pick from an academic menu consisting of forty-one majors, most of which are available as minors as well. There are 1,948 undergraduates on campus, but there is not a single graduate student to be found, which means that, beginning freshman year, the full resources of this school are already at your disposal.

Inside the Classroom

In typical liberal arts fashion, students are required to complete one course in every major discipline: physical and biological sciences, mathematics, social sciences, literature, creative arts, philosophy/religion, and history. There are also requirements in foreign language, writing, and technology. For a laid-back group, there is no shortage of academic ambitions as over one-quarter of undergrads complete a double major. Many also complete a thematic minor that is offered in distinct areas including Modern Greece and Its Background, Non-Violence, or Psychoanalysis: Theories of the Unconscious.

The student-faculty ratio is an inviting 10:1, and 69% of classes contain fewer than 20 students; 19% contain fewer than ten. Conn College's faculty has a reputation for being wholly committed to teaching and forging meaningful relationships with students. Evidence of a personalized experience can be found in the numbers—93% of 2022 grads completed a capstone project, 34% engaged in an individual study with a professor's guidance, and 36% reported giving a public presentation or performance during their undergraduate career. Slightly less than half of students elect to study abroad in 40 countries, with Denmark, Italy, and the United Kingdom being the most common destinations.

Consistently named a "top producer" of Fulbright Scholars, Conn College saw seven students win the prestigious award in 2022. Many recent Fulbright winners majored in the school's strong programs in international relations or region-specific programs (e.g., Hispanic Studies, Slavic Studies). Other well-regarded majors include neuroscience, psychology, English, dance, and theatre. In terms of the most frequently conferred degrees, the social sciences at large lead the way (30%), followed by biology (17%), visual and performing arts (9%), psychology (8%), and computer science (5%).

Outside the Classroom

This gorgeous 750-acre campus is wedged between two large bodies of water and features its own hiking trails and arboretum. The gender breakdown still skews strongly in one direction; men make up only 38% of the undergraduate population. Three-quarters of the student body participate in competitive sports. For a tiny school, it manages to field 28 intercollegiate sports teams (NCAA Division III) as well as a number of intramural squads. Outside of athletic clubs, there are roughly seventy student organizations on campus, highlighted by six popular a cappella groups. There are no fraternities or sororities at Conn College, but 97% of the student body lives on campus in one of 23 residence houses. A close-knit community, Camels come together for some notable campus-wide events like Floralia, Harvestfest, or the massive Seinfeld-inspired Festivus celebration. Public transportation options are plentiful, and the campus and surrounding area are easily bikeable. Even with the relatively close proximity to bigger cities like Boston, New York, and Providence, the school itself estimates that 80% of its students stay put on the weekends, making campus a vibrant place seven days a week.

Career Services

The Hale Center for Career Development has seven full-time staff members who specialize in employer relations, general advising, prelaw advising, and connecting students with internships. With a 278:1 student-to-advisor ratio, Conn College sports a higher level of support than many other schools featured in this guide. Its four-year career program assures that the only interaction with the office isn't a harried and panicked "What do I do now?" conversation right before graduation. Advisors visit the required first-year seminar courses and begin to engage students right away, encouraging them to keep in touch via one-on-one advising sessions as well as by attending sponsored events like Sundays with Alumni, workshops, and joint career fairs such as the Liberal Arts Recruiting Connection in Boston that features on-site interviews with more than thirty companies.

Rising seniors are eligible to spend their summers in a school-funded internship. That's right— all students are guaranteed $3,000 to help fund an internship experience anywhere in the world. Plenty are advertised on CamelLink, but advisers will also work individually with students to unearth additional opportunities. In a typical year, a terrific 76% of grads have completed an internship funded through the Hale Center and 98% of that group reported that the experience enhanced their career prospects. It's a testament to the career services staff that 90% of alumni said that the career office was instrumental in helping them find jobs. A stunning 95% of students use this exemplary career services office at some point during their four years on campus.

Professional Outcomes

One year after graduating, 95% of alumni are employed or in graduate school. Connecticut College produces an interesting blend of career pathways. A solid 20% of recent grads entered the finance industry, but a large swath also veered toward education (17%); art, design, and entertainment (11%); and health care (11%). Those in banking frequently find homes at Bank of America, JPMorgan Chase & Co., and Morgan Stanley. On the public service/health side, three of the largest employers are AmeriCorps, Fulbright, and Sloan Kettering Cancer Center. Other companies employing twenty or more alumni include Pfizer, Massachusetts General Hospital, Deloitte, and UBS. Camels end up working predominately in New York (33%) and Massachusetts (22%), but New London/Norwich, Connecticut; DC; San Francisco; and Hartford claim sizable numbers of alumni as well.

Conn College students are known for being grad school ready as a surprising (given the small size of the school) 27 alumni earn their doctoral degrees each year. Examining the graduate school attendees from recent graduating classes, it is common for multiple students to land at prestigious schools such as NYU, Columbia, and Yale as well as nearby state schools like UMass and UConn. In recent years, graduates have earned spots at just about every top law school in the country including Harvard, Emory, Columbia, Penn, Duke, and Northwestern. Those pursuing medical and dental degrees do so at the likes of Tufts University School of Medicine, NYU School of Medicine, and the University of Texas School of Medicine.

Admission

The school admitted 40% of applicants in the Class of 2026 admissions cycle. Over the prior five years, its acceptance rate has hovered in the 35-40% range; its low ebb was 32% in 2010. Conn College is test-optional, and unlike most test-optional colleges, a fairly larger percentage of applicants elected not to submit a standardized test score as part of their applications. For those who did, the middle 50% range for attending students is 1180-1390 on the SAT and 28-32 on the ACT.

While test scores occupy the "considered" category for the Conn College admissions staff, rigor of coursework, grades, class rank, and character/personal qualities are deemed "most important." Academic performance needs to be strong, but you don't need to be perfect to be considered as 72% are in the top 25% of their high school class and 35% cracked the top 10%. The average GPA for the Class of 2026 was 3.81. Legacy students have an edge and have access to special Admission 101 sessions hosted by the college while they are still in high school. Conn College offers two rounds of early decision, and for those who consider it a top choice, it would be wise to consider partaking. A healthy 50%+ of early applicants were accepted in one recent cycle, accounting for more than two-fifths of the freshman class. In essence, this is not a school with a strict formula for admission. It tends to attract a distinguished applicant pool but does not require Ivy-level qualifications for acceptance. Those who apply early face the best odds.

Worth Your Money?

For a very sizable 50% of the student population, 100% of financial need is met to the tune of $47,000 per year, making attending Conn College possible for lower- and middle-income students. This is a school that the rich pay close to full price ($83k) to attend, and the not-rich get generous aid packages. Still, the average debt load carried by alumni is higher than the national average. Therefore, middle- to upper-income students without a solid financial aid offer should carefully consider their future plans before investing in the school.

FINANCIAL
Institutional Type: Private
In-State Tuition: $64,812
Out-of-State Tuition: $64,812
Room & Board: $17,885
Books & Supplies: $1,000

Avg. Need-Based Grant: $46,784
Avg. % of Need Met: 100%

Avg. Merit-Based Award: $24,168
% Receiving (Freshmen w/o Need): 44%

Avg. Cumulative Debt: $38,564
% of Students Borrowing: 50%

CAREER
Who Recruits
1. Amazon
2. JLL
3. Morgan Stanley
4. Deloitte
5. UBS

Notable Internships
1. Sony Music Entertainment
2. Smithsonian
3. J. Crew

Top Employers
1. Pfizer
2. Google
3. Fidelity Investments
4. JPMorgan Chase
5. Bank of America

Where Alumni Work
1. New York City
2. Boston
3. Norwich, CT
4. Washington, DC
5. San Francisco

Earnings
College Scorecard (10-YR Post-Entry): $70,044
PayScale (Early Career): $63,400
PayScale (Mid-Career): $108,900
PayScale 20-Year ROI: $578,000

RANKINGS
Money: 4
U.S. News: 46, Liberal Arts Colleges
Wall Street Journal/THE: 225
Washington Monthly: 42, Liberal Arts Colleges

OVERGENERALIZATIONS
Students are:
Wealthy
Preppy
Politically liberal
Homogenous
Artsy

COLLEGE OVERLAPS
Bates College
Colby College
Hamilton College
Skidmore College
Trinity College

New York, New York | 212-353-4120

Tuition-free from its founding in 1859 until 2013, The Cooper Union is home to 899 talented undergraduate students concentrating in art, architecture, and engineering. While tuition has returned (at least until 2029), CU remains an immensely popular destination for its unique programmatic offerings and world-class faculty; hence, it has an intimidating acceptance rate of 22%.

Inside the Classroom

The Irwin S. Chanin School of Architecture offers a five-year bachelor's program. The School of Art offers a Bachelor of Fine Arts degree with concentrations in painting, sculpture, drawing, film and video, graphic design, photography, and printmaking. The Albert Nerken School of Engineering offers Bachelor of Engineering degrees in chemical, civil, electrical, and mechanical engineering. All undergraduates must pursue a core curriculum consistent with founder Peter Cooper's insistence on not ignoring the humanities and social sciences in the pursuit of a practical education. As such, a four-semester sequence is required of all students that includes a freshman seminar focusing on poetry and drama as well as three history/sociology courses that follow a chronological sequence from the 1500s to modern day.

No matter your area of study at CU, students report receiving a high degree of attention and mentorship from faculty. With 57% of class sections containing fewer than 20 students, learning is an intimate endeavor. Roughly 20% elect to study abroad through one of the school's six- to eight-week summer offerings. Engineering students can travel to Spain, Iceland, or Germany while art students have additional options in he Netherlands, France, England, and Sweden. Undergraduate research opportunities are most common in the School of Engineering where all students must complete a senior project.

Accounting for 56% of the student body, engineering is the subject in which the largest number of degrees are conferred followed by visual arts (28%) and then architecture (16%). All three schools shine in the eyes of employers as well as other institutions of higher education. Graduates of The Cooper Union obtain prestigious fellowships and scholarships at impressive rates. CU has enjoyed 39 Fulbright scholars since 2001, 13 National Science Foundation Graduate Research Fellowships since 2004, and typically sweeps all four annual Royal Society of Arts-Architecture Student Design Awards.

Outside the Classroom

Most of campus is located in three large buildings: The Foundation Building, 41 Cooper Square, and one freshman-only residence hall where 20% of undergraduates reside. Yet, being located in the heart of the East Village, your "campus" is really all of New York City. When they aren't up all night working on projects, students can enjoy the array of restaurants, shops, theaters, and museums within easy walking distance of the school or hop one of the nearby subway stops for access to Midtown Manhattan as well as the outer boroughs. CU does have five club sports teams—men's and women's basketball, men's and women's volleyball, and a coed soccer squad. Two fraternities and one sorority have local chapters, but they fall well short of being a dominant force in the social sphere. Over 80 student-run organizations are active on campus including music and drama troupes, a student newspaper, cultural clubs, and professional societies that participate in intercollegiate competitions.

Career Services

The Center for Career Development employs two full-time professional staff members, equating to a 450:1 student-to-advisor ratio that allows for plentiful personalized attention. Undergraduates are always free to book forty-five-minute one-on-one sessions focusing on areas including résumé and cover letter writing, portfolio development, job and internship search strategies, interview preparation, grad school applications, and applications to competitive fellowship and scholarship programs. Current students and alumni can utilize Handshake for a wealth of job postings. Employers attend the fall and spring career fairs and stop by campus for recruiting sessions and on-campus interviews.

The Cooper Union for the Advancement of Science and Art

E-mail: admissions@cooper.edu | Website: cooper.edu

The office organizes a multitude of targeted information sessions and networking opportunities for CU students. Recent examples include a roundtable discussion with gallerists and curators, a graduate school information session with Carnegie Mellon, and lunch with alumni. Opportunities for experiential learning are facilitated by career services staff. For instance, art students can partake in the Professional Internship Program for Art that provides undergraduates with a stipend to work at one of a dozen partner NYC-based museums and galleries. Thanks to a full calendar of intimate events catering to art, architecture, and engineering, The Cooper Union's Center for Career Development serves its students admirably.

Professional Outcomes

Due to the exceptionally low numbers of graduates from Cooper Union each year, it is hard to say that large numbers of alumni cluster in any particular company. However, it is fair to state that CU graduates regularly find their way into the most desirable firms within their respective disciplines. Recent graduates of the School of Architecture found homes at many of the world's largest architecture firms such as AECOM, Gensler, Perkins Eastman, and HOK as well as any desirable boutique firm one can name. School of Art alumni can be found at every great museum of art in the county, including the MoMA and the Met, and at prestigious media outlets such as The New Yorker and The New York Times. Engineering grads waltz into an endless list of top companies including Deloitte, ExxonMobil, Google, Goldman Sachs, IBM, and SpaceX. Among engineering grads, 95% land a job or grad school placement within six months of earning their degree.

Forty percent of CU graduates continue their education at top-ranked graduate programs. In the last few years, Cooper Union diploma-holders have gone on to advanced study in architecture at Columbia, Harvard, MIT, Princeton, the Rhode Island School of Design, Penn, and Yale. Art students have been accepted to US-based programs at Cornell, Georgetown, NYU, and Pratt, and internationally at The Glasgow School of Art; Oslo Academy of Art; and Goldsmiths, University of London. Engineering students pursuing master's and doctorate degrees have landed spots at Carnegie Mellon, Johns Hopkins, Stanford, Berkeley, and Vanderbilt.

Admission

Among those seeking a spot in the Class of 2026, only 336 of the 1,508 applicants to The Cooper Union gained acceptance, a 22% acceptance rate which was higher than the 15% acceptance rate the previous cycle. This is a self-selecting group of students, many of whom have slotted CU as their number one choice, a fact affirmed by the school's solid 54% yield rate. The median SAT score was 1460 and the median ACT was 32. Successful applicants to all three programs generally had A/A- averages. The average GPA was 3.7 for those entering the school in 2022-23.

The two categories rated as "most important" to one's admissions prospects at CU are GPA and talent/ability. The admissions office recommends that all applicants "take a well-rounded high school program, preferably in advanced coursework." Program-specific recommendations include that "engineering students should also be well prepared in calculus, chemistry, and physics. Art and architecture applicants should take visual art classes" and that architecture applicants should take pre-calculus in high school. Additional application components are required by the various programs. School of Art students must complete a Hometest and submit a portfolio. Those applying to the School of Architecture must complete a studio test. While standardized test scores differ greatly across the three schools, all successful applicants to Cooper Union boast solid academic credentials along with demonstrated gifts in their area of interest. Those seeking to study art or architecture will face a holistic review process; those applying to study engineering will be judged more heavily by their test scores.

Worth Your Money?

After over 100 years of providing tuition-free education to undergraduate students, Cooper Union controversially decided, in light of a depleted endowment, to begin charging tuition. While plans exist to progressively reduce tuition over the next decade before returning to a tuition-free policy, those entering the school now encounter an annual tuition bill of almost $45k per year. However, the school does remain extremely generous with aid, awarding every admitted student a scholarship valued at $22,275 per year. While it's not as great as receiving a world-class education gratis, Cooper Union remains worth every dollar and is, undoubtedly, worth your money.

FINANCIAL
Institutional Type: Private
In-State Tuition: $46,820
Out-of-State Tuition: $46,820
Room & Board: $18,650
Books & Supplies: $1,800

Avg. Need-Based Grant: $45,274
Avg. % of Need Met: 96%

Avg. Merit-Based Award: $28,198
% Receiving (Freshmen w/o Need): 52%

Avg. Cumulative Debt: $25,393
% of Students Borrowing: 29%

CAREER
Who Recruits
1. AECOM
2. Bloomberg
3. General Motors
4. AT&T
5. Credit Suisse

Notable Internships
1. Con Edison
2. Bloomberg LP
3. PepsiCo

Top Employers
1. Con Edison
2. Google
3. Bloomberg LP
4. IBM
5. Amazon

Where Alumni Work
1. New York City
2. San Francisco
3. Los Angeles
4. Boston
5. Philadelphia

Earnings
College Scorecard (10-YR Post-Entry): $76,855
PayScale (Early Career): $73,700
PayScale (Mid-Career): $139,800
PayScale 20-Year ROI: $1,050,000

RANKINGS
Money: 5
U.S. News: 2, Regional Colleges North
Wall Street Journal/THE: Not Ranked
Washington Monthly: 1, Bachelor's Colleges

OVERGENERALIZATIONS
Students are:
Diverse
More likely to venture off campus
Decided upon their chosen major
Less likely to party
Always studying

COLLEGE OVERLAPS
Carnegie Mellon University
Cornell University
Georgia Institute of Technology
New York University
Rhode Island School of Design

Cornell University

Ithaca, New York | 607-255-5241

By a wide margin, Cornell boasts the largest undergraduate enrollment of any school in the Ivy League at 15,735 students, 5,000+ more than the next largest school, the University of Pennsylvania. Located in Ithaca, a certifiable college town in the Finger Lakes region of Upstate New York, Cornell's campus is a seemingly endless 745 acres, and that is not including the adjacent Botanic Gardens owned by the university. A diverse array of academic programs includes 80 majors and 120 minors spread across the university's seven schools/colleges: the College of Agriculture and Life Sciences; College of Architecture, Art and Planning; College of Arts and Sciences; SC Johnson College of Business; College of Engineering; College of Human Ecology; and School of Industrial and Labor Relations.

Inside the Classroom
Most degrees conferred in 2022 were in computer science (17%), engineering (13%), business (13%), and biology (13%). Required courses within the College of Arts & Sciences include two first-year writing seminars, mastery of a foreign language, and ten distributional requirements. While that sounds like a substantial number of mandated classes, the school does allow certain courses to simultaneously fill more than one distributional requirement.

Classes are a bit larger at Cornell than at many other elite institutions. Still, 55% of sections have fewer than 20 students. Introductory courses sometimes take place in larger lecture halls, so 24% of courses have an enrollment of more than forty students. Undergraduates do give their professors generally high marks: 88% report being satisfied with the instruction they have received, 48% report completing a thesis/research project, and 53% conducted research with a faculty member. Members of Big Red can choose from study abroad opportunities in more than forty countries, and roughly one-third participate.

The SC Johnson College of Business houses two undergraduate schools, both of which have phenomenal reputations. The Cornell School of Hotel Administration is one of the finest such programs in the world, and the Charles H. Dyson School of Applied Economics and Management cracks most lists of the top 10 business programs in the United States. The School of Engineering offers 14 areas of specialization and is held in high regard by employers and prestigious graduate schools. Highly desired postgraduate scholarships are procured by Cornell grads at a steady rate. The university has 30+ Rhodes Scholars to its credit as well as a regular flow of Fulbright, Schwarzman, Goldwater, and Truman Scholarship award winners.

Outside the Classroom
Ithaca has as much Upstate New York natural splendor as you can handle, from Lake Cayuga to parks to the many breathtaking ravines and gorges. (You've likely seen the "Ithaca is Gorges" T-shirt.) Yet, thanks to frigid weather and the absence of a major metropolis nearby, campus itself and the nearby neighborhoods are where the action is. With over a 15% participation rate across the 50+ fraternity and sorority chapters on campus, Greek life dominates much of the social scene. Freshmen are required to live in university housing, although a substantial 48% percent of undergrads live off campus. Student-run organizations can be found for almost anything your mind can fathom. Over 1,000 clubs are active. The Cornell Concert works to bring major acts to campus that suit a variety of tastes. The university also succeeds in luring a fair share of impressive guest speakers to campus each year. *The Cornell Daily Sun*, founded in 1880, is one of the finest student papers in the country, and the dining hall cuisine and libraries (Hogwarts-esque Uris in particular) receive high marks. Athletics feature 37 men's and women's teams competing against NCAA Division I competition as well as countless club and intramural opportunities.

Career Services
The Career Services Department has 55 full-time staff members, excluding office assistants, who are spread across the various colleges within the university. Those individuals serve as career counselors, internship co-op coordinators, recruiting coordinators, and graduate school advisors in specified disciplines. The 286:1 student-to-advisor ratio is better than average compared to other schools featured in this guide. Among large universities, Cornell's level of support is unparalleled.

Career fairs at Cornell are two-day affairs involving hundreds of Fortune 500, government, and nonprofit employers. In recent years, the fall University Career Fair Days have drawn over 6,200 students and 250 employers. In the previous academic year, 17% found their jobs through an internship or volunteer experience, 13% through on-campus recruiting, and 8% through career fairs. In an average year, students make over 14,000 advising appointments, and more than 12,000 students attend programs and presentations. Hundreds of students take advantage of job-shadowing opportunities offered during winter and spring breaks. Most importantly, in an average year, roughly 90% of surveyed students have completed, or plan to complete, an internship/practicum.

Professional Outcomes

Breaking down the 2020 graduates of the College of Arts and Sciences, the largest school at Cornell, 68% entered the workforce, 28% entered graduate school, 1% pursued other endeavors such as travel or volunteer work, and the remaining 3% were still seeking employment six months after receiving their diplomas. The top sectors attracting campus-wide graduates in 2020 were financial services (18%), technology (17%), consulting (15%), and education (10%). Starting salary data varies greatly across schools as well as by major. For example, the average Dyson graduate earns $81k in base pay, while the average A&S graduate starts at $75k. College of Engineering students enjoy an average starting salary of $99k+ with a heavy representation at Google, Amazon, Microsoft, and Goldman Sachs.

Of the students from A&S going on to graduate school, 15% were pursuing JDs, 5% MDs, and 22% PhDs. Popular destinations included staying at Cornell (especially computer science majors), other Ivies, Stanford, MIT, universities in the UC system, or abroad at Oxford, Cambridge, the University of Toronto, or the University of St. Andrews. Harvard is the No. 1 destination for biology majors, and Stanford attracted the highest number of chemistry graduates. The six most frequently attended law schools by Big Red alumni were Columbia, NYU, Penn, Harvard, NYU, Fordham, and Cornell itself. Those entering medical school most frequently studied at NYU, Penn, WashU, UChicago, and the University of Michigan.

Admission

The deluge of over 71,000 applications for the Class of 2026 was an all-time high for the school. An acceptance rate of 7% was lower than the previous year's 9% figure. For further comparison, Class of 2016 applicants gained acceptance at a 16% clip. At Cornell, applicants must apply to one of the eight colleges or schools (counting Dyson and the Hotel School separately), and acceptance rates vary among schools. For example, in one recent admissions cycle, only 5% of applicants were accepted into the Dyson School of Applied Economics and Management while the College of Human Ecology admitted 17%.

Most (82%) Cornell freshmen in 2022-23 placed in the top 10% of their high school class. The Class of 2026 entered with mid-50% ranges of 1470-1550 on the SAT and 33-35 on the ACT. Children of alumni comprise approximately 15% of the student body, and legacy students are believed to have a significant edge, although the school has not been willing to release any statistics in that area. The seven criteria deemed most important by the admissions office are rigor of coursework, grades, recommendations, essays, extracurriculars, talent/ability, and character/personal qualities. Having joined the other Ivy League institutions with single-digit acceptance rates, becoming part of Big Red is only a possibility for the crème de la crème of college applicants.

Worth Your Money?

Graduates emerge from their four years of study with an average debt load that sits right around the national average. Like many other elite universities, Cornell does not award any merit aid, instead focusing its generosity on students who could not otherwise afford the school. As a result, the $83,000 annual cost of attendance is greatly reduced for students who demonstrate financial need. These students have 100% of their need met to the tune of a $52,000 grant. Alumni enjoy starting salaries far superior to those from your average college, making Cornell a phenomenal investment, even if you need to take out sizable loans to attend.

FINANCIAL
Institutional Type: Private
In-State Tuition: $66,014
Out-of-State Tuition: $66,014
Room & Board: $18,554
Books & Supplies: $1,354

Avg. Need-Based Grant: $52,413
Avg. % of Need Met: 100%

Avg. Merit-Based Award: Not Reported
% Receiving (Freshmen w/o Need): Not Reported

Avg. Cumulative Debt: $28,408
% of Students Borrowing: 37%

CAREER
Who Recruits
1. Four Seasons Hotel and Resorts
2. WeWork
3. Uber
4. Accor
5. Hilton

Notable Internships
1. American Express
2. Lyft
3. PayPal

Top Employers
1. Google
2. Amazon
3. Microsoft
4. IBM
5. Facebook

Where Alumni Work
1. New York City
2. San Francisco
3. Boston
4. Washington, DC
5. Los Angeles

Earnings
College Scorecard (10-YR Post-Entry): $98,321
PayScale (Early Career): $75,800
PayScale (Mid-Career): $139,600
PayScale 20-Year ROI: $1,034,000

RANKINGS
Money: 5
U.S. News: 12, National Universities
Wall Street Journal/THE: 24
Washington Monthly: 10, National Universities

OVERGENERALIZATIONS
Students are:
Environmentally conscious
Competitive
Always admiring the beauty of their campus
Working hard and Playing hard
Highly motivated

COLLEGE OVERLAPS
Brown University
Columbia University
Princeton University
University of Pennsylvania
University of Michigan

Hanover, New Hampshire | 603-646-2875

ADMISSION
Admission Rate: 6%
Admission Rate - Men: 7%
Admission Rate - Women: 6%
EA Admission Rate: Not Offered
ED Admission Rate: 21%
ED Admits as % of Total Admits: 31%
Admission Rate (5-Year Trend): -4%
% of Admits Attending (Yield): 62%
Transfer Admission Rate: 7%

SAT Reading/Writing (Middle 50%): 740-780
SAT Math (Middle 50%): 760-800
ACT Composite (Middle 50%): 33-35

% Graduated in Top 10% of HS Class: 95%
% Graduated in Top 25% of HS Class: 98%
% Graduated in Top 50% of HS Class: 100%

Demonstrated Interest: Considered
Legacy Status: Considered
Racial/Ethnic Status: Considered
Admission Interview Offered: Yes

ENROLLMENT
Total Undergraduate Enrollment: 4,458
% Full-Time: 100%
% Male: 51%
% Female: 49%
% Out-of-State: 97%
% Fraternity: 35%
% Sorority: 36%
% On-Campus (All Undergraduate): 85%
Freshman Housing Required: Yes

% African-American: 6%
% Asian: 14%
% Hispanic: 10%
% White: 48%
% Other: 2%
% International: 13%
% Low-Income: 15%

ACADEMICS
Student-to-Faculty Ratio: 7 to 1
% of Classes Under 20: 61%
% of Classes 20-49: 33%
% of Classes 50 or More: 6%
% Full-Time Faculty: 81%
% Full-Time Faculty w/ Terminal Degree: 96%

Top Programs
Biology
Computer Science
Economics
Engineering
Government
History
Mathematics
Neuroscience

Retention Rate: 98%
4-Year Graduation Rate: 84%
6-Year Graduation Rate: 95%

Curricular Flexibility: Somewhat Flexible
Academic Rating: ★★★★★

The smallest school in the Ivy League, Dartmouth plays home to 4,458 undergraduate students on its remote, 237-acre New Hampshire campus. Dartmouth has long wrestled with its reputation as one of the most conservative (purely in a relative sense) of the Ivy League universities as well as one of the top party schools. Regardless, there are few arguments against the academic superiority of the college that sports 60+ majors and a stunning breadth of course selections for an institution of its size.

Inside the Classroom
Dartmouth offers a unique year-round academic calendar with four ten-week terms that allow students maximum flexibility as they pursue internships, paid work, research opportunities, or travel abroad. Undergraduates design their own individual "D-Plan." Needing thirty-five credits for graduation, individuals are free to take anywhere from two to four courses per term. (Most students take three.) Typically, students are expected to spend 12 of the 15 terms during their natural four-year period on campus, including Sophomore Summer, a mandatory term for rising juniors. All freshmen must take a writing requirement and a first-year seminar course, both designed as intensive workshops to elevate student writing to Dartmouth's high standards.

The learning environment at Dartmouth is extraordinarily intimate. Not only do 61% of course sections have under twenty students, but 18% have single-digit enrollments. The student-to-faculty ratio is an outstanding 7:1. Undergraduate research opportunities abound with roughly 60% of students participating at some point. Further, close to 90% of those participants report having a satisfying experience working with a faculty member in that capacity. The rate of satisfaction is hardly surprising as Dartmouth's faculty consistently rates at the top of rankings/surveys regarding quality of instruction. An extensive study abroad program offers 40+ Dartmouth faculty-led academic experiences around the world, and over 50% of all students partake.

Top programs offered by Big Green include biology, economics, neuroscience, and government. The social sciences are the most popular, accounting for 32% of degrees conferred, followed by computer science (10%), mathematics (9%), engineering (9%), and biology (7%). In recent years, an average of 10-15 Dartmouth grads have been offered Fulbright Scholarships annually. With 60+ Rhodes Scholars to its credit, Dartmouth is the sixth-highest producer in the history of the award. The Truman Foundation lists Dartmouth as one of its Honor Institutions as many grads have been awarded its $30,000 prize to pursue graduate study in a public service field.

Outside the Classroom
The presence of Greek life at Dartmouth is powerful with over 40% of the student population belonging to fraternities and sororities. In fact, the school sports one of the highest percentages of Greek-affiliated undergraduates in the entire Northeast; female upperclassmen join sororities at a 49% clip, and 46% of men sign up for fraternity life. Over 30 intercollegiate Division I sports are on tap along with two dozen intramural sports and over 35 club sports. Roughly three-quarters of Dartmouth men and women participate in some form of athletics. Other highlights include *The Dartmouth*, America's oldest school newspaper, 160+ student-run clubs and organizations, and the Dartmouth Outing Club, the largest collegiate outdoor recreation club in the country. The college owns over 30,000 acres of New Hampshire land that can be enjoyed by students for camping, skiing, hiking, and similar activities. Eighty-four percent of the student body and 100% of freshmen live on campus. Dorms earn rave reviews from students, and all are supervised by full-time, live-in community directors. Big Green is living up to its nickname as a green campus with a number of sustainability ventures including transportation, eco-friendly energy options, and its own organic farm/student-operated farmer's market. If you come from an urban environment, the remote feel of Hanover may induce some culture shock, yet Boston is only a two-hour drive away.

Career Services
The Center for Professional Development (CPD) has 12 full-time staff members (including those housed in the engineering department) who focus on either career advising or employer relations. The 371:1 student-to-advisor ratio is in the average range for schools included in this guide. However, also available to advise students are the thousands of alumni who volunteer their time as members of the Dartmouth Career Network. Employer Connection Fairs draw over 1,000 students and feature a strong corporate presence. One recent Fall Engineering Career Fair attracted 50+ companies including Microsoft, DraftKings, Mastercard, and Wayfair. Students

E-mail: admissions.office@dartmouth.edu | Website: dartmouth.edu

are given a DartBoard account that allows them to access event notifications, on-campus recruiting opportunities, and thousands of internships. In 2021-22, the office conducted 20 customized workshops on topics such as My First Resume and overcoming "imposter syndrome."

In part because of its unique academic calendar, Dartmouth does an exceptional job facilitating undergraduate internships. A stunning 96% of recent grads participated in at least one internship experience. Many major corporations have elected to become employer partners with the college, a designation that includes, among other things, annual recruiting on campus. Many of those are financial institutions that also grace the list of top employers of Dartmouth grads. (Please see "Professional Outcomes" below.) This alignment of on-campus recruiting and offers of employment at Dartmouth is most impressive.

Professional Outcomes

A great reputation along with a passionate alumni network that is 80,000 strong leads Dartmouth grads to successful transitions into graduate school and the world of work. A recent Cap & Gown survey found 63% of graduating seniors already employed, while 21% were headed to graduate school and 9% were still weighing their options. Finance is a popular arena for graduates with 16% of recent alumni going in that direction. Thus, it is little surprise that included in the top ten employers of Dartmouth grads are a number of investment banks including Goldman Sachs, Morgan Stanley, Bain & Company, Citibank, and Deutsche Bank. Another 27% enter the world of consulting. While many start in finance and consulting, a large number of grads plan to enter academia or a career in government down the road. Dartmouth grads will not struggle financially. Right off the bat, 52% of graduates make more than $70,000 in salary. Upon graduation, the majority of the student body migrates to major cities with notably high concentrations in Chicago, DC, New York, Seattle, San Francisco, and Mountain View, California.

Those pursuing graduate and professional degrees often trade one Ivy for another. Harvard, Columbia, and Princeton are three of the most frequent landing spots for Dartmouth grads. Many others continue their studies in one of Dartmouth's own graduate programs or head to other top institutions such as the University of Cambridge, Duke, Carnegie Mellon, or UC Berkeley. Among recent grads, 18% were chasing a law degree, 12% intended to obtain a medical degree, and 9% enrolled in PhD programs.

Admission

Like many highly selective schools, Dartmouth's popularity is at an all-time high. The college's yield—the percentage of accepted students who choose to attend—is 62%. In 2022, Dartmouth sported a single-digit acceptance rate for the fifth year in a row at 6%. There were 28,336 total applicants for the Class of 2026. Five years ago, the admit rate was double today's clip; a decade ago, the acceptance rate was three times the 2022-23 figure.

The mean SAT is up to 1528 and the mean ACT is 34. Finishing at the top of your class is a must; 95% hail from the top 10% of their high school graduating class. Legacy students have a fairly strong but not overwhelming presence on campus, comprising close to 10% of the student body. Seventeen percent of freshmen are the first in their families to attend college. Alumni interviews are offered but not required. Essays and recommendations are rated as "very important" by the admissions staff. Bottom line: many pine to be part of this Ivy League institution, but earning a spot on the bucolic Hanover campus has never been tougher. Those who wish to experience its renowned teaching faculty and intimate learning environment, rich with hands-on opportunities, will need to bring stellar credentials to the table.

Worth Your Money?

The Class of 2026 received an average annual scholarship award of $67k, a figure that meets 100% of every single student's demonstrated financial need. Most other students will pay the full cost of attendance—$87,793—as there is no merit aid offered at Dartmouth. Big Green is unlikely to cost you large amounts of green unless you can comfortably afford it. For that reason, coupled with the stellar postgraduate outcomes you would expect from an Ivy, Dartmouth is, without question, worth the price.

FINANCIAL
Institutional Type: Private
In-State Tuition: $65,511
Out-of-State Tuition: $65,511
Room & Board: $18,759
Books & Supplies: $1,005

Avg. Need-Based Grant: $62,937
Avg. % of Need Met: 100%

Avg. Merit-Based Award: $0
% Receiving (Freshmen w/o Need): 0%

Avg. Cumulative Debt: $25,195
% of Students Borrowing: 33%

CAREER
Who Recruits
1. Partenon
2. Nomura
3. Oliver Wyman
4. Bridgewater
5. Trinity Partners

Notable Internships
1. PNC
2. Bain & Company
3. ICM

Top Employers
1. Google
2. Goldman Sachs
3. Amazon
4. Morgan Stanley
5. Facebook

Where Alumni Work
1. Boston
2. New York City
3. San Francisco
4. Washington, DC
5. Los Angeles

Earnings
College Scorecard (10-YR Post-Entry): $95,540
PayScale (Early Career): $77,600
PayScale (Mid-Career): $149,800
PayScale 20-Year ROI: $1,020,000

RANKINGS
Money: 5
U.S. News: 18, National Universities
Wall Street Journal/THE: 21
Washington Monthly: 28, National Universities

OVERGENERALIZATIONS
Students are:
Outdoorsy
Collaborative
Teeming with school pride
Working hard and Playing hard
Tight-knit (possess a strong sense of community)

COLLEGE OVERLAPS
Brown University
Cornell University
Duke University
Princeton University
Yale University

Davidson College

Davidson, North Carolina | 704-894-2230

Strolling around Davidson's lush campus, taking in the historic buildings and intellectually engaged student body, it's easy to forget that you are situated about twenty miles north of Charlotte, North Carolina, and not in the heart of New England. The 1,927 students who grace this undergrad-only institution are high achievers who take academics and their school's more-than-just-lip-service Honor Code seriously.

Inside the Classroom
With its small size, the impressive part of the college is the exceptional quality of its offerings, not the breadth of them, as only 37 majors are available. Additional interdisciplinary majors also can be accessed for those seeking another pathway. However, the majority of students stick to traditional areas of concentration with economics, biology, political science, and psychology being the most popular. Required courses include eight classes under the umbrella category of Ways of Knowing that feature, among others, history, rhetoric, quantitative thought, and the visual performing arts. Additional mandated coursework in foreign language, writing, diversity, justice/equality, and physical education must be completed by all students, regardless of major.

The student-to-faculty ratio is 9:1, which allows the college to ensure that 62% have fewer than twenty students and 24% have enrollments you can count on two hands. Overall, the average number of students per class is only 18. Study abroad is encouraged, and approximately 65% elect to study in one of 125 programs around the globe. Undergrads working side-by-side with their professors is commonplace as over 60% of faculty have published with student coauthors at some point.

Top programs at Davidson include psychology, political science, chemistry, and English; biology is also quite popular, accounting for 12% of degrees conferred in 2022. However, any degree from Davidson is a credential from one of the most respected liberal arts colleges in the country. In fact, it regularly cracks top ten lists of best liberal arts schools and best teaching faculty. Students are no strangers to accolades either; six students were named Fulbright finalists in 2023. In recent years, others have won Boren, Truman, Watson, and Princeton in Africa fellowships/scholarships. In addition, 23 alumni have won Rhodes Scholarships.

Outside the Classroom
"Typical" is not a word that applies to any facet of campus life at Davidson. For example, team sports participation is required at the varsity, club, or intramural level. The ten men's and nine women's varsity teams compete in NCAA Division I with the successful men's basketball team atop the popularity charts. Davidson's 14 Greek houses are all under the purview of one entity, Patterson Court, which ensures that fraternities, sororities, and eating houses all have a social/charitable mission and abide by a common set of rules. Participation is extremely high as 28% of male students and 50% of females join a Patterson Court house. Students also run over 200 clubs, including Davidson Outdoors, which organizes kayaking, hiking, and climbing trips around the globe as well as in the school's own backyard. The Lake Norman campus, a 110-acre waterfront property only seven miles from the main campus, is reserved for exclusive use by Davidson students. The college's Union Board, the largest student organization, puts on well-attended events including concerts, trivia nights, and movie screenings on a regular basis. The surrounding town of Davidson features many attractions such as an array of student-friendly coffee shops and restaurants as well as a local farmer's market. Those seeking off-campus nightlife and cultural experiences can make that easy twenty-minute drive south to Charlotte.

Career Services
The Matthews Center for Career Development is staffed by 11 full-time staff members. That works out to a student-to-advisor ratio of 175:1, much lower (i.e., better) than the average institution included in this book. Despite the administrative titles, all members of the staff get hands-on with career counseling. In the 2022-23 school year, 84% of undergrads engaged with the CCD, including 4,139 one-on-one advising appointments. Over 120 employers recruited on campus including Amazon, Google, Bain, IBM, Deloitte, and Cigna.

One nice aspect of the CCD is its systematic four-year development model that outlines recommended activities for students at all phases of their undergraduate education. As freshmen, Davidson students are encouraged to get comfortable with Handshake and get one-on-one assistance with resume writing. From there, students receive career coaching and help locating internships, and can participate in the Senior Bootcamp. Almost 80% of recent grads had at least one internship experience. The newly launched Insider Series brings professionals in a host of fields (e.g., sports marketing, advertising, and writing careers) to campus to impart career advice. Participation in Career Treks and group visits to corporations and nonprofit agencies has increased significantly in recent years.

Professional Outcomes

Looking at the outcomes data for 2022 grads, 70% landed jobs within six months of graduation, 26% were enrolled in a graduate program, and 3% were still seeking employment. Remaining in North Carolina after graduation is a popular choice, but many grads migrate to New York and DC as well. The top three industries favored by graduates are (in order), financial services, education, and consulting. Employers of the largest number of Davidson grads include Carolina Healthcare System, Teach for America, the NIH, Wells Fargo, and Bank of America.

Of those who attended grad school, the highest number were in healthcare-related programs (including MDs), law school, and laboratory sciences. Significant numbers of students pursue advanced degrees at other Southern gems including Vanderbilt, Emory, Duke, Wake Forest, and UNC. In fact, over a five-year period, the college sent more law school-bound alumni to UNC Law School (22), Duke (10), and Emory (7) than any other institution. There is also a fair showing of Ivy League acceptances in all graduate disciplines among Wildcat alumni.

Admission

In selecting their Class of 2026, Davidson received a modest 5,621 applications and accepted 17%, one percentage point lower than the previous year. For perspective, in 2013, the school accepted 26% of applicants, so the school has become a bit more selective in recent years. On standardized tests, enrolled students have a middle 50% score of 1360-1490 on the SAT and 31-33 on the ACT. However, Davidson did begin a test-optional pilot in 2021, so there has been less of an emphasis on test results recently. The average GPA of an enrolled student is 3.82, and 69% finished in the top 10% of their class; 94% finished in the top quartile.

The college has a unique set of admissions criteria atop its list. According to the admissions office, it places the most weight on rigor of coursework, recommendations, volunteer work, and character/personal qualities. Applying via binding early decision greatly improves your odds. Class of 2026 members who applied ED were accepted at a 43% rate, roughly three times the mark of their regular decision peers. Almost 64% of the incoming class was filled through the early round, one of the highest figures you will find at any school. One of the most selective liberal arts schools in the South, those offered admission typically sport excellent grades/test scores, although components of the process are genuinely holistic.

Worth Your Money?

Half of Davidson undergraduates qualify for need-based aid, an area in which the university is notably generous. Every student who qualifies for financial aid sees 100% of demonstrated need met, and the average total financial aid package is over $57k. At just under $77,000 in annual cost of attendance, Davidson's list price is a touch lower than many other schools of its ilk, and, even better, most students do not pay the full amount. With a record of solid graduate outcomes to boot, Davidson is absolutely worth your money.

FINANCIAL
Institutional Type: Private
In-State Tuition: $60,050
Out-of-State Tuition: $60,050
Room & Board: $16,400
Books & Supplies: $1,000

Avg. Need-Based Grant: $52,898
Avg. % of Need Met: 100%

Avg. Merit-Based Award: $29,885
% Receiving (Freshmen w/o Need): 4%

Avg. Cumulative Debt: $23,409
% of Students Borrowing: 22%

CAREER
Who Recruits
1. ESPN
2. Barings
3. Deloitte
4. EY
5. BlackArch Partners

Notable Internships
1. Cancer Treatment Centers of America
2. U.S. House of Representatives
3. POLITICO

Top Employers
1. Wells Fargo
2. Bank of America
3. University of North Carolina
4. US Army
5. Deloitte

Where Alumni Work
1. Charlotte
2. New York City
3. Washington, DC
4. Atlanta
5. Raleigh

Earnings
College Scorecard (10-YR Post-Entry): $77,379
PayScale (Early Career): $61,300
PayScale (Mid-Career): $124,100
PayScale 20-Year ROI: $463,000

RANKINGS
Money: 4.5
U.S. News: 16, Liberal Arts Colleges
Wall Street Journal/THE: 30
Washington Monthly: 23, Liberal Arts Colleges

OVERGENERALIZATIONS
Students are:
Always studying
Politically balanced
Athletic/active
Homogenous
Crazy about the Wildcats

COLLEGE OVERLAPS
Duke University
Emory University
University of North Carolina at Chapel Hill
University of Virginia
Vanderbilt University

Denison University

Granville, Ohio | 740-587-6276

ADMISSION
Admission Rate: 22%
Admission Rate - Men: 22%
Admission Rate - Women: 22%
EA Admission Rate: Not Offered
ED Admission Rate: 31%
ED Admits as % of Total Admits: 13%
Admission Rate (5-Year Trend): -15%
% of Admits Attending (Yield): 25%
Transfer Admission Rate: 35%

SAT Reading/Writing (Middle 50%): 630-710
SAT Math (Middle 50%): 640-750
ACT Composite (Middle 50%): 29-32

% Graduated in Top 10% of HS Class: 72%
% Graduated in Top 25% of HS Class: 85%
% Graduated in Top 50% of HS Class: 100%

Demonstrated Interest: Considered
Legacy Status: Considered
Racial/Ethnic Status: Not Reported
Admission Interview Offered: Yes

ENROLLMENT
Total Undergraduate Enrollment: 2,330
% Full-Time: 100%
% Male: 48%
% Female: 52%
% Out-of-State: 74%
% Fraternity: 17%
% Sorority: 43%
% On-Campus (All Undergraduate): 99%
Freshman Housing Required: Yes

% African-American: 6%
% Asian: 3%
% Hispanic: 7%
% White: 60%
% Other: 2%
% International: 17%
% Low-Income: 14%

ACADEMICS
Student-to-Faculty Ratio: 9 to 1
% of Classes Under 20: 67%
% of Classes 20-49: 33%
% of Classes 50 or More: 0%
% Full-Time Faculty: 76%
% Full-Time Faculty w/ Terminal Degree: 97%

Top Programs
Biology
Communication
Economics
History
International Studies
Political Science
Psychology

Retention Rate: 88%
4-Year Graduation Rate: 82%
6-Year Graduation Rate: 82%

Curricular Flexibility: Less Flexible
Academic Rating: ★★★★↓

#CollegesWorthYourMoney

Ohio is loaded with top-notch liberal arts schools with the two most famous undoubtedly being Kenyon and Oberlin. Those two cast long shadows, often stealing some of the light from another stellar college of 2,330 undergraduates located in the quiet village of Granville, 35 miles east of the state capital of Columbus. Parents of college-bound teens who were somewhat familiar with Denison back in their own college search days will remember a school that, in the 1990s, received roughly 2,000 applications per year and had an acceptance rate of 85%. The number of applications has since quadrupled, and the acceptance rate tied an all-time low of 22% for the Class of 2026.

Inside the Classroom
As you would expect from a liberal arts college, the General Education Program at this school is full of competencies and divisional requirements that students must address. This is not a university where foreign language can be evaded; rather, students must complete the third semester of their chosen language. Courses within general areas like the fine arts, the sciences (including lab), the humanities, and social sciences must be checked off as well as more specific mandates in areas such as power and justice and two writing-inten- sive courses.

Boasting a 9:1 student-to-faculty ratio, face time with your professors is never hard to come by. In fact, 67% of sections contain fewer than 20 students. All students have the opportunity to engage in undergraduate research, such as through the Summer Scholar Independent Research Program, which has 130 student partic- ipants each year. Off-campus opportunities, including those in the study abroad realm, are pursued by roughly 80% of the student body at some point during their four undergraduate years.

You won't find business or engineering among the most popular majors for a very solid reason—the school doesn't offer them. However, Denison's outstanding economics department does offer a financial economics concentration as well as Bloomberg Module Certification (BMC), a key credential for students pursuing jobs and internships in the financial industry. The greatest number of degrees are conferred in the social sciences (21%), business (9%), biology (9%), and communication (9%). Denison students apply in droves for competitive national scholarships. The school was named a Top Fulbright Producer, having an astonishing 10 winners a few years ago—a truly remarkable number given the size of the university. Over the last decade, students and alumni also have received multiple National Science Foundation Graduate Research Fellowships, Critical Language Scholarships, and Boren Scholarships.

Outside the Classroom
This 931-acre campus offers university-owned housing to all undergraduates; 99% live on campus all four years. For a liberal arts school, Greek life is surprisingly prevalent, with 17 total fraternities/sororities that attract 25% of the male population and 44% of female students. Denison offers 160+ clubs and student organizations, 40+ intramural sports, and 24 NCAA DIII varsity sports teams. More than 600 campus leadership positions in various endeavors are available. With an annual student government budget of one million dollars, anything is possible. Despite the massive spread of the grounds, the buildings are all within walking distance of one another. Highlights of the campus include a 350-acre biological reserve and the Denison Golf Club, one of the finest public courses in the Midwest. The Campus Series of lectures, performances, and exhibitions bring fascinating people to campus from Yo-Yo Ma to Madeline Albright to Robert Ballard, the discoverer of the Titanic wreckage. Rural Ohio may not be a hotbed of excitement, but the on-campus life is more than lively enough to keep most students sufficiently entertained. Stir-crazy individuals can get to Columbus in half an hour by car; Cleveland and Cincinnati are both over two hours away.

Career Services
With 24 professional employees working at the Knowlton Center for Career Exploration, Denison has been able to assemble one of the most supportive career guidance programs in the country with a 97:1 counselor-to-student ratio. It has multiple staff members working in employer relations and as career coaches, including in discipline-specific advising roles such as a prelaw advisor.

E-mail: admission@denison.edu | Website: denison.edu

Professional success and living a fulfilling life can be two very separate achievements, but not at Denison. According to alumni, 94% feel that Denison prepared them for professional success after college, and 89% feel that the school helped them toward a rich and fulfilling life— professionally, personally, and civically. During freshman year, the Knowlton Center helps facilitate the type of self-discovery that leads to such phenomenal postgraduate outcomes. For example, in September of one's first semester, the office hosts a First-Year Pre-Medicine meeting to give an overview of how to become a quality med school applicant over the next four years. For those more toward the end of their undergraduate journey, career center staff put on separate graduate school fairs for a variety of subjects, including social work, psychology, computer science, education, and environmental science. Whatever your aims may be, the Knowlton Center for Career Exploration almost certainly offers relevant programming for you.

Professional Outcomes

Denison does an excellent job tracking the long-term outcomes for its graduates, something many schools do not even attempt. Through this process, it can say with certainty that five years after graduating 99% of alumni are currently employed or in graduate school. Ninety-two percent of grads achieve this successful result within six months of leaving the university. More than 25 alums have held jobs at companies such as JPMorgan Chase, Morgan Stanley, UBS, PNC, Deloitte, Wells Fargo, IBM, and Microsoft. Some graduates stay somewhat local in the Columbus, Cleveland, or Cincinnati areas, but large clusters of alumni can be found in New York City; Chicago; Washington, DC; Boston; and San Francisco. The median salary for Denison alumni five years after graduating is $57,000.

Within five years of receiving their bachelor's degree, over three-fifths of Denison alumni have already earned an advanced degree or are presently in a graduate program. Those applying to Doctor of Osteopathic Medicine programs fared phenomenally well; in recent years, as many as 75% of those applying gained acceptance. Medical schools attended by recent graduates included Harvard Medical School, the University of Michigan Medical School, and the David Geffen School of Medicine at UCLA. In that same time frame, those seeking a legal education have entered law schools such as Ohio State, Fordham, and Temple University.

Admission

With just a 22% acceptance rate, Denison has become a highly-selective institution. Approximately 80% of accepted students came from outside the state of Ohio, and 17% of this cohort were international students from 72 countries. The average SAT score is 1360 and the mean ACT score is 31. Students at this university tend to have finished in at least the top quarter of their high school class; 85% have earned this distinction while 72% placed in the top 10%.

Denison is "seeking students who have demonstrated a seriousness toward their academic life and who, in addition, would bring a variety of interests, characteristics, and personal qualities to our dynamic campus community." The committee places the heaviest emphasis on an applicant's GPA, rigor of coursework, recommendations, and essays. An interview, extracurricular participation, and talent/ability are rated as "important." Standardized test scores are "considered" if submitted, but the school has been test-optional since 2008. Applying via early decision will give you a massive edge at this institution. In the 2022-23 admissions cycle, ED applicants were accepted at a 31% clip, far better than the rate of regular decision applicants. If you are on the fence about applying, the lack of an application fee may just entice you.

Worth Your Money?

Including an allowance for personal expenses and books, the estimated cost of attendance at Denison for the 2023-24 school year is $79,400. Don't have that kind of change lying around? No problem. This school meets 100% of demonstrated need, which translates to an average need-based grant of $43k. The average merit scholarship is in the amount of $20k. However, with the majority of students graduating with liberal arts or social science degrees, prospective attendees should engage in proper financial planning to make sure they are not biting off more than they can chew.

FINANCIAL
Institutional Type: Private
In-State Tuition: $64,000
Out-of-State Tuition: $64,000
Room & Board: $15,400
Books & Supplies: $1,000

Avg. Need-Based Grant: $42,799
Avg. % of Need Met: 100%

Avg. Merit-Based Award: $20,137
% Receiving (Freshmen w/o Need): 42%

Avg. Cumulative Debt: $31,610
% of Students Borrowing: 44%

CAREER
Who Recruits
1. DreamWorks
2. JPMorganChase
3. Cisco
4. Pitney Bowes
5. Orix

Notable Internships
1. Vector Marketing
2. John Hancock
3. Epic

Top Employers
1. JPMorgan Chase
2. Ohio State University
3. Morgan Stanley
4. UBS
5. Deloitte

Where Alumni Work
1. Columbus, OH
2. New York City
3. Chicago
4. Washington, DC
5. Boston

Earnings
College Scorecard (10-YR Post-Entry): $60,673
PayScale (Early Career): $56,900
PayScale (Mid-Career): $121,000
PayScale 20-Year ROI: $492,000

RANKINGS
Money: 4
U.S. News: 39, Liberal Arts Colleges
Wall Street Journal/THE: 317
Washington Monthly: 60, Liberal Arts Colleges

OVERGENERALIZATIONS
Students are:
Dressed to impress
Ready to party
Career-driven
Wealthy
Politically balanced

COLLEGE OVERLAPS
The College of Wooster
Dickinson College
Kenyon College
Lafayette College
Miami University - Oxford

Greencastle, Indiana | 765-658-4006

ADMISSION
Admission Rate: 66%
Admission Rate - Men: 62%
Admission Rate - Women: 70%
EA Admission Rate: 69%
ED Admission Rate: 50%
ED Admits as % of Total Admits: 2%
Admission Rate (5-Year Trend): -1%
% of Admits Attending (Yield): 14%
Transfer Admission Rate: 31%

SAT Reading/Writing (Middle 50%): 570-670
SAT Math (Middle 50%): 570-690
ACT Composite (Middle 50%): 24-31

% Graduated in Top 10% of HS Class: 45%
% Graduated in Top 25% of HS Class: 78%
% Graduated in Top 50% of HS Class: 97%

Demonstrated Interest: Considered
Legacy Status: Considered
Racial/Ethnic Status: Not Considered
Admission Interview Offered: Yes

ENROLLMENT
Total Undergraduate Enrollment: 1,752
% Full-Time: 100%
% Male: 49%
% Female: 51%
% Out-of-State: 55%
% Fraternity: 65%
% Sorority: 57%
% On-Campus (All Undergraduate): 97%
Freshman Housing Required: Yes

% African-American: 6%
% Asian: 3%
% Hispanic: 8%
% White: 59%
% Other: 1%
% International: 21%
% Low-Income: 16%

ACADEMICS
Student-to-Faculty Ratio: 9 to 1
% of Classes Under 20: 80%
% of Classes 20-49: 20%
% of Classes 50 or More: 0%
% Full-Time Faculty: 76%
% Full-Time Faculty w/ Terminal Degree: 98%

Top Programs
Cellular and Molecular Biology
Communication
Computer Science
Economics
English
Global Health
Kinesiology
Music

Retention Rate: 89%
4-Year Graduation Rate: 73%
6-Year Graduation Rate: 83%

Curricular Flexibility: Somewhat Flexible
Academic Rating: ★★★↙

#CollegesWorthYourMoney

A small school with a 180-year history and 700-million-dollar endowment, DePauw University provides a fantastic, personal level of education to just 1,752 undergraduates. Greencastle, IN, may not be a worldwide draw, but the university located there certainly is. Extremely small classes, faculty accessibility, and ample opportunity for experiential learning attract students from around the world with 21% being international students from 39 countries. Another 55% of students come from out of state. Perhaps the school's own words capture the spirit of the institution best: "DePauw prepares you for a life of meaning and means . . . You will be taught by extraordinary professors in small, exciting classes; live and study with peers whose diversity enriches the community; and supported as you pursue your academic and experiential passions."

Inside the Classroom
Freshmen begin with a strong First-Year Seminar program that is designed to create a sense of intellectual community and develop skills in writing, thinking, reading, and thoughtful discussion. On the back end, seniors have a Senior Capstone Experience that varies in its requirements by department. In between, all undergrads have to meet two sets of distributional requirements—Liberal Arts Foundations (arts and humanities, science and math, and social science)—and Global and Local Awareness that includes a newly instituted, two-semester language requirement as well as one course under the Power, Privilege, and Diversity umbrella.

No matter which of the 40+ majors you pursue at DePauw, you will enjoy the benefits of small class sizes and face time with faculty. A 9:1 student-to-faculty ratio and the fact that only four class sections in the whole university enroll more than 29 students assures that. Even more impressive, 32% of courses enroll single-digit numbers of students, and 80% enroll fewer than 19.

Ninety-seven percent of young alumni surveyed expressed satisfaction with the quality of the school's faculty, and 30% of Tigers have assisted with a faculty member's research by senior year. With the fourth highest percentage of study abroad participants of any school in the country, DePauw sends nearly all of its students to a foreign locale at some point during their four years of study.

The greatest number of DePauw undergrads earn degrees in the social sciences (17%), biology (10%), the visual/performing arts (9%), communication/journalism (8%), and computer science (6%). The school has functioned as a full-blown Fulbright factory; in one recent six-year run, it produced the eighth most Fulbright students of any school in the country.

Outside the Classroom
A 100% residential campus leads to a level of closeness that is difficult to manufacture otherwise. Greek life is a huge component of the social scene with 65% of men and 57% of women becoming affiliated with 25 fraternities and sororities. If that isn't your scene, no worries; there are 100+ other clubs. With 21 Division III teams, close to 30% of students compete on a Tiger squad. The popular DePauw After Dark series features late-night activities including game nights, open mic, karaoke, dance parties, and other alcohol-free events. Plenty of volunteer opportunities are available throughout Putnam County, including at local schools, shelters, museums, and retirement communities. Campus itself consists of 36 buildings laid out on 175 acres, but the adjoining 520-acre DePauw Nature Park makes the grounds feel even more expansive. The park offers all the flora, fauna, and hiking trails you could desire, and the main campus is included on many "Most Beautiful Campuses" lists. While Greencastle is fairly remote, Indianapolis is less than an hour away.

Career Services
Within the Hubbard Center for Student Engagement, 10 professionals are dedicated to career services roles that include employer relations coordinator, prelaw advisor, health professions advisor, and associate dean of experiential learning. This exceptional 175:1 counselor-to-student ratio is among the best of any school featured in this guide. As a result, the school connects with students throughout their undergraduate years. The center offers three signature programs: the Sophomore Series, which helps find meaningful internships and study abroad experiences; the Junior Jumpstart, which prepares students for the upcoming job/grad school search; and Senior Offerings, which helps soon-to-be graduates plan a fulfilling and fruitful post-college life.

More than 80% of recent grads had at least one internship experience. In addition, employers regularly travel to Greencastle to participate in career and internship fairs, industry panels, information sessions, and on-campus interviews. One recent Graduate & Professional School Fair attracted 40 institutions. There have been recent complaints in the school's newspaper about the lack of Fortune 500 employers that recruit on DePauw's campus, but the university does partner with other Indiana-based schools to put together larger events, such as the Indiana Means Business Career Fair, that attract major corporations. In sum, the Hubbard Center provides oodles of personalized attention that leads to tangible results for the school's undergraduates.

Professional Outcomes

The university's "Gold Commitment" guarantees that all grads will land at their next destination within six months, or they will be provided with an entry-level professional opportunity or an additional tuition-free semester. Fortunately, few struggle to find employment; the top 10 employers of DePauw grads are Eli Lilly and Company, Salesforce, West Monroe Partners, Indiana University Health, Roche, Teach for America, IBM, Northern Trust Corporation, AT&T, and Procter & Gamble. The university had a third-party survey conducted with employers that found DePauw grads were viewed as superior to their peers in the areas of writing research, communication, and critical thinking, among many others. Alumni can be found in the highest concentrations in Indianapolis, Chicago, Terre Haute, New York City, and Denver.

Tigers applying to graduate and professional schools experience a similar level of success. Of medical school applicants who earned a 3.6 GPA and scored in the 80th percentile on the MCAT, 90% are accepted to at least one institution. Law school applicants find a home at an 80% clip. Looking at a sampling of individual graduate/professional school outcomes, you'll find students pursuing a PhD in informatics at Indiana University, a PhD in biophysics at Notre Dame, and master's degrees at schools including Yale and Northwestern.

Admission

Compared to many schools of similar quality, nothing about DePauw's admissions data should be terrifying. In constructing the Class of 2026, the university admitted 3,756 of the 5,708 individuals who applied, an acceptance rate of 66%. In addition, the school became test optional in 2019, prior to the pandemic, meaning that those lacking high SAT/ACT results still have a pathway into the school. Last cycle, 34% of enrolled freshmen included an SAT score in their applications while 19% included an ACT result. The middle-50% range was 1160-1360 on the SAT and 24-33 on the ACT. Forty-five percent of that group placed in the top 10% of their high school class, 78% were in the top quartile, and 97% were in the top half; the average GPA was 3.92.

The greatest emphasis is placed on an applicant's level of rigorous coursework and GPA. DePauw views class rank, essays, and recommendations as "important" and "considers" just about everything else, from extracurricular activities to an admissions interview. The school does offer an ED I deadline of November 1 and an EDII option by February 15th. They accepted 50% of ED applicants last year. Without much of an edge from an admissions standpoint, applying ED to this university probably doesn't make great strategic sense unless you are both on the borderline academically and view DePauw as your clear number-one choice.

Worth Your Money?

DePauw cracks just about every reputable list of schools that return a student's investment and facilitate social mobility. This is a particularly remarkable feat for a school with no engineering program and only 1% who earn business/marketing degrees. The school has displayed a genuine commitment to making an undergraduate education "affordable and accessible." Almost three-fifths of students receive need-based financial aid with the average annual package exceeding $46k. The average merit scholarship for freshmen with no financial need is over $35,000. That level of generosity makes the $72k cost of attendance far more manageable for most families and leads to below-average graduate debt levels.

FINANCIAL
Institutional Type: Private
In-State Tuition: $57,070
Out-of-State Tuition: $57,070
Room & Board: $14,850
Books & Supplies: $950

Avg. Need-Based Grant: $42,267
Avg. % of Need Met: 88%

Avg. Merit-Based Award: $35,090
% Receiving (Freshmen w/o Need): 48%

Avg. Cumulative Debt: $24,216
% of Students Borrowing: 75%

CAREER
Who Recruits
1. Roche Holding AG
2. EY
3. Abbott Laboratories
4. Indiana University Health
5. Liberty Mutual Insurance

Notable Internships
1. MillerCoors
2. KeyBanc Capital Markets
3. The ALS Association

Top Employers
1. Eli Lilly and Company
2. Salesforce
3. Indiana University Health
4. Amazon
5. Accenture

Where Alumni Work
1. Indianapolis
2. Chicago
3. New York City
4. Denver
5. St. Louis

Earnings
College Scorecard (10-YR Post-Entry): $66,577
PayScale (Early Career): $62,300
PayScale (Mid-Career): $111,100
PayScale 20-Year ROI: $613,000

RANKINGS
Money: 4.5
U.S. News: 46, Liberal Arts Colleges
Wall Street Journal/THE: 92
Washington Monthly: 67, Liberal Arts Colleges

OVERGENERALIZATIONS
Students are:
Tight-knit (possess a strong sense of community)
Working hard and playing hard
More likely to rush a fraternity/sorority
Always admiring the beauty of their campus
Politically balanced

COLLEGE OVERLAPS
Allegheny College
Denison University
Juniata College
Kenyon College
The College of Wooster

Dickinson College

Carlisle, Pennsylvania | 717-245-1231

ADMISSION
Admission Rate: 35%
Admission Rate - Men: 31%
Admission Rate - Women: 38%
EA Admission Rate: Not Offered
ED Admission Rate: 58%
ED Admits as % of Total Admits: 9%
Admission Rate (5-Year Trend): -14%
% of Admits Attending (Yield): 20%
Transfer Admission Rate: 37%

SAT Reading/Writing (Middle 50%): 640-723
SAT Math (Middle 50%): 620-703
ACT Composite (Middle 50%): 29-32

% Graduated in Top 10% of HS Class: 49%
% Graduated in Top 25% of HS Class: 82%
% Graduated in Top 50% of HS Class: 94%

Demonstrated Interest: Very Important
Legacy Status: Considered
Racial/Ethnic Status: Important
Admission Interview Offered: Yes

ENROLLMENT
Total Undergraduate Enrollment: 2,125
% Full-Time: 100%
% Male: 42%
% Female: 58%
% Out-of-State: 72%
% Fraternity: 4%
% Sorority: 25%
% On-Campus (All Undergraduate): 99%
Freshman Housing Required: Yes

% African-American: 5%
% Asian: 5%
% Hispanic: 7%
% White: 65%
% Other: 1%
% International: 12%
% Low-Income: 14%

ACADEMICS
Student-to-Faculty Ratio: 9 to 1
% of Classes Under 20: 78%
% of Classes 20-49: 22%
% of Classes 50 or More: 0%
% Full-Time Faculty: 80%
% Full-Time Faculty w/ Terminal Degree: 96%

Top Programs
Biology
Economics
Environmental Studies
Foreign Languages
History
International Business and Management
International Studies
Law & Policy

Retention Rate: 88%
4-Year Graduation Rate: 80%
6-Year Graduation Rate: 83%

Curricular Flexibility: Somewhat Flexible
Academic Rating: ★★★★

#CollegesWorthYourMoney

Set in the small town of Carlisle, Pennsylvania, Dickinson College is a liberal arts school with a strong academic reputation that dates back to the earliest days of the United States. In fact, it was founded the same week the United States signed the Treaty of Paris that ended the Revolutionary War. Today, the 2,125 undergraduate students who call Dickinson home are an increasingly diverse group, both in terms of academic/career interests and demographically. In recent years, the school has doubled its rate of international students to 12% and raised the presence of underrepresented minorities from 15% in 2013 to one-quarter today. The school does have a notable gender gap to the tune of a 58/42 split in favor of women.

Inside the Classroom

Freshmen are matched with a professor-advisor and engage in a mandatory first-year seminar intended to hone critical thinking, analysis, and research skills. From there, students must embark on an extensive trek through required coursework in quantitative reasoning, the humanities and arts, the social sciences, laboratory science, foreign language, and four physical education blocks. There are additional boxes to check in the areas of US diversity, global diversity, and sustainability.

As students immerse themselves in one of 46 areas of concentration, Dickinson supports them with a 9:1 student-to-faculty ratio and average class size of fifteen, with 78% of classes being capped at 19 students. This type of intimacy allows the school to advertise that: "Not only will you have the opportunity to conduct advanced research as an undergraduate that most wouldn't experience until graduate school, you'll also have the chance to work alongside faculty in the process." The majority of students also elect to venture to other continents as part of their undergraduate experience. Offering study abroad opportunities with 16 global programs, more than 50 study abroad options, and boasts a 60% participation rate.

By discipline, the greatest number of degrees are conferred in the social sciences (27%), biology (12%), business (10%), psychology (7%), and foreign languages (5%). The college's foreign language program, which features 13 offerings—including Arabic, Hebrew, and Portuguese—is recognized as one of the top programs in the country. International studies, history, and environmental studies also have particularly strong reputations. Dickinson students are known as a globetrotting and service-oriented bunch. Thus, it is fitting that the college is a leading producer of Fulbright scholars (4 in 2023 alone) and Peace Corps volunteers.

Outside the Classroom

Dickinson is located in central Pennsylvania about 20 miles from the state capital of Harrisburg. Carlisle may be a small town, yet there are a reasonable number of nearby shopping/dining options, including dozens of restaurants within walking distance. The school's small-town location means that a good deal of social life takes place on campus where 99% of students reside in college-owned housing. Greek life has a strong but not dominant presence with only 4% of men joining fraternities but 25% of women joining sororities. More than 120 student clubs exist with the highest concentrations in the performing arts and club sports. For those serious about athletics, the Red Devils compete in NCAA Division III in 11 men's and 12 women's sports. Environmental sustainability is important to the administration and students alike, and with its own organic farm and pledge to be climate neutral, the college is regularly ranked as one of the top eco-friendly colleges in the country.

Career Services

The Career Center has 11 professional employees who play advising, pre-professional counseling, and employer relations roles. That works out to a 193:1 student-to-advisor ratio, which is significantly better than average when compared to other schools featured in this guide. One counselor is dedicated to pre-health advising and another guides prelaw students.

Dickinson does not host its own career fairs but does endorse two nearby gatherings, the Capital Region Internship Fair at Penn State Harrisburg and the Not-for-Profit Networking Fair in Philadelphia. However, there are other areas where this office excels. For example, a tremendous 92% of recent grads completed an internship, service-learning, or research apprenticeship at some point over their four years of study. The college also launched an externship program in which students can spend between two and ten days over winter break shadowing alums in their workplaces. In short, it is hard to go through Dickinson without completing relevant, hands-on learning opportunities that lead to successful postgraduate outcomes.

Professional Outcomes

One year after graduating, 95% of Dickinson grads have found jobs or full-time volunteer work, or have enrolled in graduate school. The most popular industries are, in order, business and industry, education, health and medical services, and nonprofits. Red Devils head to a wide range of organizations/employers, with multiple recent grads headed to the US Army, the Peace Corps, Teach for America, and, on the other end of the spectrum, the Vanguard Group. Many other well-known financial, pharmaceutical, and consulting companies are represented on the list of recent graduate destinations, as are a host of other nonprofit organizations. Across all graduating years, companies employing more than 25 Dickinson alumni include Deloitte, IBM, Morgan Stanley, JPMorgan Chase & Co., Merck, EY, PNC, PwC, Google, and Amazon. It's interesting that more alumni can be found in New York City than in Pennsylvania.

Within five years of receiving their diplomas, 55-60% of recent grads have entered or finished graduate school. For the Class of 2022, many graduate school-bound new alums found homes in state universities; however, a sizable number of prestigious acceptances were sprinkled in including Columbia, Johns Hopkins, Northwestern, and the University of Chicago. Law school applicants are accepted at a rate of 94% with some applicants finding success at the Boston University School of Law, Penn State Dickinson School of Law, and Duke University School of Law. Of students recommended for medical school by the college last academic year, 95% are accepted into at least one institution.

Admission

The admit rate for the Class of 2026 was 35%, down from 48% just last year. Standardized test scores for admitted students have remained fairly constant over the years, and the majority do submit them even though the school went test-optional a long time ago. The mid-50% range is 1288-1413 on the SAT. In terms of class rank, 49% of freshmen hail from the top 10% of their high school cohort, and 82% finish in the top 25%; only 6% did not finish in the top half of their class.

Dickinson shows love to students who love them as 58% of early decision applicants were offered admission in 2022-23. It is unusual for a college to include "demonstrated interest" as one of the most important factors in admissions decisions, but Dickinson does exactly that. This strategy helped to raise the school's yield rate to 20% from just 18% in the recent past. A handful of other soft factors also sit atop the list: volunteer work, talent/ability, and character/personal qualities. Despite its status as a highly selective institution, intelligent students with a blemish still have a chance to find a home here. With its test-optional policy, those who excelled in the classroom but struggled on Saturday mornings with a No. 2 pencil in their hand are still in the running as are those with the opposite imperfection—strong SAT-takers who bloomed late as serious-minded students.

Worth Your Money?

An impressively high 80% of Dickinson students are awarded some level of aid or scholarship. Almost 100% of demonstrated need is met, and the average institutional grant is for $48k. This helps to cut into a list price cost of attendance of $83k. The amount of debt incurred by the average Dickinson student is less than that of the average college student in the United States. If you were borrowing $100k+ to study the liberal arts, we would caution against selecting this school without first exploring more cost-effective options. However, for those taking on modest amounts of student loans, this is a college worth attending for the intimate class environment and solid graduate outcomes.

FINANCIAL
Institutional Type: Private
In-State Tuition: $63,450
Out-of-State Tuition: $63,450
Room & Board: $16,500
Books & Supplies: $1,324

Avg. Need-Based Grant: $48,199
Avg. % of Need Met: 99%

Avg. Merit-Based Award: $21,542
% Receiving (Freshmen w/o Need): 24%

Avg. Cumulative Debt: $27,462
% of Students Borrowing: 63%

CAREER
Who Recruits
1. Gartner
2. Amazon
3. Booz Allen Hamilton
4. PwC
5. PNC

Notable Internships
1. BlackRock
2. IBM
3. Cushman & Wakefield

Top Employers
1. US Army
2. Deloitte
3. IBM
4. Morgan Stanley
5. JPMorgan Chase

Where Alumni Work
1. New York City
2. Philadelphia
3. Washington, DC
4. Boston
5. Harrisburg, PA

Earnings
College Scorecard (10-YR Post-Entry): $72,568
PayScale (Early Career): $59,700
PayScale (Mid-Career): $104,000
PayScale 20-Year ROI: $393,000

RANKINGS
Money: 4.5
U.S. News: 46, Liberal Arts Colleges
Wall Street Journal/THE: Not Ranked
Washington Monthly: 21, Liberal Arts Colleges

OVERGENERALIZATIONS
Students are:
Globally-minded
Environmentally conscious
Involved/invested in campus life
Collaborative
Wealthy

COLLEGE OVERLAPS
Bucknell University
Franklin & Marshall College
Gettysburg College
Lafayette College
Lehigh University

Drexel University

Philadelphia, Pennsylvania | 215-895-2400

ADMISSION
Admission Rate: 80%
Admission Rate - Men: 78%
Admission Rate - Women: 81%
EA Admission Rate: 97%
ED Admission Rate: 92%
ED Admits as % of Total Admits: 1%
Admission Rate (5-Year Trend): +1%
% of Admits Attending (Yield): 10%
Transfer Admission Rate: 54%

SAT Reading/Writing (Middle 50%): 610-700
SAT Math (Middle 50%): 620-730
ACT Composite (Middle 50%): 27-32

% Graduated in Top 10% of HS Class: 37%
% Graduated in Top 25% of HS Class: 69%
% Graduated in Top 50% of HS Class: 93%

Demonstrated Interest: Considered
Legacy Status: Considered
Racial/Ethnic Status: Not Considered
Admission Interview Offered: No

ENROLLMENT
Total Undergraduate Enrollment: 12,482
% Full-Time: 92%
% Male: 50%
% Female: 50%
% Out-of-State: 50%
% Fraternity: 11%
% Sorority: 8%
% On-Campus (All Undergraduate): 21%
Freshman Housing Required: Yes

% African-American: 8%
% Asian: 23%
% Hispanic: 8%
% White: 44%
% Other: 2%
% International: 9%
% Low-Income: 25%

ACADEMICS
Student-to-Faculty Ratio: 9 to 1
% of Classes Under 20: 55%
% of Classes 20-49: 37%
% of Classes 50 or More: 8%
% Full-Time Faculty: 54%
% Full-Time Faculty w/ Terminal Degree: 86%

Top Programs
Actuarial Science
Animation
Construction Management
Design
Engineering
Information Systems
Nursing

Retention Rate: 89%
4-Year Graduation Rate: Not Reported
6-Year Graduation Rate: 74%

Curricular Flexibility: Somewhat Flexible
Academic Rating: ★★★✦

#CollegesWorthYourMoney

Building your campus adjacent to an Ivy League school like the University of Pennsylvania is a solid recipe to end up a higher education afterthought. Yet Drexel, established in 1891, has carved out its own solid reputation as a private research university specializing in engineering, business, and nursing, all bolstered by a groundbreaking and distinctive co-op program that just celebrated its one-hundredth anniversary. The 13,881 Drexel Dragon undergrads come to the University for its rigorous programs as well as the emphasis placed on experiential learning. They leave, by and large, with well-paying jobs in their area of interest. Practical, career-minded teens find a good partner institution in Drexel University.

Inside the Classroom
There are 80+ undergraduate majors to choose from at Drexel, and the academic culture lets you get down to brass tacks quickly. Other than a Composition & Rhetoric course and introductory classes that provide an overview of university life and the co-op experience, most students dive right into their major-specific coursework as freshmen. Business students take courses like Foundations of Economics, Principles of Economics, and Introduction to Analysis. Engineering students are plopped right into chemistry, calculus, and Introduction to Engineering Design and Data Analysis. The robust co-op program sees just about every single undergraduate participate. Students can choose between a five-year plan that includes three co-op experiences or a traditional four-year pathway that allows for one co-op placement. The school runs year-round on a quarter calendar to accommodate students on co-ops.

Drexel offers a reasonable 9:1 student-to-faculty ratio with commensurately reasonable class sizes. Fifty-two percent of sections contain 19 or fewer students, and just a sliver under 9% of sections contain fifty or more. Drexel students are encouraged to begin seeking undergraduate research opportunities "as early as the freshman year." An array of research-oriented co-ops exist at local hospitals, museums, and pharmaceutical companies as well. With the emphasis on co-op education, it can be difficult to carve out time to study abroad while at Drexel. In a typical year, roughly 900 students manage to study internationally at one of 60 locations. Co-ops in foreign countries are another way to access the benefits of this type of experience.

Looking at the number of degrees conferred by discipline, the big three at Drexel are business (25%), health professions (21%), and engineering (17%). Visual and performing arts (9%), computer science (8%), and biology (4%) round out the list of majors with a sizable representation. The Westphal College of Media Arts & Design has a growing reputation, as do programs in engineering. Also on the rise is Drexel's number of winners of prestigious postgraduate fellowships. In 2023, ten students were chosen as Fulbright Semifinalists and three former Drexel undergrads took home National Science Foundation Graduate Research Fellowships.

Outside the Classroom
Set on a 96-acre urban campus in University City, the section of Philadelphia that also includes the University of Pennsylvania, Drexel has 82% of freshmen residing in university-owned housing. However, less than one-quarter of the overall student body live on campus. Greek life draws 11% of male and 8% of female students. There are 18 NCAA Division I sports teams that compete in the Colonial Athletic Association. Club and intramural sports are huge with over 9,000 participants each year. The Drexel Recreation Center is an 18,000-square-foot facility with all of the fitness amenities one could desire. There are 300+ active student organizations on campus and a ton more opportunities for fun in the surrounding area. Drexel students get in free at the Academy of Natural Sciences, the oldest museum of its kind in the country, and can just as easily walk to World Café Live and catch a free concert with a big-name artist every Friday afternoon. Famed art museums, major sporting events, and an excellent food and bar scene are all within a short distance of campus. Student groups like the Campus Activities Board organize group trips to amusement parks and Broadway plays, and host block parties and other special events on campus.

Career Services
The Steinbright Career Development Center is staffed by 13 full-time staff members who serve as career counselors, prelaw/pre-health advisors, and employer relations specialists. However, there are 28 additional professional employees dedicated to the co-op program, bringing the total to 41 staff members who work with undergraduates on career-related matters. That works out to a 339:1 ratio, a respectable figure for a university of Drexel's size and scope. Its three annual career fairs are well attended by employers, but student attendance is lower than one would expect. A recent Fall Career Fair drew 220+ employers and almost 1,700 students, the Spring Career Fair attracted 100+ companies/organizations and 900+ students, and the Engineering Career Fair saw 135 employers and 625 students in attendance.

When it comes to career services at Drexel, the co-op experiences are, to quote Philadelphia-area native Reggie Jackson, "The straw that stirs the drink." Among surveyed graduates, 88% had a co-op experience that was relevant to their current job, and 92% were satisfied with their positions. More importantly, 53% of students received a job offer from one of their co-op employers. Placements are available in 21 states and 45 countries, and partner organizations include major players like Goldman Sachs, Lockheed Martin, and Exelon. The strength of this one-of-a-kind co-op program combined with strong employment statistics earns the Steinbright Career Development Center high marks from our staff.

Professional Outcomes

One year after graduating, 97% of the Class of 2021 (most recent available) had arrived at their next destination; 81% were employed, and 13% had matriculated into graduate or professional school. The largest employers of Drexel alumni are Comcast, Merck, Vanguard, and Johnson & Johnson. There are also at least one hundred Dragons within GlaxoSmithKline, JP Morgan Chase, SAP (software), Amazon, Microsoft, IBM, Accenture, Deloitte, Google, and EY. Nine times as many graduates remain in Philadelphia as go to the second most popular post-graduation destination of New Jersey. The average starting salary for Drexel grads with a full-time job was $64,774.

The predominately career-driven group that attends the university does not immediately move on to graduate schools in large numbers. However, those who do have produced some solid results, particularly those applying to medical and law school. Drexel's medical school acceptance rate was 60%, roughly 20 points higher than the national average. It offers an accelerated BS/MD program with its own Drexel University College of Medicine. Seventy-six percent of law school applicants ultimately found a home for their legal education. Recent grads have landed at prestigious law schools at Harvard, the University of Michigan, Vanderbilt, and the University of Pennsylvania as well as a number of local options including Drexel's own law school that opened in 2006.

Admission

Drexel's 37,040 applicants for a place in the freshman class of 2022-23 overwhelmingly received favorable admissions news—80% were accepted. That healthy percentage is the norm at Drexel as acceptance rates have been in the 70-80% range for some time. Its yield rate, the number of accepted students who actually enroll, is around 10%. This is because, for many, Drexel is not their first choice. Still, those who end up attending have a strong academic profile. Freshmen in the Class of 2026 possessed a mid-50% SAT of 1240-1420 and an ACT of 27-32. Thirty-seven percent placed within the top 10% of their high school class and 69% were in the top quartile.

Admissions decisions are made in a manner consistent with Drexel's STEM focus—the hard numbers are of utmost importance. GPA, class rank, test scores (although the school is test-optional), and the rigor of one's high school coursework are deemed "very important" while soft factors like recommendations, essays, and character/personal qualities occupy the second tier. With such a low yield rate, the university looks favorably upon those who will commit to it through binding early decision. The ED acceptance rate in 2021 was 92%. In short, Drexel is a rare school with a pre-professional focus that is not terribly difficult to get into. Those with solid but imperfect grades should find a welcome home here.

Worth Your Money?

Drexel graduates earn 12% above the national average which, even given the focus on business, engineering, and nursing, is still an impressive achievement. That salary boost is needed thanks to the $78,000+ annual cost of attendance, although 99% of incoming freshmen receive some level of aid. Fortunately, the co-op experience is top-notch and frequently leads to gainful employment in one's area of study. Students do not pay tuition during their co-op year and, in fact, are paid a median six-month salary of almost $20k. This college is unique and connected enough to be worth the high price tag, particularly for students pursuing more pre-professional majors.

FINANCIAL
Institutional Type: Private
In-State Tuition: $60,663
Out-of-State Tuition: $60,663
Room & Board: $17,550
Books & Supplies: $1,200

Avg. Need-Based Grant: $32,759
Avg. % of Need Met: 79%

Avg. Merit-Based Award: $20,347
% Receiving (Freshmen w/o Need): 36%

Avg. Cumulative Debt: $34,140
% of Students Borrowing: 65%

CAREER
Who Recruits
1. Seer Interactive
2. Bentley Systems
3. Johnson & Johnson
4. Spark Therapeutics
5. Lockheed Martin

Notable Internships
1. KPMG
2. Anthropologie
3. Delancy Street Partners

Top Employers
1. Lockheed Martin
2. Comcast
3. Merck
4. Vanguard
5. Johnson & Johnson

Where Alumni Work
1. Philadelphia
2. New York City
3. Washington, DC
4. San Francisco
5. Baltimore

Earnings
College Scorecard (10-YR Post-Entry): $79,785
PayScale (Early Career): $66,700
PayScale (Mid-Career): $118,800
PayScale 20-Year ROI: $762,000

RANKINGS
Money: 4
U.S. News: 98, National Universities
Wall Street Journal/THE: 54
Washington Monthly: 136, National Universities

OVERGENERALIZATIONS
Students are:
Career-driven
More likely to venture off campus
Independent
Always working
Goal-oriented

COLLEGE OVERLAPS
Pennsylvania State University - University Park
Rutgers University - New Brunswick
Rochester Institute of Technology
Temple University
University of Pittsburgh

Duke University

Durham, North Carolina | 919-684-3214

ADMISSION
Admission Rate: 6%
Admission Rate - Men: 6%
Admission Rate - Women: 6%
EA Admission Rate: Not Offered
ED Admission Rate: 16%
ED Admits as % of Total Admits: 26%
Admission Rate (5-Year Trend): -4%
% of Admits Attending (Yield): 55%
Transfer Admission Rate: Not Reported

SAT Reading/Writing (Middle 50%): 730-770
SAT Math (Middle 50%): 760-800
ACT Composite (Middle 50%): 34-35

% Graduated in Top 10% of HS Class: 94%
% Graduated in Top 25% of HS Class: 98%
% Graduated in Top 50% of HS Class: 100%

Demonstrated Interest: Considered
Legacy Status: Considered
Racial/Ethnic Status: Considered
Admission Interview Offered: Yes

ENROLLMENT
Total Undergraduate Enrollment: 6,640
% Full-Time: 100%
% Male: 48%
% Female: 52%
% Out-of-State: 81%
% Fraternity: Not Reported
% Sorority: Not Reported
% On-Campus (All Undergraduate): 82%
Freshman Housing Required: Yes

% African-American: 9%
% Asian: 21%
% Hispanic: 11%
% White: 37%
% Other: 4%
% International: 10%
% Low-Income: 12%

ACADEMICS
Student-to-Faculty Ratio: 5 to 1
% of Classes Under 20: 71%
% of Classes 20-49: 22%
% of Classes 50 or More: 7%
% Full-Time Faculty: 95%
% Full-Time Faculty w/ Terminal Degree: 94%

Top Programs
Biology
Economics
English
Engineering
Mathematics
Neuroscience
Political Science
Public Policy

Retention Rate: 98%
4-Year Graduation Rate: 91%
6-Year Graduation Rate: 96%

Curricular Flexibility: Somewhat Flexible
Academic Rating: ★★★★

#CollegesWorthYourMoney

Duke is a place where students can be, at once, fanatical, face-painted members of the Cameron Crazies as well as studious, career-minded young people in an Ivy League-caliber academic environment. In fact, Duke is now more selective than several Ivies, which is no surprise given the university's unique combination of academic prestige and extracurricular excitement. Over 6,600 undergrads are joined by more than 11,400 graduate students on this picturesque, 8,800-acre campus in Durham, North Carolina.

Inside the Classroom
The academic offerings at Duke include 53 majors, 52 minors, and 23 interdisciplinary certificates. More than 4,000 undergraduate courses run each semester in the College of Arts & Sciences alone. Rarely do students concentrate solely on one major—82% either double major, add a minor, or pursue an additional certificate. Undergraduates encounter a good number of unique academic requirements. All freshmen in the Trinity College of Arts & Sciences must take a first-year seminar and first-year writing course. Before graduation, each individual must take two small group learning experiences that can involve an independent study and/or constructing a thesis. Foreign language and multiple courses under the umbrellas of Areas of Knowledge and Modes of Inquiry also must be tackled.

Class sizes are on the small side—71% are nineteen or fewer, and almost one-quarter are less than ten. A stellar 5:1 student-to-faculty ratio helps keep classes so reasonable even while catering to five figures worth of graduate students. The Undergraduate Research Support Office does great work connecting students with opportunities to conduct research, either over the summer or during the regular school year. All told, more than half of undergraduates conduct research. More Duke students pursue a semester abroad than students at any other top ten research institution—roughly half elect to venture off to one of the school's 300 partner programs scattered around the world.

Duke has a sterling reputation for academics across the board. The Department of Biology is world-class and a leading producer of successful medical school applicants. Programs in economics, English, and public policy consistently earn top rankings as well. Computer Science is the most popular area of concentration (11%), followed by economics (10%), public policy (9%), biology (8%), and computer engineering (7%). Blue Devils win prestigious postgraduate fellowships on a regular basis. Named a top producer of Fulbright Scholars for the last decade, Duke churned out 14 winners in 2023. The university has produced an incredible 50+ Rhodes Scholars in its illustrious history, more than Emory and Vanderbilt combined.

Outside the Classroom
When you enter campus through Duke Gardens, it can feel like you're strolling through a perfectly manicured Disney theme park; everything is pristine and aesthetically pleasing. Thus, no one is anxious to live anywhere other than the university's grounds and 100% of freshmen and 80%+ of the entire student body live on campus. With 35 recognized Greek chapters, fraternities and sororities have historically played a major role in the social life at Duke. However, a number of Greek organizations have disaffiliated in recent years; less than a quarter currently belong to a still-affiliated organization as of 2023. Those who occupy dorms are generally pleased, and the food at Duke is universally praised. Big-time sports are a staple of life on campus as the Blue Devils compete in twenty-three sports in NCAA Division I's vaunted Atlantic Coast Conference. Since the beloved Coach K took over in 1980, the men's basketball squad has made the Final Four a dozen times and has won five national championships. One of the most popular non-sports-related, campus-wide events is the annual Last Day of Classes (LDOC) celebration, which draws a large percentage of the student body for activities, beverages, and music. More than 400 student organizations run on campus, including a high-performing mock trial team and The Chronicle, an award-winning student newspaper with a seven-figure budget. The culture of volunteering is strong with an 80% participation rate; Blue Devils perform community service in the city of Durham in programs like Engineers Without Borders.

Career Services
The Career Hub at Duke is staffed by 28 undergraduate career advisors, employer relations specialists, and event coordinators, calculating to a student-to-advisor ratio of 236:1, which is in the average range when compared to other schools in its weight class. Yet, this "mediocrity" is not indicative of anything less than outstanding career services offerings. This assessment can be delivered by one quick fact: An astounding 95% of graduating seniors who had lined up their first jobs were hired by companies that work in some capacity with the Duke Career Center.

Undergrads each have their own assigned career counselor, and the school recommends establishing a relationship as a freshman. Two-thirds of graduates reported meeting with a career center staff member at least once over their four years of study. Regular events held include Practice Interview Day, Ignite Your Internship Search, and the Fall Career Fair which includes over one hundred top companies, many of which recruit and offer interviews on campus. Bottom line—the Career Center at Duke is among the best in the country at preparing students for high-paying employment and admission into prestigious graduate/professional programs.

Professional Outcomes

At graduation, approximately 70% of Duke diploma-earners enter the world of work, 20% continue into graduate schools, and 2% start their own businesses. The industries that attract the largest percentage of Blue Devils are tech (21%), finance (15%), business (15%), healthcare (9%), and science/research (6%). Companies employing a minimum of three Duke grads per year include Google, Capital One, Amazon, Microsoft, Oracle, Goldman Sachs, Morgan Stanley, Accenture, and a host of other top-shelf corporations in the areas of technology, finance, and consulting. One-third of Duke alumni elect to stay in North Carolina. New York, California, DC, and Massachusetts follow in popularity. The top foreign destinations for employment are the United Kingdom and China. Duke students, on average, do exceptionally well financially.

Of the 20% headed into graduate school, a hefty 22% are attending medical school, 18% are in PhD programs, and 12% are entering law school. The med school acceptance rate is 85%, more than twice the national average. Eventually, 84% of Duke undergraduates will go on to earn an advanced degree. A typical graduating class sees around 150 members apply to law school, scoring an average of 165 on the LSAT, among the highest in the country. Those applicants find their way into just about every top-ranked law school in existence. In the last few years, Blue Devils have pursued a JD at Stanford Law School, University of Chicago Law School, and Harvard Law School, among others.

Admission

Getting into Duke is an Ivy League-level, single-digit proposition. The applicant pool vying for a place in the Class of 2026 saw only 6% gain acceptance. That isn't a new trend. Rather, Duke has had an admit rate under 10% for the last decade. Among freshmen in 2022-23, 37% submitted ACT scores and had a 50th percentile range of 34-35; the SAT range was 1490-1570. An intimidating 94% of Blue Devils graduated in the top 10% of their high school class, and 98% were in the top quartile.

Early decision applicants saw a far more favorable acceptance rate—21%—than in the regular round; close to half of the freshman class is typically cemented during this early round. However, it is worth keeping in mind that athletes and legacy students are typically admitted in the early round, which certainly helps prop up the acceptance rate. Additionally, legacy students comprise 10-13% of the student body in any given year, and they typically apply ED. The Duke Admissions Committee considers eight factors as "very important" in admissions decisions: rigor of classes, grades, test scores, essays, recommendations, extracurricular activities, talent/ability, and character/personal qualities. Like the Ivies, Duke routinely rejects valedictorians and teens with perfect standardized test scores. Successful applicants will have exceptional academic credentials, attention-grabbing essays, and special talents that set them apart from a crowded field of aspiring Blue Devils.

Worth Your Money?

Duke's annual cost of attendance is $85,238, but over half pay less than that amount. Members of the undergraduate student body who qualify for need-based financial aid receive annual aid packages of $62,000 per year, meeting 100% of their demonstrated need. In fact, 21% of freshmen attend tuition-free. The university has one of the 15 largest endowments in the United States ($12 billion) and puts it to good use, making Duke affordable to those from non-wealthy families. Essentially, the approximately 50% of students who come from wealthy (or upper-middle-class) families pay the bulk of the sticker price while those from lower-to-middle-income homes get significant tuition reductions. Even if you had to take on a lot of debt to attend Duke, this is one school that will almost certainly pay you back many times over; alumni salaries and employment prospects are that strong.

FINANCIAL
Institutional Type: Private
In-State Tuition: $66,172
Out-of-State Tuition: $66,172
Room & Board: $19,066
Books & Supplies: $536

Avg. Need-Based Grant: $58,019
Avg. % of Need Met: 100%

Avg. Merit-Based Award: $74,057
% Receiving (Freshmen w/o Need): 2%

Avg. Cumulative Debt: $24,990
% of Students Borrowing: 24%

CAREER
Who Recruits
1. 4170 Trading LLC
2. Cornerstone Advisors LLC
3. National Security Agency
4. Xerox
5. Qualtrics

Notable Internships
1. Carlyle Group
2. CNBC
3. Instagram

Top Employers
1. Google
2. Amazon
3. Microsoft
4. Facebook
5. Goldman Sachs

Where Alumni Work
1. Raleigh
2. New York City
3. Washington, DC
4. San Francisco
5. Boston

Earnings
College Scorecard (10-YR Post-Entry): $97,418
PayScale (Early Career): $76,800
PayScale (Mid-Career): $142,500
PayScale 20-Year ROI: $1,014,000

RANKINGS
Money: 5
U.S. News: 7, National Universities
Wall Street Journal/THE: 16
Washington Monthly: 6, National Universities

OVERGENERALIZATIONS
Students are:
Working hard and playing hard
Crazy about the Blue Devils
Always admiring the beauty of their campus
Career-driven
Highly motivated

COLLEGE OVERLAPS
Cornell University
Northwestern University
Princeton University
University of North Carolina at Chapel Hill
University of Pennsylvania

Elon, North Carolina | 336-278-3566

Nestled in the centralized Piedmont region of North Carolina, Elon University is home to 6,337 undergraduates and is—most fittingly for a school whose mascot is the Phoenix—a school on the rise. Not yet an uber-selective school (roughly three-quarters of applicants get in), this modestly sized university is known for its quality undergraduate teaching, experiential learning opportunities, and unparalleled study abroad program. Individualized attention is available at every turn, particularly from a well-staffed and highly effective Career Services Department.

Inside the Classroom

Students choose from 70 majors and can add a number of interesting minors like adventure-based learning, coaching, and multimedia authoring. Regardless of one's area of concentration, all Elon undergrads must work through an extensive core curriculum that is made up of six interrelated parts: two first-year foundations courses focused on developing writing and critical thinking skills; an experiential learning component that requires studying abroad, interning, or conducting independent research; foreign language (can be exempted through AP tests); a total of thirty-two credits in the arts and sciences; eight credit hours of advanced coursework outside one's major; and a capstone seminar as a senior. Ninety-eight percent of students elect to take a one-credit freshman course entitled Elon 101 that, among other things, helps new students map out a graduation plan.

Elon's 11:1 student-to-faculty ratio leads to an average class size of 20 students; 51% of sections contain fewer than 20 students. A whopping 77% of students elect to study abroad, the highest participation rate in the country among master's-granting institutions. There are limitless options for overseas study including official Elon Centers Abroad in Shanghai, Dunedin, London, and Florence. Chances for working closely with faculty on research projects are also plentiful; 23% of students participate in faculty-mentored research.

Though Elon possesses solid offerings in many disciplines, programs in finance, communication, exercise science, and the performing arts receive the most praise. The areas in which the greatest number of degrees are conferred are business (29%), journalism/communication (20%), social sciences (8%), the visual and performing arts (6%), and psychology (6%). Elon is recognized as a top producer of Fulbright Scholars, seeing eight fellowship winners in 2022; it had 45 winners between 2013 and 2018. Recent graduates also have received a Truman Scholarship, a Goldwater Scholarship, and grants from the National Science Foundation.

Outside the Classroom

Sixty-two percent of undergrads live on the school's 656-acre grounds. Greek life is a dominant force on the Elon social scene with 39% of women joining sororities and 20% of men signing up for fraternity life. The 59/41 gender breakdown in favor of women is certainly a factor in social life. It also should be noted that Elon has been rated as one of the LGBTQ-friendlier schools in the country. An athletically inclined student body participates in seventeen NCAA Division I sports as well as twenty-one intercollegiate club teams and eighteen intramural sports. Elon students are known for being involved in their college community as nearly 90% contribute some level of volunteer service, and 59% hold some type of leadership role in a student organization. There are 250 student-run clubs, including a student-run television station and an award-winning weekly newspaper, The Pendulum. The Elon Speakers Series sees an incredible list of notable figures visit campus each year. In the last few years, it has welcomed David Cameron, Anita Hill, and Bob Woodward. The town of Elon is not the world's most exciting place, but those with access to a car are no more than an hour from the larger cities of Durham, Raleigh, and Winston-Salem.

Career Services

The Student Professional Development Center (SPDC) at Elon University has 19 professional employees (not counting a number of graduate fellows and apprentices) who play advising, pre-professional counseling, and employer relations roles. That works out to a 336:1 student-to-advisor ratio, which is better than average when compared to other schools featured in this guide. This office has sufficient resources to offer individualized services and coordinate large events such as fall and spring job fairs that attract over 90 employers and over 1,000 students. The center also regularly offers smaller events, such as the Accounting Meet and Greet, which attracts fifteen firms and 120 undergraduate students. Its Graduate & Professional School Fair brings representatives from fifty institutions to campus each October. In total, 250+ employers attend career fairs during a given academic year.

Thanks to the efforts of the Student Professional Development Center, 87% of 2022 grads completed an internship during their four undergraduate years and the majority of those internships led directly to a job offer. Recently, Elon students have interned at a range of employers including Pfizer, Booz Allen Hamilton, Mercedes-Benz, and the American Red Cross. Companies known to recruit at Elon and/or offer on-campus interviews include Walt Disney Co., ESPN, Oracle, Credit Suisse, EY, PwC, Goldman Sachs, and ABC News. The SPDC facilitates close to 6,000 one-on-one advising appointments per year, an absolutely remarkable number given the modest size of the school.

Professional Outcomes

Results of a survey administered nine months after graduation found that 96% of the Class of 2022 had found employment, a graduate school, or an internship. That is a significant improvement from a decade ago when only 83% of graduates had found their next postsecondary or employment home nine months after receiving their diplomas. Of those accepting employment, a magnificent 94% reported that their job directly related to their area of study. Top employers of recent Elon graduates include Bloomberg, Deloitte, EY, Google, Goldman Sachs, Red Ventures, and Wells Fargo. Geographically, alumni are dispersed all over the map. A mere 25% of graduates remained in the Tar Heel State while 17% migrated to New York and 14% to Massachusetts. The starting salaries for Elon graduates vary greatly by discipline. For example, recent business grads enjoyed a median salary of $61k while communications majors earned $47k.

Just under one-quarter of recent grads gained acceptance into graduate/professional school. Many remain at Elon or continue at other Carolina-based schools such as UNC-Chapel Hill, Wake Forest, East Carolina University, or North Carolina State. Class of 2022 members gained acceptance into prestigious graduate schools such as Boston College, Duke, NYU, Penn, and Georgetown. Applicants to medical school typically gain acceptance at the same rate as the national average. In recent years, that figure fluctuated between 33-52%. That group of students earned average MCAT scores that placed them in the 75th percentile. Few graduates in recent years have been accepted into the top medical schools in the country.

Admission

Elon admitted 78% of the 17,551 applicants for a place in the 2022-23 freshman class, up from 74% the previous cycle. First-year students possessed a mid-50th percentile SAT score of 1175-1330 and an ACT range of 25-30. Only 20% of admitted students finished in the top 10% of their high school class, and 50% finished in the top quartile. Interestingly, a decade ago, the acceptance rate was a much stingier 42%, but the credentials of accepted students were roughly the same. In that time, the quality of applicants has remained consistent, but the school's yield rate has declined from 33% to 13%, leading to more offers of acceptance in order to meet enrollment goals.

The admissions committee rates four factors as having the greatest importance: rigor of secondary curriculum, GPA, recommendations, and essays. Attributes such as character/personal qualities, extracurricular activities, and demonstrated interest round out the next tier of considered factors. Applying early decision offers a sizable advantage as 90% were accepted in the early round. A school whose reputation is ascending, Elon, for now, remains a welcoming landing spot for teens with solid but unspectacular transcripts. Applying early further increases your odds but may be unnecessary as an admissions strategy unless you are a borderline applicant.

Worth Your Money?

As far as private universities go, a list price of $60,657 (COA) isn't outlandish. The cost of Elon is approximately $15,000 less than comparable private institutions; however, they do not meet a high percentage of demonstrated financial need, which leads to slightly above-average cumulative debt totals for graduates. Elon isn't a bargain for most students, but it is a solid deal for a school that provides ample individualized attention and has largely positive student outcomes.

FINANCIAL
Institutional Type: Private
In-State Tuition: $44,536
Out-of-State Tuition: $44,536
Room & Board: $14,478
Books & Supplies: $900

Avg. Need-Based Grant: $18,291
Avg. % of Need Met: 63%

Avg. Merit-Based Award: $8,036
% Receiving (Freshmen w/o Need): 32%

Avg. Cumulative Debt: $33,774
% of Students Borrowing: 39%

CAREER
Who Recruits
1. Walt Disney Company
2. SAS
3. Oracle
4. Net Suite
5. Vanguard

Notable Internships
1. ABC's The View
2. Aflac
3. Merrill Lynch

Top Employers
1. Wells Fargo
2. Bank of America
3. EY
4. PwC
5. IBM

Where Alumni Work
1. Winston-Salem, NC
2. New York City
3. Raleigh
4. Washington, DC
5. Charlotte

Earnings
College Scorecard (10-YR Post-Entry): $66,617
PayScale (Early Career): $58,200
PayScale (Mid-Career): $99,400
PayScale 20-Year ROI: $418,000

RANKINGS
Money: 4
U.S. News: 133, National Universities
Wall Street Journal/THE: 232
Washington Monthly: 200, National Universities

OVERGENERALIZATIONS
Students are:
Preppy
Wealthy
Career-driven
More likely to rush a fraternity/sorority
Always admiring the beauty of their campus

COLLEGE OVERLAPS
Clemson University
James Madison University
University of North Carolina at Chapel Hill
University of Richmond
University of South Carolina

Emerson College

Boston, Massachusetts | 617-824-8600

Positioned in Boston's historic Theater District, Emerson College is a school of 4,149 undergraduate students, all united in their desire to make a mark in a creative field like film, television, or marketing/advertising. All 26 majors offered by the school have some element of performance or artistry and include highly unique academic concentrations such as comedic arts, sports communication, and musical theater. Like many other schools situated in downtown Boston, Emerson has become a more popular destination in recent years and, thus, the credentials needed to earn an invitation to this East Coast paradise for creative minds have been raised.

Inside the Classroom
No matter what artistic or performance-based field one is attending Emerson for, exposure to a broad liberal arts core is assured through the series of mandatory courses all students must embark upon. Freshmen take foundations courses in oral and written communication. In subsequent years, students must complete courses classified as aesthetics, global diversity, US diversity, ethics and values, history and politics, interdisciplinary, literary, scientific, social and psychological, and quantitative reasoning. Those in the school's Honors Program can add a senior thesis and a number of small seminar courses to the checklist of graduation requirements.

Emerson has a 15:1 student-to-faculty ratio and 69% of courses seat fewer than 20 students. Professors are generally accessible as evidenced by 83% of seniors rating their interactions with faculty as being "satisfactory" or "very satisfactory." Overall, 81% were "satisfied" or "very satisfied" with their educational experience at the college. Opportunities to study in other cities, both foreign and domestic, can be had through Emerson-sponsored external programs in Los Angeles, DC, The Netherlands, Prague, Spain, Beijing and Shanghai, Ireland, Mexico, Austria, Greece, and France.

The Journalism and Communications Studies programs rank among the top in the country. Emerson's various degree offerings in the film/television realm will open doors thanks to the school's LA affiliations and connected alumni network. By sheer popularity, the top majors are film/video production, journalism, marketing, theater arts, and creative writing. Seniors will, on occasion, win a prestigious national scholarship/fellowship, but very few apply, as Emerson grads enter the workforce in overwhelming numbers.

Outside the Classroom
Undergrads are fairly evenly divided between living in one of the school's five residential spaces and off-campus housing. While finding a cheap dwelling in Beantown is impossible (studio apartments start at $2k per month), the college offers resources to help students find the most reasonably priced options available. Despite the school's 65% women, 35% men gender breakdown, there are actually more fraternities at Emerson than sororities. Yet, Greek life is anything but a dominant part of the social scene. United more by their creative passions than official affiliations, the 100+ student-run clubs tend to be more of a draw, especially the student publications—highlighted by Ploughshares, a literary journal—film groups, theater, comedy troupes, Emerson TV, and WERS FM, the acclaimed campus radio station. Close to 200 undergrads participate in the school's 14 NCAA Division III sports teams known as the Lions, but sports are a secondary interest for the bulk of the student body. Perhaps the best part about Emerson's campus is that it's located in the heart of downtown Boston. Everything you could ever want is within a short walk or T ride of the college. This list includes the Museum of Fine Arts, Loews Theater (which offers free film screenings to students), Fenway Park, and Boston Common, as well as countless restaurants, cafes, and bars.

Career Services
Emerson's Career Development Center (CDC) has nine professional employees who work in advising and employer engagement capacities. This works out to a 461:1 student-to-advisor ratio, which is about average when compared to many of the other small-to-midsize colleges featured in this guide. The office places an emphasis on helping students carve out Career Design Pathways which, beginning freshman year, help connect on-campus events and opportunities to "students' long-term planning and professional development." Some components of this program take place online, but face-to-face counseling is also encouraged. In a single recent academic year, the office engaged 54% of the student population (2,912 total appointments).

Internship fairs are hosted by the college each fall and spring and draw representatives from an impressive array of arts and media employers such as The Boston Globe, the Boston Ballet, Converse (for advertising/marketing), and a number of Boston-area media companies/stations.

The CDC's emphasis on helping students find internships pays off, with 70% of undergraduates landing at least one internship experience; the majority actually completed more than one. Of those in this category, 90%+ find their internships helpful in preparing them for their eventual first post-college job. Further, one-third of interns were offered a job with their host employer. Overall, a survey of recent graduates found that approximately 80% of them found the Career Development Center helpful.

Professional Outcomes

Within six months of leaving Emerson, 61% of recent grads were employed, 4% were enrolled in graduate school, and 35% were still seeking their next landing spot. The film, TV, and music sector is the area employing the largest number of recent alumni (24%), followed by journalism (15%), nonprofit (13%), and marketing & advertising (7%). Top employers of the Class of 2020 include the Walt Disney Company, Warner Media, Sinclair Broadcast Group, and CNN. Many members of the alumni network can be found working at Netflix and at a number of local radio and television stations throughout the New England region.

The majority of graduates remain in the state of Massachusetts, with California, New York, Connecticut, and Texas attracting most of those electing to relocate. The average full-time salary for employed grads is $40,255. This figure is impressive when you consider the school's lack of a STEM program and emphasis on preparing students for careers in more creative and, generally, lower-paying jobs. Upon completing their undergraduate education, only about 1 in 20 students decide to immediately begin pursuing an advanced degree. Obviously, if you want to be a scientist or medical doctor, Emerson doesn't offer the right academic programs. Of those entering a master's program, the bulk stay put, pursuing a master's at Emerson in an area like writing for film and television, creative writing, or journalism.

Admission

A more selective school than it was just a few short years ago, Emerson admitted 43% of its 12,109 applicants seeking a spot in the Class of 2026, an improvement from the 33% seen three years prior. Emerson shares an applicant pool with many other Boston-based schools, many of which may rank higher on applicants' lists. As a result, the yield rate is 19%, a higher mark than in previous years after adding an early decision option last cycle.

The admissions committee wants to see "how students have challenged themselves academically, balancing hard work with extracurricular activities." This is reflected in the average freshman's GPA of 3.7. In terms of class rank, 33% of freshmen finished in the top 10% of their high school class, and 68% were in the top quarter. In 2017, Emerson implemented a test-optional policy. While Emerson, like just about every other school in downtown Boston, is growing increasingly more difficult to get into, it will still open its door to students not at the very top of their class. Strong students with solid grades in rigorous courses and standardized test scores in the 85th-90th percentile will find success, particularly those with a nice extracurricular resume and portfolio.

Worth Your Money?

Emerson's 2022-23 tuition is $52,896, and room and board will set you back another $20k. The school does award some level of financial aid to 51% of undergrads. The average award for a freshman is $35k—very few see 100% of their need met. An Emerson education is unlikely to come cheap but, for those entering fields in performing arts or film, the training you will receive and connections you will make will definitely make this school worth the high cost.

FINANCIAL
Institutional Type: Private
In-State Tuition: $55,392
Out-of-State Tuition: $55,392
Room & Board: $20,310
Books & Supplies: $1,250

Avg. Need-Based Grant: $27,887
Avg. % of Need Met: 62%

Avg. Merit-Based Award: $13,299
% Receiving (Freshmen w/o Need): 23%

Avg. Cumulative Debt: $21,883
% of Students Borrowing: 56%

CAREER
Who Recruits
1. CNN
2. Penguin Random House
3. United Talent Agency
4. Spotify
5. The Daily Beast

Notable Internships
1. The Boston Globe
2. Vogue China
3. Discovery Studios

Top Employers
1. NBC Universal
2. Netflix
3. Northeastern University
4. MIT
5. Apple

Where Alumni Work
1. Boston
2. New York City
3. Los Angeles
4. San Francisco
5. Washington, DC

Earnings
College Scorecard (10-YR Post-Entry): $58,491
PayScale (Early Career): $54,200
PayScale (Mid-Career): $105,600
PayScale 20-Year ROI: $304,000

RANKINGS
Money: 3.5
U.S. News: 13, Regional Universities North
Wall Street Journal/THE: Not Ranked
Washington Monthly: 297, Master's Universities

OVERGENERALIZATIONS
Students are:
Artsy
Career-driven
More likely to venture off campus
Politically liberal
LGBTQ-Friendly

COLLEGE OVERLAPS
Boston University
Fordham University
Ithaca College
New York University
Syracuse University

Emory University

Atlanta, Georgia | 404-727-6036

ADMISSION
Admission Rate: 11%
Admission Rate - Men: 13%
Admission Rate - Women: 11%
EA Admission Rate: Not Offered
ED Admission Rate: 26%
ED Admits as % of Total Admits: 25%
Admission Rate (5-Year Trend): -11%
% of Admits Attending (Yield): 38%
Transfer Admission Rate: 19%

SAT Reading/Writing (Middle 50%): 700-760
SAT Math (Middle 50%): 730-790
ACT Composite (Middle 50%): 32-34

% Graduated in Top 10% of HS Class: 81%
% Graduated in Top 25% of HS Class: 97%
% Graduated in Top 50% of HS Class: 100%

Demonstrated Interest: Not Considered
Legacy Status: Considered
Racial/Ethnic Status: Considered
Admission Interview Offered: No

ENROLLMENT
Total Undergraduate Enrollment: 7,101
% Full-Time: 99%
% Male: 43%
% Female: 57%
% Out-of-State: 84%
% Fraternity: 20%
% Sorority: 20%
% On-Campus (All Undergraduate): 62%
Freshman Housing Required: Yes

% African-American: 9%
% Asian: 24%
% Hispanic: 11%
% White: 33%
% Other: 1%
% International: 17%
% Low-Income: 18%

ACADEMICS
Student-to-Faculty Ratio: 9 to 1
% of Classes Under 20: 58%
% of Classes 20-49: 30%
% of Classes 50 or More: 12%
% Full-Time Faculty: 87%
% Full-Time Faculty w/ Terminal Degree: 96%

Top Programs
Applied Mathematics and Statistics
Biology
Business
Chemistry
English
Political Science
Neuroscience and Behavioral Biology
Philosophy

Retention Rate: 95%
4-Year Graduation Rate: 83%
6-Year Graduation Rate: 90%

Curricular Flexibility: Somewhat Flexible
Academic Rating: ★★★★★

#CollegesWorthYourMoney

Widely viewed as a "Southern Ivy," Emory University hosts 7,101 elite undergraduates on its Atlanta-based campus. To be more geographically precise, the prestigious school, which boasts the sixteenth largest endowment of any university in the United States, is located in the Druid Hills section of Atlanta, home to the Centers for Disease Control as well as one of the wealthiest neighborhoods in the entire state of Georgia. This midsize university offers a diverse array of majors (80+) and minors (60+), and 30% of Emory students pursue more than one area of study.

Inside the Classroom
All freshmen must complete a first-year seminar in which they are tasked with stretching their critical thinking and research skills as they explore one of a series of fascinating topics in an intimate setting with a faculty member. The immersion and support don't stop there; all freshmen also must take a one-credit advising program called PACE (Pre-Major Advising Connections at Emory) in which they work with a faculty advisor and peer mentor to explore academic pathways. Ultimately, the greatest number of students go on to earn degrees in the social sciences (15%), biology (14%), business (14%), health professions (12%), and mathematics (9%).

One unique feature of Emory is that one of its undergraduate divisions, Oxford College (about 45 minutes away), functions as a small liberal arts college for freshmen and sophomores. Oxford students knock out many of their lower-level courses before declaring a major and attending upper-level courses at Emory. No matter which school you attend, hands-on learning opportunities abound. Over half of Emory's student body works directly with a faculty member on academic research and 58% of courses have class sizes of under twenty students. Studying abroad is a fairly common feature of an Emory education, with 40% of students traveling to one of 100 international destinations.

Emory is notable for its renowned Woodruff School of Nursing and Goizueta School of Business. It also routinely rates well in biology, neuroscience, creative writing, and political science. Undergrads at Emory have a strong history of winning national awards; the school boasted 16 Fulbright Scholars in 2023 alone and has produced 21 Rhodes Scholars in its history. Further, Emory churns out more Teach for America candidates than any other midsize school in the United States, and it is also a leading producer of students who join the Peace Corps upon graduation.

Outside the Classroom
Last year, 99% of freshmen and 62% of all undergraduates resided in university-owned housing. Many also live in Greek houses as 20% of men pledge fraternities and 20% of women join sororities. Emory claims 480 student-run clubs and sports teams, and Oxford College adds another eighty to that diverse list. Volunteer Emory organizes twenty to thirty service trips per week, and over 80% of students participate in one or more of the opportunities for community service each year. If you are looking for top-of-the-line collegiate athletics, Emory may not be a great fit. Despite the absence of nationally televised football games, roughly 400 non-scholarship athletes
compete in a variety of Division III athletic competitions. Another 600+ students compete in one or more of Emory's club sports, which include everything from flag football to golf to swimming. Impressive amenities, such as two Olympic-size swimming pools and a rock climbing arena, also are available for recreational use. Notable campus-wide events include Wonderful Wednesdays, a weekly open-invite celebration that can include anything from a petting zoo to a volunteer fair to an annual town hall with former President Jimmy Carter. Off campus, there is something for everyone with Atlanta's nightlife and natural beauty (a nature trail begins on Oxford's campus) right in your backyard.

Career Services
The Career Center at Emory is staffed by 10 full-time professional employees as well as four additional full-time staff members who exclusively serve business majors at Goizueta. That equates to a student-to-advisor ratio of 507:1, in the average range when compared to the other institutions included in this book. Spring and fall job fairs are well attended (over 1,000 students each), and approximately 200 companies recruit on campus each year. Each year, more than 12,000 jobs and internships are posted on Handshake, 350+ events are held, and 1,500 one-on-one counseling sessions take place.

E-mail: admission@emory.edu | Website: emory.edu

Typical career-prep services are available to undergraduate students. Resumes, cover letters, and personal statements can be submitted online for editing by a staff member with fairly quick turnaround times. Through Emory Connects, alumni can connect virtually with current students to share career advice. At any time, students can access alumni as well as internship opportunities through their Handshake account. Emory Connects: Career Discovery Days provides students with job-shadowing opportunities in the Atlanta area.

Professional Outcomes

Shortly after graduation, 66% of 2022 grads were already employed, and 96% had arrived at their next destination. The top employers of recent Emory grads include Deloitte, Epic, ScribeAmerica, Meta, Morgan Stanley, and Cloudmed. Past graduating classes have had a significant number of Eagles (the school's lesser-known mascot) land at Deloitte, PwC, the Home Depot, and The Coca-Cola Company. Teach for America is the 15th largest employer of the last graduating class. While a healthy number of Emory grads found employment in Georgia, the top destinations for the Class of 2022 included non-Southern locales in New York City, DC, LA, Chicago, and Philadelphia. Graduates of the Goizueta Business School found strong starting salaries with an average of $81k. The previous year, Emory College grads enjoyed an average salary of $63k.

A healthy number of Emory grads pursue further education upon graduation. In the last few years, multiple Emory grads/alums received acceptance letters from the following top law schools: Columbia, Berkeley, Michigan, Northwestern, and Georgetown. Med school acceptances included Duke, Johns Hopkins, Vanderbilt, and USC. Overall, the most commonly attended graduate schools included Emory itself, Columbia, Duke, Northwestern, NYU, Penn, Harvard, and BU. Emory is quite strong in premed and saw 375 students apply to medical schools in 2023, an astounding number for a midsized school.

Admission

Emory received 33,179 applications for the Class of 2026; only 3,767 were accepted, an overall acceptance rate of 11%, down from 19% two years prior. Enrolled students in the Class of 2026 possessed a mid-50% ACT range of 32-34 and a range of 1450-1530 on the SAT. The average GPA on a 4.0 scale was 3.84, and less than 1% of students possessed a GPA under a 3.25. While high test scores and near-perfect grades (81% were in the top 10% of their high school classes) are close to prerequisites, Emory does employ a holistic review process that carefully considers letters of recommendation, essays, and how you spent your time outside the classroom.

It is a fairly common strategy for students to submit applications to both Emory and Oxford. The latter is slightly less selective and typically sports an acceptance rate a few points higher than its counterpart. It is also important to note that 66% of first-year students at Emory were admitted through early decision, and the ED acceptance rate was 26%, more than double the regular round rate. Thus, if Emory is your first choice, applying early may be a good idea. In sum, Emory is a highly selective, elite school where competition for a spot on campus is growing more difficult every year. Nothing short of straight A's in a rigorous selection of courses, along with a 1450+ SAT score, puts you in good standing to earn a place in one of the South's most prestigious universities.

Worth Your Money?

Almost all Emory students who qualify for financial aid see 100% of their demonstrated need met by the university. Forty-six percent of undergraduates receive need-based aid and 19% receive Pell Grants. The remaining students pay the full $79k annual cost of attendance. Emory does a tremendous job of opening its doors to students from every socioeconomic background as the median family income for current students (estimated by tax return data) is much lower than many other private institutions of its ilk. Given that grads enjoy top-shelf employment prospects and generous financial aid, Emory is likely to be worth every dollar it will cost you.

FINANCIAL
Institutional Type: Private
In-State Tuition: $60,774
Out-of-State Tuition: $60,774
Room & Board: $18,972
Books & Supplies: $1,250

Avg. Need-Based Grant: $51,828
Avg. % of Need Met: 100%

Avg. Merit-Based Award: $27,933
% Receiving (Freshmen w/o Need): 5%

Avg. Cumulative Debt: $25,895
% of Students Borrowing: 32%

CAREER
Who Recruits
1. American Express
2. SunTrust
3. Turner Construction
4. Macy's
5. BNP Paribas

Notable Internships
1. ExxonMobil
2. Booz Allen Hamilton
3. BlackRock

Top Employers
1. Centers for Disease Control
2. Deloitte
3. EY
4. PwC
5. Google

Where Alumni Work
1. Atlanta
2. New York City
3. Washington, DC
4. San Francisco
5. Boston

Earnings
College Scorecard (10-YR Post-Entry): $81,802
PayScale (Early Career): $68,400
PayScale (Mid-Career): $125,800
PayScale 20-Year ROI: $763,000

RANKINGS
Money: 4.5
U.S. News: 24, National Universities
Wall Street Journal/THE: 42
Washington Monthly: 50, National Universities

OVERGENERALIZATIONS
Students are:
Service-oriented
Diverse
Working hard and playing hard
Career-driven
Lacking school spirit

COLLEGE OVERLAPS
Duke University
Johns Hopkins University
New York University
University of Pennsylvania
Vanderbilt University

Fairfield University

Fairfield, Connecticut | 203-254-4100

ADMISSION
Admission Rate: 52%
Admission Rate - Men: 53%
Admission Rate - Women: 52%
EA Admission Rate: 56%
ED Admission Rate: 83%
ED Admits as % of Total Admits: 3%
Admission Rate (5-Year Trend): -9%
% of Admits Attending (Yield): 19%
Transfer Admission Rate: 8%

SAT Reading/Writing (Middle 50%): 620-680
SAT Math (Middle 50%): 620-690
ACT Composite (Middle 50%): 28-31

% Graduated in Top 10% of HS Class: 30%
% Graduated in Top 25% of HS Class: 67%
% Graduated in Top 50% of HS Class: 92%

Demonstrated Interest: Important
Legacy Status: Considered
Racial/Ethnic Status: Considered
Admission Interview Offered: Yes

ENROLLMENT
Total Undergraduate Enrollment: 4,757
% Full-Time: 99%
% Male: 42%
% Female: 58%
% Out-of-State: 80%
% Fraternity: Not Offered
% Sorority: Not Offered
% On-Campus (All Undergraduate): 76%
Freshman Housing Required: Yes

% African-American: 1%
% Asian: 2%
% Hispanic: 7%
% White: 81%
% Other: 5%
% International: 2%
% Low-Income: 7%

ACADEMICS
Student-to-Faculty Ratio: 12 to 1
% of Classes Under 20: 41%
% of Classes 20-49: 57%
% of Classes 50 or More: 2%
% Full-Time Faculty: 49%
% Full-Time Faculty w/ Terminal Degree: 91%

Top Programs
Accounting
Communication
English
Finance
Marketing
Nursing
Politics

Retention Rate: 91%
4-Year Graduation Rate: 82%
6-Year Graduation Rate: 83%

Curricular Flexibility: Less Flexible
Academic Rating: ★★★✦

#CollegesWorthYourMoney

If you're seeking a high-caliber Catholic/Jesuit institution and don't have the grades and test scores for Georgetown, Holy Cross, Boston College, or Fordham, say hello to a new friend named Fairfield University. This school may not have the national name recognition of its Jesuit brethren but, rest assured, this Connecticut university of 4,757 undergraduates has its share of stellar students and no shortage of connections to the nearby corporate world of New York City, including many of Wall Street's premier firms.

Inside the Classroom
No matter which of the 43 majors you happen to be pursuing, a significant amount of time will be spent fulfilling the required Magis Core Curriculum. Totaling 45 credits (15 courses), students must complete Introduction to Rhetoric and Composition and Introduction to Philosophy as well as coursework in math, history, religious studies, modern or classical language, and additional forays into the behavioral and social sciences, literature, natural sciences, and visual and performing arts. Business majors, of which there are many (stats to follow), take a whole extra set of mandated coursework including Calculus, Introduction to Microeconomics, and Introduction to Macroeconomics.

A 12:1 student-to-faculty ratio is fully felt in the classroom as courses average only 20 students per section. While 41% come in under that marker and only a smattering of sections contain 40+ students, the greatest number of courses have enrollments in the 20-29 range. Each year, 300+ faculty-directed undergraduate research projects are completed and shown off at the university's Annual Research and Creative Accomplishments Symposium. Study abroad programs have a 30% participation rate, and opportunities are available to travel to 60+ programs across 40 countries on five continents.

Fairfield is primarily known for its business program, which serves as a pipeline to many of the top financial/accounting/consulting firms in the country. A whopping 42% of degrees conferred are from the highly respected Dolan School of Business. Next in popularity are majors within the health professions (18%) and the social sciences (8%)—both areas also receive high marks at Fairfield. Fulbright winners have trailed off in recent years, but the school has had as many as nine in a single year in the not-too-distant past. However, landing fellowships is rarely the postgraduate goal of this business-minded group.

Outside the Classroom
Housing is guaranteed for all four years and three-quarters of students elect to live on the school's 200-acre campus. Demographically, two things at Fairfield stand out. One, the lack of ethnic diversity is real—81% of current students identify as white—and second, women make up nearly three-fifths of the undergraduate population. As at many Jesuit institutions, Greek life doesn't exist here, but there are plenty of social opportunities around; for many years, Fairfield made appearances on top party school lists, but today it cracks prominent lists measuring schools with the happiest students and best quality of life. With 20 NCAA Division I teams, Fairfield certainly has plenty of sports to offer. While the Stags' fan base is quiet compared to a place like fellow Jesuit school Boston College, it is still significant that 10% of the student body are Division I athletes. There are over 100 clubs and activities to enjoy, including twenty intramural sports and twenty-five club teams. Being just sixty miles from NYC is an advantage not only for networking but also for weekend trips. Campus itself cannot unreasonably be assigned adjectives like "idyllic" and "stunning." Its location on the Connecticut coast turns the nearby beach into an extension of campus; in fact, 400 seniors each year live in beachfront homes and apartments.

Career Services
The University Career Center staff at Fairfield is comprised of eight full-time employees who work in employer development, recruitment, and experiential learning and internship coordination. The 595:1 student-to-advisor ratio is only average compared to the schools featured in this guidebook, but that does not appear to prevent this staff from directly touching the lives of almost every student. The office hosts four career fairs per year, including general expos in the fall and spring and smaller affairs specific to nursing and law school. One recent Fall Career Fair was attended by 120+ employers and 700+ students; companies in attendance included EY, KPMG, PwC, Morgan Stanley, and Epsilon.

Events including mock interviews, job shadowing, industry nights, resume-writing workshops, and employer presentations occur on a regular basis. The Stags4Hire platform (powered by Handshake) connects students with job opportunities and can help book on-campus interviews. Almost half of recent grads reported that they found their first job through on-campus recruiting/interviewing opportunities during their senior year. Among that same cohort, 600+ individuals participated in internships, and almost one-quarter cited that experience as directly leading to their first full-time employment opportunity. Taking full advantage of their proximity to NYC, Fairfield's career services staff provides all of the internship and employment opportunities one could hope for.

Professional Outcomes

Fairfield's Class of 2022 found its next destination within six months of graduating at a hard-to-beat 98% clip. Healthcare/nursing was the most commonly entered industry (32%), followed by financial services (19%), marketing (12%), science/biotech (7%), and accounting (5%). Many major investment banks, accounting firms, and consulting companies employ large numbers of Fairfield alumni. For example, PwC, Deloitte, Morgan Stanley, JP Morgan Chase & Co., EY, UBS, and Merrill Lynch all employ one hundred or more Stags, and Fairfield grads also have strong representation at IBM, Goldman Sachs, Citi, and Prudential. Thus, it's no wonder that the average starting salary is a healthy $67,054, not including bonuses. Connecticut is not the primary destination for graduates. Rather, New York City attracts the greatest number of alumni with Boston second and Hartford a distant third.

Thirty percent of 2022 grads enrolled directly in graduate or professional school. The breakdown of programs was as follows: business (55%), engineering (13%), and education (10%). The university produces roughly thirty graduates per year who go on to earn their degrees in medicine and dentistry. Medical schools where recent grads have been admitted include Johns Hopkins, Georgetown, and the Albert Einstein College of Medicine. Those headed to law school do so at a range of institutions that includes elite schools like Fordham, Boston College, and Cornell. Graduate schools pursued and attended by Stag alumni run the gamut of selectivity, but those with high GPAs are in the running for a place in elite graduate institutions.

Admission

Applications to the Class of 2026 set a record for the school as over 13,359 lined up for the chance to become a Stag; 52% were admitted, still an unintimidating acceptance rate despite the school's rising reputation. Fairfield is a test-optional school and the vast majority of 2022-23 freshmen were admitted sans test scores. For those who did submit, the mid-50% SAT range was 1260-1360 and the ACT range was 28-31. Thirty percent finished in the top 10% of their high school class and 67% were in the top quartile, but 8% did not land in the top half, giving hope to late bloomers with some blemishes on their transcripts. The average GPA was 3.75, but plenty of students with lower GPAs received acceptance letters; in fact, 15% of accepted students had lower than a 3.25.

The four factors the committee lists as being of supreme importance are rigor of curriculum, GPA, recommendations, and the essay. On the next tier of still "important" factors are an interview, extracurricular activities, first-generation status, character/personal qualities, talent/ability, work experience, volunteer work, and demonstrated interest. It's definitely a good idea to visit campus and interview in order to let the university know you are serious about attending. Fairfield only has a 19% yield rate, meaning that 81% of those accepted into the school do not ultimately enroll. Applying early decision is a good way to punch your ticket to campus as those going the ED route enjoyed an 83% acceptance rate.

Worth Your Money?

On the surface, Fairfield, being a not terribly selective, high-priced private school, is an unlikely candidate for this guide. Yet, Fairfield succeeds where many others in its class fail. For one, thanks to generous merit and need-based aid, even parents in high-income brackets can expect to pay less than the sticker price of $74k. Ninety-five percent of students receive some type of aid, and, with strong graduate outcomes and connections to major corporations, this university could make financial sense for students of all income levels, especially if they have business-related aspirations. However, it is worth noting that the average cumulative debt for Fairfield grads is a bit higher than the national average. Fortunately, high starting salaries make most loans manageable.

FINANCIAL
Institutional Type: Private
In-State Tuition: $56,360
Out-of-State Tuition: $56,360
Room & Board: $17,500
Books & Supplies: $1,175

Avg. Need-Based Grant: $34,712
Avg. % of Need Met: 86%

Avg. Merit-Based Award: $19,178
% Receiving (Freshmen w/o Need): 60%

Avg. Cumulative Debt: $41,297
% of Students Borrowing: 59%

CAREER
Who Recruits
1. FBI
2. Deloitte
3. Ipsos
4. McIntyre Group
5. TEKsystems

Notable Internships
1. Major League Baseball
2. PwC
3. Deutsche Bank

Top Employers
1. PwC
2. Deloitte
3. Morgan Stanley
4. UBS
5. EY

Where Alumni Work
1. New York City
2. Boston
3. Hartford, CT
4. Philadelphia
5. Washington, DC

Earnings
College Scorecard (10-YR Post-Entry): $95,393
PayScale (Early Career): $67,700
PayScale (Mid-Career): $128,500
PayScale 20-Year ROI: $757,000

RANKINGS
Money: 4
U.S. News: 124, National Universities
Wall Street Journal/THE: 124
Washington Monthly: 206, National Universities

OVERGENERALIZATIONS
Students are:
Homogenous
Ready to party
Career-driven
Wealthy
Politically conservative

COLLEGE OVERLAPS
Boston College
Fordham University
Loyola University Maryland
Providence College
Quinnipiac University

Florida State University

Tallahassee, Florida | 850-644-6200

ADMISSION
Admission Rate: 25%
Admission Rate - Men: 25%
Admission Rate - Women: 25%
EA Admission Rate: Not Reported
ED Admission Rate: Not Offered
ED Admits as % of Total Admits: Not Offered
Admission Rate (5-Year Trend): -24%
% of Admits Attending (Yield): 31%
Transfer Admission Rate: 28%

SAT Reading/Writing (Middle 50%): 620-690
SAT Math (Middle 50%): 590-680
ACT Composite (Middle 50%): 26-31

% Graduated in Top 10% of HS Class: 65%
% Graduated in Top 25% of HS Class: 87%
% Graduated in Top 50% of HS Class: 99%

Demonstrated Interest: Not Considered
Legacy Status: Not Considered
Racial/Ethnic Status: Not Considered
Admission Interview Offered: No

ENROLLMENT
Total Undergraduate Enrollment: 32,936
% Full-Time: 90%
% Male: 43%
% Female: 57%
% Out-of-State: 13%
% Fraternity: 17%
% Sorority: 23%
% On-Campus (All Undergraduate): 20%
Freshman Housing Required: No

% African-American: 8%
% Asian: 3%
% Hispanic: 23%
% White: 58%
% Other: 1%
% International: 2%
% Low-Income: 24%

ACADEMICS
Student-to-Faculty Ratio: 17 to 1
% of Classes Under 20: 66%
% of Classes 20-49: 24%
% of Classes 50 or More: 10%
% Full-Time Faculty: 80%
% Full-Time Faculty w/ Terminal Degree: 96%

Top Programs
Accounting
Crimonology
Exercise Physiology
Industrial Engineering
Motion Picture Arts
Marketing
Music
Theatre

Retention Rate: 94%
4-Year Graduation Rate: 74%
6-Year Graduation Rate: 84%

Curricular Flexibility: Somewhat Flexible
Academic Rating: ★★★★

#CollegesWorthYourMoney

Founded in 1851, FSU is one of the state's oldest institutions of higher education as well as one of the nation's finest public research universities. A wide range of baccalaureate degrees—103 to be precise—are available to the school's 32,936 undergraduate students, a group possessing increasingly impressive academic credentials with every passing year. Bound by excellent academics and athletics, FSU's student body and alumni are, with good reason, proud to call themselves Seminoles.

Inside the Classroom
The greater university is comprised of sixteen distinct colleges, and all except the College of Law and College of Medicine offer undergraduate degree programs. All students must meet a number of state and university requirements as they progress through their four years of study. Regardless of academic concentration, thirty-six semester hours of coursework are mandated in the areas of quantitative and logical thinking, English composition, natural sciences, social sciences/history, humanities, cultural practices/ethics, and two semesters of foreign language.

The student-to-faculty ratio is 17:1, which translates into somewhat larger class sizes. Ten percent of sections contain more than fifty students, and 4% have more than 100. However, that is balanced by the 66% of sections that contain fewer than twenty students. Undergraduate research is taken advantage of by one-quarter of students, and the school plans to greatly expand such offerings in the coming years. An abundance of study abroad choices include special summer programs in Panama, Florence, London, and Valencia, Spain. FSU has 60 academic programs available in 20 locations throughout the world; 2,700+ students per year participate.

FSU boasts a number of standout academic programs including those in the College of Motion Picture Arts, the premier film school in the region. The College of Business is extremely well-regarded in the corporate world as its real estate, marketing, accounting, management, and insurance programs are all highly ranked. Twenty-three percent of degrees conferred fall under the business umbrella. The social sciences (15%), psychology (8%), biology (8%), and homeland security (6%) are next in popularity. More Seminoles have landed prestigious postgraduate fellowships in recent years than ever. Nine graduates took home Fulbright Scholarships in 2022 and 15 captured Gilman Scholarships in 2023.

Outside the Classroom
Florida State could easily be called Extrovert U—93% of undergrads participate in at least one on-campus activity. Just about everyone cheers on the Seminole football team as well as seventeen other NCAA Division I teams competing in the esteemed Atlantic Coast Conference (ACC). Forty sports clubs and a thriving intramural program draw widespread participation. The Bobby E. Leach Center offers students recreational amenities including a sixteen-lane pool and indoor track, and all of the exercise equipment one could ever desire. While campus is a sizable 477 acres, only 20% of undergrads—almost exclusively freshmen—live on-site. Greek life is a driving force on campus despite a temporary ban in 2017 after a tragic hazing death. The school has a 23% participation rate across its twenty-six sororities and a 17% participation in its fraternities. Those seeking non-Greek, non-sports activities can pick from one of more than 750 recognized student organizations. Approximately 70% of students become engaged in community service projects at some point during their four years. Club Downunder, a student-run venue in town, brings notable comedy and musical acts to Tallahassee on a regular basis. The Student Life Cinema plays free movies for students six nights a week. Tallahassee offers plenty of nightlife and cultural opportunities and can be easily accessed via public transit.

Career Services
The Career Center at Florida State University employs 40 full-time staff members (not including office assistants) who work in career advising, employer relations, and experiential learning. This student-to-advisor ratio of 823:1 is below average compared to the other institutions included in this book. Of course, the size and scope of the operation are massive, and FSU's Career Center does a solid job of reaching a healthy number of the 33,000 undergraduate students through a variety of means. They even made an incredible 16,220 career advising contacts in a single year.

The university puts on twenty job fairs per year that attract close to 1,000 employers and 3,600 students. Annually, the office puts on 500+ programs/workshops drawing a total audience of greater than 27,000. An impressive 71% of the Class of 2022 completed an internship. Approximately 45% of graduates who found employment credited the Career Center with providing them the lead. Many big-time corporations recruit on campus, including PepsiCo, KPMG, and PricewaterhouseCoopers. Close to 2,500 mock interviews are conducted in an average year. Despite a high student-to-counselor ratio, Florida State's Career Center deploys its resources efficiently, reaching an extremely high percentage of the student body.

Professional Outcomes

Eighty-three percent of job-seeking Seminole grads receive at least one offer of employment within three months of graduation. The top five sectors employing 2022 grads are (in order) finance, technology, marketing, health, and engineering. Employers hiring the greatest number of FSU alumni include Apple, Northrop Grumman, EY, General Motors, and Deloitte. Geographically, the greatest number of alumni remain in Florida but large numbers also relocate to Massachusetts, Georgia, Texas, New York, and California.

Roughly one-third of 2022 Florida State grads elected to immediately pursue admission into an advanced degree program; 75% of those who apply receive at least one acceptance. A typical graduating class sees over 100 students accepted into medical schools and over 200 accepted into law schools. Students enjoy graduate school acceptances at a wide range of state and private universities with some recent alumni landing at prestigious institutions including Emory, Johns Hopkins, MIT, Northwestern, Georgetown, Vanderbilt, and the University of Chicago.

Admission

The acceptance rate into Florida State's Class of 2026 dipped below the 37% mark seen for the Class of 2025 yet again, hitting 25% as the university received a record 78,088 applications. Less than a decade ago, the university received fewer than 30,000 applications and accepted more than half. Enrolled freshmen possessed middle-50% SAT scores of 1220-1360 and ACT scores of 26-31. For perspective, a decade ago, the ranges were 1090-1270 and 23-28, indicating a notable increase in the academic caliber of the average first-year student. A solid 65% of FSU freshmen finished in the top 10% of their high school class; 87% were in the top quarter. A weighted GPA of 4.0 or higher was possessed by 87% of first-year students in 2022-23 and the average GPA was a 4.29.

The admissions committee ranks the rigor of an applicant's secondary school record above all other factors but also strongly weights GPA, standardized test scores (the SAT is the more commonly submitted test), talent/ability, and state residency (out-of-state applicants face tougher prospects and are admitted at half the rate of in-staters). While FSU does not offer a binding early decision option, it does have three deadlines—resident-only early action in October, regular decision in December, and rolling decision in March. For nonresidents, the December deadline is preferable as this early round typically sees higher acceptance rates. Over 80% of attendees are residents of the Sunshine State, and admissions standards are more lax for residents than outsiders. With draws like elite sports, beautiful weather, and an excellent academic reputation, the number of applicants to FSU is likely to continue to rise. Candidates should be mindful of the increasingly selective admissions process and the need to post strong ACT/SAT scores and grades, above all else.

Worth Your Money?

An in-state cost of attendance of just under $26,000 puts places like FSU in the "absurd bargain" category. While the school rarely meets full demonstrated need, it does give average need-based awards of over $10k to qualifying undergrads. Even for the roughly 20% of students who do not have residency status, the out-of-state COA is a reasonable $40k. Attending Florida State and paying $38k per year is especially appealing if you are entering a field in which grads enjoy high average starting salaries like computer science ($66k), engineering ($68k), or math and sciences ($64k).

FINANCIAL
Institutional Type: Public
In-State Tuition: $6,517
Out-of-State Tuition: $21,683
Room & Board: $12,740
Books & Supplies: $1,000

Avg. Need-Based Grant: $10,551
Avg. % of Need Met: 71%

Avg. Merit-Based Award: $3,369
% Receiving (Freshmen w/o Need): 8%

Avg. Cumulative Debt: $18,866
% of Students Borrowing: 36%

CAREER
Who Recruits
1. Grant Thorton LLC
2. Enterprise
3. Aldi
4. Northrop Grumman
5. KPMG

Notable Internships
1. Equifax
2. Walt Disney Company
3. Royal Carribean Cruises

Top Employers
1. IBM
2. Raymond James
3. JPMorgan Chase
4. Amazon
5. Microsoft

Where Alumni Work
1. Tallahassee, FL
2. Miami
3. Tampa
4. Orlando
5. Atlanta

Earnings
College Scorecard (10-YR Post-Entry): $57,007
PayScale (Early Career): $55,100
PayScale (Mid-Career): $100,800
PayScale 20-Year ROI: $458,000

RANKINGS
Money: 4.5
U.S. News: 53, National Universities
Wall Street Journal/THE: 102
Washington Monthly: 54, National Universities

OVERGENERALIZATIONS
Students are:
Crazy about the Seminoles
Laid-back
Friendly
Ready to party
Diverse

COLLEGE OVERLAPS
University of Alabama
University of Central Florida
University of Florida
University of Miami
University of South Florida

Bronx, New York | 718-817-4000

ADMISSION
Admission Rate: 54%
Admission Rate - Men: 48%
Admission Rate - Women: 58%
EA Admission Rate: 58%
ED Admission Rate: 67%
ED Admits as % of Total Admits: 1%
Admission Rate (5-Year Trend): +8%
% of Admits Attending (Yield): 10%
Transfer Admission Rate: 50%

SAT Reading/Writing (Middle 50%): 660-730
SAT Math (Middle 50%): 660-750
ACT Composite (Middle 50%): 30-33

% Graduated in Top 10% of HS Class: 37%
% Graduated in Top 25% of HS Class: 75%
% Graduated in Top 50% of HS Class: 96%

Demonstrated Interest: Considered
Legacy Status: Considered
Racial/Ethnic Status: Considered
Admission Interview Offered: No

ENROLLMENT
Total Undergraduate Enrollment: 10,098
% Full-Time: 98%
% Male: 40%
% Female: 60%
% Out-of-State: 59%
% Fraternity: Not Offered
% Sorority: Not Offered
% On-Campus (All Undergraduate): 47%
Freshman Housing Required: No

% African-American: 5%
% Asian: 13%
% Hispanic: 18%
% White: 50%
% Other: 1%
% International: 7%
% Low-Income: 21%

ACADEMICS
Student-to-Faculty Ratio: 14 to 1
% of Classes Under 20: 52%
% of Classes 20-49: 48%
% of Classes 50 or More: 1%
% Full-Time Faculty: 37%
% Full-Time Faculty w/ Terminal Degree: 94%

Top Programs
Communication and Culture
English
Film and Television
Finance
International Studies
Marketing
Performing Arts
Psychology

Retention Rate: 89%
4-Year Graduation Rate: 79%
6-Year Graduation Rate: 83%

Curricular Flexibility: Somewhat Flexible
Academic Rating: ★★★↲

#CollegesWorthYourMoney

With campuses in both Manhattan and the Bronx, Fordham University, a private Jesuit school with 175+ years of tradition, has hit new heights of popularity and prestige in recent years; it shows no signs of slowing down. As one of the top 25 most expensive schools in the United States, paying for Fordham may be even more challenging than getting accepted. Yet, for those who can afford it, this is a wonderful place to live and learn for four years. Of course, paying back loans becomes easier when you enter a high-paying field like business, which accounts for roughly one-quarter of all degrees conferred.

Inside the Classroom
The university offers more than seventy majors, minors, and pre-professional programs. On their way to earning 124 credits, and regardless of concentration area, all Rams (minus many pursuing a Bachelor of Science) are required to tackle from one to four semesters of foreign language. Freshmen must complete an advanced composition course, Computational Reasoning, Philosophy of Human Nature, Faith and Critical Reason, and one seminar course that focuses on enhancing students' written and oral communication abilities. As students progress to sophomore, junior, and senior years, they are required to tackle additional courses in philosophy, literature, life science, theology, the performing arts, natural science, and ethics.

Fordham's 14:1 student-to-faculty ratio leads to an average class size of 23 students. Some classes will be on the smaller side as 52% of sections contain nineteen or fewer students. Rarely will an undergrad end up in a classroom of more than forty students. A substantial 36% of the student body spends a semester abroad at one of the school's 125 programs in 50+ countries. The undergraduate research program has awarded 1.5 million dollars to students over the last decade and recently saw thirty-eight undergrads obtain coauthor status on professor-published work in a single year.

The university's theater and dance programs are world-renowned for sending countless alumni to Broadway and Hollywood. Gabelli is a top-rated business program with standout programs in international business and finance and serves as a pipeline to many large firms. Other popular areas of study include communications (10%), visual and performing arts (7%), psychology (6%), and biology (5%). Another point of pride is the phenomenal number of graduates who earn competitive national scholarships and fellowships. All-time, Fordham has produced 200+ Fulbright Scholars as well as 650+ total prestigious national scholarships in one recent five-year span.

Outside the Classroom
The undergraduate experience will differ depending on whether you attend the Rose Hill Campus in the Bronx or the Lincoln Center campus in Manhattan. At Lincoln Center, there are two large high-rises that offer every convenience imaginable. Of course, Manhattan has all of the culture, shopping, dining, and entertainment you could ever dream of. The Bronx campus offers 14 residential buildings and is near the New York Botanical Garden, the Bronx Zoo, Yankee Stadium, and Little Italy. Between the two sites, just under half of the student body lives on campus. Greek life at Fordham is a complete non-factor—the university does not have any fraternities or sororities. Instead, 170 student-run organizations provide opportunities for social bonding. Athletics are popular as the Rams field twenty-three teams in NCAA Division I and also run twenty-four club and intramural sports. Over 4,000 students participate in community service each year, contributing over one million collective hours. The school's newspaper, The Observer, enjoys a loyal readership and has garnered widespread praise. Yet, no feature of campus life will play a bigger role in the Fordham experience than its Big Apple location, which opens the doors to limitless possibilities on a daily basis.

Career Services
The Career Services office at Fordham is staffed by 14 professional employees who specialize in areas that include undergraduate counseling and employer relations. There are an additional 10 career services professionals housed in the Gabelli School of Business. That 421:1 student-to-advisor ratio is slightly higher than many of the other schools featured in this guide. In order to reach the masses, the office puts on four career fairs in the fall and two in the spring. Some are specific to areas like finance, STEM, or government while others are more general. The school attempts to engage with students beginning in their freshman year, encouraging first-years to meet one-on-one with an advisor, attend a resume/cover letter workshop, and take personality assessments.

A phenomenal 89% of recent graduates completed at least one internship during their undergraduate years. An examination of how recent graduates found their jobs reveals the following breakdown: internships (16%), Handshake/Career Services (11%), and the alumni network (1%). The vast majority found employment primarily through non-school resources. Yet plenty of opportunities exist to expand one's contacts by taking advantage of the Ram alumni network of over 200,000 individuals embedded in top companies across the globe. Despite a less-than-ideal student-to-counselor ratio and a low percentage of students attributing their job acquisition to the direct efforts of career services, Fordham grads do enjoy better-than-average employment and graduate school outcomes.

Professional Outcomes

Class of 2022 graduates found employment, graduate school, or other meaningful activities at a 96% clip within six months of receiving their degrees. Nearly two-thirds of this group landed employment and enjoyed an average salary of $70,000, higher than the national average. Financial services was, by a large margin, the most common industry followed by advertising, media and communications, health care, and accounting. Significant numbers of 2022 grads found homes at major companies including PwC (36), Ernst & Young (29), KPMG (24), Morgan Stanley (22), and Deloitte (21). A sizable number of graduates also moved into working for nonprofit organizations such as the Jesuit Volunteer Corps, AmeriCorps, or the Peace Corps.

Those aiming for graduate school found homes at a variety of excellent institutions. The greatest number of recent graduates landed at Fordham, NYU, and Columbia. Some also gained acceptance into Penn, Georgetown, Boston University, and George Washington. Law school applicants were successful 95% of the time, a rate 17% higher than the national average. In recent years, Fordham alumni have gone on to Harvard Law School, University of Pennsylvania Law School, Cornell Law School, and Northwestern University School of Law. Those applying to professional health programs, including medical school, gained acceptance at a 76% rate compared to the national average of 45%.

Admission

Fordham offered admission to 54% of the over 47,203 applicants vying for a place in the Class of 2026 versus 46% three years prior. Those who ultimately enrolled possessed a median test score of 1400 and a mean high school GPA of 3.71 on a 4.0 scale. In 2014, a 1400 would have placed you well above the 75th percentile of all Fordham freshmen. Thirty-seven percent of freshmen finished in the top 10% of their high school cohort, and 76% placed in the top quarter; 4% did not place in the top half.

The admissions committee prioritizes the usual factors of rigor of coursework and GPA. In part because it serves as a safety school for many elite students aiming for Ivies or Ivy equivalents, Fordham has an exceptionally low yield rate—10% of admitted students actually enroll. Therefore, demonstrating your genuine interest in attending and applying early decision are strategic moves that serious applicants should consider. ED applications to the university are surprisingly low, but acceptance rates are higher than during the regular cycle—67% for the Class of 2026. Like many schools in Manhattan, Fordham's rising popularity can be best summed up by the real estate cliché of location, location, location. Always a school that required students to have reasonably strong credentials, Fordham is entering a new stratum and is now a viable option for very accomplished students.

Worth Your Money?

An annual total cost of attendance exceeding $85,000 sounds prohibitive, but 90% of incoming students receive some form of aid and the average need-based grant was $31k. Unfortunately, only a small number see 100% of their need covered by the university, but starting salaries tend to be solid, making it worth incurring a moderate amount of debt, particularly for students pursuing study within Fordham's strongest programs, most notably business.

FINANCIAL
Institutional Type: Private
In-State Tuition: $61,567
Out-of-State Tuition: $61,567
Room & Board: $23,075
Books & Supplies: $1,088

Avg. Need-Based Grant: $31,090
Avg. % of Need Met: 71%

Avg. Merit-Based Award: $18,694
% Receiving (Freshmen w/o Need): 6%

Avg. Cumulative Debt: $35,123
% of Students Borrowing: 55%

CAREER
Who Recruits
1. EY
2. Teach for America
3. Standard Motor Products
4. Enterprise
5. Northwestern Mutual

Notable Internships
1. The Philadelphia Zoo
2. NBCUniversal
3. Spotify

Top Employers
1. NYC Department of Education
2. Teach for America
3. NBCUniversal
4. JPMorgan Chase
5. US Army

Where Alumni Work
1. New York City
2. Washington, DC
3. Boston
4. Los Angeles
5. Philadelphia

Earnings
College Scorecard (10-YR Post-Entry): $78,820
PayScale (Early Career): $63,700
PayScale (Mid-Career): $124,800
PayScale 20-Year ROI: $613,000

RANKINGS
Money: 4
U.S. News: 89, National Universities
Wall Street Journal/THE: 185
Washington Monthly: 291, National Universities

OVERGENERALIZATIONS
Students are:
Politically active
More likely to venture off campus
Only a short drive from home (i.e., Most come from NY or nearby states)
Lacking school spirit
Wealthy

COLLEGE OVERLAPS
Binghamton University (SUNY)
Boston College
Boston University
New York University
Villanova University

Franklin & Marshall College

Lancaster, Pennsylvania | 717-358-3953

Situated on the pastoral hills of Lancaster County, Pennsylvania—most famous for its large Amish community—Franklin & Marshall has carved out its own stellar reputation ever since its two namesake colleges merged in 1853. An undergraduate population of 1,990 gets to choose from a generous liberal arts menu that features 60 distinct academic programs. Never content to rest on its laurels, F&M just completed a $200 million fund-raising campaign entitled "Now to Next" that is designed to take this already excellent school to even greater heights. The campaign exceeded its target goal by more than $16 million.

Inside the Classroom
The educational experience at F&M is guided by its "Connections" curriculum, a series of requirements divided into three phases: Introduction, Exploration, and Concentration. Freshmen must take two small, intensive seminar classes that immerse them in the world of intellectual discourse, academic writing, and the art of oral presentation. Next, students tackle courses in the arts, humanities, social and natural sciences, foreign language, and non-Western cultures. As a culminating experience, students complete a capstone project that may involve research alongside a professor.

Franklin & Marshall's student-faculty ratio is 10:1, and 58% of classes have fewer than 20 students enrolled; 40% are in the 20-49 range. The average classroom contains 18 students. Juniors are encouraged to spend a semester abroad, and 50% oblige, jetting off to locations from Argentina to Vietnam. Grants through the Hackman Scholars program allow approximately seventy-five students to conduct research with faculty each summer. Many more Diplomats research with faculty through other means during the academic year and, by graduation, 65% of students have engaged in a one-on-one research experience with a faculty mentor.

The greatest number of degrees conferred at the college are in the social sciences, interdisciplinary studies, biology, and business. Programs in public health and environmental science receive high marks, as does F&M's interdisciplinary major in Business, Organizations and Society (BOS). In addition, students in the official premed program and related majors have experienced a high degree of success in earning acceptance into medical school. F&M students also find success when it comes to securing prestigious fellowships—nine earned Fulbright Scholarships in 2023 while other recent graduates were recently awarded fellowships from Public Policy and International Affairs, Princeton in Asia, and Princeton in Africa.

Outside the Classroom
Lancaster, Pennsylvania, may be notable primarily for its Amish population, but there is a surprisingly large downtown area replete with a full array of shopping, eating, and entertainment options. Those seeking the excitement of a bigger city will have a bit of a car ride ahead of them—Philly is 80 miles away. Being in a relatively remote locale, the center of social life at F&M is on campus where 98% of the student population resides. Greek life is a big part of the Franklin and Marshall tradition, dating back to the school's founding, and it enjoys a robust participation rate of 17% for men and 24% for women. Participation in athletics is also central to campus life. Being a small school and fielding twenty-seven sports teams, mostly in NCAA Division III, translates to over 30% of the student body being comprised of varsity athletes. Outside of sports and frats/sororities, there are roughly one hundred active, student-run organizations that cover everything from a cappella to seven student-run publications. The vast majority of incoming freshmen performed community service in high school, and that practice continues while at F&M through numerous volunteer groups as well as through Greek organizations.

Career Services
The Office of Student and Post Graduate Development (OSPGD), a mouthful to say, is staffed by 12 full-time professionals. That works out to a 166:1 student-to-advisor ratio, which is better than average compared to other schools featured in this guide. Noteworthy for a small liberal arts school, F&M employs expert advisors who specialize in healthcare professions and law school advising so that undergrads on those tracks can receive specialized guidance. In a single academic year, an impressive 2,500+ (more than one per student) one-on-one advising sessions are conducted.

Students seeking a personal touch in advising will appreciate the OPSGD's availability to meet one-on-one to discuss internship opportunities, professional pathways, or graduate school planning. A commendable 93% of seniors engaged with the office each year. Annual Job and Internship Fairs draw roughly eighty employers, and 100+ employers recruit at some point on campus during a single year. The office puts on about 200 events each year with a total attendance of over 3,200. With each student's Handshake account, they also can access a database of 800+ alumni and parent mentors more than happy to dispense career advice. With a high level of engagement and positive graduate outcomes, the OSPGD receives a positive rating from our staff.

Professional Outcomes

Shortly after graduation, 95% of 2022 F&M grads are either employed or continuing their educational journey. The most frequently pursued industries are finance (18%), education (9%), research (9%), and healthcare (8%). Students find work at a cornucopia of interesting companies and organizations from HBO to the Selective Mutism Research Institute to Sotheby's. Across all graduating years, the companies with the greatest number of Diplomats on staff are Morgan Stanley, Deloitte, Vanguard, EY, Merrill Lynch, IBM, Wells Fargo, and Citi. Sixty-two percent of graduates stay in the Northeast and 20% head down South. There are more alumni living in New York City than in Philadelphia. The median salary for Class of 2022 grads was $56,000.

F&M boasts excellent results for premed students. Over a three-year period, 91% of students with at least a 3.4 GPA and a strong MCAT score were accepted into medical school. That includes admission into schools of medicine at Harvard, Yale, Johns Hopkins, Penn, and Georgetown. Those seeking a legal education head to universities such as Villanova, Harvard, William & Mary, NYU, Yale, Tulane, and UC Berkeley. Of the 27% of 2022 graduates furthering their education, there is a genuine mix of prestigious and less prestigious graduate programs, but it is fair to say that excelling at F&M at least puts you in the running for a spot at a top graduate school.

Admission

F&M saw 8,923 applications pour in for a place in the Class of 2026, and 36% were accepted; two years ago, only 30% were admitted. The implementation of a full-blown test-optional strategy could be behind the massive spike. The Class of 2026 possessed mid-50% standardized test scores of 1300-1440 on the SAT and 30-32 on the ACT. F&M continues to place the highest value on rigor of coursework, GPA, class rank, and character/personal qualities. On that last factor, it particularly values athletic participation/leadership; an insanely high percentage of incoming students played a varsity sport in high school. Fifty-two percent of freshmen in the 2022-23 academic year finished in the top 10% of their high school cohort; 78% were in the top 25%.

F&M faces stiff competition for students as it must compete with a high number of other excellent liberal arts schools in PA and the surrounding states. Its yield rate (the percentage of accepted students who enroll) is only 15%, which means the admissions staff is particularly interested in qualified applicants for whom F&M is a top choice. Thus, it is no surprise that the early decision acceptance rate is 58%, far more favorable than that of the regular round; more than half of the 2022-23 freshman cohort came through the ED round. Not a school with a formulaic admissions algorithm, F&M students do typically share two common traits—excellent high school grades and strong interest in attending the college.

Worth Your Money?

Attending Franklin & Marshall will cost you $87k+ per year unless you are among the 58% of undergraduates who demonstrate financial need, in which case you see 100% of your financial need met. The average grant is more than $54,000. Merit-based aid is not offered. Overall, F&M does an admirable job of making the school affordable for those from a wide range of socioeconomic backgrounds. However, middle-to-upper income students who cannot comfortably afford F&M's price and who fail to qualify for significant need-based aid should consider their desired path after college before committing. For everyone else, investing in an F&M degree is likely worth the money.

FINANCIAL
Institutional Type: Private
In-State Tuition: $68,380
Out-of-State Tuition: $68,380
Room & Board: $15,568
Books & Supplies: $1,200

Avg. Need-Based Grant: $53,945
Avg. % of Need Met: 100%

Avg. Merit-Based Award: $11,547
% Receiving (Freshmen w/o Need): <1%

Avg. Cumulative Debt: $29,998
% of Students Borrowing: 54%

CAREER
Who Recruits
1. W.B. Mason
2. The JDK Group
3. Travelers
4. ScribeAmerica
5. S&T Bank

Notable Internships
1. New Jersey Office of the Governor
2. Acacia Finance
3. Audible

Top Employers
1. Morgan Stanley
2. Deloitte
3. UBS
4. Vanguard
5. EY

Where Alumni Work
1. New York City
2. Philadelphia
3. Lancaster, PA
4. Washington, DC
5. Boston

Earnings
College Scorecard (10-YR Post-Entry): $80,452
PayScale (Early Career): $61,600
PayScale (Mid-Career): $129,700
PayScale 20-Year ROI: $568,000

RANKINGS
Money: 4.5
U.S. News: 35, Liberal Arts Colleges
Wall Street Journal/THE: Not Ranked
Washington Monthly: 25, Liberal Arts Colleges

OVERGENERALIZATIONS
Students are:
Diverse
Always studying
Competitive
Involved/invested in campus life
Wealthy

COLLEGE OVERLAPS
Bucknell University
Dickinson College
Gettysburg College
Lafayette College
Lehigh University

Needham, Massachusetts | 781-292-2222

ADMISSION
Admission Rate: 19%
Admission Rate - Men: 12%
Admission Rate - Women: 39%
EA Admission Rate: Not Offered
ED Admission Rate: Not Offered
ED Admits as % of Total Admits: Not Offered
Admission Rate (5-Year Trend): +6%
% of Admits Attending (Yield): 45%
Transfer Admission Rate: 100%

SAT Reading/Writing (Middle 50%): 720-770
SAT Math (Middle 50%): 770-790
ACT Composite (Middle 50%): 35-35

% Graduated in Top 10% of HS Class: NR
% Graduated in Top 25% of HS Class: NR
% Graduated in Top 50% of HS Class: NR

Demonstrated Interest: Very Important
Legacy Status: Considered
Racial/Ethnic Status: Important
Admission Interview Offered: Yes

ENROLLMENT
Total Undergraduate Enrollment: 386
% Full-Time: 92%
% Male: 50%
% Female: 50%
% Out-of-State: 87%
% Fraternity: Not Offered
% Sorority: Not Offered
% On-Campus (All Undergraduate): 99%
Freshman Housing Required: Yes

% African-American: 3%
% Asian: 21%
% Hispanic: 10%
% White: 42%
% Other: 6%
% International: 7%
% Low-Income: 15%

ACADEMICS
Student-to-Faculty Ratio: 8 to 1
% of Classes Under 20: 51%
% of Classes 20-49: 47%
% of Classes 50 or More: 2%
% Full-Time Faculty: 74%
% Full-Time Faculty w/ Terminal Degree: 93%

Top Programs
Electrical and Computer Engineering
Engineering
Mechanical Engineering

Retention Rate: 99%
4-Year Graduation Rate: 82%
6-Year Graduation Rate: 94%

Curricular Flexibility: Somewhat Flexible
Academic Rating: ★★★★★

#CollegesWorthYourMoney

Perhaps the most highly-regarded school of its size in the entire United States, The Franklin W. Olin College of Engineering was founded in the early 2000s as an experimental, cutting-edge training ground for budding engineers. Today, this Boston-area institution has an undergraduate enrollment of 386 students who are every bit as brilliant as the talent at Caltech or MIT. Academically, there is only one item on the menu here but, boy, is it delicious. Every single degree conferred at Olin has "engineering" in its name: electrical and computer engineering, mechanical engineering, or general engineering with a concentration area such as bioengineering, computing, or design and robotics.

Inside the Classroom

No matter one's major, all students must take a collection of core courses that the college deems essential to its mission, giving its students the engineering toolkit needed to "have a positive impact in the real world." Those required classes are tied to three interconnected themes: Design and Entrepreneurship, Modeling and Analysis, and Systems and Control. Students also work through a concentration in either the arts and humanities or entrepreneurship that can be completed at partner colleges Brandeis, Wellesley, or Babson. Unlike most engineering schools where students knock out a laundry list of math and science requirements before taking a deep dive into their engineering-specific coursework, Olin students take three such courses in their first semester.

Many classes are taught in a studio environment to encourage collaboration, and a number of courses are co-taught by professors from different disciplines. Classes are generally reasonably small; 51% of class sections contain fewer than twenty students. The school's terrific 8:1 student-to-faculty ratio translates into an enormous amount of individualized attention and invitations to participate in research. Students can easily track down current research projects and contact information on the school's website and can obtain funding for their efforts via the Undergraduate Research Fund. Additionally, students can elect to take advantage of study abroad programs in 35 foreign locations. Half of students ultimately do spend a semester in a foreign country, a notably high percentage for an engineering school.

As chronicled in more detail in our "Professional Outcomes" section, the Franklin W. Olin College of Engineering may not be a household name for the average American, but employers and elite graduate schools adore its graduates every bit as much as those from Stanford or Carnegie Mellon. For such an incredibly small school, Olin graduates annually take home a number of prestigious awards. In fact, the school has already produced 20+ Fulbright students in its short history. Eight recent grads were named Grand Challenge Scholars by the National Academy of Engineers.

Outside the Classroom

Not far from Wellesley and Babson, Olin College of Engineering's Needham locale places it less than 20 miles outside of Boston. It features a 70-acre campus lined with buildings as new as the college itself. Nearly all students reside on campus in one of two residence halls. No frats or sororities operate at this institution. There are no NCAA sports because it would be interesting to field teams from a pool of 386 engineering geniuses. However, thanks to agreements forged with nearby schools, Olin students can participate in intramural leagues at Babson or Wellesley. Additionally, Olin does field its own intercollegiate soccer and ultimate Frisbee teams. Fans of the outdoors can connect with hiking trails on campus as well as around Needham and the town of Wellesley. There are plenty of student-run clubs with an engineering/innovation emphasis, including the Olin robotic sailing team that competes in global competitions, Olin Baja—a vehicle design competition, and AERO—a drone and plane designing team. Historic Needham is a safe suburb with plenty of restaurants, shops, museums, and cultural events.

Career Services

The Office of Postgraduate Planning consists of three professional employees, equating to a superior student-to-advisor ratio of 129:1, among the best of any school in the country. The office's mission is aligned with that of the school's—to assist future engineers in finding meaningful opportunities for hands-on training. This mission is accomplished to the tune of 100% of recent grads having had a technical internship or research experience; 91% had more than one such experience. The Fall Career Fair is attended by more than 50 top companies. Given that this works out to about one company for every two seniors, this attendance is extraordinary and speaks to how desirable Olin students are in the eyes of employers.

With only 16 years' worth of graduates, the total alumni base has barely crossed the 1,000 mark—but the industry connections made via the school's Corporate Partners Program open countless doors. In the past year, undergrads landed internships at organizations including Tesla, Bose, GE, Microsoft, and Google. Thanks to a focus on experiential learning, ample industry connections, and exceptional starting salaries for grads, Olin's career services is held in high esteem by our staff.

Professional Outcomes

For a school exclusively graduating engineers, it isn't a surprise that alumni tend to find good-paying jobs. The average starting salary for recent graduates is in excess of $93,000. Electrical and computer engineers earn the most while mechanical engineers are at the "low" end of the spectrum. Over the past decade, the companies employing the greatest number of alumni are Google, Microsoft, athenahealth, Apple, and Amazon. In recent years, Epic, Tesla, and Meta all hired more than one Olin graduate. While a majority of graduates find work in Massachusetts, a large number also migrate to California where Silicon Valley welcomes them with open arms.

Olin College of Engineering undergrads have gone on to prestigious graduate engineering programs in impressive numbers. Since 2006, more than twenty graduates have gone to Stanford, MIT, and Harvard. The school also has sent double-digit numbers of alumni to Carnegie Mellon, Cornell, and Berkeley. Perusing the lists of graduate school acceptances, it is rare that anyone attends anything less than one of the world's most prestigious institutions. The majority of those hopping right into advanced studies are pursuing PhDs.

Admission

The 74 freshmen in the Class of 2026 are an impressive group, no matter the metric. With an average unweighted GPA of 3.91 and middle 50% standardized test scores of 1500-1550 on the SAT and the median score is a 35 on the ACT, Olin students are nothing shy of Ivy caliber. In selecting the 2022-23 freshman class, the school's acceptance rate was 19%, but it has dipped as low as 13% in recent years.

Applicants can rest assured that they will be viewed in three dimensions as a number of factors beyond grades and test scores are considered "very important" to the admissions committee. Those include essays, recommendations, interview, extracurricular activities, talent/ability, character/personal qualities, and level of demonstrated interest in the college. In fact, those considerations all rate ahead of standardized test results. Yet, consideration of those traditional factors is only half of the acceptance process. Each year, roughly 225-250 applicants are selected by Olin College of Engineering to visit during a Candidates' Weekend—a process closer to how most schools hire faculty than select their undergraduates. The prospective students are put through a design challenge, an individual interview, and a group exercise to help evaluate which students would bring the most to and benefit the most from the Olin College of Engineering. Getting into Olin is a marathon; it is not a school you even apply to unless you are 100% committed to attending. Elite academic prowess is only one of many prerequisites for consideration to join this small but potent engineering juggernaut.

Worth Your Money?

The total annual cost of attendance (COA) at Franklin W. Olin is $86,474, but no one pays that price as 100% of enrolled students are awarded an Olin Tuition Scholarship of $27k. Forty-four percent also receive need-based assistance, and the grant and scholarship amounts can be as high as the full annual COA. Even if you don't receive one of the larger aid packages, you're always safe investing in a college where the average starting salary exceeds the annual cost of attending. Olin is such a school, and with engineering being the only pathway, you are just about guaranteed a solid return on your educational investment.

FINANCIAL
Institutional Type: Private
In-State Tuition: $61,802
Out-of-State Tuition: $61,802
Room & Board: $19,820
Books & Supplies: $216

Avg. Need-Based Grant: $54,775
Avg. % of Need Met: 99%

Avg. Merit-Based Award: $28,399
% Receiving (Freshmen w/o Need): 56%

Avg. Cumulative Debt: $19,911
% of Students Borrowing: 34%

CAREER
Who Recruits
1. Cognex Corporation
2. Ford Motor Company
3. General Electric
4. Watts
5. Tableau

Notable Internships
1. Ford Motor Company
2. Raytheon
3. Tableau Software

Top Employers
1. Google
2. Microsoft
3. Apple
4. athenahealth
5. Skydio

Where Alumni Work
1. Boston
2. San Francisco
3. Seattle
4. New York City
5. Los Angeles

Earnings
College Scorecard (10-YR Post-Entry): $116,968
PayScale (Early Career): Not Reported
PayScale (Mid-Career): Not Reported
PayScale 20-Year ROI: Not Reported

RANKINGS
Money: Not Ranked
U.S. News: Not Ranked
Wall Street Journal/THE: Not Ranked
Washington Monthly: Not Ranked

OVERGENERALIZATIONS
Students are:
Tight-knit (possess a strong sense of community)
Always studying
Intellectual
Politically liberal
Passionate about their interests

COLLEGE OVERLAPS
Cornell University
Georgia Institute of Technology
Harvey Mudd College
Massachusetts Institute of Technology
University of California, Berkeley

Furman University

Greenville, South Carolina | 864-294-2034

ADMISSION
Admission Rate: 67%
Admission Rate - Men: 62%
Admission Rate - Women: 71%
EA Admission Rate: Not Reported
ED Admission Rate: 41%
ED Admits as % of Total Admits: 2%
Admission Rate (5-Year Trend): +6%
% of Admits Attending (Yield): 13%
Transfer Admission Rate: 32%

SAT Reading/Writing (Middle 50%): 640-730
SAT Math (Middle 50%): 620-725
ACT Composite (Middle 50%): 28-33

% Graduated in Top 10% of HS Class: 39%
% Graduated in Top 25% of HS Class: 75%
% Graduated in Top 50% of HS Class: 93%

Demonstrated Interest: Considered
Legacy Status: Considered
Racial/Ethnic Status: Considered
Admission Interview Offered: No

ENROLLMENT
Total Undergraduate Enrollment: 2,283
% Full-Time: 99%
% Male: 41%
% Female: 59%
% Out-of-State: 69%
% Fraternity: 26%
% Sorority: 49%
% On-Campus (All Undergraduate): 96%
Freshman Housing Required: Yes

% African-American: 6%
% Asian: 4%
% Hispanic: 6%
% White: 77%
% Other: 1%
% International: 4%
% Low-Income: 15%

ACADEMICS
Student-to-Faculty Ratio: 9 to 1
% of Classes Under 20: 78%
% of Classes 20-49: 22%
% of Classes 50 or More: 0%
% Full-Time Faculty: 80%
% Full-Time Faculty w/ Terminal Degree: 95%

Top Programs
Biology
Business Administration
Communication Studies
Philosophy
Politics and International Affairs
Public Health
Religion

Retention Rate: 87%
4-Year Graduation Rate: 78%
6-Year Graduation Rate: 83%

Curricular Flexibility: Somewhat Flexible
Academic Rating: ★★★⁀

#CollegesWorthYourMoney

Young people from 44 states and 29 countries are among the 2,283 undergraduates presently enrolled at Furman University in Greenville, South Carolina, the state's oldest private university. What draws such a diverse group of people to the foothills of the Blue Ridge Mountains is an immensely personal in-class educational opportunity with an equal focus on experiential learning and near-universal student involvement outside of the classroom. Make no mistake: this school has a "university" label, but it hosts only 160 graduate students. Furman is a top-notch, yet not uber-exclusive, Southern liberal arts school with a litany of impressive statistics from its freshman retention rate to its tremendous postgraduate outcomes.

Inside the Classroom
At Furman, undergrads have the choice of 70+ academic programs, all in the liberal arts and sciences realm. General education requirements are fairly extensive, but they also allow room for flexibility within certain umbrella categories. All undergrads must complete two writing courses, two global awareness courses, and 11 core courses. The core includes forays into the natural world, human behavior, historical analysis, interpreting texts, mathematical and formal reasoning, the visual and performing arts, and the completion of a foreign language through the 201 level. (Where you start depends on placement tests.)

The vast majority of courses at Furman take place in an intimate classroom environment. A 9:1 student-to-faculty ratio and very few graduate students lead to an average class size of just 14 students. One-fifth of sections have only a single-digit enrollment, and 99% of courses enroll fewer than 29; giant lecture halls don't even exist at this university. The school is consistently rated highly for professor accessibility and undergraduate teaching. Ninety-two percent of the recent grads participated in at least one of what the university calls a "high impact practice," which includes a research experience, an internship, or a term studying abroad.

Standout programs at this school include business, public health, and politics and international affairs. The social sciences are the area in which most degrees are conferred (13%) followed by business (10%), communication/journalism (9%), and biology (8%). Furman is a prolific producer of Fulbright Scholars having seen four members of the Class of 2022 capture the award. In the school's history, it has produced 50+ Fulbright Scholars and six Rhodes Scholars.

Outside the Classroom
Pretty much everyone lives on campus, either in the dorms or Greek houses; 99% of the entire undergraduate student body lives in college-owned housing. There are seven sororities and five fraternities on campus that attract 49% of women and 26% of men. Furman's 18 Division I athletic teams, 20+ club teams, and ample intramural leagues ensure that just about everyone is involved in some recreational activity. The 96,000-square-foot Trone Student Center serves as a hub for the school's 150+ student organizations. The school features everything from a notably active student government to a popular Esports club. However, the largest organization is the Heller Service Corps, which facilitates community service participation for over 1,800 students each year. Furman's beautifully designed 750-acre campus is among the nation's most admired. On-campus features include a lake, a 16,000-seat football stadium, an 18-hole golf course, a pool, and a newly renovated science complex that features a planetarium. The city of Greenville (population 73,000) also receives high grades for its affordable housing, "foodie" reputation, and endless opportunities for outdoor recreation.

Career Services
The Malone Center for Career Engagement has eight professional employees who work in advising and employer engagement capacities. This works out to a 285:1 student-to-advisor ratio, which is very solid compared to similarly sized institutions featured in this guide. As such, the staff are able to genuinely encourage each student to stop by to explore careers or grad programs, and the center offers almost daily events. In one week in September, the center hosts a prelaw workshop on how to apply to law school, an alumni chat on careers in consulting, and a seminar on pitching yourself to startups.

Thanks in part to the fact that it provides 1:1 assistance in the internship search, a solid 72% of students complete at least one such experience during their four years. The Malone Center's ability to facilitate so many meaningful internships yields dividends in terms of future employment satisfaction. The Class of 2021 boasted an 89% satisfaction rate in terms of their postgraduate employment plans, and 95% of those continuing their education were pleased with those plans. Paladins also enjoy helping other Paladins, and an alumni network of 30,000+ active members can assist current students as they search for ways to get a foot in the door of just about any industry/company.

Professional Outcomes

Recent first destination surveys reveal some highly encouraging results, starting with the fact that 95% of grads quickly achieved positive outcomes with 49% employed, 35% continuing their education, 4% working and attending graduate school, 3% engaged in volunteer work or joining the military, and only 5% still seeking employment. The greatest number of students entered the education/nonprofit sector (18%), followed by marketing/sales (18%), health care (13%), accounting/finance (11%), and business/consulting (10%). Companies that employ a large number of Paladin alums include Wells Fargo, EY, Deloitte, Bank of America, Michelin, and PwC. Recent grads have also found their way to SpaceX, the PGA Tour, and the US Department of Commerce. Furman alumni can be found in large numbers in the Greenville, South Carolina, area, as well as Atlanta; Charlotte; Washington, DC; and New York City.

Furman graduates tend to pursue an advanced or professional degree very quickly after earning their bachelor's degree. Among recent grads, 27% were studying in a health-related field, 14% were pursuing a business degree, 13% were in a science and engineering program, and 7% were in law school. Over the past decade, medical school applicants from the university with at least a 3.5 GPA have been accepted into at least one program at a 79% clip, almost double the national average. Since 2006, the school has seen alumni matriculate at elite medical schools including Columbia, Duke, Harvard, Johns Hopkins, and Yale. Prelaw students have found similar success, enjoying a 90% acceptance rate and beginning their legal training at the likes of UVA, Berkeley, and Duke.

Admission

Out of 7,510 applications received for a place in the Class of 2026, Furman offered 5,033 students an invitation to join the 2022-23 freshman class. This equates to an acceptance rate of 67%. Only 13% of accepted students went on to enroll. Middle-50% SAT scores were 1280-1435; the ACT range was 27-32. The average GPA was 3.66. Thirty-nine percent of last year's freshmen hailed from the top decile of their high school class, and 75% placed in the top quartile.

Furman places the greatest emphasis on the rigor of one's secondary school record, followed by class rank, GPA, essays, extracurricular activities, and character/personal qualities. Furman is a test-optional institution but will consider any submitted scores (29% of attending students submitted SATs, and 31% submitted ACTs). Additional factors that will be considered by the admissions committee are recommendations, an interview, talent/ability, legacy, first-generation status, racial/ethnic status, volunteer work, work experience, and the level of an applicant's interest. Applying early decision is one way to communicate that you are passionate about becoming a Paladin, yet, it wasn't of much help to Class of 2026 applicants—just 41% of ED applicants gain acceptance. If your devotion isn't quite at ED-level, applying early action is a wise move.

Worth Your Money?

Furman's total cost of attendance for the 2023-24 academic year, including tuition, room and board, books, transportation, and personal expenses, is an estimated $74k. Thirty-five percent of recent grads borrowed money to pay tuition, and the average cumulative debt is right around the national average. We would not recommend borrowing more than that to attend Furman unless you were majoring in business or had a clear plan that would lead to a high enough starting salary to make debt repayment manageable. Fortunately, the school does provide average merit awards of $27k and need-based awards of $40k, making Furman a more affordable choice for some.

FINANCIAL
Institutional Type: Private
In-State Tuition: $58,312
Out-of-State Tuition: $58,312
Room & Board: $15,868
Books & Supplies: $1,000

Avg. Need-Based Grant: $39,590
Avg. % of Need Met: 88%

Avg. Merit-Based Award: $26,764
% Receiving (Freshmen w/o Need): 46%

Avg. Cumulative Debt: $34,145
% of Students Borrowing: 35%

CAREER
Who Recruits
1. Wells Fargo
2. Merrill Lynch
3. S&P Global
4. Prisma Health
5. PwC

Notable Internships
1. Manhattan Institute
2. W.W. Norton
3. Salesforce

Top Employers
1. Greenville County Schools
2. Wells Fargo
3. US Army
4. Prisma Health
5. Clemson University

Where Alumni Work
1. Atlanta
2. Charlotte
3. Washington, DC
4. New York City
5. Columbia, SC

Earnings
College Scorecard (10-YR Post-Entry): $60,889
PayScale (Early Career): $55,400
PayScale (Mid-Career): $109,200
PayScale 20-Year ROI: $470,000

RANKINGS
Money: 4
U.S. News: 46, Liberal Arts Colleges
Wall Street Journal/THE: 233
Washington Monthly: 87, Liberal Arts Colleges

OVERGENERALIZATIONS
Students are:
More likely to rush a fraternity/sorority
Politically conservative
Wealthy
Involved/invested in campus life
Working hard and playing hard

COLLEGE OVERLAPS
Clemson University
Elon University
University of South Carolina
Wake Forest University
Wofford College

George Mason University

Fairfax, Virginia | 703-993-2400

If you had to describe George Mason University in five adjectives or less, large, public, affordable, career-focused, and politically conservative (the Koch brothers are/were major donors) would be apt selections. Outsiders sometimes find the number of GMU students surprising; there are 39,000+ of them, 27,014 of whom are undergraduates. The high number of commuters can hide the actual scope of the university, which features ten undergraduate schools and colleges and approximately seventy distinct academic programs. You can get a sense of the pre-professional feel of the student body simply by examining the areas where the greatest number of degrees are conferred. Business (20%) is followed by computer and information sciences (13%), the social sciences (8%), health professions (8%), and homeland security (8%).

Inside the Classroom
Mason aims to make every one of its graduates an "engaged citizen and well-rounded scholar who is prepared to act." Toward that goal, it requires a journey through the "Mason Core," a forty-three-credit collection of foundation, exploration, and integration requirements. Among the mandatory topics one must tackle are written communication, oral communication, and quantitative reasoning as well as information technology, literature, arts, natural sciences, and other liberal arts staples. That trek will take you the equivalent of three full semesters. The Honors College requires twelve additional credits.

As a result of a 16:1 student-to-faculty ratio and 12,000 graduate students, class sizes at GMU are rarely small, but it tends to be a mixed bag, and many sections do feature relatively modest numbers. Fifty-two percent of sections enroll nineteen or fewer students, 13% have fifty or more students, and the remaining sections lie in between. More intimate educational experiences can be sought in the form of undergraduate research, which roughly half of all students ultimately engage in (in some form). There are plenty of summer research opportunities, but you can also take courses designated as Discovery of Scholarship, Scholarly Inquiry, or Research & Scholarship Intensive that offer built-in supervised research. Presently, only 10% of GMU students study abroad, but the school does sponsor 140+ programs, including travel to the school's own international campus in South Korea.

The Volgenau College of Engineering, which houses a top-tier Information Technology Department, and the School of Business are both extremely reputable in the eyes of prospective employers, and the school's Northern Virginia location allows many connections with industry to be forged via internships and face-to-face recruiting opportunities. Recent grads have also captured a growing number of prestigious fellowships and scholarships. A few years back, five students won Fulbright Scholarships; a solid number have also captured Boren Awards in recent years.

Outside the Classroom
In the 2022-23 school year, 21% of the overall undergraduate population resides in on-campus housing. There are many students who commute and/or live in (sometimes) cheaper off-campus housing in Arlington, Falls Church, Annandale, or Manassas. Because roughly 80% of GMU students are Virginia residents, they are usually in fairly close proximity to their families. Greek life exists but doesn't dominate; 3% of men join frats, and 4% of women join sororities. While DC isn't exactly in your backyard at Mason, it is like having a beautiful park right down the street. The heart of the city is only fifteen miles from campus. Meanwhile, the 677 wooded acres that comprise the school's grounds are home to 500+ student-run clubs. There are hundreds of events to attend for free at the Center for the Arts, organic gardens that can be fully utilized by students, two pools, and loads of intramural and club sports. On the more serious athletic front, the Patriots' 500+ student-athletes compete in 22 NCAA Division I sports with a men's basketball team good enough to have made a Final Four run this millennium. The Hub Student Center is another place where a student body with a large contingent of commuters can coalesce and mingle, but surveys indicate that, at present, the social scene at Mason has room for improvement. Seniors offer much lower ratings of indicators like "sense of belonging" and "involvement in campus activities" than the quality of academic instruction they received.

Career Services
George Mason University Career Services employs 25 professionals (not including office assistants, the webmaster, or peer advisors). Roles include employer outreach, industry advisor, career counselor, and career fair manager. That works out to a 1,080:1 student-to-advisor ratio, poorer than the average ratio when compared to other institutions included in this guidebook but not altogether unusual for a school of Mason's size. The career services staff still manages to help more than 20,000 unique students each year—close to 80% of all undergraduate students—which is impressive.

This level of outreach helps to explain why, among employed Class of 2022 members, 89% were in jobs that aligned with their career goals. Some connections are made through fall and spring career fairs that draw 150 employers and 1,500+ students each semester. In total, 700+ employers recruit at Mason, and more than 180 career programs and hiring events were held last year. The internship outlook is aided by the prime location of the university as well as cultivated relationships with many companies. There are 15 Fortune 500 companies and, of course, every government agency within a stone's throw. Roughly three-fifths of students land at least one internship. Over 200,000 Mason alumni, who are mainly concentrated in the Beltway area, also greatly aid the job and internship hunt.

Professional Outcomes

Six months after receiving their degrees, 87% of the class of 2022 had accepted a job offer or started work in a graduate program. The most commonly entered industries were consulting/finance, government, technology, healthcare, and education. GMU grads flow into major consulting firms like Booz Allen Hamilton, Deloitte, and Accenture, financial institutions like Capital One and Freddie Mac, and engineering/tech firms like General Dynamics, IBM, and Microsoft. Recent graduates also secured employment at Disney, MITRE, KPMG, NASA, and the United States Senate. The vast majority of recent grads stay in the area as 86% work in DC, Virginia, or Maryland. New York City and San Francisco also have sizable numbers of Mason alumni. Including bonuses, the median first-year salary for a GMU grad is $72,000.

George Mason is presently conducting a feasibility study for creating its own medical college. In the meantime, it offers two guaranteed admissions, joint-degree programs with Virginia Commonwealth University and George Washington University. George Mason does have its own institution for legal education—the Antonin Scalia Law School—and it offers a 3+3 bachelor's/JD program. Across all disciplines, Mason graduates tend to pursue advanced degrees either at Mason itself or at other area schools including George Washington, American University, or the University of Maryland. They have also sent a fair number of students to elite graduate programs at NYU, UVA, Emory, and Berkeley.

Admission

At 90%, George Mason has one of the highest acceptance rates of any school featured in this guide, making it an excellent choice for someone with less-than-stellar credentials but a desire to attend a school with tremendous resources. The school is test-optional and the majority of enrolled students take advantage of the policy. The mid-50% ranges were 1140-1350 on the SAT and 25-31 on the ACT. Only 15% of 2022-23 freshmen placed in the top 10% of their high school class, 43% were in the top quartile, and 77% were in the top half. The average GPA was 3.7, but approximately one-third were below 3.5, giving hope to those who may have hit some bumps along their academic road.

GMU values the rigor of one's high school courses and the GPA earned above all else. Intangibles like talent & ability come next. There are no interviews offered as part of the process, nor is there an option for binding early decision. An early action deadline of November 1 will get students a decision by December 15. Entry to Mason is competitive, but compared to many other schools of its class, the bar is easier to clear.

Worth Your Money?

As a state resident, George Mason is an unequivocal steal at just a shade under $14,000 in tuition. Out-of-staters will pay more than three times as much, making it a question of (a) will Mason provide me with significantly better academics/job prospects than public universities in my own state, and (b) will my potential area of study warrant the extra cost? For example, an applicant from Pennsylvania intent on majoring in education would be unlikely to get a solid return on investment depending, of course, on the degree of merit and need-based aid.

FINANCIAL
Institutional Type: Public
In-State Tuition: $13,812
Out-of-State Tuition: $37,976
Room & Board: $15,151
Books & Supplies: $1,278

Avg. Need-Based Grant: $9,616
Avg. % of Need Met: 70%

Avg. Merit-Based Award: $6,787
% Receiving (Freshmen w/o Need): 12%

Avg. Cumulative Debt: $31,190
% of Students Borrowing: 53%

CAREER
Who Recruits
1. CoStar
2. BAE Systems
3. Andersen Tax
4. Boeing
5. Black Horse

Notable Internships
1. Verizon
2. Cisco
3. BAE Systems

Top Employers
1. Booz Allen Hamilton
2. Deloitte
3. Northrop Grumman
4. Capital One
5. Freddie Mac

Where Alumni Work
1. Washington, DC
2. New York City
3. Richmond, VA
4. San Francisco
5. Baltimore

Earnings
College Scorecard (10-YR Post-Entry): $69,958
PayScale (Early Career): $63,500
PayScale (Mid-Career): $115,100
PayScale 20-Year ROI: $704,000

RANKINGS
Money: 4.5
U.S. News: 105, National Universities
Wall Street Journal/THE: 95
Washington Monthly: 91, National Universities

OVERGENERALIZATIONS
Students are:
Diverse
More likely to go home on weekends
Career-driven
Lacking school spirit
Practical

COLLEGE OVERLAPS
James Madison University
University of Maryland, College Park
University of Virginia
Virginia Commonwealth University
Virginia Tech

Washington, District of Columbia | 202-994-6040

ADMISSION
Admission Rate: 49%
Admission Rate - Men: 52%
Admission Rate - Women: 47%
EA Admission Rate: Not Offered
ED Admission Rate: 66%
ED Admits as % of Total Admits: 6%
Admission Rate (5-Year Trend): +8%
% of Admits Attending (Yield): 22%
Transfer Admission Rate: 34%

SAT Reading/Writing (Middle 50%): 670-740
SAT Math (Middle 50%): 660-750
ACT Composite (Middle 50%): 31-34

% Graduated in Top 10% of HS Class: 44%
% Graduated in Top 25% of HS Class: 78%
% Graduated in Top 50% of HS Class: 96%

Demonstrated Interest: Considered
Legacy Status: Considered
Racial/Ethnic Status: Considered
Admission Interview Offered: No

ENROLLMENT
Total Undergraduate Enrollment: 11,482
% Full-Time: 95%
% Male: 37%
% Female: 63%
% Out-of-State: 96%
% Fraternity: 9%
% Sorority: 12%
% On-Campus (All Undergraduate): 62%
Freshman Housing Required: Yes

% African-American: 8%
% Asian: 14%
% Hispanic: 13%
% White: 50%
% Other: 2%
% International: 9%
% Low-Income: 16%

ACADEMICS
Student-to-Faculty Ratio: 12 to 1
% of Classes Under 20: 57%
% of Classes 20-49: 32%
% of Classes 50 or More: 10%
% Full-Time Faculty: 44%
% Full-Time Faculty w/ Terminal Degree: 95%

Top Programs
Communication
Criminal Justice
Finance
Interior Architecture
International Affairs
International Business
Political Science
Public Health

Retention Rate: 90%
4-Year Graduation Rate: 79%
6-Year Graduation Rate: 84%

Curricular Flexibility: Somewhat Flexible
Academic Rating: ★★★★

#CollegesWorthYourMoney

Appropriately located only four blocks from the White House, the university named after our nation's first president educates 11,482 undergraduate students and an additional 14,500 graduate students. One of the pricier schools in the United States, George Washington University, nevertheless, has rarely been in higher demand since its founding in 1821. Thanks to the popularity of DC as a college setting and a number of highly regarded academic programs, GW has become increasingly selective, catering to a more talented group of students today than it did at the turn of the millennium.

Inside the Classroom

GW undergraduates choose from 75+ majors spread across nine colleges: the Columbian College of Arts & Sciences, Corcoran School of the Arts & Design, School of Business, School of Engineering & Applied Science, Elliot School of International Affairs, School of Media & Public Affairs, School of Medicine & Health Sciences, School of Nursing, and the Milken Institute School of Public Health. All GW students must complete one course in mathematics or statistics, one course in natural and/or physical laboratory sciences, two courses in social sciences, one course in humanities, and two writing-intensive courses. From there, another set of college/major-specific requirements follow, but general education requirements tend not to be overly restrictive.

The school's 12:1 student-to-faculty ratio translates to a mix of small, medium, and large undergraduate sections. Twelve percent of courses have single-digit enrollments, 10% have over 50 students, and the majority fall in the 10 to 29 range. In recent years, the university has invested in increasing the number of undergraduate research experiences available to its students through the GW Center for Undergraduate Research and Fellowships. The efforts are paying off as 400 undergrads now present at the GW Research Days, a two-day event held in April. Close to half of Colonials study abroad for one semester in Europe (65%), Asia (10%), Latin America (8%), Africa (7%), or Australia (6%).

Standout programs at GW include political science, international affairs, communications, and public health. Any degree earned from the university will serve students well when they vie for positions at top companies and elite graduate schools. The social sciences (31%) are the area in which the greatest number of degrees are awarded followed by health professions (17%), business (15%), biology (5%), and computer science (5%). A service-oriented institution, GW is proudly the number one producer of Peace Corps volunteers among mid-size universities, and it also churns out Teach for America members at one of the highest rates in the country. Eighteen students were named Fulbright Scholars in 2023, and GW sported a higher Fulbright acceptance rate than Harvard, Princeton, or Columbia in recent years.

Outside the Classroom

Freshmen and sophomores are required to live in one of 26 residence halls situated on the university's two campuses. Three-quarters of freshmen reside at the main Foggy Bottom campus, and the other 25% of first-years live at the Mount Vernon campus which is three miles away in Northwest DC. In a typical year, only 9-12% of students are Greek-affiliated, making fraternities and sororities only modestly powerful social forces at GW. The school's robust sports program includes 27 NCAA Division I teams. An additional 1,000 students participate in club sports, and the intramural programs scoop up the rest of the athletically inclined undergrads. The 500+ registered student organizations collectively offer 1,200 leadership positions, and 87% of undergraduates are involved with at least one group. Noteworthy guest speakers appear with regularity through the GW Speaker Series. Of course, what's on campus is only the first layer of recreational opportunities at George Washington. The Foggy Bottom campus is only a few miles from the National Mall and many of the best museums in the country. As a bridge between the school and outside city, GW's flexible meal plans allow you to visit ninety partner restaurants, cafes, and grocery stores around DC. At GW, your life outside the classroom can involve every corner of the District of Columbia.

Career Services

The Center for Career Services is staffed by 32 full-time employees, including nine individuals with the title of career coach as well as other professionals focusing on employer relations and graduate school advising. These figures include separate career centers for business and engineering schools. That calculates to a student-advisor ratio of 359:1, within the average range of institutions profiled in this guide.

Personalized career coaching is readily available. The office receives high marks from students as 95% of recent grads agreed that career programs had helped enhance their career development. Sixty-five percent of Class of 2022 grads participated in at least one internship. In a single school year, more than 900 employers engage with current GW students and more than 36,000 global connections were available within the GW Alumni Association LinkedIn group.

Internships are completed by two-thirds of undergraduates and over half are either paid or awarded a stipend for their work. Thanks to the university's far-reaching connections and prime location, internships are procured at thousands of different companies/organizations each year, from the US Congress to the Smithsonian to the NFL Players Association. The school also enjoys an alumni base of over 250,000 which leads to ample opportunities for networking. In sum, the Center for Career Services does a solid job facilitating internships and utilizing its DC locale and huge, well-connected alumni base to produce decent outcomes for its graduates.

Professional Outcomes
Within six months of leaving GW, 96% of the Class of 2022 had found their way to gainful employment or graduate school while 4% were still job hunting. Of the 68% of grads already in the workplace, 68% were in a for-profit industry, 25% had entered a nonprofit position, and 8% were working in government. Fifty-two percent of grads earned a starting salary in excess of $60k, while an additional 35% earned between $40k and $60k. Over three-quarters of recent grads remained in the Mid-Atlantic region with the West and Mountain regions a distant second.

A healthy 27% of those earning their diplomas in 2022 immediately turned their attention to earning an advanced degree. Among that group were 76% seeking master's degrees, 11% entering law school, 5% pursuing a medical degree, and 3% entering a doctoral program. Looking at recent grads, 1,107 students have continued their studies at George Washington. The next most commonly attended institutions were Columbia University (93), Georgetown (89), Johns Hopkins (78), NYU (56), and American University (54).

Admission
Of the 27,266 Class of 2026 hopefuls, GW admitted 13,354 for an acceptance rate of 49%. That number has shown volatility over current attendees' lifetimes, hitting as low as 32% in 2010 and as high as 80% in 1998 when today's seniors were still years away from being born. Freshmen during the 2022-23 school year earned excellent grades in high school as 44% finished in the top 10% of their class, and 78% landed in the top 25%. Of those submitting standardized test results, the middle-50% of SAT scores were 1340-1470 and 31-34 on the ACT.

The admissions committee rates two factors—rigor of secondary school record and GPA—as carrying the greatest weight in the process. The next tier of factors includes the essay, volunteer work, recommendations, talent/ability, and extracurricular activities. GW has been test-optional since 2015, and a fair number of applicants do actually forgo submitting standardized test scores. Over the past two decades, GW has grown into a highly selective and sought-after university in one of the country's hottest cities. Still, this institution is in a dogfight for top students and rewards those who apply early, accepting 66% of ED applicants to the Class of 2026.

Worth Your Money?
Attending a private college in the fifth most expensive US city isn't going to come cheap. GW will set you back $86k per year for the total cost of attendance. For the 42% of students who qualify for need-based financial aid, an average annual award of $40,000 at least puts a dent in the total costs. George Washington grads emerge with higher-than-average debt loads, thus prospective students need to carefully determine whether this school is a good financial fit for them, given their individual circumstances. Students pursuing study in the areas of business, communication, politics, and policy enjoy better prospects for a strong ROI.

FINANCIAL
Institutional Type: Private
In-State Tuition: $64,990
Out-of-State Tuition: $64,990
Room & Board: $16,300
Books & Supplies: $1,400

Avg. Need-Based Grant: $39,874
Avg. % of Need Met: 94%

Avg. Merit-Based Award: $23,844
% Receiving (Freshmen w/o Need): 28%

Avg. Cumulative Debt: $32,730
% of Students Borrowing: 44%

CAREER
Who Recruits
1. Becton, Dickinson and Co.
2. Consumer Financial Protection Bureau
3. Westat
4. Turner Construction
5. Gunnison Consulting

Notable Internships
1. United States Senate
2. NBC News
3. Macy's

Top Employers
1. Booz Allen Hamilton
2. Deloitte
3. IBM
4. U.S. House of Representatives
5. Capital One

Where Alumni Work
1. Washington, DC
2. New York City
3. San Francisco
4. Boston
5. Philadelphia

Earnings
College Scorecard (10-YR Post-Entry): $87,548
PayScale (Early Career): $66,000
PayScale (Mid-Career): $133,600
PayScale 20-Year ROI: $757,000

RANKINGS
Money: 4
U.S. News: 67, National Universities
Wall Street Journal/THE: 58
Washington Monthly: 40, National Universities

OVERGENERALIZATIONS
Students are:
Politically active
Politically liberal
More likely to venture off campus
Career-driven
Decided upon their chosen major

COLLEGE OVERLAPS
American University
Boston University
Georgetown University
New York University
Northeastern University

Georgetown University

Washington, District of Columbia | 202-687-3600

The nation's oldest Catholic and Jesuit university also happens to be one of the best institutions in the country and one of the premier training grounds for future political bigwigs. Spired campus buildings, cobblestone walkways, and tree-lined streets give Georgetown an elegant aesthetic and an air of sophistication that perfectly matches the rigorous educational experience and conservative/traditional campus vibe.

Inside the Classroom

The university's 7,900 undergraduates and 13,084 graduate students are divided among nine schools/colleges, but only four are open to undergrads. Applicants to Georgetown must select one of these four schools: Georgetown College, McDonough School of Business, the Walsh School of Foreign Service, or the School of Nursing & Health Studies. Core requirements vary by school but are fairly extensive. For example, Georgetown College requires one course in the humanities and writing and two courses per discipline in theology, philosophy, math/science, social science, foreign language, and diversity for a total of 14 required courses. There are forty-four majors within Georgetown College, seven business-oriented majors within McDonough, four tracks in the nursing school, and eight majors within the Walsh School of Foreign Service.

For a large university with a heavy presence of graduate students, Georgetown maintains a personalized and intimate learning environment. The student-faculty ratio is 11:1, and 60% of classes enroll fewer than 20 students. While some classes are a bit larger, only 7% cross the 50-student threshold. There are many ways that students can seek funding for independent research projects or become an assistant to faculty members via the Georgetown Undergraduate Research Opportunities Program. Summer research can lead to the completion of a senior thesis that can be presented at the College Academic Council Research Colloquium every spring. Each year, 1,000+ Hoya undergrads participate in one of the school's 200+ study abroad programs that are spread across 50+ countries.

Those desiring to join the world of politics or diplomacy are in the right place. The Government and International Affairs programs are among the best in the country. For those with their eyes on a finance career, McDonough is one of the most esteemed business schools one can find. The greatest number of degrees are conferred in the social sciences (38%) followed by business (20%), interdisciplinary studies (8%), and biology (7%). Georgetown is regularly a top producer of distinguished fellowship winners. In 2023, it produced 49 Fulbright Scholars, placing it first in the nation. It typically also sees multiple Truman, Boren, Gilman International, and Marshall Scholars from each graduating class.

Outside the Classroom

The scenic and safe Georgetown area of DC is littered with high-end restaurants and shops. Only a short Metro ride away, the opportunities for museums, live music, fine cuisine, sporting events, and pulsating nightlife are endless. Almost four-fifths of undergrads live on campus. The 23 NCAA Division I sports teams are part of the fabric of Hoya life, particularly the men's basketball team. More than 2,500 students participate in intramural sports, utilizing the school's superb facilities that include Yates Field House. Due to the clash of values between the Jesuits and Greek life, fraternities and sororities are not recognized by the school, but they have enjoyed a recent rise in popularity despite their unofficial status. Religion is a guiding force at the university in some ways; however, the great majority of undergrads are not practicing Catholics. The campus ministry is popular, and many students are part of faith-based or secular volunteer organizations. In total, there are over 200 active student organizations that offer an array of clubs focused on spirituality, culture, academics, and the arts. The Georgetown University Lecture Fund brings an incredible lineup of luminaries from the realms of politics, entertainment, business, media, and social activism to speak on campus.

Career Services

The Cawley Career Education Center is manned by eleven professionals (not counting office managers and administrative assistants). Additional career services professionals housed within various schools brings the total to 19. That gives it a student-to-advisor ratio of 416:1, below average compared to many comparable institutions included in this book. Yet, that does not translate to poor delivery of services. In fact, the staff boasts roughly 14,000 interactions with undergraduate students each year, almost twice the population of the student body; by graduation, over 90% have engaged with the career center. In a given year, counselors spend approximately 800 collective hours meeting one-on-one with students to discuss professional pathways and dole out career/graduate school advice.

In a single school year, Georgetown arranged for 2,400 interviews on campus and attracted more than 1,800 attendees at both its fall and spring career expos. Over 200 corporate, government, and nonprofit employers met with students at those events. Additionally, sixty-five companies visited campus to host information sessions with undergraduates. With a strong and active alumni base, the Hoya Gateway is a platform through which students can connect with 13,000 alumni. Despite not having an elite student-advisor ratio, Cawley's extensive counseling offerings/events, proficiency with facilitating on-campus recruiting by top-level employers, and tremendous student outcomes earned it top grades from our staff.

Professional Outcomes

Within six months of graduating, 75% of members of the Class of 2022 entered the workforce, 19% went directly into a graduate or professional program of study, and 3% were still seeking employment. In past years, the number of fresh alums entering grad school has been significantly greater—as high as 24%. The Class of 2022 sent massive numbers of graduates to a number of major corporations including JPMorgan Chase (22), Citi (21), BOA (18), Morgan Stanley (16), and EY (10) as well as a number of other international financial institutions. As one might ascertain from this list of companies, four of the most popular industries were investment banking (14%), consulting (12%), healthcare (8%), and financial services (6%). By far, New York and remaining in DC are the two most popular postgraduate destinations, although a fair number also migrate to Virginia, California, Massachusetts, Texas, and Maryland. The financial picture for Georgetown graduates is rosy. Average starting salaries fall well above the national average. In 2022, McDonough grads enjoyed starting compensation that averaged $97k.

Over the past decade, medicine and law have been the top two graduate fields chosen by Hoya alumni. Each year, roughly 40 to 55 grads entered law school, and another 40 to 55 entered med school. An incredibly high percentage elect to remain at Georgetown—52 members of the Class of 2022 entered graduate school at their alma mater. The number two choice was Columbia with 11 students and Harvard came in third attracting seven Hoyas. The other schools on that list are almost exclusively elite institutions including UCLA, Oxford, Duke, Cornell, NYU, Berkeley, and the University of Chicago.

Admission

Like many other prestigious universities, Georgetown has seen all-time highs in applications received and all-time low acceptance rates in recent years. Of the 26,638 applications, 3,257 were admitted for an acceptance rate of 12%, a less encouraging figure than the 17% two years prior. For enrolled freshmen in 2022-23, the mid-50% range was 1410-1540 on the SAT and 32-35 on the ACT. Grades must be equally exceptional for serious consideration; 84% of enrolled students finished in the top 10% of their high school class. The profile of students admitted today has much in common with those admitted five years ago.

Georgetown does not have an early decision option but does offer nonbinding early action. However, this EA round is restricted and you cannot apply ED anywhere else. Also noteworthy, the university does not allow Score Choice, the option that permits applicants to select which standardized scores are reported to prospective schools and which are not. The admissions office rates eight factors as being "very important" to admissions decisions including grades, test scores, essays, and recommendations. An admissions interview and extracurriculars rate as "important." The most selective school in the DC Metro area, Georgetown attracts growing lines of extremely well-qualified candidates each year. There are few admissions surprises here. Test scores around the 97th percentile and near-perfect grades in an AP-heavy course load are virtually required.

Worth Your Money?

A year at Georgetown will cost you approximately $85,000 (tuition + room & board) if you do not receive any financial aid. Like many similarly elite institutions, it is more focused on providing sizable grants to those with true financial need. More than one-third of enrolled undergrads receive need-based aid and Georgetown meets 100% of demonstrated need, which works out to an average annual grant of roughly $49k. Unless you plan to enter a low-paying field and need to take on an excessive amount of debt, this school is well worth paying for as the Georgetown name will open doors for you well into adulthood.

FINANCIAL
Institutional Type: Private
In-State Tuition: $65,082
Out-of-State Tuition: $65,082
Room & Board: $20,458
Books & Supplies: $1,000

Avg. Need-Based Grant: $49,384
Avg. % of Need Met: 100%

Avg. Merit-Based Award: Not Reported
% Receiving (Freshmen w/o Need): Not Reported

Avg. Cumulative Debt: $25,512
% of Students Borrowing: 34%

CAREER
Who Recruits
1. BMO Capital Markets
2. AlphaSights
3. RBC Capital Markets
4. Capital One
5. Charles River Associates

Notable Internships
1. U.S. Securities and Exchange Commission
2. Vanguard
3. Goldman Sachs

Top Employers
1. Deloitte
2. Google
3. PwC
4. Citi
5. Goldman Sachs

Where Alumni Work
1. Washington, DC
2. New York City
3. San Francisco
4. Boston
5. Los Angeles

Earnings
College Scorecard (10-YR Post-Entry): $101,797
PayScale (Early Career): $71,600
PayScale (Mid-Career): $141,700
PayScale 20-Year ROI: $947,000

RANKINGS
Money: 5
U.S. News: 22, National Universities
Wall Street Journal/THE: 12
Washington Monthly: 15, National Universities

OVERGENERALIZATIONS
Students are:
Wealthy
Politically active
Dressed to impress
Career-driven
Working hard and playing hard

COLLEGE OVERLAPS
Cornell University
Duke University
Northwestern University
University of Pennsylvania
University of Notre Dame

Georgia Institute of Technology

Atlanta, Georgia | 404-894-4154

ADMISSION
Admission Rate: 17%
Admission Rate - Men: 14%
Admission Rate - Women: 23%
EA Admission Rate: Not Offered
ED Admission Rate: Not Offered
ED Admits as % of Total Admits: Not Offered
Admission Rate (5-Year Trend): -6%
% of Admits Attending (Yield): 42%
Transfer Admission Rate: 36%

SAT Reading/Writing (Middle 50%): 670-760
SAT Math (Middle 50%): 700-790
ACT Composite (Middle 50%): 31-35

% Graduated in Top 10% of HS Class: 87%
% Graduated in Top 25% of HS Class: 98%
% Graduated in Top 50% of HS Class: 99%

Demonstrated Interest: Not Considered
Legacy Status: Not Considered
Racial/Ethnic Status: Considered
Admission Interview Offered: No

ENROLLMENT
Total Undergraduate Enrollment: 18,415
% Full-Time: 93%
% Male: 60%
% Female: 40%
% Out-of-State: 34%
% Fraternity: 5%
% Sorority: 8%
% On-Campus (All Undergraduate): 44%
Freshman Housing Required: No

% African-American: 8%
% Asian: 30%
% Hispanic: 8%
% White: 38%
% Other: 1%
% International: 10%
% Low-Income: 14%

ACADEMICS
Student-to-Faculty Ratio: 22 to 1
% of Classes Under 20: 29%
% of Classes 20-49: 41%
% of Classes 50 or More: 30%
% Full-Time Faculty: 85%
% Full-Time Faculty w/ Terminal Degree: 94%

Top Programs
Architecture
Business
Chemistry
Computer Science
Engineering
Industrial Design
Mathematics
Physics

Retention Rate: 97%
4-Year Graduation Rate: 56%
6-Year Graduation Rate: 92%

Curricular Flexibility: Less Flexible
Academic Rating: ★★★★

#CollegesWorthYourMoney

Downtown Atlanta is home to one of the world's undisputed best public technological institutes. The Georgia Institute of Technology, more commonly referred to as Georgia Tech, educates 18,416 undergraduates as well as another 26,000+ graduate students who are on track to be the next generation of leaders in engineering, computer science, and related fields. While still catering to locals (approximately 60% are Georgia residents), Tech has managed to grow its national reputation in recent years and has blossomed from a top public tech university to simply a top tech university.

Inside the Classroom
Georgia Tech is divided into six colleges: the College of Design, the College of Computing, the College of Engineering, the College of Sciences, Ivan Allen College of Liberal Arts, and Scheller College of Business. Altogether, 130 majors and minors are available to undergraduates; all students are held to a stringent list of core requirements that is partially governed by the state. Must-take courses include Constitution & History, Communication Outcomes, Quantitative Outcomes, and Introduction to Computing as well as requirements in humanities/fine arts/ethics, social sciences, and wellness (physical education).

Being a large research university, the student-to-faculty ratio is a less-than-ideal 22:1, leading to some larger undergraduate class sections. In fact, 49% of courses had enrollments of more than thirty students in 2022-23. On the other end of the spectrum, 8% of sections had single-digit enrollments. While not all of your professors will know you by name, there are plenty of ways that motivated students can strike up meaningful faculty-student relationships. For example, 30% of aerospace engineering majors collaborate on research with their professors. In the School of Chemical and Biomolecular Engineering, that figure rises to 60%. Fifty-two percent of Tech students have gone abroad by the time they graduate, with a growing number electing to complete internships in a foreign land rather than academic coursework. In a given year, 130+ undergraduate students participate in a global internship.

Georgia Tech's engineering and computer science programs are at the top of any "best programs" list. The Scheller College of Business boasts top programs in management information systems, production/operation management, quantitative analysis, and supply chain management/logistics. The architecture school also receives national recognition. In terms of total number of degrees conferred, the most popular areas of study are engineering (51%), computer science (21%), and business (9%). Those pursuing prestigious scholarships have done well in recent years. In 2023, three students won Fulbright Scholarships. Others have succeeded at taking home Astronaut, Udall, Truman, and Marshall Scholarships. Three undergrads from one major—electrical engineering—won National Science Fellowships in a single recent year.

Outside the Classroom
Georgia Tech's 400-acre, wooded campus contains the vast majority of freshmen (94%), but only 44% of the overall student body lives in the school's forty residence halls. The rest find apartments or housing in surrounding neighborhoods like Buckhead, Home Park, Westside, or Atlantic Station. The Yellow Jackets field seventeen varsity intercollegiate athletic teams. The school's nine men's and eight women's teams participate in the Atlantic Coast Conference (ACC). Add 20+ intramural sports, 40+ sports clubs, and one of the largest outdoor recreation programs around, and the result is an extremely athletically-inclined student body. Those who aren't involved with sports typically find another place to connect, whether it's in one of the more than 400 student organizations or 50+ Greek organizations. Tech is a Greek-heavy school with 22% of freshmen men and 26% of freshmen women belonging to a fraternity or sorority. Campus provides plenty of chances for social engagement, but those seeking more can enjoy all that Atlanta has to offer.

Career Services
The Georgia Tech Career Center employs 18 full-time staff members (not counting IT professionals and office assistants) who work with undergraduate students. That collection of career advisors, employee relations specialists, and graduate school counselors works out to a student-to-counselor ratio of 1,023:1, below average compared to the pool of institutions included in this book. Despite this unremarkable number, GT is able to put on impressive, large-scale events that enhance student outcomes. The Fall Career Fair is the school's largest, featuring over 400 employers including Accenture, Capital One, GM, and Intel, and 7,000 students attend each year. The school also forges formal corporate partnerships with big-time companies including Google, Airbnb, Qualcomm, Northrop Grumman, and ConocoPhillips. Corporations routinely host information sessions on campus.

Internships and co-op programs receive some of the highest marks in the country. Thirty-five percent of undergrads choose to enter the school's three-semester co-op program, which leads to a five-year degree, while many others complete a one- or two-semester internship. In an average year, the Career Center places over 1,000 students in internships and another 1,300+ in co-op programs. Individualized appointments are encouraged as early as freshman year to begin planning potential career and graduate school pathways. Overall, Georgia Tech's career services does a fantastic job of funneling undergraduates into the world's premier employers at high starting salaries.

Professional Outcomes

More than three-quarters of recent grads had already procured employment by the time they were handed their diplomas. The median salary reported by that group was $80,000. The highest median salaries went to graduates of the School of Computer Science. By mid-career, Georgia Tech alumni enjoy one of the highest average salaries of all public university alumni in the country. You will find graduates at every major technology company in the world. Just examining those who have LinkedIn profiles, massive numbers of Yellow Jackets work at Google, Microsoft, Amazon, IBM, Apple, Facebook, and Uber. The bulk of graduates remain in the Atlanta metro area. The next three most popular destinations are San Francisco, New York City, and Washington, DC.

At the time of their exit surveys, roughly 20% of grads planned on pursuing an advanced degree within the next year. Many remain on campus to earn advanced engineering degrees through Georgia Tech, but the school's reputation is such that gaining admission into other top programs including MIT, Carnegie Mellon, Berkeley, Stanford, and Caltech is an achievable feat. Those same schools are institutions where Tech alumni have gone on to work as professors and researchers.

Admission

Only 17% of applicants to the Class of 2026 were admitted, one point lower than the prior year. Freshmen during the 2022-23 school year possessed middle-50% scores of 1370-1530 on the SAT and 31-35 on the ACT, and 98% had a GPA of over 3.75; the average GPA was over the 4.0 mark. A staggering 87% of first-year students hailed from the top 10% of their high school classes; 97% were in the top 25%. Only a decade ago, the university admitted 63% of applicants, and the average ACT score was lower than the 25th percentile mark today. Clearly, this school is infinitely more difficult to get into than it was only a short time ago.

Two factors can give you an advantage in your quest to gain acceptance at Tech: (1) you are from Georgia and (2) you are female. Last cycle, the acceptance rate for Peach State residents was 35%, much higher than the out-of-state figure (14%). The acceptance rate for Class of 2026 female applicants was 23% versus only 14% for male applicants. The early action acceptance rate is typically nearly identical to the regular decision figure. For all applicants, the admissions committee places the most emphasis on seven factors: the rigor of one's high school coursework, GPA, extracurricular activities, essays, character and personal qualities, geographical residence, and state residency. Getting into Georgia Tech has become a harrowing enterprise and is a wholly different experience than for previous generations.

Worth Your Money?

Georgia residents are looking at an annual cost of attendance of $29k which, when you consider that the median starting salary is well over two times that amount, makes Georgia Tech an exceptional bargain. Even better, merit aid is generously distributed, including via the Stamps President's Scholars Program, which gives a free ride to 40 highly qualified applicants each year. Need-based aid is granted to 35% of students with the average amount in the range of $14k. Only a small percentage of aid recipients see 100% of their demonstrated need met. Even if you received limited aid and/or were paying out-of-state tuition, which brings the COA to $50k, Tech would still prove a worthwhile investment of your time and money.

FINANCIAL
Institutional Type: Public
In-State Tuition: $11,764
Out-of-State Tuition: $32,876
Room & Board: $15,244
Books & Supplies: $800

Avg. Need-Based Grant: $13,687
Avg. % of Need Met: 57%

Avg. Merit-Based Award: $5,903
% Receiving (Freshmen w/o Need): 7%

Avg. Cumulative Debt: $27,451
% of Students Borrowing: 32%

CAREER
Who Recruits
1. SunTrust Bank
2. Caterpillar
3. The Chlorox Company
4. Equifax
5. Rockwell Automation

Notable Internships
1. NASA
2. Procter & Gamble
3. Uber

Top Employers
1. Google
2. Microsoft
3. Amazon
4. Home Depot
5. Apple

Where Alumni Work
1. Atlanta
2. San Francisco
3. New York City
4. Washington, DC
5. Seattle

Earnings
College Scorecard (10-YR Post-Entry): $96,375
PayScale (Early Career): $79,000
PayScale (Mid-Career): $145,300
PayScale 20-Year ROI: $1,105,000

RANKINGS
Money: 5
U.S. News: 33, National Universities
Wall Street Journal/THE: 39
Washington Monthly: 78, National Universities

OVERGENERALIZATIONS
Students are:
Always studying
Competitive
Diverse
Nerdy
Intense

COLLEGE OVERLAPS
Carnegie Mellon University
Cornell University
University of California, Berkeley
University of Georgia
University of Michigan

Gettysburg College

Gettysburg, Pennsylvania | 717-337-6100

ADMISSION
Admission Rate: 56%
Admission Rate - Men: 54%
Admission Rate - Women: 59%
EA Admission Rate: Not Reported
ED Admission Rate: 55%
ED Admits as % of Total Admits: 9%
Admission Rate (5-Year Trend): +10%
% of Admits Attending (Yield): 20%
Transfer Admission Rate: 39%

SAT Reading/Writing (Middle 50%): 680-720
SAT Math (Middle 50%): 670-720
ACT Composite (Middle 50%): 28-32

% Graduated in Top 10% of HS Class: 47%
% Graduated in Top 25% of HS Class: 76%
% Graduated in Top 50% of HS Class: 99%

Demonstrated Interest: Considered
Legacy Status: Considered
Racial/Ethnic Status: Not Considered
Admission Interview Offered: Yes

ENROLLMENT
Total Undergraduate Enrollment: 2,241
% Full-Time: 100%
% Male: 49%
% Female: 51%
% Out-of-State: 73%
% Fraternity: 26%
% Sorority: 32%
% On-Campus (All Undergraduate): 95%
Freshman Housing Required: Yes

% African-American: 5%
% Asian: 3%
% Hispanic: 12%
% White: 67%
% Other: 3%
% International: 8%
% Low-Income: 21%

ACADEMICS
Student-to-Faculty Ratio: 10 to 1
% of Classes Under 20: 70%
% of Classes 20-49: 29%
% of Classes 50 or More: 0%
% Full-Time Faculty: 77%
% Full-Time Faculty w/ Terminal Degree: 97%

Top Programs
Business, Organizations, and Management
English
Globalization Studies
Health Sciences
History
Political Science
Public Policy
Sociology

Retention Rate: 90%
4-Year Graduation Rate: 78%
6-Year Graduation Rate: 83%

Curricular Flexibility: Somewhat Flexible
Academic Rating: ★★★★

#CollegesWorthYourMoney

The oldest existing Lutheran College in the US, Gettysburg College was already 31 years old when President Lincoln delivered his now-famous address from the newly opened Soldiers' National Cemetery. Much like the address itself, the college has garnered more admiration through the passage of time. (Lincoln's speech was widely panned at the time.) In fact, another distinguished president, Dwight Eisenhower, actually served on the school's board of trustees, greatly raising the national profile of the school during his tenure. Today, Gettysburg College offers 65 academic programs to 2,241 undergraduates.

Inside the Classroom

The goals of the Gettysburg curriculum emphasize inquiries and integrations over the mere checking of boxes in a host of academic disciplines. All undergrads are expected to engage in inquiries within the humanities (1 course), the arts (1 course), the social sciences (1 course), and natural sciences (2 courses). While completing these courses, the college wants each student to demonstrate (1) integrative thinking, (2) communication skills, and (3) informed citizenship. Freshmen start their postsecondary careers in a first-year seminar and conclude their experience with a capstone course within their major. Additional requirements include two diversity courses and at least two courses in a second language.

If you want to learn in a large group setting at Gettysburg, you'll have to join a battlefield tour. A student-to-faculty ratio of 10:1 allows for incredibly small class sizes; the average is 18, and 70% of sections enroll fewer than 20 students. Undergraduate research opportunities are accessible to students in all academic departments. Overall, more than 50% of students get a chance to work on academic/laboratory research with one of their professors and nearly 60% of Gettysburgians elect to study abroad for a semester or longer. The school has formal partnerships in countries like China, Tanzania, and Senegal.

By a substantial margin, the social sciences are the most common choice of major at Gettysburg, accounting for 26% of all degrees conferred. Other frequently selected disciplines include biology (16%), business/marketing (9%), psychology (7%), and the visual and performing arts (5%). This is not a school with one or two standout departments, but one with many solid academic programs. Prestigious scholarship organizations typically pluck at least a few Gettysburg grads each year—recent students have been honored as Fulbright and Beinecke Scholarship recipients.

Outside the Classroom

Just about every single undergraduate resides in on-campus housing at the college; 99% of freshmen live in dorms while 95% of the student population stays on the grounds for all four years. Greek life has an equally massive presence for both men and women as fraternities and sororities attract roughly one-third of all undergrads. Gettysburg sponsors 24 varsity sports, a dozen for men and a dozen for women that play at the Division III level. Additionally, there are nine club teams, and the college has a reputation as a school where just about everyone plays intramural sports. The school has over 140 student-run clubs and 85% of the student body is engaged in some type of extracurricular activity. While campus is a hub of activity, the town itself can be a bit slow except, of course, for Civil War history buffs. The greatest number of students hail from within a few hours of campus—Pennsylvania, New Jersey, New York, Maryland, and Connecticut. Trips home or other excursions are always within reasonable driving distance. Baltimore is 55 miles from campus while Washington, DC, can be reached in an hour and a half, Philadelphia in two hours, and New York City in three and a half hours.

Career Services

The Center for Career Engagement (CCE) is staffed by nine professional staff members who specialize in career mentoring, direct counseling, and employer relations. The CCE's student-to-advisor ratio of 249:1 is in the better-than-average range compared to all institutions included in this book. This solid level of support results in the office working "with every student from the moment they step on campus to graduation." Utilizing a four-year career framework, the CCE helps students discover, create, experience, and connect their way to a satisfying postgraduate outcome.

A wealth of real-world experience is at the fingertips of Gettysburg undergrads including internships, 3-5-day externships, job shadowing, and multiday career treks and immersion trips. Seventy-seven percent of students complete at least one full-blown internship. The alumni network includes over 30,000 individuals who are known for their willingness to help current students and recent grads. The CCE hosts one large Job & Internship Fair each fall, but employer meet and greets, workshops, virtual events, and on-campus interviews take place year-round. Thanks to the multitude of available opportunities for career exploration and networking, just about all newly minted graduates quickly find their place in life.

Professional Outcomes

One year after receiving their diplomas, 98% of recent grads landed their first job or had enrolled in graduate/professional school. Large numbers of Gettysburg alumni are employed by major corporations and financial institutions like Vanguard, Morgan Stanley, Wells Fargo, Deloitte, Merrill Lynch, JPMorgan Chase, Google, Accenture, Pfizer, and UBS. Even though the college is closer to Philadelphia, New York City is actually the number one destination for alums. Philly is second. The next most common destinations are Washington, DC; Baltimore; Boston; Harrisburg; and San Francisco. According to PayScale, the school ranks 73rd among all American colleges for early-career and mid-career salaries.

Five years after graduation, 36% of surveyed Gettysburg grads had earned an advanced degree, and another 12% were presently enrolled in a graduate program. The college has produced an impressive (for its size) 1,272 doctoral-degree earners since 1966, 51st among all baccalaureate colleges. Medical school applicants possessing at least a 3.5 GPA and an MCAT above 510 enjoy an 88% acceptance rate. Prelaw students have found law school homes at the likes of NYU, Temple University, Villanova University, Penn, and Georgetown University.

Admission

The school receives 5,800 applications per year and accepted more prospective students than it rejected last year; the most recent acceptance rate was 56%. The average freshman had an excellent high school career, as 47% finished in the top 10% and 76% placed in the top quartile. Those who did elect to submit standardized test scores performed well; the middle-50% ACT score was 28-32, and on the SAT, students ranged from 680-720 on the reading and writing section and 670-720 on the math section.

Gettysburg was fairly early to the test-optional party, making standardized testing optional for all domestic applicants in 2006. Its holistic review process places the most stock in the rigor of each applicant's secondary school record, GPA, essays, and recommendations. Factors considered "important" include class rank, test scores, an interview, extracurricular activities, talent/ability, character/personal qualities, and volunteer work. In the school's own words, the admissions office is "very interested in individuals of character who will make positive contributions to the campus community and beyond. In estimating such qualities, we rely on what students say about themselves through essays, along with the recommendations from secondary school counselors and teachers. In-depth involvement in extracurricular and community service activities both inside and outside of school is favorably considered in the admissions process."

Worth Your Money?

The small class sizes and oodles of individual attention offered by the college do come at a cost—tuition alone is $64,230, and the full annual cost of attendance is close to $80k. Fortunately, Gettysburg does give out over $90 million in merit and need-based grants; 60% of the student body receives a portion of this money. While the mean debt load at graduation is slightly above the national average, Gettysburg does offer enough financial aid to make this school accessible to less-than-wealthy students. That being said, those planning on borrowing a sizable chunk of the COA should be pursuing a major that will see quick financial returns. Otherwise, a less pricey option may fit better into your life plan.

FINANCIAL
Institutional Type: Private
In-State Tuition: $64,230
Out-of-State Tuition: $64,230
Room & Board: $15,530
Books & Supplies: $1,000

Avg. Need-Based Grant: $48,852
Avg. % of Need Met: 90%

Avg. Merit-Based Award: $25,327
% Receiving (Freshmen w/o Need): 23%

Avg. Cumulative Debt: $33,421
% of Students Borrowing: 62%

CAREER
Who Recruits
1. Vanguard
2. Morgan Stanley
3. T. Rowe Price
4. Deloitte
5. Accenture

Notable Internships
1. Deloitte
2. Bank of America
3. U.S. House of Representatives

Top Employers
1. Vanguard
2. Morgan Stanley
3. Wells Fargo
4. Deloitte
5. Merrill Lynch

Where Alumni Work
1. New York City
2. Philadelphia
3. Washington, DC
4. Baltimore
5. Boston

Earnings
College Scorecard (10-YR Post-Entry): $72,638
PayScale (Early Career): $61,800
PayScale (Mid-Career): $129,500
PayScale 20-Year ROI: $656,000

RANKINGS
Money: 4.5
U.S. News: 63, Liberal Arts Colleges
Wall Street Journal/THE: 146
Washington Monthly: 72, Liberal Arts Colleges

OVERGENERALIZATIONS
Students are:
Working hard and playing hard
Homogeneous
Preppy
Wealthy
Tight-knit (possess a strong sense of community)

COLLEGE OVERLAPS
Bucknell University
Dickinson College
Franklin & Marshall College
Lafayette College
Muhlenberg College

Admission Rate: 70%
Admission Rate - Men: 66%
Admission Rate - Women: 73%
EA Admission Rate: Not Offered
ED Admission Rate: Not Offered
ED Admits as % of Total Admits: Not Offered
Admission Rate (5-Year Trend): +5%
% of Admits Attending (Yield): 18%
Transfer Admission Rate: 66%

SAT Reading/Writing (Middle 50%): 610-700
SAT Math (Middle 50%): 600-710
ACT Composite (Middle 50%): 26-31

% Graduated in Top 10% of HS Class: 37%
% Graduated in Top 25% of HS Class: 74%
% Graduated in Top 50% of HS Class: 95%

Demonstrated Interest: Considered
Legacy Status: Considered
Racial/Ethnic Status: Considered
Admission Interview Offered: Yes

ENROLLMENT
Total Undergraduate Enrollment: 5,084
% Full-Time: 99%
% Male: 46%
% Female: 54%
% Out-of-State: 52%
% Fraternity: Not Offered
% Sorority: Not Offered
% On-Campus (All Undergraduate): 53%
Freshman Housing Required: Yes

% African-American: 1%
% Asian: 7%
% Hispanic: 13%
% White: 65%
% Other: 3%
% International: 4%
% Low-Income: 14%

ACADEMICS
Student-to-Faculty Ratio: 12 to 1
% of Classes Under 20: 42%
% of Classes 20-49: 57%
% of Classes 50 or More: 1%
% Full-Time Faculty: 57%
% Full-Time Faculty w/ Terminal Degree: 90%

Top Programs
Accounting
Biology
Business Administration
Engineering
Kinesiology and Physical Education
Nursing
Public Relations

Retention Rate: 93%
4-Year Graduation Rate: 80%
6-Year Graduation Rate: 87%

Curricular Flexibility: Less Flexible
Academic Rating: ★★★★

#CollegesWorthYourMoney

Thanks to its success on the basketball court over the past two decades, most Americans have heard the name Gonzaga. However, if you ask them where the school is located, very few will correctly answer "Spokane, Washington." Just shy of 5,100 undergraduates attend this midsize Jesuit university that offers 53 undergraduate majors and 68 minors. This school caters to strong students (the average unweighted high school GPA is 3.73), but it is not overly exclusive as more than 75% of applicants gain acceptance. For anyone seeking the benefits of a Jesuit education, there is much to like about what Gonzaga University has to offer.

Inside the Classroom

The school's core curriculum is guided by the question, "As students of a Catholic, Jesuit, and Humanistic University, how do we educate ourselves to become women and men for a more just and humane global community?" In year one, students also take courses covering the categories of writing, reasoning, communication and speech, scientific inquiry, and mathematics. Sophomores take classes on Christianity/Catholicism and philosophy, and juniors delve into ethics and comparative religion. Two new additions to the school's mandated courses are a first-year seminar and a core integration seminar taken toward the end of a student's undergraduate experience.

An enviable 12:1 student-to-faculty ratio leads to an average class size of 18 students, and the school rates well in surveys of undergraduate instructional quality. Less than 2% of course sections enroll more than 50 students. The Center for Undergraduate Research & Creative Inquiry was launched last decade to facilitate an increased number of student-faculty collaborations. Opportunities for research exist not only in the natural sciences but also in the arts, humanities, and social sciences. Sixty-three percent of Zags choose to study abroad during their college experience, including at the university's flagship program in Florence, Italy.

Business/marketing is the area of study that attracts the most Zag undergrads; 24% earn degrees in that discipline. The next most common areas of degree conferment are biology (12%), engineering (11%), communication/journalism (7%), and psychology (7%). The School of Engineering & Applied Science is rated extremely high among non-doctoral, degree-granting institutions, and the School of Business Administration has a solid national reputation. The university does not produce a large number of competitive postgraduate scholarship winners but does usually see at least a couple of Fulbrights awarded to seniors each year.

Outside the Classroom

The 152-acre campus is located right along the Spokane River less than one mile from the downtown business district. Last year, 98% of freshmen resided in university-owned housing, and 53% of the undergraduate population, as a whole, did the same. As is typical at Jesuit institutions, there are no Greek organizations on campus. The 18 intercollegiate sports teams are a point of pride, particularly the men's basketball team that has reached the Sweet Sixteen eight times. Intramural athletics are also huge with 53% of undergraduates participating in 30 different sports; another 700 students are members of club teams. There are also more than 150 student-initiated clubs including 30 academic honor societies, 30 pre-professional clubs, 20 political groups, 15 cultural clubs, and 10+ volunteer organizations. So-termed "SpikeNites" occur every Saturday night, offering events such as movie night, ice skating, bingo, and bubble soccer. GU Outdoors offers students the chance to engage in skiing, snowboarding, hiking, backpacking, fishing, rock climbing, and kayaking in the beautiful natural areas that surround Gonzaga's campus. A student newspaper is published 28 times during each academic year, and iZAG internet radio runs 24/7. Being located in the heart of Washington's second-largest city while also being surrounded by endless natural beauty presents enough opportunity for fun on its own. Add in Gonzaga's above-average sense of school spirit and student community, and the result is a generally happy bunch.

Career Services

Nine professional employees make up the Career and Professional Development Office at Gonzaga University, working in areas such as alumni engagement, employer relations, and in various advising capacities. This equates to a 565:1 student-to-counselor ratio, which is a fairly standard figure for a midsized university. Zags are treated to five on-site career fairs each year: the Accounting Career Fair, Post Graduate Service Fair, All Majors Career & Internship Fair, Engineering & Computer Science Career & Internship Fair, and the FUSE Career Fair.

A total of 300+ employers recruit on campus in a given year. Companies visiting Gonzaga included Adidas, CBRE Group, HP, JPMorgan, McKinstry, PepsiCo, and Salesforce. The Gonzaga Alumni Mentoring Program (GAMP) matches current students with mentors based on geographical locations and career interests. This organization also arranges TREKS to New York, the Bay Area, Seattle, and Portland each year to meet with alumni who work at 30 of those areas' top corporations. The university has placed great emphasis on increasing the number of undergraduates who participate in at least one internship during their four years of study. Way back in 2008, just 34% of students did so; today, the overwhelming majority of undergrads land internships. All of these efforts leave Gonzaga alumni enjoying the best employment rate of any school in the state.

Professional Outcomes

The most recent grads enjoyed a largely gentle landing as they left their Spokane campus home and flew on to their next destination—this cohort enjoyed a 95% success rate. Seventy-six percent of those surveyed found full-time employment within six months, with a large number of grads getting hired by Providence Health & Services (16), UW Medicine (14), and Boeing (12). Additional companies that employ large numbers of Zag alumni include Microsoft, Starbucks, Nike, and Nordstrom. The average starting salary for 2022 grads was $67,911. The most popular cities for newly minted grads are Seattle and Spokane followed by Portland, San Francisco, and Los Angeles.

Of the 17% of 2022 grads who entered a graduate/professional degree program, the most popular institutions were Gonzaga (54), the University of California (5), Arizona State (3), and Boston University (3). Recent grads pursuing a legal education have matriculated into law school at the University of Minnesota, Villanova University, and UCLA. Gonzaga sees around 50 students apply to medical schools each year. While the university does not have its own medical school, it does have a partnership with the UW School of Medicine.

Admission

Gonzaga is certainly a selective school but not one that should send shivers down the spines of prospective applicants. Of the 9,886 applicants vying for a place in the Class of 2026, a healthy 70% received invitations to join the university (up from 62% three years prior). Only 18% of this group actually went on to enroll in the university. The freshman class of 2022-23 brought with it an impressive set of high school credentials, with an average GPA of 3.73 and 37% earning a place in the top decile of their graduating cohort. The middle 50% ACT composite score was 26-31; on the SAT, the range was 1210-1400. However, it is important to note that the majority of enrolled students did not submit scores.

Three factors sit atop the list in terms of how the Gonzaga committee evaluates applicants: rigor of secondary school record, GPA, and character/personal qualities. Essays, recommendation letters, extracurricular activities, and talent/ability are deemed "important" when making admissions decisions. This school definitely looks favorably upon applicants who demonstrate significant interest in the university. With a relatively low yield rate (the 18% mentioned a moment ago), and no early action or early decision options, Gonzaga is anxious to admit any students who have indicated a likelihood of enrolling.

Worth Your Money?

The sticker price of a Gonzaga education is less than many other Jesuit schools featured in our guide (e.g., Boston College, Fairfield University, and Santa Clara University). The $52,540 annual tuition and projected annual cost (including personal expenses, transportation, etc.) is under $75k. Including both need and merit-based aid, the average package handed out by the school is around $32,000; in total, the school meets 78% of eligible students' needs. Those seeking the perks of a private college can get what they are looking for at Gonzaga, and the school can provide value, particularly for those who are career-oriented and will jump into a solid starting salary.

FINANCIAL
Institutional Type: Private
In-State Tuition: $53,500
Out-of-State Tuition: $53,500
Room & Board: $15,080
Books & Supplies: $1,382

Avg. Need-Based Grant: $11,706
Avg. % of Need Met: 81%

Avg. Merit-Based Award: $18,198
% Receiving (Freshmen w/o Need): 51%

Avg. Cumulative Debt: $28,601
% of Students Borrowing: 50%

CAREER
Who Recruits
1. EY
2. Booz Allen Hamilton
3. CALIBRE
4. CIA
5. American Continental Group

Notable Internships
1. Seattle Seahawks
2. KPMG
3. Columbia Records

Top Employers
1. Boeing
2. Amazon
3. Microsoft
4. US Army
5. Nike

Where Alumni Work
1. Seattle
2. Spokane
3. Portland
4. San Francisco
5. Canada

Earnings
College Scorecard (10-YR Post-Entry): $76,325
PayScale (Early Career): $63,300
PayScale (Mid-Career): $117,500
PayScale 20-Year ROI: $622,000

RANKINGS
Money: 4.5
U.S. News: 93, National Universities
Wall Street Journal/THE: 136
Washington Monthly: 147, National Universities

OVERGENERALIZATIONS
Students are:
Crazy about the Bulldogs
Service-oriented
Friendly
Homogenous
Tight-knit (possess a strong sense of community)

COLLEGE OVERLAPS
Loyola Marymount University
Santa Clara University
Seattle University
University of Portland
University of Washington - Seattle

Grinnell College

Grinnell, Iowa | 641-269-3600

ADMISSION
Admission Rate: 11%
Admission Rate - Men: 9%
Admission Rate - Women: 12%
EA Admission Rate: 51%
ED Admission Rate: 51%
ED Admits as % of Total Admits: 27%
Admission Rate (5-Year Trend): -18%
% of Admits Attending (Yield): 41%
Transfer Admission Rate: 15%

SAT Reading/Writing (Middle 50%): 680-750
SAT Math (Middle 50%): 700-780
ACT Composite (Middle 50%): 31-34

% Graduated in Top 10% of HS Class: 66%
% Graduated in Top 25% of HS Class: 90%
% Graduated in Top 50% of HS Class: 98%

Demonstrated Interest: Considered
Legacy Status: Considered
Racial/Ethnic Status: Considered
Admission Interview Offered: Yes

ENROLLMENT
Total Undergraduate Enrollment: 1,759
% Full-Time: 100%
% Male: 47%
% Female: 53%
% Out-of-State: 91%
% Fraternity: Not Offered
% Sorority: Not Offered
% On-Campus (All Undergraduate): 88%
Freshman Housing Required: Yes

% African-American: 4%
% Asian: 8%
% Hispanic: 8%
% White: 53%
% Other: 3%
% International: 20%
% Low-Income: 17%

ACADEMICS
Student-to-Faculty Ratio: 9 to 1
% of Classes Under 20: 64%
% of Classes 20-49: 36%
% of Classes 50 or More: 0%
% Full-Time Faculty: 83%
% Full-Time Faculty w/ Terminal Degree: 97%

Top Programs
Anthropology
Biology
Chemistry
Economics
History
Physics
Political Science
Sociology

Retention Rate: 90%
4-Year Graduation Rate: 84%
6-Year Graduation Rate: 88%

Curricular Flexibility: Very Flexible
Academic Rating: ★★★★✓

#CollegesWorthYourMoney

Long a bastion of progressive, free-thinking liberal arts education, Grinnell College, set in remote Iowa, has never been a more popular destination in its more than 170-year history than it is today. Rising numbers of applications and shrinking acceptance rates have raised the caliber of the 1,759 young people who currently occupy campus.

Inside the Classroom

Grinnell offers 42 areas of study and over 500 courses each semester, and students have an immense deal of autonomy with course selection. In fact, nothing better epitomizes the school's philosophy than its list of graduation requirements that are more a list of the maximum number of courses a student can take in any one area rather than a list of minimal expectations. The only required course is the First-Year Tutorial, a ten- to fourteen-student, writing-intensive seminar with topics ranging from the artist Kendrick Lamar to the comic strip Calvin & Hobbes. Outside of that one course, your education is personally crafted through the college's Individually-Advised Curriculum that sees students working closely with a faculty advisor to make the most of their educational journey.

Thanks to a 9:1 student/faculty ratio and no competition from graduate students, 64% of classes have fewer than twenty students, and roughly one-quarter of sections have single-digit student enrollments. Participating in research is a normal part of an undergraduate education at Grinnell. Overall, roughly three-fifths of Grinnell undergrads participate in one on- or off-campus research experience that was not simply built into their coursework. Some entered Mentored Advanced Projects, which see faculty work closely with students on scholarly or creative works while others conducted research at another location such as Duke University, Georgetown University, or Carnegie Mellon University. International study is also a fairly common part of a Grinnell education with over 50% of students studying abroad. The Grinnell-in-London program is a popular option, offering a semester's worth of courses on English politics, history, and theater.

A top producer of PhDs in both the sciences and the social sciences, Grinnell has strong offerings across the board, with programs in biology, chemistry, physics, economics, and history receiving particularly high praise. The largest number of degrees are conferred in the social sciences, foreign languages, biology, and computer science. A fast riser, the computer science program now graduates 60+ students per year versus only 15 just a handful of years ago. Grinnell students fare extraordinarily well at obtaining competitive scholarships. Just about every single year, Grinnell students and alumni capture Watson, Fulbright, and Schwarzman fellowships and scholarships. Grinnell is one of the top Fulbright-producing institutions in the country; students have earned as many as ten in a single recent year.

Outside the Classroom

Eighty-eight percent of students live on campus in small residence halls that house between 50 and 60 students. Grinnell has a long tradition of being fraternity- and sorority-free, instead favoring an "inclusive and open-minded" social scene. One-third of students engage in varsity athletics; the school fields 20 NCAA Division III teams that compete in the Midwest Conference. Intramurals draw heavy participation with soccer, volleyball, flag football, and basketball being among the most popular. Two-thirds of students participate in community service projects, and opportunities include teaching at a local prison, a buddies program for nearby children, and Alternative Breaks in impoverished areas around the United States. There are more than 100 student organizations as silly and relaxed as the Zombie Movie Club or as serious as the local chapter of the Roosevelt Institute Campus Network. With its remote location amidst the cornfields of Iowa, there's not much to explore in the surrounding area. Fortunately, campus itself is a nurturing and lively place.

Career Services

For a school of just over 1,750 students, the Center for Careers, Life, and Service (CLS) employs an astounding 22 full-time staff members that include those specializing in career advising, employer relations, internships, and fellowships and awards. That equates to a student-to-advisor ratio of 80:1, better than every other school that is featured in this guide. The personalized attention that staffing level affords enables the CLS to adhere to its core belief that "one's impact, satisfaction, and sense of purpose are maximized when one is able to align their values, strengths, and curiosities." To that aim, students are assigned a CLS exploratory advisor before they even set foot on campus. In a typical year, the office boasts 7,000 one-on-one advising contacts with students, which works out to almost four per student!

While its somewhat remote location and small student body make it tough to host a large-scale career fair, the school compensates by hosting/facilitating 180+ smaller events each year including career treks, workshops, alumni panels, and networking receptions. Close to 80 companies recruit on campus per year. Grinnell does a solid job facilitating internship experiences with a 61% participation rate among recent graduates. Internships were procured around the globe including stops at BMW China, Amazon Japan, the White House, the United Nations, Facebook, and IBM. Thirty-five percent of the employed grads state that their first job was exactly what they wanted to be doing, and 50% view their position as a "good stepping stone." Grinnell's CLS offers unparalleled support and has an excellent track record of helping students secure valuable internships, meaningful first jobs, and graduate school acceptances.

Professional Outcomes

Upon graduation, 62% of Grinnell students head into the workforce, 26% to graduate school, 2% to postgraduate service, and 2% earned fellowships. Multiple recent grads accepted positions with JPMorgan, Epic, and Google while others were hired by desirable organizations that included the Federal Reserve Board, Deloitte, the Brookings Institute, Goldman Sachs, and the Centers for Disease Control. The most commonly entered fields by 2022 grads were IT/computing (18%), research/science (13%), education (11%), and healthcare (11%). The mean salary of those employed was roughly $64,397, and the median was $57,500. Massachusetts and Illinois attracted the highest number of graduates, slightly more than Iowa itself. New York and Minnesota were the next most popular locations for Grinnell grads.

Close to 40% of those entering graduate school pursue PhDs or master's degrees in the hard sciences, 8% head to law school, and 3% were bound for medical school; 88% of all applicants were accepted into their first or second choice program. Recent law school acceptances included top-tier institutions like Harvard and the University of Chicago. Others were admitted to various advanced degree programs at Cambridge, Yale, Carnegie Mellon, and Cornell University. Overall, 86% of law school applicants received at least one acceptance, and 66% of medical school applicants were successful, which was 25 points above the national average.

Admission

In the last few years, the acceptance rate has jumped around between 20 and 29%, dipping to 11% during the Class of 2026 cycle. That is far more selective than Grinnell was only a short time ago. For example, in the 2010-11 cycle Grinnell accepted 43% of applicants. That year, it received only 2,969 applications, but it received 9,997 for a place in the Class of 2026. Standardized test scores of attending freshmen are higher as well—the median SAT score is 1460 and the median ACT score is 33. Nearly two-thirds of Grinnell students hail from the top 10% of their high school classes; 90% were in the top quartile.

Admissions factors rated by the committee as being "very important" are rigor of secondary curriculum, GPA, class rank, and recommendations. The four categories that fall under "important" are standardized test scores, extracurricular activities, and talent/ability. Most members of the Class of 2026 were deeply involved during high school, with 65% participating in community service, 62% in the arts, and 62% in athletics, while 55% held jobs. Applying through early decision yields a major advantage as 53% of applicants receive positive news, far higher than the regular rate. Early decision applicants comprised 67% of the incoming class in 2022-23, meaning that a large number of spots are already filled by the time the regular cycle rolls around. Even with Grinnell's transformation into a highly sought-after liberal arts college, the process remains holistic. Grades and test scores certainly matter, but unique talents and high school involvement play a major role as well. We can't stress enough how advantageous applying early is for students dead-set on studying at this now-elite Iowa school.

Worth Your Money?

The cost of attendance at Grinnell College is $82,890, but 91% of students receive some level of aid and 64% receive need-based aid for an average award of $56k+. Further, Grinnell manages to meet the full demonstrated need of 100% of aid-eligible students. Starting salaries are generally on the lower side coming out of this college, which is perhaps attributed to the many Grinnellians in the academic and nonprofit sectors; however, that isn't a big deal for most, thanks to the generosity of the aid packages being distributed. The average graduate comes out of Grinnell with under $20,000 of debt, a very manageable sum.

FINANCIAL
Institutional Type: Private
In-State Tuition: $64,862
Out-of-State Tuition: $64,862
Room & Board: $15,878
Books & Supplies: $800

Avg. Need-Based Grant: $56,274
Avg. % of Need Met: 100%

Avg. Merit-Based Award: $19,690
% Receiving (Freshmen w/o Need): 26%

Avg. Cumulative Debt: $14,738
% of Students Borrowing: 55%

CAREER
Who Recruits
1. Epic Systems
2. Morningstar
3. Nationwide
4. Teach for America
5. Google

Notable Internships
1. U.S. Forest Service
2. MasterCard
3. Restorative Justice Project

Top Employers
1. Google
2. Amazon
3. Epic
4. U.S. State Department
5. Wells Fargo

Where Alumni Work
1. Des Moines, IA
2. Chicago
3. New York City
4. Washington, DC
5. Minneapolis

Earnings
College Scorecard (10-YR Post-Entry): $62,529
PayScale (Early Career): $58,300
PayScale (Mid-Career): $108,500
PayScale 20-Year ROI: $419,000

RANKINGS
Money: 4.5
U.S. News: 11, Liberal Arts Colleges
Wall Street Journal/THE: 266
Washington Monthly: 26, Liberal Arts Colleges

OVERGENERALIZATIONS
Students are:
Always studying
Politically liberal
Quirky
Less concerned with fashion or appearance
Environmentally conscious

COLLEGE OVERLAPS
Carleton College
Kenyon College
Macalester College
Oberlin College
Vassar College

Hamilton College

ADMISSION
Admission Rate: 12%
Admission Rate - Men: 11%
Admission Rate - Women: 12%
EA Admission Rate: Not Offered
ED Admission Rate: 34%
ED Admits as % of Total Admits: 22%
Admission Rate (5-Year Trend): -12%
% of Admits Attending (Yield): 41%
Transfer Admission Rate: 8%

SAT Reading/Writing (Middle 50%): 700-760
SAT Math (Middle 50%): 720-780
ACT Composite (Middle 50%): 33-34

% Graduated in Top 10% of HS Class: 86%
% Graduated in Top 25% of HS Class: 98%
% Graduated in Top 50% of HS Class: 100%

Demonstrated Interest: Considered
Legacy Status: Considered
Racial/Ethnic Status: Considered
Admission Interview Offered: Yes

ENROLLMENT
Total Undergraduate Enrollment: 2,075
% Full-Time: 100%
% Male: 45%
% Female: 55%
% Out-of-State: 72%
% Fraternity: 20%
% Sorority: 13%
% On-Campus (All Undergraduate): 100%
Freshman Housing Required: Yes

% African-American: 3%
% Asian: 9%
% Hispanic: 10%
% White: 65%
% Other: 1%
% International: 7%
% Low-Income: 18%

ACADEMICS
Student-to-Faculty Ratio: 9 to 1
% of Classes Under 20: 72%
% of Classes 20-49: 28%
% of Classes 50 or More: 1%
% Full-Time Faculty: 75%
% Full-Time Faculty w/ Terminal Degree: 96%

Top Programs
English
Economics
Environmental Studies
Mathematics and Statistics
Philosophy
Physics
Public Policy
World Politics

Retention Rate: 94%
4-Year Graduation Rate: 89%
6-Year Graduation Rate: 92%

Curricular Flexibility: Very Flexible
Academic Rating: ★★★★⏜

#CollegesWorthYourMoney

Recent years have been kind to Alexander Hamilton. His legacy has sparked a mega-hit Broadway musical and a Pulitzer Prize-winning biography, and the liberal arts college in Clinton, New York, that bears his name—Hamilton College—has achieved new heights of prestige, claiming a place among the best liberal arts schools in the United States.

Inside the Classroom
The 2,075 undergraduate students can choose from 45 areas of concentration, but education at Hamilton is about so much more than merely choosing a major. The unique open curriculum is immensely flexible and caters to student passions and curiosity over a rigid list of required courses. While there are no distributional requirements, certain skill areas must be addressed as you work your way through the thirty-two courses needed for graduation. That includes three writing-intensive courses, one quantitative/symbolic reasoning course, one physical education course, and an area of concentration that includes a senior project.

The student-to-faculty ratio is 9:1, and without any pesky graduate students to get in the way, face time with professors is a regular occurrence. In fact, 28% of all classes have nine or fewer students; 72% have nineteen or fewer. Each summer, approximately 120 students engage in high-level undergraduate research with a faculty member. Many Hamilton students study off campus for a semester, although those locations are not always foreign countries. Many participate in domestic study programs in NYC, DC, or Boston while others take advantage of international opportunities like the school's own renowned Chinese language program in Beijing or one of one hundred other approved programs around the globe. Each year, 35-45% of juniors study abroad.

Economics, government, and biology are among the strongest and most popular majors; other standout programs include public policy, mathematics, and environmental studies. Thirty percent of students earn social science degrees, with biology (13%), visual and performing arts (9%), physical science (7%), and foreign languages (7%) next in line. Hamilton students fare extremely well in the competition for prestigious national fellowships, capturing a shocking number when considering the small size of each graduating class. In 2023, students won six Fulbright Scholarships, two Gilman Scholarships, and the school has produced Critical Language Scholarship winners in recent years.

Outside the Classroom
Just about everyone lives in university housing—100% in 2022-23 to be precise—leading to a cohesive atmosphere on the college's 1,350-acre campus. Greek life is strange in that it is nonresidential, following a series of reforms over the past decade. While a growing number of Hamilton students belong to a fraternity (20%) or sorority (13%), those organizations do not play nearly as prominent a role on campus as they once did. The school's 29 teams (15 women's, 14 men's) compete as the Colonials in the New England Small College Athletic Conference (NESCAC) with other elite liberal arts schools Amherst, Bates, Bowdoin, Middlebury, Tufts, Wesleyan, and Williams. There are 700 student-athletes donning the buff-and-blue colors, accounting for 35-40% of the total student body. Add that total to the 17 club and 12 intramural teams and it can feel like just about everyone is, technically, an athlete. Yet, with 200+ active student organizations, there are plenty of ways to get involved outside of competitive team sports. The Hamilton Association for Volunteering, Outreach, and Charity (HAVOC) attracts hundreds of civic-minded students each year. The Hamilton Outing Club is the largest club on campus and organizes weekend camping/hiking/skiing trips to the Adirondacks as well as more exotic locations around the world. Amazing speakers come to town as part of the Sacerdote Great Names Series. In recent years, Hamilton has hosted David Cameron, Jimmy Carter, Desmond Tutu, Jon Stewart, and Colin Powell.

Career Services
The Maurice Horowitch Career Center is staffed by 12 professionals with expertise in career development, employer development, and health professions advising. That works out to a 173:1 student-to-advisor ratio, which is significantly stronger than most schools featured in this guide. Each student is assigned a career advisor who works with that student throughout the four-year journey. On the job-finding front, the center assists "students in developing skills in self-assessment, career exploration, resume preparation, interviewing, and uncovering job leads that will empower them to proactively manage their own careers." Yet, that is all steeped in the belief that career planning is a developmental process that unfolds over a lifetime.

The college does not host any large-scale career expos, but numerous employers do visit campus each year to host informational sessions or to recruit/interview candidates. Hamilton's Career Center does a superb job assisting students with finding opportunities for experiential learning. A whopping 84% of recent grads had at least two internships over the course of the four years. Alumni are highly supportive of current students and are willing to present on campus or offer job-shadowing experiences; 75% of alumni in a recent survey stated they would be happy to supply current students with career advice. Hamilton's 23,200 alumni rank in the top 1% when measured by the percentage that donate to their alma mater. Students can join Handshake to find internship and career possibilities and My Hamilton to network with alumni. Despite not hosting a notable career fair, the individualized attention and care that Hamilton shows its undergrads results in tremendously overall positive postgraduate and career outcomes.

Professional Outcomes

Examining the 491 graduates in Hamilton's Class of 2022, an enviable 97% wasted no time landing jobs, graduate school acceptances, or fellowships. The most commonly entered industries were finance (17%), education (13%), business (12%), and science/tech (11%). Among the employers welcoming multiple recent graduates aboard were Wayfair, Goldman Sachs, Teach for America, Dana Farber Cancer Institute, Kantar Consulting, and Deutsche Bank. New York City, Boston, and DC were the most popular destinations.

Only 17% of 2022 graduates went directly into an advanced degree program. In one recent year, 33% of Hamilton grads were studying a STEM field, 22% were in the social sciences, 17% pursued a health care degree, and 5% went to law school. Law school acceptances over the past few years have included Georgetown, the University of Virginia, NYU, Penn, Yeshiva University, Washington University, Boston College, and Boston University. Medical school/veterinary school acceptances in that same period have included Columbia University, Penn, Temple, Tufts, SUNY, the University of Rochester, and Boston University. Other Hamilton graduates have been accepted into master's programs at Stanford, Cornell, USC, the University of Chicago, Vanderbilt, and others. Clearly, a degree from Hamilton opens doors to some of the world's top graduate/professional programs.

Admission

Hamilton saw 9,899 applicants vie for a coveted spot in the Class of 2026, but only 12% of that group made the cut, a decrease of 2% from the previous cycle. Many applicants provide SAT or ACT scores, but this institution is test-optional. The mid-50% range on the SAT was 1440-1520 and 33-34 on the ACT. The vast majority of students finished near the top of their high school class; 86% were in the top decile and 98% placed in the top quartile. Hamilton's admissions statistics have remained highly consistent over the past decade, so the level of selectivity should not come as a surprise to anyone.

The admissions committee's top priorities are an applicant's GPA, class rank, and the rigor of their coursework. Essays, recommendations, character/personal qualities, and an interview comprise the second tier of key factors. Because Hamilton is competing for applicants with a host of other elite liberal arts schools, it favors those willing to commit via binding early decision; the acceptance rate for early applicants is roughly three times that (34%) of those in the regular pool. Further, early acceptances make up 41% of the freshman class, leaving only a limited number of seats in the spring. To be a competitive applicant you should be in the top 10% of your graduating class and have standardized test scores in the 95th percentile or higher. If you're on the cusp and Hamilton is your top choice, definitely apply ED.

Worth Your Money?

If you have a genuine need for financial aid to make your education possible, Hamilton will usually answer the bell. In the 2022-23 academic year, the college awarded half of its undergraduates an average grant of $51k, taking some of the sting out of the $82,430 sticker price for full cost of attendance. In 2008, Hamilton ceased offering merit aid to admitted applicants, a rare and admirable practice in the world of higher education. With 100% of its focus on making college affordable to lower- and middle-class students, higher-earning families can expect to pay full freight. Still, this school, with its minuscule class sizes, truly exceptional academics, and powerful network is, in the end, worth the money for most teens.

FINANCIAL
Institutional Type: Private
In-State Tuition: $65,740
Out-of-State Tuition: $65,740
Room & Board: $16,690
Books & Supplies: $800

Avg. Need-Based Grant: $50,645
Avg. % of Need Met: 100%

Avg. Merit-Based Award: $0
% Receiving (Freshmen w/o Need): 0%

Avg. Cumulative Debt: $22,699
% of Students Borrowing: 45%

CAREER
Who Recruits
1. Merrill Lynch
2. NERA Economic Consulting
3. Isaacson Miller, Inc.
4. Teach for America
5. Kantar Consulting

Notable Internships
1. Credit Suisse
2. CNBC
3. UBS

Top Employers
1. Morgan Stanley
2. Goldman Sachs
3. Google
4. Wayfair
5. Citi

Where Alumni Work
1. New York City
2. Boston
3. Washington, DC
4. San Francisco
5. United Kingdom

Earnings
College Scorecard (10-YR Post-Entry): $77,214
PayScale (Early Career): $66,100
PayScale (Mid-Career): $111,100
PayScale 20-Year ROI: $872,000

RANKINGS
Money: 4.5
U.S. News: 16, Liberal Arts Colleges
Wall Street Journal/THE: 88
Washington Monthly: 15, Liberal Arts Colleges

OVERGENERALIZATIONS
Students are:
Tight-knit (possess a strong sense of community)
Wealthy
Politically active
Working hard and playing hard
Athletic/active

COLLEGE OVERLAPS
Bowdoin College
Colby College
Colgate University
Cornell University
Middlebury College

Harvard University

Cambridge, Massachusetts | 617-495-1551

ADMISSION
Admission Rate: 3%
Admission Rate - Men: 3%
Admission Rate - Women: 3%
EA Admission Rate: Not Reported
ED Admission Rate: Not Offered
ED Admits as % of Total Admits: Not Offered
Admission Rate (5-Year Trend): -2%
% of Admits Attending (Yield): 83%
Transfer Admission Rate: 1%

SAT Reading/Writing (Middle 50%): 730-780
SAT Math (Middle 50%): 760-800
ACT Composite (Middle 50%): 34-36

% Graduated in Top 10% of HS Class: 92%
% Graduated in Top 25% of HS Class: 98%
% Graduated in Top 50% of HS Class: 100%

Demonstrated Interest: Not Considered
Legacy Status: Considered
Racial/Ethnic Status: Considered
Admission Interview Offered: Yes

ENROLLMENT
Total Undergraduate Enrollment: 7,240
% Full-Time: 100%
% Male: 48%
% Female: 52%
% Out-of-State: 85%
% Fraternity: Not Offered
% Sorority: Not Offered
% On-Campus (All Undergraduate): 97%
Freshman Housing Required: Yes

% African-American: 9%
% Asian: 23%
% Hispanic: 12%
% White: 34%
% Other: 1%
% International: 13%
% Low-Income: 19%

ACADEMICS
Student-to-Faculty Ratio: 7 to 1
% of Classes Under 20: 71%
% of Classes 20-49: 17%
% of Classes 50 or More: 13%
% Full-Time Faculty: 86%
% Full-Time Faculty w/ Terminal Degree: 93%

Top Programs
Biology
Chemistry
Economics
Government
Mathematics
Physics
Psychology
Statistics

Retention Rate: 92%
4-Year Graduation Rate: 87%
6-Year Graduation Rate: 98%

Curricular Flexibility: Somewhat Flexible
Academic Rating: ★★★★

#CollegesWorthYourMoney

The oldest university in the United States, founded 140 years before the United States itself was even a concept, is also the most iconic and, in many ways, revered institution of higher learning. Worldwide, Harvard is the envy of other universities and the dream destination for countless teenage geniuses and overachievers. For 7,240 young people, the Ivy League university in Cambridge, Massachusetts, is their reality, and learning from Nobel Laureates, Pulitzer Prize winners, and global leaders in every field is an everyday occurrence.

Inside the Classroom

There are 50 undergraduate fields of study referred to as concentrations; many are interdisciplinary. More than 3,700 courses are on the menu, so learning options are extensive. Core requirements are minimal outside of expository writing (which all freshmen must conquer), proficiency in a foreign language (which must be achieved by the end of sophomore year), and a trek through the program in general education. The latter requirement ensures that undergrads are exposed to four main areas: aesthetics and culture; ethics and civics; histories, societies, and individuals; and science and technology in society. Roughly half of students complete some type of senior thesis, but there are no requirements in that area.

Even with a graduate population of over 14,000 to cater to, undergraduate class sizes still tend to be breathtakingly intimate, with 42% of sections having single-digit enrollments and 71% being capped at nineteen. Graduates report an almost 90% satisfaction rate with the experience within their academic concentration. Summer research experiences are taken advantage of by over one-third of the student body. Approximately 55-60% of students study abroad at a number of locations in South America, Africa, Europe, or Asia.

Economics, government, and computer science are the three most popular areas of concentration at Harvard. Those programs, along with ones in biology, chemistry, physics, math, statistics, sociology, history, English, and psychology all sit atop most departmental ranking lists. The university also occupies the top position in the all-time Rhodes Scholar rankings with 385 to its credit, more than the combined total from Stanford, Penn, Dartmouth, Brown, MIT, Cornell, and Columbia. Other prestigious postgraduate fellowships are awarded to Harvard students with regularity including the Fulbright, which is typically captured by 12-25 students per year. The list of all-time alumni accolades could go on forever and includes almost 100 Nobel Laureates and eight US presidents.

Outside the Classroom

Possessing a bottomless endowment, the school never needs to cut corners on any programs, campus infrastructure, or amenities—and it shows. Freshmen live together at a centralized campus location adjacent to the famed Harvard Yard and then, as sophomores, move into one of twelve stately, upper-class houses, each with its own set of traditions and sense of community. Greek life, once thriving, has taken a dip in recent years after university officials enacted new regulations to deter membership in single-sex clubs. Students who participate forfeit eligibility for leadership positions in athletics or student government and will not be recommended for prestigious scholarships. Fortunately, a bevy of other social clubs exist in the form of 500 student-run organizations including the history-rich Hasty Pudding Club and the Phillips Brooks House Association that runs eighty-six volunteer organizations. Of course, studying is also a popular "hobby," and the Harvard Library is the largest academic library in the world and boasts a staff of nearly 800. The Harvard Crimson is a premier college newspaper with a long and storied history—Franklin Roosevelt and John F. Kennedy are among its alums—and The Harvard Lampoon is one of the world's oldest humor magazines, one that has helped launch talents ranging from John Updike to Conan O'Brien. Athletics also play a prominent role in Harvard's culture, both past and present, as the school fields 42 NCAA Division I sports teams, evenly split between men's and women's squads. Cambridge itself is a bustling hub of culture, nightlife, and entertainment. Downtown Boston is only a 12-minute ride away on the city's easily accessible public transit system.

Career Services

The Office of Career Services has 24 professional staff members (excluding students, assistants, and IT staff) who are dedicated to tasks including employer relations, career counseling, and summer funding opportunities. The 302:1 student-to-advisor ratio is superior when compared to other schools featured in this guide. And, the closer you look into Harvard's career services, locating any feature that is less than superior is a nearly impossible task.

In a single recent year, this office hosted 340+ events that were attended by 12,000+ students. It also organizes twenty independent career fairs, each targeting a particular sector that attracts more than 6,000 net attendees. Harvard's career services staff logs 6,600 advising appointments per year and manages to engage with 70% of the total undergraduate student body. On-campus recruiting occurred on a regular basis with more than 140 employers, including just about any big-name company you can think of, conducting over 3,500 interviews on-site in Cambridge. More than three-quarters of students participate in a summer internship during their four years of study. In short, career services are what you would expect from America's preeminent university—exceptional.

Professional Outcomes

The Crimson Class of 2022 saw 15% of students head directly into graduate/professional school. Of the graduates entering the world of work (virtually everyone else), 58% were entering either the consulting, finance, or technology field. Over 1,000 Harvard alumni presently work for Google and over 500 for Microsoft, McKinsey & Company, and Goldman Sachs. More than 250 are employed at Amazon, Facebook, and Bain & Company. Post-graduation, Harvard students tend to cluster in three main states—New York, California, and Massachusetts. Those three states collectively reel in 60% of newly minted alumni. Remuneration is excellent with 63% of graduates reporting starting salaries over $70k and 30% taking home $110k+ in base pay. By mid-career, grads have the second-highest median salaries in the Ivy League.

Turning our attention to those moving on to graduate school, Harvard grads with at least a 3.5 GPA typically enjoy acceptance rates into medical school of 90% or greater, demolishing the national average. Harvard grads tend to trade one high prestige school for another when pursuing an advanced degree. Many also stay close to home—Harvard Medical School (HMS), Harvard Law School, and the Graduate School of Arts & Sciences all accept more Harvard College graduates than those from any other single institution. It is estimated that approximately one-fifth of the HMS student body already spent four years in Cambridge as an undergraduate.

Admission

Harvard's admission rate for the Class of 2026 was 3%, down slightly from the prior year's 4%. For historical context, at the turn of the millennium, 12% of applicants were welcomed aboard. The mid-50% SAT range for enrolled freshmen in 2022-23 was roughly 1490-1580; and 96% of students scored above a 700 on the Math section of the exam. It's not shocking that 92% of students admitted earned a place in their high school class's top decile. An insanely high number—83%—of admitted students elect to enroll. In other words, Harvard is second choice for few students.

The admissions staff does not rank any factor as being "very important" or even "important." All of the usual factors—grades, SATs, essays, and so on—are "considered." Demonstrated interest is not considered, which is unsurprising in light of the aforementioned yield rate. Legacy students comprise roughly one-third of the student body and enjoy an acceptance rate five times that of non-legacy applicants. For information about the role of race in admissions at Harvard, simply consult any newspaper. Getting into Harvard is the subject of plenty of (mostly awful) movies for a reason—it is a mammoth task set against harrowing odds. Even valedictorians with perfect test scores are not immune from rejection. However, impeccable credentials of that nature will at least allow you the opportunity to roll the dice with a realistic chance of success.

Worth Your Money?

Asking if Harvard is worth the money is a bit like John C. Reilly's character in Stepbrothers, Dale Doback, asking if bonito fish are big. Yes, Dale, bonito fish are big, and Harvard is worth the $79,450 annual cost of attendance. Merit aid does not exist at the university but, thanks to a $51 billion endowment, the 56% of the undergraduate population that is eligible for financial aid sees 100% of its need met; no family making under $65,000 per year will pay a dime. Harvard is one of the rare schools where the average graduate's salary exceeds the annual cost of attendance, so even if you did have to take out loans to attend, it would be more than worth the expense.

FINANCIAL
Institutional Type: Private
In-State Tuition: $59,076
Out-of-State Tuition: $59,076
Room & Board: $20,374
Books & Supplies: $1,000

Avg. Need-Based Grant: $65,053
Avg. % of Need Met: 100%

Avg. Merit-Based Award: $7,379
% Receiving (Freshmen w/o Need): <1%

Avg. Cumulative Debt: $13,683
% of Students Borrowing: 15%

CAREER
Who Recruits
1. Putnam Investments
2. Akuna Capital
3. Atlantic Media
4. Vertica
5. Environmental Defense Fund

Notable Internships
1. McKinsey & Company
2. NASA Jet Propulsion Laboratory
3. Jane Street Capital

Top Employers
1. Google
2. Microsoft
3. Goldman Sachs
4. McKinsey & Company
5. IBM

Where Alumni Work
1. Boston
2. New York City
3. San Francisco
4. Washington, DC
5. Los Angeles

Earnings
College Scorecard (10-YR Post-Entry): $95,114
PayScale (Early Career): $80,900
PayScale (Mid-Career): $156,200
PayScale 20-Year ROI: $1,231,000

RANKINGS
Money: 5
U.S. News: 3, National Universities
Wall Street Journal/THE: 6
Washington Monthly: 1, National Universities

OVERGENERALIZATIONS
Students are:
Always studying
Diverse
Intense
Teeming with school pride
Self-motivated

COLLEGE OVERLAPS
Columbia University
Massachusetts Institute of Technology
Princeton University
Yale University
Stanford University

Harvey Mudd College

Claremont, California | 909-621-8011

To the average college-bound teen, Harvey Mudd may not have the name recognition that other schools of its caliber enjoy. While it may sound a bit like a Depression-era comic strip, the smallest of the colleges within the illustrious Claremont Consortium (Pomona, Claremont McKenna, Scripps, and Pitzer are the others) is routinely rated one of the best liberal arts colleges in the entire country and one of the top STEM institutions in the world.

Inside the Classroom
Only 906 undergraduate students occupy this tiny 33-acre campus; however, it is surrounded by the aforementioned affiliated colleges, giving the experience a less claustrophobic feel. Only six majors are offered: biology, chemistry, computer science, engineering, mathematics, and physics. All are incredibly strong. Students also have the option to combine certain disciplines into what amounts to a double major. In preparing a small army of future engineers and scientists, Harvey Mudd has been at the forefront of preaching a balanced education. The school requires a significant amount of coursework in the humanities, backing up its stated belief that "technology divorced from humanity is worse than no technology at all."

Class sizes are not always as tiny as the school itself. While 62% of courses have an enrollment under 20, another 32% enroll between 20 and 39 students. Regardless, Mudd prides itself on offering graduate-level research opportunities and experiential learning to all undergrads. The college backs up its philosophical stance with cold, hard cash, allocating three million dollars annually to facilitate student-faculty research. Students can participate during the school year or during the Summer Undergraduate Research Program that entails 10 weeks of full-time laboratory work. The Clinic Program groups juniors and seniors and lets them work on a real-world problem for corporate or agency sponsors for 1,200 to 1,500 hours over the course of one year. It is not uncommon for participants to end up with their names on a patent.

The college routinely produces winners of scholarships from the National Science Foundation, the Astronaut Scholarship Foundation, the Department of Energy, the Department of Defense, the Watson Fellowship, and the Mindlin Prize for Innovative Ideas in Science. The faculty also regularly receive accolades for their teaching. Per capita, the college is the second leading producer of future PhDs in the country (behind Caltech).

Outside the Classroom
Campus life at Mudd is, in part, defined by the fact that you are not confined to one campus. After all, Pomona, Pitzer, Scripps, and CMC all share the same 560 acres of land, not to mention a whole lot else. Overall, 98% of undergrads elect to live on campus all four years. For athletics, Harvey Mudd, Claremont, and Scripps combine forces to compete in 21 NCAA Division III men's and women's sports. Club and intramural sports from ultimate Frisbee and equestrian to roller hockey and water polo are available as well. Both cross-consortium and Mudd-only clubs and activities are plentiful and diverse, ranging from a poker club to a lettuce-eating competition (seriously). With Los Angeles just a half-hour drive away, Claremont is located in close proximity to all of the restaurants, museums, theaters, and even Disneyland, if you so desire. Mudd's dorms are known for having distinct personalities, but one common thread is that the college is known, in general, to be a friendly and accepting place.

Career Services
HMC's Career Services Office only has three full-time professional staff members working on grad school/career advising and employer recruitment. That equates to a 302:1 student-to-advisor ratio, which is about average for a school in this guide, but easily meets the needs of HMC's small student population. Career Services is highly accessible to students, and it even offers walk-in hours from 1 to 4 p.m. each weekday. Staff members are more than happy to offer one-on-one attention, and students take advantage as the office holds roughly 900 sessions per year, just over one per student.

Harvey Mudd hosts a Fall Software Fair, a Fall General STEM Fair, and a Spring Fair that can be attended by all members of the consortium, which can draw as many as 235+ employers per year. The three fairs draw almost 2,000 student participants per year. Companies that recruit on campus comprise a who's who of tech royalty: Google, Microsoft, Meta, Space X, and Uber. In fact, many of those companies, along with other major corporations, conducted interviews on HMC's campus—228 in one recent academic year alone. Undergrads routinely land summer internships at an equally impressive array of technology companies. In examining the breakdown of where Mudd grads end up receiving job offers, there is a clear correlation with the employer relations efforts of the Career Services Office. Overall, HMC's career services earns top grades from the College Transitions staff.

Professional Outcomes

Seventy-two percent of the Class of 2022 planned on entering a job right after receiving their bachelor's degree. The highest number of recent Harvey Mudd graduates are scooped up by the following companies (in order of representation): Meta, Microsoft, and Caltech. Across all graduating years, significant numbers of alumni also can be found at Apple, Raytheon, Intel, Boeing, and the NASA Jet Propulsion Laboratory. Software and technology is, by far, the career field of choice with aerospace a distant second. The most common job titles held immediately out of college are software engineer, firmware engineer, and electrical engineer. Graduates average an impressive $117,500 starting salary, a phenomenal number even when accounting for the preponderance of STEM majors. By some measures, that is the highest starting salary of any institution in the United States.

Many Harvey Mudd grads—20% in 2022—go directly into graduate school programs. Last year's grads pursued advanced degrees at schools such as Caltech, Princeton, and UPenn. Others attended Duke, Cornell, Carnegie Mellon, Stanford, Georgetown, and Brown. The most pursued graduate fields of study at those elite schools are computer science, mathematics, physics, and mechanical engineering. A healthy 69% of those attending grad school are presently working toward a PhD.

Admission

A decade ago, over 30% of applicants to Harvey Mudd were accepted. In recent years, HMC's admit rate has hovered in the 13 to 15% range; it was 13% for applicants aspiring to join the Class of 2026. In examining the recent admissions history at this school, it is important to note that the profile of the average accepted student has not changed significantly and, unlike many other elite colleges across the United States, the number of applicants has not skyrocketed in the past few years. Early decision applicants made up 41% of the 2022-23 freshman class, which means applying early may be a good idea if Mudd is your top choice. The ED rate was 19%, which was significantly higher than in the regular round.

In a typical year, 90%+ of accepted applicants finished in the top 10% of their high school class, and every single student placed at least in the top 25%. Valedictorians and salutatorians make up approximately 40% of the student body. While test-optional for now, standardized test scores typically need to be high to garner serious consideration. The mid-50% range on standardized tests for freshmen in 2022-23 was 1480-1560 on the SAT and 34-36 on the ACT. The school lists essays, GPA, course rigor, and recommendations as being "very important" factors in admissions decisions. In sum, Harvey Mudd is not a school that you add to your college list on a whim. It is an institution for those with a proven track record within the realm of science and engineering. Excellent grades in AP/IB course work, along with standardized test scores well above the 95th percentile, are just about prerequisites for serious consideration.

Worth Your Money?

At $89,115 per year, a degree from Harvey Mudd won't come cheap, but the majority of undergraduates do not pay the full cost. Almost 70% of students receive some type of financial aid and the average award is $49k; last year, 13% of freshmen qualified for merit awards. As a result, HMC helps many students from lower- and middle-income families attend the school. While that does result in a postgraduate debt load in the average range, alumni enjoy such strong job prospects that paying back loans will not be overly worrisome. No matter your circumstances, if you have a chance to go to Mudd, start packing your bags.

FINANCIAL
Institutional Type: Private
In-State Tuition: $66,255
Out-of-State Tuition: $66,255
Room & Board: $21,710
Books & Supplies: $800

Avg. Need-Based Grant: $48,675
Avg. % of Need Met: 100%

Avg. Merit-Based Award: $14,147
% Receiving (Freshmen w/o Need): 20%

Avg. Cumulative Debt: $22,789
% of Students Borrowing: 48%

CAREER
Who Recruits
1. Palantir
2. The Aerospace Corporation
3. Oracle
4. Boeing
5. Farmers Insurance

Notable Internships
1. Google
2. Salesforce
3. PayPal

Top Employers
1. Google
2. Microsoft
3. Apple
4. Northrop Grumman
5. Facebook

Where Alumni Work
1. Los Angeles
2. San Francisco
3. Seattle
4. San Diego
5. New York City

Earnings
College Scorecard (10-YR Post-Entry): $128,215
PayScale (Early Career): $97,700
PayScale (Mid-Career): $166,600
PayScale 20-Year ROI: $1,511,000

RANKINGS
Money: 4.5
U.S. News: 16, Liberal Arts Colleges
Wall Street Journal/THE: Not Ranked
Washington Monthly: 1, Liberal Arts Colleges

OVERGENERALIZATIONS
Students are:
Always studying
Politically liberal
Nerdy
Tight-knit (possess a strong sense of community)
Friendly

COLLEGE OVERLAPS
California Institute of Technology
Carnegie Mellon University
Massachusetts Institute of Technology
Stanford University
University of California, Berkeley

Haverford College

Haverford, Pennsylvania | 610-896-1350

ADMISSION
Admission Rate: 14%
Admission Rate - Men: 13%
Admission Rate - Women: 15%
EA Admission Rate: Not Offered
ED Admission Rate: 41%
ED Admits as % of Total Admits: 24%
Admission Rate (5-Year Trend): -6%
% of Admits Attending (Yield): 45%
Transfer Admission Rate: 14%

SAT Reading/Writing (Middle 50%): 700-760
SAT Math (Middle 50%): 730-780
ACT Composite (Middle 50%): 33-35

% Graduated in Top 10% of HS Class: 96%
% Graduated in Top 25% of HS Class: 100%
% Graduated in Top 50% of HS Class: 100%

Demonstrated Interest: Considered
Legacy Status: Considered
Racial/Ethnic Status: Considered
Admission Interview Offered: Yes

ENROLLMENT
Total Undergraduate Enrollment: 1,421
% Full-Time: 100%
% Male: 46%
% Female: 54%
% Out-of-State: 86%
% Fraternity: Not Offered
% Sorority: Not Offered
% On-Campus (All Undergraduate): 96%
Freshman Housing Required: Yes

% African-American: 5%
% Asian: 12%
% Hispanic: 13%
% White: 49%
% Other: 1%
% International: 11%
% Low-Income: 14%

ACADEMICS
Student-to-Faculty Ratio: 9 to 1
% of Classes Under 20: 72%
% of Classes 20-49: 27%
% of Classes 50 or More: 1%
% Full-Time Faculty: 79%
% Full-Time Faculty w/ Terminal Degree: 98%

Top Programs
Anthropology
Astronomy
Biology
Chemistry
English
Mathematics
Physics
Political Science

Retention Rate: 94%
4-Year Graduation Rate: 83%
6-Year Graduation Rate: 91%

Curricular Flexibility: Very Flexible
Academic Rating: ★★★★✦

#CollegesWorthYourMoney

Serving 1,421 remarkably accomplished undergraduate students, Haverford College, situated on Philly's ritzy Main Line, has 190 years of history and a reputation as one of the best liberal arts colleges in the country. Affectionately known as "The Ford," the college is part of the Tri-College Consortium with nearby Bryn Mawr and Swarthmore, which also happen to be among the crème de la crème of liberal arts schools. Students can take courses at those two schools as well through Penn's Wharton School of Business via an additional alliance known as the Quaker Consortium.

Inside the Classroom
Haverford offers 31 majors, 32 minors, 12 concentrations, and eleven consortium programs—areas of study that can be pursued at partner campuses. All students must fulfill a first-year writing requirement, a two-course language requirement, and a quantitative or symbolic reasoning requirement, and students need to take an uncredited physical education course prior to their junior year. Every student produces a senior thesis, a work of original research/scholarship under the close supervision of a faculty member. Teens seeking a relatively open curriculum that encourages exploration and the pursuit of one's unique passions will adore Haverford.

The school's 9:1 student-to-faculty ratio and exclusive emphasis on undergraduate education lead to exceptionally intimate classes, 33% of which have fewer than 10 students, and 72% have fewer than 20. Plenty of summer research opportunities exist in which students can work alongside faculty, and some STEM students conduct and present original research through the Undergraduate Science Research Symposium. The study abroad program has a 49% participation rate, and students can choose from 70+ programs in 30+ countries.

The most popular areas of study at Haverford include the social sciences (24%), biology (14%), psychology (11%), physical sciences (10%), computer science (9%), and mathematics (7%). All majors are highly respected in the eyes of graduate institutions and potential employers, but programs in English, physics, and political science receive especially high marks. Science majors and those on a premed track gain acceptance to prestigious PhD programs and medical schools at an eye-popping rate (95%). Graduates are also no strangers to competitive national awards/fellowships. In the school's history, it claims 20 Rhodes Scholars, and in 2023 alone, Haverford seniors and alumni captured four Fulbright Scholarships.

Outside the Classroom
Last year, 96% of students lived on this stunningly beautiful 216-acre campus; first-years are assigned to one of four residence halls. There are no fraternities or sororities at Haverford. Even with such a tiny student body, Haverford fields 23 varsity sports teams that compete in NCAA Division III. Combined with the seven club sports teams, 33% of undergrads participate in varsity athletics. The college's 145 student-run organizations include an array of pre-professional and service-oriented groups as well as plenty of recreational/performance options such as the Martial Arts Alliance, contemporary dance, and a number of a cappella groups. HAVOC is an outdoor adventure group that has a strong membership. The mock trial team placed second in the nation in 2017. Fellow Tri-Co member schools Bryn Mawr and Swarthmore offer plenty of additional chances for social connection, both formal and informal. All that the city of Philadelphia has to offer is only eight miles away. The Main Line area itself offers plenty of dining, cultural, and entertainment choices. The college's Honor Code and governing Honor Council are central to life at Haverford. Tenets of the code include un-proctored exams, no RAs in dorms, and tolerance of people of all backgrounds and orientations.

Career Services
The Center for Career & Professional Advising (CCPA) employs seven individuals who specialize in career counseling, prelaw advising, and health professions advising. With a 203:1 student-to-advisor ratio, Haverford compares favorably against most of the other colleges featured in this guide. The resources are deployed efficiently; in a given year, the CCPA engages in 1,500+ advising sessions, reaches 84% of the student body in some capacity, and makes a great effort to reach first-year students. In fact, close to 90% of freshmen report engaging with the office. The level of personalized advising is also evident by the annual number of resume critiques, 550+.

In hosting 150 information sessions and workshops per year, there are almost daily opportunities for students to sharpen their pre-professional skills and connect with potential employers. Large- scale career fairs are typically a joint effort of the Tri-College Consortium, along with Bryn Mawr and Swarthmore. Haverford alone draws more than one hundred employers to campus for its career fairs. The CCPA funds more than 140 internships per year and helps facilitate 190 on-campus interviews. Additionally, the college has more than 1,000 alumni association volunteers who provide hundreds of job-shadowing and externship experiences to current students. The CCPA delivers ample personalized attention to undergraduates and does an unsurpassed job assisting students with acceptance into top graduate schools.

Professional Outcomes

Six months after leaving Haverford, 63% of the Class of 2022 had found employment, 19% had enrolled in graduate school, and 9% were still job hunting. Among the employed, business was the most common industry (28%), followed by education (18%), science & technology (15%), and healthcare (14%). Employers hiring multiple recent Haverford grads include Epic, JP Morgan Chase Bank, Boston Consulting Group, Goldman Sachs, the National Institutes of Health, and the Children's Hospital of Philadelphia. Mid-career salaries are comparable to other elite liberal arts schools such as Wesleyan, Colby, and Swarthmore, and staying in the Philly metro area is the number one choice of alumni. New York City, various international destinations, Boston, and DC are next in popularity.

Of the 19% of 2022 grads who elected to continue their education, the most commonly entered fields of study were STEM (51%) and medicine/health (15%). Graduate schools accepting the highest number of recent alumni include Yale, Columbia, the University of Chicago, Penn, Stanford, and Duke. Those applying to medical school have extraordinary success as the college's 95% rate of acceptance is more than double the national average. Haverford undergrads average MCAT scores in the 85th percentile of all test takers. In the last three years, 100% of those applying to law school received at least one letter of acceptance. Of that group, roughly one-third were accepted into a top fifteen law school, and 94% had found homes at a top one hundred law school.

Admission

Admissions saw 5,657 applications received for a place in the Class of 2026 and only 14% were accepted; this was lower than the previous cycle's 18% figure. A staggering 96% of enrolled freshmen earned a place in the top 10% of their high school class and sported a mid-50% test score of 1410-1530 on the SAT and 33-35 on the ACT. A handful of years ago, the acceptance rate was a slightly higher 22%, but the academic profile of the average admitted applicant was similar to that of a 2022-23 freshman.

According to the admissions committee, the most important factors in the decision-making process are: rigor of coursework, GPA, essays, recommendations, extracurricular activities, and character/personal qualities. Class rank, talent/ability, test scores, work experience, and volunteer work make up the second rung of considered data points. Applying early decision can be a significant advantage. In the most recent cycle, ED applicants were accepted at a far more generous 41% clip and comprised 54% of that year's incoming freshmen. Even with a self-selecting applicant pool that results in modest application numbers, Haverford is an exceptionally difficult school to gain acceptance into. The 14% acceptance rate is almost misleadingly encouraging, and applicants sizing up their chances will be better informed by the high level of academic achievement displayed by successful applicants. Applying ED should be given serious consideration if Haverford is among your top choices.

Worth Your Money?

Haverford's annual cost of attendance is among the highest in the country at $86,540, but, on the positive end, it meets 100% of demonstrated need for those who qualify. The total average annual grant is almost $61,000 and given to 43% of attending students, helping make the school affordable for those not in the highest income brackets. If you can afford the upfront costs, or if you receive a sufficiently sized financial aid award, becoming part of this elite institution will likely prove worth the investment in the long run.

FINANCIAL
Institutional Type: Private
In-State Tuition: $68,020
Out-of-State Tuition: $68,020
Room & Board: $18,520
Books & Supplies: $1,209

Avg. Need-Based Grant: $60,937
Avg. % of Need Met: 100%

Avg. Merit-Based Award: $0
% Receiving (Freshmen w/o Need): 0%

Avg. Cumulative Debt: $16,354
% of Students Borrowing: 24%

CAREER
Who Recruits
1. Chatham Financial
2. FDIC
3. Janney Montgomery Scott
4. Boston Consulting Group
5. Analysis Group

Notable Internships
1. Boston Consulting Group
2. Spotify
3. U.S. House of Representatives

Top Employers
1. Google
2. Children's Hospital of Philadelphia
3. Facebook
4. US State Department
5. Deloitte

Where Alumni Work
1. New York City
2. Philadelphia
3. Washington, DC
4. Boston
5. San Francisco

Earnings
College Scorecard (10-YR Post-Entry): $78,330
PayScale (Early Career): $65,400
PayScale (Mid-Career): $141,200
PayScale 20-Year ROI: $719,000

RANKINGS
Money: 4.5
U.S. News: 21, Liberal Arts Colleges
Wall Street Journal/THE: 41
Washington Monthly: 5, Liberal Arts Colleges

OVERGENERALIZATIONS
Students are:
Always studying
Politically liberal
Collaborative
Intellectual
Involved/invested in campus life

COLLEGE OVERLAPS
Amherst College
Brown University
Swarthmore College
University of Pennsylvania
Wesleyan University

Hobart and William Smith Colleges

Geneva, New York | 315-781-3622

ADMISSION

Admission Rate: 68%
Admission Rate - Men: 66%
Admission Rate - Women: 71%
EA Admission Rate: 82%
ED Admission Rate: 74%
ED Admits as % of Total Admits: 5%
Admission Rate (5-Year Trend): +4%
% of Admits Attending (Yield): 13%
Transfer Admission Rate: 44%

SAT Reading/Writing (Middle 50%): 610-700
SAT Math (Middle 50%): 600-700
ACT Composite (Middle 50%): 27-32

% Graduated in Top 10% of HS Class: 29%
% Graduated in Top 25% of HS Class: 53%
% Graduated in Top 50% of HS Class: 87%

Demonstrated Interest: Considered
Legacy Status: Considered
Racial/Ethnic Status: Considered
Admission Interview Offered: Yes

ENROLLMENT

Total Undergraduate Enrollment: 1,559
% Full-Time: 99%
% Male: 49%
% Female: 51%
% Out-of-State: 50%
% Fraternity: 12%
% Sorority: 5%
% On-Campus (All Undergraduate): 87%
Freshman Housing Required: Yes

% African-American: 7%
% Asian: 2%
% Hispanic: 9%
% White: 66%
% Other: 4%
% International: 8%
% Low-Income: 24%

ACADEMICS

Student-to-Faculty Ratio: 9 to 1
% of Classes Under 20: 75%
% of Classes 20-49: 25%
% of Classes 50 or More: 0%
% Full-Time Faculty: 91%
% Full-Time Faculty w/ Terminal Degree: 98%

Top Programs
Architectural Studies
Economics
Environmental Studies
History
International Relations
Media and Society
Philosophy
Political Science

Retention Rate: 87%
4-Year Graduation Rate: 68%
6-Year Graduation Rate: 75%

Curricular Flexibility: Very Flexible
Academic Rating: ★★★★

#CollegesWorthYourMoney

As the "s" at the end of the name Hobart & William Smith Colleges implies, there are two "coordinate colleges" on the same campus that share the same resources, curriculum, and faculty. Those who identify as men enter Hobart College, founded in 1822, and those identifying as women matriculate into William Smith College, founded in 1906. The schools began offering coeducational classes in 1942 and the two institutions have only become more interwoven in the intervening years. The schools do still possess their own distinct deans, student governments, and athletic departments. For a small school of only 1,559 undergrads, the offerings are wide with 45 majors and 68 minors.

Inside the Classroom

HWS students take four courses per semester and 32 over the course of their undergraduate years. All are greeted by a comprehensive orientation program that includes a First-Year Seminar in the first semester. From there, students map out a course of study that addresses a series of "Aspirational Goals of Curriculum." Those include developing an experiential understanding of scientific inquiry, a critical and experiential understanding of the artistic process, and a critical understanding of cultural differences. Additional encounters with a "Writing Entrenched Curriculum" are built into a course of study as a senior capstone experience.

The average class size is just 16 students, and 100% of courses are taught by full-time faculty; the student-to-faculty ratio is an excellent 9:1. That ratio has a tremendous impact on faculty accessibility, as evidenced by the fact that 96% of students report having a discussion with a professor outside the classroom. Every student participates in at least one of the following: community service, service learning, or community-based research. Possessing one of the strongest study abroad programs you'll find at any American college, 60% of HWS undergraduates take a semester of study in one of nearly 50 locations around the globe.

The social sciences account for the greatest number of degrees conferred each year, typically more than 25%. The next most popular areas of concentration are in biology, psychology, journalism, and the physical sciences. The most popular major (within the social sciences) is economics, and many graduates in that area go on to work for prominent banking institutions. (See more details in the "Professional Outcomes" section.) The school also places a strong emphasis on global exploration and the procurement of prestigious national fellowships. Recent students have captured Fulbright, Udall, Critical Language, Goldwater, and Truman Scholarships.

Outside the Classroom

Almost 60% of Hobart and William Smith undergrads hail from out of state and all, even the locals, live on campus as freshmen. Most continue that practice even as upperclassmen with 87% of all students residing in campus housing. There are seven fraternities recognized by the school but just one sorority. Not surprisingly, based on those numbers, the percentage of men participating in Greek life exceeds the number of women at 6% versus 2%. The sense of community is strong at HWS, and the student body performs over 80,000 hours of collective service each year. There are 90+ organizations as well as a number of popular campus-wide events that include the annual Caribbean Student Association's Masquerade Ball and events organized by the Campus Activities Board, such as hot air balloon rides over the quad and Open Mic nights. On the athletics front, the Hobart Statesmen participate in 11 intercollegiate sports, all of which play at the NCAA Division III level, with the exception of a Division I men's lacrosse squad. Meanwhile, the William Smith Herons compete in 12 intercollegiate sports. The schools also offer a full array of club sports including alpine skiing, a step team, and mixed martial arts. The town of Geneva is in the heart of New York's Finger Lakes region, an area known for its gorgeous natural landscape and insane concentration of wineries. (There are 10,000 acres of vineyards in a 9,000-square-mile area.)

Career Services

The Salisbury Center for Career, Professional, and Experiential Education is staffed by six professional employees, which calculates to a 260:1 student-to-counselor ratio, a figure comparable to many other schools of similar size. Where the center stands out begins with its Pathways Program that delineates a series of steps and activities for each student to engage in from freshman through senior year. Students are encouraged to attend regular resume-writing workshops and cover-letter clinics, or to schedule a one-on-one appointment with a career assistant.

Any student who is in good academic standing and completes the aforementioned Pathways Plan is eligible for the Guaranteed Internship Program, a unique feature of the Salisbury Center. For unpaid interns, the school will supply up to $1,300 to help offset some of the living costs interns will incur. Recent internship sites include Yahoo, Comedy Central, Bank of America, Lockheed Martin, HBO Films, and Ralph Lauren. The 23,000 living alumni generally like to stay connected to their alma mater and are known for their willingness to mentor current undergraduates. Job-shadowing opportunities can be arranged through corporate contacts or alumni connections. In sum, this is a career services office that takes pride in reaching all students, beginning from the moment they set foot on campus.

Professional Outcomes

In a typical year, approximately two-thirds of HWS grads immediately enter the world of full-time employment while 15% jump right into pursuing a graduate or professional degree. Looking at all living alumni, companies employing the greatest number of grads include Morgan Stanley, Fidelity Investments, Merrill Lynch, Bozzuto (real estate), JP Morgan, Google, UBS, JPMorgan Chase, and Citi. The greatest concentration of alumni can be found in New York City; Boston; Rochester; Washington, DC; Philadelphia; and San Francisco.

On the graduate and professional school front, HWS alumni fare quite well, including at many of the top programs in the country. For example, nearly 100% of law school applicants are accepted, including at top-ranked Yale, the University of Chicago, and the University of California, Berkeley law schools. Medical and dental school applicants are equally successful. In fact, in a single recent year, four alums enrolled at dental schools that included Harvard, Penn, and Boston University. In the last few years, grads have matriculated into medical school at the likes of Penn State College of Medicine and Columbia University's College of Physicians and Surgeons.

Admission

There were 5,082 applicants for a place in the Class of 2026, and 3,475 (68%) were accepted. The average high school GPA of enrolled students was 3.61, and 53% ranked in the top 25% of their class. Many of those students took advantage of the school's test-optional policy that has been in place since 2006; only 22% submitted SAT scores (the median score was 1320), and 9% included ACT results (the median score was 31). It is important to note that 23% of entering first-years possessed a GPA of 3.25 or lower, so this school is not closed off to B students.

Hobart and William Smith Colleges rate the rigor of an applicant's curriculum and GPA as the top factors in admissions decisions. Other factors that loom large are class rank, essays, recommendations, extracurricular activities, work experience, volunteer experience, and an admissions interview. The personal interview is only required for those seeking particular scholarships, but the 25-minute Q&A is recommended for all candidates as "last year's applicants who interviewed had a much higher acceptance rate to HWS." If you are a borderline applicant, going early decision may be a wise move. Almost 40% of the Class of 2026 was filled via early decision, and the ED acceptance rate was 74%.

Worth Your Money?

Hobart and William Smith Colleges have an intimidating tuition sticker price of $63k, and room and board will set you back another $17k. However, few undergrads pay anything close to $80k+ per year. In fact, over 90% of current students are granted some form of financial aid. HWS ranks well in terms of ROI, and its graduates earn slightly higher mid-career salaries than graduates of other New York-based liberal arts schools including Vassar, Ithaca, and Skidmore. It is worth noting that the average student graduates with a debt load that exceeds the national average, so we cannot recommend this school for a cost-conscious student without a clear path to a solid-earning career path.

FINANCIAL
Institutional Type: Private
In-State Tuition: $63,268
Out-of-State Tuition: $63,268
Room & Board: $17,334
Books & Supplies: $1,300

Avg. Need-Based Grant: $44,873
Avg. % of Need Met: 84%

Avg. Merit-Based Award: $27,397
% Receiving (Freshmen w/o Need): 28%

Avg. Cumulative Debt: $37,668
% of Students Borrowing: 72%

CAREER
Who Recruits
1. HSBC
2. Goldman Sachs
3. NYC Department of Education
4. Citi
5. UBS

Notable Internships
1. Hallmark Channel
2. New York Stock Exchange
3. Morrill Lynch

Top Employers
1. Morgan Stanley
2. Fidelity Investments
3. Merrill Lynch
4. JPMorgan Chase
5. Google

Where Alumni Work
1. New York City
2. Boston
3. Rochester, NY
4. Washington, DC
5. Philadelphia

Earnings
College Scorecard (10-YR Post-Entry): $68,706
PayScale (Early Career): $59,700
PayScale (Mid-Career): $121,600
PayScale 20-Year ROI: $471,000

RANKINGS
Money: 4
U.S. News: 70, Liberal Arts Colleges
Wall Street Journal/THE: 186
Washington Monthly: 32, Liberal Arts Colleges

OVERGENERALIZATIONS
Students are:
Outdoorsy
Environmentally conscious
Always admiring the beauty of their campus
Tight-knit (possess a strong sense of community)
Collaborative

COLLEGE OVERLAPS
Colgate University
Connecticut College
Hamilton University
Skidmore College
Union College

Hofstra University

Hempstead, New York | 516-463-6700

Looking at Hofstra University today, one sees a private university of 6,110 undergraduate students spread across a gorgeous and imposing Long Island campus. Its roots as a commuter school for Long Island residents have long since faded from view as the student body is now comprised of close to 40% out-of-state and international students. While still a common safety school choice for high-achieving Northeasterners aiming for schools like Fordham and Boston University, Hofstra's national reputation is undoubtedly on the rise. It remains an excellent academic institution with tremendous resources to help students find their way to a successful career. Even better, it also is accessible to students with imperfect academic profiles—at least for now.

Inside the Classroom

There are 165 programs for undergraduates spread across the various colleges housing liberal arts, engineering, business, communications, and nursing/health professions. While the core curriculum varies from school to school, most Hofstra students are required to complete coursework in the humanities, natural sciences, history, philosophy, foreign language, quantitative reasoning, two introductory writing courses, and two advanced writing courses. In total, there are thirty-three credits worth of distributional requirements for students in the College of Liberal Arts and Sciences. First-year seminars are courses reserved for freshmen that enroll nineteen or fewer students, focus on a specific topic of interest, and help new students acclimate to college-level work.

The average undergraduate class size is 21, and the student-faculty ratio is a favorable 13-to-1. The great bulk of courses enroll between 10 and 29 students; 12% are single-digit enrollment courses, and only 2% of sections contain more than 50 students. Opportunities to participate in undergraduate research are managed by each department separately. Students in the Honors College have an easier time procuring opportunities as supervised independent research is built into the program. Full-length study abroad opportunities are offered in locations that include Amsterdam, China, Florence, Rome, and Ireland. Many students prefer short-term international sessions offered in January (three weeks) or summer (five weeks).

The Zarb School of Business draws 19% of the student body for good reason; it is a well-regarded business school with strong connections to many major banks and consulting firms. It also boasts one of the nation's best simulated trading rooms. The Lawrence Herbert School of Communication is widely known in the media industry, and Hofstra students enter in large numbers—14% of the total degrees conferred are in communication/journalism. Health professions (13%), social sciences (9%), and engineering (8%) are third, fourth, and fifth in popularity, respectively. Winning national postgraduate fellowships is not a major focus of Hofstra seniors. They have won an occasional Fulbright Scholarship, Critical Language Scholarship, and Gilman Scholarship in recent years.

Outside the Classroom

In 2022-23, only 57% of freshmen and 41% of the overall undergraduate student body lived on campus in one of 35 residence halls. There are traditional dorms as well as high-rise options that, collectively, offer single, double, triple, quad, and suite-style living options. Within the limits of the 240-acre campus are eighteen eateries, six theaters, an arboretum, a bird sanctuary, and an art museum that houses 5,000 works and artifacts. Hofstra's gorgeous, tree-lined grounds are deservedly included on many "most beautiful campus" lists. The school's fraternities and sororities attract 5% of men and 8% of women, creating an atmosphere with a noticeable Greek presence, but not a suffocating one. The sports teams, for many years known as the Flying Dutchmen, now compete as the Pride at the NCAA Division I level in the Colonial Athletic Association. There are 21 varsity sports—ten men's and eleven women's teams. There are 200 student-run clubs at Hofstra, including plenty of performance, cultural, or pre-professional options, and a big-time collegiate radio station, WRHU, which also serves as the radio home of the National Hockey League's New York Islanders. Hempstead is not the safest area or most desirable part of town, but this is made up for by having an amenity-filled campus and being only a twenty-five-minute drive from famed Jones Beach in Long Island and, of course, being only a 40- to 50-minute trip from all that New York City has to offer.

Career Services

Hofstra's Center for Career Design & Development is manned by eight professionals with expertise in career coaching, corporate outreach, and diversity and inclusion initiatives. That works out to a 764:1 student-to-advisor ratio, which is higher than the average school in this guide but not awful when compared to other midsize universities. The Fall Career and Internship Fair is attended by 130+ employers, and the center routinely offers in-person and online workshops, field trips to companies, networking events, and on-campus interview days with employers. More than 1,500 students attend career fairs at Hofstra each year.

Drawing employers to campus and placing current students with big-name organizations is aided by the school's location and the tight connections that the Career Center has forged with New York City employers. Hofstra's internship numbers for undergraduates are particularly strong. With the help of career services staff members, 67% of Hofstra students participate in at least one internship, and the average student completes 2.23 such experiences. Recent grads interned at hundreds of organizations including Berkshire Hathaway, Last Week Tonight with John Oliver, ABC News, and the Securities and Exchange Commission. Current students can also benefit from connecting with the 128,000 active alumni, over 1,000 of whom are active volunteers for the school and more than willing to assist with career exploration and the job search.

Professional Outcomes

Within six months of exiting with their diplomas, 92% of recent grads had found employment or a graduate school destination; 80% were employed and 33% were pursuing an advanced degree, which includes some overlap as many individuals were doing both. Northwell Health, the largest health care provider in New York State, is also the largest employer of Hofstra alumni. Other companies employing more than one hundred Flying Dutchmen/Pride alums include JPMorgan Chase, Citi, PwC, Morgan Stanley, EY, Deloitte, Estee Lauder, and NBC Universal. Recent grads have gone on to a number of interesting careers with professional sports teams, major media outlets, and political groups. The median starting salary was $62,000 with 19% of the class bringing home less than $40k and 50% making over $60k. Just about everyone stays in the Greater New York City area with Boston, Philly, and DC picking up the crumbs.

Grad school is a common next step for those receiving their Hofstra degree as 33% enrolled within months of receiving their bachelor's degree. Recent grads have matriculated into a wide array of graduate and professional schools including every SUNY and CUNY institution as well as many elite universities like Columbia, Yale, Carnegie Mellon, NYU, Berkeley, and Brown. The school offers its undergraduates a 4+4 BS/MD option in conjunction with its own Zucker School of Medicine. Other medical schools attended by recent grads include the Albert Einstein College of Medicine, Icahn School of Medicine, and SUNY Downstate.

Admission

Sixty-nine percent of the 23,577 applicants competing for a spot in the Class of 2026 were accepted, but a minuscule 10% of those accepted actually enrolled in the university. Of those who became 2022-23 freshmen, 95% had over a 3.0 GPA, 32% were in the top 10% of their high school class, and 52% were in the top 25%. The mid-50% SAT score was 1190-1370, and the average ACT range was 26-31. The university's degree of selectivity has remained constant in recent years. Acceptance rates and grades from the early 2010s are comparable to those today. Standardized test scores have risen, but much of that can be attributed to going test-optional (more on that in a moment).

The five factors viewed as the most important by the admissions committee are GPA, class rank, rigor of secondary school record, recommendations, and the essay. Hofstra went test-optional in 2014 and presently, around 40% of applicants still submit standardized test scores. Interviews are listed as "important" but are not a required part of the process. Extracurricular activities, talent/ability, and character/personal qualities also play a major factor in the process. For a school that has such a low yield rate (the percent of accepted students who enroll), it is surprising that it does not offer a binding early decision option, but it does offer early action. Hofstra remains a realistic option for B students who take some advanced coursework in high school.

Worth Your Money?

Hofstra is an expensive school, registering a $74,000 annual cost of attendance, but it is somewhat generous with financial aid, offering an average annual award of $30k. The Long Island location can make this school worth the money for those with a clear plan of how to take advantage of the school's New York City connections. Students without a pre-professional focus and for whom costs are a concern should also consider more affordable options.

FINANCIAL
Institutional Type: Private
In-State Tuition: $55,450
Out-of-State Tuition: $55,450
Room & Board: $18,560
Books & Supplies: $1,000

Avg. Need-Based Grant: $27,110
Avg. % of Need Met: 71%

Avg. Merit-Based Award: $23,346
% Receiving (Freshmen w/o Need): 29%

Avg. Cumulative Debt: $29,261
% of Students Borrowing: 60%

CAREER
Who Recruits
1. Cox Media Group
2. Stanley Black & Decker
3. Raytheon
4. Partners Healtcare
5. Boston Children's Hospital

Notable Internships
1. The Tonight Show
2. The Carlyle Group
3. CNN NY News Bureau

Top Employers
1. Northwell Health
2. JPMorgan Chase
3. Citi
4. Morgan Stanley
5. PwC

Where Alumni Work
1. New York City
2. Boston
3. Philadelphia
4. Washington, DC
5. Los Angeles

Earnings
College Scorecard (10-YR Post-Entry): $68,703
PayScale (Early Career): $60,000
PayScale (Mid-Career): $123,100
PayScale 20-Year ROI: $617,000

RANKINGS
Money: Not Ranked
U.S. News: 185, National Universities
Wall Street Journal/THE: 306
Washington Monthly: 422, National Universities

OVERGENERALIZATIONS
Students are:
Diverse
Career-driven
Collaborative
Social
Liberal

COLLEGE OVERLAPS
Boston University
Drexel University
Fordham University
Pennsylvania State University - University Park
Stony Brook University (SUNY)

ADMISSION
Admission Rate: 53%
Admission Rate - Men: 50%
Admission Rate - Women: 55%
EA Admission Rate: 64%
ED Admission Rate: 48%
ED Admits as % of Total Admits: 2%
Admission Rate (5-Year Trend): +12%
% of Admits Attending (Yield): 24%
Transfer Admission Rate: 62%

SAT Reading/Writing (Middle 50%): 540-650
SAT Math (Middle 50%): 510-640
ACT Composite (Middle 50%): 20-26

% Graduated in Top 10% of HS Class: 27%
% Graduated in Top 25% of HS Class: 63%
% Graduated in Top 50% of HS Class: 90%

Demonstrated Interest: Considered
Legacy Status: Considered
Racial/Ethnic Status: Not Considered
Admission Interview Offered: No

ENROLLMENT
Total Undergraduate Enrollment: 9,809
% Full-Time: 92%
% Male: 28%
% Female: 72%
% Out-of-State: 88%
% Fraternity: 8%
% Sorority: 6%
% On-Campus (All Undergraduate): 54%
Freshman Housing Required: Yes

% African-American: 65%
% Asian: 3%
% Hispanic: 6%
% White: 0%
% Other: 15%
% International: 4%
% Low-Income: 42%

ACADEMICS
Student-to-Faculty Ratio: 14 to 1
% of Classes Under 20: 46%
% of Classes 20-49: 44%
% of Classes 50 or More: 11%
% Full-Time Faculty: 70%
% Full-Time Faculty w/ Terminal Degree: 81%

Top Programs
Biology
Business
Communications
Computer Science
Criminology
Health
Nursing
Political Science

Retention Rate: 89%
4-Year Graduation Rate: 61%
6-Year Graduation Rate: 66%

Curricular Flexibility: Somewhat Flexible
Academic Rating: ★★★

#CollegesWorthYourMoney

Referred to by students as "The Mecca," Howard University is widely viewed as the premier institution among all historically black colleges and universities (HBCUs) in the country. Founded in 1867, the university contains 13 schools and colleges, including law and medical schools, and it serves 9,800+ undergraduates. HU's remarkable alumni list includes Toni Morrison, Thurgood Marshall, Kamala Harris, Chadwick Boseman, and Zora Neale Hurston.

Inside the Classroom
The university-wide core curriculum, in place for over two decades, is comprised of 23-27 credit hours' worth of coursework, although mandated classes vary slightly by academic program. Every HU grad will take two courses in English Composition and one in Afro-American Studies. Most students take one class in each of the following categories: college mathematics, freshman orientation, physical education, humanities, social sciences, and natural sciences. Some students also complete courses in philosophy, science, writing, foreign language, and speech.

A strong 12:1 student-to-faculty ratio allows for generally small class sizes, even with over 3,000 graduate students also in attendance. Sixty-seven percent of undergraduate course sections enroll fewer than 30 students, and just 11% enroll more than 50 students. Undergraduate opportunities are available in all disciplines, both internally and externally. In the hard sciences alone, HU undergrads have worked on research in "the synthesis of inorganic nanoparticles, determining the amount of particulate matter in the atmosphere, using computational algorithms to design nanoscale materials, developing novel medicines to fight cancer, and even designing biomaterials." Not many students take advantage of the study abroad program; a typical year sees roughly 60 students take a semester in one of 20 international destinations.

The three most popular major choices at Howard are business (15%), communication and journalism (15%), and biology (9%). The Howard University School of Business is highly respected by global corporations as well as top MBA programs. The Afro-American Studies and English departments also are strong. Additional areas in which a high percentage of bachelor's degrees are conferred include the social sciences (12%), health programs (9%), and engineering (5%). Prestigious national scholarship organizations regularly select HU grads. The school has seen four total Rhodes Scholars named and it produces more than five Fulbright Scholars in an average year.

Outside the Classroom
Just about every single freshman—95%—live on Howard's 257-acre Washington, DC, campus. More than half of all undergraduates can be found residing in university-owned housing. The university's four first-year halls are separated by gender, but the four halls that house sophomores through seniors are open to both men and women. The percentage of students participating in Greek life tends to be in the single digits each year. Nineteen varsity athletic teams compete as the Bison at the NCAA Division I level for basketball and the Division IAA level for all other sports; the basketball squad has appeared in the March Madness tourney just twice. Overall, there are 200+ registered student organizations, including a long-running TV and radio station that each reach a large audience. Homecoming Weekend in October is a monumental event at Howard, one that attracts over 100,000 visitors and features events like YardFest, a massive outdoor concert featuring superstar artists. HU has its own Metro stop, a convenience that opens the entire DC area to its students. Whether for the purposes of entertainment, cultural exploration, or historical appreciation, you can't ask for a better university location.

Career Services
The Center for Career and Professional Success (CCPS) has seven professional employees, including members dedicated to career coaching, employer relations, and experiential learning. With additional staff housed within the School of Business' Center for Career Excellence, the student-to-advisor ratio checks in at 980:1, higher than the majority of midsize institutions included in this book. Still, HU's career services delivers a plethora of outstanding resources, workshops, and networking opportunities that help Bison enjoy exceptional career outcomes. (See more details in the next section.)

The university hosts multiple career fairs each year, some discipline specific and others broader and open to all majors. The combination of the desirable applicant pool and DC location help to make those events worthwhile affairs that are well-attended by scores of top employers. Smaller workshops, panels, and information sessions take place virtually every day of the academic year. Howard also helps current students connect with former ones via the Alumni Services Portal. With such an active and deeply involved alumni network, Bison grads are known for taking time to help undergraduates as they look to blaze their own trails.

Professional Outcomes

If you name a desirable company in the tech, banking, or consulting industries, chances are it will employ more than a handful of Bison. In fact, over 100 alumni presently work for Amazon, Microsoft, Google, IBM, Accenture, Deloitte, Wells Fargo, and Apple. Large numbers of Bison also roam the corporate offices of JPMorgan Chase, Capital One, Facebook, and Goldman Sachs. It is similarly easy to locate Howard grads in just about any major American city. The heaviest concentrations can be found in Washington, DC; New York City; Atlanta; Los Angeles; Baltimore; Philadelphia; Chicago; San Francisco; and Houston.

Howard graduates typically earn fantastic results when applying to graduate and professional schools. For example, HU produces more African American medical school applicants than any other institution in the United States. In addition to Howard's own College of Medicine, those training to be doctors also go on to study at elite DC-based programs including the Georgetown University School of Medicine and the George Washington School of Medicine. HU offers a BS/MD program that allows applicants to complete an undergraduate and medical degree in just six years (as opposed to eight). Some future lawyers remain on campus to attend the Howard University School of Law while other recent grads are accepted into prestigious programs at Emory, Tulane, Harvard, Penn, and NYU. Simply put, if you post strong grades as an undergraduate at Howard, you will have no trouble finding another excellent school at which to earn an advanced degree.

Admission

Howard received more than 19,000 applications from those seeking an offer to join the Class of 2026 and accepted 54%; that was far more favorable than the 35% mark of the previous year. Among those who went on to enroll, the average unweighted high school GPA was 3.65, and the mid-50% standardized test scores were 20-26 on the ACT and 1060-1270 on the SAT. Twenty-seven percent placed in the top decile of their graduating class, and 10% fell outside the top half. This school does not offer interviews to undergraduate students, so the best ways to forge a personal connection with admissions staff are through the two required letters of recommendation and via an optional essay that allows applicants to discuss their major of interest.

GPA and the rigor of an applicant's curriculum sit atop the list of factors deemed "very important" by the admissions committee. Soft factors including essays, recommendations, and character/personal qualities are "important." Howard also considers class rank, test scores, legacy status, extracurriculars, talent/ability, first-generation status, and demonstrated interest. It offers both an early decision and a nonbinding early action deadline. It is worth noting that EA applicants tend to fare much better than those waiting until the regular decision deadline and, interestingly, even better than those applying ED.

Worth Your Money?

Howard's list price is extremely reasonable by modern standards, even before financial awards are factored in. At $32,878 in tuition and total direct costs of under $56k annually, it makes sense that Howard alumni carry a below-average cumulative debt compared to the national average. Median mid-career earnings are solid and higher than those at other prominent HBCUs like Morehouse or Spelman. All things considered, this school is definitely worth every dollar for just about every undergraduate who attends.

FINANCIAL
Institutional Type: Private
In-State Tuition: $33,344
Out-of-State Tuition: $33,344
Room & Board: $16,474
Books & Supplies: $1,360

Avg. Need-Based Grant: $11,430
Avg. % of Need Met: 28%

Avg. Merit-Based Award: $14,162
% Receiving (Freshmen w/o Need): 10%

Avg. Cumulative Debt: $29,646
% of Students Borrowing: 53%

CAREER
Who Recruits
1. IBM
2. JPMorganChase
3. AT&T
4. PwC
5. Amazon Web Services

Notable Internships
1. National Security Agency
2. The Washington Post
3. American Airlines

Top Employers
1. Amazon
2. Microsoft
3. Google
4. Deloitte
5. Wells Fargo

Where Alumni Work
1. Washington, DC
2. New York City
3. Atlanta
4. Los Angeles
5. Baltimore

Earnings
College Scorecard (10-YR Post-Entry): $59,441
PayScale (Early Career): $60,500
PayScale (Mid-Career): $107,900
PayScale 20-Year ROI: $482,000

RANKINGS
Money: 3
U.S. News: 115, National Universities
Wall Street Journal/THE: 315
Washington Monthly: 388, National Universities

OVERGENERALIZATIONS
Students are:
Politically liberal
Career-driven
Working hard and playing hard
Teeming with school pride
Dressed to impress

COLLEGE OVERLAPS
American University
Hampton University
Morehouse College
Spelman College
University of Maryland, College Park

Illinois Institute of Technology

Chicago, Illinois | 312-567-3025

A rare school that educates more advanced degree-seekers than undergraduate students, the Illinois Institute of Technology—traditionally referred to as IIT but rebranded in 2001 as Illinois Tech—is a private research university with just over 3,100 undergrads and 40+ undergraduate majors, mostly in the realms of engineering, business, computer science, and architecture. Located on Chicago's South Side, this school has a large international presence with 70+ countries represented as well as a large percentage of undergraduates present with serious financial need. This is significant because Illinois Tech has a reputation not just for producing grads who earn excellent salaries but for facilitating social and economic mobility as well.

Inside the Classroom
Undergraduates study in one of six undergraduate divisions: the Armour College of Engineering, the College of Architecture, the College of Science, the Lewis College of Human Sciences, the School of Applied Technology, or the Stuart School of Business. The university has four learning goals associated with its core curriculum: (1) commitment to positive change in their communities, nations, and the world; (2) the ability to think critically and view problems as opportunities for innovation; (3) the ability to collaborate professionally and ethically; and (4) communicate effectively. Toward those aims, one must take three courses in the humanities, three in the social or behavioral sciences, three in science or engineering, one computer science course, and thirty-six hours of coursework with a substantial focus on oral or written communication. A 600 SAT reading score will get you out of introductory writing.

The student-to-faculty ratio is 13:1, but with so many graduate students to serve, undergraduate course sections are not small across the board; rather, they vary from single-digit enrollment in 22% of sections to 40+ students in 17% of courses. Yet, an Illinois Tech education provides many opportunities for students to have close contact with faculty. For example, the Interprofessional Projects (IPRO) Program features "teams of students from a variety of majors that develop solutions to real-world problems using design-centered methodology and innovative thinking." Completing two IPROs is a graduation requirement. The Elevate program connects students with undergraduate research and other experiential learning opportunities as early as freshman year. There are over 40 study abroad programs in which IIT students can participate, although as with most technical institutions, the bulk of undergrads remain on campus for all four years.

The most popular major is computer science followed by architecture and mechanical engineering. Overall, 47% of the degrees conferred are in engineering, 25% in computer science, and 12% in architecture. The School of Applied Technology offers one of the most respected information technology programs in the country and serves as a pipeline to many top tech companies. The College of Architecture has a similarly sterling national reputation. Programs in engineering and computer science are also strong.

Outside the Classroom
In an average year, Illinois Tech's 120-acre urban campus is home to around two-fifths of the undergraduate population. Freshmen and sophomores are required to live on campus, but commuters who live with their parents and transfers are often granted exemptions. There are two traditional dormitories and two "villages" that are collections of smaller residence halls. S.R. Crown Hall and the McCormick Tribune Campus Center are architecturally unique, and the campus as a whole sometimes cracks "most beautiful" lists. Many students self-identify as "nerds," and the rigorous academics and male-heavy population (only around one-third of students are female) can limit social life. Greek life has a moderate presence on campus drawing 9-10% of the student body. There are 17 varsity intercollegiate sports teams—nine men's and eight women's—many of which compete in NCAA Division III. More than 150 student-run organizations are available, and the BOG serves as a popular hub thanks to its free, eight-lane bowling alley and abundance of arcade games. Campus is only three miles south of downtown Chicago and about one mile from Guaranteed Rate Field where the Chicago White Sox play baseball. Plenty of bars, jazz clubs, museums, zoos, and an aquarium are a short distance from campus.

Career Services
The main Career Services Office at IIT consists of seven professional employees, but the Stuart School of Business has its own separate office with two full-time employees bringing the school's total to nine career services professionals. That works out to a student-advisor ratio of 347:1, within the average range of schools profiled in this book. Freshmen are encouraged to begin working with a career counselor during their first semester. In addition to the professional staff members, a number of peer counselors also are available to those looking to get the jump on vocational exploration.

Staff members are always willing to assist with "résumé and cover letter writing, networking advice, company research assistance, mock interviews, (and) dinner/business etiquette workshops." Two-day career fairs are held on campus each semester, and more than 150 employers attend, including industry giants Amazon, Goldman Sachs, NBCUniversal, and Grainger. The school claims 80,000+ living alumni, many of whom are concentrated in tech companies in Chicago, making networking conditions favorable. That can come in handy when pursuing for-credit internships or co-ops during the school year or the summer term. However, the school does not release information about what percentage of students complete one or more internships or what percentage of the undergraduate student body is serviced by the office in any capacity in a given year.

Professional Outcomes

Ninety percent of Illinois Tech grads in 2022 already enjoyed a positive career/grad school outcome within six months of earning their degree. Alumni can be found in sizable numbers within major corporations including Motorola, Amazon, Microsoft, Google, Apple, Accenture, JPMorgan Chase, IBM, EY, and Cisco. The Greater Chicago area plays home to more than half of IIT alumni with San Francisco, New York City, and Seattle all attracting fairly large numbers of Scarlet Hawks. Starting salaries as well as mid-career compensation figures are the strongest in the state of Illinois and among the highest anywhere when compared to other highly selective private universities; the median starting salary is $73,650.

Those continuing to graduate school often stay at Illinois Tech, which offers degrees in engineering, science, architecture, business, design, human sciences, applied technology, and law. The next most frequently attended institutions include Carnegie Mellon, Northwestern, UIUC, and Boston University with computer science, mechanical engineering, and architecture being the three most popular fields of advanced study. For premed students, the medical school acceptance rate is "often above the national average." A dual degree program is offered in partnership with Midwestern University's Chicago College of Osteopathic Medicine. Recent students have earned a place at top medical schools like the Northwestern University Feinberg School of Medicine, New York University School of Medicine, and the University of Michigan Medical School.

Admission

With an acceptance rate of 61%, the Illinois Institute of Technology is not looking to shut the door on those with imperfect credentials, yet some of that hefty number is attributed to self-selection. The mid-50% SAT range of 2022-23 freshmen is 1230-1390 and the ACT range is 28-32. Fifty-six percent of freshmen earned a place in the top 10% of their respective high school class, 79% were in the top quartile, and 99% were in the top 50%. All of those numbers, including the overall acceptance rate, are similar to those from five years ago, despite a spike in the total number of applications.

Like most engineering-focused schools, the hard numbers are paramount when it comes to making admissions decisions. Standardized test scores, GPA, and the level of rigor of one's coursework are of the utmost importance while factors such as class rank and recommendations are also given weight by the committee. Female applicants enjoy slightly better admissions prospects with an acceptance rate of 68% compared to men at 58%. There are EA and ED options at this school, the latter just having been added to the menu recently. Applying on the early side is your best bet regardless of whether IIT is your number one choice or one of many irons in the fire.

Worth Your Money?

On paper, the cost of attendance at IIT is greater than $74,000 per year. However, 98% of students receive some type of aid, and even families with an income above $110,000 receive an average scholarship and grant combo adding up to almost half of the tuition cost. As a result, the school is a worthy investment for most as solid-paying tech, finance, and architecture jobs in the Chicago area await your arrival post-graduation.

FINANCIAL
Institutional Type: Private
In-State Tuition: $51,763
Out-of-State Tuition: $51,763
Room & Board: $16,528
Books & Supplies: $1,200

Avg. Need-Based Grant: $41,790
Avg. % of Need Met: 89%

Avg. Merit-Based Award: $31,179
% Receiving (Freshmen w/o Need): 34%

Avg. Cumulative Debt: $31,572
% of Students Borrowing: 53%

CAREER
Who Recruits
1. Webber, LLC
2. Wise Equation Solutions
3. W.W. Grainger
4. AVG Automation
5. CCC Information Services

Notable Internships
1. BMW
2. Salesforce
3. Motorola

Top Employers
1. Amazon
2. Motorola
3. Google
4. Microsoft
5. Apple

Where Alumni Work
1. Chicago
2. San Francisco
3. Houston
4. New York City
5. Seattle

Earnings
College Scorecard (10-YR Post-Entry): $82,793
PayScale (Early Career): $70,300
PayScale (Mid-Career): $127,000
PayScale 20-Year ROI: $879,000

RANKINGS
Money: 4
U.S. News: 98, National Universities
Wall Street Journal/THE: 23
Washington Monthly: 120, National Universities

OVERGENERALIZATIONS
Students are:
More likely ot venture off campus
Competitive
Nerdy
Career-driven
Diverse

COLLEGE OVERLAPS
DePaul University
Loyola University Chicago
Marquette University
University of Illinois at Chicago
University of Illinois at Urbana-Champaign

Indiana University Bloomington

Bloomington, Indiana | 812-855-0661

ADMISSION
Admission Rate: 82%
Admission Rate - Men: 82%
Admission Rate - Women: 83%
EA Admission Rate: Not Reported
ED Admission Rate: Not Offered
ED Admits as % of Total Admits: Not Offered
Admission Rate (5-Year Trend): +6%
% of Admits Attending (Yield): 24%
Transfer Admission Rate: 68%

SAT Reading/Writing (Middle 50%): 590-690
SAT Math (Middle 50%): 590-710
ACT Composite (Middle 50%): 27-32

% Graduated in Top 10% of HS Class: 31%
% Graduated in Top 25% of HS Class: 64%
% Graduated in Top 50% of HS Class: 93%

Demonstrated Interest: Not Considered
Legacy Status: Not Considered
Racial/Ethnic Status: Considered
Admission Interview Offered: No

ENROLLMENT
Total Undergraduate Enrollment: 35,660
% Full-Time: 98%
% Male: 50%
% Female: 50%
% Out-of-State: 40%
% Fraternity: 20%
% Sorority: 20%
% On-Campus (All Undergraduate): 34%
Freshman Housing Required: Yes

% African-American: 4%
% Asian: 9%
% Hispanic: 8%
% White: 68%
% Other: 0%
% International: 5%
% Low-Income: 17%

ACADEMICS
Student-to-Faculty Ratio: 18 to 1
% of Classes Under 20: 37%
% of Classes 20-49: 47%
% of Classes 50 or More: 16%
% Full-Time Faculty: 83%
% Full-Time Faculty w/ Terminal Degree: 90%

Top Programs
Accounting
Criminal Justice
Kinesiology
Finance
Marketing
Music
Psychology
Sport Management

Retention Rate: 90%
4-Year Graduation Rate: 72%
6-Year Graduation Rate: 80%

Curricular Flexibility: Somewhat Flexible
Academic Rating: ★★★

#CollegesWorthYourMoney

From coast to coast, flagship public universities have seen their admissions standards skyrocket in recent years. Students for whom the University of Maryland, the University of Wisconsin, or any school within the University of California system would have been a safety school a decade ago now find themselves sweating out admissions decisions each spring. Fortunately, this is not so at Indiana's famed Bloomington campus where more than three-quarters of applicants who apply still receive a friendly Midwestern welcome, and both the quality and price of the education that await are exceptionally solid. That combination of accessibility, quality, and variety—IU offers 200+ majors—draws more out-of-state and international students than you might expect. Only 54% of the 2023 freshman class was from in state and 5% were international students.

Inside the Classroom

Unlike many large universities made up of numerous schools and colleges, Indiana is not overeager to assign and confine you to a particular program. Upon entering IU, freshmen are housed within the University Division, and they remain there for one or two years in order to figure out their academic direction. This gives all freshmen time to begin wrestling with the Common Ground Curriculum that involves completing courses in six areas: English composition, mathematical modeling, arts and humanities, social and historical studies, natural and mathematical sciences, and world languages and cultures. Of note for any foreign language averse students, there are ways to fill the latter requirement without learning another language. Students who are members of the Hutton Honors College also typically need to complete a senior thesis within their academic departments.

The university's 18:1 student-to-faculty ratio is not bad for a school of Indiana's size, and it does make an effort to keep undergraduate classes on the small side. While there are a number of introductory courses that transpire in giant lecture halls, 37% of all sections contain no more than 19 students. Experiential learning opportunities are available to those who seize them; over one-quarter of arts and sciences students completed research with a faculty member. On the study abroad front, roughly the same percentage of A&S graduates spent a semester in a foreign country. In total, the school offers 380 programs in 70 countries and 20 languages.

Business/marketing is the most popular major accounting for 30% of the total degrees conferred. Kelley is an acclaimed business school that draws immense national respect, ranking up there in prestige with Goizueta (Emory), McDonough (Georgetown), and its neighbor to the north, Mendoza (Notre Dame). Indiana, notably, did not offer an engineering program until recently, likely making Purdue a better local public option for anyone entering that field of study. However, IU's computer science degree program has tight ties to top tech companies, and it is the school's third most frequently conferred degree at 8%. The other degrees most commonly awarded are in biology (9%) and journalism (8%). Plenty of students from all academic backgrounds capture competitive postgraduate scholarships. In 2021, thirteen students captured Fulbrights and two won Boren Awards.

Outside the Classroom

The university housed 98% of freshmen but only 34% of the overall undergraduate student body on its sprawling 1,936-acre campus in 2022-23. Living options include 13 residence halls, 11 apartment complexes, and more than 20 residential thematic communities. For everyone else, there are plenty of affordable off-campus apartments within close proximity. Fraternities and sororities play an enormous role in social life as 20% of men and 20% of women join Greek organizations; there are 70 to choose from. There are 24 varsity sports, and many boast Big Ten championships, yet one shines above the rest as Hoosier hoops is nothing short of a religion in Bloomington, and you'll never find one of the 17,222 seats within Assembly Hall unfilled during men's basketball games. For those looking for lower-key athletics, there are more than seventy club and intramural sports at your disposal. Overall, Indiana University is home to more than 750 student organizations featuring clubs ranging from calligraphy to bass fishing. Bloomington gets high marks as a safe and enjoyable college town, and there are always events going on whether it's a free show at the spectacular Musical Arts Center or a community service opportunity—students donate a total of 225,000 hours per year. Indianapolis is a 50-mile highway drive away, making it an option for a quick weekend getaway.

Career Services

The university has a main Career Development Center for those who enter undecided as well as discipline-specific career services offices housed within each undergraduate college. There are 82 full-time staff members dedicated to career advising, experiential education, and employer relations. The university's overall 435:1 student-to-counselor ratio is one of the best for a public institution of Indiana's immense size. This staff's output is astounding whether measured by its 23,000+ one-on-one counseling sessions per year or its large-scale efforts that include booking almost 1,800 companies to attend the school's many career fairs.

Sixty-one percent of recent grads completed at least one internship. Over 2,000 employers recruit at Bloomington including EY, PwC, Deloitte, Oracle, JPMorgan Chase & Co., Microsoft Corporation, Anheuser-Busch, Epic Systems, Procter & Gamble, and Grainger, Inc. Just a quick glance at the university calendar reveals a frenetic pace of career fairs taking place in the fall of one recent school year, including targeted events for those interested in business, media, social services, finance, public health, internships, the creative arts, and the hard sciences. Any way you measure it, the IU career services staff's output is prodigious and helps set undergraduates up for successful postgraduation transition.

Professional Outcomes

Indiana University tracks the postgraduate outcomes from each undergraduate school. Looking at the College of Arts & Sciences, by far the largest group of students, Class of 2022 grads reached their next employment or graduate school destination at a 94% rate within six months of receiving their degrees. Sixty percent had procured their first jobs, and 29% of students were in grad school; only 5% of those looking for jobs were unable to land one in that time. The most frequently entered industries (from A&S) were education, healthcare, retail, arts, and business The median starting salary for A&S grads was $41,000. In the Kelley School of Business, 97% were placed successfully within six months, and the median starting salary was $67,000. School of Informatics, Computing & Engineering grads had comparable starting salaries and a similar 95% success rate. Among the largest employers of Hoosier alumni are local pharmaceutical giant Eli Lilly, EY, Amazon, PwC, Salesforce, Deloitte, IBM, Oracle, Microsoft, Accenture, and Google. Indianapolis, Chicago, Bloomington, and New York City are the locales where you can find the greatest concentration of Indiana graduates.

Among the most frequently attended graduate schools by recent grads are Indiana Bloomington (including its own law and medical schools), Purdue, Loyola Chicago, Northwestern, and Columbia. Indiana is a premed factory with 286 applicants applying to med school in 2022-23 alone. Impressively, the well-regarded Indiana University School of Medicine was the second most frequently attended graduate school overall. That was aided by the fact that the in-state acceptance rate at this medical school is almost 50%, six times higher than the out-of-state rate. The university also operates two separate law schools, one in Indianapolis and one in Bloomington, and both draw large numbers of IU undergraduates. A combined BA/JD program can be completed in six years.

Admission

Of all the flagship universities profiled in this book, Indiana has the most relaxed admissions standards as 82% of those who applied for a place in the Class of 2026 were welcomed aboard. The school became test-optional in 2020, but the majority of applicants still submit scores. The mid-50% ranges for freshmen in 2022-23 were 1180-1400 on the SAT and 27-32 on the ACT; the average GPA was 3.8 and 31% finished in the top 10% of their high school class. More encouraging for less-than-perfect applicants is the fact that 36% of undergrads did not place in the top quartile of their graduating cohort, and 25% of students possessed cumulative GPAs under 3.6.

With roughly 50,080 applications to wade through, the admissions committee must first rely on the easy-to-assess credentials of class rank, GPA, and level of academic rigor. The application essay is "important," but factors like extracurricular activities, recommendations, test scores, and volunteer work are merely "considered." While there is no binding early decision option available, IU does offer an early action round with a deadline of November 1, also the deadline for the most complete scholarship consideration.

Worth Your Money?

Indiana residents enjoy not only a reasonable tuition cost that is a touch under $12,000 but also a modest room-and-board price as well when compared to other schools of roughly the same quality. For comparison, room and board alone at Notre Dame would cost an extra $16,000 over four years. Nonresidents should consider their aid package and program of study (business-related fields are your best bet) before packing off to Bloomington, as out-of-state rates are approaching that of many private colleges. Hoosiers cannot go wrong heading to Bloomington for their bachelor's degree, no matter what field of interest they plan to study.

FINANCIAL
Institutional Type: Public
In-State Tuition: $11,790
Out-of-State Tuition: $40,482
Room & Board: $12,404
Books & Supplies: $690

Avg. Need-Based Grant: $13,473
Avg. % of Need Met: 67%

Avg. Merit-Based Award: $7,717
% Receiving (Freshmen w/o Need): 30%

Avg. Cumulative Debt: $28,449
% of Students Borrowing: 40%

CAREER
Who Recruits
1. Macy's
2. Anheuser-Busch
3. Grant Thornton LLC
4. Oracle
5. Insight Global

Notable Internships
1. The Economist
2. Grant Thornton LLP
3. Bain & Company

Top Employers
1. Eli Lilly and Company
2. EY
3. Amazon
4. PwC
5. Salesforce

Where Alumni Work
1. Indianapolis
2. Chicago
3. Bloomington, IN
4. New York City
5. Washington, DC

Earnings
College Scorecard (10-YR Post-Entry): $61,279
PayScale (Early Career): $57,900
PayScale (Mid-Career): $105,200
PayScale 20-Year ROI: $531,000

RANKINGS
Money: 4.5
U.S. News: 73, National Universities
Wall Street Journal/THE: 154
Washington Monthly: 72, National Universities

OVERGENERALIZATIONS
Students are:
Crazy about the Hoosiers
Friendly
Ready to party
Always admiring the beauty of their campus
Always saying nice things about Bloomington, IN

COLLEGE OVERLAPS
The Ohio State University - Columbus
Pennsylvania State University - University Park
Purdue University - West Lafayette
University of Illinois at Urbana-Champaign
University of Michigan

Ithaca College

Ithaca, New York | 607-274-3124

It's easy to feel a bit overshadowed when your name is Ithaca College and you aren't even the most well-known school in Ithaca, New York—that honor, of course, goes to Cornell University. Yet, Ithaca has had no problem carving out its own niche as a terrific liberal arts option for creative types that might not have straight A's or standardized test scores fully representative of their abilities. When your official institutional origin story begins with "Founded by a homesick violinist…" and you claim more nearby waterfalls (150) than affiliated Greek houses (0), you are genuinely a special, charming, and unique institution of higher learning. There is truly something for everyone both academically and socially at this beloved Upstate New York school that educates 4,600 undergrads.

Inside the Classroom
Ithaca has five schools that specialize in business, communications, humanities and sciences, health sciences and human performance, and music. Each school moves students through their Integrative Core Curriculum (ICC) where students pick one of six themes (e.g. Identities, Power & Justice, etc.) to guide their exploration across the traditional disciplines of quantitative literacy, the natural and social sciences, writing, humanities, and the creative arts. More than 80 distinct undergraduate degrees are offered at this school and all end with an ICC Capstone experience that involves self-reflection and making connections to educational and life experiences.

You won't find yourself in many classes with more than 29 of your fellow undergraduates as 82% of sections fall below that marker. Twenty percent of sections enroll fewer than 10 students, a reality made possible by an enviable 11:1 student-to-faculty ratio. Students consistently rate professors as being of high quality and committed to undergraduate instruction and Ithaca rates very well nationally according to these qualities. The college is committed to facilitating undergraduate research in all disciplines, including the fine arts, music, and theater, and hosts the National Conference on Undergraduate Research which is attended by 3,000 students and their mentors from around the country. The Department of Biology offers four different research courses during the school year, as well as a bevy of summer opportunities. Study abroad terms are also highly accessible—Ithaca sends 500+ students to international destinations each year.

Bombers most frequently earn degrees in the disciplines of communication/journalism (24%), the visual and performing arts (18%), health professions and related programs (15%), business/marketing (11%), and the social sciences (5%). The programs with the strongest national reputations are those in communications, film, and the performing arts. Prestigious national scholarship/fellowship organizations recognize Ithaca grads to some extent each year. Typically, the school produces between one and five Fulbright winners annually as well as occasional Boren, Gilman, Goldwater, and Udall awards.

Outside the Classroom
The town of Ithaca wins wide praise as one of the best college towns in America. Whether you enjoy live music, theater, natural beauty, watersports, or great dining, this progressive, aesthetically-pleasing town has something to offer you. The 670-acre campus is set on beautiful Lake Cayuga and offers expansive views in every direction. While there are no official Greek institutions here (only music-centered organizations), there are sororities and fraternities that are unrecognized by the college. Formal Greek life was ended in the 1980s after hazing incidents made national headlines. Eighty percent of students live on campus. The split between those that hail from New York and elsewhere is around 50/50. The Bombers compete in 27 sports in the NCAA Division III Liberty League against other New York-based liberal arts schools like St. Lawrence, Skidmore, Union, and Vassar. Club sports are offered at two levels—competitive and recreational—and 20% of the student body participates in intramural sports. There are 200+ student organizations recognized by the Office of Student Engagement including the popular newspaper, *The Ithacan*, as well as 25 different service-oriented clubs.

Career Services
With eight professional employees in Ithaca College's Career Services office, the ratio of counselors to students works out to 575:1, a sub-average figure compared to many liberal arts schools featured in CWYM. However, they do manage to maintain recruiting relationships with over 6,000 employers and made 140,000 internship and job opportunities available to students and alumni in the last academic year. Some career fairs are local and on-campus such as the Fall Industry Focused Business and Management Career Fair while others are done through collaboration with groups like the Western NY Career & Internship Fair. All told, 265 companies attended career fairs last year.

Alumni connections can prove very helpful as 75,000+ Bombers around the globe are active alumni members. As a result of these connections, 80% of those in Park School of Communications land at least one internship while at Ithaca and more than half of those individuals landed their first post-graduate job directly as a result of that experience. The School of Business sees close to 90% of its students complete one or more internships. Alumni also routinely return to campus to put on career service programming. These types of events include: Life on the Big Stage: Careers in Theatre; Communicating in a Virtual World; and Nonprofit Management 101.

Professional Outcomes

Within nine months of graduating, 52% of one recent graduating cohort had already found their first post-college job and 22% were still seeking employment. Media companies like ESPN and NBCUniversal Media are among the largest employers of Ithaca alumni along with corporations like IBM, Morgan Stanley, Google, Salesforce, and Amazon. Other companies that hired multiple recent grads include Deloitte, ScribeAmerica, Viacom, and Major League Baseball. The Greater New York City Area houses the highest number of Ithaca diploma-holders followed by Boston, Ithaca itself, Los Angeles, Philadelphia, and Washington, DC.

Just shy of one-quarter of recent Ithaca grads immediately entered a graduate/professional degree program. This varied greatly by college as those in the School of Health Sciences and Human Performance continued their studies at a 65% clip, while just 18% of business students did the same. The most common move is to continue in a graduate program at Ithaca College, but more than five students enrolled at nearby Cornell University and multiple grads traveled to Columbia University, Syracuse University, Boston University, and Northwestern University. Ithaca students applying to medical school enjoy a slightly above-average acceptance rate of 45%. Over the past five years, medical school acceptances included the University of Pennsylvania, the University of Minnesota, and a variety of New York State medical schools. Law school hopefuls have found homes at the likes of American University, NYU, and the University of Pittsburgh in recent years.

Admission

Ithaca is not among the schools featured in this book that possess admissions standards that will make even a valedictorian sweat bullets. The college admitted 9,359 of the 12,446 individuals who applied to be part of the Class of 2026; this 75% acceptance rate was slightly lower than the 76% accepted in the previous cycle. The college went test-optional a decade ago and many accepted students do take advantage of the policy—28% of enrolled freshmen submitted SATs and 7% included ACT results. The mid-50% standardized test scores were 1213-1360 on the SAT and 28-32 on the ACT. Not everyone admitted ranked near the top of their class. In fact, just 23% of first-year students in 2022-23 were in the top decile, 54% were in the top quartile, and 85% were in the top half.

Of the three factors that Ithaca's admissions department considers to be "very important," only one is a surprise. The standard duo of rigor of secondary school record and GPA is joined by demonstrated interest, meaning that the college is very interested to know if they are one of your top choices or merely a "safety school." This is primarily because Ithaca is a popular "safety" choice as only 14% of those admitted actually go on to enroll. As such, they greatly value those who apply early decision; the ED acceptance rate is 94%. Interestingly, the non-binding early action rate is also extremely high. Clearly, students with less strong credentials should consider applying early to Ithaca.

Worth Your Money?

Almost three-quarters of freshmen are awarded some form of financial aid from Ithaca College, lowering the list tuition price of $50k for most attendees. Room & board fees add approximately $16k to the bill. The average need-based financial aid package offered was over $30k, making an Ithaca education quite affordable for those who are awarded significant amounts of merit or need-based aid. However, the bulk of Bombers do end up borrowing money to fund their undergraduate educations and the average cumulative debt is more than $10k over the national average. Those with unmet financial need who also lack a clear pathway to a steady post-graduation income should weigh Ithaca against other options.

FINANCIAL
Institutional Type: Private
In-State Tuition: $49,883
Out-of-State Tuition: $49,883
Room & Board: $16,030
Books & Supplies: $850

Avg. Need-Based Grant: $31,497
Avg. % of Need Met: 89%

Avg. Merit-Based Award: $19,757
% Receiving (Freshmen w/o Need): 32%

Avg. Cumulative Debt: $36,314
% of Students Borrowing: 72%

CAREER
Who Recruits
1. ADP
2. Netflix
3. IBM
4. ESPN
5. Citi

Notable Internships
1. MLB Network
2. MGM Resorts
3. Estee Lauder Companies

Top Employers
1. Cornell University
2. NBCUniversal
3. Amazon
4. ESPN
5. IBM

Where Alumni Work
1. New York City
2. Boston
3. Ithaca, NY
4. Los Angeles
5. Philadelphia

Earnings
College Scorecard (10-YR Post-Entry): $62,403
PayScale (Early Career): $56,400
PayScale (Mid-Career): $115,800
PayScale 20-Year ROI: $447,000

RANKINGS
Money: 4
U.S. News: 13, Regional Universities North
Wall Street Journal/THE: 311
Washington Monthly: 111, Master's Universities

OVERGENERALIZATIONS
Students are:
Environmentally conscious
Politically liberal
Career-driven
Decided upon their chosen major
Creative

COLLEGE OVERLAPS
Colgate University
College of the Holy Cross
Fairfield University
Hobart and William Smith Colleges
Vassar College

James Madison University

Harrisonburg, Virginia | 540-568-5681

ADMISSION
Admission Rate: 78%
Admission Rate - Men: 73%
Admission Rate - Women: 82%
EA Admission Rate: 79%
ED Admission Rate: Not Offered
ED Admits as % of Total Admits: Not Offered
Admission Rate (5-Year Trend): +3%
% of Admits Attending (Yield): 20%
Transfer Admission Rate: 77%

SAT Reading/Writing (Middle 50%): 580-670
SAT Math (Middle 50%): 560-650
ACT Composite (Middle 50%): 23-29

% Graduated in Top 10% of HS Class: 15%
% Graduated in Top 25% of HS Class: 31%
% Graduated in Top 50% of HS Class: 85%

Demonstrated Interest: Not Considered
Legacy Status: Considered
Racial/Ethnic Status: Considered
Admission Interview Offered: No

ENROLLMENT
Total Undergraduate Enrollment: 20,346
% Full-Time: 95%
% Male: 43%
% Female: 57%
% Out-of-State: 19%
% Fraternity: 4%
% Sorority: 5%
% On-Campus (All Undergraduate): 32%
Freshman Housing Required: Yes

% African-American: 5%
% Asian: 6%
% Hispanic: 8%
% White: 75%
% Other: 2%
% International: 1%
% Low-Income: 14%

ACADEMICS
Student-to-Faculty Ratio: 16 to 1
% of Classes Under 20: 37%
% of Classes 20-49: 51%
% of Classes 50 or More: 12%
% Full-Time Faculty: 70%
% Full-Time Faculty w/ Terminal Degree: 86%

Top Programs
Accounting
Communication Studies
Finance
Health Services Administration
Hospitality Management
Industrial Design
Public Policy and Administration
Sport and Recreation Management

Retention Rate: 90%
4-Year Graduation Rate: 78%
6-Year Graduation Rate: 82%

Curricular Flexibility: Somewhat Flexible
Academic Rating: ★★★

#CollegesWorthYourMoney

Over 80 years ago, before adopting the namesake of our nation's fourth president, the college went by the slightly less memorable handle, "The State Normal and Industrial School for Women." Men were actually not enrolled until after World War II, and the school still has close to a 58/42 gender split today. More than three-quarters of James Madison University's 20,346 undergraduates are Virginia natives, yet this well-regarded public institution draws plenty of out-of-staters to its often-praised, beautiful Shenandoah Valley campus. Unquestionably a university with a rising national reputation as well as the distinction as one of the top public schools in the region, JMU offers 75+ undergraduate degrees to a very happy student population; surveyed undergrads report a stunning 93% satisfaction rate.

Inside the Classroom
General Education: The Human Community, JMU's core curriculum, requires students to complete 41 credit hours in coursework covering five "clusters." The clusters are (1) Skills for the 21st Century, (2) Arts & Humanities, (3) The Natural World, (4) Social and Cultural Processes, and (5) Individuals in the Human Community. Many majors require students to demonstrate proficiency in foreign language at the intermediate level. This can entail taking between 2-4 courses, but teens who took advanced foreign language coursework in high school can test out of the requirement. All told, a minimum of one math and two science classes are needed to meet graduation requirements.

A 17:1 student-to-faculty ratio does not fully capture how generally modest class sizes tend to be at the university. Thirty-seven percent of sections enroll fewer than 19 students and the average class size is 25 students. On the other end of the spectrum, there are some larger lecture-hall size courses; 17% of sections contained 40 or more students. Therefore, it's no shock that every measure of professor quality at JMU reveals high levels of student satisfaction. Students in the Honors College are guaranteed a research experience alongside faculty, and the school does publish its own peer-reviewed undergraduate research journal. For decades, JMU has also been a leader in study abroad participation, with some of the highest numbers of participants of any college in the country. In fact, it presently ranks first among all master's-granting institutions with almost 1,500 participants annually.

A quality nursing program leads to JMU conferring a large number of health degrees. Overall, 19% of all degrees awarded are in this area. Next in popularity are business/marketing (15%), communication/journalism (9%), and the social sciences (8%)—majors within each discipline are strong. James Madison is the most prolific producer of Fulbright Scholars of any master's-level university in the entire country. In 2022, there were 11 recent alumni studying abroad on Fulbrights. Dukes also captured multiple National Graduate Research Fellowships, Goldwater Scholarships, and Boren Fellowships these past two years.

Outside the Classroom
Not only is the campus typically found on any "most beautiful" list, but JMU also ranks high for housing, food, Greek life, and the party scene. While it sounds trite, it is accurate to say that the average student at this school can be described as "happy." Purple and gold colors can be spotted all around campus as this passionate student body supports its school's 18 varsity sports teams. Teams compete at the NCAA Division I level, with the exception of football, where the Dukes participate in the Football Championship Subdivision. Greek life is fairly pervasive, drawing in 12-14% of 2022-23 freshmen to the 30+ Greek chapters at JMU. Ninety-eight percent of freshmen reside on campus, but the majority of upperclassmen—68% of the total population—reside in off-campus housing. The school offers an Off-Campus Housing Service to help students locate safe and affordable apartments and houses. More than 450 student-run clubs translate to there being something for just about everyone. There are plenty of community service, faith-based, a cappella, and intramural sports options. Harrisonburg is situated about a two-hour drive from both Washington, DC, and Richmond. To help students without a car get home on breaks, JMU offers a shuttle service to and from the Charlottesville airport, Amtrak station, and Greyhound bus station.

Career Services
There are 30 professional employees engaged in career service-related duties at the main University Career Center. There are also three professionals housed within the College of Business. This works out to a fairly weak 617:1 student-to-counselor ratio, higher than the average school featured in this guide. Still, face-to-face meetings with career counselors are available to current students and recent grads. Resume development is the most common focus of counseling sessions. There are a number of other less personalized resources that Dukes have access to. The university adopted Handshake a few years back, giving students access to 250,000 employers. The Class of 2022 saw 63% complete at least one internship.

In addition to a larger two-day general career fair that draws 150-200 employers and 600-800 students, JMU also hosts career-specific fairs in the areas of accounting, science and engineering, nursing, teaching, and media arts and design. For those considering extending their educational journey beyond a bachelor's, the school also hosts a Graduate & Professional School Fair that features 120 programs. The university has a good number of local and national corporate partners that leads to quality connections for internship and job leads. For example, Verizon, MITRE, AT&T, and Intuit all have some type of affiliation with JMU. A gigantic alumni association with more than 144,000 members can also help to complement the services of this relatively understaffed career services department.

Professional Outcomes

Within six months of graduating, 75% of 2022 grads had obtained full-time employment, 22% were continuing their education, and 4% were still figuring out their next step. More than 25 recent grads were hired by each of KPMG and Deloitte. Fifteen or more found employment at Booz Allen Hamilton, EY, and RSM. Fifty-eight percent of 2022 grads remained in Virginia, and large numbers also settled in Washington, D.C.; Pennsylvania; Maryland; and New York. Overall, Dukes found employment at 1,610 organizations around the world and the average starting salary was $57,615.

Among the almost one-quarter of recent grads who matriculated directly into a graduate school program, the most popular location was JMU itself. Almost 300 stayed put at their alma mater. More than 20 students attended UVA, George Mason and Virginia Commonwealth, and 5+ were accepted at NYU, Virginia Tech, and George Washington. Others were accepted into elite graduate programs at Duke, Emory, William & Mary, and Yale. Fifty-seven members of the Class of 2023 applied to medical school and, while current acceptance rates are unavailable, past applicants were accepted at a 44% clip, which is right around the national average. Past prelaw students found success in gaining acceptance to colleges of law three-quarters of the time, attending schools such as American, Georgetown, and Washington and Lee.

Admission

This is one of the best schools you can find that accepts over three-quarters of those who apply. Applicants for a place in the Class of 2026 found success in 78% of cases. James Madison is a test-optional institution, yet the majority of accepted applicants still do include an SAT or ACT score. The mid-50% scores for 2022-23 freshmen were 1160-1310 on the SAT and 23-29 on the ACT. Just 3% of those admitted had an SAT composite score of under 1000; 8% possessed a score above 1400. This is one school where you don't need perfect grades in order to gain admission. Only 15% of the Class of 2026 ranked in the top 10% of their high school cohort, 31% placed in the top quartile, and 85% finished in the top half.

Academic GPA and the rigor of one's secondary school record were the only two factors rated as "very important" by the JMU committee. First-generation status and state residency were ranked as being "important," and "considered" elements of the application included standardized test scores, application essay, talent/ability, recommendation letters, extracurricular activities, legacy status, geographical residence, volunteer work, and paid work experience. There is no binding early decision policy at JMU; however, there is an early action option that does not provide any notable edge in the admissions process. In sum, the application process here is very straightforward and "focuses primarily on high school courses and grades."

Worth Your Money?

The in-state tuition at JMU of $13,850 is among the best values in the entire country. The total in-state cost allows you to get an undergraduate degree for around $130k without any financial aid, which qualifies as an exceptional deal in today's higher education world. JMU wisely keeps out-of-state costs within reason; the list price COA for a nonresident is a very fair $49,482. This makes the university a very attractive option for large numbers of students from outside Old Dominion. No matter your intended major or residency status, JMU is a school that will be worth the money for most graduates.

FINANCIAL
Institutional Type: Public
In-State Tuition: $13,576
Out-of-State Tuition: $30,790
Room & Board: $12,584
Books & Supplies: $1,176

Avg. Need-Based Grant: $8,364
Avg. % of Need Met: 37%

Avg. Merit-Based Award: $7,208
% Receiving (Freshmen w/o Need): 2%

Avg. Cumulative Debt: $31,333
% of Students Borrowing: 49%

CAREER
Who Recruits
1. KPMG
2. GGV Capital
3. Freddie Max
4. Ethos Group
5. Verizon

Notable Internships
1. Smithsonian
2. Carmax
3. Baltimore Orioles

Top Employers
1. Capital One
2. Booz Allen Hamilton
3. Deloitte
4. EY
5. Accenture

Where Alumni Work
1. Washington, DC
2. Charlottesville, VA
3. Richmond, VA
4. New York City
5. Norfolk, VA

Earnings
College Scorecard (10-YR Post-Entry): $65,172
PayScale (Early Career): $61,700
PayScale (Mid-Career): $111,300
PayScale 20-Year ROI: $648,000

RANKINGS
Money: 4.5
U.S. News: 124, National Universities
Wall Street Journal/THE: 152
Washington Monthly: 75, National Universities

OVERGENERALIZATIONS
Students are:
Crazy about the Dukes
Friendly
Ready to party
Athletic/active
Teeming with school pride

COLLEGE OVERLAPS
George Mason University
Pennsylvania State University - University Park
University of Delaware
University of Virginia
Virginia Tech

Johns Hopkins University

Baltimore, Maryland | 410-516-8171

ADMISSION
Admission Rate: 7%
Admission Rate - Men: 8%
Admission Rate - Women: 7%
EA Admission Rate: Not Offered
ED Admission Rate: 15%
ED Admits as % of Total Admits: 30%
Admission Rate (5-Year Trend): -6%
% of Admits Attending (Yield): 51%
Transfer Admission Rate: 6%

SAT Reading/Writing (Middle 50%): 740-770
SAT Math (Middle 50%): 780-800
ACT Composite (Middle 50%): 34-35

% Graduated in Top 10% of HS Class: 99%
% Graduated in Top 25% of HS Class: 100%
% Graduated in Top 50% of HS Class: 100%

Demonstrated Interest: Not Considered
Legacy Status: Not Considered
Racial/Ethnic Status: Not Reported
Admission Interview Offered: No

ENROLLMENT
Total Undergraduate Enrollment: 6,044
% Full-Time: 100%
% Male: 46%
% Female: 54%
% Out-of-State: 86%
% Fraternity: 14%
% Sorority: 20%
% On-Campus (All Undergraduate): 37%
Freshman Housing Required: Yes

% African-American: 9%
% Asian: 27%
% Hispanic: 20%
% White: 21%
% Other: 1%
% International: 15%
% Low-Income: 21%

ACADEMICS
Student-to-Faculty Ratio: 6 to 1
% of Classes Under 20: 78%
% of Classes 20-49: 16%
% of Classes 50 or More: 6%
% Full-Time Faculty: 61%
% Full-Time Faculty w/ Terminal Degree: 73%

Top Programs
Biology
Chemistry
Computer Science
Engineering
English
International Studies
Mathematics
Physics

Retention Rate: 97%
4-Year Graduation Rate: 89%
6-Year Graduation Rate: 94%

Curricular Flexibility: Somewhat Flexible
Academic Rating: ★★★★★

#CollegesWorthYourMoney

High schoolers who dream of entering the medical profession look to North Baltimore as their Mecca—more specifically, to Johns Hopkins University, Charm City's prestigious, midsized research institution. Yet, four years at Johns Hopkins is so much more than merely a prelude to seven years of medical school. With 53 majors as well as 51 minors, JHU excels in everything from its bread-and-butter medical-related majors to international relations and dance. Of the five undergraduate schools within the university, the vast majority of students reside in either the Krieger School of Arts and Sciences or the Whiting School of Engineering. However, the Carey School of Business, School of Education, and Peabody Institute also award bachelor's degrees.

Inside the Classroom
All Hopkins bachelor's-seekers must meet distributional requirements covering the basics: humanities, natural sciences, social and behavioral sciences, quantitative and mathematical sciences, and engineering. Writing-intensive courses also are mandated regardless of one's major. Students are encouraged to broaden their horizons by double majoring or selecting a minor, and 60% do so. First-year experience courses help to transition students to the school and second-year experience courses assist with community-building and career planning.

Boasting an enviable 6:1 student-to-faculty ratio and with 78% of course sections possessing an enrollment under 20, face time with professors is a reality. That presents a phenomenal opportunity to learn directly from a group that includes four Nobel Laureates, four Medal of Science winners, and two recipients of the Presidential Medal of Freedom. Fitting for America's first research university, 70% of JHU undergraduates complete a research experience while working closely with a faculty member. Each year, hundreds of students receive significant funding for independent projects through the Hopkins Office for Undergraduate Research.

Universally respected by employers and graduate schools alike, many departments carry a high level of clout, including biomedical engineering, chemistry, English, and international studies. Biology, neuroscience, and computer science, which happen to be the three most popular majors, can also be found at the top of the national rankings. In 2023, there were 20 Fulbright Scholars named from the university. Johns Hopkins grads also are competitive in landing Luce, Truman, Marshall, Goldwater, and National Science Foundation Graduate Research Fellowships.

Outside the Classroom
The 140-acre Homewood campus located in North Baltimore is the site of the School of Engineering and the School of Arts & Sciences. The dorms located at Homewood house most underclassmen and feature dining halls that garner generally high praise. Despite the excellent chow, upperclassmen tend to outgrow university-owned housing; in a typical year, only 45% of students live on campus. The 25 Greek organizations each have their own charitable focus and attract 14% of women and 20% of men. Nicknamed the Blue Jays, athletes compete in twelve men's and ten women's sports in NCAA Division III. Over 400 student organizations are active at JHU. Groups centered on community service tend to be the most popular. The Center for Social Concern connects students with over seventy-five local organizations. For those interested in a medical career, you'll have the chance to volunteer in one of fifteen local hospitals, including Johns Hopkins' own facilities. Popular traditions include the three-day Spring Fair, the nation's largest student-run fair. Famous guest speakers from all walks of life regularly visit campus and draw engaged audiences. Homewood is only a few miles from the bustle of Baltimore's Inner Harbor so, even though the area immediately surrounding campus isn't the most inviting, culture and nightlife can easily be found.

Career Services
The newly-renamed Life Design Lab at Homewood is staffed by 36 full-time professional employees who work with and on behalf of undergraduates in the areas of career development, employer engagement, internship coordination, and event planning. This figure does not include administrative assistants, IT, graduate advisors, or marketing professionals. Possessing a student-to-advisor ratio of 168:1, JHU is superior to the vast majority of the institutions included in this book.

Johns Hopkins University

In a typical year, the Life Design Lab engages roughly 2,000 undergraduates in one-on-one career coach appointments. More than 90 employers, including many Fortune 1000 companies, conduct 700+ interviews on campus. Over 15,000 jobs and internship opportunities were available on Handshake. Homewood hosts three major career fairs each year: the flagship Fall Career Fair with more than 150 employers, the STEM & Innovation Career Fair with forty targeted companies attending, and the spring Nonprofit Career Fair which also focuses on internship procurement. All told, 170 companies attend career fairs annually at JHU, and approximately 250 companies recruit on campus. The university also provides a number of internships that are built into each academic department. These include credit-bearing options in orthopedic surgery, film and media studies, business, and computational biology. An exceptional 75% of undergraduates complete one internship over their four years of study; it is not unusual to complete two. Another 40% of students embark on shadowing experiences.

Professional Outcomes

The Class of 2022 saw 94% of graduates successfully land at their next destination within six months of exiting the university; 66% of graduates entered the world of employment and a robust 19% went directly to graduate/professional school. Of those entering the workforce, the most popular industries were research, consulting, engineering, data & analytics, and health care. Johns Hopkins University and its affiliated medical institutions were the largest employers of recent graduates. Other prominent companies landing more than a handful of fresh JHU alums were Goldman Sachs, Amazon, Booz Allen Hamilton, Google, and Microsoft. Across all graduating years, you'll find hundreds of Hopkins grads working for IBM, Lockheed Martin, and Apple. The median starting salary across all majors was $80,000 for the Class of 2022, significantly higher than the previous year.

Johns Hopkins' sterling reputation also helps land its undergrads at premier graduate schools. Engineering is the most popular graduate field and medical school is not a rare postsecondary destination either. The overall admit rate to medical schools is a healthy 80%. Law school grads also found homes at an above-average 97% clip. Johns Hopkins itself is the most frequently attended graduate school, and it's not even close, with over 100 grads per year continuing their educations in Baltimore. The next most frequently attended institutions included Columbia, Harvard, Yale, and MIT.

Admission

If Johns Hopkins' aim in the 2020s was to become one of a dozen or so elite universities with a single-digit admissions rate, then this was the decade when the champagne corks popped. Only 7% of undergraduates were admitted into the Class of 2026 compared to 8% the prior year. That follows a pattern of declining acceptance rates in recent years. For historical context, the school admitted one-quarter of applicants only a decade ago. The SAT middle-50% range in 2008 was 1320-1480; today it is 1520-1560. Given that the former 75th percentile SAT score is now beneath the 25th percentile score, it's pretty clear that Johns Hopkins has grown increasingly competitive in recent years. For those taking the ACT, the mid-50% is 34-35.

Current students landed in the top 10% of their high school classes at a 99% clip, so impeccable grades in the most competitive curriculum available are pretty much a prerequisite for consideration. The average unweighted GPA for 2022-23 freshmen was 3.93, meaning that more than one or two imperfections on a transcript can be a disqualifier. Leadership qualities and community service are also highly valued. In the university's own words, it is "looking for students who can think beyond their limits, who don't see 'impossible' as a roadblock, and who will not only elevate themselves but also those around them." Early decision applicants will see improved odds as their acceptance rate is close to double that of the regular round (15% last year). Further, 57% of the Class of 2026 was accepted via ED. Always a highly selective school, Johns Hopkins is now in the upper-upper tier of selectivity along with the Ivies, Stanford, and a small cadre of elite liberal arts colleges. Only those with first-rate test scores and transcripts need apply.

Worth Your Money?

If your family is in a lower-to-mid-tier income bracket, Johns Hopkins will provide you with every dollar of financial aid you need to attend the university. Presently, over half of the undergraduate population benefits from that generosity with an average need-based grant of $57k. The annual cost of attendance is over $86,000, and while families making more than $200k per year can expect to pay close to full price, roughly 90% of families making less than that amount receive grants. Even for those taking out loans to attend, JHU is the type of school that it is almost always OK to pay up for. With fantastic job and professional school prospects down the road, the $340,000+ investment will be well worth it in the long run.

FINANCIAL
Institutional Type: Private
In-State Tuition: $63,340
Out-of-State Tuition: $63,340
Room & Board: $19,840
Books & Supplies: $1,345

Avg. Need-Based Grant: $57,350
Avg. % of Need Met: 99%

Avg. Merit-Based Award: $24,474
% Receiving (Freshmen w/o Need): 7%

Avg. Cumulative Debt: $17,712
% of Students Borrowing: 34%

CAREER
Who Recruits
1. Dean & Company
2. Bloomberg
3. Lockheed Martin
4. Bain & Company
5. McKinsey & Co.

Notable Internships
1. Twitter
2. NASA Jet Propulsion Laboratory
3. National Institutes of Health

Top Employers
1. Booz Allen Hamilton
2. Google
3. Deloitte
4. IBM
5. Microsoft

Where Alumni Work
1. Baltimore
2. Washington, DC
3. New York City
4. San Francisco
5. Boston

Earnings
College Scorecard (10-YR Post-Entry): $89,551
PayScale (Early Career): $73,500
PayScale (Mid-Career): $125,800
PayScale 20-Year ROI: $894,000

RANKINGS
Money: 4.5
U.S. News: 9, National Universities
Wall Street Journal/THE: 99
Washington Monthly: 13, National Universities

OVERGENERALIZATIONS
Students are:
Diverse
Always studying
Competitive
Intellectually curious
Always admiring the beauty of their campus

COLLEGE OVERLAPS
Cornell University
Duke University
Princeton University
University of California, Berkeley
University of Pennsylvania

Juniata College

Huntingdon, Pennsylvania | 814-641-3420

ADMISSION
Admission Rate: 76%
Admission Rate - Men: 73%
Admission Rate - Women: 79%
EA Admission Rate: Not Reported
ED Admission Rate: 67%
ED Admits as % of Total Admits: 2
Admission Rate (5-Year Trend): +5%
% of Admits Attending (Yield): 15%
Transfer Admission Rate: 68%

SAT Reading/Writing (Middle 50%): 570-670
SAT Math (Middle 50%): 550-660
ACT Composite (Middle 50%): 26-30

% Graduated in Top 10% of HS Class: 23%
% Graduated in Top 25% of HS Class: 50%
% Graduated in Top 50% of HS Class: 84%

Demonstrated Interest: Not Considered
Legacy Status: Considered
Racial/Ethnic Status: Considered
Admission Interview Offered: No

ENROLLMENT
Total Undergraduate Enrollment: 1,177
% Full-Time: 100%
% Male: 47%
% Female: 53%
% Out-of-State: 30%
% Fraternity: Not Offered
% Sorority: Not Offered
% On-Campus (All Undergraduate): 94%
Freshman Housing Required: Yes

% African-American: 5%
% Asian: 2%
% Hispanic: 8%
% White: 72%
% Other: 1%
% International: 8%
% Low-Income: 29%

ACADEMICS
Student-to-Faculty Ratio: 11 to 1
% of Classes Under 20: 68%
% of Classes 20-49: 31%
% of Classes 50 or More: 1%
% Full-Time Faculty: 97%
% Full-Time Faculty w/ Terminal Degree: 97%

Top Programs
Biology
Business
Chemistry
Communication
Education
Environmental Science and Studies
Peace and Conflict Studies
Psychology

Retention Rate: 84%
4-Year Graduation Rate: 66%
6-Year Graduation Rate: 75%

Curricular Flexibility: Somewhat Flexible
Academic Rating: ★★★

#CollegesWorthYourMoney

If you stop at just about any exit along the Pennsylvania Turnpike in the eastern part of the state, you'll find a Wawa, a Sheetz in the west, and a quality liberal arts college statewide. Okay, perhaps that's a slight exaggeration, but 13 of US News' Top 100 liberal arts schools are, in fact, within the Keystone State. One is Juniata College in Huntingdon, approximately halfway between Pittsburgh and the state capital of Harrisburg. It offers a terrific education and experience to around 1,200 undergraduates. Of equal interest, especially to those with more B's than A's on their transcript and/or a less-than-flush 529 account, are two key stats: Juniata accepts over two-thirds of those who apply, and it offers tens of thousands of dollars in aid per year to almost every student who attends.

Inside the Classroom

The intellectual foundation of the Juniata academic experience comes from its core curriculum, which is composed of these three themes: Connect, Engage, and Discern. Collectively, those experiences are designed to help students answer the following three essential questions:

- How will I choose to live my life?
- How, and with what tools at my disposal, will I understand the world?
- How will I choose to act in the world?

The journey begins with eight credits in First-Year Experience courses designed to support freshmen in their transition to college life by building resiliency and pondering what a "life of meaning" would look like. Four to five classes fall under the "Ways of Knowing" umbrella and help students learn to view issues through an interdisciplinary prism. "Self and the World" classes (10-17 credits) explore concepts of ethics, diversity, and how to operate in a community. Lastly, all Juniata undergrads complete a senior capstone that can take various forms, such as the creation of a portfolio highlighting key learning experiences, community engagement, research, or internships.

A stunning 95% of graduates report engaging in some form of hands-on learning in their time at the college. The 10:1 student-to-faculty ratio may lag slightly behind some other small liberal arts schools featured in this guide, but professors are deployed with enhancing the undergraduate experience in mind. As a result, there are only a handful of classes that enroll 40+ students, and 68% enroll fewer than 20. One marker of Juniata's success in providing personalized attention to undergrads is the fact that a stunning 94% of those who ultimately graduate do so in four years or less. Study abroad placements are available in 26 countries spread across six continents, and roughly 40% of students take advantage.

Biology is easily the most common major as it accounted for 22% of degrees conferred in 2022; next in line were natural resources and conservation (12%), education (12%), and the physical sciences (7%). The Biology and Environmental Science departments are two of the school's standouts, and the medical school acceptance rates (more on that later) offer evidence of Juniata's strength in the hard sciences. For such a small college, Juniata has produced an exceptional number of prestigious national fellowship winners including Gilman Scholars, Goldwater Scholars, and Fulbright Fellows.

Outside the Classroom

Juniata's rural, 800-acre campus includes a 315-acre nature preserve and a 365-acre Environmental Studies Field Station. The main campus is 110 acres and contains Juniata's 50 residential and academic buildings. Ninety-four percent of undergraduates lived in campus housing during the 2022-23 school year, and 97% of first-year students did the same. No Greek life is permitted. Juniata does field 20 NCAA Division III athletic teams and offers a full complement of club and intramural options. The school has had 135 All-American honorees. The Kennedy Sports + Recreation Center has two gymnasiums, a six-lane swimming pool, racquetball/handball courts, and all of the personal fitness equipment you could want. By car, Juniata is 40 minutes from Penn State University, 2.5 hours from Harrisburg, and 3.5 hours from Philadelphia or Washington, DC. While you won't find big-city fun near campus, Huntingdon is home to Raystown Lake, and activities like boating, swimming, hiking, and biking are never hard to find. Downtown is far from a bustling metropolis, but it does contain a movie theater, a bowling alley, and a handful of restaurant and café options.

Career Services

The Career Services Department at Juniata College is staffed only by a director and assistant director, which equates to a 590:1 student-to-counselor ratio. Despite limited manpower, the office manages to offer "academic classes, workshops, internship programs, job fairs, and full-time job search and graduate/professional school assistance in both group and individual settings." Juniata College Career Day is held every February and attracts employers including Raytheon, Farmers Insurance, and the Pennsylvania Department of Revenue. More than 100 employers attend each year. Being such a small school in a somewhat remote location, Juniata is also a member of two larger consortium-coordinated fairs, one in Pittsburgh and one in the state capital of Harrisburg.

The school does not release statistics regarding the percentage of undergraduates that land one or more internships, but it does offer some unique programs designed to make internship dreams come true. For example, Super Internship Awards of up to $5,000 are granted to help students defray housing and supplemental living expenses as they pursue meaningful summer internships. As an additional resource, there are 900 parent and alumni members of the Juniata Career Team who are happy to share career experiences and advice with current students.

Professional Outcomes

Ninety-six percent of Juniata students are employed or attending graduate school six months after diplomas are awarded. More than ten alumni work for the University of Pittsburgh Medical Center, Merck, Geisinger, WellSpan Health, and the US Army. In the last few years, grads have landed positions at the Walt Disney Company, the National Football League, Boeing, Google, Showtime, and The Wall Street Journal. The majority of Juniata alumni stay in the Keystone State with heavy concentrations in State College, Philadelphia, Pittsburgh, and Harrisburg, but sizable pockets also can be found in Washington, DC, and New York City.

The college only offers a handful of graduate programs itself, so most individuals pursuing advanced degrees do so elsewhere. Recent acceptances include Columbia, Wake Forest, Johns Hopkins, and MIT; clearly, top-shelf graduate and professional schools are on the table for Juniata grads. With a 90% acceptance rate for premedical and other graduate programs in the health professions, Juniata is a choice institution for future doctors, nurses, dentists, veterinarians, and other health professionals. Medical school acceptance rates in isolation have been in the 74%-100% range in a given year. Acceptances include many top medical programs such as Duke, Dartmouth, Harvard, the University of Pennsylvania, and the University of Virginia.

Admission

Juniata received just 2,563 applications for its Class of 2026; the school accepted over three-quarters of that group. A test-optional school, 27% of those who applied included an SAT score with their application to go along with 4% who submitted an ACT result. The middle 50% SAT range was 1120-1340, and the ACT range was 26-30. Only 21% of enrolled freshmen earned a place in the top decile of their high school class, 49% were in the top quarter, and 10% were outside the top half. The average weighted GPA was 3.67, but more than 20% of those attending had a weighted GPA under 3.25. Translation: you can be a B student and still gain acceptance at Juniata.

According to the admissions committee, GPA is the most important factor in a student's application. The rigor of high school coursework, essay, talent/ability, character/personal qualities, and extracurricular activities make up the "important" factors. If that breakdown hasn't already spelled this out clearly, Juniata gives each application a genuinely holistic review. This is by no means an institution where grades and test scores alone determine an applicant's fate. A quality essay and interview can open doors for students with flawed transcripts. Few apply early decision to Juniata, but the vast majority who do find success.

Worth Your Money?

A sticker price of $69,948 for tuition, fees, and room and board does little to inform prospective students of what they are likely to pay for a Juniata education. Amazingly, 100% of freshmen received some form of aid. Almost three-quarters of undergrads received an average of $41k in need-based aid. The average debt carried by a Juniata graduate is close to the mean national debt load. As long as that debt fits comfortably into your life plans (grad school, salary in field of interest, geographic destination), Juniata can be an excellent value.

FINANCIAL
Institutional Type: Private
In-State Tuition: $56,402
Out-of-State Tuition: $56,402
Room & Board: $13,546
Books & Supplies: $1,000

Avg. Need-Based Grant: $37,387
Avg. % of Need Met: 89%

Avg. Merit-Based Award: $34,081
% Receiving (Freshmen w/o Need): 27%

Avg. Cumulative Debt: $37,827
% of Students Borrowing: 65%

CAREER
Who Recruits
1. Charles River Laboratories
2. Pfizer
3. Vanguard
4. Merck
5. Lincoln Financial Group

Notable Internships
1. Children's Hospital Pittsburgh
2. National Electronics Museum
3. The Philadelphia Zoo

Top Employers
1. Penn State University
2. UPMC Healthcare
3. Merck
4. WellSpan Health
5. Geisinger

Where Alumni Work
1. State College, PA
2. Philadelphia
3. Harrisburg, PA
4. Washington, DC
5. New York City

Earnings
College Scorecard (10-YR Post-Entry): $59,092
PayScale (Early Career): $53,400
PayScale (Mid-Career): $103,500
PayScale 20-Year ROI: $434,000

RANKINGS
Money: 4
U.S. News: 82, Liberal Arts Colleges
Wall Street Journal/THE: Not Ranked
Washington Monthly: 38, Liberal Arts Colleges

OVERGENERALIZATIONS
Students are:
Tight-knit (possess a strong sense of community)
Friendly
Homogenous
Less likely to party
Academically driven

COLLEGE OVERLAPS
Allegheny College
Dickinson College
Gettysburg College
Kenyon College
Muhlenberg College

Kalamazoo College

Kalamazoo, Michigan | 269-337-7166

ADMISSION
Admission Rate: 80%
Admission Rate - Men: 77%
Admission Rate - Women: 82%
EA Admission Rate: 90%
ED Admission Rate: 75%
ED Admits as % of Total Admits: 1%
Admission Rate (5-Year Trend): +7%
% of Admits Attending (Yield): 13%
Transfer Admission Rate: 34%

SAT Reading/Writing (Middle 50%): 610-700
SAT Math (Middle 50%): 590-670
ACT Composite (Middle 50%): 26-32

% Graduated in Top 10% of HS Class: 35%
% Graduated in Top 25% of HS Class: 67%
% Graduated in Top 50% of HS Class: 92%

Demonstrated Interest: Considered
Legacy Status: Considered
Racial/Ethnic Status: Considered
Admission Interview Offered: No

ENROLLMENT
Total Undergraduate Enrollment: 1,210
% Full-Time: 98%
% Male: 44%
% Female: 56%
% Out-of-State: 32%
% Fraternity: Not Offered
% Sorority: Not Offered
% On-Campus (All Undergraduate): 64%
Freshman Housing Required: Yes

% African-American: 5%
% Asian: 6%
% Hispanic: 16%
% White: 61%
% Other: 2%
% International: 4%
% Low-Income: 25%

ACADEMICS
Student-to-Faculty Ratio: 11 to 1
% of Classes Under 20: 72%
% of Classes 20-49: 28%
% of Classes 50 or More: 0%
% Full-Time Faculty: 68%
% Full-Time Faculty w/ Terminal Degree: 89%

Top Programs
Biology
Chemsitry
Community and Global Health
Economics and Business
Foreign Languages
Physics
Political Science
Psychology

Retention Rate: 86%
4-Year Graduation Rate: 71%
6-Year Graduation Rate: 80%

Curricular Flexibility: Somewhat Flexible
Academic Rating: ★★★⯪

#CollegesWorthYourMoney

A liberal arts institution of 1,210 undergraduate students, Kalamazoo College in southern Michigan is one of the 100 oldest colleges in the United States, having been founded in 1833. However, the school's ascendance into the national spotlight can be traced to 1996 when the school was included in Loren Pope's popular book, Colleges That Change Lives. This is, indeed, an institution of higher learning that grants undergrads a personalized and bountiful four years of education—a stellar 70% graduate in four years. And you will be pleased to learn that Kalamazoo accepts more than three-quarters of those who apply.

Inside the Classroom

For more than half a century, the "K-Plan" has maintained the same core components: career service internships, foreign study, and an individualized senior project. In addition, all students complete three Shared Passages courses that include a First-Year Seminar, a Sophomore Seminar, and a Senior Seminar. On the foreign language front, every undergrad has to achieve intermediate proficiency, defined as completing a third language course at the 201 level. Outside of those staples, much of a student's curricular choices remain flexible and can be worked out with an advisor prior to the start of each semester.

As you would expect at a small liberal arts college, class sizes are relatively small with 70% of sections enrolling 19 or fewer. The student-to-faculty ratio of 11:1 is solid and is down from 13:1 two years prior. Regardless, plenty of opportunities exist for conducting undergraduate research in addition to the aforementioned senior project requirement, and the Chemistry, Physics, Biology, and Psychology departments all provide a wealth of resources toward that aim. This institution places enormous value on international experience, and 70% of undergrads engage in an immersive experience overseas, one of the highest figures of any school in the United States.

The social sciences is the discipline in which the greatest number of degrees were conferred in 2022 (16%). It was followed by biology (14%), the physical sciences (12%), business (12%), and psychology (10%). And computer science degrees accounted for 5%, impressive for a liberal arts school. Kalamazoo was named a Top Producer of Fulbright Recipients in 2023 when ten students and alumni captured that distinction. Recent students also have captured Boren and Critical Language scholarships.

Outside the Classroom

Kalamazoo is roughly 140 miles from both Chicago and Detroit but only 35 miles from Lake Michigan. In a typical non-pandemic year, 100% of freshmen and three-fifths of all undergrads live on the small, approximately 60-acre hilltop campus. There are six residence halls and a number of Living Learning Housing Units. There is no Greek life to speak of at Kalamazoo, so the party scene tends to be on the quiet side. Intercollegiate sports do exist, but they are not a huge focal point. There are 18 varsity teams that participate in the NCAA Division III Michigan Intercollegiate Athletic Association. There are only around 75 registered student organizations including a weekly student newspaper, a college radio station, and organizations for Jewish students, Pacific Islanders, and African Americans. Kalamazoo itself is a small city of approximately 73,000 that includes the Kalamazoo Institute of the Arts, the Kalamazoo Valley Museum, and the Kalamazoo Nature Center that features 1,100 acres of trails to explore.

Career Services

The Center for Career and Professional Development (CCPD) features six professional employees as well as eight undergraduate career associates. Only counting professional staff, the school offers a 202:1 student-to-counselor ratio, far better than the average liberal arts college in this book. Seventy-one percent of graduates end up participating in at least one program organized by the CCPD. Those include career workshops, networking receptions, individualized career coaching, externships, and career treks. Every incoming freshman is introduced to the school's career services and the concept of a "four-year career exploration plan."

The college hosts a separate Grad School Fair and Employer Fair each fall. It also participates in a larger fair held at Western Michigan University that features 150+ employers each February. First-generation and low-income students can receive up to $4,000 in stipends from the CCPD for unpaid internship experiences. K-Treks send students to visit companies in San Francisco; New York City; Washington, DC; and Chicago. Passions to Professions events afford students the chance to enjoy a meal while connecting with a current professional in their field of interest.

Professional Outcomes

By the December following their graduation, 92% of recent grads were already engaged in their next meaningful phase of life. The employers nabbing the greatest number of Hornets included Pfizer, General Motors, Ford Motor Company, Google, the Henry Ford Health System, Charles River Laboratories, Deloitte, Amazon, and Spectrum Health. Many live in the greater Detroit area, but significant numbers of alumni can be spotted in Chicago; the UK; New York City; Washington, DC; San Francisco; and Los Angeles.

Fifteen percent of recent diploma-earners had already enrolled in graduate or professional school within six months of officially earning their bachelor's degree; almost half begin pursuing an advanced degree within five years. Recent grads have matriculated at schools including the University of Michigan, Columbia, Johns Hopkins, and a number of other nearby Michigan-based institutions. An exceptional number of Kalamazoo alumni go on to earn a doctoral degree. To be precise, the school places in the second percentile (per capita) among all US colleges and universities in that regard. Over the last few years, alumni have enrolled in law schools including Michigan State, Marquette, the University of Texas, and USC. Kalamazoo boasts an incredible 68% graduate acceptance rate into medical school; recent grads have entered med school at the Central Michigan University College of Medicine and Western Michigan University Homer Stryker MD School of Medicine.

Admission

Eighty percent of applicants to the Class of 2026 were offered admission, an identical figure to the previous year. Having gone test-optional in 2015, the post-pandemic years brought no great changes when only 38% of applicants submitted an SAT score and 5% submitted an ACT result. Among the enrolled members of the Class of 2026 who submitted standardized test scores, the mid 50% range was 1200-1370 on the SAT and 26-32 on the ACT; the average scores were 30 and 1285. Thirty-five percent of this cohort placed in the top decile of their high school class, and 92% ranked in the top quartile. The average high school GPA for first-time students was 3.8.

The Kalamazoo Admissions Committee strongly considers each applicant's GPA, level of curricular rigor, and extracurricular activities; the application essay and recommendations are also given a good deal of weight. The committee assures applicants that the school utilizes "a holistic review process to fully assess your candidacy for admission" and that "all materials you submit will be given careful consideration." Interviews can be scheduled with the admissions office or alumni interviewer, and taking advantage of that opportunity is a good idea as demonstrated interest is a considered factor in the admissions process. In the 2022-23 admissions cycle, 40 students submitted early decision applications, and 26 were granted admission.

Worth Your Money?

You can pretty much ignore the list price of tuition at Kalamazoo College as 98% of students receive some level of need-based or merit-based aid. The listed cost of attendance of $72,151 is sliced significantly by average need-based packages of $41k and merit scholarships that range from $36k-$44k per year. The average cumulative debt upon graduation is right around the national average. If debt load can be kept reasonable, Kalamazoo presents an opportunity to receive a beautifully personal education. If the cost fits into your plan (including future grad school costs), then it is absolutely worth your money.

FINANCIAL
Institutional Type: Private
In-State Tuition: $56,562
Out-of-State Tuition: $56,562
Room & Board: $11,340
Books & Supplies: $825

Avg. Need-Based Grant: Not Reported
Avg. % of Need Met: Not Reported

Avg. Merit-Based Award: $32,179
% Receiving (Freshmen w/o Need): 27%

Avg. Cumulative Debt: $31,811
% of Students Borrowing: 64%

CAREER
Who Recruits
1. Spectrum Health
2. Charles River Laboratories
3. General Motors
4. Kalamazoo Public Schools
5. Ford Motor Company

Notable Internships
1. Stryker
2. Newmind Group
3. US Senate

Top Employers
1. Michigan State University
2. Stryker
3. Michigan Med
4. Pfizer
5. Ford Motor Company

Where Alumni Work
1. Detroit
2. Kalamazoo
3. Chicago
4. United Kingdom
5. Grand Rapids, MI

Earnings
College Scorecard (10-YR Post-Entry): $60,627
PayScale (Early Career): $54,600
PayScale (Mid-Career): $111,500
PayScale 20-Year ROI: $492,000

RANKINGS
Money: 4.5
U.S. News: 70, Liberal Arts Colleges
Wall Street Journal/THE: 141
Washington Monthly: 56, Liberal Arts Colleges

OVERGENERALIZATIONS
Students are:
Globally-minded
Politically liberal
Always studying
Passionate about social justice
Involved/invested in campus life

COLLEGE OVERLAPS
Albion College
DePauw University
Hope College
Kenyon College
The College of Wooster

Kenyon College

Gambier, Ohio | 740-427-5776

ADMISSION
Admission Rate: 34%
Admission Rate - Men: 29%
Admission Rate - Women: 38%
EA Admission Rate: Not Offered
ED Admission Rate: 44%
ED Admits as % of Total Admits: 8%
Admission Rate (5-Year Trend): 0%
% of Admits Attending (Yield): 19%
Transfer Admission Rate: 33%

SAT Reading/Writing (Middle 50%): 700-760
SAT Math (Middle 50%): 670-760
ACT Composite (Middle 50%): 31-34

% Graduated in Top 10% of HS Class: 63%
% Graduated in Top 25% of HS Class: 86%
% Graduated in Top 50% of HS Class: 97%

Demonstrated Interest: Important
Legacy Status: Considered
Racial/Ethnic Status: Considered
Admission Interview Offered: Yes

ENROLLMENT
Total Undergraduate Enrollment: 1,885
% Full-Time: 100%
% Male: 44%
% Female: 56%
% Out-of-State: 88%
% Fraternity: 8%
% Sorority: 8%
% On-Campus (All Undergraduate): 99%
Freshman Housing Required: Yes

% African-American: 3%
% Asian: 5%
% Hispanic: 8%
% White: 66%
% Other: 1%
% International: 12%
% Low-Income: 11%

ACADEMICS
Student-to-Faculty Ratio: 10 to 1
% of Classes Under 20: 73%
% of Classes 20-49: 26%
% of Classes 50 or More: 1%
% Full-Time Faculty: 82%
% Full-Time Faculty w/ Terminal Degree: 96%

Top Programs
English
History
International Studies
Neuroscience
Performing Arts
Political Science
Sociology

Retention Rate: 89%
4-Year Graduation Rate: 84%
6-Year Graduation Rate: 88%

Curricular Flexibility: Very Flexible
Academic Rating: ★★★★

#CollegesWorthYourMoney

When your list of notable alumni includes Paul Newman, Allison Janney, National Humanities Medal recipient E.L. Doctorow, and largely forgotten US President Rutherford B. Hayes, it's clear that your college is a unique and special place. Kenyon College in rural Gambier, Ohio, has a history of excellence in drama, English, and across the broader liberal arts that produces passionate and talented alumni who are ready, willing, and able to carve out their legacies within their chosen disciplines.

Inside the Classroom

Kenyon offers 50 majors, minors, and concentrations that allow students to complete their education with few non-departmental core requirements. All undergrads must demonstrate proficiency in a foreign language (AP opt-out is available) and take a quantitative reasoning course, but other than that, a Kenyon education is open and flexible. A senior capstone awaits all would-be graduates and can take many forms, but the project must demonstrate a student's skills in writing, speaking, collaborating, and "distinguishing the essential from the trivial." This latter requirement epitomizes Kenyon's emphasis on critical thought throughout one's four years of study.

The student-faculty ratio is 10-to-1, and the average class size is 15. Twenty-nine percent of classes are even more intimate, offering single-digit enrollments. Close relationships develop with faculty and often lead to opportunities to engage in undergraduate research. Summer research programs available to students include the Kenyon Summer Scholars Program, a joint program with Ohio State, and the Summer Science Program that sees more than thirty student-professor pairs collaborate on research for an eight- to ten-week period. A stunning 100% of recent alumni state that they learned to write better while at Kenyon. Roughly half of each junior class packs up its bags and heads off to a distant land for a semester abroad. Students choose from more than 190 programs in 50 countries across Africa, Asia, Australia, Europe, and the Americas; the school also sponsors programs in England and Rome.

English, economics, psychology, political science, and the visual and performing arts are all popular majors. As alluded to earlier, the drama program is one of the country's finest and has a lengthy alumni list of recognizable actors and performers. It's rare to identify an institution's English program as having an elevated reputation in the minds of employers and graduate schools, but Kenyon's would be one of the exceptions. For a relatively small school, Kenyon graduates procure nationally competitive scholarships and fellowships at an exceptional clip. In 2022, the college had eight Fulbright winners and a Goldwater recipient. It has been a top Fulbright producer for the last decade.

Outside the Classroom

Kenyon's 1,000-acre campus is located 45 miles from bustling Columbus and includes a 500-acre nature preserve. All students live on campus, and freshmen are clustered in special residence halls near the Gund Commons. Facilities receive rave reviews from students—the Kenyon Athletic Center includes tennis courts, a pool, and an indoor track. Eight percent of male Kenyon undergraduates are involved in Greek life as are 8% of women, but, uniquely, fraternities and sororities are situated within residence halls, leading to a more integrated experience. Close to one-third of students are on the roster of one of the school's 20 NCAA Division III athletic teams (ten men's and ten women's). Plenty of club and intramural sports are available for those seeking a less formal sports pursuit. Intramurals include offbeat games like cornhole and capture the flag. Beyond Greek organizations and sports teams, there are 150 student organizations to consider including five a cappella groups, numerous community service opportunities, and the Kenyon College Dance & Dramatics Club that puts on high-quality student productions. Nature lovers can hike the six miles of trails in the school's own preserve along the Kokosing River or join the Outdoors Club that takes backpacking and whitewater rafting trips to more adventurous locations such as the Monongahela National Forest of West Virginia.

Career Services

The Career Development Office (CDO) employs eight professional staff members who work in career development or graduate school advising. With a 236:1 student-to-advisor ratio, Kenyon provides a higher-than-average level of support when compared against the other institutions in this guidebook. While it doesn't host a large-scale career fair, it does offer employer/graduate school information sessions at a rate of fifteen to twenty per month.

The CDO's strengths lie in its willingness to give individualized attention to students and its involved alumni network. The online Kenyon Career Network helps link current students to alumni working in their field of interest; there are 8,000 alumni (in 200 industries) willing to offer their advice and assistance. Job-shadowing opportunities are plentiful, and experiences have included trips to The New York Times, Random House, and the Federal Reserve Bank of Chicago. The office is adept at helping students find internships, and recent grads have had stints with organizations such as the Museum of Modern Art, the San Diego Padres, and the Library of Congress. Ninety-six percent of students engage in an internship or job shadowing experience. In recent years, 65-75% of employed graduates reported that their jobs were related to their desired career path. Only two-thirds of graduates reported that Kenyon was effective at preparing them for the work of employment. Those indicators suggest that not all graduates are fully satisfied with the career services delivered at this school.

Professional Outcomes

Ninety-two percent of grads find their next step within six months of graduation. Popular fields for Kenyon grads include education, health care, marketing, nonprofit management, research, and writing and editing. Due to Kenyon's small size and the diversity of its academic programs, it lacks dense concentrations of alumni at particular companies. Economics majors often land as financial analysts or advisors at firms including BlackRock, Wells Fargo, JP Morgan, or Goldman Sachs. English and journalism majors end up at a diverse array of publishing houses, talent agencies, news organizations, and consulting companies. New York City, DC, Columbus, Chicago, and Boston are the five cities drawing the greatest numbers of Kenyon alumni. Early career salaries for Kenyon grads are modest, but that can partially be explained by the fact that many alumni pursue lengthy graduate/professional programs that typically pay financial dividends later in life.

Eighteen percent of grads enroll directly in graduate school, and within five years of completing their undergraduate education at Kenyon, 50% have already finished an advanced degree program and 70% are enrolled in one. Law and business school applicants find success at a 99% clip and, among medical school candidates with a minimum GPA of 3.25+, the acceptance rate is a phenomenal 90%. Recent grads have been welcomed into top law schools at Yale, NYU, Berkeley, Stanford, UVA, Michigan, and the University of Chicago. Future doctors are currently training at prestigious medical schools including Johns Hopkins, Duke, Harvard, Tufts, Vanderbilt, and Northwestern. A successful undergraduate career at Kenyon will make possible admission into the finest graduate and professional schools in the world. Across all disciplines, 98% of those applying to an advanced degree program are accepted by one of their top three choices.

Admission

A rarity among elite liberal arts schools, Kenyon's acceptance rate has risen in recent years. The Class of 2019 acceptance rate hit an all-time low of 24%, but the Class of 2026 rate was a significantly friendlier 34%. The latest incoming freshman class possessed an average GPA of 3.9 and mid-50% scores of 1380-1490 on the SAT and 31-34 on the ACT. Three years ago, when the acceptance rate was ten points lower, the SAT range was 1240-1420; the average GPA was the same. Therefore, one can conclude that the profile of the average Kenyon student has not changed much in recent years.

The admissions committee values four factors above all others: rigor of courses, GPA, recommendations, and essays. Test scores, class rank, the interview, talent/ability, extracurricular activities, character/personal qualities, and the level of an applicant's interest make up the next rung of important considerations. Facing stiff competition from other elite liberal arts schools, Kenyon very much wants to know if you truly want to go there. Applying early decision is the ultimate sign of devotion, and that act is rewarded. Forty-four percent of ED applicants were accepted, and they comprise a good portion of each incoming class. Kenyon is looking for academically curious and talented students who are actively involved in their schools/communities. Excellent grades are a must, and demonstrating interest is more valuable here than at your average college. If your heart is set on Kenyon, strongly consider demonstrating your loyalty by applying early.

Worth Your Money?

Current Kenyon students who qualify for financial aid see 100% of their need met. To help lower the $83,740 cost of attendance, 65% of undergrads receive some form of financial aid, including 43% who receive a need-based scholarship. This school is definitely worth your money but, as when considering any institution, we would caution against taking on an excessive amount of debt if you are pursuing a major that is unlikely to lead to fiscal stability upon graduation.

FINANCIAL
Institutional Type: Private
In-State Tuition: $69,330
Out-of-State Tuition: $69,330
Room & Board: $14,410
Books & Supplies: $860

Avg. Need-Based Grant: $51,445
Avg. % of Need Met: 100%

Avg. Merit-Based Award: $15,854
% Receiving (Freshmen w/o Need): 29%

Avg. Cumulative Debt: $24,719
% of Students Borrowing: 38%

CAREER
Who Recruits
1. GBQ Partners
2. DHL Supply Chain
3. Skylight Financial Group
4. TEKsystems
5. Verizon

Notable Internships
1. Penguin Random House
2. Guggenheim Museum
3. Morgan Stanley

Top Employers
1. JPMorgan Chase
2. Cleveland Clinic
3. Google
4. Amazon
5. US State Department

Where Alumni Work
1. New York City
2. Washington, DC
3. Columbus, OH
4. Chicago
5. Boston

Earnings
College Scorecard (10-YR Post-Entry): $63,557
PayScale (Early Career): $58,800
PayScale (Mid-Career): $117,400
PayScale 20-Year ROI: $350,000

RANKINGS
Money: 4.5
U.S. News: 39, Liberal Arts Colleges
Wall Street Journal/THE: 298
Washington Monthly: 92, Liberal Arts Colleges

OVERGENERALIZATIONS
Students are:
Wealthy
Politically liberal
Involved/invested in campus life
Always admiring the beauty of their campus
Quirky

COLLEGE OVERLAPS
Grinnell College
Hamilton College
Middlebury College
Oberlin College
Vassar College

Lafayette College

Easton, Pennsylvania | 610-330-5100

Nearing its 200th birthday, this elite liberal arts school named after the Revolutionary War hero the Marquis de Lafayette offers a rare blend of an intimate academic experience mixed with big- time sports and prominent Greek life. Roughly 2,700 students comprise the student body at this undergraduate-only liberal arts school in quiet Easton, Pennsylvania. Undergrads are a high-caliber lot, possessing academic credentials equal to those of archrival Lehigh University.

Inside the Classroom
Lafayette offers 51 areas of study over four academic divisions: engineering, humanities, natural sciences, and the social sciences. It also allows for self-designed majors such as behavioral economics, environmental issues and policy, or nanoscience. All undergrads delve into a first-year seminar during the fall of their freshman year, a course designed to strengthen writing, thinking, and speaking abilities. Other required components of the school's common course of study include a year of foreign language, a quantitative reasoning course, two classes under the umbrella of global and multiculturalism, and at least a singular foray into each of the college's academic divisions.

One-on-one attention from professors is a reality at Lafayette, thanks to a 10:1 student-to-faculty ratio and no graduate students to compete with. A solid 62% of sections contain fewer than twenty students; 11% enroll nine or fewer. By the time senior year is nearing its completion, slightly more than half of students have completed a research experience with a faculty member. The school invests almost half a million dollars annually in funding undergraduate research. A majority of students also have studied for a semester in a foreign country as 60-65% of graduates elect to study abroad in one of 50 locations. In addition to semester-long options, Lafayette offers truncated study abroad opportunities during semester breaks.

Of the degrees conferred in 2022, social sciences (34%) and engineering (19%) were the disciplines in which the largest number of degrees were earned. The engineering program is one of the best in the country among non-doctoral granting institutions. Economics was the next most commonly conferred degree and is also one of Lafayette's strongest. Other popular and well-regarded programs include psychology, international affairs, and film studies. On the whole, Lafayette students fare well with employers and top graduate schools but also experience success when applying for prestigious fellowships. Named a top Fulbright producer, Lafayette had five winners in 2023. In recent years, it has had graduates land Gilman, Goldwater, and Udall Scholarships.

Outside the Classroom
In sleepy Easton, over 90% of undergrads lay their heads at night inside college-owned housing. Greek life, which was under a microscope after a 2012 hazing death, has survived and thrived, still drawing 24-30% of the student body into fraternities and sororities. Athletics are also a central part of the Lafayette experience as the Leopards compete in 23 NCAA Division I sports as well as in more than fifty club and intramural programs. Games against rival Lehigh garner a high level of interest. Over 200 student-run organizations are active. For those interested in the performing arts, over 20 such clubs are on the menu. There are 40+ cultural and/or service organizations that help contribute a collective 20,000 annual hours of charitable engagement. Nature lovers aren't far from the Pocono Mountains, which offer all of the hiking, snowboarding, skiing, tubing, and fishing you can handle. Almost equidistant (in terms of travel time) between New York City and Philadelphia, big-city fun is only a car ride away. Easton is a small town with plenty of history and some nice eateries, but campus is the hub of the social experience.

Career Services
The recently renamed Gateway Career Center is staffed by 13 professional employees (not counting office assistants) who work in career counseling, employer relations, internship coordination, or graduate school advising. That 210:1 student-to-advisor ratio is significantly better than average when compared to other schools featured in this guide. Thanks to such generous staffing, counselors can offer distinct services to students at every phase of their college education. In a single year, this group hosts 180 workshops and programs and engages 1,300+ students in almost 5,000 total career- and graduate school-related activities.

Large-scale events, such as the Fall Career Fair, attract more than sixty employers including Goldman Sachs, ExxonMobil, and Fidelity Investments. The Gateway Career Center does an excellent job guiding students into internships and other meaningful opportunities for hands-on learning. By senior year, 80% of Lafayette undergrads have completed an internship, externship, or other field experience. A robust 40% of recent grads found their jobs directly through campus recruiting and/or the alumni network. On-campus interviews take place October-November and again from February-April. With a high level of personalized offerings and excellent career and graduate school outcomes, the Gateway Career Center accomplishes its mission on behalf of its undergraduates.

Professional Outcomes

Within six months of graduation, a stellar 98% of the Class of 2022 had already landed full-time jobs or were enrolled in graduate/professional school. The most commonly procured jobs are in business development, education, operations, engineering, sales, finance, and research. Companies employing large numbers of Lafayette alumni include Merck, IBM, Morgan Stanley, Citi, Merrill Lynch, JP Morgan Chase Co., Deloitte, and EY. Despite being a Pennsylvania institution, Philadelphia is the second most popular landing spot for alumni; New York City attracts nearly three times as many Leopards. Large pockets of alumni also can be found in DC, Boston, and San Francisco.

Those attending graduate school frequently land at some of the top programs in the country within their respective disciplines. Recent economics majors have entered business/econ programs at Stanford, the University of Chicago, and Yale. Government majors have gone on to study at Penn, Harvard, and GW. Chemistry majors go on to pursue PhDs at institutions such as Tulane, Princeton, and Emory. Medical school applicants with a 3.6 GPA or above enjoy a 72% acceptance rate, and dental school candidates find homes at an 89% clip. Recent graduates have matriculated into medical schools at Georgetown, UVA, Brown, Dartmouth, and Boston University. Law school applicants found homes at a perfect 100% rate, and those acceptances included many top law schools.

Admission

The 10,500 students jostling for a spot in the Lafayette Class of 2026 were granted acceptance at a 34% rate; last year's class was admitted at a 41% clip. The Class of 2026 possessed a mid-50% SAT range of 1350-1460, an ACT range of 30-33, and an average unweighted GPA of 3.56. In a typical year, over 20 incoming freshmen were the valedictorian or salutatorian of their high school classes; 53% hailed from the top 10%, and 75% from the top quarter. On the other hand, they do leave room for some late bloomers with lower cumulative GPAs; 5% earned less than a 3.0.

In the eyes of the admissions committee at Lafayette, two factors receive the highest level of consideration—rigor of coursework and GPA. The next tier of factors includes test scores, class rank, essays, recommendations, extracurricular activities, the interview, character/personal qualities, and talent/ability. Those applying early decision were accepted at a 43% clip and accounted for more than half of entering freshmen in the 2022-23 academic year. Lafayette is a competitive institution but not out of reach for students with SAT scores in the 1300s and/or a less-than-pristine transcript. Applying early yields a strong advantage in the admissions process as the acceptance rate is higher, and a large chunk of the spots in the freshman class are already occupied by the time applicants enter the regular round.

Worth Your Money?

The annual bill to attend Lafayette exceeds $80,000. The good news is that those who are awarded a grant see 100% of their need met, one of only approximately 70 schools in the country to do so. With 60 million dollars budgeted annually, this school takes care of those from lower-income backgrounds and cumulative debt figures are right around the national average. The school's excellent offerings in engineering and strong networks in Philly and NYC lead to generally high starting salaries, making it possible for most to pay their student loans without too much economic pain.

FINANCIAL
Institutional Type: Private
In-State Tuition: $61,824
Out-of-State Tuition: $61,824
Room & Board: $19,084
Books & Supplies: $1,000

Avg. Need-Based Grant: $47,475
Avg. % of Need Met: 100%

Avg. Merit-Based Award: $26,074
% Receiving (Freshmen w/o Need): 14%

Avg. Cumulative Debt: $28,840
% of Students Borrowing: 39%

CAREER
Who Recruits
1. Gilbane Building
2. Crayola
3. SMC Partners
4. MarketAxess
5. Whiting-Turner Contracting

Notable Internships
1. Disney Streaming Services
2. RCA Records
3. Cisco

Top Employers
1. Merck
2. IBM
3. Morgan Stanley
4. Citi
5. Deloitte

Where Alumni Work
1. New York City
2. Philadelphia
3. Allentown, PA
4. Boston
5. Washington, DC

Earnings
College Scorecard (10-YR Post-Entry): $94,200
PayScale (Early Career): $72,600
PayScale (Mid-Career): $138,500
PayScale 20-Year ROI: $890,000

RANKINGS
Money: 4.5
U.S. News: 30, Liberal Arts Colleges
Wall Street Journal/THE: Not Ranked
Washington Monthly: 28, Liberal Arts Colleges

OVERGENERALIZATIONS
Students are:
Athletic/Active
Working hard and playing hard
Preppy
Tight-knit (possess a strong sense of community)
Motivated

COLLEGE OVERLAPS
Bucknell University
Colgate University
Franklin & Marshall College
Gettysburg College
Villanova University

Lawrence University

Appleton, Wisconsin | 920-832-6500

The history of Lawrence University, a tiny liberal arts school in Appleton, Wisconsin, is as unique as its present-day educational offerings. One of the earliest (ninth, to be precise) coeducational colleges in the United States and one of the top music conservatories anywhere, the 1,426 undergraduates on campus today enjoy an intimate academic environment in which the largest number of degrees conferred are in the performing arts. It is the only school in the nation whose college of arts and sciences and music conservatory are both 100% populated by undergraduates. There are 65 majors and minors as well as the option to complete a five-year double major from both the conservatory and A&S; like we said, LU is unique.

Inside the Classroom
Operating on a trimester calendar, the academic year is comprised of ten-week fall, winter, and spring sessions. For more than seventy years, part of the LU core curriculum has been a yearlong Freshman Studies program that explores questions like "What is the best sort of life for human beings? Are there limits to human knowledge? How should we respond to injustice and suffering?" in a small, seminar-style classroom. From there, Lawrence undergrads encounter a dose of humanities, natural science, social science, and fine arts offerings and must show competency in a foreign language, quantitative reasoning, and a writing/speaking-intensive course. Every graduate completes a Senior Experience that can take the form of a paper, performance, portfolio, or exhibition.

An 8:1 student/faculty ratio allows for extremely small class sizes—the majority of sections contain only two to nineteen students, and many independent study/1:1 music instruction courses also are available. With Lawrence being a "university" in name only, undergraduate research opportunities are wide open. Professors are expected to allow undergraduates access to their research studies; for example, every member of the Chemistry Department has to run an active research group. The Lawrence University Research Fellows (LURF) program offers a stipend during ten-week, research-focused terms. All told, close to two-thirds of LU students gain hands-on research experience at some point during their four years of study. The college strongly encourages students to study abroad, and roughly 40% take the plunge. Sponsored opportunities include the London Lawrence Center or the Francophile Seminar in Dakar, Senegal.

The visual and performing arts (23%), the social sciences (16%), and biology (14%) comprise the most popular areas of study at LU. The world-renowned Conservatory of Music enrolls approximately 350 undergraduates. Extremely strong natural science programs allow the university to be a top producer of future STEM PhDs. It is also a top producer of Fulbright Scholars, with five to its credit in a single recent year. Other prestigious fellowships won by recent students include a Watson Fellowship and a Goldwater Scholarship.

Outside the Classroom
In the 2022-23 school year, Lawrence's 88-acre campus housed 100% of freshmen and 95% of the undergraduate student body in five residence halls. The Greek presence is minimal with 4% of men affiliated with frats and 4% of women who are members of sororities. One-quarter of the population are NCAA Division III varsity athletes competing on one of the ten men's or nine women's squads known as the Vikings. Non-sports events that draw many participants include Fall Festival, Winter Carnival, and the Great Midwest Trivia Contest, a 50-hour marathon that has drawn national media attention. There are over one hundred clubs and activities, and virtually every student on campus is involved in at least one. Volunteer organizations are popular, and students give a collective 10,000 hours per year. Three or four times per year, campus will close for an hour while everyone flocks to Memorial Chapel for convocation where a famous speaker like Maya Angelou or David Sedaris will address the student body. If the Appleton campus that overlooks the Fox River doesn't provide enough natural beauty for you, the college also owns 425+ acres on the shores of Lake Michigan that can be utilized for hiking, ice skating, and camping. With a population of around 75,000, Appleton is a safe and enjoyable small town that contains ample bars, restaurants, and shops. The town is only about a thirty-minute drive from Green Bay and about ninety minutes from Milwaukee.

Career Services
The Career Center employs eight full-time staff members in employer and alumni relations, career advising, and pre-professional advising and major fellowships. That student-to-advisor ratio of 178:1 is strong when compared to other colleges featured in this guide, and it allows the career services staff to carve out time even for freshmen. All first-years are encouraged to come in for at least a fifteen- or twenty-minute counseling session. The center's stated mission is "preparing students for lives of achievement, responsible and meaningful citizenship, lifelong learning, and personal fulfillment," and it offers ample one-on-one counseling toward those aims.

Many students pursue internships with nonprofit institutions, charitable organizations, and museums, although several recent undergrads have landed positions at Apple, Google, and JPMorgan Chase. In part due to the school's small size and location, recruiting or on-campus interviewing visits from major employers are not frequent occurrences, and the school does not host a major job fair. Unfortunately, LU does not publicize data such as the percentage of students who land an internship, the number of in-person counseling sessions per year, or information about employers visiting campus. In the absence of such information and given the low starting salaries of recent graduates, it appears that some improvement may be needed in those areas.

Professional Outcomes

Of the 350 graduates in one recent graduating class, an impressive 99% had already reached their next employment or postsecondary destination. Among the 73% of that group who had landed their first jobs, business/finance, social services/nonprofit, the arts, health care/pharmaceutical, and media/communications were the most popular industries. Companies presently employing more than a dozen Lawrence alumni include Amazon, Epic Systems, Wells Fargo, Northwestern Mutual, US Bank, and UnitedHealth Group. Most students continue to reside in the Midwest after graduating. Greater Chicago; Oshkosh, Wisconsin; Greater Minneapolis-St. Paul; and Greater Milwaukee boast the greatest number of alums.

Over the last few years, graduates have gone on to master's and doctoral programs at a wide range of universities on the prestige spectrum. Highlighting that list are elite schools Carnegie Mellon, Duke, Dartmouth, Emory, Georgetown, University of Pennsylvania, and Washington University in St. Louis. Medical school acceptance rates fluctuate between 67% and 75%— significantly higher than the national average, even in down years. Recent graduates have matriculated into medical schools at Johns Hopkins, the University of Chicago, Northwestern, Boston University, and the University of Wisconsin. According to the National Science Foundation, Lawrence produces the fourteenth most future science and engineering PhDs among liberal arts colleges.

Admission

It's hard to find a school of better quality that has a higher acceptance rate than Lawrence's 72%. Even for less-than-perfect high schoolers, odds of admission are pretty strong. While 37% did place in the top 10% of their graduating class and 49% possessed a GPA of greater than 3.75, many others brought more middling credentials to the table. The average GPA for admitted students is 3.65, and 35% did not land in the top 25% of their high school cohort. This school does not require SATs or ACTs but, among those who elected to submit scores anyway, the mid-50% range was 1200-1440 on the SAT and 27-32 on the ACT.

Lawrence was early to the test-optional party, jettisoning mandatory standardized test submission in 2006. As a result, GPA, rigor of coursework, class rank, talent/ability, and character/personal qualities are perched atop the list of most important factors. The application essay, recommendations, extracurricular activities, and an interview, which is recommended but not required, make up the second rung of "important factors." Few apply early decision; only 68 did so in 2022, and 47 were accepted. A safety school for many applying to even more prestigious Midwestern liberal arts institutions, only 17% of those admitted actually enroll. Thus, it is advantageous to communicate your genuine interest in attending throughout the application process.

Worth Your Money?

The sticker price (including room and board and all fees) at Lawrence is $67,299, but few receive an annual bill for that amount. In fact, 99% of Lawrentians receive some type/level of financial aid, including 64% who received need-based aid. Because the most commonly studied fields at LU are not among the highest paying, students need to adjust the value of loans they are willing to take out accordingly. That said, this school provides an amazing educational experience, particularly for those interested in performance and academia, and it typically provides enough financial aid to make a Lawrence degree affordable.

FINANCIAL
Institutional Type: Private
In-State Tuition: $55,461
Out-of-State Tuition: $55,461
Room & Board: $11,838
Books & Supplies: $900

Avg. Need-Based Grant: $39,389
Avg. % of Need Met: 93%

Avg. Merit-Based Award: $31,925
% Receiving (Freshmen w/o Need): 34%

Avg. Cumulative Debt: $27,817
% of Students Borrowing: 57%

CAREER
Who Recruits
1. M3 Insurance
2. Enterprise Holdings
3. Hauser Advertising
4. McAdam Financial
5. Air Wisconsin Airlines, LLC

Notable Internships
1. American Museum of Natural History
2. Uber
3. EY

Top Employers
1. US Bank
2. Epic
3. Northwestern Mutual
4. Target
5. Wells Fargo

Where Alumni Work
1. Chicago
2. Oshkosh, WI
3. Minneapolis
4. Milwaukee
5. New York City

Earnings
College Scorecard (10-YR Post-Entry): $50,848
PayScale (Early Career): $53,100
PayScale (Mid-Career): $109,500
PayScale 20-Year ROI: $405,000

RANKINGS
Money: 3.5
U.S. News: 75, Liberal Arts Colleges
Wall Street Journal/THE: 366
Washington Monthly: 77, Liberal Arts Colleges

OVERGENERALIZATIONS
Students are:
Economically diverse
Tight-knit (possess a strong sense of community)
Collaborative
Intellectual
Quirky

COLLEGE OVERLAPS
Beloit College
Grinnell College
Macalester College
Oberlin College
St. Olaf College

Lehigh University

Bethlehem, Pennsylvania | 610-758-3100

Emblematic of the American economy as a whole, the once-great industrial town of Bethlehem, Pennsylvania, is now highlighted by a research university known for preparing the next generation of problem-solving engineers. Lehigh University is a research powerhouse that caters to only 5,624 undergraduate students, allowing for lots of individualized attention from expert faculty in world-class facilities. There are five colleges within the larger university: the College of Arts & Sciences, the College of Business, the College of Education (graduate students only), the College of Health, and the prestigious Rossin College of Engineering and Applied Science.

Inside the Classroom
Despite its modest size, Lehigh offers more than one hundred majors, minors, and programs. Academic requirements vary by school but, notably, none possess a foreign language mandate. In the College of Arts & Sciences, students must complete two semesters of Composition & Literature, a First-Year Seminar, one math course, and eight credits in each of the humanities, natural sciences, and social sciences. The core curricula in the College of Business & Economics includes foundational courses in decision-making and business principles as well as introductory coursework in accounting, economics, marketing, management, and finance (no matter which of those concentrations you choose). Lastly, all business students must complete a senior capstone project. Within the Rossin College of Engineering and Applied Science, undergrads must knock out ten credits of English and economics and thirteen credits in the humanities. There are also two innovative programs that require a foray into other disciplines—the Integrated Business & Engineering Honors Program (IBE) and the Integrated Degree Engineering, Arts & Sciences Honors Programs (IDEAS).

Lehigh has a 10:1 student-to-faculty ratio, but classes aren't as tiny as one might expect with such favorable staffing numbers. The average class size is 26 but, on the plus side, 45% of courses have enrollments of 19 or fewer. Undergraduate research is commonplace, particularly within the engineering school. Each year, 40% of engineering students gain faculty-led research experience. Additionally, 40% of graduates engage in some type of international experience, whether it's a semester of academic study abroad or a foreign-based internship. Roughly half of those students took courses in one of 250 study abroad programs approved by the university.

With a highly ranked engineering school, it's easy to view Lehigh as primarily a techie haven. Surprisingly, the majority of students pursue other programs, with Lehigh's well-regarded business school drawing the most majors (29%); 22% graduate with a degree in engineering and 12% study computer science. Competitive fellowship and scholarship programs look favorably upon the university. Thirty undergrads and alumni were awarded Gilman Scholarships over the last few years, and multiple students win National Science Foundation Fellowships in a given year.

Outside the Classroom
Lehigh's three contiguous campuses account for 1,600 picturesque acres. Last year, 61% of students lived on campus, and 97% of first-year students resided in college-owned housing. The school plans to add 1,000 undergraduate students by 2026 and is presently building additional on-campus housing to accommodate the increased student population. Even with a large number of students living off campus, this is an incredibly involved student body with 93% involved in some type of extracurricular activity. Greek life is a powerful force with 26% of women joining sororities and 18% of men pledging a fraternity. On the athletics front, the Mountain Hawks compete in 23 intercollegiate sports, mostly in the NCAA Division I Patriot League. An additional 40+ intramural and club teams claim another 2,900 participants annually. On the non-sports front, there are 200+ student organizations at Lehigh and over 250 art events on campus annually. Service-oriented clubs are popular and account for 65,000 collective hours of community service per year. Bethlehem is known more for its industrial history as a hub of steel production than for thrilling nightlife, but students with a car can get to Philly in an hour and a half or New York City in a little over two hours.

Career Services
The Center for Career and Professional Development (CCPD) is staffed by 15 professional employees (not counting student interns) who work in career counseling, employer engagement, or graduate school advising. That 375:1 student-to-advisor ratio is within the average range of universities profiled in this guide. Yet, by almost any metric, the level of support offered to the school's undergraduates is of superior quality.

The CCPD entices more than 6,900 attendees to its events (more than the entire undergraduate population). The fall and spring career expos draw large student crowds and are attended by as many as 140 employers, including many major corporations. Counselors hold almost 2,500 one-on-one advising sessions and achieve 12,000+ total engagements through in-person and online interaction. Perhaps most impressive is the number of on-campus interviews conducted per year—2,700+—more than double the number of graduating seniors. Lehigh's career services staff also does a superb job facilitating internships and other valuable immersive experiences. An exceptional 94% of grads complete at least one internship or externship. Lehigh's Center for Career and Professional Development provides a top-notch level of service to its undergraduate clientele, and those efforts translate into stellar employment and graduate school outcomes.

Professional Outcomes

Recent grads quickly found its way toward the next productive step in their lives with 97% landing jobs or grad school placements within six months of leaving Lehigh. Among graduates of the School of Business and Economics, the top industries entered were financial services, accounting, consulting, and computer software. Top employers of recent business degree earners include Amazon, CitiGroup, Deloitte, EY, KPMG, Morgan Stanley, and PwC. Rossin College of Engineering and Applied Science graduates flocked to companies such as ExxonMobil, GE, Google, IBM, Lockheed Martin, Merck, and Microsoft. Arts & Sciences graduates secured employment at places like CBS, People Magazine, and the National Institutes of Health. Across all schools, the average starting salary for a recent grad is $67,000 with computer science majors on the high end at $86k and math and natural sciences majors on the low end at $47k.

Among recent diploma-earners heading straight to graduate/professional school, roughly 30% were studying engineering, one-quarter were pursuing business degrees, 10% were training for health professions, and a smaller number entered law schools including Boston University, Georgetown, and Yale. In a typical year, a phenomenal 90%+ of medical school applicants earn at least one acceptance, and recent med school acceptances included Boston University School of Medicine, Harvard School of Dental Medicine, and Johns Hopkins School of Medicine. Those pursuing a master's or a PhD did so at Columbia, MIT, Stanford, UPenn the University of Michigan, and a number of other first-class universities.

Admission

Lehigh had an all-time low 22% acceptance rate for those jockeying for a spot in the Class of 2022. Fortunately, for prospective students, the Class of 2026 received 15,163 applications and accepted 37%, quite a jump in a short three-year period. Freshmen entering Lehigh for the 2022-23 school year possessed middle-50% scores of 1350-1480 on the SAT and 30-33 on the ACT. Eighty-five percent of the non-test-optional students possessed an ACT score of 30 or better. Fifty-seven percent of the Class of 2026 placed in the top decile of their high school class, and 87% were in the top quartile.

Only two factors sit perched atop the list of criteria considered by the Lehigh admissions committee: rigor of courses and GPA. Class rank, test scores, essays, recommendations, extracurricular activities, talent/ability, work experience, character/personal qualities, and demonstrated interest are on the next rung of factors deemed "important." On the subject of demonstrated interest, Lehigh places high value on an applicant's level of commitment to attending the university. To quantify that importance, early decision applicants are admitted at a rate of 66%. Early decision applicants comprised 57% of the incoming class. Women face slightly better odds, sporting an acceptance rate 5% higher than male applicants.

Worth Your Money?

Those who don't qualify for financial aid will not receive much help from Lehigh in covering the $72k cost of attendance; however, 46% of undergrads do receive some degree of financial aid, and 90% of families making less than $75,000 received grants and scholarships equal to or greater than the cost of tuition. With extremely high starting salaries, this school is likely to pay you back, particularly if you major in the business/engineering realm.

FINANCIAL
Institutional Type: Private
In-State Tuition: $62,180
Out-of-State Tuition: $62,180
Room & Board: $16,470
Books & Supplies: $1,000

Avg. Need-Based Grant: $50,287
Avg. % of Need Met: 98%

Avg. Merit-Based Award: $16,317
% Receiving (Freshmen w/o Need): 5%

Avg. Cumulative Debt: $37,147
% of Students Borrowing: 45%

CAREER
Who Recruits
1. Knowles Corporation
2. Mineral Technologies Inc.
3. SIG
4. Tge LiRo Group
5. Crayola

Notable Internships
1. Prudenial Financial
2. Barclays
3. Visa

Top Employers
1. Merck
2. EY
3. PwC
4. IBM
5. Deloitte

Where Alumni Work
1. New York City
2. Allentown, PA
3. Philadelphia
4. Boston
5. Washington, DC

Earnings
College Scorecard (10-YR Post-Entry): $100,559
PayScale (Early Career): $74,600
PayScale (Mid-Career): $147,300
PayScale 20-Year ROI: $1,006,000

RANKINGS
Money: 4.5
U.S. News: 47, National Universities
Wall Street Journal/THE: 14
Washington Monthly: 52, National Universities

OVERGENERALIZATIONS
Students are:
Working hard and playing hard
More likely to rush a fraternity/sorority
Politically balanced
Career-driven
Only a short drive from home (i.e., Most come from PA or nearby states)

COLLEGE OVERLAPS
Cornell University
Bucknell University
Lafayette College
Pennsylvania State University - University Park
University of Michigan

Lewis & Clark College

Portland, Oregon | 503-768-7040

ADMISSION
Admission Rate: 69%
Admission Rate - Men: 69%
Admission Rate - Women: 68%
EA Admission Rate: 81%
ED Admission Rate: 72%
ED Admits as % of Total Admits: 1%
Admission Rate (5-Year Trend): -2%
% of Admits Attending (Yield): 14%
Transfer Admission Rate: 61%

SAT Reading/Writing (Middle 50%): 650-720
SAT Math (Middle 50%): 610-680
ACT Composite (Middle 50%): 29-32

% Graduated in Top 10% of HS Class: 43%
% Graduated in Top 25% of HS Class: 75%
% Graduated in Top 50% of HS Class: 94%

Demonstrated Interest: Considered
Legacy Status: Considered
Racial/Ethnic Status: Considered
Admission Interview Offered: Yes

ENROLLMENT
Total Undergraduate Enrollment: 2,210
% Full-Time: 99%
% Male: 35%
% Female: 65%
% Out-of-State: 86%
% Fraternity: Not Offered
% Sorority: Not Offered
% On-Campus (All Undergraduate): 68%
Freshman Housing Required: Yes

% African-American: 3%
% Asian: 5%
% Hispanic: 11%
% White: 69%
% Other: 1%
% International: 4%
% Low-Income: 19%

ACADEMICS
Student-to-Faculty Ratio: 13 to 1
% of Classes Under 20: 54%
% of Classes 20-49: 45%
% of Classes 50 or More: 1%
% Full-Time Faculty: 46%
% Full-Time Faculty w/ Terminal Degree: 96%

Top Programs
Biology
English
Environmental Studies
History
International Affairs
Psychology
Rhetoric and Media Studies
Sociology and Anthropology

Retention Rate: 84%
4-Year Graduation Rate: 67%
6-Year Graduation Rate: 75%

Curricular Flexibility: Somewhat Flexible
Academic Rating: ★★★

#CollegesWorthYourMoney

Moving swiftly past the countless bad puns we could begin with about Lewis & Clark College being a great place to "explore" various disciplines or begin an "expedition" toward your future career, let's move into the key reasons why this Oregon-based liberal arts school of 2,210 undergraduates is worth your consideration. For starters, the school is so committed to helping graduate students in four years that if you need an extra semester, it's on the house. The 29 majors and 33 minors are offered in a setting that is widely praised for the strength of its undergraduate teaching. For those without perfect high school grades and/or an aversion to standardized tests, there is even better news; this test-optional school accepts more than three-quarters of those who apply.

Inside the Classroom
The standard course at L&C is worth four credits, and students take 16 credits each 15-week semester. All freshmen complete a two-part First-Year Seminar over their first two semesters on campus. Foreign language proficiency up to the 201 level is required; students can place out through the completion of a standardized exam. Additional credits must be earned in the following categories: Bibliographic Research in Writing; the Creative Arts; Culture, Power & Identity; Global Perspectives; Historical Perspectives; the Natural Sciences; and Physical Education and Well-Being (two one-credit courses).

There are 200 full-time faculty members for the 2,200+ undergraduate students, which leads to a 13:1 student-to-faculty ratio. Seventeen percent of courses unfold in small, seminar-style environments of no more than nine students, and 54% of classes seat no more than 19. Only 15% of all sections enroll more than 29 students. Studying abroad is the norm at this school with 60% of Pioneers studying overseas in one of more than 30 programs. Research apprenticeships are a bit less commonplace, but they can be procured through the Rogers Science Research Program, a 10-week summer program that accepts 35% of applicants. Other department-specific opportunities exist, such as within the Biology Department where students can serve as research apprentices to professors for credit and, later in their undergraduate experience, assume a more collaborative role with a faculty member.

The greatest number of students earn degrees in the social sciences (22%) followed by psychology (14%), biology (14%), visual and performing arts (9%), and natural resources and conservation (6%). Some participate in the colleges 3+3 program that expedites the process of earning an undergraduate and law degree (from the Lewis & Clark Law School) or the five-year BA + Master of Arts in Teaching program that leads to licensure. The school's emphasis on creating global citizens is further evidenced by the fact that the school is regularly named a top producer of Fulbright winners; four students and alumni were named in 2023.

Outside the Classroom
While it is a private college, almost 90% of attendees hail from within the Beaver State. Even though many undergrads live close to home, 97% of freshmen and 68% of all students live in on-campus housing. A fairly large gender divide exists at Lewis & Clark as 65% of undergraduates are female. There are no fraternities or sororities, nor is there a huge emphasis on athletics. However, there are still 350 student-athletes who are members of 19 NCAA Division III teams. More than 100 student-led clubs include plenty of intramural sports for less serious athletes. The 134-acre campus is situated in southwest Portland in the College View section of the city. It sits adjacent to the 645-acre Tryon Creek State Natural Area and, for lovers of nature, the opportunities are endless. The popular College Outdoors program takes students all around the Pacific Northwest for backpacking, white-water rafting, hiking, nature meditation, and more. Those seeking culture, shopping, entertainment, and excellent cuisine will find it in Portland. Within a ten-mile radius, you'll be able to access the Portland Museum of Art, the famous Powell's Books, and Saturday Market, the largest weekly open-air crafts fair in the United States.

Career Services
Five professionals are employed within the Lewis & Clark Career Center including a director, two associate directors, an employer relations specialist and—most interestingly—a "diplomat in residence" who helps enrich the experience of students interested in disciplines/careers with a global flavor. The career center's 442:1 student-to-counselor ratio is solid, and plenty of individualized support is available for major and career exploration, internship procurement, job search planning, and the graduate school search and application process. As a bonus, you also have access to a number of peer career advisors.

The school is in Oregon's largest city (the 25th largest in the US), so it makes landing meaningful internships and connecting with prospective employers a relatively easy task. Each semester, the center promotes hundreds of career-related events from information sessions to resume workshops to full-blown career fairs in the fall and spring. In one recent spring fair, the school saw 78 employers connect with 575 students. As the following section of our profile will show, the Lewis & Clark Career Center is succeeding in connecting its graduates to some of the most prominent and desirable employers in the region.

Professional Outcomes

Half a year after receiving their diplomas, 95% of recent grads had arrived at their next destination with 80% obtaining employment, 13% entering graduate or professional school, and 2% engaged in service work. Among those landing their first professional jobs, 35% were in the business/industry sector, 23% in education, 9% in STEM, and 7% in health care. More than two dozen alumni are employed at major companies, many of which have offices in the Pacific Northwest. Those include Nike, Kaiser Permanente, Intel, Microsoft, Amazon, Wells Fargo, and Google. Portland, San Francisco, Seattle, Los Angeles, New York City, and Denver are the cities where Pioneers most frequently settle after earning their diplomas.

Many entering graduate school do so in state at the University of Oregon or Oregon State University, but recent grads also have gone on to pursue MBAs at the University of Southern California, UCLA, Northwestern, and Columbia. Some students pursuing a legal education funnel into the Lewis & Clark College of Law while others have gained acceptance at top law schools including Harvard, Cornell, NYU, and Stanford. Premed students have gone on to study at the Emory University School of Medicine, the Vanderbilt University School of Medicine, and Johns Hopkins University School of Medicine.

Admission

An early adopter of a test-optional policy back in 1991, Lewis & Clark has long utilized a holistic evaluation process for prospective undergraduates. At present, at least two admissions counselors review each application to search for "evidence indicating you're capable of academic success here at L&C and determining what you will contribute to the entering class." As evidenced by the 69% acceptance rate for the Class of 2026, admissions staff here are not focused on piling up rejections and, consequently, instead of prestige-grabbing low acceptance rates, it offers a direct evaluation of whether a student can be successful once accepted. For a school that accepts more than two-thirds of applicants, enrolled students possess some stellar credentials including an average weighted GPA of 3.72; only 2% earned a GPA under 3.0. Among those who submitted standardized test scores (the majority did not), the mid-50% ranges were 1270-1400 on the SAT and 29-32 on the ACT.

This admissions staff is primarily concerned with a student's performance in a rigorous high school curriculum. It also places a good deal of weight on essays, recommendations, extracurricular activities, talent/ability, character/personal qualities, volunteer work, and work experience. The staff also considers an in-person or virtual interview that is recommended but not required. Interviewing is a good way to demonstrate interest, which L&C does consider in its admissions process. The school is not most applicants' first choice; the yield rate is a meager 14%. Only 75 students in the Class of 2025 cohort applied via early decision, but 54 were accepted.

Worth Your Money?

With 86% of Lewis & Clark students receiving some type of financial assistance—aid packages range from $1,000 to $60,000—the sticker price cost of attendance of roughly $77k becomes easier to swallow. The school meets 90% of a student's demonstrated financial need, which can make the school affordable for many. In the end, L&C graduates carry a debt load right around the national average. We would not recommend taking out enormous amounts of debt to attend this institution, particularly since the bulk of degrees earned are not in areas that see an immediate, early career return on investment.

FINANCIAL
Institutional Type: Private
In-State Tuition: $62,350
Out-of-State Tuition: $62,350
Room & Board: $15,002
Books & Supplies: $1,050

Avg. Need-Based Grant: $44,193
Avg. % of Need Met: 91%

Avg. Merit-Based Award: $25,806
% Receiving (Freshmen w/o Need): 38%

Avg. Cumulative Debt: $30,914
% of Students Borrowing: 48%

CAREER
Who Recruits
1. Wells Fargo
2. Oregon Health Authority
3. Nike
4. Intel
5. Kaiser Permanente

Notable Internships
1. US Global Leadership Coalition
2. The Innocence Project
3. Overcup Press

Top Employers
1. Portland Public Schools
2. Oregon Health & Science
3. Nike
4. Kaiser Permanente
5. Intel Corporation

Where Alumni Work
1. Portland
2. Seattle
3. San Francisco
4. Los Angeles
5. St. Louis

Earnings
College Scorecard (10-YR Post-Entry): $52,151
PayScale (Early Career): $53,900
PayScale (Mid-Career): $104,500
PayScale 20-Year ROI: $309,000

RANKINGS
Money: 3.5
U.S. News: 93, Liberal Arts Colleges
Wall Street Journal/THE: Not Ranked
Washington Monthly: 65, Liberal Arts Colleges

OVERGENERALIZATIONS
Students are:
Environmentally conscious
Outdoorsy
Politically liberal
Homogenous
Always admiring the beauty of their campus

COLLEGE OVERLAPS
Occidental College
Reed College
University of Puget Sound
Whitman College
Willamette University

Loyola Marymount University

Los Angeles, California | 310-338-2750

If you encounter a map of all of the four-year colleges and universities in the United States (possibly on your counselor's wall, next to the "Hang in there" cat poster), you'll notice that the Greater Los Angeles area is blown up in its own special window; there are simply too many excellent schools concentrated in this area to label them all without first zooming in. Given this reality, Loyola Marymount University, a midsize Jesuit school of roughly 7,300 undergraduate students, sometimes fails to get the acclaim it deserves. In reality, those immersed in LMU's 55 majors and 58 minors are doing so at an institution that is rising in the rankings.

Inside the Classroom

There are six undergraduate schools and colleges within the larger university: the Bellarmine College of Liberal Arts, the Frank R. Seaver College of Science and Engineering, the College of Communication & Fine Arts, the School of Film & Television, the College of Business Administration, and the School of Education. All Lions are required to take the same 13 courses that comprise the school's core. This includes First-Year Seminar, as well as a march through such areas as Rhetorical Arts; Quantitative Reasoning; Creative Experience; Faith and Reason; and Nature of Science, Technology, and Mathematics.

Faculty here are heralded for their warmth and accessibility, a sentiment backed by an 11:1 faculty-to-student ratio. Fifty-seven percent of courses enroll 19 or fewer students, and 99% enroll fewer than 39 individuals. Science laboratories are a noted point of pride, and research opportunities, in STEM as well as the humanities, are abundant. There are four programs through which students can access on-campus research opportunities, including the Summer Undergraduate Research Program. Each year, a healthy number of undergrads (usually 500+) elect to study abroad in more than 20 different countries including Ghana, the Netherlands, and New Zealand.

The greatest number of degrees conferred in 2022 were in the area of business/marketing (25%), followed by the visual and performing arts (15%), the social sciences (14%), journalism (9%), and psychology (9%). Programs in film and television, theatre arts, and business typically receive the highest praise. LMU undergrads have begun to capture more prestigious national fellowships in recent years, taking home Goldwater, Gilman, and Fulbright Scholarships; a steady flow of seniors is also accepted into Teach for America each year.

Outside the Classroom

If you want a traditional, campus-centric college experience, then LMU is your place. A whopping 93% of undergraduate students reside on school grounds during a typical year. There are 200+ active student-run organizations, including many in the realm of community service. The school's Jesuit influence places strong emphasis on volunteering, and the student body contributes 200,000 service hours annually. Naturally, being such a strong school for film and television, the school's television network, ROAR, is an award winner. The school is also one of the more eco-friendly around, regularly cited by environmental organizations for its commitment in areas such as recycling and solar rooftops. Loyola Marymount athletics features 22 men's and women's Division I sports teams that compete within the West Coast Conference. Greek life is quite popular, attracting 16% of men and 26% of women; there are 20+ total combined frats and sororities. No one complains about the university's location in the Westside area of Los Angeles, overlooking the picturesque Playa Vista. The 142-acre grounds easily place on just about every list you can find of "Most Beautiful Campuses." Lovely Manhattan Beach is only 5-15 minutes away from the dorms.

Career Services

With 14 professional employees in its Career and Professional Development (CPD) office, Loyola Marymount offers a 521:1 counselor-to-student ratio, slightly higher than average compared to other midsize universities featured in this guide. There are also a number of peer advisors and graduate assistants that make regular one-on-one connections a genuine possibility. Staff are always happy to help with career exploration, resume development, internship assistance, interview prep, and more. The office affords students access to over 525,000 companies via Handshake and offers a number of special events like Career Chats, Pathways in Entertainment, Seaver Connect, and a Graduate Summit for those interested in pursuing a career in academia.

In general, more than two-thirds of LMU students land internships, which many take for credit. The school's location near Silicon Beach gives prime access to tech giants as well as over 500 start-ups. The annual Career Expo draws 100+ employers to campus, including the LA Clippers, Warner Music Group, Wells Fargo, Honda, and PlayStation. Motivated students can also embark on Career Treks through New York, Seattle, and the Bay Area. An involved alumni network, almost 105,000 strong, is available to help with mentorship, internships, or just an informal career exploration session. Thanks to its connected alumni, employer outreach, and strong internship coordination, the CPD appears to be doing its job in launching successful grads.

Professional Outcomes

Just 2% of LMU graduates in 2022 were still looking for work six months after completing their degrees. Seventy-four percent had procured employment, 23% were in graduate school, and 2% were engaged in some type of service program. By sector, 81% entered for-profit companies, 13% joined nonprofit organizations, and 4% were hired by government agencies. Many of the top tech, accounting, and entertainment companies presently employ more than 50 Lions. These include Northrop Grumman, Google, Netflix, Amazon, NBCUniversal Media, Apple, PwC, Sony Pictures Entertainment, Facebook, EY, and Salesforce. It's no wonder that the most common income bracket for grads to find themselves in is $60k-$70k and the second most common is $70k+. Roughly 60% of alumni remain in the Greater Los Angeles area. The next most popular destinations are San Francisco, Orange County, San Diego, and New York.

Recent alumni have gone on to further their education in a range of disciplines at Brown University, Stanford University, NYU, and Georgetown University. In the last few years, premed students have been admitted into medical schools such as Duke University School of Medicine, the David Geffen School of Medicine at UCLA, Saint Louis University School of Medicine, and Harvard Medical School, along with countless other top institutions. Over the last decade, 74% of applicants ultimately matriculated into medical or dental school. Those on a prelaw track have found homes at law schools such as Boston College, UC Davis, and the University of Southern California, as well as Loyola's own well-regarded legal training ground.

Admission

With an acceptance rate of 41% for the Class of 2026, LMU saw a 5% decrease from the prior year's clip. This group sported an average GPA of 3.96, and 34% of those enrolled in the Class of 2026 placed in the top decile of their high school class. 74% were in the top quartile, and 94% were in the top half. On standardized tests, this cohort possessed mid-50th percentile scores of 1280-1430 on the SAT and 28-32 on the ACT. However, it is important to note that the vast majority of enrolled students applied without submitting a standardized test result.

Academic GPA is the lone factor rated as "very important" in rendering admissions decisions. Coming in as "important" were the rigor of an applicant's coursework, application essay, talent/ability, and character/personal qualities. Class rank, recommendation letters, extracurricular activities, first-generation status, legacy status (100+ freshmen each year are legacies), volunteer work, standardized test scores, and paid work experience are "considered." Seniors have the option to apply by November 1, either as an early action or early decision applicant. There was a significant advantage to applying early for a place in the Class of 2026 as 61% were accepted.

Worth Your Money?

An LMU education won't come cheap for many as the estimated COA for the 2023-24 school year was $84,208. However, 85% of undergrads do receive some form of financial aid—a total of 147 million dollars went to grants and scholarships in one recent academic year. Strong starting salaries for the majority of graduates also help to ensure positive financial outcomes postgraduation. Less than 1% of alumni end up defaulting on their loans, a positive indicator that the school's grads are succeeding in the real world. For those entering business, a tech field, or the film/television industry, LMU is very likely to be worth the cost of attendance.

FINANCIAL
Institutional Type: Private
In-State Tuition: $58,489
Out-of-State Tuition: $58,489
Room & Board: $19,287
Books & Supplies: $938

Avg. Need-Based Grant: $26,301
Avg. % of Need Met: 71%

Avg. Merit-Based Award: $12,098
% Receiving (Freshmen w/o Need): 42%

Avg. Cumulative Debt: $32,828
% of Students Borrowing: 43%

CAREER
Who Recruits
1. Disney
2. Kaiser Permanente
3. Morgan Stanley
4. AT&T
5. Epson

Notable Internships
1. Tesla
2. 3M
3. LucasFilm

Top Employers
1. LA Unified School District
2. Teach for America
3. Northrop Grumman
4. Google
5. Amazon

Where Alumni Work
1. Los Angeles
2. San Francisco
3. Orange County, CA
4. San Diego
5. New York City

Earnings
College Scorecard (10-YR Post-Entry): $71,771
PayScale (Early Career): $63,200
PayScale (Mid-Career): $129,700
PayScale 20-Year ROI: $562,000

RANKINGS
Money: 3.5
U.S. News: 93, National Universities
Wall Street Journal/THE: 269
Washington Monthly: 268, National Universities

OVERGENERALIZATIONS
Students are:
Environmentally conscious
Laid-back
Always admiring the beauty of their campus
Social
More likely to venture off campus

COLLEGE OVERLAPS
Chapman University
Santa Clara University
University of California, San Diego
University of California, Santa Barbara
University of San Diego

Loyola University Maryland

Baltimore, Maryland | 410-617-5012

ADMISSION
Admission Rate: 83%
Admission Rate - Men: 84%
Admission Rate - Women: 83%
EA Admission Rate: 92%
ED Admission Rate: Not Offered
ED Admits as % of Total Admits: Not Offered
Admission Rate (5-Year Trend): +8%
% of Admits Attending (Yield): 16%
Transfer Admission Rate: 42%

SAT Reading/Writing (Middle 50%): 600-690
SAT Math (Middle 50%): 580-670
ACT Composite (Middle 50%): 26-33

% Graduated in Top 10% of HS Class: 25%
% Graduated in Top 25% of HS Class: 56%
% Graduated in Top 50% of HS Class: 84%

Demonstrated Interest: Not Considered
Legacy Status: Considered
Racial/Ethnic Status: Considered
Admission Interview Offered: No

ENROLLMENT
Total Undergraduate Enrollment: 3,977
% Full-Time: 99%
% Male: 45%
% Female: 55%
% Out-of-State: 69%
% Fraternity: Not Offered
% Sorority: Not Offered
% On-Campus (All Undergraduate): 79%
Freshman Housing Required: No

% African-American: 10%
% Asian: 4%
% Hispanic: 14%
% White: 66%
% Other: 1%
% International: 2%
% Low-Income: 18%

ACADEMICS
Student-to-Faculty Ratio: 13 to 1
% of Classes Under 20: 49%
% of Classes 20-49: 51%
% of Classes 50 or More: 1%
% Full-Time Faculty: 75%
% Full-Time Faculty w/ Terminal Degree: 77%

Top Programs
Accounting
Communication
Education
Finance
Management

Retention Rate: 87%
4-Year Graduation Rate: 75%
6-Year Graduation Rate: 81%

Curricular Flexibility: Less Flexible
Academic Rating: ★★★

College consumers can sometimes find the Loyola brand hard to grasp. After all, there is Loyola University Chicago, Loyola University New Orleans, Loyola Marymount University in Los Angeles, and the school we are profiling here—Loyola University Maryland—and none of the schools is affiliated in any way with the others. While all honor St. Ignatius, the Jesuit founder, Loyola University Maryland is its own distinct entity and is a rare school where the acceptance rate and six-year graduation rate both hover around 80%. Offering 30+ undergraduate programs through its three schools, Loyola College (arts and sciences), the Sellinger School of Business and Management, and the School of Education, Loyola services an undergraduate population of 3,977, only about 30% of whom are Maryland residents.

Inside the Classroom
Consistent with the Jesuit ideology of cura personalis, Loyola has created a liberal arts curriculum designed to help develop the whole person and produce well-rounded citizens. This extensive seventeen-course set of requirements includes writing, history, literature, foreign language, social sciences, fine arts, mathematics, theology, philosophy, ethics, and diversity. Students in the small but excellent Honors Program follow an identical path but complete their core curriculum within honors-only sections.

A 13:1 student-to-faculty ratio leads to average class sizes of only twenty students. The vast majority of courses enroll between ten and twenty-nine students, 11% have a single-digit enrollment, and of 887 total sections, only 13 contained forty or more undergraduates. Students are encouraged to apply for undergraduate research opportunities such as the Hauber Summer Research Fellowship Program which, in one recent year, gave 12 students in the natural and applied sciences fields a chance to conduct ten weeks of independent research. Biology majors can enroll in two courses that facilitate experiential research opportunities. Those with wanderlust will find plenty of kindred spirits and no shortage of options; there are 20 countries that students can choose from as study abroad options, and the participation rate exceeds 60%, one of the highest figures of any master's-granting school in the nation.

Roughly one-third of the degrees conferred are in the area of business/marketing, making it, by far, the school's most popular area of concentration. Next are communication/journalism (11%), the social sciences (9%), psychology (9%), and biology (7%). The Sellinger School of Business and Management has a solid reputation beyond the immediate region, and the Department of Communication has an excellent record of placing students within media organizations. The school's push for international study translated to a record number of Fulbright Scholars with eight winners in a single recent year. Additionally, seven current students captured Gilman Scholarships.

Outside the Classroom
If you are looking for a school where just about everyone lives in a tight-knit community on campus, then the Loyola Maryland experience is for you. In the 2022-23 school year, freshmen occupied university-owned dorms at a 92% clip, and 79% of the total student body resided on this 81-acre wooded campus that isn't what you'd expect to find in the middle of Baltimore. Loyola's 17 residence halls are some of the best-rated college accommodations in the entire country. As is the case at many Jesuit institutions, there are no sororities or fraternities at this school, but there are 200+ clubs. Service is popular as 80% of the student body engages in some type of charitable endeavor. Religion plays a major role as students are predominately Catholic—27% attended Catholic/Jesuit high schools. Loyola has a strong athletics program that features 17 NCAA Division I teams that play in the Patriot League. Johns Hopkins is its biggest rival, and the annual lacrosse showdown is a big deal. There are also 26 club teams, and 20% of students participate in intramural leagues. Recreational amenities include a ten-lane pool, rock climbing wall, and indoor track. Not known as a big party school, there are plenty of safe commercial pockets in the city of Baltimore worth exploring, and DC is only an hour away for weekend trips.

Career Services
The Rizzo Career Center at Loyola Maryland is manned by eight professionals with expertise in career counseling and employer outreach. That works out to a 497:1 student-to-advisor ratio, which is within the average range of colleges featured in this guide. However, they also train 12 student ambassadors who each specialize in a different academic discipline. This office also keeps careful track of its own statistics that paint a picture of a supportive and highly available career services staff offering ample opportunity to connect with relevant employers.

In a single recent school year, the office held over 2,200 counseling appointments and attracted 2,000+ students to networking events, workshops, career fairs, and information sessions. For a small university, it's highly impressive that over 100 companies and organizations interviewed seniors on campus. In total, 300 unique employers visit campus. A helpful alumni base 70,000+ strong is also willing to lend a hand to those about to launch their careers. If you're looking to land a position far from Baltimore, Loyola Maryland's Career Center has reciprocity with twenty-eight other Jesuit institution's career centers around the country. The school also has forged many strong internship partners. For example, within the Department of Writing, partners include nine publications and ten nonprofits that regularly take Loyola interns. Career fairs enjoyed official sponsors such as Bank of America, Dixon Hughes Goodman (the largest accounting firm in the South), and CareFirst BlueCross BlueShield. In sum, the Loyola Career Center directly connects with more than half of the undergraduate student body each year and facilitates a solid number of industry connections, making it a highly useful resource for all current students.

Professional Outcomes

Members of the Class of 2022 found their way to their next employment, volunteer, or grad school home within six months of receiving their diplomas at a stellar 97% clip. Major companies and organizations employing members of this cohort include Accenture, Booz Allen Hamilton, Bloomberg, Goldman Sachs, NASA, the National Institutes of Health, the New York Giants (NFL), Sony/ATV Music Publishing, and Walt Disney Company. Employers of the overall greatest number of alumni include T. Rowe Price, Northrop Grumman, Morgan Stanley, JPMorgan Chase, PwC, EY, Black & Decker, and Deloitte. The average starting salary for a Loyola graduate is $57k with social sciences majors bringing home a mean salary of $50k and degree-earners in business averaging $63k. Baltimore, New York City, DC, Philly, and Boston woo the most Greyhound alumni.

Thirty-two percent of the members of the Class of 2022 immediately enrolled in graduate or professional school after completing their undergraduate work at Loyola Maryland. Some members earned a spot at elite graduate institutions like Georgetown, Johns Hopkins, Yale, Northwestern, and the University of Pennsylvania. Over the last decade, the percentage of successful law school applicants has vacillated between 77% and 93%, and Loyola grads are currently pursuing their legal education at Villanova, George Washington, UC Berkeley, and the University of Maryland. Over the past few years, medical school applicants who obtained a committee letter supporting their candidacy enjoyed an 87% acceptance rate. Recent acceptances include some of the top medical schools in the country such as Brown, Tufts, and Harvard Medical School.

Admission

Getting into Loyola is not a harrowing process, even if you hit a few bumps along your academic road. The acceptance rate for a place in the Class of 2026 was an unintimidating 83%, and that doesn't show any signs of falling as the school has only a 16% yield rate; in other terms, 84% of those who are accepted ultimately enroll at another institution. Loyola is test-optional, and most 2022-23 freshmen chose not to submit scores—29% included SATs and 5% included ACTs as part of their applications. The mid-50% scores were 26-33 on the ACT and 1185-1350 on the SAT. The average high school GPA earned by entering members of this class was 3.66, and while 25% ranked in the top decile of their graduating class and 56% were in the top quartile, 16% did not even rank in the top 50%, giving hope to those without glowing transcripts.

This committee means what it says when it declares that it does "not use a formula or have strict cutoffs. Instead, the admission office's goal is to conduct a balanced and individual review, taking a number of factors into account." At the top of that list are GPA, rigor of secondary school record, and character/personal qualities. Extracurricular activities, recommendations, essays, volunteer work, and talent/ability also receive strong consideration. Loyola is a school where bright but perhaps late-blooming teens can find a welcoming institution that will offer a top-notch Jesuit education.

Worth Your Money?

Living on campus brings the total annual sticker price to more than $73,000, a steep price to pay for any school. At that cost, it is hard to justify attending Loyola University Maryland if you are in a situation where you will need to take out large loans; the average Greyhound's debt is above the national average. However, it is worth applying to see what kind of aid package you receive as 99% of all students do receive some form/level of financial aid. Freshmen who qualify for need-based aid pay an average net price of $26k. If the total cost of attendance is comparable to other institutions to which you are accepted, a degree from this university can certainly make it worth your money.

FINANCIAL
Institutional Type: Private
In-State Tuition: $55,480
Out-of-State Tuition: $55,480
Room & Board: $16,880
Books & Supplies: $800

Avg. Need-Based Grant: $15,208
Avg. % of Need Met: 83%

Avg. Merit-Based Award: $23,189
% Receiving (Freshmen w/o Need): 36%

Avg. Cumulative Debt: $37,594
% of Students Borrowing: 61%

CAREER
Who Recruits
1. Legg Mason
2. Baltimore Orioles
3. T. Rowe Price
4. Cisco
5. Stanley Black & Decker

Notable Internships
1. LGT Capital Partners
2. National Bank of Canada
3. Fidelity Investments

Top Employers
1. T. Rowe Price
2. Northrop Grumman
3. Morgan Stanley
4. JPMorgan Chase
5. PwC

Where Alumni Work
1. Baltimore
2. New York City
3. Washington, DC
4. Philadelphia
5. Boston

Earnings
College Scorecard (10-YR Post-Entry): $81,216
PayScale (Early Career): $64,200
PayScale (Mid-Career): $125,800
PayScale 20-Year ROI: $796,000

RANKINGS
Money: 4.5
U.S. News: 7, Regional Universities North
Wall Street Journal/THE: Not Ranked
Washington Monthly: 24, Master's Universities

OVERGENERALIZATIONS
Students are:
Politically conservative
Preppy
Only a short drive from home (i.e., Most come from nearby states)
Tight-knit (possess a strong sense of community)
Career-driven

COLLEGE OVERLAPS
Fairfield University
Fordham University
Providence College
University of Maryland, College Park
Villanova University

Macalester College

St. Paul, Minnesota | 651-696-6357

One might expect a small liberal arts school in Minnesota to be set in a remote tundra, its own little universe surrounded by a stark landscape and frigid air. In the case of Macalester College, the frigid air would be accurate, but this collection of 2,175 undergraduate students is a rarity in the liberal arts world—it is situated in the metropolis of St. Paul on the border of Minneapolis. While typically lagging slightly behind rival Carleton College in most rankings, Macalester is every bit in the same league, boasting a strong reputation for rigorous academics that draws worldwide attention as evidenced by the fact that students from 58 countries are part of the Class of 2027.

Inside the Classroom

International students aren't flocking to Mac for the weather or Great Plains scenery; they are here for the academic reputation. Students can choose from roughly 40 majors and over 800 courses that are offered each academic year. Requirements for all students are fairly straightforward and include a first-year course that is a small, writing-intensive seminar, courses in each of the school's four divisions—Fine Arts, Humanities, Social Studies, and Natural Science and Mathematics, and courses in multiculturalism and internationalism. Perhaps the most notable mandate is in foreign language where proficiency equivalent to four semesters of study must be demonstrated.

Being an undergraduate-only institution, Macalester students enjoy the full benefits of the school's 10:1 student-to-faculty ratio. The average class size is only 17 students, and 14% of class sections have single-digit enrollments. Only 1% of the overall courses contain more than forty students, so the chances are high that you will never be in a course where the professor does not know your name. That level of intimacy leads to plentiful chances to be part of faculty-led research, including through the Collaborative Summer Research Program that provides stipends for student-faculty research ventures. In total, 54% of students participate in some form of undergraduate research. Study abroad opportunities, typically twelve weeks in length, are taken advantage of by 60% of Macalester undergrads.

As an elite liberal arts institution with no attached graduate schools, Macalester possesses strong offerings across many different disciplines. Programs in economics, international studies, and mathematics are among the best anywhere. In addition, science majors of all varieties benefit from the school's strong premed program and reputation for preparing future PhD scientists. Prestigious postgraduate fellowships are routinely awarded to Mac seniors. In the last decade, grads have walked away with 60+ Fulbright Scholarships, including nine such awards in 2023 alone. In that same time, students and alumni have procured a Rhodes Scholarship, 40+ National Science Foundation Fellowships, as well as a number of Watson Fellowships, Goldwater Scholarships, and Truman Scholarships.

Outside the Classroom

Due to the limited availability of college-owned housing, only 58% of Macalester students live on campus. However, 100% of freshmen live in one of four residence halls for first-years; sophomores, who are also required to live on campus, have their own dorms as well. There is no Greek life here, so undergrads find other ways to forge deep bonds. With twenty-one sports teams and roughly 400 student-athletes, one-quarter of the student population dons a Scots jersey as they compete in NCAA Division III. Intramurals and club teams also draw heavy participation, leading to a majority of Mac students being involved in some type of formalized athletics. There are also 100+ student-run organizations, including eleven musical ensembles, student theater groups with 125 participants, three student publications, including the popular Mac Weekly, and a campus radio station, WMCN. The LGBTQ+ population on campus is notably large—25% identify in that category. This cozy 53-acre campus provides ample activity, but access to the city's nightlife is quite easy by car. The Mall of America is less than a fifteen-minute drive from the college, and students also enjoy Minnesota's pro sports scene, museums, restaurants, and nightlife.

Career Services

The Career Development Center is staffed by eleven professionals, equating to a student-to-advisor ratio of 198:1, significantly better than the average college included in this book. That level of support allows the CDC to implement its four-phase process of "explore, design, connect, launch," which ultimately results in favorable outcomes for graduates. In a single school year, the CDC enticed 100+ employers to recruit on campus and held 1,900 one-on-one advising appointments. Even more telling is the fact that 99% of students stated that they were satisfied with their counseling session.

Internships and/or mentored research experiences are enjoyed by almost three-quarters of Macalester undergraduates. Internships, specifically, are obtained and completed by approximately 60% of students. In a given year, almost 400 students engage in credit-bearing internships at organizations as varied as the US Department of State, EY, Minnesota Public Radio, the New York University School of Medicine, and Lockheed Martin. This strong internship program sets up students for a successful transition into a meaningful first job. Among recent grads who found employment within six months of leaving, 92% said their first job was congruent with their interests. While Macalester grads do not all go on to earn high starting salaries, they do find fulfilling jobs aligned with their interests and have success entering and completing top graduate/professional degree programs.

Professional Outcomes

Six months after graduating, 95% of the Macalester Class of 2022 had found employment, graduate school, or a fellowship. Fifty-four percent of those finding employment landed with for-profit corporations, 17% with educational institutions, 15% with nonprofit organizations, and 13% with federal, state, or local government. Employers of recent grads include ABC News, Google, Goldman Sachs, Dow Chemical Company, McKinsey & Company, the ACLU, the National Cancer Institute, and National Geographic. Across all sectors, the average starting salary for recent grads was above $62k. Geographically, 53% of grads elected to stay in the North Star State while many others migrated to the West Coast (15%) or East Coast (13%).

Sixty percent of Mac grads pursue an advanced degree within six years of earning their bachelor's; 90% believe that the college prepared them well for graduate/professional school. Among recent grads, most frequently attended graduate schools such as the University of Washington–Seattle, University of Wisconsin-Madison, Harvard, Georgetown, NYU, and Johns Hopkins. In recent years, 100% of Macalester grads who applied to graduate school received at least one acceptance, and the school ranks 24th in the country for having the most grads (per capita) who went on to earn PhDs. Among students with at least a 3.5 GPA and decent MCAT scores, 90% were admitted to at least one medical school. Recent medical school acceptances include Tufts University, Northwestern, Brown, and Washington University in St. Louis. The most popular medical school attended by alumni is the University of Minnesota - Twin Cities.

Admission

Macalester received 8,434 applications for admission into the Class of 2026, and it admitted 28%, three points lower than the previous year. Of that group, 23% went on to enroll in the school. Freshmen in the 2022-23 cohort sported mid-50% SATs of 1350-1490 and an ACT range of 30-34. Fifty-six percent of this group placed in the top decile of their high school class and 90% were in the top quartile.

The admissions committee ranks the rigor of one's secondary programming and GPA earned as the two most critical factors in the process. The second rung of still "important" factors is comprised of recommendations, essays, extracurricular activities, and character/personal qualities. The school adopted a permanent test-optional policy in 2021. Macalester insists that it does not consider demonstrated interest in the admissions process, an unusual move for a school with a relatively low yield rate (the percentage of accepted students who go on to enroll). That being said, applying via early decision is a wise choice for those committed to attending the college as the ED acceptance rate is 53%. Attracting students from all fifty states and almost 100 countries, this school's Minnesota locale draws talented applicants from around the world. Lots of AP courses and excellent grades should set up candidates for success.

Worth Your Money?

Just under two-thirds of the Macalester student population receives need-based aid for an average grant of more than $50k per year. Unfortunately, if you don't qualify for need-based aid, do not expect much in the way of merit aid—most likely, you'll be paying close to the full annual cost of attendance of $79,890. With so many graduates pursuing advanced degrees, average early career earnings aren't spectacular, but Mac is still a school with phenomenal long-term career outcomes and a very wise investment for students who can afford the price without racking up higher-than-average debt.

FINANCIAL
Institutional Type: Private
In-State Tuition: $64,908
Out-of-State Tuition: $64,908
Room & Board: $14,982
Books & Supplies: $926

Avg. Need-Based Grant: $50,236
Avg. % of Need Met: 100%

Avg. Merit-Based Award: $18,034
% Receiving (Freshmen w/o Need): 24%

Avg. Cumulative Debt: $21,841
% of Students Borrowing: 58%

CAREER
Who Recruits
1. ScribeAmerica
2. ESRI
3. BMO Capital Markets
4. Twin Cities Public Television
5. Airbnb

Notable Internships
1. Minnesota Wild
2. U.S. Bank
3. U.S. House of Representatives

Top Employers
1. Wells Fargo
2. UnitedHealth Group
3. Target
4. Epic
5. 3M

Where Alumni Work
1. Minneapolis
2. New York City
3. San Francisco
4. Washington, DC
5. Chicago

Earnings
College Scorecard (10-YR Post-Entry): $62,762
PayScale (Early Career): $57,300
PayScale (Mid-Career): $103,700
PayScale 20-Year ROI: $373,000

RANKINGS
Money: 4.5
U.S. News: 27, Liberal Arts Colleges
Wall Street Journal/THE: 231
Washington Monthly: 22, Liberal Arts Colleges

OVERGENERALIZATIONS
Students are:
Environmentally conscious
Politically liberal
Politically active
Less likely to party
Diverse

COLLEGE OVERLAPS
Brown University
Carleton College
Grinnell College
University of Chicago
Wesleyan University

Marist College

Poughkeepsie, New York | 845-575-3226

ADMISSION
Admission Rate: 63%
Admission Rate - Men: 60%
Admission Rate - Women: 64%
EA Admission Rate: 77%
ED Admission Rate: 77%
ED Admits as % of Total Admits: 2%
Admission Rate (5-Year Trend): +20%
% of Admits Attending (Yield): 19%
Transfer Admission Rate: 64%

SAT Reading/Writing (Middle 50%): 610-690
SAT Math (Middle 50%): 599-670
ACT Composite (Middle 50%): 25-30

% Graduated in Top 10% of HS Class: 19%
% Graduated in Top 25% of HS Class: 48%
% Graduated in Top 50% of HS Class: 84%

Demonstrated Interest: Considered
Legacy Status: Not Considered
Racial/Ethnic Status: Not Considered
Admission Interview Offered: No

ENROLLMENT
Total Undergraduate Enrollment: 5,475
% Full-Time: 97%
% Male: 41%
% Female: 59%
% Out-of-State: 48%
% Fraternity: 3%
% Sorority: 3%
% On-Campus (All Undergraduate): 62%
Freshman Housing Required: No

% African-American: 4%
% Asian: 3%
% Hispanic: 13%
% White: 73%
% Other: 1%
% International: 2%
% Low-Income: 16%

ACADEMICS
Student-to-Faculty Ratio: 16 to 1
% of Classes Under 20: 51%
% of Classes 20-49: 49%
% of Classes 50 or More: 0%
% Full-Time Faculty: 41%
% Full-Time Faculty w/ Terminal Degree: 80%

Top Programs
Business Administration
Communication
Criminal Justice
Fashion Design
Fashion Merchandising
Information Technology and Systems
Political Science

Retention Rate: 87%
4-Year Graduation Rate: 73%
6-Year Graduation Rate: 83%

Curricular Flexibility: Somewhat Flexible
Academic Rating: ★★★

#CollegesWorthYourMoney

Competing for attention in the world of New York State institutions of higher education must feel like raising your hand to volunteer while surrounded by equally eager-to-contribute NBA centers. As a school serving 5,475 undergraduates, Marist College is overshadowed by smaller and more selective options that include Hamilton, Colgate, Vassar, and Skidmore as well as the more famous larger universities Cornell, Rochester, and Syracuse—and that's not even considering schools in New York City. Yet, there are many reasons you should get to know Marist, an accessible school for solid-but-imperfect high schoolers that succeeds in providing a world-class education to undergraduates who go on to land enviable internships with regularity, study abroad at exceptional rates, and, as a whole, experience tremendous postgraduate success.

Inside the Classroom
Marist offers 47 distinct bachelor's programs but is ultimately a true liberal arts institution that requires its undergrads to complete a core curriculum. As freshmen, students engage in a first-year seminar and a course called Writing for College, both of which incorporate themes related to "Cultural Diversity, Nature & the Environment, Civic Engagement, and/or Quantitative Reasoning." There are thirty-six credits worth of distributional courses of study including ethics and justice, fine arts, history, literature, mathematics, natural science, philosophy, and social science. Additionally, although this can overlap with distributional requirements, students must also tackle a four-course "Pathway," choosing from twenty-three courses including African Diaspora Studies, Gender Studies, and Public Health Studies.

Marist has a 16:1 student-to-faculty ratio—few sections are single-digit seminars or large lectures but 51% of sections are under 20 students. On the less-than-ideal side, the majority of Marist's professors are adjuncts. On the plus side, undergrads enjoy the real-world knowledge brought by those non-tenure-track professors, and few complain about availability outside the classroom. Marist is supportive of undergraduate research, particularly in the hard sciences where completion of a research project is often a graduation requirement. Marist sees 50% of its students study abroad as part of the college's robust international program that is rated among the best in the country.

The School of Management and the School of Communication are quite popular as business (33%) and communication (15%) are, by far, Marist's two most commonly conferred degrees. They are also among Marist's strongest. It is also noteworthy that the School of Mathematics and Computer Science has had a joint study program with IBM for more than three decades. This intensive collaboration frequently leads to employment at IBM after graduation. With many grads entering corporate America, applications to prestigious national fellowship programs are sparse, but a few students have captured Fulbrights in the last two years.

Outside the Classroom
Sixty-six percent of the undergraduate population at Marist live on campus in a combination of corridor, suite, apartment, and townhouse-style residences. The 150+ acre campus is spectacularly set on the shores of the Hudson River. On the border of what arguably qualifies as "Upstate" New York, Poughkeepsie is about an hour and a half drive from the heart of New York City. On campus, there are three fraternities and four sororities with around 300 members, giving Greek life a modest presence of roughly 3% of the undergraduate population. Playing in NCAA Division I, the Red Foxes field twenty-three varsity sports teams. For less serious athletes, there are eleven club teams as well as an extensive intramural program that draws an incredible 65% of students. Overall, there are more than eighty student-run clubs and organizations. The Hudson Valley offers plenty worth exploring, from the ample natural beauty ripe for hiking and canoeing to the commerce of the popular Poughkeepsie Galleria Mall. While the school's Catholic origins are no longer officially linked to the school, the largest student group at Marist is the Campus Ministry that has a membership of 1,300 students. At 59% female, there is a noticeable gender gap at this school.

Career Services
The Center for Career Services (CCS) at Marist is staffed by five professionals with expertise in career coaching, employer relations, and graduate school advising. That works out to a 1,095:1 student-to-advisor ratio that is much higher than the average school in this guide. We do, however, take it as a positive sign that the Student Services Department (which includes the CCS) received a thumbs-up from 94% of grads. As the CCS states, "It's never too early to begin the process of learning how your interests and passions turn into long-term career aspirations." To back up that ideal, the CCS offers daily walk-in hours, scheduled one-on-one career counseling appointments, and weekly workshops on topics like resumes, cover letters, interviewing, and building a personal brand online.

Large events take place regularly, including the two annual Career and Internship Fairs that 127 companies attended in one recent year. Last year, the office conducted 2,960 one-on-one career advising sessions. An annual Graduate School Forum brings forty graduate and professional schools to campus to meet with prospective students. The CCS also maintains an active Alumni Career Network of 1,663 former students in a variety of fields who are willing to volunteer their time to mentor. Efforts such as those lead to an extremely healthy 83% internship participation rate for Marist undergrads. Over 1,100 internships are completed annually at organizations including the Brooklyn Nets (NBA), CBS, Goldman Sachs, HBO, Morgan Stanley, Seventeen Magazine, and Madison Square Garden. Success in helping its students secure experiential and networking opportunities ends up leading to positive career and graduate school outcomes for the vast majority of students.

Professional Outcomes

Red Foxes strutting across the graduation stage from 2018-2022 went on to find employment or a graduate school home at a terrific 95% rate by the time they filled out their first-destination survey. Major employers of Marist alums include IBM, which presently employs close to 700 individuals, as well as JP Morgan Chase, EY, Macy's, Citi, Morgan Stanley, Deloitte, and NBC Universal Media. Members of the Class of 2022 headed to a number of media powerhouses including ViacomCBS, NBC Sports, and MSNBC as well as other major companies Adidas, Coach, Lockheed Martin, Northrop Grumman, and Moody's. The Greater New York City area draws approximately two-thirds of grads; Boston, Atlanta, Albany, and Hartford attract their own slivers of each graduating class. Mid-career median salaries are in the same range as other excellent schools in this guide such as UC Santa Barbara, Texas A&M, Colby, and American University.

In terms of selectivity, recent grads have gone on to attend a wide range of institutions including elite universities Cornell, Penn, Harvard, Columbia, and Oxford. Over the last decade, 78% of medical school applicants were accepted to at least one institution, a figure that is roughly double the national average. Acceptances have included Georgetown Medical School, Albany Medical College, New York Medical College, SUNY Upstate Medical Center at Syracuse, Medical College of Virginia, and the Albert Einstein School of Medicine. Recent law school acceptances have included William & Mary, the University of Texas, and Northeastern University.

Admission

Last cycle, Marist received 10,966 applications, accepted 63%, and saw 19% of those accepted ultimately go on to enroll. The Class of 2026 possessed a median SAT score of 1280 and a 28 on the ACT. In the classroom, this cohort earned an average high school GPA of 3.6, and only 19% of its members placed in the top decile of their high school class. Not only can students gain acceptance into Marist without a pristine transcript, but the college also became test-optional back in 2011. In the years since it went test-optional, the average scores have predictably gone up a bit because those with lower scores simply do not submit. The other qualifications, such as GPA and class rank, have remained fairly constant over the last decade.

According to the admissions office, Marist applicants "should rank in the top half of their graduating class and hold a recalculated average of 3.3 or better." The school also likes to see some honors and/or Advanced Placement courses on an applicant's transcript. Evidence of leadership and extracurricular participation is valued by the committee as well. With lots of liberal arts competition both Upstate and around New York City, Marist finds itself fighting for quality freshmen each year. Thus, committing to the school via early decision gives you a massive edge in the admissions game; for the Class of 2026, the college accepted an overwhelming 77% of ED applicants.

Worth Your Money?

Tuition fees plus room and board bring the total sticker price to close to $64,000, making a four-year degree a $256,000 venture. Fortunately, through a combination of merit and need-based aid, the net price ends up under $41k per year, even for families in the top income brackets. In total, 90% of Marist students receive some form of aid. While not cheap by any means, Marist has the type of NYC corporate connections that can eventually open doors to lucrative and interesting careers that will likely return your investment.

FINANCIAL
Institutional Type: Private
In-State Tuition: $46,110
Out-of-State Tuition: $46,110
Room & Board: $20,260
Books & Supplies: $1,225

Avg. Need-Based Grant: $23,766
Avg. % of Need Met: 79%

Avg. Merit-Based Award: $15,499
% Receiving (Freshmen w/o Need): 36%

Avg. Cumulative Debt: $41,731
% of Students Borrowing: 60%

CAREER
Who Recruits
1. IBM
2. EY
3. KPMG
4. UBS
5. The Met

Notable Internships
1. ESPN
2. Sony Music Entertainment
3. American Red Cross

Top Employers
1. IBM
2. JPMorgan Chase
3. EY
4. Macy's
5. Citi

Where Alumni Work
1. New York City
2. Boston
3. Atlanta
4. New York City
5. Hartford, CT

Earnings
College Scorecard (10-YR Post-Entry): $74,865
PayScale (Early Career): $60,700
PayScale (Mid-Career): $108,900
PayScale 20-Year ROI: $512,000

RANKINGS
Money: 4
U.S. News: 10, Regional Universities North
Wall Street Journal/THE: Not Ranked
Washington Monthly: 152, Master's Universities

OVERGENERALIZATIONS
Students are:
Friendly
Politically balanced
Only a short drive from home (i.e., Most come from NY or nearby states)
Preppy
Career-driven

COLLEGE OVERLAPS
Fairfield University
Fordham University
Loyola University Maryland
Syracuse University
University of Connecticut

Marquette University

Milwaukee, Wisconsin | 414-288-7302

ADMISSION
Admission Rate: 87%
Admission Rate - Men: 86%
Admission Rate - Women: 88%
EA Admission Rate: Not Offered
ED Admission Rate: Not Offered
ED Admits as % of Total Admits: Not Offered
Admission Rate (5-Year Trend): -2%
% of Admits Attending (Yield): 14%
Transfer Admission Rate: 77%

SAT Reading/Writing (Middle 50%): 590-670
SAT Math (Middle 50%): 580-690
ACT Composite (Middle 50%): 26-31

% Graduated in Top 10% of HS Class: 29%
% Graduated in Top 25% of HS Class: 61%
% Graduated in Top 50% of HS Class: 92%

Demonstrated Interest: Considered
Legacy Status: Considered
Racial/Ethnic Status: Not Considered
Admission Interview Offered: No

ENROLLMENT
Total Undergraduate Enrollment: 7,528
% Full-Time: 98%
% Male: 44%
% Female: 56%
% Out-of-State: 64%
% Fraternity: 4%
% Sorority: 10%
% On-Campus (All Undergraduate): 41%
Freshman Housing Required: Yes

% African-American: 5%
% Asian: 6%
% Hispanic: 16%
% White: 67%
% Other: 1%
% International: 2%
% Low-Income: 22%

ACADEMICS
Student-to-Faculty Ratio: 13 to 1
% of Classes Under 20: 50%
% of Classes 20-49: 40%
% of Classes 50 or More: 9%
% Full-Time Faculty: 56%
% Full-Time Faculty w/ Terminal Degree: 89%

Top Programs
Accounting
Biomedical Sciences
Criminology & Law Studies
Engineering
Exercise Physiology
Information Systems
Nursing
Supply Chain Management

Retention Rate: 89%
4-Year Graduation Rate: 66%
6-Year Graduation Rate: 83%

Curricular Flexibility: Somewhat Flexible
Academic Rating: ★★★

#CollegesWorthYourMoney

In adopting the slogan "Be the Difference" twenty years ago, Marquette University succinctly captured the spirit of this midsized, private, Jesuit institution in Milwaukee, WI. The undergraduate population of just over 7,500 is one of the most community service-focused groups in the country, and the school takes great pride in its prioritization of undergraduate teaching. Marquette is a school that accepts B students and then strives to deliver the proverbial A+ educational experience. In a world where many schools are obsessed with increasing their number of applications and decreasing their acceptance rates, Marquette should be commended for focusing on what actually happens on campus.

Inside the Classroom
Like many Jesuit institutions, the core curriculum includes multiple courses on morality and ethics. During a "Discovery" phase, students pick a theme that is meaningful to them and take four courses that align with that theme across the humanities, natural sciences and mathematics, and social science. Later on, students engage in a "Culminating" course that focuses on their future vocational path and ability to work for justice in the world. This set of requirements gives students a ton of disciplinary flexibility under an overarching philosophical/moral framework.

With a 13:1 student-to-faculty ratio, the university is able to keep 50% of class sections at 19 or fewer students. The average lower-division class size is 33, and the average upper-division course enrolls 25. Opportunities for hands-on training are available, including in the Biomedical Sciences Summer Research Program or via other discipline-specific postings available each semester. With 80+ partnerships throughout the world, 30% of Golden Eagles study abroad.

The College of Business Administration conferred 26% of total undergraduate degrees in 2022. The next most popular disciplines were biology (14%), engineering (11%), the social sciences (11%), and health professions and related programs (9%). Marquette does not have one program that stands out reputation-wise, but most popular majors are regarded as solid and fare well according to graduate outcome measures (more on that later). The school does not produce large numbers of prestigious fellowship winners, but it does typically see two to three students capture Fulbright Scholarships each year.

Outside the Classroom
Ninety-one percent of freshmen and 41% of the overall student body live on the 107 acres situated near the downtown Milwaukee neighborhood of University Hill. Unlike many Jesuit institutions, there is a bit of a Greek presence on campus that attracts 4-10% of undergrads. The Golden Eagles' 14 NCAA Division I and 250+ student-athletes provide plenty for sports fans to cheer about. The men's basketball team shares an arena with the Milwaukee Bucks and has produced 45 NBA players. There is also a thriving club and intramural sports scene that includes plenty of fun for the less athletically inclined with activities including cornhole, Jenga, and kickball. Close to 300 clubs and organizations include thirteen service-oriented organizations. Overall, 80% of undergrads participate in community service. Each semester, 1,200 students get involved in the community via credited courses that fall under the Service-Learning umbrella. In terms of demographics, there is a notable gender gap with the Class of 2026 being 56% female. The majority of students are Catholic, but 43% are not, so there is room for students of all faiths. A high number (21%) of Marquette students are legacy students, continuing a family tradition of attending the school.

Career Services
The Career Services Center (CSC) is staffed by eight professionals, most of whom work as career counselors or employer relations specialists; two additional staff members operate out of the Business Career Center. While this 753:1 student-to-counselor ratio seems a bit high, the office also has five individuals serving as graduate assistants and interns. Further, there are complementary career services offices housed within the various colleges. Together, the 15 members of the CSC work hard to ensure that Golden Eagles end up in fulfilling postgraduate placements. The evidence suggests they are succeeding as 97% of employed graduates said their current job related to their overarching career goals.

E-mail: admissions@marquette.edu | Website: marquette.edu

The school brings employers to campus through events such as the Business Career & Internship Fair, the Engineering Job Fair, and the Helping Professions Career & Internship Fair. It also provides opportunities through membership in the Wisconsin Private College Career Consortium. Individual attention is always at your fingertips as undergrads can schedule 50-minute sessions at any point in their journey or drop in for a quick 10-15-minute meeting. The career services staff is also happy to set you up with an alumni mentorship in your field of interest by tapping into the alumni network of over 115,000. Employers regularly travel to campus to engage with students and even offer formal on-campus interviews; 70 employers do so annually within the College of Business Administration alone.

Professional Outcomes

Sixty-six percent of the Class of 2022 enjoyed full-time employment within six months of graduation, although that figure varied widely by discipline. Within the College of Business Administration, 82% had landed a job, and 77% of College of Engineering grads did the same. In contrast, this figure was just 40% for Arts & Sciences grads. The largest employers of Golden Eagle alumni include GE Healthcare, Northwestern Mutual, Rockwell Automation, Baird, Johnson Controls, and the Harley-Davidson Motor Company. Other Midwestern powerhouses, including Kohl's Medtronic and Milwaukee Tool, also employ hundreds of Marquette graduates. Slightly over half of 2022 grads stayed put in the state of Wisconsin while 25% went south to Illinois, and 6% settled in another Midwestern state.

One-quarter of 2022 diploma-earners elected to continue their education in graduate or professional school. Among that group, 53% were pursuing a master's degree, 27% were pursuing a medical or health-related degree, 11% entered law school, and 3% began a PhD program. Marquette does not offer an official pre-law major, but last year it sent students from various academic backgrounds to the likes of Boston University School of Law, Northwestern Pritzker School of Law, University of Chicago Law School, and USC's Gould School of Law. Marquette saw 78 seniors apply to medical school during the 2022-23 school year, and students earned acceptances at the Baylor College of Medicine, the UW-Madison School of Medicine, and the University of Michigan Medical School.

Admission

Of the 15,883 applications received for the 2022-23 freshman class, 13,851—87%—were accepted, one of the highest rates of any university featured in our guide. The admissions process at Marquette is not designed to keep the bulk of applicants out but to make sure that those admitted possess the skills needed to excel at the university. For a school with such a high admit rate, the middle-50% ACT score range was an impressive 26-31, and the SAT range was 1180-1350. Just under one-third of those enrolled in the Class of 2026 placed in the top 10% of their high school class, and 61% fell within the top quartile. Marquette went test optional at the start of the pandemic, but that decision had been made pre-COVID and will be in place for the long haul.

The factors at the top of a Marquette admissions officer's list are an applicant's GPA and rigor of coursework. Even though it is test optional, standardized tests still qualify as an "important" factor along with essays, extracurricular activities, and volunteer work. The university does not offer interviews and, interestingly for a Jesuit school, does not consider religious affiliation in the admissions process. In addition to possessing one of the highest acceptance rates of any school in this guide, Marquette is also among the few to offer rolling admissions. While you can apply anytime, submitting by the December 1 priority deadline is recommended to maximize your chances.

Worth Your Money?

Approximately 90% of Golden Eagles qualify for some level of financial aid, which helps knock down the tuition that is listed at just shy of $49k. The full cost of attendance is approximately $65k. The average need-based scholarship is $30k, and the school delivers merit-based aid to a large chunk of students who don't qualify for need-based aid. Those awards average about $20k. Like many other non-highly selective private schools, whether Marquette is worth your tuition money may come down to your intended major and level of aid awarded. Those entering the excellent engineering, business, CS, or nursing programs will likely be making a sound investment, regardless of other variables.

FINANCIAL
Institutional Type: Private
In-State Tuition: $48,700
Out-of-State Tuition: $48,700
Room & Board: $15,740
Books & Supplies: $720

Avg. Need-Based Grant: $30,225
Avg. % of Need Met: 85%

Avg. Merit-Based Award: $20,078
% Receiving (Freshmen w/o Need): 39%

Avg. Cumulative Debt: $36,244
% of Students Borrowing: 57%

CAREER
Who Recruits
1. Microsoft
2. Kohler Co.
3. Abbott Laboratories
4. Miwaukee Tool
5. Rockewell Automation

Notable Internships
1. KPMG
2. Milwaukee Bucks
3. MillerCoors

Top Employers
1. Northwestern Mutual
2. GE Healthcare
3. Rockwell Automation
4. Baird
5. Johnson Controls

Where Alumni Work
1. Milwaukee
2. Chicago
3. Minneapolis-St. Paul
4. New York City
5. Madison, WI

Earnings
College Scorecard (10-YR Post-Entry): $76,417
PayScale (Early Career): $62,200
PayScale (Mid-Career): $114,100
PayScale 20-Year ROI: $612,000

RANKINGS
Money: 4.5
U.S. News: 86, National Universities
Wall Street Journal/THE: 56
Washington Monthly: 104, National Universities

OVERGENERALIZATIONS
Students are:
Service-oriented
Only a short drive from home (i.e., Most come from WI or nearby states)
Career-driven
Crazy about the Golden Eagles
Working hard and playing hard

COLLEGE OVERLAPS
DePaul University
Indiana University Bloomington
Loyola University Chicago
University of Denver
University of Pittsburgh

Massachusetts Institute of Technology

Cambridge, Massachusetts | 617-253-3400

A beacon of egalitarianism and meritocracy, the Massachusetts Institute of Technology is less about legacy and more about the future. MIT doesn't care who your grandfather was or how far you can throw a football; it is seeking the world's sharpest and most innovative minds in engineering, the sciences, mathematics, and related fields who, one day, will create the world the rest of us will merely inhabit. Graduate students account for the majority of students enrolled at MIT, but the 4,657 undergraduates pursue one of 57 majors and 59 minors at this world-class research institution that continues to be one of the world's most magnetic destinations for math and science geniuses.

Inside the Classroom

There are five separate schools within MIT: the School of Architecture and Planning; the School of Engineering; the School of Humanities, Arts, and the Social Sciences; the Sloan School of Management; and the School of Science. There are a number of broad academic requirements across all five schools including an eight-subject humanities, arts, and social sciences requirement and a six-subject science requirement that includes two terms of calculus, two terms of physics, one term of chemistry, and one term of biology. Additionally, students must complete two courses under the designation of "restricted electives" in science and technology, a laboratory requirement, and a physical education course.

The student-to-faculty ratio is an astonishing 3-to-1, and even with a substantial focus on graduate programs, the class sizes are intimate. Over two-fifths of all class sections have single-digit enrollments, and 70% of courses contain fewer than twenty students. MIT is known for having one of the best formalized undergraduate research programs in the country. The Undergraduate Research Opportunities Program (UROP) operates year-round and helped connect 93%+ of students to a research experience with an MIT faculty member. Studying abroad is strongly encouraged, and the school offers some fantastic opportunities through programs such as MIT Madrid, Imperial College London Exchanges, and departmental exchange programs in South Africa, France, and Japan; almost half participate.

The highest numbers of degrees conferred in 2022 were in the following majors: engineering (31%), computer science and engineering (28%), mathematics (10%), and the physical sciences (7%). Just about every program at MIT sits at or near the top of any rankings. The most sought-after employers and grad schools aggressively recruit alumni. Graduates win nationally competitive fellowships and scholarships on a routine basis. In 2022, two students were awarded Marshall Scholarships; in 2022, eleven of the 45 finalists for Hertz Fellowships were MIT grads.

Outside the Classroom

The campus' 166 acres include twenty-six acres of playing fields, 20 acres of green spaces and gardens, and 18 student residences that house the 93% of students who live on campus, a requirement for freshmen. It may be a bit of a surprise that the school's 35+ fraternities, sororities, and living groups attract 44% of male students and 25% of females. Around half live in frat/sorority/living group housing, and the other half reside in dorms. Falling victim to stereotypes, one might not immediately assume that MIT would have an athletically-inclined student body. However, the school fields 33 varsity sports teams, most of which compete in NCAA Division III against other New England colleges. The intramural program is bursting at the seams with over 4,000 participants annually. Another 800 students are members of thirty-three club teams. Plenty of culture/creativity can be found on campus in one of MIT's twelve museums and galleries (the MIT Museum draws 150,000 visitors each year). There are also more than sixty arts, dance, music, and writing organizations for students. The school is devoted to environmental sustainability, and the campus and surrounding area are designed for a car-free lifestyle that remains highly convenient. With over 40 bike-sharing stations, six subway stations, and 30 bus routes in the surrounding area, students can navigate Cambridge with ease. Harvard's campus is less than one mile away, and downtown Boston is easy to reach. For reference, Fenway Park is less than two miles from campus.

Career Services

MIT Career Advising and Professional Development (CAPD) has 25 professional staff members who are directly involved in employer relations, career counseling, and graduate school advising. That 186:1 student-to-advisor ratio is far better than many other schools featured in this guide. The office provides top-notch individualized counseling and also puts on phenomenal large-scale events. The MIT Fall Career Fair is an unmatched event that sees around 450 companies and 5,000 students attend. If you can think of a desirable tech/finance company, chances are it has a booth at the event. Even the less-epic Spring Career Fair attracts seventy employers including Northrop Grumman, Wayfair, Bank of America, the Walt Disney Company, and Cisco.

With assistance from the CAPD, 82% of recent MIT undergraduates completed at least one internship. Almost one-quarter of those participating in internships received a full-time job offer from that same organization. The CAPD played a direct role in helping many others land jobs through various means as 53% found employment through career fairs and 47% through CAPD and faculty members. In a single year, the CAPD hosted 130 different employers, which led to a collective 2,600 interviews held on campus. An additional 1,000+ employers posted 2,600 unique jobs online in an effort to lure MIT seniors. MIT students sell themselves, so career services staff have a role akin to managing the '27 Yankees. Still, the office does a world-class job of setting up its highly desired undergrads with premium opportunities.

Professional Outcomes

The Class of 2023 saw 29% of its members enter the world of employment and 43% continue on their educational paths. By industry, the highest percentage of recent graduates found jobs in information technology (31%), scientific services (20%), healthcare (17%), and finance (14%). The top employers included Accenture, Amazon, Microsoft, Goldman Sachs, Google, General Motors, the US Navy, Apple, Bain & Company, and McKinsey. The mean starting salary for an MIT bachelor's degree holder was $95,000, and the median was $90,000.

The most frequently attended graduate schools are a who's who of elite institutions including MIT itself, Stanford, Caltech, Harvard, and the University of Oxford. Also making the list were Princeton, Columbia, Northwestern, the University of Chicago, the University of California Berkeley, and the University of Michigan. The most common degree being pursued by recent grads was a master's of engineering (39%) and the second most common degree was a PhD (38%). Only 6% were entering medical/dental/veterinary school, and 1% were headed to law school. Medical school acceptance rates typically land in the 80-95% range for grads/alumni, more than double the national average.

Admission

Applicants for a place in the Class of 2026 encountered a murderous 4% acceptance rate. Freshmen entering MIT in the fall of 2022 possessed mid-50% SATs of 1520-1570 and ACTs of 35-36. Students were almost unanimously from the top 10% of their high school classes. MIT offers a nonbinding early action option with a November 1 deadline, but it yields little in the way of an admissions edge. The acceptance rate for the early round is usually almost identical to that of the regular round.

The MIT admissions committee rates character/personal qualities as "very important," and just about everything else—rigor of courses, GPA, test scores, essays, recommendations, interview, extracurricular activities—in the next tier of importance. While a nice nod to the importance of character, every one of the aforementioned factors ranked as merely "important" has to be close to perfect for it to even enter the equation. Legacy status is not considered at MIT, a rarity among elite universities, meaning that the alumni connection of your mother, grandfather, or brother plays zero role in helping you gain admission. Despite a large intercollegiate sports program, athletic prowess plays a minimal role in admissions decisions as well. MIT is as close to a true meritocracy as you can find in the world of higher education. The most brilliant and innovative minds from around the globe are admitted regardless of family name or lacrosse skills. Rather, a sparkling academic record, near-perfect test scores, and impressive STEM-focused experiences/accomplishments outside the classroom will rule the day.

Worth Your Money?

Yes…need more? Going to MIT is punching your ticket to any number of lucrative careers. If you need financial assistance, this school will meet 100% of your demonstrated need; the average grant is roughly $60,000. The full cost of attendance is $82,730.

FINANCIAL
Institutional Type: Private
In-State Tuition: $60,156
Out-of-State Tuition: $60,156
Room & Board: $19,390
Books & Supplies: $880

Avg. Need-Based Grant: $60,345
Avg. % of Need Met: 100%

Avg. Merit-Based Award: $0
% Receiving (Freshmen w/o Need): 0%

Avg. Cumulative Debt: $25,556
% of Students Borrowing: 15%

CAREER
Who Recruits
1. Hudson River Trading
2. Nvidia
3. Five Rings Technology
4. Stripe
5. AB InBev

Notable Internships
1. Jane Street Capital
2. Airbnb
3. Shell

Top Employers
1. Google
2. Apple
3. Microsoft
4. Amazon
5. IBM

Where Alumni Work
1. Boston
2. San Francisco
3. New York City
4. India
5. United Kingdom

Earnings
College Scorecard (10-YR Post-Entry): $124,213
PayScale (Early Career): $93,700
PayScale (Mid-Career): $167,200
PayScale 20-Year ROI: $1,468,000

RANKINGS
Money: 5
U.S. News: 2, National Universities
Wall Street Journal/THE: 2
Washington Monthly: 3, National Universities

OVERGENERALIZATIONS
Students are:
Always studying
Diverse
Intellectually curious
Self-motivated
Intense

COLLEGE OVERLAPS
Columbia University
California Institute of Technology
Harvard University
Princeton University
Stanford University

Miami University - Oxford

Oxford, Ohio | 513-529-2531

Unless you are from Ohio, telling someone that you attend Miami University will likely lead to images of palm trees, gorgeous white sand beaches, and world-famous nightclubs. Such is the fate of this excellent public university located in southwestern Ohio. The town of Oxford may not be South Beach, but it provides a home to almost 17,000 undergraduates and boasts a No. 1 ranking among Ohio-based public universities for both return on investment and four-year graduation rate.

Inside the Classroom
The Global Miami Plan appears to be, at first glance, a labyrinthine set of requirements that involves foundational courses, thematic sequences, intercultural perspectives, experiential learning, and a capstone. Despite the categorical overload, the core curriculum at Miami is actually fairly straightforward and allows for a good deal of flexibility within a series of umbrella categories. Students in all 100+ of the school's majors tackle 27 credits worth of foundational courses in English, the humanities, natural sciences, STEM, and global perspectives. The experiential learning and capstone requirements help ensure that Miami grads engage in activities like service-learning, research, or portfolio projects.

A freshman retention rate of 89% is excellent for a public university, and the strength of undergraduate teaching gets high marks. In part, this is made possible by a reasonable 15:1 student-to-faculty ratio, lower than Ohio State. As at most publics, classes certainly aren't tiny, but Miami U. keeps the majority of courses—65% to be precise—at an enrollment of 29 or fewer. Each year, more than 2,800 undergrads work with professors on research, and some become coauthors of academic papers and/or find themselves presenting at academic conferences. The school also ranks in the top five among public institutions for the percent of students who elect to study abroad; a phenomenal 55% of undergrads elect to study away from Oxford.

Almost one-quarter of Miami University graduates earn a degree in business/marketing, making it, by far, the most popular area of academic concentration. Other commonly pursued majors include the social sciences (9%), health professions (9%), communication/journalism (8%), biology (6%), parks and recreation (6%), and education (6%). The Farmer School of Business and the College of Engineering and Computing both have terrific national reputations. The university also offers standout programs in architecture, sports management, and kinesiology. The school's overall profile is also on the rise in the eyes of prestigious scholarship-granting organizations; in 2023, five RedHawks were selected as Fulbright Scholars. The school also recently produced multiple winners of Astronaut Scholarships, Boren Scholarships, Critical Language Scholarships, Gilman Scholarships, and Goldwater Scholarships.

Outside the Classroom
Set on 2,100 rural acres, Miami is a school that houses just about all of its freshmen on campus and sees the majority of upperclassmen live in off-campus housing; in 2022-23, just shy of 80% lived on campus. Greek life soaks up a massive percentage of the population, with 30% of women joining sororities and 20% of men affiliated with a fraternity. Just about every student in Oxford laces up athletic sneakers, cleats, or skates to participate in one of 18 Division I sports, 50+ club teams, or 600 intramural teams with 3,000 total annual participants. Facilities for these endeavors are top-notch and include the Recreational Sports Center with two swimming pools and an indoor jogging track (70% of students participate in Rec Center programming), the Goggin Ice Center, which contains two ice rinks, and the Outdoor Pursuit Center, which offers hiking, canoeing, camping, and rafting opportunities. Oxford may be a small town a full hour away from Cincinnati, but few students complain thanks to an ample selection of extracurriculars, a thriving Greek/party scene, and a notably beautiful campus.

Career Services
The Center for Career Exploration & Success (CCES) employs 21 professional employees with roles in the areas of career counseling (by academic discipline), employer relations, and event coordination. This figure includes advisors who are housed within the Farmer School of Business and, in total, works out to an 803:1 counselor-to-student ratio. The wealth of resources Miami devotes to career assistance led to the office putting on 300+ career programs per year. An impressive 3,326 members of the Class of 2022 engaged with the CCES in their freshman year.

E-mail: admission@miamioh.edu | Website: miamioh.edu

Seven out of every ten recent Miami U graduates completed an internship (or other field experience) during their time on campus. In a single recent year, students participated in 870 live mock interviews, and 14,000+ logged onto Handshake. An astounding 592 companies came to Oxford to recruit and conducted a grand total of 3,056 on-campus interviews. Undoubtedly a result of all of this hard work, over three-quarters of recent grads are employed in their field of study, and 90%+ are employed in a position that requires a college degree.

Professional Outcomes

The overall success rate for the Class of 2022 was 99%, roughly the same as for the previous two cohorts. Fifty-five percent of recent Miami grads were employed and by mid-career, alumni enjoy a median salary of $118k. Staying in Ohio is a common postgraduate choice with 46% of grads doing so, but Chicago; New York City; Washington, DC; and Denver are also popular landing spots. The companies attracting the greatest number of RedHawk alumni are Procter & Gamble, EY, Fifth Third Bank, JPMorgan Chase, Deloitte, PNC, PwC, and Amazon.

Over one-quarter of recent grads elected to continue their education in graduate or professional school. Miami boasts a strong premed program that resulted in 63% of medical school applicants gaining acceptance over the last four years. Those with a 3.2 GPA and no less than the 50th percentile score on any section of the MCAT had an even more favorable 73% acceptance rate. Recent medical school acceptances include the University of Michigan Medical School, the University of Cincinnati College of Medicine, and Case Western Reserve University School of Medicine. Miami seniors are accepted into law schools at a 95% clip, above the national average, and have recently matriculated at schools like Boston College, Wake Forest, and Ohio State University.

Admission

Miami University saw 30,367 applications roll in during the previous admissions cycle and accepted 88% from this pool, down from 89% the previous year. Many of those accepted were using the university as a safety school as only 15% of this group actually went on to enroll. Those who did enroll in the freshman class of 2022-23 possessed a middle-50th percentile ACT score of 24-29 and SAT score of 1170-1350. Seventy percent scored above 1200 on the SAT. The average weighted GPA was 3.89, over one-third placed inside the top 10% of their high school class, and 64% were in the top quartile. This public university actually attracts many out-of-state students—typically around 35% of the undergraduate student population.

Utilizing a holistic admissions process, Miami University considers eight factors as being "very important": rigor of secondary school record, class rank, GPA, standardized test scores, application essay, recommendations, talent/ability, and character/personal qualities. "Considered" factors include extracurricular activities, first-generation status, legacy status (13% percent of admitted students were sons, daughters, or siblings of alumni), geographical residence, state residency, volunteer work, and paid work experience. If you are a borderline applicant, applying early decision can be an effective strategy. Yet, the ED acceptance rate of 87% of ED is actually a touch lower. However, if you possess credentials around the median figures, this move is not necessary as Miami University is very likely to accept you in the regular round.

Worth Your Money?

Miami University is not a public school that offers dirt-cheap (relatively speaking) tuition prices. In fact, the tuition will cost you $17,808, around $4,000 more a year than at Ohio State. With housing and meals, the annual cost of attendance rises to $34k for residents and $57k for out-of-staters. The average debt load for graduates is just shy of $30k, about average by national standards and just a couple thousand more than the total for alumni of the aforementioned Ohio State. Overall, close to 90% of first-year students receive aid that does not need to be paid back. In sum, this school is reasonably priced for in-state students, but for nonresidents who are on a budget, heading to Oxford may only make sense if you are planning on pursuing a business degree.

FINANCIAL
Institutional Type: Public
In-State Tuition: $17,055
Out-of-State Tuition: $38,127
Room & Board: $15,558
Books & Supplies: $1,240

Avg. Need-Based Grant: $13,088
Avg. % of Need Met: 60%

Avg. Merit-Based Award: $11,782
% Receiving (Freshmen w/o Need): 49%

Avg. Cumulative Debt: $29,434
% of Students Borrowing: 43%

CAREER
Who Recruits
1. Textron
2. Deloitte
3. EY
4. Oracle
5. Fifth Third Bank

Notable Internships
1. Wells Fargo
2. E&J Gallo
3. Cleveland Clinic

Top Employers
1. Procter & Gamble
2. EY
3. Fifth Third Bank
4. JPMorgan Chase
5. Deloitte

Where Alumni Work
1. Cincinnati
2. Chicago
3. Columbus, OH
4. Cleveland
5. New York City

Earnings
College Scorecard (10-YR Post-Entry): $55,590
PayScale (Early Career): $61,000
PayScale (Mid-Career): $118,400
PayScale 20-Year ROI: $659,000

RANKINGS
Money: 4
U.S. News: 133, National Universities
Wall Street Journal/THE: 303
Washington Monthly: 255, National Universities

OVERGENERALIZATIONS
Students are:
Politically conservative
Homogeneous
Ready to party
Always admiring the beauty of their campus
Preppy

COLLEGE OVERLAPS
Indiana University Bloomington
The Ohio State University - Columbus
Ohio University
Pennsylvania State University - University Park
University of Wisconsin - Madison

Michigan State University

East Lansing, Michigan | 517-355-8332

Established in 1855, the Agricultural College of the State of Michigan was the prototype for the original land-grant institutions that forever changed the college landscape in the United States. Since then, it has been through six iterations, five of which saw the inclusion of the word "agriculture" in the school's name; the last—Michigan State University— was adopted in 1964. Today, this highly regarded state institution boasts over 200 programs—undergraduate, graduate, and professional—across 17 degree-granting colleges. Even better, it remains accessible to solid but not elite-level applicants, accepting more than 85% of those who apply.

Inside the Classroom
In addition to many school-specific requirements within its individual colleges, all Spartans must complete a mathematics course, two writing-intensive courses (Tier 1 and 2), and 24 credits worth of integrative studies courses. This includes a lower- and upper-level humanities course, a sequence within the social, behavioral, or economic sciences, and eight credits worth of lab-based biological or physical science. Some majors require students to become proficient in a foreign language while others do not have a language requirement. Over 4,000 students are admitted to the MSU Honors College, which offers a more flexible curriculum, smaller classes, and increased interaction with faculty.

A 17:1 student-to-faculty ratio rates in the average range for public universities of MSU's size and scope. Class sizes are a genuine mix of small seminars and giant lecture halls. Fifty-five percent of undergraduate course sections contain fewer than 30 students; just 23% enroll more than 50. Undergraduate research opportunities do exist for those bold enough to pursue them; 36% of recent grads completed one such experience. Around 25% of undergrads study abroad at one of 260 programs located in 60+ countries.

A strong business program attracts the greatest number of undergrads; 16% of the degrees conferred in 2022 were in the business/marketing category. The next most common degrees were earned in communication/journalism (12%), engineering (11%), and the social sciences (8%). Those academic departments all rank well nationally as well. MSU produced nine Fulbright Scholars in 2023 as well as multiple Goldwater Scholars and Critical Language Scholars in recent years.

Outside the Classroom
Three miles from the state capital of Lansing, MSU's campus is a seemingly never-ending 5,300-acre property, populated by 563 buildings. The 27 residence halls are occupied by 43% of the overall student body; 95% of freshmen live on campus. There are more than 900 student groups from which to choose, including a widely circulated student newspaper, The State News, and the popular Impact 89FM radio station that broadcasts to the wider Lansing community. There are 50+ Greek-letter organizations, but they do not dominate the social scene. All told, 11% of men join fraternities, and 12% of women join sororities. Athletics at Michigan State are a huge focal point as the Spartans field 25 varsity squads (12 men's and 13 women's), including a stellar basketball team that has made 25 straight March Madness appearances and has earned ten trips to the Final Four. East Lansing, as a college town, rates among the very best in the country. Among the cultural jewels on campus are the Wharton Center for Performing Arts, the MSU Museum, the Broad Art Museum, the Abrams Planetarium, the Breslin Student Events Center, and the 7.5 acres of horticultural gardens. School spirit is plentiful, sports are celebrated, and there is no shortage of ways to connect with peers.

Career Services
Michigan State's Career Services Network has 40 professional employees who work as discipline-specific career consultants, employer-relations specialists, and internship coordinators. This works out to a 980:1 student-to-advisor ratio, which is higher than the average university featured in this guide, but it is not unusual for a school of MSU's size. The office hosts more than a dozen career fairs per year with massive numbers of employers attending. Even the relatively niche School of Hospitality Business Fair attracts 80+ employers. The office is also glad to provide virtual or one-on-one assistance with career exploration, resume and cover letter writing, LinkedIn profile creation, or interview practice.

A commendable 76% of Class of 2022 members completed at least one internship while attending MSU. Many are able to find internships or their first jobs through MSU Connect, which helps undergrads locate mentors from the 500,000-member network of Spartan alumni. Workshops hosted or coordinated by the Career Services Network are available on an almost daily basis where students can participate in virtual sessions with a variety of employers, learn about internship opportunities, or work on skills related to the nuts and bolts of the job search process. In sum, MSU is able to provide solid career services offerings and, even with minimal hand-holding, internship and post-graduation outcome numbers suggest it is producing very strong results.

Professional Outcomes

Within months of strutting across the graduation stage, 56% of Class of 2022 members had landed full-time employment, 27% were pursuing advanced degrees, and 6% were still looking for a job. The top employers of this group included big names like General Motors, Ford Motor Company, Deloitte, Epic Systems, Target, PepsiCo, and Microsoft. The median starting salary earned was $60,000. Sixty-two percent of fresh alumni remained in Michigan, 10% situated in Illinois, and New York, Texas, and California each attracted 2-3% of graduates.

Of the more than one-quarter of 2022 graduates who continued their education, the most popular choice was to stay in Lansing and continue at Michigan State. The next most commonly attended schools included the University of Michigan, New York University, Columbia University, and Boston University. Michigan State ranks as the undergraduate institution with the 29th highest number of applicants to medical school in the 2022-23 cycle. Law schools attended by recent grads include the likes of Cornell, Northeastern, Notre Dame, Boston College, and the University of Michigan. Plenty of undergraduates on the premed and prelaw tracks end up attending Michigan State University College of Osteopathic Medicine and Michigan State University College of Law.

Admission

The university received 53,341 applications for a place in the Class of 2026 and admitted 88% of all who applied. Twenty-one percent of those who were admitted ended up becoming Spartans. The mid-50% standardized test ranges were 1110-1320 on the SAT and 24-30 on the ACT. Twenty-six percent of 2022-23 freshmen placed in the top 10% of their high school class, 58% earned a spot in the top quartile, and 92% landed in the top half. The average GPA was an impressive 3.8, and 29% of those entering the university possessed a 4.0 or better.

The two most heavily weighted factors in admissions decisions are academic GPA and the application essay. The rigor of one's secondary school record registers as "important," as do extracurricular activities, talent/ability, character/personal qualities, geographical residence, and the level of an applicant's interest. MSU is fully test-optional. The school does not offer a binding early decision option but does have an early action deadline of November 1. According to the school, applying EA "does not make it easier to gain admission to MSU, and the Office of Admissions promises no special privileges to early action candidates in the admissions review, such as giving your application a higher priority or a more lenient review."

Worth Your Money?

Residents of the Great Lake State face a reasonable annual cost of attendance of $28k, meaning that a bachelor's degree can be obtained at list price for right around $110k. Even at full price, this presents an affordable option by the standards of today's postsecondary market. Roughly half of freshmen receive financial aid, but the average award covers just 60% of the determined need. The close to one-quarter of undergraduates from outside the state pay a COA that is almost exactly double the in-state amount. At $220k, MSU may not be the most cost-effective option, and nonresidents would likely be better off seeking out public options within their home state.

FINANCIAL
Institutional Type: Public
In-State Tuition: $15,372
Out-of-State Tuition: $41,958
Room & Board: $10,990
Books & Supplies: $1,254

Avg. Need-Based Grant: $11,341
Avg. % of Need Met: 60%

Avg. Merit-Based Award: $6,864
% Receiving (Freshmen w/o Need): 14%

Avg. Cumulative Debt: $31,591
% of Students Borrowing: 50%

CAREER
Who Recruits
1. Ford Motor Company
2. Neogen Corporation
3. Nexient
4. Proctor & Gamble
5. DTE Energy

Notable Internships
1. The Detroit News
2. UFC
3. Ralph Lauren

Top Employers
1. General Motors
2. Ford Motor Company
3. FCA Fiat Chrysler
4. Quicken Loans
5. Amazon

Where Alumni Work
1. Detroit
2. Chicago
3. Grand Rapids, MI
4. New York City
5. San Francisco

Earnings
College Scorecard (10-YR Post-Entry): $64,566
PayScale (Early Career): $59,700
PayScale (Mid-Career): $105,900
PayScale 20-Year ROI: $563,000

RANKINGS
Money: 4.5
U.S. News: 60, National Universities
Wall Street Journal/THE: 57
Washington Monthly: 45, National Universities

OVERGENERALIZATIONS
Students are:
Crazy about the Spartans
Diverse
Ready to party
Independent
Supportive

COLLEGE OVERLAPS
Indiana University Bloomington
Purdue University - West Lafayette
University of Illinois at Urbana-Champaign
University of Michigan
University of Wisconsin - Madison

Middlebury College

Middlebury, Vermont | 802-443-3000

ADMISSION
Admission Rate: 13%
Admission Rate - Men: 14%
Admission Rate - Women: 12%
EA Admission Rate: Not Offered
ED Admission Rate: 42%
ED Admits as % of Total Admits: 27%
Admission Rate (5-Year Trend): -4%
% of Admits Attending (Yield): 39%
Transfer Admission Rate: 8%

SAT Reading/Writing (Middle 50%): 700-760
SAT Math (Middle 50%): 710-780
ACT Composite (Middle 50%): 33-35

% Graduated in Top 10% of HS Class: 73%
% Graduated in Top 25% of HS Class: 96%
% Graduated in Top 50% of HS Class: 100%

Demonstrated Interest: Considered
Legacy Status: Considered
Racial/Ethnic Status: Important
Admission Interview Offered: Yes

ENROLLMENT
Total Undergraduate Enrollment: 2,773
% Full-Time: 99%
% Male: 47%
% Female: 53%
% Out-of-State: 95%
% Fraternity: Not Offered
% Sorority: Not Offered
% On-Campus (All Undergraduate): 95%
Freshman Housing Required: Yes

% African-American: 5%
% Asian: 7%
% Hispanic: 12%
% White: 56%
% Other: 1%
% International: 11%
% Low-Income: 17%

ACADEMICS
Student-to-Faculty Ratio: 9 to 1
% of Classes Under 20: 59%
% of Classes 20-49: 40%
% of Classes 50 or More: 1%
% Full-Time Faculty: 91%
% Full-Time Faculty w/ Terminal Degree: 97%

Top Programs
Architecture
Biochemistry
Economics
Environmental Studies
International & Global Studies
Neuroscience
Performing Arts
Political Science

Retention Rate: 93%
4-Year Graduation Rate: 86%
6-Year Graduation Rate: 93%

Curricular Flexibility: Somewhat Flexible
Academic Rating: ★★★★✓

#CollegesWorthYourMoney

Located between the Green Mountains and the Adirondacks, Middlebury College is heading toward the summit of Northeastern liberal arts colleges. In the same conversation as (although always ranked just behind) Williams and Amherst, Middlebury's 2,700+ undergraduate students are an exceptionally accomplished crew. Even the frigid Vermont winters do little to take away from the beauty of the college's historic 350-acre campus or the natural grandeur of the surrounding area. A quintessential New England liberal arts college aesthetically, "Midd" also plays that role when it comes to the classroom experience.

Inside the Classroom

Offering 50 departments and programs in which to major and minor, the college requires all students to complete one course in seven of the following eight categories: literature, the arts, philosophical and religious studies, historical studies, physical and life sciences, deductive reasoning and analytical processes, social analysis, and foreign language. Undergrads also must complete four additional courses that meet the cultures and civilization requirement. Mandatory writing-intensive seminars must be tackled—one as a freshman and the second by the end of the sophomore year.

The school's 9:1 student-faculty ratio allows 100% of courses to be taught by professors, not graduate assistants. Most classes are small; the mean class size is 16, and 14% of sections contain fewer than ten students. The Summer Research at Middlebury program funds 130 students annually to work alongside faculty in a variety of disciplines. Each year, more than 50% of juniors take a semester abroad in one of 75 programs in 40 countries. The college's robust international program includes Middlebury Schools Abroad in Argentina, Brazil, Cameroon, Chile, China, France, Germany, India, Israel, Italy, Japan, Jordan, Morocco, Russia, Spain, the United Kingdom, and Uruguay.

Middlebury is renowned for its Language Department as well as its programs in economics and international studies. Graduate schools know the value of a Middlebury education (see med school acceptance rates below). The college also produces a large number of national fellowship/scholarship winners. In 2023, graduates/alumni took home two Critical Language Scholarships, seven Fulbright Scholarships, and a host of other prestigious honors.

Outside the Classroom

Implementing the Oxford/Cambridge system of residential housing, all Middlebury undergraduates are required to live in one of more than 60 on-campus buildings. First-year students are assigned to one of five larger Commons where they will reside until the end of their sophomore year. More than thirty faculty/staff members regularly eat in the Commons, allowing for classroom discussions to continue over a meal. That leaves no room for Greek life, which vanished two decades ago (limited "social houses" do remain). With thirty-one varsity sports teams competing in the NCAA New England Small College Athletic Conference, the Middlebury Panthers put a sizable portion of its undergraduate population—28%—in uniform. Less committed athletes can enjoy a full array of club and intramural sports as well as the school's eighteen-hole golf course, 3.5-mile jogging trail, 2,200-seat ice hockey rink, or six-lane indoor track. Midd offers more than 200 student-run organizations with options in all the usual realms—performing arts, spiritual, social, student government, and more. Outdoor activity clubs that engage in climbing, hiking, kayaking, skiing, and camping are among the most popular groups. Student theater productions are also well attended. The town of Middlebury is tiny and quiet, so some students make the just-under-an-hour drive to Burlington. Montreal, Canada, is the closest cosmopolitan destination with Boston and New York more than three hours away.

Career Services

The Center for Careers and Internships is staffed by 13 full-time staff members who specialize in areas such as employer relations, career advising, health professions and STEM advising, and internships and early engagement. Its 213:1 student-to-advisor ratio places it among the most supportive career services offices of any college profiled in this guide. Middlebury's career counselors are almost always found actively engaging undergraduates in career/grad school planning. In a given year, they coordinate 125 events and workshops, and advisors hold 3,000 individual student sessions.

For a school of modest size, Middlebury brought an impressive 90 employers to campus to host information sessions and facilitated 750 on-campus interviews in a single recent year. They helped Class of 2022 members find internships at a 75% clip and contributed $850,000 to help fund unpaid summer work experiences. More than 25,000 opportunities for jobs and internships are posted online. Further, a generous alumni base is more than willing to assist current Panthers—more than 5,800 alums in a range of professions wait to connect on Midd2Midd. In sum, Middlebury gets extremely high marks from our team, as grads regularly find their way to careers they find meaningful and fulfilling, including many at some of the country's best companies.

Professional Outcomes

Six months after graduating, 81% of the Class of 2022 had landed jobs, 12% were in graduate school, and 4% were still searching for employment. The most commonly held jobs fell under the categories of financial services (19%), consulting (14%), science and healthcare (14%), and media and technology (12%). Interestingly, the number of Middlebury grads entering tech-related fields has grown by over 50% in the last handful of years. Google and Facebook are now two of the leading employers of alumni alongside Morgan Stanley, Goldman Sachs, Deloitte, Amazon, and JP Morgan. More than 100 alumni work in the US State Department and more than two dozen presently work for Apple, Microsoft, McKinsey, and Credit Suisse. New York City, Boston, Washington, DC, and San Francisco claim the greatest numbers of Panther alumni.

Middlebury students with solid grades will be viewed favorably by graduate and professional schools should they wish to continue their education. Graduate schools attended by recent alumni include Columbia, Georgia Tech, Harvard Law School, Oxford, Stanford, and Yale. Recent grads who applied to medical school were accepted at a 93% clip. Over the last decade, the most frequently attended medical schools include Tufts, Boston University, Geisel (Dartmouth), and NYU. The law school acceptance rate is 89%.

Admission

Middlebury College admitted 13% of the 12,952 applicants for a place in the Class of 2026, down from 22% two admissions cycles prior. Of those receiving an acceptance letter, 39% went on to enroll at the college. The middle-50% standardized test scores of those who enrolled were 1420-1520 on the SAT and 33-35 on the ACT. Formerly one of the rare test-flexible institutions, Middlebury shifted to a full-blown test-optional policy in 2020. Last cycle, only roughly half of enrolled students submitted an ACT or SAT score with their application.

Six factors sit atop the pecking order as applicants are being evaluated by the admissions committee: rigor of secondary coursework, GPA, class rank, extracurricular activities, talent/ability, and character/personal qualities. Test scores, recommendations, essays, and racial/ethnic status comprise the second tier of "important" factors. Those who commit to the college through binding early decision are rewarded with a 42% acceptance rate, more than three times that of the regular cycle. The college continues to use a genuinely holistic approach in the admissions process, and the test-optional policy can be useful for a certain type of applicant. Even when considering the "special" students being accepted via the early round, ED still provides borderline applicants with an increased chance at getting in.

Worth Your Money?

Middlebury's list price is about the going rate for elite liberal arts institutions with a total annual cost of attendance of $87k. However, if you qualify for need-based aid (as 49% of students do), the college will meet your full level of need; the average grant is $58,000. As with most schools that meet a student's full demonstrated need, there isn't much, if any, merit aid money to go around. A school of superior quality, Middlebury rates as a rare liberal arts school that will pay you back multiple times over the course of your life, even if the upfront costs are steep.

FINANCIAL
Institutional Type: Private
In-State Tuition: $65,280
Out-of-State Tuition: $65,280
Room & Board: $18,600
Books & Supplies: $1,000

Avg. Need-Based Grant: $58,084
Avg. % of Need Met: 100%

Avg. Merit-Based Award: $32,272
% Receiving (Freshmen w/o Need): <1%

Avg. Cumulative Debt: $17,792
% of Students Borrowing: 48%

CAREER
Who Recruits
1. Analysis Group
2. Goldman Sachs
3. Oak Hill Advisors
4. ScribeAmerica
5. CIA

Notable Internships
1. Tesla
2. Bain & Company
3. Merrill Lynch

Top Employers
1. Google
2. Goldman Sachs
3. Morgan Stanley
4. Amazon
5. Deloitte

Where Alumni Work
1. New York City
2. Boston
3. Washington, DC
4. San Francisco
5. Glen Falls, NY

Earnings
College Scorecard (10-YR Post-Entry): $69,022
PayScale (Early Career): $66,100
PayScale (Mid-Career): $128,000
PayScale 20-Year ROI: $645,000

RANKINGS
Money: 4.5
U.S. News: 11, Liberal Arts Colleges
Wall Street Journal/THE: 131
Washington Monthly: 19, Liberal Arts Colleges

OVERGENERALIZATIONS
Students are:
Outdoorsy
Wealthy
Politically liberal
Well-rounded
Preppy

COLLEGE OVERLAPS
Amherst College
Brown University
Dartmouth College
Tufts University
Williams College

Mount Holyoke College

South Hadley, Massachusetts | 413-538-2023

Stately, majestic, and Hogwarts-esque are three of the most common adjectives used to describe the grounds of Mount Holyoke College, an exclusively female liberal arts school located in South Hadley, Massachusetts. Situated ninety miles west of Boston, MHC is home to 2,220 undergraduates and is part of the Five College Consortium with nearby Amherst, Smith, Hampshire, and UMass Amherst. With fifty departmental and interdepartmental majors as well as the option to design your own major, MHC students, nicknamed "Lyons" after the college's founder, are free to follow their academic passions, an attribute that helps explain the incredible percentage of alumni who go on to earn PhDs.

Inside the Classroom

By liberal arts college standards, Mount Holyoke requires a minimal amount of core coursework. While working toward the completion of the 128 credits needed for graduation, students must complete one class in each of the humanities, sciences, social sciences, and mathematics. A freshman seminar focused on sharpening writing skills is mandatory as is one semester of foreign language study, one course focused on multicultural perspectives, and physical education. Thanks to membership in the Five College Consortium, undergrads can take a good number of courses at one of the other institutions but must complete two of their final three years of study on the MHC campus.

Professors are known for their accessibility and commitment to undergraduate education. Thanks to a 10-to-1 student-to-faculty ratio, 75% of sections contain fewer than twenty students; 12% are single-digit seminar classes. Opportunities to research and publish alongside faculty are definitely available, and many 200- and 300-level courses have independent research baked-in as a requirement. Across all disciplines, more ambitious students can arrange summer research internships with professors. More than one hundred study abroad options are on the table, but preferred MHC-affiliated programs are definitely worth considering. Those targeted college-run programs include Globalization, Development, and Environment in Costa Rica; Economic Transformation and Business in Shanghai; and the Associated Kyoto Program, which allows students to attend a full academic year of classes in Japan.

MHC isn't a school where one or two programs are more popular and/or more respected than the rest. Rather, strong programs are found across a variety of fields—for example, in biology, English, and international relations. Among undergrads, the greatest number of degrees are awarded in the social sciences (25%), biology (11%), psychology (11%), the visual and performing arts (9%), and natural resources and conservation (6%). Fellowships award season is usually kind to Mount Holyoke grads. In 2022, MHC students took home five Fulbright Scholarships, and, in recent years have captured Davis Projects for Peace and Boren Awards.

Outside the Classroom

Ninety-five percent of undergraduates live on campus in one of 18 residential halls. The last time sororities existed on campus was in 1910 when they were dissolved for being "undemocratic." The college's 13 sports teams compete in NCAA Division III, including a stellar equestrian program. Of the over 100 student organizations, a cappella and glee are among the most popular along with volunteerism in many forms. Each year, over half of MHC students volunteer at local schools, hospitals, YMCAs, and other community organizations. Speakers, including many authors, appear frequently on campus to give well-attended talks. Thanks again to membership in the Five College Consortium, social opportunities are expanded to include those offered at Smith, UMass, Amherst, and Hampshire. Campus, which is almost always cited as one the nation's prettiest, is a spacious 800 acres that features notable man-made highlights such as the MHC Art Museum, a fitness center that is less than a decade old, and an eighteen-hole golf course in addition to natural highlights such as two lakes and several hiking trails. South Hadley is a small town exploding with quaint New England charm. Those seeking more adventure can make the two-hour trip to Boston.

Career Services

The Career Development Center (CDC) is staffed by eight professionals (not counting admin assistants) who work directly with, or on behalf of, students in the following capacities: career counseling, internships, experiential learning, and external relations. That 274:1 student-to-advisor ratio is superior to many of the schools featured in this guidebook. Ample individualized attention is at the fingertips of undergraduates—30-minute advising sessions are available as often as once per week for current students or three times per year for recent graduates. The CDC does not host many large events itself; rather, it takes advantage of the school's geographic location and takes part in events such as the Smith College Life Sciences & Technology Fair, the UMass Amherst Computer Science & Engineering Fair, and the MIT Asian Career Fair.

Through an approach dubbed the "Lynk," Mt. Holyoke strives to systematically assist students in connecting their curriculum to their future careers. That goal is accomplished through the offering of experiential learning opportunities, internship connections (funding is guaranteed), industry site visits, and networking with past students who have entered fields of interest. In one recent year, the office engaged with 63% of the student body and 39% met one-on-one with a career advisor. An impressive (particularly during a pandemic) 82% of Class of 2022 grads participated in summer internships, research, or shadowing experiences. Overall, the CDC excels in helping young women find their next destination, as evidenced by a low percentage of students still seeking employment six months out and the strength of its graduate school preparation (more in a moment). Even with salaries on the lower end and a dearth of on-campus recruiting, the Mount Holyoke Career Development Center works hard to connect its students to fulfilling and relevant career paths.

Professional Outcomes

Six months after commencement, 62% of 2022 grads had found employment, 23% had entered graduate/professional school, 5% had landed fellowships/internships, and only 5% were still searching for jobs (down from 9% two years prior). Education was the most frequently entered field (32%). It was followed by healthcare (14%) and technology, science, and engineering (12%). The top Lyon employers of recent grads included Bank of America, BlackRock, Citigroup, the National Institutes of Health, and Boston Children's Hospital. Microsoft, IBM, Harvard University, and Amazon also employ a healthy number of Lyons. Given the number of grads entering the public sector or pursuing graduate degrees, it isn't shocking that average salary statistics for alumni tend to be on the low side. Plenty of alumni also can be found in New York, California, or international locales.

Ten years after graduation, 75% of alumnae have enrolled in graduate or professional school. The college produces an exceptional number of future STEM PhDs. In a ten-year period, it saw 171 of its graduates go on to earn doctorates in hard sciences. In recent years, the law school acceptance rate has fluctuated between 75% and 100%. Recent acceptances include Harvard Law School, Boston College, University of Michigan, and Stanford; 66% of recent law school applicants attended a top 20 program. Medical school acceptance rates tend to be above average, and recent graduates have attended Johns Hopkins, Tufts, Emory, Columbia, UVA, and Washington University. Across all disciplines, the graduate schools accepting the most recent alumni included Yale, Cornell, NYU, and Duke. Massachusetts-based Simmons, UMass Amherst, and Mt. Holyoke itself also cracked the list.

Admission

The 4,894 applicants fighting for membership in the Class of 2026 were accepted at a 40% rate, a decline from the Class of 2025's 52% mark. Just under 30% of those who were accepted ultimately enrolled in the college. The academic profile of the typical Mt. Holyoke student is quite different than what you would expect to find at a college that has seen a 50% acceptance rate in recent years. The middle-50% range for SATs was 1370-1500 (though many apply test-optional), and 57% of those attending placed in the top decile of their high school class; 76% were in the top quartile. Over three-quarters of students earned GPAs of 3.75 or higher and the average GPA was a robust 3.89.

Four factors reign supreme in the eyes of the admissions committee: rigor of coursework, GPA, recommendations, and essays. Factors such as class rank, the interview, extracurricular activities, talent/ability, character/personal qualities, volunteer work, and work experience also are deemed "important" in the evaluation process. Missing from this list are standardized test scores because Mount Holyoke is a test-optional school. A self-selecting applicant pool leads to a deceptively high(ish) acceptance rate. Yet, the women who are offered admission at Mount Holyoke tend to be high achieving with impressive high school transcripts to their names. Those sure that this is the Seven Sisters school for them can typically gain a significant advantage by applying early. However, the advantage was relatively small last year, as just 62% of 2022 ED applicants were admitted.

Worth Your Money?

Mt. Holyoke has an annual cost of attendance approaching the $83,000 mark, yet thanks to the generosity of its aid offers, many pay far less. In fact, almost two-thirds of the undergraduates at the college qualify for need-based aid, and the average grant is $47k, a figure that covers 100% of demonstrated need for every single recipient. Further, the school is not stingy with merit aid either, helping to make the school a touch more affordable for those who are not wealthy but ineligible for need-based aid. While many graduates don't immediately land high-paying jobs, the swarms of alumni earning advanced degrees do just fine financially in the long run.

FINANCIAL
Institutional Type: Private
In-State Tuition: $64,142
Out-of-State Tuition: $64,142
Room & Board: $18,838
Books & Supplies: $1,000

Avg. Need-Based Grant: $46,978
Avg. % of Need Met: 100%

Avg. Merit-Based Award: $21,813
% Receiving (Freshmen w/o Need): 14%

Avg. Cumulative Debt: $23,715
% of Students Borrowing: 59%

CAREER
Who Recruits
1. ESPN
2. Life Technologies
3. Forester Capital, LLC
4. NERA Economic Consulting
5. Analysis Group

Notable Internships
1. United States Senate
2. Nike
3. The Coca-Cola Company

Top Employers
1. Google
2. MassMutual
3. Microsoft
4. Amazon
5. Goldman Sachs

Where Alumni Work
1. New York City
2. Boston
3. Springfield, MA
4. Washington, DC
5. San Francisco

Earnings
College Scorecard (10-YR Post-Entry): $54,415
PayScale (Early Career): $56,400
PayScale (Mid-Career): $101,600
PayScale 20-Year ROI: $298,000

RANKINGS
Money: 4
U.S. News: 34, Liberal Arts Colleges
Wall Street Journal/THE: 282
Washington Monthly: 16, Liberal Arts Colleges

OVERGENERALIZATIONS
Students are:
Politically liberal
Always studying
Less likely to party
Tight-knit (possess a strong sense of community)
Passionate about social justice

COLLEGE OVERLAPS
Barnard College
Bryn Mawr College
Smith College
Vassar College
Wellesley College

New York University

New York, New York | 212-998-4500

ADMISSION
Admission Rate: 12%
Admission Rate - Men: 12%
Admission Rate - Women: 13%
EA Admission Rate: Not Offered
ED Admission Rate: Not Reported
ED Admits as % of Total Admits: Not Reported
Admission Rate (5-Year Trend): -16%
% of Admits Attending (Yield): 49%
Transfer Admission Rate: 20%

SAT Reading/Writing (Middle 50%): 720-770
SAT Math (Middle 50%): 750-800
ACT Composite (Middle 50%): 33-35

% Graduated in Top 10% of HS Class: 94%
% Graduated in Top 25% of HS Class: 100%
% Graduated in Top 50% of HS Class: 100%

Demonstrated Interest: Considered
Legacy Status: Considered
Racial/Ethnic Status: Considered
Admission Interview Offered: No

ENROLLMENT
Total Undergraduate Enrollment: 29,401
% Full-Time: 97%
% Male: 41%
% Female: 59%
% Out-of-State: 67%
% Fraternity: 2%
% Sorority: 4%
% On-Campus (All Undergraduate): 36%
Freshman Housing Required: No

% African-American: 8%
% Asian: 20%
% Hispanic: 17%
% White: 22%
% Other: 4%
% International: 26%
% Low-Income: 19%

ACADEMICS
Student-to-Faculty Ratio: 8 to 1
% of Classes Under 20: 58%
% of Classes 20-49: 32%
% of Classes 50 or More: 9%
% Full-Time Faculty: 43%
% Full-Time Faculty w/ Terminal Degree: 96%

Top Programs
Business and Political Economy
Computer Science
Film and Television
Finance
International Relations
Journalism
Mathematics
Performing Arts

Retention Rate: 93%
4-Year Graduation Rate: 78%
6-Year Graduation Rate: 87%

Curricular Flexibility: Somewhat Flexible
Academic Rating: ★★★★✦

#CollegesWorthYourMoney

A genuine melting pot, even by the standards of the city in which it is located, New York University's campus is graced by talented young people of every ethnicity, from every socio-economic status, and from every corner of the globe. All told, there are over 59,000 students presently enrolled at NYU, 29,400 of whom are undergraduates. With more than 230 areas of undergraduate study, the talents and passions of this student body are as diverse as its demographic makeup.

Inside the Classroom

NYU is divided into a number of smaller (but still quite large) colleges organized by discipline. Schools with undergraduate programs include the College of Arts & Sciences; Tisch School of the Arts; Tandon School of Engineering; Steinhardt School of Culture, Education, and Human Development; Silver School of Social Work; Rory Meyers College of Nursing; Stern School of Business; College of Global Public Health; and the Gallatin School of Individualized Study where students can create their own liberal arts course of study. There are five parts to NYU's Core Curriculum that must be tackled by all arts and sciences students. Within other colleges, alterations are made in some areas. The Core is comprised of (1) a research- and writing-focused first-year seminar capped at eighteen students, (2) a course in expository writing, (3) two years of language study, (4) Foundations of Contemporary Culture, and (5) Foundations of Scientific Inquiry.

With over 29,000 graduate students and a similar number of undergrads, you might expect undergraduate courses to be held in large lecture halls, even with an 8:1 student-to-faculty ratio. However, NYU manages to run a commendable 58% of its classes with an enrollment under 20 students; only 9% of courses contain more than 50 students. The school puts a great deal of money into undergraduate research, and it has been running an Undergraduate Research Conference for over forty years. Summer research opportunities are plentiful, including through the School of Engineering's ten-week summer research program for rising juniors and seniors. With more than 4,400 students studying in foreign countries each year, NYU sends more undergrads abroad than any other US university.

While all schools within NYU have solid reputations that will open doors to top corporations and grad schools alike, Stern holds the distinction as one of the top undergraduate business programs in the country. For those entering film, dance, drama, or other performing arts, Tisch is as prestigious a place as you can find to study, and the alumni list is full of Hollywood legends. In recent years, NYU has seen an increase in the number of students winning highly competitive postgraduate scholarships. In 2022, Fulbright Scholarships were awarded to 16 undergraduates; three students captured Critical Language Scholarships from the US Department of State the previous year.

Outside the Classroom

Campus life at NYU is best described in one word: diverse. The make-up of the student body is 26% international, the highest percentage of any US school, as its students hail from 110 countries. With sizable Asian, Latino, and African American populations, only about one-fifth of the students are classified as white. Life outside the classroom is every bit as diverse as the demographics as NYU truly has something for everyone. The school's 22 dorms provide housing for 36% of undergrads. With eleven men's and ten women's varsity teams competing in NCAA Division III sports as well as an extensive club and intramural program, NYU has enough opportunity to satisfy the athletically inclined but is far from a "sports school." Greek life is also available but tempered with single-digit participation rates in sororities and fraternities. There are 300 student organizations open to all students as well as hundreds more school-specific clubs (e.g., Stern-only, Tandon-only). Performance-based groups abound and often sport incredible alumni lists such as those from the Hammerkatz sketch comedy, Tisch New Theater, and WNYU radio. Plenty of quirky, niche options also are available such as the uber-popular Milk and Cookies Club. The university's Greenwich Village location means all that New York City has to offer is at your fingertips. International cuisine, Broadway shows, world-renowned museums, top musical and comedy acts, and shopping can all be part of your daily existence.

Career Services

The Wasserman Center for Career Development has 51 professional staff members who work in areas such as career counseling, recruitment, and student employment. That 576:1 student-to-advisor ratio is a bit higher than the average school featured in this guide. Catering to the career services needs of 29,401 undergrads is a massive task. Fortunately, NYU's staff is up to it, hosting large-scale events such as the Fall Job & Internship Fair as well as other industry-specific events throughout the year including real estate, nursing, government, and hospitality and tourism.

Of the employed members of the Class of 2022, 90% utilized Wasserman's resources. Among the resources rated "most helpful" by job/internship seekers were NYU CareerNet, NYU Connections, and the NYU On-Campus Recruiting Program. The top summer internship destinations include PwC, EY, Credit Suisse, Accenture, Barclay's, Bank of America, and Wells Fargo. A solid 52% of recent grads received two or more job offers. More than half a million alumni are situated in companies and organizations around the world, leaving no shortage of networking opportunities.

Professional Outcomes

Within six months of graduating, 94% of NYU Class of 2022 graduates had successfully landed at their next destination. Of that group, 78% were employed and 21% were in graduate school. The top industries for employment were healthcare (11%), internet and software (9%), finance (8%), and entertainment (8%). Large numbers of alumni can be found at major corporations such as Google, Deloitte, Morgan Stanley, Goldman Sachs, IBM, JP Morgan Chase, Citi, and Amazon. The mean starting salary is $76,336 with a mean signing bonus of $9,567. New York is (by more than ten times) the most popular destination over number two choice California. New Jersey, DC, and Massachusetts were next in attracting the highest numbers of recent alumni.

Of the 21% of the Class of 2022 attending graduate school, 17% were studying business, 15% were seeking degrees in the arts, sciences, and humanities, and 6% went to law school. Elite graduate and professional schools are very much within the grasp of an NYU alum, including the university's own top-ranked Stern School of Business, School of Law at New York University, and the School of Medicine at New York University (Langone). In 2023, there were 277 medical school applicants.

Admission

Acceptance rates at NYU have experienced a rapid decline in recent years. In 2013, a solid 35% of applicants were accepted; for the Class of 2026, that figure was just 12%. In total, the university received 100,662 applications for a place in the Class of 2026. This cohort boasted a mid-50% SAT score of 1470-1560, an all-time high for an incoming class at NYU; the ACT mid-50% range was 33-35. The average unweighted GPA was 3.8 and 95% of entering freshmen typically place in the top decile of their high school class; every single individual was at least in the top quartile.

The overwhelming volume of applicants makes an in-depth, personalized admissions process unfeasible. Rather, the committee relies primarily on hard numbers like GPA, class rank, and standardized test scores. Participation in a highly rigorous course load is also a must, and special talents/abilities are given serious consideration. NYU does offer an early decision round that yields more favorable acceptance rates than those in the regular round; however, they have been quite secretive about the hard numbers in recent years. Warning: This is a school where high school guidance counselors, thinking of NYU-bound students they worked with a few years ago, may not be aware of the increased selectivity demonstrated by the university in the last few years.

Worth Your Money?

NYU is not as generous with financial aid as many other elite schools that strive to meet 100% of demonstrated student need. In fact, only a small percentage of those who qualify for aid see all of their need met and the average annual grant for those found eligible is $43k. The overall cost of attendance is $90,222, and merit aid awards are extremely uncommon and typically for very low amounts. The university is an exceptional place to learn, but for $360k in total costs, you'll need to weigh your expected future salary (based on the field you intend to enter) versus the amount of debt you are willing to take on. Of course, if you are aiming to study at any New York City school, the living costs will be on the high side, but the benefits may be great.

FINANCIAL
Institutional Type: Private
In-State Tuition: $60,438
Out-of-State Tuition: $60,438
Room & Board: $24,102
Books & Supplies: $1,494

Avg. Need-Based Grant: $43,014
Avg. % of Need Met: 99%

Avg. Merit-Based Award: $28,536
% Receiving (Freshmen w/o Need): 6%

Avg. Cumulative Debt: $26,388
% of Students Borrowing: 33%

CAREER
Who Recruits
1. Infosys
2. BNP
3. Netflix
4. PayPal
5. Eileen Fisher

Notable Internships
1. United Nations
2. Credit Suisse
3. NYU Langone Health

Top Employers
1. Google
2. JPMorgan Chase
3. Citi
4. Morgan Stanley
5. Amazon

Where Alumni Work
1. New York City
2. Los Angeles
3. San Francisco
4. Washington, DC
5. Boston

Earnings
College Scorecard (10-YR Post-Entry): $79,812
PayScale (Early Career): $67,900
PayScale (Mid-Career): $132,100
PayScale 20-Year ROI: $698,000

RANKINGS
Money: 4
U.S. News: 35, National Universities
Wall Street Journal/THE: 166
Washington Monthly: 105, National Universities

OVERGENERALIZATIONS
Students are:
More likely to venture off campus
Politically liberal
Independent
Career-driven
Lacking community

COLLEGE OVERLAPS
Boston University
Cornell University
University of California, Berkeley
University of Michigan
University of Pennsylvania

North Carolina State University

Raleigh, North Carolina | 919-515-2434

ADMISSION
Admission Rate: 47%
Admission Rate - Men: 42%
Admission Rate - Women: 52%
EA Admission Rate: 48%
ED Admission Rate: Not Offered
ED Admits as % of Total Admits: Not Offered
Admission Rate (5-Year Trend): -4%
% of Admits Attending (Yield): 33%
Transfer Admission Rate: 46%

SAT Reading/Writing (Middle 50%): 620-700
SAT Math (Middle 50%): 625-740
ACT Composite (Middle 50%): 24-31

% Graduated in Top 10% of HS Class: 46%
% Graduated in Top 25% of HS Class: 85%
% Graduated in Top 50% of HS Class: 99%

Demonstrated Interest: Considered
Legacy Status: Considered
Racial/Ethnic Status: Considered
Admission Interview Offered: No

ENROLLMENT
Total Undergraduate Enrollment: 26,254
% Full-Time: 94%
% Male: 50%
% Female: 50%
% Out-of-State: 10%
% Fraternity: 11%
% Sorority: 15%
% On-Campus (All Undergraduate): 36%
Freshman Housing Required: Yes

% African-American: 6%
% Asian: 9%
% Hispanic: 8%
% White: 68%
% Other: 2%
% International: 3%
% Low-Income: 20%

ACADEMICS
Student-to-Faculty Ratio: 16 to 1
% of Classes Under 20: 37%
% of Classes 20-49: 46%
% of Classes 50 or More: 17%
% Full-Time Faculty: 85%
% Full-Time Faculty w/ Terminal Degree: 92%

Top Programs
Architecture
Agricultural Science
Animal Science
Design
Engineering
Fashion and Textile Management
Sport Management
Statistics

Retention Rate: 94%
4-Year Graduation Rate: 65%
6-Year Graduation Rate: 85%

Curricular Flexibility: Less Flexible
Academic Rating: ★★★✔

#CollegesWorthYourMoney

Of the University of North Carolina System's seventeen campuses, UNC-Chapel Hill, the flagship, understandably has the highest national profile by a wide margin. Yet, those in the know are aware that North Carolina State University (NC State) has emerged as a highly competitive and elite academic institution in its own right. Located in the state capital of Raleigh, NC State is at the heart of the Research Triangle—in fact, the school is one of its vertices, with the aforementioned UNC-Chapel Hill and Duke University accounting for the others. Some would be surprised to learn that among those enrolled in 2022, the median SAT score was 1340 and a typical entering class includes 200+ valedictorians and salutatorians.

Inside the Classroom
The general education program requires all students to conquer 39 credits of mandated coursework in the following areas: mathematical science, natural sciences, humanities, social sciences, health and exercise studies, US diversity, interdisciplinary studies, global studies, and technology fluency. Everyone also engages in an Introduction to Writing class and the demonstration of foreign language proficiency, but it's extremely easy to opt out of a foreign language if you choose, as long as you took two years of courses in the same language in high school.

Thanks to a reasonable 16:1 student-to-faculty ratio, you won't exclusively have classes in enormous lecture halls. Rather, NC State offers its undergraduates a mix of experiences with 64% of sections enrolling 29 or fewer students and 14% enrolling 50 or more. The Office of Undergraduate Research works diligently to connect star students to faculty research projects, which leads to over 600 student presentations at spring/summer poster sessions. The "Speed-Data-ing" program brings together 250 underclassmen to learn about current research being conducted by NC State professors. The university has put a good deal of emphasis on raising its study abroad participation rate in recent years, and those efforts have been fruitful; 20% of undergraduates now study abroad, and there has been a massive increase in participation by underrepresented students over the past decade.

Engineering is the most popular area of concentration as 24% of Class of 2022 graduates earned a degree in that field. Business/marketing comes in second at 17% followed by biology (10%) and agriculture (7%). NC State has an exceptional regional reputation and an expanding national one with the College of Engineering now found near the top of many rankings. Programs in design, architecture, and animal science are also very strong. Wolfpack members also are gaining the attention of the most prestigious postgraduate fellowship organizations. In a typical year, multiple students capture National Science Foundation Graduate Research Fellowships, Goldwater Scholarships, Fulbright Scholarships, and Gilman Scholarships.

Outside the Classroom
Freshmen overwhelmingly reside on campus; that figure was 97% in the 2022-23 school year. Among all undergraduates, just over one-third live on campus in one of twenty residence halls that are a mix of suite, hotel, and traditional buildings. Greek houses draw their fair share of the population with 15% of women joining sororities and 11% of men pledging fraternities. More than 550 athletes participate as part of the 23 varsity athletic teams that have combined to capture four national championships, including the legendary 1983 NCAA champion men's basketball team. Wolfpack fans are a rabid bunch, and they rank in the top ten for hoops attendance in the United States. The Talley Student Union is the central hub for 600+ student organizations including a daily newspaper, a popular college radio station, and plenty of cultural, performance-based, political, and pre-professional organizations. The school's 2,110-acre campus is within a few miles of many of Raleigh's finest attractions including North Carolina's state art, natural history, and history museums; multiple parks and arboretums; and the beautiful Lake Johnson Park.

Career Services
The NCSU Career Development Center employs 21 professionals who function as career identity coaches, career counselors, employer relations specialists, and pre-professional advisors. There are numerous other departments within individual colleges that employ another five career services staff members to bring the total of full-time, professional employees to twenty-three, which works out to a 1,250:1 student-to-advisor ratio, higher than the average school featured in this guidebook.

Still, 50% of recent grads reported receiving counseling in the Career Development Center, and the vast majority found the experience to be a positive one. A solid two-thirds of graduating seniors stated that their first job was "directly related" to their major, a sign that career counseling staff are pointing students in the right direction. In the Poole College of Management, the co-op/internship completion rate was 85%. Co-op participation is encouraged, and students can complete up to three alternating semesters of paid work experience. NC State offers 1,000 different work rotations, making it one of the largest university co-op programs in the country. Major employers are regular visitors to campus, and career expos such as the Engineering Career Fair, Poole College of Management Career & Internship Fair, and the Ag & Sciences Career Expo collectively draw hundreds of top hiring organizations to Raleigh. Being situated in the Triangle means that many big-time companies are nearby and loaded with Wolfpack alumni.

Professional Outcomes

Fifty-four percent of students graduating in May 2022 reported that they had already accepted full-time jobs before they even received their diplomas. Members of that class who obtained a full-time job reported an average starting salary of $62,024 (with a slightly higher median). Around 70% remain in the state of North Carolina for work, with a large percentage situated in the Research Triangle area of Raleigh, Durham, and Chapel Hill. San Francisco, DC, New York City, and Atlanta also attracted a fair number of graduates. Including all graduating years, the companies employing the largest number of Wolfpack alumni are Cisco, Red Hat, SAS (major NC-based software companies), IBM, Lenovo, Amazon, Microsoft, Intel, Google, Deloitte, Facebook, and Salesforce. Many recent graduates also work for the university itself and for the Wake County Public School System.

Upon graduation, 27% of Class of 2022 members indicated that their plan was to attend graduate/professional school. In past years, close to half of all grads continue their educational journey at NC State, and 70% attend a school in North Carolina. An encouraging 88% of recent graduates stated that they were attending their first-choice institution. The most commonly pursued degree was a master's (67%) followed by a professional degree (18%) and a doctoral degree (15%). Each year, roughly 300 NC State students apply to medical school and another 150 to dental school. Recent med school acceptances include prestigious programs at Duke, UNC-Chapel Hill, UVA, Wake Forest, and Emory. Between 75 and 80% of those recommended by the Health Professions Advising Center are accepted into at least one medical school. Law candidates find similar positive results, and schools like Yale, Duke, UNC-Chapel Hill, and Washington & Lee regularly visit NC State to recruit.

Admission

The present iteration of NC State is highly selective, which may come as a shock even to an older relative who attended the university. In fact, the 25th percentile SAT score of attending freshmen in 2022-23 is close to the 75th percentile figure from a decade prior. The acceptance rate is now 47%, and the applicant pool is more competitive than ever. Those attending possess impressive mid-50% standardized test ranges of 24-31 on the ACT and 1260-1420 on the SAT, with a similar number of students submitting results from both exams. They also earned the grades to match those test scores with an average GPA of 3.84. A solid 46% hailed from the top 10% of their high school class, and 85% placed in the top quartile.

With more than 35,000 applicants annually, NC State admissions officers rely heavily on factors like SAT scores, GPA, class rank, and the rigor of one's course load. Most other factors are mere considerations, unlikely to exert significant influence on the decision. There are no early action or early decision options at NC State, but we recommend that every serious applicant submits by the Nov. 1 priority deadline rather than waiting until mid-January. Thirty-three percent of those accepted ultimately enroll in the school compared with over 50% in 2000 when the school drew one-third as many applicants. Despite the lower yield rate, it is fair to say that NC State is a more desirable landing spot than ever for high-achieving North Carolina residents.

Worth Your Money?

When an annual tuition bill is in the four figures, it instantly qualifies as an absurd bargain. NC State's tuition is actually around one-sixth the cost of North Carolina private schools like Duke, Davidson, or Wake Forest. For the roughly 15% of Wolfpack members not from in state, thanks to low housing costs, the total cost of attendance is not obscene, coming in at under $50k. Therefore, the value of this degree for a nonresident would be context-dependent—engineering, computer science, and design students are more than likely to see favorable returns. For a resident, it's a no-brainer investment.

FINANCIAL
Institutional Type: Public
In-State Tuition: $9,105
Out-of-State Tuition: $31,976
Room & Board: $13,719
Books & Supplies: $869

Avg. Need-Based Grant: $10,883
Avg. % of Need Met: 76%

Avg. Merit-Based Award: $5,032
% Receiving (Freshmen w/o Need): 7%

Avg. Cumulative Debt: $24,042
% of Students Borrowing: 47%

CAREER
Who Recruits
1. John Deere
2. Smithfield
3. GSK
4. Allstate
5. SAS

Notable Internships
1. Barclays
2. Red Hat
3. Cisco

Top Employers
1. Cisco
2. SAS
3. IBM
4. Lenovo
5. Red Hat

Where Alumni Work
1. Raleigh
2. Charlotte
3. Winston-Salem, NC
4. Washington, DC
5. San Francisco

Earnings
College Scorecard (10-YR Post-Entry): $65,211
PayScale (Early Career): $62,200
PayScale (Mid-Career): $114,200
PayScale 20-Year ROI: $638,000

RANKINGS
Money: 4.5
U.S. News: 60, National Universities
Wall Street Journal/THE: 106
Washington Monthly: 85, National Universities

OVERGENERALIZATIONS
Students are:
Crazy about the Wolfpack
Decided upon their chosen major
Competitive
Career-driven
Politically balanced

COLLEGE OVERLAPS
Clemson University
Pennsylvania State University - University Park
University of North Carolina at Chapel Hill
University of South Carolina
Virginia Tech

Northeastern University

ADMISSION
Admission Rate: 7%
Admission Rate - Men: 6%
Admission Rate - Women: 8%
EA Admission Rate: Not Reported
ED Admission Rate: 33%
ED Admits as % of Total Admits: 14%
Admission Rate (5-Year Trend): -20%
% of Admits Attending (Yield): 41%
Transfer Admission Rate: 30%

SAT Reading/Writing (Middle 50%): 700-760
SAT Math (Middle 50%): 740-790
ACT Composite (Middle 50%): 33-35

% Graduated in Top 10% of HS Class: 76%
% Graduated in Top 25% of HS Class: 95%
% Graduated in Top 50% of HS Class: 99%

Demonstrated Interest: Considered
Legacy Status: Not Considered
Racial/Ethnic Status: Considered
Admission Interview Offered: No

ENROLLMENT
Total Undergraduate Enrollment: 20,980
% Full-Time: 100%
% Male: 44%
% Female: 56%
% Out-of-State: 73%
% Fraternity: 10%
% Sorority: 15%
% On-Campus (All Undergraduate): 47%
Freshman Housing Required: Yes

% African-American: 6%
% Asian: 19%
% Hispanic: 11%
% White: 42%
% Other: 1%
% International: 14%
% Low-Income: 12%

ACADEMICS
Student-to-Faculty Ratio: 16 to 1
% of Classes Under 20: 66%
% of Classes 20-49: 28%
% of Classes 50 or More: 7%
% Full-Time Faculty: 73%
% Full-Time Faculty w/ Terminal Degree: 94%

Top Programs
Communication Studies
Computer Science
Criminal Justice
Engineering
Environmental and Sustainability Sciences
International Affairs
Neuroscience
Nursing

Retention Rate: 98%
4-Year Graduation Rate: 0%
6-Year Graduation Rate: 90%

Curricular Flexibility: Somewhat Flexible
Academic Rating: ★★★★✦

#CollegesWorthYourMoney

If Northeastern University was a middle-aged person headed to a twentieth high school reunion, it would easily earn the distinction of the least recognized individual in the room. Few institutions have undergone such a substantial metamorphosis in such a short time. Beginning in the 1990s, NU decided to reverse-engineer the US News rankings and make a grab for increased prestige. At the time, the school was ranked the 162nd-best university in the nation. By 2020, it had cracked the top fifty. Today, the average undergraduate student possesses a 4.2 GPA and better than a 1487 on the SAT, literally 400+ points higher than two decades ago. You read that correctly—400 points!

Inside the Classroom
On the menu for this suddenly top-flight breed of undergrads are all the trappings of a major research university, including 290 majors and 180 combined majors available at Northeastern's nine colleges and programs. All students are required to walk the NUpath, the school's core curriculum that is "built around essential, broad-based knowledge and skills—such as understanding societies and analyzing data—integrated with specific content areas and disciplines." There are eleven components to the NUpath that involve forays into the natural and designed world, creative expression and innovation, culture, formal and quantitative reasoning, societies and institutions, analyzing data, differences and diversity, ethical reasoning, writing across audiences, integrating knowledge and skills through experience, and a capstone course as you near completion of your chosen major(s).

More than two-thirds of Husky classrooms contain nineteen or fewer students, and 11% have single-digit enrollments. Large lecture hall courses crammed with undergrads are rare at this school—only 6% of sections sport a student enrollment of fifty or more. A well-deployed 16:1 student-to-faculty ratio makes these cozy class sizes possible. Since 2006, Northeastern has added an incredible 650+ tenured and tenure-track faculty members. Undergraduate research opportunities exist in all departments, and experiential learning of some type is had by virtually all graduates, thanks to the school's illustrious and robust co-op program. NU students have not only become more accomplished but also more worldly. In a given year, 3,800+ students have a global experience in one of 80+ countries, and 500+ students participate in a co-op program overseas.

The D'Amore-McKim School of Business is a top-ranked school and offers one of the best international business programs anywhere, and both the College of Engineering and College of Computer Science are highly respected as well. Criminal justice, architecture, and nursing are three other majors that rate near the top nationally. Business/marketing (24%) and engineering (20%) account for the largest percentage of degrees conferred. Health-related professions (9%), biology (9%), and the social sciences (8%) round out the list of most popular majors. Northeastern grads are faring better than ever in procuring nationally competitive scholarships these days. In recent years, students have taken home Fulbright Scholarships as well as National Science Foundation Graduate Research Fellowships.

Outside the Classroom
Northeastern is split down the middle in terms of those who live in on-campus housing and those who do not. All freshmen and sophomores are required to live in the dorms, and most have at least one or two roommates. Campus offers six large quad areas and twenty eateries. Greek life is fairly strong with 10% of men and 15% of women joining frats and sororities. The 73-acre urban campus is situated in the true heart of downtown Boston and within one mile of Fenway Park, Newbury Street, and the Museum of Fine Arts. With such a premier location, the beloved city of Boston is truly an extension of your campus, but there are also plenty of university-sponsored activities to keep you busy. Out of 500 student clubs and organizations, the Northeastern University Hus-skiers and Outing Club (NUHOC), student government, and 40 club sports teams are among the most popular. In total, 3,000 students participate in club and intramural sports. Spectator sports are not a focal point of NU life—the football program was dissolved in 2009— but of the sixteen existing NCAA Division I squads, the Huskies hockey team reigns supreme. The spirit of volunteerism is huge at NU as students have contributed a collective 1.4 million+ hours since 2006.

Career Services
Twenty-six counselors, employer relations specialists, and experiential learning coordinators comprise the NU Employer Engagement and Career Design Office (EECD), which doesn't count admin assistants or IT professionals. Working out to a student-to-advisor ratio of 627:1, NU offers a high level of support for an institution with more than 16,000 undergraduates. Northeastern University has long held a reputation as one of the premier career services providers in the nation, and it's not hard to see why.

Career counselors receive incredibly high reviews from students as 96% report progress on their career goals after only one session; 100% felt it was worth their time to return for a follow-up. The EECD has forged relationships with over 3,000 employers and, through its employer-in-residence program, representatives from those organizations spend up to one day per week for an entire year interacting with students, making personal connections, and offering career tips. A typical Fall Career Fair is attended by 260 employers and the Spring Engineering and Technology Career Fair usually draws 4,000+ students and 140 companies. Perhaps the most impactful role of this office is to facilitate co-op placements. Ninety-five percent of NU graduates spend at least one semester in a co-op placement, and 50% of students receive a job offer from their co-op partner; 3,000+ employers participate each year.

Professional Outcomes

Nine months after leaving Northeastern, 97% of students have landed at their next employment or graduate school destination. Huskies entering the job market are quickly rounded up by the likes of State Street, Fidelity Investments, IBM, and Amazon, all of whom employ 500+ Northeastern alums. Between 200 and 500 employees at Wayfair, Google, Amazon, Oracle, IBM, and Apple have an NU lineage. Whether or not they originally hailed from New England, the vast majority of graduates remain in the Greater Boston area. Next in popularity are New York City, San Francisco, DC, Los Angeles, Philadelphia, and Seattle. Starting salaries are above average (55% make more than $60k), in part due to the stellar co-op program, and compensation is in the same range as other highly selective schools including Fordham and Boston University.

The five graduate schools most frequently attended by NU grads include Boston University, Columbia University, Harvard, NYU, and Northeastern University itself. The highly ranked Northeastern University School of Law also takes a large number of its own undergraduates. More than one alum is currently enrolled at such law schools as Wake Forest, Brooklyn Law School, and Boston College. While Northeastern does not have its own medical college, many graduates go on to attend top institutions. Multiple recent grads are currently attending such medical schools as UMass, Harvard, UConn, and Tufts. The medical school acceptance rate is 73%, significantly better than the national average.

Admission

Only 7% of the 91,000 applicants vying for a place in the 2022-23 freshman class received a letter of acceptance. Among those who submitted test scores, the mid-50% SAT was 1450-1535 and the ACT range was 33-35. Slightly over three-quarters of those enrolled placed in the top 10% of their high school class. A decade ago, the school received only 34,000 applications, and a far less menacing 41% were let through the door. Freshmen in 2009-10 possessed middle 50% SAT scores of 1200-1370. Any way you measure it, the level of selectivity is far greater than even in the most recent past.

An applicant's GPA, rigor of courses, standardized test scores, essays, and recommendation letters are all categorized as "very important" admissions factors by this committee. Admissions officers at Northeastern place soft factors such as extracurricular activities, talent/ability, character, personal qualities, volunteer work, and work experience on the next rung of "important" categories. Northeastern's desirability and prestige have risen at a lightning pace, making it exactly the type of school that even a well-intentioned school counselor or parent can easily misjudge in terms of the current odds of gaining admission. This is a school that generally only accepts students with standardized test scores in the top 2% and who have virtually flawless transcripts. Applying via binding early decision is definitely a serious consideration. Of the 2,707 who did so last year, 33% were successful.

Worth Your Money?

Northeastern has a list price cost of attendance in excess of $86,000 per year, and the need-based aid situation was less than ideal in the past. However, the Northeastern Promise, a pledge to meet 100% of demonstrated need, has resulted in over 330 million dollars per year in financial aid awards. In short, this school is worth your money if you are aiming to enter a high-paying field and/or have parents who can afford the hefty tuition payments. Then, the connections the school provides are worth a substantial amount. However, middle-class students set on entering public service would likely not see their investment returned and could accumulate a good deal of debt along the way.

FINANCIAL
Institutional Type: Private
In-State Tuition: $63,141
Out-of-State Tuition: $63,141
Room & Board: $20,880
Books & Supplies: $1,000

Avg. Need-Based Grant: $40,623
Avg. % of Need Met: 100%

Avg. Merit-Based Award: $14,204
% Receiving (Freshmen w/o Need): 30%

Avg. Cumulative Debt: $32,559
% of Students Borrowing: 46%

CAREER
Who Recruits
1. IBM
2. Siemens
3. Staples
4. Coleman
5. Northwestern Mutual

Notable Internships
1. Wayfair
2. Vogue
3. Tesla

Top Employers
1. State Street
2. Fidelity Investments
3. Amazon
4. IBM
5. Wayfair

Where Alumni Work
1. Boston
2. New York City
3. San Francisco
4. Washington, DC
5. Los Angeles

Earnings
College Scorecard (10-YR Post-Entry): $88,842
PayScale (Early Career): $69,200
PayScale (Mid-Career): $115,600
PayScale 20-Year ROI: $729,000

RANKINGS
Money: 4.5
U.S. News: 53, National Universities
Wall Street Journal/THE: 138
Washington Monthly: 139, National Universities

OVERGENERALIZATIONS
Students are:
Career-driven
Diverse
Independent
More likely to venture off campus
Less connected to each other

COLLEGE OVERLAPS
Boston University
Cornell University
George Washington University
New York University
University of Michigan

Northwestern University

Evanston, Illinois | 847-491-7271

ADMISSION
Admission Rate: 7%
Admission Rate - Men: 7%
Admission Rate - Women: 7%
EA Admission Rate: Not Offered
ED Admission Rate: 22%
ED Admits as % of Total Admits: 30%
Admission Rate (5-Year Trend): -2%
% of Admits Attending (Yield): 55%
Transfer Admission Rate: 13%

SAT Reading/Writing (Middle 50%): 730-770
SAT Math (Middle 50%): 760-800
ACT Composite (Middle 50%): 33-35

% Graduated in Top 10% of HS Class: 96%
% Graduated in Top 25% of HS Class: 99%
% Graduated in Top 50% of HS Class: 100%

Demonstrated Interest: Considered
Legacy Status: Considered
Racial/Ethnic Status: Considered
Admission Interview Offered: Yes

ENROLLMENT
Total Undergraduate Enrollment: 8,659
% Full-Time: 99%
% Male: 46%
% Female: 54%
% Out-of-State: 74%
% Fraternity: 12%
% Sorority: 13%
% On-Campus (All Undergraduate): 55%
Freshman Housing Required: Yes

% African-American: 7%
% Asian: 21%
% Hispanic: 14%
% White: 37%
% Other: 3%
% International: 11%
% Low-Income: 20%

ACADEMICS
Student-to-Faculty Ratio: 7 to 1
% of Classes Under 20: 78%
% of Classes 20-49: 16%
% of Classes 50 or More: 7%
% Full-Time Faculty: 88%
% Full-Time Faculty w/ Terminal Degree: 98%

Top Programs
Biology
Communication Studies
Economics
Engineering
Journalism
Performing Arts
Political Science
Social Policy

Retention Rate: 98%
4-Year Graduation Rate: 87%
6-Year Graduation Rate: 95%

Curricular Flexibility: Somewhat Flexible
Academic Rating: ★★★★★

#CollegesWorthYourMoney

Like the neighboring University of Chicago, Northwestern University is a highly selective academic institution that operates on a quarter system and is located in Illinois, but the similarities end there. Where UChicago has a reputation as a breeding ground for future academics/researchers, Northwestern's vibe is more pre-professional, athletic, and Greek-inclined, but the 8,659 undergraduates who attend must bring equally flawless academic credentials to the table—otherwise, they will find themselves among the 93% of applicants left outside the gates.

Inside the Classroom

Northwestern is home to six undergraduate schools: Weinberg College of Arts and Sciences; McCormick School of Engineering and Applied Science; School of Education and Social Policy; School of Communication; Medill School of Journalism, Media, Integrated Marketing Communications; and Bienen School of Music. Academic requirements vary by school. Weinberg, which enrolls half of all Wildcats, requires two first-year seminars, the demonstration of proficiency in a foreign language and in writing as well as two courses each in six intellectual divisions. Overall, coursework requirements are extensive but do allow for choice.

The quarter system allows students to take four courses at a time rather than the typical five. Even so, the academic demands are intense, and Northwestern students work hard for their grades. Fortunately, the academic experience is far from an anonymous endeavor. The university has a phenomenal 6:1 student-faculty ratio, and a spectacular 45% of class sections have nine or fewer students enrolled; 78% have fewer than twenty enrollees. Faculty receive generally favorable reviews from undergraduate students and are rated as being highly accessible outside of the classroom. Fifty-seven percent of recent grads had the chance to conduct research with a faculty member at some point during their undergraduate years.

The social sciences account for the greatest numbers of degrees conferred (19%), followed by communications/journalism (13%), engineering (11%), biology (7%), computer science (7%), the visual and performing arts (7%), and psychology (7%). Medill is widely regarded as one of the country's best journalism schools. The McCormick School of Engineering also achieves top rankings, along with programs in economics, social policy, and theatre. Students from all majors bring home prestigious postgraduate fellowships at an enviable rate. In 2022 alone, the school produced 17 Fulbright Scholars and four Goldwater Scholars. In total, Wildcats take home a ridiculous 200+ competitive national/global scholarships per year.

Outside the Classroom

Northwestern, like its elite peers Duke, Stanford, and USC, offers top-level academics without sacrificing any of the major college frills like football and frat parties. With the recent lifting of a temporary Greek ban, fraternities and sororities now again exert a significant degree of influence over the social scene. Athletics are also a strong part of the university's culture with eight men's and eleven women's teams competing in NCAA Division I. The Wildcats are the lone private school competing in the Big Ten Conference, which is otherwise made up of athletic powerhouses like Penn State, Ohio State, and Michigan. NU undergrads report that 92% are "deeply involved" with a student organization or athletic team. Nearly half the student population reported that same level of involvement with a community service project. Of the school's almost 480 student-run clubs, pre-professional organizations, service-oriented groups, and The Daily Northwestern—named the nation's top student paper by the Society of Professional Journalists—are among the most popular. Evanston is roughly thirty to forty-five minutes from downtown Chicago (depending on traffic). One of the famous North Shore suburbs of Chicago, Evanston is an affluent city with plenty of high-end restaurants and coffee shops. Natural beauty is easy to find as the school owns a lakefront beach that is on campus. More than half of students (and 99% of freshmen) elect to live in on-campus housing, which is highlighted by 16 residence halls, each accommodating anywhere from 25-500 students.

Career Services

Northwestern Career Advancement (NCA) employs 20 full-time professionals who work directly with or on behalf of undergraduate students. That includes career counselors, career advisors, and employer relations staff but does not include graduate advisors, interns, or IT specialists. The student-to-advisor ratio of 433:1 puts NU in the average range compared to other institutions included in this book. Career counselors keep extensive walk-in hours and arrange a number of career-related events, large and small, from the two-day Fall Internship and Job Fair with over 150 employers to more intimate workshops and employer information sessions that are held throughout the year.

A phenomenal 89% of graduates reported they engaged in at least one experiential learning opportunity. When looking specifically at internships, 71% reported landing at least one summer of paid or unpaid experience. The Northwestern Network Mentorship Program now has 5,000 alumni across ninety industries and sixty-six countries ready and willing to help current students with their career planning. The NCA has corporate partnerships with a host of top-notch companies including Accenture, Deloitte, PwC, Capital One, and JP Morgan.

Professional Outcomes

Six months after graduating, 69% of the Class of 2022 had found employment, 27% were in graduate school, and only 2% were still looking for work. The four professional fields attracting more than 10% of Wildcat alumni were consulting (18%), engineering (18%), business/finance (16%), and communications/marketing/media (13%). Employers included an impressive group of media outlets including the BBC, NBC News, *The Washington Post*, and NPR. Across all other industries, Wildcats had strong representation at all of the usual corporate giants including Boeing, Google, IBM, Deloitte, PepsiCo, Northrop Grumman, and Goldman Sachs. More than 50% of graduates remained in the Midwest. Across all majors, the average starting salary was $73k; engineering and applied sciences students averaged $92k and the lowest income belonged to communications students who earned $61k.

Of the recent alums headed straight to graduate school, 18% were pursuing medical degrees, 13% were beginning PhD programs, and 6% were entering law school. Engineering, medicine, and business were the three most popular graduate areas of concentration. Recent grads have pursued advanced degrees at all eight Ivy League schools. Stanford, MIT, Carnegie Mellon, UChicago, and Oxford were among a host of other elite institutions. Northwestern is a prolific producer of future MDs; 241 applied in the 2022-23 school year alone.

Admission

Continuing a decade-long decline in acceptance rates, Northwestern matched its all-time low of 7% for the Class of 2026. The profile of the average freshman in the 2022-23 school year was a mid-50% SAT of 1500-1560 and an ACT of 33-35. A decade ago, when 26% of applicants were accepted, the ACT range was a significantly lower 30-32. The percentage of freshmen in the top 10% of their high school class also increased during that time, jumping from 85% to 96%.

According to the admissions office, rigor of courses, GPA, and class rank are among the eight factors that are "very important" in the admissions process. Ordinarily, standardized tests also enter this stratosphere of importance, but they were not weighted equally during the pandemic. Last year, early decision applicants comprised 53% of the incoming classes and enjoyed increased chances of getting in with a 22% acceptance rate in the ED round. Northwestern has always been a highly selective school, but the bar has been raised even higher in recent years. Those who wish to find a home on this picturesque North Shore campus next fall must bring excellent credentials to the table and should strongly consider applying early decision.

Worth Your Money?

The average Northwestern graduate who took out loans owes $34k, which is a tad more than the national average. This is to be expected at a school that costs roughly $91,000 per year and does not award much merit aid. Yet, 45% of undergraduates do receive financial aid and the university meets 100% of demonstrated need. With very few exceptions, this is a school worth paying for. Even in programs such as journalism that do not generally lead to high-paying first jobs, the networks you will gain at Northwestern are likely to end up paying career dividends many decades down the road.

FINANCIAL
Institutional Type: Private
In-State Tuition: $65,997
Out-of-State Tuition: $65,997
Room & Board: $20,334
Books & Supplies: $1,686

Avg. Need-Based Grant: $60,889
Avg. % of Need Met: 100%

Avg. Merit-Based Award: $9,028
% Receiving (Freshmen w/o Need): 3%

Avg. Cumulative Debt: $34,309
% of Students Borrowing: 29%

CAREER
Who Recruits
1. Nielsen
2. Aldi
3. AQR
4. Roland Berger
5. Flow Traders

Notable Internships
1. Brookings Institute
2. HSBC
3. BlackRock

Top Employers
1. Google
2. Accenture
3. Amazon
4. Microsoft
5. Deloitte

Where Alumni Work
1. Chicago
2. New York City
3. San Francisco
4. Los Angeles
5. Washington, DC

Earnings
College Scorecard (10-YR Post-Entry): $85,796
PayScale (Early Career): $68,800
PayScale (Mid-Career): $128,000
PayScale 20-Year ROI: $765,000

RANKINGS
Money: 4
U.S. News: 9, National Universities
Wall Street Journal/THE: 25
Washington Monthly: 31, National Universities

OVERGENERALIZATIONS
Students are:
Working hard and playing hard
Career-driven
Over-achievers
Busy
Less likely to interact with different types of students

COLLEGE OVERLAPS
Cornell University
Duke University
University of Chicago
University of Michigan
University of Pennsylvania

Oberlin College

Oberlin, Ohio | 440-775-8411

A Midwestern version of Oregon's Reed College in terms of the originality and progressive leanings of the student body, Oberlin College in Ohio is an extremely strong provider of a liberal arts education. Known primarily for its top-ranked Conservatory of Music and as a factory for future PhDs, particularly in the hard sciences, Oberlin enrolls 2,986 undergraduates. Boasting over 40 majors, the college provides an educational setting where professors in just about all of your classes will not only know your name but, amazingly, perhaps even your goals and interests.

Inside the Classroom
As part of the curriculum exploration requirement, two courses each are required in each of the college's three divisions: Arts & Humanities, Mathematics & Natural Sciences, and the Social Sciences. Two of the thirty-two total courses taken must be classified as writing and another two as meeting the Quantitative & Formal Reasoning requirement. Three additional courses must have a Cultural Diversity designation. Students are encouraged—but not required—to become proficient in a foreign language. Overall, Oberlin's mandated coursework is not cumbersome, especially compared to many liberal arts schools of its ilk.

Thanks to its almost entirely undergraduate student population, the effects of Oberlin's 9:1 student-to-faculty ratio are fully felt. Of all the courses at the college, 79% had 19 or fewer students enrolled, and professors are generous with their time in an academic environment conducive to the formation of mentorships. Undergraduate research opportunities are not hard to locate. In fact, according to the school, "Many students coauthor articles with faculty, which are published in scholarly journals and presented at national meetings." The Office of Study Away helps arrange for 300 students per year to study in a foreign land. School-run opportunities such as Oberlin-in-London are on the table as are 100 affiliated programs.

The greatest number of degrees conferred are typically in music, political science, biology, psychology, and history. The Conservatory of Music has a worldwide reputation as one or more of its representative alumni are in every major ensemble in the United States. Programs in the natural sciences have sterling reputations, leading to remarkable medical school acceptance rates and the aforementioned number of future PhD scientists and researchers. Highly competitive postgraduate fellowship-granting organizations adore Oberlin grads. In 2023, thirteen grads and alumni were named Fulbright Scholars, and the school routinely produces Gilman, Critical Language, Goldwater, and Marshall winners as well.

Outside the Classroom
If you understand Oberlin's vibe it will not surprise you that there are no frats or sororities on campus. Instead, Oberlin requires students to live in either college-owned housing or student-run co-ops all the way through graduation. Some co-ops offer "theme living" centered on commonalities such as an obsession with sci-fi, disability status, sustainability/environmental concerns, or a love of ancient Mediterranean culture. With more than 175 clubs and organizations, 21 varsity teams, and dozens of intramural and club sports, just about every one of Oberlin's undergraduate students is involved in something. The Yeomen and Yeowomen compete within NCAA Division III with 350 athletes competing at that level. If you happen to like live classical music, you're in luck—the school's conservatory puts on hundreds of concerts each year. Guest speakers, often intellectuals and authors, regularly attract large crowds at Oberlin. There are a wealth of organizations catering to political/social causes and musical/theatrical performance as well as seven student-run publications. To generalize, most Oberlin students are politically liberal and enjoy challenging social norms. Most students stick around campus, and the small town of Oberlin's quaintness is best exemplified by its claim of having one of the last single-screen movie theaters in the country. For those with access to a car, Cleveland is only a forty-minute drive away.

Career Services
The Career Development Center employs eight professional staff members who work in career development or graduate school advising (not counting technical support or administrative assistants). With a 373:1 student-to-advisor ratio, Oberlin provides an average level of career services support than many comparable liberal arts schools featured in this guide. While the office does encourage one-on-one appointments and walk-ins, large-scale events like career fairs are lacking, and on-campus recruiting by major employers is not a routine occurrence.

Oberlin College

E-mail: college.admissions@oberlin.edu | Website: oberlin.edu

Beginning a few years ago, Oberlin began hosting Career Communities covering nine sectors (e.g., entrepreneurship and innovation, professions in music, and science and technology). Up to thirty juniors and seniors can join each community, which includes a guaranteed summer internship and a set of industry-specific mentors. Each community meets as a group six times per semester. Oberlin helps to arrange summer and winter term internships for all interested students, primarily through the use of its online resources. The Oberlin Alumni Database is a platform from which current students can seek job advice from alumni. The office also recommends connecting with thousands of alumni via LinkedIn. New programs such as the Career Communities show Oberlin's commitment to expanding its career services offerings.

Professional Outcomes

Recent graduates found employment within six months of graduating at a 74% clip; 17% enrolled in graduate school, and just 5% were still seeking employment. Multiple recent grads were hired by Google, Netflix, and Sony Pictures. In part because so many students go on to enter careers in research and academia, median salaries are quite low in the early career stage of life. However, it is important to note that many Oberlin graduates do go on to remunerative careers. New York is home to the highest number of alumni followed by San Francisco, Cleveland, DC, and Boston.

Over the last few years, multiple students have gone on to pursue advanced degrees at Harvard, Stanford, MIT, Brown, Columbia, Princeton, and the University of Michigan. Graduates fare well in gaining acceptance into med school, sporting a 70% success rate, far above the national average. Recent grads have enrolled in medical school at the University of Pennsylvania, Baylor College of Medicine, and SUNY Upstate Medical University. Law school applicants have enjoyed a 97% acceptance rate and have found homes at the likes of Yale, Indiana, and Wake Forest. Oberlin also has a reputation for churning out future PhDs and, in fact, is among the top 20 schools (per capita) across all disciplines in producing graduates who go on to earn their doctoral degrees.

Admission

Thirty-five percent of the 11,066 applicants for a place in the Class of 2026 were successful, but that number doesn't fully tell the story of how competitive the Oberlin admissions process really is. Twenty-three percent of those accepted went on to enroll in the college. Of those who joined the college, the mid-50% SAT was roughly 1360-1530, the ACT range was 30-33, and 53% placed in the top decile of their graduating class. The average weighted GPA was 3.7 and approximately half of freshmen possessed a 3.75 or better GPA.

GPA, class rank, and the rigor of one's secondary school record are the three factors weighted most heavily in the process. Secondary factors include essays, recommendations, talent/ability, character/personal qualities, and the seemingly polar opposite categories of legacy and first-generation status. Over the last five years, those who apply via early decision enjoy a 66% acceptance rate and account for roughly one-third of each incoming class. Oberlin is definitely a college where the self-selecting applicant pool results in a deceptively high acceptance rate. Make no mistake—you need to bring extremely strong grades to the table (only a small percentage of enrolled high school freshmen possessed GPAs under 3.25). Applying early is a worthwhile maneuver for those clamoring to spend the next four years in rural Ohio at this liberal arts gem.

Worth Your Money?

Oberlin is in the exclusive club of colleges that meets 100% of all undergraduates' demonstrated need. Last year, the school administered some form of aid to 80% of undergrads with an average grant of $32,000. With an annual cost of attendance of $83,588, those "discounts" are most appreciated, especially because many graduates pursue careers that are not among the most lucrative and/or require many additional years of education beyond the bachelor's degree. Admitted students should consider their future plans before committing. However, Oberlin's top-notch academics and generous aid make it a worthy investment for most.

FINANCIAL
Institutional Type: Private
In-State Tuition: $64,646
Out-of-State Tuition: $64,646
Room & Board: $18,942
Books & Supplies: $1,908

Avg. Need-Based Grant: $45,718
Avg. % of Need Met: 100%

Avg. Merit-Based Award: $18,794
% Receiving (Freshmen w/o Need): 38%

Avg. Cumulative Debt: $30,446
% of Students Borrowing: 45%

CAREER
Who Recruits
1. Cleveland Clinic
2. Sony Pictures
3. City Year
4. Epic
5. Microsoft

Notable Internships
1. Gotham Group
2. Colgate-Palmolive
3. Fidelity Investments

Top Employers
1. Google
2. Apple
3. Amazon
4. Microsoft
5. IBM

Where Alumni Work
1. New York City
2. San Francisco
3. Cleveland
4. Boston
5. Washington, DC

Earnings
College Scorecard (10-YR Post-Entry): $52,483
PayScale (Early Career): $58,000
PayScale (Mid-Career): $103,900
PayScale 20-Year ROI: $259,000

RANKINGS
Money: 3.5
U.S. News: 51, Liberal Arts Colleges
Wall Street Journal/THE: Not Ranked
Washington Monthly: 111, Liberal Arts Colleges

OVERGENERALIZATIONS
Students are:
Environmentally conscious
Politically liberal
Politically active
Quirky
Hippies or hipsters

COLLEGE OVERLAPS
Grinnell College
Kenyon College
Macalester College
Vassar College
Wesleyan University

Occidental College

Los Angeles, California | 323-259-2700

A rare liberal arts dynamo in an urban setting, Occidental College, one of the oldest schools on the West Coast, is home to 1,942 undergraduate students. Situated only eight miles from downtown Los Angeles, Occidental attracts a diverse set of talented and community-oriented young people. Non-higher-education aficionados may have first heard of the college when Barack Obama burst onto the political scene; he attended the school through sophomore year before transferring to Columbia University. Along with the Claremont Colleges, the school known affectionately as Oxy is among the best liberal arts institutions west of the Mississippi.

Inside the Classroom

Forty-five majors, minors, and programs are on tap, but all students must plow through the Oxy Core Program, which is designed to "encourage critical thinking, problem-solving, effective communication and productive engagement with issues of difference, diversity and community." Before students even arrive on campus, they must complete a summer reading assignment centered on an annual theme. Once class commences, students engage in the Cultural Studies Program, two small seminar courses intended to introduce students to collegiate-level writing and discourse.

Oxy offers an enviable 9:1 student-to-faculty ratio and an average class size of 19 students. Only one class contained over 40 students, and 95% enrolled fewer than thirty. The Undergraduate Research Center facilitates a plethora of hands-on experiences including a ten-week mentored summer program and limitless chances to pursue independent and course-based academic research during the regular school year. At the end of the summer, 100+ students present their research findings. Over two-thirds of undergraduates become global citizens during their time at Occidental through international internships and fellowships or through participation in the study abroad program. Faculty-led programs are available at a variety of destinations around the globe including Italy, Costa Rica, China, the Czech Republic, and Austria. Its partnership with the United Nations provides a one-of-a-kind opportunity for a cohort of students to live in New York, intern at the UN, and take courses with Occidental professors at the same time.

The most popular degree programs at Oxy, all of which carry strong reputations with employers and top-tier graduate schools, are economics, biology, sociology, psychology, diplomacy and world affairs, mathematics, and urban and environmental policy. Over 30% of all degrees conferred are in the social sciences, 11% are in biology, and 10% are in the visual and performing arts. Prestigious postgraduate scholarship programs look kindly on those with a degree from Oxy. Ten Rhodes Scholars graduated from the school that has been a top ten producer of Fulbright Fellowships for the last decade; six seniors/alumni took home Fulbrights in 2023 alone.

Outside the Classroom

Hardly your typical urban campus, Occidental's 120 acres are among the most notably beautiful higher education homes in the entire country. Countless Hollywood productions (e.g., Clueless, 90210) have selected Occidental as a filming location. The amenities are more in line with a private resort than a typical college. It features a 25,000-square-foot facility only for tennis, a thirty-four-meter-deep pool only for water polo, and dining services that serve restaurant-quality cuisine. Four-fifths of the student population resides in one of the school's 13 residence halls, and there are seven Greek organizations that attract a modest membership. Roughly 25% of undergrads compete on one of 20 NCAA Division III sports teams. Tigers also have the option of joining eight club sports teams or any number of intramural athletic leagues. A full array of student organizations exists as well—over 100—with everything from Oxy TV to a microfinance club. Wandering off campus and into the Eagle Rock and Highland Park sections of Northeast Los Angeles provides easily accessible entertainment, and downtown LA is only a short drive away, which is relevant because 60% of Oxy students bring a car to school. In addition, destinations including Venice Beach and Disneyland are less than an hour away.

Career Services

The Hameetman Career Center (HCC) has four full-time professional staff members working in career advising, pre-health advising, and national/international fellowship application guidance. The HCC's 486:1 student-to-advisor ratio is better than average when compared to other colleges featured in our guidebook. Additionally, the center trains four career peer advisors to assist their fellow undergrads. The six core services provided by the office are "(1) career education and career advice; (2) access to internships; (3) pre-law advice; (4) employer, alumni, and parent engagement; (5) job search; and (6) employer recruiting events." It conducts close to 1,000 one-on-one advising appointments per year.

One recent Oxy Career Fair was attended by 40+ employers and 692 students. Hosting more than 200 events each year, the HCC also brings 120 employers to campus each year for recruiting purposes. Seventy-five percent of recent grads obtain internships. Organizations hosting Oxy interns in recent years include Mercedes-Benz Shanghai, the Office of the Mayor of Los Angeles, *The Los Angeles Times*, and the NASA Jet Propulsion Laboratory. This office aims to reach students in their freshman year and first presents their services to incoming students at orientation with an eye toward preparing them for a productive first summer experience. Impressive employment and graduate enrollment statistics indicate that its approach works, earning Occidental's Hameetman Career Center praise from current and former students alike.

Professional Outcomes

One year after graduation, 95% of Occidental alumni are employed, pursuing graduate studies, or engaged in both simultaneously. By sector, the largest numbers of grads enter community service/education (25%), STEM (23%), and business (20%). Among the largest employers of Oxy alumni are the Los Angeles Unified School District, Kaiser Permanente, Microsoft, NASA Jet Propulsion Laboratory, Google, Morgan Stanley, and Amazon. Also on the list are a number of universities that employ Occidental grads after they earn advanced degrees. Most Tigers remain on the prowl in California—mainly LA or San Fran, although there are large alumni clusters on the East Coast, especially in New York City and DC. Starting salaries for recent Occidental grads were $52k.

Close to three-quarters of Oxy alumni eventually earn one or more advanced degrees. Recent graduates have gone on to continue their educations at Harvard, Stanford, NYU, University of Chicago, UCLA, USC, and UC Berkeley. Those pursuing law degrees have done so at Stanford, USC, UCLA, University of Pennsylvania, Yale, Columbia, Vanderbilt, and Emory. Each year, Occidental sees roughly 20 graduates and alumni accepted into medical school, including many of the finest universities in the country. In short, graduate and professional schools respect the college's reputation and know that those who post an impressive undergraduate GPA have fully earned it.

Admission

Of the 6,305 applicants vying for a place in Occidental College's 2022-23 freshman class, 39% were admitted, and 531 ultimately enrolled. Members of the Class of 2026 held a mean unweighted GPA of 3.70, mid-50% SAT range of 1380-1490, and ACT range of 31-34. Students were generally active outside the classroom as 76% of freshmen played a sport in high school, 80% volunteered in their community, and 39% played a musical instrument. Fifty-four percent placed within the top decile of their high school graduating class; 83% landed in the top quarter.

An admissions review from the Occidental staff is a genuinely holistic process. As the committee states, "Creative, soulful, funny, introspective—all words to describe some of our most memorable applicants, but the common thread is always authenticity." That philosophy is supported by GPA, rigor of secondary school record, and the application essay as the triumvirate of admissions factors designated as "most important." Men may receive a slight edge in the admissions process as they make up only 41% of the student body, but the admit rate for men and women is generally comparable. Those applying early decision received a "Yes" 59% of the time. The college has a fairly low yield rate of 21%, which means that it is always on the lookout for students who demonstrate interest and view the school as their number one choice.

Worth Your Money?

An education at Occidental is a phenomenal and highly personalized experience. Of course, providing such an intimate and supportive learning environment costs money. As a result, the annual cost of attendance is $81,730. Fortunately, those with significant financial need will see 100% of their need met by the school. That translates to over half of incoming freshmen receiving grants of $44k, helping to make the Occidental experience far more affordable and a worthy investment. Middle-income students without a significant financial aid offer should consider their career plans before agreeing to attend.

FINANCIAL
Institutional Type: Private
In-State Tuition: $63,446
Out-of-State Tuition: $63,446
Room & Board: $18,284
Books & Supplies: $1,240

Avg. Need-Based Grant: $45,440
Avg. % of Need Met: 100%

Avg. Merit-Based Award: $14,556
% Receiving (Freshmen w/o Need): 14%

Avg. Cumulative Debt: $27,879
% of Students Borrowing: 51%

CAREER
Who Recruits
1. NASA Jet Propulsion Laboratory
2. Northwestern Mutual
3. Aflac
4. Bank of America
5. Teach for America

Notable Internships
1. Calvin Klein
2. Paramount Pictures
3. Pfizer

Top Employers
1. Kaiser Permanente
2. Google
3. NASA Jet Propulsion Laboratory
4. Microsoft
5. Amazon

Where Alumni Work
1. Los Angeles
2. San Francisco
3. New York City
4. Seattle
5. Orange County, CA

Earnings
College Scorecard (10-YR Post-Entry): $68,355
PayScale (Early Career): $60,300
PayScale (Mid-Career): $125,300
PayScale 20-Year ROI: $428,000

RANKINGS
Money: 4
U.S. News: 35, Liberal Arts Colleges
Wall Street Journal/THE: Not Ranked
Washington Monthly: 41, Liberal Arts Colleges

OVERGENERALIZATIONS
Students are:
Politically liberal
Diverse
Opinionated
Less likely to party
Involved/investsed in campus life

COLLEGE OVERLAPS
Colorado College
Macalester College
Pitzer College
Pomona College
Whitman College

Columbus, Ohio | 614-292-3980

Anyone who has ever seen a college football game, even a flicker of one while flipping channels on a Saturday afternoon, will immediately associate the name Ohio State with gray football helmets covered in buckeye leaves. Yet, football is hardly the only draw at the great state of Ohio's flagship university, one of the top public research institutions anywhere. More than 46,000 undergraduate students now grace the Columbus campus, 79% of whom are Ohio natives, 21% of whom are from out of state, and 10% of whom are international students. As you will see in the "Admissions" section below, if you want to gain access to OSU, you'd better be one of the better students in your high school graduating class.

Inside the Classroom

With 200+ undergraduate majors and 18 schools and colleges housed within OSU, curricular requirements vary among the many academic programs. However, all Buckeyes must take a liberal arts core that includes writing, quantitative skills, natural science, literature, visual and performing arts, history, social science, and a foreign language. From there, it's all about completing your major, but students can find electives in just about anything you can imagine because the university offers 12,000+ courses.

A 17-to-1 student-to-faculty ratio leads to fairly large classes as only 40% of sections enroll fewer than 20 students, so expect a fair number of courses in a large lecture hall setting. In fact, 18% of courses contain 50 or more undergraduate students. Still, aggressive students can find opportunities to work closely with faculty. The Office of Undergraduate Research & Inquiry helps 800 students participate in the annual Denman Undergraduate Research Forum and 50+ students receive funding from OSU for summer research. All told, approximately 20% of students gain research experience. The same percentage of undergraduates elect to study abroad in one of 200 programs spread across 70 countries, the highest figure of any Big Ten university.

Business sees the greatest percentage of degrees conferred at 18% followed by engineering (15%), health professions (10%), and the social sciences (9%). It makes sense that so many flock to the business and engineering schools as they are among the highest-rated undergraduate programs in their respective disciplines. Top companies adore new Buckeye grads, and hundreds of alums can be found at some of the top tech companies, banks, and accounting firms in the United States. In recent years, the university has produced between five and eleven Fulbright Scholars annually and as many as six Boren Scholars, thirteen Gilman Scholars, four Goldwater Scholars, and eleven National Science Foundation Graduate Research Fellowship honorable mentions.

Outside the Classroom

There's a little something for everyone on this anything-but-little 1,665-acre campus that ranks third largest in the United States in sheer size. If you are seeking Greek life, you can find it—11% of women join sororities and 8% of men enter fraternities. The sports scene is epic in scope whether you are a casual athlete wanting to join one of the 60+ club teams and numerous intramural leagues or one of the 1,000+ big-time athletes on the Buckeyes' 36 varsity teams. Football Saturdays are "kind of a big deal" as more than 102,000 fans of the Scarlet and Gray pack Ohio Stadium. In total, 1,400 student organizations are awaiting your participation on the Columbus campus alone. Only 32% of students live in university-owned housing so, for many, sports and club activities are a way to stay connected. Many aspects of OSU campus life receive rave reviews in surveys—from the food to general happiness to LGBTQ friendliness, the university gets a giant thumbs up from its own students. Ohio's capital city is almost equidistant from Cincinnati and Cleveland, about a two-hour car ride. However, Columbus itself has much to offer, recently being ranked by several publications, including US News and Time, as among the best places to live in the United States. For those craving nature, skiing, camping, and hiking opportunities can be found less than an hour away.

Career Services

Buckeye Careers is a university-wide office staffed by four professionals, yet the bulk of the counseling takes place within discipline-specific career services offices housed within individual colleges. Including career coaches and other professional staff from the College of Arts & Sciences (14), College of Engineering (9), Fisher School of Business (6), and smaller undergraduate schools, there are 42 professional members on the OSU career services team. The university's overall 1,098:1 student-to-counselor ratio is poor compared to many other schools in this guide, but there are myriad facts and figures that suggest the university is preparing students for successful post-graduation outcomes.

A recent Career and Internship Fair was attended by over 200 employers and more than 4,000 students, 93% of whom rated the event as helpful. The Fisher School of Business has its own career fair that brings 185 companies to campus in the fall and another 130 in the spring. In a typical year, an eye-popping 35+ career fairs are held. A solid 69% of 2021 Ohio State graduates completed at least one internship. Within the Fisher School of Business, 95% of graduates participated in an internship or other intensive work experience; Fisher also conducts over 1,100 mock interviews per year. A solid 73% of grads believe the university prepared them well for the job market. Despite less-than-desirable staffing levels, Ohio State University's career services is well-run and manages to have a positive impact on students' lives.

Professional Outcomes

Upon receiving their diplomas, a solid number of Class of 2022 graduates were entering the world of employment (56%) while 17% were already accepted into graduate or professional school. Hordes of Buckeyes can be found in the offices of many of the nation's leading companies. More than 2,000 alumni work for JPMorgan Chase, more than 1,000 are employed by Amazon, and more than 600 work for Google and Microsoft. Roughly half of graduates settle in for the long haul in the Columbus area, and many others remain in the state, residing in Cleveland or Cincinnati. New York, Chicago, DC, and San Francisco also attract a fair number of alumni.

Of the more than one-quarter of recent grads directly matriculating into graduate or professional school, many continue in one of OSU's own 102 doctoral programs, 127 master's programs, or excellent law and medical schools. In the last few years, law school-bound graduates have earned admission at universities including UVA, Penn, Fordham, Harvard, George Washington, Georgetown, Case Western, and Cornell. Close to 550 graduates applied to medical school in 2023, and some have gone on to prestigious medical institutions like Harvard Medical School, Duke University School of Medicine, and Johns Hopkins School of Medicine. In sum, Ohio State grads attend a wide variety of graduate schools, and they can absolutely earn their way into some of the best institutions in the world.

Admission

Fifty-three percent of the 65,189 applicants for a place in the Class of 2026 gained acceptance, but that figure hardly tells the whole story of just how selective the flagship Columbus campus has become. The ACT is, by far, the more commonly submitted test, and members of the 2022-23 freshman class possessed a mid-50% ACT composite score of 29-32; the SAT range was 1310-1480. Even more shocking is the fact that 70% of enrolled students finished in the top 10% of their high school classes; 97% were in the top quartile. Ohio State has become significantly more competitive in recent years. A decade ago, it received fewer than half as many applications as it does today.

The OSU admissions staff promises a holistic review of each application but does rank the concrete factors of class rank, standardized test scores, GPA, and rigor of curriculum as "very important" in the process. Essays, extracurricular activities, talent/ability, first-generation status (few schools give this factor so much weight), volunteer work, and work experience get second billing. In a broad sense, OSU seeks individuals who are "not only smart but willing to lead; who see strength in diversity of people and ideas; who seek collaboration when solving problems; and who make use of all opportunities to figure out what kind of impact they want to have in the world." An influx of out-of-staters and international students has caused the school to make huge jumps in selectivity. As a result, Buckeye State residents need to be A/A- students with standardized test scores in at least the 90th percentile to be on solid footing.

Worth Your Money?

Ohio residents have a cost of attendance of $27,000+ per year, making the cost of a four-year degree from a well-respected university very reasonable. The out-of-state cost of attendance is over $53,000 per year. Roughly one-quarter of undergrads receive a small merit aid award, but as is typical at public institutions, the need-based aid tends to be a bit more substantial. Over 40% of current students receive some level of aid with an average award of $16k. In state, OSU is an easy choice and a spectacular value; out of state, it may be worth paying for certain top programs, particularly those that lead to careers with above-average starting salaries.

FINANCIAL
Institutional Type: Public
In-State Tuition: $12,485
Out-of-State Tuition: $36,722
Room & Board: $13,966
Books & Supplies: $1,012

Avg. Need-Based Grant: $14,002
Avg. % of Need Met: 69%

Avg. Merit-Based Award: $7,124
% Receiving (Freshmen w/o Need): 22%

Avg. Cumulative Debt: $25,599
% of Students Borrowing: 44%

CAREER
Who Recruits
1. Abercrombie & Fitch
2. Cargill
3. Nestle
4. Sherwin-Williams
5. Marriott International

Notable Internships
1. Sun National Bank
2. Walt Disney World
3. U.S. Department of State

Top Employers
1. JPMorgan Chase
2. Nationwide
3. Cardinal Health
4. Amazon
5. IBM

Where Alumni Work
1. Columbus, OH
2. Cleveland
3. Cincinnati
4. New York City
5. Chicago

Earnings
College Scorecard (10-YR Post-Entry): $58,596
PayScale (Early Career): $60,500
PayScale (Mid-Career): $103,800
PayScale 20-Year ROI: $533,000

RANKINGS
Money: 4.5
U.S. News: 43, National Universities
Wall Street Journal/THE: 222
Washington Monthly: 68, National Universities

OVERGENERALIZATIONS
Students are:
Crazy about the Buckeyes
Teeming with school pride
Ready to party
Collaborative
Diverse

COLLEGE OVERLAPS
Indiana University Bloomington
Miami University - Oxford
Pennsylvania State University - University Park
Purdue University - West Lafayette
University of Michigan

University Park, Pennsylvania | 814-865-5471

"We are Penn State," the signature slogan of Pennsylvania State University, is one of the more recognizable chants echoing across any college campus in the United States. Over 40,000 undergraduates reside in State College, nicknamed Happy Valley, a moniker that has weathered scandal and continues to be a destination point for Pennsylvanians as well as many out-of-staters and international students who make up 43% of today's student population. Not only does PSU have one the world's largest and most passionate alumni bases, but it also possesses as diverse an academic menu as you will find anywhere with its 275 majors and a number of top-ranked programs in a host of disciplines.

Inside the Classroom
There are 45 credits worth of general education requirements that you'll need to fulfill whether you are studying turfgrass science, toxicology, or telecommunications—all actual majors at PSU. Fifteen of those credits will come through introductory courses in writing, speaking, and quantification, and thirty will come via explorations of the humanities, natural sciences, social and behavioral sciences, the arts, and health and wellness. First-year engagement courses help students hone study and research skills and introduce freshmen to resources around campus. Students also must take courses that satisfy the categories of writing across the curriculum, United States cultures, and international cultures, but those can overlap with the aforementioned forty-five credits worth of distributional mandates.

Unlike some public research universities that can have student-to-faculty ratios greater than 20:1, PSU boasts a solid 15:1 ratio. That level of support allows 61% of classes to have an enrollment below thirty students. Still, you will take some intro courses in massive lecture halls, and 16% of sections enroll more than 50 undergraduates. Even at such a large institution, it is possible to get involved in undergraduate research. Eberly College of Science professors are running upwards of 3,000 research projects per year, and the school has a well-maintained and up-to-date database of undergraduate research positions. All told, 10% of graduates report having engaged in undergraduate research. Over 2,600 Penn Staters avail themselves of study abroad opportunities in one of 300+ programs in 50+ countries each year.

Penn State University's College of Engineering is rated exceptionally well on a national scale, cracking the top 25 on just about everyone's list, and even hits the top ten in some sub-disciplines such as industrial and biological engineering. It's no wonder that engineering is the most popular field of study at the university, accounting for 15% of the degrees conferred. The Smeal College of Business is equally well-regarded, also earning high rankings in everything from supply chain management to accounting to marketing. This school not only ranks among the top undergraduate public business colleges in the United States but among all colleges, and it attracts 15% of total degree-seekers. In addition to gaining positive attention from the engineering and business communities, PSU is viewed favorably by prestigious national fellowship organizations. In recent years, as many as ten students were named Fulbright Semifinalists and one or more have captured Boren, Critical Language, Astronaut, Marshall, and Goldwater Scholarships in the last three years.

Outside the Classroom
Only 34% of Nittany Lions technically lived in university-owned housing in 2022-23, but that doesn't quite capture the cohesive spirit of the PSU community. Greek life is a moderate social force at the school as 5% of men join frats and 7% of women become members of sororities. A tragic hazing death a few years back led to a shutdown of one fraternity and increased administrative scrutiny of the practices of others. Unfortunately, the school is no stranger to national controversy. Yet, even after the infamous Sandusky scandal, Penn State football is a tradition like no other as 106,000 pack into Beaver Stadium to watch the Lions battle with Big Ten rivals like Ohio State, Michigan, and Nebraska. Thon, an annual charity dance marathon, is one of the grandest and most impressive events on campus, raising over $15 million to fight childhood cancer in 2023. With over 1,000 clubs and activities to choose from, it's hard not to find your niche at Penn State. Campus itself covers almost 8,000 acres and contains its own arboretum, the Palmer Art Museum, and the famous (and delicious) Penn State Creamery. State College may be in the middle of nowhere, but it truly is the ultimate college town, walkable and brimming with terrific restaurants, bars, and shops.

Career Services
Not counting graduate assistants and office managers, there are 30 full-time employees occupying the Bank of America Career Services Center at University Park. However, there are additional offices that serve specialty groups such as the Career Resources & Employer Relations department housed within the College of Engineering, which is staffed by seven professionals, and the Smeal College of Business, which has nine career services employees.

Eleven other staff members are spread across campus in other departments. Based on this grand total of 57 career counselors, internship coordinators, employer relations specialists, and related positions, the student-to-counselor ratio is 723:1, higher than most of the schools featured in this guide, but not at all bad for a school of PSU's size.

Career fairs, such as the major one held each fall, are massive undertakings, some featuring 300+ companies. The Fall Career Fair is four days in length, and that time is divided to cover technical jobs, nontechnical jobs, internships, and interviews. It also offers many smaller (but still large) targeted fairs in areas such as nursing, education, graduate school, small business and startups, and impact (nonprofits). The majority of graduates, over 60%, report participating in at least one internship while at University Park. More than one recent graduate held an internship position at companies like Amazon, Pfizer, and Xerox. PSU does not publish statistics on how many students take advantage of career services offerings, but it is clear that this staff facilitates powerful, door-opening opportunities for those proactive enough to seek them out.

Professional Outcomes

By the day of graduation, 70% of Nittany Lions have found their next employment or graduate school home; within some of the university's many colleges, that rate is even higher. Three months after receiving their diplomas, 98% of Smeal College of Business grads already have their next step lined up. They flock in large numbers to some of the nation's best finance, accounting, consulting, and technology firms. More than 500 PSU alumni are currently working at each of IBM, Deloitte, PwC, Amazon, EY, JPMorgan Chase, Microsoft, Google, and Oracle. Hundreds more work at Citi, Salesforce, and Meta. Philadelphia, New York City, Pittsburgh, DC, San Francisco, Boston, and Los Angeles all have a strong PSU alumni presence. Three-quarters of 2022 graduates employed full-time earned starting salaries of greater than $50k.

Medical school acceptance rates for PSU graduates hover around 60%, well above the national average, an impressive figure when considering that over 280 students applied in 2022-23. Seventy percent of those accepted into medical school enroll at Pennsylvania-based institutions including the Penn State College of Medicine. Overall, PSU alumni are presently enrolled in 60 medical schools throughout the country. Likewise, many prelaw students go on to pursue legal educations at one of the university's two law schools (Penn State Law and Dickinson Law), other strong local options like Temple or Villanova, or prestigious national universities like the University of North Carolina, Stanford, Cornell, or Wake Forest.

Admission

The 85,784 Nittany Lion hopefuls seeking a place in the Class of 2026 were accepted at a 55% rate, a figure that somewhat undersells how competitive gaining admission right out of high school truly is (transferring later is easier). For some, Penn State is a clear number-one choice and often a family tradition; for other Pennsylvania students, it occupies mere safety status. Overall, the yield rate—the percentage of accepted students who go on to enroll—is 19%. Freshmen who entered the university in 2022-23 possessed mid-50% SAT/ACT scores of 1220-1380 and 26-31, respectively. With 33% of freshmen having earned a place in the top 10% of their high school class and 68% in the top quartile, most Penn State admits sport strong grades, generally a mix of A's and B's in at least some AP and honors courses.

The only "very important" factor in the admissions process is GPA. The rigor of one's high school coursework sits alone in the next tier of still "important" factors. Soft factors like essays, extracurricular activities, work experience, talent/ability, and character/personal qualities as well as state residency status and ethnicity are "considered" in candidate evaluation. An early option allows students to submit an application by November 1. After that, admission is rolling, but you should absolutely meet the priority date of November 30.

Worth Your Money?

PSU's in-state tuition cost of roughly $20k and total cost of attendance of $33,000 isn't as cheap as, for example, schools in New York's SUNY system that have a COA approximately $10k cheaper. A non-Keystone State resident would pay a COA of over $54,000, which would not make sense in most circumstances. However, denizens of Pennsylvania residents will generally reap the benefits of this flagship institution's strong reputation and incomprehensibly vast alumni network.

FINANCIAL
Institutional Type: Public
In-State Tuition: $19,835
Out-of-State Tuition: $38,651
Room & Board: $12,984
Books & Supplies: $1,840

Avg. Need-Based Grant: $8,438
Avg. % of Need Met: 69%

Avg. Merit-Based Award: $5,420
% Receiving (Freshmen w/o Need): 10%

Avg. Cumulative Debt: $44,008
% of Students Borrowing: 53%

CAREER
Who Recruits
1. Google
2. Grant Thorton LLP
3. Oracle
4. PNC
5. Accenture

Notable Internships
1. Anheuser-Busch
2. Morgan Stanley
3. Aramark

Top Employers
1. IBM
2. PwC
3. Amazon
4. Johnson & Johnson
5. EY

Where Alumni Work
1. Philadelphia
2. New York City
3. Pittsburgh
4. State College, PA
5. Washington, DC

Earnings
College Scorecard (10-YR Post-Entry): $61,185
PayScale (Early Career): $71,700
PayScale (Mid-Career): $123,500
PayScale 20-Year ROI: Not Reported

RANKINGS
Money: 3.5
U.S. News: 60, National Universities
Wall Street Journal/THE: 220
Washington Monthly: 146, National Universities

OVERGENERALIZATIONS
Students are:
Crazy about the Nittany Lions
Ready to party
Teeming with school pride
Only a short drive from home (i.e., Most come from PA or nearby states)
Outgoing

COLLEGE OVERLAPS
The Ohio State University - Columbus
Purdue University - West Lafayette
University of Maryland, College Park
University of Michigan
University of Pittsburgh

Pepperdine University

Malibu, California | 310-506-4392

ADMISSION
Admission Rate: 49%
Admission Rate - Men: 52%
Admission Rate - Women: 47%
EA Admission Rate: 47%
ED Admission Rate: Not Offered
ED Admits as % of Total Admits: Not Offered
Admission Rate (5-Year Trend): +9%
% of Admits Attending (Yield): 17%
Transfer Admission Rate: 34%

SAT Reading/Writing (Middle 50%): 650-730
SAT Math (Middle 50%): 635-750
ACT Composite (Middle 50%): 28-32

% Graduated in Top 10% of HS Class: 41%
% Graduated in Top 25% of HS Class: 74%
% Graduated in Top 50% of HS Class: 95%

Demonstrated Interest: Not Considered
Legacy Status: Considered
Racial/Ethnic Status: Considered
Admission Interview Offered: Yes

ENROLLMENT
Total Undergraduate Enrollment: 3,662
% Full-Time: 94%
% Male: 42%
% Female: 58%
% Out-of-State: 44%
% Fraternity: 18%
% Sorority: 33%
% On-Campus (All Undergraduate): 63%
Freshman Housing Required: Yes

% African-American: 4%
% Asian: 14%
% Hispanic: 18%
% White: 46%
% Other: 2%
% International: 9%
% Low-Income: 19%

ACADEMICS
Student-to-Faculty Ratio: 13 to 1
% of Classes Under 20: 74%
% of Classes 20-49: 24%
% of Classes 50 or More: 2%
% Full-Time Faculty: 43%
% Full-Time Faculty w/ Terminal Degree: 89%

Top Programs
Advertising
Business Administration
Communication
International Studies
Psychology
Public Relations
Sports Medicine
Theatre

Retention Rate: 89%
4-Year Graduation Rate: 76%
6-Year Graduation Rate: 86%

Curricular Flexibility: Less Flexible
Academic Rating: ★★★★

#CollegesWorthYourMoney

The incongruity of a resort-like university located in Malibu that only lifted its ban on dancing in the late 1980s is hard to reconcile. Maybe the most beautiful campus in the world, Pepperdine is also a bastion of evangelical Christianity and largely conservative politically. On the academic menu for the 3,662 undergrads at Seaver College (the school's undergraduate wing) are 46 majors and 47 minors with the most commonly conferred degrees being in business/marketing (29%), communication/journalism (17%), general social sciences (11%), psychology (8%), and parks and recreation (7%). Only 2% pursue degrees in religion, but its influence is interwoven into the fabric of both the academic experience and the social scene.

Inside the Classroom
Among the 19 courses that constitute Pepperdine's general education requirements for all undergraduates are three classes under the umbrella of Christianity and Culture. Other mandated areas of study include the American experience, Western cultures, human institutions and behavior, world civilizations, fine arts, mathematics, laboratory science, and speech and rhetoric. First-year seminars are intended to sharpen skills in the areas of communication, critical thinking, and learning how to "apply the university's Christian mission." Those seminars tackle big-picture topics that include science and religion, the nature of conscience, and the pain of betrayal. Students must continually update a writing portfolio that is formally evaluated as the junior writing portfolio when students reach their third year of study.

A 13:1 student-to-faculty ratio is solid, and faculty are fully deployed with the aim of creating an intimate liberal arts classroom setting. The average class contains 19 students, and 23% of courses will contain fewer than ten students. There are three formal programs for undergraduate research: the Summer Undergraduate Research Program, the Cross-disciplinary/Interdisciplinary Undergraduate Research Program, and the Academic Year Undergraduate Research Initiative. Close to 80% of Seaver students study abroad and build global experience in locations such as Buenos Aires, Florence, London, and Shanghai.

The Graziadio Business School has a strong reputation that penetrates far beyond the school's home state. The Communication Division also registers on many national ranking lists. Thanks in part to the school's focus on international experience, five 2023 graduates won Fulbright Scholarships. Recent grads also have, on occasion, been awarded Gilman, Boren, and National Science Foundation fellowships.

Outside the Classroom
The university's 835-acre grounds can be found in the number one or two position in just about any nationwide ranking of "most beautiful campuses." Given its size and luxurious feel, it's a bit strange that only 63% of the undergraduate population lives on campus; however, 99% of freshmen do reside in university-owned housing. Dorms and on-campus apartments are single-sex, and overnight visitors of the opposite sex are prohibited. The alcohol policies are also enforced more than at your average college. Gender-wise, Seaver has a 58/42 split in favor of women, 33% of whom join sororities while 18% of men join fraternities. A relatively athletic undergraduate student body participates on seventeen NCAA Division I sports teams (the Waves) that have produced an impressive 50+ Olympians in the school's history. There are plenty of intramural and club teams as well as four fitness centers and an Olympic-size swimming pool. One hundred and ten student organizations are active, and more than 1,000 on-campus events are hosted each semester. A focus on service leads three-fifths of students to engage in volunteer work with over 80,000 hours contributed each year. Pepperdine is nestled in the Santa Monica Mountains only minutes from some of the world's premier surfing beaches. As another bonus, campus is only 30 miles west of Los Angeles, so Hollywood is just a short car ride away.

Career Services
Pepperdine Career Services employs eight full-time professional staff members (not counting office managers) working as counselors, industry specialists, events managers, and employer relations coordinators. That works out to a 458:1 student-to-counselor ratio, within the average range of institutions profiled in this book. This department offers a solid blend of one-on-one counseling and large-scale events such as industry-specific career fairs in business, health and sciences, nonprofit and government, and arts/entertainment/media. There is also a more generalized Spring Career Expo attended by 50+ employers and graduate schools.

Two-thirds of recent grads had at least one internship. Career Services posted 10,000 internships last year and facilitated 125 job shadowing opportunities. Last year, over 120 employers recruited on-site at Pepperdine, conducting information sessions as well as on-campus interviews. The alumni network is always happy to be involved in assisting current students. Over 5,000 alumni volunteer to work with undergraduates directly, and 124,000 living alumni can be found around the globe. A formalized Career Coaching Program has set up 500 students with alumni mentors who have guided them through each stage of the career exploration and development process since its inception in 2001. An above-average level of next-step support and reasonably successful student outcomes make Pepperdine Career Services a strong-performing outfit.

Professional Outcomes

Members of the Seaver Class of 2022 landed at their next destination within six months of graduating at an 86% clip, with 63% employed full-time, 18% admitted to graduate school, and 1% in a full-time service or military role. Of those entering the world of work, 87% were in the for-profit sector, 12% were with nonprofit/government entities, and 1% were pursuing entrepreneurial ventures. Disney, Morgan Stanley, Northrop Grumman, and Wells Fargo have hired the most recent graduates. Other companies employing fifty or more alumni include Kaiser Permanente, Apple, Google, and Amazon. Many graduates remain in California as Los Angeles and Orange County are the two most common landing spots. Other West Coast locales, including San Diego, San Francisco, and Seattle, also sport sizable numbers of alums.

Class of 2022 graduates were admitted to graduate/professional school at a 72% rate. Training in a medical field was the choice of 17% of that group while 21% matriculated into law school and 11% pursued MBAs. In a typical year, twenty to thirty grads apply to medical school, and 70-80% are successful. Recent students have gained acceptance to medical schools at Georgetown; Emory; USC; University of California, San Diego; and Washington University in St. Louis. Those going the law school route study at many fine institutions including Pepperdine's own law school. In the last few years, others have been admitted to Harvard Law School, UCLA School of Law, and NYU School of Law. No matter your postgraduate pursuit, a solid transcript and a Pepperdine degree will leave you with many strong graduate/professional school options.

Admission

In the Class of 2026 admissions cycle, the university admitted 49% of the 11,466 applicants, an improvement (from any applicant's perspective) over the mark of 32% just three years earlier. Applicants who accepted a place in the freshman class had a 28-32 ACT range, a 1290-1460 SAT range, and an average GPA of 3.75. "Only" 41% of that cohort placed in the top 10% of their high school class, a somewhat low figure compared to many other elite universities. Further, 26% did not place in the top quartile, so there is some leeway here for students with imperfect academic transcripts.

There are seven factors rated as "very important" by the admissions committee, most notably religious affiliation; Pepperdine, as noted earlier, is a Christian school. The other more common critical factors are rigor of coursework, GPA, application essay, extracurricular activities, talent/ability, and character/personal qualities. Recommendations and volunteer work make up the second rung of still "important" factors. The yield rate (percent of those accepted who actually enroll) is only 17%, which means that Pepperdine is definitely interested to know if you are a student who truly places the university at the top of your college list. Since it offers only early action and does not have a binding early decision program, demonstrating interest is a good idea if you are serious about this school. Admissions standards at Pepperdine today are almost identical to those of five years ago. It remains a niche institution for devout Christians with strong academic credentials.

Worth Your Money?

Pepperdine's annual cost of attendance is over $90,000, making it one of the most expensive colleges in the country. The average need-based grant amount is over $43k, almost slicing the COA in half, and the average amount of debt incurred by Pepperdine grads is right around the national average. There aren't exactly dozens of academically competitive, conservative Christian universities with a beachfront view, so, if that's the description of your ideal school, Pepperdine will likely be worth your money, especially if you have plans to enter the fields of business or communication.

FINANCIAL
Institutional Type: Private
In-State Tuition: $66,742
Out-of-State Tuition: $66,742
Room & Board: $23,270
Books & Supplies: $1,000

Avg. Need-Based Grant: $45,119
Avg. % of Need Met: 77%

Avg. Merit-Based Award: $17,145
% Receiving (Freshmen w/o Need): 32%

Avg. Cumulative Debt: $28,962
% of Students Borrowing: 47%

CAREER
Who Recruits
1. PennyMac
2. Disney
3. Universalizer
4. Sony Pictures Entertainment
5. REX-Real Estate Exchange Inc.

Notable Internships
1. United Nations
2. U.S. Securities and Exchange Commission
3. Farmers Insurance

Top Employers
1. Boeing
2. Kaiser Permanente
3. Wells Fargo
4. Walt Disney
5. Amazon

Where Alumni Work
1. Los Angeles
2. Orange County, CA
3. San Francisco
4. San Diego
5. New York City

Earnings
College Scorecard (10-YR Post-Entry): $78,224
PayScale (Early Career): $63,400
PayScale (Mid-Career): $112,200
PayScale 20-Year ROI: $607,000

RANKINGS
Money: 4
U.S. News: 76, National Universities
Wall Street Journal/THE: 100
Washington Monthly: 189, National Universities

OVERGENERALIZATIONS
Students are:
Less likely to party
Always admiring the beauty of their campus
Religious
Tight-knit (possess a strong sense of community)
Goal-oriented

COLLEGE OVERLAPS
Loyola Marymount University
Southern Methodist University
University of California, San Diego
University of California, Santa Barbara
University of San Diego

Pitzer College

Claremont, California | 909-621-8129

Every member school within the Claremont Consortium has its own distinct personality—Harvey Mudd is for engineering geniuses, Scripps is a highly selective women's college, Pomona and CMC are premier liberal arts colleges that battle East Coast schools Swarthmore, Amherst, and Williams for the top spot in the national rankings. Then there is Pitzer College, a liberal arts powerhouse in its own right with an emphasis on service learning and global engagement that has experienced logarithmic leaps in selectivity itself since the dawn of the new millennium. Cozy in size, hosting a mere 1,212 students, Pitzer still manages to offer 40+ majors and 20 minors and, as a bonus, students are free to take more than 2,000 courses across the consortium.

Inside the Classroom
Graduating from Pitzer involves the completion of 32 courses, including a minimum of 11 required courses that are part of meeting the college's educational objectives. That involves two courses in the humanities and fine arts, two in the behavioral and social sciences, and one each in written expression, quantitative reasoning, and the natural sciences. Sequences covering social justice/social responsibility and intercultural understanding also must be completed. The class on social justice requires active community engagement. First-year experience courses are taught on a variety of topics, and are capped at fifteen students.

A 10:1 student-to-faculty ratio and no graduate student presence lead to an average class size of 16 students, and 69% of sections enroll 19 or fewer students. In 2022-23, only one course section was larger than 39 students. Finding mentorship is doable in this atmosphere and can lead to undergraduate research opportunities such as those at the Keck Science Department, which also services CMC and Scripps students. Those opportunities can occur in the summer or during senior year while completing a required thesis. With one of the highest study abroad percentages of any school at 75%, Pitzer runs eight foreign programs and offers access to 32 international exchange programs.

The most popular majors at Pitzer are interdisciplinary studies (18%), the social sciences (18%), and psychology (8%). Nearly all programs have the full admiration of graduate/professional schools as well as prestigious scholarship programs, but majors within the social and behavioral sciences (e.g., psychology and sociology) typically draw the most praise. In a single recent year, seven seniors and recent alumni captured Fulbrights, three were named Napier Fellows, and two students won Gilman Scholarships. Students also captured one Goldwater Scholarship, a National Science Foundation Graduate Research Fellowship, a Princeton in Asia Fellowship, and a Davis Projects for Peace Award. Not bad for a school with around 250 graduates per year.

Outside the Classroom
Last year, 100% of Pitzer freshmen and 75% of all students lived in six dorms on the school's 31-acre campus. Dorms receive glowing reviews as environmentally responsible housing, and their farm-to-table program is ranked as one of the best in the country. From those two facts, you're likely picking up on the school's ethos and can guess that it does not have fraternities or sororities. Pitzer does have a joint athletics department with Pomona College that features twenty-one NCAA Division III varsity sports teams known as the Sagehens. There are 250+ clubs students can join, many of which are of the cross-college variety. Every single member of the Pitzer community gives back through service. In total, students, faculty, and staff commit approximately 100,000 hours to community-based projects each year. Activism carries over to student government, which is consistently passionate and vocal whether the issue is undergraduate housing costs or a recent ban on studying abroad in Israel. Pitzer Outdoor Adventure (POA) is also immensely popular and regularly leads its large membership on hiking, cycling, climbing, camping, and surfing trips. Those seeking big-city fun will relish the fact that the City of Angels can be reached in less than an hour.

Career Services
Career Services at Pitzer has only four full-time professional staff members, yet being such a small college, that number still works out to a solid 303:1 student-to-advisor ratio, better than the average college featured in our guidebook. For such a tiny operation, the level of outreach is spectacular as 75% of freshmen engage with career services. Overall, approximately two-thirds of the student body utilize career services, and 33% take advantage of walk-in counseling appointments each year. It hosts roughly ninety events per year that attract almost 800 student participants. Of the almost 400 students who receive one-on-one counseling each year, 96% had a positive experience. The office also puts on 60+ workshops that draw 600+ student participants.

Being part of the Claremont Consortium has as many advantages with regard to career development as it does with regard to academics. Over 350 companies recruit annually at the 5Cs, and Pitzer students enjoy full access to networking and on-campus interviews. The office also does an excellent job financially supporting students' job exploration endeavors. Roughly fifty students per year receive financial assistance from the Pitzer Internship Fund, which enables students to complete unpaid or low-paid experiential learning opportunities. Roughly 50 students engage in a job-shadowing experience with an alum over winter break. Overall, this is an accessible office that greatly benefits from its affiliation with its neighboring schools.

Professional Outcomes

Upon receiving their degrees, 59% of 2022 Pitzer graduates had already found full-time employers, 16% were headed to graduate school, and 9% were entering fellowship, internship, or service programs. Among those employed, the most popular industries were tech/sustainability (25%), finance/business (17%), entertainment/arts (16%), health, medicine, and research (15%), and education (12%). Employers presently issuing paychecks to more than ten Pitzer alumni include Google, Kaiser Permanente, the Los Angeles Unified School District, and Accenture. Graduates tend to be a globetrotting bunch, and the 11,000 living alumni can be found all over the map, although roughly half settle in Los Angeles or San Francisco. Median salaries, even ten years after graduation, are on the lower end of selective colleges. While plenty of Pitzer grads go on to pursue high-paying finance and tech jobs, many others choose PhD programs, medical school, or fellowship programs abroad that can delay financial returns.

Recent grads have headed to prestigious graduate schools including Vanderbilt, Oxford, Emory, Columbia, Georgetown, NYU, and Cornell. For premed students, the college offers a Joint Medical Program with the Western University of Health Sciences, admitting up to six students each year. The W.M. Keck Science Department services Scripps, Claremont McKenna, and Pitzer, so all students have access to an excellent premed curriculum and facility. Those heading to law school in recent years have matriculated into a wide range of institutions that includes Notre Dame, UC Berkeley, Georgetown, Santa Clara, and Loyola Marymount University.

Admission

Applicants to the Class of 2026 were admitted at only an 10% clip, a rate similar to five years ago but far below that of 2005 when the admit rate was 39%. Even that 39% figure represented a sharp decline from a more forgiving admissions era in the 1990s. An early adopter of test-optional policies, Pitzer stopped requiring SAT or ACT scores in 2003, and it is now a test-blind institution, which means that they do not consider ACT, SAT, or AP scores in the admissions process. It's within the realm of high school performance that successful Pitzer applicants set themselves apart. Fifty-two percent placed within the top 10% of their graduating class, and 76% were in the top quartile. The average GPA for an entering member of the Class of 2026 was 3.98.

The admissions process at Pitzer is highly personalized, and each application receives a lengthy review. A rigorous high school course load, a high GPA, a strong essay, and the demonstration of solid and unique character/personal qualities are at the forefront of the decision-making process. Recommendations, volunteer work, talent/ability, and extracurricular activities are also important factors. If you are a borderline applicant who is serious about getting in, applying early decision may be the way to go; 40% of ED applicants were accepted into the Class of 2026.

Worth Your Money?

Pitzer has notably generous financial aid as 35% of undergraduates received an average annual package of $50k, meeting 100% of students' demonstrated need. That assistance helps greatly lessen the blow of a $62k list tuition price and $87k cost of attendance. While median salaries are on the low side, being part of the world-renowned Claremont Consortium allows access to premier facilities and professors and opens doors to the most competitive grad schools, fellowships, and, should you choose, major corporations. You wouldn't want to pay $350,000 for a humanities degree without a clear plan for how to pay back those loans. Again, thanks to merit aid and need-based awards from the school, you are unlikely to be asked to pay anything approaching the full sticker price.

FINANCIAL
Institutional Type: Private
In-State Tuition: $62,692
Out-of-State Tuition: $62,692
Room & Board: $21,374
Books & Supplies: $1,100

Avg. Need-Based Grant: $49,525
Avg. % of Need Met: 100%

Avg. Merit-Based Award: $7,422
% Receiving (Freshmen w/o Need): 2%

Avg. Cumulative Debt: $19,715
% of Students Borrowing: 36%

CAREER
Who Recruits
1. City Year
2. Apple
3. Amazon
4. JumpStart
5. Accenture

Notable Internships
1. FX Networks
2. Collins Aerospace
3. Apple

Top Employers
1. Kaiser Permanente
2. Los Angeles Unified School District
3. Google
4. Wells Fargo
5. Accenture

Where Alumni Work
1. Los Angeles
2. San Francisco
3. New York City
4. Seattle
5. Portland, OR

Earnings
College Scorecard (10-YR Post-Entry): $64,269
PayScale (Early Career): $58,700
PayScale (Mid-Career): $100,200
PayScale 20-Year ROI: $279,000

RANKINGS
Money: 4
U.S. News: 39, Liberal Arts Colleges
Wall Street Journal/THE: Not Ranked
Washington Monthly: 51, Liberal Arts Colleges

OVERGENERALIZATIONS
Students are:
Environmentally conscious
Politically liberal
Politically active
Wealthy
Service-oriented

COLLEGE OVERLAPS
Colorado College
Lewis & Clark College
Oberlin College
Occidental College
Whitman College

Pomona College

Claremont, California | 909-621-8134

Considered the preeminent institution among the Claremont Consortium, Pomona College in Claremont, California, is much like the elite liberal arts schools of the Northeast—Williams and Amherst—only with perfect weather, gorgeous beaches, and Disneyland in relatively close proximity. Pomona also boasts one of the lowest acceptance rates in the country, one that is on par, from a selectivity standpoint, with Yale, Columbia, Brown, and MIT. That said, if you are one of the rare individuals capable of gaining entrance, you won't find a better or more rigorous liberal arts education anywhere.

Inside the Classroom
There are 48 majors and minors to select from with the most popular being social sciences (23%), biology (13%), and computer science (12%). More than 600 courses are on the menu at Pomona alone, but students can access any of the Claremont Consortium's 2,700 courses. Everyone begins with a critical inquiry seminar as a freshman and must complete coursework designated as writing intensive, speaking intensive, and analyzing difference. Breadth of study requirements demand that undergrads complete one course in the following six categories: criticism, analysis, and contextual study of works of the human imagination; social institutions and human behavior; history, values, ethics, and cultural studies; physical and biological sciences; mathematical and formal reasoning; and creation and performance of works of art and literature. There are literally eight ways to meet the college's foreign language requirement including AP scores and passing three semesters of language, but all eight demand the demonstration of proficiency.

The school's 217 full-time professors are dedicated to the task of undergraduate education. Pomona's 8:1 student-to-teacher ratio leads to an average class size of only 15 students. There are only 10 of 461 courses that ran in 2022-23 that contained more than 40 students. Small classes also lead to the forging of student-professor bonds that help over 50% of the undergraduate population conduct research alongside a faculty member. Each summer, 200 students remain on campus for such an endeavor. Close to 50% of Pomona students travel abroad to one of 59 programs in 34 countries.

All of the college's academic offerings are highly respected by employers, graduate/professional schools, and national fellowship/scholarship competitions. Majors in economics, international relations, chemistry, and mathematics receive especially high marks. One-quarter of Pomona students apply for at least one competitive fellowship. As many as 13 students have won Fulbrights in a single year. Two captured Watson Scholarships in 2022, and a remarkable 11 grads and alumni were awarded National Science Foundation Graduate Research Fellowships in 2023.

Outside the Classroom
Pomona's bustling campus is spread across 140 acres and contains 15 residence halls and three dining halls; 97% of students live in campus housing. There are two co-ed fraternities on campus that student members themselves describe as "just a bunch of dorks that hang out sometimes." Pomona partners with Pitzer to field more than 21 varsity teams who play as the Sagehens in NCAA Division III; 20% of the student body are members of a varsity team, and many others participate in club and intramural athletics. Student life at Pomona is, in part, defined by the multitude of opportunities to enjoy the resources of the other Claremont Colleges—Pitzer, Scripps, Harvey Mudd, and CMC. More than 250 clubs can be accessed by students of any of the five schools. On the Loose is a popular outdoors club that organizes 150 excursions into natural settings each year. Students can tend to their own plots at an on-campus organic farm, perform for the Claremont Colleges Ballroom Dance Company, write for the Student Life newspaper, or connect with volunteer opportunities through the Draper Center for Community Partnerships. While campus itself receives rave reviews, few complain about the school's enviable location either. Less than an hour from campus, students can access all of the fun Los Angeles has to offer as well as some of the most beautiful beaches in the country.

Career Services
The Career Development Office (CDO) has eight full-time professional staff members working on grad school/career advising, employer relations, and experiential learning coordination. The CDO's 224:1 student-to-advisor ratio is significantly better than the average college featured in our guidebook. Pomona's staff puts its resources to good use, engaging 80% of freshmen through lunches where the CDO's offerings are introduced. Each year, the office engages in over 1,800 one-on-one counseling appointments, more than one per enrolled undergraduate student. Two-thirds of seniors directly engage with counselors.

On a more global scale, Pomona students can connect with more than 8,500 employers through the school's membership in three consortia groups: the Claremont Consortium, the Career and Internship Connection, and the Liberal Arts Career Network. More than 520 employers engage in on-campus recruiting at Pomona each year, including many that attend winter break recruiting programs. Unique internship opportunities are available such as the Pomona College Internship Program (PCIP), which funds students to intern domestically in places like DC or New York or abroad in cities like Bangkok or Tokyo. Roughly 170 students are awarded PCIP positions each school year. By senior year, roughly 90% of students have participated in at least one internship, and 70% have completed two or more. Thanks to loads of individualized attention and ways to connect directly with top employers and graduate schools, Pomona's career services is highly regarded by our staff.

Professional Outcomes

Seventy-one percent of the Class of 2022 had entered the working world within six months of exiting the college. Whether entering the corporate world or a nonprofit position, Pomona grads are adored by employers. Overall, the largest number of Pomona alumni can be found in the offices of Google, Kaiser Permanente, Microsoft, Amazon, and Meta. Recently, economics degree-earners have landed jobs at Goldman Sachs, Wells Fargo, Morgan Stanley, or Accenture. Majors in the hard sciences frequently landed at top research laboratories and hospitals. The three most popular geographical landing spots were Los Angeles, San Francisco, and New York City. Mid-career salaries are middle-of-the-pack among elite schools and are commensurate with other highly selective liberal arts schools like Williams, Middlebury, and Colby.

Of the 21% of Class of 2022 members who were accepted directly into graduate school, the most frequently attended institutions were a not-too-shabby list which included the University of Cambridge, Duke, Harvard, Caltech, UChicago, and Stanford. When Pomona students go to law school, they attend only the best. Thirty percent of alumni were admitted into top-five law schools; nearly three-quarters were admitted into top-fourteen schools. Med school applicants are admitted at an 85% clip, and in recent years, more than one Pomona graduate has enrolled in medical school at USC, UCLA, University of Washington, and Emory University. In short, attending Pomona as an undergraduate will put you in a direct pipeline to the world's best graduate/professional schools.

Admission

Pomona now sits among the most ultra-selective schools in the world after admitting only 7% of the 10,666 students fighting for a spot in the Class of 2026. The mid-50% ranges for enrolled students were 1480-1540 and 33-35. Students submitted SAT and ACT scores at a fairly even rate. Ninety-one percent placed in the top 10% of their high school class. International admits hailed from 60 countries, and 48% of enrolled domestic applicants were students of color. A relatively high yield rate of 55% indicates that teens who apply to Pomona are likely to attend the college if accepted.

Getting in is a genuinely holistic process that strongly weighs wide-ranging factors including rigor of curriculum, GPA, class rank, essays, recommendations, extracurricular activities, talent/ability, and character/personal qualities. Class of 2026 ED applicants were admitted at a rate of 14%, which suggests that ED does provide an admissions edge. In 1914, the school's president declared, "Let only the eager, thoughtful, and reverent enter here." Over a century later, those criteria hold true with the addendum of near-perfect test scores and placement atop your high school graduating class. Like other schools with single-digit acceptance rates, there is an element of randomness that can leave valedictorians and possessors of 1500+ SAT scores wondering why they were rejected.

Worth Your Money?

Pomona may have a sky-high sticker price, but it does everything in its power to make attending the school a possibility for students who otherwise could not afford it. In meeting 100% of the need of every eligible student, it awards an average of $59k per year to 52% of its undergraduate population. For everyone who can afford the $88k+ annual cost of attendance, that will be the actual cost because Pomona does not award merit aid. If you are offered a rare chance to attend Pomona, you should take advantage. With a superior reputation in academic and corporate circles alike, this college is definitely worth your money.

FINANCIAL
Institutional Type: Private
In-State Tuition: $62,326
Out-of-State Tuition: $62,326
Room & Board: $20,374
Books & Supplies: $1,100

Avg. Need-Based Grant: $63,102
Avg. % of Need Met: 100%

Avg. Merit-Based Award: $15,141
% Receiving (Freshmen w/o Need): <1%

Avg. Cumulative Debt: $20,181
% of Students Borrowing: 26%

CAREER
Who Recruits
1. Kaiser Permanente
2. Saatchi & Saatchi
3. UPS
4. JPMorgan Chase
5. AlphaSights

Notable Internships
1. Los Angeles Review of Books
2. U.S. Senate
3. Spotify

Top Employers
1. Google
2. Microsoft
3. Kaiser Permanente
4. Amazon
5. Facebook

Where Alumni Work
1. Los Angeles
2. San Francisco
3. New York City
4. Seattle
5. Washington, DC

Earnings
College Scorecard (10-YR Post-Entry): $74,305
PayScale (Early Career): $70,200
PayScale (Mid-Career): $131,300
PayScale 20-Year ROI: $786,000

RANKINGS
Money: 4.5
U.S. News: 4, Liberal Arts Colleges
Wall Street Journal/THE: 49
Washington Monthly: 9, Liberal Arts Colleges

OVERGENERALIZATIONS
Students are:
Politically liberal
Intellectually curious
Friendly
Less concerned with fashion or appearance
Teeming with school pride

COLLEGE OVERLAPS
Brown University
Claremont McKenna College
Stanford University
University of Southern California
Williams College

Princeton University

Princeton, New Jersey | 609-258-3060

The fourth-oldest college in the United States is also an institution whose very name rings of wealth, privilege, and power—Princeton University. A charter member of the so-called Big Three alongside Harvard and Yale, Princeton has the smallest undergraduate population of that elite trio, but that doesn't stop it from churning out a disproportionate number of leaders and luminaries. Alumni include three current members of the US Supreme Court, 18 Nobel Prize winners, business giants like Jeff Bezos and Steve Forbes, and countless other influential politicians, actors, writers, and scientific geniuses. We're hardly breaking new ground here—suffice to say that Princeton is Princeton.

Inside the Classroom

Once noted for its policy of grade deflation, Princeton ended that practice nearly a decade ago, and GPAs have been on the rise since, providing a source of relief to current and future undergraduates. The majority of students are required to take a freshman writing seminar, one course in each of epistemology and cognition, ethical thought and moral values, historical analysis, and quantitative reasoning as well as two courses in each of literature and the arts, social analysis, and science and technology. All students must demonstrate proficiency in a foreign language. Central to a Princeton education is the culminating senior thesis project that is developed through one-on-one mentorship with a faculty member.

An absurdly low 5:1 student-to-faculty ratio does, as you might expect, translate to tiny class sizes for undergraduates. Just under three-quarters of class sections have an enrollment of 19 or fewer students, and 31% have fewer than ten students. Princeton is known for its commitment to undergraduate teaching, and students consistently rate professors as accessible and helpful. The Office of Undergraduate Research assists Tigers in locating faculty members with whom they can jointly conduct research in the summer or during a regular term. The university offers more than one hundred study abroad programs in over 40 countries; over half of its students take advantage.

As evidenced by the partial list of Princeton alumni, graduates of the university find themselves well-received by the worlds of employment and top graduate schools. That goes for recipients of any degree, but the Engineering Department is widely recognized as one of the country's best as is the School of Public and International Affairs (formerly Woodrow Wilson). Prestigious scholarship programs love to go Tiger hunting. Students and alumni regularly make off with as many as 14 Fulbright Scholarships in a given year and also earn multiple Truman, Gaither, Goldwater, and Schwarzman scholarships.

Outside the Classroom

An attractive and historic 500-acre campus plays home to 95% of Princeton undergraduates, who are guaranteed housing for all four years. Freshmen and sophomores are required to live in one of six Residential College houses, each staffed by a live-in faculty member and full administrative team intent on creating a "strong sense of community, collaboration, and mutual respect, and to support individual initiative and personal growth."

Sports are serious at Princeton as the Tigers field 38 varsity men's and women's squads that compete in NCAA Division I, and the school is the all-time leader in Ivy League titles. A sizable 18% of undergraduate students compete at that level, and many others join one of the thirty-seven club sports teams. There are no officially recognized Greek organizations on campus, but that doesn't mean fraternities and sororities do not exist. In fact, 15-20% of the undergraduate population joins a Greek organization, and many more go through the "Bicker" process in an attempt to gain entry into one of the university's storied and exclusive "Eating Clubs" that are located in mansions on what is known as "The Street." The 135-member Ivy Club, immortalized by F. Scott Fitzgerald in This Side of Paradise, is Princeton's version of a Skull and Bones secret society. For everyone else, there are 500 student organizations that include popular dance troupes, singing groups, fifteen chaplaincies, The Daily Princetonian (one the oldest collegiate papers), and the 500-member American Whig-Cliosophic Society, which is the oldest debate team in the country and was actually founded by James Madison. Princeton's location 55 miles from both Philadelphia and New York City means that big-city fun is always only a reasonable car or train ride away.

Career Services

The Center for Career Development at Princeton University has 26 professional staff members (excluding peer career advisors and assistants) who are dedicated to tasks such as prelaw advising, employer engagement, career advising, and alumni engagement. That 215:1 student-to-advisor ratio is superior to the average college featured in this guide. In addition to loads of individualized attention, Princeton also offers large-scale events such as the Fall & Spring HireTigers Career Fair which features one hundred top employers, and the school's online Handshake system sees over 42,000 applications for 6,500 jobs and internships each year.

An endless stream of impressive data supports the excellent work of the CCD office. In a given year, counselors engage students in 5,500 one-on-one advising sessions and attract over 11,000 attendees at close to 400 unique career services events. Approximately 3,800 students participated in student-alumni engagement programs, and 46% of undergraduate participants reported that those sessions helped influence their postgraduate plans. More than 3,100 on-campus employer interviews take place each year. Highly personalized career and graduate school advising, along with ample resources and a supportive alumni base, assure graduating Tigers that a multitude of wonderful pathways await them post-commencement.

Professional Outcomes

Over 95% of a typical Tiger class has found their next destination within six months of graduating. Large numbers of recent grads flock to the fields of business and engineering, health/science, & tech. Companies presently employing hundreds of Tiger alumni include Google, Goldman Sachs, Microsoft, McKinsey & Company, Morgan Stanley, IBM, and Meta. The average salary reported by the graduates entering the business and financial operations field is over $70k while the school's grads holding computer/mathematical positions averaged over $100k. Those finding jobs in education, health care, or social services generally made less than $40k. The majority of grads remain in the Northeast and Mid-Atlantic regions, but approximately 10% head to international destinations such as China, the United Kingdom, and South Korea.

Between 15-20% of graduating Tigers head directly to graduate/professional school. Princeton alumni typically choose equally prestigious graduate schools to attend. Members of one recent class flocked in the largest numbers to Stanford (21), Penn (11), Princeton (11), Harvard (11), Cambridge (11), Columbia (10), and Oxford (10). The most frequently pursued degree was a master's (51%) followed by a PhD (28%), MD (7%), and JD (7%). In recent years, Princeton undergrads have received acceptances into medical school 82-90% of the time, more than double the national average.

Admission

On the surface, Princeton's 6% acceptance rate for the Class of 2026 is extremely intimidating, as are the middle-50% of enrolled freshman test scores of 1510-1570 for the SAT and 34-35 for the ACT. Taking a granular look only makes things worse. The average unweighted GPA of entering first-years was 3.95 and 68% had a perfect 4.0. Candidates with lower than a 3.75 GPA or a 1400 SAT score are accepted only on very rare occasions.

The committee ranks nine factors as being most important in making admissions decisions: rigorous curriculum, GPA, class rank, essays, recommendations, standardized test scores, extracurricular activities, talent/ability, and character/personal qualities. Sorry, Risky Business fans, but alumni interviews are merely "considered." The single-choice early action (SCEA) acceptance rate is usually around 15-16%. There are a fair number of legacy admits, particularly in the early round. Overall, 10% of recent incoming freshmen had Tiger lineage. Any way you slice it, getting into Princeton is a harrowing undertaking that will, more often than not, result in failure, even for some of the most accomplished applicants. Those who are successful typically have near-perfect to perfect test scores and GPAs and a "hook" to seal the deal.

Worth Your Money?

If you qualify for financial aid, your family won't pay a dime more than it can afford. That is the case for the 61% of current undergrads who qualify for need-based aid; they receive an annual award of $63k. The university does not award merit aid. The average student graduates from Princeton with around $10k in debt, less than one-third the national average. Of course, graduates also regularly walk into financially rewarding positions, so taking on any amount of debt to attend this school would absolutely be worth the sacrifice.

FINANCIAL
Institutional Type: Private
In-State Tuition: $59,710
Out-of-State Tuition: $59,710
Room & Board: $19,380
Books & Supplies: $1,050

Avg. Need-Based Grant: $62,876
Avg. % of Need Met: 100%

Avg. Merit-Based Award: $0
% Receiving (Freshmen w/o Need): 0%

Avg. Cumulative Debt: $12,500
% of Students Borrowing: 17%

CAREER
Who Recruits
1. Bain & Company
2. Schlumberger
3. MIT Lincoln Laboratory
4. Blackstone Group
5. Uber

Notable Internships
1. US Department of State
2. Jane Street
3. Bain & Company

Top Employers
1. Google
2. Goldman Sachs
3. Microsoft
4. McKinsey & Company
5. Facebook

Where Alumni Work
1. New York City
2. San Francisco
3. Washington, DC
4. Boston
5. Philadelphia

Earnings
College Scorecard (10-YR Post-Entry): $110,433
PayScale (Early Career): $81,800
PayScale (Mid-Career): $161,500
PayScale 20-Year ROI: $1,200,000

RANKINGS
Money: 5
U.S. News: 1, National Universities
Wall Street Journal/THE: 1
Washington Monthly: 5, National Universities

OVERGENERALIZATIONS
Students are:
Always studying
Intense
Intellectually curious
Ambitious
Always admiring the beauty of their campus

COLLEGE OVERLAPS
Columbia University
Harvard University
Stanford University
University of Pennsylvania
Yale University

Providence College

Providence, Rhode Island | 401-865-2535

Large for a liberal arts institution, Providence College, a Catholic and Dominican-affiliated private school in Rhode Island, is home to 4,200+ undergraduates. Of the approximately 50 majors on tap, the most popular offerings are all within the School of Business, which helps draw 88% of its students from out of state, but more than two-thirds do hail from New England. High school students with strong academic credentials who want to avoid the single-digit acceptance rat race at many other liberal arts institutions in the region would do well to look to PC, which takes around half of all applicants each year.

Inside the Classroom
Providence is the only school in the nation run by Dominican friars, a reality that has a strong influence over the core curriculum that emphasizes an understanding of "faith and reason." Toward that aim, undergrads take four courses under the heading Development of Western Civilization, two in theology, two in philosophy/ethics, and one class in each of the fine arts, natural sciences, social sciences, and quantitative reasoning. A foreign language requirement is not part of the core curriculum, but some degree programs do require two semesters of study in this area.

It's highly unlikely that you'll find yourself surrounded by 50+ peers in more than a single course during your time at Providence—just 2% of undergraduate courses meet this criteria while 95% of classes enroll 29 students or fewer; the average class size is 19. The student-to-faculty ratio of 11:1 is low enough to make individual connections possible, including undergraduate research experiences that 36% of recent grads reported having the chance to engage in. With more than 300 study abroad programs, the opportunity to spend a semester just about anywhere in the world is on the table.

Outside of business-centric institutions like Babson College and Bentley University, you won't find many schools that confer a higher percentage of their total bachelor's degrees in business than Providence College (39%). The next most common majors are the social sciences (14%), biology (9%), psychology (9%), and health-related professions (6%). PC students have begun to capture an increasing number of prestigious postgraduate scholarships, and Providence has been named a top producer of Fulbright students multiple times in recent years.

Outside the Classroom
Situated in the Elmwood section of Rhode Island's capital city, this gated, 105-acre campus offers the tranquility of a remote locale, yet it is only miles away from all of the cultural and recreational offerings you might desire. On campus, where two-thirds of undergrads and 98% of freshmen reside, there are 100 student organizations including WDOM, one of the nation's best college radio stations as well as the long-running newspaper, The Cowl. There are no Greek organizations allowed at PC. The Concannon Fitness Center provides 13,850 square feet of dedicated fitness space for student use, and the Taylor Natatorium boasts a six-lane, 25-meter swimming pool. More serious athletes may be competing for one of 19 NCAA Division I teams with the Friars playing in the Big East for most sports, but the uber-competitive Hockey East for that sport. (PC won a hockey national title a decade ago.) The town of Providence is loaded with shopping, art, film, and concert options, and it also offers hiking and biking plus beautiful beaches that are only a short drive away. A weekend road trip to Boston takes only about an hour.

Career Services
The Chirico Career Center at Providence College is staffed by 12 professional employees, leading to a solid 357:1 student-to-counselor ratio. The staff is deployed effectively in planning large-scale events like the Fall Career Expo, which attracts 1,500+ students annually. Counselors are also available any time for a career coaching appointment, drop-in visit, mock interview, resume polish-up, or Handshake tutorial. It's no wonder the center was named one of the best college career services offices by the National Association of Colleges and Employers in 2021.

A stunning 94% of recent grads completed an internship or other career-appropriate experience (e.g., student teaching). This wealth of hands-on opportunities no doubt contributes to the fact that 81% of alumni state they are satisfied with their current positions. Few schools, if any, do a better job connecting current students to alumni in their areas of interest. Through their Find a Friar Series held in January, 800+ students connect with 100+ alumni over 20 events that target various majors/future careers. Another 140 students spend winter break participating in job shadowing.

Professional Outcomes

Ninety-six percent of Class of 2022 graduates were employed or in graduate school within six months of graduating. Among the employed, 94% were working in their field of interest, and the mean starting salary was $58,009. The greatest number of students enter the financial management/consulting/sales sector followed by marketing, healthcare, and engineering & scientific research. More than 50 alumni are presently employed by Fidelity Investments, PwC, Morgan Stanley, EY, IBM, Citi, and Dell Technologies. Recent grads also have been hired by Apple, Brown Brothers Harriman, Hasbro, and the US House of Representatives. The most common geographic landing spots for graduates are (in order) Boston; Providence; New York City; Hartford; and Washington, DC.

In a typical year, around 18% of graduates immediately enrolled in full-time graduate or professional degree programs. Those pursuing a graduate degree do so at a wide range of schools including prestigious institutions such as Brown, Columbia, Johns Hopkins, NYU, and Notre Dame. For applicants deemed "qualified" by PC faculty, the medical school acceptance rate fluctuates between 80% and 100%. Recent grads have attended schools such as the Zucker School of Medicine at Hofstra, Rutgers University, and Albany Medical College. Pre-law advising is available and, in the past few years, alumni have matriculated into Fordham Law School, the Georgetown University Law Center, and Tulane University Law School.

Admission

Of 11,129 applicants to the Class of 2026, PC accepted 53%, up from a 47% acceptance rate three years ago. The school has been test-optional for over 10 years, so it is little surprise that last cycle only 56% submitted an SAT score; another 13% included ACT results. The mid-50th percentile among those who did elect to submit scores was 1130-1330 on the SAT and 25-31 on the ACT. Looking at class rank, 39% of the Class of 2026 placed in the top decile of their high school class while 77% were in the top quartile. The average GPA was 3.57, and only 6% possessed a GPA under 3.0.

Three factors are of paramount importance as the committee reviews your application: rigor of postsecondary record, GPA, and your essay. Another three factors are viewed on the next tier of importance: recommendations, character/personal qualities, and extracurricular activities. On that last note, the admissions office states, "It is important to remember that we are much more interested in the quality and depth of your involvement rather than the quantity." If, based on the above admissions statistics, you feel that you are a borderline applicant and consider PC to be among your top choices, applying early decision is a good bet. The ED acceptance rate for the Class of 2026 was 87%.

Worth Your Money?

With a stated cost of attendance of $78k, which is all too standard for New England-based private colleges, many families and students might mistakenly believe that Providence College is out of their price range. Yet, students with a 3.8 unweighted GPA in a rigorous curriculum often receive a merit-based scholarship of somewhere between $20k and $30k. In fact, 30% of admitted students land an award in that range. With average need-based grants of $36k also being awarded to a majority of incoming freshmen, few pay that $78k figure. Still, this school is not a perfect fit for everyone as evidenced by the fact that graduate debt at PC is higher than the national average. Unless you were majoring in the business program (or another field with strong starting salaries), we would not recommend taking on that level of debt in order to attend.

FINANCIAL
Institutional Type: Private
In-State Tuition: $60,848
Out-of-State Tuition: $60,848
Room & Board: $17,150
Books & Supplies: $1,150

Avg. Need-Based Grant: $35,600
Avg. % of Need Met: 92%

Avg. Merit-Based Award: $21,383
% Receiving (Freshmen w/o Need): 16%

Avg. Cumulative Debt: $41,907
% of Students Borrowing: 72%

CAREER
Who Recruits
1. EY
2. CVS Health
3. UBS
4. Amazon Web Services
5. Takeda

Notable Internships
1. CBRE
2. Citizens Bank
3. Dell

Top Employers
1. Fidelity Investments
2. PwC
3. Citizens
4. CVS Health
5. Morgan Stanley

Where Alumni Work
1. Boston
2. Providence
3. New York City
4. Hartford, CT
5. Washington, DC

Earnings
College Scorecard (10-YR Post-Entry): $79,628
PayScale (Early Career): $63,500
PayScale (Mid-Career): $119,100
PayScale 20-Year ROI: $571,000

RANKINGS
Money: 4.5
U.S. News: 1, Regional Universities North
Wall Street Journal/THE: 135
Washington Monthly: 76, Master's Universities

OVERGENERALIZATIONS
Students are:
Politically conservative
Ready to party
Homogeneous
Preppy
Tight-knit (possess a strong sense of community)

COLLEGE OVERLAPS
Boston College
College of the Holy Cross
Fairfield University
Loyola University Maryland
Villanova University

West Lafayette, Indiana | 765-494-1776

After dominating Wabash College in an 1892 football contest, a newspaper reporter labeled the brutes from Purdue University as "burly boiler makers." It was intended to be derogatory—a dig at an engineering and agricultural education—but it was almost immediately embraced by not only the football team but the entire university. As the twenty-first century has progressed, Purdue University, the public STEM university in Indiana, has grown to where it now educates 37,949 undergraduates and another 12,935 graduate students and draws bright techie teens from well beyond the Hoosier State's 92 counties. Indiana residents comprise only 40% of the total student population at Purdue, and 18% are international students.

Inside the Classroom

Waves of new students crash onto Purdue's West Lafayette campus each year, filling up ten discipline-specific colleges in the pursuit of 200+ undergraduate majors. Yet, whether you are a member of the College of Engineering or the College of Education, you'll have to complete the same core curriculum, a thirty-credit concoction that lists among its ingredients written communication, information literacy, oral communication, science, quantitative reasoning, human behavior, and human cultures. The school's renowned Honors College welcomes 700+ freshmen each fall and offers small class sizes, honors housing, and special leadership opportunities.

But class sizes are reasonable for all students, not only those in the Honors College. For a school of immense size, Purdue offers a reasonable 14:1 student-to-faculty ratio that leads to 38% of course sections having an enrollment of 19 or fewer. You can also expect a balance of larger lectures; 20% of courses enroll more than fifty students. Undergraduate research opportunities are afforded to around 2,000 students per year. Undergrads can connect with professors on research projects during the academic year or apply to participate in a Summer Research Fellowship. A similar number, 2,400 students per year, elect to study abroad at one of 300 programs in 50 countries.

Engineering and engineering technologies majors earn 34% of the degrees conferred by the university. It makes sense that so many take advantage. After all, Purdue's College of Engineering cracks the top ten on almost every list of best engineering schools. The Krannert School of Management is also well-regarded by employers around the country; 11% of degrees conferred are in business. Other popular majors include computer science (10%) and agriculture (5%)—both are incredibly strong. Nationally competitive scholarships have been captured by recent grads of all academic backgrounds, including as many as six Fulbright Scholarships per year and a multitude of National Science Foundation Graduate Research Fellowships.

Outside the Classroom

Male-heavy to the tune of 57% (a typical STEM disproportionality), roughly two-fifths of the Purdue undergraduate student body lives on campus. Freshman housing is only guaranteed to those who sign a housing contract by early May; 93% of first-year students followed through in 2022-23. There are over ninety fraternity and sorority houses, and 15% of men and 17% of women partake in Greek life. Nearly 1,000 clubs and activities are available, and among those who participate, two-thirds cited their involvement as one of the major reasons they remain at the university. A hard-to-fathom 18,000 students participate in one of forty intramural sports—there are 300 flag football teams alone. There is also no shortage of big-time sports to consume as a fan. A top-ranked marching band helps cheer on the eighteen NCAA Division I squads that compete in the Big Ten Conference. Purdue has sent thirty players to the NBA, and the football team has appeared in eighteen postseason bowl games. Campus food receives favorable reviews as does the sprawling 2,000-acre campus and its proximity to traditional college-town fare and basic entertainment. In addition, Indianapolis can be reached within about an hour by car, and Chicago is a nice weekend destination that is only a two-hour drive away.

Career Services

There are 20 professional staff members (not counting administrative assistants) occupying the offices of Purdue University's Center for Career Opportunities & Pre-Professional Advising (CCO). The majority have the title of career services consultant while others specialize in pre-professional advising. There are also 25 student advisors. The university's overall 1,897:1 student-to-counselor ratio is quite high compared to most other schools profiled in this guidebook. Fortunately, the center is adept at organizing large-scale events, connecting with industry leaders, and facilitating experiential learning and networking opportunities for its undergraduate students.

The Industry Roundtable, held every September, is the largest student-run career fair in the United States, drawing 400 companies and 12,000+ students. A business-specific career fair attracts another 2,000 students, the Agricultural Career Fair brings one hundred companies to campus, and Purdue also offers fairs for aviation, civil engineering, hospitality/tourism, aerospace, and construction management. This robust operation brings a total of 1,400 employers to campus each year for recruiting and/or on-campus interviews. Internship numbers are equally impressive—82% of recent grads engaged in at least one internship experience during their four years of study; over one-quarter completed more than one. Catering to the career services needs of almost 38,000 undergraduates with limited staff may be a logistical battle, but it is one that Purdue's CCO is managing to win. What it lacks in the ability to hand-hold, it makes up for in the scope of offerings and the positive career results for graduates.

Professional Outcomes

Shortly after receiving their diplomas, 70% of 2022 grads headed to the world of employment, 24% were continuing their educational journey in graduate/professional school, and a mere 2% were still seeking employment. The top industries entered by Purdue graduates in recent years are (1) health care, pharmaceuticals, and medical devices; (2) finance, insurance, and consulting; (3) manufacturing and machinery; (4) airline, aviation, and aerospace. Companies employing the greatest number of 2021 graduates were, in order: Amazon, Deloitte, PepsiCo, Labcorp, Lockheed Martin, and Microsoft. The average starting salary was an exceptional $68k across all degree programs. The majority of alumni remain in Indiana with Chicago, San Francisco, New York, and DC rounding out the five next most common destinations.

Purdue enjoys professional school acceptance rates that are "slightly above" the national averages. In 2023, the school saw 191 of its seniors apply to medical school, and many went on to attend the Indiana University School of Medicine and other Midwestern institutions including the University of Minnesota and the University of Illinois. Given the academic concentrations of many undergrads, law school is not an immensely popular choice. Interestingly, Purdue purchased an unaccredited online law school in 2017, which was recognized by the American Bar Association in 2020. Looking at all grad school applicants, 538 graduates in the most recent graduating class who continued their educations did so in state. Illinois, New York, and California all attracted 40+ graduate/professional students to top institutions like NYU, UC Berkeley, and the University of Chicago.

Admission

Purdue – West Lafayette received 68,309 applications for a spot in the Class of 2026 and admitted 53% of wannabe Boilermakers, down from 69% the prior year. Of those who were admitted and ultimately enrolled, the median SAT score was 1330 and the median ACT score was 31. Math scores are generally stronger than reading scores—43% of freshmen scored above a 700 on the SAT math section while only 31% hit that same target on the reading section. Fifty-three percent placed in the top 10% of their high school class, and 82% were in the top quartile, giving a glimmer of hope to applicants with a few blemishes on their transcripts and who aren't looking to pursue either engineering or computer science. Earning entry into these majors can prove considerably more difficult.

The university's admissions staff looks foremost at the hard numbers of GPA and standardized test scores as well as the rigor of your high school curriculum. First-generation status is among the categories occupying the next rung of "important" factors. It is joined by essays, extracurricular activities, recommendations, and character/personal qualities. Women enjoyed a 64% acceptance rate compared to 45% for male applicants. There is no binding early decision option, but there is an early action round with a November 1 deadline. Overall, acceptance rates at Purdue are definitely on the decline. In 2007, the school received approximately 20,000 applications and accepted 79% of the pool. Despite the rise in selectivity, Purdue remains one of the top STEM-focused universities that accepts solid but imperfect applicants.

Worth Your Money?

Tuition for Hoosier State residents remains a tremendous bargain at a hair under $10k. Nonresidents will pay $29k in tuition which, given the graduates' employment and salary data, is still not a bad price. Like most STEM-oriented schools, Purdue is highly likely to return your investment many times over. The only person for whom this school would not make complete sense is an out-of-state applicant taking loans to pursue a non-STEM/business degree.

FINANCIAL
Institutional Type: Public
In-State Tuition: $9,992
Out-of-State Tuition: $28,794
Room & Board: $10,030
Books & Supplies: $1,160

Avg. Need-Based Grant: $12,378
Avg. % of Need Met: 64%

Avg. Merit-Based Award: $5,631
% Receiving (Freshmen w/o Need): 8%

Avg. Cumulative Debt: $30,861
% of Students Borrowing: 39%

CAREER
Who Recruits
1. Cognex Corporation
2. Endress + Hauser
3. Lockheed Martin
4. General Motors
5. General Electric

Notable Internships
1. Caterpillar
2. Qualcomm
3. PepsiCo

Top Employers
1. Amazon
2. Microsoft
3. IBM
4. Google
5. Apple

Where Alumni Work
1. Indianapolis
2. Lafayette, IN
3. Chicago
4. San Francisco
5. New York City

Earnings
College Scorecard (10-YR Post-Entry): $68,414
PayScale (Early Career): $66,500
PayScale (Mid-Career): $112,800
PayScale 20-Year ROI: $731,000

RANKINGS
Money: 4.5
U.S. News: 43, National Universities
Wall Street Journal/THE: 115
Washington Monthly: 59, National Universities

OVERGENERALIZATIONS
Students are:
Crazy about the Boilermakers
Career-driven
Competitive
Practical
Not afraid to work hard

COLLEGE OVERLAPS
Indiana University Bloomington
The Ohio State University - Columbus
Pennsylvania State University - University Park
University of Illinois at Urbana-Champaign
University of Michigan

Reed College

Portland, Oregon | 503-777-7511

"A band of fierce intellectuals and the distinctive institution that nurtures them. All in for rigorous scholarship and the joy of intellectual pursuit." Thus reads the X profile of an elite liberal arts school of 1,523 undergraduates located in Portland, Oregon—the one-and-only Reed College. It would be difficult to create a statement that more aptly sums up this unique institution that, for many, serves primarily as a prelude to a PhD program.

Inside the Classroom
Twenty-six academic departments collectively offer 38 majors, 13 of which are interdisciplinary (e.g., history-literature or mathematics-economics). One of the most storied features of a Reed education is the mandatory, year-long freshman Humanities 110 course that comprehensively explores Greco-Roman culture and its many influences. However, five years ago, after a series of student-led protests over the course's "Eurocentrism," the school agreed to alter the course to include the study of other cultures. As with the aforementioned X statement, that anecdote also helps paint a picture of the Reed experience.

Grades at the college are, paradoxically, both (a) difficult to earn and (b) completely unknown to the students themselves. To ensure that the emphasis in the classroom remains on learning for learning's sake, grades are issued but not shared with students until graduation. The average GPA earned is 3.2, and only 12 students have graduated with a perfect 4.0 in the last three decades. The educational experience is highly personalized, and students work directly with their professors. Class sizes average 16 students, and the student-to-faculty ratio is 10:1. Study abroad opportunities exist at 50+ partner university programs in twenty-three countries. The college funds a number of undergraduate research opportunities for students to work alongside faculty, and all students are required to complete their own senior thesis, which is essentially a mini-dissertation under the guidance of a faculty advisor.

The areas in which the highest number of degrees are conferred are the social sciences (22%), biology (11%), the health professions (9%), and the physical sciences (7%). All majors are viewed favorably by elite graduate programs that are fully aware of the exceptional level of rigor baked into every academic program at the college. English, math, and physics receive particularly strong praise. Competitive fellowship and scholarship programs are also acutely aware of Reed's excellence and pluck up graduates at exceptionally high rates. In its history, Reed grads have won 32 Rhodes Scholarships, 60+ Watson Fellowships, and 170+ National Science Foundation Fellowships.

Outside the Classroom
Downtown Portland is only ten minutes away, making Reed's location in the southeastern corner of the city ideal for finding culture, the arts, and entertainment. Public transportation is easy to navigate, so just about anything that the uber-progressive City of Roses has to offer is accessible. One hundred percent of freshmen in 2022-23 lived on campus and 67% of the total student body resided in university-owned housing. Others live in affordable off-campus housing that is easy to locate in the immediate area. There are no fraternities or sororities at Reed, nor is there any semblance of highly competitive athletics. There are, however, five intercollegiate club teams in which athletically inclined students may wish to participate. While most Reedies would say their primary outside-the-classroom activity is "studying," there are ninety student-run organizations from which to choose, including KRRC, the campus radio station; Quest, the student body's independent newspaper; and typical "Reedish" groups like the Sky Appreciation Society. Renn Fayre, an annual campus-wide, weekend-long party for graduating seniors is an out-of-control event that is truly beloved by students. Notable amenities include a recently renovated ski cabin on Mt. Hood that students are free to use as well as the Watzik Sports Center, which boasts a pool, sauna, and climbing wall.

Career Services
The Center for Life Beyond Reed (CLBR) employs six full-time staff members, giving it a 254:1 student-to-advisor ratio that is better than average for a college included in this guidebook. The guiding mission of the office, since a rebranding a decade ago, is to help students "try to connect the intellectual passions they cultivate during their time here to successful careers."

On the practical side, the CLBR offers six full-day senior boot camps where students can receive help with resumes, online professional profiles, interview techniques, and helpful contacts in students' areas of interest. In recent years, it has increased engagement with freshmen and sophomores, encouraging earlier 1:1 advising sessions. Handshake and the Reed Career Network are the places online to find a job or internship, or connect with alumni. Winter Shadow internships allow current students to join alumni in their places of business. With an intense focus on preparing the next generation of academics and researchers, the campus is not swarming with corporate recruiters, yet Reed does maintain some productive relationships with employers—Microsoft, for example, contributed $500,000 toward the development of the college's computer science program. Acknowledging its immense level of success in placing students at elite graduate and professional schools, the CLBR serves its unique student population well in spite of below-average starting salaries (more on that in a moment).

Professional Outcomes

An examination of Reed's alumni database reveals that the three most common occupational pathways are business (28%), education (25%), and self-employment (19%). Included among the most frequent current employers are Microsoft Corporation, Kaiser Permanente, Portland Public Schools, Intel Corporation, the US Department of State, National Institutes of Health, and Apple. Because of the incredible number of students who flock to academia (more on this later), many institutions of higher education are also employers of large numbers of Reed alumni. Early-to-mid-career salary figures are generally low even by liberal arts standards. However, it is important to place that fact in proper context because that is the age when many Reed alumni may be completing an advanced degree.

Reed is rarely the final stop on a student's academic journey. In College Transitions' analysis of National Science Foundation data, Reed was the No. 6 producer of future PhD holders across all academic disciplines as determined by the percentage of graduates attaining that degree. This puts them right beside the likes of Caltech, Swarthmore, and MIT. MBAs were earned at institutions that include Penn, Georgetown, Columbia, and UChicago. Reedies who went the legal route obtained their JDs primarily from top-tier law schools. Recent med school applicants have enjoyed a 68% acceptance rate over the past decade, and many have attended similarly impressive universities as those in other fields already mentioned.

Admission

Reed College's 31% acceptance rate does not do its level of selectivity justice, not that the college cares. Admirably, this institution has long been anti-rankings and has no interest in PR efforts to drum up more applicants for the purpose of enhancing its status. It receives 9,000 applications per year. Its students are a self-selecting crew who choose to apply to this unique liberal arts school in Portland, Oregon. The middle-50% range for enrolled students is right around 1320-1500 on the SATs and 30-33 on the ACTs. Grades/class rank numbers are impressive but do not automatically exclude those with an imperfect transcript; 62% finished in the top 10% of their high school class, 81% were in the top 25%, and only 2% placed outside of the top half.

The Reed Admissions Office only designates three factors as being "very important" in its evaluation process: rigor of secondary school record, grades, and essays. Factors deemed "important" are standardized test scores, class rank, interview, demonstrated interest, and recommendations. This is a college that, like Wesleyan on the opposite coast, is looking for intellectual risk-takers whose passion comes through in their writing and in conversation. Applying early usually helps, although last year 33% of ED applicants were accepted, a similar clip as during the regular round. Teens who are destined to be Reedies are the ones who fall in love with the school in the first place. Brilliant young people with an open mind who eschew convention will be thrilled to find a home here. Of course, strong credentials will help to make that goal a reality.

Worth Your Money?

At a cost of $78,000 and little available in the way of merit aid, many pay a steep price for attending this institution. Over 50% of Reed students do qualify for need-based aid and receive average annual aid packages of $52k. Undoubtedly, the academic experience here is uniquely wonderful and a perfect fit for a certain type of budding intellectual. Yet, if you don't qualify for need-based aid and don't come from a wealthy family, you would have to make sure that the $312,000 bill for tuition would make sense as part of your life plan. Interestingly, the average student loan debt among Reed graduates is lower than the national average.

FINANCIAL
Institutional Type: Private
In-State Tuition: $64,760
Out-of-State Tuition: $64,760
Room & Board: $15,950
Books & Supplies: $1,050

Avg. Need-Based Grant: $46,643
Avg. % of Need Met: 100%

Avg. Merit-Based Award: $0
% Receiving (Freshmen w/o Need): 0%

Avg. Cumulative Debt: $26,500
% of Students Borrowing: 43%

CAREER
Who Recruits
1. TerraCotta Group LLC
2. First Book
3. Cranial Technologies
4. Teach for America
5. Wayfair

Notable Internships
1. Melville House Publishing
2. RTI International
3. Whitney Museum of American Art

Top Employers
1. Google
2. Microsoft
3. Apple
4. Intel
5. Amazon

Where Alumni Work
1. Portland, OR
2. San Francisco
3. New York City
4. Seattle
5. Los Angeles

Earnings
College Scorecard (10-YR Post-Entry): $52,236
PayScale (Early Career): $61,600
PayScale (Mid-Career): $120,100
PayScale 20-Year ROI: $312,000

RANKINGS
Money: 3
U.S. News: 67, Liberal Arts Colleges
Wall Street Journal/THE: Not Ranked
Washington Monthly: 112, Liberal Arts Colleges

OVERGENERALIZATIONS
Students are:
Always studying
Politically liberal
Intellectually curious
Quirky
Hippies or hipsters

COLLEGE OVERLAPS
Brown University
Carleton College
Lewis & Clark College
Swarthmore College
University of Chicago

Rensselaer Polytechnic Institute

Troy, New York | 518-276-6216

Founded 200 years ago, Rensselaer Polytechnic Institute is America's first technological research university and still one of its best. Fittingly situated on the eastern bank of the Hudson River in the Industrial Revolution hotspot of Troy, New York, RPI is the proud home of 5,895 of the brightest and most innovative technical undergraduate minds anywhere. This is merely perpetuating a long history of producing high achievers in the tech world. Including both faculty and alumni, Rensselaer claims 85 members of the National Academy of Engineering, five members of the National Inventors Hall of Fame, and a Nobel Prize winner in physics.

Inside the Classroom
There are five undergraduate schools within the larger university: the School of Architecture; the Lally School of Management; the School of Science; the School of Engineering; and the School of Humanities, Arts, and Social Sciences. All students take what is known as the HASS Core, a six-course, twenty-four-credit foray into the humanities and social sciences. New in 2021-22 were the HASS Integrative Pathways, designed to help students go more in-depth in a secondary area of interest. Beyond that, the academic programs are tailored to different schools and degree programs. There is no foreign language requirement, although the school does offer coursework in Mandarin Chinese for interested students.

The student-to-faculty ratio at RPI is 12:1, and with only about 1,200 graduate students to serve, there is plenty of time and attention left for undergraduates. Students will encounter various class sizes over the course of their four years of study. A solid 54% of sections contain fewer than 20 students; 10% will have 50 or more students. Being a research institution, RPI attracts $103 million in research funding each year, meaning that the school's 420+ faculty members are constantly in the middle of projects that require student assistance. Students can participate during the academic year for credit or during the summer when select individuals receive $4,000 to work full-time in a lab. International study is also encouraged at one of the school's affiliate universities in thirteen countries including Australia, Finland, and Singapore.

Engineering is the most commonly conferred degree area, accounting for 45% of graduates. Computer and information sciences was second (21%), followed by math/statistics (5%), engineering technology (5%), and biology (4%). The School of Engineering has a brilliant reputation with employers worldwide and is always near the top of the rankings for its programs in mechanical, aerospace, computer, electrical, and biomedical engineering. Physics, architecture, and computer science are also strong. Graduates do not apply to prestigious fellowship programs in droves, but the school does capture an occasional Fulbright or Truman Scholarship. RPI does, however, typically produce more than one annual National Science Foundation Graduate Research Fellowship winner.

Outside the Classroom
The school's 296-acre suburban campus houses 56% of the student body; many upperclassmen seek off-campus apartments or join fraternities or sororities. Sixteen percent of men and 12% of women elect to join Greek organizations. Those numbers are down after several chapters were suspended or dissolved in recent years. For a technical school, RPI boasts a highly athletic student body. Three-fifths of incoming freshmen participated in varsity athletics in high school, and two-fifths were the captains of their squads. There are 23 varsity men's and women's sports teams, twenty-two of which compete in NCAA Division III. The exception is men's hockey, which is one of the oldest and best teams in the entire country, having produced a long list of NHL stars over the years. Including the university's thriving intramural and club programs, 80% of RPI students are involved in athletics. With over 200 student organizations, students have their pick of non-sports/Greek sources of camaraderie. For example, the RPI Players has put on 300 theatrical shows over its 90-year history, and there are nineteen service-oriented groups that serve the local community. In addition, fitness classes run by professional instructors are available just about every day at the Mueller Center. Troy itself may lack excitement, but the state capital of Albany is only ten miles away, and scenic retreats like the Berkshires or Catskills are under two hours away.

Career Services
The Center for Career and Professional Development consists of 14 professional employees, which calculates to a student-to-advisor ratio of 421:1, a bit higher than the average school featured in this guide. However, that less-than-ideal statistic is not at all representative of the exceptional work done by RPI's career services staff. Other numbers tell a different story, such as the 225 annual events and the close to 2,000 one-on-one counseling appointments that take place. And that doesn't even include the employer recruiting numbers that are even more eye-popping.

In a given year, career fairs draw 250 employers to campus, and 100+ employers conduct 1,900 on-campus interviews. Companies also hosted 130 information sessions for RPI students that same year. Companies that recruit on campus include Cisco, the Blackstone Group, Deloitte, Johnson & Johnson, and Credit Suisse. Rensselaer Alumni Connect is a platform with over 2,500 active users, 79% of whom are willing to introduce others to connections while 83% are willing to answer industry-specific questions. Internship and co-op opportunities abound, and large numbers of students land co-op positions at Hasbro (27), NASA Jet Propulsion Laboratory (10), and Walt Disney World (7). Thanks to an endless parade of recruiters flowing into campus, high starting salaries, and plenty of individualized attention, the CCPD has earned a reputation for stellar work.

Professional Outcomes

As they receive their diplomas, 54% of RPI grads have already landed a job, 32% have committed to a graduate school, and 10% are still seeking their next destination. The largest numbers of grads were hired by companies that included Google, Microsoft, Deloitte, General Dynamics, Boeing, and IBM. Massive numbers of alumni hold leadership positions in corporations like Google, Pratt & Whitney, General Motors, GE, and Microsoft. Geographically, 64% of graduates remain in the Northeast, 16% head to the West—primarily to Silicon Valley—and 6% land in the Southeast. Recent grads enjoy starting salaries in excess of $81k.

Of the 32% of grads who entered an advanced degree program, many headed to some of the nation's best schools. Recent grads have been accepted by the likes of Carnegie Mellon University, Duke University, Massachusetts Institute of Technology, Northwestern University, Texas A&M, and the University of Chicago. Those intent on medical school have the option to apply to RPI's seven-year BS/MD program with affiliate Albany Medical College. Recent medically minded grads have enjoyed acceptances at the likes of Harvard Medical School and Cornell University College of Veterinary Medicine. Those intent on law school also have the option of a combined degree, in this case, a BS/JD at either Albany or Columbia University.

Admission

RPI received fewer applications from Class of 2026 hopefuls than the previous year—16,863 in 2021. While the acceptance rate of 65% will do little to scare off prospective students, the composition of the 2022-23 freshman class was an impressive one. The median SAT score was 1440, a solid 54% placed in the top 10% of their high school class, and 87% were in the top quarter. In a typical year, close to 100 students earned either valedictorian or salutatorian status. The average GPA of an entering freshman was 3.9.

There is nothing opaque about the way in which applicants are evaluated by the Rensselaer admissions committee. The most strongly weighted factors are GPA, class rank, and the rigor of one's high school coursework. Of secondary importance are application essays, recommendations, extracurricular activities, and character/personal qualities. Unusual for a tech school, males and females have fairly similar acceptance rates. Applying early decision provides an advantage; ED acceptance rates are usually a bit higher than the RD rates. Rensselaer Polytechnic Institute is looking for students with GPAs above 3.75 in most or all honors and AP courses and who scored in the 95th percentile on standardized tests. The criteria are fairly simple.

Worth Your Money?

Rensselaer's annual cost of attendance is a pretty high $82,404; the good news is that starting salaries for graduates just about match that sum. Over one-third of entering students do get an offer of merit aid that averages almost $29k, and more than half of attendees qualify for a need-based aid package with an average value of $49k. Attending a STEM-heavy school like RPI is almost always a good bet for getting an excellent return on your educational investment, even if the up-front cost is quite high.

FINANCIAL
Institutional Type: Private
In-State Tuition: $61,884
Out-of-State Tuition: $61,884
Room & Board: $17,530
Books & Supplies: $1,310

Avg. Need-Based Grant: $17,068
Avg. % of Need Met: 72%

Avg. Merit-Based Award: $28,970
% Receiving (Freshmen w/o Need): 31%

Avg. Cumulative Debt: $41,523
% of Students Borrowing: 53%

CAREER
Who Recruits
1. U.S. Nuclear Regulatory Commission
2. Etsy
3. GlobalFoundries
4. Apprenda
5. American Airlines

Notable Internships
1. Regeneron Pharmaceuticals
2. NASA
3. Pfizer

Top Employers
1. IBM
2. Pratt & Whitney
3. Google
4. Boeing
5. GE

Where Alumni Work
1. New York City
2. Albany, NY
3. Boston
4. San Francisco
5. Washington, DC

Earnings
College Scorecard (10-YR Post-Entry): $100,141
PayScale (Early Career): $76,700
PayScale (Mid-Career): $140,500
PayScale 20-Year ROI: $992,000

RANKINGS
Money: 4.5
U.S. News: 60, National Universities
Wall Street Journal/THE: 34
Washington Monthly: 109, National Universities

OVERGENERALIZATIONS
Students are:
Nerdy
Diverse
Career-driven
STEM-focused
Tight-knit (possess a strong sense of community)

COLLEGE OVERLAPS
Carnegie Mellon University
Cornell University
Georgia Institute of Technology
Purdue University - West Lafayette
Worcester Polytechnic Institute

Rhodes College

Memphis, Tennessee | 901-843-3700

Rhodes College's Memphis location places it among the rare liberal arts schools located in an urban setting. (Occidental in Los Angeles is another such school featured in this guide.) Just four miles from the world-famous Beale Street, Rhodes, founded in 1848, is one of the top colleges in the region. A progressive, service-oriented student body of just over 1,996 students flock to Rhodes for its small classes, awesome location, and nurturing environment that leads many on the path to top graduate and professional programs.

Inside the Classroom
The school offers 50 majors and minors and a great deal of academic autonomy along the way. The foundation requirements can be met by roughly 400 varied courses that cover target areas such as written communication, becoming an active and engaged citizen, gaining proficiency in a second language, and understanding scientific approaches to the natural world. As part of this experience, students choose between two signature courses: The Search for Values in the Light of Western Religion and History and Life: Then and Now, both of which were developed after World War II. Freshmen also must engage in the first-year experience requirement—an integrative, year-long program focused on becoming an active student-citizen—as well as a first-year writing seminar.

A 9:1 student-to-faculty ratio leads to an amazingly intimate average class size of only 14 students. Only 5% of course sections contain more than 29 students. Eighty-five percent of the 195 full-time faculty members hold the highest degree available in their fields, so you will not be taught by TAs or adjuncts. A great deal of resources are committed to undergraduate education. For example, Rhodes puts an astounding sum of money into its physical science programs, having committed $34 million to a new science center five years ago. As a result, the school produces an incredible number of PhDs (more on this under "Professional Outcomes"). Three-quarters of students at this institution engage in some form of undergraduate research. Opportunities to collaborate with faculty on research projects are plentiful in every academic discipline, and the annual Undergraduate Research and Creativity Symposium is a chance to show off student projects. An affiliation with St. Jude's Children's Research Hospital leads to intensive summer research opportunities for those in the hard sciences. A solid 75% of students elect to study abroad or at off-campus sites, and the school offers many Rhodes faculty-led locations around the world.

While the sciences may be the area for which Rhodes receives the greatest recognition, business, psychology, and international studies are also strong and attract large numbers of undergrads. In a single recent year, seniors and alumni have captured an incredible 11 Fulbright Scholarships and have won Watson, Luce, and NSF Fellowships.

Outside the Classroom
This 123-acre wooded oasis in midtown Memphis is home to 71% of all undergraduates. Students are required to live in residence halls for their first two years. Most residence halls are intimate places of under one hundred students where everyone knows everyone. A 58/42% breakdown in favor of women certainly has an impact on student life. Greek life is a defining characteristic of social life at Rhodes with 33% of women joining a sorority and 29% of men pledging a fraternity. Participation in sports is also common with twenty-one men's and women's varsity teams competing in NCAA Division III athletics. The Bryan Campus Life Center offers ample facilities for recreational sports and fitness. For non-jocks, there are more than one hundred student-run organizations, and over 80% of students engage in community service activities. The mock trial team is exceptionally strong in national competitions. With the Lynx Lair serving as a hub for food and social events as well as frequent concerts, lectures, and films, there is rarely a dull moment at Rhodes. Of course, with Memphis as your backyard, there are always exciting excursions for entertainment, culture, or dining. The Memphis Zoo, the Memphis Brooks Museum of Art, and the National Civil Rights Museum are only a few miles away. Campus is walker-friendly, but bikes are popular as well. The city of Memphis has over 200 miles of bike infrastructure to help ensure safety.

Career Services
The Career Services Office at Rhodes has four full-time staff members. Rhodes' 499:1 student-to-advisor ratio does not compare favorably to other liberal arts schools featured in this guide, but the push for personalized service is evident everywhere you look. The school encourages meeting one-on-one with advisors two or three times in the freshman year as well as during sophomore year. Few schools promote that level of contact so early in a student's undergraduate career.

Every fall, representatives from over one hundred graduate and professional schools travel to Rhodes' campus to attend the Graduate School Exposition. One recent Career Fair was attended by over 50 employers, including many national corporations such as AutoZone, Raymond James, and St. Jude's Research Hospital. Approximately 75% of undergraduates complete at least one internship. Those numbers are bolstered by career services partnerships with over one hundred local, national, and global employers. Many of the 13,000 alums are willing to lend a hand to a current student or recent grad seeking to network.

Professional Outcomes

Within one year of receiving their diplomas, 98% of Rhodes grads have found their way into the world of employment or are pursuing an advanced degree program. Among the companies employing the largest number of alumni are St. Jude's Children's Hospital, Deloitte, EY, FedEx, Raymond James, and PwC. Mid-career salaries are the second-highest among any Tennessee institution, behind only Vanderbilt. Greater Memphis is where most graduates remain. Many others situate themselves in Greater Nashville, Atlanta, DC, New York, or Dallas.

Close to 90% of those applying to graduate school get into their top-choice institution. Medical and law school applicants are accepted at higher rates than the national average. Those with a 3.4 GPA and above the 57th percentile on the MCAT are accepted into medical school at an impressive 86% clip and, overall, enjoy a 65% acceptance rate. Three years ago, an impressive forty-four graduates were accepted into med school. Rhodes is in the top 11% of science PhD-producing undergraduate schools in the country, and is ranked among the top 50 PhD producers in several social science disciplines as well, including economics, political science, and psychology. Recent graduates have been accepted into programs at elite universities including Brown, Columbia, Georgetown, Harvard Law School, New York University School of Law, and Yale Divinity School. Medical schools attended by recent grads include Tufts, Dartmouth, Boston University, Wake Forest, and UVA.

Admission

With a 48% acceptance rate for a place in the Class of 2026, Rhodes College is a rare school that provides an elite education without putting applicants through a harrowing admissions process with dreadfully unfavorable odds. The 5,932 hopefuls who submitted applications were a strong bunch, but those who were successful didn't have to sport a perfect transcript. The median SAT was 1380 and the median ACT is 30. Eighty-three percent of admitted freshmen held a weighted GPA of 3.75 or higher, 54% finished in the top decile of their high school class, and 81% were in the top quartile. The average GPA of incoming 2022-23 freshmen was 3.7.

Rigor of secondary school record, GPA, and class rank sit atop the list of most important factors in the eyes of the admissions office. Factors considered as "important" include standardized test scores, essays, recommendations, character/personal qualities, legacy status, and racial/ethnic background. Only 17% of those accepted actually enrolled; thus, the college values those who demonstrate interest, particularly in the form of committing through early decision. As a result, 58% of ED applicants were accepted in 2022. In their own words, Rhodes uses a "holistic approach to evaluate every facet of your application to get a better sense of the whole you." Obviously, the school is looking for students with strong grades in a demanding curriculum, but students do not need to have perfect test scores and grades for consideration at this fine liberal arts institution.

Worth Your Money?

Rhodes' sticker-price cost of attendance of almost $68,000 isn't particularly tough to swallow, at least when considered against the cost of many comparable institutions. Yet, Rhodes still delivers need-based aid to almost 50% of its students, who receive an average scholarship or grant award of $37k. The school meets 92% of total demonstrated need. Given the cost that most people actually pay, Rhodes College is a fairly priced option that will afford you a one-of-a-kind educational experience.

FINANCIAL
Institutional Type: Private
In-State Tuition: $54,892
Out-of-State Tuition: $54,892
Room & Board: $12,910
Books & Supplies: $1,125

Avg. Need-Based Grant: $36,842
Avg. % of Need Met: 95%

Avg. Merit-Based Award: $30,149
% Receiving (Freshmen w/o Need): 48%

Avg. Cumulative Debt: $21,967
% of Students Borrowing: 39%

CAREER
Who Recruits
1. St. Jude's Children's Research Hospital
2. Raymond James
3. Methodist Healthcare
4. PeaceCorps
5. Teach for America

Notable Internships
1. Graystar Real Estate
2. Christie's
3. FedEx

Top Employers
1. St. Jude Children's Research Hospital
2. Deloitte
3. EY
4. Raymond James
5. FedEx

Where Alumni Work
1. Memphis
2. Nashville
3. Atlanta
4. Washington, DC
5. New York City

Earnings
College Scorecard (10-YR Post-Entry): $69,215
PayScale (Early Career): $55,100
PayScale (Mid-Career): $116,500
PayScale 20-Year ROI: $348,000

RANKINGS
Money: 4
U.S. News: 56, Liberal Arts Colleges
Wall Street Journal/THE: 178
Washington Monthly: 105, Liberal Arts Colleges

OVERGENERALIZATIONS
Students are:
More likely to rush a fraternity/sorority
Working hard and playing hard
Politically liberal
Involved/invested in campus life
Always admiring the beauty of their campus

COLLEGE OVERLAPS
Furman University
Tulane University
Sewanee - The University of the South
Vanderbilt University
Wake Forest University

Rice University

Houston, Texas | 713-348-7423

With 4,494 undergraduates, Rice is at once a powerhouse research institution and a place where world-class instruction is the norm. The university's illustrious faculty includes multiple Nobel Prize and National Medal of Science winners as well as countless recipients of any prestigious fellowship or award that one can name. And the best news is that undergraduates have the chance to learn from that distinguished lot.

Inside the Classroom
Rice offers more than 50 majors across six broad disciplines: engineering, architecture, music, social science, humanities, and natural science. Double majoring is more common at Rice than at your average university; roughly 20% of students graduate with a double major. Speaking of majors, there is a greater diversity of majors than one might assume at a STEM-famous school. The most commonly conferred degrees are in engineering (16%), the social sciences (12%), biology (11%), computer science (10%), and parks and recreation (8%).

Boasting a student-to-faculty ratio of 6:1, Rice offers a spectacularly intimate learning experience. Class sizes are ideally small with 66% containing fewer than 20 students and a median class size of only fourteen. Undergraduate research opportunities abound with approximately 70% of graduates participating in academic research during their four years. Those experiences are open to freshmen through the Century Scholars Program and to all underclassmen through the Rice Undergraduate Scholars Program. Study abroad options are available in seventy countries, including collaborative programs with some of the top schools in the world including The London School of Economics, Oxford, and Cambridge; approximately 30% of Rice students elect to spend a semester in another country.

Programs in architecture, biochemistry, math, and music are incredibly strong, while the School of Architecture and the George R. Brown School of Engineering are among the highest-ranking schools in their disciplines. It is also notable that Rice is doing its part to close the STEM gender gap; the school is among the national leaders in producing female engineers, and one-third of computer science majors are female, almost twice the national average. When it comes to procuring scholarships and fellowships upon graduation, Owls fare well, regularly producing Fulbright Scholars, Marshall Scholars, Watson Fellows, Hertz Fellows, and an occasional Rhodes Scholar (a dozen in its history).

Outside the Classroom
Central to student life at Rice is the Oxford/Cambridge-style (or more familiarly, Yale-style) residential college system. Upon matriculation, students are assigned to one of eleven residential colleges that contain their own dorms, dining halls, common areas, and faculty sponsors. Each college has its own student-run government, unique traditions, and social events. Those seeking a strong Greek life will have to look elsewhere as Rice has always operated free of fraternities and sororities. Rice does not have a particularly fervent sports culture either despite seven men's and seven women's varsity teams competing in NCAA Division I. The most notable squad is the baseball team, which is always competing for national titles. Opportunities for intramural and club team participation are vast and include sports like aikido, badminton, and water polo. Student-run clubs are plentiful as well with over 300 to select from. The Rice Thresher, the student newspaper, is widely read and regularly wins national awards. While campus life is abuzz with activity, many venture into the city of Houston to enjoy the nightlife and cultural events in such close proximity.

Career Services
The Rice Center for Career Development (CCD) is staffed by 12 full-time professional employees, which equals a student-to-advisor ratio of 375:1, better than average when compared with the other institutions included in this book. Additional peer career advisors, embedded in each residential college, offer services such as resume reviews or assistance with locating internship opportunities. Internship opportunities can also be discovered at the Career and Internship Expo, which is attended by more than one hundred employers—it's no wonder 88% ultimately procure one or more internships. An incredible 4,800 interactions took place between employers and students at one recent Fall Expo alone.

The university does a phenomenal job of connecting with students, completing 2,200 appointments with undergrads. Further, 485 new employers were added to Handshake each month. The CCD also facilitates Owl Edge Externships, job-shadowing experiences that last from one day to a full week; over 1,000 students landed an externship or engaged in job shadowing. Overall, an astounding 99% of surveyed students reported that they would recommend the CCD to a friend. In short, it is hard to imagine a career services office accomplishing more for its undergraduates than the CCD does for students at Rice.

Professional Outcomes

Six months after graduation, 12% of Rice grads are still seeking employment. The overwhelming majority have found careers or a graduate school home. Companies that are known to pluck more than their fair share of employees each year from Rice's senior class include Deloitte, Capital One, JP Morgan Chase, Google, and Microsoft. Over one hundred alumni are also current employees of companies such as Shell, ExxonMobil, Chevron, Amazon, Accenture, and Meta. Median starting salaries for Rice grads far exceed national averages. Across all majors, the average starting salary is $73k. That encompasses engineering majors at the high end and humanities majors at the low end. Texas is among the most common destinations for recent grads, but many also flock to California, New York, Wisconsin, and Washington State.

One-third of graduates move directly into graduate or professional school. That group fares well in gaining admission to elite graduate institutions; Harvard, Yale, Stanford, MIT, Columbia, and Berkeley are among the schools that absorb the highest number of Rice applicants. Rice is also known for producing a strong number of successful medical school applicants each year. A robust 28% of graduate school attendees are enrolled in medical school. Baylor College of Medicine and the med schools in the UT system are popular destinations for future doctors. Other recent grads are presently attending Harvard Medical School, Duke University School of Medicine, and Stanford Medical School.

Admission

Rice's acceptance rate for the Class of 2026 tied the all-time low figure of 9%. The number of applications received by the university topped 31,000, and that figure has more than doubled in the last decade. The ACT mid-50% range is 34-36; the median SAT was 1530. A decade ago, that was close to the 75th percentile score for entering freshmen. This is a clear indicator that Rice's diminishing acceptance rate is, in fact, indicative of an increasingly selective student profile.

Early decision applicants, as would be expected, enjoy a better acceptance rate of 19%, but an applicant's bona fides still need to meet the university's sky-high standards. Rice lists more factors as being "very important" than most elite schools, granting this designation to rigor of courses, GPA, class rank, test scores, essays, recommendations, talent/ability, and character/personal qualities. An intimidating 89% of Rice students placed in the top 10% of their high school class, and 97% were in the top quartile. Five years ago, Rice instituted an expedited system of reviewing applications; it now takes two admissions officers fewer than ten minutes to review each candidate and assign a numerical rating, a 5 being the highest. With that in mind, to have a realistic chance of getting in, the admissions staff shouldn't have to dig very deep to find reasons to say "Yes." A quality essay and glowing recommendations will help, but you'll need a sparkling academic profile and in-range test scores to make it through the first wave.

Worth Your Money?

For the 57% of students who qualify for some form of financial aid, Rice delivers by meeting 100% of every individual's demonstrated need. That equates to $53k per year, which certainly helps make the $78,000 annual cost (including personal expenses) of attendance more affordable. Graduates not only encounter incredibly high starting salaries, but they also have less debt, on average, than the average college graduate in the United States. In fact, close to three-quarters of undergrads leave the school owing not a cent. Needless to say, Rice is worth the cost of admissions no matter who you are or how much you have to pay.

FINANCIAL
Institutional Type: Private
In-State Tuition: $58,128
Out-of-State Tuition: $58,128
Room & Board: $15,900
Books & Supplies: $1,400

Avg. Need-Based Grant: $57,380
Avg. % of Need Met: 100%

Avg. Merit-Based Award: $19,528
% Receiving (Freshmen w/o Need): 4%

Avg. Cumulative Debt: $19,623
% of Students Borrowing: 18%

CAREER
Who Recruits
1. DMC, Inc.
2. INT Software
3. Quantlab
4. Oxy
5. Chevron

Notable Internships
1. The Blackstone Group
2. Jane Street
3. Houston Rockets

Top Employers
1. Google
2. Shell
3. ExxonMobil
4. Chevron
5. Microsoft

Where Alumni Work
1. Houston
2. San Francisco
3. Dallas
4. Austin
5. New York City

Earnings
College Scorecard (10-YR Post-Entry): $87,254
PayScale (Early Career): $77,900
PayScale (Mid-Career): $141,600
PayScale 20-Year ROI: $1,007,000

RANKINGS
Money: 5
U.S. News: 17, National Universities
Wall Street Journal/THE: 64
Washington Monthly: 95, National Universities

OVERGENERALIZATIONS
Students are:
Diverse
Playing hard but working harder
Friendly
More likely to interact with different types of students
Teeming with school pride

COLLEGE OVERLAPS
Cornell University
Duke University
Northwestern University
Stanford University
The University of Texas at Austin

Rochester Institute of Technology

Rochester, New York | 585-475-6631

ADMISSION
Admission Rate: 67%
Admission Rate - Men: 66%
Admission Rate - Women: 68%
EA Admission Rate: Not Offered
ED Admission Rate: 79%
ED Admits as % of Total Admits: 8%
Admission Rate (5-Year Trend): +10%
% of Admits Attending (Yield): 19%
Transfer Admission Rate: 49%

SAT Reading/Writing (Middle 50%): 630-710
SAT Math (Middle 50%): 640-740
ACT Composite (Middle 50%): 29-33

% Graduated in Top 10% of HS Class: 44%
% Graduated in Top 25% of HS Class: 79%
% Graduated in Top 50% of HS Class: 95%

Demonstrated Interest: Important
Legacy Status: Considered
Racial/Ethnic Status: Considered
Admission Interview Offered: Yes

ENROLLMENT
Total Undergraduate Enrollment: 13,940
% Full-Time: 97%
% Male: 66%
% Female: 34%
% Out-of-State: 51%
% Fraternity: 3%
% Sorority: 2%
% On-Campus (All Undergraduate): 49%
Freshman Housing Required: Yes

% African-American: 5%
% Asian: 12%
% Hispanic: 9%
% White: 62%
% Other: 2%
% International: 4%
% Low-Income: 28%

ACADEMICS
Student-to-Faculty Ratio: 13 to 1
% of Classes Under 20: 48%
% of Classes 20-49: 48%
% of Classes 50 or More: 5%
% Full-Time Faculty: 70%
% Full-Time Faculty w/ Terminal Degree: 73%

Top Programs
Computer Science
Engineering
Film and Animation
Game Design and Development
Imaging Science
Industrial Design
Management Information Systems
Photographic Arts

Retention Rate: 87%
4-Year Graduation Rate: 29%
6-Year Graduation Rate: 72%

Curricular Flexibility: Less Flexible
Academic Rating: ★★★

#CollegesWorthYourMoney

Since 1829, the Rochester Institute of Technology has been more than simply a technical school that churns out large quantities of engineers each year. With additional strengths in art and animation and design, this institution genuinely desires to "shape the future and improve the world through creativity and innovation." Even by STEM-focused school standards, the training at RIT is highly focused on career readiness and launches students into hands-on learning opportunities from the start of their freshman year. Large compared to other schools of its ilk like RPI and WPI, Rochester Institute of Technology educates 14,000 undergraduates. Half are from New York State, but students from all over the United States as well as one hundred countries brave the frigid Upstate New York weather in order to attend this accessible school that offers many standout programs and some of the best connections to industry of any school in the country.

Inside the Classroom
The co-op program is the fourth oldest in the country, and just about all students complete a one- or two-semester paid learning experience after finishing their first two years of academic study. There are nine undergraduate colleges at RIT, and while all have distinct course requirements, the school's signature general education curriculum touches every single student. Students earning a bachelor of science degree in engineering, for example, need to take 60 credit hours of general education courses—including first-year writing—and a number of perspectives courses that cover categories such as social, ethical, global, artistic, mathematics, scientific principles, and natural science inquiry. One immersion sequence that involves a three-course deep dive into a particular topic also must be built into every undergrad's program.

RIT's 13:1 student-to-faculty ratio and a genuine commitment to undergraduate teaching lead to a respectable 48% of sections enrolling fewer than 20 students, and only 5% of courses contain more than 50 students. Additionally, RIT provides an array of undergraduate research opportunities including the Biological Sciences Research Scholars Program, the Chemistry Research Scholars Program, Economics Undergraduate Research, and the Undergraduate Research Symposium that sees 200+ students give presentations in a given academic year. Ample opportunities exist to study abroad, but few undergraduates elect to take advantage.

The most popular majors at this school are engineering & engineering technologies (34%), computer and information sciences (20%), visual and performing arts (10%), and business (9%). The Gleason College of Engineering and the Golisano College of Computing and Information Sciences are top-of-the-line. The latter houses RIT's game design program, which is the best on the entire East Coast. Strong film, art, and design programs also churn out successful graduates. Few pursue postgraduate fellowships, but the school does produce roughly one Fulbright Scholar and two Goldwater Scholars each cycle.

Outside the Classroom
RIT guarantees housing to freshmen and can accommodate about half the total undergraduate population in a mix of residence halls, apartments, the RIT Inn and Conference Center, Greek housing, and the Global Village. Like too many institutes of technology, the male-to-female ratio is heavily skewed at 2-to-1, which certainly has an impact on aspects of campus life. There are thirty fraternities and sororities on campus, but in the scope of such a large school, Greek life only draws single-digit participation. While RIT doesn't award athletic scholarships, it does field twenty-four NCAA varsity sports teams including Division I men's and women's ice hockey as well as many highly competitive Division III teams. RIT is so competitive, in fact, rumors have swirled about a step-up to Division I. There are 300 clubs and organizations, including an extensive intramural sports program that signs up roughly half of the student body, and plenty of opportunities for competitive or friendly gaming; video games are a way of life here. One of the greenest campuses around with a focus on sustainability, the 1,159 acres owned by the school offer federally designated wetlands, ample native plantings and wildlife, and a 200-acre area where most buildings are concentrated. There's enough to do on campus and in the classroom to mitigate the impact of an otherwise unexciting locale.

Career Services
The Office of Career Services and Cooperative Education (OCSCE) is staffed by 22 professional staff members (not counting office assistants) who play roles such as career advisor, employer engagement and partnerships coordinator, and alumni relations coordinator. Rochester Institute of Technology's 634:1 student-to-advisor ratio is higher than the average school featured in this guide, but it unquestionably has sufficient personnel to get the job done. Large-scale, university-wide career fairs are put on twice per year, drawing 500 companies and 8,800 students. Numerous boutique fairs cater to groups such as future accountants, civil engineers, and teachers. On a more personal level, the office also arranges "tailored orientations, workshops, and one-on-one advisement. It also plans and promotes events such as career fairs, workshops, and speakers from industry," and that's only the tip of the iceberg.

The co-op program, more than a century old, saw 4,100 participants participate in a co-op last year, with employers from all 50 states and 40 countries. The list of co-op and internship partners is incredible— Boeing, the CIA, EY, Fisher-Price, Walt Disney World, SpaceX, NASA, Google, and literally dozens of other equally impressive organizations. RIT has thousands of employer partners. The off-the-charts employer relations accomplishments do not stop there; the career services staff posts 48,000 jobs and hosts 900+ job interviews. In sum, the Rochester Institute of Technology offers an exceptional level of support to its undergraduates through its robust co-op program as well as all of the one-on-one attention you could desire.

Professional Outcomes

Within six months of graduation, 95% of recent grads had found employment or a full-time graduate program. Major companies presently employing more than 500 RIT alums include Xerox and Paychex, both with offices in Rochester. Between 200 and 450 employees of IBM, Microsoft, Apple, Intel, Amazon, Google, and Cisco were educated at RIT. Many graduates remain in the Upstate New York area while large numbers of other RIT alumni flock to New York City, Boston, DC, and San Francisco. Median income levels by mid-career are in the same neighborhood as fellow New York institutions including the University of Rochester, Fordham, and Syracuse. Starting salary figures vary greatly by major with College of Business grads landing a median starting salary of $63k and computer science majors of $102k right out of school.

In a typical year, 8-12% of graduates elect to pursue an advanced degree. While only a small number of RIT grads head directly to grad school, those who do typically head to some of the world's best, such as Carnegie Mellon, Duke, Harvard, Johns Hopkins, MIT, Rhode Island School of Design, Penn, UVA, and the University of Michigan. The number of seniors applying to medical school has risen in recent years and is now between 40 and 45 applicants annually. Historically, the school has an 80-85% acceptance rate, but that number includes non-MD graduate programs in the health professions. Recent graduates have landed at top medical schools including Columbia University Vagelos College of Physicians and Surgeons, Emory University School of Medicine, Geisel School of Medicine at Dartmouth, and Georgetown University School of Medicine.

Admission

Applicants to the Rochester Institute of Technology benefit from a fairly generous acceptance rate that is typically in the mid-to-high 50% range; in 2022-23, that spiked to an even friendlier 67%. Students apply to individual colleges within the larger university, and standards vary somewhat from program to program. Overall, the average entering GPA was 3.7 and the median SAT score was 1350. Over two-fifths placed in the top decile of their high school class, over three-quarters were in the top quartile, and all but 5% ranked in the top half.

This admissions committee looks, first and foremost, for applicants who engaged in a rigorous high school course load and achieved a solid mix of A's and B's. The five factors that make up the second tier of admissions considerations are standardized test scores, class rank, recommendations, character/personal qualities, and the essay. It is important to note that the school is now test-optional, but only for applicants to the College of Liberal Arts. RIT's yield rate is only 21%, meaning that the school is eager to know if students have genuine interest. In 2022, almost 1,700 individuals applied via early decision, and RIT rewarded their pledge of loyalty with a 79% ED acceptance rate.

Worth Your Money?

Yes. That's the short answer for anyone coming to RIT to study engineering or computer science. The school keeps the sticker price reasonable at $56k for tuition and under $76k total cost of attendance. Every single incoming first-year student receives some type of financial assistance each year; the average need-based grant is $35k. Those coming for liberal arts, business, or an art and design degree would have to weigh RIT's offer against their other options to find the most sensible deal.

FINANCIAL
Institutional Type: Private
In-State Tuition: $57,016
Out-of-State Tuition: $57,016
Room & Board: $15,516
Books & Supplies: $1,100

Avg. Need-Based Grant: $34,827
Avg. % of Need Met: 90%

Avg. Merit-Based Award: $15,856
% Receiving (Freshmen w/o Need): 24%

Avg. Cumulative Debt: $38,111
% of Students Borrowing: 72%

CAREER
Who Recruits
1. General Electric
2. Google
3. Microsoft
4. Intel
5. IBM

Notable Internships
1. GE Aviation
2. Electronic Arts
3. L.L. Bean

Top Employers
1. Xerox
2. Paychex
3. IBM
4. Microsoft
5. Apple

Where Alumni Work
1. Rochester, NY
2. New York City
3. Boston
4. Washington, DC
5. San Francisco

Earnings
College Scorecard (10-YR Post-Entry): $69,250
PayScale (Early Career): $67,600
PayScale (Mid-Career): $110,900
PayScale 20-Year ROI: $685,000

RANKINGS
Money: 3.5
U.S. News: 98, National Universities
Wall Street Journal/THE: 196
Washington Monthly: 314, National Universities

OVERGENERALIZATIONS
Students are:
Career-driven
Nerdy
Diverse
Accepting
Decided upon their chosen major

COLLEGE OVERLAPS
Clarkson University
Drexel University
Rensselaer Polytechnic Institute
University at Buffalo (SUNY)
Worcester Polytechnic Institute

Rose-Hulman Institute of Technology

Terre Haute, Indiana | 812-877-8213

ADMISSION
Admission Rate: 73%
Admission Rate - Men: 71%
Admission Rate - Women: 79%
EA Admission Rate: 80%
ED Admission Rate: Not Offered
ED Admits as % of Total Admits: Not Offered
Admission Rate (5-Year Trend): +12%
% of Admits Attending (Yield): 16%
Transfer Admission Rate: 49%

SAT Reading/Writing (Middle 50%): 620-720
SAT Math (Middle 50%): 670-763
ACT Composite (Middle 50%): 27-33

% Graduated in Top 10% of HS Class: 60%
% Graduated in Top 25% of HS Class: 89%
% Graduated in Top 50% of HS Class: 99%

Demonstrated Interest: Considered
Legacy Status: Considered
Racial/Ethnic Status: Considered
Admission Interview Offered: No

ENROLLMENT
Total Undergraduate Enrollment: 2,169
% Full-Time: 99%
% Male: 76%
% Female: 24%
% Out-of-State: 69%
% Fraternity: 31%
% Sorority: 46%
% On-Campus (All Undergraduate): 60%
Freshman Housing Required: Yes

% African-American: 4%
% Asian: 8%
% Hispanic: 5%
% White: 68%
% Other: 1%
% International: 8%
% Low-Income: 8%

ACADEMICS
Student-to-Faculty Ratio: 12 to 1
% of Classes Under 20: 41%
% of Classes 20-49: 59%
% of Classes 50 or More: 0%
% Full-Time Faculty: 94%
% Full-Time Faculty w/ Terminal Degree: 98%

Top Programs
Biomedical Engineering
Chemical Engineering
Civil Engineering
Computer Science
Electrical Engineering
Mechanical Engineering

Retention Rate: 92%
4-Year Graduation Rate: 73%
6-Year Graduation Rate: 81%

Curricular Flexibility: Less Flexible
Academic Rating: ★★★★

#CollegesWorthYourMoney

When searching for the top engineering schools, you naturally encounter a number of prestigious, doctoral-granting research universities like Stanford, MIT, UC Berkeley, and Carnegie Mellon. When looking for small engineering schools, Caltech and Harvey Mudd are typically the easiest ones to locate. Likely off your radar is a small private college in Terra Haute, Indiana, that, year after year, tops the charts among engineering schools whose highest degree is a master's. The Rose-Hulman Institute of Technology offers only 22 undergraduate degree programs to 2,169 students, mostly from the Midwest, but they go on to achieve phenomenal postgraduate successes.

Inside the Classroom
Operating on the quarter system, courses are swift and rigorous, and pretty much everything you learn will be related to your major. Engineering students (the bulk of the student body) dive right in as first-semester freshmen by taking a heavy dose of math, science, and introductory engineering courses. The whole first year of study has room for only two electives in the realm of rhetoric/composition, the humanities, or social sciences. Foreign language is not among the requirements at this institution.

A student-to-faculty ratio of 12:1 and a minimal presence of graduate students bodes well for both class sizes and the number of introductory classes that are taught by full-time faculty members. The average class size is twenty, and 94% of sections are smaller than 29 students. Giant lecture halls simply don't exist at Rose-Hulman as zero of 441 sections contained more than 40 students. Undergraduate research is commonplace at this school and can be arranged through the Independent Project/Research Opportunities Program, which connects you to faculty mentors and sets you on the path toward presenting your work at the End-of-Quarter Symposium. Ten-week summer research apprenticeships also are available. International opportunities can be procured through the Global E3, a consortium of 60 engineering schools of which Rose-Hulman is a member, or through participation in Engineers Without Borders. This is a rare institute of technology that pushes its students to pursue an international experience; it even hosts an annual Study Abroad Fair as part of those efforts.

The engineering major accounts for 66% of all degrees conferred, and there's a good reason for its popularity; this program is viewed among the best by prospective employers and graduate schools, and not just in the Midwest. Rose-Hulman's reputation for excellence in engineering stretches from Silicon Valley to the East Coast. Unique undergraduate engineering programs include optical engineering and international computer science; CS, in general, is the second-most popular degree program (20%).

Outside the Classroom
Even more than your average STEM-focused school, the gender disparity is significant to the tune of a 76/24 split favoring males. (The school didn't become coed until 1995.) Greek life at Rose-Hulman is booming with 31% of men joining fraternities and 46% of women involved with the school's sororities. All but a handful of freshmen live on campus (it is a requirement). And 62% of the total undergraduate student body lives in one of ten dormitories or apartment complexes. Despite its small size, the school still fields 20 NCAA Division III sports teams, the Fightin' Engineers, who compete in the Heartland Collegiate Athletic Conference. That translates to a full quarter of the student body participating in varsity athletics. There are also ninety clubs, including a popular student newspaper, radio station, and film club plus plenty of intramural sports such as archery, ballroom dancing, scuba, and yoga. The general social hub on campus is the Mussallem Union, with well-reviewed cuisine, a giant Connect Four board, and a lakefront view—what more can you ask for? Rose-Hulman is set on a 1,300-acre property, but the majority of campus is confined to a 200-acre tract. Terra Haute isn't exactly Midtown Manhattan, but it's not that far from a number of major Midwestern destinations with trips to Indianapolis, Chicago, Louisville, Cincinnati, or St. Louis doable on a weekend.

Career Services
The Career Services and Employer Relations Office at Rose-Hulman consists of seven professional employees, which computes to a student-to-advisor ratio of 310:1, better than average when compared to other schools featured in this guide. It is also notable that this career services office puts "employer relations" right in its own title, and the statistics in that area prove that this inclusion is more than warranted.

In a given year, a stunning 800-900 companies participate in events hosted by career services or had contact with students that was facilitated by career services staff. As a school of 2,000 undergraduates, that figure is absurdly strong. In total, almost 1,400 interviews are conducted by companies on campus annually, also a ridiculously strong number when you consider there were fewer than 500 seniors. Last year, 94% of seniors had at least one opportunity for experiential learning via undergraduate research, co-op placement (50+ companies participate in the school's co-op program), or an internship. Three career fairs held annually in the fall, winter, and spring are extremely well attended by students as well as major hiring organizations. One recent fair drew a school-record 251 companies, some of which conducted on-the-spot interviews with students. In short, thanks to the vast network of employers connected to this career services office, Rose-Hulman job-seekers are not the hunters but the hunted.

Professional Outcomes

Of the 418 graduates who strutted the stage in 2022, an enviable 99% had landed at their next destination, whether employment or graduate school, within six months of exiting. Further, students in many of the school's programs enjoyed a 100% success rate. Top employers of recent graduates included Boston Scientific, Cook Group, Texas Instruments, Caterpillar, Honeywell, and Rolls Royce. Raytheon, Microsoft, and Indianapolis-based pharmaceutical giant Eli Lilly also have a strong representation of Rose Hulman-affiliated employees. The average first-year salary across all majors was $80,157, while computer science majors took home a not-too-shabby $89,000 in first-year wages. The majority of alumni remain in Indiana with Indianapolis and Terra Haute being the two favorite destinations. Smaller pockets of graduates can be found in Chicago, Cincinnati, San Francisco, and Seattle.

Twenty-one percent of 2022 grads immediately enrolled in graduate school. They head to many of the world's most distinguished universities such as Johns Hopkins, Carnegie Mellon, Duke, Northwestern, Washington University in St. Louis, Georgia Tech, Cornell, Notre Dame, and Rice University. Only a couple of students each year head to medical school. No one from the previous two classes decided to attend law school. Clearly, and not surprisingly, the records demonstrate that students come to Rose-Hulman to enter technology/engineering fields.

Admission

Rose-Hulman's acceptance rate for membership in the Class of 2026 was an unimposing 73%. Compare that to other premier institutes of technology with phenomenal job placement rates and starting salaries and you might breathe a sigh of relief. Of course, the applicant pool is a self-selecting group with an affinity for STEM learning, and that leads to an impressive freshman class academic profile. The Class of 2026 had a mid-50% SAT range of 1310-1470 and an ACT range of 27-33. Sixty percent of 2022-23 freshmen earned a place in the top 10% of their high school class while 89% were in the top quartile. Over four-fifths of students had a GPA over 3.75, and only 3% had under 3.5. Suddenly, that sigh of relief feels like a distant memory. Interestingly, the school does accept a lower percentage of applicants in some cycles. Only a few years ago, the acceptance rate was under 60% as rates can fluctuate quite a bit at a school with a small applicant pool of under 4,600 students.

Rigor of secondary coursework and grades are the two most important factors for admission followed by standardized test scores, class rank, recommendations, and extracurricular activities. The acceptance rate for female applicants is 79% compared to the rate for males of 71%. This school offers multiple early action application deadlines but no binding early decision option. In the admissions office's own words, successful applicants are "typically at the top of their high school graduating classes with scores in the 95th percentile on the SAT or ACT – plus they have taken a lot of high school science, math, and English."

Worth Your Money?

This is a rare case where an annual cost of attendance of $78,000 does little to derail the financial futures of the student population. Freshmen receiving need-based aid net an average annual award of close to $37,000; average merit aid packages for those eligible exceeded $23,000. Even without financial aid, Rose-Hulman is definitely worth the private school cost thanks to phenomenal placement rates at top companies and extremely high starting salaries, even by STEM standards.

FINANCIAL
Institutional Type: Private
In-State Tuition: $54,174
Out-of-State Tuition: $54,174
Room & Board: $17,718
Books & Supplies: $1,500

Avg. Need-Based Grant: $36,627
Avg. % of Need Met: 73%

Avg. Merit-Based Award: $23,316
% Receiving (Freshmen w/o Need): 42%

Avg. Cumulative Debt: $55,774
% of Students Borrowing: 50%

CAREER
Who Recruits
1. Archer Daniels Midland
2. Whirlpool
3. Allegant Air
4. Kinze Manufacturing
5. Ingredion Incorporated

Notable Internships
1. Rolls-Royce
2. Halliburton
3. Tesla

Top Employers
1. Eli Lilly and Company
2. Cummins Inc.
3. Rolls-Royce
4. Caterpillar Inc.
5. Google

Where Alumni Work
1. Indianapolis
2. Terra Haute, IN
3. Chicago
4. Cincinnati
5. San Francisco

Earnings
College Scorecard (10-YR Post-Entry): $97,688
PayScale (Early Career): $80,500
PayScale (Mid-Career): $146,500
PayScale 20-Year ROI: $1,068,000

RANKINGS
Money: 4.5
U.S. News: Not Ranked
Wall Street Journal/THE: 17
Washington Monthly: Not Ranked

OVERGENERALIZATIONS
Students are:
Always studying
Career-driven
Tight-knit (possess a strong sense of community)
Nerdy
Collaborative

COLLEGE OVERLAPS
Case Western Reserve University
The Ohio State University - Columbus
Purdue University - West Lafayette
Rensselaer Polytechnic Institute
Rochester Institute of Technology

New Brunswick, New Jersey | 732-445-4636

ADMISSION
Admission Rate: 66%
Admission Rate - Men: 65%
Admission Rate - Women: 68%
EA Admission Rate: Not Reported
ED Admission Rate: Not Offered
ED Admits as % of Total Admits: Not Offered
Admission Rate (5-Year Trend): +8%
% of Admits Attending (Yield): 28%
Transfer Admission Rate: 56%

SAT Reading/Writing (Middle 50%): 630-720
SAT Math (Middle 50%): 640-760
ACT Composite (Middle 50%): 28-33

% Graduated in Top 10% of HS Class: 29%
% Graduated in Top 25% of HS Class: 62%
% Graduated in Top 50% of HS Class: 91%

Demonstrated Interest: Not Considered
Legacy Status: Not Considered
Racial/Ethnic Status: Not Considered
Admission Interview Offered: No

ENROLLMENT
Total Undergraduate Enrollment: 36,344
% Full-Time: 96%
% Male: 50%
% Female: 50%
% Out-of-State: 7%
% Fraternity: Not Reported
% Sorority: Not Reported
% On-Campus (All Undergraduate): 40%
Freshman Housing Required: No

% African-American: 7%
% Asian: 33%
% Hispanic: 15%
% White: 32%
% Other: 2%
% International: 7%
% Low-Income: 26%

ACADEMICS
Student-to-Faculty Ratio: 15 to 1
% of Classes Under 20: 41%
% of Classes 20-49: 40%
% of Classes 50 or More: 19%
% Full-Time Faculty: 57%
% Full-Time Faculty w/ Terminal Degree: 54%

Top Programs
Business
Computer Science
Data Science
Criminal Justice
English
History
Pubilc Health
Supply Chain Management

Retention Rate: 93%
4-Year Graduation Rate: 70%
6-Year Graduation Rate: 84%

Curricular Flexibility: Somewhat Flexible
Academic Rating: ★★★✓

#CollegesWorthYourMoney

Rutgers-New Brunswick, the flagship campus of the school's three locations (Camden and Newark being the others), is one of the oldest universities in the country. Founded in 1766 as one of nine colleges in Colonial America, the New Brunswick campus today is a top state research university that is home to 36,344 undergraduates. Garden State residents comprise over 80% of the student body, but there has been a push in recent years to attract more out-of-staters, partially for monetary reasons. Presently, there are representatives of all 50 states and 81 countries on campus as the number of nonresidents increases each year. No matter where you're from, you'll enjoy the benefits of Rutgers' massive operation that is divided into 17 schools and colleges, collectively offering 100+ undergraduate majors.

Inside the Classroom
Core requirements are variable across different programs, but members of the School of Arts & Sciences, by far the university's largest college, have a ten- to fourteen-course core. Mandates include fulfilling coursework in areas such as diversities and inequalities, our common future, natural sciences, social and historical analysis, arts and humanities, writing and communication, and quantitative and formal reasoning. In the School of Engineering, first-year coursework will look quite different as students must conquer courses that include General Chemistry for Engineers, Calculus, Analytical Physics, and Introduction to Computers for Engineers; non-STEM coursework is minimal for engineering students. A host of first-year initiatives, including Byrne Seminars and First-Year Interest Group Seminars, leads to a freshman retention rate of 93%, a tremendous achievement for a public university.

Reasonable for a school of its size and scope, Rutgers possesses a 15:1 student-to-faculty ratio. As a result, it can offer a sizable number of smaller, seminar-style courses to undergraduates. Forty-one percent of class sections have an enrollment of nineteen or fewer students compared to only 19% of sections that contain more than 50 undergrads. Rutgers offers 180 study abroad programs in fifty countries, but few take advantage; the participation rate is a paltry 2%. Undergraduate research, on the other hand, attracts more takers. The Aresty Research Center serves as a clearinghouse that matches undergraduates with faculty members conducting research in an area of interest; there are presently 1,500 faculty partners. An annual Undergraduate Research Symposium has showcased thousands of student projects in its 15+ years of existence.

The areas of study in which the greatest number of degrees are conferred are business (20%), computer science (12%), engineering (10%), health professions (10%), biology (9%), and social sciences (7%). Rutgers Business School sends many majors to top Wall Street investment banks, and programs in computer science, public health, and criminal justice have a terrific national reputation. Competitive scholarship and fellowship organizations also show lots of love to Scarlet Knights. Students and alumni received 19 Fulbright Scholarships in 2023 and the school has also had Goldwater, Schwarzman, Gates-Cambridge, and Truman Scholars in recent years.

Outside the Classroom
Rutgers-New Brunswick's sprawling 2,685-acre campus is divided into five distinct, interconnected campuses. Despite one of the largest undergraduate housing operations of any school in the United States, only 40% of students live on campus in one of 136 residence hall buildings or university-owned apartment complexes. The Greek scene is on the rise at Rutgers as the school now has over 3,800 members of 80+ fraternities and sororities, all of which are located off campus. The Scarlet Knights compete in NCAA Division I athletics in ten men's and fourteen women's sports. Highpoint.com Stadium is the only Division I football stadium in the NY/NJ region, but it rarely fills its 52,000-seat capacity. Rutgers students would rather play sports as a member of one of 50+ club teams or intramural leagues than watch them. The school's five fitness and recreation centers attract more than 5,000 visitors per day; ten outdoor fields and parks also are available for student use. There are also 500+ student-run organizations, including a top-ranked Model UN team and the Rutgers University Dance Marathon, which raises close to $500,000 for pediatric illnesses each year. Rutgers' excellent location makes weekend trips to Philly, New York, or the Jersey Shore a painless one-hour car ride.

Career Services
Forty-five professional employees staff the Rutgers University Career Services (UCS) Office in areas such as career exploration, career development, and employer relations. The university's overall student-to-counselor ratio of 808:1 is higher than the average school featured in this guidebook, but not alarmingly so when compared to other large public universities. Despite the monumental task of connecting with 36,000 students, the UCS has made some inroads as it currently interacts, in some form, with 56% of the student population each year. In a single recent year, the UCS conducted 4,800+ one-on-one advising appointments.

There are plenty of large-scale offerings designed to benefit the student population. Career fair attendance is solid with 3,400 students connecting with 300 companies in the fall and 4,700 engaging with 230 employers in the spring. Each year, 600+ unique employers visit career fairs and there are more than 3,400 on-campus interviews conducted with Rutgers seniors. The CareerKnight online database of job and internship opportunities receives hundreds of thousands of annual hits. The Road to Wall Street mentoring program led to over 90% of participants landing competitive summer internships. Job search boot camps draw solid reviews as 100% of attendees said they have a better awareness of the next steps in the process as a result of attending. With 585,000 alumni, there is always a Scarlet Knight networking opportunity in your field of interest. Roughly two-fifths of graduates say that the Rutgers UCS contributed to their career success.

Professional Outcomes

Upon graduation, 82% of Rutgers students have their next stop squared away, whether it's a first job or graduate school. Sixty-seven percent of the Class of 2022 were headed directly to the world of employment, where the companies hiring the largest number of grads included Amazon, Johnson & Johnson, L'Oréal, and JP Morgan Chase. Investment banks like Goldman Sachs and Citi also employ hundreds of alumni. More than 300 current employees of Verizon, Bristol-Myers Squibb, Novartis, Amazon, Pfizer, and Google also have Scarlet Knight lineage. The median starting salary across all majors was $70,000. The median starting salary for engineering majors was $75,000 while arts and sciences grads brought home $65k. The bulk of graduates, approximately 85%, end up settling in New Jersey/the Greater New York area. Philadelphia, DC, and San Francisco are next in popularity.

Only 9% of 2022 grads matriculated into full-time graduate or professional school. The most frequently attended universities were Rutgers, NYU, Columbia, Penn, and Johns Hopkins University. Of the 532 recent graduates who applied to medical school, 49% gained acceptance, a bit above the national average. Those sporting a 3.5 GPA or higher were even more successful, gaining acceptance at a 67% clip. Ninety-two of those individuals who were accepted matriculated into one of Rutgers' two medical colleges. Recent prestigious acceptances included Duke, Georgetown, Cornell, UVA, and Stanford. Future lawyers also end up in droves at Rutgers' own highly reputable law school as well as at Villanova, Fordham, and Notre Dame.

Admission

Unlike at so many other premier flagship universities around the nation, the acceptance rate at Rutgers-New Brunswick has not plummeted in recent years. Those seeking entry into the Class of 2026 were given the thumbs up 66% of the time. Still, the quality of the applicant pool has risen dramatically over the 2000s. Freshmen in the 2022-23 school year had an average SAT score of 1362 and an average ACT of 30. Just under 30% of current students placed in the top 10% of their high school class, and 62% landed in the top 25%. Five years ago, the acceptance rate at the university was comparable, but average test scores were far lower.

The factors deemed most important by the admissions committee are GPA, standardized test scores, and rigor of secondary curriculum. Extracurricular involvement is the lone category dubbed "important." Rutgers does offer an early action deadline of November 1, but no binding early decision plan is available. An average in the B+/A- range and standardized test scores in the 85th percentile put you firmly in play for an invitation to attend the New Brunswick campus right out of high school. Otherwise, a start at the Camden or Newark campus may be the only option. Out-of-state applicants may find slightly more relaxed admission standards, given the university's push to recruit applicants from outside New Jersey.

Worth Your Money?

Rutgers doesn't have the endowment to meet anything close to your full level of financial need, but it does award grants averaging $13k to 36% of current undergraduates. The in-state cost of attendance is $38k, which is not a bad deal for a flagship public school in the Northeastern United States. Out-of-state students would pay close to $49k per year COA, which would be a curious move for students not receiving aid, given the likelihood that better deals would be available.

FINANCIAL
Institutional Type: Public
In-State Tuition: $17,239
Out-of-State Tuition: $36,001
Room & Board: $14,715
Books & Supplies: $1,391

Avg. Need-Based Grant: $13,412
Avg. % of Need Met: 46%

Avg. Merit-Based Award: $10,324
% Receiving (Freshmen w/o Need): 2%

Avg. Cumulative Debt: $26,105
% of Students Borrowing: 47%

CAREER
Who Recruits
1. Aerotek
2. Automatic Data
3. Enterprise Holdings
4. Insight Global
5. Robert Half

Notable Internships
1. Colgate-Palmolive
2. NBCUniversal
3. New York Giants

Top Employers
1. Johnson & Johnson
2. Verizon
3. Bristol-Myers Squibb
4. JPMorgan Chase
5. Novartis

Where Alumni Work
1. New York City
2. Philadelphia
3. Washington, DC
4. San Francisco
5. Boston

Earnings
College Scorecard (10-YR Post-Entry): $69,748
PayScale (Early Career): $64,600
PayScale (Mid-Career): $122,000
PayScale 20-Year ROI: $740,000

RANKINGS
Money: 4.5
U.S. News: 40, National Universities
Wall Street Journal/THE: 162
Washington Monthly: 62, National Universities

OVERGENERALIZATIONS
Students are:
Diverse
Only a short drive from home (i.e., Most come from NJ or nearby states)
Ready to party
Self-sufficient
Career-driven

COLLEGE OVERLAPS
Boston University
New York University
Pennsylvania State University - University Park
The College of New Jersey
University of Maryland, College Park

San Diego State University

ADMISSION
Admission Rate: 39%
Admission Rate - Men: 36%
Admission Rate - Women: 41%
EA Admission Rate: Not Offered
ED Admission Rate: Not Offered
ED Admits as % of Total Admits: Not Offered
Admission Rate (5-Year Trend): +4%
% of Admits Attending (Yield): 22%
Transfer Admission Rate: 37%

SAT Reading/Writing (Middle 50%): Test-Blind
SAT Math (Middle 50%): Test-Blind
ACT Composite (Middle 50%): Test-Blind

% Graduated in Top 10% of HS Class: 27%
% Graduated in Top 25% of HS Class: 64%
% Graduated in Top 50% of HS Class: 92%

Demonstrated Interest: Not Considered
Legacy Status: Not Considered
Racial/Ethnic Status: Not Considered
Admission Interview Offered: No

ENROLLMENT
Total Undergraduate Enrollment: 31,724
% Full-Time: 89%
% Male: 43%
% Female: 57%
% Out-of-State: 14%
% Fraternity: 10%
% Sorority: 12%
% On-Campus (All Undergraduate): 26%
Freshman Housing Required: Yes

% African-American: 4%
% Asian: 13%
% Hispanic: 35%
% White: 34%
% Other: 3%
% International: 3%
% Low-Income: 29%

ACADEMICS
Student-to-Faculty Ratio: 24 to 1
% of Classes Under 20: 31%
% of Classes 20-49: 49%
% of Classes 50 or More: 20%
% Full-Time Faculty: 48%
% Full-Time Faculty w/ Terminal Degree: 84%

Top Programs
Art
Communication
Construction Management
Criminal Justice
International Business
Kinesiology
Psychology

Retention Rate: 89%
4-Year Graduation Rate: 54%
6-Year Graduation Rate: 76%

Curricular Flexibility: Less Flexible
Academic Rating: ★★★

#CollegesWorthYourMoney

They say that a rising tide lifts all boats. As the University of California system has become ultra-competitive over the past decade, the California State University system has seen many of its schools become beneficiaries of an overflow of uber-qualified applicants. San Diego State University, offering a highly affordable education in a gorgeous and temperate setting, is one such institution. A diverse school of 31,724 undergraduates, one-third of its students are Hispanic, and roughly the same percentage are first-generation students. Most hail from the Golden State, but 3% of the population are international students representing one of 92 countries. Don't be scared off by the low acceptance rate (38%); you don't need straight A's in high school to gain access to this excellent research university that boasts nearly 160 undergraduate majors, minors, and pre-professional programs.

Inside the Classroom
The general education requirements at SDSU are the breadth portion of one's educational experience and will comprise approximately one-third of an undergraduate's time at the university. Forty-nine units are required, including nine units of communications and critical thinking courses; thirty-one units of foundational study in the humanities; social and behavioral sciences; and natural sciences and quantitative reasoning; and nine units in "explorations" that are upper-division courses you cannot begin until junior year. After completing sixty credits, all students must take and pass a writing placement assessment. Some majors require you to learn a language other than English while some, like engineering, do not. Lastly, there is a mandated course called American Institutions in which you must demonstrate your knowledge of the California government, the US Constitution, and American history.

Like many other schools in the California State University system, cheap tuition and heavy enrollment lead to a high student-to-faculty ratio. San Diego State sports a 24:1 ratio and, consequently, classes tend to be on the large side. Twenty-eight percent of course sections enroll more than 40 students, and only 31% of sections contain fewer than 20 students. To help connect students to faculty mentors and undergraduate research opportunities, the school maintains a useful database of current professors seeking assistance. Summer research programs and an annual Undergraduate Research Symposium provide additional experiences in that realm. An incredible 650 study abroad programs can be accessed and the school ranks fifth in the country in terms of the sheer number of students taking a semester in a foreign country.

Business/marketing accounts for 21% of the degrees conferred, making it the school's most popular area of study. Next in line are engineering (9%), psychology (8%), and the social sciences (7%). You won't find the engineering or computer science programs at the top of any rankings lists, but that doesn't have much of an impact on employment, thanks to the booming local tech and startup scene. Because of its emphasis on international study, many graduates go on to win fellowships that take them all around the globe. SDSU has had as many as nine Fulbright award winners in recent years, and it often has multiple recipients of Boren, Critical Language, and Gilman Scholarships. SDSU also has had several undergraduates receive National Science Foundation Graduate Research Fellowships over the last few years.

Outside the Classroom
On-campus housing is limited, and preference is given to freshmen—who take advantage at a 75% percent clip. Overall, only 26% of undergraduates resided in university-owned housing last year. However, there is plenty to bond the student body and create cohesion on campus. Ten percent of men and 12% of women belong to the university's 50+ fraternities and sororities. In addition to Greek life, annual campus-wide events like AzFest and Homecoming Weekend unify the 31,000+ undergrads, as do basketball and football games. The Aztecs field nineteen NCAA Division I sports teams, and famous alumni athletes include Marshall Faulk (NFL), Tony Gwynn (MLB), and 2019 NBA Finals MVP Kawhi Leonard. There are 300+ student organizations including KCR College Radio, which has a long history and large listenership, intramural sports that draw thousands of participants, and the Aztec Unity Project, which is committed to local community service projects. Viejas Arena, where the Aztecs play basketball, doubles as a major concert venue and draws world-famous artists. San Diego weather, sunsets, and seventeen miles of coastline are all free benefits of attending SDSU. Additionally, there are multiple beaches less than ten miles from campus. The Aquaplex is, essentially, a free resort on campus for student use. It features two outdoor pools and a twenty-person spa; such is life at San Diego State.

Career Services

The main San Diego State Career Services Office employs 35 full-time professional staff members (not counting administrative assistants) working as internship coordinators, career counselors, employer outreach specialists, and experiential learning specialists. There are an additional four staff members working out of the Fowler College of Business, bringing the campus-wide total to 39, which works out to an 813:1 student-to-counselor ratio, poorer than the average school profiled in this book.

SDSU offers four large-scale career fairs in the fall semester and another four fairs in the spring semester. One hundred ten employers attend the Fall Career and Internship Fair, and the Nonprofit and Education Career Fair in the spring draws thirty employers. In addition, the Graduate & Professional School Fair draws representatives from 90+ institutions. Roughly 40% of recent graduates reported completing at least one internship or co-op. Workshops are offered on a regular basis on useful topics such as Applying for Federal Jobs, Personal Branding Using Social Media, and Planning for Graduate School. Career counselors specialize in a variety of fields and encourage 50-minute one-on-one career exploration sessions or fifteen-minute walk-in appointments. The Aztec Mentor Program connects juniors and seniors to alumni in their fields of interest for a minimum of eight hours of mentorship. In sum, programmatic offerings by SDSU's Career Services Office are impressive, but they do not publicize statistics on how many counseling sessions take place or how many on-campus interviews with employers occur each year.

Professional Outcomes

At the time of receiving their degrees, roughly 75% of newly minted SDSU graduates already have their next phase of life planned. Thirty-four percent of recent grads had secured full-time employment, 21% were engaged in military service/volunteer work/part-time employment, and 17% were entering graduate or professional school. Qualcomm is the largest employer of Aztec alumni, and they are followed by Apple, Amazon, Google, and a number of other Silicon Valley-based tech companies. All of the most common geographic landing spots for alumni are within California borders; San Diego keeps a large chunk of grads while Los Angeles, San Francisco, and Orange County also have fairly strong representation.

In 2023-24, there were 78 SDSU graduates applying to medical school and, while the university lacks its own affiliated hospital/medical schools, many future physicians do remain in the state of California at universities like UC San Diego, UC Davis, UC Riverside, UCLA, and Western University of Health Sciences; others move out of state to the University of Michigan, Tufts, and the University of South Carolina. Likewise, many law students remain in state at schools such as the University of San Diego School of Law, the Thomas Jefferson School of Law, Loyola Law School, Santa Clara School of Law, and UC Davis. SDSU offers a prelaw society, mock trial team, and targeted prelaw advising to those considering a legal education.

Admission

Only 39% of the 77,250 applicants for a place in the Class of 2026 were accepted into the university; 22% of that group went on to enroll at SDSU. Despite the intimidating acceptance rate, there is plenty of room at this school for solid but less-than-perfect applicants. Since all CSU schools have adopted a test-blind policy, they will not consider SAT or ACT scores in the admissions process. Twenty-seven percent of the most recent cohort placed within the top 10% of their high school class, 64% were in the top quartile, and 92% landed in the top half. While 71% of Class of 2026 members possessed a high school GPA of 3.75 or above, 12% earned under a 3.5.

The admissions committee needs to work quickly to sift through the deluge of applications it receives each year. As a result, it reviews standardized test scores, GPA, rigor of courses, state residency, and literally nothing else. Soft factors like essays, recommendations, and extracurricular activities play no role in the admissions process at San Diego State. There is no early action or early decision option at SDSU, but the application deadline is quite early—November 30th last admission cycle. In spite of the low acceptance rate, students should be able to accurately gauge their odds given the relatively formulaic evaluation process. Those placing in the top 25% of their high school class can feel good about their chances.

Worth Your Money?

The process to qualify for residency status has tightened in recent years, making it almost certain that international and non-California residents will pay roughly $47,000 per year total cost of attendance. In-state COA is estimated at $34k, with only $8,290 of that figure covering basic tuition. Thus, those living at home or commuting can attend the university at an absurdly low cost. Like the other 22 schools in the California State University System, SDSU is affordable and, with its excellent ties to industry, job prospects for most graduates are bright.

FINANCIAL
Institutional Type: Public
In-State Tuition: $8,290
Out-of-State Tuition: $20,170
Room & Board: $21,630
Books & Supplies: $908

Avg. Need-Based Grant: $10,575
Avg. % of Need Met: 68%

Avg. Merit-Based Award: $4,074
% Receiving (Freshmen w/o Need): 1%

Avg. Cumulative Debt: $21,212
% of Students Borrowing: 35%

CAREER
Who Recruits
1. Bainbridge
2. Cox Communications
3. GoSite
4. ASML
5. Marriott International

Notable Internships
1. BAE Systems
2. Cushman & Wakefield
3. U.S. Senate

Top Employers
1. Qualcomm
2. Apple
3. EY
4. Amazon
5. Intuit

Where Alumni Work
1. San Diego
2. Los Angeles
3. San Francisco
4. Orange County, CA
5. Germany

Earnings
College Scorecard (10-YR Post-Entry): $61,522
PayScale (Early Career): $60,000
PayScale (Mid-Career): $110,400
PayScale 20-Year ROI: $558,000

RANKINGS
Money: 4.5
U.S. News: 105, National Universities
Wall Street Journal/THE: 169
Washington Monthly: 94, National Universities

OVERGENERALIZATIONS
Students are:
Diverse
Open-minded
Working hard and playing hard
Social
Laid-back

COLLEGE OVERLAPS
Cal Poly, San Luis Obispo
California State University, Long Beach
University of California, Riverside
University of California, Irvine
University of California, San Diego

Santa Clara University

Santa Clara, California | 408-554-4700

ADMISSION
Admission Rate: 52%
Admission Rate - Men: 47%
Admission Rate - Women: 57%
EA Admission Rate: 81%
ED Admission Rate: 83%
ED Admits as % of Total Admits: 4%
Admission Rate (5-Year Trend): -2%
% of Admits Attending (Yield): 19%
Transfer Admission Rate: 45%

SAT Reading/Writing (Middle 50%): 640-720
SAT Math (Middle 50%): 650-760
ACT Composite (Middle 50%): 29-33

% Graduated in Top 10% of HS Class: 39%
% Graduated in Top 25% of HS Class: 74%
% Graduated in Top 50% of HS Class: 96%

Demonstrated Interest: Considered
Legacy Status: Considered
Racial/Ethnic Status: Important
Admission Interview Offered: No

ENROLLMENT
Total Undergraduate Enrollment: 6,115
% Full-Time: 98%
% Male: 52%
% Female: 48%
% Out-of-State: 44%
% Fraternity: Not Offered
% Sorority: Not Offered
% On-Campus (All Undergraduate): 53%
Freshman Housing Required: Yes

% African-American: 3%
% Asian: 21%
% Hispanic: 18%
% White: 40%
% Other: 2%
% International: 6%
% Low-Income: 11%

ACADEMICS
Student-to-Faculty Ratio: 12 to 1
% of Classes Under 20: 44%
% of Classes 20-49: 56%
% of Classes 50 or More: 0%
% Full-Time Faculty: 63%
% Full-Time Faculty w/ Terminal Degree: 95%

Top Programs
Accounting
Bioengineering
Communication
Computer Science and Engineering
Finance
Marketing
Public Health
Psychology

Retention Rate: 93%
4-Year Graduation Rate: 85%
6-Year Graduation Rate: 91%

Curricular Flexibility: Less Flexible
Academic Rating: ★★★★

#CollegesWorthYourMoney

If you were asked to name a premier university in the heart of California's Silicon Valley, chances are your immediate answer would be Stanford. Yet, those who aren't likely to be among the 4% of accepted applicants at Stanford might want to turn their attention to the Valley's second most prestigious school, one that has over ten times the acceptance rate. Santa Clara University is a Jesuit school with a growing national reputation; right now, 52% of undergraduates still hail from California, and major tech firms love to recruit at this excellent institution located in their own backyard.

Inside the Classroom

Students can pursue 50 degrees offered by three undergraduate colleges: the College of Arts & Sciences, the School of Engineering, and the Leavey School of Business. Santa Clara's core curriculum is designed to provide "a humanistic education that leads toward an informed, ethical engagement with the world." To accomplish that, students must take (1) foundations courses in critical thinking and critical writing, cultures and ideas, a second language, mathematics, and religion, theology, and culture; (2) explorations courses in ethics, civic engagement, diversity, additional religion/theology courses, and all of the traditional prerequisites in the natural sciences, social sciences, and the arts; and (3) integrations courses in advanced writing, experiential learning for social justice, and a pathways class that requires students to make connections across disciplines. It's a tall order that involves a certain amount of religious study and doesn't leave a ton of room for electives.

Santa Clara caters to 6,115 undergraduate students as well as another 3,063 graduate students but, thanks to a 12:1 student-to-faculty ratio, it keeps classes reasonably sized. While you won't find many single-digit enrollment seminars, 44% of course sections do contain fewer than 20 students. Undergraduate research is built into many academic programs, particularly in the sciences, and students can partner with willing professors for credited research opportunities. In addition, study abroad ventures are available on all six continents fit for human habitation, and more than 500 students take advantage each year.

The most commonly conferred degrees are in business (31%), engineering (15%), and the social sciences (13%). The Leavey School of Business offers highly ranked management information systems, accounting, and entrepreneurship degree programs. The engineering program is respected by employers, and computer science students fare extraordinarily well in the Silicon Valley job market, which happens to be one of the most competitive in the world. Graduates of SCU do not seek prestigious fellowships in droves, but many of those who do are successful. In 2021, four grads/alumni procured Fulbright Scholarships and the school regularly produces Udall Scholarship winners as well.

Outside the Classroom

The 106-acre campus houses 53% of the undergraduate student body; however, 96% of first-years do reside in university-owned dorms. There are ten fraternities and six sororities at Santa Clara, and although none of them are affiliated with the university (they were dropped in 2001), Greek life still plays a significant social role. For a school of its size, athletics are surprisingly serious at SCU as the Broncos compete at the NCAA Division I level and field nineteen intercollegiate teams. Intramural sports draw an astonishing 3,800 participants every year on 500 teams in sports ranging from soccer to ping-pong. Almost every student is involved in at least one (if not two or three) of the 125 organizations presently operating. The Ruff Riders, a booster organization, is one of the largest groups of its kind with over 1,000 members. Into the Wild is another popular club that plans outdoor excursions to locations such as Big Sur, the beaches of Santa Cruz, and Lake Tahoe. World-class recreational facilities exist on campus for fitness enthusiasts such as the 45,000-square-foot Malley Fitness Center and the Sullivan Aquatic Center. The university's Silicon Valley location means that plenty of high-end cultural, dining, and entertainment options are at your fingertips, and San Francisco is only an hour away by car.

Career Services

Santa Clara's Career Center has ten full-time professional staff members working as career development specialists, employer relations specialists, and coordinators of experiential learning. The 612:1 student-to-advisor ratio is slightly higher than average when compared with the other institutions featured in this guide. However, the center has many strengths, particularly its deep connections to major Silicon Valley companies. Each year, the Fall Career Fair draws many top employers (including tech companies) as well as over 1,000 undergraduates. Another STEM-specific fair in October brings in another 650 students in search of jobs. Across the school's six annual career fairs, 470 employers manned booths and spoke with SCU students.

More than 6,000 employers recruit Santa Clara undergraduates through a mix of Career Center programs and the online job board available through the Handshake platform, and 65% of students utilize their accounts. Over 900 on-campus interviews take place each academic year. Recruiting companies include Disney, Tesla, Apple, Oracle, Cisco, Kaiser Permanente, and NBC Universal. Almost four-fifths of those completing an SCU degree completed at least one internship position during their time at the university. This school boasts an alumni network 105,000 strong, and many are willing to assist current students with finding their first job. Thanks to the strength of its employer recruiting efforts and internship program, SCU's Career Center gets high marks from our staff.

Professional Outcomes

Within six months of receiving their degrees, 91% of Santa Clara graduates have landed jobs, started graduate school, or committed to a full-time service program. Of those employed, the five most commonly entered industries are business development, engineering, education, entrepreneurship, and sales. The companies presently employing the greatest number of Bronco alumni are all tech giants including Cisco, Apple, Google, Oracle, Meta, and Adobe. The median starting salary for all grads is $67,000 with engineering majors enjoying the highest compensation ($83k), and social sciences grads on the low end ($51k). Roughly two-thirds of alumni remain in the Bay Area. Other West Coast destinations such as Los Angeles, Seattle, Portland, Sacramento, and San Diego also attract a fairly large number of grads.

Many graduates who continue their education at the master's or doctoral level do so at one of Santa Clara's own excellent grad programs; the same goes for law school. Over the last fifteen years, 90% of SCU medical school applicants with a minimum MCAT score of 505 and a GPA of 3.5 or higher have been accepted by at least one institution. However, many fail to meet those criteria as only 40% of overall applicants in that period have been accepted, slightly lower than the national average. The three most frequently attended medical schools are fellow Jesuit institutions Creighton, Georgetown, and Loyola (Chicago). A look at where recent grads were pursuing additional education includes a wide range of schools such as UCLA, Berkeley, USC, the University of Washington, and Duke University.

Admission

Growing in popularity, Santa Clara crossed the 16,000 application mark for the fifth straight year with the Class of 2026. A seemingly soft 52% of applicants were granted admission, but a glance at the profile of the average accepted applicant is more informative as to the school's level of selectivity. Of those who enrolled in the university, the middle-50% SAT range was a solid 1290-1480. Thirty-nine percent placed in the top decile of their high school class, and 74% finished in the top quartile; the average unweighted GPA was 3.7. Notably, only 19% of admitted students went on to enroll in the freshman class of 2022-23.

The admissions committee ranks three categories as most important: rigor of secondary school record, GPA, and essays. The list of factors ranked as "important" is far longer and includes class rank, recommendations, volunteer work, racial/ethnic status, first-generation status, legacy status, and extracurricular activities. Due to the aforementioned low yield rate, Santa Clara is always happy to have strong applicants who are willing to commit to the school. As a result, a whopping 83% of early decision applicants gain admission. Santa Clara University is a school that is attracting more applicants every year as its national reputation climbs to new heights. A deceptively high acceptance rate does not do full justice to the caliber of undergraduate it currently attracts. Borderline candidates who have a strong desire to attend should definitely consider applying early decision.

Worth Your Money?

At $82,000 in total annual cost of attendance (including indirect costs), Santa Clara is an expensive proposition any way you slice it. However, qualifying students receive need-based grants that average close to $33,000, and 73% of all undergrads receive some type of financial aid. A Santa Clara degree won't come cheap, but that's okay for business and engineering students who will be heading to high-paying careers in Silicon Valley. Those intending to pursue majors in less immediately lucrative disciplines need to calculate whether the finances make sense for them to attend this school.

FINANCIAL
Institutional Type: Private
In-State Tuition: $59,241
Out-of-State Tuition: $59,241
Room & Board: $17,967
Books & Supplies: $1,152

Avg. Need-Based Grant: $33,465
Avg. % of Need Met: 79%

Avg. Merit-Based Award: $16,589
% Receiving (Freshmen w/o Need): 36%

Avg. Cumulative Debt: $25,193
% of Students Borrowing: 35%

CAREER
Who Recruits
1. Stryker Corporation
2. Gap Inc.
3. Tesla
4. Teach for America
5. Kiva

Notable Internships
1. McAfee
2. Yelp
3. Vera Wang

Top Employers
1. Cisco
2. Apple
3. Google
4. Oracle
5. Facebook

Where Alumni Work
1. San Francisco
2. Los Angeles
3. Seattle
4. Sacramento
5. Portland, OR

Earnings
College Scorecard (10-YR Post-Entry): $99,012
PayScale (Early Career): $75,800
PayScale (Mid-Career): $154,700
PayScale 20-Year ROI: $942,000

RANKINGS
Money: 4.5
U.S. News: 60, National Universities
Wall Street Journal/THE: 75
Washington Monthly: 153, National Universities

OVERGENERALIZATIONS
Students are:
Working hard and playing hard
Wealthy
Athletic/active
Dressed to impress
Always admiring the beauty of their campus

COLLEGE OVERLAPS
Loyola Marymount University
University of California, Davis
University of California, San Diego
University of California, Santa Barbara
University of San Diego

Sarah Lawrence College

Bronxville, New York | 914-395-2510

Founded in 1926 as the affiliated women's college of Vassar, Sarah Lawrence College became coeducational in 1968, although 80% of the current student body are women. Situated in high-end Westchester County just outside of New York City, the school of just over 1,500 is a dream locale for free-thinking, politically engaged, and highly motivated young people. Of course, enjoying this liberal arts utopia comes at a price; SLC's list price places it among the nation's most expensive colleges.

Inside the Classroom

Offering programs in 50 disciplines, the college does not seek to confine its program of study. Instead, it encourages students to follow their own intellectual curiosity. Seeking to promote "experimentation, exploration, and the constant quest for knowledge in every form," Sarah Lawrence offers an extremely open curriculum. All first-years must take a seminar course and dabble in three of the four disciplines: humanities, history and the social sciences, science and mathematics, and creative and performing arts. Over their four years, students must earn 10 credits in three of those four disciplines; otherwise, students are free to follow their passions.

An 11:1 student-to-faculty ratio only tells part of the story as the ratio becomes 1:1 during bi-weekly individual conferences with your professors. Oodles of personalized attention and one-on-one interaction with dedicated professors are available. One-quarter of classes sport single-digit enrollments and a jaw-dropping 87% of sections contain 19 or fewer students. In addition to receiving grades, students also receive detailed written evaluations of their performance in each class as well as an assessment of their "critical abilities." Undergraduate research is a staple of the SLC experience as every student engages in some level of academic research directly with a faculty member. One example is the Summer Undergraduate Research Program in Science & Mathematics, which provides paid, 10-week research opportunities alongside professors. An expansive study abroad program includes partnerships with the University of Leeds (England), Tsuda University in Tokyo, Kansai Gaidai University in Osaka (Japan), and a Tanzania/South Africa/Zimbabwe three-part trip that is co-run with Pitzer College. Close to half of all SLC undergrads participate in one of the smorgasbord of study abroad options.

Sarah Lawrence graduates are recognized as serious scholars and fare well in their quests to obtain admission to many of the nation's top graduate/professional programs. There are no majors that shine above the others—in fact, 100% of degrees conferred fall under the umbrella of liberal arts. Given the vibe of the student body and the international flavor of the school, it is somewhat surprising that Sarah Lawrence grads do not typically win many graduate fellowships or scholarships; the school has had only around a dozen Fulbright winners since the turn of the millennium.

Outside the Classroom

Seventy-six percent of Sarah Lawrence undergraduates, and just about all freshmen, live on campus in one of 23 residence halls that provide luxurious accommodations by collegiate housing standards. The college's wooded, 44-acre campus is only 15 miles from the heart of New York City; Midtown Manhattan is just a 30-minute train ride away. The gender breakdown of 80/20 in favor of women certainly dictates some aspects of social life. There is no Greek life whatsoever at SLC. Women's sports outnumber men's sports eight to six (there is also a coed equestrian team) and the Gryphons compete in NCAA Division III; there are over 125 students competing in varsity athletics. There are over 120 student organizations with many in the identity-based or activism categories. About 20 clubs are dedicated to performance (theatrical and musical) and another 20 to student publications. Amenities at the school are off the charts and include a 60,000-square-foot visual arts center, brand-new dining facilities, and the inviting Esther Raushenbush Library that will make you feel you have gone back in time (in a good way).

Career Services

The Career Services team at Sarah Lawrence is made up of four professional staff members who cater to the needs of 1,465 undergraduates. The office has a 366:1 student-to-advisor ratio, in the average range for this guidebook. Just as with the faculty, career advisors have the reputation of always being willing to sit down for an intimate chat. Events such as the Spring Career and Internship Fair are intimate, usually hosting about 15 employers. However, Sarah Lawrence is one of the 17 members of Career Internship Connections, an annual collegiate hiring event that includes undergrads from Pomona, Carnegie Mellon, and Tufts.

The office does a decent job of helping students obtain internships. The school's online database contains 250 active listings of internship opportunities, and each year about 300 students procure an opportunity. Almost 60% of grads held one internship during their four years of study. Being located in New York City opens doors to desirable internships at places like ELLE magazine, the Guggenheim Museum, Simon & Schuster, NBCUniversal, and the New York City Ballet.

Professional Outcomes

Many of the largest employers of Sarah Lawrence alumni are institutions of higher learning, including the college itself, NYU, Columbia University, the New School, and Fordham. Other leading employers include public sector entities like the NYC Department of Education and hospitals like Sloan Kettering, NYU Langone Health, and New York Presbyterian Hospital. As you can deduce from the names of the most popular employers, the vast majority of graduates remain in New York City. The next most frequent landing spots are Los Angeles, San Francisco, Boston, and DC.

Part of the reason for the aforementioned uninspiring salary numbers is the fact that 70% of Sarah Lawrence alumni go on to earn advanced degrees, thus delaying their prime earning years. Of those pursuing further education, 51% obtain professional degrees, 27% concentrate in a humanities field, and 13% focus on the creative or performing arts. Alumni go on to attend many impressive graduate institutions around the globe including The London School of Economics, Oxford, Harvard, Yale, and Brown. Recent graduates engaged in legal studies have enrolled at Cornell Law School, University of Michigan School of Law, Georgetown University Law Center, New York University Law School, Columbia University School of Law, and others.

Admission

The acceptance rate for the Sarah Lawrence Class of 2026 was a fairly unintimidating 50%. Only 931 of the 5,186 seniors who applied were men, and they were accepted at a slightly more favorable 53% clip. While Sarah Lawrence is a test-optional college, the median SAT score for enrolled freshmen was 1360 and the average ACT was 30. Twenty-nine percent of freshmen finished in the top 10% of their high school class, 55% in the top 25%, and 88% in the top half. The average GPA was 3.8.

Just as Sarah Lawrence is known for giving its students loads of one-on-one attention, the application process is personal also. The admissions committee cites three factors as being of paramount importance: rigor of coursework, the application essay, and recommendations. The second tier of considered criteria includes GPA and "soft" factors such as extracurricular activities, talent/ability, and character/personal qualities. Imperfections in a student's high school resume can be compensated for through thoughtful essays and a strong in-person interview. Being male helps, as does professing your love for the school in the form of an ED application. Sarah Lawrence has been test-optional since 2013, and many students take advantage—only 15% of applicants submit SAT scores, and 6% submit ACT scores. Due to a low yield rate—just 15% of admitted applicants enroll—the college loves those who commit via early decision, and it admits 59% of ED applicants.

Worth Your Money?

With a list price of more than $81,000, Sarah Lawrence can quickly end up in a prospective family's "Can't afford it" pile. However, it does meet approximately four-fifths of demonstrated need among those who qualify. Even better, more than 75% of undergrads receive some type of financial aid, and the average package is over $40k. While over one-third of graduates do owe money, the average debt load is less than the national average. Clearly, most attendees of this college end up on solid financial footing after leaving Bronxville, but cost-conscious students will want to plan well to make sure they account for potentially (sector-dependent) low starting salaries and the cost of future advanced degrees.

FINANCIAL
Institutional Type: Private
In-State Tuition: $63,678
Out-of-State Tuition: $63,678
Room & Board: $17,546
Books & Supplies: $600

Avg. Need-Based Grant: $39,557
Avg. % of Need Met: 83%

Avg. Merit-Based Award: $25,661
% Receiving (Freshmen w/o Need): 31%

Avg. Cumulative Debt: $25,918
% of Students Borrowing: 62%

CAREER
Who Recruits
1. Montefiore Health System
2. The New York Times
3. NYC Department of Education
4. Invitae
5. Penguin Random House

Notable Internships
1. ACLU
2. Netflix
3. US House of Representatives

Top Employers
1. New York University
2. NYC Dept of Education
3. Columbia University
4. Self Employed
5. Montefiore Health

Where Alumni Work
1. New York City
2. Los Angeles
3. San Francisco
4. Boston
5. Washington, DC

Earnings
College Scorecard (10-YR Post-Entry): $47,659
PayScale (Early Career): $56,900
PayScale (Mid-Career): $113,100
PayScale 20-Year ROI: $306,000

RANKINGS
Money: 3
U.S. News: 100, Liberal Arts Colleges
Wall Street Journal/THE: Not Ranked
Washington Monthly: 146, Liberal Arts Colleges

OVERGENERALIZATIONS
Students are:
Intellectually curious
Politically liberal
Nonconformist
Artsy
Homogenous

COLLEGE OVERLAPS
Bard College
Fordham University
New York University
Skidmore College
Vassar College

Scripps College

Claremont, California | 909-621-8149

ADMISSION
Admission Rate: 28%
Admission Rate - Men: Not Applicable
Admission Rate - Women: 28%
EA Admission Rate: Not Offered
ED Admission Rate: 40%
ED Admits as % of Total Admits: 12%
Admission Rate (5-Year Trend): -5%
% of Admits Attending (Yield): 30%
Transfer Admission Rate: 11%

SAT Reading/Writing (Middle 50%): 710-760
SAT Math (Middle 50%): 680-750
ACT Composite (Middle 50%): 32-34

% Graduated in Top 10% of HS Class: 69%
% Graduated in Top 25% of HS Class: 94%
% Graduated in Top 50% of HS Class: 100%

Demonstrated Interest: Not Considered
Legacy Status: Considered
Racial/Ethnic Status: Considered
Admission Interview Offered: Yes

ENROLLMENT
Total Undergraduate Enrollment: 1,081
% Full-Time: 100%
% Male: Not Applicable
% Female: 100%
% Out-of-State: 57%
% Fraternity: Not Applicable
% Sorority: Not Offered
% On-Campus (All Undergraduate): 97%
Freshman Housing Required: Yes

% African-American: 4%
% Asian: 13%
% Hispanic: 13%
% White: 54%
% Other: 1%
% International: 3%
% Low-Income: 12%

ACADEMICS
Student-to-Faculty Ratio: 10 to 1
% of Classes Under 20: 76%
% of Classes 20-49: 25%
% of Classes 50 or More: 0%
% Full-Time Faculty: 76%
% Full-Time Faculty w/ Terminal Degree: 99%

Top Programs
Area Studies
Art
Biology
English
Environmental Analysis
Media Studies
Politics
Psychology

Retention Rate: 90%
4-Year Graduation Rate: 77%
6-Year Graduation Rate: 86%

Curricular Flexibility: Somewhat Flexible
Academic Rating: ★★★★

#CollegesWorthYourMoney

While the East Coast is swarming with high-end women's colleges such as Wellesley, Smith, Bryn Mawr, Barnard, and Mt. Holyoke, there is only one such jewel resting closer to the Pacific Ocean. Scripps College, a member of the five-school Claremont Consortium, is the West Coast's lone elite all-female institution, making it a highly desirable destination for young women seeking a classic liberal arts education in a nurturing and supportive academic environment without the lonely, harsh winters of the Northeast.

Inside the Classroom
There are 65+ majors available to Scripps undergrads, including some that are accessible through membership in the Consortium. Curricular requirements at Scripps are extensive, requiring a three-semester dive into interdisciplinary humanities coursework that tackles the essential question of "What makes a community?" through a combination of lectures, seminar-style discussions, and a self-designed project. All undergraduates must demonstrate competency in mathematics, foreign language, and writing. Along the way, one course must be taken in each of the four divisions: fine arts, natural sciences, letters, and social sciences. Within one's major, a minimum of eight courses must be tackled, culminating in the completion of a senior thesis, which 100% of graduates must complete.

A 10:1 student-to-faculty ratio at a school with zero grad students breeds an intimate learning atmosphere where professors are genuinely dedicated to educating the 1,081 undergrads on campus. A lack of competitiveness should not be mistaken for a lack of rigor. Scripps is loaded with driven students, 15% of whom elect to double major. As part of the required senior thesis, many undergraduates also have the chance to assist professors with academic/scientific research. Due to the absence of graduate students who would gobble up such positions, research opportunities are readily available for credit during the academic year as well on a full-time basis during the summer; the Scripps Undergraduate Research Fellowship is one such program. Study abroad programs in 40 countries are taken advantage of by nearly two-thirds of the student body, giving Scripps one of the highest participation rates of any college in the United States.

The top five areas of concentration are the social sciences (18%), biology (14%), natural resources/conservation (8%), psychology (7%), and area, ethnic, and gender studies (6%). Each possesses a very strong reputation. Regardless of your major, however, graduate/professional schools know that earning a degree from Scripps is no small achievement. Prestigious scholarship committees also look kindly upon the school as Scripps is regularly a top twenty-five producer of Fulbright winners, taking home an incredible (considering the size of each graduating class) eight awards in 2023. Recent grads have also taken home Watson Fellowships and a Davis Projects for Peace Fellowship.

Outside the Classroom
At Scripps, 97% of students live on the school's modestly sized 30-acre campus in one of eleven immaculately maintained dorms or in thematic housing options catering to those with goals and interests in common such as the STEM Living Learning Community and the Wellness Community. There are no sororities at Scripps. Sports exist but are a combined effort with Harvey Mudd and Claremont McKenna that, collectively, field 11 NCAA Division III teams. Fitness and recreational facilities are shared with Pitzer, Pomona, Harvey Mudd, and CMC. That means students have access to four swimming pools, four fitness centers, and a dozen playing fields. There are roughly 30 Scripps-only student-run organizations, but there are also more than 250 clubs that can be accessed by students of any of the five schools. One of the more notable social hubs is the Motley Coffeehouse, founded in 1974 and run entirely by Scripps students. In fact, the feminist, environmental, and social justice vibe makes its coffeehouse a perfect embodiment of the college's values and ethos. The college also boasts its own art museum, the Williamson Gallery, which contains works by many notable American artists. Of course, cultural options are hardly confined to the campus limits with Los Angeles only a forty-five-minute car ride away.

Career Services
The Career Planning & Resources Office (CP&R) has two full-time professional staff members working as career counselors. Scripps' 541:1 student-to-advisor ratio is in the average range for a college featured in our guidebook. It may be a small office, but you won't find a more proactive career services staff at any college in the country as the CP&R meets with 80-85% of freshmen within the students' first three weeks on campus. Larger events are typically joint affairs with the other esteemed members of the Claremont Consortium.

Scripps takes pride in its facilitation of student internships and has the stats to prove it; 85% of graduates held at least one internship, and close to one-quarter completed three or more. Internship locations of note include 20th Century Fox, the California Department of Justice, and the Smithsonian. Career Treks whisk Scripps students off to metropolitan areas around the country to meet with alumni who are working in the same field of interest. Former students are always willing to lend a hand to current ones and can connect with soon-to-be grads through the Alumni Book, a compilation of student resumes. A week-long Emerging Professionals Program featuring alumni, recruiters, and CP&R counselors can be accessed for free. The office also offers a Financial Literacy Program to teach undergraduates about everything from budgeting to investing to filing taxes.

Professional Outcomes

Scripps women land jobs at some of the world's leading companies after receiving their diplomas. The top employers of Scripps alumni include Google, Kaiser Permanente, and Amazon. Many go on to work for universities, particularly after earning additional degrees (more on this in a moment). Schools employing significant numbers of Scripps alumni include Pomona, Scripps, Stanford, UCLA, and UC San Diego. Recent graduates also have entered positions at BlackRock, CBS, Goldman Sachs, Meta, and Pfizer. Median salaries by mid-career are quite a bit lower than fellow Consortium member schools Pomona and Claremont McKenna, but they are comparable to other elite women's colleges such as Bryn Mawr. Most Scripps alumni remain on the West Coast with the largest percentage in Los Angeles followed by San Francisco, Seattle, Portland, San Diego, and Orange County. The most popular East Coast destinations are New York City, DC, and Boston.

An advanced degree is in the cards for most Scripps grads and it isn't usually too far in the future—two-thirds complete a graduate/professional program within five years of receiving their bachelor's degrees. Recent grads have pursued further study at institutions such as Caltech, Harvard, MIT, Vanderbilt, Oxford, Brown, Northwestern, and Tufts. Scripps knows what it's doing when it comes to premed, thanks to its Post-Baccalaureate Premedical Program that boasts a 98% acceptance rate; traditional undergrads also fare well above the national average. Those eyeing law school also find favorable results; recent grads have been accepted at top-tier law schools such as Emory, Georgetown, the University of Chicago, Berkeley, and the University of Michigan.

Admission

Thirty percent of the 3,099 women who applied for a place in the Class of 2026 were accepted. An equal thirty percent of accepted students went on to enroll. Freshmen in 2022-23 possessed a middle 50% score of 1410-1510 on the SAT and 32-34 on the ACT. An impressive 69% came from the top decile of their high school class; 94% placed in the top quarter. Ninety percent sported a GPA of 3.75 or greater; only 4% earned less than a 3.5. The average GPA of an entering first-year student was 4.28. In 2020, the school announced the implementation of a test-optional policy which remains in place today.

The admissions committee seeks "to build a community of curious and engaged students who are eager to contribute their diverse interests, backgrounds, and experiences to our academic and residential community." As such, they weigh five factors as being "very important" to admissions decisions: rigor of coursework, GPA, class rank, essays, and character/personal qualities. Applying early decision at Scripps does yield an edge; 40% of ED applicants were accepted into the Class of 2026. Those accepted in the early round comprised two-fifths of the incoming freshman class.

Worth Your Money?

At a bit over $87,000, the sticker price cost of attendance for Scripps College is undoubtedly on the high side. However, the undergraduates who are determined eligible for need-based aid all see 100% of their need met; the average grant is $45k. Graduates leave with a debt total that is less than the national average. If attending Scripps is financially feasible for your family, the quality of the educational experience and networks/resources offered by the Consortium make this school worth some level of sacrifice.

FINANCIAL
Institutional Type: Private
In-State Tuition: $63,434
Out-of-State Tuition: $63,434
Room & Board: $21,330
Books & Supplies: $800

Avg. Need-Based Grant: $48,098
Avg. % of Need Met: 100%

Avg. Merit-Based Award: $17,662
% Receiving (Freshmen w/o Need): 19%

Avg. Cumulative Debt: $17,171
% of Students Borrowing: 28%

CAREER
Who Recruits
1. DaVita
2. Nielsen
3. Pfizer
4. Nordstrom
5. Brancart & Brancart

Notable Internships
1. ACLU
2. Louis Vuitton
3. KPMG

Top Employers
1. Google
2. Kaiser Permanente
3. Amazon
4. Microsoft
5. Seattle Children's

Where Alumni Work
1. Los Angeles
2. San Francisco
3. Seattle
4. New York City
5. Portland, OR

Earnings
College Scorecard (10-YR Post-Entry): $70,465
PayScale (Early Career): $59,900
PayScale (Mid-Career): $105,100
PayScale 20-Year ROI: $327,000

RANKINGS
Money: 4
U.S. News: 35, Liberal Arts Colleges
Wall Street Journal/THE: Not Ranked
Washington Monthly: 113, Liberal Arts Colleges

OVERGENERALIZATIONS
Students are:
Politically liberal
Intellectually curious
Passionate
Social Justice-Oriented
Always admiring the beauty of their campus

COLLEGE OVERLAPS
Claremont McKenna College
Pitzer College
University of California, Los Angeles
University of Southern California
Wellesley College

Sewanee - The University of the South

Sewanee, Tennessee | 931-598-1238

ADMISSION
Admission Rate: 52%
Admission Rate - Men: 47%
Admission Rate - Women: 57%
EA Admission Rate: 79%
ED Admission Rate: 60%
ED Admits as % of Total Admits: 3%
Admission Rate (5-Year Trend): +5%
% of Admits Attending (Yield): 17%
Transfer Admission Rate: 51%

SAT Reading/Writing (Middle 50%): 643-710
SAT Math (Middle 50%): 590-670
ACT Composite (Middle 50%): 27-32

% Graduated in Top 10% of HS Class: 32%
% Graduated in Top 25% of HS Class: 66%
% Graduated in Top 50% of HS Class: 91%

Demonstrated Interest: Considered
Legacy Status: Considered
Racial/Ethnic Status: Not Considered
Admission Interview Offered: Yes

ENROLLMENT
Total Undergraduate Enrollment: 1,613
% Full-Time: 99%
% Male: 47%
% Female: 53%
% Out-of-State: 79%
% Fraternity: 57%
% Sorority: 61%
% On-Campus (All Undergraduate): 99%
Freshman Housing Required: Yes

% African-American: 4%
% Asian: 1%
% Hispanic: 6%
% White: 81%
% Other: 3%
% International: 5%
% Low-Income: 15%

ACADEMICS
Student-to-Faculty Ratio: 10 to 1
% of Classes Under 20: 66%
% of Classes 20-49: 34%
% of Classes 50 or More: <1%
% Full-Time Faculty: 72%
% Full-Time Faculty w/ Terminal Degree: 95%

Top Programs
Biology
Economics
English
Environment & Sustainability
History
International & Global Studies
Politics

Retention Rate: 89%
4-Year Graduation Rate: 74%
6-Year Graduation Rate: 80%

Curricular Flexibility: Somewhat Flexible
Academic Rating: ★★★✦

#CollegesWorthYourMoney

People flying over the historic campus of the University of the South, sometimes referred to as "Sewanee," might, in a moment of panic, fret that they had accidentally hopped aboard an international flight and were passing directly over Oxford or Cambridge. This breathtaking campus that includes 13,000 acres of natural beauty known affectionately as "The Domain" is situated on Tennessee's Cumberland Plateau. The pretty packaging is not misleading; the University of the South delivers a powerful academic punch, and it isn't quite as picky as many other top schools as to who gets to step into the ring. While designated a "university," Sewanee is really more of a liberal arts college of 1,704 undergrads and fewer than one hundred graduate students.

Inside the Classroom
Offering 37 majors and 42 minors, undergrads are exposed to a wide scope of liberal arts study, no matter their area of concentration. All students must complete a designated writing-intensive course by the end of their sophomore year as well as coursework fulfilling six "learning objectives." Literary analysis, understanding the arts, and seeking meaning require one course each while multiple classes are required in exploring past and present, the scientific and quantitative view, and language and global studies. Two physical education and wellness classes also must be tackled prior to graduation.

A 10:1 student-to-faculty ratio and a limited number of grad students mean that undergraduate teaching remains the primary focus at Sewanee. The average class size is 17 students, and 66% of course sections have an enrollment under 20. Opportunities to conduct research with faculty members are not only plentiful but also often funded by the university. Recent students have collaborated on fascinating research projects on topics such as Adolescent Substance Use Perception in Southern Appalachia; Synthesis of New, More Effective Anti-Cancer Metallopharmaceuticals; and Corporate Political Contributions and Stock Returns. Study abroad options that are a summer, a semester, or a full year in length are embarked upon by roughly half of all Sewanee students. European Studies and British Studies are two of the most popular global programs offered by the college.

The degrees most commonly conferred are in economics (12%), psychology (11%), political science (10%), biology (10%), and English (9%). All are strong, but Sewanee's English Department has a leading national reputation. Thanks to the Tennessee Williams Writers-in-Residence program, accomplished authors from around the globe come to teach at Sewanee, and English majors routinely continue their studies at the likes of Princeton, Yale, Duke, and the University of Chicago. The school has also historically had success in helping its students procure the most distinguished graduate fellowships. Sewanee is routinely named a top producer of Fulbright Scholars and over 50 students have claimed Watson Scholarships since they were first made available in 1968. Incredibly, the school claims 27 Rhodes Scholars in its history, more than Amherst, Emory, or Middlebury.

Outside the Classroom
Just about the entire student body, 99% to be precise, lives in the dorms or in other on-campus housing. Greek life is extremely popular at Sewanee as the eleven fraternities and ten sororities attract an overwhelming 80% of undergraduates in rushing. When it's all said and done, 61% of women and 57% of men end up Greek affiliated. Involvement in some type of sport is also common. Eleven men's and thirteen women's Division III athletic teams are joined by 30% of the student population. Another eight club teams and plenty of intramural sessions draw many more. More than ninety student-run organizations are active with the most popular being the Student Government Association, the Order of Gown (focusing on campus spirit and traditions), and the Student Activity Board. If climbing, caving, hiking, biking, or canoeing is more your style, then the Sewanee Outing Program (SOP) is a must-join organization. In addition to taking outdoorsy road trips, the SOP also takes full advantage of the pristine beauty of the aforementioned Domain. With Chattanooga only an hour away and Nashville an hour-and-a-half car ride from campus, Sewanee students can access big-city fun on the weekends.

Career Services
Sewanee Career Readiness employs ten full-time staff members. That equates to a student-to-staff ratio of 161:1, in the average range compared to the other institutions included in this book. The CLD does manage to reach 97% of students by the time they graduate, and a hard-to-beat 99% report being satisfied by the guidance they receive. Events such as the annual Graduate and Professional School Fair draw reps from more than 35 programs including Tulane, Vanderbilt, and UGA's law schools, Wake Forest's MBA program, and Emory's School of Theology. An annual Beyond the Gates event sees close to fifty alumni from all walks of professional life spend a weekend mentoring current juniors and seniors as they ready themselves for the job search.

Via the Sewanee Pledge, the university guarantees funding for one unpaid internship or research experience for every single student. Each year, more than 200 such stipends are granted for unpaid internships alone and, in summer 2022, the university spent $500k toward this aim. Over 150 Sewanee-exclusive internship opportunities are posted each year, creating a favorable environment for students to gain the inside track on desirable opportunities. Recent students have interned at Style Magazine, Accenture, the World Wildlife Fund, and the US Forest Service. The alumni network includes 18,000 individuals who are happy to help current students. The Sewanee Career Readiness office, thanks to a high level of connection and personalized counseling, succeeds in assisting the bulk of graduates reach their next destination.

Professional Outcomes

Within six months of their commencement ceremony, 95% of 2022 Sewanee grads have found some form of employment or have begun their graduate studies. Sixty-eight percent have obtained full-time employment with the highest number of grads entering the sectors of business/finance (97); health care (51); and government, politics, and law (36). Organizations employing recent graduates include Booz Allen Hamilton, Sony Pictures, Warby Parker, BlackRock, and Massachusetts General Hospital. The largest number of total alumni can be found at Wells Fargo, Deloitte, Regions Bank, and Vanderbilt University Medical Center. Many alumni remain in the South after graduation as Nashville, Atlanta, and Chattanooga are the most frequent destinations. However, DC and New York City also contain large pockets of grads.

The majority of those in the Class of 2022 who pursued advanced degrees entered master's programs, followed by medical school, law school, and PhD programs. Elite graduate school acceptances included Johns Hopkins, Georgetown, Vanderbilt, and Washington University in St. Louis. Law schools attended included Baylor U, the College of William & Mary, and Notre Dame. Medical school acceptances in the last several years included East Carolina University and the University of Texas. In recent years, law school acceptance rates have been in the 90-95% range and medical school admit rates have hovered around 80-85%, double the national average.

Admission

Sewanee is a rare top school that, even in the 2020s, still lacks a menacing acceptance rate—its 52% is about as friendly as you will find among top colleges. The entering Class of 2026 held strong academic credentials, sporting median standardized test scores of 1305 on the SAT and 30 on the ACT (the school is test-optional). You don't need to be at the top of your high school class to gain admittance as only 32% placed in the top decile and 66% in the top quartile. The school's selectivity level is similar to that of a full decade ago.

A test-optional school, the University of the South places a strong emphasis on the rigor of one's secondary school record, GPA, and recommendations. Second billing is granted to the application essay, extracurricular activities, character/personal qualities, volunteer work, and work experience. A relatively low yield rate of 17% means that over four-fifths of those accepted enroll elsewhere. While the university does not rank demonstrated interest as an important factor in admissions decisions, the committee certainly appreciates those who apply via binding early decision. In fact, 60% of those applying ED are accepted. A fine and distinctive education can be yours at this exceptionally beautiful Tennessee campus without the typical crucible of admissions-related stress found at many of the schools featured in this book.

Worth Your Money?

The overall cost of attendance of $69k represents a less-than-exorbitant sticker price in the world of small liberal arts schools. This is particularly true since 98% of new students receive an average award of over $34k. If your family has limited funds (like most), you'll want to see how much merit and need-based aid you are awarded before making a decision on whether Sewanee is the right choice for your wallet.

FINANCIAL
Institutional Type: Private
In-State Tuition: $53,704
Out-of-State Tuition: $53,704
Room & Board: $15,338
Books & Supplies: $1,200

Avg. Need-Based Grant: $36,856
Avg. % of Need Met: 92%

Avg. Merit-Based Award: $22,906
% Receiving (Freshmen w/o Need): 45%

Avg. Cumulative Debt: $33,670
% of Students Borrowing: 36%

CAREER
Who Recruits
1. Springbot
2. JumpCrew
3. Showtime Networks
4. Accenture
5. Harris Williams & Co.

Notable Internships
1. UBS
2. Wells Fargo
3. U.S. Senate

Top Employers
1. Wells Fargo
2. Regions Bank
3. CBRE
4. Deloitte
5. Capital One

Where Alumni Work
1. Nashville
2. Atlanta
3. Chattanooga, TN
4. Washington, DC
5. New York City

Earnings
College Scorecard (10-YR Post-Entry): $59,529
PayScale (Early Career): $57,100
PayScale (Mid-Career): $114,200
PayScale 20-Year ROI: $37,000

RANKINGS
Money: 4
U.S. News: 51, Liberal Arts Colleges
Wall Street Journal/THE: Not Ranked
Washington Monthly: 98, Liberal Arts Colleges

OVERGENERALIZATIONS
Students are:
Outdoorsy
More likely to rush a fraternity/sorority
Working hard and playing hard
Poitically balanced
Tight-knit (possess a strong sense of community)

COLLEGE OVERLAPS
Furman University
Rhodes College
University of Georgia
Wake Forest University
Washington & Lee University

Skidmore College

Saratoga Springs, New York | 518-580-5570

Founded as a women's college at the turn of the twentieth century, Skidmore still serves more women than men today, but going co-ed isn't the most notable shift that has occurred at this private liberal arts college in Upstate New York. The school's 2,758 undergrads, affectionately known as "Skiddies," have become an increasingly higher-achieving lot as the school has transformed from selective to highly selective over the past decade. What has remained is its reputation as a free-spirited institution with an extremely accessible and student-friendly faculty.

Inside the Classroom
An undergraduate-only institution, there are 40+ majors to choose from with the most popular being business, English, psychology, political science, economics, studio art, theater, biology, and environmental studies. All students begin by completing a first-year experience that is highlighted by participation in the Scribner Seminars, where students begin to grasp the level of rigor that will be expected as they launch their collegiate studies. Foundations courses include Applied Quantitative Reasoning, Global Cultural Perspectives, Language Study, and Writing. Inquiry courses include Artistic Inquiry through Practice, Humanistic Inquiry and Practice, and Scientific Inquiry through Practice. It's hard to earn a diploma without completing some type of culminating project; 75% complete a senior capstone, 53% engage in independent study, and 32% produce a senior thesis or advanced research project.

With no graduate students around to suck up professorial attention, undergrads reap the full benefits of the school's student-to-faculty ratio of 8-to-1. Skidmore's average class size is only 16 students, and 98% of sections have fewer than thirty students. Nineteen percent of sections enroll only single digits. Each year, roughly 500 students—20% of the student body—engage in research with a faculty mentor, including eighty students who participate in the Summer Student-Faculty Research Program. Internships and service-learning courses are a normal part of the Skidmore experience. Three-fifths of students study abroad at one of 120 programs in 45 countries, a rate of participation that places it at the very top in the nation.

Known for its superior undergraduate teaching, a Skidmore degree will carry enough prestige to open doors to top employers and graduate schools, particularly in the aforementioned areas that are among the most popular majors. The social sciences (17%), business (14%), visual and performing arts (13%), and biology (12%) are the most common areas of study. The school produces a surprisingly modest number of competitive postgraduate scholars and fellows. Most years, it produces a finalist for a National Science Foundation, Goldwater, or Mitchell Scholarship, but it does not consistently take home the big prizes.

Outside the Classroom
Almost 90% of students reside in one of Skidmore's eight residence halls, which are split evenly on a North and a South campus spread over 1,000 enchanting acres. The only Greek life at Skidmore can be found in courses in the classics; there are no frats or sororities in the "Skidmore bubble." An almost 60/40 split along gender lines in favor of women certainly has an impact on social life. There are nearly 130 active student-run clubs and 19 Division III varsity sports teams (10 women's and 9 men's) nicknamed the Thoroughbreds. There are plenty of club sports and intramural leagues for less serious competitors. Amenities are first-class, from the apartment-style dorms to the award-winning dining services to the 150-acre North Woods oasis that can be used for anything from meditation to skiing. Saratoga Springs is a small city of 30,000, but its funky downtown is only a ten-minute walk from campus. Skidmore is located thirty minutes from Albany and three full hours from popular road trip destinations like New York City, Boston, and Montreal. Those seeking more nature-oriented recreation can easily travel to the Berkshires, Adirondacks, or Green Mountains.

Career Services
The Career Development Center (CDC) at Skidmore College is staffed by nine professionals with counseling expertise in a variety of fields. That works out to a 306:1 student-to-advisor ratio that is solidly in the average range compared to other institutions in this guidebook. The CDC hosts an annual networking event called Career Jam that is attended by hundreds of students as well as many alumni, parents, and employers. The annual Graduate and Professional School Expo attracts representatives from roughly 45 universities to Skidmore. Students also can travel off campus to corporate destinations along the East Coast as part of the Road Trips to the Real World program.

In a single year, the CDC conducts 2,000+ one-on-one counseling sessions, brings close to 100 employers to Saratoga Springs for recruiting purposes, and facilitates more than 300 on-campus interviews. An impressive 270+ employers attend the college's job fairs. Eighty-one percent of 2022 grads participated in an internship during their time at Skidmore, and many were funded by the school. Students nab intriguing internships at places such as Tesla, NASA, the NBA, Esquire Magazine, and Memorial Sloan Kettering Cancer Center. The career services staff encourages individual meetings as early as freshman year in its effort to support "all students and alumni through the creative process of integrating their liberal arts education and experiences into a satisfying career."

Professional Outcomes

Sixty-five percent of 2022 Skidmore grads were employed within six months of completing their degrees and 26% were enrolled in graduate school. The most frequently entered industries were STEM (20%), business (17%), education (16%), health science (9%), and finance (7%). The median starting salary range for Class of 2022 grads was $40,000-$49,000. Intriguing employers of recent grads included the Metropolitan Opera, Penguin Random House, NBC Universal, Estee Lauder, and Vineyard Vines. Fairly large numbers of Skiddies can be found at major corporations including Google, Morgan Stanley, EY, Amazon, JPMorgan Chase, Fidelity Investments, and IBM. The greatest concentration of alumni can be found in Greater New York City with Boston, Albany, San Francisco, and Washington, DC, the next most popular landing spots.

Graduate acceptances procured by the Class of 2022 included Ivies like Brown, Cornell, Dartmouth, and Columbia as well as other elite institutions like Duke, the University of Virginia, and NYU. Skidmore students are accepted to medical school at a rate "far above the national average." Many recent med school-bound grads have attended NY-based schools like SUNY Upstate, SUNY Stony Brook, or the University of Buffalo. Over the last few years, grads have matriculated into law schools at Indiana University, Penn State, and the University of Miami.

Admission

For 2022-23 freshman hopefuls, only 26% were accepted and the mid-50% SAT was 1320-1440. It is important to note that Skidmore adopted a test-optional policy in 2016 (before it was "cool") that led to a spike in applications. Among enrolled freshmen, 26% submitted SAT scores and another 12% submitted ACT scores, so the majority of accepted applicants are going the test-optional route. Many students, but far from all, rank near the top of their graduating high school classes; 36% of members of the Class of 2026 placed in the top decile, and 79% earned a spot in the top quartile.

In the eyes of the admissions office, the rigor of secondary coursework is the only factor that rises to "most important" status. From there, class rank, GPA, essays, recommendations, extracurricular activities, talent/ability, character/personal qualities, work experience, volunteer work, and demonstrated interest are on equal footing as "important" factors. As a test-optional school, SATs and ACTs are relegated to "considered" status. In the most recent admissions cycle, the acceptance rate for early decision applicants was 51% and ED students made up 51% of the freshman class. A more competitive school than in the recent past, those set on Skidmore definitely should consider applying ED and should at least go out of their way to demonstrate serious interest in the college. While test-optional, strong standardized test scores can still help you win over the admissions committee.

Worth Your Money?

Need-based grants averaging $50,000 were awarded to 51% of freshmen at Skidmore in 2022-23. That helps defray some of the $83k in total costs each year for those with genuine financial need. Unfortunately, merit aid is only made available to a tiny sliver of the undergraduate population; thus, you are unlikely to get a significant tuition discount unless you qualify for a grant. If your parents can afford Skidmore, it is a wonderful place to spend four years learning and growing. On the other hand, we would not recommend taking on large amounts of debt in order to study theater, English, studio art, or any other popular but typically low-paying major without a clear postgraduate career and financial plan.

FINANCIAL
Institutional Type: Private
In-State Tuition: $64,880
Out-of-State Tuition: $64,880
Room & Board: $17,340
Books & Supplies: $1,300

Avg. Need-Based Grant: $50,000
Avg. % of Need Met: 100%

Avg. Merit-Based Award: $16,667
% Receiving (Freshmen w/o Need): <1%

Avg. Cumulative Debt: $29,389
% of Students Borrowing: 38%

CAREER
Who Recruits
1. New England Center for Children
2. M&T Bank
3. EY
4. NYS Department of Health
5. Carney Sandoe & Associates

Notable Internships
1. Scholastic
2. WHYY
3. Airbnb

Top Employers
1. Morgan Stanley
2. EY
3. JPMorgan Chase
4. Google
5. Fidelity Investments

Where Alumni Work
1. New York City
2. Boston
3. Albany, NY
4. San Francisco
5. Washington, DC

Earnings
College Scorecard (10-YR Post-Entry): $68,541
PayScale (Early Career): $58,300
PayScale (Mid-Career): $113,000
PayScale 20-Year ROI: $496,000

RANKINGS
Money: 4.5
U.S. News: 38, Liberal Arts Colleges
Wall Street Journal/THE: 245
Washington Monthly: 49, Liberal Arts Colleges

OVERGENERALIZATIONS
Students are:
Environmentally conscious
Politically liberal
Collaborative
Creative
Wealthy

COLLEGE OVERLAPS
Bates College
Hamilton College
Tufts University
Vassar College
Wesleyan University

Smith College

Northampton, Massachusetts | 413-585-2500

ADMISSION
Admission Rate: 23%
Admission Rate - Men: Not Applicable
Admission Rate - Women: 23%
EA Admission Rate: Not Offered
ED Admission Rate: 49%
ED Admits as % of Total Admits: 21%
Admission Rate (5-Year Trend): -9%
% of Admits Attending (Yield): 37%
Transfer Admission Rate: 21%

SAT Reading/Writing (Middle 50%): 700-760
SAT Math (Middle 50%): 670-760
ACT Composite (Middle 50%): 31-34

% Graduated in Top 10% of HS Class: 73%
% Graduated in Top 25% of HS Class: 95%
% Graduated in Top 50% of HS Class: 99%

Demonstrated Interest: Not Considered
Legacy Status: Considered
Racial/Ethnic Status: Considered
Admission Interview Offered: Yes

ENROLLMENT
Total Undergraduate Enrollment: 2,523
% Full-Time: 100%
% Male: Not Applicable
% Female: 100%
% Out-of-State: 82%
% Fraternity: Not Applicable
% Sorority: Not Offered
% On-Campus (All Undergraduate): 96%
Freshman Housing Required: Yes

% African-American: 5%
% Asian: 10%
% Hispanic: 12%
% White: 51%
% Other: 2%
% International: 14%
% Low-Income: 18%

ACADEMICS
Student-to-Faculty Ratio: 8 to 1
% of Classes Under 20: 69%
% of Classes 20-49: 28%
% of Classes 50 or More: 3%
% Full-Time Faculty: 95%
% Full-Time Faculty w/ Terminal Degree: 99%

Top Programs
Biology
Education & Child Study
Economics
Engineering
Geology
Government
Psychology
Statistics

Retention Rate: 89%
4-Year Graduation Rate: 83%
6-Year Graduation Rate: 89%

Curricular Flexibility: Very Flexible
Academic Rating: ★★★★✔

#CollegesWorthYourMoney

You will not find a more wide-open curriculum or liberal/progressive ethos at any women's school in the country than that of Smith College, and only a few coeducational institutions—perhaps Vassar or Wesleyan—can go toe-to-toe with Smith on both fronts. Its list of alumnae supports that claim with Gloria Steinem, Julia Child, and Sylvia Plath all being Smith grads (Nancy Reagan was the ideological oddball). From a Seven Sisters admissions standpoint, Smith is more selective than Mt. Holyoke but less selective than Wellesley, Bryn Mawr, or Barnard. Since Smith is a member of the Five College Consortium, students can cross-enroll at Mt. Holyoke, UMass, Amherst, and Hampshire. In addition to the 50 academic departments and programs and 1,000 courses offered each academic year at Smith, an additional 4,000 courses can be accessed at partner universities.

Inside the Classroom

Smith's seven major fields of knowledge are literature, historical studies, social science, natural science, mathematics and analytical philosophy, the arts, and foreign language. Forays into each are "recommended," but the only nonnegotiable requirement is one writing-intensive course in the first or second semester of the freshman year. Otherwise, graduation requirements dictate that sixty-four credits must be taken outside of one's major. What that distribution looks like is entirely up to you. Young women seeking the ultimate level of undergraduate academic freedom will adore the Smith experience.

This college of 2,523 undergraduates boasts a student-to-faculty ratio of 8:1. With only a small number of graduate students to worry about, 19% of undergraduate sections have single-digit enrollments, and 69% of total class sections enroll fewer than 20 students. Each summer, 80 Smithies spend their time working side-by-side with a professor on a research project. Around 40% of undergrads spend a semester abroad in one of 100 programs on six continents, including some programs taught in the native tongue for those proficient in a foreign language.

The social sciences are most popular at Smith, accounting for 21% of the degrees conferred, with programs in economics and government carrying very strong reputations. Next in line are biology (6%), computer science (5%), English (5%), data science (5%), and engineering science (5%). Thanks to a strong decade-long push toward increasing the number of women studying such fields as engineering, mathematics, and the hard sciences, more than two-fifths of current students are majoring in a STEM field. Smith is also the Fulbright Scholarship capital of the world producing an awe-inspiring 300+ winners since 2002. Recent students also have captured Goldwater and Udall Scholarships as well as National Science Foundation Graduate Research Fellowships.

Outside the Classroom

Every single freshman, and 96% of the total undergraduate population, lives in college-owned housing. There are 37 self-governing houses, each with its own dining hall, that accommodate between ten and one hundred students; most have a mix of freshmen through seniors. No sororities operate at this school. Smith offers 14 varsity sports that compete in NCAA Division III as well as extensive intramural and club sports programs that include oddities like Quidditch and Futsal. The Outing Club is a popular way to enjoy the area's natural beauty through hikes, canoeing trips, and rock-climbing adventures. Approximately 140 student-run organizations are available with a wide selection of cultural groups, political and student government groups, and community service clubs. Each year, 200+ volunteers dedicate 10,000+ hours of community service through the Jandon Center for Community Engagement. Smith's membership in the Five College Consortium leads to additional social and extracurricular opportunities on the campuses of Mt. Holyoke, UMass, Amherst, and Hampshire. Culture and relaxation can be found on campus at the Smith College Museum of Art or the school's own botanical garden. The town of Northampton is two hours west of Boston and features plenty of restaurants and an artsy vibe that meshes well with this particular college community.

Career Services

The Lazarus Center for Career Development at Smith is staffed by 20 professionals, including career advisors and internship and employer relations specialists. The 126:1 student-to-advisor ratio is among the very best of the schools featured in this guidebook. For a small school, it puts on a fairly large Fall Career Fair that draws 80+ companies and graduate schools. It also organizes the Spring Life Sciences, Technology & Engineering Fair that attracts 30+ employers. In addition, Smith partners with MIT and UMass Amherst to offer access to additional off-site career fairs. Membership in the Selective Liberal Arts Consortium affords the women of Smith chances to participate in interview days with major corporations in Washington, DC, and New York City.

In a given year, 700 companies recruit on campus or virtually, an exceptional figure for a small liberal arts school. More than 107,000 job and internship opportunities are posted each year on Handshake. Praxis grants of up to $4,000 are awarded to roughly 400 undergraduates per year to pursue unpaid internships. Current students also benefit from the network of 53,000 alumnae spread across 120 countries who are known for being generous with their time and offers of mentorship. While the school's starting salary numbers leave something to be desired, the Lazarus Center for Career Development excels in employer relations and procurement of prestigious scholarships, and offers ample individualized attention for those who seek it.

Professional Outcomes

Within six months after graduating, 97% of Smith alumnae have found employment. More than 25 alumnae can be found at the US Department of State, Google, IBM, Johnson & Johnson, Accenture, Fidelity Investments, Deloitte, Microsoft, JPMorgan Chase, and Amazon. Many Smith women rise to high ranks within their respective organizations and corporations. Twenty years after graduation, 10% of alumnae report holding a chief executive position, and an additional 8% are stationed in other executive-level positions. Median career incomes are on the lower side compared to other elite schools and are comparable to those of Mt. Holyoke. Surprising given its locale, Boston is only the second-most popular destination for grads. New York City is number one with Springfield (Massachusetts), San Francisco, and DC also toward the top of the list. The average salary for Class of 2022 grads was $54,571.

Within two years of graduating, 40% of alumni have already entered a graduate program, and within ten years of receiving their bachelor's degrees, 70% of Smith grads have earned or are working toward an advanced degree. The five most frequently attended graduate schools are Columbia, NYU, Harvard, Duke, and Boston University. Medical and law school acceptance rates are strong. Smith undergrads were accepted into medical school at an 80% clip last year. The law school acceptance rate is 72%.

Admission

In seeking a place in the Class of 2026, over 7,200 hopefuls applied to Smith; 23% were accepted (seven points lower than the previous year), and 37% of that group ultimately enrolled. The college went test-optional a full decade ago, but 33% of the 2022-23 freshman class submitted SAT scores, and an additional 22% included ACT results as part of their applications. The mid-50% ranges on those exams were 1390-1500 on the SAT and 31-34 on the ACT. Seventy-three percent of freshmen earned a spot in the top 10% of their high school class, and 95% placed in the top 25%; the average weighted GPA was 4.0.

As stated by the committee, "Most applications are read by two members of the admission staff, and every part of your folder reveals another facet of your life." That holistic review places the greatest emphasis on five factors: rigor of coursework, GPA, recommendations, essays, and character/personal qualities. The second rung of important factors are class rank, an interview, extracurriculars, and talent/ability. Those applying through the early decision round received a boost to their admissions prospects to the tune of a 49% acceptance rate. While not at the selectivity level of Wellesley or Barnard, Smith College has become increasingly more difficult to gain acceptance into in recent years. A sparkling high school transcript is nonnegotiable, and showing commitment through submitting an early decision application is recommended for borderline applicants who have Smith as their clear first choice.

Worth Your Money?

With a cost of attendance of $83k, a Smith degree won't come cheap for those who do not qualify for institutional aid. The good news is that the majority of undergraduates do, indeed, qualify for need-based grants that average $58,000 annually. Smith students have superb graduate/professional school and employment outcomes, making this school a solid choice for anyone who can afford it.

FINANCIAL
Institutional Type: Private
In-State Tuition: $61,568
Out-of-State Tuition: $61,568
Room & Board: $21,310
Books & Supplies: $800

Avg. Need-Based Grant: $57,547
Avg. % of Need Met: 100%

Avg. Merit-Based Award: $19,366
% Receiving (Freshmen w/o Need): 8%

Avg. Cumulative Debt: $19,595
% of Students Borrowing: 55%

CAREER
Who Recruits
1. Amazon Robotics
2. The Beacon Group
3. Woodard & Curran
4. Audible
5. Collins Aerospace

Notable Internships
1. National Institutes of Health
2. Goldman Sachs
3. Roosevelt Park Zoo

Top Employers
1. Google
2. IBM
3. Johnson & Johnson
4. Accenture
5. JPMorgan Chase

Where Alumni Work
1. New York City
2. Boston
3. Springfield, MA
4. San Francisco
5. Washington, DC

Earnings
College Scorecard (10-YR Post-Entry): $58,881
PayScale (Early Career): $57,100
PayScale (Mid-Career): $104,900
PayScale 20-Year ROI: $339,000

RANKINGS
Money: 4
U.S. News: 16, Liberal Arts Colleges
Wall Street Journal/THE: 312
Washington Monthly: 14, Liberal Arts Colleges

OVERGENERALIZATIONS
Students are:
Politically liberal
Always studying
Tight-knit (possess a strong sense of community)
Less concerned with fashion or appearance
Driven

COLLEGE OVERLAPS
Barnard College
Bryn Mawr College
Mount Holyoke College
Scripps College
Wellesley College

Southern Methodist University

Dallas, Texas | 214-768-2058

Wealthy and moderately conservative—such is the reputation of Southern Methodist University in Dallas, Texas, a midsized private institution with a loyal alumni base and plenty of financial backing. Historically, a large percentage of the school's 7,056 undergraduates come from families earning incomes in the top 5% of all families in the United States. While "Methodist" is in its name, only 17% of students identify as affiliating with that denomination; more identify as Catholic. Academically, the Cox School of Business has one of the most respected faculties in the world, but that is by no means the only high-profile academic department; the public policy, sports management, performing arts, music, and film programs shine almost as brightly. In total, SMU offers 100+ majors and 85 minors.

Inside the Classroom
The university's curriculum was revised around a decade ago and now involves fulfilling foundational, depth, and breadth requirements. While that may sound extensive, the school offers great flexibility within those categories, and many courses within one's major will naturally fulfill some of the various mandates. Seven "proficiencies and experiences" can be met through a combination of coursework and noncredit activities that address each of human diversity, information literacy, oral communication, writing, community engagement, global engagement, and quantitative reasoning.

Thanks in part to an 11:1 student-to-faculty ratio, 56% of classes enroll fewer than 20 students, and 11% of classes enroll 50+ undergraduates. Opportunities for personal connection and guidance extend beyond the classroom as 1,000 current SMU students have participated in undergraduate research or apprenticeships. Grants for independent research through an Engaged Learning Fellowship or a Summer Research Assistantship—which pays students to work alongside faculty members for twenty-nine hours per week—also are available. An annual symposium and an undergraduate-only research journal provide outlets through which you can share those valuable experiences. The 150 study abroad programs in 50 countries attract more than one-quarter of Mustangs at some point during their four years of study.

This career-minded student body gravitates toward pre-professional degrees, particularly in business (27%) and engineering (6%). SMU's Cox School of Business is top-ranked and has especially strong ties to Wall Street. Programs in engineering, sports management, and the performing arts are also very well-regarded. Most fresh SMU grads are targeting high-paying jobs or entering the graduate/professional school of their choosing, but a small number each year aim for (and win) prestigious fellowships. Mustangs are awarded between two and five Fulbright Scholarships per year, two to four Gilman Scholarships, and an occasional Goldwater or Truman Scholarship.

Outside the Classroom
Almost every freshman resides in one of the university's 11 Residential Commons (which also house sophomores), and 52% of all undergraduates call the dorms home; upperclassmen occupy six separate communities. Greek life is a huge part of the social fabric at SMU with 25% of men joining fraternities and 31% of women affiliating with a sorority. Sports are also a major force as the Mustangs field seventeen teams that compete in the American Athletic Conference against Division I competition. Impressively, SMU has won 18 conference championships in the last five years. The football tradition at SMU is strong despite a series of recruiting scandals in the '80s that led to the team being banned for the 1987 season. Now, money flows into the program legally, including the $27 million that funded a new indoor practice facility that opened in 2019. New buildings are popping up everywhere you look across campus, whether it's the 50,000-square-foot Gerald J. Ford Hall for Research and Innovation or the Crain Family Centennial Promenade running through the heart of campus. The school routinely places near the top of "most beautiful campus" lists. Those not thrilled by Greeks and sports can still choose from over 200 campus organizations or venture into Dallas as the city's downtown area is only a few miles from the school.

Career Services
The Hegi Family Career Development Center has ten full-time employees. There are also four professional staff members operating out of the Cox School of Business who work with undergraduates as well as five staff members housed within the Lyle School of Engineering. The overall student-to-counselor ratio is 371:1, a solid number when compared to midsized universities profiled in this guide. Events that take place on campus, including career fairs, draw as many as one hundred employers and 575 students. The All Majors Career Fair held in the fall attracts 50+ employers including heavy hitters like American Airlines, Southwest, Hershey's, Mary Kay, and Home Depot.

Southern Methodist University

E-mail: ugadmission@smu.edu | Website: smu.edu

SMU's connected alumni base helps sustain strong school-to-employer bonds that lead to ample internship opportunities, particularly in the Dallas area. Business majors land internships at major investment firms and banks like Goldman Sachs, Citi, and JPMorgan Chase. A tremendous 90% of Lyle School of Engineering undergraduates complete at least one internship. Services offered by the Career Development Center include one-day externships, one-on-one career counseling that staff recommends "early and often," and the facilitation of on-campus interviews with recruiters from 160 companies, including some in the Fortune 500. Becoming a Mustang enables undergraduates of all socioeconomic backgrounds to connect to industry through networking, experiential learning opportunities, and impactful corporate relationships.

Professional Outcomes

At the moment they receive their diplomas, over two-thirds of recent grads already had their first jobs or graduate school destinations in hand. Six months after graduation, that figure rose into the mid-90s. The major corporations employing the greatest number of Mustangs are Lockheed Martin, AT&T, EY, IBM, JPMorgan Chase, Microsoft, Deloitte, American Airlines, Accenture, Oracle, Amazon, and Goldman Sachs. While close to half of SMU alums stay close to their alma mater in the Dallas-Fort Worth area, many relocate to New York City, Los Angeles, San Francisco, or DC for work. The average salary for graduates of the Cox School of Business was $77k in 2022. Across all colleges and majors, the average starting salary was approximately $55,000.

In a typical year, one-quarter of seniors elect to continue their education in pursuit of a graduate or professional degree. SMU itself is a popular choice, but graduates have no shortage of options, including at the nation's top universities. Of the 98 SMU grads applying to begin medical school in one recent year, a solid 58% gained acceptance, better than the national average that year of 44%. Recent acceptances included the Baylor College of Medicine, Perelman School of Medicine at the University of Pennsylvania, the University of Texas at Austin Dell Medical School, and Vanderbilt University School of Medicine. The roughly one hundred prelaw students enjoy an annual acceptance rate hovering between 70% and 85%. Each year, 40 students enter the Pre-Law Scholars Program, which puts them on track to attend SMU's Dedman School of Law upon graduation. Other grads in recent years have entered prestigious law schools such as those at Columbia, Cornell, Duke, Penn, Stanford, and Yale.

Admission

The 16,150 applications for the Class of 2026 were a slight increase from the previous two admissions cycles and a huge jump from the roughly 8,000 applications received in 2009. Fifty-two percent of Class of 2026 applicants were accepted, and 19% of those admitted chose to attend SMU. Standardized test scores have demonstrated a strong and consistent upward trend over the past decade; in 2008, the average SAT score was 1228 and the average ACT score was 27. Today, the median SAT score is 1440 and the average ACT score is 32. Slightly over half finished in the top decile of their high school class, and 82% were at least in the top quartile. The average GPA for incoming freshmen is 3.7, and more than half of that group possessed a 3.75 or higher.

There are four "very important" factors given top priority by the SMU admissions committee: GPA, rigor of coursework, recommendations, and application essays. That holistic and deep review also grants "important" status to class rank, standardized tests, extracurricular activities, talent/ability, and character/personal qualities. Demonstrated interest is a minor factor in the process as are first-generation and legacy status. Southern Methodist University offers an early decision option with a November 1 deadline that yields a small admissions edge; ED applicants get in at a 71% clip. SMU also offers a second ED option with a January 15 deadline.

Worth Your Money?

Along with schools like Columbia, USC, and the University of Chicago, Southern Methodist University is near the top of the list of schools with the highest sticker prices in the country. The estimated total cost of attendance for an SMU student in 2023-24 was $86,130. So, is a non-Ivy worth an Ivy price tag? Perhaps, especially after accounting for financial aid. The university meets 86% of demonstrated financial need and is generous with merit scholarships, giving an average of $28k to all first-years who qualify. In total, 72% of all undergrads receive some level of grant or scholarship. Many grads from the Cox School of Business and Lyle School of Engineering start their careers with salaries that will easily cover a reasonable student loan payment.

FINANCIAL
Institutional Type: Private
In-State Tuition: $64,460
Out-of-State Tuition: $64,460
Room & Board: $18,230
Books & Supplies: $800

Avg. Need-Based Grant: $40,975
Avg. % of Need Met: 86%

Avg. Merit-Based Award: $30,532
% Receiving (Freshmen w/o Need): 40%

Avg. Cumulative Debt: $38,298
% of Students Borrowing: 25%

CAREER
Who Recruits
1. Vira Insight
2. Epsilon
3. Dell
4. Frost Bank
5. Bank of America

Notable Internships
1. Dallas Mavericks
2. Cushman & Wakefield
3. Dell

Top Employers
1. Lockheed Martin
2. AT&T
3. EY
4. IBM
5. Accenture

Where Alumni Work
1. Dallas
2. Houston
3. Austin
4. Los Angeles
5. San Francisco

Earnings
College Scorecard (10-YR Post-Entry): $76,672
PayScale (Early Career): $64,700
PayScale (Mid-Career): $122,600
PayScale 20-Year ROI: $616,000

RANKINGS
Money: 3.5
U.S. News: 89, National Universities
Wall Street Journal/THE: 175
Washington Monthly: 353, National Universities

OVERGENERALIZATIONS
Students are:
Politically conservative
Wealthy
More likely to rush a fraternity/sorority
Career-driven
Dressed to impress

COLLEGE OVERLAPS
Baylor University
Texas A&M University - College Station
Texas Christian University
The University of Texas at Austin
Vanderbilt University

Spelman College

Atlanta, Georgia | 404-270-5193

Spelman College boasts an alumnae list that includes Alice Walker and Stacey Abrams along with a lengthy list of African American women who have risen to the tops of their respective fields as poets, judges, college presidents, actresses, and professors. Rated number one among the country's 107 historically black colleges and universities (HBCUs), Spelman's 2,400 young women enjoy a highly personalized education that is steeped in tradition and overflowing with opportunity. The school's central location in a bustling and vibrant section of Atlanta leads to a bevy of internship opportunities and no shortage of recreational and cultural possibilities.

Inside the Classroom
All students begin the Spelman journey with a yearlong First-Year Experience that includes "convocations, assemblies, an e-folio module, public speaking, instruction, (and) seminars" all designed to enhance students' "social, emotional, and cultural skills development." With average second-year retention rates above 90%, this introductory program appears especially effective. In typical liberal arts fashion, core requirements in English, math, and foreign language must be met along with two semesters of African Diaspora and the World. Additional divisional requirements in the humanities, fine arts, social sciences, and natural sciences ensure that every student takes at least one course within each broad discipline.

With a student-to-faculty ratio of 10:1, you won't encounter more than a handful of large lecture halls at Spelman. Twenty-nine percent of courses have a single-digit enrollment, 66% have 19 students or fewer, and 94% of sections max out at 29 students. The school routinely ranks high in the quality of its undergraduate teaching, and faculty are viewed as being accessible. The Course-Based Undergraduate Research Experiences (CURE) program ensures that quality research apprenticeships are available to all who seek them. Spelman is in the top 30 undergraduate colleges in terms of sending the highest numbers of students abroad with 77% of recent grads having studied in a foreign destination.

The social sciences lead the way in terms of the volume of degrees conferred, representing 24% of the Class of 2022. Biology also attracts a high number of undergrads (16%) along with psychology (14%), health professions and related studies (9%), and English (7%). Not uncommon for liberal arts schools, no one program stands out above the rest, but the Spelman name is universally respected by both employers and graduate schools. Opportunities to pursue prestigious national fellowships definitely exist, and within the last seven years, multiple students have procured Goldwater, Truman, and Fulbright scholarships.

Outside the Classroom
A 39-acre campus sits in the heart of Atlanta and houses 58% of the undergraduate population. There are four National Pan-Hellenic Council sororities that are heavily focused on academic achievement and service. In addition to Greek living and dorm housing, the college offers a handful of Living Learning Communities centered around faith, social justice, service work, and intellectual leadership. Intercollegiate athletics were scrapped in 2012 in favor of a broad intramural program to help address widespread health issues faced by a large percentage of African American women. The school then constructed an 18-million-dollar, 53,000-square-foot wellness center that offers group training, aquatics, meditation, tennis and basketball courts, and an indoor track. Eighty-five student-run clubs and organizations include cultural, service, spiritual, professional, and recreational options. Additional social opportunities are available through the college's membership in the Atlanta University Center Consortium with neighboring HBCUs Clark Atlanta University and Morehouse College. The Spelman campus could not be situated more closely to the variety of activities Atlanta offers, from the State Farm Arena to the MLK National Historical Site to the Georgia Aquarium to countless theaters, restaurants, and shops.

Career Services
The Office of Career Planning and Development is staffed by four professional employees, two of whom work as career and graduate school counselors. A 593:1 student-to-counselor ratio falls within the average range of schools featured in Colleges Worth Your Money. Some recruiting events are only for Spelman students while others are hosted by all three Atlanta University Consortium schools and also are open to Morehouse and Clark-Atlanta students. Spelman hosts eight career and graduate school fairs each year. Recent events have been attended by Amazon, Lockheed Martin, Medtronic, the National Institutes of Health, and Verizon.

The 21,000+ alumnae are available as resources and mentors for current undergraduates through formal programs like the Sister 2 Sister Professional Mentoring Program, which has matched 950 alumna-student pairs since its inception. The Sister Soul Circle links alumnae and students with a focus on "self-care: mind, body, and spirit." The Office of Career Planning and Development also hosts its own formalized programs such as Freshman Reaching Excellence with Spelman's Help (FRESH), an event that introduces first-years to resume development, student intern panels, alumni panels, and the scope of career services the school offers. Spelman Women Empowered Through Professional Training (SWEPT) provides sophomores, juniors, and seniors with workshops in professionalism, teamwork, leadership, critical thinking, and global fluency. Perhaps the most impressive stat about Spelman's career services office is that over 90% of recent grads reported participating in at least one internship during their undergraduate experience.

Professional Outcomes

At the time of receiving their diploma, recent grads had full-time employment lined up 24-32% of the time and matriculated into graduate school at a 22-34% clip. Many of the employers with the largest number of Spelman alumnae are local, including the CDC, Atlanta Public Schools, Fulton County Schools, and Delta Air Lines. Other corporations with a high number of Jaguar employees include Accenture, IBM, Wells Fargo, JPMorgan Chase, Amazon, and Microsoft. The most common postgraduate destination is remaining in the Greater Atlanta Area, but large pockets of Spelman grads are also found in Washington, DC; New York City; Los Angeles; Chicago; and San Francisco.

Spelman does not offer any graduate degrees, but it frequently sends alumnae to the world's most prestigious graduate and professional programs. Many political science majors have gone on to the likes of Harvard Law School and Yale Law School. Law schools including Duke, UGA, and NYU all recruit on the Spelman campus. Spelman also partners with a number of top medical schools through the Medical School Early Assurance Program, which includes the Boston University School of Medicine, the University of Pennsylvania Perelman School of Medicine, and Vanderbilt University School of Medicine. Eighty-two Jags applied to medical school in the 2022-23 school year.

Admission

Thanks to a self-selecting applicant pool of highly qualified young women, Spelman's acceptance rate was a deceptively high 51% for the Class of 2025. However, the Class of 2026 saw just a 28% acceptance rate. But make no mistake: Spelman is a selective institution where the average enrolled freshman possesses a GPA of 3.89, and 35% finish in the top 10% of their high school class with 69% in the top quartile. The greatest number of applicants submitted SAT results, and the middle-50% score of enrolled 2022-23 freshmen was 1100-1290; the ACT range was 22-27.

Six factors rate as "very important" to the admissions committee at Spelman: rigor of course load, GPA, application essay, and character/personal qualities. Class rank, extracurricular activities, recommendations, and volunteer work are viewed as "important" and "considered factors are: talent/ability, test scores, legacy status, geographical residence, work experience, and the level of an applicant's demonstrated interest." Interestingly, of the 200 early decision applicants to the Class of 2026, only 29% were accepted. The yield rate (students admitted divided by students enrolled) was only 15%, meaning that Spelman is not the first choice for the majority who apply.

Worth Your Money?

Spelman keeps its list price cost of attendance at $46k, on the very low side for a small, private college. While 85% of current undergrads receive some level of financial aid, the school meets only 24% of the average enrolled student's demonstrated need. As a result, 92% of students borrow money to pay for college, one of the highest figures for any school in the country. As a result, average cumulative debt is a bit higher than the national mean. Spelman is an amazing place for those who can afford it, but depending on your academic/career track, it might not be worth borrowing an excessive amount to attend.

FINANCIAL
Institutional Type: Private
In-State Tuition: $25,880
Out-of-State Tuition: $25,880
Room & Board: $15,666
Books & Supplies: $1,500

Avg. Need-Based Grant: $15,592
Avg. % of Need Met: 24%

Avg. Merit-Based Award: $22,665
% Receiving (Freshmen w/o Need): 2%

Avg. Cumulative Debt: $32,004
% of Students Borrowing: 67%

CAREER
Who Recruits
1. Bank of America
2. Google
3. Accenture
4. The Coca-Cola Company
5. U.S. Department of State

Notable Internships
1. Estee Lauder Companies
2. National Park Services
3. Toyota

Top Employers
1. Atlanta Public Schools
2. CDC
3. Accenure
4. Delta Air Lines
5. Emory University

Where Alumni Work
1. Atlanta
2. Washington, DC
3. New York City
4. Los Angeles
5. Chicago

Earnings
College Scorecard (10-YR Post-Entry): $57,578
PayScale (Early Career): $65,400
PayScale (Mid-Career): $98,400
PayScale 20-Year ROI: $217,000

RANKINGS
Money: 3.5
U.S. News: 39, Liberal Arts Colleges
Wall Street Journal/THE: 179
Washington Monthly: 89, Liberal Arts Colleges

OVERGENERALIZATIONS
Students are:
Politically liberal
Competitive
Driven
Confident
Service-oriented

COLLEGE OVERLAPS
Clark Atlanta University
Georgia State University
Howard University
North Carolina A&T University
Xavier University of Lousiana

St. Lawrence University

Canton, New York | 315-229-5261

Want a trivia question that is sure to stump all of your dinner party guests? Ask them to name the oldest continuously coeducational university in the United States. The answer—St. Lawrence—is sure to surprise as its small size and Upstate New York location make it among the lesser-known liberal arts gems in the Northeast. Situated closer to Montreal than it is to Buffalo, one could argue that this 167-year-old school is harder to get to than get into. While good high school grades are a must, a holistic and test-optional admissions process makes this school accessible to those with a blemish or two on their academic records.

Inside the Classroom
For a school of just 2,145 undergraduates, the size of the campus (1,000 acres) and the scope of the offerings—74 majors and 41 minors—are quite vast. Since long before freshman-exclusive courses/experiences became a fad in the higher education world, St. Lawrence has offered its first-year program, a living and learning program that lets students in the same residence hall develop the "writing, speaking, and research skills that they will need during and after college." Students are also required to take one course in the arts, humanities, social sciences, natural science with lab, quantitative literacy, and environmental literacy. Two courses that cover the category of human diversity: culture and communication are mandated, and while foreign language courses can count here, there is no formal language requirement at this university.

Close faculty relationships are a true possibility at a school with an 11:1 student-to-faculty ratio and 68% of course sections enrolling fewer than 20 students. Only 1% of sections enroll more than 40 students. The average class size is just 16 students. An exceptional 82% of students participate in an undergraduate research experience. Study abroad programs were taken advantage of by 60% of students.

The most popular area of study is the social sciences (23%), with majors in economics, political science, and psychology drawing particularly high praise. Business (13%) and biology (9%) are also very strong. As a whole, the quality of undergraduate teaching at SLU gets high marks across the board. However, very few graduates aim for prestigious national scholarships; roughly 60 have won Fulbright Scholarships in the school's history.

Outside the Classroom
You won't find a more cohesive campus environment than that of St. Lawrence, where 99% of the undergraduate student body resides on the 1,000-acre grounds. There are 16 residence halls and six Greek chapters; fraternities draw in 18% of the male population, and sororities attract 16% of women. A plethora of sports options at various levels leads to a 31% participation rate in the 34 varsity and 25+ club and intramural teams. The Saints primarily compete against NCAA Division III competition, but the men's and women's ice hockey teams are at the Division I level. There are more than 150 student-run organizations, and 82% of undergrads participate in volunteer work. It's not unusual for the school to host speakers, bands, comedians, or free movie nights. Students rave about the wide-open, beautiful campus with unending greenspace and the excellent food that includes lots of local ingredients and ample vegetarian options. Canton is a town of roughly 7,000 people and is not located near any major American cities, but the Canadian border is just a half hour away, and Montreal and Ottawa make for popular road trips.

Career Services
With eight professional employees who work in advising and employer engagement capacities, the Center for Career Excellence is able to meet the needs of this college with a 268:1 counselor-to-student ratio. There are an additional five upperclassmen who serve as career services interns. Personalized service and one-on-one connections are encouraged, as is participation in SLU's Signature Career Programs that include Shadow-A-Saint, LINC Mentor Program, Career Success Workshops for Sophomores, and Laurentians in Residence, a program that brings alumni and parent leaders to campus for presentations and mentoring arrangements.

Over the course of your four years at the university, you will have the option to participate in SLU Connect, a program that connects students to alumni in high-powered professions in Boston; San Francisco; Albany, New York; Burlington, Vermont; and even Big Sky, Montana. The office also provides access to micro-internships, paid 5-40-hour professional assignments that allow students to dip their toes into a corporate setting. As a result of this variety of offerings, 70% of graduates complete at least one internship, and 99% engage in some type of experiential learning. Three-fifths of all freshmen report visiting the Career Services office at least once; 75% visit as sophomores. Clearly, SLU does a commendable job providing counseling as well as accessible opportunities for hands-on experiences to their undergraduates.

Professional Outcomes

A solid 95% of the Class of 2022 found their way to the world of employment or a graduate/professional program within 7-10 months of leaving the university. The most common sector was business (27%), followed by health services (17%), K-12 education (15%), and finance (14%). More than 20 alumni can be found in the offices of Morgan Stanley, Fidelity Investments, UBS, Wells Fargo, JPMorgan Chase, Goldman Sachs, and Northwestern Mutual. The most common locations for Saints to relocate to postgraduation are New York City; Boston; Utica, NY; Burlington, Vermont; and Washington, DC.

Seventeen percent of recent grads immediately entered graduate school. St. Lawrence alumni who pursue an advanced degree typically remain in the Northeast, often in the state of New York. The most commonly attended graduate schools are (in order) St Lawrence itself, Syracuse University, the University of Vermont, Boston University, and Northeastern University, along with four different SUNY campuses. Within five years of receiving their bachelor's degrees, 39% of graduates report engaging in further formal study. Twenty-five students who graduated in one recent five-year span went on to enter medical school, and 41 graduates were pursuing their law degrees in that same time frame.

Admission

St. Lawrence accepted 63% of the 5,172 applicants for the Class of 2026. A decade ago, there were only approximately 4,300 applicants and a very similar acceptance rate. An early adopter of a test-optional policy (2006), the school sees only 19% of admitted applicants submit SAT results, and 5% include an ACT score with their application. The mid-50th percentile is 1270-1380 on the SAT and 29-32 on the ACT. Thirty-one percent of 2022-23 freshmen placed in the top 10% of their high school class, and 70% landed in the top quartile. Slightly over 30% earned a 4.0 GPA or better, and more than two-thirds held at least a 3.5.

When St. Lawrence assures applicants that its admissions review process is "holistic and each application is carefully reviewed," it is more than just lip service. Rigor of high school coursework, GPA, essays, recommendations, and character/personal qualities are rated as "highly important," and class rank, the interview, and extracurricular involvement are "important." Being a test-optional institution, St. Lawrence will consider SAT/ACT results along with factors like talent/ability, first-generation status, alumni relation, geographical residence, volunteer and paid work experience, and demonstrated interest. The last factor is notable because only 20% of those accepted to the university actually go on to enroll. Those who show their devotion through a binding early decision process are accepted at a very friendly 73% clip.

Worth Your Money?

With a healthy endowment of $350 million, St. Lawrence is able to award some level of financial help to 99% of its undergraduates. The average grant to freshmen is $47,000, which helps to bring the $80,350 annual cost of attendance down to a range that is competitive with many public institutions. While this liberal arts school doesn't churn out massive numbers of engineers and finance majors who typically help a school reach a high median starting salary, a St. Lawrence education, with aid, is a unique and personalized enough experience to be worth the cost for most students.

FINANCIAL
Institutional Type: Private
In-State Tuition: $63,870
Out-of-State Tuition: $63,870
Room & Board: $16,480
Books & Supplies: $750

Avg. Need-Based Grant: $45,157
Avg. % of Need Met: 91%

Avg. Merit-Based Award: $27,466
% Receiving (Freshmen w/o Need): 24%

Avg. Cumulative Debt: $35,064
% of Students Borrowing: 62%

CAREER
Who Recruits
1. Wayfair
2. UBS
3. Northwestern Mutual
4. Brown Brothers Harriman
5. Morgan Stanley

Notable Internships
1. Center for American Progress
2. EarthWatch Institute
3. Morgan Stanley

Top Employers
1. Morgan Stanley
2. Fidelity Investments
3. Clarkson University
4. UBS
5. Wells Fargo

Where Alumni Work
1. New York City
2. Boston
3. Burlington, VT
4. Washington, DC
5. Albany, NY

Earnings
College Scorecard (10-YR Post-Entry): $68,520
PayScale (Early Career): $60,100
PayScale (Mid-Career): $113,500
PayScale 20-Year ROI: $468,000

RANKINGS
Money: 4.5
U.S. News: 59, Liberal Arts Colleges
Wall Street Journal/THE: Not Ranked
Washington Monthly: 99, Liberal Arts Colleges

OVERGENERALIZATIONS
Students are:
Outdoorsy
Environmentally conscious
Tight-knit (possess a strong sense of community)
Preppy
Involved/investsed in campus life

COLLEGE OVERLAPS
Colby College
Hamilton College
Hobart and William Smith Colleges
Union College (NY)
University of Vermont

St. Mary's College of Maryland

St. Mary's City, Maryland | 240-895-5000

In 1840, the state of Maryland approved a lottery to finance the construction of a boarding school for young women in St. Mary's City on the western shore of Chesapeake Bay. Fast-forward to 1967, and St. Mary's College of Maryland (SMCM) became a four-year baccalaureate college; in 1992 it was designated as the state's "public honors college," a title that, even today, applies to just two schools in the United States. One of the few public liberal arts colleges in the country, St. Mary's College of Maryland is now home to 1,513 undergraduate students who enjoy one of the most unique higher education bargains available.

Inside the Classroom
Offering 25 majors and 31 minors, SMCM requires a fairly standard core curriculum that begins with a First-Year Seminar designed to sharpen skills in critical thinking, information literacy, and written and oral expression. Students also must become proficient in an international language and take one course in the following six areas: the arts, cultural perspectives, humanistic foundations, mathematics, natural sciences with laboratory, and the social sciences.

A 10:1 student-to-faculty ratio is almost beyond comprehension for a public school—the average ratio nationally for all colleges (including private ones) is 18:1. As a result, 96% of course sections enroll fewer than 29 students, and 72% of classes enroll fewer than 20. Undergrads can access research opportunities through multiple avenues that include St. Mary's Projects (senior year projects that 60% of students complete), St. Mary's Undergraduate Research Fellowships (eight-week summer programs), and Research Experience for Undergraduates (paid research experiences supported by the National Science Foundation). One of the 29 study abroad programs is taken advantage of by almost half of the undergraduate population.

The college is known for its strong STEM programs; roughly 30% of all degrees conferred are in a STEM field. The social sciences accounted for 23% of the degrees earned in 2022 followed by psychology (17%), biology (13%), natural resources and conservation (8%), and the visual and performing arts (7%). While graduate schools and employers recognize the quality of Seahawk alumni, the school does not see an overwhelming number of students win nationally competitive fellowships, but it does produce an occasional Fulbright winner.

Outside the Classroom
The college's spacious 361-acre waterfront campus is conveniently located 70 miles from Washington, DC, and 95 miles from Baltimore. The majority hail from in state, but that hardly makes SMCM a commuter school. Rather, 95% of freshmen and 82% of total undergrads live on campus. There are no fraternities or sororities, but with 100+ student organizations, there are plenty of opportunities for bonding over shared experiences. The Seahawks field 19 NCAA Division III teams, which translates to an absurdly high percentage of the student body putting on at least one uniform. Competitive sailing is a particular point of pride, and the school excels in both varsity sailing and offshore sailing. Being situated on the Chesapeake Bay also leads to popular sailing and windsurfing clubs. Overall, there are 13 club sports teams, a literary magazine, preprofessional organizations for future doctors and lawyers, a cappella, and a full range of multicultural groups. It also is worth noting that the school has almost a 60/40 breakdown in favor of female students.

Career Services
The Career Development Center has seven professional employees including a director, assistant director, career advisors, and an internship coordinator. This 216:1 staff-to-student ratio is strong when compared to other public institutions featured in this book. Due to this level of support, the school can "guarantee every student the opportunity to engage in a research, internship, or international experience." Larger-scale events are tougher to orchestrate at such a small college, but each semester it does host a Career Fair that attracts 30+ employers to campus.

Recent students have landed sought-after internships with organizations such as The Washington Post, the Baltimore Orioles, CNN, the Philadelphia Museum of Art, Johns Hopkins University Hospital, Bank of America, and just about every branch/department of the US government. The CDC also helps facilitate "micro-internships" that are paid 5- to 40-hour placements. Single-day job shadowing opportunities also are available at locations including NASA, Nestle, and the National Gallery of Art. Connections with the school's 14,000 active alumni members are made through a series of formal networking events that help students make the leap from "bookbag to briefcase." St. Mary's also offers one-credit professional development courses that focus on building skills in resume writing, being interviewed, and job application strategies.

Professional Outcomes

Within six months of earning their bachelor's degrees, 96% of St. Mary's grads have landed a job or started an advanced degree. Healthcare, wellness, publishing, government, and media are the most popular industries. Top employers of Osprey alumni include JPMorgan Chase & Co., the Centers for Disease Control, BNY Mellon, Booz Allen Hamilton, the Smithsonian, and the US Department of Defense. Those entering the education sector frequently find jobs with Baltimore County Public Schools and Howard County Public Schools. You'll find the greatest concentration of SMCM grads in Washington, DC; Baltimore; New York City; Philadelphia; and Boston.

Over one-quarter of alumni begin work on their next degree within six months of graduation. Recent seniors have earned acceptances from the likes of Harvard, Yale, Rice, Penn, the University of Chicago, Vanderbilt, Cornell, and the University of Cambridge. In a typical year, 88-96% of those who apply to medical/dental/veterinary school gain at least one acceptance. Some of the most recent MD acceptances include the University of Maryland, Georgetown, Johns Hopkins, and the University of Pennsylvania. The school also provides prelaw advising to students from any academic background who aim to pursue a legal education. Recent grads have found law school homes at the University of Virginia; the University of California, Berkeley; and Columbia University.

Admission

For such a terrific college, admission into St. Mary's is within reach for a B student. From 2,934 applicants, 2,268 were offered a place in the Class of 2026. That 77% acceptance rate is identical to the clip enjoyed by the Class of 2025. Just 21% of the 410 individuals who ultimately enrolled placed in the top 10% of their high school graduating class; 47% were in the top quartile, and 83% earned a spot in the top half. The average GPA of freshmen in the 2022-23 cohort was 3.5. On the standardized testing front, the mid-50% scores were 1130-1350 on the SAT and 28-30 on the ACT.

Taking a holistic approach in evaluating each applicant, SMCM places premium value on the rigor of coursework, GPA, application essay, and recommendations. "Important" factors are class rank, extracurricular activities, talent/ability, character/personal qualities, and volunteer work. The board of trustees approved transitioning to a test-optional policy shortly before the onset of the pandemic. Last cycle, 33% of applicants submitted an SAT score, 4% submitted an ACT, and an unknown number submitted results from both exams. The school does offer an early decision plan, but few take advantage; only 39 students applied ED last cycle. Unless you are an extremely borderline applicant, there is no need to use your ED card at SMCM.

Worth Your Money?

St. Mary's lives up to its stated ideals of "affordability, accessibility, and diversity." As a National Public Honors College, Maryland residents are given a reasonable tuition break, paying just over $15k with a $31k full cost of attendance. Washington, DC, residents receive a less sizable discount, paying a COA of $41k; all other out-of-staters pay a list price COA of $47k. Almost 90% of undergrads qualify for some level of financial aid, and postgraduate cumulative debt averages are below those of the average American college. For Maryland residents, SMCM represents a unique pathway to a liberal arts education at a reasonable cost. With a bit of financial aid, this college can be a worthwhile investment for out-of-staters as well.

FINANCIAL
Institutional Type: Public
In-State Tuition: $15,236
Out-of-State Tuition: $31,312
Room & Board: $15,764
Books & Supplies: $900

Avg. Need-Based Grant: $9,913
Avg. % of Need Met: 87%

Avg. Merit-Based Award: $4,742
% Receiving (Freshmen w/o Need): 40%

Avg. Cumulative Debt: $27,106
% of Students Borrowing: 59%

CAREER
Who Recruits
1. Booz Allen Hamilton
2. Northrop Grumman
3. AstraZeneca
4. Smithsonian Institution
5. U.S. Department of Defense

Notable Internships
1. Baltimore Orioles
2. CNN
3. Bank of America

Top Employers
1. Naval Air Systems Communication
2. Booz Allen Hamilton
3. University of Maryland
4. St. Mary's County Public Schools
5. John Hopkins University

Where Alumni Work
1. Washington, DC
2. Baltimore
3. New York City
4. Philadelphia
5. Boston

Earnings
College Scorecard (10-YR Post-Entry): $60,455
PayScale (Early Career): $56,900
PayScale (Mid-Career): $104,900
PayScale 20-Year ROI: $377,000

RANKINGS
Money: 4
U.S. News: 82, Liberal Arts Colleges
Wall Street Journal/THE: Not Ranked
Washington Monthly: 83, Liberal Arts Colleges

OVERGENERALIZATIONS
Students are:
Environmentally conscious
Politically liberal
Outdoorsy
Only a short drive from home (i.e., Most come from MD or nearby states)
Less likely to party

COLLEGE OVERLAPS
Beloit College
Dickinson College
Gettysburg College
The College of Wooster
University of North Carolina at Asheville

St. Olaf College

ADMISSION

Admission Rate: 56%
Admission Rate - Men: 52%
Admission Rate - Women: 60%
EA Admission Rate: 73%
ED Admission Rate: 72%
ED Admits as % of Total Admits: 8%
Admission Rate (5-Year Trend): +13%
% of Admits Attending (Yield): 28%
Transfer Admission Rate: 25%

SAT Reading/Writing (Middle 50%): 660-730
SAT Math (Middle 50%): 640-750
ACT Composite (Middle 50%): 28-33

% Graduated in Top 10% of HS Class: 39%
% Graduated in Top 25% of HS Class: 69%
% Graduated in Top 50% of HS Class: 94%

Demonstrated Interest: Important
Legacy Status: Considered
Racial/Ethnic Status: Considered
Admission Interview Offered: Yes

ENROLLMENT

Total Undergraduate Enrollment: 3,046
% Full-Time: 100%
% Male: 42%
% Female: 58%
% Out-of-State: 50%
% Fraternity: Not Offered
% Sorority: Not Offered
% On-Campus (All Undergraduate): 93%
Freshman Housing Required: Yes

% African-American: 3%
% Asian: 6%
% Hispanic: 8%
% White: 67%
% Other: 1%
% International: 11%
% Low-Income: 21%

ACADEMICS

Student-to-Faculty Ratio: 12 to 1
% of Classes Under 20: 62%
% of Classes 20-49: 36%
% of Classes 50 or More: 2%
% Full-Time Faculty: 70%
% Full-Time Faculty w/ Terminal Degree: 95%

Top Programs
Area Studies
Biology
Chemistry
Economics
Exercise Science
Mathematics
Religion
Social Work and Family Studies

Retention Rate: 91%
4-Year Graduation Rate: 82%
6-Year Graduation Rate: 85%

Curricular Flexibility: Less Flexible
Academic Rating: ★★★★

#CollegesWorthYourMoney

Easier to gain acceptance into than neighbor/rival Carleton, St. Olaf College is a strong liberal arts school in Northfield, Minnesota, that is home to 3,046 undergraduates. Just as in 1889 when the college first opened its frost-covered doors, St. Olaf retains a strong affiliation with the Lutheran Church. Running on a 4-1-4 schedule, students take four courses during fourteen-week semesters and one course during the one month in between. Students are nicknamed Oles (pronounced OH-Leez), and they enjoy a robust academic program of 45+ major options.

Inside the Classroom

General education requirements are extensive, even by the standards of a traditional liberal arts school. This intensive regimen of coursework includes Foundation Studies, which is comprised of a first-year writing seminar, mastery of a foreign language, courses in oral communication and writing in context as well as abstract and quantitative reasoning and studies in physical movement. Freshman courses in biblical studies and theology are also mandated as well as a litany of courses across the humanities, natural sciences, and social sciences.

With a 12:1 student-to-faculty ratio and no graduate students, there is ample room for mentor-mentee relationships to flourish. Over half of all course sections contain fewer than twenty students. Graduation surveys reveal students who are immensely satisfied with the St. Olaf academic experience; 94% agreed that the faculty made them better critical thinkers. There are multiple avenues through which students can pursue research experiences. On-campus options include applying for ten-week summer stints through the Collaborative Undergraduate Research & Inquiry program, a Steen Fellowship to encourage independent research, or an independent study conducted for credit. Studying abroad is a staple of life for Oles; three-quarters spend a semester studying off campus, the vast majority at an international locale.

The most commonly conferred degrees are in the social sciences (18%), the visual and performing arts (11%), biology (11%), psychology (8%), and foreign languages (7%). Many departments at St. Olaf have exceptional national reputations including religion, mathematics, and chemistry. The most coveted fellowship and scholarship organizations definitely pay special attention to graduates of this institution. In fact, the college has produced an astounding five Rhodes Scholars since 1995 and Fulbright Scholarships were awarded to eight members of the last two graduating classes.

Outside the Classroom

With 93% of students living on campus or in college-owned housing nearby, the student body functions as a fairly cohesive unit. Students remain on campus for a variety of sound reasons. For one, dining hall cuisine is regularly rated among the country's best, and for another, no Greek life exists at St. Olaf. So-called "Honor Houses" are the closest thing to frats or sororities, but they are residences based on common academic areas of study or special interests. There are twenty-one such houses at the college, including ones focused on common bonds such as Norwegian languages, Muslim identity, or the environment. The Oles field 26 athletic teams (13 men's, 13 women's) that compete in NCAA Division III. A hefty portion of the student body—500 undergraduates—are members of a varsity sports squad. There are more than 250 clubs active at the school. Those who enjoy the outdoor life will adore the 325 adjoining acres of woodlands, wetlands, and prairie that students can freely roam. The school's location near Carleton College opens additional chances for socialization as does the fact that Minneapolis and St. Paul are both less than fifty miles away.

Career Services

The Piper Center for Vocation and Career is staffed by 13 professional employees serving roles in counseling, alumni engagement, and employer relations. Additionally, the college trains 25+ peer advisors to add an extra layer of student support. Counting only professional employees, St. Olaf sports a student-to-advisor ratio of 243:1, lower than the average school included in this book. Thanks to those favorable numbers, 73% of undergraduates meet with either a career coach or peer advisor in the most recent academic year. Among 2022 graduates, 92% reported they were adequately prepared for life beyond college.

On-campus events include an annual Recruiting Showcase featuring some of the top corporate employers of Oles and a Government and Nonprofit Career Fair open to all Minnesota college students. The college also participates in the statewide Private College and Career Fair that features 260+ employers. Opportunities for experiential learning are wide-ranging and taken advantage of by most students as 87% of recent grads completed at least one internship, job-shadowing, or field experience over the course of their four years on campus. A tight-knit and helpful alumni base regularly avails itself to assist current undergrads. Alumni events like Ole Biz, which brings over a hundred graduates to Minneapolis, invite current students to learn about ten industries while networking their hearts out. The Piper Center excels in setting students up with meaningful experiences and important alumni connections, and it has a direct line to many of the region's largest corporate employers.

Professional Outcomes

In 2022, only 2% of grads were still seeking their next step six months after graduation; the rest had entered the workforce or graduate school. The great majority of alumni remain in the Greater Minneapolis-St. Paul area (more than ten times as many as relocate to second-choice destination Chicago), which impacts what companies hire the most Oles. To name names, alumni have the largest representation at Target, UnitedHealth Group, the Mayo Clinic, Wells Fargo, Medtronic, 3M, and US Bank. Mid-career median salaries fall in the same range as other Minnesota academic powerhouses Carleton and Macalester.

While many pursuing higher education choose to stay in the Midwest, the college sends at least one graduate to the likes of Columbia, Yale, or Cornell to pursue an advanced degree every year. St. Olaf students in a premed area of concentration who have a GPA of 3.7 or better and a 510+ MCAT score gain acceptance to medical school at a solid 84% clip. The most commonly attended medical school is the University of Minnesota-Twin Cities, but recent grads have gone on to study at the University of Michigan Medical School, Washington University in St. Louis School of Medicine, and Wake Forest Medical School. Law school applicants have gone on to elite universities including Harvard, Emory, Georgetown, and UCLA. The school is also a top producer of future PhDs, placing in the top 50 among all colleges in the percentage of graduates who go on to earn doctoral degrees in their respective fields (when adjusted for enrollment size).

Admission

Fifty-six percent of those who applied for a position in St. Olaf's Class of 2026 were granted acceptance. One decade ago, the acceptance rate was 59% of an applicant pool that was only one-third the size of last year's pool. Attending freshmen in the 2022-23 school year possessed a middle-50% SAT range of 1300-1460 and a wide-ranging ACT composite of 28-33. The ACT was, by far, the test of choice; it was submitted by 37% of applicants. Fifty-seven percent of freshmen boasted GPAs of over 3.75, and the average is 3.72. Thirty-nine percent fell within the top decile of their graduating class, and 69% placed in the top quarter.

Rigorous coursework, GPA, and the application essay are of paramount importance to the admissions committee followed by a second tier of factors including class rank, recommendations, an interview, extracurricular activities, talent/ability, and character/personal qualities. The school went test-optional back in 2020. Showing a commitment to this college is typically rewarded on the admissions end and early decision applicants were accepted at 72% last cycle. Overall, St. Olaf has a yield rate of 28%, which means that just over one-quarter of accepted students actually go on to enroll. Earning admission into St. Olaf is more than a simple numbers game; a holistic approach by the committee rewards "smart, ambitious, creative people who want to be challenged." Even if you lack perfect grades or ACT scores, a candidate can still make a compelling case for acceptance into this fine Midwestern liberal arts institution.

Worth Your Money?

Total cost of attendance at St. Olaf will run you just over $72,000 per year, yet few pay that amount. Two-thirds of Oles receive some form of financial aid, and the overall value of each need-based award is $47k, ultimately making this school affordable for those with financial need. Considering the high rate of internship participation, close contact with major companies, and accessible faculty, St. Olaf is likely worth your money.

FINANCIAL
Institutional Type: Private
In-State Tuition: $56,970
Out-of-State Tuition: $56,970
Room & Board: $13,000
Books & Supplies: $1,000

Avg. Need-Based Grant: $46,941
Avg. % of Need Met: 100%

Avg. Merit-Based Award: $24,037
% Receiving (Freshmen w/o Need): 24%

Avg. Cumulative Debt: $27,181
% of Students Borrowing: 58%

CAREER
Who Recruits
1. Lewin Group
2. Cerner Corporation
3. Thomson Reuters
4. North Sky Capital
5. MatrixCare

Notable Internships
1. Game Informer Magazine
2. MITRE
3. 9/11 Tribute Museum

Top Employers
1. UnitedHealth Group
2. Target
3. Mayo Clinic
4. Wells Fargo
5. U.S. Bank

Where Alumni Work
1. Minneapolis
2. Chicago
3. New York City
4. San Francisco
5. Denver

Earnings
College Scorecard (10-YR Post-Entry): $66,260
PayScale (Early Career): $58,300
PayScale (Mid-Career): $112,100
PayScale 20-Year ROI: $376,000

RANKINGS
Money: 4.5
U.S. News: 51, Liberal Arts Colleges
Wall Street Journal/THE: Not Ranked
Washington Monthly: 29, Liberal Arts Colleges

OVERGENERALIZATIONS
Students are:
Always studying
Supportive
Politically balanced
Only a short drive from home (i.e., Most come from MN or nearby states)
Less likely to party

COLLEGE OVERLAPS
Carleton College
Gustavus Adolphus College
Lawrence University
Macalester College
University of Minnesota - Twin Cities

Stanford University

Stanford, California | 650-723-2091

ADMISSION

Admission Rate: 4%
Admission Rate - Men: 3%
Admission Rate - Women: 4%
EA Admission Rate: Not Reported
ED Admission Rate: Not Offered
ED Admits as % of Total Admits: Not Offered
Admission Rate (5-Year Trend): -1%
% of Admits Attending (Yield): 84%
Transfer Admission Rate: 2%

SAT Reading/Writing (Middle 50%): 730-780
SAT Math (Middle 50%): 770-800
ACT Composite (Middle 50%): 33-35

% Graduated in Top 10% of HS Class: 94%
% Graduated in Top 25% of HS Class: 99%
% Graduated in Top 50% of HS Class: 100%

Demonstrated Interest: Not Considered
Legacy Status: Considered
Racial/Ethnic Status: Considered
Admission Interview Offered: Yes

ENROLLMENT

Total Undergraduate Enrollment: 8,049
% Full-Time: 96%
% Male: 48%
% Female: 52%
% Out-of-State: 59%
% Fraternity: 18%
% Sorority: 23%
% On-Campus (All Undergraduate): 94%
Freshman Housing Required: Yes

% African-American: 7%
% Asian: 26%
% Hispanic: 18%
% White: 26%
% Other: 0%
% International: 11%
% Low-Income: 19%

ACADEMICS

Student-to-Faculty Ratio: 6 to 1
% of Classes Under 20: 69%
% of Classes 20-49: 20%
% of Classes 50 or More: 11%
% Full-Time Faculty: 81%
% Full-Time Faculty w/ Terminal Degree: 95%

Top Programs
Computer Science
Economics
Engineering
Human Biology
International Relations
Mathematics
Physics
Psychology

Retention Rate: 95%
4-Year Graduation Rate: 73%
6-Year Graduation Rate: 95%

Curricular Flexibility: Somewhat Flexible
Academic Rating: ★★★★★

#CollegesWorthYourMoney

Fittingly situated in the heart of Silicon Valley sits one of the tech industry's top feeder schools and one of the premier research universities in the world. Among Stanford's many quantifiable boasts and brags are the lowest acceptance rate in the country, the nation's second-largest college endowment, the best all-around athletic department in the country, the second-highest total of affiliate-won Nobel Prizes, and the highest graduate starting salaries for any non-STEM-exclusive institution. At Stanford, the list of accomplishments could go longer than a vintage John Elway (an alum) deep ball.

Inside the Classroom

Just shy of 8,049 undergrads and another 10,236 graduate students occupy this expansive campus that is the sixth-largest in the nation. For perspective on its size, 19,000 bicycle parking spots can be found on university grounds. There are three undergraduate schools at Stanford: the School of Humanities & Sciences, which houses the majority of the student body, the School of Engineering, and the School of Earth, Energy, and Environmental Sciences. All undergraduates must complete three courses in writing and rhetoric, one year of a foreign language, and a freshman course entitled Thinking Matters in which students choose from a full menu of courses covering a host of intellectual topics from Race in American Memory to How Does Your Brain Work? The Ways of Thinking, Ways of Doing requirement comprises eleven additional courses in ethical reasoning, applied quantitative reasoning, and aesthetic and interpretive inquiry. Further requirements are major-specific. Some programs require a senior capstone, research component, practicum, or, for foreign language, an oral proficiency review.

A virtually unmatched 6:1 student-to-faculty ratio sets students up for a personalized classroom experience and an incredible amount of face time with some of the leaders in their respective fields. Sixty-nine percent of classes have fewer than twenty students, and 34% have a single-digit enrollment. Stanford puts immense resources behind undergraduate research; more than $5.9 million in grant funding is allocated each year to support roughly 1,000 student research projects. Close to 900 students study abroad annually through the Bing Overseas Studies Program in 11 international cities.

The School of Engineering is one of the best in the world; all of its sub-disciplines sit atop any list of best engineering programs. Programs in computer science, physics, mathematics, international relations, and economics are arguably the best anywhere. In terms of sheer volume, the greatest number of degrees are conferred each year in the social sciences (17%), computer science (16%), engineering (15%), and interdisciplinary studies (13%). With over 100 Rhodes Scholars to its credit, Stanford ranks fourth on the all-time list. In 2023, the school produced 24 Fulbright winners, four Schwartzman Scholars, and two Truman Scholars, and in recent years has produced a multitude of winners of just about any prestigious post-grad scholarship one can name.

Outside the Classroom

Stanford is where you can receive a world-class education and experience the excitement of a typical college setting. The Cardinals have a rich sports tradition with its 16 men's and 20 women's NCAA Division I teams. The excellence the university expects in the classroom is matched on the field; the Athletic Department won the Directors' Cup, given to the most successful college athletic program, for 25 consecutive years (the streak was broken in 2021), and at least one team has won an NCAA national championship in each of the last 40+ years. With an additional forty club teams, over 900 undergraduates compete in intercollegiate athletics. Fraternities and sororities are thriving on campus with an 18-23% participation rate across twenty-nine Greek organizations. Over 600 student organizations are active including 60 student-led community service organizations, the widely circulated Stanford Daily, and a vast array of ethnic/cultural groups. Ninety-two percent of undergrads live on Stanford's sprawling 8,180-acre campus in the heart of the San Francisco Peninsula. The surrounding area of Palo Alto, America's wealthiest town, is full of natural and manmade beauty and any cultural, culinary, or entertainment delight one could seek. The university itself puts its bottomless endowment to use with immaculately manicured grounds, well-maintained dorms, state-of-the-art recreational facilities, and restaurant-quality campus dining options. Simply put, the campus aesthetics at Stanford are every bit as breathtaking as the quality of its academics.

Career Services

Stanford Career Education is Stanford's career services office. It employs 30 professional staff members who work in the Career Catalysts, Career Communities, and Career Ventures divisions. The 268:1 student-to-advisor ratio is lower than the average school featured in this guide. The three aforementioned divisions speak to the unique and comprehensive career services approach at Stanford. There is a sincere effort to get students to align their career interests with their identities and passions, cultivate a personalized network of mentors/guides, and connect directly with employers. Stanford does a fantastic job with all three phases of that process.

E-mail: admission@stanford.edu | Website: stanford.edu

In a given year, the career services staff facilitates roughly 20,000 "meaningful connections" between current students and alumni/industry professionals and initiates 37,000+ "meaningful opportunities" for undergraduates to carve out a pathway toward their employment or graduate school destination. Stanford's career services office sponsors fourteen to sixteen career fairs per year, and runs the superb Stanford Alumni Mentoring program. Major companies recruit on campus on a constant basis because (a) of the incredible talent pool and (b) the school is located in Silicon Valley, home to most of the world's largest tech companies. Stanford facilitates internships at over 700 unique sites, and close to half of all students complete two internships as part of their undergraduate education; two-thirds complete at least one. With a robust career services department and spectacular graduate outcomes (see below), Stanford Career Education earns every ounce of its stellar reputation.

Professional Outcomes

Based on the most recent data available, Stanford grads entering the working world flock to three major industries in equal distribution: business/finance/consulting/retail (19%); computer, IT (19%); and public policy and service, international affairs (19%). Among the companies employing the largest number of recent Stanford alums are Accenture, Apple, Bain, Cisco, Meta, Goldman Sachs, Google, McKinsey, Microsoft, and SpaceX. Other companies that employ hundreds of Cardinal alums include LinkedIn, Salesforce, and Airbnb. California, New York, Massachusetts, Texas, DC, and Washington State were the top six destinations for recent grads. Starting salaries for Stanford grads are among the highest in the country.

Those who are graduate school-bound often stay at Stanford with professors they already have a close working relationship with. The other dozen most popular universities attended by recent graduates include Oxford, Harvard, MIT, Yale, Columbia, the University of Chicago, and Johns Hopkins. You would be hard-pressed to find a top-ranked law or medical school that did not have Stanford alums among its ranks. In the 2023-24 school year, 162 Stanford graduates applied to medical school, and acceptance rates were nearly double the national average. In sum, if you get an undergraduate degree from Stanford, your opportunities for continuing your education will be limitless.

Admission

One of the toughest schools to get into in the United States doesn't appear to be getting less selective anytime soon. In 2022, a meager 4% of the 56,378 accomplished teens vying for a place in the Class of 2026 were offered admission. The profile of the average current student is about what you would expect at the university with the lowest acceptance rate in the country. The middle-50% SAT range for the Class of 2026 was 1500-1570 and 33-35 on the ACT. If you want to become a member of the Cardinal club, near-perfect grades are a prerequisite. Ninety-four percent of incoming freshmen had a GPA of 4.0 or above in high school, although it is important to highlight that, in one recent cycle, only 7% of applicants meeting that criterion were accepted, and only 1% of those with a 3.7 or lower made the cut. Almost all freshmen—94%—ranked in the top 10% of their high school class.

There are nine factors considered "very important" to the admissions office: rigor of courses, GPA, class rank, standardized test scores, essays, recommendations, extracurricular activities, talent/ability, and character/personal qualities. The last three from that list are of particular importance given that the first five will likely be similarly perfect from the bulk of those applying. First-generation status is not listed as a primary factor, but a healthy 21% of those admitted in 2022-23 are looking to become the first in their family to earn a degree. Stanford admissions has become the ultimate valedictorian meat grinder, now possessing a lower admission rate than MIT. With so many top-shelf applicants for a limited number of spots, it helps to have a hook—an area in which you truly excel.

Worth Your Money?

An endowment of over $36 billion helps the school cover all of the determined need of its undergraduate students. The average need-based grant is $61k+, which helps knock the $87,833 cost of attendance down to a manageable sum for the approximately 50% of students who qualify. Of course, Stanford is one of those rare universities that would be worth just about any cost.

FINANCIAL
Institutional Type: Private
In-State Tuition: $62,484
Out-of-State Tuition: $62,484
Room & Board: $19,922
Books & Supplies: $1,350

Avg. Need-Based Grant: $64,000
Avg. % of Need Met: 100%

Avg. Merit-Based Award: $26,426
% Receiving (Freshmen w/o Need): <1%

Avg. Cumulative Debt: $20,691
% of Students Borrowing: 14%

CAREER
Who Recruits
1. Masimo
2. Wealthfront
3. Calico
4. Asurion
5. Los Angeles Dodgers

Notable Internships
1. Citadel
2. SpaceX
3. United Nations

Top Employers
1. Google
2. Apple
3. Facebook
4. Microsoft
5. Amazon

Where Alumni Work
1. San Francisco
2. New York City
3. Los Angeles
4. Seattle
5. Boston

Earnings
College Scorecard (10-YR Post-Entry): $106,987
PayScale (Early Career): $87,100
PayScale (Mid-Career): $156,500
PayScale 20-Year ROI: $1,240,000

RANKINGS
Money: 5
U.S. News: 3, National Universities
Wall Street Journal/THE: 4
Washington Monthly: 2, National Universities

OVERGENERALIZATIONS
Students are:
Driven
Friendly
Teeming with school pride
Involved/invested in campus life
Well-rounded

COLLEGE OVERLAPS
Columbia University
Harvard University
Massachusetts Institute of Technology
Princeton University
Yale University

Stevens Institute of Technology

Hoboken, New Jersey | 201-216-5194

ADMISSION
Admission Rate: 46%
Admission Rate - Men: 42%
Admission Rate - Women: 55%
EA Admission Rate: Not Offered
ED Admission Rate: 59%
ED Admits as % of Total Admits: 7%
Admission Rate (5-Year Trend): +2%
% of Admits Attending (Yield): 17%
Transfer Admission Rate: 39%

SAT Reading/Writing (Middle 50%): 670-730
SAT Math (Middle 50%): 710-780
ACT Composite (Middle 50%): 31-34

% Graduated in Top 10% of HS Class: 58%
% Graduated in Top 25% of HS Class: 88%
% Graduated in Top 50% of HS Class: 98%

Demonstrated Interest: Considered
Legacy Status: Considered
Racial/Ethnic Status: Considered
Admission Interview Offered: Yes

ENROLLMENT
Total Undergraduate Enrollment: 3,988
% Full-Time: 100%
% Male: 68%
% Female: 32%
% Out-of-State: 31%
% Fraternity: 22%
% Sorority: 27%
% On-Campus (All Undergraduate): 48%
Freshman Housing Required: No

% African-American: 2%
% Asian: 19%
% Hispanic: 15%
% White: 51%
% Other: 6%
% International: 3%
% Low-Income: 21%

ACADEMICS
Student-to-Faculty Ratio: 11 to 1
% of Classes Under 20: 42%
% of Classes 20-49: 46%
% of Classes 50 or More: 12%
% Full-Time Faculty: 69%
% Full-Time Faculty w/ Terminal Degree: 97%

Top Programs
Business & Technology
Chemical Biology
Computer Science
Cybersecurity
Engineering
Information Systems
Mathematics
Quantitative Finance

Retention Rate: 93%
4-Year Graduation Rate: 65%
6-Year Graduation Rate: 87%

Curricular Flexibility: Somewhat Flexible
Academic Rating: ★★★★

#CollegesWorthYourMoney

With the Manhattan skyline visible across the Hudson River, the Stevens Institute of Technology's Hoboken, New Jersey, campus occupies prime real estate—but the school is not merely about its breathtaking panoramic view of the Big Apple. For this small but growing (just 3,988 undergrads) private research institution with a focus on engineering and business, proximity to New York City is an asset that translates into strong corporate connections, endless internship and co-op opportunities, and, ultimately, exceptional job placement rates at top companies.

Inside the Classroom

There are 35 undergraduate majors at Stevens across four undergraduate schools: the Schaefer School of Engineering & Science, the School of Business, the College of Arts and Letters, and the School of Systems and Enterprises. There is no core curriculum at Stevens as every set of requirements is school and major-dependent. The only common academic experience for all undergrads is a sequence of two College of Arts and Letters courses that every freshman must complete—Writing and Communications and Colloquium: Knowledge, Nature, Culture. Some engineering students complete a capstone senior design project that is often conducted in coordination with an industry sponsor.

Forty-nine percent of course sections contain fewer than 20 students. The student-to-faculty ratio is 11:1 but, of course, with over 5,200 graduate students some attention is diverted in their direction. Undergraduate research possibilities are plentiful and varied. Roughly 10% of each freshman class is invited to become Stevens Scholars, which guarantees a paid summer research experience with a faculty member. As a research university, the school also has close ties to industry and federally-run labs that can lead to many additional research opportunities. Co-op experiences that also can involve research are embarked upon by slightly less than one-third of students. A number of study abroad programs are available with some of the most popular destinations being the United Kingdom, Belgium, Jamaica, China, Spain, Thailand, and Greece.

Engineering is, by far, the most common undergraduate major, and all programs within the Schaefer School of Engineering & Science are strong. Programs in computer science, cybersecurity, and quantitative finance also receive praise. Over 80% of the degrees granted at Stevens are in a STEM field, and most of the remaining grads major in business, finance, and accounting. It is uncommon for Stevens grads to pursue national fellowships or scholarships as they are traditionally focused on career or graduate school as their next step after graduation.

Outside the Classroom

Last year, 48% of the undergraduate student body resided on campus in college-owned housing. Greek life is a major player on campus as fraternities and sororities attract 22% and 27% of students, respectively. Greek houses are community service-oriented and work closely with charitable organizations including Big Brothers Big Sisters, the Hoboken Shelter, and the Food Bank of New Jersey. Student-athletes participate in one of 25 NCAA Division III varsity athletic teams known as the Ducks. There are an additional sixteen intercollegiate club sports teams and a robust intramural program featuring flag football, three-on-three basketball, and floor hockey. There are over 100 clubs and activities to join. For the extremely adventurous, the Outdoor Adventure Program plans trips to locales like Costa Rica, Utah, and the Grand Canyon. The Stevens Honor System is taken seriously and permeates beyond academic life into the social realm. Students publish a weekly student newspaper and run campus radio and television stations. Hoboken is only one jam-packed square mile of land, making it immensely walkable. For those of age, the town holds the distinction of most bars per capita. Running alongside the Hudson is an aesthetically pleasing option and, perhaps best of all, New York City is only 15 minutes away.

Career Services

The Stevens Career Center is made up of 13 professional employees who work with undergraduate students as advisors, cooperative education coordinators, or in a director/assistant director capacity; the student-to-advisor ratio of 307:1 ranks in the average range when compared to other schools featured in this guide, yet Stevens' career services offerings are as strong as they come. This is a career services office that works hard to forge corporate connections and, as a result, the vast majority of seniors have secured competitive employment prior to graduation.

In a given school year, more than 300 companies recruit on campus, a phenomenal number for a school of any size, but for a small university like Stevens, that figure is astounding. It is rare for Stevens students to not complete at least one internship over their four years of study. Ninety percent of undergrads in the School of Business land internships. The co-op track is selected by 30% of all students, and that entails working a 40-hour paid work week beginning in the sophomore year. Three annual career fairs in September, December, and March each attract about 900 students. The March Career Fair alone attracts 125 companies, including the likes of IBM, Verizon, and JPMorgan Chase.

Professional Outcomes

The Class of 2022 found employment or graduate school homes at a 97% rate within six months of receiving their degree. Students entered the fields of finance (29%), technology (17%), aerospace/defense (9%), and construction (6%). Employers that hired the greatest number of Class of 2022 Stevens grads included Google, EY, Merck, Prudential, and PwC. Massive numbers of alumni (from all graduating years) can be found at major corporations including Verizon, Citi, JPMorgan Chase, Pfizer, and Johnson & Johnson. The average starting salary was $79,600. Many alumni stay local; 71% of 2022 graduates remained in New Jersey or crossed the border to New York.

Of the 33% of Stevens grads who immediately enrolled in graduate school, the vast majority were pursuing master's or PhDs. Some enrolled in doctoral programs at prestigious institutions such as Carnegie Mellon, Princeton, Columbia, and Berkeley and master's programs at NYU, MIT, Dartmouth, and Cornell. The school offers a three-three accelerated law option with Seton Hall University as well as a three-four accelerated med school program with Rutgers University. Recent medical school acceptances include Albert Einstein College of Medicine, Mount Sinai Medical School, and New York University School of Medicine.

Admission

There were 12,500 applications submitted for the 2022-23 freshman class, a sizable increase from the previous year. Of those hopefuls, 46% received an offer of acceptance compared to 53% the prior year. The median SAT score was 1450 and the average high school GPA was 3.9. Over the last couple of years, Stevens now accepts and enrolls a much greater number of students than in the past. That expansion meant that over 1,000 freshmen enrolled in the Class of 2025 while under 700 graduated just three years ago.

In addition to strong grades and standardized test scores, the admissions committee at Stevens is looking for students with a track record of "ingenuity, inventiveness, and inspiration." The school does offer admissions interviews which are evaluative in nature. Applying early is strongly encouraged if Stevens is your top choice; the acceptance rate for ED applicants is 75%. The acceptance rate for women is typically 3-6 points higher than the acceptance rate for men, yet women still make up slightly more than 30% of the student body. Stevens Institute of Technology is gaining in popularity and rapidly expanding its undergraduate enrollment. Its proximity to Manhattan, corporate connections, and stellar graduate outcomes should continue to draw larger numbers of highly qualified applicants.

Worth Your Money?

Is it good news or bad news that the average graduate's starting salary and annual cost of attendance at Stevens are nearly identical? Perhaps the adage, "You have to spend money to make money," helps answer that question. With a COA of $82k and starting salaries around the same, those paying full price will be just fine, even if they have to take out substantial loans to attend. Two-thirds of students who apply for need-based aid receive annual awards of around $32k, which still leaves a large bill left to cover. Again, the good news is that strong career outcomes help balance the upfront costs.

FINANCIAL

Institutional Type: Private
In-State Tuition: $60,952
Out-of-State Tuition: $60,952
Room & Board: $18,650
Books & Supplies: $1,200

Avg. Need-Based Grant: $33,733
Avg. % of Need Met: 72%

Avg. Merit-Based Award: $21,118
% Receiving (Freshmen w/o Need): 30%

Avg. Cumulative Debt: $41,574
% of Students Borrowing: 70%

CAREER

Who Recruits
1. MThree
2. Nasdaq
3. Bristol-Myers Squibb
4. Calgene6
5. Nielsen

Notable Internships
1. iHeartMedia
2. Merck
3. Johnson & Johnson

Top Employers
1. Verizon
2. JPMorgan Chase
3. Citi
4. Johnson & Johnson
5. Pfizer

Where Alumni Work
1. New York City
2. Philadelphia
3. San Francisco
4. Washington, DC
5. Boston

Earnings
College Scorecard (10-YR Post-Entry): $104,918
PayScale (Early Career): $80,400
PayScale (Mid-Career): $150,900
PayScale 20-Year ROI: $1,141,000

RANKINGS

Money: 4.5
U.S. News: 76, National Universities
Wall Street Journal/THE: 36
Washington Monthly: 283, National Universities

OVERGENERALIZATIONS

Students are:
Career-driven
Competitive
Only a short drive from home (i.e., Most come from NJ or nearby states)
Working hard and playing hard
More likely to venture off campus

COLLEGE OVERLAPS

Lehigh University
Northeastern University
Rensselaer Polytechnic Institute
Rutgers University - New Brunswick
Worcester Polytechnic Institute

Stony Brook University (SUNY)

Stony Brook, New York | 631-632-6868

Like many schools within the SUNY system, Stony Brook University has quietly but steadily ascended into a different tier of public universities since the turn of the millennium. In fact, back in 1999, its acceptance rate was 58%, and the 25th percentile SAT score for accepted students was 1050; in recent years, the acceptance rate has crept as low as 40%, and the 25th percentile SAT score is now 1320. Shedding its "commuter school" status has been difficult, and roughly 85% of undergrads still hail from in state; however, Stony Brook now also attracts students from 89 countries, which would have been an unthinkable feat when it opened as a teacher's college in 1957. In 2022-23, Stony Brook has an undergraduate enrollment of 17,509 as well as an extensive academic menu of 60+ majors and 80+ minors.

Inside the Classroom

There are six undergraduate colleges within the university and some, like the College of Leadership and Service or the College of Global Studies, are, perhaps, unexpected options. After a two-day compulsory orientation, the journey through the Stony Brook curriculum begins. All told, that will involve checking off double-digits worth of learning objective boxes via courses in the humanities, arts, global affairs, technology, natural science, writing, human behavior, US history, and language. Additional coursework (this can be overlapping) also must fulfill mandates related to interconnectedness, deep understanding, and lifelong learning. In sum, required coursework outside of your major will take a solid three semesters to complete but, on the plus side, there is a great deal of choice within each category for you to pursue elective areas of interest.

A 19:1 student-to-faculty ratio and 8,200 graduate students isn't exactly a recipe for small classes, but undergrads will find themselves in some first-name basis classes with 38% of all sections containing nineteen or fewer students. However, there also will be large numbers of face-in-the-crowd experiences because one-quarter of undergraduate sections enroll fifty or more students. That type of environment is not going to spoon-feed you with one-on-one faculty mentoring or the chance to participate in undergraduate research, but such experiences are available to those who show determination. In fact, more than 1,500 students have the chance to engage in undergraduate research each year. The rate of study abroad participation is low, but exciting opportunities exist for those who choose to take advantage; the school features a winter program that whisks students to Ecuador and the Galapagos.

A popular and locally well-regarded nursing program leads to the largest number of degrees being conferred in health professions (14%). Strong majors in biology (14%), math (10%), business (9%), engineering (7%), and computer sciences (6%) also draw a sizable number of Seawolves (the school's mascot). The school's reputation in the hard sciences, particularly math, chemistry, and biomedical engineering, is aided by the affiliated Stony Brook University Hospital. With regard to prestigious postgraduate scholarships, Stony Brook students have really upped their game in recent years. In 2023, four Stony Brook seniors earned National Science Foundation Graduate Research Fellowships. Further, nine students won Fulbright Awards in 2023, and the university enjoys more than one Goldwater Scholarship recipient in an average year.

Outside the Classroom

No longer the commuter-heavy school it once was, last year, 77% of freshmen and 50% of the total student population lived on campus in one of 30 residence halls or 23 apartment-style buildings. Greek life is close to invisible but has a faint heartbeat as 3% of men and women join fraternities and sororities. There are approximately 550 student-athletes competing as the Seawolves on seven men's and nine women's NCAA Division I teams. There also are 35+ club sports teams and intramural options including bowling, beach volleyball, Wiffle ball, and flag football. Over 325 clubs are on tap, including a full array of cultural, dance, charitable, and pre-professional groups. Notably strong organizations include the African Student Union, the College Democrats, and service groups like Camp Kesem and Project Sunshine. For a school without centuries of history under its belt, it does have a number of cool traditions including the annual Roth Pond Regatta where students race themed boats made of cardboard and duct tape across a campus pond. The spacious Long Island campus of 1,039 acres is located midway between Manhattan and Montauk. A train station on campus will take you the sixty miles into New York City. Parks, beaches, and shopping are all within reach, particularly for those with a car (or a friend with a car).

Career Services

The Career Center at Stony Brook University employs 26 professional staff members who are tasked with career counseling, experiential learning, and employer relations. That translates to a 673:1 student-to-counselor ratio, poorer than the average school featured in this guide. Fortunately, that figure does not appear to be preventing the school from reaching the entire undergraduate population.

In a single school year, the center conducts 6,000 one-on-one counseling sessions, and career presentations attract another 7,000 individuals; additionally, it facilitates 900,000 online transactions each year. It is also one of the only career centers to offer two credited courses on career development, one geared toward freshmen and sophomores and the other toward upperclassmen.

Stony Brook's staff helps facilitate roughly 1,200 undergraduate internships each year as well as 2,500 practicums and hundreds of clinical placements. Recently, it has adopted the practice of micro-internships, paid five- to forty-hour placements at companies ranging from Fortune 100 mega-corporations to small tech start-ups. Several job fairs take place each semester, including the Information Technology/Computer Science Job & Internship Fair, Engineering Job & Internship Fair, Business Job & Internship Fair, and the Healthcare, Research, & Human Services Job & Internship Fair. By drawing more than 400 regional and national companies to Stony Brook's campus, the Career Services Office provides ample opportunity for assertive students to make connections and land desirable jobs and internships in New York City and beyond. There were over 1,200 on-campus interviews conducted at the university last year.

Professional Outcomes

Based on the most recent data available, within two years of graduation, 61% of Stony Brook graduates are employed, 34% have entered graduate/professional school, and 5% are presently looking for their next opportunity. Graduates of the arts and sciences, social welfare, and nursing schools had the lowest reported figures of "still searching" alumni while health tech and management students had the highest. The organizations and companies employing the greatest number of Seawolves are Northwell Health, JPMorgan Chase, Google, Amazon, Citi, Morgan Stanley, Microsoft, Apple, Bloomberg, and Microsoft. Over three-quarters of alumni are settled in the Greater New York City area; sizable pockets also can be found in San Francisco, Boston, DC, and Los Angeles.

Among those pursuing further education, common choices include Stony Brook itself, other SUNY or CUNY institutions, and NYC-based powerhouses like Columbia, Fordham, and NYU. Some recent grads also have left the region to attend some of the finest schools in the world including the London School of Economics, Oxford, Caltech, Stanford, Harvard, Duke, the University of Michigan, and Yale. Traditionally, premed students with a 3.5 GPA and an MCAT in the 67th percentile gain acceptance into medical school at a 59% clip; there were 298 applicants to med school in 2023-24. The most commonly attended medical schools include Stony Brook, Downstate, Upstate, NYMC, Albany, Buffalo, Eastern Virginia, GW, Howard, Georgetown, Penn State, and Drexel. Law schools attended by recent grads include Hofstra, Boston University, Villanova, Brooklyn Law School, Wake Forest, and the Cardozo School of Law at Yeshiva University.

Admission

Members of the Class of 2026 were admitted at a 49% clip, significantly higher than the 39% of eight years ago. However, the school's popularity is definitely on the rise; it attracts double the number of applicants it did 15 years ago. Seventeen percent of those accepted ultimately enroll, a comparable figure to past years. The caliber of freshmen that Stony Brook reels in today is higher than ever. The mid-50% standardized test score ranges are 1320-1480 on the SAT and 28-34 on the ACT. SAT math scores were notably strong with 66% of this group scoring a 700 or above. Forty-seven percent of entering 2022-23 freshmen earned a spot in the top 10% of their high school class; 78% placed in the top quartile. The average high school GPA was 3.9, and 71% sported at least a 3.75.

There is nothing complicated about how admissions decisions are made at Stony Brook. With such a mass of applicants, the admissions committee primarily relies on the hard facts of standardized test scores and GPA within a rigorous course load that has a fair number of honors and AP selections. Recommendations and the application essay also are considered "important" to the evaluation process. The application deadline for everyone is January 15 as there are no early action or early decision options.

Worth Your Money?

At $7,070 in pure tuition, students living with their parents and commuting could conceivably graduate from Stony Brook for less than the cost of one semester at NYU. To top it off, more than 70% of freshmen receive financial aid. On the other hand, out-of-staters pay $26,860 in tuition, and, with living and meal costs, a degree would likely cost around $190,000 total. For the 85% of current undergraduates hailing from the state of New York, this university is an otherworldly bargain; for international students and Americans outside the state, the value would depend on financial aid and whether the program you would pursue would be likely to yield a solid starting salary.

FINANCIAL
Institutional Type: Public
In-State Tuition: $10,560
Out-of-State Tuition: $30,350
Room & Board: $18,292
Books & Supplies: $900

Avg. Need-Based Grant: $10,100
Avg. % of Need Met: 61%

Avg. Merit-Based Award: $5,619
% Receiving (Freshmen w/o Need): 11%

Avg. Cumulative Debt: $23,899
% of Students Borrowing: 46%

CAREER
Who Recruits
1. Travelers
2. North Atlantic Industries
3. GEICO
4. Broadbridge
5. Canon

Notable Internships
1. Moody's Analytics
2. Bank of America
3. Northrop Grumman

Top Employers
1. Northwell Health
2. JPMorgan Chase
3. Google
4. Citi
5. Amazon

Where Alumni Work
1. New York City
2. San Francisco
3. Boston
4. Washington, DC
5. Los Angeles

Earnings
College Scorecard (10-YR Post-Entry): $70,686
PayScale (Early Career): $63,900
PayScale (Mid-Career): $116,800
PayScale 20-Year ROI: $668,000

RANKINGS
Money: 4.5
U.S. News: 58, National Universities
Wall Street Journal/THE: 149
Washington Monthly: 156, National Universities

OVERGENERALIZATIONS
Students are:
Only a short drive from home (i.e., Most come from NY or nearby states)
Diverse
More likely to go home on weekends
Goal-oriented
Self-sufficient

COLLEGE OVERLAPS
Binghamton University (SUNY)
Rutgers University - New Brunswick
University at Albany (SUNY)
University at Buffalo (SUNY)
University of Connecticut

Swarthmore College

Swarthmore, Pennsylvania | 610-328-8300

ADMISSION
Admission Rate: 7%
Admission Rate - Men: 8%
Admission Rate - Women: 6%
EA Admission Rate: Not Offered
ED Admission Rate: 19%
ED Admits as % of Total Admits: 22%
Admission Rate (5-Year Trend): -4%
% of Admits Attending (Yield): 42%
Transfer Admission Rate: 2%

SAT Reading/Writing (Middle 50%): 710-770
SAT Math (Middle 50%): 730-790
ACT Composite (Middle 50%): 32-35

% Graduated in Top 10% of HS Class: 89%
% Graduated in Top 25% of HS Class: 100%
% Graduated in Top 50% of HS Class: 100%

Demonstrated Interest: Not Considered
Legacy Status: Considered
Racial/Ethnic Status: Considered
Admission Interview Offered: Yes

ENROLLMENT
Total Undergraduate Enrollment: 1,625
% Full-Time: 100%
% Male: 49%
% Female: 51%
% Out-of-State: 88%
% Fraternity: Not Offered
% Sorority: Not Offered
% On-Campus (All Undergraduate): 96%
Freshman Housing Required: Yes

% African-American: 9%
% Asian: 18%
% Hispanic: 14%
% White: 32%
% Other: 3%
% International: 14%
% Low-Income: 22%

ACADEMICS
Student-to-Faculty Ratio: 8 to 1
% of Classes Under 20: 70%
% of Classes 20-49: 28%
% of Classes 50 or More: 2%
% Full-Time Faculty: 86%
% Full-Time Faculty w/ Terminal Degree: 99%

Top Programs
Astronomy
Biology
Computer Science
Economics
Engineering
Mathematics
Physics
Political Science

Retention Rate: 94%
4-Year Graduation Rate: 90%
6-Year Graduation Rate: 95%

Curricular Flexibility: Somewhat Flexible
Academic Rating: ★★★★★

#CollegesWorthYourMoney

The average person in the United States may not be fully aware that Swarthmore College, located on Philadelphia's Main Line, is one of, if not the, finest liberal arts schools in the entire country. The good news is that top employers and grad schools know Swarthmore's quality well. The 1,625 undergraduate students who attend Swat are an exceptional group, having been among the 7% to gain acceptance. The college has never been more difficult to get into as applications have tripled since the turn of the millennium. A quick examination of the superb academics offered at this school is all it takes to fully understand the reasons for the long lines outside the gates.

Inside the Classroom

Despite its small size, the college offers forty undergraduate programs and runs 600+ courses each academic year. A member of the Tri-College Consortium with fellow top institutions Haverford and Bryn Mawr, students can cross-register at those institutions as well as at the University of Pennsylvania. Unusual for a school full of perfect SAT/valedictorian types, Swat also offers an honors program that involves highly independent, self-directed study that culminates with a series of oral exams. All undergrads must complete at least three courses in all three divisions: Humanities, Natural Science & Engineering, and Social Sciences. Additional requirements include three courses that are designated "writing intensive," physical education, a foreign language, and one laboratory science course.

Small, seminar-style courses are the norm at Swat—an outstanding 33% of sections enroll fewer than ten students, and 70% contain a maximum of nineteen students. Overall, the average class size is 14. Thanks to an 8:1 student-to-faculty ratio and zero grad students, professors are extremely available in and outside the classroom. As a result, two-thirds of graduates complete at least one undergraduate research or independent creative project, and the college sets aside $800,000 in funding for that express purpose. Forty percent of students elect to study abroad for a semester in one of 300 programs in 60 countries.

Social science degrees are the most commonly conferred, accounting for 24% of all 2022 graduates. Future academics and researchers would do well to look at Swat—a whopping 22% of graduates go on to earn PhDs. Future businessmen/women, engineers, and techies are also well-positioned, given Swat's incredibly strong offerings in economics, engineering, and computer science. When it comes to prestigious scholarships, Swarthmore is winning in disproportionately large numbers. In 2023, seven grads/alumni nabbed Fulbright Scholarships, four have been named Rhodes Scholars in the past decade, and undergraduates have won Gaither Fellowships, Watson Fellowships, and Luce Scholarships in recent years.

Outside the Classroom

Swarthmore is a connected and tight-knit campus community where 96% of students live in one of 18 residence halls spread across the college's 425-acre grounds. Greek life was banned in 2019. There are 22 sports teams competing in the NCAA Division III ranks, and roughly 20% of the undergraduate student body are members of one of the varsity teams. There are also plenty of intramural and club sports options, including the uber-popular ultimate Frisbee. More than one hundred campus organizations include a number of volunteer groups that attract 60% of the student body. The other Tri-Co member schools, Haverford College and Bryn Mawr, are in close proximity, further expanding the social scene at Swarthmore. The campus itself is located on the Main Line, which means there is plenty of dining and culture available, pretty much all of which comes at a high cost. Fortunately, everything the city of Philadelphia has to offer isn't far from campus. There is a regional rail line nearby affording students access to the entire city, and West Philadelphia and University City are only about a 45-minute bike ride.

Career Services

Career Services at Swarthmore College employs six individuals who specialize in career education, employer relations, and internships and technology. The 271:1 student-to-advisor ratio is better than average when compared to other colleges featured in this guidebook. As a member of the Tri-College Consortium with Haverford and Bryn Mawr as well as the Fall Recruiting Consortium with schools like Brown and William & Mary, Swarthmore students are afforded innumerable opportunities to get face time with the world's leading employers; over eighty companies recruited on campus last year. In 2022-23, they held their first-ever Career Carnival that 125 students attended.

One-on-one attention is available for anyone who wishes to take advantage of it. In one recent school year, Swat engaged 49% of the total student body, including 63% of seniors. The office conducted 1,200 counseling appointments with 460+ unique individuals to address areas such as application materials reviews (25%), interview prep (19%), job search (17%), and internship search (16%). A solid 55% of graduates completed at least one internship as part of the undergraduate experience. Locations for those experiences included some of the most desirable organizations around such as The World Bank, the FDA, and Capital One. Visitors to campus include more than one hundred alumni mentors per year as well as companies like Google, which typically spends two full days at Swat meeting with computer science students. Offering an enviable level of service to its undergraduates and producing across-the-board positive outcomes, this career services office is held in high esteem by our staff.

Professional Outcomes

Sixty-eight percent of Class of 2022 graduates had already entered the workforce shortly after graduation; the majority secured a job prior to completing their degree. Popular industries included education (17%), consulting (16%), and financial services (13%). Google is one of the leading employers of Swarthmore grads followed by Amazon, Goldman Sachs, IBM, and a number of the leading universities in the nation. The cities attracting the highest percentage of Swat alumni were NYC, Philadelphia, and Boston. The media starting salary was $60,000, a strong figure for any liberal arts school.

Eighteen percent of the 2022 senior class enjoyed acceptance into graduate school. Among those pursuing advanced degrees, the most frequently attended institutions were Harvard, Penn, Yale, Princeton, Stanford, MIT, and Cornell—not a shabby top seven. PhDs were pursued by 38% of recent grads, while 35% entered master's programs, 10% headed to law school, and 7% matriculated into medical school. The medical school acceptance rate for grads and alumni typically hovers close to 85%, an astounding number that is roughly double the national average. The school also has an early acceptance program with Thomas Jefferson University's Sidney Kimmel Medical College. Swarthmore sports a 97% acceptance rate into law schools, and the institutions attended are typically of the elite variety.

Admission

There were 14,707 applications submitted for a spot in the Class of 2026, but only 1,019 were accepted for an acceptance rate of only 7%. While the school's acceptance rate has decreased in the last decade (it was 16% ten years ago), it's unlikely that anyone will mistake Swat for anything less than one of the most selective schools in the country. Just shy of 90% of 2022-23 freshmen placed in the top decile of their graduating high school class. Mid-50% standardized test scores were 1445-1540 on the SAT and 32-35 on the ACT. For perhaps a better perspective, the median SAT score was 1500 and the median ACT score was 33.

The admissions committee ranks six factors as being of paramount importance in the admissions process: rigor of secondary coursework, class rank, GPA, application essay, recommendations, and character/personal qualities. Test scores and extracurricular activities are "considered" and they are serious about extracurriculars, particularly those involving community service; 33% of incoming freshmen were involved with a community, national, or international service organization. In a typical year, Swat enjoys a 42% yield rate meaning that it has no trouble landing a sizable percentage of those offered admission. If Swarthmore is your top choice, applying early decision is wise; it fills over half of its class through ED, and the acceptance rate is a less cutthroat 19%. Unquestionably one of the best liberal arts schools anywhere, Swarthmore will continue to sport an intimidatingly low acceptance rate well into the future.

Worth Your Money?

Swarthmore has pledged to fully meet 100% of student need, which helps explain why the 52% of freshmen who are eligible receive a sizable average grant of $63k. That certainly makes the $81,376 cost of attendance more manageable for lower-income and middle-class families. On the flip side, Swat rarely awards any merit aid whatsoever, so if your parents earn a nice living, you will likely be paying the sticker price. Of course, for a chance to attend one of the best colleges in the world, that is hardly a bad choice.

FINANCIAL
Institutional Type: Private
In-State Tuition: $62,412
Out-of-State Tuition: $62,412
Room & Board: $18,964
Books & Supplies: $760

Avg. Need-Based Grant: $60,877
Avg. % of Need Met: 100%

Avg. Merit-Based Award: $54,918
% Receiving (Freshmen w/o Need): 2%

Avg. Cumulative Debt: $25,795
% of Students Borrowing: 21%

CAREER
Who Recruits
1. Forester Capital
2. The Brattle Group
3. Apogee Adventures
4. American Enterprise Institute
5. M&T Bank

Notable Internships
1. Salesforce
2. Deutsche Bank
3. Children's Hospital of Philadelphia

Top Employers
1. Google
2. Amazon
3. Goldman Sachs
4. Apple
5. Facebook

Where Alumni Work
1. Philadelphia
2. New York City
3. San Francisco
4. Washington, DC
5. Boston

Earnings
College Scorecard (10-YR Post-Entry): $80,398
PayScale (Early Career): $70,800
PayScale (Mid-Career): $142,900
PayScale 20-Year ROI: $887,000

RANKINGS
Money: 4.5
U.S. News: 4, Liberal Arts Colleges
Wall Street Journal/THE: 11
Washington Monthly: 4, Liberal Arts Colleges

OVERGENERALIZATIONS
Students are:
Always studying
Intellectually curious
Politically liberal
Nerdy
Diverse

COLLEGE OVERLAPS
Brown University
Cornell University
Princeton University
University of Chicago
Williams College

Syracuse University

Syracuse, New York | 315-443-3611

ADMISSION

Admission Rate: 52%
Admission Rate - Men: 52%
Admission Rate - Women: 52%
EA Admission Rate: Not Offered
ED Admission Rate: 60%
ED Admits as % of Total Admits: 6%
Admission Rate (5-Year Trend): +5%
% of Admits Attending (Yield): 19%
Transfer Admission Rate: 50%

SAT Reading/Writing (Middle 50%): 630-710
SAT Math (Middle 50%): 630-720
ACT Composite (Middle 50%): 28-32

% Graduated in Top 10% of HS Class: 33%
% Graduated in Top 25% of HS Class: 67%
% Graduated in Top 50% of HS Class: 92%

Demonstrated Interest: Very Important
Legacy Status: Considered
Racial/Ethnic Status: Considered
Admission Interview Offered: Yes

ENROLLMENT

Total Undergraduate Enrollment: 15,421
% Full-Time: 97%
% Male: 46%
% Female: 54%
% Out-of-State: 65%
% Fraternity: 20%
% Sorority: 44%
% On-Campus (All Undergraduate): 53%
Freshman Housing Required: Yes

% African-American: 7%
% Asian: 7%
% Hispanic: 11%
% White: 55%
% Other: 2%
% International: 13%
% Low-Income: 16%

ACADEMICS

Student-to-Faculty Ratio: 15 to 1
% of Classes Under 20: 63%
% of Classes 20-49: 28%
% of Classes 50 or More: 9%
% Full-Time Faculty: 66%
% Full-Time Faculty w/ Terminal Degree: 93%

Top Programs
Architecture
Communications
Design
Film
Performing Arts
Policy Studies (Public Affairs)
Public Health
Sport Management

Retention Rate: 91%
4-Year Graduation Rate: 75%
6-Year Graduation Rate: 83%

Curricular Flexibility: Somewhat Flexible
Academic Rating: ★★★↓

#CollegesWorthYourMoney

A private research university of 15,421 undergraduates, Syracuse University has a reputation for more than just its instantly recognizable bright orange colors. The 'Cuse plays home to a diverse group of students, nationally-ranked sports teams, a devoted alumni network, and a broad array of academic offerings, including a number of standout programs.

Inside the Classroom

In total, 200+ majors and 100+ minors are spread across ten undergraduate schools/colleges: the School of Architecture, the College of Arts & Sciences, the School of Education, the College of Engineering & Computer Science, the Falk College of Sport & Human Dynamics, the School of Information Studies, the Whitman School of Management, the Maxwell School of Citizenship and Public Affairs, the Newhouse School of Public Communication, and the College of Visual and Performing Arts. Required courses vary significantly by school, but some common areas include two writing-intensive courses, two classes in a foreign language, and a smattering of social science, math/science, and humanities selections.

Despite a high number of graduate students also studying at SU, class sizes are kept reasonably low; 63% contain 20 students or fewer. A student-to-faculty ratio of 15:1 does mean you are likely to receive some instruction from graduate students/adjuncts along the way. The Undergraduate Research Program runs through the College of Arts & Sciences but is open to all SU students. Willing professors extend offers for research apprenticeships to highly motivated students. Recent student-assisted, faculty-led research projects include Community Theater in Kenya, The Internet's Role in the Political Process, and Cloning of Leukemia Cells. Syracuse Abroad, the university's office of study abroad programs, arranges for 45% of undergrads to spend a semester in a foreign land. There are more than a hundred programs in 60+ countries to choose from.

The most popular majors include communication/journalism (15%), the social sciences (14%), and business (12%). The School of Architecture, Maxwell School of Citizenship and Public Affairs, and Newhouse are all revered names that carry a good deal of weight in their respective fields. Newhouse, in particular, is dominant in the worlds of broadcasting and television/radio/film. Students of all academic backgrounds are competitive in procuring prestigious postgraduate fellowships, albeit at a modest clip. In a typical year, Orange graduates accept at least one Fulbright, Beinecke, SMART, Luce, Mitchell, and Astronaut Scholarship; ten students took home Fulbrights in 2023.

Outside the Classroom

Frigid temperatures and snowy conditions make for long, boring winters in Upstate New York. Thus, like many other institutions in the region, Syracuse receives the designation as a top (if not the top) "party school" on a fair number of lists. The 47 fraternities and sororities are at the heart of the lively social scene. Roughly one-third join a Greek organization. SU offers a big-time sports program with a rabid following. Many join the sea of orange in the Carrier Dome for football and basketball games; in total, there are seven men's and eleven women's NCAA Division I teams. Non-sports activities come in the form of 300+ student-run clubs, including a wide selection of performing arts troupes (there are seven a cappella organizations), pre-professional meet-ups, or The Daily Orange newspaper, which is one of the more widely read campus dailies in the country and a frequent award-winner. On campus, Marshall Street is home to a number of beloved eateries and bars and is rarely quiet. Likewise, the Quad is always abuzz with activity, especially when the weather is decent. The city of Syracuse may not be the most cosmopolitan locale, but it does feature Destiny USA, the nation's sixth-largest shopping & entertainment complex, and it's only a short ride from campus.

Career Services

For a school of over 15,000 undergraduates, SU's Career Services Office employs a central staff of six career counseling professionals as well as smaller branch offices housed within the various colleges. Collectively, there are 32 full-time staff members working in career services, which equates to a 469:1 student-to-advisor ratio—average among schools featured in this guidebook.

Flagship events include a Local Internship Fair, Fall Career Fair, and Spring Career Fair. Niche events are held year-round by the various colleges to cater to students in particular fields of study. Internship procurement varies greatly by school. The Whitman School of Management requires an internship for graduation, and three-quarters of them are paid positions. Many other undergrads must rely on the university's fervent alumni network comprised of about a quarter-million people worldwide to land a position. Within Newhouse, companies recruiting on campus include CBS News, Hearst Television, McCann, Instagram, and NBCUniversal. The school does not publish the total number of one-on-one counseling sessions held or the number of on-campus interviews facilitated by career services.

Professional Outcomes

Six months after exiting the Carrier Dome for the final time in 2022, 59% of Orangemen and women found employment (92% related to their career goals), 21% continued to graduate school, and 5% were seeking employment. The companies employing the most 'Cuse grads include major media/entertainment management companies like Conde Nast, Bloomberg, and Creative Artists Agency as well as big-name corporations like GE, KPMG, EY, Lockheed Martin, and Morgan Stanley. The average starting salary for 2022 grads was a solid $63k. Interestingly, due to the nature of the business for which it prepares its students, Newhouse grads earn a mean starting salary of only $53k. Over 60% of graduates tend to remain in the Northeast with the South coming in a distant second, attracting 7% of grads.

A fair number of those who head to graduate school remain in New York State. NYU, Hofstra, Fordham, and the University of Buffalo are among the most popular destinations to pursue an advanced degree. Elite universities such as Harvard, Johns Hopkins, Columbia, and the University of Chicago also make the list of most popular graduate schools attended. Examining the past several years of law school admissions data, it is fair to say that Syracuse does not send a high number of graduates to elite law schools. The university does not publish medical school acceptance data, but a review of recent acceptances indicates a strong relationship with nearby SUNY Upstate Medical School. In that time, the school also produced some acceptances into the nation's top medical institutions.

Admission

Most colleges with national name recognition on par with the 'Cuse have experienced an uptick in selectivity since the turn of the millennium. That Syracuse's numbers have held steady for a couple of decades makes it a refreshing oddity. In fact, last year, 52% of applicants were granted acceptance into the Class of 2026, a much friendlier number than the sub-50% rates of previous years. Standardized test scores do not have to be exceptional to gain acceptance into SU. The median SAT score for the Class of 2026 was 1340 and the median ACT score was 30. Last year's freshman class was comprised of 33% of students who finished in the top 10% of their high school class while 67% were in the top 25% and 8% failed to crack the top 50%. The average GPA for all 2022-23 freshmen was 3.75.

The Newhouse School of Public Communication is more selective than the university at large. The typical student admitted to Newhouse scored over 1300 on the SAT and earned a 3.8 GPA in high school. Whichever school you are applying to, early decision typically works in your favor, although the ED rate was actually lower than the regular decision rate last year. If you plan on applying ED, make sure you can afford it. While ED applicants get full consideration for financial aid, SU is on the expensive side, so having a chance to compare aid offers can be advantageous. Perfection is not expected by the SU Office of Admissions. It is a selective university that has room for those with B averages and/or non-eye-popping standardized test scores.

Worth Your Money?

With a list price of $85,214 (total direct cost), Syracuse University is not accessible to those on a budget without financial help. Those eligible for need-based grants receive an average award of $42k. Syracuse is worth spending up for if you have the opportunity to enter a top-flight program like Newhouse, and it's a solid choice if your parents are able to pay the full bill. Those on a budget who do not receive a generous aid package may find a better value elsewhere.

FINANCIAL
Institutional Type: Private
In-State Tuition: $63,061
Out-of-State Tuition: $63,061
Room & Board: $18,444
Books & Supplies: $1,690

Avg. Need-Based Grant: $41,818
Avg. % of Need Met: 97%

Avg. Merit-Based Award: $12,476
% Receiving (Freshmen w/o Need): 37%

Avg. Cumulative Debt: $39,319
% of Students Borrowing: 49%

CAREER
Who Recruits
1. SmartestEnergy
2. M&T Bank
3. Oppenheimer & Co.
4. City Year
5. General Electric

Notable Internships
1. Gensler
2. WeWork
3. Berkshire Hathaway

Top Employers
1. IBM
2. EY
3. Microsoft
4. JPMorgan Chase
5. Amazon

Where Alumni Work
1. New York City
2. Syracuse, NY
3. Boston
4. Washington, DC
5. Los Angeles

Earnings
College Scorecard (10-YR Post-Entry): $74,446
PayScale (Early Career): $63,000
PayScale (Mid-Career): $114,800
PayScale 20-Year ROI: $589,000

RANKINGS
Money: 4
U.S. News: 67, National Universities
Wall Street Journal/THE: 144
Washington Monthly: 51, National Universities

OVERGENERALIZATIONS
Students are:
Crazy about the Orange
More likely to rush a fraternity/sorority
Only a short drive from home (i.e., Most come from NY or nearby states)
Working hard and playing hard
More likely to join an intramural sport

COLLEGE OVERLAPS
Binghamton University (SUNY)
Fordham University
Pennsylvania State University - University Park
Rutgers University - New Brunswick
University of Connecticut

Temple University

Philadelphia, Pennsylvania | 215-204-7200

Back in the 1880s, in its earliest iteration, Temple University offered only evening classes for aspiring ministers. Today, it has 100 undergraduate programs spread across eight campuses, including locations in Rome and Japan, the oldest dental school in the country, and excellent law and medical schools. (The university health system has eight affiliated hospitals.) Like Penn State and Pitt, Temple is a "state-related university," a hybrid public/private enterprise unique to the Keystone State. The 24,106 undergraduate Owls are part of a growing institution that is in a perpetual state of expansion in North Philadelphia and has undergone dozens of major campus-altering renovations and new building projects in the last few years alone.

Inside the Classroom
The university's general education curriculum includes 11 courses and nine areas of learning that are divided into foundation and breadth courses. Intellectual Heritage I & II take students through ancient and modern philosophical texts that have shaped human thinking. Courses in world society, arts, human behavior, race and diversity, US society, science and technology, analytical reading and writing, and quantitative literacy round out the mandated coursework at Temple.

For a large university, a 12:1 student-to-faculty ratio translates to very reasonable class sizes and very few large lecture halls. Forty-two percent of classes have an enrollment of 19 or fewer students, and 71% of courses contain no more than 29 undergraduates. Undergraduate research positions are available across all 12 undergraduate schools and colleges, including a seven-month-long funded research experience called the Diamond Research Scholars program. Over 200 students present at the annual Symposium for Undergraduate Research and Creativity. The school offers plenty of study abroad opportunities, including its own programs in Spain, Japan, and Italy. A touch over 10% of undergrads take a semester in a foreign country.

The well-regarded Fox School of Business, housed in a state-of-the-art $80 million building, churns out the highest number of graduates, accounting for 22% of the total undergraduate degrees conferred. Communication/journalism and health professions are tied at 11%, followed by the visual and performing arts (8%), biology (7%), psychology (6%), and computer science (5%). Other programs that have strong national reputations include criminal justice, public health, and kinesiology. In recent years, Temple has had as many as 16 Fulbright winners. The school recently produced its first Rhodes Scholar in school history.

Outside the Classroom
Once a commuter school, Temple now plays host to 76% of freshmen but still just 19% of the overall undergraduate student body. Many students come from the city of Philadelphia or the surrounding suburbs, but 37% of domestic freshmen last year hailed from out of state, a school record. This diverse student body is not Greek-crazy as only 1% of men and women enter fraternities and sororities. On the athletic front, the Owls compete in 19 Division I sports that play in the American Athletic Conference. Home football games are played at Lincoln Financial Field, home of the Philadelphia Eagles. Less serious athletes can join one of the 31 active club sports teams that include fencing, equestrian, paintball, rugby, and ice hockey. More than 300 total student-run organizations make finding something in your niche area of interest quite probable. The school's location in economically disadvantaged North Philadelphia is not appealing to everyone, but the school generally creates a safe environment on campus. The annual number of incidents of robbery or burglary is on par with schools such as Cornell, BU, Duke, and Northwestern, none of which have widespread reputations as "dangerous" locales. Center City Philadelphia is just a few miles away for those seeking all of the culture, shopping, and dining the city has to offer.

Career Services
The Career Center has 12 full-time professional staff members, mainly with titles such as career coach, employer outreach specialist, and assistant director of internships and experiential education. There are an additional 14 employees in the Fox School of Business' Center for Student Professional Development, and additional staff members within the College of Engineering and other colleges bring the total number of career services professionals to 29, which equates to an 831:1 ratio, poorer than average when compared to other schools featured in this guide. Regardless, you can always get a same-day appointment for a resume/cover letter review, career path exploration, Handshake intro, or review of a LinkedIn profile. The Temple University Internship Program helps facilitate meaningful, paid, on-campus internships in an area of academic/career interest.

Department-specific career fairs attract many prominent local and national companies to Temple's campus. For example, the College of Science and Technology Spring Fair features companies like GSK, Comcast, NBCUniversal, Elsevier, and Eurofins Scientific. Philadelphia is home to 14 Fortune 500 companies, all of which recruit on campus. Companies that conduct on-campus interviews include Toll Brothers, AmerisourceBergen, Campbell's Soup, DuPont, Aramark, JPMorgan Chase, PwC, Cigna, and KPMG. In sum, Temple has many solid connections to big-time corporate employers and offers personalized career counseling to those who take the initiative to seek it out.

Professional Outcomes

Fifty-one percent of recent grads quickly secured employment and another 18% were enrolled in graduate school. Hundreds of Owl alumni can be found at big-time companies such as Merck, Comcast, Vanguard, GlaxoSmithKline, Johnson & Johnson, JPMorgan Chase, and Bristol Myers Squib. The highest percentage of grads reside in Philadelphia, with New York City; Washington, DC; and Los Angeles next in popularity. Within six months of graduating, 91% of Fox School of Business 2021 graduates are employed or have started their own businesses. The median salary for all graduates of that school was $57,000.

In 2023-24, there were 139 Temple undergraduates who applied to medical school—the university does not release a precise acceptance rate, but many do funnel into the university's own Lewis Katz School of Medicine. In the last three years, Temple graduates have been accepted into top law schools at Yale University, Harvard University, NYU, UPenn, the University of Chicago, and Northwestern University. In sum, Temple students pursuing advanced degrees do so at a wide range of institutions, from the most selective universities to nearby state schools.

Admission

At present, Temple still accepts more students than it rejects—the admit rate was 80% for the Class of 2026—but the academic standards continue to rise. The mid-50th percentile standardized test scores were 1130-1360 and 24-31. The university is test-optional, and the majority have been taking advantage. Twenty-seven percent of students submitted an SAT score last year; another 4% included the ACT. Students with a B+ average fare well in the admissions process. The mean high school GPA for 2022-23 freshmen was 3.42. In total, 38,666 first-year applications were received last year, an all-time high for Temple University.

While there are holistic elements to the admissions process at Temple, the most important factors are the rigor of your high school coursework and your GPA. Class rank, test scores, the essay, recommendations, extracurriculars, talent/ability/personal qualities, alumni relation, geographical residence, state residency, volunteer work, and paid work experience are all merely "considered" during the evaluation. Getting into Temple's excellent Honors Program requires another level of credentials. The average Honors student possessed a 3.9 unweighted GPA and a 1400+ on the SAT.

Worth Your Money?

As with its state-related compatriots, Temple is not an eye-popping bargain like you can find with public universities in states like California, New York, North Carolina, and Florida. However, Pennsylvania residents will find the $21k in tuition costs and $14k in room and board to be reasonable by the standards of today's marketplace. For out-of-state students, there are some situations where the $36k tuition price would be a solid value, particularly if pursuing a STEM or business degree.

FINANCIAL
Institutional Type: Public
In-State Tuition: $21,095
Out-of-State Tuition: $35,956
Room & Board: $13,612
Books & Supplies: $1,526

Avg. Need-Based Grant: $11,027
Avg. % of Need Met: 63%

Avg. Merit-Based Award: $7,169
% Receiving (Freshmen w/o Need): 16%

Avg. Cumulative Debt: $39,869
% of Students Borrowing: 74%

CAREER
Who Recruits
1. TJX Companies
2. Lockheed Martin
3. Comcast
4. Merck
5. Vanguard

Notable Internships
1. HelloFresh
2. Dow
3. JBT Corporation

Top Employers
1. Merck
2. Penn Medicine
3. Comcast
4. Vanguard
5. GSK

Where Alumni Work
1. Philadelphia
2. New York City
3. Washington, DC
4. Los Angeles
5. Allentown, PA

Earnings
College Scorecard (10-YR Post-Entry): $60,306
PayScale (Early Career): $57,300
PayScale (Mid-Career): $100,800
PayScale 20-Year ROI: $439,000

RANKINGS
Money: 4
U.S. News: 89, National Universities
Wall Street Journal/THE: 260
Washington Monthly: 180, National Universities

OVERGENERALIZATIONS
Students are:
Diverse
More likely to go home on weekends
Career-driven
Independent
Busy

COLLEGE OVERLAPS
Drexel University
Pennsylvania State University - University Park
Rutgers University - New Brunswick
University of Delaware
University of Pittsburgh - Pittsburgh Campus

College Station, Texas | 979-845-1060

ADMISSION
Admission Rate: 63%
Admission Rate - Men: 64%
Admission Rate - Women: 61%
EA Admission Rate: Not Reported
ED Admission Rate: Not Offered
ED Admits as % of Total Admits: Not Offered
Admission Rate (5-Year Trend): -8%
% of Admits Attending (Yield): 46%
Transfer Admission Rate: 52%

SAT Reading/Writing (Middle 50%): 570-680
SAT Math (Middle 50%): 580-710
ACT Composite (Middle 50%): 25-31

% Graduated in Top 10% of HS Class: 61%
% Graduated in Top 25% of HS Class: 88%
% Graduated in Top 50% of HS Class: 98%

Demonstrated Interest: Considered
Legacy Status: Not Considered
Racial/Ethnic Status: Not Considered
Admission Interview Offered: No

ENROLLMENT
Total Undergraduate Enrollment: 57,512
% Full-Time: 90%
% Male: 53%
% Female: 47%
% Out-of-State: 4%
% Fraternity: Not Reported
% Sorority: Not Reported
% On-Campus (All Undergraduate): 22%
Freshman Housing Required: No

% African-American: 2%
% Asian: 11%
% Hispanic: 25%
% White: 56%
% Other: 0%
% International: 1%
% Low-Income: 20%

ACADEMICS
Student-to-Faculty Ratio: 19 to 1
% of Classes Under 20: 24%
% of Classes 20-49: 49%
% of Classes 50 or More: 28%
% Full-Time Faculty: 87%
% Full-Time Faculty w/ Terminal Degree: 70%

Top Programs
Agriculture
Architecture
Business
Communication
Engineering
Kinesiology
Management Information Systems
Political Science

Retention Rate: 94%
4-Year Graduation Rate: 61%
6-Year Graduation Rate: 83%

Curricular Flexibility: Less Flexible
Academic Rating: ★★★

#CollegesWorthYourMoney

You've heard it a million times: "Everything's bigger in Texas." Perhaps the origin of that saying stems from the fact that the state is three times the size of the United Kingdom, or perhaps it was first uttered by a visitor to Texas A&M College Station's gargantuan 5,200-acre campus that is home to 57,512 undergraduates and another 16,502 graduate and professional degree- seekers, making it one of the largest higher education operations in the United States. With nineteen schools and colleges, 130+ undergraduate degree programs, and an emphasis on agriculture, engineering, and business, this public land-grant university educates an army of future professionals who carry their Aggie pride with them for life.

Inside the Classroom
The Texas Core Curriculum dictates a good amount of the coursework underclassmen must knock out, amounting to forty-two credit hours. Mandates include three classes in life and physical sciences, two classes in each of communication, mathematics, American history, government, and political science, and one class in each of language philosophy and culture, creative arts, and the social and behavioral sciences. Collectively, these courses are meant to promote six key skill areas: critical thinking, communication, empirical and quantitative, teamwork, personal responsibility, and social responsibility. Students in the University Honors College are typically required to complete a senior thesis within their departmental home.

Class sizes definitely trend large, not terribly shocking considering the 19:1 student-to-faculty ratio and a graduate school population larger than many entire universities. Only 24% of courses enroll fewer than 20 students at A&M, and 28% enroll more than 50 students. In order to forge personal connections with professors, the LAUNCH program encourages students to apply to participate in undergraduate research during the school year or the summer under the mentorship of a faculty member. Some majors—chemistry, for one— require all students to complete undergraduate research as part of their bachelor's program. A&M excels in facilitating study abroad experiences, sending over 5,000 students to 100+ countries in a typical year, the most of any public university in the United States.

As the name of the university implies, agriculture and engineering are at the core of what A&M does. Over 23,500 students are presently enrolled in the College of Engineering and 8,300 in the College of Agriculture and Life Sciences. Yet, the College of Arts & Science (19,200), the Mays Business School (6,500), and the College of Education and Human Development (4,700) are sizable presences on campus as well. The business, agriculture, and engineering programs all place well in national rankings and garner deep respect from major national corporations and graduate/professional schools. Considering its size, A&M does not produce a large number of prestigious postgraduate scholarship winners. In 2023, the school produced 17 National Science Foundation Graduate Research Fellows and regularly churns out Gilman Scholars and Critical Language Scholars.

Outside the Classroom
While the majority of freshmen live on campus, just about everyone else moves into off-campus housing by sophomore year. Housing is not guaranteed to freshmen and is awarded on a first-come, first-served basis. Fortunately, nice and affordable housing in the area is ample, and the school's database, AggieSearch, helps you locate available living spaces. There are 60+ Greek organizations on campus, which have around a 10% participation rate. Athletics are huge with 650 varsity athletes competing in twenty NCAA Division I sports, and the "Twelfth Man," the fan base, is extraordinarily passionate about its teams. For non-superstar athletes, there are thirty-four club sports squads, and over 12,000 students participate in intramural sports each year, making it one of the largest programs in the country. The Student Recreation Center contains 400,000 square feet of space for fun and fitness and boasts everything from an archery room to multiple pools. Texas A&M has 1,000 student organizations, making it impossible not to find your niche. An incredible 2,300 undergrads are involved in ROTC, and the Cadet Corps is the largest such group in the country. As the name implies, College Station is a happening college town, brimming with locally famous bars and eateries, particularly within the historic Northgate District. Situated in the so-called Texas Triangle in the central part of the state, major cities like Houston or Austin can be accessed easily by car for a weekend road trip.

Career Services
The Texas A&M Career Center was established in 1939, long before the term "career services" was even a concept at most schools. Including all college-specific career advisors, employer relations, and professional school advising staff members, there are 33 full-time professional staff members (not including office managers and admin assistants). That works out to a student-to-advisor ratio of 1,743:1, among the highest in this guidebook. Irrespective of that bloated ratio, the A&M career services staff does remarkable things for the second-largest undergraduate student body in the United States, and it publishes the numbers to prove it.

In a single school year (most recent data available), the A&M Career Center makes direct contact with 20,000 students while drawing 32,000 individuals to 150 outreach events and 40,000 to 700 workshops and other career services programs. It posts 59,000 jobs and 12,000 internship opportunities on its online database and, more importantly, it entices a stupefying 4,000 employers to actively recruit Aggie undergrads. In total, close to 60% of students had an internship, co-op, or study abroad experience while at College Station, and interns worked with 1,000 different companies. Operating on an almost unimaginable scope, Texas A&M's Career Center gets the job done.

Professional Outcomes

On graduation day, a solid 54% of soon-to-be degree-holders had already received at least one job offer, 22% were heading to graduate/professional school, and 24% were still searching for their next career step. Texas A&M supplies a number of major oil, tech, and consulting firms with a hard-to-fathom number of employees. More than 500 Aggies presently work at each of ExxonMobil, Halliburton, Chevron, EY, Amazon, Microsoft, Intel, Accenture, and PWC. More than 300 alumni work for Apple, Oracle, and Google. More than 50 engineering students from a single graduating class were hired by Lockheed Martin. Starting salaries were strong with the average College of Engineering graduate making $80,000, and the average College of Liberal Arts and College of Agriculture & Life Sciences graduate netting $51,000 and $54,000, respectively. The vast majority of graduates remain in Texas with Houston, Dallas, College Station, Austin, and San Antonio top in popularity. However, cities like San Fran, DC, New York, and Denver also have a notable Aggie representation.

Medical and dental school acceptance rates are far above the Texas state average. Aggies are admitted to medical school at a 41% clip (state average was 32%) and to dental school 49% of the time (state average was 39%). Among those applicants with a 3.6 or higher GPA and a 507+ MCAT score, 77% were accepted to medical school. Institutions where recent graduates gained acceptance included Columbia, Cornell, Wake Forest, Yale, Vanderbilt, and Northwestern. Given the engineering focus at A&M, it may surprise you that the school is the eighth-largest producer of law students in the entire country. One recent class collectively applied to 179 law schools and earned admission at 155 of them.

Admission

Texas A&M admitted a favorable 63% of those who applied for the 2022-23 freshman class. That group had a mid-50% SAT range of 1150-1390 and a 25-31 on the ACT. Texas A&M offers automatic admission to anyone in the top 10% of their high school class (public or private), and a hefty number of Class of 2026 members met that standard—61%. Overall, 88% finished at least in the top 25%. Seven years ago, the acceptance rate was a more favorable 70%, the average applicant had lower standardized test scores, and only 78% of students placed in the top quartile. Simply put, you'll need better academic credentials to get into A&M today than you would have in the recent past. This is especially so for engineering and business applicants who face the toughest admission odds and who will likely need to possess grades and standardized test scores at or above the 75th percentile.

The admissions office is looking primarily at class rank, standardized test scores, rigor of courses, GPA, extracurricular activities, and talent/ability. It also looks closely at geographical residence, which translates to 96% of the student body presently on the College Station campus hailing from the Lone Star State. With such a large applicant pool, there are no interviews offered. There is no early action or early decision offered either; the deadline is December 1 for every applicant.

Worth Your Money?

Tuition for in-state students is slightly over $12,000, and the total cost of attendance is $31k. Combine those extremely fair rates with favorable return on investment figures, and A&M is clearly one of the great values in higher education. A nonresident will pay nearly twice as much, but if you lack better in-state options close to home, a business or engineering degree from this institution will still pay for itself.

FINANCIAL
Institutional Type: Public
In-State Tuition: $12,413
Out-of-State Tuition: $40,607
Room & Board: $13,154
Books & Supplies: $900

Avg. Need-Based Grant: $12,189
Avg. % of Need Met: 73%

Avg. Merit-Based Award: $5,564
% Receiving (Freshmen w/o Need): 13%

Avg. Cumulative Debt: $24,633
% of Students Borrowing: 39%

CAREER
Who Recruits
1. Air Liquide
2. NBCUniversal
3. Ethos Group
4. Manhattan Associates
5. Nvidia

Notable Internships
1. Phillips 66
2. Novartis
3. CBRE

Top Employers
1. Haliburton
2. Deloitte
3. EY
4. Amazon
5. Intel

Where Alumni Work
1. Houston
2. Dallas
3. College Station, TX
4. Austin
5. San Antonio

Earnings
College Scorecard (10-YR Post-Entry): $70,877
PayScale (Early Career): $64,400
PayScale (Mid-Career): $125,100
PayScale 20-Year ROI: $736,000

RANKINGS
Money: 4.5
U.S. News: 47, National Universities
Wall Street Journal/THE: 38
Washington Monthly: 299, National Universities

OVERGENERALIZATIONS
Students are:
Politically conservative
Crazy about the Aggies
Religious
Working hard and playing hard
Involved/investsed in campus life

COLLEGE OVERLAPS
Purdue University
Texas Tech University
University of Texas at Dallas
University of Houston
The University of Texas at Austin

Texas Christian University

Fort Worth, Texas | 817-257-7490

ADMISSION
Admission Rate: 56%
Admission Rate - Men: 49%
Admission Rate - Women: 61%
EA Admission Rate: 65%
ED Admission Rate: 79%
ED Admits as % of Total Admits: 8%
Admission Rate (5-Year Trend): +15%
% of Admits Attending (Yield): 27%
Transfer Admission Rate: 82%

SAT Reading/Writing (Middle 50%): 580-680
SAT Math (Middle 50%): 560-680
ACT Composite (Middle 50%): 26-31

% Graduated in Top 10% of HS Class: 47%
% Graduated in Top 25% of HS Class: 77%
% Graduated in Top 50% of HS Class: 95%

Demonstrated Interest: Considered
Legacy Status: Considered
Racial/Ethnic Status: Considered
Admission Interview Offered: No

ENROLLMENT
Total Undergraduate Enrollment: 10,523
% Full-Time: 98%
% Male: 38%
% Female: 62%
% Out-of-State: 50%
% Fraternity: 43%
% Sorority: 57%
% On-Campus (All Undergraduate): 50%
Freshman Housing Required: Yes

% African-American: 4%
% Asian: 2%
% Hispanic: 17%
% White: 66%
% Other: 2%
% International: 5%
% Low-Income: 14%

ACADEMICS
Student-to-Faculty Ratio: 14 to 1
% of Classes Under 20: 39%
% of Classes 20-49: 56%
% of Classes 50 or More: 5%
% Full-Time Faculty: 58%
% Full-Time Faculty w/ Terminal Degree: 86%

Top Programs
Business
Communication Studies
Computer Information Technology
Criminal Justice
Design
Education
Nursing
Speech-Language Pathology

Retention Rate: 92%
4-Year Graduation Rate: 73%
6-Year Graduation Rate: 83%

Curricular Flexibility: Somewhat Flexible
Academic Rating: ★★★✓

#CollegesWorthYourMoney

When AddRan Male and Female College opened its doors to its first 13 matriculants in 1873, the mission of its founders—brothers Addison and Randolph Clark—could only have dreamt what their tiny institution would one day blossom into. Today, Texas Christian University is the largest religious university affiliated with the Christian church and is home to 10,500+ undergraduates and close to 1,750 graduate students. Offering 116 undergraduate majors, including several standout programs, TCU now draws more students from out-of-state or international destinations than residents of the Lone Star State.

Inside the Classroom
The core curriculum at Texas Christian is on the straightforward side, requiring students to move through the various disciplines to the tune of 39-63 credits worth of coursework. Nine credit hours are mandated in both the humanities and social sciences, six in the natural sciences, and three in the fine arts. Essential competencies also must be addressed through courses in mathematical reasoning, oral communication, written communication, and writing emphasis. The more distinctive requirements are those with the label "Heritage, Mission, Vision and Value" that address topics such as religious transitions, historical traditions, literary traditions, cultural and global awareness, and citizenship and social values.

With a 14:1 student-to-faculty ratio, classes at TCU are not all tiny, but the school manages to keep enrollment below 20 students in 39% of its class sections, and only 5% of courses seat more than 50. Of equal importance, 98% of faculty members teach undergraduate students, so you will have access to the best and brightest professors the school has to offer. For a school of close to 11,000 undergrads, TCU does an excellent job of making research apprenticeships available; 40% of biology students land such an opportunity. The study abroad program makes international study readily accessible, and two-fifths of undergrads enjoy a semester overseas.

The Neely School of Business is home to the most popular majors at TCU, which includes the highly-rated BBA in Entrepreneurship, and 27% of all degrees conferred in 2022 fell under the business umbrella. The engineering program is also well-regarded by employers, but a mere 2% of diplomas earned are in that discipline; another 4% are in computer science. Other commonly conferred degrees include communications/journalism (15%), health professions (11%), and the social sciences (9%). TCU alumni are no strangers to highly selective fellowship programs, having produced multiple Fulbright winners annually in recent years.

Outside the Classroom
This attractive 302-acre suburban campus houses 97% of freshmen in its eight first-year residence halls. Fifty percent of the total undergraduate population lives on campus, many in upperclassmen residence halls or school-owned apartments available only to juniors and seniors. Greek life is as prevalent at TCU as at any university in the country with 43% of men joining fraternities and 57% of women becoming members of a sorority. Only half of undergrads are Texas residents while the others hail from 50 states and 72 countries. TCU is a member of the Big 12 Conference, and it excels at the highest levels of competition. In fact, a few years ago, 11 of TCU's 21 teams were ranked in the top 25 nationally, and football games rarely see the stands of Amon G. Carter Stadium below its 45,000-seat capacity. For anyone seeking less serious sports or non-sports clubs, there are more than 275 organizations to choose from. TCU generally pops up on "happiest students" lists, which could be in part because of the weather. The average number of days of sunshine is 229 per year. (The US average is 205.) Fort Worth is a popular city for young people and is jam-packed with theaters, restaurants, museums, natural beauty, and one of the country's most beloved zoos. Those seeking additional big-city fun can get to Dallas in 35-40 minutes by car.

Career Services
The Center for Career and Professional Development (CCPD) at Texas Christian has ten consultants who specialize in providing career-oriented advice in disciplines such as the fine arts, nursing, science and engineering, and communication. With three additional professional staff members in the Neely School of Business, the CCPD sports a student-to-advisor ratio of 809:1, higher than the average school featured in Colleges Worth Your Money. Regardless, this office gets sparkling reviews across the board, in part because of structured activities and engagements designed to reach undergraduates during all four years of study, from the "Inquiry and Awareness" freshman phase to the "Job Search & Grad-School Planning" phase for seniors.

Thanks to the work of the CCPD, Horned Frogs shine in procuring meaningful internships with 80% obtaining at least one in their four years on campus. An eight-week course run by career services staff called "Make Your Major Work" boasts a 100% placement rate. Thanks to the school's strong reputation as well as its primo location in Fort Worth, career fairs draw hundreds of top employers to campus. The alumni base is an exceptionally passionate and active bunch that is always willing to help current undergrads. There are 135,000+ SMU alumni stationed all over the globe. Further, the CCPD offers a lifetime guarantee for career counseling services, meaning it will be as available to help you when you're 41 as it was when you were 21.

Professional Outcomes

Upon graduating from TCU, 48% of recent diploma-earners were employed, 18% had their graduate school placement lined up, and 30% were still in the throes of the job search. One year after receiving their degree, only 5% of graduates were still searching for employment. Recent alumni have been scooped up in the greatest volume by American Airlines, Deloitte, IBM, Lockheed Martin, and Medical City Hospitals. Other companies with a large TCU presence include Microsoft, CBRE, Goldman Sachs, and AT&T. Dallas, Houston, and Austin are the cities with the highest concentration of Horned Frogs, but Los Angeles, New York, and Denver each claim more than 1,000 alumni as well. Among the employed members of the Class of 2021 (most recent reported), the median starting salary was $58,900.

One-quarter of those who graduate enroll in an advanced degree program within a few years of finishing their bachelor's. The most commonly pursued areas of study were medicine/health (27%), business (21%), and psychology (13%). All ten of the most frequently attended graduate institutions are located in the state of Texas, including SMU, UT-Austin, and Texas Tech. Twelve percent of recent grads had entered law school, and 5% of advanced degree-seekers were in MD or DO programs. The university boasts an 80% medical school acceptance rate, almost twice the national average.

Admission

TCU accepted 9,087 of the 16,197 applicants for the Class of 2026, a 56% acceptance rate. The middle-50% ranges were 1140-1360 on the SAT and 26-31 on the ACT. Just over 17% of enrolled freshmen scored above a 1400 on the SAT and 33% scored below a 1200. In looking at academic performance, 47% placed in the top decile of their graduating class, 77% were in the top quartile, and 95% were in the top half. The applicant pool at TCU has grown substantially over the past two decades. Twenty years ago, the school received just over 6,000 applications and sported an acceptance rate of over 70%.

Only two factors are granted "very important" status at this university: the rigor of your high school coursework and your GPA. Six other factors are "important." Those are the essay, extracurricular activities, character/personal qualities, first-generation status, volunteer work, and paid work experience. In the school's own words, "TCU has always applied a holistic approach to application review, never relying on a single data point. As TCU professors know their students by name in the classroom, TCU applicants are considered for admission by more than a GPA or test score. We will continue to evaluate students contextually."

Worth Your Money?

The total list price for TCU in the 2023-24 school year was $72,820, but approximately 80% of incoming students receive some need-based and/or merit-based award. For the 2022-23 academic year, 41% of freshmen qualified for need-based aid that averaged $41k per student. Many who did not qualify for need-based assistance received a merit award averaging over $21,000. Considering the stellar business and engineering options on the menu, a student could pay $45k+ per year at TCU, take on some debt, and still make out well in early adulthood. However, this school is not a great financial bet for everyone. While the percentage of students borrowing money to pay tuition is fairly low, the average cumulative debt is almost $50k, far higher than the national average. For these folks, particularly native Texans, it may be preferable to take advantage of the stellar in-state public options.

FINANCIAL
Institutional Type: Private
In-State Tuition: $57,220
Out-of-State Tuition: $57,220
Room & Board: $14,800
Books & Supplies: $800

Avg. Need-Based Grant: $37,342
Avg. % of Need Met: 82%

Avg. Merit-Based Award: $20,523
% Receiving (Freshmen w/o Need): 40%

Avg. Cumulative Debt: $44,580
% of Students Borrowing: 33%

CAREER
Who Recruits
1. CBRE
2. Amazon Web Services
3. Dell
4. Microsoft
5. Deloitte

Notable Internships
1. CBS News
2. Lockheed Martin
3. EY

Top Employers
1. Lockheed Martin
2. Baylor Scott & White Health
3. Deloitte
4. BNSF Railway
5. Amazon

Where Alumni Work
1. Dallas/Fort Worth
2. Houston
3. Austin
4. New York City
5. Los Angeles

Earnings
College Scorecard (10-YR Post-Entry): $63,517
PayScale (Early Career): $60,100
PayScale (Mid-Career): $107,200
PayScale 20-Year ROI: $519,000

RANKINGS
Money: 3.5
U.S. News: 98, National Universities
Wall Street Journal/THE: 247
Washington Monthly: 352, National Universities

OVERGENERALIZATIONS
Students are:
Politically conservative
More likely to rush a fraternity/sorority
Crazy about the Horned Frogs
Friendly
Wealthy

COLLEGE OVERLAPS
Baylor University
Southern Methodist University
Texas A&M University - College Station
University of Southern California
The University of Texas at Austin

Trinity College (CT)

Hartford, Connecticut | 860-297-2180

ADMISSION
Admission Rate: 36%
Admission Rate - Men: 31%
Admission Rate - Women: 41%
EA Admission Rate: Not Offered
ED Admission Rate: 54%
ED Admits as % of Total Admits: 11%
Admission Rate (5-Year Trend): +2%
% of Admits Attending (Yield): 25%
Transfer Admission Rate: 39%

SAT Reading/Writing (Middle 50%): 660-720
SAT Math (Middle 50%): 640-750
ACT Composite (Middle 50%): 30-32

% Graduated in Top 10% of HS Class: 48%
% Graduated in Top 25% of HS Class: 74%
% Graduated in Top 50% of HS Class: 94%

Demonstrated Interest: Important
Legacy Status: Considered
Racial/Ethnic Status: Considered
Admission Interview Offered: Yes

ENROLLMENT
Total Undergraduate Enrollment: 2,167
% Full-Time: 99%
% Male: 49%
% Female: 51%
% Out-of-State: 81%
% Fraternity: 25%
% Sorority: 21%
% On-Campus (All Undergraduate): 82%
Freshman Housing Required: Yes

% African-American: 6%
% Asian: 4%
% Hispanic: 9%
% White: 61%
% Other: 2%
% International: 14%
% Low-Income: 16%

ACADEMICS
Student-to-Faculty Ratio: 8 to 1
% of Classes Under 20: 69%
% of Classes 20-49: 31%
% of Classes 50 or More: 0%
% Full-Time Faculty: 83%
% Full-Time Faculty w/ Terminal Degree: 93%

Top Programs
Anthropology
Economics
Engineering
History
International Studies
Public Policy and Law
Urban Studies

Retention Rate: 91%
4-Year Graduation Rate: 80%
6-Year Graduation Rate: 84%

Curricular Flexibility: Very Flexible
Academic Rating: ★★★★✦

#CollegesWorthYourMoney

Established as Washington College in 1823 before being renamed in 1845, Trinity College was founded as an Episcopalian alternative to Congregationalist Yale; it is the second-oldest college in the state of Connecticut. What began as a college of nine male students is today a 100-acre campus within the confines of downtown Hartford that features 2,167 full-time undergraduates, 41 majors, and more than 900 distinct courses. Famous alumni are a disparate lot who include conservative voices like George Will as well as the legendary absurdist playwright Edward Albee of *Who's Afraid of Virginia Woolf* fame.

Inside the Classroom
Freshmen learn the ropes of academic reading and writing in either a first-year seminar or via the invitation-only Gateway Program. An additional course bearing the "writing intensive" designation must be completed at some point during one's undergraduate program. All students are required to demonstrate competency as writers, quantitative thinkers, and in one foreign language. Lastly, all students must either complete a course with a global focus or participate in a study abroad program. Passing one course with a C- or better in each of the arts, humanities, natural sciences, numerical and symbolic reasoning, and the social sciences are the only other requirements in what amounts to a very open curriculum.

With a total graduate student population that doesn't even hit triple digits, the bulk of the resources are directed toward Bantam undergraduates. Thus, a student/faculty ratio of 8:1 translates to 69% of course sections boasting an enrollment of nineteen or fewer students, and the mean number of students in a class is seventeen. Working closely with faculty is a real possibility at this school where one hundred students conduct research each year alongside faculty through the Summer Research Program, and roughly two-thirds engage in some type of undergraduate research. Greater than 50% of Trinity students study abroad and have access to Trinity-exclusive programs in Shanghai and Cape Town as well as school-run programs in Paris, Barcelona, Rome, Vienna, and Trinidad.

Trinity College is well-regarded across the board with an economics department that feeds many leading investment banks and an engineering program that is among the best you will find at a small liberal arts school. Most degrees are conferred in the social sciences (36%), biology (11%), psychology (7%), and the visual and performing arts (5%). While only a small percentage of graduates pursue prestigious national fellowships, a few do typically take home Fulbrights and an occasional Watson Scholarship each year, but the school has only two Rhodes Scholars in its history.

Outside the Classroom
Last academic year, 82% of Trinity undergraduates resided on campus, and 100% of freshmen were housed in one of seven first-year exclusive dorms. Greek life is more popular among men (25% join a fraternity) than women (21% join a sorority). Competing in the New England Small College Athletic Conference within NCAA Division III, the Bantams field 30 varsity teams evenly split between men's and women's squads. Including club sports, 40% of the student body participates in intercollegiate athletics. Although sports and frats dominate the social scene, the Student Activities, Involvement, and Leadership Office (SAIL) oversees 140 student-run clubs and organizations. While the school touts the "real-world" aspect of being located in downtown Hartford, the city presently has one of the highest per-capita crime rates in the United States. Affluent students, of whom there are many at Trinity, often prefer road trips to Montreal, New York City, or Boston over their "home" city. However, the spirit of volunteerism is strong, and the Office of Community Service and Civic Engagement offers endless opportunities to work in areas such as hunger, housing, homelessness, and education.

Career Services
The Career & Life Design Center features 12 full-time staff members who specialize in areas such as strategic partnerships, prelaw advising, and pre-health career advising. That equates to a student-to-advisor ratio of 181:1, in the better-than-average range when compared to other liberal arts colleges featured in this guide. The college is one of a dozen schools in the country that uses Stanford University's Designing Your Life approach, which encourages undergraduates to shed rigid views and fears about career and, instead, use their passions, goals, and creative problem-solving skills to move toward a meaningful path. To pursue that aim, Trinity invites students to join one of six Career Communities designed for those who wish to take advantage of industry-specific career advice, internship opportunities, Career Treks, panel discussions, and Career Skills Labs.

Other perks include a Career Studio that students can stop by any time for help with tangible job search products like resumes, cover letters, or LinkedIn profiles. In addition, the Bantam Career Network functions like a private LinkedIn where current students can network with alumni in their fields of interest. During one recent fall semester, the CLDC made 1,395 connections with undergraduates, and over three-quarters utilized their Handshake accounts. Trinity has invested heavily in its career development in the last decade, and that financial commitment is starting to bear fruit. This forward-thinking center is innovating every year, and its efforts are reflected in career/graduate school outcomes, earning it top marks from our staff.

Professional Outcomes

Class of 2022 grads found a positive outcome at a 96% clip within six months of commencement. Those entering the world of employment landed jobs at desirable organizations like the New York City Ballet, NBC Universal, and Morgan Stanley, a company with a hefty share of alumni. A large Bantam presence also can be felt in the corporate offices of Citi, Merrill Lynch, Fidelity Investments, Google, IBM, and Goldman Sachs. Finance (43%), science/engineering (15%), and health and medicine (15%) were the most frequently entered fields in 2021. Starting and mid-career salaries tend to be on the higher side, ranking in the top ten among highly selective private colleges alongside many engineering-heavy schools. While a fair number of graduates remain in the Hartford area, New York City and Boston occupy the one and two slots for highest alumni concentrations.

Many Trinity grads go on to prestigious graduate schools, and 60% of alumni have entered or completed a graduate or professional program within five years. Recent graduates have matriculated into the likes of Yale Medical School, Cambridge University, and Columbia University. Medical or other health-related program applicants are successful 80% of the time and are presently enrolled at institutions such as Georgetown, Tufts, Penn, Cornell, and Boston University. Graduates eying law school earn an average LSAT of 160 (80th percentile) and enroll at a vast array of universities including top fourteen law schools like Duke, Cornell, Columbia, Stanford, and Northwestern.

Admission

The Class of 2026 saw 36% of applicants admitted, an acceptance rate quite comparable to that of the previous few cycles. In Trinity's seventh year as a test-optional school, the majority of those who ultimately enrolled took advantage of the policy, not submitting an SAT or ACT score. The median scores of those who did submit standardized test results were 1380 on the SAT and 31 on the ACT. Transcripts have to be strong but not immaculate as 48% of attendees placed in the top decile of their high school class while 74% were in the top quartile.

Rigor of secondary school record, GPA, and character/personal qualities constitute the triumvirate of most important factors. The committee genuinely values intangible qualities that research has shown lead to postsecondary success such as "grit, optimism, persistence, a willingness to take risks, and an ability to overcome adversity." A supplemental essay explaining why applicants wish to attend college in an urban setting also is recommended. The college fills almost half its freshman class via two early decision rounds. The 2025 ED cohort enjoyed a 51% acceptance rate—the school has not released its ED figures for last year's class. Trinity is a more desirable destination than ever. In 2022-23, only 25% of accepted students elected to attend, but that number has been higher in recent years. Applying ED or ED II is undoubtedly a wise strategic move.

Worth Your Money?

At $85,410 in annual costs, Trinity won't come cheap. It does not offer much in the way of merit aid, instead focusing its efforts on meeting all of the demonstrated need of students eligible for financial aid. In fact, the 60% of current undergraduates who are need-eligible receive annual grants of over $55k per year, bringing Trinity's tuition much more within reach. As a school that helps you develop professional networks and connects you to big-time employers, Trinity can be worth taking on a reasonable amount of debt in order to attend.

FINANCIAL
Institutional Type: Private
In-State Tuition: $67,420
Out-of-State Tuition: $67,420
Room & Board: $17,990
Books & Supplies: $1,000

Avg. Need-Based Grant: $55,232
Avg. % of Need Met: 100%

Avg. Merit-Based Award: $61,070
% Receiving (Freshmen w/o Need): <1%

Avg. Cumulative Debt: $33,528
% of Students Borrowing: 41%

CAREER
Who Recruits
1. Salesforce
2. CBRE
3. UBS
4. Accenture
5. Fidelity Investments

Notable Internships
1. WeWork
2. Wayfair
3. Boston Public Health Commission

Top Employers
1. Morgan Stanley
2. Google
3. Citi
4. IBM
5. Merrill Lynch

Where Alumni Work
1. New York City
2. Boston
3. Hartford
4. Washington, DC
5. San Francisco

Earnings
College Scorecard (10-YR Post-Entry): $76,456
PayScale (Early Career): $64,200
PayScale (Mid-Career): $123,200
PayScale 20-Year ROI: $694,000

RANKINGS
Money: 4.5
U.S. News: 39, Liberal Arts Colleges
Wall Street Journal/THE: 191
Washington Monthly: 40, Liberal Arts Colleges

OVERGENERALIZATIONS
Students are:
Working hard and playing hard
Wealthy
Preppy
Less likely to interact with different types of students
Always admiring the beauty of their campus

COLLEGE OVERLAPS
Boston College
Colby College
Lafayette College
Tufts University
Union College

Trinity University

San Antonio, Texas | 210-999-7207

ADMISSION

Admission Rate: 31%
Admission Rate - Men: 31%
Admission Rate - Women: 30%
EA Admission Rate: 67%
ED Admission Rate: 57%
ED Admits as % of Total Admits: 3%
Admission Rate (5-Year Trend): -7%
% of Admits Attending (Yield): 19%
Transfer Admission Rate: 35%

SAT Reading/Writing (Middle 50%): 660-730
SAT Math (Middle 50%): 650-740
ACT Composite (Middle 50%): 29-33

% Graduated in Top 10% of HS Class: 54%
% Graduated in Top 25% of HS Class: 83%
% Graduated in Top 50% of HS Class: 98%

Demonstrated Interest: Considered
Legacy Status: Considered
Racial/Ethnic Status: Not Considered
Admission Interview Offered: Yes

ENROLLMENT

Total Undergraduate Enrollment: 2,512
% Full-Time: 99%
% Male: 47%
% Female: 53%
% Out-of-State: 20%
% Fraternity: 17%
% Sorority: 27%
% On-Campus (All Undergraduate): 77%
Freshman Housing Required: Yes

% African-American: 4%
% Asian: 8%
% Hispanic: 24%
% White: 54%
% Other: 1%
% International: 5%
% Low-Income: 17%

ACADEMICS

Student-to-Faculty Ratio: 9 to 1
% of Classes Under 20: 68%
% of Classes 20-49: 32%
% of Classes 50 or More: 0%
% Full-Time Faculty: 77%
% Full-Time Faculty w/ Terminal Degree: 97%

Top Programs
Accounting
Biology
Engineering Science
English
History
Mathematical Finance
Neuroscience

Retention Rate: 91%
4-Year Graduation Rate: 67%
6-Year Graduation Rate: 78%

Curricular Flexibility: Less Flexible
Academic Rating: ★★★★

#CollegesWorthYourMoney

It is rare to see a jump in selectivity on the scale of San Antonio's top school, Trinity University, which has sliced its acceptance rate in half in only a few years. The school's meteoric rise has occurred contemporaneously with its 150th anniversary, and while the school continues to be majority Texan—three-quarters of enrollees are residents—applications from out-of-staters have risen in recent years. An increasingly gifted undergraduate student body of 2,512 enjoys the choice of 57 majors and a carefully crafted liberal arts core curriculum that is more demanding than the norm.

Inside the Classroom

The distinct Pathways Program guides the educational journey at Trinity and is defined by six curricular requirements that involve an overwhelming number of manufactured terminologies. First-year experience courses, capped at sixteen students, introduce freshmen to the rigors of university-level reading and writing. In order to fulfill the Approaches to Creation and Analysis pathway, students must complete one course in the humanities, the arts and creative disciplines, social and behavioral sciences, natural sciences, and quantitative disciplines. Undergrads must also check off each of the Core Capacities: (1) written, oral, and visual communication; (2) digital literacy; and (3) engaged citizenship. All must also tackle "the Interdisciplinary Clusters," three-course groupings with themes such as ecological civilization in Asia or constructing and deconstructing language. One physical education course and one academic major round out the complex labyrinth of mandated coursework at Trinity U.

Undergraduates are the primary beneficiaries of a 9:1 student-to-faculty ratio as the university only enrolls 180 graduate students. You won't encounter any adjuncts or teaching assistants at Trinity, and 97% of the 265 full-time faculty members hold terminal degrees in their fields. Sixty-eight percent of courses enroll fewer than 20 students and less than 1% contain more than 50. Over the summer, close to 140 students participate in intensive undergraduate research projects with faculty members. Overall, 80% of students engage in some type of hands-on learning, whether through research or an internship. Study abroad programs are taken advantage of by 35% of graduates, most of whom participate in affiliated (but not Trinity-run) offerings.

Trinity's well-regarded School of Business attracts the greatest percentage of students as finance, accounting, and business administration degrees account for 27% of the total degrees conferred. The social sciences (16%), biology (12%), foreign language (6%), and communication (5%) also have strong representation. The university's reputation within the state of Texas is strong, and many graduates further their education or begin their careers locally, but the national prestige of the school is growing by the year. That can be seen in the procurement of highly competitive national fellowships—the university has produced multiple Goldwater Scholars and Fulbright Scholars in recent years.

Outside the Classroom

With undergraduates required to live on campus for their first three years and three-quarters of all undergraduates residing on the 117-acre grounds, the formation of a tight-knit college community is almost unavoidable. Greek life is also alive and well with roughly 25% participation in a normal year; there are 17 total Greek organizations on campus. Nine men's and nine women's athletic teams compete at the Division III level, and they do so with intensity; they've captured four championships in recent years. The intramural programs scoop up pretty much everyone not playing a varsity sport with roughly three-fifths of the student body participating in intramural athletics. There are also 115 student-run organizations, including groups devoted to animal welfare, fantasy sports and analytics, and indigenous peoples. The spirit of service is strong as 1,600 students contribute 120,000+ volunteer hours annually. Trinity's campus is only three miles from downtown San Antonio, opening possibilities for all sorts of big-city fun, but having a car is useful. Austin is a popular weekend getaway that is roughly an hour-and-a-half drive from the university.

Career Services

The newly-created Center for Experiential Learning and Career Success (CELCS) is staffed by nine full-time employees (not including administrative assistants) who specialize in areas such as career counseling, experiential learning coordination, and employer relations. That equates to a student-to-advisor ratio of 279:1, in the above-average range when compared to other schools in this guidebook. Fall and spring career fairs are attended by 50+ employers each academic year, including top companies like KPMG, Booz Allen Hamilton, Valero Energy, and EY. It also regularly hosts smaller-scale events such as Lunch 'n Learns, employer information sessions, and workshops on topics such as networking, interviewing, and professional dining etiquette.

The school switched to the Handshake platform five years ago and presently has opportunities from 3,600 employers posted in its database. In a single recent school year, 65% of Trinity students participated in at least one internship during their undergraduate education. Close to 200 on-campus interviews are conducted by employers each year. There are 30,000 actively engaged Tiger alumni, and they are more than happy to provide career advice, arrange a job-shadowing experience, or offer mentorship to current students. The office also facilitates a solid number of one-on-one counseling sessions; it holds 1,000+ such appointments in a single year. The nascent CELCS is on the rise and is quickly becoming the type of career services center that the university leadership outlined in its most recent strategic plan.

Professional Outcomes

Six months after receiving their diplomas, 98% of 2022 Trinity grads were either employed full-time or matriculated into graduate school; only 2% were still seeking employment. The companies employing the largest number of alumni include USAA (a San Antonio-based financial firm), PwC, EY, Deloitte, Dell, Accenture, Morgan Stanley, and Amazon. Most Trinity grads stay in the Lone Star State with San Antonio, Houston, Dallas, and Austin being the four most common landing spots. Median salaries at mid-career are solid, ranking third in the state behind Rice and Texas A&M and just in front of UT Austin.

Recent bachelor's degree earners have been accepted into graduate school at an overall rate of 75%. Over the last five years, acceptance rates into medical school have consistently been above national averages, hovering between 55% and 75%, with the exception of one year when just 36% gained acceptance. Graduates have gone on to Dell Medical School (University of Texas), Harvard Medical School, and Tufts Medical School, among other less prestigious institutions. Law school rates have been within the 75-90% range in recent years. Among the most popular law schools attended by recent graduates are the University of Texas, Texas Tech, St. Mary's School of Law, and SMU.

Admission

Less than a decade ago, Trinity University received barely north of 4,500 applicants and admitted an unintimidating 64%; freshmen entering in 2022-23 faced an applicant pool of double that size and an acceptance rate of only 31% (the rate three years prior was 29%). Today, the mid-50% SAT score is 1310-1470 and the mid-50% ACT score is 29-33. A solid 54% of entering freshmen earned a place in the top 10% of their graduating classes and 83% were in the top quartile; the average GPA was a 3.8 on a 4.0 scale. The average profile of a student beginning at Trinity only a few years ago was significantly less impressive.

Trinity may be a small school that gives each application a "thorough review," yet the meat-and-potatoes factors of GPA, class rank, and engagement in a rigorous curriculum rest atop the list of most important considerations. The next tier of factors includes an interview, essays, recommendations, extracurricular activities, talent/ability, and character/personal qualities. There would have been little reason to apply early to this university in years past, but a sharp spike in competitiveness has put this strategic option firmly in play. In 2022-23, Trinity accepted 118 of 206 early applicants for a hyper-friendly 57% acceptance rate. Strong test scores and a B+/A- average are now prerequisites for admission to Trinity, a statement that would have been hard to believe a decade ago. If you're a borderline applicant, going the ED route makes a ton of sense.

Worth Your Money?

Amazingly, given the current landscape, a list price cost of attendance of $68,224 isn't incredibly high for a private university. Yet, the truly good news is that this sticker price is rarely what undergraduates pay. Trinity awards a merit aid discount to more than half of current students with awards ranging from $12k-$30k. Further, for students meeting the criteria for need-based grant eligibility, the average annual award is $40k. With most students receiving sizable discounts, Trinity becomes a solid value, especially when you consider that its grads bring home above-average salaries at each stage of their careers. Fifty-two percent graduate with no debt. At the same time, it should be noted that Trinity grads incur a level of debt above the national average.

FINANCIAL
Institutional Type: Private
In-State Tuition: $51,352
Out-of-State Tuition: $51,352
Room & Board: $14,472
Books & Supplies: $1,000

Avg. Need-Based Grant: $39,776
Avg. % of Need Met: 96%

Avg. Merit-Based Award: $24,974
% Receiving (Freshmen w/o Need): 53%

Avg. Cumulative Debt: $39,138
% of Students Borrowing: 48%

CAREER
Who Recruits
1. USAA
2. AXA Advisors
3. Dell
4. Capgemini
5. KPMG

Notable Internships
1. San Antonio Spurs
2. US State Department
3. Apple

Top Employers
1. USAA
2. Deloitte
3. PwC
4. EY
5. H-E-B

Where Alumni Work
1. San Antonio
2. Houston
3. Dallas
4. Austin
5. Washington, DC

Earnings
College Scorecard (10-YR Post-Entry): $67,418
PayScale (Early Career): $57,800
PayScale (Mid-Career): $112,900
PayScale 20-Year ROI: $557,000

RANKINGS
Money: 4.5
U.S. News: 59, Liberal Arts Colleges
Wall Street Journal/THE: Not Ranked
Washington Monthly: 115, Liberal Arts Colleges

OVERGENERALIZATIONS
Students are:
Driven
Always studying
Tight-knit (possess a strong sense of community
Involved/invested in campus life
Only a short drive from home (i.e., Most come from TX or nearby states)

COLLEGE OVERLAPS
Baylor University
Southern Methodist University
Texas A&M University - College Station
Texas Christian University
The University of Texas at Austin

Tufts University

Medford, Massachusetts | 617-627-3170

ADMISSION
Admission Rate: 10%
Admission Rate - Men: 10%
Admission Rate - Women: 9%
EA Admission Rate: Not Offered
ED Admission Rate: Not Reported
ED Admits as % of Total Admits: Not Reported
Admission Rate (5-Year Trend): -5%
% of Admits Attending (Yield): 50%
Transfer Admission Rate: 10%

SAT Reading/Writing (Middle 50%): 710-760
SAT Math (Middle 50%): 740-790
ACT Composite (Middle 50%): 33-35

% Graduated in Top 10% of HS Class: 87%
% Graduated in Top 25% of HS Class: 97%
% Graduated in Top 50% of HS Class: 99%

Demonstrated Interest: Considered
Legacy Status: Considered
Racial/Ethnic Status: Considered
Admission Interview Offered: Yes

ENROLLMENT
Total Undergraduate Enrollment: 6,815
% Full-Time: 98%
% Male: 44%
% Female: 56%
% Out-of-State: 71%
% Fraternity: 8%
% Sorority: 9%
% On-Campus (All Undergraduate): 61%
Freshman Housing Required: Yes

% African-American: 6%
% Asian: 16%
% Hispanic: 10%
% White: 45%
% Other: 4%
% International: 13%
% Low-Income: 12%

ACADEMICS
Student-to-Faculty Ratio: 10 to 1
% of Classes Under 20: 60%
% of Classes 20-49: 31%
% of Classes 50 or More: 9%
% Full-Time Faculty: 60%
% Full-Time Faculty w/ Terminal Degree: 95%

Top Programs
Art
Biochemistry
Data Science
Economics
Engineering
English
International Relations
Science, Technology and Society

Retention Rate: 95%
4-Year Graduation Rate: 90%
6-Year Graduation Rate: 94%

Curricular Flexibility: Somewhat Flexible
Academic Rating: ★★★★⯪

#CollegesWorthYourMoney

With 6,815 undergraduates—quite small for being one of the nation's top research universities—Tufts excels in delivering a highly personalized educational experience that is on par with its upper-echelon liberal arts rivals Williams and Amherst. In fact, like Amherst and Brown University, the school is notable for having no core curriculum. Instead, students are "encouraged to immerse themselves in the full expanse of course offerings, deepening existing interests while discovering new areas of study."

Inside the Classroom

Three schools serve Tufts' undergraduate population: the College of Arts & Sciences, the College of Engineering, and the School of the Museum of Fine Arts. The three schools combined offer more than 90 majors and minors; approximately one-third of all students double major, and half declare a minor. The school encourages freshmen and sophomores to "Go broad, then deep." Students who do not want to be tethered to a laundry list of required introductory courses will relish the freedom Tufts affords its undergrads.

The university prides itself on its undergraduate teaching, and it shows; 84% of recent grads reported feeling satisfied with their educational journey. Nearly every professor is willing to take on research assistants, and plenty of funding is available. In the College of Engineering, 60% of students have a chance to participate in a research project at some point during their collegiate experience. Classes are small, especially when considering the school's legitimate research university status. Fifteen percent of all courses see fewer than ten students enrolled, and 60% have sub-twenty enrollments. The student-to-faculty ratio is 10:1. A substantial segment of the student body, 40-45%, study abroad at one of eighty preapproved programs in locales such as Chile, Ghana, Hong Kong, and Madrid.

Well-regarded by industry and elite graduate/professional schools, a diploma in any discipline from Tufts will get you where you want to go. The most popular majors include international relations, economics, computer science, political science, and biology—all of which receive very high marks. The university does a fantastic job helping students land nationally competitive scholarships. Tufts is a leading producer of Fulbright Scholars, hitting double digits most years, and it also has seen its fair share of Goldwater, Udall, Truman, and Astronaut Scholarships in recent memory.

Outside the Classroom

Unlike some of Tufts' graduate programs, the undergraduate schools are not located in downtown Boston. However, Medford is part of the Boston metro area and is only five miles from the city limits, which makes its location far less remote than many of its rival New England colleges. Only 61% of students live on campus in one of 40 residential options ranging from traditional dorms to shared apartments. Many upperclassmen move off campus or live in fraternity or sorority houses. Close to one-quarter of the student population has traditionally gone Greek. Yet, some recent well-publicized hazing incidents led to the dissolution or suspension of many chapters that altered, at least for the time being, the influence of Greek-letter organizations on campus. Presently, only 8% of men and 9% of women are Greek-affiliated. Few Tufts students are lone wolves as a staggering 94% join at least one of the school's 300+ recognized student organizations. Opportunities for community service are plentiful. Many students are involved in athletics, whether as a member of one of the twenty-nine varsity sports teams competing in NCAA Division III, 22 club teams, or 28 intramural groups. Campus is attractive and full of perks, including the new 42,000-square-foot Tisch Sports & Fitness Center that features tennis courts, pools, squash courts, and dance studios. As a bonus, dining options are given rave reviews as every Tufts student has a favorite dish.

Career Services

With 21 full-time staff members who focus on undergraduate advising, career relations, and alumni outreach, the Tufts Career Center sports a 325:1 student-to-advisor ratio, which is within the average range of schools featured in this guide. The career services staff has done an incredible job improving its outreach over the past two decades. In 1998, only 32% of graduates were satisfied with the university's career services, but 20 years later, a healthy 83% expressed positive feelings, and annual interactions with students have risen to over 7,600.

Tufts does an exceptional job of assisting undergraduates with internship procurement. A robust 62% of 2022 Tufts graduates completed two or more internships during their time at the university; 85% completed at least one. The Fall Career Fair is attended by 185+ companies, and on-campus recruiting/interviews take place throughout the academic year. Career Treks and networking events in cities like New York and San Francisco are also regular occurrences. A recent switch from the antiquated Jumbo Jobs platform to Handshake was lauded by students. As an added long-term support, alumni have lifetime access to the spectrum of career services, including one-on-one job counseling. With a solid track record in internship participation, job placement, and graduate school outcomes, Tufts career services does an exceptional job setting its undergraduates up for the next level of success.

Professional Outcomes

Six months after earning their diplomas, 97% of 2022 Tufts graduates were employed, attending graduate school, or otherwise productively engaged. The most commonly entered fields were finance, consulting, real estate (23%); engineering and technology (22%); health, life sciences, environmental (21%); and education, advocacy, social services (11%). All of the leading finance, consulting, and technology companies sit atop the list of the most prolific employers of Tufts alums including Booz Allen Hamilton, JPMorgan, MITRE, Google, Deloitte, Amazon, Raytheon, Morgan Stanley, and BlackRock. Most Tufts alumni remain in the Boston area, but many also head to New York City, San Francisco, Seattle, DC, and Chicago.

Of the 21% of the Class of 2022 who went directly to graduate school, 85% were accepted into their first-choice institution. Included among the ten universities enrolling the highest number of Tufts alumni were MIT, Georgetown, Penn, Stanford, and Columbia. Law school applicants routinely gain acceptance into top-tier institutions. In recent years, alumni have been admitted into Harvard, Northwestern, University of Michigan, Penn, Duke, Brown, and Yale. Medical school applicants gained acceptance at a 75-90% rate, depending on the year. Those with at least a 3.5 undergraduate GPA find a med school home over 90% of the time.

Admission

The university's acceptance rate seems to have settled in the 14-16% range in recent years, but dipped to 10% for the Class of 2026 upon receiving an all-time record 34,881 applications. The vast majority of those applicants were for admittance into the School of Arts & Sciences followed by the School of Engineering, with the smallest number applying to the fine arts programs. Overall, the mid-50% SAT scores were 1460-1540 and the ACT range was 33-35. Ninety-eight percent of those enrolled possessed an ACT score of 30 or above. Last year, 87% of the freshman class finished in the top 10% of their high school class, and 97% were in the top quartile.

Tufts is looking for students who achieved top grades in AP classes, scored well on standardized tests, finished in the top 10% of their class, come highly recommended by their high school teachers, and are capable of composing a killer essay. Like many schools in its weight class, Tufts loves to scoop up a large portion of its freshman class in the early round (although they are secretive in this regard with 2022 info)—its ED acceptance rate is historically close to four times that of the regular round—and those accepted early comprise the majority of the incoming cohort. Even though it is no longer relegated to Ivy League safety status, Tufts is still understandably eager to lock down as many top candidates as possible via ED. Like all Ivy and Ivy-equivalent schools, Tufts is looking for the best and the brightest and is competing with even bigger names to haul in the best candidates. Therefore, demonstrating commitment through ED can pay dividends for qualified applicants.

Worth Your Money?

Boston is the East Coast's third-most expensive city, so perhaps it is no surprise that Tufts is on the pricey side. At $86,000 per year in cost of attendance, it is among the most expensive schools in the country. Only 36% of current undergrads qualify for need-based aid, and the average annual grant is just over $54k. Of course, many in attendance don't have to worry too much about the cost because, based on historical data, a high percentage of undergrads hail from wealthy families. It's no wonder that, despite the high costs, graduates carry a mean amount of debt slightly lower than average (compared to all college grads). Even if you have to make an economic sacrifice to attend, Tufts is a school that will expose you to many personal and professional networks that will come in handy as you enter the world of graduate school or employment.

FINANCIAL
Institutional Type: Private
In-State Tuition: $67,844
Out-of-State Tuition: $67,844
Room & Board: $17,660
Books & Supplies: $1,000

Avg. Need-Based Grant: $54,264
Avg. % of Need Met: 100%

Avg. Merit-Based Award: $1,299
% Receiving (Freshmen w/o Need): 2%

Avg. Cumulative Debt: $24,468
% of Students Borrowing: 25%

CAREER
Who Recruits
1. Gelber Group
2. Cogo Labs
3. Amazon Robotics
4. Putnam Investments
5. Oppenheimer & Co.

Notable Internships
1. Deutsche Bank
2. UBS
3. Wayfair

Top Employers
1. Google
2. Amazon
3. Microsoft
4. Deloitte
5. Facebook

Where Alumni Work
1. Boston
2. New York City
3. San Francisco
4. Washington, DC
5. Los Angeles

Earnings
College Scorecard (10-YR Post-Entry): $74,430
PayScale (Early Career): $70,700
PayScale (Mid-Career): $132,000
PayScale 20-Year ROI: $767,000

RANKINGS
Money: 4.5
U.S. News: 40, National Universities
Wall Street Journal/THE: 287
Washington Monthly: 99, National Universities

OVERGENERALIZATIONS
Students are:
Politically liberal
Wealthy
Quirky
Globally-minded
Involved/investsed in campus life

COLLEGE OVERLAPS
Brown University
Boston University
Georgetown University
New York University
Washington University

Tulane University

New Orleans, Louisiana | 504-865-5731

ADMISSION
Admission Rate: 11%
Admission Rate - Men: 10%
Admission Rate - Women: 12%
EA Admission Rate: 12%
ED Admission Rate: 68%
ED Admits as % of Total Admits: 35%
Admission Rate (5-Year Trend): -10%
% of Admits Attending (Yield): 51%
Transfer Admission Rate: 50%

SAT Reading/Writing (Middle 50%): 680-750
SAT Math (Middle 50%): 690-760
ACT Composite (Middle 50%): 31-33

% Graduated in Top 10% of HS Class: 52%
% Graduated in Top 25% of HS Class: 80%
% Graduated in Top 50% of HS Class: 94%

Demonstrated Interest: Important
Legacy Status: Considered
Racial/Ethnic Status: Considered
Admission Interview Offered: No

ENROLLMENT
Total Undergraduate Enrollment: 7,350
% Full-Time: 100%
% Male: 39%
% Female: 61%
% Out-of-State: 90%
% Fraternity: 26%
% Sorority: 54%
% On-Campus (All Undergraduate): 54%
Freshman Housing Required: Yes

% African-American: 6%
% Asian: 6%
% Hispanic: 9%
% White: 68%
% Other: 1%
% International: 6%
% Low-Income: 9%

ACADEMICS
Student-to-Faculty Ratio: 8 to 1
% of Classes Under 20: 60%
% of Classes 20-49: 33%
% of Classes 50 or More: 7%
% Full-Time Faculty: 67%
% Full-Time Faculty w/ Terminal Degree: 91%

Top Programs
Architecture
Biology
Communication
Finance
Marketing
Neuroscience
Political Science/International Relations
Sociology

Retention Rate: 93%
4-Year Graduation Rate: 81%
6-Year Graduation Rate: 86%

Curricular Flexibility: Somewhat Flexible
Academic Rating: ★★★★✦

#CollegesWorthYourMoney

In competition with Vanderbilt and Emory for King of the Southern Ivies status, Tulane University takes the bronze; yet, that is hardly a knock on this private, midsized university in the heart of New Orleans. Home to 7,350 undergraduates, Tulane successfully combines the benefits of a renowned research university with the friendly classroom atmosphere of a liberal arts college. In the wake of Hurricane Katrina, the school dedicated itself to community service, an attribute that is now deeply woven into the fabric of the university.

Inside the Classroom
Tulane offers 75 majors within five colleges, but all students, regardless of major, call Newcomb-Tulane College their home base. The school's core curriculum, which consists of thirty credits worth of courses, was redesigned a few years back to "develop information literacy, critical thinking, and personal and social responsibility." As a result, coursework is required in the areas of writing skills, formal reasoning, foreign language, mathematics and natural sciences, social and behavioral sciences, textual and historical perspectives, aesthetics and the creative arts, and a first-year seminar called the Tulane Interdisciplinary Experience Seminar (TIDES). The TIDES courses center around engaging topics, many of which have to do with local New Orleans culture/history and involve one-on-one meetings with professors and a chance to connect with a student mentor.

Despite the presence of a significant number of graduate students, the university's enviable 8:1 student-to-faculty ratio can still be felt in the classroom. The average undergraduate class size is 21 students and a solid 21% of courses have single-digit enrollments, providing a seminar-style environment. The overwhelming majority of undergraduate courses, even introductory ones, are taught by full-time professors. Exiting student surveys indicate that this focus on undergraduate education is noted; 94% rated their educational experience at Tulane as either "excellent" or "good." Those aiming to engage in undergraduate research at Tulane can find it; over 200 students per year land such opportunities in the School of Science and Engineering alone. An expansive study abroad program offers more than 120 programs in 40 countries, which is taken advantage of by 600 students each year.

Business/marketing (22%), the social sciences (20%), psychology (9%), biology (8%), and health professions (8%) are the disciplines in which most degrees are conferred. The A.B. Freeman School of Business and programs in architecture, biology, and neuroscience enjoy strong national reputations. In its history, Tulane has produced eighteen Rhodes Scholars, one fewer than Emory. The university produced 15 Fulbright Scholars in 2023. Beinecke, Boren, Truman, and Marshall Scholarships also go to Green Wave alums with regularity.

Outside the Classroom
Just over half of the undergraduate population (54%) resides on the university's 110-acre uptown campus. Ample housing exists in the nearby community that is either within walking/biking distance of campus or accessible via the university bus system. Sororities draw in 54% of the female population and fraternities attract 26% of males. Tulane offers big-time athletics with 16 NCAA Division I teams competing in the American Athletic Conference. An additional twenty-nine club sports teams and thirteen intramural leagues ensure that athletic participation is open to all. Over 200 student-run clubs currently are active with volunteer opportunities being among the most popular. Tulane undergrads contribute over 780,000 hours of volunteer service annually. Campus boasts thirty libraries/research centers, fifteen eateries, and the 156,000-square-foot Reily Student Recreation Center. The urban campus is located within the New Orleans city limits, only four miles from the bustling French Quarter, which provides students with all the culinary and cultural delights one can handle. The fact that classes shut down during Mardi Gras tells you all you need to know about life at Tulane.

Career Services
The Newcomb-Tulane College Career Services office is staffed by eight professionals who specialize in areas such as career advising, senior year experience coordination, pre-health advising, and prelaw advising. An additional 12 career services staff members are housed within the Freeman School of Business. In total, there are 23 staff members serving undergraduates in this capacity which works out to a 320:1 student-to-counselor ratio. One of this group's greatest strengths is in organizing well-attended career and grad school fairs. The Mardi Gras Invitational Job Fair brings around 150 employers to campus, the Gumbo Gathering Job Fair attracts another 130, and 115+ schools are represented at the Graduate & Professional School Fair. Additionally, they facilitated 2,600 advising appointments in a single recent year.

A one-credit course entitled Majors, Internships, and Jobs teaches resume building, interview prep, and professional social media use. Many land internships through the UCAN Intern Consortium that Tulane belongs to alongside such schools as Harvard, Notre Dame, Swarthmore, and Washington University. A nationwide alumni network that is 167,000+ members strong is another great source that current undergrads can utilize to land internships or their first paid gig. Founded in 2006, post-Hurricane Katrina, The Center for Public Service ensures that all Tulane grads engage in structured volunteer work during their four years of study. At the heart of this program is a three-credit Public Internship Program that allows students to complete sixty to seventy hours with a nonprofit organization. Thanks to an emphasis on public service and large-scale networking events, the Tulane Career Center succeeds in preparing its students for the world of work and graduate school.

Professional Outcomes

Over three-fifths of Tulane grads find employment within six months of graduation. The most popular occupations were financial analyst, management analyst, marketing specialist, and postsecondary teacher. Significant numbers of Tulane alumni can be found working in the Louisiana-based Ochsner Health System or at corporations such as Shell, EY, Google, PwC, IBM, Morgan Stanley, Deloitte, and Accenture. Thus, it is little surprise that the school's alumni enjoy the highest salaries of any college graduates from a Louisiana-based institution. Geographically, the most popular postgraduate move is to remain in the Greater New Orleans area although New York City, DC, Houston, San Francisco, and Los Angeles attract large numbers of Green Wave alumni as well.

Thirty five percent of Tulane grads eventually enroll in graduate or professional school. The four most commonly attended graduate schools by recent grads are Tulane itself, Louisiana State University, Boston University, and Johns Hopkins University. Students applying to law and medical schools, including Tulane's own institutions, fare better than the national average. Tulane undergraduates gain acceptance to medical school 58% of the time, and that figure rises to 93% for those with at least a 3.6 GPA and a score of 509 or higher on the MCAT. Recent grads have attended Columbia, Duke, and Johns Hopkins as well as the uber-selective Tulane School of Medicine. Law school hopefuls gain acceptance at an impressive 93% rate including roughly seventy admits annually into Tulane's own solidly ranked law school.

Admission

Tulane received 31,615 applications for its Class of 2026 but accepted only 11%, part of a pattern of declining admissions rates in recent years; the Class of 2021 rate was 21%. The middle-50% ACT composite score range is 31-33 and the SAT range is 1400-1500. Fifty-two percent of 2022-23 freshmen had earned a place in the top decile of their high school class, and 80% were in the top quartile. Not everyone attending Tulane had perfect grades as 25% of attendees sported an unweighted high school GPA below 3.5; the average GPA was 3.66.

With a heavy volume of applications streaming in, the Tulane Admissions Office is forced to rely on concrete factors to winnow down the pool. As a result, four factors are ranked as being most important: rigor of coursework, class rank, GPA, and standardized test scores. Essays, recommendations, and character/personal qualities receive second billing. Early decision applicants to the Class of 2026 were accepted at a 68% clip, while early action applicants earned admission at a 12% rate. Unbelievably, Tulane's regular decision rate has been just 1% (not a typo) for three straight years; so, applying EA or ED is now a near-must. An institution whose heightened selectivity in recent years may go unnoticed by applicants relying on old data or the school's reputation a decade ago, Tulane has claimed its position in the realm of highly selective research universities. Successful applicants need standardized test scores above the 95th percentile to go with A's and B's in AP/honors coursework.

Worth Your Money?

Don't let the official cost of attendance of $86,000 make you think that Tulane is beyond your financial reach because a large percentage of students receive a discount in the form of merit or need-based aid that brings that sum down to a more reasonable level. In fact, on average, Tulane covers $42k in the form of grants to the average need-eligible student. If you don't receive a sizable aid offer, the wisest move would be to evaluate (a) your other financial aid offers and (b) the amount of debt you would be likely to incur at Tulane versus the expected starting salaries for jobs related to your intended major.

FINANCIAL
Institutional Type: Private
In-State Tuition: $65,538
Out-of-State Tuition: $65,538
Room & Board: $18,088
Books & Supplies: $1,200

Avg. Need-Based Grant: $42,292
Avg. % of Need Met: 92%

Avg. Merit-Based Award: $18,997
% Receiving (Freshmen w/o Need): 33%

Avg. Cumulative Debt: $29,234
% of Students Borrowing: 27%

CAREER
Who Recruits
1. Facebook
2. Medtronic
3. Tesla
4. Starbucks
5. Amazon

Notable Internships
1. AIG
2. U.S. Senate
3. HBO

Top Employers
1. Ochsner Health System
2. Shell
3. EY
4. PwC
5. Deloitte

Where Alumni Work
1. New Orleans
2. New York City
3. Washington, DC
4. Houston
5. San Francisco

Earnings
College Scorecard (10-YR Post-Entry): $59,812
PayScale (Early Career): $60,400
PayScale (Mid-Career): $115,900
PayScale 20-Year ROI: $570,000

RANKINGS
Money: 3.5
U.S. News: 73, National Universities
Wall Street Journal/THE: 354
Washington Monthly: 431, National Universities

OVERGENERALIZATIONS
Students are:
Working hard and playing hard
Service-oriented
Always admiring the beauty of their campus
More likely to rush a fraternity/sorority
Outgoing

COLLEGE OVERLAPS
Boston University
Duke University
Emory University
University of Michigan
Vanderbilt University

Schenectady, New York | 518-388-6112

ADMISSION
Admission Rate: 47%
Admission Rate - Men: 46%
Admission Rate - Women: 47%
EA Admission Rate: 60%
ED Admission Rate: 69%
ED Admits as % of Total Admits: 5%
Admission Rate (5-Year Trend): +10%
% of Admits Attending (Yield): 15%
Transfer Admission Rate: 38%

SAT Reading/Writing (Middle 50%): 650-730
SAT Math (Middle 50%): 660-760
ACT Composite (Middle 50%): 29-33

% Graduated in Top 10% of HS Class: 62%
% Graduated in Top 25% of HS Class: 85%
% Graduated in Top 50% of HS Class: 94%

Demonstrated Interest: Considered
Legacy Status: Considered
Racial/Ethnic Status: Considered
Admission Interview Offered: Yes

ENROLLMENT
Total Undergraduate Enrollment: 2,107
% Full-Time: 99%
% Male: 56%
% Female: 44%
% Out-of-State: 67%
% Fraternity: 20%
% Sorority: 37%
% On-Campus (All Undergraduate): 92%
Freshman Housing Required: Yes

% African-American: 4%
% Asian: 6%
% Hispanic: 9%
% White: 67%
% Other: 0%
% International: 10%
% Low-Income: 13%

ACADEMICS
Student-to-Faculty Ratio: 9 to 1
% of Classes Under 20: 69%
% of Classes 20-49: 31%
% of Classes 50 or More: 0%
% Full-Time Faculty: 91%
% Full-Time Faculty w/ Terminal Degree: 98%

Top Programs
Biology
Economics
Engineering
History
Mathematics
Neuroscience
Political Science
Psychology

Retention Rate: 90%
4-Year Graduation Rate: 80%
6-Year Graduation Rate: 85%

Curricular Flexibility: Less Flexible
Academic Rating: ★★★★⬩

#CollegesWorthYourMoney

Whether intent on studying the humanities or engineering, Union College in Schenectady, New York, can perfectly meet your needs. One of the select number of schools in the country that has been in existence since the 1700s, Union, while tough to get into, has not—like many of its peer institutions—reached absurd selectivity levels in recent years. A test-optional school looking for strong but not perfect students, this rigorous, well-regarded, and exclusively undergraduate institution of 2,107 students is an excellent fit for a certain subset of high schoolers. It's not a bad option considering that, in its illustrious history, Union has produced a US president, thirteen governors, 200+ judges, seven cabinet secretaries, a National Book Award winner, and an Olympic gold medalist.

Inside the Classroom
Union operates on a trimester system of ten-week terms with an extended winter break. The Common Curriculum is both broad and highly demanding. Students begin with a First-Year Preceptorial that seeks to sharpen skills in the areas of critical reading and thinking as well as analytical writing. The Sophomore Research Seminar mandates that students participate in structured academic research early in their collegiate careers. Dutchmen also must plow through requirements in literature, natural science, quantitative and mathematical reasoning, arts and humanities, science/engineering/technology, languages and cultures, and writing across the curriculum. Union is in the exclusive club of undergraduate institutions that require all graduates to complete a senior thesis.

Class sizes at Union are favorable for creating an intimate and friendly learning environment. A 9:1 student-to-faculty ratio leads to average introductory class sizes of 24 and average upper-level class sizes of only 14. Two-thirds of course sections have an enrollment of nineteen or fewer students. Faculty-mentored research is a staple of Union's undergraduate program and is experienced by 80% of the student body in one form or another. During the Steinmetz Symposium, hundreds of students have the chance to showcase their research. Each year, over one hundred students conduct research with a faculty member for an entire summer. The school also takes immense pride in its popular study abroad program, which sees more than 60% of its students from all disciplines spend a semester of study in a foreign land.

The most commonly conferred degrees are in the social sciences (28%), biology (15%), engineering (14%), and psychology (7%), with Union's engineering program having perhaps the strongest national reputation. The school also offers a number of interdisciplinary programs and majors. A top producer of Fulbright Scholars, the Class of 2023 produced two winners as well as a Watson Fellow.

Outside the Classroom
Last year, over 90% of undergraduates resided in university-run dorms or one of 13 student-run theme houses on the 120-acre grounds. The Greek influence is massive with the eighteen sororities and fraternities (ten of which are residential) attracting 20% of men and 37% of women. Regardless of Greek affiliation, every undergrad belongs to one of seven Minerva Houses, social hubs that serve to bring students and faculty together outside the classroom for social and academic activities. On the sports front, men's and women's ice hockey takes center stage as each battles NCAA Division I competition; the other 24 squads are relegated to Division III status. In total, one-third of all Union students are members of an intercollegiate sports team. Opportunities for physical fitness also exist in the form of yoga, Pilates, dance, and aerobics classes. More than 130 student-run campus clubs are on tap, including fourteen community service groups and a number of cultural, academic, political, and performance-oriented groups. Other notables include WRUC, America's first college radio station (founded in 1920), and the *Concordiensis* student newspaper that launched in 1877. Schenectady's downtown is a short car ride away, and longer road trips include Saratoga Springs, a little more than half an hour away, and New York and Boston, which require three-hour trips.

Career Services
The Becker Career Center is staffed by six professionals, two of whom specialize in employer relations. That works out to a 351:1 student-to-advisor ratio that falls in the average range when compared to other liberal arts institutions included in this guidebook. Philosophically, the staff encourages students to follow their passions by pursuing opportunities that "pique their interest and spur their enthusiasm." The staff aims to work with students early in their undergraduate careers, regularly administering tests such as the Meyers-Briggs to freshmen. Union hosts its own career fairs but also encourages participation in larger, joint efforts with other institutions. For example, Union, Swarthmore, Bard, and Connecticut College combine for the Fall Recruiting Consortium, which attracts many major companies to Times Square.

Students are encouraged to connect with alumni via the Union Career Advisory Network. Alumni are eager to help current undergrads as evidenced by participation in events such as the Walk Down Wall Street, which includes representatives from Goldman Sachs, Barclay's Deutsche Bank, Morgan Stanley, and CITI. On-campus recruiting has doubled in the past decade and includes visits and interview opportunities with a host of desirable employers. Roughly 85% of Union students complete at least one internship during their four years. Overall, thanks to strong career outcomes and an influential alumni base, Becker does well for its graduates.

Professional Outcomes

Ninety-two percent of the Class of 2022 landed at their next destination within months of completing their degree with 71% entering full-time employment and 21% matriculating into graduate school. The most popular fields were engineering (16%), finance (15%), medicine (12%), and technology (12%). Of the pool of all living alumni, Union has the largest representation at IBM, GE, PwC, Morgan Stanley, Fidelity Investments, and Accenture. Location-wise, the strongest presence of Dutchmen/women can be found in New York City; Boston; Albany; Washington, DC; San Francisco; and Philadelphia. Median income figures by the start of mid-career are strong, ranking alongside other private institutions like Boston University, Trinity College, and Northeastern.

The 21% of students who pursue further education directly out of their undergraduate experience do so at a wide range of institutions that include many elite universities. Recent graduates have gone on to advanced business degrees at Stanford, Cornell, and UVA; advanced engineering degrees at Yale, MIT, and RPI; and science degrees at Brandeis, UCLA, and WPI. Many of those headed to medical school do so through the combined BS/MD program Union offers in conjunction with Albany Medical College, but other recent grads have gone on to study medicine at the likes of Johns Hopkins, Tufts, and Dartmouth. Likewise, many pursuing a legal education do so through the combined BA/JD program with partner Albany Law School while others have entered Harvard, Boston College, and the University of Michigan.

Admission

With an acceptance rate of 47% for the Class of 2026, Union College, while highly selective, offers strong students better odds of success than many others of its ilk. Still, those who ultimately enroll are often toward the top of their respective high school classes with 62% of 2022-23 freshmen hailing from the top decile and 85% from the top quartile. Of those who submit test scores (more on this in a moment), the mid-50% standardized test ranges are 1310-1490 on the SAT and 29-33 on the ACT.

Unless you are applying to the 3+3 Accelerated Law Program, Leadership in Medicine Program, or are a home-schooled student, Union is a test-optional institution. Yet, in the most recent admissions cycle, 38% submitted SAT results and 17% included ACT scores on their applications. Atop the list of criteria deemed "very important" in evaluating an applicant are the rigor of secondary coursework, GPA, and class rank. Soft factors like talent/ability, personal qualities, volunteer work, and extracurricular activities also play a role in evaluating candidates. If you are a student on the cusp, applying early decision is absolutely the way to go as ED applicants are given a thumbs up at a 69% clip. You don't need perfect grades to get into Union College—the average GPA for Class of 2026 enrollees was 3.7, and 33% were over a 3.75—but you do need an area of notable strength and should be engaged in a mostly AP/honors-level high school curriculum.

Worth Your Money?

Union College sports a hefty cost of attendance of $82,845 per year. However, more than 50% receive need-based financial aid for an average scholarship of $47,000, and 32% of undergrads receive a merit-based award. Like the Ivies, it meets 100% of demonstrated need for every single student. Even with the high price tag, Union is a school that opens doors and sends many graduates directly into remunerative fields such as engineering and finance.

FINANCIAL
Institutional Type: Private
In-State Tuition: $66,456
Out-of-State Tuition: $66,456
Room & Board: $16,389
Books & Supplies: $1,500

Avg. Need-Based Grant: $47,100
Avg. % of Need Met: 100%

Avg. Merit-Based Award: $16,800
% Receiving (Freshmen w/o Need): 32%

Avg. Cumulative Debt: $37,284
% of Students Borrowing: 57%

CAREER
Who Recruits
1. Rapid7
2. BioSig Technologies
3. Brown Brothers Harriman
4. Northwell Health
5. Stanley Black & Decker

Notable Internships
1. Dow Jones
2. NBCUniversal
3. AIG

Top Employers
1. IBM
2. GE
3. PwC
4. Morgan Stanley
5. GE Power

Where Alumni Work
1. New York City
2. Boston
3. Albany, NY
4. Washington, DC
5. San Francisco

Earnings
College Scorecard (10-YR Post-Entry): $74,739
PayScale (Early Career): $68,400
PayScale (Mid-Career): $131,900
PayScale 20-Year ROI: $822,000

RANKINGS
Money: 4
U.S. News: 45, Liberal Arts Colleges
Wall Street Journal/THE: Not Ranked
Washington Monthly: 85, Liberal Arts Colleges

OVERGENERALIZATIONS
Students are:
Working hard and playing hard
Politically balanced
Involved/invested in campus life
Wealthy
More likely to rush a fraternity/sorority

COLLEGE OVERLAPS
Lafayette College
Lehigh University
Rensselaer Polytechnic Institute
Trinity College
University of Rochester

United States Air Force Academy

USAF Academy, Colorado | 800-443-9266

After World War II, many leaders in the US military began to see a need for a separate service academy to train future airmen. In 1954, a location just outside Colorado Springs, CO, was selected as the site for the US Air Force Academy, and by 1959, the youngest of the five US service academies had already graduated its first class. Guided by the values of "Integrity First. Service Before Self. Excellence in All We Do," the United States Air Force Academy (USAFA) is presently home to 4,0,85 undergraduate students who receive four years of education valued at an estimated $416,000 completely free of charge.

Inside the Classroom
A unique core curriculum is designed to cover the nine USAFA institutional outcomes that include critical thinking, ethics and respect, warrior ethos, leadership, and national security. Each year, students take courses that work toward ensuring those outcomes. All students are required to take courses in English, foreign language, philosophy, physics, chemistry, computer science, engineering, political science, and physical education, among other areas. In short, this is not a school you attend for its curricular flexibility and academic exploration. On the contrary, the academics at the Air Force Academy are as regimented and demanding as the experience as a whole.

The USAFA boasts an outstanding 7:1 cadet-to-faculty ratio, and classes are accordingly modest in size with 66% of sections containing fewer than 20 students, a number that would make most traditional liberal arts schools jealous. There are plenty of opportunities to participate in research, whether at one of the 27 research centers and institutes or through the Cadet Summer Research Program, which attracts 450 cadets. Undergraduates also have the chance to participate in an international exchange program such as the Cadet Summer Language Immersion Program or Cadet Semester Study Abroad Program.

There are 32 majors, including seven with "engineering" in the title. That works out well as the Air Force Academy runs one of the premier undergraduate engineering programs in the entire country. One-third of degrees conferred in 2022 were in engineering followed by business (14%), the social sciences (13%), interdisciplinary studies (11%), and biology (6%). You might be surprised to learn that 30 members of one recent cohort won nationally competitive scholarships; there were two Rhodes Scholars, a Fulbright Scholar, and a Knight-Hennessey Scholar.

Outside the Classroom
Cadets at the USAFA do not enjoy the typical college lifestyle full of unstructured time for self-discovery. In contrast, a cadet's day begins at 5:15 each morning and ends at 11 p.m. with the playing of taps. Within those 17 hours and 45 minutes are segments designated for "personal time, military training, classes, athletics, study time, ancillary training, and meals." Every single cadet lives on the 18,500-acre Colorado Springs campus in one of two dormitories: Vandenberg Hall or Sijan Hall. Pretty much everyone shares a 13x18-foot room with one roommate. Personal items are not allowed in dorm rooms, and items like televisions, coffeemakers, and other electronics are only allowed in-room for upperclassmen. Everyone eats lunch together in Mitchell Hall, and buffet-style service is provided for breakfast, dinner, and weekend meals. Serious athletics are a part of the Air Force Academy experience for many cadets as the Air Force Falcons field 27 men's and women's Division I teams; an additional 3,000 individuals participate in the school's ten intramural programs. The town of Colorado Springs is eight miles south of campus, and Denver is 55 miles north. However, those wishing to explore the many local ski resorts, restaurants, nightclubs, theaters, and other nearby attractions will need to have earned a pass in order to leave campus. Privileges increase as cadets progress through their years at the academy.

Career Services
A traditional career services office does not exist at the United States Air Force Academy, but there are plenty of resources to help support students as they develop a vision for their future vocation and consider various areas of specialization. The primary focus of the academy is to instill the aforementioned nine traits/skills that will make all students successful in their military career as well as in the civilian employment world. This mixture of discipline, leadership, technical skill, and physical ability produces graduates who thrive professionally and financially in the decades that follow.

In recent years, between 40-60% of students entering the Academy are eligible for pilot training, and 2,500 cadets each year are introduced to concepts of flight, navigation, and operation via courses in parachuting and soaring. While cadets do not earn their pilot's wings, they do accrue flight experience that prepares them for specialized undergraduate pilot training (SUPT) after graduation. The Association of Graduates of the USAFA provides alumni with assistance in transitioning from being an Air Force pilot to a commercial pilot. Despite the absence of anyone technically operating as a "career counselor," the entire Air Force Academy successfully shepherds 100% of its cadets toward professional success in their military and civilian careers.

Professional Outcomes

As with any service academy, the bulk of graduates spend a good portion of their careers within the armed forces. In the case of USAFA grads, a minimum of a five-year commitment to the Air Force is mandatory. Many alumni spend time later in their careers working in the commercial airline industry at Delta Air Lines, United Airlines, and American Airlines. Many also work for Boeing, Northrop Grumman, Booz Allen Hamilton, and Lockheed Martin. Large numbers of USAFA alumni can be found in Washington, DC; Denver; Dallas; Los Angeles; San Antonio; Atlanta; and a number of other major US cities from coast to coast.

Since cadets are committing to years of military service postgraduation, they are not free to enroll in any graduate or professional program they choose. The roughly ten percent of each graduating class who are allowed to continue their studies will enjoy a free education at military or civilian universities in exchange for a pledge of additional years of service after earning their advanced degrees. Among one recent graduating cohort, there were 113 second lieutenants who went on to graduate school, including one to law school, 27 to the Air Force Institute of Technology, and one to study clinical psychology. There are a limited number of slots available for nursing, MD, and PhD programs within the Uniformed Services University of the Health Sciences (USUHS). In one recent class, of the fourteen grads attending medical school, 11 enrolled in the USUHS with others matriculating at Harvard, UNC-Chapel Hill, and Tulane University.

Admission

Of the 8,353 applicants seeking a spot in the Air Force Academy's Class of 2026, 11,261 made it into the candidate pool, but only 1,775 reached "Qualified Candidate" status, and just 1,071 were ultimately admitted into the USAFA. This translates to a 13% acceptance rate. The median SAT for entering members of the Class of 2026 was 1400; the ACT median was 31. Looking at class rank, 47% finished in the top decile of their high school class, 78% were in the top quartile, and 92% placed in the top half. The average unweighted GPA was 3.80.

The USAFA values these 11 factors above all others: rigor of coursework, GPA, class rank, standardized test scores, application essays, recommendations, the interview, extracurricular activities, character/personal qualities, geographical residence, and the applicant's level of demonstrated interest. Talent/ability and volunteer work also are considered "important" to the admissions committee when evaluating applicants. All Air Force Academy applicants must seek a formal nomination from one of the following sources:

- A member of the US Senate
- A member of the US House of Representatives
- The President of the United States (for children of active duty, reserve, or retired military parents only)
- The Vice President of the United States
- Your AFROTC or AFJROTC unit
- Your commander (for active service members)
- Through being a child of a deceased/disabled veteran

While the Air Force Academy doesn't need your nomination paperwork until January 31 of your senior year, it is advisable to reach out to your members of Congress (MOC) during 11th grade. All applicants also must pass a Candidate Fitness Assessment and a medical examination.

Worth Your Money?

Again, an Air Force Academy education is valued at an estimated $416,000, and yet cadets don't pay a dime. Of course, you are committing to a minimum of eight years (five of which must be active duty) of paid service as an officer in the US Air Force. Overall, if a career in the US military is your goal, then a gratis degree from an academically elite institution with an exceptional engineering program is a no-brainer.

FINANCIAL
Institutional Type: Public
In-State Tuition: $0
Out-of-State Tuition: $0
Room & Board: $0
Books & Supplies: $0

Avg. Need-Based Grant: Not Applicable
Avg. % of Need Met: Not Applicable

Avg. Merit-Based Award: Not Applicable
% Receiving (Freshmen w/o Need):
Not Applicable

Avg. Cumulative Debt: Not Applicable
% of Students Borrowing: Not Applicable

CAREER
Who Recruits
1. United States Air Force
2. United Airlines
3. Lockheed Martin
4. Boeing
5. Northrop Grumman

Notable Internships
1. Not Applicable
2. Not Applicable
3. Not Applicable

Top Employers
1. US Military
2. United Airlines
3. Lockheed Martin
4. Boeing
5. Northrop Grumman

Where Alumni Work
1. Colorado Springs, CO
2. India
3. Washington, DC
4. Denver
5. Dallas/Fort Worth

Earnings
College Scorecard (10-YR Post-Entry): NR
PayScale (Early Career): $80,100
PayScale (Mid-Career): $148,600
PayScale 20-Year ROI: $1,121,000

RANKINGS
Money: Not Ranked
U.S. News: 7, Liberal Arts Colleges
Wall Street Journal/THE: Not Ranked
Washington Monthly: Not Ranked

OVERGENERALIZATIONS
Students are:
Politically conservative
Athletic/Active
Less likely to party
Crazy about the Falcons
More likely to interact with different types
of students

COLLEGE OVERLAPS
Norwich University
The Citadel
United States Coast Guard Academy
United States Military Academy
United States Naval Academy

United States Military Academy

ADMISSION
Admission Rate: 12%
Admission Rate - Men: 13%
Admission Rate - Women: 9%
EA Admission Rate: Not Offered
ED Admission Rate: Not Offered
ED Admits as % of Total Admits: Not Offered
Admission Rate (5-Year Trend): +2%
% of Admits Attending (Yield): 78%
Transfer Admission Rate: Not Offered

SAT Reading/Writing (Middle 50%): 610-710
SAT Math (Middle 50%): 610-740
ACT Composite (Middle 50%): 27-33

% Graduated in Top 10% of HS Class: 43%
% Graduated in Top 25% of HS Class: 69%
% Graduated in Top 50% of HS Class: 92%

Demonstrated Interest: Important
Legacy Status: Not Considered
Racial/Ethnic Status: Considered
Admission Interview Offered: Yes

ENROLLMENT
Total Undergraduate Enrollment: 4,393
% Full-Time: 100%
% Male: 77%
% Female: 23%
% Out-of-State: 94%
% Fraternity: Not Offered
% Sorority: Not Offered
% On-Campus (All Undergraduate): 100%
Freshman Housing Required: Yes

% African-American: 11%
% Asian: 10%
% Hispanic: 13%
% White: 62%
% Other: 0%
% International: 1%
% Low-Income: No Pell Recipients

ACADEMICS
Student-to-Faculty Ratio: 7 to 1
% of Classes Under 20: 98%
% of Classes 20-49: 2%
% of Classes 50 or More: 0%
% Full-Time Faculty: 81%
% Full-Time Faculty w/ Terminal Degree: 49%

Top Programs
Cyber Science
Engineering
Engineering Psychology
International Affairs
Kinesiology
Law and Legal Studies
Management
Systems and Decision Sciences

Retention Rate: 96%
4-Year Graduation Rate: 85%
6-Year Graduation Rate: 86%

Curricular Flexibility: Less Flexible
Academic Rating: ★★★★⁴

#CollegesWorthYourMoney

During the Revolutionary War, George Washington identified a plateau on the west bank of the Hudson River, about 50 miles north of New York City, as the single most important strategic position in all of nascent America. Despite the best treasonous efforts of Benedict Arnold to hand over the newly fortified lands to the British, the Continental Army never lost control of West Point, and it has remained the longest continuously occupied military post in the United States. In 1802, President Thomas Jefferson turned West Point into the United States Military Academy (USMA) where, for hundreds of years, it has churned out a steady flow of American military leaders. Cadets who attend receive a completely free education and emerge as second lieutenants with an eight-year commitment to the military. Yet, to secure that opportunity, prospective West Pointers must overcome a complex admissions process with an Ivy-ish, single-digit acceptance rate.

Inside the Classroom
Twenty-four courses make up the core academic program at West Point, although there are an additional three mandatory engineering courses for non-engineering majors. Whereas certain majors may be able to avoid extensive math/science coursework at most universities, the USMA has everyone taking at least one class in each of the following: chemistry, physics, modeling, calculus, statistics, and computing. There are 37 majors at West Point, and students must conquer a minimum of 13 courses within their area of study.

Professors at the USMA have a reputation as being some of the most accessible and dedicated in all of higher education. A 7:1 student-to-faculty ratio is also among the better figures you'll see. This level of support and availability helps lead to an outstanding 97% first-year student retention rate. Almost 98% of class sections at West Point enroll fewer than 20 students. Big, impersonal, lecture-based courses simply do not exist at the academy. Plenty of research opportunities exist within each department. For example, the Advanced Individual Academic Development (AIAD) Program in the Department of Chemistry and Life Science provides numerous two-to-four-week research apprenticeships all around the United States. Those looking to leave the country for a semester at sea are free to do so; West Point sends 150 cadets each year to one of 20 nations.

West Point is one of the best undergraduate engineering colleges in the entire United States and has standout programs in civil engineering, computer engineering, electrical engineering, and mechanical engineering. The academy's reputation with civilian employers and graduate schools is stellar across the board. The same goes for prestigious postgraduate fellowships as West Point grads capture a good number of Marshall, Schwarzman, and Fulbright scholarships in an average year; it also produced four Rhodes Scholars in the past two years.

Outside the Classroom
Rise at 6:55 a.m. for breakfast, attend class until 11:45 a.m.….that level of regimentation continues all the way until taps at 11:30 p.m. with lights out at midnight. Attending a service academy involves committing to a unique college experience unlike the open expanse of free time with a couple classes mixed in that is enjoyed by the average American residential college student. Instead of a dorm room, cadets live in barracks with the rest of their company. There are 36 companies, each comprised of senior leaders (firsties), juniors (cows) in midlevel leadership positions, and sophomores (yearlings) who oversee a team of freshmen (plebes). As you progress through the years, you are afforded more privileges, such as being able to eat off campus. There are 130+ extracurricular activities, including military-relevant clubs for marksmanship and parachuting along with more typical college offerings including a Film Forum and Latin Dance Club. Every cadet is required to participate in a sport at the intercollegiate, club, or intramural level and take advantage of the academy's 500,000+ square feet of fitness facilities. The Army Black Knights compete in 24 Division I sports with football games being especially popular, highlighted by the annual Army-Navy game. On the weekends, cadets can venture into the scenic Hudson Valley to hike or utilize West Point's own golf course or ski slope.

Career Services
West Point does not have a career counseling department like you would find at a standard university. Instead, the overarching goal is to prepare individuals to be a "soldier, servant of the nation, and leader of character—and to incorporate these roles into their own emerging professional identities." Individuals with those qualities will be prepared when they begin their US Army careers as second lieutenants and beyond when they transition into civilian life.

As seniors, cadets learn which branch (area of specialization) they will enter to begin their military careers. Individual preferences and the needs of the Army will both be considered when making those assignments. Common branches include Infantry, Aviation, Signal Corps, Military Intelligence, Engineers, Finance, and Cyber. The West Point Association of Graduates offers career services to alumni transitioning from military service to civilian employment. As we will see in the "Professional Outcomes" section that follows, USMA alumni go on to a phenomenal level of success in their professional lives, landing positions with the country's most coveted employers for salaries that are far above average.

Professional Outcomes

West Point graduates must honor their eight-year commitment (five years of active duty, three in the reserves), and many continue their military careers beyond those requirements. Of course, civilian employers are keenly interested in USMA graduates for obvious reasons—their experience, leadership, and training are unique and invaluable in the private sector. As a result, large numbers of alumni can be found in the offices of Amazon, Microsoft, Deloitte, Meta, Google, ExxonMobil, Johnson & Johnson, McKinsey & Company, and Goldman Sachs. Mean mid-career pay is in excess of $125,000, significantly more than the average university can claim. The highest concentrations of alums are located in New York City; Washington, DC; Dallas; Atlanta; Seattle; Boston; and Houston.

With military duties to fulfill, only a small percentage of cadets matriculate directly into graduate programs. Each year, up to 2% of graduates (roughly 20 individuals) are allowed to attend medical school. Many attend the Uniformed Services University of the Health Sciences, but other recent grads have entered medical training at UCLA, Yale, and Stanford. After two years of active duty in the Army, alumni can apply to law schools and, if accepted, can have the government cover the tuition. Recent West Point grads have attended many of the top law schools in the country.

Admission

Of the 12,559 applicants seeking a spot in the West Point Class of 2026, only 3,400 ended up receiving nominations. From there, the pool was sliced in half as the admissions committee found 1,771 of that group to be "qualified" physically and academically. Another round of scrutiny cleaved the number of men and women to a mere 1,501 which equates to a 12% acceptance rate. The acceptance rate two years ago was a less favorable 8%. The median SAT score for this cohort was 1350, and the ACT scores ranged from 27 to 33. Turning to class rank, 64% finished in the top 20% of their high school class. There were 70 valedictorians and 32 salutatorians in the Class of 2026 cohort.

When applying to West Point, you are required to obtain a congressional nomination from one of the following:
- A member of the US Senate
- A member of the US House of Representatives
- The Vice President of the United States
- The governor or resident commissioner of Puerto Rico
- The Secretary of the Army

While getting more than one congressional nomination will not benefit you, it behooves applicants to apply to both of their senators as well as their local House of Representatives member as doing so will increase the overall odds of obtaining at least one nomination. Each member of Congress (MOC) is given five nomination slots per year across all five service academies; each senator is given the same.

While West Point doesn't need your nomination paperwork until January 31 of your senior year, it is advisable to start the process of reaching out to your MOC during 11th grade. Interviews are mandatory and are a critical component of any application. Interviews last around 30-45 minutes and are typically conducted by a field force representative, academy liaison officer, or ROTC professor of military science. Additionally, you must pass a Candidate Fitness Assessment and a physical examinationX.

Worth Your Money?

As long as you are committed to military service after graduation, there is no way that a free education from a top-ranked institution could be anything less than the deal of all deals. With significant numbers of engineering, computer science, and business degrees conferred each year, many grads bring highly marketable skills to the table. For the 12% of those who are able to gain admission to West Point, a lucrative career is likely waiting down the road.

FINANCIAL
Institutional Type: Public
In-State Tuition: $0
Out-of-State Tuition: $0
Room & Board: $0
Books & Supplies: $0

Avg. Need-Based Grant: Not Applicable
Avg. % of Need Met: Not Applicable

Avg. Merit-Based Award: Not Applicable
% Receiving (Freshmen w/o Need):
Not Applicable

Avg. Cumulative Debt: Not Applicable
% of Students Borrowing: Not Applicable

CAREER
Who Recruits
1. Deloitte
2. Microsoft
3. McKinsey & Company
4. Amazon Web Services
5. JPMorgan Chase

Notable Internships
1. Not Applicable
2. Not Applicable
3. Not Applicable

Top Employers
1. US Military
2. Amazon
3. US Dept of Defense
4. Microsoft
5. Deloitte

Where Alumni Work
1. New York City
2. Washington, DC
3. Dallas/Fort Worth
4. Atlanta
5. Seattle

Earnings
College Scorecard (10-YR Post-Entry): NR
PayScale (Early Career): $84,200
PayScale (Mid-Career): $154,300
PayScale 20-Year ROI: $1,267,000

RANKINGS
Money: Not Ranked
U.S. News: 8, Liberal Arts Colleges
Wall Street Journal/THE: Not Ranked
Washington Monthly: Not Ranked

OVERGENERALIZATIONS
Students are:
Politically conservative
Athletic/Active
Less likely to party
Crazy about the Black Knights
More likely to interact with different types of students

COLLEGE OVERLAPS
Norwich University
The Citadel
United States Air Force Academy
United States Coast Guard Academy
United States Naval Academy

United States Naval Academy

Annapolis, Maryland | 410-293-1858

ADMISSION
Admission Rate: 11%
Admission Rate - Men: 11%
Admission Rate - Women: 11%
EA Admission Rate: Not Offered
ED Admission Rate: Not Offered
ED Admits as % of Total Admits: Not Offered
Admission Rate (5-Year Trend): +3%
% of Admits Attending (Yield): 85%
Transfer Admission Rate: Not Offered

SAT Reading/Writing (Middle 50%): 600-720
SAT Math (Middle 50%): 600-720
ACT Composite (Middle 50%): 25-32

% Graduated in Top 10% of HS Class: 62%
% Graduated in Top 25% of HS Class: 84%
% Graduated in Top 50% of HS Class: 97%

Demonstrated Interest: Very Important
Legacy Status: Considered
Racial/Ethnic Status: Considered
Admission Interview Offered: Yes

ENROLLMENT
Total Undergraduate Enrollment: 4,450
% Full-Time: 100%
% Male: 72%
% Female: 28%
% Out-of-State: 93%
% Fraternity: Not Offered
% Sorority: Not Offered
% On-Campus (All Undergraduate): 100%
Freshman Housing Required: Yes

% African-American: 6%
% Asian: 9%
% Hispanic: 14%
% White: 59%
% Other: 1%
% International: 1%
% Low-Income: No Pell Recipients

ACADEMICS
Student-to-Faculty Ratio: 8 to 1
% of Classes Under 20: 71%
% of Classes 20-49: 29%
% of Classes 50 or More: 0%
% Full-Time Faculty: 94%
% Full-Time Faculty w/ Terminal Degree: 67%

Top Programs
Chemistry
Cyber Operations
Engineering
Oceanography
Mathematics
Physics
Political Science
Quantitative Economics

Retention Rate: 97%
4-Year Graduation Rate: 88%
6-Year Graduation Rate: 91%

Curricular Flexibility: Less Flexible
Academic Rating: ★★★★★

#CollegesWorthYourMoney

With the motto *"Ex Scientia Tridens"* ("Through Knowledge, Sea Power"), the United States Naval Academy (USNA), sometimes referred to simply as "Navy," dates back to the 1850s, but it wasn't until 1933 that the Annapolis, MD, institution began awarding bachelor's degrees. Before long, it had cultivated a number of top engineering/STEM programs and, in 1976, became a coeducational institution, finally shaping into the modern form of the Naval Academy that 13,000 applicants line up for a chance to attend each year. Today's version of the USNA accepts only 11% from a strong pool of aspiring midshipmen, a level of selectivity that is comparable to Ivy League universities and top liberal arts colleges.

Inside the Classroom
From the get-go, you'll get a sense of what you are in for at the Naval Academy through Plebe Summer, which can be thought of as a first-year orientation on steroids. For seven weeks, plebes undergo highly rigorous mental and physical training designed to prepare them for the challenges ahead. On the academic front, all undergraduates take six courses in engineering and weapons, nine math and science courses, eight humanities and social science courses, a four-semester foreign language sequence (Chinese, Japanese, Arabic, and Russian are available), four courses under the umbrella of leadership education and development, and four seamanship and navigation courses that include practicums.

Close to three-quarters of course sections will contain fewer than 20 students, and the student-to-faculty ratio is a stellar 7:1. Undergraduate research can be accessed through research-focused courses, design projects, or the Trident Scholar Research Program, an independent study conducted during senior year. Many midshipmen have the chance to study abroad, and up to 450 do each year through programs like the Language Study Abroad Program. The range of destinations is wide with recent students studying Arabic for full semesters in Morocco, Oman, Israel, Qatar, and Egypt.

The Naval Academy has some of the top-ranked undergraduate engineering programs in the world with standout reputations in aerospace, computer, electrical, and mechanical engineering. By rule, at least 65% of students complete degrees in a STEM discipline. Midshipmen routinely capture the most sought-after scholarships and fellowships in the country. The academy had its 56th all-time Rhodes Scholar in 2023, and it also claimed recent Gates, Cambridge, Fulbright, Truman, Schwarzman, and Marshall recipients.

Outside the Classroom
By design, "The four years at Annapolis are very challenging, tightly structured, and designed to push you well beyond your perceived limits." That means college life for a midshipman will be far more regimented and involve far fewer choices than for an average American undergraduate. Every USNA student is part of a battalion, and the academy's six battalions are divided into 30 companies. Those company-mates will be the individuals you drill with, eat next to, and sleep near for four years. Much of the Naval Academy experience outside the classroom will involve that core group. A typical weekday schedule involves a 5:30 a.m. start for a personal fitness workout and ends with an 8-11 p.m. study period. Even with the ample demands of this highly structured routine, midshipmen still have a bevy of extracurricular activities to choose from, including everything from a debate team to gospel choir to women's ice hockey. All midshipmen must participate in either a club, intramural, or varsity sport. For intercollegiate sports, there are 18 men's teams, 12 women's squads, and three coed units, and many compete at the Division I level against the likes of Boston University, Colgate University, and Holy Cross. While the schedule inside and outside the classroom leaves little room for downtime, leave is typically granted for major holidays, a brief spring break, and three weeks of summer vacation.

Career Services
In a typical college, career counselors are available to administer personality tests, talk over potential careers, and connect you to internship and employment opportunities, but the United States Naval Academy is not a typical college. Midshipmen can select up to six preferred service assignments from 24 career choices and submit those requests in late August of their senior year. No matter what professional goals midshipmen choose to pursue, the academy ensures that they gain proficiency in ten attributes including selflessness, professionalism, inclusiveness, and resiliency—characteristics that will lead to success in all future endeavors.

One recent graduating class saw the greatest number of 1st Class midshipmen (seniors) receive assignments as surface warfare officers (259), Navy pilots (228), US Marine Corps ground (161), submarine (138), and US Marine Corps pilots (91). In smaller numbers, others are assigned to career paths in intel, special operations, cryptologic warfare, and additional specialty areas. Nearly 30% of USNA grads join the Marine Corps in some capacity each year. Naval officers who are moving from military to civilian employment can access events such as the Service Academy Career Conference, which is held four times per year.

Professional Outcomes

USNA grads have a mandatory five-year commitment to the Navy or Marine Corps. Upon entering civilian employment/life, Naval Academy alumni flock to companies that include Lockheed Martin, Northrop Grumman, Booz Allen Hamilton, Amazon, Microsoft, Meta, and McKinsey and Co. Given such job market success, it is hardly surprising that USNA grads enjoy some of the highest average salaries of any alumni group in the country. The most popular cities in which alumni settle include Washington, DC; Baltimore; San Diego; Norfolk; New York City; Seattle; and San Francisco.

While graduate school is not a common route directly after obtaining a bachelor's degree, the Naval Academy does send around two dozen newly minted alumni to civilian universities to complete master's degrees through the Immediate Graduate Education Program. Recent graduates went on to such prestigious institutions as Cambridge, MIT, and Stanford. Roughly 10-20 graduates per year are granted a waiver to attend medical school on the government's dime. The vast majority of graduating midshipmen become ensigns in the Navy or second lieutenants in the Marine Corps.

Admission

Of the 12,927 applicants seeking a spot in the Naval Academy's Class of 2026, fewer than half ended up receiving nominations. Another round of scrutiny sliced the number of men and women left standing to a mere 1,390, which equates to an 11% overall acceptance rate. Two years ago, Class of 2024 hopefuls were admitted at a lower 9% rate. The mid-50% SAT range for entering members of the Class of 2026 was 1230-1430; the ACT range was 27-33. Looking at the class rank data for that same cohort, 43% finished in the top decile of their high school class, 69% in the top quartile, and 92% in the top half.

The USNA values six factors above all others: rigor of coursework, GPA, the interview, extracurricular activities, character/personal qualities, and standardized test scores. Interviews are mandatory and are a critical component of any application. Interviews are conducted with a Blue and Gold Officer (BGO) in your home state. Students should contact their BGO immediately upon receiving their official candidate letter.

Naval Academy applicants must seek a formal nomination from one of the following:
- A member of the US Senate
- A member of the US House of Representatives
- The President of the United States (for children of active duty, reserve, retired military parents only)
- The Vice President of the United States
- Your NROTC or NJROTC unit
- Your commander (for active service members)
- Through being a child of a deceased/disabled veteran

While the Naval Academy doesn't need your nomination paperwork until January 31 of your senior year, it is advisable to start the process of reaching out to your members of Congress (MOC) during 11th grade. It is also important to note that all applicants must pass a Candidate Fitness Assessment as well as a medical examination.

Worth Your Money?

To receive an education of this quality for free is a spectacular deal for anyone passionate about pursuing a career in the Navy or Marine Corps. When entering civilian life, USNA alumni enjoy some of the highest average salaries of any school in the country. As long as you are ready for the intensity of four years as a midshipman and at least five postgraduate years in the Navy, this institution is an unbeatable value.

FINANCIAL
Institutional Type: Public
In-State Tuition: $0
Out-of-State Tuition: $0
Room & Board: $0
Books & Supplies: $0

Avg. Need-Based Grant: Not Applicable
Avg. % of Need Met: Not Applicable

Avg. Merit-Based Award: Not Applicable
% Receiving (Freshmen w/o Need): Not Applicable

Avg. Cumulative Debt: Not Applicable
% of Students Borrowing: Not Applicable

CAREER
Who Recruits
1. Amazon Web Services
2. Deloitte
3. Google
4. Booz Allen Hamilton
5. Bank of America

Notable Internships
1. Not Applicable
2. Not Applicable
3. Not Applicable

Top Employers
1. US Military
2. Booz Allen Hamilton
3. Northop Grumman
4. Lockhead Martin
5. Amazon

Where Alumni Work
1. Washington, DC
2. Baltimore
3. San Diego
4. Norfolk, VA
5. New York City

Earnings
College Scorecard (10-YR Post-Entry): NR
PayScale (Early Career): $83,700
PayScale (Mid-Career): $160,100
PayScale 20-Year ROI: $1,216,000

RANKINGS
Money: Not Ranked
U.S. News: 3, Liberal Arts Colleges
Wall Street Journal/THE: Not Ranked
Washington Monthly: Not Ranked

OVERGENERALIZATIONS
Students are:
Diverse
Athletic/Active
Crazy about the Midshipmen
Less likely to party
More likely to interact with different types of students

COLLEGE OVERLAPS
Norwich University
The Citadel
United States Air Force Academy
United States Coast Guard Academy
United States Military Academy

University at Buffalo (SUNY)

Buffalo, New York | 716-645-6900

You can make all the jokes you want about the city of Buffalo (cold jokes from relatives never get old), and you can call the university bearing the city's name a "commuter school" if you want, but they don't care. SUNY University at Buffalo is the most popular destination within the colossal State University of New York system, boasting an undergraduate population of 20,761. Well-regarded and highly affordable business, engineering, and computer science programs lure an increasingly more selective group of freshmen each year. It is primarily New York residents who come to Buffalo for its robust academic offerings that include 140 undergraduate degree programs. However, the university ranks in the top 30 nationwide for percentage of international students at 15%.

Inside the Classroom
Totaling 40 credits, the UB curriculum will take the equivalent of almost three full semesters to complete. The program begins freshman year with a small seminar that emphasizes critical thinking and discussion. Next, students will knock out foundations courses in communication literacy, quantitative literacy, scientific literacy, and diversity learning followed by nine credits (each) from thematic and global pathways. Lastly, as a senior, students will complete a one-credit capstone course. Those in the university's Honors Program also must complete twenty-four credits in honors-only courses.

Despite a favorable 12:1 student-to-faculty ratio, undergraduate class sizes do tend to be rather large at the University at Buffalo. Only 39% of course sections enroll fewer than 20 students, and 20% of courses contain fifty or more students. The Center for Undergraduate Research and Creative Activity (CURCA) can help make a huge university feel a bit smaller by connecting students with faculty mentors for research endeavors. The center advertises that "100 percent of students have the opportunity to participate in research," thus, it is fair to say that procuring opportunities is simply a matter of being proactive. Likewise, for those interested in spending a semester at a foreign university, UB offers 1,000 study abroad programs across all seven continents (Antarctica, anyone?).

A good number of Buffalo students flock to the school's strongest offerings with 17% of the degrees conferred coming from the School of Management and 16% from the School of Engineering and Applied Sciences. Other commonly conferred degrees are in the social sciences (12%), psychology (11%), biology (10%), and health professions (8%). There has been a slight uptick in recent years in undergraduates capturing prestigious post-graduate scholarships and fellowships. Eleven seniors/alumni won Fulbright Scholarships in 2023 while others have netted Gilman and Critical Language Scholarships.

Outside the Classroom
Even though a sizable number of UB students commute from home or nearby rental homes/apartments, the school does bring nearly 70% of freshmen to live in university-owned housing that features 12 residence halls and five apartment communities. Greek life has only a faint heartbeat, attracting 1-2% of men and women. Want to see a big-name speaker live? The UB Speakers Series has enticed the likes of Hillary Clinton, Malcolm Gladwell, and John Oliver to trek to Buffalo in recent years. There are 300+ student organizations to choose from at the university, and there are many campus-wide events that energize the Bulls community such as Fall Fest, Spring Fest, and Oozefest, which is the muddiest game of volleyball you will ever play. The sports scene is on the rise as the school now supports sixteen NCAA Division I athletic teams that compete in the Mid-American Conference. In the school's own words, the City of Good Neighbors is home to "a vibrant arts scene, quaint neighborhoods, remarkable restaurants, and an affordable cost of living." On campus, the Crossroads Culinary Center is rated the best in the entire SUNY system.

Career Services
The central Career Design Center at UB employs 11 professional staff members who hold titles such as career counselor, employer relations manager, and employer and alumni relationship associate. The Ciminelli Family Career Resource Center within the School of Management is staffed by nine full-time employees who work with or on behalf of undergraduate students. That translates to a 1,038:1 student-to-counselor ratio, which is significantly higher than the average school featured in this guide, but it is to be expected at a public university of Buffalo's size. The good news is that in a single academic year, almost 11,000 students utilize the Career Center by attending a job fair, a workshop, or making an individual appointment for career coaching; another 16,000 students used Bullseye, the office's online networking app.

Career Center staff could improve outreach efforts as only about 10% of the undergraduate student population seek direct career counseling services each year. However, the center did succeed in bringing many top employers to campus for expos such as the STEAM Job + Internship Fair which draws 100+ employers and 2,000+ students each fall. The Spring Job + Internship Fair also brings out 100+ employers and around 1,300 students. Unfortunately, those efforts ultimately result in fewer than 500 on-campus interviews each year. Based on the most recent data available, close to 60% of students engage in at least one internship, co-op, or other experiential learning placement during their four years at the university. Like much else at the University of Buffalo, the career services spoils go to those who aggressively track down and utilize the available resources.

Professional Outcomes

Within six months of graduating, 94% of School of Management degree-holders in the Class of 2022 had found employment or were enrolled in a graduate program. The median base salary for those who found jobs was $55,000 (business grads only). UB graduates are well-represented in the corporate offices of many top finance, accounting, consulting, and technology companies. More than one hundred alumni of the school are currently employed at the likes of M&T Bank, Citi, Amazon, Microsoft, Google, JPMorgan Chase, PwC, Apple, Deloitte, and Cisco. The greatest number of alumni remain in the Buffalo area but many relocate to New York City, San Francisco, DC, and Boston.

There were 150 SUNY Buffalo graduates in 2023 who applied to medical school. Including those applying to osteopathic schools, a GPA of 3.5-3.7 and an MCAT score in the 505-510 range typically led to successful results. Recent graduates are currently attending medical schools at Virginia Commonwealth University and Boston University with the greatest percentage heading to the four SUNY medical training grounds at the Stony Brook, Buffalo, Upstate, and Downstate locations. Many law school attendees also stay within the SUNY system, including Buffalo's own home for legal education, but other recent grads have entered such schools as Duke, Wake Forest, and Notre Dame. That pattern is also true for those pursuing master's and doctoral degrees. Graduating with honors from UB can absolutely put elite graduate and professional schools in play, but the bulk of students select local public options.

Admission

SUNY University at Buffalo receives the largest number of applications of any school in the state system—over 30,000—and the school accepted 68% of those aiming to join the Class of 2026. Perfect grades aren't necessary, but you need a pretty sound transcript. Twenty-nine percent of attending students placed in the top 10% of their high school class, and 62% finished in the top quartile. The average GPA was 3.8, and the median SAT score for a freshman in 2022-23 was 1290 while the median ACT score was 29.

So many applicants, so little time—it's a recipe for a formulaic admissions process, and that's exactly what the University at Buffalo utilizes. At the top of the list are standardized test scores, GPA, and the rigor of one's coursework followed by the still-important factors of class rank and recommendations. In the end, 20% of those admitted go on to enroll. Roughly 350 students per year are admitted into the Honors College, and preference is given to those who apply earlier in the rolling process. For all applicants, we highly recommend meeting the school's priority deadline.

Worth Your Money?

Total cost of attendance for a New York resident comes to about $32,000 per year, which accounts for direct and indirect living expenses—an excellent deal for the quality of education the school provides. For those from out of state, costs climb to $52,000 per year, making attending UB a curious choice for those with more affordable options. Over 11,000 undergraduates are determined needy each year, and the school awards an average annual need-based grant of $8,500. For New York residents, SUNY Buffalo is, unequivocally and independent of circumstance, worth your money.

FINANCIAL
Institutional Type: Public
In-State Tuition: $10,781
Out-of-State Tuition: $30,571
Room & Board: $16,754
Books & Supplies: $1,300

Avg. Need-Based Grant: $8,606
Avg. % of Need Met: 49%

Avg. Merit-Based Award: $4,097
% Receiving (Freshmen w/o Need): 5%

Avg. Cumulative Debt: $26,103
% of Students Borrowing: 56%

CAREER
Who Recruits
1. ACV Auctions
2. Salesforce
3. Facebook
4. PwC
5. Apple

Notable Internships
1. Walt Disney World
2. Wegman's Food Markets
3. HSBC

Top Employers
1. M&T Bank
2. Citi
3. Amazon
4. Ingram Micro
5. Microsoft

Where Alumni Work
1. Buffalo, NY
2. New York City
3. Rochester, NY
4. San Francisco
5. Singapore

Earnings
College Scorecard (10-YR Post-Entry): $65,856
PayScale (Early Career): $58,800
PayScale (Mid-Career): $102,000
PayScale 20-Year ROI: $511,000

RANKINGS
Money: 4
U.S. News: 76, National Universities
Wall Street Journal/THE: 121
Washington Monthly: 149, National Universities

OVERGENERALIZATIONS
Students are:
Diverse
Only a short drive from home (i.e., Most come from NY or nearby states)
More likely to go home on weekends
Independent
Self-motivated

COLLEGE OVERLAPS
Binghamton University (SUNY)
Stony Brook University (SUNY)
Syracuse University
University at Albany (SUNY)
University of Pittsburgh

University of Arizona

Tucson, Arizona | 520-621-3237

ADMISSION
Admission Rate: 87%
Admission Rate - Men: 85%
Admission Rate - Women: 88%
EA Admission Rate: Not Offered
ED Admission Rate: Not Offered
ED Admits as % of Total Admits: Not Offered
Admission Rate (5-Year Trend): +3%
% of Admits Attending (Yield): 20%
Transfer Admission Rate: 67%

SAT Reading/Writing (Middle 50%): 570-680
SAT Math (Middle 50%): 570-690
ACT Composite (Middle 50%): 21-29

% Graduated in Top 10% of HS Class: 39%
% Graduated in Top 25% of HS Class: 66%
% Graduated in Top 50% of HS Class: 89%

Demonstrated Interest: Important
Legacy Status: Not Considered
Racial/Ethnic Status: Not Considered
Admission Interview Offered: No

ENROLLMENT
Total Undergraduate Enrollment: 40,407
% Full-Time: 77%
% Male: 44%
% Female: 56%
% Out-of-State: 44%
% Fraternity: 4%
% Sorority: 8%
% On-Campus (All Undergraduate): 22%
Freshman Housing Required: No

% African-American: 4%
% Asian: 5%
% Hispanic: 27%
% White: 48%
% Other: 4%
% International: 5%
% Low-Income: 28%

ACADEMICS
Student-to-Faculty Ratio: 18 to 1
% of Classes Under 20: 33%
% of Classes 20-49: 52%
% of Classes 50 or More: 15%
% Full-Time Faculty: 86%
% Full-Time Faculty w/ Terminal Degree: 92%

Top Programs
Business
Engineering
Film & Television
Geosciences
Physics
Political Science
Psychology
Public Health

Retention Rate: 85%
4-Year Graduation Rate: 54%
6-Year Graduation Rate: 66%

Curricular Flexibility: Somewhat Flexible
Academic Rating: ★★★

#CollegesWorthYourMoney

Residents of many states are lucky to have one university that (1) charges a reasonable tuition, (b) accepts the vast majority of students, even those with a B average, and (c) provides a high-quality educational and social experience for its undergraduates. Arizona is lucky to not only have Arizona State University (featured in this book) but the University of Arizona as well. A genuinely diverse school—25% of the undergraduate student body identifies as Hispanic, and students hail from all 50 states and roughly 100 countries—UArizona is noted for its success in improving social mobility. It also happens to have a terrific national reputation, a status that attracts many nonresidents to its exquisite Tucson campus. In fact, over 40% of current Wildcats are from out of state and are willing to pay a large premium to attend the school of 40,407 undergraduates and another 10,700+ graduate students.

Inside the Classroom
The UA general education requirements entail conquering foundations courses (first-year writing, mathematics, second language), tier one courses (traditions and cultures, individuals and societies, natural sciences), tier two courses (humanities, arts, etc.), and one course that falls under the umbrella of diversity emphasis. Students in the Honors College must also complete at least 30 honors units prior to graduation, which includes a thesis/capstone project.

An 18:1 student-to-faculty ratio leads to a mix of smaller and larger course sections with 33% of classes having an enrollment of under 20 and 15% possessing 50 or more students. UArizona promotes opportunities for hands-on learning and faculty mentors through a variety of undergraduate research programs including the Summer Research Institute, Undergraduate Biology Research Program, and Collaborative Research in the Chemical Sciences. Opportunities to study abroad and earn UA credits at partner universities abound. There are 12 such programs available at locations as varied as London, Jakarta, and Phnom Penh.

With more conferred degrees than any other discipline, business/marketing (15%) is the most popular major choice at UArizona. Other common pursuits include biology (9%), health professions (9%), and engineering (7%). Majors within business, engineering, and the geosciences all have excellent national reputations. For those pursuing prestigious fellowships/scholarships, the university has its own Office of Nationally Competitive Scholarships. There have been years in which the school has produced double-digit numbers of Fulbright Scholars.

Outside the Classroom
This 353-acre campus is situated in a residential area of Tucson, the state's second-largest city. A touch over three-quarters of freshmen, but just 22% of the overall undergraduate student body, live in on-campus housing. Yet, in spite of this relatively low number, UArizona very much provides a quintessential big-college experience. Greek life is relatively prominent, attracting 8% of women and 4% of men, but only 25 of the 54 fraternities and sororities actually offer housing. The school is home to 500 varsity athletes who compete in 20 sports; the history of men's basketball is particularly rich and includes a 1997 NCAA title. Thirty club teams engage another 1,000 participants, and an additional 30 intramural leagues bring in thousands more. Arizona regularly garners accolades for having the nicest student recreation centers in the country. It's hard to find a Wildcat who isn't an active member of at least one organization; the school's 400 total clubs have an estimated membership of 20,000 students. Outdoor activities are accessible year-round thanks to an average annual temperature of 83 degrees. Tucson itself rates well as a fun, laid-back, bikeable city with excellent food and entertainment options.

Career Services
The Office of Student Engagement & Career Development at the University of Arizona is staffed by 25 professional employees who specialize in career education, alumni relations, employer relations, and alumni engagement. Additional career services staff members are housed with the university's various undergraduate colleges such as the College of Agriculture and Life Sciences (3) and the Eller College of Management (12), bringing the total number of staff to 40. The overall student-to-advisor ratio is 1,010:1, a high figure compared to many other institutions featured in this book.

Many large-scale events are offered by the university, including multiday, all-student career fairs in the fall and spring. Frequent employer information sessions are also offered throughout the year, as high-profile employers are more than willing to make the trek to campus to recruit UA talent. Handshake affords students access to countless job and internship opportunities, and those seeking a more personal touch can work on their resume or sales pitch with a member of the LifeLab. Job shadowing and other opportunities to connect with the 300,000 active Wildcat alumni are available to anyone who is motivated to seek them out. Within the Eller College of Management, 90% of undergraduates report participating in at least one internship. The school boasts a wealth of high-quality industry partners such as 3M, Honeywell, IBM, Johnson & Johnson, and Northrop Grumman.

Professional Outcomes

While across-the-board success rates of UArizona alumni are not published, there is enough available data for one to see the positive outcomes associated with a Wildcat education. In recent years, some of the top employers hiring Arizona grads have been Raytheon, Vanguard, PepsiCo, Amazon, KPMG, Goldman Sachs, Intel, Lockheed Martin, Nordstrom, and Texas Instruments. An astonishing 92% of employers rate Wildcats as coming to their first job with the skills needed to succeed; this is 66% higher than the national average! Graduates of the Eller College of Management enjoy a starting salary in excess of $60k. Ninety-one percent of recent graduates of the College of Engineering have already secured a job or graduate school acceptance upon receiving their bachelor's diploma; this group has an average starting salary of $74,000.

Many who go on to pursue advanced degrees do so at the University of Arizona itself, which boasts a full array of graduate/professional degree programs and features the affiliated James E. Rogers College of Law and three MD-granting medical schools, including the highly regarded University of Arizona College of Medicine – Tucson. In 2023, the university saw 340 undergraduates apply to medical schools. To get a sense of the types of graduate programs one can access with a UArizona degree, recent graduates of the College of Engineering have continued their studies in master's or PhD programs at the likes of Stanford University, the University of Cambridge, Yale University, Harvard University, Carnegie Mellon University, and Georgia Tech.

Admission

Arizona continued to post unintimidating admissions numbers in the 2022-23 cycle, accepting 87% of the 52,103 who applied. Even better, students who struggle on standardized exams can take advantage of the school's test-optional policy. Thirty-nine percent of attending students placed in the top 10% of their high school class while 66% and 89% were in the top 25% and 50%, respectively. Cumulative GPAs range widely, with 18% of students having earned a 4.0 and 15% having earned under a 3.0. The average GPA is 3.53. The mid-50th percentile ACT range is also quite wide at 21-29; on the SAT, the mid-50th percentile scores are 1140-1360.

Applications to this university are reviewed on a rolling basis. The two most important factors in the eyes of the admissions committee are GPA and the rigor of one's high school courses. Items viewed as "important" are extracurricular activities, talent/ability, character/personal qualities, and the level of an applicant's demonstrated interest. It is highly unusual for the latter category to be given so much weight, however, the University of Arizona serves as a "safety school" for many applicants (the yield rate is 20%), and therefore, they like to know when candidates have a sincere interest in attending.

Worth Your Money?

The University of Arizona continues to be a solid deal for residents of the Grand Canyon State. Including tuition, room and board, and all fees, the estimated cost per year was $33k in 2023-24. An out-of-state student would expect to pay a heftier annual total of $60,600. The average need-based scholarship is $14k, which meets an average of 64% of demonstrated need. Without financial aid, an out-of-state student would need to have a sound and specific reason for crossing state lines to pay $240k at a public university rather than exploring options closer to home. For the 44% who borrow from federal sources, the average debt carried by Wildcats upon graduation is $25k; 7% borrow an additional $43k from private lenders.

FINANCIAL
Institutional Type: Public
In-State Tuition: $12,937
Out-of-State Tuition: $37,355
Room & Board: $13,650
Books & Supplies: $900

Avg. Need-Based Grant: $13,534
Avg. % of Need Met: 70%

Avg. Merit-Based Award: $12,065
% Receiving (Freshmen w/o Need): 32%

Avg. Cumulative Debt: $25,078
% of Students Borrowing: 41%

CAREER
Who Recruits
1. KPMG
2. Moss Adams
3. Google
4. National Securty Agency
5. JPMorgan Chase

Notable Internships
1. Arizona State Legislature
2. Arizona Public Media
3. Tucson Electric Power

Top Employers
1. Amazon
2. Intel
3. Microsoft
4. Apple
5. Honeywell

Where Alumni Work
1. Tucson
2. Phoenix
3. Los Angeles
4. San Francisco
5. New York City

Earnings
College Scorecard (10-YR Post-Entry): $59,805
PayScale (Early Career): $60,500
PayScale (Mid-Career): $107,500
PayScale 20-Year ROI: $572,000

RANKINGS
Money: 4
U.S. News: 115, National Universities
Wall Street Journal/THE: 110
Washington Monthly: 96, National Universities

OVERGENERALIZATIONS
Students are:
Crazy about the Wildcats
Diverse
Ready to party
Social
Self-reliant

COLLEGE OVERLAPS
Arizona State University
Northern Arizona University
San Diego State University
University of Colorado Boulder
University of Oregon

University of California, Berkeley

Berkeley, California | 510-642-3175

The University of California, Berkeley, more commonly referred to as Berkeley or Cal, is the flagship university in the stellar and gargantuan UC system. Founded in 1868 with the motto "Fiat Lux" (Let there be light), the university today offers enlightenment to 32,831 undergraduate and 12,914 graduate students. The name Berkeley likely conjures up two immediate associations—academic prestige and the protests of the 1960s. While no longer a hotbed of youth unrest on the level of the Vietnam era, Berkeley remains a bastion of liberal thought and idealism. It is fitting that the school is the number one all-time producer of Peace Corps volunteers.

Inside the Classroom

More than 150 undergraduate majors and minors are available across six undergraduate schools: the College of Letters and Science, the College of Chemistry, the College of Engineering, the College of Environmental Design, the College of Natural Resources, and the Haas School of Business. Over two-thirds of undergrads are housed within the College of Letters and Science, which requires coursework including entry-level writing, American history and American institutions, foreign language, quantitative reasoning, and reading & composition.

Constant budget crises in the UC system haven't dented the school's reputation one iota, but the impact can be felt in measures such as the student-to-faculty ratio that, at 19:1, is significantly higher than other elite flagships like UVA or Michigan. However, that doesn't translate to across-the-board large class sizes. Rather, undergrads will encounter a mix of large lectures (20% of sections contain more than 50 students) and tiny, single-digit enrollments in seminar-style courses (22% of sections contain nine or fewer students). Undergraduate research opportunities do exist despite the school's massive size; over 55% of students assist faculty with a research project or complete a research methods course in their time at Berkeley. Study abroad opportunities are available for those who desire them, and approximately 1,800 undergrads take a semester in a foreign country each year. Locations where Berkeley faculty deliver instruction include Taiwan, Switzerland, Serbia, Peru, and the Philippines.

Thanks to its equally esteemed graduate schools, many departments have top international reputations including computer science, engineering, chemistry, English, psychology, and economics. In a typical year, 100+ grads are awarded National Science Foundation Graduate Research Fellowships, which is more than Stanford and more than Harvard and Yale combined. In 2023, there were ten Fulbright winners, five Critical Language Scholars, two Schwarzman Scholars, and one Goldwater Scholar.

Outside the Classroom

90+ percent of incoming freshmen live in university-run housing, but upperclassmen are generally left to fend for themselves. Housing is a challenging issue, and while the university is building new dormitories, it presently only has the capacity to house roughly one-quarter of the undergraduate population. A far-from-dominant Greek life attracts 4% of women but only 2% of men into 60+ active fraternities and sororities. Cal's sports program is exceptional as the Golden Bears' thirty varsity teams have won a collective 113 NCAA championships in the school's history; they mostly compete in the Pac-12 Conference. With 1,000+ clubs and activities, there is truly something for everyone, including many political and public service organizations. Roughly 5,300 undergraduate students volunteer their time to community service projects, and the campus has a genuine focus on sustainability; 87% of students walk, bike, or take public transit, and the school has a goal of producing zero non-recycled waste. Being a few miles north of Oakland and a few miles east of San Francisco, big-city fun is never far away. Berkeley itself is replete with awesome restaurants (including, of course, many vegan options), a botanical garden, a marina, an art museum, and a 2,000-acre park.

Career Services

With 35 full-time employees dedicated to undergraduates, the UC Berkeley Career Center has a 938:1 student-to-counselor ratio, much higher than most of the schools featured in this guide but comparable to the other University of California institutions. What the center lacks in its ability to connect one-on-one it makes up for by putting together large-scale events that bring 350+ employers to campus every year. There are large career fairs in the fall and spring, and many industry-specific affairs are held as well including the Social Impact Career Fair, Investment Banking Forum, Law & Graduate School Fair, and the Civil & Environmental Engineering Career Fair.

ADMISSION
Admission Rate: 11%
Admission Rate - Men: 9%
Admission Rate - Women: 14%
EA Admission Rate: Not Offered
ED Admission Rate: Not Offered
ED Admits as % of Total Admits: Not Offered
Admission Rate (5-Year Trend): -6%
% of Admits Attending (Yield): 46%
Transfer Admission Rate: 24%

SAT Reading/Writing (Middle 50%): Test-Blind
SAT Math (Middle 50%): Test-Blind
ACT Composite (Middle 50%): Test-Blind

% Graduated in Top 10% of HS Class: 98%
% Graduated in Top 25% of HS Class: 100%
% Graduated in Top 50% of HS Class: 100%

Demonstrated Interest: Not Considered
Legacy Status: Not Considered
Racial/Ethnic Status: Not Considered
Admission Interview Offered: No

ENROLLMENT
Total Undergraduate Enrollment: 32,831
% Full-Time: 95%
% Male: 44%
% Female: 56%
% Out-of-State: 15%
% Fraternity: 2%
% Sorority: 4%
% On-Campus (All Undergraduate): 27%
Freshman Housing Required: No

% African-American: 2%
% Asian: 35%
% Hispanic: 20%
% White: 20%
% Other: 3%
% International: 13%
% Low-Income: 27%

ACADEMICS
Student-to-Faculty Ratio: 19 to 1
% of Classes Under 20: 50%
% of Classes 20-49: 30%
% of Classes 50 or More: 21%
% Full-Time Faculty: 70%
% Full-Time Faculty w/ Terminal Degree: 69%

Top Programs
Biological Sciences
Business
Chemistry
Computer Science
Data Science
Economics
Engineering
English

Retention Rate: 96%
4-Year Graduation Rate: 82%
6-Year Graduation Rate: 93%

Curricular Flexibility: Somewhat Flexible
Academic Rating: ★★★★✦

#CollegesWorthYourMoney

A survey of employed graduates reveals that the efforts of the career center directly contributed to their job attainment. Specifically, 17% found their first job through on-campus recruiting, 15% directly from an internship, 14% via a career fair or information session, and 13% through Cal's Handshake platform. A hard-to-beat alumni network of 450,000 individuals—100,000 are dues-paying members of the alumni association—can assist you throughout your career. More than 4,500 students attend webinars and in-person events hosted by alums. The average student received two job offers. Overall, despite a high counselor-to-student ratio, Cal's career services provide plenty of opportunities for undergrads to connect with top employers, resulting in students landing positions that align with their career goals while also paying the bills.

Professional Outcomes

Upon graduating, 49% of Cal's Class of 2022 members had already secured employment, 20% were headed to graduate school, and 30% were still seeking their first jobs. Business is the most popular sector, attracting 62% of employed grads; next up are industrial (17%), education (8%), and nonprofit work (7%). Thousands of alumni can be found in the offices of Google, Apple, and Meta, and 500+ Golden Bears are currently employed by Oracle, Amazon, and Microsoft. Most alumni are concentrated in the San Francisco Bay area with Los Angeles, New York, Seattle, DC, Boston, and the United Kingdom next in popularity. The median starting salary was an astonishing $86,459 across all majors.

Because almost 8,000 students earn bachelor's degrees each year, it's hard to pinpoint the most commonly attended graduate/professional schools with literally hundreds of institutions absorbing Berkeley undergrads. They range from the most selective Ivy League universities to a host of less selective institutions. For example, recent political science degree-earners attended graduate schools that included Stanford, Georgetown, San Francisco State, and Eastern Michigan University. Suffice it to say that earning strong grades at Berkeley will set you up for a successful graduate application process at the nation's most elite schools. In recent years, the medical school acceptance rate has hovered in the 54-67% range, and law school applicants have been successful 80-90% of the time. Among recent grads, master's degrees were the most frequently pursued degree, followed by PhDs, JDs, and MDs.

Admission

Berkeley received 128,226 applications for a place in the Class of 2026, but only 11% were offered admission. A decade prior, the university received 48,000+ applications and sported an admit rate of 22%. Acceptance rates fluctuate among three separate groups of candidates: California residents are usually admitted at a slightly higher rate than out-of-staters (2-3 points) and appear to have a massive advantage over international students whose acceptance rate is in the single digits. The school and entire UC system are now test-blind and do not consider standardized test scores in admissions decisions. As such, grades are paramount. The last time class rank was reported, an eye-popping 96% placed in the top decile of their high school class, and the average unweighted GPA was 3.9.

The committee claims that the admissions review is so holistic that it "literally hugs your application." Logistically, with nearly 128,000 applications to sift through, each embrace is surely quite short. As a result, GPA and rigor of secondary school record are presently among the "very important" criteria used to winnow down the initial pool; the essays also sit at the top of the pecking order. Becoming a Golden Bear has been a highly selective process for many decades, and now it has reached its all-time high. Flawless grades in a roster of AP and honors courses are essentially a prerequisite.

Worth Your Money?

Paying $15,891 per year in tuition to attend one of the finest institutions in the country sounds like a pipe dream, particularly considering that some private schools charge four times that. For the one-quarter or so of the undergraduate student body from out of state, the annual cost of attendance will be $73k, a far cry from the $43k COA for Californians. For the 46% of students determined eligible for need-based aid, the average award is $26k per year, making Berkeley a genuinely accessible place for lower-income students to attend without incurring unhealthy student loan debt.

FINANCIAL
Institutional Type: Public
In-State Tuition: $15,891
Out-of-State Tuition: $48,465
Room & Board: $22,402
Books & Supplies: $1,274

Avg. Need-Based Grant: $26,334
Avg. % of Need Met: 86%

Avg. Merit-Based Award: $7,288
% Receiving (Freshmen w/o Need): 6%

Avg. Cumulative Debt: $16,419
% of Students Borrowing: 28%

CAREER
Who Recruits
1. AlphaSights
2. Fisher Investments
3. Navigant
4. Putnam Associates
5. Western Digital

Notable Internships
1. Lyft
2. WeWork
3. Airbnb

Top Employers
1. Google
2. Apple
3. Facebook
4. Amazon
5. Oracle

Where Alumni Work
1. San Francisco
2. Los Angeles
3. New York City
4. Seattle
5. Boston

Earnings
College Scorecard (10-YR Post-Entry): $88,046
PayScale (Early Career): $77,400
PayScale (Mid-Career): $147,300
PayScale 20-Year ROI: $1,024,000

RANKINGS
Money: 5
U.S. News: 15, National Universities
Wall Street Journal/THE: 51
Washington Monthly: 9, National Universities

OVERGENERALIZATIONS
Students are:
Politically liberal
Driven
Diverse
Crazy about the Golden Bears
Competitive

COLLEGE OVERLAPS
Stanford University
University of California, Los Angeles
University of California, San Diego
University of California, Santa Barbara
University of Michigan

University of California, Davis

Davis, California | 530-752-2971

ADMISSION
Admission Rate: 37%
Admission Rate - Men: 32%
Admission Rate - Women: 42%
EA Admission Rate: Not Offered
ED Admission Rate: Not Offered
ED Admits as % of Total Admits: Not Offered
Admission Rate (5-Year Trend): -6%
% of Admits Attending (Yield): 18%
Transfer Admission Rate: Not Reported

SAT Reading/Writing (Middle 50%): Test-Blind
SAT Math (Middle 50%): Test-Blind
ACT Composite (Middle 50%): Test-Blind

% Graduated in Top 10% of HS Class: NR
% Graduated in Top 25% of HS Class: NR
% Graduated in Top 50% of HS Class: NR

Demonstrated Interest: Not Considered
Legacy Status: Not Considered
Racial/Ethnic Status: Not Considered
Admission Interview Offered: No

ENROLLMENT
Total Undergraduate Enrollment: 31,532
% Full-Time: 97%
% Male: 40%
% Female: 60%
% Out-of-State: 4%
% Fraternity: Not Reported
% Sorority: Not Reported
% On-Campus (All Undergraduate): 15%
Freshman Housing Required: No

% African-American: 2%
% Asian: 31%
% Hispanic: 23%
% White: 21%
% Other: 2%
% International: 15%
% Low-Income: 31%

ACADEMICS
Student-to-Faculty Ratio: 21 to 1
% of Classes Under 20: 32%
% of Classes 20-49: 37%
% of Classes 50 or More: 31%
% Full-Time Faculty: 68%
% Full-Time Faculty w/ Terminal Degree: 64%

Top Programs
Animal Science
Biological Sciences
Communication
Computer Science
Environmental Science
Engineering
English
Statistics

Retention Rate: 92%
4-Year Graduation Rate: 66%
6-Year Graduation Rate: 87%

Curricular Flexibility: Less Flexible
Academic Rating: ★★★★

#CollegesWorthYourMoney

Like so much growth in the annals of California state history, the story of UC Davis is one of a post-World War II boom that saw the state's population increase by 53% from the 1940s to the 1950s. The school's rapid rise began in 1959 when Davis officially became a general campus of the University of California system. By 1962, it launched an engineering school, and its now prestigious law and medical schools opened in 1966 and 1968, respectively. One hundred years ago, Davis was known as the University Farm and offered no degree programs. Today, it is home to 31,532 undergraduates alone and offers 100+ undergraduate majors and roughly the same number of graduate programs. As with many UC campuses, the onset of the 2010s saw application numbers spike and acceptance rates plunge. The school that was once only a farm is, today, producing crops of graduates that line corporate offices at the leading tech companies in Silicon Valley.

Inside the Classroom

There are four undergraduate schools at UCD: the College of Agricultural and Environmental Sciences, the College of Biological Sciences, the College of Engineering, and the College of Letters and Science. The university has two sets of core requirements—Topical Breadth, which mandates between twelve and twenty units in each of the arts and humanities, science and engineering, and the social sciences—and Core Literacies, which includes English composition; writing experience; oral skills; visual literacy; American cultures, governance, and history; domestic diversity; world cultures; quantitative literacy; and scientific literacy. All told, that adds up to eighty-seven units of required coursework, but the categories are broad, and pretty much any course you could take fits at least one, making those curricular requirements less limiting than they first appear.

A 21:1 student-to-faculty ratio isn't terribly inspiring, especially with a large number of graduate students stealing their share of the spotlight. While class sizes aren't small, 31% of sections enroll fewer than 20 students, and 67% of classes are kept under fifty students. There are numerous opportunities for undergraduate research through programs like the McNair Scholars Program, the Biology Undergraduate Research Program, and Sponsored Undergraduate Research programs. A solid 42% of Davis seniors report having assisted a professor with research, and 50% engage in some type of research/creative project outside the classroom. Only 1,300 students choose to study abroad each year, but offerings do include 50 programs in thirty countries with courses taught by University of California professors.

The areas of study with the largest number of degrees awarded were biology, the social sciences, psychology, and engineering. Davis attracts droves of students to programs in engineering, computer science, and animal science, all of which are nationally renowned. In recent years, Davis students have begun to capture a greater number of prestigious national awards. Eleven Fulbright Scholarships were awarded to grads and alumni in 2023, and the school has had a number of Rhodes Scholarship finalists in the last decade.

Outside the Classroom

At 5,300 acres, the Davis campus is one of the largest in the country, yet housing options are still expanding to keep up with enrollment increases. The housing capacity at the university is currently 11,000 students; freshmen are guaranteed on-campus housing, and over 90% usually take advantage. In 2021, they opened new dorms that added 3,300 beds to the West Village section of the university. The gender disparity cannot be ignored at UC Davis as women outnumber men by a 60/40 ratio. Roughly seventy Greek organizations attract 6% of the undergraduate population. There are approximately 800 student-run organizations, including award-winning academic teams that have captured the National Freescale Cup Autonomous Model Car Competition, the International Data Mining Cup, and the grand prize at the International Genetically Engineered Machines competition. On the subject of competition, the chance to participate in athletics exists no matter your level of skill. The Aggies field fourteen women's and nine men's Division I teams to go with twenty-seven intramural leagues and 40 intercollegiate club squads. Given the school's emphasis on environmental science, it should come as no shock that it is routinely voted one of the greener campuses in the United States, and over one-quarter of dining hall food is sustainably grown. Sacramento is the nearest big city, only 15 miles from campus; San Francisco is a manageable hour-long car ride away.

Career Services

The UC Davis Internship and Career Center (ICC) has 24 professional employees who work with or on behalf of undergraduate students, many of whom specialize in a particular discipline such as engineering and physical sciences, health and biological sciences, agricultural and environmental sciences, and liberal arts and business. Others play roles in the areas of internship coordination, employer relations, and recruiting. Davis has a 1,314:1 student-to-staff ratio, which is among the poorest of any university profiled in this guidebook. While the staffing may be lacking for a school with over 31,000 undergraduates, there are plenty of encouraging statistics that indicate Aggies' career prospects are in good hands.

University of California, Davis

E-mail: undergraduateadmissions@ucdavis.edu | Website: ucdavis.edu

An admirable 80% of undergraduates land at least one internship; 55% engage in two or more internships. In total, the ICC facilitates more than 10,000 internships per year. More than 500 company recruiters visit UC Davis each year looking to hire Aggies, and many major corporations attend the six large-scale career fairs that take place each year, including the Fall/Winter/Spring Internship & Career Fair, the STEM Career Fair, and the Engineering & Tech Internship & Career Fair. There are 293,000 living Aggie alumni who are embedded at many of the top companies to work for in the country. With terrific internship and recruitment statistics, the ICC overcomes its less-than-desirable staffing to be of great assistance to job-seeking graduates.

Professional Outcomes

Based on the most recent data available, one year after earning their BA or BS, 14% of Davis grads are still unemployed. Many have found homes at Silicon Valley or other California-based juggernaut employers, including about all of the world's top tech companies. The corporations employing 200 or more Aggies include Genentech, Google, Apple, Cisco, Meta, Oracle, Amazon, Microsoft, Salesforce, and LinkedIn. More than 100 Aggies are presently working for Adobe and rivals Uber and Lyft. The San Francisco Bay area is home to the largest concentration of Davis alumni followed by Sacramento, Los Angeles, San Diego, and Seattle. Median earnings rise to $112k ten years out of school.

Within one year of graduating, 39% of Aggies elect to continue their education, and 94% report that their undergraduate experience prepared them somewhere between adequately and "very well" for postgraduate study. The most popular degrees pursued are master's, MDs or other health doctorates, law, and MBA/MPA. The UC Davis School of Medicine, one of the best schools for primary care training in the country, tends to favor its own graduates, filling approximately 20% of its cohorts with homegrown students. The average undergraduate student who gained acceptance to at least one medical school possessed a 3.58 GPA and a 512 MCAT score; 488 seniors applied to med school in 2023-24. The UC Davis School of Law also draws heavily from its undergraduate schools, and many grads also find homes at other University of California schools. Currently, multiple Aggie alumni are enrolled at the likes of Harvard Law School, Duke University School of Law, and a host of other top-tier institutions.

Admission

Like all schools in the University of California system, the Davis branch has experienced an influx of applicants in the last several years. It just missed another record last cycle with 94,754 freshman applications. From that pool, 37% were welcomed aboard to form the freshman class of 2022-23 (12 points lower than the previous cycle). Most had near-perfect academic transcripts as, in one recent year, 86% were the proud owners of a 3.75 or higher unweighted GPA. The school is now test-blind and no longer factors ACT or SAT scores into their admissions decisions.

According to admissions officers, the factors most heavily weighted in the admissions process are the rigor of one's secondary courses, GPA, and the application essay. First-generation status is listed as a "considered" factor, but the number of students who are the first in their families to enter college suggests that this is a point of emphasis for the university. In fact, an astonishing 42% of current students grew up in households with parents who had not completed four-year degrees. Getting into UC Davis is harder than it used to be, and, like other University of California campuses, it requires a fairly pristine academic transcript in a rigorous curriculum.

Worth Your Money?

Over half of those attending UC Davis receive an average need-based grant of $21k. Considering that the estimated in-state cost of attendance is just under $42k, the majority of undergraduates are paying a reasonable price for a valuable degree. Estimated COA for nonresidents is $74k. For the 18% of attendees not from California, that would be an expensive venture without any financial aid, and you likely could find a better merit aid offer from a private institution.

FINANCIAL
Institutional Type: Public
In-State Tuition: $15,266
Out-of-State Tuition: $46,043
Room & Board: $18,562
Books & Supplies: $1,381

Avg. Need-Based Grant: $21,395
Avg. % of Need Met: 83%

Avg. Merit-Based Award: $4,896
% Receiving (Freshmen w/o Need): 4%

Avg. Cumulative Debt: $17,534
% of Students Borrowing: 37%

CAREER
Who Recruits
1. Airbnb
2. Lyft
3. Adobe
4. Linkedin
5. Cisco

Notable Internships
1. U.S. House of Representatives
2. Adidas
3. Credit Suisse

Top Employers
1. Kaiser Permanente
2. Genetech
3. Google
4. Apple
5. Facebook

Where Alumni Work
1. San Francisco
2. Sacramento
3. Los Angeles
4. San Diego
5. Orange County, CA

Earnings
College Scorecard (10-YR Post-Entry): $74,305
PayScale (Early Career): $66,800
PayScale (Mid-Career): $128,000
PayScale 20-Year ROI: $709,000

RANKINGS
Money: 4.5
U.S. News: 28, National Universities
Wall Street Journal/THE: 94
Washington Monthly: 21, National Universities

OVERGENERALIZATIONS
Students are:
Environmentally conscious
Diverse
Friendly
Not afraid to work hard
Outdoorsy

COLLEGE OVERLAPS
University of California, Berkeley
University of California, Irvine
University of California, Los Angeles
University of California, San Diego
University of California, Santa Barbara

University of California, Irvine

Irvine, California | 949-824-6703

A diverse school with a strong Asian and Hispanic representation that serves a phenomenally high percentage of first-generation college students, UC Irvine is, like the other schools in the University of California system, becoming more selective every year. On the eve of the millennium, as Y2K-mania reached its crescendo, Irvine was a school that accepted roughly half of its applicants and was primarily a safety school for those applying to the more prestigious UC campuses. Today, UCI is a top-of-the-list destination for 28,661 undergraduate students, half of whom are California residents, and all of whom proudly call themselves Anteaters. As the third decade of the 2000s kicks off, freshmen flock to Orange County not just for the school's premier location but for the eighty stellar undergraduate academic programs the university offers at a bargain price.

Inside the Classroom
For a school with an overwhelming number of freshmen entering its gates each year, UC Irvine takes great care to offer first-years a soft landing. The Summer Bridge Scholars Program, Freshman Edge Program, and the Freshman Seminar Series are all designed to help new students succeed, and they are effective as 92% of freshmen return for their sophomore year, a retention rate on par with many highly selective private institutions. All students take a liberal arts core that involves three courses in each of science and technology, arts and humanities, and the social sciences, two writing-intensive classes, and forays into foreign language, quantitative reasoning, multicultural issues, and international/global issues. Like most California publics, UCI operates on the quarter system, which means you'll need to get used to furiously paced ten-week periods of study.

At a school with an 18:1 student-to-faculty ratio and 7,275 graduate students to serve, you might expect all classes at Irvine to be held in hundred-seat lecture halls. We are pleased to report that this is not the case. In fact, 56% of all sections enroll 19 or fewer students, and only 21% of courses contain 50+ students. The school provides a terrific number of opportunities for undergrads to participate in some type of supervised research. More than three-fifths of students have conducted a research project, and 20% have assisted faculty in conducting research. The Undergraduate Research Opportunities Program helps students with proposal writing, developing research plans, and presenting their results at the annual spring UCI Undergraduate Research Symposium and/or publishing their results in the *UCI Undergraduate Research Journal*. Most students remain on campus for all four years as only about 1,000 individuals study abroad each year.

The most degrees at Irvine are conferred in the social sciences (16%), business (12%), psychology (11%), and biology (9%). The Samueli School of Engineering has a solid reputation as does the Bren School, the only independent computer science school in the University of California system. Programs in public health and biological sciences also earn very high marks. Between two and five graduates win Fulbright Scholarships each year, and Irvine has had an occasional Goldwater, Truman, or Marshall Scholar in the last few years, but winning prestigious national postgraduate scholarships is not a primary focus of Anteater alumni.

Outside the Classroom
It's hard to think of many more desirable locations for a college setting than Orange County, California. The Pacific Ocean is only five miles from campus, including the famed Laguna and Newport beaches. Los Angeles is within an hour's drive, San Diego is about an hour and a half, and, if you have a spare 25 minutes, you can head over to Disneyland for the afternoon. The suburban campus covers 1,474 acres, and 44% of students live in university housing. Freshmen are guaranteed two full years of housing should they choose to accept it. Around 6% percent are members of Greek life. There are 18 varsity sports teams and 400 total student-athletes. All-time, the school has produced 500 All-Americans and 50+ Olympians. Currently, there are 600+ registered campus organizations representing over nineteen categories. Aldrich Park, modeled after Central Park, is the beautiful centerpiece of Irvine's campus and the site of an annual spring fair. Campus-wide events like Shocktoberfest and Homecoming are well attended.

Career Services
The UCI Division of Career Pathways employs 20 professional employees who work with or on behalf of undergraduate students as career educators, internship coordinators, or employer engagement specialists. That 1,433:1 student-to-staff ratio is among the highest of any university profiled in this guidebook. Fortunately, the school still manages to reach a significant percentage of the undergraduate population through a variety of means as evidenced by numerous impressive data points.

University of California, Irvine

E-mail: admissions@uci.edu | Website: uci.edu

In a single recent school year, career counselors conducted 2,867 one-on-one counseling sessions, and 227 companies attended the school's various virtual career fairs that drew a collective student crowd of more than 3,300. The UCI Division of Career Pathways not only hosts general fall and spring fairs but also gatherings for STEM careers, health jobs, and law school applicants. An additional 3,000 students attended Career Pathways Panels. In a single year, companies conduct on-campus interviews with 1,300+ undergraduate students. The list of on-campus recruiters included Deloitte, KPMG, Ernst and Young, PricewaterhouseCoopers, Google, Amazon, Northrop Grumman, and Johnson & Johnson. A total of 46% of students completed internships last year; half were noncredit internships while half were for credit. The job-shadowing program, now in its sixth year, attracts nearly 300 student participants. Career services at UCI aren't perfect; it's simply too large an operation for 20 people to handle, but the office possesses strong enough corporate connections to assist grads in achieving positive postgraduate outcomes.

Professional Outcomes

Accounting, aerospace, internet and software, K-12 education, real estate, and retail are among the industries attracting the greatest number of Anteaters. Companies employing the greatest number of recent grads include Boeing, the Walt Disney Company, Google, EY, and Microsoft. Many also end up with nonprofit organizations like Teach for America and City Year. Looking at alumni from all years, hundreds of individuals can be found at each of Kaiser Permanente, Meta, Apple, Edwards Lifesciences, and Deloitte. Across all disciplines, the median salary within the first couple years of entering the working world is $69,000. Computer science graduates earn close to $120k right off the bat. Few grads leave the state of California; Orange County, Los Angeles, San Francisco, and San Diego soak up the vast majority.

Between 75 and 80% of Irvine grads plan on pursuing an advanced degree within five years of earning their bachelor's. The majority of those enrolling in graduate school do so within the state of California. Many remain at Irvine or another UC campus—Berkeley, UCLA, and San Diego are among the most popular choices. Irvine also sends graduates to Stanford and USC as well as out of state to the University of Washington and Georgia Tech. UC Irvine has a strong reputation for premed. In 2022, the university produced the 19th most medical school applicants of any institution in the country, and Anteaters possessed higher MCAT scores than the national average. The prestigious UCI School of Medicine admitted 17 of its own alumni in one recent year, which accounted for more than 15% of the incoming class. The UC Irvine School of Law is only a decade old but has already skyrocketed toward the top of the rankings. In addition to remaining in Irvine for law school, undergrads often gain acceptance to other excellent law schools within the UC system and also have earned acceptances to the likes of Harvard, Georgetown, and the University of Michigan.

Admission

An almost incomprehensible deluge of 119,199 applications rained down on the UCI admissions staff in 2022, and its acceptance rate was only 21%, a far cry from only six years prior when 41% of high school applicants were admitted. Getting into Irvine without placing in the top decile of your high school class is nearly impossible as the vast majority of freshmen earned that distinction. The average GPA for attending students was 3.95. Of course, grades and rigor are critical as Irvine is now, along with the rest of the UC system, fully test-blind.

For a school receiving six figures worth of application numbers each year, it still professes to hold seven factors as being of the highest importance: rigor of curriculum, GPA, essays, extracurricular activities, talent/ability, work experience, and volunteer work. Interestingly, first-generation status is listed as merely "considered," yet the school's undergraduate population is comprised of an incredible 46% of first-generation students. While racial/ethnic status is "not considered" in admissions, one-third of the student population are underrepresented minorities.

Worth Your Money?

An annual tuition (plus fees) of under $17,000 for California residents helps explain the rising popularity of Irvine as well as the other UC campuses. No matter your intended major, this in-state rate represents a genuine bargain. Out-of-state residents without plans to pursue computer science or engineering should think twice before committing three times that amount in tuition costs alone. You would likely be better off pursuing options in your home state or private options with merit aid.

University of California, Los Angeles

Los Angeles, California | 310-825-3101

Among the most selective public universities in the country, UCLA is also the most diverse campus on the planet. The undergraduate student body is 35% Asian, 21% Hispanic, and 9% international, not to mention 30%+ first-generation college students, making UCLA a fascinating place to pursue one of 125 majors in 100+ academic departments. More than 32,423 undergraduates enjoy a whopping 3,800 course offerings that include programs in over 40 languages, many of which—such as Armenian, Old Norse, and Sanskrit—you won't find offered at your average university.

Inside the Classroom
The general education curriculum requires that every student explore three foundational areas: the arts and humanities, society and culture, and scientific inquiry. That entails completing ten courses. Additionally, in order to graduate you'll need to meet requirements in foreign language, writing, and diversity. The school's Capstone Initiative has sought to bring a culminating senior academic endeavor to as many students as possible. As of 2023, more than 60 majors at UCLA require a capstone experience that results in the creation of a tangible product under the mentorship of faculty members.

Close to half of classrooms contain fewer than twenty Bruins, but those taking introductory courses will find themselves in a fair number of lecture halls with a hundred or more students. Professors are given impressively high marks for a research university of UCLA's size. Over 90% of the graduates of the College of Letters and Science rate their professors as being both intellectually challenging and accessible. By senior year, 40% of undergraduates have participated in a research experience. There are multiple undergraduate research journals in which students can publish their original works as well as a Research Poster Day each May when students can present. Every year, one-quarter of the undergraduate population elects to study abroad, a sharp increase from only a few years ago. UCLA has 115 partner universities in 40+ countries around the globe.

By volume, the most commonly conferred degrees are in the social sciences (25%), biology (16%), psychology (11%), mathematics (8%), and engineering (7%). Departmental rankings are high across the board in areas such as computer science, engineering, film, fine and performing arts, mathematics, political science, and many more. The school also produces a reasonable number of postgraduate scholarship winners each year.

Outside the Classroom
If you can't find your niche at UCLA, it can hardly be blamed on the school that offers over 1,000 clubs and student organizations; 74% of students join at least one. There is no shortage of opportunities to volunteer in the surrounding Los Angeles community—the Volunteer Center, Center for Community Learning, and Community Programs Office offer countless avenues for civic involvement. Greek life is readily available with more than sixty fraternities and sororities on campus, but it is hardly smothering; only 11% of men and 13% of women are Greek affiliated. UCLA's sports scene boasts storied basketball and baseball teams, big-time football, and 121 all-time championships across 25 Division I men's and women's sports. Ninety-seven percent of freshmen reside on campus, and 58% of the entire student body lives in university-owned housing. As bountiful as campus life is at UCLA, the excitement that can be found in the surrounding neighborhoods is truly limitless. Within a few miles of campus, undergrads can venture to Venice Beach, Santa Monica, Malibu, or Beverly Hills. In short, you won't find too many Bruins complaining of boredom.

Career Services
With 29 full-time employees dedicated to undergraduates, the UCLA Career Center has a 1,118:1 student-to-counselor ratio, much higher than most of the schools featured in this guide. The university does host a number of major-specific job fairs that are attended by an impressive selection of employers. The Engineering and Technical Fair is attended by forty organizations including the CIA, Texas Instruments, Visa, and eBay. Each academic quarter, the school also hosts Hire UCLA, which is well-attended by major corporations. Perhaps, most importantly of all, over 500,000 living alumni can help you.

When it comes to finding an internship, students are not going to have their hands held throughout the entire process. The Career Center connects students with internships via Handshake, and over 60% of undergrads do eventually land one, an exceptional figure for a large, public institution. The Career Center offers services such as an online resume critique with a five-day turnaround, and students are free to schedule an appointment or drop by for career advice, a mock interview, or graduate school exploration from 9 a.m. to 4 p.m. on weekdays. Additional events are organized by the UCLA Career Center just about every day. For example, over the course of one random week in October, the center hosted a resume workshop, an engineering and tech fair, a seminar on careers in biotech, and a recruiting visit from AT&T.

Professional Outcomes

UCLA grads flow most heavily into the research, finance, computer science, and engineering sectors. The employers that snatch up the highest number of recent Bruin grads include Disney, Google (where over 2,000 alumni presently work), EY, Teach for America, Amazon, and Oracle. Hundreds also can be found in the corporate offices of Bloomberg, Deloitte, Mattel, Oracle, and SpaceX. Internships definitely help students land jobs; students who had at least one internship found employment at double the rate of their peers who did not have such an experience. The average starting salary for full-time employment exceeds $58,000 (they have not released an updated figure in several years), a solid figure considering the vast array of degrees being conferred. A good number of students stay in LA/Orange County after graduation, but the other most popular destination points include NYC, DC, Chicago, Seattle, and Boston.

Sixteen percent of recent graduates enrolled directly in a graduate/professional school. The most attended grad schools are primarily other excellent California-based institutions including Stanford, Pepperdine, USC, Berkeley, and Loyola Marymount. However, Columbia, Carnegie Mellon, and NYU also make that list. UCLA students applying to medical school have experienced acceptance rates varying from 51-59% in recent years. The most frequently attended medical schools include Duke, Boston University, Drexel, Temple, Case Western, and NYU. Over 90% of Bruins applying to law school garner at least one acceptance, a clip that is roughly 15% better than the national average. Law schools with the highest number of UCLA grads include many of the aforementioned California universities as well as Georgetown, Vanderbilt, George Washington, Duke, and American.

Admission

A decade ago, 24% of the roughly 50,000 applicants to UCLA received acceptance letters; today, the school receives the most applications of any college in the country with 149,815 in 2022, and the acceptance rate has fallen to 9% (it was 11% the year prior). Students from out-of-state usually fare better than in-state applicants and international applicants. However, last year, the numbers were almost identical. The University of California Board of Regents recently passed a measure capping out-of-state/international enrollment at 18% moving forward, which should keep that trend moving in the same direction.

Those accepted straight from high school are a high-achieving bunch as, in a typical year, a hard-to-comprehend 97% graduated in the top 10% of their high school class. UCLA is now completely test-blind so SATs and ACTs are irrelevant here. It's important to note that there is more than one way through these heavily guarded gates. UCLA is extremely transfer-friendly, offering admission to 6,130 such students in 2022 with the vast majority coming from California's system of community colleges. UCLA has joined the ranks of the uber-selective as the pool of top-of-their-class applicants continues to grow each year. While it does employ some semblance of a holistic process that considers personal qualities, likely contributions to campus life, and challenges overcome, applicants need to earn very high GPAs in a very rigorous high school curriculum to have a genuine shot at admission.

Worth Your Money?

The average UCLA graduate has almost $15,000 less in student loan debt than the average college graduate. It helps when your in-state tuition to attend one of the finest universities around is only $15k; the total annual cost of attendance is $38,517 for a resident but $71k for a nonresident. While UCLA is rarely able to meet 100% of a student's demonstrated financial need, the school is priced so reasonably that graduates emerge with little debt and sky-high job prospects. Depending on your intended major and/or financial situation, UCLA can be worth your money even as an out-of-stater, despite the elevated price.

FINANCIAL
Institutional Type: Public
In-State Tuition: $13,752
Out-of-State Tuition: $46,326
Room & Board: $17,148
Books & Supplies: $1,574

Avg. Need-Based Grant: $23,600
Avg. % of Need Met: 85%

Avg. Merit-Based Award: $6,573
% Receiving (Freshmen w/o Need): 4%

Avg. Cumulative Debt: $17,920
% of Students Borrowing: 33%

CAREER
Who Recruits
1. Bain & Company
2. Airbnb
3. Salesforce
4. Netflix
5. Oracle

Notable Internships
1. CBRE
2. Los Angeles Magazine
3. Northrop Grumman

Top Employers
1. Google
2. Apple
3. Amazon
4. Facebook
5. Microsoft

Where Alumni Work
1. Los Angeles
2. San Francisco
3. Orange County, CA
4. New York City
5. San Diego

Earnings
College Scorecard (10-YR Post-Entry): $79,826
PayScale (Early Career): $66,500
PayScale (Mid-Career): $129,300
PayScale 20-Year ROI: $781,000

RANKINGS
Money: 5
U.S. News: 15, National Universities
Wall Street Journal/THE: 74
Washington Monthly: 16, National Universities

OVERGENERALIZATIONS
Students are:
Working hard and playing hard
Diverse
Always admiring the beauty of their campus
Competitive
Involved/investsed in campus life

COLLEGE OVERLAPS
New York University
University of California, Berkeley
University of California, San Diego
University of California, Santa Barbara
University of Southern California

University of California, Riverside

Riverside, California | 951-827-3411

ADMISSION
Admission Rate: 69%
Admission Rate - Men: 64%
Admission Rate - Women: 74%
EA Admission Rate: Not Offered
ED Admission Rate: Not Offered
ED Admits as % of Total Admits: Not Offered
Admission Rate (5-Year Trend): +13%
% of Admits Attending (Yield): 15%
Transfer Admission Rate: 61%

SAT Reading/Writing (Middle 50%): Test-Blind
SAT Math (Middle 50%): Test-Blind
ACT Composite (Middle 50%): Test-Blind

% Graduated in Top 10% of HS Class: 94%
% Graduated in Top 25% of HS Class: 100%
% Graduated in Top 50% of HS Class: 100%

Demonstrated Interest: Not Considered
Legacy Status: Not Considered
Racial/Ethnic Status: Not Considered
Admission Interview Offered: No

ENROLLMENT
Total Undergraduate Enrollment: 22,903
% Full-Time: 96%
% Male: 48%
% Female: 52%
% Out-of-State: 1%
% Fraternity: 2%
% Sorority: 4%
% On-Campus (All Undergraduate): 35%
Freshman Housing Required: No

% African-American: 3%
% Asian: 37%
% Hispanic: 39%
% White: 11%
% Other: 1%
% International: 4%
% Low-Income: 54%

ACADEMICS
Student-to-Faculty Ratio: 24 to 1
% of Classes Under 20: 22%
% of Classes 20-49: 44%
% of Classes 50 or More: 34%
% Full-Time Faculty: 84%
% Full-Time Faculty w/ Terminal Degree: 98%

Top Programs
Anthropology
Business
Computer Science
Creative Writing
Engineering
Global Studies
Sociology

Retention Rate: 89%
4-Year Graduation Rate: 62%
6-Year Graduation Rate: 76%

Curricular Flexibility: Less Flexible
Academic Rating: ★★★✓

#CollegesWorthYourMoney

Ethnically and socioeconomically, the University of California, Riverside is one of the most diverse schools in the United States. Enrolling 51% first-generation students and more Pell Grant recipients than the entire Ivy League combined, UCR is one of the top universities in the country (if not the top) for facilitating upward mobility as well as granting financial aid. It's no wonder that this previously unheralded tentacle of the vaunted University of California system is finally beginning to get more recognition, and, in turn, become more selective; the acceptance rate has plummeted as far as 20 points over the last decade.

Inside the Classroom
UC Riverside offers 80+ majors across five colleges: the Bourns College of Engineering; the College of Humanities, Arts, and Sciences; the College of Natural and Agricultural Sciences; the School of Business; and the School of Public Policy. Utilizing a quarter system, students must complete 180 units in order to graduate. College breadth requirements mandate that all undergrads take English composition, a foreign language, an ethnicity course, 20 units worth of natural sciences/mathematics, 20 units in the humanities, and 16 units in the social sciences.

With a 24:1 student-to-faculty ratio, you won't have the luxury of taking too many courses with a small class size. Twenty-two percent of sections enroll fewer than 20 undergrads compared to 34% that enroll 50 or more students. Faculty-mentored research opportunities are available for everyone, and the school has made expanding research participation to at least one-fifth of the undergraduate population an institutional goal. Students can pursue mentorships with professors through an undergraduate research portal. Riverside students can also take advantage of study abroad options via the system-wide UC Education Abroad Programs that have sent students to 400+ different programs in 46 countries.

There is no major at UCR that magnetically pulls in a massive chunk of the undergraduate student body. Rather, undergrads spread out to a wide array of majors with the greatest number of degrees conferred in the social sciences (20%), biology (18%), business (14%), psychology (10%), and engineering (7%). Students from all academic concentrations have begun to apply for prestigious national fellowship programs in recent years. In recent years, the school has produced a number of Fulbright Scholars, Goldwater Scholars, Marshall Scholars, and Gates-Cambridge Scholars.

Outside the Classroom
Occupying 1,900 suburban acres, UCR's campus has plenty of physical space for its undergraduates. Yet, while 68% of freshmen do take advantage of available dorms and campus apartments, just 35% of the total population reside in university-owned housing. Being unable to accommodate all students, the school does offer off-campus housing services that help undergrads locate a place to live after their first year. Greek organizations are quiet at this school, attracting just 2% of men and 4% of women. This is an extremely diverse school where only 11% of undergraduates are classified as white; 42% are Latino, and 34% are Asian. There are 17 Division I athletic teams, and over 300 student-athletes compete under the Highlander banner. The baseball team has produced more than a handful of major leaguers. For everyone else, there is an 80,000-square-foot recreational facility, plenty of intramural sports, and outdoor adventures arranged through the popular Outdoor Excursions Program. In total, there are 450+ student-run organizations. Riverside is a very eco-friendly campus having recently installed an additional 9,600 solar panels, and it has been recognized for its sustainability practices. Downtown Riverside is a vibrant area replete with dining, shopping, and cultural options. The Fox Performing Arts Center and the Riverside Municipal Auditorium host concerts, musicals, and comedic acts.

Career Services
The University of California Riverside Career Center employs 14 professionals with roles in the areas of career counseling (by academic discipline), industry outreach, and alumni engagement. This 1,636:1 counselor-to-student ratio may be less than desirable, but this office manages to reach a large chunk of the undergraduate student population as evidenced by the 200,000+ annual website visits and 12,592 in-person student contacts made in one recent year. Career fairs were attended by 436 hiring organizations; 1,550 students attended at least one job fair.

Student evaluations of the career center's planning and counseling offerings are beyond glowing—they are downright blinding. Ninety-eight percent of workshop attendees felt that the presentation met their expectations, and 99% of those receiving one-on-one counseling felt better prepared to effectively complete a job or graduate school application after their visit. In 2020-21, there were 3,195 counseling appointments, including drop-ins. A total of 7,630 students attended workshops and presentations put on by this office. Of those who found employment, 21% identified the Career Center as the way in which they found the position, and 9% cited their internship experience, leaving little doubt the services offered at Riverside are directly leading to postgraduation student success.

Professional Outcomes
Within one year of graduation, 54% of 2022 grads were employed, 15% were pursuing an advanced degree, and 29% were still seeking their next opportunity. Less than 20% of recent grads left the state, with most remaining in Southern California. The most commonly entered industries were education, business, tech, social services, the sciences, and government. The median starting salary for Class of 2022 graduates was $61k. More than 100 alumni work for major corporations like Kaiser Permanente, Amazon, Wells Fargo, Apple, Microsoft, Meta, and EY. Last year's graduates also found homes with employers such as the NASA Jet Propulsion Laboratory, SpaceX, Northrop Grumman, HP, and the Walt Disney Company.

Over one-fifth of all graduates began work on a graduate or advanced degree within one year of earning their bachelor's degree. The most common disciplines that grads pursue are education, physical/natural sciences, engineering/computer science, health professions, and arts/humanities. Four percent of graduates matriculate into law school, and 5% enroll in medical programs. In 2023, there were 288 applicants to US medical schools, and many went on to begin their studies at the UC Riverside School of Medicine, which opened its doors a decade ago. Recently enrolled law students were studying at institutions such as Loyola, UCLA, UC Davis, USC, UC Irvine, and Pepperdine.

Admission
Riverside used to be one of the UC campuses you could count on to say "yes" to anyone with decent credentials; a decade ago, it accepted 76% of applicants. First-year students applying to enter the university in the fall of 2019 were accepted at only a 56% clip. However, the Class of 2026 acceptance rate shot back up to a friendlier 69%. Terrific grades and a rank in the top 10% of one's high school class are now almost prerequisites at Riverside. The average GPA for the Class of 2026 was 3.94, and, in recent years, 94% placed in the top decile. As with all schools in the University of California system, SAT/ACT scores are no longer considered in the admissions process.

The two factors that are most important to the admissions committee are GPA and the application essays. The rigor of one's postsecondary courses is "important," and talent/ability, first-generation status, and state residency are "considered." There is nothing particularly complicated about the admissions process at UC Riverside. Strong grades and well-crafted answers to the four Personal Insight Questions should lead to a successful result.

Worth Your Money?
Like all schools in the University of California system, Riverside is worth every dollar. Tuition and fees are just $15k for the 2023-24 school year. Estimated total expenses for an in-state student residing in the dorms come to almost $41,000, but that includes health insurance, transportation, and personal expenses. Nonresidents pay a sticker price of $73k for full cost of attendance, which is close to what you would pay at an elite private liberal arts college in New England. For that price, it would take a special set of circumstances to make this school a good value for anyone lacking residency status.

FINANCIAL
Institutional Type: Public
In-State Tuition: $13,692
Out-of-State Tuition: $46,266
Room & Board: $18,925
Books & Supplies: $1,750

Avg. Need-Based Grant: $19,951
Avg. % of Need Met: 89%

Avg. Merit-Based Award: $6,320
% Receiving (Freshmen w/o Need): 2%

Avg. Cumulative Debt: $18,960
% of Students Borrowing: 55%

CAREER
Who Recruits
1. Salesforce
2. Deloitte
3. AT&T
4. Amazon Web Services
5. Kaiser Permanente

Notable Internships
1. Amazon Japan
2. Kohl's
3. Blizzard Entertainment

Top Employers
1. Kaiser Permanente
2. Amazon
3. Google
4. Wells Fargo
5. Apple

Where Alumni Work
1. Los Angeles
2. San Francisco
3. Orange County, CA
4. San Diego
5. New York City

Earnings
College Scorecard (10-YR Post-Entry): $63,645
PayScale (Early Career): $60,200
PayScale (Mid-Career): $113,200
PayScale 20-Year ROI: $549,000

RANKINGS
Money: 4.5
U.S. News: 76, National Universities
Wall Street Journal/THE: 181
Washington Monthly: 64, National Universities

OVERGENERALIZATIONS
Students are:
Diverse
Less likely to party
More likely to go home on weekends
Collaborative
Laid-back

COLLEGE OVERLAPS
Cal Poly, San Luis Obispo
California State University, Fullerton
University of California, Davis
University of California, Irvine
University of California, Santa Cruz

University of California, San Diego

La Jolla, California | 858-534-4831

ADMISSION
Admission Rate: 24%
Admission Rate - Men: 21%
Admission Rate - Women: 26%
EA Admission Rate: Not Offered
ED Admission Rate: Not Offered
ED Admits as % of Total Admits: Not Offered
Admission Rate (5-Year Trend): -10%
% of Admits Attending (Yield): 21%
Transfer Admission Rate: 59%

SAT Reading/Writing (Middle 50%): Test-Blind
SAT Math (Middle 50%): Test-Blind
ACT Composite (Middle 50%): Test-Blind

% Graduated in Top 10% of HS Class: 100%
% Graduated in Top 25% of HS Class: 100%
% Graduated in Top 50% of HS Class: 100%

Demonstrated Interest: Not Considered
Legacy Status: Not Considered
Racial/Ethnic Status: Not Considered
Admission Interview Offered: No

ENROLLMENT
Total Undergraduate Enrollment: 33,096
% Full-Time: 97%
% Male: 48%
% Female: 52%
% Out-of-State: 9%
% Fraternity: 14%
% Sorority: 14%
% On-Campus (All Undergraduate): 39%
Freshman Housing Required: No

% African-American: 3%
% Asian: 39%
% Hispanic: 23%
% White: 19%
% Other: 2%
% International: 14%
% Low-Income: 34%

ACADEMICS
Student-to-Faculty Ratio: 19 to 1
% of Classes Under 20: 44%
% of Classes 20-49: 30%
% of Classes 50 or More: 26%
% Full-Time Faculty: 88%
% Full-Time Faculty w/ Terminal Degree: 98%

Top Programs
Biological Sciences
Chemistry and Biochemistry
Cognitive Science
Communication
Computer Science
Economics
Engineering
International Studies

Retention Rate: 94%
4-Year Graduation Rate: 72%
6-Year Graduation Rate: 88%

Curricular Flexibility: Less Flexible
Academic Rating: ★★★★✦

#CollegesWorthYourMoney

Becoming a Triton used to be a disappointing consolation prize for applicants hoping to become a Bruin or a Golden Bear. While UCLA and Berkeley remain the crème de la crème of the UC system, the gap between those uber-elite jewels and UC San Diego has closed significantly in recent years as applications have sky-rocketed to over 130,000, and the profile of the average freshman has risen commensurately. In 2003, there were fewer than 20,000 undergraduates at the university; there are now over 33,000. An extremely strong academic school, UCSD offers 140+ undergraduate majors, all available for less than $18,500 per year in tuition and fees.

Inside the Classroom
There are six undergraduate colleges at UCSD that are meant, in the Oxford and Cambridge model, not to separate students by discipline but, instead, to forge flourishing small liberal arts college communities within the larger university. Core curriculum at all of the colleges includes first-year writing, advanced writing, oral communication, mathematical reasoning, quantitative reasoning, and a second language. Additionally, undergrads must complete coursework in science and technological inquiry, historical inquiry, literary inquiry, social and behavioral inquiry, artistic inquiry, theological and religious inquiry, philosophical inquiry, ethical inquiry, and diversity and social justice. Two "integration" experiences in which students make connections across disciplines also must be tackled, including one during freshman year.

Over 8,300 graduate students and a 19:1 student-to-faculty ratio are two numbers that don't bode well for those hoping for an intimate classroom experience. Yet, reality is a mixed bag. While 26% of course sections are held in larger lecture halls and contain 50+ students, 44% of undergraduate courses sport an enrollment under 20. Sixty percent of undergrads complete at least one research project as part of their coursework, and roughly one-quarter assist a faculty member with research outside of the classroom. Study abroad numbers are approaching 1,000 undergraduates per year, which is only a sliver of the total undergraduate population. Still, opportunities in forty-two countries are available for those who desire a semester of study outside of the United States.

Altogether, biology has the highest representation of all majors (19%) followed by engineering (12%), the social sciences (11%), and computer science (9%). UCSD's computer science and engineering programs have stellar reputations in the corporate and tech communities, and programs in biology, economics, and political science are among the best anywhere. In recent years, nationally competitive postgraduate fellowship programs have selected a number of Tritons, and the school has produced as many as a dozen Fulbrights per year while the Biology Department alone saw four graduates capture National Science Foundation Graduate Research Fellowships last academic year.

Outside the Classroom
In the 2022-23 school year, 80% of freshmen lived on the UCSD campus, but under 40% of the undergraduate population lived in dormitories or college-owned apartments. Fraternities and sororities have a solid but not overwhelming presence on campus, drawing 14% of men and women. Unlike UCLA and Berkeley, San Diego doesn't offer prime-time football or basketball teams; in fact, it hasn't fielded a football team since 1968. Rather, the 23 Triton squads participate in NCAA Division II and fare quite well within that less competitive environment. However, plans do exist to join Division I's Big West Conference within the next few years. A diverse student body enjoys an equally diverse array of clubs. There are over 500 to choose from with many options in the areas of student government, media, and a popular intramural sports program that has a 60% participation rate. The 180-acre campus is situated within the wealthy beachfront town of La Jolla, a thirteen-mile highway ride from downtown San Diego. While La Jolla is not a typical college town, many students live in beachfront apartments overlooking the Pacific Ocean or Mission Bay, and few complain about the heavenly weather.

Career Services
The UC San Diego Career Center has 21 full-time employees who work with or on behalf of undergraduate students, many of whom specialize in a particular discipline such as prelaw, pre-health, the social sciences, the humanities, business, or engineering. UCSD's 1,576:1 student-to-counselor ratio is toward the highest of any school featured in this guide. To compensate, it puts on a multitude of annual career fairs, many of which attract 1,000+ students. These include large-scale fairs in the fall, winter, and spring: a Graduate School Fair, an Engineering and Computing Career Fair, and an event called Impact Career Fair: Companies for a Brighter Future. Each quarter, hundreds of companies are on campus to recruit undergraduate students.

University of California, San Diego

E-mail: admissionsinfo@ucsd.edu | Website: ucsd.edu

In a single year, the school lists 8,300+ jobs/internships on Handshake, and those efforts led to roughly 80% of graduates having participated in an experiential learning activity—internship, research, or community service. Thirty-minute one-on-one appointments can be scheduled, but scoring one of those appointments, particularly with a "good fit" counselor, can be a challenge. Students, via op-eds in the school paper, have been clamoring for an increased number of advisors to accommodate the growing number of undergraduate students at the university. Thanks to the rising prestige of the school, UCSD students have enjoyed increasingly positive postgraduation outcomes, but there is still room to increase the level of support offered.

Professional Outcomes

Employers of recent graduates included the Walt Disney Company, Tesla, NBC Universal, PwC, Northrop Grumman, and EY. More than 1,000 current Google employees are UC San Diego alumni, and Qualcomm, Amazon, and Apple all employ 500+ each. The median early career salary is $65,000 across all majors, placing the university in the top 10 public universities in the country. UCSD also fares well in measures of its return-on-investment potential. The bulk of grads remain in San Diego or relocate to Los Angeles or San Francisco.

UC San Diego is a school from which you can matriculate into any graduate program you desire—if you bring the requisite transcript and test scores. In 2023, there were 646 seniors applying to medical school—the sixth-most in the nation. Though Tritons appear to experience average to slightly below-average levels of success—roughly 39-40% of applicants have been admitted in recent years—low(ish) acceptance rates are likely attributable to the fact that UCSD includes all undergraduate applicants in their tally, not just those who achieve a certain GPA threshold or receive an official endorsement from a premed advisor. Prelaw students most frequently head to California-based institutions such as the University of San Diego School of Law, California Western School of Law, Thomas Jefferson School of Law, and Santa Clara University School of Law. However, recent grads also found law school homes at the University of Chicago, Pepperdine, UCLA, Notre Dame, and Fordham.

Admission

A tsunami of 131,254 applications for a place in the Class of 2026 flooded the inboxes of the UC San Diego admissions office, more than doubling the number of applications received a decade ago; the admit rate was 24%, down ten points from the prior year. An incredible 100% of the Class of 2026 placed in the top 10% of their graduating class. The average unweighted high school GPA was a hard-to-beat 3.9. The average weighted GPA was 4.16 and 86% of enrolled freshmen were above the 4.0 mark. Less than 2% of successful applicants sported a GPA under 3.75. It is also important to note that UCSD is now test-blind, meaning standardized testing is not considered in the admissions process.

When you are attracting 130,000 applicants, a microscopic exploration of every application is not a realistic expectation. Thus, it makes sense that the three "very important" factors considered by the admissions committee are level of rigor, GPA, and essays. If the person advising you on college admissions (counselor, parent, family friend) hasn't been paying close attention to the spike in applications and selectivity, UC San Diego can easily become an institution that should be a "reach" or "target" school, but could be mistakenly assigned the title of "safety school." In reality, a pristine academic transcript is a must for most applicants.

Worth Your Money?

For the roughly 20% of undergraduates who come from outside the state, the University of California, San Diego has an annual cost of attendance of $72k. Residents, on the other hand, enjoy a COA of $40k. More than half of current students receive some level of financial aid; the average award is $24k. Staying within the UC system is always an excellent choice for residents, and while the school is getting expensive for outsiders, it may still prove to be a degree that returns your investment, particularly if you aim to work in the tech industry.

FINANCIAL
Institutional Type: Public
In-State Tuition: $16,056
Out-of-State Tuition: $48,630
Room & Board: $17,325
Books & Supplies: $1,308

Avg. Need-Based Grant: $24,176
Avg. % of Need Met: 86%

Avg. Merit-Based Award: $12,701
% Receiving (Freshmen w/o Need): 4%

Avg. Cumulative Debt: $19,230
% of Students Borrowing: 39%

CAREER
Who Recruits
1. Nordson Corp
2. Sherwin Williams
3. IQVIA
4. Hulu
5. Netflix

Notable Internships
1. Inuit
2. Dow Jones
3. American Express

Top Employers
1. Google
2. Qualcomm
3. Apple
4. Amazon
5. Illumina

Where Alumni Work
1. San Diego
2. San Francisco
3. Los Angeles
4. Orange County, CA
5. New York City

Earnings
College Scorecard (10-YR Post-Entry): $82,255
PayScale (Early Career): $69,300
PayScale (Mid-Career): $135,300
PayScale 20-Year ROI: $869,000

RANKINGS
Money: 5
U.S. News: 28, National Universities
Wall Street Journal/THE: 103
Washington Monthly: 20, National Universities

OVERGENERALIZATIONS
Students are:
Environmentally conscious
Diverse
Nerdy
Academically driven
Lacking social outlets

COLLEGE OVERLAPS
University of California, Berkeley
University of California, Irvine
University of California, San Diego
University of California, Santa Barbara
University of Southern California

University of California, Santa Barbara

Santa Barbara, California | 805-893-2881

When your campus is bordered on three sides by the Pacific Ocean and the weather is 70-75 degrees virtually year-round, it would be easy for academics to become an afterthought. While the University of California, Santa Barbara does, indeed, have a well-earned reputation as a "party school," the 23,460 undergraduate students are, today, a higher-achieving lot than ever, and they flock to UCSB for the 90 undergraduate majors and slew of top-ranked departments every bit as much as the sand and surf.

Inside the Classroom

The College of Letters and Science, the College of Engineering, and the College of Creative Studies all have different core curricular requirements. There is some crossover in terms of mandated courses in all three schools that include English, reading, and composition; literature; art; social science; and culture and thought. College of Letters and Science grads also must complete classes in foreign language and science, mathematics, and technology. Classes covering the special subject areas of European traditions, ethnicity, world cultures, and quantitative relationships are also part of some academic programs.

The student-to-faculty ratio at UC Santa Barbara is a decent 17:1, and the school does an excellent job of keeping undergraduate class sizes on the small side. In fact, more than half of sections contain fewer than 20 students, and 72% enroll 29 or fewer. Undergraduate research opportunities definitely exist for those willing to forge relationships with faculty outside the classroom. A solid 56% of graduates report engaging in some type of independent study or research. It's not as easy to inspire Gauchos to leave their campus paradise for a semester in a foreign land—only around 20% of students participate in study abroad.

The social sciences are the most popular area of study, accounting for 27% of the total degrees conferred. Biology (10%), math (9%), and psychology (9%) are next in popularity. The school has highly regarded programs in communication, computer science, engineering, physics, environmental science, and the performing arts. Santa Barbara graduates do not tend to apply for prestigious postgraduate fellowships in overwhelming numbers, but the school did produce three Fulbright winners in 2023.

Outside the Classroom

Freshmen live on the UCSB campus at a 90% clip; overall, 38% of the undergraduate student population resides in university-owned housing. Santa Barbara's glorious 1,000-acre campus is set against the Pacific Ocean, and multiple beaches are literally in your backyard (you can actually hear the ocean while you're studying). Of course, keeping focused is a challenge with the perfect weather, beautiful surroundings, and the fact that, no matter what rankings list you check, UCSB is one of the top party schools in the entire country. The town of Isla Vista is almost exclusively a college town with a laid-back vibe full of free spirits and free-flowing hard liquor. Fraternities and sororities have a presence but do not dominate the social scene; only 7% of men and 13% of women join Greek organizations. Just about everyone on campus is involved in athletics in some way as there are twenty-nine club sports teams and a stunning 18,000 intramural participants each year. Nineteen varsity teams compete in NCAA Division I's Big West Conference. The baseball program is, perhaps, the most notable, making regular tournament appearances and having produced many MLB players in its almost one-hundred-year history. There are also over 500 student clubs and numerous campus-wide events, including the famous (or infamous) annual Halloween celebration on Isla Vista. Fifty-seven percent of students found time to engage in community service.

Career Services

USCB Career Services is run by 16 professional employees who function as discipline-specific career counselors, employment specialists, graduate school counselors, and internship/experience managers. That 1,466:1 student-to-staff ratio is much higher than the average school in this guidebook, but that is not particularly alarming for a public university of Santa Barbara's size. Career services certainly keeps busy, hosting nearly 300 workshops that, collectively, drew 2,400 students in a single recent year and also met one-on-one with 3,000+ individuals through scheduled appointments and another 3,500 through drop-ins. Four job and internship fairs held over the course of the year attract 350+ employers and 4,600+ students. Additionally, staff posts 38,000+ jobs on Handshake for undergraduate consumption.

ADMISSION
Admission Rate: 26%
Admission Rate - Men: 23%
Admission Rate - Women: 28%
EA Admission Rate: Not Offered
ED Admission Rate: Not Offered
ED Admits as % of Total Admits: Not Offered
Admission Rate (5-Year Trend): -7%
% of Admits Attending (Yield): 17%
Transfer Admission Rate: 58%

SAT Reading/Writing (Middle 50%): Test-Blind
SAT Math (Middle 50%): Test-Blind
ACT Composite (Middle 50%): Test-Blind

% Graduated in Top 10% of HS Class: 100%
% Graduated in Top 25% of HS Class: 100%
% Graduated in Top 50% of HS Class: 100%

Demonstrated Interest: Not Considered
Legacy Status: Not Considered
Racial/Ethnic Status: Not Considered
Admission Interview Offered: No

ENROLLMENT
Total Undergraduate Enrollment: 23,460
% Full-Time: 97%
% Male: 44%
% Female: 56%
% Out-of-State: 8%
% Fraternity: Not Reported
% Sorority: Not Reported
% On-Campus (All Undergraduate): 38%
Freshman Housing Required: No

% African-American: 2%
% Asian: 20%
% Hispanic: 26%
% White: 31%
% Other: 2%
% International: 12%
% Low-Income: 28%

ACADEMICS
Student-to-Faculty Ratio: 17 to 1
% of Classes Under 20: 57%
% of Classes 20-49: 25%
% of Classes 50 or More: 19%
% Full-Time Faculty: 88%
% Full-Time Faculty w/ Terminal Degree: 100%

Top Programs
Actuarial Science
Communication
Computer Science
Engineering
Environmental Studies
Global and International Studies
Performing Arts
Physics

Retention Rate: 92%
4-Year Graduation Rate: 73%
6-Year Graduation Rate: 85%

Curricular Flexibility: Somewhat Flexible
Academic Rating: ★★★★♪

#CollegesWorthYourMoney

This office is continuing to aggressively expand the number of employers who recruit on campus. Bain & Company, Goldman Sachs, US Bank, and Kaiser Permanente all have begun visiting Santa Barbara for information sessions, career fairs, and on-campus interviews. Internship experiences are supported through programs like the Intern Scholarship Program, which issues $1,500 grants to help offset the costs of unpaid placements. An encouraging 45% of those who land an internship end up being hired by that organization on a full-time basis. Overall, this office does a nice job of bringing top employers to campus with regularity and hosts almost daily workshops such as Engineering Boot Camp, Internships 101, "So You Want to be a Researcher?," and Conversations about Careers in Mental Health.

Professional Outcomes

Within six months of earning their diplomas, 84% of Gauchos have found employment, and only 7% of those seeking their first jobs have yet to nail down a position. The most popular industries entered are science/research (16%), engineering/computer programming (14%), business (13%), finance/accounting (11%), and sales (10%). Among the top employers of recent graduates are Google, EY, KPMG, Oracle, Amazon, IBM, and Adobe. Large numbers of UCSB alumni also can be found on the payrolls of Apple, Meta, Microsoft, and Salesforce. A fairly even split of Gauchos can be found in the Greater Los Angeles area and San Francisco. Many also remain in Santa Barbara or head to other Golden State locales like Sacramento, Orange County, or San Diego. Two years after graduating, UCSB alumni make an average salary of $55k, and more than half make $100k by mid-career.

Seventy-five percent of Santa Barbara grads stated they intend to pursue a graduate or professional degree at some point. Of those jumping directly into an advanced degree program, 9% are continuing at UCSB, 23% at a University of California location, 16% at a school within the California State University system, 22% at a private school in California, and 36% at out-of-state institutions. In 2023, there were 260 applicants to medical schools from UCSB, and acceptance rates were in line with the national average. Recent acceptances included prestigious medical schools such as Harvard, Cornell, Tufts, Georgetown, Johns Hopkins, Dartmouth, Wake Forest, UVA, UNC-Chapel Hill, and Duke. Those applying to law school or other graduate programs also gained entrance to a wide range of schools, including the most prestigious in the country.

Admission

A line 111,006 students long formed for a place in the UC Santa Barbara Class of 2026; 26% were admitted, and 17% of those accepted ultimately enrolled at the university. Those entering the university in 2022-23 earned an average high school GPA of 4.29, and 95% had a GPA of over 3.75. The school is now test-blind (along with the rest of the UC system). Among those who submitted a class rank, 100% typically place in the top 10%. A decade ago, Santa Barbara was a much easier university to get into. At that time, the acceptance rate was close to 50%. It's important that current applicants do not mistake the UCSB of ten years ago for the highly selective school it is today.

For a university approaching six figures worth of applicants, it is a bit surprising that it lists the application essays as being "very important," a designation only given to one other factor: GPA. Rigor of one's high school course load is ranked as "important," and factors like work experience, extracurricular activities, state residency, and first-generation status are "considered." As is the standard with schools in the University of California system, there is no early action or early decision; rather, the regular deadline is on the early side. You must submit your application by November 30.

Worth Your Money?

Cheap tuition (around $14k) plus expensive California living brings the overall cost of attendance to a touch over $41,000 per year. As with all of the schools in the University of California system, even if you received zero aid, UC Santa Barbara would still be a solid investment if you live in state. An out-of-state student would pay $74k per year in tuition, meaning that budget-conscious teens and families would likely have much better private or in-state options. The school caps nonresident enrollment at 18% (it currently sits below that mark), but that population has been rising in recent years, so there are many people willing to spend $296,000 on a public school education—a move that we do not recommend unless financial resources are unlimited and/or you happen to be majoring in engineering or computer science.

FINANCIAL
Institutional Type: Public
In-State Tuition: $14,881
Out-of-State Tuition: $45,658
Room & Board: $16,515
Books & Supplies: $1,344

Avg. Need-Based Grant: $22,834
Avg. % of Need Met: 84%

Avg. Merit-Based Award: $8,183
% Receiving (Freshmen w/o Need): 3%

Avg. Cumulative Debt: $17,242
% of Students Borrowing: 40%

CAREER
Who Recruits
1. Arista Networks
2. Deckers Brands
3. Peace Corps
4. Raytheon
5. West Coast Financial, LLC

Notable Internships
1. SpaceX
2. U.S. House of Representatives
3. Telsa

Top Employers
1. Google
2. Apple
3. Oracle
4. Amazon
5. Microsoft

Where Alumni Work
1. Los Angeles
2. San Francisco
3. Santa Barbara, CA
4. San Diego
5. Orange County, CA

Earnings
College Scorecard (10-YR Post-Entry): $70,326
PayScale (Early Career): $63,600
PayScale (Mid-Career): $131,400
PayScale 20-Year ROI: $710,000

RANKINGS
Money: 4.5
U.S. News: 35, National Universities
Wall Street Journal/THE: 122
Washington Monthly: 67, National Universities

OVERGENERALIZATIONS
Students are:
Working hard and playing hard
Always admiring the beauty of their campus
Social
Diverse
Open-minded

COLLEGE OVERLAPS
University of California, Berkeley
University of California, Davis
University of California, Irvine
University of California, Los Angeles
University of California, San Diego

University of California, Santa Cruz

Santa Cruz, California | 831-459-4008

ADMISSION
Admission Rate: 47%
Admission Rate - Men: 42%
Admission Rate - Women: 51%
EA Admission Rate: Not Offered
ED Admission Rate: Not Offered
ED Admits as % of Total Admits: Not Offered
Admission Rate (5-Year Trend): -4%
% of Admits Attending (Yield): 12%
Transfer Admission Rate: 61%

SAT Reading/Writing (Middle 50%): Test-Blind
SAT Math (Middle 50%): Test-Blind
ACT Composite (Middle 50%): Test-Blind

% Graduated in Top 10% of HS Class: 96%
% Graduated in Top 25% of HS Class: 100%
% Graduated in Top 50% of HS Class: 100%

Demonstrated Interest: Not Considered
Legacy Status: Not Considered
Racial/Ethnic Status: Not Considered
Admission Interview Offered: No

ENROLLMENT
Total Undergraduate Enrollment: 17,502
% Full-Time: 96%
% Male: 50%
% Female: 50%
% Out-of-State: 4%
% Fraternity: 4%
% Sorority: 5%
% On-Campus (All Undergraduate): 51%
Freshman Housing Required: No

% African-American: 2%
% Asian: 23%
% Hispanic: 28%
% White: 32%
% Other: 2%
% International: 5%
% Low-Income: 32%

ACADEMICS
Student-to-Faculty Ratio: 23 to 1
% of Classes Under 20: 27%
% of Classes 20-49: 46%
% of Classes 50 or More: 27%
% Full-Time Faculty: 84%
% Full-Time Faculty w/ Terminal Degree: 98%

Top Programs
Anthropology
Astrophysics
Computer Science
Earth Sciences
Engineering
Environmental Studies
Film & Digital Media
Physics

Retention Rate: 88%
4-Year Graduation Rate: 62%
6-Year Graduation Rate: 77%

Curricular Flexibility: Somewhat Flexible
Academic Rating: ★★★✦

#CollegesWorthYourMoney

Along with several fellow previously unheralded UC campuses, Santa Cruz has, in recent years, gained recognition as one of the top 35 public universities in the entire country. In addition to high-level academics and an ever-increasingly accomplished pool of applicants (the average GPA of accepted students is now over 4.0), UCSC is surrounded by panoramic views of the Pacific and towering redwoods, and is minutes away from beaches. And, oh yeah, its athletic teams have one of the greatest nicknames in college sports—the Banana Slugs. But, don't worry, there is nothing sluggish about this often overlooked university that plays host to 17,502 bachelor's degree pursuers and 73 undergraduate majors.

Inside the Classroom
UCSC students study within one of the following academic divisions: arts, humanities, physical and biological sciences, social sciences, and the Jack Baskin School of Engineering. All first-year students take a course called College 1 their first semester that prepares them for the "styles of critical reading, thinking, and engagement that [they] will encounter throughout [their] university experience." The composition requirement is met through one or two writing courses, depending on the outcome of a placement test. In addition to these entry-level courses, students must check off a number of general education mandates in areas such as cross-cultural analysis, ethnicity and race, interpreting arts and media, math and formal reasoning, and statistical reasoning.

Santa Cruz has a student-to-faculty ratio of 23:1, one of the highest figures of any school featured in this guide. An identical percentage of classes contain 50+ students (27%) as under 20 students (27%). Fortunately, thanks in part to a relatively small number of graduate students (roughly 1,976), there are still opportunities to work side-by-side with faculty. In fact, a commendable 75% of undergraduates conduct research during their four years at Santa Cruz. A few years ago, the school pledged to raise the number of students participating in study abroad programs to 50%, and encourages all students to take advantage of the well-established UC programs situated all around the globe.

Biology is the university's most popular major; 15% of all degrees conferred in 2022 were in this discipline. Fourteen percent of degrees were in the social sciences, 13% were granted in computer and information sciences, and 12% in psychology. CS is one of UCSC's most respected programs. A notable number of Slugs volunteer with organizations like the Peace Corps and City Year following graduation. They also produce occasional winners of Fulbrights and other prestigious fellowships/scholarships such as Gilman Scholarships.

Outside the Classroom
Ninety-nine percent of freshmen normally reside in on-campus housing, but among the total undergraduate student body, that figure falls to just below 51%. Still, this is the highest number of any school within the University of California system. Overall, 4% of men and 5% of women enter Greek life. The UCSC campus is a vast 2,000 acres, regularly receiving praise as one of the country's most aesthetically pleasing colleges. This includes the 409-acre Natural Reserves that serve as a living laboratory for budding scientists. The Banana Slugs may have the greatest team name in college sports, but they are—unlike Cal and UCLA—light-years from being an athletic powerhouse. Fifteen varsity teams compete at the NCAA Division III level. The school is home to 200 student-run clubs covering the standard categories of politics, performance, academics, and hobbies. From beach bonfires to strolls on the boardwalk to visits to the local farmer's market, there is also plenty to do in the surrounding area. The student body is, in general, very liberal and very laid back. If you're looking for a Greek-heavy, sports-crazed campus, look elsewhere.

Career Services
The University of California Santa Cruz Career Center employs 18 professionals (including positions that are presently vacant) with roles in the areas of career counseling, employer engagement, and event planning. Their 972:1 counselor-to-student ratio is high, but not that different from other UC branches. In a typical year, UCSC holds more than a handful of career fairs that are attended by as many as 50 employers and 450 students; the Graduate and Professional School Fair draws representatives from approximately 100 universities.

According to the most recent survey of career center utilization, 33% take advantage of one-on-one advising sessions, 27% of graduates attend career fairs, and 21% attend at least one workshop. The last time the center reported data on how often students came to the office for advising sessions, almost 4,000 individual appointments were made in a calendar year, and the average student satisfaction rating was 4.5 out of 5 stars. A solid 59% of Santa Cruz grads completed at least one internship; 18% had two. Students utilize Handshake to view tens of thousands of job and internship postings. An alumni network that is 140,000 strong can aid in this process as well.

Professional Outcomes

Within three months of earning their degree, 29% of UCSC grads have found employment, another 17% are starting graduate programs, and 34% are still seeking employment. Proximity to Silicon Valley helps open doors to companies like Google, Apple, Meta, Genentech, and Cisco, which all employ over 250 alumni. More than 100 alums can also be found in the offices of Amazon, Salesforce, Microsoft, Adobe, and LinkedIn. The majority of grads live in the San Francisco area, with large numbers also concentrated in Los Angeles, San Diego, Sacramento, and New York City. Among graduates from the last five years, over half make more than $40k.

Among those recent grads who hadn't yet started an advanced degree program, three-fifths stated that they planned to do so within the next five years. In the 2023 academic year, 113 Slugs applied to medical school, and many have gone on to attend, with schools in the UC system being popular landing spots. Recent grads who have entered law school have gone on to attend fellow California-based schools like Berkeley, UCLA, Santa Clara, Pepperdine, and Loyola as well as institutions like Tulane, Northeastern, and Baylor. While the quality of graduate school acceptances of Santa Cruz grads varies, many high achievers do get accepted into elite programs. For example, recent grads have matriculated into graduate programs at Stanford, Rice, USC, and Columbia University.

Admission

Everyone knows about how selective UCLA and Berkeley are, some are catching on to the elevated admissions standards at San Diego and Santa Barbara, but few understand just how competitive admission now is for every UC branch campus, including Santa Cruz. The good news is that UCSC's acceptance rate is still 47%, one of the "easier" UC schools to gain admission into as a first-year applicant. The average GPA for incoming 2022-23 freshmen was 3.98 and 87% earned a 3.75 or better. In one recent year, 94% of accepted students placed in the top decile of their graduating high school class.

Four factors are viewed as "highly important" to the admissions committee: GPA, application essays (the UC personal insight questions), state residency, and the rigor of your coursework. Standardized tests have been phased out of UC admissions, with a test-blind policy having recently gone into effect. The following factors are viewed as "important": extracurricular activities, talent/ability, character/personal qualities, first-generation status, and geographical residence. An applicant's volunteer or paid work experience is "considered." The school does not consider class rank, recommendations, legacy status, or one's level of demonstrated interest.

Worth Your Money?

One simple question to ask when determining if a school is worth your money is, "Is it in the University of California system?" If the answer is "Yes"—and you are a California resident—then you are getting one of the premier bargains in the world of higher education. Sure, living in California is expensive in every other regard, but the tuition for the 2023-24 academic year is only $14,640. Those from outside the Golden State are charged an extra $31,026 nonresident tuition fee. There are circumstances where paying this amount would still be worth it (e.g., for a technology and information management degree), but in most cases, this school makes the most sense for locals. Close to 70% of all students received some type of financial aid through the university.

FINANCIAL
Institutional Type: Public
In-State Tuition: $15,288
Out-of-State Tuition: $47,862
Room & Board: $18,785
Books & Supplies: $1,315

Avg. Need-Based Grant: $23,731
Avg. % of Need Met: 85%

Avg. Merit-Based Award: $7,554
% Receiving (Freshmen w/o Need): 6%

Avg. Cumulative Debt: $20,895
% of Students Borrowing: 43%

CAREER
Who Recruits
1. Fortinet
2. FDIC
3. Moss Adams
4. Deloitte
5. Capital Insurance Group

Notable Internships
1. Gesher Consulting Group
2. Genentech
3. Tech4Good

Top Employers
1. Google
2. Apple
3. Facebook
4. Amazon
5. Genentech

Where Alumni Work
1. San Francisco
2. Los Angeles
3. San Diego
4. Sacramento
5. New York City

Earnings
College Scorecard (10-YR Post-Entry): $64,166
PayScale (Early Career): $63,400
PayScale (Mid-Career): $116,600
PayScale 20-Year ROI: $583,000

RANKINGS
Money: 4
U.S. News: 82, National Universities
Wall Street Journal/THE: 241
Washington Monthly: 133, National Universities

OVERGENERALIZATIONS
Students are:
Outdoorsy
Politically liberal
Always admiring the beauty of their campus
Easy-going
Friendly

COLLEGE OVERLAPS
University of California, Davis
University of California, Irvine
University of California, Riverside
University of California, San Diego
University of California, Santa Barbara

University of Chicago

Chicago, Illinois | 773-702-8650

ADMISSION
Admission Rate: 5%
Admission Rate - Men: 6%
Admission Rate - Women: 5%
EA Admission Rate: Not Offered
ED Admission Rate: Not Reported
ED Admits as % of Total Admits: Not Reported
Admission Rate (5-Year Trend): -4%
% of Admits Attending (Yield): 85%
Transfer Admission Rate: 7%

SAT Reading/Writing (Middle 50%): 740-780
SAT Math (Middle 50%): 760-800
ACT Composite (Middle 50%): 34-35

% Graduated in Top 10% of HS Class: 99%
% Graduated in Top 25% of HS Class: 100%
% Graduated in Top 50% of HS Class: 100%

Demonstrated Interest: Not Considered
Legacy Status: Considered
Racial/Ethnic Status: Not Considered
Admission Interview Offered: No

ENROLLMENT
Total Undergraduate Enrollment: 7,470
% Full-Time: 100%
% Male: 53%
% Female: 47%
% Out-of-State: 81%
% Fraternity: Not Reported
% Sorority: Not Reported
% On-Campus (All Undergraduate): 61%
Freshman Housing Required: Yes

% African-American: 7%
% Asian: 20%
% Hispanic: 16%
% White: 32%
% Other: 2%
% International: 16%
% Low-Income: 15%

ACADEMICS
Student-to-Faculty Ratio: 5 to 1
% of Classes Under 20: 77%
% of Classes 20-49: 16%
% of Classes 50 or More: 7%
% Full-Time Faculty: 89%
% Full-Time Faculty w/ Terminal Degree: 98%

Top Programs
Data Science
Economics
English
History
International Relations
Mathematics
Psychology
Sociology

Retention Rate: 99%
4-Year Graduation Rate: 89%
6-Year Graduation Rate: 96%

Curricular Flexibility: Less Flexible
Academic Rating: ★★★★★

#CollegesWorthYourMoney

Once a bastion of uncompromising intellectuals lovingly referred to as "the place where fun comes to die," the University of Chicago has undergone a transformational rebranding over the past decade. Still a destination point for an army of 7,470 brilliant young people, it now boasts an acceptance rate in the same league with Ivies like Brown and Yale (40% were accepted as recently as 2005) and, while still as academically rigorous as any institution in the country, it has worked to expand its previously unidimensional appeal.

Inside the Classroom

There are 53 majors at the University of Chicago, but close to half of all degrees conferred are in four majors: economics, biology, mathematics, and political science. Economics alone is the selection of roughly one-fifth of the undergraduate population, in large part because the university does not, for reasons of philosophy and tradition, offer a traditional business major. The University of Chicago runs on a quarter system that equates to four ten-week sessions in which students take three or four classes at a time. Given the legendarily heavy workload at the school, the truncated terms can lead to a good deal of stress and an excessive number of all-night study sessions. All undergraduates must plow through the school's Core curriculum that requires an introduction to the tools of inquiry in every discipline: math and science (6 combined courses), humanities (6 courses), and social science (3 courses). Many elect to take nothing but core courses for their entire freshman year.

A 5:1 student-to-faculty ratio means that classrooms remain fairly intimate, and face time with the renowned faculty is a reality. More than three-quarters of UChicago undergraduate sections have an enrollment of nineteen or fewer students. Undergraduate research opportunities are ubiquitous as 80% of students end up working in a research capacity alongside a faculty member. A solid 60% of undergrads study abroad at one of the 74 programs offered in 31 cities around the world.

No matter your area of concentration, a degree from UChicago will carry a great deal of weight in the eyes of employers and graduate/professional schools alike. All of the areas previously mentioned as the most popular majors have particularly sterling reputations with a global reach. On that topic, if you name a prestigious post-graduate award or fellowship, chances are the University of Chicago is one of the most frequent producers. Perhaps most astoundingly, between faculty and alumni, UChicago boasts ninety affiliated Nobel Prizes (eight are currently on faculty) over the school's illustrious history. Lastly, it is one of the top 10 Rhodes-producing institutions in the country, laying claim to 50+ Scholars all-time.

Outside the Classroom

With its campus based in the Hyde Park neighborhood on Chicago's South Side, students have access to a vibrant metropolis within walking distance of their dorms. Countless museums, restaurants, bookshops, parks, and theaters are never more than a stone's throw away. Given UChicago's reputation as a haven for hardcore intellectuals, it may come as a surprise that there are nineteen official Greek organizations on campus with a participation rate of 15-20%. Athletes, nicknamed the Maroons, participate in NCAA Division III; there are twenty varsity teams that are evenly split between the genders. No athletic scholarships are offered, and athletics, in general, capture a limited degree of student attention. Yet, a hard-to-comprehend 70% of the student body participates in the school's extensive intramural and club sports programs. Over 350 undergraduate-run clubs are active, including a number of improv and theater groups (the university is the birthplace of modern improv), community service organizations, and publications. DOC is the nation's oldest student-run film society and screens films on a daily basis. On-campus housing consists of seven residence halls divided into 39 houses designed to nurture a sense of community. Freshmen are required to participate in the university housing system, but a large percentage of upperclassmen—61% of the total student body—reside in off-campus housing.

Career Services

The university pours ample resources into career services, employing 60 full-time consultants who have highly specialized areas of expertise including business careers, law school planning, healthcare careers, journalism, STEM, and start-ups. Boasting a student-to-advisor ratio of 125:1, UChicago has one of the absolute best ratios of any institution included in this book. It also puts its extensive staff to work on behalf of undergraduate students. To help quantify that statement, the staff engaged students in more than 12,000 one-on-one advising appointments in a single recent school year.

An exceptional 80% of freshmen engage with the Career Advancement Office. Through the Metcalf Internship Program, massive numbers of students procure internship positions at top companies around the globe. In a given year, UChicago students secure more than 3,000 internships with more than 850 organizations. Undergraduates participate in excess of 500 employer site visits around the world—which are known as Career Treks—as well as 600 externships. The university forges strong connections with employers who are eager to conduct on-campus interviews with students; it currently has over one hundred full-time recruiting partners, including a laundry list of Fortune 1000 companies. Incredibly, 1,000+ distinct employers recruited at the school during the last academic year. Unmatched in terms of sheer personnel power and deeply committed to personalized, expert student counseling, UChicago's Career Advancement Office is a leader in the career services realm.

Professional Outcomes

On commencement day, 99% of the Class of 2023 already had their next step lined up, whether that involved entering the world of employment or continuing their higher education odyssey in graduate school. Business and financial services (30%) and STEM (12%) are the two sectors that scoop up the most graduates, but public policy and consulting also were well-represented. Some of the most popular employers of recent grads include Google, JPMorgan, Goldman Sachs, McKinsey & Company, Bank of America, Citi, and Accenture. While many graduates go on to lucrative careers, average early career incomes lag a bit behind many other schools of its ilk due to the heavy number of students pursuing advanced degrees.

University of Chicago grads are highly sought after by elite graduate universities. The top seven destinations for recent graduates are Yale, Columbia, Penn, MIT, Stanford, UCLA, and Johns Hopkins. Top law schools swoon at the sight of applicants from UChicago; 97% of applicants to Top 20 institutions gain admittance. In one recent cycle, twenty-four grads were accepted by NYU, sixteen by UChicago itself, fourteen by Columbia, twelve by Harvard, and eight by Stanford. Med school applicants found an identical level of success with 80% earning acceptance, close to double the national average. A fairly substantial 36% of graduates remain in the Midwest after finishing their degrees, 35% migrate to the Northeast, and 13% make the journey west.

Admission

The University of Chicago admitted 5% of applicants for admission into the Class of 2026, placing the school in a selectivity stratosphere with Stanford, Yale, and Columbia. If you had predicted that figure at the turn of the millennium, sideways glances would have surely followed. In 2005, the university admitted 40% (not a typo) of applicants and still followed the beat of its own drummer, offering what was known as "The Uncommon App" and maintaining a reputation for welcoming waves of uber-serious bookworms. Changes in leadership and a decade of aggressive marketing practices (soliciting applications from unqualified students) led to a flood of new applicants and a sharp decline in the admit rate.

The average SAT score for enrolled students is now 1545, although the school announced in 2018 that it was going test-optional. Skeptics believe that one of the motivations for the policy change was to drum up even more applicants to eventually reject, further enhancing its selectivity. Interestingly, the incoming profile of a UChicago student isn't that much different from what it was when it was "easier" to get into; the average SAT score 15 years ago was in the mid-1400s and 99% of incoming students finished in the top 10% of their high school class. In sum, UChicago still takes similarly talented academic superstars now, accepting 5% of applicants, as it did when it accepted eight times that figure. The difference is that instead of attracting a self-selecting pool, it now attracts hordes of applicants, the vast majority of whom are destined for rejection.

Worth Your Money?

If you are among the 34% of current UChicago students who qualify for financial aid, then you are in luck. The school covers 100% of demonstrated need, which leads to an average annual grant of $62k. Thank goodness for that because the university has one of the highest costs of attendance of any school in the country at $89,040. Fortunately, if you need to pay back some epic loans, you should be able to do so by landing at one of the many top corporations to which the university funnels its graduates. If the University of Chicago is just a stop on the academic road, alumni do incredibly well in gaining acceptance into top graduate and professional schools. Either way, this school is worth your money, even at a relatively obscene list price.

FINANCIAL
Institutional Type: Private
In-State Tuition: $65,619
Out-of-State Tuition: $65,619
Room & Board: $19,221
Books & Supplies: $1,800

Avg. Need-Based Grant: $61,561
Avg. % of Need Met: 100%

Avg. Merit-Based Award: Not Reported
% Receiving (Freshmen w/o Need): Not Reported

Avg. Cumulative Debt: $28,068
% of Students Borrowing: 14%

CAREER
Who Recruits
1. Kraft Heinz
2. Nielson
3. Boston Consulting Group
4. AQR Capital Management
5. Kaufmanm Hall & Associates

Notable Internships
1. Instagram
2. The Blackstone Group
3. Jane Street

Top Employers
1. Google
2. Goldman Sachs
3. JP Morgan
4. Facebook
5. Accenture

Where Alumni Work
1. Chicago
2. New York City
3. San Francisco
4. Washington, DC
5. Boston

Earnings
College Scorecard (10-YR Post-Entry): $78,439
PayScale (Early Career): $70,700
PayScale (Mid-Career): $131,700
PayScale 20-Year ROI: $732,000

RANKINGS
Money: 5
U.S. News: 12, National Universities
Wall Street Journal/THE: 37
Washington Monthly: 32, National Universities

OVERGENERALIZATIONS
Students are:
Always studying
Intellectually curious
Diverse
Intense
Quirky

COLLEGE OVERLAPS
Columbia University
Harvard University
Northwestern University
Princeton University
University of Pennsylvania

University of Colorado Boulder

Boulder, Colorado | 303-492-6301

What do you get when you place a great college town at the foothills of the Rocky Mountains and fill it with 31,103 fun-loving undergraduates? The University of Colorado Boulder is the answer to this question, and is now the higher education choice of more than just locals; the university draws an increasing number of out-of-state students who now comprise close to half of the total student body. It also draws thousands of international students from 100+ countries who travel to pursue one of 90 bachelor's degree programs at one of seven schools and colleges.

Inside the Classroom
Five years ago, CU Boulder adopted a new set of general education requirements that takes 46 credits to fulfill. The bulk of these mandates are distributional, with Buffaloes being required to earn 12 credits in each of arts and humanities, social sciences, and natural sciences. Skills requirements include foreign language proficiency, quantitative reasoning, and written communication. Members of the Arts & Sciences Honors Program are required to write and defend an honors thesis.

An 18:1 student-to-faculty ratio suggests that small course sections would be a rarity at CU Boulder, but, in reality, class sizes are a mixed bag. Forty-one percent of classes actually have fewer than 20 students, while 19% of courses enroll 50 or more students. Opportunities to connect with faculty for research opportunities span all majors and fields of study. The school also offers $1,000-$2,000 grants for assistantships where students assist professors with active research and $1,500-$3,000 for original student projects. Over 1,800 students per year participate in the credit-bearing Education Abroad program that offers hundreds of destinations within 60 countries around the world. Participation in this program has almost doubled in the last decade.

Business/marketing is the discipline where the greatest number of degrees (15%) were conferred in 2022. Engineering (13%), biology (12%), social sciences (12%), and journalism (10%) each account for a sizable percentage of bachelor's degrees awarded. The College of Engineering & Applied Science and the Leeds School of Business both possess excellent national reputations. Many students pursue and capture prestigious national scholarships. In a typical year, CU Boulder claims one or more Goldwater Scholars, Truman Scholars, and Fulbright Scholarships; students won nine Fulbrights in 2022 and six more in 2023.

Outside the Classroom
Freshmen are required to live on campus, and pretty much everyone else lives in off-campus housing in the Boulder area. The Off-Campus Housing and Neighborhood Relations Office assists students with the search for post-first-year housing. Known for their focus on Greek life, CU Boulder students join sororities in large numbers, with around 13% of men and 22% of women pledging. The Buffs field 17 varsity sports teams that compete at the NCAA Division I level in the Pac-12 Conference. Folsom Field attracts almost 50,000 fans per game for football games, and the men's basketball squad made four appearances in March Madness in the 2010s. The university has 450+ student-run clubs with outdoor recreation-oriented organizations among the most sought-after. Boulder ranks as one the very best college towns in the United States thanks to its exceptional public transportation system, bike-friendly layout, bar and restaurant scene, and the 36,000 acres of nature surrounding campus that afford opportunities for hiking, camping, skiing, snowboarding, and more. Pearl Street is rarely a dull place, offering street performers and raucous game-day pep rallies. Those looking for additional adventure can hop on US-36 and arrive in downtown Denver in half an hour.

Career Services
There are 29 professional employees working out of the Career Services office within the Division of Student Affairs. Another 13 staff members work within the Leeds School of Business as career advisors. This total of 42 career services workers equates to a 741:1 student-to-counselor ratio, not at all a bad showing for a school of CU Boulder's immense size. This high level of support does, in fact, lead to a direct positive impact on Buffs as they move toward graduation. For recent graduates, CU Career Services/Handshake was cited as one of the top five ways that seniors found their first jobs.

Thanks to the work of industry coaches within Leeds, nearly 80% of business students pursue one or more internships, and 80 companies attended 200+ on-campus engagements with undergrads. Across all departments, information sessions and career fairs are held regularly. In one recent year, the career services staff arranged a dizzying number of virtual meetups in a single recent year, featuring the likes of Bain & Company, EY, Teach for America, Deloitte, and Northwestern Mutual. There were also multiple opportunities to connect with alumni in various industries, work on personal branding, or join a Women in Finance Forum. No matter your area of academic and future career concentration, CU Boulder's career services staff will make sure you have ample chances to explore, connect, and prosper.

Professional Outcomes

Ninety-one percent of recent grads were working or in graduate school six months after graduating from CU Boulder. The greatest number of recent Buffalo grads can be found roaming the offices of Lockheed Martin, Ball Aerospace, Deloitte, Qualcomm, Northrop Grumman, KPMG, Charles Schwab, and Boeing. More than 100 alumni can also be found at companies like Google, Oracle, Amazon, Apple, and Microsoft. Within the first six months after graduation, Boulder alumni earn an estimated median salary of $54k. The Greater Denver area plays home to the greatest percentage of Boulder grads followed by San Francisco, New York City, Los Angeles, and Seattle.

Twenty percent of newly minted grads immediately jumped into a graduate or professional degree program, and 80% were accepted into their first-choice school. The majority of those continuing on to an advanced degree program did so at either CU Boulder or CU Denver. The private University of Denver, the University of Washington – Seattle, Johns Hopkins, and Berkeley were the next most frequent graduate school destinations. The university produced 178 medical school applicants in 2023, including those who applied to the University of Colorado School of Medicine.

Admission

CU Boulder is a school that offers a quality education without needing to first survive a harrowing admissions process. Those entering the university in 2022-23 encountered an acceptance rate of 79%. Middle-50% SAT composite scores of attending freshmen were 1170-1380, and the mean SAT score was 1270. ACT middle-50% scores were 26-31 with a mean score of 28. In the classroom, Class of 2026 members earned an average GPA of 3.68 with 26% placing inside the top 10% of their class; 54% finished in the top quartile.

Academic GPA and the rigor of one's secondary school record were the two factors rated as "very important" by the University of Colorado Boulder. Standardized test scores used to be a strong consideration, but the school is presently test-optional. Factors viewed as "important" are essays, recommendations, extracurricular activities, talent/ability, character/personal qualities, and first-generation status. Legacy status, geographical residence, state residency, ethnic status, and volunteer/paid work experience are all in the "considered" category. This school is easier to get into as a resident of the Rocky Mountain State; in-staters typically enjoy a big edge in the admissions process. However, the acceptance rates were actually fairly even in the 2022-23 cycle. Ultimately, slightly more in-state students go on to enroll in the university than those from outside of Colorado.

Worth Your Money?

The total estimated annual cost for an in-state student in 2023-24 is $35,518; non-Coloradans living in the US have a COA of $55,190, and international students have a COA of $64,620. This price makes the University of Colorado Boulder an excellent investment for anyone paying in-state tuition and, potentially, a reasonable destination for a nonresident looking for a top business or engineering program in a desirable geographic location. This school is held in enough esteem by major corporations across various industries to open doors for Buffaloes as they enter the workforce.

FINANCIAL
Institutional Type: Public
In-State Tuition: $13,622
Out-of-State Tuition: $41,966
Room & Board: $16,950
Books & Supplies: $1,800

Avg. Need-Based Grant: $13,657
Avg. % of Need Met: 72%

Avg. Merit-Based Award: $10,199
% Receiving (Freshmen w/o Need): 34%

Avg. Cumulative Debt: $29,179
% of Students Borrowing: 36%

CAREER
Who Recruits
1. NBC Universal
2. Chevron
3. Ball Aerospace
4. Zayo Group
5. Amazon Web Services

Notable Internships
1. Apple
2. Medtronic
3. Twitter

Top Employers
1. Google
2. Amazon
3. Oracle
4. Apple
5. Microsoft

Where Alumni Work
1. Denver
2. San Francisco
3. New York City
4. Los Angeles
5. Seattle

Earnings
College Scorecard (10-YR Post-Entry): $65,273
PayScale (Early Career): $62,400
PayScale (Mid-Career): $119,900
PayScale 20-Year ROI: $616,000

RANKINGS
Money: 3.5
U.S. News: 105, National Universities
Wall Street Journal/THE: 246
Washington Monthly: 159, National Universities

OVERGENERALIZATIONS
Students are:
Environmentally conscious
Ready to party
Outdoorsy
Wealthy
Laid-back

COLLEGE OVERLAPS
Colorado State University
University of Arizona
University of Denver
University of Oregon
University of Washington - Seattle

University of Connecticut

Storrs, Connecticut | 860-486-3137

ADMISSION
Admission Rate: 55%
Admission Rate - Men: 48%
Admission Rate - Women: 59%
EA Admission Rate: Not Offered
ED Admission Rate: Not Offered
ED Admits as % of Total Admits: Not Offered
Admission Rate (5-Year Trend): +7%
% of Admits Attending (Yield): 18%
Transfer Admission Rate: 69%

SAT Reading/Writing (Middle 50%): 610-710
SAT Math (Middle 50%): 610-730
ACT Composite (Middle 50%): 28-33

% Graduated in Top 10% of HS Class: 50%
% Graduated in Top 25% of HS Class: 84%
% Graduated in Top 50% of HS Class: 98%

Demonstrated Interest: Not Considered
Legacy Status: Not Considered
Racial/Ethnic Status: Considered
Admission Interview Offered: No

ENROLLMENT
Total Undergraduate Enrollment: 18,983
% Full-Time: 98%
% Male: 47%
% Female: 53%
% Out-of-State: 24%
% Fraternity: 10%
% Sorority: 11%
% On-Campus (All Undergraduate): 64%
Freshman Housing Required: Yes

% African-American: 7%
% Asian: 13%
% Hispanic: 15%
% White: 51%
% Other: 1%
% International: 8%
% Low-Income: 25%

ACADEMICS
Student-to-Faculty Ratio: 16 to 1
% of Classes Under 20: 53%
% of Classes 20-49: 29%
% of Classes 50 or More: 18%
% Full-Time Faculty: 81%
% Full-Time Faculty w/ Terminal Degree: 91%

Top Programs
Accounting
Animal Sciences
Education
Exercise Science
Finance
Industrial Engineering
Nursing
Pharmacy

Retention Rate: 93%
4-Year Graduation Rate: 74%
6-Year Graduation Rate: 84%

Curricular Flexibility: Somewhat Flexible
Academic Rating: ★★★★

#CollegesWorthYourMoney

New England is so overflowing with superior institutions of higher education that it is genuinely a challenge to travel more than a few miles through Massachusetts or Connecticut without accidentally bumping into one of the top colleges on the planet. However, that surplus of elite universities is balanced by a notable dearth of stellar public institutions. For applicants seeking such a school, you'll have to travel to the sleepy town of Storrs, Connecticut, a half-hour east of Hartford, where you'll find a regional giant with a national reputation. The main campus of the University of Connecticut is home to 18,983 undergraduates, fourteen schools and colleges, and 115+ undergraduate majors. While 71% of the student body are state residents, there are also individuals hailing from 46 states and 80 countries presently enrolled, and the percentage of outsiders has been on the rise in recent years.

Inside the Classroom

Whether you enter the School of Business, School of Engineering, School of Fine Arts, or other undergraduate college at Storrs, you will encounter a core curriculum of basic requirements. In an effort to ensure "that a balance between professional and general education be established and maintained in which each is complementary to and compatible with the other," UConn mandates two courses in each of arts and humanities, social science, science and technology, and diversity and multiculturalism. Further, students must demonstrate competencies in information literacy, quantitative reasoning, writing, and a second language via additional coursework.

Considering the university's 16:1 student-to-faculty ratio and 8,020 graduate and professional students, one might expect all UConn courses to contain a vast sea of undergraduate faces. However, the school does a nice job creating a balance of classroom experiences with 53% of sections enrolling fewer than 20 students and only 18% containing more than fifty. To help forge even deeper connections with faculty, the Office of Undergraduate Research encourages students to schedule advising sessions to apply for both internal and external research posts. There are also formal programs to target including the Work-Study Research Assistant Program, the Honors Program, or the University Scholar Program that make research a centerpiece of the educational experience. Hundreds of study abroad options are on the table, and the university has taken steps to increase the rate of participation, which currently sits around 15%.

From a sheer volume standpoint, the four most commonly conferred undergraduate degrees are in business (15%), engineering (12%), the social sciences (12%), and health professions/nursing (12%). In terms of prestige and national reputation, programs in business, pharmacy, and nursing carry a good deal of weight. Speaking of reputation, UConn's growing stature has helped its students capture an increasing number of highly competitive scholarships in 2023 including ten Fulbright Scholarships, two Goldwater Scholarships, one Truman Scholarship, and a Udall Scholarship.

Outside the Classroom

Unlike many universities of its size, a healthy 64% of undergraduates live on UConn's 4,100-acre campus (at least in a non-pandemic year). Freshmen are not required to live on campus, but 96% do. Overall, four semesters of housing are guaranteed to all entering students, and there are plenty of traditional apartments, suites, and residential learning communities available. At UConn, you will be treated to one of the best college athletic programs in the country. Husky fans are a fervent bunch, and of the twenty-four varsity teams, nothing captures the attention of all of campus quite like the basketball squads. Since 1999, the men's hoops squad has captured four NCAA titles, and the women's team has won an astounding ten championships. Greek life draws 10% of men and 11% of women. In total, there are 700 student clubs and five cultural centers. Amenities include an on-campus movie theater, an ice rink, and a 191,000-square-foot recreation center that opened in 2019. Volunteer spirit is strong as students contribute a collective 1.3 million hours of community service each year. Major cities like Hartford, Providence, and Boston are close enough for a weekend jaunt.

Career Services

There are 32 full-time employees at the University of Connecticut Center for Career Development (CCD) who serve as career consultants, corporate relations specialists, experiential learning coordinators, and operations specialists. There are an additional six career consultants who work in the School of Business and School of Engineering, bringing the total of professional staff to 38. (That does not include the career services staff members located at UConn's branch campuses.) The CCD's 500:1 student-to-advisor ratio is slightly higher than the average school in this guidebook, but it is pretty solid for a school with close to 19,000 undergraduates.

The vast majority of Huskies utilize career services at some point in their four years, and that rate is higher among students with successful postgraduate outcomes; 79% of recent graduates took advantage of the CCD's services. Experiential learning—including internships—was completed by 80% of graduates. The school forges strong ties to national as well as local companies. In fact, the seventeen Fortune 500 companies located in Connecticut all recruit on the Storrs campus. There are a number of career fairs throughout the year with the largest being the fall career fairs (All-University & STEM) that bring in 150 employers each per day and attract more than 2,000 students. Overall, the UConn CCD provides quality assistance to those it is able to reach, and its industry connections, particularly those with Connecticut-based companies, are strong.

Professional Outcomes

Ninety percent of the graduating Class of 2022 had reached a positive outcome (job, grad school, military, volunteer position) within six months of earning their degrees. Among the 59% who had found employment, the largest numbers landed at Aetna, Cigna, PwC, The Hartford, Travelers, and Raytheon Technologies. Historically, massive numbers of alumni also have been employed by Pratt & Whitney, Pfizer, IBM, and Deloitte. A sampling of the top job titles held by recent grads included financial analyst, consultant, engineer, nurse, sales consultant, and business analyst. Huskies can be found in the largest packs in New York City and Greater Hartford—72% who attended a Connecticut high school remain in the state post-graduation. Boston, DC, San Francisco, and Philadelphia also have their fair share of UConn alumni. The median starting salary across all majors was a superb $62,400.

Many of the 30% of 2022 graduates who immediately entered a graduate or professional program did so at their home university, which caters to a total of 8,300 grad students. In 2022, there were 247 Huskies who applied to medical school. Recent acceptances include many elite medical institutions including the University of Pennsylvania, Georgetown, the University of Chicago, Vanderbilt, and UVA. As many as 25 undergraduates per year matriculate into the University of Connecticut School of Medicine. Law acceptances in the past few years include an impressive list of the nation's top institutions such as Harvard, Yale, William & Mary, Cornell, Columbia, and Boston College.

Admission

UConn accepted 55% of the 40,894 Class of 2026 hopefuls, representing the lowest acceptance rate in school history and quite a departure from the UConn of a generation ago. In 2000, it received one-third as many applications and admitted more than 80% of in-state applicants. The median SAT of freshmen arriving at the Storrs campus was 1340; a decade ago, a 1290 would have put you in the 75th percentile of attending students. Even with the changes to the SAT since that time, that is still an indicator of a major jump in selectivity. Fifty percent of the entering class in 2022-23 finished in the top decile of their graduating cohort, and 84% placed within the top quartile. That group included an astonishing 144 valedictorians and salutatorians.

For a suddenly swamped admissions office, the most important factors in evaluating applicants are the quickest to break down: standardized test scores, GPA, class rank, and the overall rigor of one's high school curriculum. First-generation status, essays, recommendations, extracurricular activities, volunteer work, character/personal qualities, and talent/ability are secondary considerations. There are no early action or early decision options at UConn; everyone faces the same January 15 deadline, but applicants should submit by the December 1 priority deadline for their best chance at merit aid offerings.

Worth Your Money?

For Constitution State residents, UConn is a rock-solid deal at $16k for tuition and a total cost of attendance hovering around $34k. Those in the other New England states can attend at a discount for around $43k, but those from outside the region will see an annual COA of $57k. This school is a no-brainer for state residents as it's hard to get a combination of a cheaper/better education in the Northeast. For everyone else, the value of the degree would depend on the intended area of study. However, those not eligible for a discount of some kind could very likely locate better deals within their home states.

FINANCIAL
Institutional Type: Public
In-State Tuition: $20,366
Out-of-State Tuition: $43,034
Room & Board: $13,996
Books & Supplies: $990

Avg. Need-Based Grant: $15,912
Avg. % of Need Met: 63%

Avg. Merit-Based Award: $11,200
% Receiving (Freshmen w/o Need): 19%

Avg. Cumulative Debt: $27,408
% of Students Borrowing: 52%

CAREER
Who Recruits
1. CGI Inc.
2. ScribeAmerica
3. Mercer
4. USDA
5. Fidelity Investments

Notable Internships
1. iHeartMedia
2. UBS
3. New York Yankees

Top Employers
1. Pratt & Whitney
2. Travelers
3. The Hartford
4. Aetna
5. Cigna

Where Alumni Work
1. New York City
2. Hartford, CT
3. Boston
4. Washington, DC
5. San Francisco

Earnings
College Scorecard (10-YR Post-Entry): $76,076
PayScale (Early Career): $64,700
PayScale (Mid-Career): $111,000
PayScale 20-Year ROI: $652,000

RANKINGS
Money: 4.5
U.S. News: 58, National Universities
Wall Street Journal/THE: 46
Washington Monthly: 83, National Universities

OVERGENERALIZATIONS
Students are:
Ready to party
Crazy about the Huskies
Only a short drive from home (i.e., Most come from CT or nearby states)
Involved/invested in campus life
Seeking the quintessential college experience

COLLEGE OVERLAPS
Boston University
Northeastern University
Pennsylvania State University - University Park
Syracuse University
University of Massachusetts Amherst

University of Delaware

Newark, Delaware | 302-831-8123

The state of Delaware may take its share of abuse as a place with few attractions (see Wayne's World), but the state's public university is a pretty happening place. The University of Delaware's charming, almost 2,000-acre Newark campus is surrounded by one of the most lively college towns in America. Known for passionate Division I sports fans, a robust Greek life, and a number of well-regarded academic departments, the U of D is attractive to students from all over the US and the world. In fact, the majority of the school's 18,066 undergraduates come from outside of the First State, including international students from 100+ different countries.

Inside the Classroom
No matter which of the school's 150 bachelor's degree programs one pursues, there are 21 credits worth of requirements one must complete. This includes a First-Year Experience course that is a discussion-based, seminar-style class designed to provide a soft landing for freshmen, a discovery learning experience that involves an instructional venture outside of the traditional classroom, and one class each in the realms of multiculturalism; creative arts and humanities; history and cultural change; social and behavioral science; and mathematics, natural sciences, and technology.

Even when including graduate students in the calculation, the University of Delaware's student-to-faculty ratio is only 12:1, an excellent figure for a public institution. Blue Hens do find themselves in an occasional larger lecture hall as 17% of sections enroll 50+ students, but 62% of all courses enroll fewer than 30 students. Those who are ambitious and aggressive can unearth research opportunities at U of D; 400 students participate in the Undergraduate Research and Service Scholar Symposium. The university has the oldest study abroad program in the nation. At almost 100 years old, the program entices more than 30% of undergraduates to spend a semester in one of 40 foreign countries.

Nearly one-third of Delaware students pursue a degree in either business (21%) or engineering (9%), two of the school's highest-ranked departments. Nursing is also popular, with 11% of degrees conferred being in the health professions. Other frequently pursued majors include the social sciences (10%), biology (7%), and education (5%). Plenty of seniors apply for and land prestigious postgraduate fellowships; 11 Blue Hens landed Fulbright Scholarships in 2023, and students have also captured Truman, Schwarzman, and Critical Language Scholarships in recent years.

Outside the Classroom
U of D's vast campus features plenty of university-run housing in which 92% of freshmen and 40% of the entire student body reside. Fraternities attract 16% of the undergraduate population, and sororities draw 21% of all women. Greek culture is alive and well in Newark and is a significant force in the campus social scene. Out of the 21 NCAA Division I teams, the football squad is most popular and often draws crowds of close to 20,000. A full array of intramural sports and 36 club teams exist for less-gifted athletes. The club team offerings include bass fishing, figure skating, and trap and skeet. Overall, there are 400+ clubs of all varieties to choose from. The school dates back to the 1740s and is littered with iconic buildings, old and new, such as Memorial Hall, the Morris Library, and the Whitney Athletic Center. Being located halfway between Washington, DC, and New York City and right outside of Philadelphia makes the school a reasonable drive from a number of desirable urban locations.

Career Services
The Career Center at the University of Delaware has a professional staff of 23 members who work in areas such as event coordination, employer relations, and discipline-specific career advising. The Lerner College of Business & Economics has an additional eight staff members, bringing the total to 31. This works out to a 609:1 counselor-to-student ratio, better than just about every other large public university in the country. Even more importantly, the center succeeds in achieving a very high level of student engagement. In fact, 79% of all undergraduates utilized career services resources in 2022-23. In that same academic year, 1,793 students participated in 149 career readiness programs, workshops, and classroom presentations.

Of the over 2,500 students who came into the office for 1:1 career coaching or resume assistance, 96% rate the appointments positively. The center also does a stellar job connecting undergrads to internship and job opportunities, posting more than 127,000 such opportunities last year. Top companies flock to the 17 career fairs and meetups that take place annually in Newark; 660 unique employers visited campus in 2022-23. Companies that regularly recruit Blue Hens include Capital One, Agilent Technologies, BlackRock, Siemens, DowDuPont, Deloitte, Northrop Grumman, PwC, Intel, and Bank of America. In sum, U of D has an exceptional career services staff that is highly effective at connecting with just about every single student on campus.

Professional Outcomes

Blue Hens who strutted across the graduation stage in 2022 quickly found their next destination at a 94% clip. Sixty-six percent of graduates were employed, with 74% taking jobs at for-profit companies, 16% at nonprofits, 7% in K-12 education, and 4% with a government entity. The greatest number of newly minted alums were hired by JPMorgan Chase & Co. (58), KPMG (31), EY (32), ChristianaCare (30), and Deloitte (17). The median starting salary for this cohort was $62,000 with a 25th percentile salary of $48,000 and a 75th percentile salary of $71,000. The top five states where Class of 2022 diploma receivers landed were Delaware (647), New York (380), Pennsylvania (349), New Jersey (232), and Maryland (138).

Of the 28% immediately pursuing an advanced degree, 62% entered master's programs, 20% entered a professional program such as law, medicine, physical therapy, or pharmacy, and 9% began their doctoral studies. The most frequent higher education landing spots were the U of D itself (283) followed by Thomas Jefferson University (48), NYU (20), and Widener (20). More than ten individuals also matriculated into programs at elite institutions such as UPenn, Johns Hopkins University, and NYU. The University of Delaware saw 102 seniors apply for medical school in 2023, and the most commonly attended medical schools were the Philadelphia College of Osteopathic Medicine, Temple University, Thomas Jefferson University, Rutgers University, and Rowan University. Temple, Rutgers, Widener, and Drexel were the top law school selections for recent grads, but it also sent students to Georgetown University, the College of William & Mary, and UNC-Chapel Hill.

Admission

The applicant pool for the Class of 2026 was 35,228 students large, and 72% were ultimately granted admission. Delaware was test-optional for the Class of 2026, but it still saw 62% of applicants submit SAT scores while 10% submitted ACT results. The middle-50% scores are 1210-1350. The range for composite ACT scores is 26-31. Twenty-nine percent of 2022-23 first-year students placed in the top 10% of their graduating high school class, 64% were in the top quartile, and 92% were in the top half. Seventy percent of this group possessed high school GPAs of 3.75 or above. The average GPA for an entering freshman was 3.96.

Three factors reign supreme in the admissions process: rigor of secondary school record, GPA, and state residency. Of secondary importance are standardized test scores, application essays, recommendations, extracurricular activities, talent/ability, character/personal qualities, volunteer work, and paid work experience. "Considered" elements of one's application include class rank, first-generation status, legacy status, geographical residence, racial/ethnic status, and the level of an applicant's demonstrated interest. This school does not conduct formal interviews as part of the admissions process. Those applying to the Honors College will face additional scrutiny, with past accepted students sporting 4.0+ GPAs and SATs in the 1400s.

Worth Your Money?

With an in-state tuition of around $14k, the University of Delaware represents a solid value for residents of the First State. The full cost of attendance is close to $34,000 per year, making it comparable in price to the in-state costs of public universities in the surrounding states of Pennsylvania, New Jersey, and Maryland. Nonresidents will pay $57k per year for the privilege of becoming a Blue Hen, a price that may make sense for students with a clear postgraduation career plan and no solid in-state options of their own.

FINANCIAL
Institutional Type: Public
In-State Tuition: $16,080
Out-of-State Tuition: $39,720
Room & Board: $14,838
Books & Supplies: $1,000

Avg. Need-Based Grant: $13,189
Avg. % of Need Met: 63%

Avg. Merit-Based Award: $9,674
% Receiving (Freshmen w/o Need): 28%

Avg. Cumulative Debt: $38,234
% of Students Borrowing: 60%

CAREER
Who Recruits
1. Thomas Jefferson University Hospital
2. GlaxoSmithKline
3. BKD Leaders
4. Allan Myers
5. PwC

Notable Internships
1. Northwestern Mutual
2. Philadelphia Phillies
3. Christiana Trust

Top Employers
1. JPMorgan Chase
2. DuPont
3. Citi
4. Merck
5. Capital One

Where Alumni Work
1. Philadelphia
2. New York City
3. Washington, DC
4. Baltimore
5. Boston

Earnings
College Scorecard (10-YR Post-Entry): $71,861
PayScale (Early Career): $63,200
PayScale (Mid-Career): $113,700
PayScale 20-Year ROI: $677,000

RANKINGS
Money: 4.5
U.S. News: 76, National Universities
Wall Street Journal/THE: 86
Washington Monthly: 97, National Universities

OVERGENERALIZATIONS
Students are:
Always admiring the beauty of their campus
Ready to party
Homogeneous
Outgoing
Only a short drive from home (i.e., Most come from DE or nearby states)

COLLEGE OVERLAPS
James Madison University
Pennsylvania State University - University Park
Rutgers University - New Brunswick
University of Connecticut
University of Maryland, College Park

University of Denver

Denver, Colorado | 303-871-2036

A midsize private university of 6,160 students, the University of Denver has a rich history by West Coast standards, having been founded a full 14 years before Colorado was even granted statehood. With over 200 total degree programs, small class sizes, and a commitment to hands-on learning and international experience, DU is becoming a terrific destination point for quality students whose credentials fall short of perfection.

Inside the Classroom

Utilizing a quarter system, the university requires all undergraduate students to conquer an extensive Common Curriculum that ultimately comprises roughly half of one's total credits. This journey includes a first-year seminar, first-year writing and rhetoric courses, demonstrated proficiency in a foreign language, eight courses designated as "Ways of Knowing," and, lastly, a culminating writing-intensive advanced seminar.

Small classes are the norm at the University of Denver as 55% of sections contain no more than 19 students, and 80% enroll a maximum of 29 individuals. The student-to-faculty ratio is 8:1, allowing the school to stay committed to its mission of focusing on experiential learning. The Undergraduate Research Center helps facilitate connections between intellectually curious undergrads and faculty mentors. Three years ago, the school launched an annual Research and Scholarship Showcase to celebrate the original work of its students. You won't find many schools more committed to encouraging their undergraduates to study abroad. An astonishing 70% of DU students spend a semester or summer in a foreign country, which has, in certain years, seen it ranked No. 1 in study abroad percentage. It offers 150 programs across 50 countries.

The Daniels College of Business is highly respected by employers and attracts the greatest number of undergraduates. Thirty-two percent of the degrees conferred in 2022 were in business/marketing, 16% were in the social sciences, 9% in biology, 9% in psychology, 8% in communication/journalism, and 7% in the visual and performing arts. Four to six students per year capture Fulbright Scholarships. Whether it's the reputation of various academic departments or the university's reputation with prestigious national fellowship organizations, DU's reputation is unquestionably on the rise.

Outside the Classroom

Ninety-five percent of freshmen and 51% of all undergrads reside on the University of Denver's 125-acre campus just south of downtown Denver. The buildings are a mix of nineteenth-century and new construction, as the university splurged on building projects during the first decade of the new 2000s. Greek life has a strong heartbeat at this school with 16% of men joining fraternities and 20% of women affiliated with sororities; 22 chapters in total have houses on campus. The 17 Pioneer athletic teams all compete in NCAA Division I, with ice hockey being the most popular spectator sport with eight all-time championships and 75+ Pioneer alumni going on to play in the National Hockey League. There are also 32 club sports teams, 23 intramural leagues, and a world-class gym, the Coors Fitness Center, which includes an Olympic-sized pool, racquet sports, and recreational ice skating. Over 150 other clubs exist for students to pursue their non-sports passions, including all types of performance groups that collectively put on 400+ performances per year. Few complain about this school's location just miles from the heart of Denver, one of the country's most popular cities. Whether hiking in the Rocky Mountains, enjoying the walkable urban area, or taking advantage of the campus' numerous amenities, DU students are rarely bored.

Career Services

Career & Professional Development at the University of Denver is staffed by 15 professional staff members who specialize in discipline-specific career coaching, alumni relations, and employer relations. This equates to a student-to-advisor ratio of 410:1, which is a solid figure, particularly for a non-liberal arts college. The impact of this exceptional level of investment in career services truly pays off, both for the university and its well-supported undergraduates. There is rarely a day when the office is not hosting a skill-building boot camp or an information session with a prominent corporation. Even in the summers, this office remains highly engaged and available.

ADMISSION
Admission Rate: 78%
Admission Rate - Men: 76%
Admission Rate - Women: 79%
EA Admission Rate: 90%
ED Admission Rate: 62%
ED Admits as % of Total Admits: 1%
Admission Rate (5-Year Trend): +20%
% of Admits Attending (Yield): 11%
Transfer Admission Rate: 60%

SAT Reading/Writing (Middle 50%): 620-710
SAT Math (Middle 50%): 600-690
ACT Composite (Middle 50%): 28-32

% Graduated in Top 10% of HS Class: 41%
% Graduated in Top 25% of HS Class: 68%
% Graduated in Top 50% of HS Class: 94%

Demonstrated Interest: Considered
Legacy Status: Considered
Racial/Ethnic Status: Considered
Admission Interview Offered: No

ENROLLMENT
Total Undergraduate Enrollment: 6,160
% Full-Time: 95%
% Male: 45%
% Female: 55%
% Out-of-State: 70%
% Fraternity: 16%
% Sorority: 20%
% On-Campus (All Undergraduate): 51%
Freshman Housing Required: Yes

% African-American: 3%
% Asian: 4%
% Hispanic: 13%
% White: 69%
% Other: 2%
% International: 3%
% Low-Income: 15%

ACADEMICS
Student-to-Faculty Ratio: 8 to 1
% of Classes Under 20: 55%
% of Classes 20-49: 38%
% of Classes 50 or More: 7%
% Full-Time Faculty: 47%
% Full-Time Faculty w/ Terminal Degree: 90%

Top Programs
Communication Studies
Finance
Hospitality Management
International Studies
Music
Psychology
Real Estate

Retention Rate: 85%
4-Year Graduation Rate: 70%
6-Year Graduation Rate: 76%

Curricular Flexibility: Somewhat Flexible
Academic Rating: ★★★

#CollegesWorthYourMoney

For the Class of 2022, 81% percent of DU grads participated in at least one internship during their four years. A jaw-dropping 92% of the Class of 2022 engaged with the office. In citing their job source, 12% landed their job directly from an internship experience, 9% utilized the DU job board, and 6% connected with their future employer at a DU career event. By any measure, the DU career services personnel do a superb job at preparing their students for real-world success.

Professional Outcomes

Ninety percent of 2022 Pioneer grads successfully entered the world of employment or graduate school within six months of earning their bachelor's degree. The 59% who landed their first job primarily remained in Colorado (69%) while 8% headed to the West Coast and 5% settled in the mid-Atlantic region. The mean starting salary of Denver grads was $62k. Top employers of recent grads included KPMG, Brown Brothers Harriman, Lockheed Martin, Epic, and Oracle. Other corporations employing 70 or more University of Denver alums include CenturyLink, Charles Schwab, Comcast, Deloitte, Amazon, Google, and Microsoft.

Twenty-seven percent of 2022 graduates elected to continue their education in a graduate program, including the University of Denver's own 12 schools and colleges that offer master's, doctoral, and professional degrees. This includes the Sturm College of Law, which welcomes many of its own grads along with alumni of 150+ other institutions. In recent years, other Pioneers have gone on to pursue legal studies at the University of Colorado, Northeastern, the University of Virginia, and the University of Minnesota. On the medical school front, there are generally around 50 applicants from the university each year. Unfortunately, the school does not release its annual acceptance rate.

Admission

Seventy-eight percent of the 22,694 applicants for a place in the 2022-23 freshman class received offers of admission; this was 14% higher than the previous year. The mid-50th percentile standardized test scores were 1240-1390 on the SAT and 28-32 on the ACT; the median figures were 1310 and 30, respectively. Forty-one percent of Class of 2026 members hailed from the top 10% of their high school class, 68% from the top 25%, and only 6% fell outside of the top half. The average GPA was 3.80, and 45% possessed a weighted GPA of 4.0 or higher.

The rigor of your high school coursework and your GPA are deemed the "most important" factors by UD. Test scores, essays, recommendations, talent/ability, character/personal qualities, and extracurricular activities are "important." First-generation status (16% of one recent freshman class met this criterion), alumni relation, geographical residence, racial/ethnic status, volunteer work, work experience, and the level of an applicant's interest are all "considered." This school has an extraordinarily low yield rate of 11%, meaning that only one in ten accepted students go on to enroll. Therefore, it is undoubtedly a good idea to make it clear to the university if it is your top choice. It is a bit strange that early decision applicants were admitted at only a 62% clip in 2022, but it is likely that the average ED candidate was far weaker academically than the average candidate in the regular cycle.

Worth Your Money?

A full-time student living on campus will pay $79,193 for the privilege. Unless money is no object for your family, we cannot recommend paying full price to attend this school. On the plus side, UD is generous with need-based aid, dishing out an average award of $41k. It offers plenty of merit aid as well. All told, 84% of incoming freshmen receive some type of financial aid. If you are receiving a reasonable aid package, this school can definitely be worth your money, particularly if you are pursuing a business, engineering, or computer science degree.

FINANCIAL
Institutional Type: Private
In-State Tuition: $59,340
Out-of-State Tuition: $59,340
Room & Board: $17,049
Books & Supplies: $1,000

Avg. Need-Based Grant: $40,501
Avg. % of Need Met: 85%

Avg. Merit-Based Award: $21,438
% Receiving (Freshmen w/o Need): 53%

Avg. Cumulative Debt: $31,313
% of Students Borrowing: 44%

CAREER
Who Recruits
1. Zayo Group
2. Arrow Electronics
3. U.S. Department of State
4. Google
5. Wells Fargo

Notable Internships
1. Brookings Institute
2. AARP
3. NBA

Top Employers
1. Denver Public Schools
2. Lockheed Martin
3. Walt Disney Company
4. Charles Schwab
5. Deloitte

Where Alumni Work
1. Denver
2. New York City
3. San Francisco
4. Los Angeles
5. Chicago

Earnings
College Scorecard (10-YR Post-Entry): $68,764
PayScale (Early Career): $60,300
PayScale (Mid-Career): $114,000
PayScale 20-Year ROI: $498,000

RANKINGS
Money: 4
U.S. News: 124, National Universities
Wall Street Journal/THE: 229
Washington Monthly: 250, National Universities

OVERGENERALIZATIONS
Students are:
Outdoorsy
Environmentally conscious
Wealthy
More likely to venture off campus
Homogenous

COLLEGE OVERLAPS
Colorado State University
Santa Clara University
University of Colorado Boulder
University of San Diego
University of Washington - Seattle

University of Florida

Gainesville, Florida | 352-392-1365

At a time when flagship state schools are being overrun by out-of-state and international students willing to pay full freight, the University of Florida stands strong as an almost exclusive landing spot for Sunshine State residents—to the tune of 90%. Gator Nation could almost be its own small nation with 34,552 undergraduates, 20,000+ graduate students, and roughly 450,000 living alumni. It's not hard to see why top Florida-based teens target UF as their number-one choice. One of the top-ranked state universities in the US can still be accessed by residents for an annual tuition under $7,000 at a time when many elite (and not so elite) schools are eight times higher in cost.

Inside the Classroom

With 16 colleges and 100 undergraduate majors to choose from, the educational experiences of UF students are exceptionally diverse. That includes one of the country's largest honors programs at 3,400 students; classes within this program are capped at 25. All Gators must chomp through a blend of state and university core academic requirements that include coursework in composition, humanities, mathematics, biological and physical sciences, social and behavioral sciences, and classes with "international" and "diversity" designations.

A 16:1 student-to-faculty ratio and a massive number of graduate students lead to some fairly large undergraduate course sections. Yet, the school impressively offers 53% of sections with an enrollment of fewer than 20 students. The Center for Undergraduate Research offers a University Research Scholars program as well as summer opportunities, hosts its own Undergraduate Research Symposium, and publishes its own UF Journal of Undergraduate Research. One-third of all undergrads have such an experience. The school has connections to 1,100 study abroad programs that are taken advantage of by more than 2,200 undergrads each year.

The Warrington College of Business and the Wertheim College of Engineering are highly respected, and a degree from either will yield one of the more absurd returns on investment in all of postsecondary education. Therefore, it's no surprise that those two programs confer the greatest percentage of degrees—12% and 14%, respectively. Biology (11%), the social sciences (11%), and health professions (8%) are next in popularity. The procurement of highly competitive fellowships and postgraduate scholarships is not a focal point of the university, but Gators do claim their fair share. Eleven students in 2023 were Fulbright winners, and as many as 27 students have won National Science Foundation Graduate Research Fellowships in recent years.

Outside the Classroom

Not leading off with a discussion of campus life at UF with football would be an egregious case of burying the lede. The 90,000 orange-and-blue adorned fans crammed into Ben Hill Griffin Stadium, more commonly referred to as "The Swamp," captures the lifeblood of the University of Florida. And it's not only football that is a point of athletic pride in Gainesville. UF is ranked alongside Stanford and UCLA as one of the best overall sports programs in the country. Twenty of the school's 21 teams compete in the ultra-competitive SEC Conference, and the Gators have earned an astounding 42 all-time national championships. Outside of varsity sports, there are 1,000 student organizations, and 76% of students are engaged in campus activities for a minimum of an hour per week. There are sixty intramural sports leagues, two large fitness centers, and two lakes for swimming, boating, and relaxation. Due to a dearth of school-owned housing, only around one-quarter of students live on campus, almost all freshmen. Many move into Greek houses as 17% of men and 24% of women enter fraternity and sorority life. Gainesville is constructed as a Southern college-town-by-numbers experience with all the requisite components of beautiful weather, an overwhelming number of restaurants, bars, and shops, plenty of parties, and, of course, the sports-crazed atmosphere.

Career Services

Unlike many schools of UF's size that have a network of smaller career services offices housed within various colleges, the centralized University of Florida Career Connections Center (C3) serves more than 55,000 current students and alumni. At C3, 35 professionals are available to assist you with career counseling, internship coordination, and networking. The university's overall student-to-counselor ratio of 987:1 is high compared to many other schools featured in this guidebook. Still, there are many positive, measurable things occurring at this career services center. In fact, 78% of recent grads would recommend career services to a friend.

In 2022-23, the Career Connections Center made 53,242 student connections. Staff put on countless planning workshops, attracted over one million website visits, and brought 900+ employers to career fairs, leading to almost 12,000 engagements. Close to 60% of graduates report at least one internship experience during their four years of study. Around one-quarter of employed grads reported a job fair as being a resource that helped them land their first jobs, and 10% cited the Career Connections Center. Despite limited staffing for individualized counseling to reach almost 35,000 undergrads, UF does a nice job putting on large-scale events and bringing a vast array of companies onto campus to recruit and interview.

Professional Outcomes

At the time they received their diplomas, 66% of the Class of 2022 had already procured a first job. The top occupational areas for recent graduates were engineering (13%), health care (13%), computer science (5%), and marketing (4%). Across the entirety of the alumni base, impressive numbers of Gators can be found at many of the nation's most desirable corporations. In fact, more than 200 UF grads are currently employed by Google, EY, Raymond James, Deloitte, Apple, Amazon, Microsoft, Oracle, and PwC. Many graduates remain in the Gainesville area or spread out to other Florida cities including Miami, Tampa Bay, Orlando, Jacksonville, or West Palm Beach. However, substantial numbers of alumni also can be found in Atlanta, New York, DC, and San Francisco. Grads of the College of Business Administration earn median starting salaries—including bonuses—of $80k, computer science majors earn $100k, and psychology majors earn $51k; the average salary for all 2022 grads was $69k.

Of those seeking full-time graduate studies upon receiving their diplomas, a master's degree was the most popular pursuit (63%) followed by law school (11%). The premed program is solid as UF sends the third-most undergrads to medical school of any university in the country, behind only UCLA and UT Austin. Students with strong GPAs and MCAT scores feed directly into the university's own highly ranked College of Medicine. Law school applicants enjoy an 85% acceptance rate. The most commonly attended institution was UF's own law school where 80+ recent graduates matriculated. Three students entered each of Harvard and the University of Chicago and two went to Yale while Columbia, NYU, and Penn all welcomed four Gators each into their prestigious law schools.

Admission

Over 64,000 students submitted applications to the University of Florida for a spot in the 2022-23 freshman class; the admit rate was 23%. The typical Class of 2026 admitted student possessed a 3.93 unweighted GPA, an SAT score of 1400, and an ACT score of 31. Students tend to rank near the top of their high school class as 84% placed in the top decile of their graduating cohort and 98% finished in the top 25%. Five years ago, the acceptance rate was a far friendlier 47%, and the 75th percentile SAT score was lower than the average SAT score among 2026 admits, confirmation that the sinking acceptance rate is indicative of a genuine rise in the school's level of selectivity.

With such a mammoth pile of applications to weed through, one would expect the admissions committee to place the greatest value on hard numbers like standardized test scores, GPA, and class rank. However, of those three factors, the UF Admissions Office only rates GPA as being "very important" to the process. Other considerations listed as "very important" are more in line with those of an elite liberal arts school: rigor of secondary coursework, application essay, extracurricular activities, talent/ability, character/personal qualities, and volunteer work. Grades are king for Gainesville hopefuls; last year, 96% had a GPA of 3.75 or above on a 4.0 scale.

Worth Your Money?

A $6,380 annual tuition cost in the modern era of universally exorbitant tuition looks like a misprint at first glance. Amazingly, the University of Florida, even at full price—room and board and all fees—would only set you back $23k per year assuming, of course, that you qualify as a Florida resident. The sliver of students coming to Gainesville from out of state pay more than double that amount, but UF still ultimately proves a bargain. If you live in Florida and can get into the university, start packing your bags because you simply won't find a better value.

FINANCIAL
Institutional Type: Public
In-State Tuition: $6,381
Out-of-State Tuition: $28,658
Room & Board: $11,500
Books & Supplies: $1,060

Avg. Need-Based Grant: $11,913
Avg. % of Need Met: 99%

Avg. Merit-Based Award: $3,000
% Receiving (Freshmen w/o Need): 5%

Avg. Cumulative Debt: $18,991
% of Students Borrowing: 25%

CAREER
Who Recruits
1. L3 Harris Technologies
2. OMP
3. Citrix
4. Procter & Gamble
5. KPMG

Notable Internships
1. Jet Blue
2. The Walt Disney Company
3. Kellogg Company

Top Employers
1. Amazon
2. Intel
3. Microsoft
4. Google
5. PwC

Where Alumni Work
1. Gainsville, FL
2. Miami
3. Tampa
4. Orlando
5. Jacksonville

Earnings
College Scorecard (10-YR Post-Entry): $69,468
PayScale (Early Career): $60,300
PayScale (Mid-Career): $110,500
PayScale 20-Year ROI: $613,000

RANKINGS
Money: 5
U.S. News: 28, National Universities
Wall Street Journal/THE: 15
Washington Monthly: 22, National Universities

OVERGENERALIZATIONS
Students are:
Crazy about the Gators
Working hard and playing hard
Seeking the quintessential college experience
Ambitious
Social

COLLEGE OVERLAPS
Florida State University
University of Central Florida
University of Georgia
University of Miami
University of South Florida

University of Georgia

Athens, Georgia | 706-542-8776

ADMISSION
Admission Rate: 43%
Admission Rate - Men: 38%
Admission Rate - Women: 46%
EA Admission Rate: Not Reported
ED Admission Rate: Not Offered
ED Admits as % of Total Admits: Not Offered
Admission Rate (5-Year Trend): -11%
% of Admits Attending (Yield): 37%
Transfer Admission Rate: 75%

SAT Reading/Writing (Middle 50%): 620-710
SAT Math (Middle 50%): 600-710
ACT Composite (Middle 50%): 27-32

% Graduated in Top 10% of HS Class: 61%
% Graduated in Top 25% of HS Class: 92%
% Graduated in Top 50% of HS Class: 99%

Demonstrated Interest: Not Considered
Legacy Status: Not Considered
Racial/Ethnic Status: Not Considered
Admission Interview Offered: No

ENROLLMENT
Total Undergraduate Enrollment: 30,714
% Full-Time: 94%
% Male: 42%
% Female: 58%
% Out-of-State: 15%
% Fraternity: 23%
% Sorority: 36%
% On-Campus (All Undergraduate): 35%
Freshman Housing Required: Yes

% African-American: 6%
% Asian: 12%
% Hispanic: 7%
% White: 68%
% Other: 1%
% International: 1%
% Low-Income: 18%

ACADEMICS
Student-to-Faculty Ratio: 17 to 1
% of Classes Under 20: 49%
% of Classes 20-49: 40%
% of Classes 50 or More: 11%
% Full-Time Faculty: 81%
% Full-Time Faculty w/ Terminal Degree: 94%

Top Programs
Animal Science
Biology
Business
Exercise & Sport Science
International Affairs
Journalism & Mass Communication
Psychology
Public Health

Retention Rate: 95%
4-Year Graduation Rate: 71%
6-Year Graduation Rate: 87%

Curricular Flexibility: Somewhat Flexible
Academic Rating: ★★★✦

#CollegesWorthYourMoney

Founded in 1785 as the first state-sponsored university in the country, UGA has since grown into a vast operation that boasts seventeen distinct colleges and schools that offer 125+ majors. Those who make scenic Athens their undergraduate home are free to pursue concentrations in anything from the traditional disciplines to more exotic fields such as avian biology, furnishings and interiors, and turfgrass management. Becoming a Bulldog is infinitely more difficult than a generation ago, but that's an understandable marketplace adjustment for a school that is of extraordinarily high quality, about as sports-conscious as any you'll come across, and that offers as low a tuition as you can hope to find anywhere in the country.

Inside the Classroom
Students cover all of the basics through the school's Core Curriculum, which requires two or more courses in each of English, math, science, world language/culture, and social science along with one course in quantitative reasoning. Freshmen at UGA all participate in a First-Year Odyssey seminar led by a faculty member and capped at eighteen students. Within that intimate setting, students have the opportunity to explore one of 300 thought-provoking topics including Chocolate Science, Death and Dying, Pets in Modern Society, and The Psychology of Harry Potter. Freshmen also have the choice of signing up for Residential Learning Communities, a program that allows dorm residents with similar interests to take classes together. The University of Georgia is the largest undergraduate institution in the country to mandate hands-on learning for every single graduate. UGA students must fulfill that requirement by completing one from a lengthy menu of internships, service options, or research opportunities.

The school's student-to-faculty ratio is 17:1, and, with 9,893 graduate students to also serve, not all of your coursework will be conducted in a cozy setting. Still, 49% of sections enroll fewer than 20 students compared with 11% of sections that enroll 50 or more. No matter your major, UGA encourages you to conduct research with a member of the school's faculty. The Center for Undergraduate Research Opportunities (CURO) awards grants to 500 students per year, and in a typical year, a robust 550+ students presented at the CURO Symposium. Meanwhile, the Office of Global Engagement helps 2,000 students annually find which of the 100+ study abroad programs (many of which are led by UGA faculty) is right for them.

Business is the most commonly conferred undergraduate degree, accounting for 29% of diplomas earned. It is followed by biology (10%), social sciences (8%), communication & journalism (8%), and psychology (7%). Top-ranked programs include animal science, business, communications, and public and international affairs. The school has seen an increase in its number of Fulbright Scholars, producing 11 in 2023. Among public institutions, UGA also has been one of the top three producers of Rhodes Scholars over the previous two decades.

Outside the Classroom
Ninety-eight percent of freshmen, but only 35% of the student body, reside in university-owned housing. As you would expect at a school with over 30,000 undergraduates, there is a full smorgasbord of over 700 clubs and activities from which to choose. The Center for Leadership and Service connects 12,500 students with over 228,000 volunteer hours. Fraternities and sororities have a strong presence with sixty-two Greek-letter organizations on campus that draw 23% of men and 36% of women. If you want to follow Division I athletics, UGA's perennial powerhouse football team draws 92,746 fans to Sanford Stadium each week in autumn. The school fields competitive men's and women's teams in a variety of other sports as well as a diverse selection of over seventy club and intramural teams. For non-athletic competitors, UGA's debate team has qualified for the National Debate Tournament for 25 consecutive years, and its chess team routinely wins state championships. The bottom line is that no matter your passion, you'll be able to find kindred spirits at UGA.

Career Services
The University of Georgia Career Center employs 32 full-time staff members including administrators, career consultants, and employer relations team members. That equates to a student-to-advisor ratio of 960:1, higher than average compared to the pool of institutions included in this book, but about average for an institution of its size. While individualized attention can occasionally be a challenge, the career center does regularly host job and internship fairs, and virtual Q&A sessions with employers are hosted on X. Annually, over 1,000 companies engage in on-campus recruiting through one of the university's major-specific fairs. It's no wonder that 87% of 2022 grads' first jobs aligned with their career aspirations and 31% cited the Career Center as the most helpful resource in their successful job hunt.

Students can sign up at any time for a mock interview with a career consultant. The center also offers a more formalized series of career prep events called "Arch Ready," referencing the iconic campus landmark. Those events cover topics such as major selection, career exploration, and resume writing. The career center does engage companies to become internship partners for students, but data on the percentage of UGA undergrads that land internships is unavailable; what is known is that more than one-quarter of Bulldogs who secured an internship did so through the career center. A robust alumni network will help recent grads connect with other Bulldogs anywhere in the world. Last year, 2,998 unique employers hired UGA grads, resulting in a wide-reaching alumni presence in business, government, and educational institutions.

Professional Outcomes

UGA's career outcomes rate (the percent of students employed or continuing their education six months after graduation) was 96% for the Class of 2022. Popular employers include Accenture, PricewaterhouseCoopers, the Walt Disney Company, and Deloitte. Sixty-nine percent of 2022 grads stayed in the state of Georgia with the cities of Dallas, Houston, Chicago, DC, New York City, and San Francisco also among the top destinations. UGA does an excellent job of tracking graduates' starting salary data by school/major. That data allows prospective students to properly calibrate their financial expectations based on area of study. For instance, engineering grads in the Class of 2022 had a median starting salary of $65k while graduates of the Grady College of Journalism and Mass Communication reported a median income of $50k.

In 2022, a solid 24% of graduates elected to jump directly into a full-time advanced degree program. The most commonly attended graduate/professional schools included elite institutions such as Columbia, Duke, Emory, Georgia Tech, Penn, UVA, and Johns Hopkins. In a given year, roughly half of the Bulldogs applying to medical school gain acceptance. Recent graduates are currently studying medicine at local schools, such as the Mercer University School of Medicine, as well as prestigious medical training grounds like Emory, Harvard, and Washington University.

Admission

Like many flagships around the country, the University of Georgia has grown increasingly competitive in recent years. The university received 39,354 applications in 2022, more than triple the number received in 2005. The acceptance rate for a place in the Class of 2026 was 43%. Freshmen in 2022-23 possessed an ACT mid-50% score of 26-32 and 1220-1400 on the SAT. A strong academic profile is also essential—65% of successful applicants were in the top 10% of their class, and 93% were in the top quartile. Perhaps the most intimidating statistic is that the average GPA is 4.12.

A scholarship program guaranteeing free tuition to any valedictorian or salutatorian from a Georgia high school has led to 5% of the student body being comprised of students holding those illustrious distinctions. The UGA Admissions Office says, "More than any other single factor, the grades you earn in your high school courses play the most important role in determining your competitiveness for admission to UGA." A rigorous high school course load is a must as 96% of admitted students took at least one AP, IB, or dual enrollment class. In sum, this public jewel has become a destination point for the Peach State's top high school students. Knowledgeable applicants should use caution in underestimating the level of competition for spots on the picturesque Athens campus.

Worth Your Money?

You would be hard-pressed to locate a better value for a college diploma from a highly respected institution than what you would get at UGA. In-state residents pay under $10k in tuition and, thanks to cheap living in Athens, only $28k in total cost of attendance. Out-of-staters pay a not unreasonable total annual cost of $48k. The school awards an average need-based grant of $11k to 34% of current students. It's little wonder that the average amount of debt for a University of Georgia grad is well under the national average. In short, this school is worth the money for any type of degree; even nonresidents can find a solid value here.

FINANCIAL
Institutional Type: Public
In-State Tuition: $11,180
Out-of-State Tuition: $30,220
Room & Board: $11,246
Books & Supplies: $1,002

Avg. Need-Based Grant: $10,659
Avg. % of Need Met: 78%

Avg. Merit-Based Award: $3,024
% Receiving (Freshmen w/o Need): 4%

Avg. Cumulative Debt: $22,532
% of Students Borrowing: 36%

CAREER
Who Recruits
1. Mailchimp
2. State Farm
3. Yelp
4. Boston Consulting Group
5. Home Depot

Notable Internships
1. Anthropologie
2. Delta Air Lines
3. TJX Companies

Top Employers
1. Home Depot
2. Delta
3. EY
4. Coca Cola
5. Deloitte

Where Alumni Work
1. Atlanta
2. Athens, GA
3. New York City
4. Washington, DC
5. Charlotte

Earnings
College Scorecard (10-YR Post-Entry): $63,405
PayScale (Early Career): $59,500
PayScale (Mid-Career): $110,000
PayScale 20-Year ROI: $535,000

RANKINGS
Money: 4.5
U.S. News: 47, National Universities
Wall Street Journal/THE: 170
Washington Monthly: 93, National Universities

OVERGENERALIZATIONS
Students are:
Crazy about the Dawgs
More likely to rush a fraternity/sorority
Politically balanced
Seeking the quintessential college experience
Driven

COLLEGE OVERLAPS
Clemson University
Georgia Institute of Technology
University of Florida
University of North Carolina at Chapel Hill
University of South Carolina

University of Illinois at Chicago

Chicago, Illinois | 312-996-4350

ADMISSION
Admission Rate: 79%
Admission Rate - Men: 74%
Admission Rate - Women: 82%
EA Admission Rate: 91%
ED Admission Rate: Not Offered
ED Admits as % of Total Admits: Not Offered
Admission Rate (5-Year Trend): +2%
% of Admits Attending (Yield): 23%
Transfer Admission Rate: 62%

SAT Reading/Writing (Middle 50%): 560-660
SAT Math (Middle 50%): 550-680
ACT Composite (Middle 50%): 24-30

% Graduated in Top 10% of HS Class: 23%
% Graduated in Top 25% of HS Class: 53%
% Graduated in Top 50% of HS Class: 89%

Demonstrated Interest: Not Considered
Legacy Status: Not Considered
Racial/Ethnic Status: Not Considered
Admission Interview Offered: No

ENROLLMENT
Total Undergraduate Enrollment: 21,807
% Full-Time: 91%
% Male: 47%
% Female: 53%
% Out-of-State: 4%
% Fraternity: 4%
% Sorority: 4%
% On-Campus (All Undergraduate): 13%
Freshman Housing Required: No

% African-American: 8%
% Asian: 21%
% Hispanic: 36%
% White: 23%
% Other: 2%
% International: 7%
% Low-Income: 50%

ACADEMICS
Student-to-Faculty Ratio: 18 to 1
% of Classes Under 20: 34%
% of Classes 20-49: 47%
% of Classes 50 or More: 19%
% Full-Time Faculty: 73%
% Full-Time Faculty w/ Terminal Degree: 91%

Top Programs
Biology
Computer Science
Criminology
Industrial Design
English
Engineering
Finance
Psychology

Retention Rate: 80%
4-Year Graduation Rate: 40%
6-Year Graduation Rate: 62%

Curricular Flexibility: Very Flexible
Academic Rating: ★★★

#CollegesWorthYourMoney

With no racial or ethnic majority among the student population, the University of Illinois at Chicago is one of the most genuinely diverse institutions of higher learning in the United States. It is also the largest school in the Greater Chicago area with almost 22,000 undergraduates and 11,900 graduate and professional students. Undergrads pursue one of 95 bachelor's programs offered through the 11 (of 16) colleges within UIC that grant undergraduate degrees. The university, in its present form, is only 40 years old, and with its combination of desirable location and quality academics, it is sure to continue to rise up the rankings in the coming decade.

Inside the Classroom
The general education core covers six categories: analyzing the natural world, understanding the individual and society, understanding the past, understanding the creative arts, exploring world cultures, and understanding US society. Students must demonstrate proficiency as writers by either completing two English composition courses or demonstrating their skills on standardized tests. Four semesters of a foreign language is among the graduation requirements within the College of Liberal Arts and Sciences, but second language mandates vary by college. For the approximately 1,500 students in the Honors College, at least one honors activity must be completed each semester, and an honors capstone project is required during senior year.

As would be expected at a modestly priced state school with a plethora of graduate school programs, the student-to-faculty ratio is a mediocre 18:1, and some classes, particularly those of the introductory variety, will be conducted in expansive lecture halls. Yet, while 19% of classes at UIC do, indeed, enroll more than 50 students, close to two-thirds enroll fewer than 29. Ten percent of courses are taught by teaching assistants, but 88% of full-time faculty here have a PhD. Opportunities to engage in undergraduate research will not be handed to you, as at some liberal arts colleges, but the Undergraduate Research Experience, a university-wide program, does connect motivated students with faculty researchers in their field of interest. Those interested in studying abroad have access to 200+ programs in 50 countries.

The most popular majors at this school are business/marketing (16%), health professions (13%), and engineering (13%). The next most commonly conferred degrees are in biology (12%), psychology (9%), and the social sciences (5%). The business, engineering, and computer science programs all have a solid national reputation, regularly cracking "Top 100" lists in their respective disciplines. UIC is not, at this time, a prolific producer of prestigious national fellowship winners.

Outside the Classroom
One of the more diverse schools in the country by any measure, the University of Illinois at Chicago boasts large Hispanic, African American, and Asian populations as well as a sizable number of older students; 9% of undergrads are over the age of 25. There are a good deal of commuters and students who live in off-campus housing from the very beginning of their college journey; just 31% of freshmen and 13% of total undergraduates live in the dorms. Greek life is modest in size with just 4% of students electing to join one of the 17 sororities or 17 fraternities. Playing as the Flames, the university fields 20 NCAA Division I sports teams, and all tickets are free to students. Even with approximately half of the student body home for the weekends, there is still plenty to do on this 240-acre urban campus. There are limitless opportunities to participate in intramural sports and a 214,000-square-foot Outdoor Field Complex on which to play them. The Credit Union 1 Arena is a 9,500-seat multipurpose stadium on the university's campus that plays host to a wide range of cultural, musical, dramatic, and athletic events. Being located in the heart of one of America's most beloved cities also has many advantages. Within a couple miles of campus are sights like the Art Institute of Chicago, the Chicago Riverwalk, and, of course, plenty of world-famous pizza places.

Career Services
There are multiple career services offices within the University of Illinois at Chicago. First, there is a catch-all Career Services office staffed by 18 professionals. The Engineering Career Center employs an additional four individuals. The Business Career Center offers nine career services professionals, and the College of Liberal Arts and Sciences Career Development office has another two. All told, 33 professional staff members work in career services on behalf of UIC undergraduates, equating to a less-than-ideal 661:1 student-to-advisor ratio. Still, this figure is not uncommon at a university of this size, and career services staff put on plenty of large-scale events to accommodate the heavy flow of undergraduates.

Each year, the school hosts eight major career fairs, including the UIC Graduate and Professional School Fair, attended by reps from 200+ colleges and universities, and the All Majors Career Fair, which attracts 100+ major companies. Fifty-four percent of 2022 UIC grads reported completing at least one internship during their time on campus, an impressive percentage for a public school with such high enrollment. The Engineering Career Center is always happy to discuss your career search one-on-one, review a resume, or offer useful workshops such as "Preparing for Technical Interviews with Google." The Business Career Center excels at connecting students to paid internships and on-campus interviews with some of the world's most sought-after employers.

Professional Outcomes

The Class of 2022 had a 97% success rate six months after graduation, and 14% enrolled in graduate school. Students on the engineering, applied sciences, and public health tracks found employment or a graduate school home at the highest rates; education, architecture, and liberal arts majors had the poorest short-term outcomes. By volume, the largest employer of University of Illinois at Chicago grads is Chicago Public Schools. More than 100 alumni can also be found employed by Allstate, Amazon, Accenture, Microsoft, IBM, Google, Deloitte, and Meta. Over 90% of recent grads began their careers within the state of Illinois; in the long run, the Greater Chicago area remains the most popular area of residence with San Francisco, New York City, Los Angeles, and Washington, DC, next on the list. The average salary for a 2022 grad was a solid $64k.

Recent graduates of UIC went on to enroll at top graduate schools such as Boston University, New York University, Northwestern University, and the University of Chicago. Many elected to continue their studies within the University of Illinois system at either the Urbana-Champaign or Chicago campus. Last year, 261 seniors applied to medical schools around the country including the university's own University of Illinois College of Medicine. Many prelaw students matriculate into UIC's John Marshall School of Law while other recent grads have gone on to attend the University of Chicago, Boston College, Northwestern, and the University of Illinois College of Law (Urbana-Champaign).

Admission

The University of Illinois at Chicago saw 23,562 applicants in the most recent admissions cycle; 79% were accepted, making for a less stressful process than at many other schools featured in this guide. The SAT was the more commonly submitted of the two major standardized tests (29% vs. 6%) and the middle-50th percentile SAT score was 1120-1320. The middle-50th percentile on the ACT was a wide-ranging 24-30. Only 23% of freshmen earned a place in the top 10% of their graduating class compared to 59% at the Urbana-Champaign campus. Fifty-three percent of freshmen placed in the top quartile, and 89% were in the top half of their high school cohort.

Utilizing a straightforward and numbers-based admissions process, the UIC committee leans most heavily on the rigor of one's secondary school record and GPA. The only other factors that are even considered are essays, recommendations, test scores, and extracurricular activities. Applicants to the College of Engineering are held to a higher standard, as accepted students sported a middle-50% SAT range of 1240-1450. Those admitted to the College of Education scored in the 1050-1220 range. There is no early decision option at this school, but students do have the option to apply early action by November 1.

Worth Your Money?

The university rates among the best in the country for social mobility, providing the opportunity for those born into lower-income households to achieve more favorable economic standing in their adult lives. UIC charges $16k in tuition and fees for Illinois residents, and even though the school only meets 54% of demonstrated need, the average graduate leaves UIC with only an average level of debt. Out-of-staters pay a reasonable tuition of $33,000 which, if studying within the well-regarded College of Business Administration or College of Engineering, is a price worth paying, particularly if the city of Chicago appeals to you as a postsecondary home.

FINANCIAL
Institutional Type: Public
In-State Tuition: $17,811
Out-of-State Tuition: $32,833
Room & Board: $14,400
Books & Supplies: $1,400

Avg. Need-Based Grant: $16,204
Avg. % of Need Met: 54%

Avg. Merit-Based Award: $6,899
% Receiving (Freshmen w/o Need): 6%

Avg. Cumulative Debt: $22,414
% of Students Borrowing: 43%

CAREER
Who Recruits
1. MWH Global
2. Siemens
3. Mayo Clinic
4. GrubHub
5. Allstate

Notable Internships
1. Northrop Grumman
2. Motorola
3. ScribeAmerica

Top Employers
1. Chicago Public Schools
2. Rush University Medical Center
3. AbbVie
4. Amazon
5. JPMorgan Chase

Where Alumni Work
1. Chicago
2. San Francisco
3. New York City
4. Los Angeles
5. Washington, DC

Earnings
College Scorecard (10-YR Post-Entry): $64,108
PayScale (Early Career): $61,500
PayScale (Mid-Career): $109,900
PayScale 20-Year ROI: $532,000

RANKINGS
Money: 4.5
U.S. News: 82, National Universities
Wall Street Journal/THE: 55
Washington Monthly: 57, National Universities

OVERGENERALIZATIONS
Students are:
Diverse
Career-driven
More likely to go home on weekends
Independent
Focused

COLLEGE OVERLAPS
DePaul University
Illinois Institute of Technology
Illinois State University
Loyola University Chicago
University of Illinois at Urbana-Champaign

University of Illinois at Urbana-Champaign

Champaign, Illinois | 217-333-0302

ADMISSION

Admission Rate: 45%
Admission Rate - Men: 38%
Admission Rate - Women: 53%
EA Admission Rate: Not Offered
ED Admission Rate: Not Offered
ED Admits as % of Total Admits: Not Offered
Admission Rate (5-Year Trend): -17%
% of Admits Attending (Yield): 28%
Transfer Admission Rate: 50%

SAT Reading/Writing (Middle 50%): 660-740
SAT Math (Middle 50%): 680-790
ACT Composite (Middle 50%): 29-34

% Graduated in Top 10% of HS Class: 59%
% Graduated in Top 25% of HS Class: 89%
% Graduated in Top 50% of HS Class: 99%

Demonstrated Interest: Not Considered
Legacy Status: Not Considered
Racial/Ethnic Status: Considered
Admission Interview Offered: No

ENROLLMENT

Total Undergraduate Enrollment: 35,120
% Full-Time: 98%
% Male: 53%
% Female: 47%
% Out-of-State: 14%
% Fraternity: 21%
% Sorority: 27%
% On-Campus (All Undergraduate): 50%
Freshman Housing Required: Yes

% African-American: 6%
% Asian: 22%
% Hispanic: 14%
% White: 39%
% Other: 1%
% International: 14%
% Low-Income: 25%

ACADEMICS

Student-to-Faculty Ratio: 21 to 1
% of Classes Under 20: 39%
% of Classes 20-49: 42%
% of Classes 50 or More: 19%
% Full-Time Faculty: 100%
% Full-Time Faculty w/ Terminal Degree: 94%

Top Programs
Agriculture
Business
Chemistry
Computer Science
Engineering
Information Sciences
Psychology
Statistics

Retention Rate: 93%
4-Year Graduation Rate: 72%
6-Year Graduation Rate: 85%

Curricular Flexibility: Less Flexible
Academic Rating: ★★★★

#CollegesWorthYourMoney

The University of Illinois at Urbana-Champaign, the mammoth, highly ranked research university with an iconic Midwestern campus, serves as the beloved home to 35,120 increasingly accomplished undergraduates. The university's humble beginnings as an industrial college upon its founding in 1867 are now nothing more than a distant, long-obliterated memory. Illinois' flagship institution 135 miles south of Chicago has fifteen schools and colleges, eight of which cater to undergraduate students. There are 150 academic programs including 15 in the acclaimed Grainger College of Engineering alone.

Inside the Classroom

As at many large universities, curricular mandates vary by school. The College of Liberal Arts & Sciences, by far UIUC's largest school, has a long list of must-takes including four classes in a foreign language, two English composition courses, and two courses in each of humanities and arts, natural sciences and technology, and social and behavioral sciences. A few years ago, three cultural studies courses were added as requirements: Western Cultures, Non-Western Cultures, and US Minority Cultures.

Illinois' student-to-faculty ratio of 21:1 is among the highest of any school in this guide, but the school still manages to keep 39% of sections capped at 19 students. Further, 29% of undergraduates work with a faculty member on a research project; another 22% have some type of fieldwork, practicum, or clinical experience. Unique opportunities for experiential learning abound at Research Park, an on-campus technology hub that hosts more than one hundred major corporations and 2,100 employees who use the space as an incubator of innovation and a place to collaborate with Illinois faculty and students. Also strong, particularly for a school of UIUC's size, is the 33% participation rate for the school's study abroad programs, which offer over 350 sites in 50 countries.

In sheer volume of degrees conferred, engineering and business/marketing are tied at 19%, followed by the social sciences (9%) and psychology (6%). The aforementioned Grainger College of Engineering, a top-ten school on any list, has a direct pipeline to top firms and tech companies. The Gies College of Business is also strong, particularly the Accounting Department, which is also a feeder to the world's best accounting firms. Prestigious scholarship competitions are similarly fond of Illinois grads—nine of the Fulbright Scholarship applicants from the university won awards, a performance comparable to elites such as Berkeley, Dartmouth, and Tufts. Twenty-six students captured National Science Foundation Graduate Research Fellowships in 2023.

Outside the Classroom

The University District is one of the only campuses in the United States better measured by miles than acres. The school's 354 buildings are contained on 3.3 square miles. Everything at UIUC is massive in scale. Twenty-four residence halls are home to half of all undergraduates, mostly freshmen, as all first-years are required to live on campus. Including private certified housing units and frat and sorority houses, approximately half of undergrads reside on campus. Student life is dominated by 96 Greek organizations that scoop up 27% of female and 21% of male undergraduates. The twenty-one NCAA Division I sports teams are also a major focal point at this school. The Fighting Illini football team plays before crowds of 60,000+ at Memorial Stadium. An unfathomable 470,000 square feet of recreational spaces offer everything from indoor tracks to a leisure pool with a slide to an inline skating rink. With roughly 800 student-run organizations, it's hard not to find your niche somewhere. One doesn't even have to venture off university grounds to find robust cultural opportunities as the four theaters in the Krannert Center for the Performing Arts annually host more than 350 performances by students as well as touring professionals. The Krannert Art Museum boasts 10,000 original works. Those looking to road trip to a major city can reach St. Louis, Chicago, or Indianapolis in two to three hours by car.

Career Services

Eighteen professional employees staff The Career Center at Illinois (TCC) with roles such as career counselor, health career advisor, employer relations, and professional development for international students. However, additional career services support can be found within the Gies College of Business (three professional staff); the Grainger College of Engineering (5); the School for Information Sciences (1); the Department of Economics (1); and the College of Agricultural, Consumer & Environmental Sciences (1). All told, the University of Illinois at Urbana-Champaign possesses an overall student-to-career staff ratio of 1,211:1, which is higher than the average university featured in this book.

University of Illinois at Urbana-Champaign

Serving 35,000+ undergraduate students is a monumental task, but it's one that UIUC successfully meets by offering a wide array of services and large-group activities. The TCC serves roughly one-quarter of the student population each year. Staff conducts 2,500+ one-on-one advising sessions, completes nearly 5,000 resume/cover letter/LinkedIn page reviews, hosts 430+ employers and graduate/professional schools at career fairs, and facilitates roughly 750 on-campus interviews. In total, 73% of Class of 2022 graduates completed at least one internship while at Illinois, and 90% participated in some type of experiential learning. Job shadowing, application boot camps, career fair preparation workshops, and etiquette dinners are only a small sampling of opportunities provided by the TCC to students proactive enough to take advantage. Despite the sheer numbers challenge of serving every student, UIUC Career Services provides many excellent programs that lead to impressive career and graduate school outcomes.

Professional Outcomes

Ninety-five percent of the members of the graduating Class of 2022 had landed at their next destination within six months of graduation. Employed (full-time) graduates represented 57% of the total cohort, and the most popular sectors were finance, consulting, healthcare, electronics, and education. Among the corporations that landed 20 or more 2022 Illini grads were KPMG, Deloitte, Epic Systems, EY, PwC, and Amazon. More than 15 newly minted grads landed at companies like Medline Industries, JPMorgan Chase, and United Airlines. The average salary across all majors for 2022 grads was an extremely solid $75,000. Two-thirds of graduates remained in the Land of Lincoln; California, Massachusetts, Missouri, and Washington State welcomed the greatest percentages of migrating alumni.

A notably high 38% of Class of 2022 graduates matriculated directly into an advanced degree program with 68% pursuing a master's degree. More than 850 students stayed put at the University of Illinois and over 15 Class of 2022 graduates enrolled in prestigious universities such as Columbia, Northwestern, Stanford, NYU, and the University of Michigan. Clearly, Illinois grads are extremely competitive candidates at all of the country's elite graduate programs. Medical school applicants fare decently with acceptance rates around 10% higher than the national average, and recent grads have trained at Rush University Medical College, Washington University School of Medicine in St. Louis, the University of Michigan Medical School, and Johns Hopkins. Law school applicants attend many fine institutions including the University of Illinois' own highly ranked law school.

Admission

The University of Illinois at Urbana-Champaign accepted 45% of the 47,527 applicants battling for a place in the Class of 2026. This was a steep drop from the 60% clip experienced by the Class of 2025 and the newest Illini are a high-achieving lot. Those admitted for the 2022-23 school year had mid-50% standardized test scores of 1340-1530 on the SAT and 29-34 on the ACT. Fifty-nine percent placed in the top decile of their graduating classes, and 89% hailed from the top quartile. Applicants to UIUC's Grainger College will need to possess grades and test scores well above the aforementioned averages. Standards for entry into a computer science major are similar to those encountered at an Ivy.

The admissions committee places the greatest emphasis on the rigor of one's secondary school record and the GPA earned. Standardized test scores, essays, extracurricular activities, and talent/ability are considered "important" to the decision-making process. It also states that those who submit their applications by November 1 "may [have] the best chance for being admitted to our most selective programs and special attention for admission to honors programs and for merit awards." There is no reason not to apply to UIUC by the early deadline because it is a nonbinding proposition and gives you the best odds at admission.

Worth Your Money?

Almost three-quarters of undergraduates enrolled in this university are from within the state of Illinois, entitling them to an affordable education. One of the few American schools to charge different tuition rates to business/engineering majors than education/social work majors, residents enjoy an average cost of attendance between $35k and $40k per year. Nonresidents are offered a COA of $55k to $65k, lower than most private institutions, making the University of Illinois at Urbana-Champaign a viable option for some out-of-staters, particularly those planning to enter the corporate or tech world. Around half of entering freshmen are determined eligible for need-based financial aid with an average award of $20k.

FINANCIAL
Institutional Type: Public
In-State Tuition: $17,572
Out-of-State Tuition: $36,068
Room & Board: $13,938
Books & Supplies: $1,200

Avg. Need-Based Grant: $19,965
Avg. % of Need Met: 77%

Avg. Merit-Based Award: $7,287
% Receiving (Freshmen w/o Need): 12%

Avg. Cumulative Debt: $22,811
% of Students Borrowing: 41%

CAREER
Who Recruits
1. Micron
2. Crowe Horwath
3. Shell
4. Phillips 66
5. BP America

Notable Internships
1. Ford Motor Company
2. Uber
3. State Farm

Top Employers
1. Google
2. Microsoft
3. Amazon
4. EY
5. IBM

Where Alumni Work
1. Chicago
2. Urban-Champaign, IL
3. San Francisco
4. New York City
5. Los Angeles

Earnings
College Scorecard (10-YR Post-Entry): $77,368
PayScale (Early Career): $68,300
PayScale (Mid-Career): $123,600
PayScale 20-Year ROI: $753,000

RANKINGS
Money: 5
U.S. News: 35, National Universities
Wall Street Journal/THE: 35
Washington Monthly: 24, National Universities

OVERGENERALIZATIONS
Students are:
Diverse
Competitive
Career-driven
Working hard and playing hard
More likely to rush a fraternity/sorority

COLLEGE OVERLAPS
Indiana University Bloomington
Northwestern University
Purdue University - West Lafayette
University of Michigan
University of Wisconsin - Madison

University of Iowa

Iowa City, Iowa | 319-335-3847

ADMISSION
Admission Rate: 86%
Admission Rate - Men: 87%
Admission Rate - Women: 85%
EA Admission Rate: Not Reported
ED Admission Rate: Not Offered
ED Admits as % of Total Admits: Not Offered
Admission Rate (5-Year Trend): 0%
% of Admits Attending (Yield): 23%
Transfer Admission Rate: 73%

SAT Reading/Writing (Middle 50%): 570-670
SAT Math (Middle 50%): 560-670
ACT Composite (Middle 50%): 22-28

% Graduated in Top 10% of HS Class: 33%
% Graduated in Top 25% of HS Class: 65%
% Graduated in Top 50% of HS Class: 93%

Demonstrated Interest: Not Considered
Legacy Status: Not Considered
Racial/Ethnic Status: Not Considered
Admission Interview Offered: No

ENROLLMENT
Total Undergraduate Enrollment: 21,973
% Full-Time: 93%
% Male: 44%
% Female: 56%
% Out-of-State: 37%
% Fraternity: 13%
% Sorority: 17%
% On-Campus (All Undergraduate): 28%
Freshman Housing Required: No

% African-American: 3%
% Asian: 5%
% Hispanic: 9%
% White: 75%
% Other: 3%
% International: 2%
% Low-Income: 16%

ACADEMICS
Student-to-Faculty Ratio: 16 to 1
% of Classes Under 20: 50%
% of Classes 20-49: 36%
% of Classes 50 or More: 14%
% Full-Time Faculty: 88%
% Full-Time Faculty w/ Terminal Degree: 89%

Top Programs
Accounting
Economics
Engineering
English and Creative Writing
Exercise Science
Nursing
Psychology
Statistics

Retention Rate: 88%
4-Year Graduation Rate: 55%
6-Year Graduation Rate: 73%

Curricular Flexibility: Somewhat Flexible
Academic Rating: ★★★

#CollegesWorthYourMoney

In the classic film *Field of Dreams*, an Iowa farmer hears a magical voice from the depths of a cornfield delivering the cryptic message, "If you build it, he will come." Perhaps the founders of the state's flagship school heard a similar mysterious message of encouragement before the University of Iowa opened its doors in 1855. Like Kevin Costner's ghost-trodden baseball diamond in *Field of Dreams*, UI was a genuine original from the very start. It was the first public university in America to admit men and women on an equal basis, the first to award advanced degrees in writing, theater, and music, and the first to open dental and law schools west of the Mississippi River. Today, Iowa ranks among the top 35 public institutions in the United States and draws undergraduates from all over the country and the world; over 40% of the nearly 22,000 undergraduates hail from out of state.

Inside the Classroom

Completing the College of Liberal Arts and Sciences (CLAS) Core involves a minimum of 35 credit hours plus up to four classes in a foreign language, depending on a student's level of proficiency. This includes at least one course in the following categories: rhetoric; interpretation of literature; quantitative or formal reasoning; social sciences; diversity and inclusion; historical perspectives; international and global issues; literary, visual, and performing arts; and values and culture. Two courses in the natural sciences are required. However, not all majors are required to complete the CLAS Core. For example, students in the College of Engineering only have 15 mandated general education credits.

The 15:1 student-to-faculty ratio is not suggestive of an intimate learning environment, yet the University of Iowa still manages to keep over half of its undergraduate sections at an enrollment of 19 or fewer students. Just 14% of sections enroll 50 or more undergrads. Increasing the number of undergraduate research opportunities available is part of the university's strategic plan. At present, about 30% of UI undergrads conduct or assist research. In a given year, more than 1,300 University of Iowa students studied abroad; all told, 17% of graduates study abroad for a semester at some point during their four years at the university.

By a wide margin, the most commonly conferred degree at UI is business (24%), with parks and recreation (10%), social sciences (8%), health professions (8%), engineering (7%), and communication & journalism (5%) next in popularity. The Tippie College of Business has a strong reputation, and the English and creative writing major allows students access to some of the same resources as the Iowa Writers' Workshop, the top-rated MFA program in the entire country. Highly competitive national postgraduate scholarships are won by Iowa grads with astonishing regularity. In 2023, there were 15 students and alumni who captured Fulbright Scholarships. Recent grads have also been awarded Boren Awards, Critical Language Scholarships, and National Science Foundation Fellowships.

Outside the Classroom

On-campus housing is primarily reserved for freshmen as 91% of first-years live in the dorms compared to only 28% of the total undergraduate student body. There is a fairly sizable Greek/party culture on campus for those who wish to partake; 17% of women join sororities, and 13% of men join fraternities. There are 27 total fraternities and 22 sorority chapters at the university. There are more women than men at this school by a 56% to 44% margin. There are plenty of big-time sports with 22 varsity teams competing in the Big Ten Conference alongside athletic powerhouses like Penn State, Ohio State, and the University of Michigan. If you are not among the 800+ athletes competing at this high level, there are countless intramural sports from archery tag to pickleball. In total, there are more than 500 student-run clubs covering every niche interest under the sun. The Campus Activities Board brings major acts to the school, typically for cheap ticket prices, and the popular Dance Marathon attracts more than 2,000 participants to help raise money to combat childhood cancer. Iowa City is safe and walkable with plenty of museums, restaurants, and natural beauty. It has, in the past, been rated the top college town in the country as well as one of the most livable cities.

Career Services

The Pomerantz Career Center employs 24 professional staff members who work in areas such as experiential education, employer relations, and career advising. This works out to a 915:1 counselor-to-student ratio, weaker than many schools in this guidebook, but not that unusual or alarming for a university of Iowa's size. In fact, in a single year, the University of Iowa managed to conduct individual counseling sessions with over 5,000 students (including peer advisor sessions) and deliver career-related workshops and programs to another 4,900+.

This staff does exceptional work bringing employers to campus to set up at job fairs and even conduct on-campus job interviews—a total of 600 employers recruit at the university each year. Four major career fairs attract 3,500 students and hundreds of companies, including major corporations like Epic, Chase, BMO Financial Group, Aramark, and 3M. Overall, 72% of Class of 2022 grads reported participating in at least one internship. A testament to both the career center as well as the school's academic advising, 91% of Hawkeyes finding employment did so in a position that is related to their academic study. The University of Iowa is not a place where every undergraduate fully takes advantage of personalized career counseling, but there are enough supports in place to ensure that career guidance and connections are available to those who seek them out.

Professional Outcomes

96% of those who graduated from the University of Iowa in 2022 found their first job or advanced degree program within six months of receiving their diploma. Healthcare is the most commonly entered industry, attracting 23% of employed graduates, followed by entertainment/the arts (14%), finance and insurance (11%), and marketing/PR (10%). Companies that presently employ hundreds of Iowa alumni include Wells Fargo, Collins Aerospace, Principal Financial Group, Amazon, Accenture, and Microsoft. The median salary for 2022 grads was $50,000. While many graduates end up in Iowa City, Des Moines, and Cedar Rapids, the most popular landing spot is actually Chicago. The average median mid-career income is comparable to other Midwestern publics like Iowa State, Michigan State, and the University of Minnesota.

Twenty-eight percent of recent graduates have gone right from undergraduate to graduate school. Remaining at the University of Iowa was the most common choice, with 76% of grad school attendees staying put in Iowa City. Other students enrolled in the likes of Drake University, Loyola University Chicago, DePaul University, and the University of Illinois. The school saw 185 of its undergraduates apply to medical school in 2022, including to its own highly ranked Carver College of Medicine. Those interested in law school can elect to pursue the 3+3 program in conjunction with UI's own law school.

Admission

An 86% acceptance rate is about as friendly as it gets among schools included in this guide, and that's the exact percentage of applicants granted acceptance into the Class of 2026. Just 23% of this group elected to enroll and officially become Hawkeyes. Sixty-three percent of 2022-23 applicants submitted an ACT score, and the mid-50th percentile range was 22-28; the SAT range was 1140-1340. One-third of enrolled students finished in the top 10% of their high school class, and 65% placed in the top quartile. Sixty-one percent of all undergrads earned a 3.75 or above GPA while in high school; the average GPA is 3.82.

The admissions process at the University of Iowa is about as straightforward and no-frills as it gets. Rigor of high school coursework, GPA, class rank, and standardized test scores are rated as "highly important," and recommendations, talent/ability, character/personal qualities, and state residency are "considered." Applications are reviewed on a rolling basis beginning in early fall, and the final deadline for submissions isn't until May 1. In sum, applying to UIowa is not particularly stressful; the review process is transparent and predictable, and the result—the educational experience—is excellent. That's not a bad combination.

Worth Your Money?

For residents of the Hawkeye State, tuition alone at the university is $11k, and with housing and meals, the annual cost rises to over $24k. Nonresidents pay approximately $46k in total cost of attendance. There are no reciprocity agreements with nearby states. At the in-state cost, this school qualifies as a genuine bargain; at the out-of-state cost, a case can certainly be made that it is worth $184k over four years, but that would depend on one's intended major and family financial circumstances. The school does offer limited merit-based scholarships, but far more individuals qualify for need-based aid; the average package is roughly $10,000.

FINANCIAL
Institutional Type: Public
In-State Tuition: $10,964
Out-of-State Tuition: $32,927
Room & Board: $12,616
Books & Supplies: $950

Avg. Need-Based Grant: $10,413
Avg. % of Need Met: 75%

Avg. Merit-Based Award: $6,363
% Receiving (Freshmen w/o Need): 27%

Avg. Cumulative Debt: $31,771
% of Students Borrowing: 49%

CAREER
Who Recruits
1. Cottingham & Butler
2. Bristol Myers Squibb
3. State Farm
4. HNI Corporation
5. TEKsystems

Notable Internships
1. Athene
2. Principal Financial Group
3. Workiva

Top Employers
1. University of Iowa Health Center
2. Wells Fargo
3. John Deere
4. Collins Aerospace
5. Amazon

Where Alumni Work
1. Iowa City
2. Chicago
3. Des Moines
4. Cedar Rapids
5. Minneapolis

Earnings
College Scorecard (10-YR Post-Entry): $62,670
PayScale (Early Career): $58,400
PayScale (Mid-Career): $108,400
PayScale 20-Year ROI: $541,000

RANKINGS
Money: 4.5
U.S. News: 93, National Universities
Wall Street Journal/THE: 160
Washington Monthly: 103, National Universities

OVERGENERALIZATIONS
Students are:
Outdoorsy
Crazy about the Hawkeyes
Homogeneous
Laid-back
Friendly

COLLEGE OVERLAPS
Indiana University Bloomington
Iowa State University
University of Illinois at Urbana-Champaign
University of Minnesota
University of Wisconsin - Madison

University of Maryland, College Park

College Park, Maryland | 301-314-8385

ADMISSION
Admission Rate: 44%
Admission Rate - Men: 41%
Admission Rate - Women: 48%
EA Admission Rate: 48%
ED Admission Rate: Not Offered
ED Admits as % of Total Admits: Not Offered
Admission Rate (5-Year Trend): -1%
% of Admits Attending (Yield): 23%
Transfer Admission Rate: 59%

SAT Reading/Writing (Middle 50%): 670-740
SAT Math (Middle 50%): 690-780
ACT Composite (Middle 50%): 30-34

% Graduated in Top 10% of HS Class: 66%
% Graduated in Top 25% of HS Class: 90%
% Graduated in Top 50% of HS Class: 99%

Demonstrated Interest: Not Considered
Legacy Status: Not Considered
Racial/Ethnic Status: Considered
Admission Interview Offered: No

ENROLLMENT
Total Undergraduate Enrollment: 30,353
% Full-Time: 93%
% Male: 51%
% Female: 49%
% Out-of-State: 22%
% Fraternity: 11%
% Sorority: 14%
% On-Campus (All Undergraduate): 38%
Freshman Housing Required: No

% African-American: 13%
% Asian: 23%
% Hispanic: 10%
% White: 42%
% Other: 4%
% International: 3%
% Low-Income: 19%

ACADEMICS
Student-to-Faculty Ratio: 18 to 1
% of Classes Under 20: 47%
% of Classes 20-49: 37%
% of Classes 50 or More: 17%
% Full-Time Faculty: 73%
% Full-Time Faculty w/ Terminal Degree: 91%

Top Programs
Business
Computer Science
Communication
Criminology and Criminal Justice
Economics
Engineering
Physics
Public Health

Retention Rate: 95%
4-Year Graduation Rate: 74%
6-Year Graduation Rate: 88%

Curricular Flexibility: Somewhat Flexible
Academic Rating: ★★★★

#CollegesWorthYourMoney

It's a highly affordable research university with a respected name and a big-time sports program that, oh yeah, happens to be only minutes from Washington, DC, so it's no shock that the University of Maryland, College Park has become an increasingly popular college destination. A school that has been on the rise since it became the state's flagship campus in 1988, College Park today enrolls teens from all 50 states and international students from 116 countries, although three-quarters of the undergraduate population are residents. This university enrolls 30,353 undergraduates who can select from 100+ majors across twelve colleges. Real terrapins may be turtles that are hyper-aggressive carriers of salmonella, but the Maryland variety is an accomplished group of young scholars who, in overwhelming numbers, go on to do great things post-graduation.

Inside the Classroom

Depending on which college and program you are part of, the sequence and pace at which you will fill the school's general education requirements will vary. The requirements themselves will not. There are forty-one credits of required coursework that include twelve credits in communications, six in the arts and humanities, six in behavioral and social sciences, seven in biological and physical sciences, seven in interdisciplinary or emerging issues, and three in mathematics. Maryland offers one of the best Honors Colleges, and those able to gain acceptance (the average SAT is 1490) must complete three honors seminars and two additional honors courses.

Despite an 18:1 student-to-faculty ratio and a heavy concentration of graduate students, many undergraduate course sections at the University of Maryland are held in intimate classroom settings. In fact, 46% of sections enroll fewer than twenty students. Of course, you will also have your share of packed introductory lecture courses; 17% of classes enroll 50 or more students. Undergraduate research opportunities are within reach as 39% of graduates complete one, including 8% who complete a summer research experience. The Maryland Center for Undergraduate Research also facilitates numerous opportunities throughout the year and hosts an annual Undergraduate Research Day at which 350+ students make presentations. A reasonable number of students also pursue a semester overseas. Over 1,500 students elect to study abroad at one of 400+ destinations.

Collectively, the social sciences account for 13% of degrees awarded by the University of Maryland with criminology, government and politics, and economics among the most popular majors. However, computer science is actually in the top spot with 18% of undergraduate degrees conferred. It is followed by engineering (13%), business (11%), and biology (8%). The Robert H. Smith School of Business, the A. James Clark School of Engineering, and the Merrill College of Journalism all command respect from employers and graduate schools, as do programs in computer science and criminology. Maryland's reputation also helps its graduates win highly competitive national fellowships. In a typical year, College Park students capture multiple Boren Awards, Fulbrights, Critical Language Scholarships, Goldwater Scholarships, and Churchill Scholarships.

Outside the Classroom

Last year, campus was home to 88% of Terrapin freshmen and 38% of the overall undergraduate student body. Only first-year students are guaranteed housing. Greek life is prominent with 57 fraternities and sororities active on campus. Major sports are a thriving enterprise at the University of Maryland as the school boasts twenty Division I teams, including a basketball team that won the NCAA tournament 20 years ago and plays in March Madness pretty much every year. There are 650+ clubs, including many in the realm of improv, comedy, and pre-professional as well as an intramural program so expansive it offers both competitive and recreational levels. Also notable are The Mighty Sound of Maryland, a big-time marching band, and the strength of the volunteering spirit that sees the U of M community contribute a collective two million hours per year. Suburban Maryland isn't the most exciting place you could hope for, but, fortunately, Washington, DC, is only a short Metro ride away.

Career Services

There are 28 full-time staff members working out of the centralized University Career Center with 16 undergraduate-focused employees stationed in the Robert H. Smith School of Business, five in the A. James Clark School of Engineering, and another five career counselors housed within other colleges and departments. That brings the grand total of professional career services staff members at College Park to 54, equating to a 562:1 student-to-counselor ratio, below average compared to the average school in this book, but strong for a school with over 30,000 undergraduates.

A superb 75% of 2022 graduates reported completing at least one internship, and more than one was the norm with 33% completing two internships and 29% completing three. Among those who desired to turn their internship into a full-time gig post-graduation, 78% received an offer of employment. The jobs landed by all graduates were closely aligned with students' career goals, another testament to the work of this office. To be precise, 94% of job holders reported that their position either directly aligned with their career goals or was a proper stepping-stone toward their ultimate goal. The school puts on several career fairs, including a fall event that draws 3,500 students and a Computer Science Career & Internship Fair that, alone, brings 125 companies to campus. Additionally, you can turn to the 414,000 Terrapin alumni to help you open a door into just about any hiring organization you can conjure up. Terrific internship numbers, on-campus recruiting, and overall student outcomes make this a world-class career services outfit.

Professional Outcomes

Class of 2022 graduates from the University of Maryland had, within six months of graduating, successfully found their next life step 96% of the time. Of the 67% of that cohort who found employment, the companies/organizations hiring the greatest number of 2022 grads were Northrop Grumman, Deloitte, Amazon, and EY. Taking all alumni into account, more than 200 individuals with a University of Maryland affiliation presently work for Meta, Apple, and Google. By far the most popular landing spot for alumni is the Greater Washington, DC, area with Baltimore, New York City, San Francisco, and Philadelphia next in line. The median starting salary self-reported by Class of 2022 grads was $71,648; the mid-50% range was $55k-$83k.

Twenty-one percent of Class of 2022 members headed directly to graduate and professional school to begin work on an advanced degree. Of that contingent, 11% entered doctoral programs, 5% were on the path to becoming medical doctors, and 5% entered law school. By a wide margin, continuing at the University of Maryland was the top choice; the greatest number of survey respondents reported remaining at their home institution. Other popular schools were George Washington University, Johns Hopkins, Georgetown, and Columbia. Medical school acceptance rates for Maryland students are excellent—over 60% in recent years, which is roughly 20 points higher than the national average. The medical schools where the largest number of alumni matriculate are the University of Maryland, George Washington University, New York Medical College, and Drexel University. Over the past few years, law school applicants earned 15+ acceptances to Georgetown, Michigan, Emory, Cornell, Columbia, and Harvard.

Admission

Applicants for a freshman spot at College Park in 2022-23 were accepted at a rate of 44%; a year earlier, the admit rate was 52%. The mid-50% standardized test scores for the Class of 2026 were 1370-1510 on the SAT and 31-34 on the ACT. Sixty-six percent of enrolled students earned a spot in the top 10% of their high school class, and 90% were in the top quartile. The average weighted GPA was 4.43. Those class rank and GPA numbers are similar to those of ten years ago, but SAT scores are significantly higher today, even when accounting for the impact of a temporary test-optional policy.

With 56,637 applicants, this admissions committee needs to look first at cold, hard numbers, which is why GPA and the presence of a rigorous course load are ranked as "very important" factors. Class rank, the essay, recommendations, state residency, first-generation status, and talent/ability make up the next rung of "important" factors. There is no binding early decision option at Maryland; the early action deadline of November 1 will get you an answer by January 31. In sum, getting into Maryland's flagship university's main campus pretty much requires a 3.75 or higher GPA and standardized test scores above the 90th percentile.

Worth Your Money?

In-state tuition is a shade over $11,000, and the total cost of attendance for those living on campus is $31k. Out-of-staters pay over three times the tuition rate, which leads to a total cost of attendance of $62k+ to become a Terrapin. Getting literally any degree at the in-state rate is a no-brainer. For nonresidents, you would have to have a compelling reason to cross state lines to pay $248,000+. However, if you are eyeing the exceptional programs in business, engineering, or computer science, that sum may be worth the education and connections you will gain.

FINANCIAL
Institutional Type: Public
In-State Tuition: $11,505
Out-of-State Tuition: $40,306
Room & Board: $15,417
Books & Supplies: $1,250

Avg. Need-Based Grant: $14,041
Avg. % of Need Met: 68%

Avg. Merit-Based Award: $7,214
% Receiving (Freshmen w/o Need): 15%

Avg. Cumulative Debt: $30,420
% of Students Borrowing: 36%

CAREER
Who Recruits
1. AIG Retirement Services
2. Carrier Corporation
3. Corvel Corporation
4. Federal Aviation Administration
5. Lockheed Martin

Notable Internships
1. Adobe
2. Nike
3. U.S. State Department

Top Employers
1. Booz Allen Hamilton
2. Deloitte
3. IBM
4. Capital One
5. Google

Where Alumni Work
1. Washington, DC
2. Baltimore
3. New York City
4. Philadelphia
5. San Francisco

Earnings
College Scorecard (10-YR Post-Entry): $76,997
PayScale (Early Career): $67,200
PayScale (Mid-Career): $118,600
PayScale 20-Year ROI: $762,000

RANKINGS
Money: 4.5
U.S. News: 46, National Universities
Wall Street Journal/THE: 140
Washington Monthly: 80, National Universities

OVERGENERALIZATIONS
Students are:
Diverse
Crazy about the Terrapins
Working hard and playing hard
Career-driven
Goal-oriented

COLLEGE OVERLAPS
George Washington University
Pennsylvania State University - University Park
University of Maryland, College Park
Baltimore County
University of Michigan
Virginia Tech

University of Massachusetts Amherst

Amherst, Massachusetts | 413-545-0222

ADMISSION
Admission Rate: 64%
Admission Rate - Men: 54%
Admission Rate - Women: 72%
EA Admission Rate: 61%
ED Admission Rate: Not Offered
ED Admits as % of Total Admits: Not Offered
Admission Rate (5-Year Trend): +6%
% of Admits Attending (Yield): 19%
Transfer Admission Rate: 70%

SAT Reading/Writing (Middle 50%): 630-720
SAT Math (Middle 50%): 630-760
ACT Composite (Middle 50%): 29-33

% Graduated in Top 10% of HS Class: 29%
% Graduated in Top 25% of HS Class: 65%
% Graduated in Top 50% of HS Class: 94%

Demonstrated Interest: Considered
Legacy Status: Not Considered
Racial/Ethnic Status: Not Reported
Admission Interview Offered: No

ENROLLMENT
Total Undergraduate Enrollment: 24,391
% Full-Time: 95%
% Male: 49%
% Female: 51%
% Out-of-State: 18%
% Fraternity: 6%
% Sorority: 5%
% On-Campus (All Undergraduate): 58%
Freshman Housing Required: Yes

% African-American: 5%
% Asian: 13%
% Hispanic: 8%
% White: 59%
% Other: 3%
% International: 7%
% Low-Income: 20%

ACADEMICS
Student-to-Faculty Ratio: 18 to 1
% of Classes Under 20: 47%
% of Classes 20-49: 35%
% of Classes 50 or More: 18%
% Full-Time Faculty: 82%
% Full-Time Faculty w/ Terminal Degree: 95%

Top Programs
Architecture
Business
Computer Science
Nursing
Psychology
Public Health Sciences
Sociology
Sport Management

Retention Rate: 90%
4-Year Graduation Rate: 76%
6-Year Graduation Rate: 83%

Curricular Flexibility: Somewhat Flexible
Academic Rating: ★★★✓

#CollegesWorthYourMoney

Sesame Street's iconic "One of These Things (is not like the others)" song comes to mind when examining the Five College Consortium in Western Massachusetts. The group consists of tiny, elite liberal arts schools Amherst College, Mount Holyoke, Smith, Hampshire, and . . . UMass? That's right, UMass, a school that has 24,391 undergraduate students, another 7,838 graduate students, and 110 majors offered across eight undergraduate colleges. While UMass Amherst students are free to cross-register in any course at the affiliated liberal arts havens, there is plenty to like on the grounds of the Commonwealth's flagship campus. The home of the Minutemen and Minutewomen boasts the highly ranked and affordable Isenberg School of Management as well as revered academic programs in sports management, architecture, computer science, and nursing.

Inside the Classroom
Whether you end up in the Isenberg School of Management, the College of Engineering, or the School of Public Health and Health Sciences, you will encounter the same set of general education requirements that, fortunately, are not as overbearing as at many state universities. A ten-course, thirty-credit jaunt through writing, math, analytical reasoning, the physical sciences, and the social world is all it takes to knock out the full run of nonnegotiable coursework. The Commonwealth Honors College at UMass Amherst has high admissions standards (average 1418 SAT and 4.3 GPA) and even higher graduation standards, requiring additional honors coursework and the completion of a senior thesis.

The student-to-faculty ratio is 18:1, leading to undergraduate class sizes that are all over the map. You will encounter a number of smaller sections during your time at UMass as 47% of courses enroll fewer than 20 students; however, 18% of sections contain more than 50 students, so you also will have some larger lecture hall classes. In spite of some gigantic classes where you'll feel anonymous, a stunning 96% of graduates report being satisfied with their academic experience. Further, a substantial and encouraging 30% report engaging in some type of undergraduate research. For a large university, UMass also enjoys fairly wide participation in its study abroad program. Every year, 1,200 students spend a semester in one of more than 70 countries.

UMass has a fairly even spread of students across its various areas of concentration. Of all degrees conferred in 2022, business/marketing diplomas accounted for 14%. That was followed by biology (11%), social sciences (10%), psychology (8%), health professions (7%), engineering (7%), and computer science (7%). UMass produced an impressive number of national postgraduate scholarship winners in 2023, including 12 Fulbright Scholars and three Goldwater Scholars. In one recent year, one grad was one of only fifteen Churchill Scholars named in the nation.

Outside the Classroom
Last year, 98% of freshmen lived on the 1,450-acre Amherst campus, and over 58% of the entire student body lives in university-owned housing, a relatively high figure for a state university. There are fifty-two separate residence halls. Those residing off campus typically find rentals in the surrounding towns of Amherst, Hadley, and Sunderland. Men and women both join fraternities and sororities at a 5-6% clip. Twenty-one NCAA teams compete at the Division I level, mostly within the Atlantic 10 Conference. Involvement is spread around with 38% of students joining at least one student-run club, 24% playing varsity, club, or intramural sports, and 13% participating in community service. There are 200+ registered student organizations, and UMass students can participate in any club or activity at the other colleges within the Consortium. Amherst garners consistent praise as one of the top college towns in the United States because, in its own accurate words, it offers "a perfect blend of New England natural beauty and cosmopolitan culture and energy." Even on-campus dining gets rave reviews. Road trips to Boston (90 miles) or New York City (175 miles) are possible despite the somewhat remote feel of the Western Massachusetts locale.

Career Services
There are three central career service administrators at UMass Amherst, but the majority of service providers are housed within eight career service departments in the various undergraduate colleges. Obtaining an exact count of the number of advisors was, unfortunately, not possible, but to provide some reference point for counselor availability, the business school has seven advisors and a student-to-counselor ratio of roughly 500:1, very strong compared to the other large public universities featured in this guide. Job fair offerings are plentiful, and top employers are more than willing to make the trip to Amherst to recruit top students. In a single recent year, the office hosted 18 career fairs and held 60+ on-campus recruitment events in the fall alone.

Overall, Minutemen and women feel that UMass adequately prepares them for beyond graduation; close to 80% of graduates are either "very satisfied" or "somewhat satisfied" with the way the university prepared them for the world of work. Two-thirds of recent graduates had some type of practicum, internship, co-op experience, or clinical assignment. Routine internship and co-op placements include the Boston Red Sox, CNN, IBM, MTV, Disney World, The Boston Globe, Sheraton, and United Technologies. With 330,000+ alumni heavily concentrated in the Boston and Springfield areas, it's hard to walk down a New England street without bumping into a UMass alum. This supportive network, coupled with respected academic programs, helps the career services staff succeed in opening doors for qualified graduates.

Professional Outcomes

Six months after graduating, 65% of newly minted 2022 grads were employed full-time and 26% were attending graduate school part-time. The most populated industries are health/medical professions (13%), internet & software (10%), biotech & life sciences (4%), and higher education (4%). Companies presently employing 100+ Minutemen and Minutewomen include Oracle, Mass Mutual, Amazon, IBM, Google, Intel, Microsoft, PwC, Wayfair, and Apple. Boston is the most popular landing spot for graduates; it's followed by Springfield, Massachusetts; New York City; San Francisco; Washington, DC; and Los Angeles.

If you achieve stellar grades while an undergraduate at UMass, you will have a full array of graduate/professional school options awaiting you. Medical school applicants with a 3.6 GPA and an MCAT score in at least the 74th percentile are admitted to medical school more than 76% of the time. That rate was even higher when you include the criteria of having clinical experience and being open to osteopathic programs. Many recent graduates have attended medical school at UMass Medical School while others have gained acceptance to medical or dental school at Harvard, the University of Chicago, the University of Michigan, and the University of Pennsylvania. Similarly, prelaw students flock to UMass' own legal training ground or other Massachusetts-based options like Suffolk Law, but recent grads also have matriculated into elite institutions like William & Mary, Northeastern, or Boston University.

Admission

Sixty-four percent of the 45,451 applicants to UMass Amherst gained entry into the Class of 2026. A popular safety school for Massachusetts residents, only 19% of those who were accepted ultimately enrolled in the university. The mid-50% scores were 1280-1450 and the equivalent ACT range was 29-33. Just under 30% of students hailed from the top 10% of their high school class, and 65% were in the top quartile. The university received only half as many applicants at the dawn of the new millennium. The entering Class of 2000-01 had mid-50% SAT scores of 1010-1240, and only 52% were in the top quartile of their graduating class. Clearly, admissions standards are much higher now than a generation ago.

GPA and the level of rigor of one's coursework are the two factors weighed as "very important" by the admissions committee. The school is presently test-optional. Also "important" are class rank, essays, recommendations, extracurricular activities, talent/ability, character/personal qualities, first-generation status, work experience, and the level of an applicant's interest. It is rare to see a large public university even consider demonstrated interest in admissions decisions, so make sure you take advantage by reaching out to a UMass admissions officer, visiting campus, or attending an admissions event in your area.

Worth Your Money?

At full price, UMass Amherst will set a Massachusetts resident back $36k per year; an out-of-stater will pay $58k. Bay State residents are getting a terrific deal attending UMass and shouldn't hesitate to pull the trigger, regardless of their financial situation or intended academic path. With a bit of aid, it is possible to receive a four-year education at a solid institution for under six figures in total cost of attendance. Those out of state will likely find better deals elsewhere unless they are eligible for the New England Regional Students Program, which allows residents of other New England states to attend at a discount if their intended academic program is not offered by public colleges in their home state.

FINANCIAL
Institutional Type: Public
In-State Tuition: $17,357
Out-of-State Tuition: $39,293
Room & Board: $15,437
Books & Supplies: $1,000

Avg. Need-Based Grant: $14,078
Avg. % of Need Met: 79%

Avg. Merit-Based Award: $7,724
% Receiving (Freshmen w/o Need): 28%

Avg. Cumulative Debt: $31,480
% of Students Borrowing: 60%

CAREER
Who Recruits
1. HubSpot
2. Facebook
3. Salesforce
4. Wayfair
5. Apple

Notable Internships
1. PepsiCo
2. AIG
3. TJX Companies

Top Employers
1. Oracle
2. MassMutual
3. IBM
4. Amazon
5. Google

Where Alumni Work
1. Boston
2. Springfield, MA
3. New York City
4. San Francisco
5. Washington, DC

Earnings
College Scorecard (10-YR Post-Entry): $65,645
PayScale (Early Career): $62,300
PayScale (Mid-Career): $109,400
PayScale 20-Year ROI: $584,000

RANKINGS
Money: 4.5
U.S. News: 67, National Universities
Wall Street Journal/THE: 190
Washington Monthly: 90, National Universities

OVERGENERALIZATIONS
Students are:
Outgoing
Involved/invested in campus life
Ready to party
Always saying nice things about Amherst, MA
Politically liberal

COLLEGE OVERLAPS
Boston University
Northeastern University
Syracuse University
Pennsylvania State University - University Park
University of Connecticut

University of Miami

Coral Gables, Florida | 305-284-4323

The sunny paradise of Coral Gables, just south of Miami, is home to the University of Miami—commonly referred to as UM or "the U." It is easily identifiable by its team name, the Hurricanes, with its distinctive orange, green, and white colors. This private research institution of 12,504 undergrads, which boasts a number of top academic programs and world-renowned faculty, struggled to be taken seriously as a world-class university for many decades. Having been dubbed "Sun Tan U" in the 1940s and suffering through revelations about its morally bereft football program of the 80s and 90s was a lot to overcome, yet Miami has finally arrived as an unquestioned member of higher education's elite. More selective than ever, Miami has more than gridiron glory to brag about as we enter the third decade of the millennium.

Inside the Classroom

In an effort to ensure the acquisition of "essential intellectual skills and exposure to a range of intellectual perspectives and academic disciplines," UM mandates general education requirements via the Cognates Program. So-termed cognates are, at a minimum, three-course clusters that the faculty has determined share a focus or thematic elements. The three main areas of cognates are arts and humanities; people and society; and science, technology, engineering, and mathematics. Students fulfill one cognate through their major area of study and also must complete the other two broad areas. Hurricanes also must blow through two English composition courses and one quantitative skills class. Other than that, the core academic requirements at Miami are not prohibitive.

Students rate their teachers and their overall UM experience extremely favorably. A noteworthy 92% of graduates report being satisfied with their education while 82% were satisfied with their major. The student-to-faculty ratio is 13:1, and even though there are 7,000 graduate students to serve, class sizes are reasonable. Fifty-two percent of all course sections contain fewer than 20 students, and only 7% of sections sport enrollments of more than 50 undergrads. Study abroad opportunities are vast and include university-run programs in Rome, Shanghai, India, Paris, Prague, the Galapagos, Cape Town, and Buenos Aires. Undergraduate research posts can be had, but the onus is on the student to contact a professor directly, apply for placement through the Office of Research and Community Outreach, or apply for a summer research grant. In total, 37% of recent grads participated in research.

The University of Miami confers the greatest number of degrees in business/marketing (21%), health professions (13%), biology (11%), the social sciences (9%), communication (9%), and engineering (8%). The Miami Business School and the College of Engineering enjoy solid national reputations, and programs in music, marine science, communications, and architecture sit high atop many rankings. UM graduates fared well at procuring highly competitive awards including multiple Fulbright and Goldwater Scholarships over the past few years.

Outside the Classroom

Ninety-two percent of freshmen live on the University of Miami's 239-acre main campus in Coral Gables, but 63% of the total undergraduate student body lives off campus. Fraternities attract 19% of male students and also sororities draw 19% of female students, creating a strong Greek presence within the social scene; there are close to three dozen active Greek organizations. Of course, the U's most galvanizing force is its famous (and at times infamous) football team as well as sixteen other varsity sports squads that compete in the powerhouse Atlantic Coast Conference in NCAA Division I. Approximately 500 students participate in varsity athletics. The school is trying to move away from its "Sun Tan U" reputation, and it certainly has in terms of academic rankings, yet the South Beach atmosphere continues to earn Miami "top party school" status in many publications' rankings. For non-partiers, the school also offers 300+ clubs, thirty service organizations, an active student government, and an award-winning student-run cable channel. On-campus amenities border on luxurious with the Herbert Wellness Center being one of the finest collegiate gyms around. Students also enjoy an arboretum, the Lowe Art Museum, the Ring Theatre, which launched stars like Sly Stallone and Ray Liotta, and close proximity to the beach.

Career Services

The Toppel Career Center is staffed by 15 full-time professional employees (not counting admin assistants or office managers) who focus on employer relations, career counseling, and internship coordination. A student-to-advisor ratio of 834:1 is higher than average when set against the other institutions included in this book. Still, this office reaches the bulk of the population as 87% of 2022 graduates utilized Toppel at some point in their four years of study. The most utilized services were (1) resume and cover letter review, (2) career expo and fairs, (3) job and internship listing search, and (4) one-on-one career advising.

A laundry list of impressive organizations/companies that visit Coral Gables to recruit and conduct on-campus interviews includes PepsiCo, American Airlines, Meta, Adidas, EY, and the Miami Marlins. In a single year, 175 companies attend the annual Career Expo, and 2,500 students participate. Perhaps most impressively, 80% of 2022 grads landed an internship. Counselors held 1,791 individual advising sessions. Career services also review 1,100 resumes, conduct over 800 practice interviews, and take roughly 600 professional headshots for students to use in their job searches. That frenetic pace and strong outreach lead to mostly positive postgraduate outcomes for newly minted Hurricane alumni.

Professional Outcomes

The Hurricane Class of 2022 saw 98% of its members secure post-grad plans within six months, with 64% employed full-time and 34% in graduate school. Companies employing 2022 graduates included Deloitte, Citrix, NBCUniversal, Bank of America, JPMorgan Chase, Citi, and Morgan Stanley. Across the entire alumni base, 100+ Canes also can be found in the offices of Google, IBM, PwC, Apple, and Microsoft. Across all majors, the median starting salary was an impressive $63k. Miami, New York, DC, Chicago, and Los Angeles were the primary destinations of choice for 2022 grads.

The most frequently attended graduate schools included a mix of prestigious institutions, Miami itself, and other Sunshine State universities. In order, the schools of choice for one recent cohort were Miami (186), Nova Southeastern (15), Columbia (13), NYU (12), Boston University (10), and George Washington (10). Those graduating in 2022 also earned acceptance into the likes of Harvard, Duke, Yale, and Johns Hopkins. Premed students have the advantage of accumulating clinical hours within the University of Miami Health Systems or any of six other hospitals not far from campus. In a typical year, the U's own Miller School of Medicine takes 40+ of its own exiting undergraduates, and over 90% of "highly recommended" applicants find a medical school home somewhere in the country.

Admission

Miami received an all-time record 49,167 applications for a place in the Class of 2026. The 19% acceptance rate for those jockeying for a spot in the 2022-23 freshman class was significantly lower than the 28% acceptance rate the previous year. The middle-50% ranges were 1330-1450 on the SAT and 30-33 on the ACT for current freshmen. Sixty-two percent of 2022-23 first-years earned a place in the top 10% of their high school class while 88% placed in the top quartile. The average high school GPA for attending students was 3.8.

Six categories top the list of most important factors in making admissions decisions—GPA, rigor of coursework, class rank, standardized test scores, application essays, and extracurricular activities. Due to the massive number of applicants, the university does not offer interviews as part of the evaluation process. The U offers an early decision round where 57% of applicants are let through the gates, but only about one-third of the freshman class is filled through ED. Aspiring Hurricanes will see their activities reviewed and their essays read carefully as part of a holistic process. Yet, at a school receiving so many applications, you will need to bring strong grades and within-range test scores.

Worth Your Money?

The U's direct cost of attendance is over $83,000, over three times the in-state COA for the University of Florida or Florida State. To compete for the top students, the university dishes out merit aid to a high percentage of students at an annual average of $22k. It also grants need-based aid to over half of all students with an average annual grant of $36k. If your family has unlimited funds, or if you receive a solid aid package, Miami is definitely a school that can make a lot of sense from an investment standpoint. If you are on a budget, paying full freight could lead to an unpleasant financial situation early in one's adult life.

FINANCIAL
Institutional Type: Private
In-State Tuition: $59,926
Out-of-State Tuition: $59,926
Room & Board: $21,580
Books & Supplies: $1,328

Avg. Need-Based Grant: $14,041
Avg. % of Need Met: 68%

Avg. Merit-Based Award: $22,323
% Receiving (Freshmen w/o Need): 31%

Avg. Cumulative Debt: $20,000
% of Students Borrowing: 33%

CAREER
Who Recruits
1. SpaceX
2. adidas
3. Hilton
4. Ball Aerospace
5. CIA

Notable Internships
1. Lincoln Financial Group
2. Cato Institute
3. Viacom

Top Employers
1. Microsoft
2. IBM
3. Citi
4. Apple
5. PwC

Where Alumni Work
1. Miami
2. New York City
3. Los Angeles
4. West Palm Beach, FL
5. Washington, DC

Earnings
College Scorecard (10-YR Post-Entry): $71,739
PayScale (Early Career): $61,500
PayScale (Mid-Career): $106,500
PayScale 20-Year ROI: $476,000

RANKINGS
Money: 3.5
U.S. News: 67, National Universities
Wall Street Journal/THE: 90
Washington Monthly: 323, National Universities

OVERGENERALIZATIONS
Students are:
Always saying nice things about Coral Gables
Diverse
Working hard and playing hard
Dressed to impress
Open-minded

COLLEGE OVERLAPS
Boston University
Emory University
New York University
Tulane University
University of Florida

University of Michigan

Ann Arbor, Michigan | 734-764-7433

ADMISSION
Admission Rate: 18%
Admission Rate - Men: 20%
Admission Rate - Women: 15%
EA Admission Rate: Not Reported
ED Admission Rate: Not Offered
ED Admits as % of Total Admits: Not Offered
Admission Rate (5-Year Trend): -9%
% of Admits Attending (Yield): 47%
Transfer Admission Rate: 37%

SAT Reading/Writing (Middle 50%): 670-750
SAT Math (Middle 50%): 680-780
ACT Composite (Middle 50%): 31-34

% Graduated in Top 10% of HS Class: 19%
% Graduated in Top 25% of HS Class: 41%
% Graduated in Top 50% of HS Class: 77%

Demonstrated Interest: Considered
Legacy Status: Not Considered
Racial/Ethnic Status: Not Considered
Admission Interview Offered: No

ENROLLMENT
Total Undergraduate Enrollment: 32,695
% Full-Time: 96%
% Male: 48%
% Female: 52%
% Out-of-State: 39%
% Fraternity: 8%
% Sorority: 16%
% On-Campus (All Undergraduate): 27%
Freshman Housing Required: No

% African-American: 4%
% Asian: 18%
% Hispanic: 8%
% White: 51%
% Other: 5%
% International: 8%
% Low-Income: 18%

ACADEMICS
Student-to-Faculty Ratio: 15 to 1
% of Classes Under 20: 56%
% of Classes 20-49: 25%
% of Classes 50 or More: 19%
% Full-Time Faculty: 80%
% Full-Time Faculty w/ Terminal Degree: 90%

Top Programs
Business
Communication and Media
Computer Science
Economics
Engineering
English
Political Science
Psychology

Retention Rate: 97%
4-Year Graduation Rate: 81%
6-Year Graduation Rate: 93%

Curricular Flexibility: Somewhat Flexible
Academic Rating: ★★★★✦

#CollegesWorthYourMoney

What do you get when you combine one of the best college towns in the country with one of the premier research universities in the world, and stir in a passionate sports scene? The answer is the first public university in the Northwest Territories. Originally dubbed the "Catholepistemiad of Detroit," it is now known by the catchier name of the University of Michigan. Brilliant teens flock to Ann Arbor for 280+ undergraduate degree programs across fourteen schools and colleges, and their success can be measured in countless ways, whether you look at the 97% freshman retention rate or the fact that more current Fortune 100 CEOs are alums of the Ross School of Business than any other school on the planet.

Inside the Classroom
All applicants must apply to one of the fourteen schools right off the bat. The College of Literature, Science, and the Arts (LSA) serves the majority, and those accepted are held to school-specific rather than university-wide academic requirements. However, all Wolverines ultimately end up with broad academic requirements in the areas of English, foreign language, natural sciences, and social sciences. Freshmen in the LSA take a first-year seminar that is capped at eighteen students and affords an immediate opportunity to connect with a professor in an area of academic interest. LSAers also have the option to sign up for a "theme semester" in which major topics such as India in the World or Understanding Race are explored in and outside the classroom through activities such as museum visits, guest lectures, and film screenings.

With 32,695 undergrads, it's not surprising that undergrads will end up sitting in some large lecture halls. Michigan sports a 15:1 student-to-faculty ratio, and 19% of classes contain 50 or more students, but a solid 56% of classes offer a more intimate experience with fewer than 20 students. Opportunities to conduct independent research or work in a laboratory beside a faculty member can be found. The Undergraduate Research Opportunity Program draws in 1,200-1,400 participants each year. For students in all academic programs at Michigan, study abroad opportunities are taken advantage of at high rates. In fact, the university is fourth in the nation in the number of students it sends to study in foreign lands.

In general, the faculty is exceptional and overflowing with award-winning researchers. Michigan finds itself atop any ranking of best public research universities. The Ross School of Business offers highly rated programs in entrepreneurship, management, accounting, and finance. The College of Engineering is also one of the best in the country. By sheer numbers, the school confers more engineering degrees (15%) than in any other discipline. Computer science is next (14%), followed by the social sciences, which attract 11% of the student body. Graduating Wolverines are routinely awarded prestigious scholarships to continue their studies. In 2023, the school produced 15 Fulbright Scholars, and has had Rhodes Scholars in many recent years.

Outside the Classroom
Ann Arbor is a prototypical college town, the type you would show to a Martian who wanted to know what a quintessential American college was like. Vibrant, stimulating, and extremely safe, the 3,200-acre campus and surrounding town are ideal places to spend four years. When your football stadium seats more than 100,000, that's a pretty solid indicator that the sports scene is thriving. Donning the iconic maize and blue jerseys, Michigan's twenty-seven Division I sports teams have enjoyed a ridiculous level of success. A substantial but not overwhelming 8% of men and 16% of women belong to one of the 50+ fraternities and sororities on campus. A hard-to-comprehend 1,600 student organizations exist. If you can conceive it, Michigan probably already offers it, and more than 80% of the student body participates in at least one club or activity. Intramural and club sports also enjoy wide participation. The Ginsberg Center for Community Service and Learning is popular, and roughly half of Wolverines have engaged in volunteer experiences. Only 27% live on campus, almost all of whom are freshmen.

Career Services
The University of Michigan Career Center employs 35 full-time staff members (including staff working out of the engineering and business programs) as well as a handful of peer advisors. Only counting the full-time employees, UM has a student-to-advisor ratio of 934:1, higher than the average school featured in this guide. Thus, hand-holding is limited, but appointments with peer advisors are available for mock interviews and resume assistance. One-on-one appointments with a professional career counselor can be scheduled to discuss finding internships and jobs. The career center reaches more students through hosting workshops, putting on more than 200 per year with a total attendance exceeding 6,000 undergrads.

Staffing may be less than desired, but on the plus side, Michigan's alumni network is one of the largest and most powerful in the nation. With over half a million loyal alums spread across one hundred countries, there is always a fellow Wolverine willing to dispense advice, facilitate a job-shadowing experience or internship (around three-quarters land one), or help you get your foot in the door in the industry of your choosing. Also working in the school's favor is the fact that Michigan grads are highly sought after by major employers who are happy to travel to Ann Arbor for recruiting purposes. The Ross School of Business alone arranges for hundreds of companies to recruit on campus each year, including all of the big boys: Goldman Sachs, Deutsche Bank, EY, and Morgan Stanley. At UM, counselors are not going to personally hunt you down to take personality inventories and create a killer LinkedIn profile, but large-scale resources are available that will get motivated students on the right path to their next destination.

Professional Outcomes

Within three months of exiting Ann Arbor, 89% of the graduates of the College of Literature, Science, and the Arts are employed full-time or attending graduate school. Healthcare, education, law, banking, research, nonprofit work, and consulting are the most popular sectors in which LSA alums launch their careers. Ross School of Business graduates fare quite well on the open market; within three months, 99% are employed with a median salary of $90k. The companies listed above that recruit on campus are among the top employers of recent grads along with PwC, Deloitte, and Amazon. Engineering grads have similar success with 96% employed or in grad school within six months for an average salary of $84k. The companies employing the greatest number of alumni across all years include General Motors, Ford, Google, Microsoft, Apple, and Meta.

As with employers, elite graduate and professional schools also hold a Michigan diploma in high esteem. University of Michigan grads applying to law school are well prepared, averaging an LSAT score in the 80th percentile; more than half obtain at least one acceptance. Those aiming for medical school have average MCATs above the 85th percentile and get accepted at a 54% clip, a rate more than 10% higher than the national average. Last year, 863 Wolverines applied to medical school, one of the highest numbers of any school in the United States. In short, if you succeed at Michigan, there isn't a graduate or professional school in existence that will be beyond your reach.

Admission

Over 84,000 wanna-be Wolverines submitted applications last cycle. The overall acceptance rate for a place in the Class of 2026 was 18%, but in-state applicants typically fare far better, often enjoying acceptance rates around double that of nonresidents. The SAT range of current Michigan students is 1350 to 1530, and the ACT range is 31-34. For comparison, in 2014, the SAT range was 1280-1480, and the ACT range was 29-33, which tells us that admission into this popular flagship university may be a touch more difficult now than in the recent past.

The school ranks the two most important admissions factors as "rigor of secondary school record" and "GPA." Average Michigan students earned a 3.90 GPA on a 4.0 scale in the most challenging courses available to them. Standardized test scores are listed as a secondary factor alongside recommendations, personal qualities, and first-generation status. The University of Michigan has more than doubled its number of applications received in the last decade, and gaining acceptance is genuinely more challenging than ever. Top students who hail from in state will face better odds than out-of-staters who need to bring an impeccable academic record to the table to garner serious consideration.

Worth Your Money?

The average amount of debt held by a University of Michigan graduate is slightly below the national average. For residents of the Great Lakes State, the school is in the "ridiculous value" category—at least by the standards of an out-of-whack marketplace. Michigan's total cost of attendance for in-state students is $35k; the out-of-state price is over $76k. Michigan is able to meet 90% of qualifying students' need and the average award is $23k. This is truly exceptional for a public institution and is only one of the many reasons this top-flight university is worth your money.

FINANCIAL
Institutional Type: Private
In-State Tuition: $17,786
Out-of-State Tuition: $57,273
Room & Board: $13,171
Books & Supplies: $1,092

Avg. Need-Based Grant: $14,078
Avg. % of Need Met: 79%

Avg. Merit-Based Award: $6,027
% Receiving (Freshmen w/o Need): 11%

Avg. Cumulative Debt: $28,487
% of Students Borrowing: 35%

CAREER
Who Recruits
1. Hudson's Bay
2. BP America
3. Bain & Company
4. United Talent
5. News America Marketing

Notable Internships
1. Uber
2. Nike
3. Lockheed Martin

Top Employers
1. General Motors
2. Ford Motor Company
3. Google
4. Amazon
5. Microsoft

Where Alumni Work
1. Detroit
2. New York City
3. Chicago
4. San Francisco
5. Washington, DC

Earnings
College Scorecard (10-YR Post-Entry): $79,580
PayScale (Early Career): $70,200
PayScale (Mid-Career): $119,400
PayScale 20-Year ROI: $776,000

RANKINGS
Money: 5
U.S. News: 21, National Universities
Wall Street Journal/THE: 28
Washington Monthly: 23, National Universities

OVERGENERALIZATIONS
Students are:
Crazy about the Wolverines
Always studying
Politically active
Driven
Always saying nice things about Ann Arbor

COLLEGE OVERLAPS
Cornell University
Michigan State University
Northwestern University
University of California, Berkeley
University of Pennsylvania

University of Minnesota - Twin Cities

Minneapolis, Minnesota | 612-625-2008

ADMISSION
Admission Rate: 75%
Admission Rate - Men: 72%
Admission Rate - Women: 78%
EA Admission Rate: Not Reported
ED Admission Rate: Not Offered
ED Admits as % of Total Admits: Not Offered
Admission Rate (5-Year Trend): +25%
% of Admits Attending (Yield): 24%
Transfer Admission Rate: 56%

SAT Reading/Writing (Middle 50%): 640-730
SAT Math (Middle 50%): 650-770
ACT Composite (Middle 50%): 27-32

% Graduated in Top 10% of HS Class: 41%
% Graduated in Top 25% of HS Class: 76%
% Graduated in Top 50% of HS Class: 98%

Demonstrated Interest: Not Considered
Legacy Status: Considered
Racial/Ethnic Status: Considered
Admission Interview Offered: No

ENROLLMENT
Total Undergraduate Enrollment: 39,248
% Full-Time: 93%
% Male: 46%
% Female: 54%
% Out-of-State: 25%
% Fraternity: Not Reported
% Sorority: Not Reported
% On-Campus (All Undergraduate): 23%
Freshman Housing Required: No

% African-American: 8%
% Asian: 12%
% Hispanic: 6%
% White: 61%
% Other: 2%
% International: 6%
% Low-Income: 22%

ACADEMICS
Student-to-Faculty Ratio: 16 to 1
% of Classes Under 20: 40%
% of Classes 20-49: 42%
% of Classes 50 or More: 18%
% Full-Time Faculty: 68%
% Full-Time Faculty w/ Terminal Degree: 93%

Top Programs
Business
Chemistry
Computer Science
Data Science
Economics
Engineering
Mathematics
Psychology

Retention Rate: 92%
4-Year Graduation Rate: 73%
6-Year Graduation Rate: 84%

Curricular Flexibility: Less Flexible
Academic Rating: ★★★✓

#CollegesWorthYourMoney

Home to 39,248 undergraduates, the University of Minnesota Twin Cities can easily be overshadowed by its neighboring flagships (Wisconsin, Michigan, and Illinois). Yet, UMTC deserves its fair share of the Midwestern limelight, thanks in part to a number of academic programs rising toward the top of national rankings and the university's positioning as a direct pipeline to the nineteen Fortune 500 companies located within state borders. While a massive out-of-state tuition increase over the last eight years has slowed down the tidal wave of nonresident applicants, international students and out-of-staters still make up around 25% of the undergraduate student body. The average Gopher today boasts significantly better academic credentials than previous generations at the university. In fact, four-year graduation rates have doubled since 1997, a testament to both the improved caliber of student as well as increased institutional support.

Inside the Classroom
There are 150 majors on tap across eight freshman-admitting undergraduate colleges, but all students are subjected to the same twenty-three-credit Diversified Core as well as fifteen credits worth of Designated Themes. Those combined thirty-seven credits include forays into the art/humanities, social sciences, physical sciences, mathematics, literature, and history. More targeted topics include civic life and ethics, diversity and social justice in the US, the environment, global perspectives, and technology and society. All freshmen also must take a first-year writing course and one other course designated as "writing intensive" later in their educational journey. Students in the university's Honors Program must complete eight honors courses and a culminating senior thesis.

Despite a massive number of graduate students, this school generally keeps class sizes in check. A 16:1 student-to-faculty ratio is deployed effectively so that 65% of sections enroll 29 or fewer students. On the other end of the spectrum, 18% of courses enroll 50 or more students, so you can expect some highly impersonal lecture-based introductory courses while in the Twin Cities. No matter your field of study, you can utilize UM's well-maintained database of upcoming faculty research projects as a way to connect directly with the professor of your choice; more than 250 undergraduates participate in a campus-wide undergraduate research program each summer. An outstanding 24% of UMTC students study abroad during their academic career with the most popular destinations being Spain, Italy, France, the United Kingdom, and Germany.

The most commonly conferred degrees at the university are in biology (13%), business & marketing (11%), engineering (10%), the social sciences (10%), computer science (9%), and psychology (8%). The College of Science and Engineering and the Carlson School of Management have strong national reputations and offer top-ranked programs in accounting, business, and every branch of engineering. The quality of the chemistry, economics, psychology, and political science departments is also well-known by elite graduate schools. The school's reputation also helps those applying for prestigious postgraduate scholarships. Fifteen students won Fulbright Scholarships in 2022, and Minnesota also produced a number of Udall, Gilman, Critical Language, and Astronaut Scholars in recent years.

Outside the Classroom
In past years, nine of every ten freshmen resided on the 1,200-acre Twin Cities campus in one of nine residence halls or eight apartment complexes; pretty much everyone else lived in off-campus housing as only 23% of the entire student body goes to sleep in university-owned domiciles. Roughly 10% of undergrads participate in Greek life, so fraternities and sororities play a fairly major role in social life. The Golden Gophers compete in 23 varsity sports; the most successful programs are the men's and women's ice hockey teams. Over 1,000 student organizations are active including nine student-run cultural centers, dozens of intramural sports, and a popular Outdoors Club. Arts and culture can be found right on campus at the school's own art, design, and natural history museums as well as the nearby Minneapolis Sculpture Garden, Guthrie Theater, Walker Art Center, and Minneapolis Institute of the Arts. Natural beauty also can be enjoyed on university grounds that contain 10,000 trees in the extensive Mississippi National River and Recreation Area, an area that also features miles of bike paths. For shopping or just hanging out, the famed Mall of America is only a fifteen-minute ride away. The Minneapolis and St. Paul campuses that together form UMTC are only three miles apart, and the best of both cities can be enjoyed from that advantageous central location.

Career Services
Instead of having one centralized career services office at the Twin Cities campus, the university has smaller offices housed within each of its undergraduate colleges. The College of Liberal Arts Career Services Office leads the way with 18 full-time professional employees for a total of 63 across all colleges. That 623:1 ratio is within the average range when compared to other institutions profiled in this guidebook.

However, for a school of UMTC's size, that level of support is exceptionally strong. Whether students are in the College of Science and Engineering, the Carlson School of Management, or the School of Nursing, there will be a team of experts in the areas of career counseling, graduate/professional school advising, internship coordination, and employer relations ready to work directly on your behalf.

Career fairs are similarly segmented by discipline with annual offerings targeting those entering computer science, government, business, accounting, and health management. The College of Engineering (CSE) Career Fair draws around 3,500 students in the fall and 1,700 in the spring. The spring CSE event featured 175 companies such as Dell, Hewlett Packard, Tesla, Wells Fargo, and BAE Systems. Having 496,000 living alumni, many of whom are local, is a huge advantage for carving out internships and other networking opportunities. The Carlson School of Management has a Long-Term Mentoring and Flash Mentoring program in which it will hand-pick a professional mentor from the business community to assist you. Between a sizable and friendly alumni base and a number of tight industry connections to Minnesota-based businesses, the Career Services Office at UMTC offers a wealth of opportunities to its undergraduates.

Professional Outcomes

The top seven companies snatching up the largest number of Gophers are all companies headquartered in the state of Minnesota: Medtronic (the largest medical device manufacturer in the world), Target, 3M, United Health Group, US Bank, and Cargill (the company with the highest revenue in the United States). Therefore, it is easy to see why roughly 70% of grads remain in the Greater Minneapolis-St. Paul area. San Francisco, New York, Chicago, and Seattle also attract some graduates each year, and non-Minnesota-based companies like Intel, Microsoft, Google, Apple, and Meta all employ hundreds of Twin Cities alumni. The mean starting salary for recent grads was $50k.

With 130 graduate programs in science, art, engineering, agriculture, medicine, and the humanities, the University of Minnesota retains many of its graduates as they pursue their next degrees. However, some of the top graduate programs in the country routinely welcome UM grads. Future doctors benefit from the BA/MD program in conjunction with the University of Minnesota Medical School. The university produces 360+ applicants to medical school every year, and many go on to study within their home state, but, in recent years, Gophers also have been accepted to prestigious medical institutions like Emory, the University of Wisconsin, and Columbia University.

Admission

UMTC saw 75% of those seeking a place in the Class of 2026 gain acceptance, up from 57% three years prior. Minnesota is predominately an ACT state, and 39% of the 2022-23 applicants submitted results from that exam (versus 8% for the SAT), scoring a mid-50% range of 27-32. Those submitting SAT scores had mid-50% scores of 1300-1470. Forty-one percent of those attending the university placed in the top 10% of their high school class, and 76% earned spots in the top quarter. The applicant pool here has grown stronger over the last decade, but admission is only slightly more competitive now than it was a decade ago.

The only factors rated as "very important" by the admissions committee are rigor of coursework, GPA, and class rank. Essays, recommendations, and interviews are not considered in the process. Freshmen accepted into the University of Minnesota Twin Cities are admitted directly into one of seven undergraduate colleges. The schools requiring the highest grades and test scores are biological sciences, management, and science and engineering (CSE). In fact, the ACT range for those admitted into the School of Engineering is 29-34 compared with the 25-29 mid-50% range for those admitted into the College of Education and Human Development.

Worth Your Money?

In-state tuition of $17k and reasonable room-and-board fees make the list price approximately $36,000 for those from the Land of 10,000 Lakes. After financial aid, even families making over $110,000 end up paying less than $25k. That makes UMTC a strong value for Minnesota teens no matter their area of academic pursuit. While out-of-state costs will run your four-year total bill to $228k, the return-on-investment numbers are the strongest of any school in Minnesota. The Carlson School of Management and the College of Science and Engineering are so highly regarded that a degree from either is probably worth a private university-level price tag.

FINANCIAL
Institutional Type: Public
In-State Tuition: $16,488
Out-of-State Tuition: $36,402
Room & Board: $13,178
Books & Supplies: $1,000

Avg. Need-Based Grant: $13,570
Avg. % of Need Met: 77%

Avg. Merit-Based Award: $5,676
% Receiving (Freshmen w/o Need): 10%

Avg. Cumulative Debt: $26,576
% of Students Borrowing: 51%

CAREER
Who Recruits
1. Enterprise Holdings
2. The Hertz Corporation
3. Aerotek
4. Thomson Reuters
5. Century Link

Notable Internships
1. Minnesota Timberwolves
2. Pratt & Whitney
3. U.S. State Department

Top Employers
1. Medtronic
2. Target
3. 3M
4. UnitedHealth Group
5. U.S. Bank

Where Alumni Work
1. Minneapolis
2. San Francisco
3. Chicago
4. New York City
5. Los Angeles

Earnings
College Scorecard (10-YR Post-Entry): $65,087
PayScale (Early Career): $62,400
PayScale (Mid-Career): $112,200
PayScale 20-Year ROI: $623,000

RANKINGS
Money: 4.5
U.S. News: 53, National Universities
Wall Street Journal/THE: 168
Washington Monthly: 34, National Universities

OVERGENERALIZATIONS
Students are:
Crazy about the Golden Gophers
Athletic/Active
Politically liberal
Always saying nice things about the Twin Cities
Goal-oriented

COLLEGE OVERLAPS
The Ohio State University - Columbus
Purdue University - West Lafayette
University of Illinois at Urbana-Champaign
University of Michigan
University of Wisconsin - Madison

University of North Carolina at Asheville

Asheville, North Carolina | 828-251-6481

ADMISSION
Admission Rate: 74%
Admission Rate - Men: 73%
Admission Rate - Women: 75%
EA Admission Rate: 78%
ED Admission Rate: 78%
ED Admits as % of Total Admits: 7%
Admission Rate (5-Year Trend): -6%
% of Admits Attending (Yield): 16%
Transfer Admission Rate: 94%

SAT Reading/Writing (Middle 50%): 600-680
SAT Math (Middle 50%): 540-650
ACT Composite (Middle 50%): 21-28

% Graduated in Top 10% of HS Class: 16%
% Graduated in Top 25% of HS Class: 43%
% Graduated in Top 50% of HS Class: 78%

Demonstrated Interest: Considered
Legacy Status: Considered
Racial/Ethnic Status: Considered
Admission Interview Offered: No

ENROLLMENT
Total Undergraduate Enrollment: 2,914
% Full-Time: 90%
% Male: 42%
% Female: 58%
% Out-of-State: 12%
% Fraternity: 2%
% Sorority: 1%
% On-Campus (All Undergraduate): 48%
Freshman Housing Required: Yes

% African-American: 5%
% Asian: 2%
% Hispanic: 8%
% White: 75%
% Other: 4%
% International: 1%
% Low-Income: 32%

ACADEMICS
Student-to-Faculty Ratio: 11 to 1
% of Classes Under 20: 72%
% of Classes 20-49: 27%
% of Classes 50 or More: 1%
% Full-Time Faculty: 74%
% Full-Time Faculty w/ Terminal Degree: 85%

Top Programs
Art
Atmospheric Science
Environmental Studies
Management
Mass Communication
Health and Wellness Promotion
New Media
Psychology

Retention Rate: 73%
4-Year Graduation Rate: 44%
6-Year Graduation Rate: 61%

Curricular Flexibility: Somewhat Flexible
Academic Rating: ★★★

#CollegesWorthYourMoney

Outside of the service academies, you won't find many highly regarded public liberal arts colleges in the United States. However, you will find one shining example in the reputational shadows of one of the nation's premier public universities: the University of North Carolina Asheville. Also part of the illustrious North Carolina state college system, the Asheville branch provides a unique and quality undergraduate education for 2,914 students at a bargain-basement price. Of the 30+ bachelor's degree programs, a standout Art & Art History Department attracts scores of talented young painters, sculptors, and photographers.

Inside the Classroom

Every undergrad is required to engage with the Liberal Arts Core that includes a First-Year Seminar, Academic Writing and Critical Inquiry, 12 credits in the humanities, and up to four semesters of foreign language. (Students can test out of this requirement.) Students also must take a minimum of one course in laboratory science, scientific perspectives, quantitative perspective, the social sciences, arts and ideas, and "diversity-intensive." A senior capstone looms as a graduation requirement and can be fulfilled by enrolling in one of two courses—Critical Perspectives on Contemporaneity or Cultivating Citizenship in a Global World. A major paper will be completed in either class.

Asheville's 11:1 student-to-faculty ratio may be the same as for the average liberal arts school (11:1), but it is far below the average ratio (17:1) for a public school. Thanks to the almost exclusive emphasis on undergraduate instruction as well as those favorable numbers, 97% of courses enroll 29 or fewer students. The average class size is just 14 students. One area where this college flat-out excels is in connecting students to hands-on undergraduate research opportunities; a stunning 65% of students complete original research in their field of study. The majority of students do not study abroad during their four years, but 20% do take a semester in an international location.

The aforementioned stellar art program conferred the greatest percentage of degrees in 2022 (16%), followed by psychology (14%), the social sciences (10%), and business (9%). Engineering and computer science degrees accounted for a combined 19%. Over 50 students in school history have won Fulbright Awards, so we can conclude that competitive national fellowship organizations do not ignore this tiny public school within the UNC system.

Outside the Classroom

While 87% of undergraduates hail from North Carolina, few commute. In fact, 95% of freshmen live in the dorms as does 48% of the overall student population. There are 16 residence halls spread across this 365-acre campus. Greek life is technically alive, but it has a faint heartbeat; only 1-2% of students are affiliated with fraternities and sororities. There are 16 NCAA Division I teams at UNC Asheville, and plenty of intramural options are available among the 70+ clubs and activities on campus. As at many liberal arts institutions, the gender divide is notable, falling just shy of a 60:40 ratio in favor of female students. While anecdotal in nature, it is fair to state that the student body is particularly liberal, social justice-minded, and LGBTQ-friendly. Community engagement and service-learning opportunities are plentiful and popular; all student organizations are required to complete at least 10 hours of community service per semester. The Sherrill Center, the largest facility on campus, serves as a social hub with its fitness center, café, and meditation room. The Kimmel Arena, also part of the Sherrill Center, is a 3,800-seat facility that hosts anything from concerts to lectures to sporting events. Asheville itself has an artsy and laid-back vibe where you'll find 30+ art galleries, plenty of live music, and endless culinary delights.

Career Services

There are five core members of the UNC Asheville Career Center team: a director of career education, an assistant director of employer relations, a student engagement coordinator, a career coach, and an associate director for experiential learning. There are also multiple peer mentors. Not counting the peer volunteers, the student-to-counselor ratio is 583:1, higher than the average liberal arts school featured in this guide, but not alarmingly high for a public college. The department was recognized a few years back with the Member's Choice Award from the National Association of Colleges and Employers for the creation of its NextFest, a series of innovative career fairs that draw more than 300 students and an ever-growing number of employers per event. There are three NextFest events in a typical school year.

The career center staff helps engage undergraduates by offering themed, week-long skill-building offerings such as Cover Letter Week and Interview Workshop & Mock Interview Week plus individual workshops on topics like budgeting and salary negotiation. Even those who avoid such events are exposed to career service-related programming through classroom workshops planned in collaboration with faculty members. While close to 90% of Asheville grads engage in at least one "high-impact learning practice" (such as undergraduate research, service learning, or studying abroad), less than one-third complete a formal internship. Facilitating more of those opportunities is an area where improvement is desired.

Professional Outcomes

Employers snagging the greatest number of Bulldog alumni include Mission Health, Wells Fargo, Lowe's, Bank of America, Thermo Fisher Scientific, and a number of local school districts. A fair number of grads also find employment at Duke Energy Company, the US Environmental Protection Agency, Apple, EY, PwC, and the National Oceanic and Atmospheric Administration. The majority of graduates settle around various cities in North Carolina—Asheville itself, Raleigh-Durham, Charlotte, and Greensboro—but there also are clusters of alumni in Greenville, SC; New York City; and Washington, DC. Being a liberal arts college with a focus on the arts, you won't find this institution near the top of any ROI ranking system or average alumni salary lists, but Asheville does rate well when it comes to generating a high degree of social mobility.

The school does offer pre-health advising to those who aim to attend medical school; UNC–Asheville's own school of medicine opened its doors in 2009 and takes in some of its own undergrads each year. The biology major, which accounts for 5% of degrees conferred, is designed in part for those with an eye on becoming physicians, pharmacists, veterinarians, and physical therapists. Recent graduates interested in legal studies have entered law school at the likes of American University Washington College of Law, UNC Law School, and Temple University Beasley School of Law. While many pursue graduate schools at other public universities within North Carolina, nothing is off the table with a degree from UNC Asheville.

Admission

This is not a school that attracts massive numbers of applicants; just over 4,500 applied for membership in the Class of 2026, and the acceptance rate was a hefty 74%, a bit lower than the 82% figure for the Class of 2025. Only 16% of those who were accepted went on to enroll. Among that group, students submitted SAT and ACT results in relatively even numbers, and the mid-50% ranges were 1160-1340 on the SAT and 21-28 on the ACT. Only 16% of entering 2022-23 freshmen placed in the top decile of their high school class, 43% were in the top quartile, and 22% were outside the top half. The average unweighted GPA was 3.53, and 10% possessed a GPA under 3.0.

While presently test-optional, Asheville typically views standardized test scores among the most important admissions factors alongside rigor of coursework, GPA, class rank, essays, and recommendations. This holistic review process also puts significant weight on an applicant's extracurricular activities, talent/ability, and character/personal qualities. The school also attempts to discern any "other contributions that an individual might bring to the UNC Asheville community." In sum, UNC Asheville definitely qualifies as an institution that is realistically accessible to "B" students while still providing a high-quality undergraduate experience for an affordable price.

Worth Your Money?

The total direct costs for Tar Heel State residents was just $21,256 in 2023-24, a tremendous bargain. If you do live in state, you can stop reading this section; even without any aid, UNC Asheville is unequivocally "worth your money." Out-of-staters pay roughly double the in-state figure, but that can still be a fair price, particularly with more than half of undergrads receiving an average need-based grant of $9k. As a result, the average cumulative debt accrued by Asheville graduates is below the national average.

FINANCIAL
Institutional Type: Public
In-State Tuition: $7,461
Out-of-State Tuition: $24,809
Room & Board: $11,018
Books & Supplies: $1,200

Avg. Need-Based Grant: $8,183
Avg. % of Need Met: 80%

Avg. Merit-Based Award: $2,716
% Receiving (Freshmen w/o Need): 16%

Avg. Cumulative Debt: $23,246
% of Students Borrowing: 58%

CAREER
Who Recruits
1. Bank of America
2. Eaton
3. Wells Fargo
4. Atrium Health
5. RTI International

Notable Internships
1. Northwestern Mutual
2. Volvo
3. National Archives

Top Employers
1. Buncombe Public Schools
2. Mission Health
3. Wells Fargo
4. NC State University
5. Bank of America

Where Alumni Work
1. Asheville
2. Raleigh
3. Charlotte
4. Winston-Salem, NC
5. Greenville, SC

Earnings
College Scorecard (10-YR Post-Entry): $44,906
PayScale (Early Career): $47,900
PayScale (Mid-Career): $79,100
PayScale 20-Year ROI: $136,000

RANKINGS
Money: 3.5
U.S. News: 139, Liberal Arts Colleges
Wall Street Journal/THE: Not Ranked
Washington Monthly: 55, Liberal Arts Colleges

OVERGENERALIZATIONS
Students are:
Environmentally conscious
Outdoorsy
Politically liberal
Service-Oriented
Always saying nice things about Asheville

COLLEGE OVERLAPS
Appalachian State University
Elon University
North Carolina State University
University of North Carolina at Chapel Hill
University of North Carolina at Wilmington

University of North Carolina at Chapel Hill

Chapel Hill, North Carolina | 919-966-362

In 1789, a full thirty years before Thomas Jefferson founded UVA, our young nation's first public university was chartered. Four years later, the first cornerstone was laid smack dab in the middle of the new state of North Carolina, right next to a hill upon which sat New Hope Chapel. In that moment, simultaneously, the University of North Carolina and the town of Chapel Hill were born. Fast-forward 230+ years and UNC-Chapel Hill is one of the most prestigious flagship public schools in the country with 355,000+ proud alumni, the vast majority of whom were born and bred in the university's home state. That fact can be attributed to a thirty-year-old state law mandating that at least 82% of each freshman class be comprised of in-state students.

Inside the Classroom
Massive in its scope, the lovely and affluent town of Chapel Hill is home to 20,210 undergraduates and around 12,000 graduate/professional students. Undergraduates can choose from 74 bachelor's degree programs in a number of schools and colleges, the largest of which is the College of Arts & Sciences. The general education curriculum is called Making Connections and involves checking boxes in the areas of English composition and rhetoric, foreign language, quantitative reasoning, physical and life sciences, social and behavioral sciences, and the humanities and fine arts.

The student-to-faculty ratio is 15:1, and few courses are held in giant lecture halls; 87% of classes have fewer than 50 students. In fact, you'll have a number of intimate, seminar-style courses as part of your undergraduate education as 44% of classes have a student enrollment under 20. UNC sends more than one-third of graduates abroad to one of 70 countries at some point in their educational career. For a school of such massive size, an impressive 60% of students end up completing some type of research experience as undergraduates.

The social sciences (15%), biology (12%), media/journalism (9%), computer science (8%), and business (6%) are the areas in which the most degrees are conferred. The Kenan-Flager Business School is internationally renowned and requires separate admission through UNC's Assured Admission program or through an application process following freshman year. Other strong programs include those in chemistry, journalism, psychology, and public policy. However, an undergraduate degree of nearly any kind from UNC will open doors in the world of employment as well as for those seeking entrance into top graduate programs around the country. In its illustrious history, UNC-Chapel Hill has produced 54 Rhodes Scholars and 40+ Luce Scholars. In 2023, twenty-one students were named Fulbright Scholars, in the top ten highest total among public research universities. It also has a high rate of success in helping students procure NSF Graduate Research Fellowships.

Outside the Classroom
The University of North Carolina-Chapel Hill requires that all freshmen live in one of the school's 32 residence halls. However, only 44% of the total undergraduate population lives on campus while many others live in apartments/houses in Chapel Hill or surrounding Durham or Carrboro. Still, there are many unifying experiences that bring the campus together, none more so than UNC men's basketball. Nothing short of a local religion, it sees 22,000 pack the Dean Smith Center to root for the Tar Heels; games against rival Duke are an unforgettable experience. In sum, there are 28 varsity sports teams as well as a robust network of 50 club and intramural sports. Fourteen to sixteen percent of UNC undergrads join a fraternity or sorority, but Greek life at UNC is unusually diverse, inclusive, and service-oriented. On average, its students collectively contribute 35,000 hours of community service per year. More than 800 student activities are running on the Chapel Hill campus, highlighted by the popular twenty-four-hour UNC Dance Marathon fundraiser, an involved student government, a host of cultural and professional organizations, and the widely-read Daily Tar Heel, which has a distribution of 20,000.

Career Services
UNC's University Career Services Office employs 14 full-time staff members who work with undergraduates, excluding individuals who work as administrative assistants. That equates to a student-to-advisor ratio of 1,444:1, significantly worse than average compared to the other institutions included in this book. Other schools within the larger university do have smaller career services offices, but they primarily serve graduate students. Despite less-than-ideal personnel numbers, the staff does create solid outcomes for graduates.

University of North Carolina at Chapel Hill

E-mail: unchelp@admissions.unc.edu | Website: unc.edu

In one recent year, 344 companies attended 17 career fairs and almost 200 employers held information sessions in Chapel Hill. In a single recent academic year, the department held 8,500 counseling appointments and posted 68,000 jobs and internships on Handshake. The Carolina Career Partners Program helps connect local companies to undergraduate job candidates. Of those students directly entering the world of employment, 80% landed at least one internship while at UNC, and, in one-third of those cases, the internship eventually led to a job with that same organization. All of the basic career services—resume assistance, practice interviews, 1:1 career counseling, and job and internship postings through Handshake—are available to undergraduates.

Professional Outcomes

Six months after leaving Chapel Hill, 97% of 2022 grads had entered employment, military service, or graduate school; 2% were still seeking employment. Among the for-profit companies that hire the most graduates are Wells Fargo, IBM, Cisco, Deloitte, EY, Google, Microsoft, Amazon, Oracle, McKinsey & Company, and Goldman Sachs. In the nonprofit sector, a large number of Tar Heels are snatched up by AmeriCorps, NIH, Teach for America, and the Peace Corps. The vast majority of graduates hang their diplomas somewhere in the state of North Carolina while New York, Georgia, Texas, Florida, and Illinois also attracted 20 or more graduates in a typical year. The average starting salary for a UNC-Chapel Hill grad is $70,619.

Last year, a healthy 18% of students enrolled directly in graduate/professional school. Some of the most commonly attended graduate schools are other Carolina-based institutions such as East Carolina University, Appalachian State, UNC-Greensboro, or—on the elite/local front—Duke and Wake Forest. Other prestigious schools frequented by UNC alums include Columbia and Harvard. UNC Chapel Hill had 502 applicants to medical school in 2023, the 10th-highest total in the nation. Recent graduates have gone on to study medicine at institutions such as Harvard Medical School, Duke University School of Medicine, UNC School of Medicine, and the Wake Forest School of Medicine.

Admission

Gaining admission into UNC-Chapel Hill is a completely different ballgame for North Carolina residents than it is for those hailing from any of the other 49 states or a foreign country. In-state applicants for admission into the Class of 2026 had a 44% success rate; all others faced harsher competition as the out-of-state acceptance rate was 7%. While many other flagship state institutions such as Michigan, Wisconsin, and UVA have substantially increased their number of nonresidents in recent years, UNC does not have the authority to follow suit as out-of-state enrollment is capped at 18%. The overall Class of 2026 acceptance rate was 17%.

Of those who enrolled, the median SAT was 1440 and 32 on the ACT. Just under three-quarters of enrolled students placed in the top 10% of their high school class, and 12% were either the valedictorian or salutatorian. Among the most important factors are the rigor of coursework, test scores, essays, recommendations, and extracurricular activities. While in-state applicants need to be strong in all of those areas, out-of-state applicants need to be exceptional, well above the mean. In sum, the fork in the residency road sends applicants down two significantly different admissions gauntlets. For out-of-staters, higher standardized test scores and/or a "hook" can help to set you apart. In-state applicants with in-range credentials have a much friendlier but still selective process awaiting them.

Worth Your Money?

One of the most incredible bargains in all of American higher education, residents of the Tar Heel State pay less than $10k in tuition and only $26,118 in annual cost of attendance. Those from out of state pay around $57k per year, not a bad price for an education at one of the premier universities in the country. UNC-Chapel Hill is, by leaps and bounds, the most generous UNC school when it comes to need-based aid. The university grants an average annual award of $18k to those it declares eligible, meeting 100% of the demonstrated need for all qualifying students. Whether you are headed to Chapel Hill as a resident or out-of-stater, you will get your money's worth at this school.

FINANCIAL
Institutional Type: Public
In-State Tuition: $8,998
Out-of-State Tuition: $39,338
Room & Board: $13,016
Books & Supplies: $1,290

Avg. Need-Based Grant: $17,676
Avg. % of Need Met: 100%

Avg. Merit-Based Award: $6,127
% Receiving (Freshmen w/o Need): 5%

Avg. Cumulative Debt: $20,680
% of Students Borrowing: 33%

CAREER
Who Recruits
1. Greystar
2. Lincoln Financial Group
3. PNC Bank
4. Comcast
5. Fidus Investments

Notable Internships
1. Vanguard
2. Adobe
3. The Walt Disney Company

Top Employers
1. Wells Fargo
2. IBM
3. Cisco
4. Deloitte
5. EY

Where Alumni Work
1. Raleigh
2. Charlotte
3. Winston-Salem, NC
4. New York City
5. Washington, DC

Earnings
College Scorecard (10-YR Post-Entry): $67,765
PayScale (Early Career): $60,400
PayScale (Mid-Career): $104,300
PayScale 20-Year ROI: $557,000

RANKINGS
Money: 5
U.S. News: 22, National Universities
Wall Street Journal/THE: 83
Washington Monthly: 17, National Universities

OVERGENERALIZATIONS
Students are:
Crazy about the Tar Heels
Always saying nice things about Chapel Hill
Working hard and playing hard
Teeming with school pride
Seeking the quintessential college experience

COLLEGE OVERLAPS
Duke University
North Carolina State University
University of Michigan
University of Virginia
Vanderbilt University

University of Notre Dame

Notre Dame, Indiana | 574-631-7505

ADMISSION
Admission Rate: 13%
Admission Rate - Men: 14%
Admission Rate - Women: 12%
EA Admission Rate: 21%
ED Admission Rate: Not Offered
ED Admits as % of Total Admits: Not Offered
Admission Rate (5-Year Trend): -6%
% of Admits Attending (Yield): 60%
Transfer Admission Rate: 27%

SAT Reading/Writing (Middle 50%): 700-760
SAT Math (Middle 50%): 720-790
ACT Composite (Middle 50%): 32-35

% Graduated in Top 10% of HS Class: 92%
% Graduated in Top 25% of HS Class: 99%
% Graduated in Top 50% of HS Class: 100%

Demonstrated Interest: Considered
Legacy Status: Considered
Racial/Ethnic Status: Important
Admission Interview Offered: No

ENROLLMENT
Total Undergraduate Enrollment: 8,971
% Full-Time: 100%
% Male: 51%
% Female: 49%
% Out-of-State: 93%
% Fraternity: Not Offered
% Sorority: Not Offered
% On-Campus (All Undergraduate): 79%
Freshman Housing Required: Yes

% African-American: 4%
% Asian: 6%
% Hispanic: 13%
% White: 64%
% Other: 1%
% International: 6%
% Low-Income: 13%

ACADEMICS
Student-to-Faculty Ratio: 9 to 1
% of Classes Under 20: 60%
% of Classes 20-49: 31%
% of Classes 50 or More: 9%
% Full-Time Faculty: 87%
% Full-Time Faculty w/ Terminal Degree: 90%

Top Programs
Architecture
Biological Sciences
Business
Engineering
English
Philosophy
Physics
Political Science

Retention Rate: 98%
4-Year Graduation Rate: 94%
6-Year Graduation Rate: 96%

Curricular Flexibility: Somewhat Flexible
Academic Rating: ★★★★★

#CollegesWorthYourMoney

As iconic for its educational quality as for its storied gridiron glory, Notre Dame is the dream destination for Catholic students with Ivy-level academic qualifications. Over four-fifths of the 8,971 undergraduate students possess a Catholic religious identity, reinforcing the school's values and traditions. Academically, a robust selection of 75 majors is offered across six undergraduate colleges: the School of Architecture, the College of Arts and Letters, the Mendoza School of Business, the College of Engineering, the Keough School of Global Affairs, and the College of Science (which includes a premed track).

Inside the Classroom

Required coursework is comprehensive and includes four courses covering Catholic theology and philosophy. The Moreau First Year Experience is a two-semester course designed to help freshmen "integrate their academic, co-curricular, and residential experiences." Freshmen also take University Seminar, one of two writing-intensive courses mandated by the school. Six additional mandatory liberal arts courses assure that students at least dip their toes into the study of quantitative reasoning, science and technology, history, literature, and the social sciences.

A solid 60% of courses enroll fewer than 20 students, and 15% have single-digit numbers. Just 9% of courses have an enrollment of more than 50 undergrads. A 9:1 student-to-faculty ratio is top-notch and also represents an improvement over the 12:1 ratio of a decade ago. The Center for Undergraduate Scholarly Engagement offers hundreds of opportunities for conducting research, both individually and alongside faculty; more than one-third of graduates ultimately partake. One of the top universities for study abroad participation, 75% of Notre Dame undergrads select one of 50+ programs in 26 countries; the satisfaction rate for study abroad experiences is above 90%.

The top areas in which degrees were conferred in 2022 were: business (20%), the social sciences (18%), engineering (12%), and biology (8%). Mendoza has a reputation as one of the country's best business schools and, to a slightly lesser extent, the College of Engineering often ranks highly on "best of" lists as well. Prestigious fellowships are won by the Irish in droves. After collecting 17 Fulbrights in 2023, it is one of the top producers in the whole United States. The National Science Foundation granted honors to 26 students and alumni in 2023. The list goes on and on with multiple Gilman, Gates Cambridge, Critical Language, and Truman Scholarships in recent years.

Outside the Classroom

Every single freshman and 79% of all undergrads live in one of the school's 30 residence halls. As the centers of spiritual and recreational life, the residence halls serve a major role on a campus that is free of sororities and fraternities. Notre Dame also has no athletic program . . . just kidding! Sports are a way of life at the home of the Fighting Irish, whether you are a member or mere fan of one of the twenty-three NCAA Division I teams. Of course, the famed football program has a tradition unlike any other, and 81,000 pack the stands of Notre Dame Stadium each fall Saturday to cheer for the eleven-time national champions. One of the best intramural programs in the country and extensive recreational facilities ensure widespread athletic participation; the outdoor five-on-five basketball tournament draws 700 participating teams each year. If it's not sports, Irish men and women are engaged in some other meaningful activity; there are more than 500 student-run organizations active at the school. The 1,250-acre campus is as scenic as they come and includes two beautiful lakes, one famous golden dome, and all of the lush foliage one can absorb. South Bend is not a small college town but a city with a population of over 300,000. Within the immediate vicinity of campus are over 50 restaurants, 70 shops, and four museums.

Career Services

The Center for Career Development (CCD) is staffed by 31 professional employees who work in career advising, employer relations, or event coordination and who impact undergraduate students (additional career services branches aimed at graduate students were not included in this figure). That equates to a 289:1 student-to-advisor ratio, which is in the better-than-average range when compared with other schools featured in this guide, but it is much stronger than most schools of Notre Dame's size. In short, this office works hard on behalf of its students, bringing to mind the classic Lou Holtz line, "No one has ever drowned in sweat."

More than three-quarters of students participate in at least one internship during their undergraduate years. Career fairs are attended by 450+ employers annually, including many major corporations known for employing large numbers of Fighting Irish alumni. Overall, more than 500 companies conduct approximately 7,000 job interviews on campus each academic year. The building in which the CCD is housed features 45 interview/ meeting rooms that have seen their fair share of "welcome aboard" handshakes. An alumni base 150,000+ strong, many of whom have attained leadership positions in the field, are eagerly awaiting an opportunity to help current students and graduating seniors. Having one of the most connected, passionate, and loyal alumni networks in your corner is no small advantage. Tremendous corporate connections and graduate school/ employment results for recent grads led to the Notre Dame CCD receiving high marks from our staff.

Professional Outcomes

A spectacular 97% of 2022 Notre Dame graduates were employed within six months of completing their degrees. Of the 69% who directly enter the world of employment, the most common industries are financial services (21%), consulting (17%), technology (12%), and health services (9%). Massive numbers of alumni can be found in the offices of some of the nation's most desirable private employers including Deloitte, EY, PwC, IBM, Accenture, Booz Allen Hamilton, Google, Microsoft, Amazon, Goldman Sachs, JPMorgan, and McKinsey & Co. With so many entering the world's top finance & consulting firms, it isn't shocking that early-career salaries tend to be high; as of 2022, the median figure was $76,000, a mark that is significantly higher than the national average for college grads. The highest concentration of alumni can be found in the Greater Chicago area followed by the Greater New York City area, South Bend itself, DC, San Francisco, and Boston.

Of the 20% of first-year alums who went directly into their graduate/professional studies, 18% were pursuing medical degrees and 9% were studying law. Medical school applicants had a much higher rate of success than the national average; the Irish acceptance rate generally hovers around 80%. Recent grads went on to attend institutions such as Harvard Medical School, the Indiana University School of Medicine, the Icahn School of Medicine at Mt. Sinai, the Medical College of Wisconsin, and Albert Einstein Medical College. Presently, Notre Dame grads can be found at some of the nation's top law schools such as Columbia, Duke, Harvard, Notre Dame, Boston College, UVA, and the University of Chicago. Those attending graduate schools in other fields can be found at comparably elite institutions all over the globe.

Admission

Of the 26,509 applicants to the Class of 2026, only 3,421 were accepted for a rate of 13%, down from 15% the previous cycle. The yield rate—admitted applicants who enrolled—was an impressively high 60%. Notre Dame hopefuls will need to finish at the very top of their high school class, and we don't just mean in the top decile. A hard-to-fathom 40% of accepted students typically hail from the top 1% of the class and 92% of accepted students placed in the top 10%. The SAT mid-50% range has reached similarly intimidating heights; it currently sits at approximately 1450-1550. The ACT, which is submitted by 31% of applicants, has a mid-50% composite range of 32-35.

The admissions committee rates rigor of secondary coursework and character/personal qualities above all other factors. Class rank, GPA, recommendations, essays, extracurricular activities, and talent/ability are all "important." Religious affiliation does matter at Notre Dame as 82% of admits identify as Catholic. Being a legacy applicant can help—14% of one recent cohort of incoming freshmen were children of alumni. Both religious affiliation and legacy status are factors "considered" by the committee. In recent years, the admissions standards at Notre Dame have approached Ivy League levels. Ten years ago, the acceptance rate was a much friendlier 27%, and the 25th percentile SAT mark was a full 80 points lower than it is today. Those with serious ambitions to spend four years in South Bend need to be in the top 1-2% in both academic performance and standardized test scores. Otherwise, you'll find yourself in the Rudy Ruettiger category as a long shot.

Worth Your Money?

Notre Dame has a high cost of attendance at over $83,000 per year. However, this is a school that funnels undergrads into high-paying jobs and top professional schools, leading to high lifetime earnings and the expansion and enhancement of one's personal and professional networks. Those receiving need-based aid receive an average annual grant of $51k, helping to make the school a very worthy investment and accessible to students from all socioeconomic backgrounds.

FINANCIAL
Institutional Type: Private
In-State Tuition: $62,693
Out-of-State Tuition: $62,693
Room & Board: $17,378
Books & Supplies: $1,250

Avg. Need-Based Grant: $50,894
Avg. % of Need Met: 100%

Avg. Merit-Based Award: $14,112
% Receiving (Freshmen w/o Need): 4%

Avg. Cumulative Debt: $28,625
% of Students Borrowing: 36%

CAREER
Who Recruits
1. Salesforce
2. Boston Consulting Group
3. Facebook
4. JPMorgan Chase
5. McKinsey & Co.

Notable Internships
1. Saks Fifth Avenue
2. Citizens Bank
3. Citadel Securities

Top Employers
1. Deloitte
2. EY
3. PwC
4. IBM
5. Accenture

Where Alumni Work
1. Chicago
2. New York City
3. South Bend, IN
4. Washington, DC
5. San Francisco

Earnings
College Scorecard (10-YR Post-Entry): $93,220
PayScale (Early Career): $73,000
PayScale (Mid-Career): $143,800
PayScale 20-Year ROI: $914,000

RANKINGS
Money: 5
U.S. News: 20, National Universities
Wall Street Journal/THE: 32
Washington Monthly: 12, National Universities

OVERGENERALIZATIONS
Students are:
Crazy about the Irish
Service-oriented
Politically conservative
Religious
Driven

COLLEGE OVERLAPS
Boston College
Duke University
Georgetown University
Northwestern University
Vanderbilt University

University of Oregon

Eugene, Oregon | 541-346-3201

ADMISSION
Admission Rate: 86%
Admission Rate - Men: 84%
Admission Rate - Women: 88%
EA Admission Rate: Not Reported
ED Admission Rate: Not Offered
ED Admits as % of Total Admits: Not Offered
Admission Rate (5-Year Trend): +3%
% of Admits Attending (Yield): 17%
Transfer Admission Rate: 69%

SAT Reading/Writing (Middle 50%): 580-690
SAT Math (Middle 50%): 560-680
ACT Composite (Middle 50%): 24-30

% Graduated in Top 10% of HS Class: 26%
% Graduated in Top 25% of HS Class: 57%
% Graduated in Top 50% of HS Class: 86%

Demonstrated Interest: Not Considered
Legacy Status: Not Considered
Racial/Ethnic Status: Considered
Admission Interview Offered: No

ENROLLMENT
Total Undergraduate Enrollment: 19,565
% Full-Time: 94%
% Male: 44%
% Female: 56%
% Out-of-State: 49%
% Fraternity: 16%
% Sorority: 17%
% On-Campus (All Undergraduate): 29%
Freshman Housing Required: Yes

% African-American: 3%
% Asian: 7%
% Hispanic: 15%
% White: 62%
% Other: 1%
% International: 2%
% Low-Income: 29%

ACADEMICS
Student-to-Faculty Ratio: 19 to 1
% of Classes Under 20: 37%
% of Classes 20-49: 44%
% of Classes 50 or More: 19%
% Full-Time Faculty: 75%
% Full-Time Faculty w/ Terminal Degree: 96%

Top Programs
Architecture
Art and Design
Biology
Business
Education
Environmental Science
Product Design
Sociology

Retention Rate: 86%
4-Year Graduation Rate: 61%
6-Year Graduation Rate: 74%

Curricular Flexibility: Somewhat Flexible
Academic Rating: ★★★

#CollegesWorthYourMoney

In 1859, as the territory of Oregon was officially granted statehood, the United States Congress instructed the state's founders that they would need to establish a public university. It took almost 15 years from that point for construction to begin on the first buildings to grace the 18-acre property that would become the University of Oregon. Today, this flagship university in the city of Eugene draws students from all over the US and even the world. In fact, 49% of Ducks hail from another state or another country. All told, 19,565 undergraduates and another 3,600 graduate students proudly wear the distinctive green and yellow color scheme that has become an unmistakable symbol of this excellent public institution.

Inside the Classroom
No matter which of the close to 80 undergraduate degrees you are pursuing, all Ducks complete coursework in the areas of arts and letters; social science; science; global perspectives; and US: difference, inequality, and agency. Those pursuing a BA degree need to demonstrate proficiency in a second language, which can be fulfilled through three semesters of coursework. Graduates of BS programs will need to demonstrate proficiency in either mathematics or computer science. First-year experience programs (FIGS) are not mandatory at the school, but they are recommended by 95% of students who have completed them.

The student-to-faculty ratio at UO is 19:1, which leads to a mix of class sizes. 37% contain fewer than 20 students while 19% of sections are larger, with 50 or more students; the median class size is 20 students. Most impressively, a healthy 80% of undergraduate students engage in some type of research activity. The Undergraduate Research Opportunity Program excels at connecting students to mentor professors on campus as well as external research opportunities. Ducks study abroad in 80 countries, and roughly one-quarter of students do so at some point during their undergraduate years.

Students flock in large numbers to the social sciences at this university as 19% of undergraduate degrees conferred fall under this umbrella. The next most popular academic pursuits are communication/journalism (14%), business (14%), psychology (9%), biology (8%) and the visual and performing arts (7%). The Lundquist College of Business and the College of Education have strong national reputations. Oregon students apply for prestigious national scholarships in droves and sport inspiring numbers of Gilman Scholars (18 in 2023) and multiple Fulbright Scholars virtually every year.

Outside the Classroom
Freshmen are pretty much the only students who live in campus housing; 93% of first-years do so. Greek life attracts 17% of women into sororities and 16% of men into fraternities. Enthusiasm for the athletic teams is off the charts. Eighteen Division I teams compete in the Pac-12; the men's basketball team has become a regular March Madness qualifier, and the popular Ducks football team plays before 54,000+ raucous fans. Thirty-six club and intramural sports are also available including jiu-jitsu, Nordic skiing, and triathlon. There are 300+ student groups and organizations in total at the university, including a strong number with an environmental theme. An environmentally conscious student body enjoys the ample natural beauty of both the 295-acre campus and the surrounding area of Eugene. Students love to ski, raft in the local rivers, and bike just about everywhere. Eugene is the third-ranked city for bicycling in the United States. Immediately surrounding campus, students can visit various farmer's markets, enjoy locally grown food, and visit museums. Portland is a road trip that can be accomplished in under two hours, but many undergrads are happy to stay put in a town that sits atop national rankings for green space, clean air, and transportation options.

Career Services
There are 15 employees working out of the main University of Oregon Career Center. Another nine professionals work within the Lundquist College of Business to bring the total number of career services workers to 24, which equates to an 815:1 student-to-counselor ratio, above average for schools included in this book, but not notably poor when compared to other large public universities. In the department's own words, "Whether you need help deciding on a profession, finding a job or internship, practicing for interviews, or writing your resume, we strive to provide guidance in all aspects of career and postgraduate life."

Career staff members at OU execute many career and graduate school fairs throughout the year. Employers in attendance include Kaiser Permanente, the US Department of Health and Human Services, Comcast, and the Portland Trailblazers. Attendance at career fairs has been rising in recent years and has increased to over 1,000 attendees; the fall fair draws 100+ companies to Eugene. The UO Alumni Association works to keep the 250,000 Duck alumni around the globe connected, which is a resource that can prove invaluable during an internship or job hunt.

Professional Outcomes

Members of the Class of 2022 already had their next destination lined up at graduation with 78% already employed or entering graduate school. For 73% of that group, their outcomes related directly to the degree that they had just completed. There are many positive indicators hinting that a UO degree is quite valuable in the job market. More than 1,000 Oregon alumni work for Nike, and hundreds of others occupy offices at Intel, Amazon, Microsoft, Adidas, Google, Apple, and Salesforce. Portland and Eugene, Oregon, are the most common places to settle after graduation, but plenty of Ducks flock to San Francisco, Seattle, Los Angeles, and New York City. The median starting salary for a 2022 graduate was $51,000.

Many newfound bachelor's holders continue their education right at OU in one of 150 degree and certificate programs, including a fair number entering the University of Oregon School of Law and the OHSU School of Medicine. A total of 112 Ducks applied to medical school last year, a comparable number to Oregon State University. The school finds itself on the list of undergraduate schools represented in the most recent Yale Law School admissions cycles. Oregon is a reputable enough public university that access to elite graduate and professional programs is certainly on the table for high achievers.

Admission

A grand total of 37,154 students applied for freshman admission, and the vast majority were let through the gates—86% to be precise. The University of Oregon is a test-optional institution, but those who elected to submit had a middle-50% composite score of 1140-1370 on the SAT and 24-30 on the ACT. The majority of entering first-years possessed GPAs above a 3.5; a 4.0 GPA was achieved by 33%, and another 22% earned a 3.75-3.99. The average was a 3.76.

Rigor of secondary school record and GPA are the only two "very important" factors in the admissions process; application essays sit alone in the next tier of "important" categories. Oregon will consider all other "soft" factors, but it does not offer interviews or assign any weight to legacy status or demonstrated interest. Those seeking admission into the Clark Honors College must prepare for a more challenging process. The average unweighted GPA for accepted students is 3.91, and the average SAT score is around the 90th percentile. Roughly 800 students are members of the Honors College.

Worth Your Money?

The annual in-state tuition & fees of $15,669 represent a reasonable deal for Beaver State residents; everyone else will pay almost triple that amount—$43,302. Financial aid is not particularly generous at this school as only an average of 51% of determined need is actually met. Still, students emerge with an average debt total slightly below the national average. As with most public schools, if money is an issue for your family, we recommend checking out public universities within your home state. Given the quality of the business and computer science programs, paying more to attend UO in some circumstances could be a reasonable investment.

FINANCIAL
Institutional Type: Public
In-State Tuition: $14,751
Out-of-State Tuition: $41,194
Room & Board: $15,840
Books & Supplies: $1,320

Avg. Need-Based Grant: $11,207
Avg. % of Need Met: 47%

Avg. Merit-Based Award: $6,725
% Receiving (Freshmen w/o Need): 13%

Avg. Cumulative Debt: $24,823
% of Students Borrowing: 42%

CAREER
Who Recruits
1. Apex Systems
2. Insight Global
3. Fisher Investments
4. Wayfair
5. Oracle

Notable Internships
1. Google
2. Nike
3. Bloomberg LP

Top Employers
1. Nike
2. Intel
3. Amazon
4. Microsoft
5. adidas

Where Alumni Work
1. Portland, OR
2. Eugene, OR
3. San Francisco
4. Seattle
5. Los Angeles

Earnings
College Scorecard (10-YR Post-Entry): $57,157
PayScale (Early Career): $56,000
PayScale (Mid-Career): $104,700
PayScale 20-Year ROI: $419,000

RANKINGS
Money: 4
U.S. News: 98, National Universities
Wall Street Journal/THE: 210
Washington Monthly: 150, National Universities

OVERGENERALIZATIONS
Students are:
Politically liberal
Crazy about the Ducks
Outdoorsy
Environmentally Conscious
Ready to party

COLLEGE OVERLAPS
Arizona State University
University of Arizona
Oregon State University
University of Colorado Boulder
University of Washington - Seattle

University of Pennsylvania

Philadelphia, Pennsylvania | 215-898-7507

ADMISSION
Admission Rate: 7%
Admission Rate - Men: 6%
Admission Rate - Women: 7%
EA Admission Rate: Not Offered
ED Admission Rate: 16%
ED Admits as % of Total Admits: 34%
Admission Rate (5-Year Trend): -2%
% of Admits Attending (Yield): 68%
Transfer Admission Rate: 5%

SAT Reading/Writing (Middle 50%): 730-770
SAT Math (Middle 50%): 770-800
ACT Composite (Middle 50%): 34-35

% Graduated in Top 10% of HS Class: 93%
% Graduated in Top 25% of HS Class: 98%
% Graduated in Top 50% of HS Class: 100%

Demonstrated Interest: Not Considered
Legacy Status: Considered
Racial/Ethnic Status: Considered
Admission Interview Offered: Yes

ENROLLMENT
Total Undergraduate Enrollment: 9,760
% Full-Time: 100%
% Male: 46%
% Female: 54%
% Out-of-State: 81%
% Fraternity: 20%
% Sorority: 21%
% On-Campus (All Undergraduate): 60%
Freshman Housing Required: Yes

% African-American: 8%
% Asian: 28%
% Hispanic: 10%
% White: 31%
% Other: 5%
% International: 13%
% Low-Income: 17%

ACADEMICS
Student-to-Faculty Ratio: 8 to 1
% of Classes Under 20: 59%
% of Classes 20-49: 21%
% of Classes 50 or More: 20%
% Full-Time Faculty: 80%
% Full-Time Faculty w/ Terminal Degree: 95%

Top Programs
Business
Cognitive Science
Communication
Computer Science
Engineering
English
Philosophy
Political Science

Retention Rate: 97%
4-Year Graduation Rate: 88%
6-Year Graduation Rate: 96%

Curricular Flexibility: Somewhat Flexible
Academic Rating: ★★★★

#CollegesWorthYourMoney

Once known for its insecurity over being frequently confused with Penn State and having a reputation in snooty circles as a "second-tier Ivy," the University of Pennsylvania has long since brushed that dirt off its shoulders. Today, Penn boasts twice as many applicants as a decade ago, and, with a 7% acceptance rate, it is now a dream destination for many of the brightest students around the world—and we mean world. Sixteen percent of first-years were residents of foreign countries. The 9,760 Quaker undergrads on campus in 2022-23 were pursuing ninety distinct degrees across four schools: the College of Arts & Sciences, the College of Applied Science and Engineering, the College of Nursing, and, of course, arguably the top business school anywhere—Wharton.

Inside the Classroom
The Core Curriculum at UPenn is based on seven Sectors of Knowledge: society, history and tradition, arts and letters, humanities and social sciences, the living world, the physical world, and natural sciences and mathematics. In fulfilling those requirements, students take mandatory courses in foreign language, writing (seminar), quantitative data analysis, formal reasoning, cross-cultural analysis, and diversity in the United States. The greatest number of students pursue degrees in business (19%), social sciences (14%), biology (11%), health sciences (9%), engineering (9%), and computer science (9%).

Penn has an 8:1 student-to-faculty ratio, but with a focus on research and 13,614 graduate students, not every undergraduate section is a tiny seminar. However, the university does boast an exceptional 26% of courses with an enrollment under ten and 59% with an enrollment under twenty—quite an achievement for a school of Penn's massive size. It also offers multiple ways for undergrads to conduct research, whether through independent studies or working side-by-side with faculty members. It is a testament to its focus in this area that the university publishes 11 distinct journals featuring original undergraduate research. Penn ranks first among Ivies in study abroad participation rate; each year, over 2,500 students head off to earn a semester's credit in one of 50 countries.

While Wharton is the ultimate name-drop, the Penn engineering program garners more quiet respect. Outstanding programs abound throughout the university, in fields ranging from computer science to philosophy. Graduates of UPenn are, in general, met with high-paying jobs at desirable companies and entry into the best graduate and professional schools in existence. Prestigious national scholarship and fellowship programs adore Penn grads just the same. Penn grads won Rhodes Scholarships each year from 2019-22. In a typical year, the school produces multiple Fulbright Scholars, Schwarzman Scholars, Truman Scholars, and National Science Foundation Graduate Research Fellowship recipients.

Outside the Classroom
All freshmen, but only 60% of students, live in university-owned housing at Penn. One reason for the lack of upperclassmen interest in dorms is the popular Greek system that attracts over 20% of undergrads into one of fifty frat and sorority houses. The Quakers compete in 33 NCAA Division I sports in the Ivy League; over 1,000 members of the student body are varsity athletes. Many more participate in club and intramural athletics. There are multiple fitness centers including a 120,000-square-foot facility that includes an Olympic-size swimming pool, rock climbing wall, and sauna. The school also hosts the Penn Relays, the longest-running collegiate track meet in the country, which draws 100,000 spectators annually. With 450+ student organizations active at Penn, there is a group that caters to wherever your talents and interests lie, whether that is in the performance, community service, or cultural identity realms. The school's newspaper, The Daily Pennsylvanian, has a staff of 250 students and has garnered many awards. Penn's West Philly campus is comprised of 215 buildings on 299 attached acres and contains plenty of green space. The urban setting affords students the benefits of walkability and easy trips to any part of the sixth-largest city in the United States.

Career Services
The University of Pennsylvania's Career Services Office has 34 professional staff members who are dedicated to undergraduate counseling, on-campus recruiting, and maintaining digital resources like Handshake. The 287:1 student-to-advisor ratio is average compared to other schools featured in this guide but strong for a school of Penn's size. Close to 20 annual career fairs are held, some of which are industry-specific (engineering, finance, nursing) while others are themed, such as the Common Good Career Fair; the Creative Career Fair; or the Startup, VC, and Data Analytics Fair.

Rising sophomores, juniors, and seniors find themselves in paid internships at some of the world's top employers in droves. To quantify that, recent grads, between their junior and senior year, found positions at a 90% clip, including 20+ at Goldman Sachs and Morgan Stanley. Penn also excels at facilitating on-campus interviews; more than 300 companies conduct interviews on campus each year. A sizable 39% of 2022 grads found their position directly through Career Services. Ample support is also provided for those applying to medical, law, or graduate school. An equal emphasis on large-scale events such as industry-specific job fairs and one-on-one counseling leads to phenomenal graduate outcomes (more ahead).

Professional Outcomes

Seventy-five percent of Class of 2022 Quaker grads were employed within six months following degree completion, another 18% were in graduate school, and 3% were still planning their next educational/career move. Finance was the sector attracting the highest percentage of grads (30%) followed by consulting (20%), technology (15%), and healthcare (10%). Employers hiring the greatest number of 2022 graduates included JPMorgan, Boston Consulting Group, McKinsey, Bain & Company, Meta, and Goldman Sachs. The median starting salary for all graduates is $80,000. Among elite colleges, Penn alumni enjoy the highest mid-career salaries of any school except MIT. Unsurprisingly, the Philadelphia Metro area has the strongest concentration of alumni, but New York is a close second. San Francisco and DC also have a strong Quaker presence.

For those continuing their educational journeys, the most popular move is to remain at Penn—over 100 recent graduates made that decision. The next most attended graduate schools were Columbia and Harvard. Students gain acceptance to medical school at a terrific rate—80% versus the national average of 44%. Medical schools that have taken more than five Penn grads in the last five years include Emory University, Temple University, Harvard Medical School, the Icahn School of Medicine at Mt. Sinai, and Penn's own uber-elite Perelman School of Medicine, which sports a 4% acceptance rate. The acceptance rate into law school is 83%, which is made lower by the fact that the vast majority are aiming for top-tier schools. The most attended law schools in recent years are NYU School of Law, Penn Law School, Fordham University School of Law, Columbia University School of Law, and Harvard Law School.

Admission

Penn received 54,588 applications for a place in the Class of 2026, the fourth-highest figure of any Ivy League university behind Cornell, Harvard, and Columbia. They admitted 7% of that pool and the median SAT for those who went on to enroll was 1540; the median ACT was 35. A nearly unanimous 93% of admitted Quakers earned a place in the top decile of their graduating high school class, and the average unweighted GPA was 3.9. In the past decade, the average admitted applicant's SAT score has increased by over 50 points, and the grades/class rank has stayed the same. Back then, the school received less than half as many applications, and the acceptance rate was a far more forgiving 18%.

According to the admissions committee, rigor of secondary school record, GPA, standardized test scores, essays, recommendations, and character/personal qualities are deemed "very important" to the evaluative process. Factors classified as "important" are class rank, the interview, extracurricular activities, and talent/ability. Eighteen percent of 2022-23 freshmen were the first in their families to attend college. Just over 1,200 students were admitted via early decision; the ED round saw a 16% acceptance rate, and close to half of the Class of 2026 was filled by those welcomed through binding early acceptance. As is the case with so many top-shelf elite institutions, Penn rejects more students than ever, including thousands of teens who would have waltzed into the university a generation ago. Applying ED is a no-brainer if you want to gain a slight edge.

Worth Your Money?

Penn's total cost of attendance is $89,000+ per year and, unless you qualify for need-based financial aid, that is the price you will pay because the university does not award merit aid. It does, however, meet 100% of demonstrated need for all eligible students, awarding annual grants averaging $58k. Even if you are required to pay the full sticker price, Penn's starting salaries are such that even substantial loans will not be crippling to the vast majority of grads.

FINANCIAL
Institutional Type: Private
In-State Tuition: $66,104
Out-of-State Tuition: $66,104
Room & Board: $18,496
Books & Supplies: $1,358

Avg. Need-Based Grant: $58,232
Avg. % of Need Met: 100%

Avg. Merit-Based Award: $0
% Receiving (Freshmen w/o Need): 0%

Avg. Cumulative Debt: $27,705
% of Students Borrowing: 18%

CAREER
Who Recruits
1. Children's Hospital of Philadelphia
2. Teach for America
3. Facebook
4. Boston Consulting Group
5. JPMorgan Chase

Notable Internships
1. Pfizer
2. Gensler
3. HBO

Top Employers
1. Google
2. Amazon
3. Microsoft
4. Goldman Sachs
5. Facebook

Where Alumni Work
1. Philadelphia
2. New York City
3. San Francisco
4. Washington, DC
5. Boston

Earnings
College Scorecard (10-YR Post-Entry): $112,761
PayScale (Early Career): $78,300
PayScale (Mid-Career): $153,100
PayScale 20-Year ROI: $1,142,000

RANKINGS
Money: 5
U.S. News: 6, National Universities
Wall Street Journal/THE: 7
Washington Monthly: 4, National Universities

OVERGENERALIZATIONS
Students are:
Competitive
More likely to rush a fraternity/sorority
Career-driven
Working hard and playing hard
Diverse

COLLEGE OVERLAPS
Brown University
Cornell University
Columbia University
Duke University
Harvard University

University of Pittsburgh - Pittsburgh Campus

Pittsburgh, Pennsylvania | 412-624-7488

ADMISSION
Admission Rate: 49%
Admission Rate - Men: 45%
Admission Rate - Women: 52%
EA Admission Rate: Not Offered
ED Admission Rate: Not Offered
ED Admits as % of Total Admits: Not Offered
Admission Rate (5-Year Trend): -11%
% of Admits Attending (Yield): 17%
Transfer Admission Rate: 46%

SAT Reading/Writing (Middle 50%): 640-720
SAT Math (Middle 50%): 640-750
ACT Composite (Middle 50%): 29-33

% Graduated in Top 10% of HS Class: 56%
% Graduated in Top 25% of HS Class: 89%
% Graduated in Top 50% of HS Class: 99%

Demonstrated Interest: Important
Legacy Status: Not Considered
Racial/Ethnic Status: Considered
Admission Interview Offered: No

ENROLLMENT
Total Undergraduate Enrollment: 19,928
% Full-Time: 97%
% Male: 43%
% Female: 57%
% Out-of-State: 36%
% Fraternity: 11%
% Sorority: 14%
% On-Campus (All Undergraduate): 42%
Freshman Housing Required: No

% African-American: 5%
% Asian: 14%
% Hispanic: 7%
% White: 63%
% Other: 2%
% International: 5%
% Low-Income: 17%

ACADEMICS
Student-to-Faculty Ratio: 13 to 1
% of Classes Under 20: 42%
% of Classes 20-49: 42%
% of Classes 50 or More: 17%
% Full-Time Faculty: 78%
% Full-Time Faculty w/ Terminal Degree: 94%

Top Programs
Biology
Biomedical Engineering
Business
Chemistry
English
Neuroscience
Philosophy
Psychology

Retention Rate: 93%
4-Year Graduation Rate: 69%
6-Year Graduation Rate: 84%

Curricular Flexibility: Somewhat Flexible
Academic Rating: ★★★★

#CollegesWorthYourMoney

A generation ago, you wouldn't see many teens from outside Pennsylvania clamoring to attend the University of Pittsburgh. In fact, for everyone other than western Pennsylvania residents, Penn State was the clear number one public university in the Keystone State. Fast-forwarding to today, Pitt attracts undergraduates from all 50 states and many countries around the globe. The home of the Panthers has ascended to the status of a premier public research university; its 19,928 undergraduate students rank near the top of their respective high school classes and possess average standardized scores in the 90th percentile. Those in the Swanson School of Engineering sport SATs in the 97th percentile, and the top-ranked Honors College requires 99th percentile and above.

Inside the Classroom

The university takes great care in welcoming new students to campus and ensuring a smooth transition. First-year mentors are available to help orient new students to campus life. Academic Foundations is a one-credit course that serves as an insider's guide to Pitt, and first-year seminar classes are centered on a theme of interest with a capped enrollment of nineteen students. Pitt admits freshmen to the Dietrich School of Arts & Sciences, the College of Business Administration, the Swanson School of Engineering, and the School of Nursing. Core coursework is mandated as follows: composition, two writing-intensive classes, algebra, quantitative and formal reasoning, two second language courses, and a class with a diversity designation. A total of nine courses in the humanities, social sciences, and natural sciences are required for all Dietrich School of Arts & Sciences students.

For a large public university, Pitt has a strong 13:1 student-to-faculty ratio and, as a result, it offers many smaller course sections to go along with some classes in large lecture halls. Forty-two percent of sections have an enrollment of under twenty students while 17% enroll more than 50. Plenty of personal connection with professors is available to those who seek it. Undergraduate research opportunities are granted to more than half of all students. There are 350 study abroad programs in 75 countries, and many take advantage; the participation rate in the College of Business Administration is 55%.

The University of Pittsburgh is respected nationally by both top companies and prestigious graduate/professional institutions. Its engineering and business schools are rated top 50 in most rankings and are among the most commonly chosen fields of study. Premed offerings are also top-notch, with majors in the health professions (12%), biology (11%), psychology (9%), and computer science (9%) rounding out the list of most popular majors. Pitt grads are no strangers to nationally competitive scholarships. In 2023, nine students captured Fulbright Scholarships, and an additional six Pitt students and alumni were the recipients of National Science Foundation Graduate Research Fellowships.

Outside the Classroom

A 132-acre urban campus houses roughly two-fifths of the school's undergraduate student population. The Oakland neighborhood where the school is located is safe, walkable, and brimming with culture and fun. The Carnegie Museums of Art and Natural History and innumerable bars and eateries, including plenty of international options, are close by. The city, often rated as one of the "most livable in America," is truly an extension of campus, but campus itself isn't too shabby either. Pitt does guarantee housing to most students for three full years, and it is currently building dorms containing thousands of additional beds. Eleven percent of men and 14% of women join Greek life, giving it a notable but not smothering presence. There are 400+ student organizations, and popular activities include the Pitt Dance Marathon, which raises over $300,000 annually for the Children's Hospital of Pittsburgh. Intramural sports also are popular, and seemingly everyone participates. The university boasts an award-winning Robotics & Automation Society, Hillel Chapter, Hindu Students Council, and Society for Women Engineers. Pitt's nineteen varsity teams compete at the highest levels of NCAA Division I, and the football team shares a stadium with the Steelers and attracts over 41,000 fans per game.

Career Services

There are 28 full-time employees at Pitt's Career Center, housed within the Office of Student Affairs. Members of the team serve as career consultants, employer development specialists, internship coordinators, and alumni engagement specialists. The office's 712:1 student-to-advisor ratio is greater than the average school in this guidebook but not alarming for a public university of its size. In fact, the University of Pittsburgh measures up well when it comes to the raw data in the areas of student engagement and employer relations.

In a single year, counselors conducted 4,500+ one-on-one advising sessions and booked over 400 total employers to attend their Fall Career + Internship Fair, which includes separate days for engineering and computer science students. In total, 474 employers recruited at Pitt in one recent year, and 760 on-campus interviews were held. Companies recruiting on campus include EY, Amazon, Epic Systems, Lockheed Martin, Vanguard, Cigna, and Deloitte. Tight employer partnerships led to internships being completed by more than half of recent graduates. However, those who complete the Internship Prep Program, a combination of workshops and individual appointments hosted by the Career Center, are guaranteed an internship or comparable experiential learning activity. With well-cultivated regional and national employer connections, Pitt students are given every opportunity to secure employment at a solid median starting salary or attend a graduate school consistent with their personal and professional goals.

Professional Outcomes

Within a few months of receiving their degrees, 94% of 2022 grads entered full-time employment or graduate or professional school on a full-time basis. Only 6% were still seeking employment. Engineering, nursing, business, and information sciences majors were the most likely to be employed full-time upon graduation. Those majors had 73-86% employment rates while other majors tended to flock to graduate school in large numbers. The employers scooping up the highest number of grads in one recent year included the University of Pittsburgh Medical Center (170), PNC (57), BNY Mellon (36), and Deloitte (19). Actual panthers may be solitary creatures, but Pitt Panthers flock in notable quantities to major corporations. More than one hundred alumni presently work for Dick's Sporting Goods, Amazon, Google, Microsoft, and Uber. Starting salaries fluctuate across the nine undergraduate schools. The median starting salary for graduates of the Swanson School of Engineering was $65,000 while College of Business Administration students earned $50,000 and Dietrich School of Arts & Sciences grads were paid just shy of $37,000. Pittsburgh, Philly, New York, and DC host the most alumni.

With so many fine graduate programs at the University of Pittsburgh itself, many newly minted grads stay put to continue their education. For one recent class, Pitt was the most popular graduate location by a wide margin, attracting 456 students. Next in popularity were Penn (19), Duquesne (17), and Carnegie Mellon (12). Five or more attended Columbia, Duke, UVA, and Boston University. Undergraduate applicants can apply to the Guaranteed Admissions Program that earns them conditional acceptance to the University of Pittsburgh School of Medicine, one of the best medical schools in the entire US. Recent Pitt graduates have gone on to attend law schools at George Washington University, the University of Chicago, and UVA as well as Pennsylvania-based options like Temple, Duquesne, and Pitt itself.

Admission

Pitt received 53,072 applications to join the Class of 2026 and allowed entrance to 49%, down from 67% the year prior. However, in a typical year, only 20% of accepted applicants ultimately enter the freshman class as many Pennsylvania residents applying to ultra-selective schools use Pitt as a safety school. However, there is nothing that comes close to screaming "safety school" when examining the academic credentials of current undergraduates. With median test scores of 1370 on the SAT and 31 on the ACT, today's Panthers are high achievers. The average GPA is 4.1, 56% hailed from their graduating classes' top decile, and 89% placed in the top quartile.

At the top of the admissions office checklist are the rigor of one's courses and GPA. The essay and character/ personal qualities are the only other factors ranking at or above the "important" level. There is no early action or early decision option at Pitt, but the university does employ a rolling admission policy; applying early is a must if you wish to maximize your admission prospects. The Pitt Honors College has become one of the premier honors programs in the country. SAT scores for admitted honors students are generally in the 1450-1500 range and the average GPA is 4.39. The school accepts between 300 and 400 students each year. Prior to the turn of the new millennium, Pitt was a school that would admit "B" students. Twenty years ago, only 29% of the entering Arts & Sciences students were top-10% finishers, and the average SAT in the nursing program was a 1060. Today, Pitt takes "A" students who took AP courses and registered strong standardized test scores.

Worth Your Money?

Pitt's in-state tuition is $20,000-$25,000 per year (depending on major); for out-of-state students, that number climbs to $44k for majors like business. Families making over $75,000 a year are not going to receive much need-based aid and will pay somewhere near full price. Only a sliver of incoming Panther freshmen nets any merit aid at all. Based on that data, it is fair to say that Pitt is worth the price of admission for any Keystone State resident, no matter what degree you may be pursuing. There is a lot to like about Pitt for out-of-state and international students, but the cost will be higher.

FINANCIAL
Institutional Type: Public
In-State Tuition: $21,524
Out-of-State Tuition: $39,890
Room & Board: $13,420
Books & Supplies: $584

Avg. Need-Based Grant: $15,310
Avg. % of Need Met: 59%

Avg. Merit-Based Award: $9,233
% Receiving (Freshmen w/o Need): 5%

Avg. Cumulative Debt: $38,460
% of Students Borrowing: 59%

CAREER
Who Recruits
1. American Eagle
2. Allegheny Health Network
3. FedEx
4. EPIC Systems
5. Norfolk Southern

Notable Internships
1. Boston Consulting Group
2. NASA Jet Propulsion Laboratory
3. CVS

Top Employers
1. PNC
2. BNY Mellon
3. Deloitte
4. Dick'sSporting Goods
5. Amazon

Where Alumni Work
1. Pittsburgh
2. Philadelphia
3. New York City
4. Washington, DC
5. San Francisco

Earnings
College Scorecard (10-YR Post-Entry): $61,744
PayScale (Early Career): $62,300
PayScale (Mid-Career): $106,200
PayScale 20-Year ROI: $556,000

RANKINGS
Money: 4
U.S. News: 67, National Universities
Wall Street Journal/THE: 307
Washington Monthly: 124, National Universities

OVERGENERALIZATIONS
Students are:
Teeming with school pride
Always saying nice things about Pittsburgh
Crazy about the Panthers
Career-driven
Working hard and playing hard

COLLEGE OVERLAPS
Boston University
New York University
The Ohio State University - Columbus
Pennsylvania State University - University Park
University of Maryland, College Park

University of Richmond

Richmond, Virginia | 804-289-8640

Considering that, in 1861, many of the University of Richmond faculty went off to fight for the Confederacy whose capital was only miles from campus, it may come as a surprise that now the school is a diverse and progressive assemblage of young people from all 50 US states and more than 70 foreign countries. With 3,145 undergraduates, the school is at once modest in size and robust in its academic and student life offerings; there are over sixty undergraduate majors at the university and many standout programs, including the one-of-a-kind Jepson School of Leadership Studies as well as a host of respected pre-professional pathways.

Inside the Classroom

A distinctive general education curriculum includes a first-year seminar as well as the initial leg of a three-course wellness curriculum (the freshman course covers topics like alcohol education). From there, undergrads must demonstrate proficiency in a foreign language and then march through one course in each of historical studies, literary studies, natural sciences, social analysis, symbolic reasoning, and visual and performing arts. The list of required courses is relatively short, affording students a nice amount of academic freedom and exploration.

Don't let the "university" designation fool you; Richmond is all about undergraduate education. The student-to-faculty ratio is 8:1, the average class size is sixteen students, and not a single course is taught by a teaching assistant. Twenty-one percent of classes have single-digit enrollment numbers, and 76% of sections contain fewer than 20 students. Half of all Richmond students participate in an intensive research experience with a faculty member prior to graduation, and students can have those summer opportunities funded through the Richmond Guarantee, which sees the university fund research apprenticeships as well as internships. More than 650 students receive such funding every summer. Going abroad is the norm at UR—65% take a semester or full year of study in one of seventy programs in 30 countries.

The highly regarded Robbins School of Business is responsible for granting 37% of the degrees conferred by the university, a staggering number that dwarfs any other field of study. Homeland security/law enforcement attracts 9% of the student body, and biology (premed is strong) accounts for 8% of degrees earned. The international relations, political science, and history departments also have excellent reputations. Applicants to prestigious fellowships fare quite well. In 2023, eight students won Fulbrights and four won Goldwater Scholarships the prior year.

Outside the Classroom

The University of Richmond's 350-acre campus houses 86% of the undergraduate population, and 99% of freshmen live on campus, creating a cohesive student body. Fifteen Greek organizations on campus rule the social scene with 26% of women joining sororities and 18% of men entering fraternity life. The Spiders compete in 17 NCAA Division I sports within the highly competitive Atlantic Ten Conference, an astounding fact considering the size of the school's liberal arts college. There are 175 student-run organizations, including thirty club sports teams, fourteen religious groups, and seven honors societies. Intramural leagues are run out of the award-winning Weinstein Center for Recreation, which contains a six-lane, twenty-five-yard swimming pool, racquetball/squash courts, and an indoor jogging track. UR's food services are regularly ranked high on lists of best college cuisine. School-run buses and shuttles make getting around a breeze. Campus is located only six miles from downtown Richmond, and longer road trips to DC (90 miles), the Atlantic Ocean, or the Blue Ridge Mountains make for an easy weekend getaway.

Career Services

The Office of Alumni and Career Services is staffed by 16 full-time professional employees (not counting administrative coordinators) who hold positions like career advisor, employer relations coordinator, and director of experiential learning and assessment. That equates to a student-to-advisor ratio of 197:1, in the superior range when compared to the other institutions included in this book. It's no wonder that 97% of Richmond grads report being "generally satisfied" or "very satisfied" with their education one year after graduation, a good indicator of contentment with early career outcomes.

University of Richmond

E-mail: admission@richmond.edu | Website: richmond.edu

Richmond's career services office operates with a four-year plan that connects students to advisors during freshman year. Over three-quarters of recent grads met with an advisor during their senior year. The Spider-Connect system and alumni connections helped 78% of grads land at least one internship during their four years of study. There are 50+ regional alumni groups located around the United States and abroad, creating opportunities to build bridges and find mentorships in just about any major city. Career expos on campus typically attract fifty employers, and major corporations regularly travel to Richmond to recruit and interview current seniors. Spider Road Trips and Spider Shadowing are other avenues to hands-on job exploration opportunities. With strong industry connections, more-than-adequate staffing, and a number of innovative career exploration programs, the Office of Alumni and Career Services does well for its undergraduate students.

Professional Outcomes

One year after receiving their degrees, 96% of Richmond grads who are seeking employment have found jobs. The most popular sectors are financial services/insurance (17%), accounting (7%), consulting (6%), healthcare (6%), teaching (6%), and sales/business development (6%). Companies where you can find at least 50 Richmond alumni employed include Capital One (which employs 380+ Spiders), Deloitte, PwC, Wells Fargo, EY, Dominion Energy, Morgan Stanley, Altria, Google, and Accenture. The average salary range one year out of school is $55,000-$59,000. The majority of students remain in the Richmond area after finishing at the university; however, large pockets of alumni can be found in New York City, DC, Philadelphia, and Boston. Richmond is a school with strong connections to industry in every region of the United States.

Within a year of graduation, approximately one-quarter of alumni enroll in a graduate or professional degree program. The school boasts an impressive list of recent acceptances into high-end law schools such as Harvard, Duke, the University of Chicago, Vanderbilt, Yale, UVA, and the University of Michigan. Even more notable is Richmond's success in helping students get accepted into medical school. In one recent five-year period, a phenomenal 77% of those who applied were accepted, a figure that blows away the national average. Medical schools attended by those students included Brown, Dartmouth, UNC, Stanford, Emory, and Harvard.

Admission

Of the 14,364 who applied for a place in the Class of 2026, only 3,501 were welcomed to the university, working out to an acceptance rate of 24%, an all-time low for the University. The mid-50% standardized test scores also reached record levels of 1425-1510 on the SAT and 32-34 on the ACT. Fifty-six percent of entering freshmen hailed from the top 10% of their high school class, and 86% placed in the top quartile. The average unweighted GPA was 3.78. A decade ago, 39% of applicants gained acceptance, and the SAT range was 1170-1370, a clear signal that Richmond has significantly increased its level of selectivity in recent years.

The admissions committee holds GPA and the rigor of one's secondary school courses as the two most important factors in evaluating an applicant. Seven categories make up the second tier of still "important" factors. Those are standardized test scores, class rank, essays, recommendations, extracurricular activities, character/personal qualities, and talent/ability. Leadership and engagement in high school are sincerely valued by this committee as one recent entering class included 279 athletic captains/class presidents, 23 Eagle Scouts, and 95 who worked part-time for at least 15 hours per week. Applying through early decision or early action is a good idea as the school is looking for applicants for whom Richmond is a genuine top choice. The school's yield rate is 24%, meaning 76% of admitted applicants head elsewhere. Thus, it's no wonder that 42% of the Class of 2026 was admitted via ED and those students enjoyed a 44% acceptance rate compared to 15% in the regular round.

Worth Your Money?

Richmond's cost of attendance exceeds $81,000, making a four-year degree list price of $324,000. UR focuses most of its generosity on those with true financial need, issuing average annual grants of $51k to 37% of the undergraduate student body. Further, Richmond meets 100% of the demonstrated need for those who qualify for financial aid. A uniquely intimate undergraduate setting and solid starting salaries (particularly for business grads) make Richmond worth your money, despite the high price tag.

FINANCIAL
Institutional Type: Private
In-State Tuition: $62,600
Out-of-State Tuition: $62,600
Room & Board: $16,210
Books & Supplies: $1,000

Avg. Need-Based Grant: $51,209
Avg. % of Need Met: 100%

Avg. Merit-Based Award: $27,128
% Receiving (Freshmen w/o Need): 22%

Avg. Cumulative Debt: $27,352
% of Students Borrowing: 37%

CAREER
Who Recruits
1. Baker Tilly
2. BB&T Corporation
3. Dominion Energy
4. John Hancock
5. MAXIMUS

Notable Internships
1. Cushman & Wakefield
2. The Cohen Group
3. Citi

Top Employers
1. Capital One
2. Deloitte
3. Wells Fargo
4. PwC
5. EY

Where Alumni Work
1. Richmond
2. New York City
3. Washington, DC
4. Philadelphia
5. Boston

Earnings
College Scorecard (10-YR Post-Entry): $80,715
PayScale (Early Career): $64,000
PayScale (Mid-Career): $117,000
PayScale 20-Year ROI: $770,000

RANKINGS
Money: 4.5
U.S. News: 25, Liberal Arts Colleges
Wall Street Journal/THE: Not Ranked
Washington Monthly: 35, Liberal Arts Colleges

OVERGENERALIZATIONS
Students are:
Working hard and playing hard
Involved/invested in campus life
Preppy
Goal-oriented
Always admiring the beauty of their campus

COLLEGE OVERLAPS
Boston College
College of William & Mary
Georgetown University
University of Virginia
Wake Forest University

University of Rochester

Rochester, New York | 585-275-3221

Since its founding in 1850, the University of Rochester has established a national reputation as a strong research university. The adoption of its Renaissance Plan in 1995 instituted a uniquely open curriculum for a STEM-focused university, smaller class sizes, and a heavy investment in modernizing campus. Paying dividends today, those changes helped the school blossom into a world-class school that is home to 6,767 undergraduates and another 5,430 graduate students. U of R's 160 undergraduate programs offer students a chance at a rigorous yet flexible educational experience at a small liberal arts college within a renowned research institution.

Inside the Classroom

There are literally no required subjects at the University of Rochester's College of Arts, Sciences, and Engineering. Instead, students must, over their four years of study, take one writing-focused course of their choosing and twelve-credit clusters of courses in two of the following categories (whichever two do not encompass the student's major): humanities, social sciences, and natural sciences and engineering. Those course clusters are designed to ensure "substantive and integrated study," and there are 250+ to choose from, ensuring a high degree of autonomy in selecting one's academic path. The overarching goal of the curriculum is to best reflect the school's ideals of curiosity, competence, and community.

Rochester has maintained a 9:1 student-to-faculty ratio despite graduating more undergraduate students in recent years than ever before. You will encounter some large lecture halls for introductory courses, but the most common class size is 10 to 19 students; 66% of sections enroll fewer than 20. An impressive 77% of students are involved in undergraduate research, a strong indicator that opportunities for intimate learning experiences are plentiful. Approximately one-third of students take a semester abroad in one of the 45+ countries the university has an affiliation with.

Excellence is everywhere you look at Rochester. The Eastman School of Music is one of the best music conservatories in the United States. The Hajim School of Engineering & Applied Sciences is a top 50 institution. Other strong majors include mathematics, economics, and political science—each will open doors in their respective fields. And graduates are no strangers to prestigious fellowship programs. In a typical year, Rochester produces more than a handful of Fulbright Scholarship winners, as well as large numbers of National Science Foundation Graduate Research Fellowship recipients.

Outside the Classroom

In an average year, 70% of undergrads reside in university-owned housing on the school's 154-acre main campus that is nestled around a bend of the Genesee River. First-years and sophomores are required to live on campus. The school's 33 fraternities and sororities entice 12-13% of the undergraduate student body into joining. Most Greek participants—85%—also are engaged with other student organizations. Twenty-one NCAA Division III sports teams play as the Yellowjackets while the university also boasts one of the largest club sports systems with 40 registered club sports and over 1,100 members. There are more than 250 clubs with which undergrads can become involved including the Campus Times, a student-run newspaper in print since 1873, and a selection of top-notch a cappella groups. There are plenty of campus-wide events such as Yellowjacket Weekend, a carnival that marks the start of the academic year, and great musical acts, speakers, and activists are regularly booked to provide cultural and entertainment opportunities without straying from school grounds. Harsh weather can make for long winters, but campus is always humming with some type of appealing activity. The closest major American city is Buffalo, but for the more adventurous, Toronto, Canada, is less than three hours by car.

Career Services

The Gwen M. Greene Career Center for Career Education and Connections is staffed by 19 professionals with expertise in career education and advising, employer development, and event coordination. That number does not include the many peer advisors or administrative assistants. The University of Rochester's 356:1 student-to-advisor ratio is about average for institutions featured in this guide. Still, it manages to mostly achieve its stated aim of assisting students "in achieving their individual career goals while providing them with the resources and tools they need to develop connections between their aspirations, academic pursuits, and co-curricular experiences."

ADMISSION
Admission Rate: 39%
Admission Rate - Men: 33%
Admission Rate - Women: 44%
EA Admission Rate: Not Offered
ED Admission Rate: 43%
ED Admits as % of Total Admits: 8%
Admission Rate (5-Year Trend): +5%
% of Admits Attending (Yield): 21%
Transfer Admission Rate: 41%

SAT Reading/Writing (Middle 50%): 680-750
SAT Math (Middle 50%): 710-790
ACT Composite (Middle 50%): 31-34

% Graduated in Top 10% of HS Class: 62%
% Graduated in Top 25% of HS Class: 90%
% Graduated in Top 50% of HS Class: 98%

Demonstrated Interest: Important
Legacy Status: Considered
Racial/Ethnic Status: Considered
Admission Interview Offered: Yes

ENROLLMENT
Total Undergraduate Enrollment: 6,767
% Full-Time: 97%
% Male: 47%
% Female: 53%
% Out-of-State: 57%
% Fraternity: 13%
% Sorority: 12%
% On-Campus (All Undergraduate): 73%
Freshman Housing Required: Yes

% African-American: 5%
% Asian: 16%
% Hispanic: 8%
% White: 40%
% Other: 3%
% International: 24%
% Low-Income: 17%

ACADEMICS
Student-to-Faculty Ratio: 9 to 1
% of Classes Under 20: 66%
% of Classes 20-49: 22%
% of Classes 50 or More: 13%
% Full-Time Faculty: 72%
% Full-Time Faculty w/ Terminal Degree: 93%

Top Programs
Biology
Business
Mathematics
Music
Neuroscience
Optics
Political Science
Psychology

Retention Rate: 92%
4-Year Graduation Rate: 82%
6-Year Graduation Rate: 87%

Curricular Flexibility: Very Flexible
Academic Rating: ★★★★↙

#CollegesWorthYourMoney

The Greene Center engages more than 500 organizations annually in recruiting and career education programs. The Spring Career and Internship Fair draws 40+ employers to campus including the US Department of State, Epic Systems, the FBI, Citi, and Johnson & Johnson. The center also offers regular events, typically multiple workshops and information sessions per week. Sample recent events included a CV and resume workshop, a night with Kraft Heinz leadership, and a virtual career conversation about innovation in the workplace. Staff is happy to meet one-on-one to help students select and secure an internship that will be meaningful to their career development process. A near-perfect 95% of Yellowjackets complete at least one internship during their undergraduate years; 75% complete two or more. You can also apply for a $1,000 to $2,500 alumni grant to help fund a summer internship that might not otherwise be possible. There are a significant number of opportunities for students to engage with UR alumni through structured programs, networking, and courses offered by the Greene Center.

Professional Outcomes

Six months after receiving their diplomas, 97% of Class of 2022 grads had achieved positive outcomes with 57% employed and a notably high 38% already pursuing an advanced degree. Popular industries included internet and software (14%), healthcare (14%), and investment banking (6%). Top employers of 2022 grads included Google (12), Goldman Sachs (11), Epic Systems (9), and Deloitte (8). Looking across all graduating years, significant numbers of Rochester alumni also can be found in the offices of Amazon, IBM, Apple, and Microsoft. The average starting salary for the most recent cohort of grads was an impressive $82,325; that figure was over $105k for graduates of the Hajim School of Engineering and close to $69k for those in the School of Arts and Sciences. Upstate New York, New York City, Boston, DC, San Francisco, and Philadelphia play home to the greatest number of alumni.

With close to half of grads jumping directly into a graduate program, many continue their studies at the University of Rochester (99) or at other elite institutions such as Columbia (25), Boston University (12), USC (12), Cornell (10), NYU (9), and Johns Hopkins (9). The university has an excellent premed reputation, and acceptance rates into MD programs are significantly higher than the national average. Thanks to the Rochester Early Medical Scholars program, some premed students are already on an eight-year pathway toward the completion of a medical degree at the University's School of Medicine and Dentistry. In a single recent year, neighboring SUNY Buffalo took three Rochester grads, and other grads headed to the Sidney Kimmel Medical College and Albany Medical College. Recent grads have matriculated into a wide range of law schools including top-tier institutions like William & Mary, Emory, Boston University, the University of Wisconsin, and Indiana University.

Admission

The fight for a place in the Class of 2026 saw applications approach 20,000 and the acceptance rate land at 39%; this was actually friendlier than the 30% mark three cycles before. Those who enrolled possessed an average GPA of 3.76 and a median SAT score of 1460. In 2020, the university moved from test-flexible to test-optional and has remained as such. Undergraduate applicants to the college may now decide which exam, if any, is an accurate representation of their ability and potential for success. Over three-fifths of enrolled freshmen finished in the top 10% of their high school class.

Interviews are strongly recommended as part of this holistic admissions process that seeks to "identify curious, capable, and engaged students from across the globe." In addition to stellar grades in a highly rigorous academic program, the committee wants to see evidence of leadership through extracurricular involvement as well as strong character/personal qualities. Last cycle, an all-time high of 614 students was accepted via early decision, and the ED acceptance rate was 43%, giving early applicants slightly better odds than those in the regular round. In sum, Rochester has never been more difficult to get into, so there is far less room for error than there was a generation ago.

Worth Your Money?

Including tuition, fees, room and board, and other estimated expenses, the total projected cost of attendance at this school is $85,858 per year. The good news is that, of those who apply for need-based aid, 94% see their full financial need met. While a $344,000 sticker price for a bachelor's degree is steep, the majority of students receive sizable discounts via need-based or merit aid. The average net price paid by families, even those in the top income bracket, is $47k; those in the lowest brackets paid far less. Further, significant starting salaries and corporate connections allow Yellowjackets to get a running start toward financial stability. For those who know what they want from their education (i.e., certain about major and career-oriented), the University of Rochester is worth your money.

FINANCIAL
Institutional Type: Private
In-State Tuition: $64,384
Out-of-State Tuition: $64,384
Room & Board: $18,788
Books & Supplies: $1,310

Avg. Need-Based Grant: $50,333
Avg. % of Need Met: 98%

Avg. Merit-Based Award: $15,918
% Receiving (Freshmen w/o Need): 24%

Avg. Cumulative Debt: $29,386
% of Students Borrowing: 47%

CAREER
Who Recruits
1. Instagram
2. The Martin Agency
3. Goldman Sachs
4. CarMax
5. Citi

Notable Internships
1. Wegman's Food Markets
2. Lockheed Martin
3. SpaceX

Top Employers
1. Google
2. Apple
3. IBM
4. Amazon
5. Microsoft

Where Alumni Work
1. Rochester, NY
2. New York City
3. Boston
4. Washington, DC
5. San Francisco

Earnings
College Scorecard (10-YR Post-Entry): $75,226
PayScale (Early Career): $67,300
PayScale (Mid-Career): $122,600
PayScale 20-Year ROI: $644,000

RANKINGS
Money: 4
U.S. News: 47, National Universities
Wall Street Journal/THE: 126
Washington Monthly: 84, National Universities

OVERGENERALIZATIONS
Students are:
Diverse
Nerdy
Intellectually curious
Not afraid to work hard
Involved/investsed in campus life

COLLEGE OVERLAPS
Boston College
Carnegie Mellon University
Cornell University
Northeastern University
Tufts University

University of San Diego

San Diego, California | 619-260-4506

ADMISSION
Admission Rate: 53%
Admission Rate - Men: 49%
Admission Rate - Women: 55%
EA Admission Rate: Not Offered
ED Admission Rate: Not Offered
ED Admits as % of Total Admits: Not Offered
Admission Rate (5-Year Trend): +3%
% of Admits Attending (Yield): 16%
Transfer Admission Rate: 63%

SAT Reading/Writing (Middle 50%): Test-Blind
SAT Math (Middle 50%): Test-Blind
ACT Composite (Middle 50%): Test-Blind

% Graduated in Top 10% of HS Class: 30%
% Graduated in Top 25% of HS Class: 68%
% Graduated in Top 50% of HS Class: 96%

Demonstrated Interest: Considered
Legacy Status: Not Considered
Racial/Ethnic Status: Considered
Admission Interview Offered: No

ENROLLMENT
Total Undergraduate Enrollment: 5,669
% Full-Time: 98%
% Male: 43%
% Female: 57%
% Out-of-State: 40%
% Fraternity: 19%
% Sorority: 30%
% On-Campus (All Undergraduate): 46%
Freshman Housing Required: Yes

% African-American: 4%
% Asian: 8%
% Hispanic: 24%
% White: 47%
% Other: 3%
% International: 6%
% Low-Income: 20%

ACADEMICS
Student-to-Faculty Ratio: 12 to 1
% of Classes Under 20: 43%
% of Classes 20-49: 57%
% of Classes 50 or More: 0%
% Full-Time Faculty: 49%
% Full-Time Faculty w/ Terminal Degree: 94%

Top Programs
Accountancy
Business
Communication Studies
Engineering
Finance
Industrial Engineering
International Relations
Psychology

Retention Rate: 90%
4-Year Graduation Rate: 71%
6-Year Graduation Rate: 81%

Curricular Flexibility: Less Flexible
Academic Rating: ★★★✓

#CollegesWorthYourMoney

For anyone outside of the Golden State, it is easy to confuse the University of California, San Diego with the University of San Diego. Not only are the names similar, but they are just a 15-minute drive away from one another. Both are excellent schools, but the latter is a private, midsized university of approximately 5,700 undergraduate students while the former is a large public institution and part of the UC system. A Catholic university, USD was founded a few years after World War II and rapidly grew into a school with eight academic divisions, including its own law school. In addition to a number of fine (and popular) departments, the school is also admired for its aesthetics—the 180-acre grounds have been named the nation's most beautiful campus by more than one major publication.

Inside the Classroom
The San Diego core constitutes 14-17 classes, a sizable portion of one's undergraduate experience. Freshmen are required to take First-Year Writing and Mathematical Reasoning as well as begin work on a foreign language, which they must take up until the 201 level (as many as four courses). The school's Catholic affiliation necessitates a dive into theological and religious inquiry, philosophical inquiry, and ethical inquiry. Other explorations into areas such as artistic inquiry, scientific and technological inquiry, and literary inquiry are also required. Lastly, all students must complete an advanced integration as a senior, which takes the form of a culminating project or learning experience.

You will find nary a large lecture course anywhere in this school. In fact, 99% of courses at USD contain 39 or fewer students. However, only 43% enroll fewer than 20 students. This university's student-to-faculty ratio is 12:1. If you desire to participate in undergraduate research, there is a faculty member willing to work with you, "regardless of major or class standing." Students can participate through a number of formal on-campus programs like the Summer Undergraduate Research Experience or the McNair Scholars Program, which provides faculty mentors and stipends as support. The 75 available study abroad programs attract an exceptional 70% of Toreros. The takeaway here is that it is almost impossible to get through a USD education without engaging in at least one hands-on program.

Business and accounting are the academic programs that receive the most acclaim at USD; they also attract, by some margin, the most undergraduates. Thirty-eight percent of degrees conferred fall under the business umbrella. The next most popular fields are biology (13%), social sciences (10%), engineering (10%), and psychology (8%). Competitive postgraduate fellowships are not a focal point of this institution—they do not regularly produce a significant number of recipients.

Outside the Classroom
Forty-six percent of 2021-22 freshmen hailed from out of state, and all were welcomed to a campus that has a high level of first-year cohesion; 93% live on campus in 11 separate living areas. Looking at the undergraduate student body as a whole, only two-fifths live in school-provided housing. Greek organizations soak up a fair number of students—18% of men and 30% of women. There are nine national fraternity chapters at the school and nine sorority chapters. Sports at the Division I level are engaged in by 17 teams. There are also 23 club teams as well as many recreational clubs and fitness classes. Ample faith-based and community service-oriented clubs are available as are a student-run newspaper, television station, and radio station. The amenities at USD are rated as highly as the overall gorgeousness of the grounds. Campus dining nets rave reviews for its quality and diversity of cuisines—Pavilion Dining offers authentic Mexican, Thai, Vietnamese, Mediterranean, and made-to-order sushi. Famed Mission Beach, Petco Park, the San Diego Zoo, endless shopping and dining options, and breathtaking natural sites like La Jolla Cove are all just minutes from campus.

Career Services
The well-staffed Career Development Center (CDC) at the University of San Diego employs 16 professional employees with roles in the areas of career counseling (by academic discipline), experiential learning, employer experience coordination, and alumni engagement. This excellent 354:1 counselor-to-student ratio allows the CDC to produce great results such as 87% of graduates participating in at least one experiential learning activity (e.g., internship, community service, or research opportunity).

In a single year, this office manages to hold 3,100+ in-person counseling appointments and bring 300+ employers and 1,500+ students to job fairs and information sessions. Over 10,000 contacts are made by students with employers via Handshake; there are more than 20,000 jobs and internships posted each year. Roughly 350 students embarked on Torero Treks where undergraduates visit alumni employed by major corporations in New York, Seattle, Portland, and Los Angeles. One-on-one assistance is always available whether you are sitting down with a counselor for a Myers-Briggs assessment as a freshman, getting connected with an alum for an internship heading into the summer after sophomore year, or polishing your resume prior to a job fair senior year. The University of San Diego has notably supportive career services offerings, well above the average of schools featured in this guide, and these efforts directly translate into positive professional outcomes.

Professional Outcomes

Half a year after being handed their diplomas, 90% of recent University of San Diego graduates have found their next destination. Sixty-five percent of graduates were employed at a diverse range of employers such as PwC, The Walt Disney Company, the San Diego Padres, NBC Universal, and Tesla. Large numbers of alumni are also entrenched at the likes of Apple, Google, EY, Amazon, and Salesforce. The median starting salary for a USD grad entering the job market last year was a healthy $65k. Nearly one-quarter entered the world of sales, marketing, finance, or accounting. The greatest number of alumni from all years can be found clustered in San Diego, with Los Angeles, San Francisco, Orange County, and New York the top runners-up.

Of the 23% of recent grads who immediately began pursuit of an advanced degree, 36% were studying business, 16% were in engineering programs, and another 17% were in health programs. Toreros gained acceptance into a wide range of universities, including some of the most prestigious in the country such as Cornell, Northwestern, the University of Michigan, Yale, Columbia, Stanford, and Johns Hopkins. Medical school acceptances included the Boston University School of Medicine, the Indiana University School of Medicine, and the New York University School of Medicine. Law schools attended included UCLA, the University of Chicago, and the University of Michigan.

Admission

Accepting 53% of applicants, the University of San Diego is one of those rare schools that hasn't become more selective in recent years. At present, the university is test-blind, meaning that SAT and ACT scores play no role whatsoever in the admissions process. Freshmen in the 2022-23 school year earned an average weighted high school GPA of 4.01, and 57% achieved greater than a 4.0. Thirty percent of this group placed in the top 10% of their class, and 68% landed in the top quartile.

When making admissions selections, this school places the greatest emphasis on high school class rigor and GPA. Factors rated as "important" were as follows: class rank, essay, recommendations, extracurricular activities, talent/ability, character/personal qualities, and volunteer work. Showing that you have genuine interest in attending is a must as this school has only a 16% yield rate. It does not offer an early decision option, so if USD is your first choice, make that known through direct communication with the admissions office and by applying on or before the December regular decision deadline.

Worth Your Money?

USD does not come cheap, as the annual cost of attendance for 2023-24 is just a couple hundred bucks shy of $77k. The financial aid situation at this school is decent; 53% of undergraduates receive need-based aid with an annual average award of $38k. Solid starting salaries for graduates entering certain industries can make San Diego a viable option for those receiving minimal aid. For those entering the accounting/auditing, engineering and design, finance and banking, real estate, or technology fields, remuneration is likely to be high enough to be able to comfortably pay down any educational debt accrued.

FINANCIAL
Institutional Type: Private
In-State Tuition: $56,444
Out-of-State Tuition: $56,444
Room & Board: $18,084
Books & Supplies: $938

Avg. Need-Based Grant: $40,327
Avg. % of Need Met: 85%

Avg. Merit-Based Award: $19,532
% Receiving (Freshmen w/o Need): 19%

Avg. Cumulative Debt: $25,208
% of Students Borrowing: 51%

CAREER
Who Recruits
1. NBC Universal
2. General Atomics
3. Boeing
4. PwC
5. Tesla

Notable Internships
1. Adobe
2. San Diego Padres
3. San Diego Zoo

Top Employers
1. US Navy
2. Northrop Grumman
3. UC San Diego
4. Qualcomm
5. Wells Fargo

Where Alumni Work
1. San Diego
2. Los Angeles
3. San Francisco
4. Orange County, CA
5. New York City

Earnings
College Scorecard (10-YR Post-Entry): $78,234
PayScale (Early Career): $64,000
PayScale (Mid-Career): $122,400
PayScale 20-Year ROI: $613,000

RANKINGS
Money: 4.5
U.S. News: 98, National Universities
Wall Street Journal/THE: Not Ranked
Washington Monthly: 102, National Universities

OVERGENERALIZATIONS
Students are:
Environmentally conscious
Always saying nice things about San Diego
Friendly
Wealthy
Dressed to impress

COLLEGE OVERLAPS
Loyola Marymount University
Pepperdine University
Santa Clara University
University of California, San Diego
University of San Francisco

University of South Carolina

Columbia, South Carolina | 803-777-7700

ADMISSION
Admission Rate: 64%
Admission Rate - Men: 59%
Admission Rate - Women: 67%
EA Admission Rate: Not Reported
ED Admission Rate: Not Offered
ED Admits as % of Total Admits: Not Offered
Admission Rate (5-Year Trend): -8%
% of Admits Attending (Yield): 24%
Transfer Admission Rate: 66%

SAT Reading/Writing (Middle 50%): 600-690
SAT Math (Middle 50%): 580-690
ACT Composite (Middle 50%): 27-32

% Graduated in Top 10% of HS Class: 26%
% Graduated in Top 25% of HS Class: 58%
% Graduated in Top 50% of HS Class: 92%

Demonstrated Interest: Not Considered
Legacy Status: Not Considered
Racial/Ethnic Status: Not Considered
Admission Interview Offered: No

ENROLLMENT
Total Undergraduate Enrollment: 27,343
% Full-Time: 97%
% Male: 44%
% Female: 56%
% Out-of-State: 38%
% Fraternity: 26%
% Sorority: 31%
% On-Campus (All Undergraduate): 31%
Freshman Housing Required: Yes

% African-American: 9%
% Asian: 4%
% Hispanic: 6%
% White: 74%
% Other: 1%
% International: 2%
% Low-Income: 13%

ACADEMICS
Student-to-Faculty Ratio: 18 to 1
% of Classes Under 20: 42%
% of Classes 20-49: 44%
% of Classes 50 or More: 15%
% Full-Time Faculty: 64%
% Full-Time Faculty w/ Terminal Degree: 89%

Top Programs
Criminology and Criminal Justice
Exercise Science
Finance
Information Science
International Business
Public Health
Sport and Entertainment Management

Retention Rate: 89%
4-Year Graduation Rate: 69%
6-Year Graduation Rate: 78%

Curricular Flexibility: Somewhat Flexible
Academic Rating: ★★★

#CollegesWorthYourMoney

Tired of competing for the USC acronym with the University of Southern California, the University of South Carolina has adopted its own abbreviated identity: UofSC. This newfound shortened identity is attached to a school with a long and storied history, having been founded during the Jefferson administration. The modern version of the UofSC is a massive enterprise, enrolling 27,343 undergraduate students and operating sixteen total colleges and schools within the larger university. This includes a law school and two medical schools.

Inside the Classroom
Voted the best first-year experience of any public college, the University of South Carolina knows how to welcome freshmen to Columbia. In fact, it essentially invented the first-year experience back in the early '70s. Today, the University 101 course fosters "a sense of belonging" and "promote(s) engagement in the curricular and co-curricular life of the university." The Carolina Core makes sure that all UofSC graduates are exposed to 10 essential areas such as scientific literacy; effective, engaged, and persuasive written communication; foreign language; and information literacy. These required areas of study account for at least 36 credit hours, depending on one's foreign language proficiency when entering the university. Students can elect to take up to two "overlay" courses that fulfill two requirements at once, creating a bit more overall curricular flexibility. Honors students must take 45 credits in designated honors courses and complete a thesis. The South Carolina Honors College is extremely hard to get into (more later) and is one of the finest in the entire country.

An 18:1 student-to-faculty ratio ensures that classes with single-digit enrollment will be a rarity during one's educational journey. Still, 70% of all sections contain 29 or fewer students, and only 15% enroll more than 50 individuals. The Office of Undergraduate Research will help ambitious students locate a mentor professor in their discipline, pursue funding sources, and compete for school-based undergraduate research awards. Study abroad opportunities are also there for all who seek them; close to 2,000 students study abroad each year, and UofSC runs its own programs with faculty members in Costa Rica, the Galapagos, and Tuscany, Italy.

With the superb Darla Moore School of Business available, it's no surprise that 32% of students avail themselves of the opportunity to earn a degree in the business/marketing realm. The school's international business program recently took home the top spot in the US News rankings. Other disciplines in which the greatest number of degrees are conferred include health services (11%), biology (10%), engineering (6%), and communication and journalism (6%). A top producer of Fulbright students, the university also had four Gilman Scholars in 2023.

Outside the Classroom
Greek life and athletics are dominant forces in the culture at this 359-acre main campus in downtown Columbia. Across all varsity programs, the Gamecocks draw 1.3 million fans annually and have won 11 individual and team national championships in the last decade. Thirty-one percent of all undergraduate women are members of sororities, and 26% of men join fraternities. The vast majority of freshmen, 96%, reside in the dorms while only 31% of the overall student population remains on campus. You can certainly find a big-school party scene at UofSC, but there is much more to daily life at this school. The Leadership and Service Center supports over 550 student-run clubs in the categories of intramural sports, games, dance, academics, and more. Carolina Productions coordinates on-campus entertainment and manages to book major live acts and screenings of hit movies. Located within a mile of the statehouse, the campus is situated right in the heart of the city. Everything from art museums to escape rooms to music venues is within a short walk from the dorms.

Career Services
There are 25 professional staff members within the University of South Carolina Career Center, many of whom focus on career counseling, experiential education, and employer relations. An additional five career personnel are housed within the Darla Moore Office of Career Management. This 911:1 ratio is significantly higher than the average school selected for this guidebook. Fortunately, resources are plentiful to put on meaningful large-scale events like career fairs. Discipline-specific fairs include those focused on STEM, corporate careers, government and public service, health and wellness, and professional schools and graduate programs. Handshake can be utilized at any point in time to locate internships and begin the job hunt. On-campus interview opportunities are arranged through this platform as well.

Students have access to unique programs like the Carolina Internship Program, which allows undergrads to complete an internship or co-op during the school year while maintaining full-time student status. South Carolina grads who completed an internship while at the school reported earning $7k more in annual starting salary than those who did not. The School of Business has forged partnerships with companies such as FedEx, Ipsos, Crayola, ESPN, and Coca-Cola. Staff are always willing to assist with the internship/job search, prep for interviews, explore graduate school options, or help sharpen your resume. Overall, this university is not going to hold your hand through the career development process, but those who are assertive and proactive will find all the resources they need to prepare for their postgraduation launch.

Professional Outcomes

Seventy-nine percent of recent grads landed at their next destination within six months. The average starting salary for Gamecocks is over $55,000 (based on the most recent available data – the school has not released 2022 figures). The top employers of recent classes included KPMG, IBM, Aramark, Bank of America, Vanguard, PwC, and Marriott. Additional companies employing 100 or more UofSC-affiliated alumni are Wells Fargo, Amazon, Colonial Life, EY, Merrill Lynch, and Microsoft. Suffice it to say no matter at which multinational corporation you are seeking employment, you are likely to find a solid number of South Carolina alumni. While over 40% of graduates remain in South Carolina, many also relocate to Charlotte; Atlanta; Washington, DC; and New York City. Within the Darla Moore School of Business, 87% of 2023 grads were employed within three months and the average starting salary is $69k.

As is the case at many large public universities, the majority of those continuing their studies in a graduate/professional degree program did so right at the University of South Carolina. Duke and Wake Forest are also frequent landing spots for those seeking an advanced degree. In 2023, there were 230 applicants to various med schools from the university. Seventy-nine percent of honors students who apply to medical school are accepted. The most frequently attended medical school was the Medical University of South Carolina. The most commonly attended law school was the University of South Carolina Law School.

Admission

The University of South Carolina's 64% acceptance rate for the Class of 2026 should be encouraging for students looking for an excellent public institution that does not close its doors to students with SATs below the 90th percentile of all test takers. In fact, midrange scores are 1200-1380 on the SAT and 27-32 on the ACT. For academic performance, the school does expect a little bit closer to perfection as the average GPA is 3.66. Twenty-six percent of 2022-23 freshmen placed in the top decile of their high school class, and 58% were in the top quarter. Those admitted to the Honors College possess an average weighted GPA of 4.77 and an SAT range of 1410-1520.

Two factors are paramount in the eyes of South Carolina admissions officers: rigor of secondary school record and GPA. If you check both boxes, your admission is virtually assured. There are zero factors deemed "important" to the process, and "considered" factors include test scores, class rank, essays, recommendations, extracurricular activities, talent/ability, character/personal qualities, first-generation status, state residency, racial/ethnic status, and volunteer/paid work experience. The committee also states that it values factors like military experience, writing ability, and "the applicant's potential for contribution to a diverse educational environment." Students can choose to apply early action by the October 15 deadline, but there is little admissions-related advantage to doing so.

Worth Your Money?

South Carolina residents pay a total cost of attendance of $38,700 while nonresidents, who make up 47% of the most recent freshman class, pay $61,000. The Palmetto State charges more for its public colleges than many fellow Southern states like North Carolina and Florida. Still, by nationwide standards, UofSC's price is not, by any means, out of bounds. Those who qualify for need-based financial aid receive an average grant of roughly $7,500. If you live in a neighboring state with a more affordable price tag, then there are limited circumstances where crossing state lines would make sense. For residents, South Carolina is a solid investment that generally leads to positive postgraduation outcomes.

FINANCIAL
Institutional Type: Public
In-State Tuition: $12,688
Out-of-State Tuition: $33,928
Room & Board: $11,780
Books & Supplies: $1,226

Avg. Need-Based Grant: $7,467
Avg. % of Need Met: 76%

Avg. Merit-Based Award: $7,031
% Receiving (Freshmen w/o Need): 42%

Avg. Cumulative Debt: $31,695
% of Students Borrowing: 53%

CAREER
Who Recruits
1. Collins Aerospace
2. Seibels
3. Boeing
4. Prisma Health
5. Cigna

Notable Internships
1. Becton, Dickinson and Co.
2. Enterprise Holdings
3. Sands Investment Group

Top Employers
1. Wells Fargo
2. Bank of America
3. Amazon
4. PwC
5. Boeing

Where Alumni Work
1. Columbia, SC
2. Charlotte
3. Greenville, SC
4. Charleston, SC
5. Atlanta

Earnings
College Scorecard (10-YR Post-Entry): $57,734
PayScale (Early Career): $55,200
PayScale (Mid-Career): $93,900
PayScale 20-Year ROI: $339,000

RANKINGS
Money: 4
U.S. News: 124, National Universities
Wall Street Journal/THE: 274
Washington Monthly: 188, National Universities

OVERGENERALIZATIONS
Students are:
Politically conservative
Crazy about the Gamecocks
More likely to rush a fraternity/sorority
Laid-back
Social

COLLEGE OVERLAPS
Clemson University
College of Charleston
North Carolina State University
University of Alabama
University of Georgia

University of Southern California

Los Angeles, California | 213-740-1111

ADMISSION

Admission Rate: 12%
Admission Rate - Men: 13%
Admission Rate - Women: 12%
EA Admission Rate: Not Offered
ED Admission Rate: Not Offered
ED Admits as % of Total Admits: Not Offered
Admission Rate (5-Year Trend): -4%
% of Admits Attending (Yield): 41%
Transfer Admission Rate: 24%

SAT Reading/Writing (Middle 50%): 710-760
SAT Math (Middle 50%): 740-790
ACT Composite (Middle 50%): 32-35

% Graduated in Top 10% of HS Class: 73%
% Graduated in Top 25% of HS Class: 94%
% Graduated in Top 50% of HS Class: 99%

Demonstrated Interest: Not Considered
Legacy Status: Considered
Racial/Ethnic Status: Considered
Admission Interview Offered: No

ENROLLMENT

Total Undergraduate Enrollment: 20,699
% Full-Time: 98%
% Male: 48%
% Female: 52%
% Out-of-State: 39%
% Fraternity: 0%
% Sorority: 0%
% On-Campus (All Undergraduate): 36%
Freshman Housing Required: No

% African-American: 6%
% Asian: 25%
% Hispanic: 17%
% White: 30%
% Other: 2%
% International: 13%
% Low-Income: 21%

ACADEMICS

Student-to-Faculty Ratio: 9 to 1
% of Classes Under 20: 62%
% of Classes 20-49: 26%
% of Classes 50 or More: 12%
% Full-Time Faculty: 59%
% Full-Time Faculty w/ Terminal Degree: 90%

Top Programs
Business
Cinematic Arts
Communication
Computer Science
Design
Engineering
International Relations
Performing Arts

Retention Rate: 95%
4-Year Graduation Rate: 79%
6-Year Graduation Rate: 92%

Curricular Flexibility: Somewhat Flexible
Academic Rating: ★★★★✦

#CollegesWorthYourMoney

A few decades back, if you told someone "in the know" about college admissions that the University of Southern California would eventually be in the same league with UC Berkeley, they would likely have concluded that an asteroid was headed for the San Francisco Bay area. At that time, USC was stereotyped as a lily-white school for wealthy underachievers that accepted the majority of applicants. Today, the home of the Trojans is one of the premier private research universities in the country, enriched by a diverse pool of students from around the globe and, at times in recent years, sporting a lower acceptance rate than Georgetown, Tufts, Washington University in St. Louis and—to bring things full circle—Berkeley.

Inside the Classroom

There are 140 undergraduate majors and minors within the Dornsife College of Arts & Sciences alone, the university's oldest and largest school. Graduation requirements are a fairly run-of-the-mill assortment of selections across the major disciplines. By degrees conferred, the most popular areas of study are business (22%), social sciences (11%), visual and performing arts (11%), communications/journalism (9%), and engineering (8%).

At an institution with 20,699 undergraduates and 28,246 graduate students, you would not expect to find many tiny seminar courses with single-digit enrollments, but 18% of classes at USC do, in fact, meet that standard. The bulk of courses offered are in the ten to nineteen range, but you also will find yourself in a fair share of large lecture halls in your time at USC. Still, there is little anonymity in a Trojan education. Aided by a favorable 9:1 student-to-faculty ratio, the school does an excellent job facilitating undergraduate research opportunities. Each school/college has a course entitled Directed Research 490 in which students work closely with a faculty supervisor and earn between two and eight credits as well as countless opportunities to get their hands dirty in academic research.

All programs within the Marshall School of Business and Viterbi School of Engineering are highly acclaimed and have far-reaching reputations with employers and elite grad schools (more on both later). Programs in communication, the cinematic arts, and the performing arts carry sterling reputations as well. Students are quite competitive in the race for elite postgraduate fellowships. The Class of 2023 saw 22 Fulbright awards, and the school has produced multiple NSF Graduate Research Fellows, Gilman Scholars, Boren winners, and Critical Language Scholarship recipients.

Outside the Classroom

While most Trojans live on campus as freshmen, the majority of upperclassmen reside in the surrounding neighborhoods and commute to school. That is not entirely a matter of choice; USC offers limited university-owned housing options, only enough to accommodate 36% of its undergraduate population. Fortunately, the school recently opened eight new residential houses which, collectively, increased its capacity substantially. Greek life is thriving at USC with a 20-30% participation rate in over sixty sororities/fraternities, which, thanks to a recent ban, are unaffiliated with the University. The Trojans' beloved football team takes center stage each fall, attracting 93,000 fans each Saturday. There are nineteen additional NCAA Division I sports teams fielded by the university as well as a massive club sports operation with 2,500+ participants. Over 850 student organizations are active, including popular choices like student government, cultural groups, and performance troupes. USC's LA location ensures that there is never a dearth of excitement and adventure. Within a few miles of campus are countless museums, the Staples Center, multiple theaters, and all the nightlife you could desire. Being in LA has other perks—major musical acts and guest speakers from Barack Obama to alum Will Ferrell appear at the university on a regular basis. The Visions & Voices program provides free cultural events multiple times per week that draw rave reviews from the student body.

Career Services

The University of Southern California Career Center only represents a portion of the career counseling received by Trojan undergrads as additional, more specialized experts are embedded within every undergraduate college. For example, seven professionals provide counseling only to engineering students, and six work exclusively with Annenberg students. In total, there are 51 full-time staff members working in counseling, employer relations, and recruiting, equating to a 406:1 student-to-counselor ratio, within the average range of institutions profiled in this book. Yet, that ratio may be the only thing that could be labeled ordinary about this highly accomplished Career Center.

On-campus recruiting at USC is extraordinary with 275 employers granting on-site interviews. In a single year, undergraduate students engaged in 4,400+ job interviews at the university. The companies recruiting on campus make for an impressive list, even if you only highlighted those that start with "A"—Adobe Systems, Accenture, Amazon, Apple, and AT&T. Outreach efforts are successful as career services engages with 6,400 students via 1:1 counseling appointments and has just shy of 10,000 attendees at workshops and other events. Large events include the Fall Career Fair that brings 200+ employers to campus, and every school has its own concentrated fairs in areas such as architecture, engineering, and pre-law. A strong alumni network of more than 480,000 is another useful resource for fresh graduates.

Professional Outcomes

USC sees 96% of students experience positive postgraduation outcomes within six months of earning their bachelor's degree. The median salary earned across all undergraduate colleges is an astounding $79k. The top five industries entered by members of that cohort were finance, consulting, advertising, software development, and engineering. Presently, there are between 300 and 1,500 alumni employed at each of Google, Amazon, Apple, Microsoft, KPMG, Goldman Sachs, and Meta. Half of all alumni reside in the Los Angeles area while San Francisco, Orange County, and New York City are next in popularity.

The graduate/professional schools enrolling the greatest number of 2022 USC grads include NYU, Georgetown, Harvard, Stanford, Pepperdine, and UCLA. Further, the University of Southern California is one of the most prolific producers of students accepted into the T14 law schools. The good news doesn't stop there; the university also ranks as one of the leading producers of students accepted into top MBA programs like Wharton, Booth, and Tuck. There were 348 medical school applicants in 2023.

Admission

USC admissions (and those at several other schools) made front-page headlines for months on end five years ago as part of the "Varsity Blues" scandal that saw famous actresses and powerful businesspeople cheating and bribing their way into the university. Interestingly, you probably wouldn't have seen people cheating their way into USC a decade ago. Admission into USC has become significantly more challenging in recent years. Last year, of 69,062 wanna-be Trojans, only 8,304 were accepted, equating to a 12% admit rate. Three cycles ago, USC sported an all-time low acceptance rate of 11%. The SAT range of the Class of 2026 was 1460-1540, and the ACT range was 32-35. On a 4.0 scale, the average high school GPA was 3.87. Those figures are slightly higher than in previous years.

There are no unusual factors designated as "most important" by the admissions staff, but rigor of curriculum, grades, test scores, essays, and recommendations reign supreme. USC does not have an early action/early decision option, so all candidates are in the same boat. Legacy students, called "scions," make up a significant portion of the student body—10-15% of current students are the son or daughter of an alum. There is definitely an edge available for those with Trojan lineage. Those from a generation ago, including USC alumni now hoping to shepherd their own children into their alma mater, may find the current level of selectivity a complete and utter shock. For additional perspective, twenty years ago, 45% of applicants were accepted, and the average SAT score was over 200 points lower than it is for today's enrollees.

Worth Your Money?

At over $91,000, there is nothing shocking about the annual cost of attendance at USC; it's pretty standard these days for a private university. Where it does seem outrageously high is when you see that amount is twice the cost of any of the elite University of California schools such as Berkley or UCLA. Nearly two-thirds of current undergrads receive some form of financial aid and all students who qualify for need-based grants see their need fully met. Further, many USC grads go on to lucrative careers that are enhanced by the school's employer/graduate school connections as well as those of the well-connected alumni base.

FINANCIAL
Institutional Type: Private
In-State Tuition: $68,237
Out-of-State Tuition: $68,237
Room & Board: $19,198
Books & Supplies: $1,200

Avg. Need-Based Grant: $45,764
Avg. % of Need Met: 100%

Avg. Merit-Based Award: $17,585
% Receiving (Freshmen w/o Need): 22%

Avg. Cumulative Debt: $26,534
% of Students Borrowing: 32%

CAREER
Who Recruits
1. FTI Consulting
2. Moss Adams
3. Cornerstone Research
4. Nike
5. Universal Creative

Notable Internships
1. Dow Jones
2. Tesla
3. The Blackstone Group

Top Employers
1. Google
2. Amazon
3. Apple
4. Microsoft
5. Facebook

Where Alumni Work
1. Los Angeles
2. San Francisco
3. Orange County, CA
4. New York City
5. San Diego

Earnings
College Scorecard (10-YR Post-Entry): $89,884
PayScale (Early Career): $70,400
PayScale (Mid-Career): $133,300
PayScale 20-Year ROI: $759,000

RANKINGS
Money: 4.5
U.S. News: 28, National Universities
Wall Street Journal/THE: 22
Washington Monthly: 47, National Universities

OVERGENERALIZATIONS
Students are:
Crazy about the Trojans
Working hard and playing hard
Diverse
Social
Teeming with school pride

COLLEGE OVERLAPS
Cornell University
New York University
Stanford University
University of California, Berkeley
University of California, Los Angeles

Austin, Texas | 512-475-7399

ADMISSION
Admission Rate: 31%
Admission Rate - Men: 27%
Admission Rate - Women: 36%
EA Admission Rate: Not Offered
ED Admission Rate: Not Offered
ED Admits as % of Total Admits: Not Offered
Admission Rate (5-Year Trend): -5%
% of Admits Attending (Yield): 49%
Transfer Admission Rate: 34%

SAT Reading/Writing (Middle 50%): 620-730
SAT Math (Middle 50%): 610-770
ACT Composite (Middle 50%): 27-33

% Graduated in Top 10% of HS Class: 87%
% Graduated in Top 25% of HS Class: 96%
% Graduated in Top 50% of HS Class: 99%

Demonstrated Interest: Not Considered
Legacy Status: Not Considered
Racial/Ethnic Status: Considered
Admission Interview Offered: No

ENROLLMENT
Total Undergraduate Enrollment: 41,309
% Full-Time: 94%
% Male: 43%
% Female: 57%
% Out-of-State: 5%
% Fraternity: 13%
% Sorority: 15%
% On-Campus (All Undergraduate): 18%
Freshman Housing Required: No

% African-American: 5%
% Asian: 24%
% Hispanic: 28%
% White: 33%
% Other: 1%
% International: 4%
% Low-Income: 25%

ACADEMICS
Student-to-Faculty Ratio: 18 to 1
% of Classes Under 20: 39%
% of Classes 20-49: 37%
% of Classes 50 or More: 24%
% Full-Time Faculty: 82%
% Full-Time Faculty w/ Terminal Degree: 91%

Top Programs
Architecture
Biochemistry
Business
Communication
Computer Science
Engineering
Geosciences
Psychology

Retention Rate: 96%
4-Year Graduation Rate: 72%
6-Year Graduation Rate: 88%

Curricular Flexibility: Somewhat Flexible
Academic Rating: ★★★★

#CollegesWorthYourMoney

A ridiculously affordable flagship university that also happens to be one of the top public schools in the United States, the University of Texas at Austin serves up a quality undergraduate education on a massive scale. The school's 41,309 undergraduates enjoy a dizzying 150+ distinct degree programs and 12,000+ annual course offerings. Austin itself is a progressive city that has wide appeal, even to coastal dwellers; however, thanks to the automatic admission granted to all Texas students in the top 6% of their high school class, the university remains 90% Texas residents.

Inside the Classroom

Each year, 175 freshmen are admitted into the elite Plan II Honors Program, an interdisciplinary major created in 1935. One of the best honors programs in the country, Plan II students enjoy small class sizes and are required to complete a senior thesis. The school also offers its Liberal Arts Honors Program to an additional 130 students each year. All students must complete forty-two credit hours in the statewide Core Curriculum. That entails a first-year Signature Course in a small seminar environment, two English composition courses, one humanities course, two classes in American and Texas government, two in US history, one in the behavioral and social sciences, one in mathematics, three in the natural sciences, and one in the visual and performing arts.

An 18:1 student-to-faculty ratio and over 11,000 graduate students on campus render across-the-board tiny class sizes an impossibility. Still, an encouraging 39% of course sections enroll nineteen or fewer students; 24% of classes are filled with over 50 students. Opportunities for undergraduate research vary by school. An impressive 90% of engineering students conduct research or intern during their four years of study; others must compete for slots in programs such as the Freshman Research Initiative and Summer Research Scholars, or use the Eureka database to find individual professors offering research assistantships. A robust study abroad program boasts 400 offerings in 100+ foreign countries, and sees between 3,400 and 4,400 students participate each year.

The Cockrell School of Engineering is one of the most heralded undergraduate engineering schools around, while The McCombs School of Business cracks just about any top ten list and dominates in the specialty areas of accounting and marketing. UT's computer science department is also top-ranked, and regularly sends graduates to the world's best tech companies (see more below). In terms of sheer volume of degrees conferred, engineering is tied with biology (12%) followed by communication (11%), business (11%), and the social sciences (8%). Prestigious fellowship organizations love UT Austin grads just as much as employers do; in 2023, the school produced an impressive 17 Fulbright Scholars.

Outside the Classroom

You won't find many schools in this book where so few undergraduates live on campus. Last year, 18% of the total student body—and 63% of freshmen—resided on the 431-acre campus. The bulk of students live in three nearby neighborhoods: Downtown Austin, East Austin, and West Campus (which is not actually part of campus). There are more than 70 Greek organizations at UT Austin with sororities attracting 15% of women and fraternities enlisting 13% of men. Sports are a way of life at this institution. Approximately 500 student-athletes compete on twenty teams in NCAA Division I competition. UT has captured almost 200 Big 12 Championships across all sports in its history. Texas Memorial Stadium packs in 100,000+ on football Saturdays. In excess of 1,100 student organizations include hundreds of intramural and club sports options and a sprawling media network of newspapers, magazines, television, and radio stations to ensure that no interest goes unaccounted for. The city of Austin, a liberal enclave in a conservative state, is a perennial darling of "Best Places to Live" and "Best College Towns" lists. Few complain of boredom in a city with all the live music, good food, and culture one can handle.

Career Services

There are 15 career centers on the UT Austin campus, 11 of which cater to undergraduate students, as well as the Vick Center for Strategic Advising and Career Counseling, which serves undeclared students. With 51 full-time employees devoted to undergrads across those eleven career centers, the university offers an 810:1 student-to-counselor ratio, higher than many of the schools featured in this guide yet slightly better than average among universities close to UT's size. In the end, 79% of Longhorn alumni state that they found career services to be somewhere between "somewhat helpful" and "very helpful."

The scope of the offerings is overwhelming, as would be expected at a school with more than 41,000 undergraduates. For example, one recent Fall Science and Technology Career Fair drew 200 employers and 2,500 students. The Spring Communication Job & Internship Fair welcomes up to eighty-five employers and 1,000 students. In a single year, the McCombs College of Business Career Expo featured 180+ corporations.

Over one hundred employers engage in on-campus recruiting/interviewing with Texas Engineering students every year. An impressive 70% of Liberal Arts graduates complete at least one internship. Like many universities of its size, UT Austin cannot offer the hand-holding provided by many smaller liberal arts colleges, but it does provide plenty of on-campus networking opportunities for those bold enough to take advantage.

Professional Outcomes

Within the College of Liberal Arts, six months after graduating, 68% of Longhorns are employed, 24% have entered graduate school, and 6% are still seeking their next opportunity. The for-profit sector attracts 65% of those employed while 19% enter public sector employment and 16% pursue jobs at a nonprofit. At a school with nearly half a million living alumni, there is no shortage of major corporations that employ more than 500 UT Austin grads. In the tech realm, Google, Meta, Oracle, Microsoft, IBM, and Apple all meet that qualification, and giants such as Accenture, Amazon, and Uber also employ hundreds of Longhorns. Austin remains home to the largest number of graduates with the Houston, Dallas, and San Antonio areas next in popularity. Plenty of alumni also can be found in New York City and San Francisco. Starting salaries were solid and, as would be expected, fluctuated significantly by major. Engineering majors took home a median income of $79k, business majors took home $70k, and fine arts majors made in the $30k range.

University of Texas at Austin undergraduates go on to pursue advanced degrees in massive numbers with one-quarter electing to continue their educational journey right after completing their bachelor's. Many pursue advanced study at UT Austin itself, which offers more than one hundred graduate programs. Medical school acceptance rates were a very strong 57%, which is above the national average. The sheer volume of med school applicants is incredible; 965 applied in 2023 alone, the second most in the country. The university's own Dell Medical School is a common destination as are other Texas-based institutions like UT-Houston, UT-San Antonio, and Baylor. Others land at premier medical schools—including Harvard, Georgetown, and UVA—each year. No matter what advanced degree you choose to pursue, an impressive UT Austin transcript can open doors to any institution in the country.

Admission

Longhorn hopefuls totaled 59,767 in the most recent admissions cycle, roughly 30,000 more than at the break of the new millennium. At that time, the acceptance rate exceeded 60%; it is now only 31%. Among 2022-23 freshmen, the median standardized test scores were 1430 on the SAT and 32 on the ACT. The vast majority were situated in the top 10% of their high school classes—in one recent year, 86% earned such a distinction—and 96% were in the top quartile. The UT system has kept "outsiders" from making up a large percentage of the student body as 90% of current students hail from the Lone Star State. The school's policy of automatically accepting students from the top 6% of any Texas high school keeps quality homegrown freshmen pouring through the gates. There were an astounding 781 valedictorians and salutatorians in one recent cohort. Applicants to UT's business, computer science, and engineering majors will face the stiffest competition; earning entry typically requires Ivy-like credentials, especially if you're from out of state.

The university ranks pretty much every admissions factor as "considered," but it's safe to say that with such an onslaught of applications each year, the hard numbers of standardized test scores, GPA, and class rank are most essential. There is no early round at UT Austin, so all applicants are in the same boat. The school has no interest in demonstrated interest on the part of applicants because it enjoys a relatively high yield rate approaching 50%. While the school accepts roughly 2,300 transfer students per year, that's only 34% of those who apply. That differs greatly from many other elite state universities where transferring is much easier than getting admitted directly out of high school. The University of Texas at Austin is the flagship school of the UT system and among the largest genuinely elite schools in the entire country. Texas residency, top-of-the-class academic performance, and solid test scores give you the best chance to get in.

Worth Your Money?

An annual in-state cost of attendance of $31k-$34k for a UT Austin degree is one of the best bargains anywhere in the country. In addition, 46% of undergrads qualify for need-based aid with average grants that are a hair under $14,000. Out of state, the sticker price for full COA is $62k-$69k, not an unreasonable sum for what you'll receive, particularly if you are majoring in business, engineering, or computer science. If you are a resident of Texas, there are no qualifiers—UT Austin is unquestionably worth every dollar.

FINANCIAL
Institutional Type: Public
In-State Tuition: $11,698
Out-of-State Tuition: $41,070
Room & Board: $13,058
Books & Supplies: $724

Avg. Need-Based Grant: $13,616
Avg. % of Need Met: 81%

Avg. Merit-Based Award: $4,152
% Receiving (Freshmen w/o Need): 5%

Avg. Cumulative Debt: $21,809
% of Students Borrowing: 41%

CAREER
Who Recruits
1. Shell
2. General Electric
3. Affigen, LLC
4. Merck
5. SnapStream

Notable Internships
1. Visa
2. Uber
3. Boeing

Top Employers
1. IBM
2. Google
3. Microsoft
4. Accenture
5. Amazon

Where Alumni Work
1. Austin
2. Houston
3. Dallas
4. San Antonio
5. San Francisco

Earnings
College Scorecard (10-YR Post-Entry): $72,713
PayScale (Early Career): $65,900
PayScale (Mid-Career): $121,800
PayScale 20-Year ROI: $731,000

RANKINGS
Money: 4.5
U.S. News: 32, National Universities
Wall Street Journal/THE: 118
Washington Monthly: 87, National Universities

OVERGENERALIZATIONS
Students are:
Crazy about the Longhorns
Diverse
Always saying nice things about Austin
Working hard and playing hard
Politically liberal

COLLEGE OVERLAPS
Southern Methodist University
Rice University
Texas A&M University - College Station
University of Michigan
University of California, Berkeley

University of Utah

Salt Lake City, Utah | 801-581-8761

The oldest state school west of the Missouri River, the University of Utah dates back to 1850 when it was founded as the University of Deseret. As the 21st century rolls along, the over 26,000 undergraduate Utes continue to enjoy an institution that is widely recognized for its Eccles School of Business and College of Engineering. The university's 16 colleges and schools house 100 undergraduate programs and 90 graduate degree programs that draw students from all 50 states and 80+ countries. Unlike BYU, this flagship public university is a genuine mix of Mormons (roughly one-third) and non-Mormons, giving it a more secular and liberal vibe than BYU.

Inside the Classroom
No matter which college or major you choose, you will have to move through lower-division courses in writing, quantitative reasoning, math, statistics/logic, and American institutions. Eight classes under the "Intellectual Exploration" umbrella come next, covering the areas of fine arts, humanities, physical/life sciences, and social/behavioral sciences. Additionally, everyone pursuing a bachelor of arts completes at least two years of a foreign language, and all bachelor of science students complete two "quantitative intensive" courses. A degree will necessitate the completion of 122 credit hours with at least 40 in upper-division coursework.

For a school with an 18:1 student-to-faculty ratio and plenty of graduate students, Utah's classes are, for the most part, reasonably small. Forty-four percent of courses enroll 19 students or fewer while 17% are on the larger side, enrolling 50 or more students. Those seeking more personalized mentorship can pursue opportunities through the Office of Undergraduate Research, which connects with 2,700+ students per year and, in one recent year, saw 590 individuals become Undergraduate Research Opportunities Program (UROP) Scholars; 230 members of that group went on to present at the Undergraduate Research Symposium. More than 600 undergraduates at the University of Utah leave campus to study abroad each year in one of over 40 countries. The school has aggressively sought to disseminate information about study abroad programs in recent years, and those efforts have led to an increase in participation.

The business, engineering, and computer science programs all enjoy impressive reviews from just about any publication that ranks schools by discipline. Those three areas of study also happen to be three of the most frequently entered programs with 13% of degrees conferred in business, 9% in engineering, and 8% in computer science. Other popular majors include the social sciences (14%), psychology (8%), communication/journalism (6%), and health professions (6%). Utes do not pursue competitive scholarships in massive numbers, but the school did see four Fulbright Scholarship winners and a phenomenal 17 National Science Foundation Graduate Research Fellowship winners last year.

Outside the Classroom
The university's Salt Lake City campus covers more than 1,500 acres and offers breathtaking vistas of the surrounding 15,000-foot-tall Wasatch Mountains. What it does not offer is the capacity to house a high percentage of its students on campus; just 59% of freshmen live in the school's six first-year dormitories. There are seven apartment complexes for upperclassmen and graduate students, but only a sliver of the total population resides in them. The university does run an off-campus housing website to help undergrads find places to live. Only 7-8% of undergrads join Greek life; many more form bonds through the school's 600+ clubs and organizations. Competing in the Pac-12, the Utes are a force to be reckoned with. The men's basketball team is in the NCAA's top ten for all-time victories, and it has sent countless players to the NBA. The football team is also a powerhouse whose average attendance has been greater than the stadium's capacity for over a decade straight. Many show their school spirit by joining the raucous "Muss" (Mighty Utah Student Section) and taking part in Crimson Nights, popular school-wide parties held in the A. Ray Olpin Student Union.

Career Services
Twenty-six professional employees work directly with or on behalf of undergraduate students within the University of Utah Career & Professional Development Center (CPDC). Its 1,014:1 student-to-counselor ratio is nothing unusual for a large public university, but the office does a fantastic job utilizing its personnel. For example, eleven employees' sole job responsibilities are to provide career coaching to undergraduates; an additional three coaches work exclusively with graduate students. In one recent school year, career coaches met individually with 2,600+ students. The office also hosted 10 career fairs/expos that attracted 730+ hiring organizations and over 5,000 undergraduate attendees. Staff also took the center's show directly into the classroom, engaging with 4,400 students in over 160 classroom workshops.

Fifty-six percent of Utah grads report landing at least one internship, 16% gain two such experiences, and 14% procure three or more. Roughly half of those experiences are paid internships. Notable organizations where multiple Utes have interned in recent years include Amazon, the American Heart Association, Citigroup, Disney, Symantec, the US Department of Veterans Affairs, and the Utah Jazz. More than 15,000 students log on to Handshake to explore the more than 30,000 jobs and internships posted in a single academic year.

Professional Outcomes

Sixty-three percent of recent graduates planned to enter full-time employment within six months of earning their bachelor's degree while one-quarter were jumping directly into an advanced degree program. More than four-fifths of those graduating planned to remain in the state of Utah, but there are significant numbers of alumni clustered in San Francisco, Los Angeles, and Seattle. Employers hiring the greatest number of Utes include Intermountain Healthcare, Goldman Sachs, Amazon, Microsoft, Adobe, Pluralsight, and Lucid. Additional companies of note that hired three or more recent grads include Apple, Deloitte, eBay, Fidelity Investments, Lockheed Martin, Northrop Grumman, and PwC. The average starting salary is $65,786, and the median is $58,240.

Turning our attention to the outcomes for the 25% headed to graduate/professional school, the university typically sees anywhere from 200 to 350 seniors apply to medical school each year. Their success rate has been as low as 36% and as high as 38% in recent years. In one five-year period, the school sent 202 students to its own University of Utah School of Medicine, 13 to the St. Louis University School of Medicine, and 16 to the University of Colorado School of Medicine. Utes also enjoyed multiple med school acceptances to the likes of Harvard, Tufts, Tulane, Columbia, and Dartmouth. Looking at law school applicants, 73% of the 200+ seniors and alumni applying a couple of years ago were accepted into at least one school; the average LSAT score was 155, and the SJ Quinney College of Law at the University of Utah welcomes many of its own graduates.

Admission

Living in a world where elite universities grab headlines with 8.9% acceptance rates, it's always nice to come across a quality institution that accepts 89% of those who apply. Utah received over 21,072 applications to the Class of 2026, down from 24,000+ three cycles prior. The acceptance rate for the Class of 2023 was 62%, 27% lower than for the more recent cohort. Among those who submitted standardized test results, the ACT was far more popular than the SAT, and the mid-50% ACT range was 22-29; the SAT range was 1200-1380. The average GPA for enrolled freshmen was 3.66, and 10% earned a perfect 4.0.

In evaluating applicants, Utah looks foremost at the academic GPA and the level of rigor of the secondary school record. The school is presently test-optional. As a result, standardized test scores are merely "considered" alongside other secondary criteria including class rank, extracurricular activities, and talent/ability. The admissions committee also considers items like familial responsibilities, extraordinary circumstances, and a "significant commitment to community engagement, citizenship, and leadership." There is an early action option for the University of Utah, but it does not offer a binding early decision option.

Worth Your Money?

For a resident of the Beehive State, tuition and fees add up to less than $10k, and living on campus will set you back another $14k. As crazy as this sounds, the fact that even those receiving no aid can graduate from the University of Utah for under $100,000 qualifies the school as a major bargain in today's terms. Tuition for out-of-state students is three times that figure, but it can still return value, particularly since the university's areas of greatest academic strength—business, CS, and engineering—also tend to yield higher-paying early career jobs. Whether looking at in-state or out-of-state fees, there is no cheaper school in the Pac-12 or Big Ten than Utah.

FINANCIAL
Institutional Type: Public
In-State Tuition: $9,103
Out-of-State Tuition: $31,861
Room & Board: $12,398
Books & Supplies: $1,100

Avg. Need-Based Grant: $10,483
Avg. % of Need Met: 61%

Avg. Merit-Based Award: $7,643
% Receiving (Freshmen w/o Need): 24%

Avg. Cumulative Debt: $20,236
% of Students Borrowing: 33%

CAREER
Who Recruits
1. Adobe
2. Goldman Sachs
3. Intermountain Healthcare
4. Amazon Web Services
5. Qualtrics

Notable Internships
1. Northrop Grumman
2. Thatcher Group
3. Northwestern Mutual

Top Employers
1. Intermountain Healthcare
2. Amazon
3. Goldman Sachs
4. Microsoft
5. Adobe

Where Alumni Work
1. Salt Lake City, UT
2. Provo, UT
3. San Francisco
4. Los Angeles
5. India

Earnings
College Scorecard (10-YR Post-Entry): $64,456
PayScale (Early Career): $68,100
PayScale (Mid-Career): $125,900
PayScale 20-Year ROI: $572,000

RANKINGS
Money: 4.5
U.S. News: 115, National Universities
Wall Street Journal/THE: 43
Washington Monthly: 58, National Universities

OVERGENERALIZATIONS
Students are:
Politically balanced
Outdoorsy
Religious
Only a short drive from home (i.e., Most come from UT or nearby states)
Always saying nice things about Salt Lake City

COLLEGE OVERLAPS
Arizona State University
Brigham Young University
Utah State University
University of Arizona
University of Colorado Boulder

University of Virginia

Charlottesville, Virginia | 434-982-3200

When Thomas Jefferson helped to found the University of Virginia in 1819, our nation's third president did more than just assist in securing the funds—he also personally designed some of the campus' now-famous architecture, planned the curriculum, and recruited the first faculty members. As the so-called "father" of the school, Jefferson would undoubtedly be thrilled with what his progeny has gone on to achieve. Two hundred years after its first cornerstone was laid, UVA has become one of the most iconic public universities in the United States where state residents can get an Ivy-level education at a bargain price.

Inside the Classroom

Undergrads can study within one of seven colleges/schools: the College of Arts & Sciences, the School of Engineering and Applied Science, the McIntire School of Commerce, the School of Architecture, the School of Nursing, the Batten School of Leadership & Public Policy, and the Curry School of Education. Within the College of Arts & Sciences, undergraduates must complete 30 credits worth of Area Requirements broken down as follows: Natural Science and Mathematics (12), Social Sciences (6), Humanities (6), Historical Studies (3), and Non-Western Perspectives (3). Further Competency Requirements include a First Writing Requirement, a Second Writing Requirement, and a Foreign Language Requirement. The 225-250 students per freshman class who are selected for the Echols Scholars Program are not bound by any competency or area requirements.

The University of Virginia sports a 14:1 student-to-faculty ratio, a very strong figure for a large public institution. As such, the school is able to offer many small classes like you would find at an elite liberal arts college. In fact, 15% of sections boast a single-digit enrollment and 48% contain 19 or fewer students. Undergraduate research opportunities can be challenging to uncover at any large school where graduate students get the prime spots, yet, UVA does offer a multitude of opportunities. To cite examples, every single engineering major completes one major research project, the biology department has 230 students each semester participating in research, and physics students are given the chance to get their names on published work. The classroom at UVA extends well beyond Charlottesville as one-third enjoy a semester abroad in one of 65 countries around the world.

The two most commonly conferred degree areas are in liberal arts/general studies (22%) and the social sciences (14%). Engineering (11%), business/marketing (8%), and biology (7%) are next in sheer popularity. The McIntire School of Commerce has a glowing reputation in the finance/accounting realm and the School of Engineering and Applied Science is just as highly respected. Other notable departmental strengths include computer science, economics, and political philosophy, policy, and law. Cavaliers are extremely competitive in the pursuit of prestigious national scholarships as well. In a single recent school year, UVA produced 22 Fulbright Scholars, five Critical Language Scholars, and a Marshall Scholar.

Outside the Classroom
Last year, just 38% of all students lived on UVA's campus, although 99% of freshmen resided on the school's vast 1,682-acre grounds. Greek life is popular as 35% sign up for fraternity and sorority life. The Cavaliers compete in 27 varsity sports teams (13 men's and 14 women's) in the Atlantic Coast Conference. Approximately 2,100 students are members of 65 club sports teams and many others participate in intramural athletics. As you would expect at such a large institution, there are 1,000+ clubs available in everything from acrobatics to high-powered rocketry; the process of joining some of the more competitive clubs can be fierce (i.e., the University Judiciary Committee). A cappella is a beloved pastime at the school and there are countless groups to consider. Outside of being the site of a disturbing rally in 2017, Charlottesville is generally considered to be one of the most student-friendly college towns. There is no shortage of culture, craft breweries, and outdoor recreation opportunities. Plenty of Jefferson and Madison-related history can be explored nearby and a trip to the state capital of Richmond will take you just over an hour. Those looking to fly home for the holidays will enjoy the convenience of having the Charlottesville-Albemarle Airport just eight miles from campus.

Career Services
The UVA Career Center employs 30 full-time staff members giving them a student-to-advisor ratio of 583:1, which is in the average range compared to schools in this guide and a very respectable level of support for a school of the University of Virginia's size. This well-resourced office encourages one-on-one appointments, has ample drop-in hours and daily "Coffee Chats with Career Counselors," and hosts regular "Career Communities" that help students interested in a specific field like Business & Technology or Science and Sustainability.

The majority of Class of 2022 grads learned about their first job through a career services-affiliated source such as Handshake or an internship. On that front, 528 recent respondents reported having one internship while at UVA while 441 held two and 294 held three. The university hosts large-scale general career fairs in the fall and spring as well as many discipline-specific events. The Engineering, Science, and Technology Career Fair attracts over 2,000 students and 230 companies each year. There are close to a quarter of a million Cavalier alumni and many are happy to help current students find internships and employment or offer some level of mentorship. Each year, more than 1,000 alums return to campus for this purpose.

Professional Outcomes

Upon receiving their degree, 95% of the Class of 2022 immediately joined the workforce or headed directly to graduate school; 5% of graduates were still looking for their next destination. Industries attracting the greatest number of freshly-minted graduates were internet & software, higher education, and management consulting. The companies that scooped up the greatest number of 2022 graduates were Capital One (85), Deloitte (46), Amazon (38), and Bain & Co. (26). The average starting salary for those finding employment was a robust $90k. Large numbers of recent graduates migrate to Washington, DC, and New York City, and many others head to Boston, San Francisco, Seattle, Charlotte, and Atlanta.

Among the 2022 grads who decided to continue their education, 248 enrolled in an advanced degree program at UVA—the next most popular destinations were Columbia University (21), Virginia Commonwealth University (18), Johns Hopkins (13), and UPenn (10). In recent years, medical school acceptance rates for Cavaliers have beaten national averages. In the last six years, UVA applicants to MD programs have enjoyed between a 52-60% acceptance rate versus the national average range of 42-45%. Virginia grads head to a wide range of medical colleges including the nation's best like Johns Hopkins, Emory, Cornell, Harvard, Tufts, and Georgetown.

Admission

The University of Virginia received 50,941 applications for a place in its Class of 2026, more than double the number received in 2005. Just 19% of this group were welcomed into the freshman class of 2022-23. Those who went on to attend the university possessed mid-50% SAT scores of 1400-1540; the ACT range was 32-34. Eighty-five percent of freshmen earned a place in the top decile of their high school class and 96% landed in the top quartile. The average weighted GPA was a stunning 4.35.

Six factors are rated by the UVA committee as being "very important" to the admissions process, headlined by state residency. In the regular decision cycle, the school offers admission to 13% of locals but just 8% of those hailing from outside of the state. In seeking to maintain at least a two-thirds majority of Virginians, the student body is presently comprised of two-thirds state residents. Other highly ranked factors included rigor of secondary school record, class rank, GPA, recommendations, and character/personal qualities. Criteria ranked as still "important" include standardized test scores, the application essay, extracurricular activities, and talent/ability. Early decision was just added back into the equation two years ago and the acceptance rate for the Class of 2026 was 45%.

Worth Your Money?

A rare public university that meets 100% of all students' demonstrated financial need, UVA serves up an average of $35k per year to qualifying freshmen. Roughly one-third of students take out loans and the mean amount of debt for those individuals is less than the average college graduate in the country. Residents of Virginia pay an annual cost of attendance of just $39k while out-of-state undergrads are met with a COA of almost $77,000. This school, with its sparkling national reputation and strong graduate outcomes, is worth your money either way, but the real bargain is enjoyed by those whose taxes help fund the university.

FINANCIAL
Institutional Type: Public
In-State Tuition: $22,323
Out-of-State Tuition: $58,950
Room & Board: $14,700
Books & Supplies: $1,480

Avg. Need-Based Grant: $30,370
Avg. % of Need Met: 100%

Avg. Merit-Based Award: $5,389
% Receiving (Freshmen w/o Need): 7%

Avg. Cumulative Debt: $26,211
% of Students Borrowing: 33%

CAREER
Who Recruits
1. Yext
2. Pariveda
3. Oak Hill Advisors
4. Altria
5. Harris Williams & Co.

Notable Internships
1. Strategic Investment Group
2. NBCUniversal
3. Proctor & Gamble

Top Employers
1. Capital One
2. Deloitte
3. EY
4. Google
5. Accenture

Where Alumni Work
1. Washington, DC
2. Charlottesville, VA
3. New York City
4. Richmond, VA
5. San Francisco

Earnings
College Scorecard (10-YR Post-Entry): $80,584
PayScale (Early Career): $69,800
PayScale (Mid-Career): $131,700
PayScale 20-Year ROI: $909,000

RANKINGS
Money: 5
U.S. News: 24, National Universities
Wall Street Journal/THE: 84
Washington Monthly: 42, National Universities

OVERGENERALIZATIONS
Students are:
More likely to rush a fraternity/sorority
Working hard and playing hard
Involved/invested in campus life
Always saying nice things about Charlottesville
Crazy about the Cavaliers

COLLEGE OVERLAPS
College of William & Mary
Duke University
University of North Carolina at Chapel Hill
University of Pennsylvania
Virginia Tech

Seattle, Washington | 206-543-9686

Under the perpetually rainy skies and in the birthplace of grunge, Starbucks, and modern romantic comedies rests the flagship campus of the University of Washington system, home to 36,872 undergraduate students, only around 60% of whom benefit from the uber-affordable in-state rate. International and out-of-state students have begun flocking to UW in recent years to enjoy the literally dozens of top-ranked academic programs and the deep connections to a handful of corporations located nearby that also happen to be some of the most desirable employers anywhere on the planet. With thirteen colleges/schools with undergraduate programs, 180+ majors, and 6,500 courses, UW can meet the needs of just about anyone.

Inside the Classroom

UDub's quarter-based academic calendar keeps students on their toes as most students take three or four classes in each of the 10-week fall, winter, and spring quarters. A strong honors program gives students access to smaller classes, but you'll likely need a 1450+ SAT score to access the program. Core curricular requirements vary by school. Some undergraduate colleges require a foreign language, but others do not. However, all students complete coursework in three Areas of Knowledge: visual, literary, and performing arts; individual societies; and the natural world. Freshmen can enroll in First-Year Interest Groups or Collegium Seminars that offer small classes and engaging topics.

The university does have a relatively high 21:1 student-to-faculty ratio that makes consistently small undergraduate class sizes a logistical impossibility. Over one-third of sections contain 40 or more students compared to 28% of sections that contain fewer than 20. Still, there are opportunities for personal connections with professors as evidenced by the fact that 55% of graduates complete a faculty-mentored research project. The study abroad rate of participation has climbed steadily since the turn of the millennium; roughly one-fifth now spend a semester in a foreign locale.

The most commonly earned degrees at the University of Washington are in the social sciences (13%), biology (12%), computer science (11%), and business (8%). There are simply too many stellar majors for there to be too large a concentration in any one or two areas. The College of Engineering, which includes the revered Paul G. Allen College of Computer Science & Engineering, is one of the absolute best in the nation, but UW also boasts strong programs in everything from business to social work to environmental science. Employers adore Huskies, but so do competitive scholarship organizations. In 2023, an impressive 12 grads and alumni were awarded Fulbrights and the school has produced 35 Rhodes Scholars in its illustrious history.

Outside the Classroom

A solid 83% of UDub students who live on campus rate the experience as "excellent." Unfortunately, only a paltry 29% of the undergraduate student body actually do so, and, even among freshmen, just under 70% reside in the dorms. Some find housing in one of the school's 70 Greek organizations that attract 13% of men and 12% of women. Most live in houses and apartments in the University District of the city; downtown Seattle is a short car or bus ride away. Students come together to take part in the 1,000+ student organizations including the Aerial Robotics Club or the Creating a Company Club. Whatever your pleasure, the Husky Union Building (HUB) is, indeed, a great place to get involved. Heck, it even has its own bowling alley. If bowling isn't athletic enough for you, enjoy the 22 varsity sports teams that compete in the Pac-12 Conference. Football reigns supreme as UDub boasts the largest stadium in the Pacific Northwest, and it is known to reach deafening noise levels on fall Saturdays. Recreation is aided by state-of-the-art fitness facilities that include a pool, rock climbing wall, driving range, and Waterfront Activities Center on Lake Washington. Gear for hiking, boating, and camping can be rented from the UWild Gear Garage.

Career Services

There are 12 full-time employees at the Career and Internship Center, which is housed within the Division of Student Life. Additional staff members serving undergraduate students can be found within the School of Engineering and School of Business to bring the total of career counselors to 24, a relatively small number considering that they serve more than 36,000 undergraduate students. The resulting 1,536:1 student-to-advisor ratio is among the worst of any school featured in this book; however, unlike some understaffed career services offices (at schools that do make the cut for inclusion in this guide), the CIC at the University of Washington has no shortage of brag-worthy accomplishments.

UW's Career and Internship Center brings close to 400 employers to the Seattle campus each school year. In addition to the hard-to-match local corporations (chronicled in the next section), companies like Wells Fargo, Adobe Systems, Tesla, Bloomberg, Comcast, and Dell recruit and/or conduct interviews on campus. Career fairs are plentiful throughout the year and include specialty expos for data science, engineering, and business. In part due to the prime Seattle location, internships are not hard to locate; 78% of 2022 grads completed at least one internship, and many completed two or three. An excellent 89% of recent grads classified their first job as being "career-related." Thanks to some extremely impressive corporate connections and an alumni base that is embedded in some of the country's most desirable employers, UW's career services successfully overcomes its numbers disadvantage.

Professional Outcomes

A few months after graduation, 73% of Class of 2022 graduates had found employment, 17% had continued their education in graduate/professional school, and 5% were still hunting for their first job. The most popular employers of the Class of 2022 included Google, Amazon, Microsoft, Boeing, and KPMG. Including all living alumni, more than 6,000 Huskies currently work for Bill Gates, and more than 4,000+ work for each of Boeing and Amazon. Meta, Apple, Nordstrom, Starbucks, and Tableau Software all employ at least 400 UDub alums. The Greater Seattle area is far and away the home of choice for UW grads, followed in popularity by San Francisco, Portland, Los Angeles, and New York.

Of those headed to graduate school, just over half remain in state, mostly at the University of Washington itself to become one of the school's 16,222 graduate students. Seventy-five percent of graduate students were pursuing an MS/MA degree and 20% entered doctoral programs. Large numbers of 2022 grads also packed their bags for Columbia, Johns Hopkins, and USC. The University of Washington has one of the best medical schools in the country, and 95% of accepted med students come from Washington, Wyoming, Alaska, Montana, and Idaho, thus giving UW graduates an inside track. The University of Washington School of Law is a top 50 institution that gives UW undergrads an excellent at-home option for a legal education. However, multiple graduates have also gone on to study law at Stanford, Harvard, and Fordham in recent years.

Admission

UW-Seattle admitted 48% of the 52,488 applicants desiring to join the Husky Class of 2026. On the SAT, the mid-50% range of 2022-23 freshmen was 1320-1500; the ACT range was 29-34. An impressive 75% of attending undergrads sported high school GPAs of 3.75 and above, and the average GPA was 3.83. Interestingly, the admissions standards for residents, out-of-staters, and international students are similar. However, differences do exist across desired majors, with applicants to programs in engineering and computer science facing the toughest odds. Other than a rise in SAT scores, not a ton has changed at UW admissions in the past decade. Back in 2009, the acceptance rate was a somewhat comparable 61% and the average GPA was almost identical, but the 25th percentile SAT score was 1100 compared to 1320 today.

UW officially became a test-optional institution five years ago. Predictable factors like GPA and rigor of high school coursework are designated as "very important" by the admissions committee, but so is the application essay, a surprise given the volume of applications received. Extracurricular activities occupy the realm of "important" factors alongside talent/ability, first-generation status, work experience, and volunteer experience. The committee also recommends "taking full advantage of senior year, demonstrating a positive grade trend," and "exercising significant responsibility in a family, community, or employment situation or through activities."

Worth Your Money?

With an annual in-state tuition of just under $13,000 and a direct pipeline to many of the world's top corporations that happen to have their headquarters in Washington State, UDub is a can't-miss option if you get the hometown discount. Many nonresidents, particularly those pursuing computer science, engineering, and business, also find a good value, even at a total cost of attendance for four years of about $260k. Students pursuing other majors may do better looking at other reputable yet less pricey options.

FINANCIAL
Institutional Type: Public
In-State Tuition: $12,643
Out-of-State Tuition: $41,997
Room & Board: $17,982
Books & Supplies: $900

Avg. Need-Based Grant: $19,107
Avg. % of Need Met: 74%

Avg. Merit-Based Award: $4,090
% Receiving (Freshmen w/o Need): 10%

Avg. Cumulative Debt: $18,136
% of Students Borrowing: 28%

CAREER
Who Recruits
1. Samsung
2. Vulcan Capital
3. Alaska Airlines
4. Liberty Mutual
5. HealthPoint

Notable Internships
1. Boeing
2. Nordstrom
3. United Nations

Top Employers
1. Microsoft
2. Boeing
3. Amazon
4. Google
5. T-Mobile

Where Alumni Work
1. Seattle
2. San Francisco
3. Portland, OR
4. Los Angeles
5. New York City

Earnings
College Scorecard (10-YR Post-Entry): $74,063
PayScale (Early Career): $67,400
PayScale (Mid-Career): $121,400
PayScale 20-Year ROI: $768,000

RANKINGS
Money: 4.5
U.S. News: 40, National Universities
Wall Street Journal/THE: 134
Washington Monthly: 14, National Universities

OVERGENERALIZATIONS
Students are:
Environmentally conscious
Politically liberal
Outdoorsy
Crazy about the Huskies
Diverse

COLLEGE OVERLAPS
Boston University
University of California, Berkeley
University of California, Los Angeles
University of California, San Diego
University of Southern California

University of Wisconsin - Madison

Madison, Wisconsin | 608-262-3961

ADMISSION
Admission Rate: 49%
Admission Rate - Men: 45%
Admission Rate - Women: 53%
EA Admission Rate: Not Reported
ED Admission Rate: Not Offered
ED Admits as % of Total Admits: Not Offered
Admission Rate (5-Year Trend): -5%
% of Admits Attending (Yield): 29%
Transfer Admission Rate: 53%

SAT Reading/Writing (Middle 50%): 660-730
SAT Math (Middle 50%): 690-780
ACT Composite (Middle 50%): 28-33

% Graduated in Top 10% of HS Class: 54%
% Graduated in Top 25% of HS Class: 87%
% Graduated in Top 50% of HS Class: 99%

Demonstrated Interest: Not Considered
Legacy Status: Not Considered
Racial/Ethnic Status: Considered
Admission Interview Offered: No

ENROLLMENT
Total Undergraduate Enrollment: 37,230
% Full-Time: 95%
% Male: 47%
% Female: 53%
% Out-of-State: 46%
% Fraternity: 9%
% Sorority: 8%
% On-Campus (All Undergraduate): 26%
Freshman Housing Required: No

% African-American: 2%
% Asian: 10%
% Hispanic: 8%
% White: 62%
% Other: 3%
% International: 10%
% Low-Income: 16%

ACADEMICS
Student-to-Faculty Ratio: 18 to 1
% of Classes Under 20: 44%
% of Classes 20-49: 34%
% of Classes 50 or More: 23%
% Full-Time Faculty: 86%
% Full-Time Faculty w/ Terminal Degree: 92%

Top Programs
Business
Chemistry
Communication Arts
Computer Science
Economics
Engineering
Political Science
Psychology

Retention Rate: 95%
4-Year Graduation Rate: 72%
6-Year Graduation Rate: 89%

Curricular Flexibility: Somewhat Flexible
Academic Rating: ★★★★

#CollegesWorthYourMoney

One of the country's best state institutions, the University of Wisconsin-Madison has become a coveted destination for a growing number of high-caliber teens far outside Wisconsin's seventy-two counties. In fact, the undergraduate student body of 37,230 is now comprised of 46% out-of-staters/foreigners. The school's over 900-acre campus is less than one mile from the Wisconsin State Capitol building and rates as one of the Midwest's most gorgeous collegiate settings. Even more attractive than the scenery are the 230+ undergraduate majors, and this tough-to-match selection includes an array of renowned academic programs that rank among the best in the United States.

Inside the Classroom

There are eight schools and colleges that serve undergraduates: the College of Letters and Science, the Wisconsin School of Business, the College of Engineering, the School of Nursing, the School of Education, the School of Pharmacy, the School of Human Ecology, and the College of Agricultural and Life Sciences. Regardless of your home school, breadth is the goal of the university's general education requirements that all Badgers must complete. As a result, thirteen to fifteen credits must be spread over three areas: the natural sciences, the behavioral and social sciences, and the humanities and arts. Required courses in ethnic studies, communications, and quantitative reasoning round out the mandated portion of a Badger education.

At UW-Madison, undergrads can expect a mix of large and small classes; 44% of sections enroll fewer than 20 students, but 23% contain more than 50 students. The student-to-faculty ratio is 18:1, and roughly 12,500 graduate students suck up their share of attention. Undergraduate research opportunities exist, but the onus is on the student to show initiative and procure the placement. However, for over 25 years, the school has hosted an Undergraduate Symposium where hundreds of students present. Participation is much higher when it comes to study abroad programs. Over 50% of students participate each year and there are 260 programs in 65 countries to choose from.

Looking for top-ranked business or engineering programs? If so, Madison is a perfect spot for you. In terms of pure percentage of degrees conferred, business (18%), biology (12%), the social sciences (11%), and engineering (10%) are the most popular. The school's guiding principle known as "The Wisconsin Idea" is that a college education should influence lives outside the confines of the classroom. Thus, it is fitting that the university is the number one producer of Peace Corps volunteers. In 2023, a phenomenal 52 students earned National Science Foundation Graduate Research Fellowships and two were named Goldwater Scholars.

Outside the Classroom

One of the best college football towns in America, it would be wrong not to lead with the rowdy, joyous atmosphere inside Camp Randall Stadium on fall Saturdays. A sea of red fills the stadium as 80,000 fans rabidly root for the Badgers and create a quintessential Midwestern college experience. Football worship, along with the other 22 Division I sports teams, unite a campus that is not exactly centralized. While the majority of freshmen reside in university-owned housing, only a touch over one-fifth of the total undergraduate population lives on campus. Fraternities and sororities are available but hardly dominate the scene as only 8-9% of Badgers join a Greek organization; still, there are sixty Greek organizations on campus with thousands of members. In excess of 900 student-run clubs and organizations are at your disposal including near-constant events hosted by the student union such as concerts, sports viewing, guest lecturers, films, and local theater productions. Nature enthusiasts don't have to travel far for hiking, boating, and birdwatching because the 300-acre Lakeshore Nature Preserve is on campus and includes four miles of shoreline along Lake Mendota. Madison is consistently ranked as one of the top college towns in the entire country because it possesses a hard-to-match combination of safety, beauty, and a booming restaurant and commercial district.

Career Services

There are ten career centers on the UW-Madison campus that, collectively, employ 53 professionals dedicated to career advising, internship coordination, employer relations, and other career-oriented tasks. The SuccessWorks initiative caters to students in the College of Letters & Sciences (which accounts for half of enrolled undergrads) and is the largest such office with twenty-one staff members. The Career Exploration Center (CEC) is a cross-college career services office serving those who are undecided on an area of study. Wisconsin also operates career services offices dedicated to pre-law and pre-health as well as discipline-specific offices housed in each undergraduate school and college. Wisconsin's overall 702:1 student-to-counselor ratio is higher than average compared to many schools featured in this guide, but that figure is relatively strong for a school of its size.

There are some impressive statistics that elevate UW-Madison from run-of-the-mill status with regard to career services offerings. For one, 87% of graduates "agreed" or "strongly agreed" that UW-Madison prepared them for the next step on their career path. More tangibly, 67% of grads report completing at least one internship during their four years of study. Career fairs are sweeping enough to accommodate an undergraduate population of 35,000+. The Fall Career & Internship Fair draws 320+ employers, including many top corporations, and over 3,600 students annually. Other fairs include a massive Spring Career & Internship Fair, the UW-Madison STEM Fair, and the Public Service Fair (also held in the spring). Thanks to plenty of targeted and accessible career guidance within every undergrad's home college and solid employment and grad school results, UW's career services are held in high regard by our staff.

Professional Outcomes

Forty-six percent of job-seeking University of Wisconsin-Madison grads had already received and/or accepted offers when they received their diplomas. The top employers of recent graduates include UW-Madison, Epic, Kohl's, Oracle, Deloitte, and UW Health. However, across all graduating years, corporations employing a minimum of 250 Badger alumni include Google, Target, Microsoft, Amazon, Apple, PwC, Accenture, and Meta. The bulk of grads settle in the Madison area, Milwaukee, Chicago, or the Greater Minneapolis-St. Paul area. Those who leave the Midwest head to locations such as New York City, DC, San Francisco, Los Angeles, and Denver.

Of the 28% of recent grads who enrolled directly in graduate/professional school, 60% stayed at UW-Madison, and more than five members of last year's class headed to each of the following prestigious institutions: Columbia, Northwestern, Carnegie Mellon, University of Chicago, Johns Hopkins, NYU, and UCLA. Clearly, an undergraduate degree from Wisconsin will serve you well when applying to elite graduate programs across the country. In 2023, there were 477 UW-Madison students applying to medical school, and, in a typical year, 55% are admitted. The University of Wisconsin-Madison's own top-ranked medical school takes a high percentage of homegrown talent as does its top-30 law school.

Admission

Forty-nine percent of the 60,260 applicants for the Class of 2026 gained entry into UW-Madison, but that figure hardly tells the tale of how selective this flagship university has become. Enrolled freshmen possessed median test scores of 1440 on the SAT and 30 on the ACT. The average high school GPA was 3.88 and 54% placed in the top decile of their graduating class; 87% were in the top quartile. A handful of years ago, the SAT range was a lower 1170-1410, which is partially attributable to SAT inflation; the acceptance rate was nearly identical to the 2022-23 figure.

The rigor of an applicant's record and GPA are rated as "very important" by UW-Madison admissions staff. Essays, recommendations, and test scores round out the list of "important" factors. There are no admissions interviews, and demonstrated interest is not considered. It's important to point out that out-of-state applicants face significantly longer odds than in-state applicants. The number of out-of-state applications for this university has grown rapidly in recent years. As a result, nonresidents should have test scores closer to the 75th percentile and rank in the top 10% of their high school classes while applicants from Wisconsin can get away with less stellar academic profiles.

Worth Your Money?

Wisconsin residents pay less than $29k per year total cost of attendance, an incredible bargain for such a high-quality educational experience with fantastic graduate outcomes. The growing number of students who come from other states or countries helps keep the UW coffers full as such students fork over $58k annually. Roughly one-third of students who applied for need-based aid received an average grant of $18k. For locals, the decision to attend Wisconsin is an easy one if you are offered admission. Outsiders still can benefit from the school's stellar reputation and vast alumni networks, but they will pay a significant sum for the privilege.

FINANCIAL
Institutional Type: Public
In-State Tuition: $11,205
Out-of-State Tuition: $40,603
Room & Board: $13,500
Books & Supplies: $1,100

Avg. Need-Based Grant: $18,070
Avg. % of Need Met: 79%

Avg. Merit-Based Award: $6,296
% Receiving (Freshmen w/o Need): 8%

Avg. Cumulative Debt: $27,495
% of Students Borrowing: 37%

CAREER
Who Recruits
1. Linkedin
2. Facebook
3. Goldman Sachs
4. Apple
5. Accenture

Notable Internships
1. U.S. Senate
2. Ford Motor Company
3. Hasbro

Top Employers
1. Google
2. Target
3. Northwestern Mutual
4. Amazon
5. Microsoft

Where Alumni Work
1. Madison, WI
2. Milwaukee
3. Chicago
4. Minneapolis
5. New York City

Earnings
College Scorecard (10-YR Post-Entry): $70,586
PayScale (Early Career): $62,900
PayScale (Mid-Career): $111,400
PayScale 20-Year ROI: $599,000

RANKINGS
Money: 5
U.S. News: 35, National Universities
Wall Street Journal/THE: 79
Washington Monthly: 11, National Universities

OVERGENERALIZATIONS
Students are:
Always saying nice things about Madison
Crazy about the Badgers
Working hard and playing hard
Assertive
Politically liberal

COLLEGE OVERLAPS
Boston University
Northwestern University
University of Illinois at Urbana-Champaign
University of Michigan
University of Minnesota - Twin Cities

Vanderbilt University

Nashville, Tennessee | 615-322-2561

With an acceptance rate that falls between Dartmouth and Cornell, Vanderbilt University in Nashville, Tennessee, has positioned itself as not only one of the South's most selective institutions but as one of the country's ultra-elite universities. Founded in 1873 by the railroad and shipping tycoon/robber baron Cornelius Vanderbilt (who had never set foot in Tennessee), this private research university is comprised of ten schools, only four of which cater to the school's 7,151 undergraduate students. Of the 70 undergraduate majors, economics, politics and government, and neuroscience are among the most popular.

Inside the Classroom
Core academic requirements known as AXLE (Achieving Excellence in Liberal Arts Education) are extensive. Those in the College of Arts and Sciences must complete three or four writing-intensive courses, including a first-year writing seminar. Thirteen additional courses are mandated in foreign language, US history, social/behavioral sciences, and mathematics and natural sciences. Juniors and seniors have the option to apply to departmental honors programs where they are then required to produce a scholarly or creative work.

With a 7:1 student-to-faculty ratio, undergraduate class sizes are kept small. In the 2022-23 school year, 26% of course sections contained nine or fewer students, and 61% contained 19 or fewer; only 9% were large lecture hall affairs of more than 50 students. Undergraduate research opportunities can be found as part of the classroom curriculum, through capstone experiences, or through the Vanderbilt University Summer Research Program. Half of all Commodores are adventurous enough to study abroad, and over 80% of those who do say the experience helped them build job skills. The university offers 120 programs in 40 countries.

Vanderbilt alumni are quickly scooped up by many of the world's most desirable and highest-paying corporations. Elite graduate, law, and medical schools are equally fond of those with a Vandy diploma. The School of Engineering has a particularly strong national reputation as do offerings in biology, economics, education, and music. Vanderbilt has been named a top producer of Fulbright Scholars, having seen 20 students win the award in 2023. Other recent graduates have captured Schwarzman, Boren, Critical Language, Luce, and Marshall Scholarships.

Outside the Classroom
Vanderbilt is a cohesive campus with 84% of all undergraduates living in the school's 30 residence halls, ten of which are exclusively for first-year students. To support its recent switch to a residential college system, the school has spent $600 million to build four new facilities over the last few years. The university's seventeen fraternity and fifteen sorority chapters attract 24% of men and 28% of women, making Greek life a rather dominant part of the social scene. Athletics also attract a big crowd; football games draw close to 40,000 fans, and thousands of students compete at some level. The university has ten varsity women's teams and six men's that compete in NCAA Division I. Additionally, there are more than 40 intramural leagues and 32 club sports that offer athletic participation to all students. Overall, there are 500+ student-led organizations presently active on campus, including roughly fifty that are focused on community service. Campus is situated only a mile and a half from downtown Nashville. Music City, USA, not only offers plenty of concerts but also all of the cultural, dining, entertainment, and shopping options one could desire.

Career Services
The Vanderbilt University Career Center is staffed by 26 full-time professionals, which equates to a student-to-advisor ratio of 275:1—in the average range compared to the liberal arts schools included in this book but quite strong for a university of Vandy's size. The center has career coaches who specialize in areas such as fellowships, STEM, economics, and the social sciences as well as three full-time staff members devoted exclusively to employer relations. The office received rave reviews from undergrads as 99% rated their interactions with career services staff positively, and there is plenty of evidence as to why.

In a given academic year, the office engages in over 2,200 coaching sessions and 1,400+ twenty-minute walk-in sessions. It hosts over 500 career programs and brings 300+ employers from all over the country to Nashville to conduct 1,800+ on-campus interviews. Large-scale events such as the Fall Career Fair attract 2,000+ students and recruiters from 140 companies including the likes of ExxonMobil, Merck, Boeing, and Booz Allen Hamilton. An abundance of legitimate internship opportunities are posted online on two platforms, HireADore and DoreWays. With more than 155,000 living alumni, many of whom remain actively connected to the school, Vanderbilt students have success networking with former Commodores. Overall, thanks to an exceptional record of guiding students into elite graduate/professional schools and tons of industry connections that help students launch their careers, it is not difficult to see why Vanderbilt's career services efforts are viewed so favorably by its own graduates.

Professional Outcomes

Six months after graduating from Vandy, 96% of the Class of 2021 were employed or in graduate school. The most commonly entered industry by recent grads was finance followed by technology, consulting, education, and engineering. Graduates landed jobs with every major financial firm, consulting company, and tech giant as well as with multiple NFL teams. In 2022, the most grads went to KPMG (31), McKinsey (21), Deloitte (20), and EY (20). Alumni across all graduating years can be found in droves at Capital One, Goldman Sachs, Bain & Company, JP Morgan Chase, Citi, and Meta. The greatest number of alumni stay in the Greater Nashville area but large pockets also assemble in New York City, Atlanta, DC, Chicago, San Francisco, and Dallas. Mid-career median salaries for Vanderbilt graduates are number one in the state by a wide margin; the median figure was $80,000 in 2022.

Among recent graduates who went directly on to pursue advanced degrees, 16% were in medical school, 13% were beginning a PhD, and 12% were in law school. Institutions where the greatest number of 2022 alumni enrolled were Vanderbilt itself (90), Columbia (16), Harvard (11), Penn (9), NYU (9), and Northwestern (8). Vanderbilt undergraduates get into med school at a solid 66% rate, and recent acceptances included Johns Hopkins, Duke, Penn, and Yale. Those pursuing a legal education from that same graduating year landed at Vanderbilt's own excellent law school as well as UVA, Harvard, Emory, and UNC-Chapel Hill. In sum, if you succeed at Vanderbilt, you will have no trouble landing at a world-class graduate or professional program.

Admission

Vanderbilt received a record 46,377 applications for a place in the Class of 2026, recording the fourth single-digit acceptance rate in the school's history (7%); the acceptance rate had bounced back up to 12% two cycles ago. For perspective, in 2000, the school received fewer than 9,000 applications and accepted 55% of applicants. In the 2022-23 admissions cycle, the ACT was the more frequently submitted test, and the mid-50% range was 34-35; the range for the SAT was 1490-1570. Just a hair under 91% of enrolled freshmen earned places in the top 10% of their high school class, and 96% placed in the top quartile. There were 230+ National Merit Scholars entering the university in a single recent year. Overall, 89% of enrolled students had GPAs above 3.75 on a 4.0 scale; the average was 3.91.

Six categories are deemed "very important" by this university's admissions committee: rigor of coursework, GPA, class rank, application essay, character/personal qualities, and extracurricular involvement. Vandy is serious about its emphasis on extracurriculars; 100% of admitted students held leadership positions in high school. Recommendations and talent/ability comprise the next tier of factors that are "important" to the process. Students applying early decision were admitted at an 18% clip, significantly higher than those applying via the regular round. In the last 20 years, Vandy has transformed from a school that accepted more than 50% of applicants to a single-digit dream crusher. The regional distinction in the "Southern Ivy" label is almost irrelevant these days. Rather, Vanderbilt is an Ivy-equivalent that happens to be located in the South, and only around one-third of the student body hails from that region.

Worth Your Money?

The full cost of attendance at Vanderbilt is $85k, but those with financial need will pay nothing near that sum. Vandy awards an average need-based grant of $63k per year, putting it among the endlessly endowed Ivy League schools as one of the most generous colleges in the country. It is a rare school that can meet 100% of demonstrated need. Unlike the Ivies, those with exceptional credentials and special talents may actually be able to procure some level of merit aid as well. Slightly over 10% of undergraduates receive an average annual merit aid award of roughly $26k. However, even if you aren't fortunate enough to be counted among this relatively small group of merit aid recipients, Vanderbilt is still worth your money.

FINANCIAL
Institutional Type: Private
In-State Tuition: $63,946
Out-of-State Tuition: $63,946
Room & Board: $20,978
Books & Supplies: $1,194

Avg. Need-Based Grant: $63,479
Avg. % of Need Met: 100%

Avg. Merit-Based Award: $26,099
% Receiving (Freshmen w/o Need): 11%

Avg. Cumulative Debt: $30,364
% of Students Borrowing: 18%

CAREER
Who Recruits
1. Vineyard Vines
2. ExxonMobil
3. Teach for America
4. AllianceBernstein
5. Defense Intelligence Agency

Notable Internships
1. UBS
2. Lyft
3. Spotify

Top Employers
1. Deloitte
2. Google
3. Microsoft
4. EY
5. Amazon

Where Alumni Work
1. Nashville
2. New York City
3. Atlanta
4. Washington, DC
5. San Francisco

Earnings
College Scorecard (10-YR Post-Entry): $84,415
PayScale (Early Career): $71,500
PayScale (Mid-Career): $129,600
PayScale 20-Year ROI: $830,000

RANKINGS
Money: 4.5
U.S. News: 18, National Universities
Wall Street Journal/THE: 13
Washington Monthly: 18, National Universities

OVERGENERALIZATIONS
Students are:
Working hard and playing hard
Always admiring the beauty of their campus
Wealthy
More likely to rush a fraternity/sorority
Preppy

COLLEGE OVERLAPS
Duke University
Emory University
Northwestern University
Rice University
University of Michigan

Vassar College

Poughkeepsie, New York | 845-437-7300

A recent three-part Malcolm Gladwell podcast was full of effusive praise for one college in Poughkeepsie, New York, that puts its money where its mouth is on the subject of making college affordable for low-income and first-generation students. Vassar deserves that type of attention for its commitment to creating a more egalitarian higher education world. Yet, this original member of the Seven Sisters that became coeducational in 1969 also has a well-deserved reputation for its exceptionally flexible and high-quality liberal arts education.

Inside the Classroom
Vassar's 2,459 undergraduate students have the choice of 50 majors and are not beholden to a core curriculum or a murderous series of freshman- and sophomore-year requirements; instead, there are only three mandates. All freshmen must take a first-year writing seminar capped at seventeen students. The second requirement is that all students must become proficient in a foreign language; among the languages offered are Korean, Hebrew, and Old English. The last is that students must take at least one course dealing with quantitative reasoning. Other than that, and, of course, one's major, there is ample room to explore electives and burgeoning intellectual passions.

The college's 369 faculty members teach every single undergraduate course offered at Vassar. A 7:1 student-to-faculty ratio leads to an average class size of 17 students, and 23% of all sections have an enrollment of nine or fewer. Professors are extremely available outside the classroom as 70% of the faculty live on or near campus, and faculty families also live within each residence hall. Opportunities to get involved in undergraduate research are taken advantage of by 300+ students each year who work side-by-side with professors on research in the sciences, social sciences, or arts and humanities. Roughly 500 students also engage in credited community-based learning in local organizations or agencies. Vassar's Undergraduate Research Summer Institute (URSI) has been operational since 1986 and offers a plethora of ten-week research experiences in everything from astronomy to computer science to psychology. Study abroad programs are taken advantage of by two-fifths of students.

In terms of number of degrees conferred, the most popular majors are in the social sciences, biology, the visual and performing arts, foreign languages, and psychology. The lack of a core curriculum makes it easy to double major if you desire. Many grads ultimately pursue further education and find elite graduate and professional programs that respect the rigor of a Vassar education. In 2023, Brewers landed nine Fulbright Scholarships, and a number of recent grads have won National Science Foundation Graduate Research Fellowships.

Outside the Classroom
Few Vassar undergraduates are eager to flee the school's idyllic 1,000-acre campus, so 97% of the student body remains in the residence halls all four years. Those seeking to live off campus need to request special permission. The nine traditional houses, one cooperative house, and three school-owned apartment complexes are situated on verdant grounds that have so many different tree varieties that the campus is technically branded an arboretum. Campus cohesion is further enhanced by the absence of Greek organizations. Men make up only 38% of the population, which can partially be attributed to the school's history as a women's college and to the realities of the demographic makeup at most liberal arts colleges. Eighteen percent of students are varsity athletes who compete as part of 29 varsity athletic squads, many of which compete at the DIII level. Club and intramural teams as well as facilities that include an elevated running track, a six-lane pool, a nine-hole golf course, and thirteen tennis courts ensure that opportunities for fitness are open to all. There are 170+ student-run organizations and 1,000+ annual campus events such as concerts, guest lectures, and visiting performers, so there is always something to do close to home. Poughkeepsie offers lots of natural beauty, a mall, and an array of affordable restaurants, although it won't be mistaken for a buzzing metropolis. Those seeking big-city life will have to make the two-hour trip to New York City or the three-hour ride to Boston.

Career Services
The Career Development Office (CDO) at Vassar College is staffed by 11 professionals who specialize in career counseling, employer relations, law/health professions advising, and alumni outreach. That works out to a 224:1 student-to-advisor ratio, a figure superior to many schools featured in this guide. Annual events organized by this office include Career Kickoff and First Year Friday, which are designed to give freshmen an overview of the career development services available. Sophomore Career Connections and Senior Week are class-specific events intended to focus students on tasks critical to their particular place in the career development process.

In addition to hosting its own events, Vassar is a member of the Selective Liberal Arts Consortium that sponsors recruiting trips to New York City and Washington, DC. The CDO is always happy to help you with your internship, but the majority of the resources in the area are on online platforms that include Handshake. An exceptional 87% of Vassar grads complete at least one internship while at the college. In a single recent school year, the CDO conducted 3,400 one-on-one advising appointments and invited thirty-one companies to recruit on campus including NERA Economic Consulting, Teach for America, and M&T Bank. In addition to helping students find their first jobs, the CDO should be lauded for the fantastic job it does in preparing students to continue their education in medical, law, or graduate school.

Professional Outcomes

Ninety-three percent of Vassar alums enjoy positive outcomes within six months of graduation. A solid number land at highly competitive companies like Google, Meta, EY, Deloitte, Microsoft, Citi, and Amazon. Elite universities such as Harvard, Penn, NYU, and Columbia are also among the top employers of former Vassar students, many of whom earn advanced degrees and enter academia. Large contingents of Brewers can be found in the Greater New York City area as well as Boston, DC, San Francisco, Los Angeles, and Philadelphia. Average mid-career salaries are toward the bottom of the pack among elite liberal arts schools but are—not coincidentally—in the same range as Reed, Oberlin, and Scripps. Like Vassar, these schools produce large numbers of advanced degree earners who do not often see high remuneration early in their careers.

Within five years of graduating, the majority of Vassar alumni pursue further education, including 20% who enroll directly in an advanced degree program upon completing their undergraduate studies. Over the last five years, medical school applicants have been admitted at an enviable 88% rate, twice the national average. The most commonly attended medical schools include Dartmouth, Tufts, Columbia, and Brown. Law school applicants experienced a superb 88% acceptance rate. Vassar ranks in the top 15 in the nation in percentage of undergraduates who go on to earn a PhD (per capita).

Admission

Vassar accepted 19% of the 11,412 applicants seeking to join the Class of 2026. The average SAT for enrolled students was 1480, and the mean ACT was 33. Seventy-seven percent were in the top decile, and 94% were in the top quartile. The average GPA is in the A/A- range. GPA and evidence of rigorous courses rest atop the list of most important factors in the eyes of the admissions committee. Essays, recommendations, extracurricular activities, talent/ability, and character/personal qualities round out a holistic process as the next most important considerations.

The college is extremely committed to providing need-based aid to low-income and first-generation students; nearly one-quarter of current students are Pell Grant recipients. With a yield rate of 32%, Vassar still treasures qualified applicants who apply on a binding early-decision basis. In the previous admissions cycle, ED applicants enjoyed a 39% acceptance rate. Vassar deserves deep admiration for its commitment to increasing access to students from all backgrounds. It has pursued those aims at the expense of hyping application numbers and, thus, increasing the perception of selectivity. As a result, those in love with this fine liberal arts institution do not face single-digit odds as they would at many other schools of its quality.

Worth Your Money?

As a result of Vassar's mission to increase access to low-income students, it does not offer any merit aid, only need-based aid, which it offers in impressively generous quantities. The blow of the list price cost of attendance of $85,220 is softened by the fact that 53% of the undergraduate student population qualifies for aid, and the school meets 100% of the demonstrated need for all students. That translates to an average grant of over $55k, making Vassar an incredibly affordable institution for those from less advantageous economic circumstances.

FINANCIAL
Institutional Type: Private
In-State Tuition: $67,805
Out-of-State Tuition: $67,805
Room & Board: $17,415
Books & Supplies: $2,250

Avg. Need-Based Grant: $54,663
Avg. % of Need Met: 100%

Avg. Merit-Based Award: $0
% Receiving (Freshmen w/o Need): 0%

Avg. Cumulative Debt: $23,809
% of Students Borrowing: 45%

CAREER
Who Recruits
1. NERA Economic Consulting
2. Teach for America
3. Peace Corps
4. M&T Bank
5. Shearman and Sterling

Notable Internships
1. U.S. House of Representatives
2. Major League Baseball
3. YouTube

Top Employers
1. Google
2. IBM
3. Morgan Stanley
4. Deloitte
5. Microsoft

Where Alumni Work
1. New York City
2. Boston
3. San Francisco
4. Washington, DC
5. Los Angeles

Earnings
College Scorecard (10-YR Post-Entry): $64,639
PayScale (Early Career): $58,700
PayScale (Mid-Career): $111,400
PayScale 20-Year ROI: $488,000

RANKINGS
Money: 4
U.S. News: 16, Liberal Arts Colleges
Wall Street Journal/THE: 284
Washington Monthly: 27, Liberal Arts Colleges

OVERGENERALIZATIONS
Students are:
Politically liberal
Opinionated
Artsy
Hippies or hipsters
Equally happy hitting the bars or hitting up a movie

COLLEGE OVERLAPS
Brown University
Cornell University
Haverford College
Tufts University
Wesleyan University

Villanova University

Villanova, Pennsylvania | 610-519-4000

Positioned twelve miles outside of Philadelphia on the swanky Main Line is Villanova University, a school that, prior to winning an NCAA basketball title in 1985, possessed only a regional reputation. Thirty years later, the prestige of its powerhouse basketball program has launched an already renowned and highly desirable school into a whole new stratosphere. Today, this midsize Catholic research university is the proud home to 6,989 enthusiastic Wildcat undergraduates. For those who can conquer its suddenly highly selective admissions process, Nova provides a world-class educational experience in a spirited collegiate atmosphere.

Inside the Classroom

Students can choose one of 55+ undergraduate programs within four schools: the College of Liberal Arts & Sciences, the Villanova School of Business, the College of Engineering, and the College of Nursing. All students must conquer the school's Core Curriculum, which is designed to ensure a "depth of study and intellectual sophistication while recognizing that learning implies different modes of inquiry." Courses in theology, ethics, and philosophy as well as the Augustine and Culture Seminar Program comprise the Core Foundational Courses. Additional requirements include all of the usual liberal arts standards (social sciences, math, foreign language, and so on), an upper-level theology course, a writing seminar, and a senior capstone.

The university sports a 10:1 student-to-faculty ratio and offers average undergraduate classes of twenty-three students. It is possible to receive a degree from the school without ever sitting in a giant lecture hall. In fact, only 5% of course sections enroll 40 or more students. As a consequence, professors are unusually available in and outside of the classroom. From the start of freshman year, opportunities for meaningful undergraduate research will be within your grasp. The Villanova Match Research Program for First Year Students allows second-semester freshmen to work as research assistants alongside distinguished faculty. The Villanova Undergraduate Research Fellows Summer Program is taken advantage of by many upperclassmen; in total, 87% of recent grads who sought out a research experience were able to find one. Wildcats study abroad in impressive numbers; the 40% participation rate places Nova among the top ten universities in the country.

Villanova's business, accounting, and engineering programs all receive a good deal of attention from ranking publications. The school's most popular degree is business with over 30% of all graduates majoring in it. The social sciences (13%), engineering (12%), and nursing (10%) are the second- through fourth-most commonly conferred degree areas. As the school's reputation reaches new heights, more students than ever are winning prestigious national awards. In 2023 alone, Villanova graduates earned 25 Fulbright Scholarships. They also routinely earn Gilman Scholarships, Goldwater Scholarships, and National Science Foundation Graduate Research Fellowships.

Outside the Classroom

Over 80% of the undergraduate student body currently lives on a 240-acre campus that is growing more beautiful and impressive by the day. Constant progress can be observed in the university's many construction projects, and we're not talking small buildings. The school recently completed on-campus housing for an additional 1,135 undergrads. The relatively new Finneran Pavilion and a brand-new performing arts center are emblematic of the administration's recent splurge. The school is home to 23 fraternities and sororities, and 25% of men and 49% of women participate in Greek life. Athletics, particularly basketball, are a way of life at Villanova. More than 500 student-athletes compete on the Wildcats' 24 NCAA Division I teams, and many more participate in the forty-four club and intramural sports options. In total, there are 250+ active extracurricular clubs, a fair number of which are centered on community service, which is a definite point of emphasis at Nova as students contribute a quarter-million service hours annually. Radnor Township isn't cheap, but it offers tons of great hangouts and places to eat. The King of Prussia Mall, the second largest in the United States, is only a few miles away. The museums, sports, restaurants, and culture of Philly are only a straight-shot, half-hour car ride away.

Career Services

The Villanova University Career Center employs 20 individuals who specialize in career counseling, prelaw advising, employer relations, and industry advising. The center also trains a large number of career assistants who are available to support their fellow undergraduates as well. Only counting professional employees, the office has a 349:1 student-to-counselor ratio, which is within the average range of schools profiled in this guide. However, by almost every other metric, this career center, like the university's famed basketball squad, measures up well against the competition.

Including graduate students, there are over 7,000 visits to the career center each school year. Over 55,000 job and internship opportunities were posted online for Wildcats to explore. On-campus recruiting is also strong with 400 companies making the trek to Villanova's grounds last year alone. A well-connected and passionate global network of 135,000 alumni is also available to help you make connections as you search for internships and employment. Most students are successful in landing an internship as 91% of 2022 grads completed at least one such experience at Nova. Large events like the Fall Career Fair draw 175+ employers to the Connelly Center. With a high level of personalized support, a robust Employer Relations Department, and excellent career outcomes for graduates (more in a moment), the Villanova University Career Center continues to do excellent work on behalf of its students.

Professional Outcomes

Within six months of commencement, Class of 2022 graduates had a placement rate of 99% with 74% entering the workforce and 21% matriculating into graduate or professional school. The most popular employers of recent grads are, not coincidentally, also companies with the largest Wildcat alumni representation. That list includes Vanguard, Verizon, PwC, JPMorgan Chase, Merck, Comcast, EY, Deloitte, and Morgan Stanley. The average starting salary across all colleges within the university was $71,363. Graduates of the engineering school earned an average salary above $75,000 while the College of Liberal Arts & Sciences figure was just over $61k. Remaining in the Philadelphia Metro area is the most popular move, but large numbers also migrate to New York City, DC, Boston, Chicago, San Francisco, and Los Angeles.

Recent grads went on to study at a number of top-flight graduate institutions. College of Engineering grads went to schools like Dartmouth, Stanford, and Notre Dame. Liberal arts grads entered programs at Harvard, Tufts, Columbia, and Penn. Nova grads enjoyed a medical school admissions rate of 70-75%, far above the national average. Among the recent graduates applying to law school, acceptances were earned at Fordham, the University of Michigan, Northeastern, Boston College, and, of course, Villanova's own Charles Widger School of Law.

Admission

The 23% of successful applicants who earned a place in the Class of 2026 were a particularly accomplished bunch. Those who enrolled possessed SATs in the range of 1390-1480 and ACTs in the range of 32-34; the average unweighted GPA was 3.89. In terms of class rank, 70% of freshmen placed in their high school classes' top decile, and 95% earned a spot in the top quartile. For perspective, in 2015, the university admitted 43% of its applicants, and the 25th percentile SAT score was an even 1200.

Rigor of coursework, GPA, and class rank comprise the factors deemed most important by the committee. Essays, recommendations, extracurricular activities, work experience, and volunteer work are among the areas that receive secondary consideration. There is no interview offered as part of the admissions process. Those applying through binding early decision were accepted at a 55% rate, providing a massive advantage over those in the regular cycle. Villanova does advertise a holistic process, but with over 23,000 applicants these days, your SATs, GPA, class rank, and other measurables need to be within range for serious consideration. Students (and their counselors) need to be aware of the year-by-year increases in selectivity as this school has transformed in the recent past.

Worth Your Money?

Villanova does not always meet a student's full amount of need, but 45% of current students do receive need-based grants that average $40k per award. The total annual cost of attendance at Nova is a touch over $85k; therefore, even with aid, becoming a Wildcat is not going to come cheap. Villanova grads do end up with a level of debt above the national average. That said, starting salaries for graduates are on the higher side, making it possible to pay back the substantial loans you may need to take out in order to attend.

FINANCIAL
Institutional Type: Private
In-State Tuition: $64,906
Out-of-State Tuition: $64,906
Room & Board: $16,896
Books & Supplies: $1,100

Avg. Need-Based Grant: $40,453
Avg. % of Need Met: 80%

Avg. Merit-Based Award: $27,402
% Receiving (Freshmen w/o Need): 7%

Avg. Cumulative Debt: $38,870
% of Students Borrowing: 37%

CAREER
Who Recruits
1. CIA
2. KPMG
3. TD Securities
4. Boston Consulting Group
5. BNY Mellon

Notable Internships
1. QVC
2. NBC Universal
3. Pratt & Whitney

Top Employers
1. Vanguard
2. Verizon
3. PwC
4. JPMorgan Chase
5. Merck

Where Alumni Work
1. Philadelphia
2. New York City
3. Washington, DC
4. Boston
5. Chicago

Earnings
College Scorecard (10-YR Post-Entry): $96,129
PayScale (Early Career): $70,700
PayScale (Mid-Career): $126,900
PayScale 20-Year ROI: $866,000

RANKINGS
Money: 4.5
U.S. News: 67, National Universities
Wall Street Journal/THE: 62
Washington Monthly: 123, National Universities

OVERGENERALIZATIONS
Students are:
Crazy about the Wildcats
Religious
Preppy
Well-rounded
Career-driven

COLLEGE OVERLAPS
Boston College
Fordham University
Georgetown University
Northeastern University
University of Notre Dame

Virginia Tech

Blacksburg, Virginia | 540-231-6267

ADMISSION
Admission Rate: 57%
Admission Rate - Men: 52%
Admission Rate - Women: 63%
EA Admission Rate: Not Reported
ED Admission Rate: 50%
ED Admits as % of Total Admits: 5%
Admission Rate (5-Year Trend): -13%
% of Admits Attending (Yield): 28%
Transfer Admission Rate: 58%

SAT Reading/Writing (Middle 50%): 610-700
SAT Math (Middle 50%): 610-720
ACT Composite (Middle 50%): 26-32

% Graduated in Top 10% of HS Class: 3%
% Graduated in Top 25% of HS Class: 77%
% Graduated in Top 50% of HS Class: 97%

Demonstrated Interest: Not Considered
Legacy Status: Considered
Racial/Ethnic Status: Very Important
Admission Interview Offered: No

ENROLLMENT
Total Undergraduate Enrollment: 30,434
% Full-Time: 97%
% Male: 57%
% Female: 43%
% Out-of-State: 29%
% Fraternity: Not Reported
% Sorority: Not Reported
% On-Campus (All Undergraduate): 33%
Freshman Housing Required: Yes

% African-American: 6%
% Asian: 12%
% Hispanic: 10%
% White: 60%
% Other: 3%
% International: 4%
% Low-Income: 15%

ACADEMICS
Student-to-Faculty Ratio: 17 to 1
% of Classes Under 20: 33%
% of Classes 20-49: 46%
% of Classes 50 or More: 21%
% Full-Time Faculty: 89%
% Full-Time Faculty w/ Terminal Degree: 88%

Top Programs
Animal Sciences
Architecture
Business
Computer Science
Engineering
Human Nutrition, Foods, and Exercise
Industrial Design
Mathematics

Retention Rate: 92%
4-Year Graduation Rate: 70%
6-Year Graduation Rate: 87%

Curricular Flexibility: Somewhat Flexible
Academic Rating: ★★★⯨

#CollegesWorthYourMoney

Sometimes, even the most epic debacles contain a silver lining. Such was the case, several years back, when Virginia Tech admitted a typical number of applicants, with an estimate that around 6,600 would enroll. When 8,000 of those admitted ended up selecting the university, the school had to offer 1,500 students financial incentives for deferring their enrollment. Logistical disaster aside, this occurrence is indicative of a positive shift—the ever-increasing popularity of an affordable state school that offers a world-class STEM and business education.

Inside the Classroom
Eight undergraduate colleges that collectively offer 110+ distinct bachelor's degrees are housed within the larger university. The Pathways curriculum was instituted in 2015 to ensure that all students were able to participate in a general education program that followed the principles of (1) integration, (2) inclusivity, and (3) relevance. Required courses force Hokies to at least dip their toes into the worlds of discourse, quantitative and computational thinking, reasoning in the natural sciences, critique and practice in design and the arts, reasoning in the social sciences, critical thinking in the humanities, and critical analysis of identity and equity in the United States.

Classes at Virginia Tech tend to be on the larger side with just 33% of sections containing fewer than 20 students while 20% enroll greater than 50 undergrads. The student-to-faculty ratio at this school is 17:1 and there are more than 7,700 graduate students to cater to. Overall, 21% of recent graduates report participating in some type of undergraduate research experience, but landing such opportunities is much easier for members of the Honors College. Each year, more than 1,200 students avail themselves of the chance to study abroad in locations such as Switzerland, New Zealand, France, and Scotland.

As one would expect, engineering is the area where the greatest number of degrees are conferred (23%), but business (20%) is actually a close second. Both disciplines are among the most respected at Tech, along with computer science. Other popular majors include the family and consumer sciences (8%), social sciences (8%), biology (8%), and agriculture (4%). The school typically has multiple Fulbright winners each year. It also produces Astronaut Scholars with regularity.

Outside the Classroom
Ninety-nine percent of freshmen, but only 33% of the overall student body, reside in on-campus housing on the school's sprawling 2,600-acre grounds. Roughly one-quarter of current undergrads hail from out of state, so the majority of the student body are Virginia residents. There are more men than women, but the 57/43 split is not as pronounced as at some other institutes of technology. Frats attract around 13% of males, and 19% of women join a sorority. More than 700 student-athletes are members of the 22 varsity sports teams that compete in the Atlantic Coast Conference at the NCAA Division I level. The Hokies' football stadium seats 66,000+ and attracts raucous crowds, so those seeking delirious football Saturdays will find VT an excellent match. Those seeking a less-competitive environment can join a club or intramural sport; there are more than 35 intramural options including activities like putt-putt, inner tube water polo, and free-throw contests. Additionally, 800 student-run organizations are presently running on campus, virtually assuring every student the chance to connect with others who share their unique interests. With large cities a few hours (or more) away, most students remain near campus on the weekends, soaking in the quintessential college town of Blacksburg, which offers a much-appreciated mix of natural beauty and restaurants, bars, and entertainment venues.

Career Services
There are 27 professional staff members within the Career and Professional Development Center (CPDC), many of whom focus on career counseling, internship/co-op coordination, and employer relations. This 1,127:1 ratio is higher than the average school selected for this guidebook. Regardless, this group ensures that Hokies have opportunities for career planning and connection on a grand scale, hosting 25+ career fairs per year and countless in-person and virtual workshops and employer information sessions. One glance at how employed members of the Class of 2022 found their first jobs, and it's clear that the CPDC is successfully executing its mission.

Twenty-six percent of recent grads report landing their first jobs directly through a connection made at a VT career fair. The CPDC had its hand either directly or indirectly in many other positive outcomes as well. Sixty-two percent of the Class of 2022 reported utilizing the career center to some extent, and only 18% stated that they "never" used any CPDC services. The majority of VT grads had some type of job-related experience during their four years in Blacksburg. Paid internships were procured by 53% of respondents, unpaid internships by 14%, and co-op placements by 5%. Overall, Virginia Tech's career services staff does a solid job reaching the majority of undergraduates, but there is room for improvement in terms of outreach.

Professional Outcomes

Within their first half-year in the real world, 56% of the Class of 2022 had found employment, 18% were in graduate school, and 19% were still looking for their next destination. One recent graduating class sent large numbers of graduates to a variety of major corporations including Deloitte (67), KPMG (44), Lockheed Martin (39), Capital One (30), EY (28), Booz Allen Hamilton (18), and Northrop Grumman (12). The top four geographic areas where Hokies settle down are all within the same region: Washington, DC; Roanoke; Richmond; and Norfolk. The median salary for 2022 graduates was $67,000 with a median bonus of $5,000.

Among recent graduates who decided to pursue an advanced degree, the greatest number did so right at VT, while 20+ traveled a couple hundred miles east to Virginia Commonwealth University, and nine freshly minted grads enrolled at George Mason University. Multiple members of the Class of 2022 went on to attend the likes of William & Mary, Columbia, Duke, and Georgia Tech. Law schools that members of this cohort are attending include UT Austin, Tulane, and the University of Maryland. In the 2023 cycle, 139 Virginia Tech seniors applied to medical school, and recent acceptances included the Baylor College of Medicine and the University of Virginia as well as dental school admissions to the University of Pennsylvania and Tufts University.

Admission

The 57% acceptance rate for applicants to join the 2022-23 freshman class is not as intimidating as the admit rates at many other strong STEM institutions. This group certainly included many high achievers—the average weighted high school GPA was 4.03, and overall, 80% of Hokie freshmen possessed a GPA of 3.75 or better. Standardized test scores of Class of 2026 members were solid but unspectacular. The mid-50% ranges were 1220-1420 on the SAT and 26-32 on the ACT. The SAT is easily the more commonly submitted test, among those who do not apply test-optional.

Virginia Tech weighs seven factors as having the greatest importance in admissions decisions: rigor of coursework, GPA, the application essay, first-generation status, geographical residence, state residency, and racial/ethnic status. While demonstrated interest is not considered, VT does appreciate students who apply early decision and awards them with a slightly higher acceptance rate. Over 70% of Hokies are state residents; the most nonresident students hail from Maryland, New Jersey, Pennsylvania, North Carolina, and New York. It is important to note that admissions are a bit more selective for out-of-state applicants.

Worth Your Money?

The in-state cost of attendance for those staying on campus is a relatively affordable $37,252 per year. Those coming from outside the state of Virginia will pay a COA of $58,750. At full price, this figure could give cost-conscious families pause; however, considering the median starting salary of $67k and heavy concentration of engineering and business majors, VT will prove worth the money for many undergraduates. As with any state school of this quality, Virginia residents can rest assured that their educational investment will be well spent, regardless of one's intended major.

FINANCIAL
Institutional Type: Public
In-State Tuition: $15,478
Out-of-State Tuition: $36,090
Room & Board: $14,888
Books & Supplies: $2,620

Avg. Need-Based Grant: $8,153
Avg. % of Need Met: 51%

Avg. Merit-Based Award: $3,348
% Receiving (Freshmen w/o Need): 10%

Avg. Cumulative Debt: $32,376
% of Students Borrowing: 46%

CAREER
Who Recruits
1. Accenture
2. MITRE
3. Dominion Energy
4. Peraton
5. L3Harris

Notable Internships
1. KPMG
2. Richmond & Towers
3. Jacobs Engineering Group

Top Employers
1. Capital One
2. Booz Allen Hamilton
3. Deloitte
4. Microsoft
5. IBM

Where Alumni Work
1. Washington, DC
2. Roanoke, VA
3. Richmond, VA
4. Norfolk, VA
5. New York City

Earnings
College Scorecard (10-YR Post-Entry): $77,621
PayScale (Early Career): $67,900
PayScale (Mid-Career): $121,800
PayScale 20-Year ROI: $784,000

RANKINGS
Money: 4.5
U.S. News: 47, National Universities
Wall Street Journal/THE: 76
Washington Monthly: 37, National Universities

OVERGENERALIZATIONS
Students are:
Crazy about the Hokies
Service-oriented
Friendly
Teeming with school pride
Working hard and playing hard

COLLEGE OVERLAPS
College of William & Mary
James Madison University
North Carolina State University
University of Maryland, College Park
University of Virginia

Wake Forest University

Founded as the Manual Labor Institute for Baptist preachers in 1834, Wake Forest has roots that sound exaggeratedly and humorously humble. Of course, the current vibe of the university could not be further from its modest beginnings, save the retention of its Southern charm. Today's Wake Forest is generally regarded as a bubble of conservatism and wealth—the average student's parental income is far higher than the average university—and, from an academic standpoint, this school is viewed as one of the top private research institutions outside the Northeast.

Inside the Classroom

All freshmen enter the Undergraduate College that offers 45 majors and 60 minors. Economics, biology, psychology, finance, and communications are the areas toward which the largest number of students gravitate. Those wishing to attend the School of Business apply prior to their sophomore year. All other concentrations are open to any student. Academic requirements include a freshman seminar, a four-credit writing seminar, foreign language, physical education, and one course in both quantitative reasoning and cultural diversity.

Sporting a student-to-faculty ratio of 10:1, classes are kept on the small side with 59% of sections enrolling fewer than 20 students. There are a fair number of courses that have twenty to thirty-nine students, but only a minuscule number that take place in large lecture halls. Close to 60% of Demon Deacons have the opportunity to engage in hands-on research for academic credit. Wake's robust study abroad options feature 400 semester, summer, and year-long programs in 200 cities in more than seventy countries worldwide. Undergrads participate at a 64-75% rate, good enough for the third-highest figure among doctoral degree-granting US universities.

Wake Forest is a school with strengths across a variety of disciplines, most notably chemistry, communication, accounting, finance, and international affairs. The most frequently conferred degrees are in business (22%), the social sciences (20%), journalism (8%), biology (8%), and psychology (7%). Overall, the institution has an excellent reputation across the board in both employment and academic circles, and Wake Forest grads are always considered for prestigious postgraduate fellowships. Seven members of the Class of 2023 were named Fulbright Scholars and the university produces a Rhodes Scholar just about every other year.

Outside the Classroom

Greek life gets top billing when it comes to describing the social scene at Wake. A sizable percentage of the student body joins a fraternity or sorority, with women joining sororities at an extraordinarily high rate (64%). Seventy-five percent of students live in university-owned housing with many off-campus upperclassmen flocking to nearby apartment complexes. The Demon Deacons are a powerhouse in NCAA Division I athletics, quite an achievement considering the university's modest size. Of the 16 varsity sports teams that compete in the vaunted ACC, men's basketball and football draw the biggest crowds. The school is brimming with less serious but still dedicated athletes as a whopping 85% of the student body participates in intramural athletics. Many non-sports options also are available as there are more than 250 active student organizations on campus, including a full array of political, religious, and performing arts groups. The quaint Southern charm of campus extends into the surrounding small city of Winston-Salem, which offers its fair share of cultural, culinary, and shopping pursuits.

Career Services

The Office of Personal and Career Development (OPCD) at Wake Forest is staffed by 34 full-time professional employees who serve as career coaches, employer relations specialists, and counselors who work on personal and professional development with alumni. That equates to a phenomenal student-to-advisor ratio of 160:1, which ranks among the best of the institutions included in this book. The OPCD is not only generously staffed but also operates with the clear mission of readying every single Demon Deacon for a meaningful next step in life.

In a single year, career coaches met with over 4,000 members of the student body to engage in 1:1 career planning sessions and/or small workshops. Career treks took students to New York City, San Francisco, and DC to meet with alumni in their places of business. Perhaps the office's most unique feature is that it runs a sequence of for-credit College-to-Career courses. Having an actual academic program dedicated to career prep affords the OPCD the chance to teach large numbers of students about matching their personalities to fulfilling careers, finding internships, developing cover letters, considering cost-of-living issues post-graduation, and so much more.

ADMISSION
Admission Rate: 21%
Admission Rate - Men: 21%
Admission Rate - Women: 22%
EA Admission Rate: Not Offered
ED Admission Rate: Not Reported
ED Admits as % of Total Admits: Not Reported
Admission Rate (5-Year Trend): -7%
% of Admits Attending (Yield): 38%
Transfer Admission Rate: 29%

SAT Reading/Writing (Middle 50%): 680-740
SAT Math (Middle 50%): 700-770
ACT Composite (Middle 50%): 31-34

% Graduated in Top 10% of HS Class: 74%
% Graduated in Top 25% of HS Class: 93%
% Graduated in Top 50% of HS Class: 98%

Demonstrated Interest: Considered
Legacy Status: Considered
Racial/Ethnic Status: Considered
Admission Interview Offered: Yes

ENROLLMENT
Total Undergraduate Enrollment: 5,447
% Full-Time: 99%
% Male: 45%
% Female: 55%
% Out-of-State: 82%
% Fraternity: 36%
% Sorority: 64%
% On-Campus (All Undergraduate): 75%
Freshman Housing Required: Yes

% African-American: 6%
% Asian: 4%
% Hispanic: 9%
% White: 66%
% Other: 1%
% International: 9%
% Low-Income: 9%

ACADEMICS
Student-to-Faculty Ratio: 10 to 1
% of Classes Under 20: 59%
% of Classes 20-49: 40%
% of Classes 50 or More: 1%
% Full-Time Faculty: 68%
% Full-Time Faculty w/ Terminal Degree: 94%

Top Programs
Accountancy
Chemistry
Communication
Economics
Finance
Health and Exercise Science
Politics and International Affairs
Psychology

Retention Rate: 94%
4-Year Graduation Rate: 85%
6-Year Graduation Rate: 89%

Curricular Flexibility: Somewhat Flexible
Academic Rating: ★★★★★

#CollegesWorthYourMoney

Almost one-quarter of graduates take at least one of those courses. Employer relations at Wake are also strong, and they host a number of well-attended job fairs. Additionally, more than 12,000 job and internship postings go up each year. All freshmen are introduced to the services offered via the OPCD Orientation that alerts students to the wealth of career-prep resources available to them from the moment they step on campus. Overall, Wake Forest's career services office is held in high regard, a view backed by the fact that almost every single graduate achieves a successful outcome within months of exiting campus.

Professional Outcomes

The members of the Class of 2022 didn't take long to arrive at their next destinations. Within six months of graduation, 97% had either landed their first professional job or were already matriculated into a graduate program. Management/consulting, investment banking, and healthcare were the top three industries. Employers landing the highest numbers of alumni included national and multinational corporations IBM, Siemens, Volvo, Goldman Sachs, Disney, Deloitte, Dell, Gucci, PepsiCo, EY, and Nike. Over 40% of graduates remain south of the Mason-Dixon Line; most of those who do exit the South head to the Mid-Atlantic region and the Northeast. By the start of mid-career, Wake Forest alumni earn the second-highest median salary of any school in North Carolina, behind Duke but ahead of Davidson and UNC-Chapel Hill.

Twenty-six percent of 2022 graduates went directly from donning their caps and gowns to pursuing advanced degrees. Students attend a wide range of schools from a selectivity standpoint, but there is a strong representation of elite institutions. As one example, an examination of recent history majors shows acceptances at elite institutions including Duke, Notre Dame, Columbia, Yale, Cornell, and Princeton. Many biology majors headed to PhD programs or into medical school at locations such as UNC, Duke, Johns Hopkins, Tufts, and Emory; Wake Forest's medical school takes in many of its own graduates. There were 145 medical school applicants in 2023 alone.

Admission

Applicants to the Class of 2026 were accepted at a 21% clip, a bit lower than a handful of years prior when 36% of applicants were successful. However, the average profile of an admitted student has barely changed in that time. Applications may be on the rise, but the requirements for admission have stayed fairly constant. Wake Forest is a test-optional school, but among those attending students who submitted scores, the middle-50% ranges were 1400-1500 on the SAT and 31-34 on the ACT. Just a shade under 75% of the freshman class finished in the top 10% of their high school class, and 93% were in the top 25%.

The above statistics jibe with factors that the admissions office self-reports as being "most important": rigor of curriculum, GPA, class rank, essay, and character/personal characteristics. If being a Demon Deacon has been your lifelong dream, then you should consider applying early decision to gain an edge on your competition. However, the last time Wake reported results, the ED acceptance rate was actually lower than that of the regular round. Landing a spot on this gorgeous Winston-Salem campus requires passing a holistic review, perhaps made even more holistic by the university's decision to jettison standardized testing back in 2008. Nonetheless, 28% of applicants still submit SAT results, and 29% submit ACT scores. Applicants should bring stellar grades to the table, possess a robust extracurricular profile, and use their ED card to their advantage (at least in most cycles).

Worth Your Money?

Wake Forest only awards need-based aid to 21% of its undergraduates, a low number compared to other top schools, but when it does offer aid, it does it right. Those who qualify see 100% of their full demonstrated need met for an average annual grant of $54k. The list price cost of attendance for Wake Forest is over $87,000, so those packages help make the school a bit more affordable for the non-wealthy. However, Wake grads still end up with debt loads that exceed the national average. Individuals required to take out a significant amount in loans should consider their career plans and other competing offers before deciding to attend Wake.

FINANCIAL
Institutional Type: Private
In-State Tuition: $64,758
Out-of-State Tuition: $64,758
Room & Board: $20,440
Books & Supplies: $1,630

Avg. Need-Based Grant: $52,174
Avg. % of Need Met: 100%

Avg. Merit-Based Award: $32,196
% Receiving (Freshmen w/o Need): 30%

Avg. Cumulative Debt: $31,476
% of Students Borrowing: 25%

CAREER
Who Recruits
1. MullenLowe Mediahub
2. Gap, Inc.
3. Horizon Media
4. Gartner
5. Goldman Sachs

Notable Internships
1. Bristol-Myers Squibb
2. Aramark
3. Sotheby's

Top Employers
1. Wells Fargo
2. EY
3. BB&T
4. PwC
5. Deloitte

Where Alumni Work
1. Winston-Salem, NC
2. New York City
3. Charlotte
4. Washington, DC
5. Raleigh

Earnings
College Scorecard (10-YR Post-Entry): $81,964
PayScale (Early Career): $65,300
PayScale (Mid-Career): $128,900
PayScale 20-Year ROI: $793,000

RANKINGS
Money: 4.5
U.S. News: 47, National Universities
Wall Street Journal/THE: 85
Washington Monthly: 48, National Universities

OVERGENERALIZATIONS
Students are:
Wealthy
Preppy
Tight-knit (possess a strong sense of community)
More likely to rush a fraternity/sorority
Working hard and playing hard

COLLEGE OVERLAPS
Boston College
Emory University
University of North Carolina at Chapel Hill
University of Virginia
University of Richmond

Washington & Lee University

Lexington, Virginia | 540-458-8710

ADMISSION
Admission Rate: 17%
Admission Rate - Men: 15%
Admission Rate - Women: 19%
EA Admission Rate: Not Offered
ED Admission Rate: 42%
ED Admits as % of Total Admits: 22%
Admission Rate (5-Year Trend): -5%
% of Admits Attending (Yield): 39%
Transfer Admission Rate: 4%

SAT Reading/Writing (Middle 50%): 700-753
SAT Math (Middle 50%): 710-780
ACT Composite (Middle 50%): 32-34

% Graduated in Top 10% of HS Class: 81%
% Graduated in Top 25% of HS Class: 98%
% Graduated in Top 50% of HS Class: 100%

Demonstrated Interest: Considered
Legacy Status: Considered
Racial/Ethnic Status: Considered
Admission Interview Offered: Yes

ENROLLMENT
Total Undergraduate Enrollment: 1,867
% Full-Time: 100%
% Male: 49%
% Female: 51%
% Out-of-State: 76%
% Fraternity: 75%
% Sorority: 71%
% On-Campus (All Undergraduate): 75%
Freshman Housing Required: Yes

% African-American: 4%
% Asian: 4%
% Hispanic: 8%
% White: 72%
% Other: 1%
% International: 6%
% Low-Income: 11%

ACADEMICS
Student-to-Faculty Ratio: 8 to 1
% of Classes Under 20: 81%
% of Classes 20-49: 19%
% of Classes 50 or More: 0%
% Full-Time Faculty: 85%
% Full-Time Faculty w/ Terminal Degree: 95%

Top Programs
Accounting
Business Administration
Economics
English
History
Journalism and Mass Communication
Philosophy
Political Science

Retention Rate: 97%
4-Year Graduation Rate: 92%
6-Year Graduation Rate: 94%

Curricular Flexibility: Less Flexible
Academic Rating: ★★★★★

#CollegesWorthYourMoney

The influence of two disparate figures in American history, George Washington and Robert E. Lee (whose name the faculty recently voted to remove from the university name), helped shape a small liberal arts school known in the eighteenth century as Liberty Hall Academy and in the nineteenth century as Washington College into today's Washington and Lee University, an elite liberal arts institution home to 1,867 undergraduates. Although dubbed a "university," the only postgraduate program is its law school. Set in the small town of Lexington, Virginia, Washington and Lee is one of the premier colleges of its modest size in all of the South, and it has remained highly selective for the entirety of the twenty-first century.

Inside the Classroom
W&L demands a high number of courses to fulfill its foundational and distributional requirements that collectively will take close to three full semesters to complete. Mandated coursework includes writing, foreign language, physical education, computer science, literature, fine arts, four arts and humanities classes, and two in each of the natural and social sciences. One experiential learning course that focuses on research/presentation/cultural competence rounds out the academic requirements that apply to all undergrads. The university offers 36 majors and 29 minors, including a fair share of interdisciplinary programs.

With an exceptionally low 7:1 student-to-faculty ratio and no graduate students to attend to, W&L undergraduates enjoy loads of attention. Over 80% of class sections contain 19 or fewer students, and less than 1% of courses enroll more than 30 students. Instructors earn rave reviews as 98% of recent grads were either "very satisfied" or "satisfied" by the quality of their professors. Students can participate in research via the Summer Research Scholars, which allows undergrads to collaborate with faculty in the field or lab. Studying abroad is a typical part of a Washington and Lee education with 70% of grads spending a semester or summer in a foreign land.

Altogether, business accounts for 23% of the degrees conferred at Washington and Lee; the social sciences (25%), biology (9%), and foreign language (6%) are also popular. The renowned Williams School of Commerce, Politics, and Economics offers outstanding business-oriented programs that feed many of the top corporations in the world. English, history, and W&L's Department of Journalism and Mass Communication are also highly respected. Given Washington and Lee's many strengths, a healthy number of students are encouraged to apply for prestigious fellowships, and a good number are successful. In 2023, thirteen undergrads were awarded Fulbrights while other recent grads have taken home Goldwater Scholarships and a William Jefferson Clinton Scholarship to study in Dubai.

Outside the Classroom
The main campus of Washington and Lee is concentrated on 50 acres, but it has an additional forty acres of playing fields and 215 acres of green space. All first-year students are required to reside in freshman-exclusive dormitories with twelve to twenty students per floor. Sophomores and juniors primarily live in dorms, apartments, or Greek houses. To say the Greek scene dominates social life is to grossly understate its reach on campus. The school's eight sororities attract 71% of female students, and a slightly higher 75% of males join the 12 fraternities on campus. The Generals play 24 NCAA Division III sports, which means that varsity athletes comprise a sizable 25% of the student body; 40% play a varsity sport for at least one year. Twenty-five intramural sports, from flag football to Wiffle ball, attract three-quarters of the student body as well as many faculty members who are eligible to participate. An impressive 90% of surveyed undergraduates were satisfied with the school's extracurricular offerings. There are 120+ clubs and organizations presently operating, including the always popular Outing Club that camps and hikes around the neighboring wilderness on weekends. Lexington is a small town with a population of around 7,400, but it does have its share of bars and restaurants. Richmond is a two-hour trip by car, and DC is a three-hour drive from campus.

Career Services
The Career and Professional Development Center (CPDC) is staffed by eight full-time professional employees, including a prelaw advisor, international advisor, assistant director of STEM programs, and assistant director of recruitment. That equates to a student-to-advisor ratio of 233:1, which is within the better-than-average range when compared to other institutions included in this book. Excellent personalized attention is provided to the tune of 960 unique student appointments (3.3 per participating student) per year. Each year, the center staff meets one-on-one with 52% of the student population, including two-thirds of seniors.

The CPDC brings 60+ employers to Lexington each year for information sessions, recruitment, and on-campus interviews. It also organizes six career exploration trips to DC and New York City that focus on finance, the arts, advertising, marketing, and STEM fields. Staff also host more than sixty career exploration and skill-building workshops on topics such as social media, Excel, and how to write a personal statement. A dazzling 85% of students complete at least one internship, fellowship, or practicum. Further, 94% of those completing such an experience found it "extremely helpful" or "somewhat helpful" in preparing for a career. With ample individualized attention and opportunities for hands-on experience, W&L's Career and Professional Development Center rates well in the eyes of our staff.

Professional Outcomes

Last year, 69% of recent graduates found employment within six months of saying goodbye to Lexington. The most frequently entered industries by recent grads were financial services, economics/finance, education, consulting, and real estate. With so many flocking to financial jobs, many top banks, accounting firms, and investment houses presently employ more than two dozen Generals including EY, Wells Fargo, Goldman Sachs, PwC, JPMorgan, Capital One, and Morgan Stanley. Washington and Lee is the rare college that sees the majority of its alumni relocate to cities in other states. DC, New York City, and Atlanta all draw more graduates than Roanoke or Richmond. Starting salaries are solid with the majority of the cohort being paid $55,000 or more while 18% brought home in excess of $75,000.

Almost one-quarter of grads immediately matriculated into a graduate or professional program upon receiving their bachelor's degrees. Within five years of graduating, many attend medical school (12%), law school (11%), and MBA programs (7%). Recent physics and engineering students have gone on to graduate study at MIT, Carnegie Mellon, Stanford, and Vanderbilt. Law schools accepting recent grads included Wake Forest, Fordham, Georgetown, Vanderbilt, and W&L's own law school. Medical school acceptances included Rutgers Medical School, LSU School of Medicine in New Orleans, and the University of Texas Medical Branch.

Admission

Of 7,224 applicants for a seat in the Class of 2026, only 1,225 were admitted for an acceptance rate of 17%; 476 ultimately enrolled. The median SAT score was 1480, and the average ACT composite was 34. Most 2022-23 freshmen hailed from the very top of their high school class with 81% placing in the top decile and 98% in the top 25%. All of the admissions statistics are almost identical to those of a decade ago. In fact, the number of applicants, acceptance rate, and achievement level of entering freshmen have remained relatively steady since the turn of the millennium.

The goal of the admissions committee is to "get to know you as well as possible through your application." The rigor of your high school curriculum is very important—95% of entering freshmen had an IB or AP background, and just shy of three-quarters studied four or more years of a foreign language. Only three other factors rated as "very important": class rank, extracurricular activities, and character/personal qualities. Applying early decision is a no-brainer for dedicated applicants as the acceptance rate was 42% in the last cycle. In fact, the school locks in 55% of its freshman class via the ED round. Washington and Lee offers a genuinely holistic admissions process. Strong grades in highly rigorous courses are nonnegotiable, but qualities like leadership and what one brings to a student community also receive strong consideration.

Worth Your Money?

While an $87k price tag might make cost-conscious families aggressively scratch Washington and Lee off their child's college list, the school is extremely generous with merit aid for exceptional students. That generosity is only trumped by the school's dedication to meeting 100% of financial need for every qualifying student. Thanks to that level of financial assistance and excellent graduate outcomes, Washington and Lee is worth the money for most attendees.

FINANCIAL
Institutional Type: Private
In-State Tuition: $64,525
Out-of-State Tuition: $64,525
Room & Board: $17,685
Books & Supplies: $2,024

Avg. Need-Based Grant: $58,623
Avg. % of Need Met: 100%

Avg. Merit-Based Award: $44,320
% Receiving (Freshmen w/o Need): 7%

Avg. Cumulative Debt: $21,269
% of Students Borrowing: 32%

CAREER
Who Recruits
1. Walker & Dunlap
2. Citi
3. Merrill Lynch
4. Berkeley Research Group
5. Morgan Stanley

Notable Internships
1. Estee Lauder Companies
2. Twitter
3. North Carolina Museum of Art

Top Employers
1. EY
2. PwC
3. Morgan Stanley
4. Wells Fargo
5. JPMorgan Chase

Where Alumni Work
1. Washington, DC
2. New York City
3. Atlanta
4. Roanoke, VA
5. Richmond

Earnings
College Scorecard (10-YR Post-Entry): $84,232
PayScale (Early Career): $69,100
PayScale (Mid-Career): $145,300
PayScale 20-Year ROI: $938,000

RANKINGS
Money: 4.5
U.S. News: 21, Liberal Arts Colleges
Wall Street Journal/THE: 44
Washington Monthly: 8, Liberal Arts Colleges

OVERGENERALIZATIONS
Students are:
Wealthy
Preppy
More likely to rush a fraternity/sorority
Tight-knit (possess a strong sense of community)
Working hard and playing hard

COLLEGE OVERLAPS
Dartmouth College
Davidson College
University of North Carolina at Chapel Hill
University of Virginia
Vanderbilt University

Washington University in St. Louis

St. Louis, Missouri | 314-935-6000

ADMISSION
Admission Rate: 11%
Admission Rate - Men: 12%
Admission Rate - Women: 11%
EA Admission Rate: Not Offered
ED Admission Rate: 26%
ED Admits as % of Total Admits: 29%
Admission Rate (5-Year Trend): -5%
% of Admits Attending (Yield): 48%
Transfer Admission Rate: 17%

SAT Reading/Writing (Middle 50%): 730-770
SAT Math (Middle 50%): 770-800
ACT Composite (Middle 50%): 33-35

% Graduated in Top 10% of HS Class: 90%
% Graduated in Top 25% of HS Class: 99%
% Graduated in Top 50% of HS Class: 100%

Demonstrated Interest: Not Considered
Legacy Status: Considered
Racial/Ethnic Status: Considered
Admission Interview Offered: Yes

ENROLLMENT
Total Undergraduate Enrollment: 8,132
% Full-Time: 95%
% Male: 46%
% Female: 54%
% Out-of-State: 89%
% Fraternity: 11%
% Sorority: 9%
% On-Campus (All Undergraduate): 70%
Freshman Housing Required: Yes

% African-American: 9%
% Asian: 20%
% Hispanic: 12%
% White: 44%
% Other: 2%
% International: 8%
% Low-Income: 17%

ACADEMICS
Student-to-Faculty Ratio: 7 to 1
% of Classes Under 20: 66%
% of Classes 20-49: 25%
% of Classes 50 or More: 9%
% Full-Time Faculty: 69%
% Full-Time Faculty w/ Terminal Degree: 90%

Top Programs
Anthropology
Architecture
Art
Biology
Business
Economics
Engineering
Mathematics

Retention Rate: 96%
4-Year Graduation Rate: 88%
6-Year Graduation Rate: 94%

Curricular Flexibility: Somewhat Flexible
Academic Rating: ★★★★★

#CollegesWorthYourMoney

Despite receiving consistently high rankings since *US News* released its first college guide in 1983, Washington University in St. Louis is, perhaps, the finest institution that is not a household name across the nation. Yet, this Midwestern research and pre-professional powerhouse is one of the most respected institutions in the eyes of Fortune 500 employers and elite graduate schools alike. Catering to 8,132 undergraduates, WashU admits students into five schools: Arts & Sciences, the Olin School of Business, the School of Engineering & Applied Sciences, and the Art of Architecture programs housed within the Sam Fox School of Design and Visual Arts.

Inside the Classroom
Arts & Sciences, which claims more than half the student body, offers more than 80 majors, and all are guided by the IQ Curriculum, the school's signature liberal arts course of study. As part of the IQ Curriculum, students must take courses in applied numeracy, social contrasts, writing, and an additional course that is classified as "writing intensive." WashU students also must complete coursework in the humanities, social sciences, natural sciences/math, and foreign language along with three "integrations" that can be completed via multi-semester, cross-disciplinary coursework. Engineering students are not beholden to all of those curricular mandates. Special programs include the University Scholars Program in Medicine, which allows students to apply for admission to both an undergraduate degree program and medical school before entering college as well as the Beyond Boundaries Program, which allows students to implement a cross-disciplinary approach with the aim of solving major global and societal problems.

The university has a 7:1 student-to-faculty ratio, and 66% of classes have fewer than 20 students; over one-quarter have single-digit enrollments. WUSTL students are known for being more collaborative than competitive and extremely hard-working as evidenced by the fact that 65% double major or pursue a minor. The Office of Undergraduate Research helps students land opportunities to research alongside faculty, primarily in the summers. A solid 59% of undergraduates report participating in a research endeavor and one-third study abroad.

Nationally recognized programs are numerous: the Olin Business School, the School of Engineering & Applied Sciences, and the College of Architecture are well-respected by employers. The Biology Department prepares many successful med school candidates, including for the university's own ultra-elite medical school. The most commonly conferred degrees are in engineering (13%), social sciences (13%), business (13%), biology (11%), and psychology (10%). Fulbright, Gilman, Luce, and Critical Language Scholarships all have been won by WashU grads in recent years, and one student was named a Rhodes Scholar in 2023.

Outside the Classroom
It sounds trite, but by almost any metric one must conclude that Washington University students seem happy. Dorms, recreational facilities, and campus food are routinely rated well. The WashU atmosphere is known for being more laid-back and friendly than that of many of its elite peers. Last year, 72% of the student body and 100% of freshmen resided on campus. WashU's 16 fraternities and 10 sororities draw 9-11% of undergrads. The Bears compete in NCAA Division III, fielding nine men's teams and ten women's squads. The athletically inclined student body also has forty-one club teams, and a simply insane three-quarters of undergraduates participate in intramural sports. In excess of 450 student-run organizations are active at WUSTL, all under the purview of the Washington University Student Union, one of the most well-funded college student governments in the country. Each semester, it funds a concert known as WILD (for Walk In, Lay Down) that features a big-time musical act, and well-attended speaker events are also organized on a regular basis. For those inclined to explore off campus, the university is located within a few miles of the St. Louis Zoo, multiple art museums, a host of great eateries, and the gorgeous Missouri Botanical Garden.

Career Services
The Washington University in St. Louis Career Center is staffed by 54 full-time professional employees who specialize in employer relations, career counseling, event planning, and pre-graduate school advising. With a student-to-advisor ratio of 151:1, WUSTL compares favorably to the other institutions included in this book. Having conducted advising sessions with 5,168 unique students in a single recent school year, the center staff does a superb job of engaging their undergraduate student population.

Eight career fairs drew a collective audience of almost 1,180 individuals and 200 employers. The center also hosted 500 low-key employer information sessions and a number of SLAMs, miniature career fairs for a particular industry where, in a bit of a role reversal, employers pitch their companies to students. An almost hard-to-fathom 400+ employers recruit on campus each year, and close to 1,100 on-campus interviews are conducted. Thanks to the strong employer connections forged by career services staff, WashU students have no trouble landing internships at major companies like CBS News, Pfizer, and AT&T, and stipends are available through the university to help offset living expenses. All told, approximately 75% of students report completing at least one internship. With ample staffing, superior outreach, and positive student outcomes, WashU's Career Center could not be doing a better job.

Professional Outcomes

The Class of 2022 sent 52% of its exiting members into the workforce and 28% into graduate and professional schools. The 30 companies employing the highest number of WashU grads feature many of the most sought-after employers in the world including Amazon, Bain, Boeing, Deloitte, Google, IBM, Goldman Sachs, and Microsoft. Of the employed members of the Class of 2022 who reported their starting salaries, 79% made more than $60k. Geographically, remaining in Missouri was the favored choice among fresh alums, but a fair number also resettled in New York and California.

The universities welcoming the largest number of Bears included the prestigious institutions of Caltech, Columbia, Harvard, Penn, Princeton, and Stanford. Others were pursuing graduate degrees at non-elite schools including Case Western, Rutgers, Colorado State, and St. Louis University. In a typical year, there were 60+ grads accepted into med school, including at WashU's own top-ranked medical school. Baylor College of Medicine attracted a large number of future physicians; students also enjoyed acceptances into Harvard Medical School, NYU School of Medicine, and the Icahn School of Medicine at Mt. Sinai.

Admission

WashU received 33,214 applications for a place in the Class of 2026, but it admitted only 11%. Ninety percent of attending students were in the top 10% of their high school class, and the middle 50% for SATs was 1500-1570 and 33-35 for the ACTs. For historical reference, in 2010, the university accepted 21% of applicants, and enrolling students possessed similar standardized test scores to those being accepted today.

Even with rising application numbers, the admissions committee carefully examines each application, granting "high importance" to soft factors including character/personal qualities, extracurricular activities, talent/ability, and volunteer/work experience. Essays also grace this list. It behooves students seriously committed to WUSTL to give serious consideration to applying early. The admission rate is 26% in the early round compared to only 9% in the regular cycle, and ED entrants comprise 57% of the freshman class. Formerly relegated to Ivy backup status, Washington University has stepped into the limelight as a destination point for the best and brightest from around the country. In fact, close to 65% of current students hail from 500+ miles away, including all 50 US states and 100 countries. This Midwestern behemoth casts a wide net, but only brings aboard the most brag-worthy fish it can find.

Worth Your Money?

A fairly standard (in the world of elite private colleges) $84k list price cost of attendance greets WashU freshmen. Undergrads who qualify for financial aid see 100% of that amount met by the university, which averages out to $58k in grant money each academic year. This school has one of the wealthiest groups of students in the country (rivaled by Colorado College and Colgate) so, for many, the price tag will not break the bank. Given that reality, WUSTL can make sense for students across a wide spectrum of socioeconomic backgrounds.

FINANCIAL
Institutional Type: Private
In-State Tuition: $62,982
Out-of-State Tuition: $62,982
Room & Board: $20,778
Books & Supplies: $762

Avg. Need-Based Grant: $58,197
Avg. % of Need Met: 100%

Avg. Merit-Based Award: $29,416
% Receiving (Freshmen w/o Need): 2%

Avg. Cumulative Debt: $21,932
% of Students Borrowing: 23%

CAREER
Who Recruits
1. Guggenheim Investments
2. Equifax
3. Cushman & Wakefield
4. Abercrombie & Fitch
5. Chicago Trading Company

Notable Internships
1. St. Louis Post-Dispatch
2. Uber
3. BlackRock

Top Employers
1. Boeing
2. Google
3. Microsoft
4. Amazon
5. Mastercard

Where Alumni Work
1. St. Louis
2. New York City
3. Chicago
4. San Francisco
5. Washington, DC

Earnings
College Scorecard (10-YR Post-Entry): $90,646
PayScale (Early Career): $70,000
PayScale (Mid-Career): $126,400
PayScale 20-Year ROI: $799,000

RANKINGS
Money: 4.5
U.S. News: 24, National Universities
Wall Street Journal/THE: 26
Washington Monthly: 27, National Universities

OVERGENERALIZATIONS
Students are:
Ambitious
Career-driven
Wealthy
Politically liberal
Playing hard but working harder

COLLEGE OVERLAPS
Duke University
Northwestern University
University of Michigan
University of Pennsylvania
Vanderbilt University

Wellesley College

Wellesley, Massachusetts | 781-283-2270

In 1995, *The New York Times* proclaimed, "More than any other college—large or small—Wellesley has groomed women who shatter the glass ceiling." Thirty years later, Barnard has surpassed Wellesley for the lowest acceptance rate among women's colleges, but Wellesley's picture-perfect campus in suburban Boston remains the premier pipeline to the boardrooms of America's most powerful companies as well as to the highest levels of politics. Students are known to be a driven bunch as committed to full engagement with campus activities as they are to the exceptionally rigorous classroom experience.

Inside the Classroom
The college's 2,447 undergraduate students can select from 50+ departmental and interdisciplinary majors, and economics, biology, and computer science are the most frequently conferred degrees. All freshmen must complete an expository writing course, and all seniors must demonstrate foreign language proficiency. In between, students are required to complete coursework in natural and physical science, mathematical modeling and problem-solving, social and behavioral analysis, language and literature, art/music/theater/film/video, epistemology and cognition, historical studies, and religion/ethics/moral philosophy. There is also a multicultural and an uncredited physical education requirement.

The student-to-faculty ratio is only 7:1, leading to an average class size of just 17 students. Thirty-six percent of course sections have single-digit enrollments while 77% have 19 or fewer students. With no graduate students to compete with, opportunities for participation in research with faculty members abound. The Summer Science Research Program is cited by many graduates as the most influential part of their educational experience. Wellesley students also regularly land research positions with the National Institutes of Health, Harvard Medical School, MIT, and The Children's Hospital of Philadelphia. The Office of International Studies facilitates the overseas study of hundreds of students each year with 45% of juniors spending a semester in one of 160 programs worldwide.

The entire undergraduate program at Wellesley is revered by top corporations and graduate schools alike. Most programs possess sterling reputations, including chemistry, computer science, neuroscience, and political science. However, the Department of Economics appears to shine most brightly, leading many into PhD programs and high-profile careers. A large number of Wellesley graduates are awarded prestigious postgraduate scholarships each year. In 2023, the school produced eight Fulbright Scholars, and has seen Gilman Scholars, Watson Fellows, Critical Languages Scholars, and Princeton in Asia Fellows in recent years.

Outside the Classroom
In the 2022-23 school year, 91% of undergraduates are denizens of the school's 21 residence halls that range in capacity from 40 to 285 students. Wellesley's 500-acre campus was described by fabled architect Frederick Olmstead as possessing "a peculiar kind of intricate beauty." Thanks to Lake Waban, a golf course, an arboretum, and botanical gardens, you will never long for gorgeous landscapes and natural beauty. There are thirteen varsity athletic teams that are members of NCAA Division III as well as eight club teams in sports that include archery, equestrian, and Nordic skiing. Athletic facilities are extensive and include the Keohane Sports Center, a pool, spin rooms, dance studios, a rock climbing wall, and just about any other fitness-related amenity one can conjure up. Wellesley women have 180 student-run organizations to choose from, including a number of dance, music, and theater groups. This is a tradition-rich school with annual events like Flower Sunday and quarterly competitions like Stepsinging, a class-vs.-class singing contest on the steps of Houghton Chapel. The town of Wellesley has coffee shops, a bookstore, and a pharmacy all within a short walk. Downtown Boston is less than half an hour away by car, but most take the T, commuter trains, or a shuttle that regularly departs from campus.

Career Services
The Wellesley Career Education Office is staffed by 27 professionals working in career counseling, internships, fellowships, experiential learning, and employer relations. For a school with 2,400+ students, the size and scope of this office are remarkable. The 91:1 student-to-advisor ratio is unmatched by any institution in the country. It's no wonder that the National Association of Colleges and Employers named Wellesley the winner of the Career Service Excellence Award among small colleges; the department has been similarly recognized multiple times by national organizations for its superior career service offerings. Staff members regularly present at national conferences and publish on the topic of career preparation.

E-mail: admission@wellesley.edu | Website: wellesley.edu

The office had a 98% satisfaction rate after in-person, one-on-one appointments; that was a dramatic improvement over the Class of 2015's satisfaction rate of 45%. Ninety-five percent of undergraduates complete at least one internship, including so-called Signature Internships with "leading cultural, educational, and scientific institutions; international agencies; media outlets; advocacy and community organizations; and businesses" around the globe. In one recent academic year, 98% of the undergraduate population engaged digitally or face-to-face with career services. The annual total of advising sessions exceeds 6,000. There were 232 seniors who were matched with an alumnae advisor in their area of interest. Unlike some of the other Seven Sister institutions, opportunities at the world's premier companies are commonplace, and salaries are higher than average. With superb resources and equally strong outcomes, the Wellesley Career Education Office deserves all of the many accolades that have been heaped upon it.

Professional Outcomes

Six months after earning their degrees, 97% of the Wellesley College Class of 2022 had already achieved positive outcomes. Of the 76% of grads who were employed, 24% were working in the finance/consulting/business fields, 17% in education, 17% in internet and technology & engineering, and 15% in healthcare/life sciences. The top employers included JPMorgan Chase, Google, Boston Children's Hospital, Goldman Sachs, and a number of top universities that included Harvard and MIT. One hundred and thirty-five members of the Class of 2022 were employed in Massachusetts, 57 in New York, 32 in California, and 20 in Washington, DC. The average starting salary for one recent cohort was a solid $63k with an average bonus of $14k.

Wellesley grads almost universally go on to elite graduate programs. Of the 20% of 2022 grads who directly entered an advanced degree program, the top dozen most common schools attended included Ivies Harvard, Columbia, Brown, Penn, and Cornell and other upper-crust institutions at Stanford, MIT, Emory, NYU, Brandeis, Boston University, and the Olin College of Engineering. Medical school applicants are generally successful; in one recent 10-year period, an average of 72% of med school hopefuls were accepted by at least one university. Three or more recent grads have been accepted into medical school at Dartmouth, Tufts, Case Western, Boston University, and Northwestern. Law school acceptance rates hover in the low-to mid 80s, a figure that is lowered by the caliber of law schools to which Wellesley grads typically apply. Law schools that accepted a minimum of three alumni in recent years include Yale, Duke, Harvard, Georgetown, Cornell, Penn, and UC Berkeley.

Admission

The 8,491 applications received for a place in the Class of 2026 was the highest total in school history; the acceptance rate was 14%. The mid-50% ranges of those enrolled were 1440-1540 on the SAT and 33-35 on the ACT, and 89% were in the top 10% of their class. Wellesley boasts a high yield rate of 51%, meaning that few apply on a whim, and nearly half of all admitted students choose to enroll in the college.

As part of its holistic review process, the admissions committee seeks "people who know that we don't know everything; who have a strong voice but listen to other voices; who have big plans but are totally open to changing them; who have taken risks, failed, and figured out a better way." As such, four factors are paramount in the evaluation process: character/personal qualities, recommendations, GPA, and rigor of one's secondary school record. The second tier of factors includes class rank, essays, talent/ability, and extracurricular activities. Applying via early decision can yield a massive advantage as 30% of applicants were accepted during the Class of 2026 ED round. In terms of pure acceptance rate, Wellesley is the second-most selective Seven Sisters school, behind only Barnard. High grades and strong test scores are required, but many softer factors weigh heavily on admissions decisions. Applicants who are involved in their high schools and communities will fare best.

Worth Your Money?

Even at an $85,000 annual cost of attendance, Wellesley is unquestionably worth the investment. You won't receive merit aid from this school, but 55% of the student population does receive need-based aid, and 100% of that group sees their need fully met. That translates to an average need-based grant of $64k. The quality of the education, mentorship, and professional networks make Wellesley, even at full price for non-STEM/business majors, the rare school that will return your money many times over.

FINANCIAL
Institutional Type: Private
In-State Tuition: $64,320
Out-of-State Tuition: $64,320
Room & Board: $19,920
Books & Supplies: $800

Avg. Need-Based Grant: $62,132
Avg. % of Need Met: 100%

Avg. Merit-Based Award: $22,306
% Receiving (Freshmen w/o Need): <1%

Avg. Cumulative Debt: $18,512
% of Students Borrowing: 41%

CAREER
Who Recruits
1. Boston Consulting Group
2. Teach for America
3. U.S. Federal Reserve
4. Massachusetts General Hospital
5. State Street

Notable Internships
1. Metropolitan Museum of Art
2. American Express
3. Dick Clark Productions

Top Employers
1. Google
2. Microsoft
3. Accenture
4. Amazon
5. Facebook

Where Alumni Work
1. Boston
2. New York City
3. San Francisco
4. Washington, DC
5. Los Angeles

Earnings
College Scorecard (10-YR Post-Entry): $75,784
PayScale (Early Career): $65,800
PayScale (Mid-Career): $114,800
PayScale 20-Year ROI: $665,000

RANKINGS
Money: 4.5
U.S. News: 4, Liberal Arts Colleges
Wall Street Journal/THE: 117
Washington Monthly: 17, Liberal Arts Colleges

OVERGENERALIZATIONS
Students are:
Always studying
Politically liberal
Highly motivated
Diverse
Always admiring the beauty of their campus

COLLEGE OVERLAPS
Barnard College
Brown University
Smith College
Tufts University
University of Pennsylvania

Wesleyan University

Middletown, Connecticut | 860-685-3000

Considered one of the "Little Ivies" and officially a member of the "Little Three" alongside Amherst and Williams, Wesleyan University in Middletown, Connecticut, has much in common with its highly selective compatriots, but it also possesses a distinctively uncompromising and independent-minded student body. One telling anecdote comes from 1998 when the administration proudly unveiled the school's new slogan, "The Independent Ivy." Many young people would love for their college to associate itself with the cache of the Ivy League, but at Wesleyan, the student response was utter disgust that led to an all-out rebellion. The students launched a vocal protest, and the higher-ups quickly dropped the slogan. That's Wesleyan in a nutshell.

Inside the Classroom
At 3,069 undergraduate students, Wes is significantly larger than many of its elite liberal arts peers. With 45 majors, 32 minors, and over 1,000 classes running each academic year, the school truly has something for everyone. The academic requirements are relatively minimal, giving undergrads a high degree of intellectual freedom. There are two stages of general education courses: stage one sees students complete two courses each in the three divisions of Humanities & Arts, Social & Behavioral Sciences, and Natural Sciences & Math. Stage two is optional for most majors but may be required to receive departmental honors at graduation.

Just under three-quarters of class sections have fewer than twenty students, allowing for close bonds/mentorships to unfold. Students rave about the accessible faculty (the faculty-to-student ratio is 7:1), and research opportunities with professors are plentiful. The undergraduate program for Research in the Sciences funds over one hundred students per year to conduct research over the summer. The university has increased its study abroad participation in recent years to the point that almost 50% of students now spend a semester overseas.

There isn't one go-to major at Wes; while the social sciences (24%), psychology (17%), the visual and performing arts (12%), and ethnic/gender studies (8%), are the most popular, none represents a massive percentage of the total degrees conferred. Nearly every program at Wesleyan is respected in the employer/graduate school communities, with offerings in economics, English, film studies, and neuroscience receiving perhaps the most praise. Wesleyan was again named a top producer of Fulbright Scholars in 2023, seeing seven student and alumni winners.

Outside the Classroom
The unofficial but popular motto, "Keep Wes Weird," perfectly sums up this iconoclastic student body's vibe and helps describe life on campus. Those looking for wild frat parties and raucous football games would be highly disappointed (and confused) walking around the Wesleyan campus. Greek life attracts a minuscule 1% of students and, other than the one-quarter of undergraduates who comprise the rosters of the school's 30 varsity sports teams, athletics are not a focal point for the average student. That being said, participation is high in intramural and club sports including ultimate Frisbee, kung fu, and WesClimb, which takes advantage of the school's own rock climbing wall. Wesleyan's other amenities include a 412-seat movie theater that screens films throughout the year, a 50-meter swimming pool, a 7,500-square-foot gymnasium, and an ice skating rink. There are more than 200 active student-run groups with large numbers in the areas of activism/politics, identity, theater, comedy troupes, and a cappella. The Center for the Arts hosts hundreds of events each year from jazz concerts to one-person shows to art exhibitions. Middletown provides a nice enough small city environment with plenty of bars and restaurants to frequent, and Hartford is only a 25-minute drive. Just about everyone lives on campus.

Career Services
The Gordon Career Center is staffed by 13 full-time staff who specialize in employer relations, general advising, health professions advising, STEM career advising, and business career advising. The 236:1 student-to-advisor ratio places it in the above-average range compared to other schools profiled in this guide. The school does not organize any large career expos/fairs; instead, it hosts events just about every day along the lines of a chat over coffee with Deloitte to a gathering entitled "Google at Wes: Laying the Foundation for Your Technical Career" featuring Wesleyan alumni who work for the tech giant.

Wesleyan University

E-mail: admissions@wesleyan.edu | Website: wesleyan.edu

Wes has partnered with a number of major employers to facilitate on-campus recruiting and interviews including Booz Allen Hamilton, LEGO (fun!), Pfizer, and Squarespace. Interested seniors participate in a job search boot camp known as Accelerate prior to engaging with those visiting companies. The WEShadow Externship programs allow current students the chance to spend anywhere from one day to one week at work with an alum. The Winter on Wyllys program is an intensive, two-week career development course available over the holidays. Data on internship participation rates and overall engagements with the career center is, at present, unavailable.

Professional Outcomes

By the end of calendar year 2022, the majority of those who received their diplomas in May had entered employment (66%). Graduate school was the next stop for 18% of new alums, and 10% were still seeking employment (down from 19% two years ago). Of those who landed jobs, the third-highest number were in arts and entertainment, which isn't shocking when your school's alumni include the likes of Lin Manuel Miranda, Michael Bay, Dana Delaney, and countless Hollywood writers and producers. Tech/engineering/sciences and education took the silver and gold. The companies employing the highest numbers of recent Wesleyan grads included Google, Epic, Analysis Group, Boston Medical Center, Booz Allen Hamilton, Accenture, and Apple. New York, Boston, San Francisco, and Hartford were the most popular post-college destinations.

Wes alumni are looked upon favorably by elite graduate and professional schools. In a recent seven-year stretch, Wesleyan grads were accepted into medical school 51-76% of the time, much higher than the national average. Those with a 3.6 GPA or higher enjoyed a superior acceptance rate. In the last five years, law school applicants were successful 76-100% of the time and fared extremely well at the most prestigious universities. One year, a gasp-worthy 64% of law school-bound seniors found a home at a top ten law school including Yale, Harvard, Stanford, Columbia, and UChicago. Those pursuing non-professional advanced degrees enrolled in a wide range of schools from elites like MIT, Stanford, and Berkeley to state universities like Rowan, Temple, and UMass.

Admission

Wesleyan admitted 14% of its 14,521 applicants into the Class of 2026, lower than the 19% mark the previous cycle. The mid-50% range on the SAT for members of the Class of 2026 was 1310-1505 and 30.5-34 on the ACT. Interestingly, this past cycle's acceptance rate was only slightly lower than that of a decade ago when the university welcomed only 15% of applicants. Yet, somehow that is fitting because Wesleyan's admissions, like its eclectic and talented students, is not unidimensional.

Unlike some other schools of its caliber, Wesleyan does not rule out those who finished outside of the top 10% of their high school class. While 79% of the Class of 2026 earned that distinction, less than 1% placed outside the top 50%. The No. 1 factor in admissions is the rigor of secondary school curriculum as it seeks young people who are "intellectual risk-takers" above all else. Standardized test scores have been made less important by Wesleyan's test-optional policy, but the vast majority of applicants submitted SAT or ACT scores in 2022. Applying early decision is definitely something you want to consider if Wesleyan is your top choice because it fills 54% of its freshman class via ED, and it has an admit rate more than triple that of the regular cycle (41% versus 12%). Getting into Wesleyan is not as formulaic a process as it is at the majority of elite institutions. Essays, recommendations, first-generation status, ethnicity, personal characteristics, and performance in the classroom are all given genuine consideration. Possessing good stats is important to your admissions chances, but so is being an engaged and passionate learner.

Worth Your Money?

Wesleyan costs $89k annually, a price similar to its elite liberal arts kin. A tiny percentage of students receive substantial merit aid, but it is need-based aid that rules the day at Wes as all qualifying students have 100% of their demonstrated need accounted for. The average grant for those individuals is $62,000. Not every student who goes to this school cruises into a six-figure job, but that's the aim of a Wesleyan education. This school is worth the cost because it assists you in finding a pathway that aligns with your passions, and it makes the school affordable for those in financial need.

FINANCIAL
Institutional Type: Private
In-State Tuition: $67,016
Out-of-State Tuition: $67,016
Room & Board: $19,034
Books & Supplies: $1,200

Avg. Need-Based Grant: $62,338
Avg. % of Need Met: 100%

Avg. Merit-Based Award: $43,394
% Receiving (Freshmen w/o Need): <1%

Avg. Cumulative Debt: $25,283
% of Students Borrowing: 28%

CAREER
Who Recruits
1. MGM Resorts International
2. Pfizer
3. Analysis Group
4. McKinsey & Co.
5. Charles River Associates

Notable Internships
1. Citadel Securities
2. ABC News
3. United Nations

Top Employers
1. Google
2. Citi
3. JPMorgan Chase
4. Accenture
5. Morgan Stanley

Where Alumni Work
1. New York City
2. Boston
3. San Francisco
4. Hartford
5. Washington, DC

Earnings
College Scorecard (10-YR Post-Entry): $72,547
PayScale (Early Career): $67,000
PayScale (Mid-Career): $129,600
PayScale 20-Year ROI: $650,000

RANKINGS
Money: 4.5
U.S. News: 11, Liberal Arts Colleges
Wall Street Journal/THE: 73
Washington Monthly: 3, Liberal Arts Colleges

OVERGENERALIZATIONS
Students are:
Passionate
Politically liberal
Play hard but work harder
Opinionated
Individualistic

COLLEGE OVERLAPS
Brown University
Cornell University
Middlebury College
Tufts University
Vassar College

Whitman College

Walla Walla, Washington | 509-527-5176

ADMISSION
Admission Rate: 48%
Admission Rate - Men: 43%
Admission Rate - Women: 51%
EA Admission Rate: Not Offered
ED Admission Rate: 44%
ED Admits as % of Total Admits: 4%
Admission Rate (5-Year Trend): -4%
% of Admits Attending (Yield): 13%
Transfer Admission Rate: 61%

SAT Reading/Writing (Middle 50%): 645-740
SAT Math (Middle 50%): 648-733
ACT Composite (Middle 50%): 30-33

% Graduated in Top 10% of HS Class: 40%
% Graduated in Top 25% of HS Class: 70%
% Graduated in Top 50% of HS Class: 95%

Demonstrated Interest: Considered
Legacy Status: Considered
Racial/Ethnic Status: Considered
Admission Interview Offered: Yes

ENROLLMENT
Total Undergraduate Enrollment: 1,493
% Full-Time: 98%
% Male: 44%
% Female: 56%
% Out-of-State: 64%
% Fraternity: 19%
% Sorority: 12%
% On-Campus (All Undergraduate): 72%
Freshman Housing Required: Yes

% African-American: 3%
% Asian: 6%
% Hispanic: 9%
% White: 61%
% Other: 2%
% International: 12%
% Low-Income: 15%

ACADEMICS
Student-to-Faculty Ratio: 9 to 1
% of Classes Under 20: 69%
% of Classes 20-49: 31%
% of Classes 50 or More: 0%
% Full-Time Faculty: 88%
% Full-Time Faculty w/ Terminal Degree: 96%

Top Programs
Art
Astronomy
Biology
Chemistry
Economics
Film and Media Studies
Philosophy
Politics

Retention Rate: 85%
4-Year Graduation Rate: 83%
6-Year Graduation Rate: 89%

Curricular Flexibility: Somewhat Flexible
Academic Rating: ★★★★

#CollegesWorthYourMoney

Due to its location in Walla Walla, Washington, there are plenty of experienced high school guidance counselors around the country who have never even heard of Whitman College. Despite a lack of instant name recognition, you'll find Whitman side-by-side in the rankings with better-known West Coast liberal arts powerhouses like Colorado College, Pitzer, and Occidental. And there's a good reason for these accolades—few colleges in the Pacific Northwest offer the intimate and supportive academic and social environment available at Whitman. The 1,493 students at Whitman, all undergrads, are a collection of high school stars who possess mid-50% SAT scores of 1310-1460 and an A/A- average in a mostly AP slate of courses. With 51 majors and 35 minors, the academic offerings at this college are robust, particularly when considering its modest size.

Inside the Classroom
The Encounters Program greets freshmen with a yearlong introduction to the liberal arts. Organized around a number of themes, these courses focus on "primary sources, discussion, writing, and the construction of knowledge across academic fields." Regardless of major, all students also must pass two courses in cultural pluralism, the humanities, the social sciences, fine arts, and the sciences as well as one course in quantitative analysis. Biology, environmental studies, geology, chemistry, economics, sociology, and politics majors are all required to complete a senior research thesis.

Whitman boasts a beautifully low 9:1 student-to-faculty ratio and hosts zero graduate students, a recipe for individualized attention. The faculty has a reputation for being extremely available, attentive, and invested in undergraduate education. Undergraduate research is so embedded into the foundation of a Whitman education that the college hosts an annual Undergraduate Conference for students to present their work. Greater than 45% of juniors study abroad in one of 80+ programs in 40 countries around the globe.

By major, the greatest number of degrees are typically conferred in the social sciences (22%), biology (15%), psychology (9%), the visual and performing arts (9%), and the physical sciences (8%). All degree programs have solid reputations, but the biology, politics, and economics departments all have an extra shine. Whitman also does an amazing job funneling students into the most prestigious postgraduate fellowship programs. Over the last decade, Whitties have captured over 60 Fulbright Scholarships, 25 National Science Foundation Fellowships, a dozen Watson Fellowships, and even one Rhodes Scholarship.

Outside the Classroom
One might assume that a school with fewer than 1,500 undergraduates would house just about everyone, especially with a spacious 117-acre campus. However, only 72% of Whitman students reside in one of the four freshman-only dorms, four upperclassmen dorms, or the eleven Interest Houses centered around commonalities like fine arts, the environment, or Asian studies. You also might expect a West Coast liberal arts school like Whitman to be Greek-free, or at least to have a minimal frat/sorority presence on campus, yet that is not at all the case. Nineteen percent of men and 12% of women join fraternities and sororities, but it is important to note that they are generally viewed as inclusive and laid-back collectives in contrast to many Greek organizations at large universities. There are 17 varsity NCAA Division III sports teams as well as 12 club and sixteen intramural squads. Forty-six percent of undergrads play intramurals, and 15% are varsity athletes. Of the close to one hundred student organizations on campus, the Outdoor Program is one of the most popular. Many students participate in its weekend hiking, kayaking, climbing, and skiing adventures. The school also had a run of award-winning debate teams within the last decade. Walla Walla is technically a city, but it's more of a quaint and charming Pacific Northwestern small town. Seattle and Portland are each over a four-hour drive.

Career Services
The Career and Community Engagement Center (CCEC) at Whitman College employs 13 professional staff members and many undergraduate employees, many of whom serve as peer advisors. The full-time professionals serve students through career coaching, community engagement, and internship coordination. Only counting those 13 professionals, the CCEC still comes out with a 115:1 student-to-advisor ratio, stronger than the vast majority of colleges profiled in this guide. Thanks to that terrific level of support, Whitties can schedule up to an hour of one-on-one career counseling whenever they like. The office lays out a Four-Phase Plan that, beginning freshman year, helps students begin, develop, refine, and own their stories through job shadowing, internships, alumni networking, job fairs, community service, graduate school exploration, and professional development.

Community service is a major part of the Whitman experience, and the SEC facilitates experiential opportunities in Walla Walla for 320 students per week. 70% of undergraduates participate each year. Many summer internships are arranged at local organizations like the Walla Walla Public Health Department, the Walla Walla Symphony, and a local minor league baseball team. The school is supportive of those wishing to spend their summers at nonprofits and funds more than 130 such internships per year. The Whitman Connect program helps link current students with the college's 18,000+ alumni, and 75 alumni and parents provide job-shadowing opportunities over spring break. Despite a dearth of national companies visiting campus and mediocre salary statistics, this office can be counted on to provide individualized nurturing and career guidance.

Professional Outcomes

After graduation, 64% of Whitman grads immediately begin their careers and 20% enroll directly in graduate programs. When you confer fewer than 400 degrees each year, you don't expect to have massive pockets of graduates joining major corporations. However, it is worth noting that twenty or more alumni currently work for Microsoft, Amazon, Boeing, Starbucks, T-Mobile, and Nordstrom. In the last few years, students have taken interesting first jobs including as a paralegal at the US Department of Justice-Antitrust Division, audio archivist at the Smithsonian, and marketing assistant at Oxford University Press. The largest number of Whitties settle in Seattle, but Portland, San Francisco, Los Angeles, New York, and Denver are other common destinations. Mid-career median pay is on the lower side among elite liberal arts schools, in the same range as Occidental, Reed, Kenyon, Vassar, and Macalester. Part of the lower median pay figure may be attributable to the high number of Whitman alumni who are continuing their educations well into their late twenties and early thirties.

Over 60% of Whitman graduates continue their educations at a wide range of graduate and professional programs (again, 20% do so right out of undergrad). In the last decade, the school has sent graduates to law schools such as Berkeley, the University of Washington, Columbia, Georgetown, Duke, the University of Pennsylvania, and the University of Chicago. In that same time, premed students have headed to elite medical programs at Northwestern, UVA, Dartmouth, and Stanford. A significant number of Whitman grads go on to earn PhDs; the school ranks in the top 25 nationwide in that department (on a per capita basis). While many attend elite graduate/professional programs, plenty of other grads head to West Coast publics like Colorado State University, Oregon State University, and Washington State University.

Admission

Whitman's 48% acceptance rate for the Class of 2026 represented a typical figure for the college (although 11 points lower than the previous year), but it should be eye-opening for any teen looking for an elite school on the West Coast. A test-optional school for almost a decade, those who submit scores have a middle-50% SAT score of 1310-1460 and 29-33 on the ACT. Forty percent hail from the top decile of their high school class, and 70% placed in the top quartile. The average GPA was a 3.68, and 56% of applicants earned above a 3.75. Whitman is the rare elite college that has become slightly easier to get into in recent years. A decade ago, the acceptance rate was a similar 46%, SAT/ACT scores were comparable, and the average GPA was actually higher.

Rigor of academic record, GPA, and the application essay form the triumvirate of "most important" factors in the eyes of the committee. Recommendations, extracurricular activities, talent/ability, and character/personal characteristics are next in order of importance. In 2022-23, the college received 255 early decision applications and welcomed 43% into the fold, meaning that there was no advantage granted to those willing to commit through ED. The admissions committee states that it is seeking "curious, inspired, and highly engaged students with a passion for learning and a wide and eclectic range of interests; the kind of independent-minded students who are motivated to take intellectual risks in order to become the kind of leaders who can make a difference in the world." The school's admissions practices seem to support that sentiment.

Worth Your Money?

The cost of attendance at Whitman is $78k, not an unexpected amount for a liberal arts college with such an intimate classroom and campus environment. Fortunately, approximately half of Whitman undergrads qualify for need-based aid with an average annual grant of more than $42k. For those who receive a generous merit or need-based offer, Whitman can absolutely be worth your money; at full price, this may not be the best choice for families lacking the funds to pay the costs upfront.

FINANCIAL
Institutional Type: Private
In-State Tuition: $61,492
Out-of-State Tuition: $61,492
Room & Board: $14,640
Books & Supplies: $1,400

Avg. Need-Based Grant: $42,642
Avg. % of Need Met: 91%

Avg. Merit-Based Award: $16,330
% Receiving (Freshmen w/o Need): 42%

Avg. Cumulative Debt: $19,217
% of Students Borrowing: 43%

CAREER
Who Recruits
1. The Spur Group
2. Peace Corps
3. Baker Boyer Bank
4. TFA
5. Pacific Northwest National Laboratory

Notable Internships
1. WebMD
2. U.S. House of Representatives
3. Bloomsbury USA

Top Employers
1. Microsoft
2. Amazon
3. Boeing
4. The Spur Group
5. T-Mobile

Where Alumni Work
1. Seattle
2. Portland, OR
3. San Francisco
4. Richland, WA
5. Los Angeles

Earnings
College Scorecard (10-YR Post-Entry): $64,442
PayScale (Early Career): $59,800
PayScale (Mid-Career): $119,700
PayScale 20-Year ROI: $403,000

RANKINGS
Money: 4
U.S. News: 46, Liberal Arts Colleges
Wall Street Journal/THE: Not Ranked
Washington Monthly: 75, Liberal Arts Colleges

OVERGENERALIZATIONS
Students are:
Politically liberal
Outdoorsy
Environmentally conscious
Tight-knit (possess a strong sense of community)
Not afraid to work hard

COLLEGE OVERLAPS
Colorado College
Lewis & Clark College
Macalester College
Occidental College
Pomona College

Willamette University

Salem, Oregon | 503-370-6303

ADMISSION
Admission Rate: 81%
Admission Rate - Men: 78%
Admission Rate - Women: 82%
EA Admission Rate: 90%
ED Admission Rate: 77%
ED Admits as % of Total Admits: 1%
Admission Rate (5-Year Trend): -8%
% of Admits Attending (Yield): 16%
Transfer Admission Rate: 53%

SAT Reading/Writing (Middle 50%): 630-710
SAT Math (Middle 50%): 600-710
ACT Composite (Middle 50%): 27-33

% Graduated in Top 10% of HS Class: 41%
% Graduated in Top 25% of HS Class: 68%
% Graduated in Top 50% of HS Class: 94%

Demonstrated Interest: Not Considered
Legacy Status: Considered
Racial/Ethnic Status: Considered
Admission Interview Offered: Yes

ENROLLMENT
Total Undergraduate Enrollment: 1,367
% Full-Time: 99%
% Male: 41%
% Female: 59%
% Out-of-State: 70%
% Fraternity: 6%
% Sorority: 7%
% On-Campus (All Undergraduate): 67%
Freshman Housing Required: Yes

% African-American: 2%
% Asian: 5%
% Hispanic: 15%
% White: 67%
% Other: 2%
% International: 1%
% Low-Income: 22%

ACADEMICS
Student-to-Faculty Ratio: 11 to 1
% of Classes Under 20: 75%
% of Classes 20-49: 25%
% of Classes 50 or More: 0%
% Full-Time Faculty: 71%
% Full-Time Faculty w/ Terminal Degree: 100%

Top Programs
Chemistry
Civic Communication and Media
Economics
Environmental Science
Exercise and Health Science
History
Japanese Studies
Mathematics

Retention Rate: 82%
4-Year Graduation Rate: 68%
6-Year Graduation Rate: 73%

Curricular Flexibility: Somewhat Flexible
Academic Rating: ★★★↲

#CollegesWorthYourMoney

Founded in 1842, the oldest university in the Western United States is not a school that the average American has likely ever heard of. Willamette University in Salem, OR, is a liberal arts institution that caters to just 1,367 undergraduates and another 548 graduate students who study in the Atkinson Graduate College of Management or the Willamette University College of Law. More than 30 distinct undergraduate majors are offered at this vastly underrated (by the general public; it fares well in national rankings) liberal arts school that accepts four times as many applicants as it rejects.

Inside the Classroom

The General Education Program at Willamette includes a College Colloquium, a small (14 students max) course for first-semester freshmen that encourages discussion and inquiry. All undergrads also complete two writing-centered courses, three world engagement classes (which encompass all foreign languages), and liberal arts distribution credits that involve one course in each of the arts and humanities, natural sciences, and social sciences. There are 31 credits required to earn a diploma (courses are worth one credit each), and no more than three credits can be completed via credited internships.

Aided by an 11:1 student-to-faculty ratio, Willamette classes are exceptionally small with 75% of sections enrolling fewer than 20 students; 20% of sections enroll fewer than 10. Undergraduate research is taken seriously, and Willamette offers more than 75 undergraduate research grants annually across all disciplines—hard sciences, humanities, and the arts. It is not uncommon for professors to invite undergrads to collaborate on scholarly projects or for a student's name to appear on a published journal article. A typical year also sees 40% of undergrads earn credit through study abroad opportunities in one of more than 40 countries.

The greatest number of degrees conferred in 2022 were in the social sciences (16%) followed by a fairly even distribution among psychology (9%), biology (9%), natural resources and conservation (8%), and foreign languages (6%). When it comes to producing postgraduate fellowship winners, Willamette is in elite company. The school joins Middlebury, Pomona, and the University of Richmond as the only four baccalaureate institutions to be named top producers of both Fulbright students and Fulbright Scholars in one recent year. Willamette often has two or more National Science Foundation Graduate Research Fellowship winners per year, and it has had a smattering of Truman and Gilman Scholars as well.

Outside the Classroom

Almost 70% of current undergraduates hail from out of state, and the vast majority of freshmen (95%) elect to live on campus while 67% of the entire undergraduate student body does the same. Six percent of men join fraternities, and 7% of women pledge a sorority. The college's 61-acre main campus houses 52 buildings, but the school also owns 305 acres of Zena Forest, which is heavily utilized by the environmental science and forestry programs. There are 20 varsity athletic teams, and although 25% of the student body participates in intercollegiate athletics, no one would mistake the Bearcats for a sports-centric institution. But it does have the distinction of fielding the first female football player, a kicker, in 1997. Overall, there are 40 intramural and club sports teams, 100+ organizations, and over 70,000 community service hours completed each year. The college is situated about one hour south of Portland, but being located in the state capital of Salem, there are plenty of noteworthy attractions in its own neighborhood; the state capitol building is across the street from the college. Oregon's third-largest art museum, multiple theaters, countless shops, bakeries, restaurants, and several beautiful parks are all within walking distance of campus.

Career Services

The Career Development staff at Willamette consists of nine professional employees, which calculates to a tremendous 152:1 student-to-counselor ratio. In addition to a director, an internship coordinator, an assistant director of career education, and a career programs coordinator, there are three undergraduate interns who are available to assist their peers. One unique feature of Willamette's career services is the existence of six career communities that students can join as early as freshman year. They link students to mentors, internship opportunities, and extracurricular activities in a chosen area of interest.

By graduation, 55% of students have completed at least one internship, and the college makes it fairly easy to receive credit for those experiences. Along the way, students complete modules in the Passport to Professionalism online program that bolsters Bearcats' general workplace readiness skills. Career Development staff are readily available to provide one-on-one assistance in the areas of interview prep, resume/cover letter development, or career exploration. The school utilizes Handshake to connect students to job and internship openings, but it also runs a platform called WUConnect that makes it easy for current undergrads to forge connections with alumni who are willing to share their expertise.

Professional Outcomes

For such a small school, you might assume that grads do not end up in large numbers in any one corporation, but that is not the case. In fact, two dozen or more alumni work for the likes of Nike, Intel, Kaiser Permanente, Microsoft, Amazon, and Wells Fargo. Portland has the highest concentration of Bearcats followed by Seattle, San Francisco, Los Angeles, and Denver. Graduates of the College of Arts & Sciences enjoy an average mid-career salary of $107k. Alumni have gone on to all kinds of interesting careers including analytics for the Houston Astros, IT engineer at Netflix, lead investigator at the National Cancer Institute, and bestselling author of young adult fiction.

Many undergraduates heading to law school stay in Salem at Willamette's College of Law; in 2021 it launched a 3+3 or 3+4 dual program that allows applicants to gain acceptance to its undergraduate school and law school simultaneously. Those seeking to enter medical, pharmacy, dental, or veterinary school benefit from the personalized attention and research opportunities provided by the college's pre-health track. Recent graduates have gone on to enroll at the University of Utah School of Medicine, the Oregon Health Science University School of Medicine, and the University of Colorado School of Medicine.

Admission

Willamette adopted a test-optional policy almost a decade ago, and a good number of the roughly 4,000 Class of 2026 applicants took advantage; only 21% submitted an SAT score, and 9% submitted an ACT result. The acceptance rate of 81% is two points higher than the previous year, and among those who submitted scores, the mid-50% range was 1240-1420 on the SAT and 27-33 on the ACT. For a school with an extraordinarily friendly acceptance rate, a look at the grades and class rank of entering 2022-23 freshmen reveals a highly impressive profile. Forty-one percent of the Class of 2026 placed in the top decile of their high school class, and 68% were in the top quartile; the average weighted GPA was 3.96. Those numbers are nearly identical to the previous year's freshman crop.

In evaluating prospective students, the admissions committee looks primarily at rigor of secondary school record, class rank, GPA, and application essays. Recommendations and interviews, which are not mandatory but are highly encouraged, are in the next tier of "important" factors. Only a small number of students apply early decision, but most are successful in gaining admission. Last year, 23 of 30 ED applicants were welcomed aboard.

Worth Your Money?

Willamette introduced a new level of "tuition transparency" a couple of years back, reducing its list tuition price by 20%. That effort to make the financial side of choosing a college less opaque is admirable, and it reduces the sticker price to $48,000—$64k with room and board included. Additionally, 99% of students receive some level of financial aid with merit scholarships of up to $20k per year awarded to candidates with stellar credentials. Just under three-fifths of students do borrow money, but the average cumulative debt load among graduates is not at all out of control. Borrowing a modest amount of money to attend Willamette is a perfectly sound move since regional industry connections and alumni salary figures are strong.

FINANCIAL
Institutional Type: Private
In-State Tuition: $48,226
Out-of-State Tuition: $48,226
Room & Board: $15,380
Books & Supplies: $1,178

Avg. Need-Based Grant: $29,802
Avg. % of Need Met: 87%

Avg. Merit-Based Award: $19,629
% Receiving (Freshmen w/o Need): 37%

Avg. Cumulative Debt: $28,722
% of Students Borrowing: 58%

CAREER
Who Recruits
1. Kaiser Permanente
2. Microsoft
3. Intel
4. Nike
5. Boeing

Notable Internships
1. Oregon State Legislature
2. Hallie Ford Museum of Art
3. Oregon State Hospital

Top Employers
1. Oregon Dept. of Justice
2. State of Oregon
3. Saalfeld Griggs PC
4. Miller Nash
5. Perkins Coie

Where Alumni Work
1. Portland
2. Seattle, WA
3. Eugene, OR
4. San Francisco
5. Washington, DC

Earnings
College Scorecard (10-YR Post-Entry): $59,621
PayScale (Early Career): $55,600
PayScale (Mid-Career): $116,100
PayScale 20-Year ROI: $385,000

RANKINGS
Money: 3.5
U.S. News: 75, Liberal Arts Colleges
Wall Street Journal/THE: Not Ranked
Washington Monthly: 86, Liberal Arts Colleges

OVERGENERALIZATIONS
Students are:
Friendly
Tight-knit (possess a strong sense of community)
Laid-back but not afraid to work hard
Politically liberal
Involved/investsed in campus life

COLLEGE OVERLAPS
Lewis & Clark College
Reed College
University of Oregon
University of Puget Sound
Whitman College

Williams College

Williamstown, Massachusetts | 413-597-2211

Massachusetts is home to many of the finest and most historic institutions of higher learning in the United States. Starting in Boston and traveling west you would encounter many schools featured in this book—MIT, Harvard, BU, BC, Northeastern, Tufts, Brandeis, Wellesley—and, eventually, the more remote campuses of Amherst and Mount Holyoke and, lastly, tucked in the Northwest corner of the state just below Vermont you would encounter the Bay State's second-oldest school and one of the most prestigious liberal arts schools in the entire country, Williams College. Set on 450 rural acres in the Berkshires, Williams educates 2,152 of the brightest and most talented undergraduates one can find. The school's 25 academic departments offer 36 majors and a number of concentrations rather than minors.

Inside the Classroom

Students only take 32 total courses—four per semester—as opposed to the standard five. A Winter Study session also runs for twenty-two days in January when students can dedicate all of their attention to one course. Prior to graduation, students must complete three courses in each of three Divisions: Languages and the Arts, Social Studies, and Science and Mathematics. Additionally, two writing-intensive courses and one course in quantitative reasoning are required. Rare for a liberal arts school of this caliber, no foreign language is required. Instead, the option exists to take a class exploring how different cultures interact with one another. While not quite as open as the curriculum at Brown or Amherst, Williams certainly gives its students their fair share of autonomy when it comes to course selection.

The college possesses an excellent 7:1 student-to-faculty ratio, and 99% of professorial attention goes to under-grads (they only run two small graduate programs). An unparalleled 40% of courses have fewer than ten students enrolled; the median class size is 12 students. Thanks to relationships built with faculty through such small classes, one Williams student said, "Students often just need to talk to a professor to find a research opportunity." However, many formal opportunities to engage in undergraduate research exist in the summer, during a semester, or as part of one's senior honors thesis. Close to 50% of the junior class connects with the International Education and Study Away program to pinpoint the study abroad opportunity that is right for them. Included on that menu is the opportunity to study at Oxford for an entire year.

The greatest number of degrees are conferred in the social sciences (26%), the physical sciences (10%), math and statistics (9%), psychology (9%), and computer science (7%). Any degree from Williams will be viewed most favorably by graduate schools and employers, but programs in economics, English, math, physics and political science are especially renowned. The college also produces a massive number of highly competitive national fellowship winners. In 2023, grads and alums won nine Fulbright Scholarships and 12 NSF Graduate Research Fellowships. In a handful of years, three graduates have been named Rhodes Scholars.

Outside the Classroom

For a supremely studious, tiny liberal enclave buried in the woods, Williams is unexpectedly sports-centric within the NCAA Division III. The Ephs (a shortened version of Ephraim Williams, the school's founder) compete in 32 varsity sports, most of which are members of the New England Small College Athletic Conference. Overall, 35% of the student body competes in intercollegiate sports, and many more join intramural athletic clubs. Fraternities were banished from campus more than 50 years ago, just before the school became co-educational. In the absence of Greek life, extracurriculars take on a larger social role as 96% of Williams undergrads are involved in at least one of the 200 outside-the-classroom organizations. Situated in the Berkshires, there is no big city that makes an easy day trip (Boston and NYC are two or three hours away), but natural beauty is ubiquitous. The largest student-run group, the Williams Outing Club, has 750 members who engage in regular hikes, campouts, and polar bear swims in the Williamstown wilderness. The vast majority of the student body lives on campus, making the school's breathtaking residence halls the epicenter of social activity. Freshmen live together in one of two large, nearly identical residence halls that form the bustling Frosh Quad. Upperclassmen reside in one of twenty-seven more modestly sized buildings.

Career Services

The '68 Center for Career Exploration (CCE) employs 14 full-time staff members who focus on career advising, alumni relations, and employer relations. Specialized help is available for those eying law school, a health profession, entrepreneurship, or a career in technology. The center's 154:1 student-to-advisor ratio is one of the best of any school featured in this guide. Major events hosted by the center's crew include the Fall Job and Internship Fair, which is attended by seventy employers including big names like Bain, Credit Suisse, Deloitte, Epic Systems, The New York Times, and T. Rowe Price. The Spring Job & Internship Fair is primarily focused on nonprofit employers.

Williams alumni are extremely available and willing to lend a hand to current students, and 71% of current students report consulting with an alum to plan their next steps after college. Additionally, alumni-sponsored internships provide 140+ undergraduates with a $3,800 stipend to pursue non-paying summer internships. The center also has introduced a new program of winter study internships with an alum. Overall, a stunning 81% of 2022 grads had at least one internship experience. On-campus interviews are brokered through the CCE, but no data is available on the number of interviews taking place or about on-campus recruiting, although a fair amount of both definitely occur. The college recently identified its tracking of alumni outcomes as being an area of weakness, and it has begun making strides toward remedying the situation. Thanks to its superhuman work getting students into top graduate schools, the '68 Center for Career Exploration still has a glowing reputation.

Professional Outcomes

The top three areas of gain that Williams graduates self-report are thinking critically, writing clearly and effectively, and the ability to learn on their own. It's hard to name three traits that speak more to one's employability, so it shouldn't come as a shock that the most desirable employers adore the school's alumni. Companies/organizations that consistently snatch up Williams graduates include Apple, Google, Goldman Sachs, McKinsey & Co., the Metropolitan Museum of Art, National Institutes of Health, and The New York Times Co. A significant number of students join the Peace Corps or are accepted into Teach for America. Business and education are the industries that attract the most students. New York City, Boston, and San Francisco are the three cities most favored by Ephs post-undergrad. Among the Class of 2022, six months after graduating, 92% were employed or continuing their educational journey. The median annual income for 2022 grads was $75,000.

For Ephs, the bachelor's degrees earned at Williams are unlikely to be their last diplomas. Approximately 75% pursue an advanced degree within five years of leaving the college. The most frequently attended graduate programs are a not-too-shabby trio of Harvard, Columbia, and Yale. The top business, law, and medical schools attracting grads are Harvard, Columbia, and Penn. Using LinkedIn data, we were able to determine that Williams College sends one of the highest percentages of graduates to prestigious medical schools of any institution in the country. It also ranked eighth overall on our list of the top producers of future PhDs and was the fourth-leading producer of economics PhDs (also by percentage).

Admission

Williams' Class of 2026 admissions data looks extremely similar to that of rival Amherst. The acceptance rate was 8% (Amherst was 7%), and the median standardized test scores of enrolled students were a 1520 on the SAT and a 35 on the ACT. Only 13% of 2022-23 freshmen were not in the top 10% of their high school class. Nothing earth-shattering has occurred in Williams' admissions standards in recent years. Like many comparably ultra-selective liberal arts colleges, the admit rate has declined; in 2011, the college accepted 17% of the applicant pool.

The admissions office views all of the meat-and-potatoes factors as holding the most weight: rigorous schedule, class rank, and GPA, but recommendations are read carefully and character/personal qualities are valued as well. The next tier of criteria includes race/ethnicity, legacy status (over 10% of admitted students are legacies, mostly of the primary variety), first-generation status (20% fit that bill), and factors like volunteer and work experience. Early decision gives you a massive edge; the acceptance rate was 31% for the Class of 2026. Williams seeks a racially and socioeconomically diverse group of uniquely talented students who will thrive in a close-knit academic community. However, few Hail Mary heaves end successfully here.

Worth Your Money?

The annual cost of attendance at Williams is, in the world of elite liberal arts schools in New England, priced at the slightly below average (amazingly) figure of $81k, but those who aren't from wealthy backgrounds will pay far less. In fact, roughly half the student population qualifies for aid, and of that group, all students have 100% of their financial need met with the average award being $66k. For the rich, the Williams bill won't sting too badly; for those in the lower-to-middle income brackets, the school will slice the cost significantly. For those in between, Williams is the caliber of school that is worth taking on debt in order to attend. Learning in seminar-style courses from some of the brightest minds around is worth paying for, and the connections you make (to peers and faculty) will stay with you for a lifetime.

FINANCIAL
Institutional Type: Private
In-State Tuition: $64,860
Out-of-State Tuition: $64,860
Room & Board: $16,300
Books & Supplies: $1,000

Avg. Need-Based Grant: $66,083
Avg. % of Need Met: 100%

Avg. Merit-Based Award: $0
% Receiving (Freshmen w/o Need): 0%

Avg. Cumulative Debt: $13,341
% of Students Borrowing: 32%

CAREER
Who Recruits
1. OC&C Strategy Consultants
2. Teach for America
3. M&T Bank
4. InterSystems
5. Trinity Industries

Notable Internships
1. WeWork
2. Late Night with Seth Meyers
3. Whitney Museum of American Art

Top Employers
1. Google
2. Goldman Sachs
3. Morgan Stanley
4. JPMorgan Chase
5. Bain & Company

Where Alumni Work
1. New York City
2. Boston
3. San Francisco
4. Washington, DC
5. Albany, NY

Earnings
College Scorecard (10-YR Post-Entry): $74,473
PayScale (Early Career): $70,600
PayScale (Mid-Career): $150,300
PayScale 20-Year ROI: $972,000

RANKINGS
Money: 5
U.S. News: 1, Liberal Arts Colleges
Wall Street Journal/THE: 31
Washington Monthly: 6, Liberal Arts Colleges

OVERGENERALIZATIONS
Students are:
Athletic and/or outdoorsy
Always studying
Well-rounded
Always admiring the beauty of their campus
Involved/investsed in campus life

COLLEGE OVERLAPS
Amherst College
Brown University
Cornell University
Dartmouth College
Middlebury College

Worcester Polytechnic Institute

Worcester, Massachusetts | 508-831-5286

ADMISSION
Admission Rate: 57%
Admission Rate - Men: 51%
Admission Rate - Women: 74%
EA Admission Rate: 65%
ED Admission Rate: 74%
ED Admits as % of Total Admits: 3%
Admission Rate (5-Year Trend): +9%
% of Admits Attending (Yield): 20%
Transfer Admission Rate: 58%

SAT Reading/Writing (Middle 50%): Test-Blind
SAT Math (Middle 50%): Test-Blind
ACT Composite (Middle 50%): Test-Blind

% Graduated in Top 10% of HS Class: 62%
% Graduated in Top 25% of HS Class: 89%
% Graduated in Top 50% of HS Class: 99%

Demonstrated Interest: Considered
Legacy Status: Considered
Racial/Ethnic Status: Considered
Admission Interview Offered: No

ENROLLMENT
Total Undergraduate Enrollment: 5,246
% Full-Time: 98%
% Male: 63%
% Female: 37%
% Out-of-State: 52%
% Fraternity: 25%
% Sorority: 27%
% On-Campus (All Undergraduate): 53%
Freshman Housing Required: Yes

% African-American: 3%
% Asian: 12%
% Hispanic: 9%
% White: 65%
% Other: 1%
% International: 7%
% Low-Income: 11%

ACADEMICS
Student-to-Faculty Ratio: 13 to 1
% of Classes Under 20: 64%
% of Classes 20-49: 24%
% of Classes 50 or More: 12%
% Full-Time Faculty: 73%
% Full-Time Faculty w/ Terminal Degree: 92%

Top Programs
Aerospace Engineering
Biomedical Engineering
Chemical Engineering
Computer Science
Industrial Engineering
Mathematical Sciences
Mechanical Engineering
Robotics Engineering

Retention Rate: 94%
4-Year Graduation Rate: 82%
6-Year Graduation Rate: 89%

Curricular Flexibility: Somewhat Flexible
Academic Rating: ★★★★

#CollegesWorthYourMoney

Worcester Polytechnic Institute, commonly referred to as WPI, is a small-to-midsize private university that is one of the fastest-growing PhD-granting schools in the United States. More than 5,200 undergraduate students and an additional 2,000+ graduate students attend school in Worcester, a city roughly 50 miles, as the crow flies, from Boston. Working on a quarter schedule, students engage in three courses for seven-week sprints as they plow through one of 50+ rigorous degree programs, primarily in engineering.

Inside the Classroom
An education at WPI is as hands-on and innovative as you will find at any university, engineering-centric or otherwise. The Interactive Qualifying Project (IQP), often completed off campus, features work in small teams on a project that "connects science and technology with social issues and human need." The Major Qualifying Project (MQP) is a unique capstone experience in which students must identify a real-world problem and find a novel solution. A host of industry partners work with students on the MQPs. Students can participate in a four-to-eight-month paid co-op experience as part of their undergraduate experience. Core academic requirements for all undergrads also include a foray into the humanities and arts as the school seeks to produce well-rounded, team-player engineers.

With a student-to-faculty ratio of 13:1, WPI does an exceptional job of keeping undergraduate classrooms cozy. In fact, a staggering 52% of its classes enroll fewer than ten students, creating an incredible level of academic intimacy. All students complete a minimum of two long-term research projects that are focused on solving real-world problems. That process begins freshman year, and by senior year, 72% have engaged in off-campus research as well. Studying abroad, like most things at WPI, is not a typical experience. Many undergrads travel to one of 50+ project centers situated on six continents where they can engage in solving real-life problems. Beginning with the Class of 2022, the school began awarding every single student $5,000 in study abroad funding with an aim toward a 90% participation rate within the next few years.

The undergraduate engineering program is respected worldwide and frequently graces lists of top schools for a variety of sub-disciplines. The most popular majors are under the engineering umbrella (63%) and computer science (16%). Those completing all of those programs find favorable conditions as they approach graduate schools, potential employers, and prestigious national scholarship organizations. WPI undergrads have won as many as 11 Gilman Scholarships in a single recent year and between two and five National Science Foundation Graduate Research Fellowships per year (plus many honorable mentions).

Outside the Classroom
Housing on campus is guaranteed only to freshmen; approximately half of all undergrads live on WPI's concentrated 95-acre campus. Many other students reside in one of the school's nineteen fraternities and sororities; 25% of men and 27% of women go Greek. It is worth noting that women make up only 37% of the undergraduate student population. Twenty varsity sports teams, evenly split between men's and women's squads, compete as the Engineers in NCAA Division III. Another forty-four combined club and intramural teams and the four-floor, state-of-the-art Sports and Recreation Center that houses a pool ensure that physical activity is accessible to all. There are 235 clubs and activities that include original offerings like underwater hockey, a Rubik's Cube club, and a lock-picking club. Hey, no one would ever argue that WPI students aren't extremely creative. Of course, there are many traditional options also on the menu, including a multitude of organizations geared toward young professionals and shared academic interests. Boston is a doable day trip, but there is plenty to do right in Worcester, including bustling Shrewsbury Street, museums, theaters, and loads of eateries. A growing urban area that still possesses the charm of a small college town, Worcester can easily be navigated via public transit.

Career Services
The Career Development Center (CDC) consists of eight professional employees, which works out to a student-to-advisor ratio of 656:1, above the average range compared to other schools featured in this guide. The staff is comprised of career counselors, corporate relations specialists, and recruiting coordinators. Students at WPI report an exceptionally high rate of satisfaction with their school's career services offerings for reasons that are obvious when you examine the basic facts.

An extraordinary 80% of all undergraduates, including freshmen and sophomores, interact with the CDC in some capacity each year. Each academic year, 400+ companies recruit on WPI's campus at career fairs, networking events, or on-campus job interviews. Annually, hundreds of students participate in summer internships or co-op placements that help them expand their network of career resources; the school's many corporate partners are always willing to take on WPI interns. In addition to strongly encouraging one-on-one counseling appointments, the office provides services like corporate tours, an employer-in-residence program, corporate information sessions, panel discussions, and a robust online system that allows students to connect with alumni and potential employers. Considering its highly accessible and broad array of offerings as well as positive professional and graduate school outcomes for alumni, the Worcester Polytechnic Institute's Career Development Center receives high marks from our staff.

Professional Outcomes

Within six months of graduation, 94% of 2022 grads had progressed beyond the seeking phase and had landed jobs or enrolled full-time in graduate school. Companies employing literally hundreds of WPI alumni of all ages include Raytheon, Pratt & Whitney, Dell, and BAE Systems. Recent graduates found jobs at companies that included Airbnb, DraftKings, Amazon Robotics, NASA, Harvard Medical School, the US Department of Defense, and SpaceX. The average starting salary crept above $74,000 and is currently among the highest of any in the country, impressive even for a school focused entirely on STEM disciplines. WPI graduates most frequently remain in Greater Boston, but significant numbers relocate to New York City, Hartford, San Francisco, and Providence.

Twenty-seven percent of recent diploma-earners elected to immediately begin work on an advanced degree. Elite graduate schools attended by recent grads included Georgia Tech, Carnegie Mellon, Johns Hopkins, Brown, and Stanford. Premed students enjoy the university's early/assured acceptance arrangements with Tufts Veterinary School, Massachusetts College of Pharmacy & Health Sciences, and Lake Erie College of Osteopathic Medicine. Recent grads have been accepted into medical school at the likes of Dartmouth, Northwestern, and Cornell.

Admission

WPI became the first top engineering university to adopt a test-optional policy way back in 2007, and it remains a rare breed among STEM-focused institutions. That decision has contributed to the school now receiving over 11,500 applications versus roughly 7,000 one decade ago. The acceptance rate for a place in the 2022-23 freshman class was 57%. Within that cohort, 62% finished in the top 10% of their high school class while 89% placed in the top quartile. The average GPA was 3.88, and over 80% of the group possessed a GPA above a 3.75.

Rigor of secondary school record and GPA are the only two factors deemed "very important" by the WPI admissions committee. Class rank, recommendations, extracurricular activities, and character/personal qualities are viewed as "important." It is worth noting that, as at most engineering schools, women enjoy a higher acceptance rate than men. At WPI, that disparity is more pronounced than is typical; female applicants gain acceptance 74% of the time, and men get in at a 51% clip. Valuing students who are "creative and curious," who "enjoy working together to get things done," and "feel pretty sure that they're leaders, not followers," the Worcester Polytechnic Institute admissions committee is looking for passionate candidates who possess strong grades in AP courses and, in many cases, superior test scores.

Worth Your Money?

If your family can afford WPI, you will likely recoup a sizable portion of the $79,000 cost of attendance. The vast majority of students do receive a merit aid package averaging $20k per year, which knocks the cost down a bit. Fortunately, with such high starting salaries for recent graduates, paying $240,000+ for an undergraduate degree from this school is not at all an unwise investment.

FINANCIAL
Institutional Type: Private
In-State Tuition: $58,870
Out-of-State Tuition: $58,870
Room & Board: $18,072
Books & Supplies: $1,200

Avg. Need-Based Grant: $30,906
Avg. % of Need Met: 82%

Avg. Merit-Based Award: $20,439
% Receiving (Freshmen w/o Need): 41%

Avg. Cumulative Debt: $32,500
% of Students Borrowing: 54%

CAREER
Who Recruits
1. PepsiCo
2. BAE Systems
3. General Electric
4. Travelers
5. Raytheon

Notable Internships
1. ExxonMobil
2. Dell
3. State Street

Top Employers
1. Raytheon
2. Pratt & Whitney
3. Dell
4. National Grid
5. Google

Where Alumni Work
1. Boston
2. New York City
3. Hartford, CT
4. San Francisco
5. Providence, RI

Earnings
College Scorecard (10-YR Post-Entry): $100,193
PayScale (Early Career): $78,800
PayScale (Mid-Career): $143,800
PayScale 20-Year ROI: $1,064,000

RANKINGS
Money: 4.5
U.S. News: 82, National Universities
Wall Street Journal/THE: 61
Washington Monthly: 282, National Universities

OVERGENERALIZATIONS
Students are:
Always studying
Nerdy
More likely to interact with different types of students
Less concerned with fashion or appearance
Involved/investsed in campus life

COLLEGE OVERLAPS
Boston University
Clarkson University
Northeastern University
Rensselaer Polytechnic Institute
Rochester Institute of Technology

Yale University

New Haven, Connecticut | 203-432-9300

World leaders, Supreme Court justices, scores of famous actors, inventors, writers, Nobel Laureates, billionaire businessmen, even fictional billionaire businessmen like The Simpsons' Mr. Burns . . . the list of Yale alumni fills multiple volumes of history books. Founded in 1701 as a more conservative, Puritan-rooted option to Harvard, the home of the Bulldogs is today, even by Ivy standards, every bit as elite as its Crimson rival of over 300 years. New Haven, Connecticut, is the destination for 6,645 undergraduates and more than 8,100 graduate students; yet, thanks to the nurturing Residential College housing system, the university serves as an intimate undergraduate home while still playing the role of a major private research university.

Inside the Classroom

There are 80 majors and 2,000 undergraduate course offerings at Yale. The social sciences (26%), biology (11%), mathematics (8%), computer science (8%), and interdisciplinary studies (7%) are the university's most popular areas of concentration. In aiming to strike a balance between freedom and control, the required coursework at Yale is modest and relatively broad. Students must take courses in the natural sciences, the humanities and arts, the social sciences, foreign language, quantitative reasoning, and writing. Most majors require a one-to-two-semester senior capstone experience. Depending on the major, students work closely with a professor toward the completion of an essay, portfolio, or research project.

The student-to-faculty ratio of 6:1 does translate to small class sizes, even with a larger number of graduate students on campus than undergrads. Over 70% of classes have an enrollment of fewer than 20 students, making for a perfect environment for teaching and learning. Undergraduate research is a staple of the Yale academic experience; 95% of science majors participate in research with faculty and, university-wide, undergraduate research fellowships are available to 90% of first-years who apply. In short, you'd have to try very hard to avoid engaging in research while an undergraduate at Yale. The number of Bulldogs electing to study abroad is typically around 70%.

Many of Yale's undergraduate programs sit atop any major rankings list. Among the crème de la crème departments are biology, economics, global affairs, engineering, history, and computer science. Any degree from Yale will get your resume/application to employers or graduate schools at the top of the pile. The same goes for applications to competitive post-college scholarships, including the uber-prestigious Rhodes Scholarship. Yalies have captured the award 250+ times, second only to Harvard in the all-time rankings. An unbelievable five students were named 2023 Rhodes Scholars.

Outside the Classroom

With 320 years of history and a $41 billion endowment, Yale's 345-acre, tree-lined campus is a blend of beautiful stone edifices and modern amenities. Perhaps the most distinctive feature of life outside the classroom at Yale is the famed Residential College system that was imported from Oxford/Cambridge over 70 years ago to facilitate a level of cohesiveness and connection typically only found at smaller liberal arts schools. Students are assigned to one of fourteen residential colleges that they will remain affiliated with for all four years. Each residence has two full-time, live-in faculty members. Greek life is not a dominant presence as only 10-20% of Yalies join a frat or sorority. So-called "secret societies," of which there are approximately 40, attract roughly half of seniors. Those include the famed Skull and Bones society, which has infiltrated American pop culture. Athletics are big-time at Yale as the Bulldogs field 35 NCAA Division I sports teams. An additional 50 club teams and 30 intramural sports are available for non-varsity athletes. Other student-run organizations include 60 cultural groups and fifty performance groups. Those seeking nature can canoe and camp on the 1,500 acres of the school's Outdoor Education Center or walk to the Yale Farm. Amenities and attractions include twelve dining halls, three on-campus museums, two theaters, and a library with 15 million holdings. Yale is situated in the middle of downtown New Haven, and the area is easily walkable. Boston and New York are each roughly a two-hour drive from New Haven.

Career Services

The Yale Office of Career Strategy (OCS) has 19 professional staff members (excluding administrative assistants and fellows who are current graduate students) who are dedicated to tasks such as employer relations, career counseling, and summer funding opportunities. The 350:1 student-to-advisor ratio is within the average range when compared to other schools featured in this book. Still, the OCS has no shortage of brag-worthy statistics attached to its name.

For starters, a jaw-dropping 87% of recent grads reported having used OCS resources in the career exploration journey. The office reports over 15,000 contacts per year with students. The OCS also hosts 13 industry-specific career fairs that attract 200 companies/organizations and close to 2,000 current students. Eighty-five top employers engaged in on-campus recruiting, and over 1,000 interviews were granted on Yale's grounds. The results are as impressive as the process—88% of recent graduates reported that they were employed in an area (at least slightly) related to their area of study. Yale students universally fill their summers with productive activities, often beginning immediately after their freshman year. By senior year, 40% have spent the previous summer at a paid internship, 16% at an unpaid internship, 11% in laboratory research, 6% in academic study, and 5% in field research.

Professional Outcomes

Shortly after graduating, 73% of the Yale Class of 2022 had entered the world of employment and 18% matriculated into graduate programs. The most common industries entered by the newly hired were finance (20%), research/education (16%), technology (14%), and consulting (12%). The mean starting salary for last year's grads was $81,769; CS majors took home a mean salary of $120k. Hundreds of Yale alums can be found at each of the world's top companies including Google, Goldman Sachs, McKinsey & Company, Morgan Stanley, and Microsoft. Geographically, New York City has the highest concentration of alumni followed by San Francisco, Boston, DC, Los Angeles, and Chicago.

Among those from the Class of 2022 pursuing graduate/professional programs, 17% were in medical school, 15% started work on a PhD, and 15% went directly from undergraduate studies to law school. Unsurprisingly, given the quality of the minds admitted into Yale, medical school applicants traditionally find a home 87% of the time, more than twice the national average. Law school applicants do just fine as well; 82% were accepted into at least one school with a substantial number continuing at Yale Law School (YLS). Roughly 10% of YLS first-years attended Yale as undergraduates. For a complete list of where Yale alumni as a whole continue their educational journeys, simply consult a list of the best graduate/professional programs in the world.

Admission

Yale received 50,060 applications for a place in the Class of 2026, but a meager 5% made it through the gates. Of those admitted, 97% placed in the top decile of their high school graduating class. The mid-50% range on the SAT was 1470-1560; the ACT span was 33-35. For an even better idea of the testing mastery (among test-submitting students) required to become a Bulldog, look to the fact that 92% had an SAT Reading score of over 700, and 95% had an SAT Math score over 700.

You can bet a school that rejects 95% of applicants relies on more than a few data points. The admissions committee ranks eight factors as being "most important": rigor of secondary record, GPA, class rank, application essay, recommendations, extracurricular activities, talent/ability, and character/personal qualities. The committee uses two overarching questions to guide its process: "Who is likely to make the most of Yale's resources?" and "Who will contribute most significantly to the Yale community?" Yale offers a unique single-choice early action (SCEA) option with a November 1 deadline. Those going that route are not bound to attend the university if accepted, but they cannot simultaneously apply ED or EA to any other school. Of the 7,288 SCEA applicants for the 2022-23 freshman cohort, 800 were admitted—an 11% success rate. Far more 2022-23 freshmen were first-generation students (18%) than legacy admits (12%). Getting into Yale is a hard-to-predict enterprise that sees many valedictorians and salutatorians bite the dust. Fantastic numbers along with a record of special talents and accomplishments that scream "future leader" will fare best.

Worth Your Money?

Yale is one of those rare schools where the contacts and networks you create while attending will make the education worth any cost. Fortunately, thanks to a $41 billion endowment, every single student who qualifies for need-based aid sees 100% of that need met by the university. The average grant is $68k, significantly reducing the sticker price cost of attendance of almost $88,000. There is no merit aid awarded by Yale, so those not in financial need will be paying full freight, but again, that will be money well spent.

FINANCIAL
Institutional Type: Private
In-State Tuition: $64,700
Out-of-State Tuition: $64,700
Room & Board: $19,180
Books & Supplies: $3,700

Avg. Need-Based Grant: $67,747
Avg. % of Need Met: 100%

Avg. Merit-Based Award: $0
% Receiving (Freshmen w/o Need): 0%

Avg. Cumulative Debt: $17,910
% of Students Borrowing: 14%

CAREER
Who Recruits
1. The New York Times
2. Uber
3. Citi
4. Bain & Company
5. Boston Consulting Group

Notable Internships
1. Netflix
2. The Blackstone Group
3. United Nations

Top Employers
1. Google
2. McKinsey & Company
3. Goldman Sachs
4. Facebook
5. Morgan Stanley

Where Alumni Work
1. New York City
2. San Francisco
3. Boston
4. Washington, DC
5. Los Angeles

Earnings
College Scorecard (10-YR Post-Entry): $95,961
PayScale (Early Career): $78,000
PayScale (Mid-Career): $151,600
PayScale 20-Year ROI: $1,106,000

RANKINGS
Money: 5
U.S. News: 5, National Universities
Wall Street Journal/THE: 3
Washington Monthly: 8, National Universities

OVERGENERALIZATIONS
Students are:
Politically liberal
More likely to interact with different types of students
Always admiring the beauty of their campus
Passionate
Equally happy hitting the bars or hitting up a movie

COLLEGE OVERLAPS
Columbia University
Dartmouth College
Harvard University
Princeton University
University of Pennsylvania

Top Colleges by Academic Program

Included in each school profile, we highlighted the academic programs that are among the very best on that particular campus. The next natural step is to look at top programs across all schools so that you can emerge with a bird's-eye picture of the premier American colleges in your program(s) or area(s) of interest. We included more than several dozen of the most popular fields of study in order to make these lists as useful and relevant to our audience as is possible.

Finally, note that although some of the colleges featured below do not offer a formal major in the area being featured, their undergraduate offerings in the subject area are so strong that they warrant inclusion on our list.

For more useful lists, including a number of majors not covered in this book, we highly recommend visiting the College Transitions Dataverse at **www.collegetransitions.com/dataverse**. Please revisit the methodology section of this book (in the front) for an extensive explanation of how we selected the programs for inclusion.

And without further ado, we present College Transitions' Top Colleges for America's Top Majors:

Accounting
Babson College
Bentley University
Boston College
Brigham Young University
Carnegie Mellon University
College of William and Mary
Emory University
Florida State University
Georgetown University
Indiana University
New York University
Ohio State University
Penn State University
University of California, Berkeley
University of Florida
University of Georgia
University of Illinois Urbana-Champaign
University of Miami
University of Michigan
University of North Carolina at Chapel Hill
University of Notre Dame
University of Pennsylvania
University of Southern California
University of Texas at Austin
University of Virginia
University of Washington
University of Wisconsin-Madison
Villanova University
Wake Forest University
Washington University

Actuarial Science
Arizona State University
Bentley University
Brigham Young University-Provo
Butler University
Carnegie Mellon University
CUNY Bernard M Baruch College
Drake University
Drexel University
Florida State University
Georgia State University
Michigan State University
New York University

Ohio State University
Pennsylvania State University
Purdue University-Main Campus
Temple University
Texas Christian University
The University of Texas at Dallas
University of California-Santa Barbara
University of Central Florida
University of Connecticut
University of Delaware
University of Georgia
University of Illinois at Urbana-Champaign
University of Iowa
University of Nebraska-Lincoln
University of Pennsylvania
University of St Thomas
University of Texas at Austin
University of Wisconsin-Madison

Aerospace Engineering
California Institute of Technology
Case Western Reserve University
Cornell University
Embry-Riddle Aeronautical University
Georgia Institute of Technology
Iowa State University
Massachusetts Institute of Technology
Ohio State University
Pennsylvania State University
Princeton University
Purdue University – West Lafayette
Rensselaer Polytechnic Institute
Stanford University
Texas A&M University – College Station
United States Air Force Academy
University of California, Los Angeles
University of California, San Diego
University of Colorado Boulder
University of Florida
University of Illinois at Urbana-Champaign
University of Maryland, College Park
University of Miami
University of Michigan
University of Minnesota – Twin Cities
University of Notre Dame

University of Southern California
University of Texas at Austin, The
University of Virginia
University of Washington – Seattle
Virginia Tech

Animal Science
Auburn University
California Polytechnic State University-San Luis Obispo
California State Polytechnic University-Pomona
Clemson University
Cornell University
Iowa State University
Kansas State University
Michigan State University
North Carolina State University
Ohio State University
Oregon State University
Pennsylvania State University
Purdue University-Main Campus
Rutgers University-New Brunswick
Texas A&M University – College Station
Texas Tech University
The University of Tennessee-Knoxville
University of California-Davis
University of Connecticut
University of Florida
University of Georgia
University of Illinois at Urbana-Champaign
University of Maryland-College Park
University of Minnesota-Twin Cities
University of Rhode Island
University of Vermont
University of Wisconsin-Madison
Virginia Tech
Washington State University
West Virginia University

Animation
Arizona State University
Brigham Young University-Provo
California Institute of the Arts
Carnegie Mellon University
Chapman University
DePaul University
Drexel University
Florida State University
George Mason University
Loyola Marymount University
New Jersey Institute of Technology
New York University
Pratt Institute
Purdue University
Rhode Island School of Design
Ringling College of Art and Design
Rochester Institute of Technology
Savannah College of Art and Design
Syracuse University
Texas A&M University
The New School
University of California, Los Angeles
University of Florida
University of Southern California
University of Texas at Dallas

Anthropology
Amherst College
Barnard College
Bowdoin College
Brown University
Columbia University in the City of New York
Dartmouth College

Duke University
Emory University
Georgetown University
Grinnell College
Harvard University
Haverford College
Northwestern University
Princeton University
Reed College
Stanford University
Tufts University
University of California-Berkeley
University of California-Los Angeles
University of California-Santa Barbara
University of California-Santa Cruz
University of Chicago
University of Florida
University of Notre Dame
University of Pennsylvania
University of Virginia
Washington University in St Louis
Wellesley College
Wesleyan University
Yale University

Applied Math
Brandeis University
Brown University
California Institute of Technology
Carnegie Mellon University
Colgate University
Columbia University in the City of New York
Emory University
Georgia Institute of Technology
Harvard University
Harvey Mudd College
Johns Hopkins University
Massachusetts Institute of Technology
New York University
Northwestern University
Rice University
Stanford University
Stevens Institute of Technology
Stony Brook University
Texas A&M University – College Station
Tufts University
University of California-Berkeley
University of California-Los Angeles
University of California-San Diego
University of California-Santa Barbara
University of North Carolina at Chapel Hill
University of Rochester
University of Southern California
University of Washington-Seattle
Virginia Tech
Yale University

Architecture
Brown University
Carnegie Mellon University
Columbia University
Cooper Union
Cornell University
Georgia Institute of Technology
Massachusetts Institute of Technology
Middlebury College
Pennsylvania State University
Princeton University
Rensselaer Polytechnic Institute
Rhode Island School of Design
Rice University
Syracuse University

Texas A&M University – College Station
University of California, Berkeley
University of California, Los Angeles
University of Cincinnati
University of Florida
University of Maryland, College Park
University of Michigan
University of Minnesota – Twin Cities
University of Notre Dame
University of Pennsylvania
University of Southern California
University of Texas at Austin, The
University of Virginia
Virginia Tech
Washington University in St. Louis
Yale University

Art (Studio)
Bard College
Brown University
California Institute of the Arts
Carnegie Mellon University
Columbia University in the City of New York
Cooper Union for the Advancement of Science and Art
Dartmouth College
Harvard University
Maryland Institute College of Art
Massachusetts College of Art and Design
Minneapolis College of Art and Design
New York University
Otis College of Art and Design
Pratt Institute
Rhode Island School of Design
Savannah College of Art and Design
School of the Art Institute of Chicago
School of Visual Arts
Stanford University
The University of Texas at Austin
Tufts University
University of California-Los Angeles
University of Chicago
University of Michigan
University of Pennsylvania
University of Southern California
Virginia Commonwealth University
Washington University in St Louis
Williams College
Yale University

Artificial Intelligence
California Institute of Technology
Carnegie Mellon University
Columbia University
Cornell University
Georgia Institute of Technology
Harvard University
Johns Hopkins University
Massachusetts Institute of Technology
New York University
Northeastern University
Princeton University
Purdue University
Rutgers University
University of California, Berkeley
University of California, Los Angeles
University of California, San Diego
University of Illinois at Urbana-Champaign
University of Maryland
University of Maryland
University of Massachusetts Amherst
University of Michigan
University of Pennsylvania

University of Texas at Austin
University of Washington
University of Wisconsin-Madison

Astronomy and Astrophysics
Amherst College
Boston University
California Institute of Technology
Carnegie Mellon University
Colgate University
Columbia University in the City of New York
Harvard University
Haverford College
Ohio State University
Princeton University
Rice University
Swarthmore College
The University of Texas at Austin
University of California-Berkeley
University of California-Los Angeles
University of California-Santa Cruz
University of Chicago
University of Colorado Boulder
University of Florida
University of Illinois at Urbana-Champaign
University of Maryland-College Park
University of Michigan
University of Virginia
University of Washington-Seattle
University of Wisconsin-Madison
Vassar College
Wellesley College
Wesleyan University
Whitman College
Williams College

Biochemistry
Amherst College
Bates College
Boston University
Bowdoin College
Brown University
Colgate University
Columbia University in the City of New York
Duke University
Grinnell College
Harvey Mudd College
Johns Hopkins University
Middlebury College
Pomona College
Princeton University
Rice University
The University of Texas at Austin
Tufts University
University of California-Los Angeles
University of California-San Diego
University of Michigan
University of Notre Dame
University of Pennsylvania
University of Washington-Seattle
University of Wisconsin-Madison
Vanderbilt University
Vassar College
Washington and Lee University
Washington University in St Louis
Wesleyan University
Yale University

Biology
Amherst College
Bowdoin College
Brown University

California Institute of Technology
Carleton College
Columbia University
Cornell University
Dartmouth College
Davidson College
Duke University
Emory University
Grinnell College
Harvard University
Haverford College
Johns Hopkins University
Massachusetts Institute of Technology
Northwestern University
Pomona College
Princeton University
Stanford University
Swarthmore College
University of California, Berkeley
University of California, Los Angeles
University of California, San Diego
University of California, Santa Barbara
University of Chicago
University of North Carolina at Chapel Hill
University of Pennsylvania
Williams College
Yale University

Biomedical Engineering
Boston University
Brown University
California Institute of Technology
Carnegie Mellon University
Case Western Reserve University
Columbia University in the City of New York
Cornell University
Dartmouth College
Duke University
Georgia Institute of Technology
Harvard University
Johns Hopkins University
Massachusetts Institute of Technology
Northwestern University
Rensselaer Polytechnic Institute
Rice University
Stanford University
The University of Texas at Austin
University of California-Berkeley
University of California-Los Angeles
University of California-San Diego
University of Maryland-College Park
University of Michigan
University of Pennsylvania
University of Southern California
University of Virginia
University of Washington-Seattle
University of Wisconsin-Madison
Washington University in St Louis
Yale University

Business Administration
Babson College
Boston College
Boston University
Carnegie Mellon University
Cornell University
Emory University
Georgetown University
Georgia Institute of Technology
Indiana University
New York University
Ohio State University

Southern Methodist University
The University of Texas at Austin
Tulane University of Louisiana
University of California-Berkeley
University of Illinois at Urbana-Champaign
University of Michigan
University of Minnesota-Twin Cities
University of North Carolina at Chapel Hill
University of Notre Dame
University of Pennsylvania
University of Richmond
University of Southern California
University of Virginia
University of Washington-Seattle
University of Wisconsin-Madison
Villanova University
Wake Forest University
Washington and Lee University
Washington University in St Louis

Chemical Engineering
Brown University
California Institute of Technology
Carnegie Mellon University
Colorado School of Mines
Columbia University in the
    City of New York
Cornell University
Georgia Institute of Technology
Johns Hopkins University
Massachusetts Institute of Technology
Northeastern University
Northwestern University
Princeton University
Purdue University-Main Campus
Rice University
Stanford University
The University of Texas at Austin
University of California-Berkeley
University of California-Los Angeles
University of California-San Diego
University of Chicago
University of Illinois at Urbana-Champaign
University of Michigan
University of Minnesota Twin Cities
University of Notre Dame
University of Pennsylvania
University of Southern California
University of Wisconsin-Madison
Vanderbilt University
Washington University in St Louis
Yale University

Chemistry
Bates College
California Institute of Technology
Carleton College
Carnegie Mellon University
College of the Holy Cross
Columbia University in the City of New York
Cornell University
Dartmouth College
Duke University
Emory University
Harvard University
Haverford College
Johns Hopkins University
Massachusetts Institute of Technology
Northwestern University
Pomona College
Princeton University
Rice University

Stanford University
United States Naval Academy
University of California-Berkeley
University of California-San Diego
University of Chicago
University of North Carolina at Chapel Hill
University of Pennsylvania
University of Virginia
Washington University in St Louis
Wellesley College
Williams College
Yale University

Civil Engineering
Carnegie Mellon University
Columbia University in the
   City of New York
Cornell University
Duke University
Georgia Institute of Technology
Johns Hopkins University
Lafayette College
Lehigh University
Massachusetts Institute of Technology
New Jersey Institute of Technology
Northeastern University
Northwestern University
Princeton University
Purdue University-Main Campus
Rice University
Rose-Hulman Institute of Technology
Stanford University
Texas A & M University – College Station
The University of Texas at Austin
United States Air Force Academy
United States Coast Guard Academy
United States Military Academy
University of California-Berkeley
University of California-Los Angeles
University of Florida
University of Illinois at Urbana-Champaign
University of Michigan
University of Notre Dame
Vanderbilt University
Virginia Tech

Communication
Boston College
Boston University
Cornell University
Fordham University
George Washington University
Michigan State University
Northeastern University
Northwestern University
Ohio State University
Penn State University
Santa Clara University
Stanford University
Syracuse University
The University of Texas at Austin
Tulane University of Louisiana
University of California-Los Angeles
University of California-San Diego
University of California-Santa Barbara
University of Florida
University of Georgia
University of Maryland-College Park
University of Michigan
University of North Carolina at Chapel Hill
University of Pennsylvania
University of Southern California

University of Washington-Seattle
University of Wisconsin-Madison
Vanderbilt University
Villanova University
Wake Forest University

Computer Science
Brown University
California Institute of Technology
Carnegie Mellon University
Columbia University
Cornell University
Duke University
Georgia Institute of Technology
Harvard University
Harvey Mudd College
Johns Hopkins University
Massachusetts Institute of Technology
New York University
Northeastern University
Princeton University
Purdue University – West Lafayette
Stanford University
Swarthmore College
University of California, Berkeley
University of California, Irvine
University of California, Los Angeles
University of California, San Diego
University of Illinois at Urbana-Champaign
University of Maryland, College Park
University of Massachusetts Amherst
University of Michigan
University of Pennsylvania
University of Southern California
University of Texas at Austin, The
University of Washington – Seattle
Yale University

Construction Management
Appalachian State University
Boise State University
Brigham Young University-Provo
California Polytechnic State University-San Luis Obispo
Clemson University
Colorado State University
Drexel University
Florida Institute of Technology
Kansas State University
Louisiana State University
Michigan State University
Michigan Technological University
Milwaukee School of Engineering
Mississippi State University
Ohio State University
San Diego State University
SUNY College of Environmental Science and Forestry
The University of Tennessee-Knoxville
University of Florida
University of Minnesota-Twin Cities
University of Nebraska-Lincoln
University of Oklahoma
University of Washington
Wentworth Institute of Technology

Criminology/Criminal Justice
American University
Appalachian State University
Arizona State University
College of New Jersey, The
Florida International University
Florida State University
George Mason University

George Washington University
Indiana University Bloomington
John Jay College of Criminal Justice
Marist College
Michigan State University
Northeastern University
Ohio State University
Pennsylvania State University
Rutgers University – New Brunswick
San Diego State University
Temple University
University at Albany (SUNY)
University of California, Irvine
University of Cincinnati
University of Delaware
University of Georgia
University of Maryland, College Park
University of Miami
University of Pennsylvania
University of Pittsburgh
University of South Carolina
University of Washington – Seattle

Data Science
California Institute of Technology
Carnegie Mellon University
Cornell University
Duke University
Johns Hopkins University
Massachusetts Institute of Technology
New York University
Northwestern University
Penn State University
Purdue University
Rutgers University
Stanford University
Tufts University
University of California, Berkeley
University of California, Irvine
University of California, Los Angeles
University of California, San Diego
University of Chicago
University of Illinois Urbana Champaign
University of Maryland, College Park
University of Michigan
University of Minnesota
University of North Carolina at Chapel Hill
University of Pennsylvania
University of Pittsburgh
University of Texas at Austin
University of Virginia
University of Wisconsin-Madison
Washington University

Drama and Theater Arts
Barnard College
Boston University
Brown University
Carnegie Mellon University
Columbia University in the City of New York
Drew University
Emerson College
Florida State University
Loyola Marymount University
Muhlenberg College
New York University
Northwestern University
Skidmore College
Southern Methodist University
SUNY at Purchase College
The Juilliard School
University of California-Irvine

University of California-Los Angeles
University of California-San Diego
University of Central Florida
University of Florida
University of Michigan
University of North Carolina School of the Arts
University of Notre Dame
University of Pennsylvania
University of Southern California
Vassar College
Washington University in St Louis
Wesleyan University
Yale University

Economics
Boston College
Brown University
Claremont McKenna College
Colgate University
Columbia University in the
  City of New York
Dartmouth College
Duke University
Georgetown University
Harvard University
Johns Hopkins University
Massachusetts Institute of Technology
Northwestern University
Princeton University
Rice University
Stanford University
Swarthmore College
Tufts University
United States Naval Academy
University of California-Berkeley
University of California-Los Angeles
University of Chicago
University of Notre Dame
University of Pennsylvania
University of Virginia
Vanderbilt University
Wake Forest University
Washington and Lee University
Washington University in St Louis
Williams College
Yale University

Education
Arizona State University
Boston College
Boston University
Bowdoin College
Brown University
Colby College
Colgate University
Duke University
Middlebury College
New York University
Northwestern University
Ohio State University
Smith College
Swarthmore College
The College of New Jersey
University of California-Irvine
University of California-Los Angeles
University of Delaware
University of Florida
University of Georgia
University of Michigan
University of Minnesota-Twin Cities
University of North Carolina at Chapel Hill
University of Washington-Seattle

University of Wisconsin-Madison
Vanderbilt University
Vassar College
Washington University in St Louis
Wellesley College
Wesleyan University

Electrical Engineering
California Institute of Technology
Carnegie Mellon University
Columbia University
Cornell University
Duke University
Georgia Institute of Technology
Johns Hopkins University
Massachusetts Institute of Technology
North Carolina State University
Northwestern University
Ohio State University
Penn State University
Princeton University
Purdue University
Rensselaer Polytechnic Institute
Rice University
Stanford University
Texas A&M University
University of California, Berkeley
University of California, Los Angeles
University of California, San Diego
University of Illinois Urbana-Champaign
University of Maryland, College Park
University of Michigan
University of Pennsylvania
University of Southern California
University of Texas at Austin
University of Washington
University of Wisconsin-Madison
Virginia Tech

English
Bates College
Boston College
Brown University
Colgate University
College of the Holy Cross
Columbia University in the
   City of New York
Dartmouth College
Duke University
Emory University
Georgetown University
Hamilton College
Harvard University
Johns Hopkins University
Northwestern University
Princeton University
Rice University
Stanford University
United States Naval Academy
University of California-Berkeley
University of California-Los Angeles
University of Chicago
University of Pennsylvania
University of Pittsburgh
University of Virginia
Vanderbilt University
Washington University in St Louis
Wellesley College
Wesleyan University
Williams College
Yale University

Environmental Engineering
Bucknell University
Clemson University
Colorado School of Mines
Colorado State University-Fort Collins
Columbia University
Cornell University
Duke University
Georgia Institute of Technology-Main Campus
Johns Hopkins University
Massachusetts Institute of Technology
North Carolina State University
Northwestern University
Purdue University-Main Campus
Rensselaer Polytechnic Institute
Stanford University
The Pennsylvania State University
The University of Texas at Austin
Tufts University
United States Military Academy
University of California-Berkeley
University of California-Davis
University of California-San Diego
University of Colorado Boulder
University of Florida
University of Michigan-Ann Arbor
University of Minnesota-Twin Cities
University of Notre Dame
University of Southern California
University of Washington- Seattle Campus
Yale University

Environmental Science/Studies
Bates College
Bowdoin College
Brown University
Colorado College
Columbia University in the City of New York
Dartmouth College
Davidson College
Dickinson College
Duke University
Hamilton College
Johns Hopkins University
Middlebury College
Northeastern University
Northwestern University
Pitzer College
Pomona College
Rice University
Scripps College
SUNY College of Environmental Science and Forestry
University of California-Berkeley
University of California-Davis
University of California-Los Angeles
University of Chicago
University of Michigan
University of Notre Dame
University of Virginia
University of Washington-Seattle
University of Wisconsin-Madison
Wellesley College
Wesleyan University

Fashion Design
Academy of Art University
Baylor University
California College of the Arts
Columbia College Chicago
Columbus College of Art and Design
Drexel University
Fashion Institute of Technology

Kent State University
Marist College
Massachusetts College of Art and Design
Oregon State University
Otis College of Art and Design
Pratt Institute
Rhode Island School of Design
Savannah College of Art and Design
SUNY Oneonta
The New School
Thomas Jefferson University
University of Cincinnati
Virginia Commonwealth University

Fashion Merchandising
Auburn University
Baylor University
Colorado State University
Cornell University
Drexel University
Fashion Institute of Technology
Florida State University
Indiana University
Iowa State University
Kent State University
Marist College
North Carolina State
Ohio State University
Savannah College of Art and Design
Texas Christian University
The New School
Thomas Jefferson University
University of Delaware
University of Georgia
University of Minnesota
University of Missouri-Columbia
University of South Carolina

Film
American University
Boston University
Chapman University
Columbia University
DePaul University
Emerson College
Emory University
Florida State University
Fordham University
Hofstra University
Ithaca College
Loyola Marymount University
New York University
Occidental College
Rochester Institute of Technology
Syracuse University
University of Arizona
University of California-Los Angeles
University of California-Santa Barbara
University of Colorado Boulder
University of Miami
University of Michigan
University of North Carolina School of the Arts
University of North Carolina Wilmington
University of Pennsylvania
University of Southern California
University of Texas at Austin
Vassar College
Wesleyan University
Yale University

Finance
Babson College
Boston College
Boston University
Carnegie Mellon University
Cornell University
CUNY Bernard M. Baruch College
Emory University
George Washington University
Georgetown University
Indiana University
Lehigh University
New York University
Ohio State University
Providence College
Santa Clara University
Southern Methodist University
The University of Texas at Austin
Tulane University of Louisiana
University of California, Berkeley
University of Illinois at Urbana-Champaign
University of Maryland-College Park
University of Michigan
University of North Carolina at Chapel Hill
University of Notre Dame
University of Pennsylvania
University of Virginia
University of Wisconsin-Madison
Villanova University
Wake Forest University
Washington University in St Louis

Geology
Bates College
Bowdoin College
Brown University
California Institute of Technology
Carleton College
Colorado College
Colorado School of Mines
Columbia University in the City of New York
Dartmouth College
Duke University
Johns Hopkins University
Massachusetts Institute of Technology
Northwestern University
Pennsylvania State University
Princeton University
Smith College
Stanford University
The University of Texas at Austin
United States Coast Guard Academy
United States Naval Academy
University of California-Berkeley
University of Chicago
University of Colorado Boulder
University of Michigan
University of Pennsylvania
University of Washington-Seattle
Vanderbilt University
Washington and Lee University
Williams College
Yale University

History
Barnard College
Brown University
Colgate University
College of the Holy Cross
College of William and Mary
Columbia University in the City of New York
Cornell University

Dartmouth College
Davidson College
Duke University
Harvard University
Johns Hopkins University
Northwestern University
Princeton University
Rice University
Stanford University
United States Military Academy
United States Naval Academy
University of California-Berkeley
University of California-Los Angeles
University of Chicago
University of North Carolina at Chapel Hill
University of Pennsylvania
University of Virginia
Vanderbilt University
Washington and Lee University
Washington University in St Louis
Wesleyan University
Williams College
Yale University

Hospitality Management
Boston University
California State Polytechnic University-Pomona
College of Charleston
Cornell University
Florida International University
Florida State University
George Washington University
Iowa State University
James Madison University
Michigan State University
New York University
Ohio State University
Pennsylvania State University
Purdue University-Main Campus
Temple University
Texas A & M University-College Station
University of Central Florida
University of Delaware
University of Denver
University of Houston
University of Massachusetts-Amherst
University of Nevada-Las Vegas
University of South Carolina
Virginia Tech
Washington State University

Industrial/Product Design
Appalachian State University
Arizona State University
Auburn University
Brigham Young University-Provo
California State University-Long Beach
Carnegie Mellon University
Clemson University
DePaul University
Drexel University
Georgia Institute of Technology
Iowa State University
James Madison University
New Jersey Institute of Technology
North Carolina State University
Ohio State University
Purdue University-Main Campus
Rochester Institute of Technology
San Jose State University
Stanford University
Syracuse University
The New School

University of Cincinnati-Main Campus
University of Houston
University of Illinois at Chicago
University of Illinois at Urbana-Champaign
University of Minnesota-Twin Cities
University of Oregon
University of Washington-Seattle
Virginia Tech
Wentworth Institute of Technology

Industrial Engineering
Auburn University
Binghamton University
California Polytechnic State University-San Luis Obispo
Clemson University
Columbia University in the City of New York
Cornell University
Florida State University
Georgia Institute of Technology
Lehigh University
North Carolina State University
Northeastern University
Northwestern University
Ohio State University
Pennsylvania State University
Purdue University-Main Campus
Rensselaer Polytechnic Institute
Texas A & M University-College Station
University of California, Berkeley
University of Connecticut
University of Illinois at Urbana-Champaign
University of Miami
University of Michigan
University of Minnesota-Twin Cities
University of Pittsburgh
University of San Diego
University of Southern California
University of Washington-Seattle
University of Wisconsin-Madison
Virginia Tech
Worcester Polytechnic Institute

Interior Design
Appalachian State University
Arizona State University
Auburn University
Baylor University
Cornell University
Drexel University
Fashion Institute of Technology
Florida State University
George Washington University
Iowa State University
Kansas State University
Michigan State University
Ohio State University
Oregon State University
Pratt Institute-Main
Purdue University-Main Campus
Rhode Island School of Design
Savannah College of Art and Design
Syracuse University
Texas Christian University
The New School
The University of Alabama
The University of Texas at Austin
Thomas Jefferson University
University of Cincinnati-Main Campus
University of Florida
University of Minnesota-Twin Cities
University of Oklahoma
University of Wisconsin-Madison
Virginia Tech

International Relations/Studies

American University
Boston College
Boston University
Brandeis University
Brown University
Carleton College
Claremont McKenna College
Colby College
Colgate University
George Washington University
Georgetown University
Hamilton College
Johns Hopkins University
Macalester College
Middlebury College
New York University
Northwestern University
Stanford University
Tufts University
United States Air Force Academy
University of California-San Diego
University of California-Santa Barbara
University of Chicago
University of Michigan
University of Notre Dame
University of Pennsylvania
University of Southern California
University of Virginia
Washington University in St Louis
Yale University

Kinesiology/Exercise Science

Auburn University
Creighton University
Florida State University
Gettysburg College
Gonzaga University
Indiana University-Bloomington
Michigan State University
Penn State University
Pepperdine University
Rice University
Rutgers University-New Brunswick
Saint Louis University
Texas A&M University-College Station
The University of Texas at Austin
United States Military Academy
University of Delaware
University of Florida
University of Georgia
University of Illinois at Urbana-Champaign
University of Iowa
University of Maryland-College Park
University of Massachusetts-Amherst
University of Miami
University of Michigan
University of Minnesota-Twin Cities
University of Pittsburgh
University of South Carolina
University of Virginia
University of Wisconsin-Madison
Wake Forest University

Management Information Systems

Carnegie Mellon University
Drexel University
Florida State University
Georgetown University
Indiana University
New York University
Ohio State University

Penn State University
Santa Clara University
Stevens Institute of Technology
Texas A&M University
The University of Texas at Austin
University of Alabama
University of Arizona
University of Delaware
University of Georgia
University of Houston
University of Illinois at Urbana-Champaign
University of Maryland
University of Michigan
University of Minnesota
University of Notre Dame
University of Oklahoma
University of Pennsylvania
University of Wisconsin-Madison

Marketing

Bentley University
Boston College
Emory University
Fairfield University
Florida State University
Fordham University
Georgetown University
Indiana University
Lehigh University
Loyola Marymount University
New York University
Ohio State University
Pennsylvania State University
Santa Clara University
The University of Alabama
The University of Texas at Austin
Tulane University of Louisiana
University of California, Berkeley
University of Florida
University of Georgia
University of Miami
University of Michigan
University of North Carolina at Chapel Hill
University of Notre Dame
University of Pennsylvania
University of Southern California
University of Virginia
University of Washington-Seattle
Villanova University
Washington University in St Louis

Materials Science and Engineering

California Institute of Technology
Carnegie Mellon University
Case Western Reserve University
Columbia University in the City of New York
Cornell University
Drexel University
Georgia Institute of Technology
Johns Hopkins University
Lehigh University
Massachusetts Institute of Technology
North Carolina State University
Northwestern University
Ohio State University
Penn State University
Purdue University-Main Campus
Rensselaer Polytechnic Institute
Stanford University
Texas A&M University – College Station
University of California-Berkeley
University of California-Los Angeles

University of Florida
University of Illinois at Urbana-Champaign
University of Maryland-College Park
University of Michigan
University of Minnesota-Twin Cities
University of Pennsylvania
University of Pittsburgh
University of Washington-Seattle
University of Wisconsin-Madison
Virginia Tech

Mathematics
Amherst College
Boston College
Bowdoin College
California Institute of Technology
Carleton College
Carnegie Mellon University
Claremont McKenna College
Columbia University in the City of New York
Cornell University
Dartmouth College
Duke University
Georgetown University
Harvard University
Harvey Mudd College
Johns Hopkins University
Massachusetts Institute of Technology
Northwestern University
Princeton University
Rice University
Stanford University
Swarthmore College
United States Naval Academy
University of California-Los Angeles
University of Chicago
University of Pennsylvania
Vanderbilt University
Wake Forest University
Washington University in St Louis
Williams College
Yale University

Mechanical Engineering
California Institute of Technology
Carnegie Mellon University
Colorado School of Mines
Columbia University in the City of New York
Cornell University
Duke University
Franklin W Olin College of Engineering
Georgia Institute of Technology
Harvard University
Johns Hopkins University
Lehigh University
Massachusetts Institute of Technology
Northeastern University
Northwestern University
Princeton University
Rensselaer Polytechnic Institute
Rice University
Rose-Hulman Institute of Technology
Stanford University
Stevens Institute of Technology
United States Military Academy
United States Naval Academy
University of California-Berkeley
University of Florida
University of Michigan
University of Notre Dame
University of Pennsylvania
Washington University in St. Louis

Worcester Polytechnic Institute
Yale University

Music
Bard College
Berklee College of Music
Boston University
California Institute of the Arts
Carnegie Mellon University
Curtis Institute of Music
Florida State University
Indiana University-Bloomington
Johns Hopkins University
Lawrence University
Manhattan School of Music
New England Conservatory of Music
New York University
Northwestern University
Oberlin College
Rice University
San Francisco Conservatory of Music
The Juilliard School
The University of Texas at Austin
University of California-Los Angeles
University of Cincinnati-Main Campus
University of Miami
University of Michigan
University of North Carolina at Chapel Hill
University of North Carolina School of the Arts
University of North Texas
University of Rochester
University of Southern California
Vanderbilt University
Yale University

Neuroscience
Amherst College
Barnard College
Boston University
Bowdoin College
Brandeis University
Brown University
Colgate University
Columbia University
Dartmouth College
Duke University
Emory University
Harvard University
Johns Hopkins University
Massachusetts Institute of Technology
Middlebury College
Northeastern University
Northwestern University
Pomona College
Princeton University
Tulane University
University of California, Los Angeles
University of California, San Diego
University of Chicago
University of Michigan
University of Pennsylvania
University of Pittsburgh
University of Rochester
University of Texas at Austin
Wellesley College
Yale University

Nursing
Baylor University
Binghamton University (SUNY)
Boston College
Case Western Reserve University

Drexel University
Duke University
Emory University
Fairfield University
Georgetown University
Marquette University
New York University
Northeastern University
Ohio State University
Pennsylvania State University
Purdue University – West Lafayette
Rutgers University – New Brunswick
Stony Brook University (SUNY)
Texas Christian University
University of California, Los Angeles
University of Delaware
University of Florida
University of Miami
University of Michigan
University of North Carolina at Chapel Hill
University of Pennsylvania
University of Pittsburgh
University of Texas at Austin, The
University of Washington – Seattle
University of Wisconsin – Madison
Villanova University

Philosophy
Bates College
Boston College
Claremont McKenna College
Colgate University
Columbia University in the City of New York
Dartmouth College
Duke University
Emory University
Georgetown University
Hamilton College
Harvard University
Johns Hopkins University
New York University
Northwestern University
Princeton University
Rice University
Stanford University
University of California-Berkeley
University of California-Los Angeles
University of California-Santa Barbara
University of Chicago
University of Notre Dame
University of Pennsylvania
University of Southern California
Vanderbilt University
Washington and Lee University
Washington University in St Louis
Wellesley College
Williams College
Yale University

Physics
Amherst College
Bates College
Brown University
California Institute of Technology
Carleton College
Carnegie Mellon University
Columbia University in the City of New York
Cornell University
Dartmouth College
Duke University
Hamilton College
Harvard University

Harvey Mudd College
Johns Hopkins University
Massachusetts Institute of Technology
Northwestern University
Pomona College
Princeton University
Rice University
Stanford University
The University of Texas at Austin
United States Naval Academy
University of California-Berkeley
University of Chicago
University of Notre Dame
University of Pennsylvania
University of Washington-Seattle
Wesleyan University
Williams College
Yale University

Political Science
Bates College
Boston College
Bowdoin College
Brown University
Colgate University
College of the Holy Cross
Columbia University in the City of New York
Cornell University
Dartmouth College
Davidson College
Duke University
Emory University
Georgetown University
Harvard University
Johns Hopkins University
Northwestern University
Princeton University
Stanford University
United States Naval Academy
University of California-Los Angeles
University of Chicago
University of Michigan
University of Notre Dame
University of Pennsylvania
Vanderbilt University
Wake Forest University
Washington and Lee University
Washington University in St Louis
Wesleyan University
Yale University

Psychology
Barnard College
Bates College
Boston College
Carleton College
Claremont McKenna College
Columbia University
Cornell University
Dartmouth College
Davidson College
Duke University
Emory University
Harvard University
Princeton University
Stanford University
University of California, Berkeley
University of California, San Diego
University of California, Santa Barbara
University of Chicago
University of Illinois at Urbana-Champaign
University of Michigan

University of Minnesota – Twin Cities
University of North Carolina at Chapel Hill
University of Pennsylvania
University of Rochester
University of Texas at Austin, The
University of Wisconsin – Madison
Washington University in St. Louis
Wellesley College
Wesleyan University
Williams College

Public Health
American University
Brown University
Cornell University
Duke University
Franklin and Marshall College
George Washington University
Georgetown University
Johns Hopkins University
Lehigh University
New York University
Northwestern University
Rutgers University-New Brunswick
Santa Clara University
The University of Texas at Austin
Tufts University
University of California-Berkeley
University of California-Irvine
University of California-San Diego
University of Florida
University of Georgia
University of Illinois at Urbana-Champaign
University of Maryland-College Park
University of Massachusetts-Amherst
University of Michigan
University of North Carolina at Chapel Hill
University of Pennsylvania
University of Rochester
University of South Carolina
University of Southern California
University of Washington-Seattle

Public Policy
Barnard College
Brandeis University
Brown University
Carnegie Mellon University
Claremont McKenna College
College of William and Mary
Cornell University
Dickinson College
Duke University
Emory University
Georgia Institute of Technology
Gettysburg College
Hamilton College
Northwestern University
Pomona College
Princeton University
Rice University
Southern Methodist University
Stanford University
Trinity College
University of California-Los Angeles
University of Chicago
University of Maryland-College Park
University of Michigan
University of North Carolina at Chapel Hill

University of Pennsylvania
University of Southern California
University of Virginia
Vanderbilt University

Robotics
Arizona State University
Carnegie Mellon University
Cornell University
Georgia Institute of Technology
Johns Hopkins University
New Jersey Institute of Technology
New York University
Northeastern University
Ohio State University
Purdue University
Rochester Institute of Technology
Stanford University
United States Military Academy
University of California, Berkeley
University of California, San Diego
University of Connecticut
University of Illinois at Urbana-Champaign
University of Maryland
University of Michigan
University of Washington
Virginia Tech
Washington University
Worcester Polytechnic Institute

Social Work
Arizona State University
Baylor University
CUNY Hunter College
Florida Atlantic University
Florida State University
Fordham University
Loyola University Chicago
Michigan State University
New York University
North Carolina State University
Ohio State University
Rutgers University-New Brunswick
Skidmore College
St Olaf College
Temple University
Texas Christian University
The University of Tennessee-Knoxville
The University of Texas at Austin
University of California-Berkeley
University of Central Florida
University of Connecticut
University of Georgia
University of Illinois at Urbana-Champaign
University of Maryland-Baltimore County
University of North Carolina Wilmington
University of Pittsburgh
University of Vermont
University of Washington-Seattle
University of Wisconsin-Madison
Virginia Commonwealth University

Sport Management
Clemson University
Florida State University
Indiana University
North Carolina State University
Ohio State University
Rice University

Rutgers University
Southern Methodist University
Syracuse University
Texas A&M University – College Station
University of Florida
University of Georgia
University of Illinois
University of Iowa
University of Massachusetts Amherst
University of Miami
University of Michigan
University of Minnesota
University of South Carolina
University of Texas at Austin

Statistics
Amherst College
Brown University
Carleton College
Carnegie Mellon University
Colby College
Columbia University in the City of New York
Cornell University
Dartmouth College
Duke University
Emory University
Harvard University
North Carolina State University
Northwestern University
Purdue University-Main Campus
Rice University
Smith College
University of California-Berkeley
University of California-Davis
University of California-Los Angeles
University of California-Santa Barbara
University of Chicago
University of Illinois at Urbana-Champaign
University of Michigan

University of North Carolina at Chapel Hill
University of Notre Dame
University of Pennsylvania
University of Washington-Seattle
Washington University in St Louis
Williams College
Yale University

Supply Chain Management
Arizona State University
Auburn University
Bryant University
Carnegie Mellon University
Clarkson University
Georgia Institute of Technology
Indiana University
Iowa State University
Lehigh University
Marquette University
Michigan State University
Ohio State University
Pennsylvania State University
Purdue University
Rutgers University-New Brunswick
Texas A&M University – College Station
Texas Christian University
The University of Tennessee-Knoxville
The University of Texas at Austin
University of Arkansas
University of California, Berkeley
University of Houston
University of Illinois at Urbana-Champaign
University of Maryland-College Park
University of Massachusetts-Amherst
University of Michigan
University of Pennsylvania
University of Pittsburgh
University of Minnesota
Washington University in St Louis

Top "Feeder" Colleges

Teens eyeing highly-competitive fields (e.g. medicine, law, finance, engineering, tech, journalism, entrepreneurship, or academia), should be aware that certain undergraduate colleges serve as "feeders," annually sending a sizable number of alumni to the crème de la crème of graduate/professional programs as well as the most desirable employers. Being aware of which colleges have a direct pipeline into the advanced degree program or corporation you aim to one day target, can help put you on the path toward making that dream a reality.

The lists that follow showcase the top 30 "feeder" schools into the most highly-ranked graduate programs/ companies for a variety of disciplines/industries. The column on the left reveals the universities that send the largest raw number of graduates into top institutions (either academic or corporate). The column on the right shows the top 30 feeders when adjusted for a school's undergraduate enrollment, which allows us to highlight schools that may be smaller in size, but that still send a consistent flow of graduates to the world's premier schools/companies.

For a more detailed look at our methodology in constructing each list, please visit the College Transitions Dataverse at **www.collegetransitions.com/dataverse**.

Top Feeders – Elite Business Schools (MBA)

Top Feeders (by Total Graduates Enrolled)

1. Harvard University
2. Cornell University
3. Northwestern University
4. University of Pennsylvania
4. University of Chicago
6. New York University
6. University of Michigan
8. Yale University
9. University of California, Berkeley
10. Stanford University
10. University of Virginia
12. Dartmouth College
12. Duke University
14. Brown University
15. University of California, Los Angeles
16. University of Notre Dame
17. University of Illinois at Urbana-Champaign
18. University of Southern California
19. Columbia University
19. Georgetown University
21. Georgia Institute of Technology
21. Princeton University
23. Vanderbilt University
24. Boston College
25. University of Maryland, College Park
26. Washington University in St. Louis
27. Pennsylvania State University – University Park
27. Tufts University
27. The University of Texas at Austin
30. University of Wisconsin – Madison

Top Feeders (Adjusted for Undergraduate Enrollment)

1. Dartmouth College
2. University of Chicago
3. Claremont McKenna College
4. Yale University
5. Williams College
6. Harvard University
7. Northwestern University
8. Stanford University
9. Duke University
10. Amherst College
11. Middlebury College
12. Brown University
13. Princeton University
14. Wellesley College
15. University of Pennsylvania
16. Colgate University
17. Swarthmore College
18. Rice University
19. Bowdoin College
20. Cornell University
21. Georgetown University
22. Pomona College
23. Vanderbilt University
24. University of Notre Dame
25. Tufts University
26. Wesleyan University
27. Columbia University
28. Colby College
29. Washington and Lee University
30. Bates College

*MBA programs incorporated into our analysis include Columbia Business School, Harvard Business School, MIT Sloan School of Management, NYU Stern School of Business, Northwestern Kellogg School of Management, Stanford Graduate School of Business, University of Chicago Booth School of Business, The Wharton School (University of Pennsylvania), UC Berkeley Haas School of Business, and Yale School of Management.

Top Feeders – Elite Law Schools (JD)

Top Feeders (by Total Graduates Enrolled)

1. Harvard University
2. University of California, Berkeley
3. Yale University
4. University of Michigan
5. Stanford University
6. New York University
7. Columbia University
8. Cornell University
9. University of Pennsylvania
10. University of California, Los Angeles
11. Princeton University
12. Duke University
13. University of Virginia
14. Georgetown University
15. Brown University
16. Dartmouth College
17. Northwestern University
18. University of Notre Dame
19. University of Chicago
20. University of Illinois at Urbana-Champaign
21. University of Southern California
22. University of North Carolina at Chapel Hill
23. Amherst College
23. The University of Texas at Austin
25. University of Florida
26. University of Wisconsin – Madison
27. Brigham Young University
28. Williams College
29. University of California, San Diego
30. Boston College

Top Feeders (Adjusted for Undergraduate Enrollment)

1. Yale University
2. Amherst College
3. Harvard University
4. Princeton University
5. Stanford University
6. Dartmouth College
7. Williams College
8. Duke University
9. Columbia University
10. Georgetown University
11. Swarthmore College
12. Haverford College
13. Brown University
14. Pomona College
15. St. John's College
16. University of Pennsylvania
17. Claremont McKenna College
18. Wesleyan University
19. Wellesley College
20. Northwestern University
21. Cornell University
22. University of Chicago
23. Brandeis University
24. Carleton College
25. University of California, Berkeley
26. Vassar College
27. University of Notre Dame
28. Colgate University
29. University of Virginia
30. Washington and Lee University

*JD programs incorporated into our analysis include Columbia University, Cornell University, Duke University, Georgetown University, Harvard University, New York University, Northwestern University, Stanford University, University of California, Berkeley, University of Chicago, University of Michigan, University of Pennsylvania, University of Virginia, Yale University.

Top Feeders – Elite Medical Schools (MD)

Top Feeders (by Total Graduates Enrolled)	Top Feeders (Adjusted for Undergraduate Enrollment)
1. Harvard University	1. Stanford University
2. Stanford University	2. Harvard University
3. Columbia University	3. Yale University
4. Yale University	4. Columbia University
5. University of Michigan	5. Duke University
6. Northwestern University	6. Princeton University
7. University of California, Berkeley	7. Johns Hopkins University
8. University of Pennsylvania	8. Massachusetts Institute of Technology
9. Duke University	9. Amherst College
10. University of California, Los Angeles	10. Northwestern University
11. Cornell University	11. California Institute of Technology
12. New York University	12. Dartmouth College
13. Johns Hopkins University	13. Haverford College
14. Princeton University	14. Williams College
15. University of North Carolina at Chapel Hill	15. Swarthmore College
16. Massachusetts Institute of Technology	16. Rice University
17. Brown University	17. Pomona College
18. Washington University in St. Louis	18. Brown University
19. Dartmouth College	19. Davidson College
20. University of Washington – Seattle	20. University of Pennsylvania
21. Emory University	21. Washington University in St. Louis
22. University of California, San Diego	22. Emory University
23. Rice University	23. Case Western Reserve University
24. The University of Texas at Austin	24. Cornell University
25. Vanderbilt University	25. Vanderbilt University
26. University of Notre Dame	26. Bowdoin College
27. Case Western Reserve University	27. University of Chicago
28. University of Chicago	28. Wellesley College
29. University of Pittsburgh	29. Wesleyan University
30. University of Virginia	30. Oberlin College

*Medical programs incorporated into our analysis include Baylor College of Medicine, Case Western Reserve University, Columbia University, Cornell University (Weill), Duke University, Emory University, Harvard University, Icahn School of Medicine at Mount Sinai, Johns Hopkins University, Mayo Clinic School of Medicine, New York University (Grossman), Northwestern University (Feinberg), Stanford University, University of California, Los Angeles, University of California, San Diego, University of California, San Francisco, University of Chicago (Pritzker), University of Michigan, University of North Carolina at Chapel Hill, University of Pennsylvania (Perelman), University of Pittsburgh, University of Washington, Vanderbilt University, Washington University, and Yale University.

Top Feeders – PhD Programs

Top Feeders (by Total PhDs earned)	Top Feeders (Adjusted for Undergraduate Enrollment)
1. University of California, Berkeley	1. California Institute of Technology
2. University of Michigan	2. Harvey Mudd College
3. Cornell University	3. Swarthmore College
4. University of Florida	4. Massachusetts Institute of Technology
5. University of Wisconsin – Madison	5. Carleton College
6. University of Illinois at Urbana-Champaign	6. Reed College
7. University of California, Los Angeles	7. Grinnell College
8. Brigham Young University - Provo	8. Williams College
9. The University of Texas at Austin	9. Haverford College
10. Pennsylvania State University – University Park	10. Pomona College
11. University of California, San Diego	11. St. John's College (MD)
12. Harvard University	12. University of Chicago
13. University of California, Davis	13. Vassar College
14. University of North Carolina at Chapel Hill	14. Bryn Mawr College
15. University of Washington – Seattle	15. Princeton University
16. Michigan State University	16. Oberlin College
17. The Ohio State University – Columbus	17. Yale University
18. Texas A&M University – College Station	18. Franklin W. Olin College of Engineering
19. University of Maryland, College Park	19. Wesleyan University
20. Massachusetts Institute of Technology	20. Amherst College
21. University of Minnesota – Twin Cities	21. Wellesley College
22. University of Virginia	22. Stanford University
23. University of Chicago	23. Whitman College
24. Purdue University – West Lafayette	24. Macalester College
25. Rutgers University – New Brunswick	25. Kenyon College
26. Stanford University	26. New College of Florida
27. University of Arizona	27. Mount Holyoke College
28. University of Pennsylvania	28. Smith College
29. Brown University	29. Dartmouth College
30. Boston University	30. Brown University

*Data collected from the National Science Foundation's Survey of Earned Doctorates (SED).

Top Feeders – Engineering

Top Feeders (by Total Graduates Employed)

1. University of Southern California
2. Georgia Institute of Technology
3. Carnegie Mellon University
4. University of California, Berkeley
5. University of Washington – Seattle
6. University of California, San Diego
7. University of Illinois at Urbana-Champaign
8. University of California, Los Angeles
9. University of California, Irvine
10. Northeastern University
11. Purdue University – West Lafayette
12. University of Michigan
13. The University of Texas at Austin
14. Cornell University
15. Columbia University
16. University of Florida
17. Texas A&M University – College Station
18. University of Maryland, College Park
19. Stanford University
20. San Jose State University
21. Penn State University – University Park
22. University of Central Florida
23. North Carolina State University
24. Cal Poly, San Luis Obispo
25. Massachusetts Institute of Technology
26. University of Pennsylvania
27. Virginia Tech
28. University of Wisconsin – Madison
29. University of Colorado Boulder
30. Rochester Institute of Technology

Top Feeders (Adjusted for Undergraduate Enrollment)

1. Carnegie Mellon University
2. Columbia University
3. California Institute of Technology
4. Massachusetts Institute of Technology
5. Georgia Institute of Technology
6. University of Southern California
7. Stanford University
8. Franklin W. Olin College of Engineering
9. Harvey Mudd College
10. Rice University
11. Northeastern University
12. Duke University
13. Cornell University
14. Santa Clara University
15. University of Pennsylvania
16. Princeton University
17. Harvard University
18. Rose-Hulman Institute of Technology
19. Johns Hopkins University
20. The Cooper Union
21. Washington University in St. Louis
22. University of California, Berkeley
23. Brown University
24. University of California, San Diego
25. Northwestern University
26. University of Washington – Seattle
27. University of Illinois at Urbana-Champaign
28. University of California, Los Angeles
29. University of California, Irvine
30. Rochester Institute of Technology

* Employers incorporated into our analysis include Amazon, Apple, Boeing, ExxonMobil, Google, Lockheed Martin, Microsoft, NASA, SpaceX, and Tesla.

Top Feeders – Entrepreneurship (via PitchBook)

Rank and Institution		Founder Count	Company Count	Capital Raised (millions, USD)
1.	Stanford University	1,448	1,258	$47.8
2.	University of California, Berkeley	1,365	1,225	$36.3
3.	Massachusetts Institute of Technology	1,125	985	$33.4
4.	Harvard University	1,100	988	$41.2
5.	University of Pennsylvania	1,021	932	$22.6
6.	Cornell University	888	824	$28.6
7.	University of Michigan	835	760	$19.1
8.	Tel Aviv University	807	673	$16.2
9.	The University of Texas at Austin	749	686	$10.2
10.	University of Illinois at Urbana-Champaign	621	575	$16.4
11.	Yale University	616	560	$15.6
12.	Technion – Israel Institute of Technology	602	509	$12.4
13.	Princeton University	593	560	$19.5
14.	University of California, Los Angeles	588	554	$15.0
15.	Columbia University	546	510	$15.3
16.	Brown University	542	496	$20.6
17.	University of Wisconsin – Madison	539	480	$8.8
18.	University of Southern California	520	480	$17.8
19.	Carnegie Mellon University	506	447	$13.6
20.	Duke University	484	461	$11.0
21.	Brigham Young University – Provo	475	378	$8.2
22.	University of Waterloo	474	375	$12.9
23.	New York University	465	431	$9.2
24.	University of Washington – Seattle	456	403	$8.4
25.	Dartmouth College	438	400	$11.3
26.	Northwestern University	434	405	$11.4
27.	University of California, San Diego	419	400	$8.7
28.	University of Colorado Boulder	405	379	$7.2
28.	University of Maryland, College Park	405	378	$6.7
30.	University of Virginia	403	380	$7.0

*Institutions and data provided by Pitchbook. Learn more at www.collegetransitions.com/dataverse/top-feeders-entrepreneurship.

Top Feeders – Finance/Wall Street

Top Feeders (by Total Graduates Enrolled)	Top Feeders (Adjusted for Undergraduate Enrollment)
1. University of Pennsylvania	1. University of Pennsylvania
2. New York University	2. Harvard University
3. Cornell University	3. Columbia University
4. University of Michigan	4. Yale University
5. Harvard University	5. University of Chicago
6. Columbia University	6. Williams College
7. University of Chicago	7. Duke University
8. University of California, Berkeley	8. Claremont McKenna College
9. University of Notre Dame	9. Middlebury College
10. Duke University	10. Princeton University
11. University of Southern California	11. Dartmouth College
12. University of Virginia	12. University of Notre Dame
13. Yale University	13. Georgetown University
14. The University of Texas at Austin	14. Washington and Lee University
15. Georgetown University	15. Cornell University
16. Brown University	16. Amherst College
17. Princeton University	17. Brown University
18. University of California, Los Angeles	18. Bowdoin College
19. Dartmouth College	19. Stanford University
20. Northwestern University	20. Vanderbilt University
21. University of North Carolina at Chapel Hill	21. New York University
22. Stanford University	22. Emory University
23. Vanderbilt University	23. Northwestern University
23. Boston College	24. Pomona College
25. Emory University	25. Massachusetts Institute of Technology
26. Middlebury College	26. Swarthmore College
27. Southern Methodist University	27. University of Virginia
28. Williams College	28. Southern Methodist University
29. Boston University	29. Colgate University
30. Rutgers University – New Brunswick	30. Boston College

*Employers incorporated into our analysis include Bank of America Merrill Lynch, Barclays, Citi, Centerview Partners, Credit Suisse, Evercore, Goldman Sachs, JP Morgan, Jefferies, Lazard, Moelis & Company, Morgan Stanley, and UBS.

Top Feeders – News/Media

Top Feeders (by Total Graduates Employed)	Top Feeders (Adjusted for Undergraduate Enrollment)
1. New York University	1. Columbia University
2. Columbia University	2. Harvard University
3. Northwestern University	3. Yale University
4. University of Maryland, College Park	4. Northwestern University
5. University of California, Berkeley	5. New York University
6. Boston University	6. Georgetown University
7. Harvard University	7. Emerson College
8. Syracuse University	8. American University
9. George Washington University	9. Princeton University
10. American University	10. Hofstra University
11. University of Missouri	11. Stanford University
12. Yale University	12. Barnard College
13. Georgetown University	13. Wesleyan University
14. University of Southern California	14. Brown University
15. University of Michigan	15. George Washington University
16. Fordham University	16. Fordham University
17. University of Florida	17. Williams College
18. Cornell University	18. Syracuse University
19. University of North Carolina at Chapel Hill	19. Ithaca College
20. Stanford University	20. Boston University
21. Hofstra University	21. Middlebury College
22. University of California, Los Angeles	22. Amherst College
23. The University of Texas at Austin	23. Wellesley College
24. Penn State University – University Park	24. University of Pennsylvania
25. University of Pennsylvania	25. Dartmouth College
26. University of Virginia	26. Duke University
27. University of Georgia	27. University of Chicago
28. Princeton University	28. Cornell University
29. Brown University	29. University of Southern California
30. University of Wisconsin – Madison	30. University of Maryland, College Park

*Employers incorporated into our analysis include the Associated Press, ABC, CBS, CNN, Fox News, MSNBC, NBC, NPR, the New York Times, the Wall Street Journal, and the Washington Post.

Top Feeders – Tech

Top Feeders (by Total Graduates Enrolled)

1. Carnegie Mellon University
2. University of Southern California
3. University of California, Berkeley
4. Georgia Institute of Technology
5. University of Illinois at Urbana-Champaign
6. University of Washington – Seattle
7. University of California, San Diego
8. University of Waterloo
9. University of California, Los Angeles
10. Stanford University
11. Columbia University
12. University of Michigan
13. Cornell University
14. Northeastern University
15. The University of Texas at Austin
16. University of California, Irvine
17. San Jose State University
18. Purdue University – West Lafayette
19. University of Toronto
20. New York University
21. Massachusetts Institute of Technology
22. University of Pennsylvania
23. University of California, Davis
24. North Carolina State University
25. University of Maryland, College Park
26. Duke University
27. Harvard University
28. University of Wisconsin – Madison
29. University of Virginia
30. Brown University

Top Feeders (Adjusted for Undergraduate Enrollment)

1. Carnegie Mellon University
2. Columbia University
3. Stanford University
4. Massachusetts Institute of Technology
5. California Institute of Technology
6. Harvey Mudd College
7. Georgia Institute of Technology
8. University of Southern California
9. Rice University
10. Harvard University
11. Duke University
12. Cornell University
13. Northeastern University
14. University of California, Berkeley
15. University of Pennsylvania
16. Princeton University
17. Brown University
18. Santa Clara University
19. Northwestern University
20. University of Illinois at Urbana-Champaign
21. Swarthmore College
22. University of California, San Diego
23. University of Washington – Seattle
24. Yale University
25. Washington University in St. Louis
26. Johns Hopkins University
27. University of Chicago
28. University of California, Los Angeles
29. University of Waterloo
30. University of Michigan

*Employers incorporated into our analysis include Adobe, Airbnb, Amazon, Apple, Dropbox, Facebook, Google, LinkedIn, Lyft, Microsoft, and Twitter.

Recommended Summer Programs

An increasing number of selective colleges now scrutinize how applicants spend their summers during high school. In response to this trend, thousands of providers–including both universities and private companies–offer academically-themed summer programs for teens. These programs vary from free-to-extremely expensive, and highly-selective-to-open enrollment. With such a bevy of options, teens will likely need expert guidance in order to successfully locate an ideal-fit program that will fully support their future academic and career dreams. The following are programs strongly recommended by the College Transitions team.

Boston University RISE
Clinical Neuroscience Immersion Experience @
  Stanford University
COSMOS University of California
Georgetown University Pre-College Online Program
Illinois Tech Elevate College Prep
  Summer Programs
JCamp
Johns Hopkins Psychology & Brain Sciences
  Summer Programs
Notre Dame Leadership Seminars
Oxford Summer Courses

Penn Carey Law Pre-College Academy
Research Science Institute (MIT)
Rice University Precollege Program
Ross Mathematics Program
Science Internship Program (SIP)
Stanford University Mathematics Camp (SUMaC)
Summer Leaders Experience
  (U.S. Military Academy)
Summer Seminar (U.S. Air Force Academy)
Summer Seminar (U.S. Naval Academy)
Telluride Association Summer Seminar

Recommended Test-Prep Providers

There are myriad reasons why a high school student might seek out a tutor or a test-prep specialist. Some teens may just be trying to pass a challenging course, while others may be looking to hold onto a perfect GPA, become proficient in a foreign language, or get a jump start on their competition by previewing an upcoming course. Likewise, on the SAT or ACT, some may be fighting and clawing to earn an average score, whereas other Ivy-focused individuals are laser-focused on nailing a perfect 1600.

No matter your aim, the most important factors to consider in shopping for the right tutor or test prep expert are that they are trustworthy, responsive, inspiring, diligent, and skilled & experienced in the area of expertise. Each of the providers on our list that follows checks each of these boxes, having earned stellar reputations in the industry.

Applerouth
www.applerouth.com
Email: info@applerouth.com
Phone: 866-789-7237

Benthall Test Prep
www.benthalltestpre.com
Email: bailey.raynor@benthalltestprep.com
Phone: 910-240-2310

Edison Prep
www.edisonprep.com
Email: edison@edisonprep.com
Phone: 404-333-8573

Mindfish
www.mindfish.com
Email: admin@mindfish.com
Phone: 720-204-1041

PrepPros
www.preppros.io
Email: info@preppros.io